A DIPLOMATIC HISTORY OF THE UNITED STATES

JOHN QUINCY ADAMS

AET. 28

From a Portrait by J. S. Copley. Reprinted from B. C. Clark's *John Quincy Adams:* "Old Man Eloquent" by permission of Little, Brown and Co.

A
DIPLOMATIC
HISTORY
OF THE
UNITED
STATES

THIRD
EDITION

Samuel Flagg Bemis

STERLING PROFESSOR OF DIPLOMATIC HISTORY AND INTER-AMERICAN RELATIONS
YALE UNIVERSITY

Henry Holt and Company · New York

PREFACE TO THE THIRD EDITION

In this new edition I have revised and corrected the text in the light of the latest scholarship, and I have abridged considerably Chapters XXXV, XXXVI, XXXVII, XXXVIII, and XLI in order to provide space for the discussion of recent events. Two new chapters, XLV and XLVI, cover American diplomacy during the Second World War and its aftermath. I have added tabulations and charts to illustrate the economics of American diplomacy and the organizations of the American states and the United Nations. Four new maps show the regional security zone defined by the Treaty of Rio de Janeiro, the zones of military occupation in Europe, the advance of Russia in Eurasia, the heartland of the world island, and the North Atlantic Area as defined in the Atlantic Treaty of 1949. The Epilogue focuses the book on the present crisis of thought and action that opens the second half of the twentieth century.

To many fellow students and colleagues I am grateful for corrections and suggestions which I have acknowledged in the notes. In addition to those persons mentioned in the Preface to the original edition, I extend my thanks to: A. M. Anderson, Lt. Commander S. R. Baraw, U.S.N., Rev. J. Neilson Barry, George P. Bohan, Jr., Manuel S. Canyes, Paul D. Dickens, William T. R. Fox, Edgar S. Furniss, Jr., Andrew Gyorgy, Richard D. Johnson, Guy P. Meredith, Vernon G. Setser, Kenneth M. Spang, Geneva W. Walsh, and Lt. Colonel Edward H. Young, U.S.A. I also wish to thank Alfred A. Knopf, Inc., for permission to reproduce in the Epilogue the sense of the historical summary of the fundamentals of United States foreign policy as expressed in my *John Quincy Adams and the Foundations of American Foreign Policy*, which they published in 1949; and Thomas Y. Crowell Company for use of some of my passages in a contribution to their publication, *World Political Geography* (New York, 1948).

S. F. B.

New Haven, Conn.
January 17, 1950

PREFACE TO THE FIRST EDITION

In presenting this volume I have tried to embody the contributions of a generation of vigorous research by scholars in many countries, increasingly from a multi-archival approach, and to give perspective and interpretation to the whole diplomatic history and foreign policy of the United States.

Footnotes are restricted to the indication of evidence or supporting scholarship and to occasional subordinate information for which there is no place in the structure of the text. I refer those who would go still further into special works and sources to the *Guide to the Diplomatic History of the United States,*[1] which serves as a comprehensive technical supplementary volume to this history. As the work has approached its contemporary chapters it has been articulated with the analyses of American foreign policy, general and regional, now taking shape in the projected studies of the Yale Institute of International Studies.

Many friends and colleagues in the field have helped me with discussions and corrections. Some have read particular chapters. I wish to acknowledge assistance from: Thomas A. Bailey, Capt. John S. Barleon, U.S.N., Robert G. Barnes, James P. Baxter, 3rd., W. C. Binkley, George H. Blakeslee, Edwin M. Borchard, Philip C. Brooks, J. C. Cady, J. C. Capt, Victor S. Clark, Anthony C. J. Davidonis, Paul Dickens, John Donaldson, C. A. Duniway, Frederick S. Dunn, T. C. Elliott, Victor J. Farrar, Willy Feuerlein, Robert W. Galvin, Grace G. Griffin, A. Whitney Griswold, Hajo Holborn, J. Franklin Jameson, Kenneth S. Latourette, Capt. L. R. Leahy, U.S.N., Dorothy M. Louraine, Frank E. Louraine, Karl Löwenstein, H. H. Martin, Lawrence Martin, James J. McTernan, Jr., Hunter Miller, Phoebe Morrison, Dana G. Munro, Roy F. Nichols, Charles O. Paullin, Dexter Perkins, Julius W. Pratt, Lowell J. Ragatz, Harry Rudin, Carlton Savage, Charles Seymour, Lester B. Shippee, E. Wilder Spaulding, Nicholas J. Spykman, Lt. Willard M. Sweetzer, U.S.N., Charles C. Tansill, Dorothy W. White, Francis White, Mary W. Williams, W. W. Willoughby, Francis Colt deWolf, Cyril Wynne. My wife, Ruth Steele Bemis, and daughter Barbara read the proof with me.

Mr. S. Whittemore Boggs, Geographer of the Department of State, Washington, D. C., has collaborated with me throughout in the preparation of the maps; he has compiled the maps and is responsible for the

[1] Samuel Flagg Bemis and Grace Gardner Griffin, *Guide to the Diplomatic History of the United States, 1775-1921* (Government Printing Office, Washington, D. C., 1935, Library of Congress).

cartography, but I am responsible for the facts and legends. I wish particularly to acknowledge the original features which he has introduced in certain maps, notably Nos. 8, 26, and 27. Mr. Boggs' colleague, Mr. F. I. Burnham, drafted the maps of the Far East and the Pacific—the area of his special knowledge and interest—and also the three colored maps. The other maps were drafted under the direction of Mr. G. W. Garland of the United States Geological Survey.

Immeasurable help has come to me from the staffs and resources of some of those great libraries of which the United States may well be proud: the William L. Clements Library at Ann Arbor, Michigan; the special library on international relations of the Carnegie Endowment for International Peace, in Washington; the Library of Congress; the Columbus Library of the Pan-American Union in Washington; the Widener Memorial Library at Harvard University; and the Sterling Memorial Library at Yale University. The Department of State has afforded me the unusual facilities available to all scholars.

S. F. B.

New London, N. H.,
July 1, 1936.

CONTENTS

PART I—FOUNDATIONS

PART II—EXPANSION

MAPS

(Designed by S. Whittemore Boggs)

MAPS

ILLUSTRATIONS

TABLES AND DIAGRAMS

PART I

FOUNDATIONS

CHAPTER I

AMERICA THE STAKES OF EUROPEAN DIPLOMACY

(1492-1775)

A DIPLOMATIC history of the United States must begin with some review of the part which the Americas, particularly North America, played in the international politics of Europe in the centuries preceding American independence.

The discovery of the New World, one of the greatest achievements in the history of mankind, marking the beginning of the modern era, coincided with and indeed was due to the appearance of strong national monarchies on the Atlantic seaboard of Europe. The newly galvanized power of nationality, still the most dynamic historical force of our own times, laid hold of the American continents at the very beginning and made them the object of European contention. They continued increasingly to be such until their separation from European sovereignty.

When Columbus sailed into the Tagus and announced to the King of Portugal that he had discovered for the monarchs of Spain some islands off the eastern coast of India and on the other side of the Atlantic, he precipitated the first and longest diplomatic controversy in American history, a dispute which involved nothing less than sovereignty over two continents and gave rise to territorial claims of Spain not to be wholly relinquished until after three centuries of diplomatic strife and intermittent warfare with rival European powers, not until the settlement in 1790 of the spectacular Nootka Sound controversy. The kings of Portugal had received from the Pope, who had assumed authority of defining the relations between Christian nations and pagan peoples, successive grants of sovereign rights and dominion over lands discovered and to be discovered by their navigators. These grants dated back to 1455. They had rewarded the explorations and pious conquests of the Portuguese in Africa which were designed to reach through to Abyssinia. They had acknowledged to the kings of Portugal exclusive rights along the coast of Africa "toward that southern shore and beyond even unto the Indies." Columbus seemed to have stumbled into these regions through the front door of an Atlantic route, a seaway previously tried

3

without success by Portuguese navigators. King John II immediately dispatched an envoy to Rome to protest this invasion.

Pope Alexander VI was himself a Spaniard. By four different bulls in 1493 he defined and redefined the respective claims of the two Iberian monarchs until finally it settled down to this: the kings of Spain were to have exclusive dominion and sovereignty over all lands not already belonging to any other Christian prince, discovered and to be discovered west and south of a line to be drawn from pole to pole 100 leagues west of the Azores and Cape Verde Islands, whether those lands should be "in western parts or in regions of the South or East or of India." [1] The kings of Portugal were to have all such lands to the east and south of the demarcation line. This line did not prove wholly satisfactory to the contending monarchs. They agreed between themselves in the treaty of Tordesillas (1494) to shift the line to 370 leagues west of the Cape Verde Islands. They supposed that this would fall about half way across the Atlantic Ocean. [2] It soon became evident that it cut off from Spanish reserves a big eastern triangle of South America, and perhaps a slice of Labrador. Labrador never became the scene of either Spanish or Portuguese activities; but because of the treaty of Tordesillas, Brazil today is a Portuguese-speaking country. The Pope confirmed by a bull (1506) this treaty of partition. Diplomatists and geographers, despite congresses and surveys, never succeeded in drawing the line of demarcation. Spain and Portugal were unable to agree on the boundaries of Brazil until 1750 when they accepted a conventional line which, very roughly, is the basis of the national limits of the present republic.

The discovery of the Pacific Ocean and Magellan's circumnavigation of the globe soon raised the question what should be the line of division in the antipodal regions. The rulers of Spain and Portugal could not agree simply to extend the demarcation line around the globe, if only because it was never settled precisely where it lay on the Atlantic side; but in 1529 they came to a practical compromise, full of import for the later diplomatic history of the United States: Portugal retained the fabulous Moluccas in the East Indies, under certain conditions of reversion never executed, and the Philippines. Spanish colonization nevertheless invaded the Philippines, and the treaty of 1750 finally acknowledged Spanish sovereignty over them. Spain held the archi-

[1] Bull of September 26, 1493.
[2] G. A. Rein, *Der Kampf Westeuropas um Nordamerika in 15. und 16. Jahrhundert* (Stuttgart-Gotha, 1925).

pelago until 1898. If this remote treaty settlement had not devised those distant islands to Spain, would the United States ever have been involved in the problems of Asiatic diplomacy? [1]

The other sovereign rulers of a still-united catholic Christendom never recognized this partnership in exclusive new-world dominion, but for a long time they were unable to contest it very formidably. At the beginning of the sixteenth century both Spain and Portugal were politically united under strong kings and unembarrassed by internal troubles, particularly religious controversies. The rival monarchies, England and France, presently were engaged in political and religious dissension, partly the aftermath of the Protestant revolt. Thus Spain and Portugal were at ease to exploit their respective spheres of the expansive domains newly discovered in the East and West Indies. Spain conquered Portugal in 1581 and with that country its overseas possessions. Whoever recognized the authority of Tordesillas and the Pope might have contended that from 1581 until 1640, when Portuguese independence was again successfully asserted, all the non-European world came under the dominion of the haughty leader of the forces of the Counter-Reformation, Philip II of Spain, and his successors.

France and England were unable to plant any enduring colonies in North America until after the close of the great Spanish war of 1585-1604. By that time they had solved the internal political and religious problems which had absorbed their energies and delayed their maritime activities. This solid political unity France maintained ever afterward, though England again broke down temporarily in the civil disturbances of 1642-1652. After these nations had successfully defended themselves against Philip II and become masters of their own national destinies, the sixteenth and seventeenth centuries witnessed a series of effective challenges by France and by England, and presently by the United Provinces of the Netherlands, to Spain's claims to colonial monopoly. From the seventeenth century forward the value of colonies and of overseas commerce came to be more and more vitally estimated. The mercantilist school of statecraft, particularly in England, incidentally in France, associated colonial dominion, trade monopoly over it, and the nursery for seapower which went with growing navigation with the colonies, as the basic elements of national strength in a world of continual strife. They not only demanded that Spain recognize their encroaching settlements and their freedom to establish others in unoccupied regions of the New World; they strove also to oblige her to

[1] See below, Chap. XXVI.

allow their subjects to trade freely within the Spanish colonial system, even to receive especial commercial monopolies there, while at the same time they proceeded to close their own colonies to foreign shipping. In time of actual war they fought with increasing eagerness to possess themselves of the enemy's colonies.

By the end of the seventeenth century France, England and the Netherlands had forced express recognition from Spain of their own colonies in America. Portugal had recovered her independence and such of her former overseas domains, including Brazil, as had not been conquered while in Spanish possession, and had opened these regions to English trade. England had taken away from the Netherlands the Dutch colonies on the Hudson and Delaware rivers. Spain had been elbowed out of half of North America. After prolonged and obstinate resistance she had been obliged to recognize specifically the right of her rivals to trade and settle in the unoccupied regions of the East and West Indies.[1] With Spain thus in process of retirement from the North American scene the stage was set for the protracted duel between France and England for the control of that continent.

Between 1688 and 1815 those two powers fought each other in six great wars. In this historic struggle it was the general policy of France and her allies—who except for the first war included Spain because of the latter's fear of the maritime power of the English—to expand on the continent of Europe and by overpowering her neighbors with her armies to break into their colonies and commerce. It was the policy of England to defeat this aggression, to control the sea with her navy and to expand her own colonial empire at the expense of France and Spain.[2] In the wars that were waged before the declaration of American independence the colonists of England and of her enemies all over the world were automatically involved in the ensuing hostilities. European international issues pulsated along the umbilical cords which bound the American colonies to their European sovereigns, and engaged Frenchmen and Englishmen in bitter warfare no matter how innocent they may have been of the remote causes of those wars; for all except the Seven Years' War began in Europe as contests for the balance of power.

[1] The various treaties in which these concessions evolved (1604, 1648, 1659, 1667, 1670, 1697, 1701) are annotated with great erudition in Frances G. Davenport's monumental publication, *European Treaties Bearing on the History of the United States and its Dependencies* (3 Vols., Washington, Carnegie Institution, 1917-1934).

[2] J. R. Seeley, *Growth of British Policy* (2 Vols., Cambridge, 1903); A. T. Mahan, *The Influence of Sea Power on History, 1660-1783* (Boston, 1897).

The War of the League of Augsburg (1688-1697) was fought by a European coalition to stay the aggressions of Louis XIV in the Low Countries, but although it brought bloodshed to North America it resulted in no changes of colonial sovereignty.

The War of the Spanish Succession (1701-1713) again thwarted the designs of Louis XIV, this time to place his grandson on the throne of Spain, to unite the two monarchies, to dominate Europe, to latinize the seas, to secure for his Bourbon successors the vast legacy of Tordesillas. On the other hand France's enemies in the event of complete victory had arranged in 1701 to take the Spanish colonies and partition France.[1] The defeat of the dynastic projects of the French King meant the preservation of the imperial future of Great Britain and the salvation of the small nations of western Europe, Portugal and the Netherlands. The ensuing peace of Utrecht (1713) was the first rearrangement of the map of North America.[2] Some commentators have gone so far as to call it the beginning of the diplomatic history of the United States, because its articles are the root of later important questions of American diplomacy. By it France renounced all claims of sovereignty over the regions adjacent to Hudson's Bay and to the island of Newfoundland (reserving certain fishing privileges along the shores thereof),[3] and recognized British possession of the original French colony of Acadia or Nova Scotia, "with its ancient boundaries" and dependencies.[4] By possession of Newfoundland and Nova Scotia, Great Britain secured a strategic control of the Gulf of St. Lawrence and the waterways lead-

[1] E. Bourgeois, *Manuel historique de politique étrangère* (4 Vols., Paris, 1900-26), Vol. I.

[2] By the treaty of St. Germain of 1632 which ended the Huguenot war between Spain and France, and England, the last two powers by implication recognized each other's colonies in North America, but no boundaries were mentioned. This was the first treaty by which any of the maritime powers recognized alien colonies in the New World.

[3] Article XIII fixed the fishing privileges: "But it shall be allowed to the subjects of France to catch fish, and to dry them on land, in that part only, and in no other besides that, of the said island of Newfoundland, which stretches from the place called Cape Bonavista to the northern point of the said island, and from thence running down by the western side, reaches as far as the place called Point Riche." See Map 27.

[4] According to the terms of the Anglo-French treaty of Utrecht (as distinct from the Anglo-Spanish treaty), a joint commission was to meet at Paris to settle the boundary between the British territory about Hudson's Bay and the French dominions of New France. The commission failed to fix the boundary, but out of British claims made in relation to it there arose later the idea—represented in cartographical fictions—of the line of 49° N.L. as the boundary between British Canada and French Louisiana, which eventually became the northern boundary of the United States, in 1818. See pp. 173, 273. Dispute over the uncertian "ancient limits" of Acadia led to much border hostilities between English and French settlers in the region of Maine and New Brunswick.

ing to New France. The control of these was to spell finally the downfall of French dominion on the continent. England also took more
than this: as another stroke against Spanish sovereignty in the New
World, it succeeded at last in getting the *asiento*, a lucrative commercial
concession recently acquired by France, and thus in driving a wedge
into Spain's trading monopoly with her own colonies while specifically
prohibiting to the French any share in Spanish-American commerce.
The famous *asiento* article of the Anglo-Spanish treaty of Utrecht
forced from Spain what that power for two hundred and fifty years
had persistently refused to allow: a company under English control
was given the monopoly of supplying African slaves to Spanish-American colonies for thirty years, and what is still more important, the
right to trade to the Indies with one ship a year of five hundred tons,
a concession which was shamelessly abused in the following years. At
the same time England received Gibraltar and Minorca. These Mediterranean fortresses later became important factors in the diplomacy
of the War of American Independence.

The abuse of the *asiento* privilege became so notorious that Spanish
cruisers sailed forth [1] to enforce the strict content of the article. Years
of acrimonious incidents, caused by the search of British ships on the
high seas—something which British policy never tolerated—eventually
wore down the peace which both powers had preserved determinedly
during the exhausted generation after Utrecht. The War of Jenkins'
Ear (1739-1748) between England and Spain developed into a European
war over the question of the Austrian succession. France entered the
maritime conflict as the family ally of Spain and became involved in
the continental struggle as Prussia's ally against the traditional French
foe, Austria. When hostilities thus became general England made an
alliance with Austria. The War of Jenkins' Ear became the War of
the Austrian Succession. In the general peace settlement which reconstructed the European balance at Aix-la-Chapelle, in 1748, the diplomatists weighed the English conquest of Louisbourg against the French
capture of Madras in India. They agreed on a mutual restoration
overseas of the *status quo ante bellum*.[2]

---

[1] Vera L. Brown, "The South Sea Company and Contraband Trade," *Am. Hist. Rev.*,
XXXI, 662.

[2] In the settlement between Great Britain and Spain, the thirty-year *asiento* contract, which would have expired in 1743, according to the terms of the treaty of 1713,
was extended for the years which had been interrupted by the war, a compromise between extinguishment of the contract and renewal over a longer period of years. The
limited term proved too short-lived for a profitable renewal of the dislocated operations

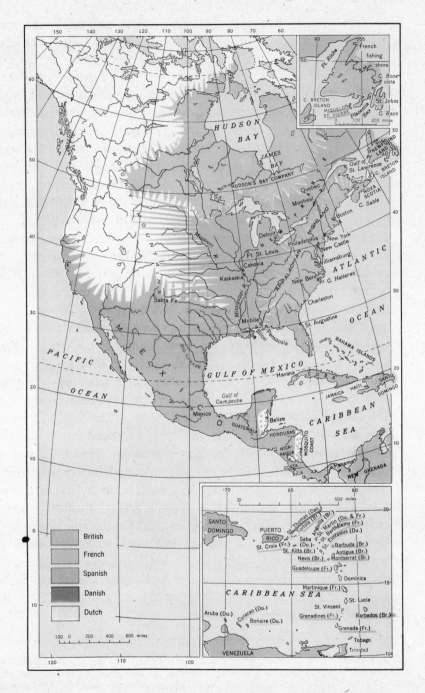

Map 1.   North America after the Peace Settlement of 1713

Another great European conflict was preparing. It was to be decisive for the future of North America. From it was to come the international situation which made possible the independence of the United States. The growth of British power and prestige, explained by the mercantilists as due to colonies and trade and the seapower based on them, finally persuaded French statesmen that in order successfully to rival England it was necessary first to strengthen the resources of France by building up a great colonial empire which would equal or overshadow the British. For a brief period France accordingly re-oriented her foreign policy. Before the Seven Years' War (1756-1763) France's policy had been mainly a European one, to which overseas adventures were incidental, if important; that is to say, it had been the traditional policy of preventing the rise of any large political entity in the Germanies and of expanding her own frontier toward the Rhine. In the previous war France had allied herself with Frederick the Great against the traditional enemy Austria. On the eve of the Seven Years' War there occurred a spectacular reversal of alliances in Europe executed by the Austrian Chancellor, Kaunitz. Austria succeeded in bringing France into a defensive alliance against Prussia; and Great Britain, the former ally of Austria, now made a pact with Prussia.

The Seven Years' War began in a collision between French and British outposts in the disputed Ohio Valley in 1753, spread to Europe, and in 1756 involved the opposing major allies, with Russia and the smaller states of central Europe shifting from side to side as the fortunes of war compelled or tempted. In the last year of the war Spain injudiciously rewrote the Bourbon Family Alliance with France, and entered the war prepared to share gains or losses of territory. The new diplomatic combinations proved France's undoing. She was bled of strength on the plains of Germany defending her useless Austrian ally from the blows of Frederick the Great of Prussia subsidized by Great Britain. She was consequently unable to withstand the onslaughts of British armies and navies which the genius of the British Prime Minister, William Pitt (Lord Chatham), marshaled in America and India. Only the insistence of the youthful George III, who came to

of the concessionaires; in 1750 Spain was able by treaty to purchase the *asiento* back from Great Britain at a cost of £100,000.

The British claimed that Spanish recognition of existing British colonies in America, by the treaty of Madrid of 1670, included the settlements of British log-cutters on the Campeche coast. Spain denied this. The Campeche settlements continued without bounds, until placed definitely under Spanish sovereignty by the treaty of Paris of 1763. They were a base for smuggling English goods from Jamaica into the Spanish provinces of Mexico and Central America.

the English throne (1760) in the midst of the war, on a tempered peace—in order to rid himself of an embarrassingly dominant war minister—saved France from complete disaster. As it was, that great monarchy was crushed, stripped of colonies, and reduced to the unprecedented and humiliating position of a second-rate power in European affairs.

The Treaty of Paris, 1763, again remade the map of North America, and it laid the territorial foundations of the future British Empire. France transferred to Great Britain, Canada and all French territory to the east of the Mississippi River, excepting New Orleans (which was the capital of the remaining French Louisiana) and the so-called island on which it stands on the east bank, and excepting also the two small islands of St. Pierre and Miquelon, in the Gulf of St. Lawrence. She was allowed to keep, unfortified, those islands as bases for the fishing "liberties" [1] (as they were now significantly denominated, as distinct from implied rights) on the coasts of Newfoundland, retained from the treaty of Utrecht. France was required to dismantle and raze her naval works in the channel port of Dunkerque, and an English commissioner was placed there to see that this article continued to be executed in good faith. In the West Indies, France retained the western part of the island of Santo Domingo, Guadeloupe and its two small dependent islands, Désirade and Marie Galante; Martinique, and Santa Lucia; and Great Britain kept her other conquests there. In India, France, compelled to accept the rôle of trader pure and simple, abandoned all political rights. In the same peace Spain ceded to Great Britain, Florida and all Spanish possessions to the east of the Mississippi; Great Britain in turn relinquished Cuba, which had been captured during the last months of the war. Spain acknowledged the right of the vexatious British log-cutting settlements "on the Bay of Honduras and other places of the territory of Spain in that part of the world" to a peaceful existence providing all fortifications were demolished. This left to the British a continuing foothold on the Isthmus of Central America, and is an historical factor in the diplomatic background of the Panama Canal.

Another provision of the treaty of Paris that was full of later importance for the diplomatic history of the United States was the regulation of the navigation of the Mississippi River. Because France retained the "island" [2] of New Orleans as a part of Louisiana, the river

---

[1] See p. 7 above for relevant stipulations of Article XIII of the treaty of Utrecht.

[2] The "island" consists of the area of low lands—about 2800 square miles—bounded by the Iberville River (really a bayou), Lakes Maurepas and Ponchartrain, the Ocean, and the Mississippi.

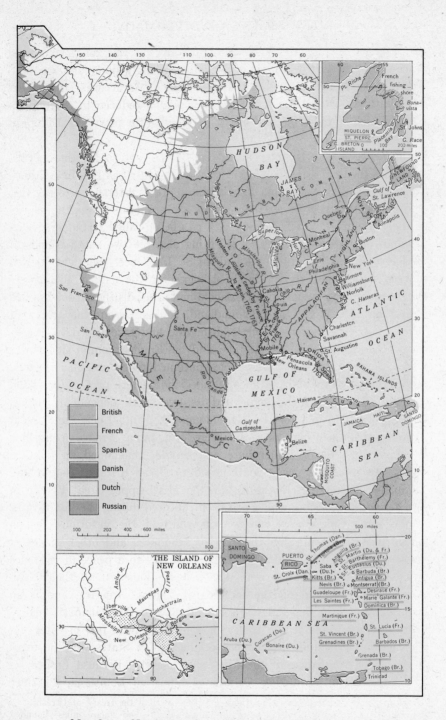

Map 2.   North America after the Peace Settlement of 1763

flowed between French banks on its last 220 miles to the sea. In order that this might not interfere with the navigation interests of British subjects upstream on the east or left bank of the remainder of the river, the treaty declared that the navigation of the Mississippi should be "equally free, as well to the subjects of Great Britain as to those of France, in its whole breadth and length, from its source to the sea, and expressly that part which is between the said island of New Orleans and the right bank of that river, as well as the passage both in and out of its mouth."

A few hours after the signature of the treaty of Paris, France transferred to Spain all of Louisiana west of the Mississippi and the "island" of New Orleans. The ostensible reason for this great cession was to compensate Spain for the loss of the Floridas. The real motive was an effort of the French Foreign Minister, the Duc de Choiseul, to induce Spain to sign the general peace promptly before the victorious English should change their minds and themselves demand Louisiana and perhaps the remaining French islands.[1] It was all the easier for the King of France to sign away the province at this time because it was a financial burden, a costly colonial "white elephant." In taking over the expensive region the Spanish ministers comforted themselves with the illusion that it might serve as a buffer in the way of future expansive forces of the "Anglo-Americans" towards the rich domains of Mexico. No one could foresee that by the end of the century Spain would be glad to rid herself of the province to the eager Napoleon Bonaparte, expecting it to continue in his hands as a buffer against the same "Anglo-Americans." Nor could the most clairvoyant of all European statesmen see further: that Bonaparte would turn around and promptly sell the same province to the very people against whose incursions he had professed it would be such a protection. Spain took over Louisiana in 1763 subject, of course, to the newly established servitude on the navigation of the Mississippi. Repossession of that vast province—for the Spanish could consider any acquisition of territory in America as repossession of regions originally under their sovereignty—temporarily enlarged the empire, and twenty years later the conquest of Florida seemed to strengthen it still more; but the French Revolution loosed forces in Europe and in America which speedily brought the final collapse.

The introductory review which has been the purpose of this chap-

[1] A. S. Aiton, "The Diplomacy of the Louisiana Cession," *Am. Hist. Rev.*, XXXVI (1931), 701-720.

ter allows us to indulge in some general reflections instructive to the reader of the diplomatic history of the United States.

The first is that North America since its discovery had become increasingly the stakes of European diplomacy in the great contests for the world balance of power. The people who lived on this continent themselves had little to say about the wars which their European sovereigns fought with each other, even though those wars automatically involved colonial subjects of kings who ruled and battled across the ocean. The lack of comprehension which the English colonists, for example, had of the causes of these dreadful conflicts in which they were engaged despite themselves, is testified by the names which they gave to them: *King William's War* (the War of the League of Augsburg), *Queen Anne's War* (the War of the Spanish Succession), *King George's War* (the War of the Austrian Succession), the *French and Indian War* (which, in contradistinction to the other wars, having started in America, was more familiar to them). They accepted their participation in these wars with undisturbed equanimity. Like the rise and fall of the tides, the movement of the heavenly bodies, or the apparent passage of time itself, it seemed ineluctable. No one questioned this dispensation of fate.

As a matter of fact, this ineligible connection of English colonists with Britain's wars was not one of the causes of the American Revolution. It remained for a newly arrived English immigrant, Thomas Paine, who was reflecting the isolationist attitude of the English Whig opposition toward continental connections,[1] to point out to the colonists that separation from British sovereignty meant also separation from Britain's wars. The conclusion was immediately irresistible. For over a century it was substantially correct. Colonial experience in being the stakes of European diplomacy, relief at the freedom from that condition which came with American independence, and determination to continue to enjoy it and to profit by it laid the foundation for that persistent policy of the United States which was crystallized in President Washington's Farewell Address and again enunciated in the Monroe Doctrine, public documents not devoid of phraseology resembling certain passages in Thomas Paine's famous pamphlet *Common Sense*.[2]

[1] Felix Gilbert has pointed out "The English Background of American Isolationism in the Eighteenth Century," in *Wm. and Mary Quarterly*, Third Series, I, No. 2 (April, 1944), 138-160.

[2] ". . . any submission to, or dependance [*sic*] on Great Britain, tends directly to involve this continent in European wars and quarrels . . . It is the true interest of America to steer clear of European contentions, which she never can do, while by her depend-

Secondly, these centuries of war and diplomatic contest reveal the characteristic foreign policies of the powers with whom the United States was to deal in the first decades of its diplomatic history. It is well to keep them in mind as we turn the pages of this volume. Spain very naturally developed a policy of procrastination and delay. She had lost so much, by discussion and contest, of her colonies and her claims that she realized no good could come by making them the object of any discussion at all. As her empire weakened she leaned on France for protection, and it became the settled tendency of Spain—like China later—to look vainly to the other powers to help her save those domains which she could not hold or govern by her own strength. France, except for the disastrous interlude of the Seven Years' War, followed a well-defined policy of seeking her advancement by maintaining the first position in Europe. Colonial and commercial advantages could be expected incidentally from the power which she might build up in the Old World.

The smaller Atlantic powers, Portugal and the Netherlands, for a short time such impressive colonial nations, dropped into the background because of the weakness of their positions in Europe. They had to buy England's protection because of their weak frontiers if they would secure their independence against Spain and France, respectively. For this they paid by colonial and commercial concessions to their powerful ally. The foreign policy of England may be simply put: aggressive expansion of her colonial empire by the use of her developing sea-power, and protection of her growing commerce against all comers. It fitted with this policy to prevent any one European state, like France, from rising to an overpowering position in Europe. British continental diplomacy uniformly has sought to marshal the weaker powers to prevent any threat to the balance by the stronger ones. By the very nature of its object, colonial expansion, British policy depended on the continued maintenance of a preponderant navy, strong enough to confront any likely combination of hostile maritime powers.

Finally, we may note the significance of France's departure in 1754 from her traditional European policy. From the days of Richelieu and Mazarin, French statesmen have striven for the first position of their nation in Europe. They have accomplished this by subduing Spain

ance on Britain, she is made the make-weight in the scale of British politics." *Common Sense.*

In his autobiography John Adams states that he resorted to similar arguments, in Congress, in 1775, for independence; but there is no supporting evidence to his recollection when a very old man of what he said forty years before.

as a dominant European power and by seeking the political pulverization of Germany.　Only once did France make the fateful blunder of
following more adventurous pathways than those mapped out by the
lucid policy of her classical statesmen.　That misadventure was responsible for the independence of the United States.　The American
Revolution and an alliance with the United States became useful to
France as a means of re-establishing her position in Europe after the
prostration of 1763.

CHAPTER II

THE FRENCH ALLIANCE

(1775-1778)

EUROPEAN diplomacy during the decade of France's prostration after the Peace of Paris of 1763 was no gentle profession. In that age of "enlightened despots," kings and their ministers of foreign affairs, and their alert diplomatists abroad, no matter how high-minded they might be in their personal and private affairs, continued to conduct their foreign relations according to the naked principles of Machiavelli, holding that a good object of state justified the employment of any means. A good end meant the advancement of one's own nation at the expense of others. These were the ways for a Prince of the eighteenth century to succeed: (1) to maintain an army and navy as strong as possible, ready to take advantage of any favorable opportunity that might present itself; (2) to watch sharply the life and affairs of other states in order to take advantage of their necessities so as (a) to make profitable and useful allies out of them, or (b) to make war on them if possible with the assistance of allies, and thus to take from them their commerce, their colonies or even their home territories and peoples. A frequent and favorite means of weakening a rival was by assisting, even stimulating, revolts and internal disorders within a kingdom. Internal convulsions with nations as with individuals tend to reduce them to impotency. A full-blown revolution, never unlikely in a despotic state and never impossible in a constitutional one, always offers opportunities to break up its power, either by recognizing the separate independence of important provinces or by actually annexing dominions and peoples. Except for loss of a needed ally no state has ever been known to grieve at the political breakup of another. Thus England and France had assisted the Dutch and the Portuguese revolts against Spain; thus Great Britain furnished secret aid to the Corsican insurrectionists; thus France intrigued with the Irish; thus Prussia, Austria and Russia meddled in the domestic politics of unhappy Poland and partitioned that independent kingdom among themselves—to cite only a few obvious illustrations. The principle of self-determination was unknown. The dominant powers, as the Spanish Minister, Alberoni, once said, cut

15

and pared the smaller states like Dutch cheeses, with no regard to the wishes of their inhabitants.

Princes practised these principles with uneven resources and subject to various handicaps and advantages, but with one constant general characteristic. At the expense of their neighbors they sought as best they could—by alliances and by wars, by inimical and subterraneous intrigues and espionage in time of peace—to advance their vital interests: Great Britain, sea-power, expanding colonial dominions, and spreading maritime commerce; France, supremacy on the continent of Europe which brought incidental expansion overseas; the Netherlands and Portugal, protection of their independence against their threatening neighbors, France and Spain, and the advancement of their commerce as much as tolerable to their powerful ally, Great Britain. They and the small Scandinavian states enjoyed when possible the war profits of neutral carriage. In central Europe, Austria and Prussia sought to overcome each other in order to build a great German state. Russia had comparatively free rein for conquests in the direction of Turkey, though France had an historic alliance with the Turks, often embarrassing to Russian ambitions.

Eighteenth-century diplomatists maintained pleasant social amenities with each other while pursuing their well-defined aims. They secretly stooped to all kinds of dissimulation, deception, espionage, bribery, treachery, robbery and even assassination. This meant that the despatches of an ambassador, even his own person, were not always safe under all circumstances in certain continental countries, despite the time-honored privileges of diplomatic immunity. In a magisterial chapter the greatest of the historians of diplomacy, Albert Sorel,[1] has depicted in sober and unforgettable passages the cut-throat nature of European international politics in the latter half of the eighteenth century when the United States first appeared among the community of independent nations. These features of diplomatic practice have not altogether faded away in our twentieth century, but possibly they have softened a little among the occidental powers. Genuine idealists like Woodrow Wilson and Lord Robert Cecil have made their appearance; assassination of diplomatists in civilized countries now is comparatively rare; and the devastating damage of war is so likely to be common to the whole occidental world that diplomatists do sometimes try to maintain peace even at great hazards. But they cannot hold back peoples spurred by pride or maddened by humiliation.

[1] *L'Europe et la révolution Française* (8 Vols., Paris, 1885-1904).

If the inarticulate masses of the French people remained unmoved by the prostration of 1763, the political leaders were profoundly affected by that defeat. France had become almost a negligible factor in European politics. She was forced to stand by unconsulted while former client states like Turkey and Poland were partitioned. At sea and overseas Britain was supreme. At every great court the British Ambassador, because of the results of the Seven Years' War, insisted on the right to pass before the French representative on ceremonial occasions. French leaders were determined to redress this balance and to retrieve the fallen position of their country. "Almost immediately after the peace of 1763 it [the French Government] sought in the tendency of the English colonies to revolt against their mother country the occasion by which we could avenge ourselves on England and tear up the treaty of Paris." So says the French historian, Henri Doniol, whose monumental publication [1] printed the revealing documents selected from the archives of the French Foreign Office. These quasi-official tomes help the historian to understand France's American policy.

Choiseul, the principal minister of Louis XV, entrusted with the portfolio of foreign affairs during and following the Seven Years' War, strove after 1763 to reorganize the battered armies of France and to restore her depleted navies, even to reinvigorate the finances of the country, the last a hopeless task under the *ancien régime*. He and his successors frankly abandoned the colonial ambitions that had been the cause of the recent disaster. They bent their energies toward quietly strengthening, wherever possible, diplomatic relations in Europe: principally by maintaining with Austria and Spain defensive alliances which could be so construed as to leave France free to make war on Great Britain at a favorable opportunity, and to building up as cordial as possible relations with Prussia lest she again become Britain's ally.[2] Choiseul was quick to see in Great Britain's dissatisfied colonies in America a possible opportunity for France to humble her traditional enemy. He maintained a succession of secret observers on the other side of the Atlantic to keep him well informed of insurrectionary tendencies in the colonies, and was greatly encouraged when some of these agents reported increasing inflammation.[3] But Choiseul left office in 1770 during a period of

[1] *Histoire de la participation de la France à l'établissement des Etats-Unis d' Amérique* (5 Vols. and a supplementary volume, Paris: Imprimerie Nationale, 1886-1892).

[2] This task was the easier because Frederick the Great nursed sore feelings against Great Britain for having made a separate peace during the Seven Years' War. P. L. Haworth, "Frederick the Great and the American Revolution," *Am. Hist. Rev.,* IX (1904), 460-478.

[3] C. H. Van Tyne, *The War of American Independence* (New York, 1929).

temporary quiescence of the American question, convinced that no worth-while insurrection would develop during his lifetime. Sooner than expected the opportunity for which he had eagerly watched came to his successor, the Count de Vergennes, who became minister of foreign affairs (1774-1787) at the accession of the new king, Louis XVI (1774-1792).

Vergennes was schooled in the prevailing European diplomacy by a long career as a diplomatist at the smaller European courts: Lisbon, Frankfort, Munich, Trèves, Hanover, Constantinople (during the Seven Years' War), and Stockholm. He was a clever and subtle states-man, tireless in his capacity for reading and writing despatches, most insinuating in guile. It had been his manner to prevail on these states by veiling the real purposes of France and persuading them that he was seeking to advance their own interests. Despite the realities of an experienced world this old-fashioned method has never failed to work when used by the proper man in the properly tempered way, as every successful salesman knows. "The surest method to succeed in a negotiation," Vergennes had once written to the foreign office from Con-stantinople, "being that of entering as much as possible into the genius and inclination of those with whom one is negotiating, it seems to me that we should hide from the Turks the real end toward which we are driving them. If we present war to them as somewhat inevitable we shall frighten them and discredit ourselves. Let us enlighten them as to their true interests; let us appear to be occupied only with what concerns them, without reference to ourselves. . . ." As minister of foreign affairs, Vergennes appeared to be working for the interests of those nations which he wished to be useful to him, among them the United States of America. Said he, later, in his instructions to the first French minister setting out for the United States: "You will show them that we are making war only for them, that it is only because of them that we are in it, that consequently the engagements we have undertaken with them are absolute and permanent, that our causes are now common causes never to be separated."[1] Because of his diplomatic suppleness and because there really was a community of interests between France and those other powers who wished ill to British supremacy, Vergennes had remarkable success in attaining his objects.[2]

Though more cautious in procedure, Vergennes' foreign policy did not

[1] Doniol, III, 281.
[2] For more extended treatment of Vergennes, and of the diplomacy of the American Revolution, 1775-1783, see my *Foundations of American Diplomacy: I, The Revolution* (N. Y., 1935).

differ much from that of Choiseul. He did not seem at first to recognize that the opportunity for revenge on England was coming into sight when in 1774 the first coercive acts again roused the English colonies in America. The person who brought this vividly to his attention was Caron de Beaumarchais, a courtier known to history as a literary genius who incidentally played at politics. He was just as much a political genius who amused himself by writing such immortal comedies as *The Barber of Seville* and *The Marriage of Figaro*. He had risen rapidly by his own qualities from the status of apprentice to his father, a watchmaker, to a position of great favor in the French Court.[1] He was in England in 1775 on a confidential and most singular mission.[2] There he came in contact with Arthur Lee, who then represented the province of Massachusetts as its colonial agent at the British capital. Lee convinced him of the serious nature of the insurrection which had commenced in America. The two men talked about France assisting the American revolutionists with arms and munitions under the guise of trade. For the neutral French Government openly to supply such aid to rebels against a putative friendly power would have been too high and direct a provocation to Great Britain. Beaumarchais eagerly wrote to Vergennes advocating such assistance to be rendered covertly. He repeatedly crossed the Channel to put memoranda before Vergennes and through the minister before the King, urging this clandestine help to the Americans. In September, 1775, Vergennes went so far as to send a French officer to the Colonies, one Bonvouloir, who had previously traveled there, to cheer them, without incriminating or committing the French Ministry, with the intimation that France did not want to get Canada back, was not unfriendly to the independence of the old colonies. He was also to suggest that American ships would be welcome and free to trade in French ports.

The proposals of Beaumarchais, including some of his inimitable phraseology, were soon embodied by Vergennes into official memoranda (since published by Doniol) which he read before the King and Council, advocating such interference. The most celebrated of these, written, it now seems certain, in the month of April, 1776, was entitled: "Reflections on the present situation of the English Colonies, and on the conduct

---

[1] L. de Loménie, *Beaumarchais and His Times* (N. Y., 1857).

[2] Beaumarchais successfully undertook the task of retrieving from a French renegade, the Chevalier d'Eon, some incriminating documents which if published, as intended by d'Eon, would have revealed secret plans of the former king, Louis XV, for a surprise attack on England. D'Eon is perhaps best remembered because of the widespread dispute during his lifetime as to his real sex.

which France ought to hold in Regard to them." It stated that despite
the great cost of suppressing the American revolt Great Britain by
preventing the loss of her colonies would be able to keep up her manufactures and her navy. If Great Britain preserved her colonies they
would always be of considerable advantage, but in losing them that
empire would suffer unmeasurable damage. England was the natural
enemy, "a rapacious, unjust and faithless enemy," possessed of an in-
variable policy for the abasement of France. Therefore the duty of
France was to seize every opportunity to weaken the power of England. Secret French assistance to the rebels would have the following
advantages: "First, it will diminish the power of England and proportionately raise that of France. Second, it will cause irreparable loss
to English trade, while it will considerably extend ours. Third, it presents to us as very probable the recovery of a part of the possessions
which the English have taken from us in America, such as the fisheries
of Newfoundland and of the Gulf of St. Lawrence, Isle Royale, etc.
We do not speak of Canada." [1] The colonies once independent, they
would set up a republican form of government by its very nature weak
and divided. That would be an assurance against any aggressive tendencies by them against European possessions in that part of the world.
He further argued disingenuously that if Great Britain were permitted
to effect a reconciliation with the Colonies the reunited empire would
then compensate itself for its recent civil losses by falling on the remaining French and Spanish—for Vergennes wished to alarm the King
of Spain into common action [2]—islands in America. Beaumarchais'
procession of strikingly phrased memoranda helped Vergennes to convince the King and the majority of the Council of Ministers to adopt
this policy, to push military and naval preparations by both France and
Spain while contriving studied friendly assurances to the British Government. Turgot, Minister of Finance, dissented. He was persuaded that
French colonies would sometime be free anyway and that it therefore
was not worth the cost of a preventive war with Great Britain to

---

[1] The reader has already noted that France retained important fishing "liberties" on
the shores of Newfoundland and in the Gulf of St. Lawrence, by the treaties of
Utrecht and of Paris. Apparently the memoir overlooked this. The negative mention
of Canada might be construed by some to mean a positive suggestion; but in the
diplomacy of the American Revolution there appears no French design on Canada.
The Franco-American alliance, it will be stated presently, reserved British continental
provinces for conquest by the United States, and for France the British islands
excepting the Bermudas.

[2] Professor E. S. Corwin has written a brilliant study of *French Policy and the American Alliance of 1778* (Princeton, 1916).

protect them against such a future danger. Reluctantly he finally acquiesced in a policy of secret assistance.[1] It was so decreed (May 2, 1776).

Louis XVI directed that one million *livres* (about $200,000) worth of munitions be provided for the colonists from the royal arsenals, through the versatile Beaumarchais, who now transformed himself into a fictitious commercial house with the stage name of Rodrigue Hortalez and Company. Charles III of Spain, royal uncle of the youthful French king, matched his nephew's contribution with another million to be distributed in the same way by the same "company." [2] Thus, before the Declaration of Independence of July 4, 1776, before any agent of the colonies had set foot on French soil, the French Government had decided to pour oil on the flames of rebellion in America in order to embarrass Great Britain and to seek the moment for revenge.

To this point we have taken altogether a European approach to American diplomacy. We may now turn to the first diplomatic activities of the United Colonies, soon to become the United States.

Smarting under the punishment of the Intolerable Acts of 1774, the Continental Congress had responded to Great Britain with an economic boycott, an expedient which we shall meet repeatedly in the early annals of American diplomacy. Their non-importation and non-exportation associations in turn encountered an act of Parliament and a royal proclamation cutting off trade with the American Colonies. Between the boycott and the punitive restrictions of Great Britain the trade of the Colonies was sealed tight. The revolted Americans needed arms and munitions which must be imported from abroad. At first they contented themselves by allowing special permits for the importation of particular cargoes which made their appearance in the ships of foreign gun-runners such as somehow appear on every revolutionary shore. Congress hesitated to throw open the ports of the country to the commerce of the world in defiance of the British navigation laws. That would have been an act tantamount to independence, and before 1776 the movement for actual independence gained little headway. Not until April 6, 1776, when such a declaration was finally under consideration, did Congress take the step of opening trade to all flags. It also appointed a committee to draw up a plan of union and another one to draft a model set of articles for treaties with foreign nations. The three great issues of

---

[1] Turgot resigned May 12.

[2] Valentín Urtazún, *Historia diplomática de América,* Vol. I. *La alianza francesca* (Pamplona, 1920).

foreign trade and treaties, independence, and confederation marched forward rapidly together. On July 2 independence was voted, and the immortal Declaration was adopted for the judgment of mankind on July
4, 1776. Articles of confederation designed to bind the states into a
federal union were reported by a committee on July 12.

Already Congress had anticipated foreign contacts by the appointment on November 29, 1775, of a secret committee "for the sole purpose
of Corresponding with our friends in Great Britain, Ireland *and other
parts of the world.*" This committee was the embryo of an American
foreign office. The original members were John Dickinson, Benjamin
Franklin, Benjamin Harrison, John Jay, and Thomas Johnson. James
Lovell was later an influential and hardworking personage in the fluctuat-
ing personnel of this committee, which presently developed into a Committee on Foreign Affairs. A group of shifting membership proved too
awkward and inefficient a medium for the conduct of diplomatic correspondence. In 1781 Congress appointed a Secretary of Foreign Affairs,
at first Robert R Livingston (1781-1783), later John Jay (1784-1790),
which conducted foreign relations until the organization of the Department of State under the present constitution.[1] The Secretary, like the
preceding committees, was the creature of Congress and directly responsible to it. The official records of the diplomacy of the United States
date back from the present day in practically unbroken series to the
files of the first Secret Committee on Correspondence.

The Secret Committee directed its first letters to Arthur Lee, still in
London and now willing to become the agent at large of the revolutionary
Continental Congress instead of representing the province of Massachusetts at the Court of London; and to Charles Frederic William
Dumas, a friendly correspondent of Franklin and student of international law who resided at The Hague. It opened a regular correspondence with these agents for the purpose of securing information as to
the disposition of foreign powers towards the United Colonies.[2] Lee
the next year became one of the first diplomatic mission of the United
States to France. Dumas remained a faithful correspondent, and a
collaborator with American diplomacy, throughout the Revolution, and
in 1783 and at times thereafter he served as *chargé d'affaires* of the
United States at The Hague, though never an American citizen. In

[1] Gaillard Hunt, *The Department of State of the United States; its History and
Functions* (New Haven and London, 1914).

[2] James B. Scott's introduction to Volume I of the *American Secretaries of State and
their Diplomacy* (N. Y., 10 Vols., 1927-1929, S. F. Bemis, ed.) contains a readable
sketch of these early contacts and a broad view of the diplomacy of the Revolution.

December, 1775, the Committee held secret conclaves with Bonvouloir, the French officer whom Vergennes had sent to make intimations and suggestions. The upshot of these conversations was a decision, March 3, 1776, to send to France a "commercial" agent to see if he could make arrangements for the purchase of military supplies on terms of credit and to make inquiries about possible French political and even military assistance. For this purpose Congress chose Silas Deane, one of its members from Connecticut, who proceeded to Paris in the guise of a merchant.

Beaumarchais and Arthur Lee had talked in London about France furnishing munitions to the revolted colonists only under the guise of trade. There is no evidence of any expectation that these would have to be paid for, and Lee understood that they would not. The creation of the fictitious house of Rodrigue Hortalez and Company by Beaumarchais certainly suggests that the commercial dress was only a disguise designed to deceive England. When Deane reached Paris he had an informal conference with Vergennes, to whom he showed his instructions. Vergennes passed him on to Beaumarchais to whom he again showed his instructions. The latter perceived that Deane was empowered to make contracts for the purchase of munitions. The ex-watchmaker immediately bound Deane to a contract, which Congress ratified, to pay for the munitions. These contraband cargoes now put in motion toward America by the energetic playwright provided General Washington's army with the indispensable requirements for the early campaigns. It is doubtful if Saratoga could have been won without them. The resourceful Beaumarchais at one time seems to have tried to get Spain to pay for them too, beyond what Charles III had advanced in the way of a million *livres,* and we know that Louis XVI had furnished first a million *livres* and then later subsidies, much of which must have gone into Rodrigue Hortalez and Company. This was in addition to the generous loans of money which France began to make to the United States in 1777. After Lee's return to America Congress became suspicious of Beaumarchais' good faith in the contract and refused to pay. The French Government would not interfere to support him. Long after the war, after Beaumarchais' death, his heirs collected from the United States 800,000 *livres* of a total claim of 3,600,000.[1] There is no reason to believe that Beaumarchais was ever out of pocket because of his fictitious munitions business, though he died in poverty. As we

[1] Ch. J. Stillé, *Beaumarchais and "the Lost Million"* (Phila., 1890).

shall see later, all French loans to the United States were repaid in full with interest.[1]

The loans and the subsidies by France and by Spain, during the American Revolution, to the United States may be tabulated at this place, for future reference:

FRANCE

Subsidies			Loans		
Date	Amount		Date	Amount	
1776	1,000,000 *livres*		1777 (Farmers		
1777	2,000,000 "		General)	1,000,000 *livres*	
1781	6,000,000 "		1778 (in 21 in-		
Interest canceled to			stallments, 1778-		
Jan. 1, 1784	1,500,000 "		1782)	18,000,000 "	
			1781 (through		
	10,500,000 *livres*		States - General		
			of the Nether-		
			lands)	10,000,000 "	
			1783	6,000,000 "	
				35,000,000 *livres*	
or (at 18.15)	$1,996,500		or (at 18.15)	$6,352,500	

SPAIN

Subsidies		Loans	
Date	Amount	Date	Amount
1776-1779 (including the 1,000,000 livres *via* Beaumarchais in 1776, and later war material)	$397,230	1778 (to Pollock and Willing)	$ 74,087
		1781-1782 (to Jay)	174,011
			$248,098

The official attitude of the French Government toward the American Revolution between 1776 and 1778 corresponded to what the publicists would call today a recognition of belligerency. Vergennes admitted the right of British cruisers to search French merchant ships for contraband provided they were not bound to neutral countries or to French colonies. Under these circumstances the French and Dutch islands became an *entrepôt* from which contraband was run into the United States. The situation was analogous to that existing during the American Civil War,[2]

---

[1] See also my article "Payment of the French Loans to the United States, 1777-1795," in *Current History*, XXIII (1926), 824-831, based largely on A. Aulard, "La dette Américaine envers la France, sous Louis XVI et sous la révolution," *Revue de Paris*, XXXII (1925), 319-338, 524-550.

[2] See p. 93.

1861-1865, when the European powers recognized the belligerency of the South, but England back in 1776 had not discovered the doctrine of continuous voyage, which was used by her so effectively during the wars of the French Revolution and Napoleon, and, in a more perfected form, by the United States during the Civil War. Though France officially reprobated the fitting out of American privateers in her ports, and officially refused to permit them to make those ports a base for hostile operations, actually she connived to make things helpful and not too inconvenient for them.

When news of the Declaration of Independence reached Paris, Vergennes went so far as to sound out Spain with a proposal to make war on Great Britain by recognizing the independence of the United States. At that time Spain and Portugal were engaged in undeclared hostilities overseas which concerned a boundary controversy in the La Plata region of South America. Grimaldi, the Spanish Foreign Minister, wished to extend the war to Europe. He looked forward to another conquest of the neighboring kingdom, and would have been glad to see Portugal's powerful ally, Great Britain, more than fully occupied. The Spanish Ministry promptly agreed in principle to Vergennes' proposals; but Vergennes withdrew his advances after news arrived of the British victory over Washington's troops at the battle of Long Island. From then on he adopted a cautious policy of watchful waiting. Naturally France would not enter the war without reasonably sure prospects of victory.

Following the Declaration of Independence the Continental Congress decided to send an official diplomatic mission to Europe, directed primarily to the French Court. The appointment of the commission, consisting of Benjamin Franklin, Arthur Lee and Silas Deane, was preceded by an agreement on a model treaty for negotiation with foreign powers, based on the report of the committee [1] for that purpose, which committee was nearly identical with the Secret Committee on Correspondence. This was the so-called "Plan of 1776," which has exerted a profound influence on the history of American diplomacy because it crystallized the policy which the United States has generally pursued throughout its history in regard to certain fundamental concepts of maritime law and neutral rights. These principles were to be incorporated in the treaties of amity and commerce expected with foreign powers, and there were

[1] John Adams, John Dickinson, Benjamin Franklin, Benjamin Harrison, and Robert Morris.

some additional articles for a particular treaty with France.[1] The maritime principles of the Plan of 1776 were picked almost word for word
out of eighteenth-century European practice as reflected in the treaties
of Utrecht and generally in the treaties of the small-navy powers: free
ships free goods, freedom of neutrals to trade in non-contraband between
port and port of a belligerent (this a repudiation of the novel British
Rule of 1756 evoked in the last war), restricted and carefully defined
lists of contraband not including foodstuffs or naval stores, and generally liberal and considerate treatment of neutral shipping. These were
the principles of maritime usage coming increasingly into favor in
Europe, particularly with enlightened publicists and the statesmen of
those powers with small naval protection. Great Britain with her sur-
passing sea-power would not admit them as prevailing international
law, though she had on occasion accepted them in particular treaties.
It was a British conviction that the greater the liberty left to neutrals in
time of war the more the smaller naval enemies could rely on neutral
shipping to replace their own vessels exposed to capture, the more
also they could be assisted by the neutral powers with supplies and
building material with which to build up their navies to a better chance
of combat with Great Britain.

The Committee rejected any idea of seeking an alliance with France.
Indeed Vergennes' own plans did not then include an American alliance,
even when he was contemplating the Franco-Spanish action against Great
Britain and Portugal. Congress at first expected to make with France
a very one-sided treaty by which that nation would recognize the independence of the United States and extend military aid and protection,
without any guaranties by the new republic not to accept any offers of
reconciliation from Great Britain and thus leave France in the lurch.
The most it was ready to do in this way was an obligation of a six
months' advance notice to France of any separate peace! Members felt
that France was so jealous of Great Britain that she would not let the
United States sink in the contest. This was a fairly shrewd analysis,
but when the moment for intervention arrived Vergennes was too astute
not to insist upon an alliance and adequate guaranties to France.

In the commission to France, which was also empowered by its instructions (September 24, 1776) to approach Spain and other powers, Franklin overshadowed his colleagues. In Congress he had been a member

[1] For notes on this plan and its application to early American (eighteenth-century)
treaties see E. C. Burnett, "Note on American Negotiations for Commercial Treaties,
1776-1786," *Am. Hist. Rev.*, XVI (1911), 579-587; and Carlton Savage, *Policy of the
United States Toward Maritime Commerce in War* (Washington, G.P.O., 1934).

of the important committees on independence, foreign correspondence, confederation, and the Plan of 1776. He was the American most familiar with European politics, and the only one with adequate diplomatic experience, which he had acquired by his previous dealings with British statesmen and by his penetrating knowledge of human nature. He was one of the two men best known in the world at that time, the other being Voltaire. His unique personality typified to French men and women the cause of an embattled nation of virtuous Cincinnati struggling for liberty against a tyrant long hateful to France. Himself a "philosopher"—as that word was understood in the quarter-century before the French Revolution—he was entirely sympathetic to the salons of French intellectuals, and he made himself easily at home there. He spoke French tolerably and was gallant in the French manner. He immediately had a good press and an adoring public. The portrait of the conqueror of the lightning soon was displayed in the shopwindows. His benevolent and winning countenance and venerable locks appeared on every fashionable lady's snuffbox. Everywhere he endeared himself to that warm-hearted public opinion [1] which, fitting in with the coolly calculated policy of the royal government, applauded the struggle of the American patriots against heavy odds. In sustaining the American position in France during the period of solicitation and in giving desirable prestige to the diplomatic delegation, the services of the venerable Doctor Franklin, still vigorous in mind, were simply prodigious. It was during these months of 1777 that enthusiastic and adventurous French officers, like young Marquis de Lafayette, entered the American military service, seeking youthful rank and personal glory. Only with his American experience did Lafayette become a convinced Republican,[2] but his departure, at which Vergennes connived, warmed French public opinion already set aglow by Franklin.

Watchful waiting by French diplomacy came to an end when the news reached Paris, December 4, 1777, of the surrender at Saratoga of General Burgoyne's British army. That American victory caused a reversal of British policy toward the revolutionists. Lord North's Government immediately prepared to send to the United States a mission with an offer of peace on the basis of home rule within the empire, something which the Colonies would have been only too glad to accept in

---

[1] Bernard Faÿ in a notable work has analyzed French public opinion and feeling toward the United States, *The Revolutionary Spirit in France and America at the End of the Eighteenth Century* (N. Y., 1927).

[2] Louis Gottschalk, *Lafayette Comes to America* (University of Chicago Press, 1935).

1775. Would they accept it now? This question Vergennes anxiously asked himself, as his alert informants brought him reports that British agents already were talking with Franklin and Deane.

It was a critical juncture. The British Ministry had sent over to Paris their secret-service ace, Paul Wentworth, who had numerous conferences with Franklin and Deane—but not with Lee—during the last weeks of December and early January, 1778. The purpose of these pourparlers was to obtain the influence of the American plenipotentiaries to support the new terms of peace which were to be offered to the "Colonies." Wentworth held out to them offers of high office and emoluments in the new loyal government which would be worked out in America. Both men refused to sell their country.[1] They purposely made no great effort to cover up their conversations. Vergennes became alarmed. He sent a despatch to Madrid to emphasize the critical nature of affairs and to suggest that Spain join France in recognizing the United States before they came to a reconciliation with Great Britain, and in making a treaty with the republic. The golden opportunity of splitting apart the British Empire might vanish forever if something positive were not done to reassure the Americans that it was worth-while to reject the British peace proposals. On December 17, 1777, before an answer could have arrived from Madrid, he precipitately promised the American delegation that he would recognize the independence of the United States and make a treaty. But the secret conferences with Wentworth continued while France tried to pursuade Spain to go along with her. On January 8 Vergennes sent his private secretary Gérard to ask Franklin and Deane what was necessary to stop their talk with the British agents. The two men replied, "A treaty and an alliance."[2] Congress had long since agreed to accept an alliance with France and Spain, if those powers could be persuaded to make one. Vergennes now consented. Some delay ensued while Spain was being further persuaded to come in with France to a triple alliance, but finally, despairing of Spanish action, the plenipotentiaries of the United States and France signed two treaties, on February 6, 1778.

The deadly earnestness of France's anti-British policy of intervention in the American war is testified to by the fact that before Vergennes actually signed the treaty with the United States there was a tempting

[1] Later, after Deane had been recalled from the mission, he returned to Europe, and in the last years of the war had mysterious contacts with the British Ministry which are not above suspicion.

[2] See my article "British Secret Service and the French-American Alliance," *Am. Hist Rev.*, XXIX (1924), 474-495.

opportunity to withdraw in favor of a traditional European aggrandizement. Upon the death of Maximilian, Elector of Bavaria, December 30, 1777,[1] Joseph II of Austria promptly occupied and annexed the major portion of that electorate. Frederick the Great of Prussia immediately went to war to prevent it. If France had been willing to support the Austrian aggression against Prussia she could have had as a reward the Austrian Netherlands—that Flanders on which for a century French kings had looked so covetously, a Flanders dampened, before and since, with the blood of hundreds of thousands of French soldiers. This would have required France to hold her peace with England. Vergennes preferred to relinquish what would have tempted a Louis XIV. Instead of taking the enticing Low Countries he chose to cripple Great Britain before that opportunity vanished. Toward Austria, then, France assumed the rôle of a benevolent mediator in order to keep the continent as quiet as possible while the maritime war was in progress. In 1779 French diplomacy, backed by the threat of Russian bayonets, successfully mediated to bring the War of the Bavarian Succession to a stalemate in the peace of Teschen. Except for the engrossment of France in the American war, Frederick the Great might have had difficulty in defending the European balance so satisfactory to him. It was not pleasing to France's Austrian ally thus to be thwarted in Bavaria. The Emperor bided his time to return the coup by a similar move against France presently in her new conflict with Great Britain.

The first of the two Franco-American treaties was a treaty of amity and commerce, which embodied most-favored-nation trading privileges and the maritime principles of the Plan of 1776. It varied very little from the articles of the plan. In signing this treaty France, of course, recognized the independence of the United States. On March 20, 1778, the King of France formally received Franklin, Deane and Lee in a notable ceremony.

The second treaty was a "conditional and defensive alliance." It provided that in case war should break out between France and Great Britain as a result of the first treaty, the two powers should fight the war together and neither would make a peace or truce with the enemy without the formal consent of the other. Nor would they "lay down their arms until the Independence of the united states shall have been formally or tacitly assured by the Treaty or Treaties that shall terminate the War." It was further stipulated that: "The essential and

---

[1] The news reached Paris by January 5, 1778. The King's Council decided on an American alliance, January 7, 1778.

direct End of the present defensive alliance is to maintain effectually the liberty, Sovereignty, and independance absolute and unlimited of the said united States, as well in Matters of Gouvernement as of commerce." Each ally was left the judge of what military efforts it might contribute. The British possessions on the continent of North America were reserved for conquest by the United States, and France similarly was given a free hand to dispose of the British islands, excepting the Bermudas. From the moment of the outbreak of the war the two allies agreed mutually to significant guaranties. The King of France guaranteed the liberty, sovereignty and independence of the United States, "absolute, and unlimited, as well in Matters of Government as commerce and also their Possessions, and the additions or conquests that their Confedération may obtain during the war, from any of the Dominions now or heretofore possessed by Great Britain in North America, conformable to the 5th & 6th articles above written,[1] the whole as their Possessions shall be fixed and assured to the said States at the moment of the cessation of their present War with England." The United States guaranteed on its part "the present Possessions of the Crown of france in America as well as those which it may acquire by the future Treaty of peace." Even if France were not eventually involved in the present war, the alliance and the guaranties were to come into effect at the conclusion of peace between the United States and Great Britain. An article provided that other powers who had received injuries from Great Britain might be admitted into the alliance on terms to be agreed upon.

France immediately communicated to the British Government the treaty of amity and commerce (but not the alliance) to see what George III would do about it. The Ministry in London already had a copy not only of that treaty but of the treaty of alliance. These had been supplied very promptly by a spy, Dr. Edward Bancroft, who had been Deane's secretary from the time of the latter's arrival in France, and who afterward served as secretary to the joint commission, later to Franklin as Minister, finally to the American peace commission of 1782-1783—all this espionage without being suspected until a century after his death. Bancroft's service had made the British Government well aware of the treacherous conduct of France behind her open assurances. With the assistance of his secret information the British naval authorities, knowing the character of their cargoes, were able to intercept some of the

---

[1] The articles which reserved conquests on the continent for the United States, in the islands for France. Text from Miller's *Treaties*.

munition ships which set out for the United States. Great Britain had not chosen to break openly with France because actual war would have been more injurious than this clandestine assistance. After receiving formal notification of the treaty of amity, George III felt obliged to dismiss the French Ambassador, but even then he did not declare war, for two reasons. A formal peace commission under Lord Carlisle was being despatched to America to propose a reconciliation according to terms laid down by an act of Parliament which had repealed the Intolerable Acts and other legislation obnoxious to the Colonies since 1763.[1] It was hoped that this commission might forestall the French action and prevent a ratification of the treaty by Congress. Further, a formal British declaration of war would have enabled France at least to invoke her defensive alliances with Austria and Spain.

The French treaties and the Carlisle peace commission raced each other across the Atlantic. The treaties won. They arrived at York, Pennsylvania, where Congress was sitting, after having been driven from Philadelphia, on May 2. They were immediately ratified, May 4. In July came a French fleet of war, with the first diplomatic representative to be accredited to the United States, Conrad Alexandre Gérard, Minister Plenipotentiary of Louis XVI. In a joyful ceremony of reception Congress and Gérard, with his staff, consumed the fancy terrapin and wines which the Carlisle commission, now arrived in America, had sent up as a preliminary amenity.

The American war continued, as France desired.

France and Great Britain drifted into hostilities without a declaration of war, by a meeting of their fleets off Ushant, June 17, 1778. A French expeditionary force arrived in the United States in 1780. As is so well known, the combination of French armies and fleets in America with General Washington's forces brought about the final fortunate victory of Yorktown. The French alliance was decisive for the cause of American independence. No American should forget that. No Frenchman ever will. But it also launched the United States into the midst of intricate European diplomatic problems.

[1] The statute prohibiting all trade and intercourse with the Colonies remained on the books, but would have ceased with a peace settlement. The "Act for the impartial administration of justice . . ." etc., in Massachusetts was not repealed until 1871. The Boston Port Act expired by its own limitations, and in effect was supplanted by the non-intercourse act applying to all the colonies in revolt.

CHAPTER III

SPAIN, THE NETHERLANDS AND THE ARMED NEUTRALITY

(1779-1781)

In the critical moment of decision after Saratoga, France had appealed to Spain for a common intervention in the War of the American Revolution. So anxious had been Vergennes not to lose the great opportunity for abasing the power of Great Britain that even before he could hear from Madrid he took the fateful step of promising the American envoys that France would recognize their country and make a treaty with it.[1] Meanwhile he delayed the business, hoping to include Spain. When the answer came from across the Pyrenees it was unfavorable. The face of affairs had changed radically for Spain since 1776, when her minister, Grimaldi, favored going into the war, along with France, against Great Britain, as an opportunity to conquer Portugal, Britain's traditional ally. She now had made a peaceful settlement with Portugal. War with Great Britain no longer held the allurement of the conquest of the neighboring kingdom. She had discouraged Arthur Lee, when the American Commission at Paris had delegated him in 1777 to solicit recognition and alliance, and turned him back on his journey; not, however, without promises of secret assistance in military supplies. A new minister of foreign affairs, Floridablanca (1777-1792), was determined not to recognize the independence of revolted colonies in America even if English colonies, for fear of the fatal example that spectacle might have for Spain's own colonies. Nor was he willing blindly to follow in the wake of French diplomatic piloting. When he heard that Vergennes had committed himself with the United States without waiting to see what Spain's answer would be, he made that a good pretext for holding aloof. Really Floridablanca wished so to maneuver things as to get specific and positive advantages for Spain out of the war.[2] It was not enough to break up the British

---

[1] J. F. Yela Utrilla, *España ante la independencia de los Estados Unidos* (2 Vols., Lérida, 1925) is to date the best book on Spanish diplomacy and the American Revolution. The second volume, of documents, to some extent serves as a Spanish supplement to Doniol, *op. cit.*

[2] Manuel Dánvila y Collado, *Reinado de Carlos III* (6 Vols., Madrid, 1893-1896), Vols. IV-V.

Empire by achieving the independence of the United States; and we repeat that Spain was opposed in principle to independence. What Spain wanted was first and foremost the recovery of Gibraltar and Minorca, snatched from her by England in the War of the Spanish Succession, then if possible Florida, Jamaica, expulsion of the English settlements from the coast of Honduras,[1] perhaps even a share in the fisheries of Newfoundland. Floridablanca at first tried to get some of this without a war by threatening the mediation of Spain between France and England to bring about peace on the basis of the *uti possidetis* in America. This would have been accompanied by a colonial status distinctly short of American independence but would have required Great Britain to accept the impossible interposition of Spain in making arrangements with her colonies. Floridablanca did not expect the British to accept this mediation, and he agreed in an alliance with France to declare war in case they did not; but as he raised the apparition of mediation he hoped that Great Britain might buy off Spanish diplomatic and military intervention by ceding Gibraltar. Then without a war he would win the fruits of one, the highest proof of success in diplomacy. Really if Great Britain had accepted the Spanish ultimatum of mediation she would have been left in a position much better than she was forced to accept in her final defeat. Fortunately for France, George III refused to accept, and on June 21, 1779, Spain, backed by a new French alliance, the convention of Aranjuez (April 12, 1779), declared war on England. Had Great Britain accepted peace on the terms of the proffered Spanish mediation France would have been sorely embarrassed because of her guaranty of the independence of the United States. She would have been obliged either to accept or to refuse. If she had accepted she would have deserted her American alliance. If she had refused she would have abandoned her Spanish affinity.[2]

By the Franco-Spanish alliance, known as the convention of Aranjuez, Spain and France agreed to fight the war until Gibraltar was secured for Spain. As a nominal equivalent France was also to secure the abolition of the servitude on Dunkerque,[3] or in place of that anything else that the King of France might indicate. Further desirable but not indispensable acquisitions were put down: for Spain, Minorca, Jamaica, Florida, ejection of the British from Honduras, a share in the fisheries of Newfoundland; for France, expulsion of the British from Newfoundland, a share in the logging preserves of Honduras, re-establishment of her old position in India; Senegal; the island of Dominica in the West Indies. Neither

---

[1] See above, p. 10.   [2] Corwin, *op. cit.*   [3] See above, p. 10.

power was to make a separate peace or enter into separate discussion of peace.

We must note the relationship of France's two alliances, with the United States (1778), and with Spain (1779). France was bound to continue the war until the independence of the United States was secured. She later became pledged to Spain, to go on until Gibraltar was recovered. Must the United States, if in fact it should establish its independence before the capture of Gibraltar, wait until that fortress were captured by Spain and France? If so, American independence had become chained by European diplomacy to the rock of Gibraltar. France's two alliances were in this respect incompatible, almost bigamous. The life-saving Franco-American alliance, by the exigencies of France's position, had involved the United States unwittingly in the toils of European diplomacy. This became one of the problems of the peace negotiations that ended the war. It became a significant chapter in the background of experience that preceded the foundations of American foreign policy.

Spain's part in the war did not fulfill the exaggerated expectations of the United States and France. Spain declined to come into the Franco-American alliance where a place had been reserved hopefully for her. She refused even to recognize the independence of the United States. She concentrated her major military efforts unsuccessfully on Gibraltar. With troops from New Orleans, Spain was able easily to occupy West Florida, but this was of no immediate [1] value to the United States nor to France. It placed the Floridas beyond any claims to them which the United States might have desired to raise at the final peace conference and enabled Spain to advance claims to a vast region on the left bank of the Mississippi which came into collision with the not unreasonable intention of the United States to make that river its western boundary. While not insisting that his American ally abandon those claims Vergennes tried to talk Congress out of them in order to stiffen the languishing military efforts of France's European ally. In America the French diplomatic representatives tended to join forces with the Spanish "observers" (not regularly accredited lest Spain commit any act that might recognize independence). For some sixteen months, from November, 1779, to March, 1781, the Spanish Ministry was engaged in covert negotiations with the enemy. Even after entering the war, Floridablanca was still trying to get Great Britain to cede Gibraltar to Spain as the price of a peace in which the United States would retain a modified

---

[1] In the long run, of course, it did prove to be advantageous to the interests of the United States to have Spain in the Floridas instead of Great Britain.

colonial status. Congress sent a plenipotentiary, John Jay, recently its president, to Spain to seek an alliance. To get it the United States would have been willing to recognize Spanish pretensions to exclusive navigation of the Mississippi. The Spanish Government refused even to recognize him, but Floridablanca found his presence useful and loaned him for his government $174,011. At least the United States considered it as a loan and later repaid it with interest, though the Spanish authorities were careful not to put it on paper lest such a document might recognize the state to which the money had been furnished.[1] They held Jay thus in dalliance hoping maybe to frighten the British into ceding Gibraltar as a pivot of general peace. Floridablanca's persistent flirtations with a British envoy at the Spanish Court, Richard Cumberland, finally drove Vergennes to map out a compromise peace—at the hands of neutral mediators—which would have left the United States in the lurch. Fortunately for American independence George III refused to let Gibraltar go or to recognize any Spanish proposals for the disposition of his colonies. The Cumberland negotiations broke down.[2] The United States and Spain were to come into opposition again in the final peace negotiations. The principal value to the United States or to France of Spain's belligerency was the moral effect of lining up another European country in the war against Great Britain.

The Netherlands were the next country to become involved in the conflict, though not of their own studied choice as had been the case with Spain. Despite some similarity of religious and political background, particularly a heroic revolt for independence, the Dutch as a people had no moving interest in the cause of American liberty. They were the bankers and traders of continental Europe.[3] They were anxious to profit by the breakdown of the British navigation laws and by the opportunity of selling supplies to belligerent countries. Their prosperity depended on their neutrality. It was this very neutrality which brought them into the war against their will.

Great Britain was able to require Portugal and the Netherlands to prohibit the export of goods directly to the revolted colonies. Nevertheless many of the contraband supplies—how much we do not know—which

---

[1] Before Spain's declaration of war, some small sums, later recognized as loans, were also furnished by the governors of Louisiana and Cuba, to assist American military operation; and subsidies of arms and supplies (in addition to the million *livres* of 1776) were supplied from Spain. For summary, see p. 24.

[2] I have described these negotiations in detail in *The Hussey-Cumberland Mission and American Independence* (Princeton, 1931).

[3] P. J. Van Winter, *Het Aandeel van den Amsterdamschen Handel aan den Opbouw van het Amerikaansche Gemeenebest* (2 Vols., The Hague, 1927-33), Vol. I.

went to the United States by way of France originated in the Netherlands. Others went disguised as neutral traffic to the Dutch colony of
St. Eustatius. This speck of an island in the Virgin group of the West
Indies speedily developed a most extraordinary and abnormal trade
because of the ease with which the forbidden traffic could filter from
there through the British navy to the southern ports of the United
States.[1] The British became increasingly stern in their demands that
the Dutch ration the colony's commerce to normal proportions and shut
out the rebel vessels. But until France entered the war the neutrality
of the Netherlands was not in serious jeopardy.

That event raised the ominous question whether the Dutch were to be
allowed to carry naval stores and shipbuilding timber to France under
protection of the neutral flag.[2] The British contended that these things
were contraband according to international law, and that neutral nations
could not carry them to a belligerent, France, unless they enjoyed
particular treaties with Great Britain that allowed this as a special
dispensation. The Netherlands did actually have a treaty with Great
Britain of 1674 which excepted those articles from the category of
contraband and also acknowledged the principle, then novel, of free
ships free goods. French practice had varied in previous wars according
to varying French interests, but the treaty by which France had
recognized the independence of the United States had accepted the
principle free ships free goods and had excluded naval stores from its
contraband list. France in 1778 wanted to extend to neutrals the
principles of this treaty in order that they might bring in the needed
ship-building materials to French arsenals in order to build up the French
navy to enable France to defeat the British fleets.[3] The British Government had a vital interest in preventing this. The French King issued a
proclamation, July 26, 1778, acknowledging the validity of the more
"liberal" principles—which were not then universally recognized international law although coming into ever wider acceptance by the small-
navy powers—but stating that if neutrals within six months should not
secure from the British Government an observance of the same practice
France would retain full freedom to adopt the British procedure.

Such contingent declarations are to be met with throughout the history

[1] J. F. Jameson, "St. Eustatius in the American Revolution," *Am. Hist. Rev.*, VIII
(1903), 683-708.
[2] H. T. Colenbrander, *De Patriottentijd, hoofdzakelijk naar buitenlandsche bescheiden*
(3 Vols., The Hague, 1897-99), is the classic history of Dutch foreign affairs, 1776-1787.
[3] French policy is clearly set forth in Paul Fauchille, *La diplomatie française et la ligue
des neutres de 1780* (1776-1783) (Paris, 1893).

of American diplomacy: during President Washington's Administration, during the Napoleonic period, during the World War. Their real motive has not been a defense of unadulterated international law. Taking advantage of uncertainties in the law of nations, their real purpose has been pretexts, on the grounds of righteous retaliation, to lay hands on the most formidable weapon of the particular belligerent which champions them. The legal uncertainty in this instance was the definition of contraband, as it was in the recent World War.

By virtue of the announced French policy and by the particular maritime treaty of 1674 between the Netherlands and Great Britain, Dutch neutral commerce on the face of things appeared amply protected, even in these essential commodities for naval building. There was, however, another century-old Anglo-Dutch treaty, the quite unequivocal treaty of alliance of 1678, which required either ally to come to the assistance of the other with stipulated forces in case of war.

If the Netherlands insisted on the extreme letter of the maritime treaty of 1674, the British Government could invoke the treaty of alliance of 1678. Instead of promptly doing this, Great Britain suggested that the two allies confer together to adapt the privileges and obligations of the two treaties to the existing situation, on the basis of a restriction of the trade in naval supplies. This the Dutch foolishly declined to do. The British now refused to let naval supplies go to France in Dutch ships. Accordingly when the conditional six months' period expired the French revoked their decree of July 26, 1778, and applied British practice to Dutch neutral commerce (not of much consequence because Great Britain controlled the North Sea) and also laid special onerous taxes on the ordinary imports into France from the Netherlands. Invidious exceptions from the taxes were made in favor of those provinces, cities and even individuals who were demanding of the States General that it furnish convoys for the debatable articles.[1] The Dutch were already convoying great fleets of merchant vessels to France, but not specifically protecting cargoes of naval stores and timbers. Ships loaded with the latter nevertheless tried to go out mixed into the convoys. After allowing one such convoy to pass unchallenged, the British Government, aware of the subterfuges, broke up the next by force and seized the suspected vessels. What with the artful French pressure, tax discriminations, and intrigue within the domestic politics of the Netherlands, and Dutch

[1] The only tolerable work in English on general relations between the United States and the Netherlands at this time is Friedrich Edler, *The Dutch Republic and the American Revolution* (Baltimore, 1911).

indignation at this British use of force, the States General voted on April 24, 1780, for unlimited convoy (i.e., including naval stores and timber), and for an increased naval armament. The French decree of July 26 was now restored for Dutch subjects. The vote of the States General for increased naval armament was too late to be effective. No

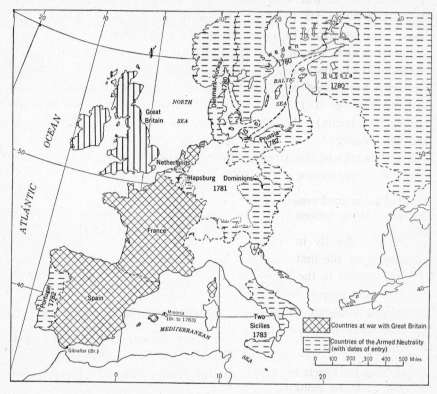

Map 3. Belligerents and Armed Neutrals in Europe, 1780-1783.

new Dutch battleships could be built until long after they would be needed.

This French diplomatic victory was a weak victory at The Hague when confronted with the resolute action which the British were prepared eventually to take. Before the last recourse Great Britain invoked, at first not as an ultimatum, the alliance of 1678. As actual British allies the Dutch could not trade with the enemy at all. As the Hollanders were confronted with this ugly situation a ray of hope appeared for them in the Armed Neutrality of 1780.

The Armed Neutrality, a notable document in the history of maritime law, was proclaimed by Catherine the Great of Russia on February 29, 1780. The proclamation embodied a set of principles for the protection of neutral commerce in time of war, which the belligerents, France, Spain and Great Britain, were invited to accept. Russia, Denmark and Sweden incorporated them in a defensive treaty which closed the Baltic Sea to war operations and announced that they would use their naval forces for the protection of their own vessels under these rules. The principal European nations upon invitation later leagued themselves with the Armed Neutrality by formal adherences: the Netherlands, January 4, 1781; Prussia, May 19, 1782 (but Frederick the Great proclaimed his code on April 10, 1781); the Empire (Holy Roman), October 9, 1781; Portugal, July 24, 1782 (after peace negotiations had begun); the Two Sicilies, February 21, 1783 (after peace had been signed).[1]

The principles of the Armed Neutrality, which were Danish in origin,[2] and even in phraseology, were:

(1) That neutral vessels may navigate freely from port to port and along the coasts of the nations at war.

This was directly in opposition to the novel British Rule of 1756[3] announced for the first time during the Seven Years' War and particularly distressing to the Danes at that time. This rule was not a matter of great controversy during the War for American Independence, but caused much dispute in the wars of the French Revolution and during the Napoleonic period, at which time we shall more conveniently note its implications.

(2) That the effects belonging to subjects of the said Powers at war shall be free on board neutral vessels, with the exception of contraband merchandise.

This was the famous principle of free ships free goods which had been a part of the American Plan of 1776, of the Franco-American treaty of 1778, and of the French proclamation of July 26, 1778. Great Britain correctly maintained that it was not universally accepted international law; but we must add that it was not an innovation like the Rule of 1756, born that year yet asserted by Great Britain as the law of nations.

---

[1] Carl Bergbohm, *Die bewaffnete neutralität, 1780-1783* (Dorpat, 1883).

[2] Thorvald Boye, *De vaebnede neutralitetsforbund* (Christiania, 1912).

[3] Namely, that a belligerent which had prohibited its colonial trade to foreign nations in time of peace could not reverse the practice in time of war in order to take advantage of the immunity of neutral carriage. Strictly speaking, this was called the Rule of the War of 1756.

Great Britain did not choose to challenge free ships free goods against the Armed Neutrals. It was not then of as vital importance to her as the question of contraband.

(3) That, as to the specification of the above-mentioned merchandise [contraband], the Empress holds to what is enumerated in the 10th and 11th articles of her treaty of commerce [of 1766] with Great Britain, extending her obligations to all the Powers at war.

The enumeration of contraband in that Russian treaty did not include naval stores or ships' timbers. Great Britain chose to stand by the treaty and let them pass free. Russian carriage of such material to France was in fact negligible. Most of it went to England. The other Armed Neutrals, in accepting the five principles of Catherine II, regulated the third according to their respective treaties with Great Britain. Only Sweden and Denmark had treaties covering the questions. They allowed naval stores and timbers to be interpreted as contraband.[1] This relieved Great Britain on that score. Next to the Dutch it was principally Danish and Swedish ships which might be carrying the questionable articles to French ports.

(4) That to determine what constitutes a blockaded port, this designation shall apply only to a port where the attacking Power has stationed its vessels sufficiently near and in such a way as to render access thereto clearly dangerous.

The only occasion for the application of this rule during the war was in regard to a loose Spanish blockade of the straits of Gibraltar. This had occasioned the capture of two Russian ships and had precipitated Catherine's declaration. In later wars the question of blockade was to become of paramount significance in American diplomacy.

(5) That these principles shall serve as a rule for proceedings and judgments as to the legality of prizes.

Spain and France immediately accepted the principles. Great Britain did not do so. She declared she would abide by her treaties with neutral powers. By following her treaties with Denmark and Sweden she was able to stop most of the naval supplies going to France without making any issue with the Armed Neutrals, some of whom did not join the League until the fag-end of the war. Aside from its moral effect the

[1] By a bit of sharp diplomatic practice the Anglo-Danish treaty was amended to this effect by a special explanatory article, July 4, 1780, just before Denmark ratified the Armed Neutrality!

Armed Neutrality was not so restraining a league as at first might have appeared. Catherine herself called it an "Armed Nullity." She hoped however that it might be a persuader for the British Ministry to accept a proposal of mediation that she was then ambitiously projecting, which we shall note in the next chapter.

Could the Netherlands, confronting Great Britain, find protection in this suddenly inspired. League of Armed Neutrality? Along with the other neutrals, they had been invited to join. They hesitated to do so, well knowing that the brunt of any hostilities between Great Britain and the Armed Neutrals would fall on themselves and their colonies. They sought first a special provision to protect their colonies against any conquest from a war in defense of the principles of Catherine II. When this proved impossible the States General voted to adhere, without qualifications, November 18, 1780. As the question was being considered in the States General, Great Britain presented an ultimatum invoking the alliance of 1678. It was rejected. Dutch adherence to the League of Armed Neutrals was formally ratified at St. Petersburg, January 4, 1781. Before then Great Britain hastily declared war, seizing upon a convenient if preposterous excuse which would put the Netherlands in a state of war ostensibly over another question than neutral rights. Outright war was preferable to a carriage of naval supplies to French ports under the protection of a league of armed neutrals.

The pretext which the British found was a curious incident in the uncertainly expanding diplomatic relations of the United States outside of France, concerning which it is proper at this point to say a brief word. The American joint commission to France had been dissolved in 1778 and Franklin appointed minister of the United States at Versailles. He continued to be the only recognized diplomatic representative before 1782. The displaced Arthur Lee, and some of his friends and relatives in Congress, felt that the United States, without feeling its way along by experience and careful appraisal of the European situation, should boldly launch out on a campaign for recognition everywhere, sending diplomatic agents to all the important courts whether their presence there was desired or not. They called this "militia diplomacy." Franklin advised against it, holding that a virgin nation ought not to go a-suitoring for alliances. Lee himself had ventured into Spain and Prussia in 1777 in search of such support, only to be actually turned back, from Spain, or to be ignominiously ignored, as was his experience in Berlin. The proponents of militia diplomacy had their way in Congress, and several agents were sent out earlier or later in the war. Ralph Izard went on a fruitless mission to the Grand Duchy of Tuscany. William Lee, brother to Arthur, journeyed to Vienna to seek a treaty with the Emperor, who was then at war with Frederick the Great, with whom W. Lee in his inexperience openly expressed the intention of making another treaty. There was no reason why either of these central European powers should antagonize Great Britain by recognizing the independence of the United States. After visiting Vienna [1] without success, W. Lee postponed his trip to Berlin until after the war of the Bavarian Succession should be over.

While sojourning at Frankfort, W. Lee had some conversations with Jean de Neuville, a somewhat irresponsible Dutchman who was acting for the burgomaster of Amsterdam. These two men drew up the draft of a treaty, modeled on the Plan of 1776 and the Franco-American treaty of commerce and amity, which they thought might be desirable to make between the Netherlands and the United States after the independence of the latter should have been recognized by Great Britain. This explanatory statement however was not attached to the treaty draft. Lee had no powers to make such a treaty with the Netherlands. The burgomaster of Amsterdam or his agent had no more power to draft treaties for the Netherlands than the mayor of New York City today has to draw up treaties for the United States. W. Lee sent the draft to Congress as an interesting suggestion,[2] not as a formal instrument.

Congress meanwhile had despatched a plenipotentiary to the Netherlands, at the instance of some individual Dutchmen who were friendly to the United States. He was Henry Laurens of South Carolina, whom the British captured at sea, with his papers, and incarcerated in the Tower of London until the last months of the war. One of the captured documents was a copy of the Lee-de Neuville treaty draft, which arrived in London just as relations with the Netherlands over the question of neutral rights were coming to a climax. The Ministry immediately accused the Dutch of having made a secret treaty with the Colonies and flaunted the draft treaty before the States General. It did no good to explain that the draft was not authorized. Great Britain was determined to declare war. George III did so, December 20, 1780, stressing the "treaty" with his revolted "Colonies," among other reasons.

---

[1] Hanns Schlitter, *Die Beziehungen Oesterreichs zu den Vereinigten Staaten von Amerika 1778-1787* (Innsbruck, 1885).

[2] F. W. van Wijk, *De republiek en Amerika, 1776-1782* (Leyden, 1921), gives the best account of these irregular negotiations.

The Armed Neutrals accepted the Dutch into their league but they refused any armed assistance to the new confederate on the ground that the war had not arisen over the question of neutral rights! The Dutch, without allies, were left face to face with British seapower, fortunately for them widely engaged with other enemies. Great Britain proceeded to capture all the enemy Dutch ships possible, thus effectively cutting off the principal artery of naval supply to France. A British fleet under Admiral Rodney swiftly descended on the island of St. Eustatius and wiped out that teeming nest of war trade. Dutch colonies in the East and West Indies were now open to capture.

After the Netherlands became engaged in the war, France succeeded in borrowing from that government 10,000,000 *livres* for the United States, guaranteeing payment therefor. But it was not until 1782, after the first peace parleys with Great Britain had commenced, that John Adams, succeeding Henry Laurens with a commission as minister plenipotentiary, was recognized. He was then able to place a loan of 5,000,000 guilders with Dutch bankers, opened to popular subscription. Presently Adams made a treaty of commerce and amity, based on the Plan of 1776 and the first Franco-American treaty. The loan from the Dutch bankers was the first of four loans between 1782 and 1788 which were the only resources which kept alive any faint spark of credit within the Confederation of the Thirteen United States [1] during the trying years of political uncertainty and reconstruction after the war. They were fully paid, with interest, according to the funding schedule, though at first it required some of the later loans to pay interest on some of the first.[2] Since 1782 relations between the United States and the

[1] The name United States of America first appears in the Declaration of Independence. The Franco-American treaties of 1778 use the phrase United States of North America, occasionally employed thereafter in official pronouncements; but Congress resolved July 11, 1778, in favor of the name United States of America, to be used on its bills of exchange, and it has been used since as the official name. See E. C. Burnett, "The Name 'United States of America'" in *Am. Hist. Rev.,* XXXI (Oct. 1925), 79-81.

The proper noun *America* is entirely proper to describe the nation comprised by the United States, and *American* to designate a citizen of the United States of America. Our South American friends have sometimes thought this presumptuous, but the fact is that the word was first used in Europe, particularly in the early diplomatic correspondence of Spain and France. Before the Revolution they spoke of *Anglo-Americans,* to distinguish from Spanish, Mexicans, Chileans, Peruvians, etc. Afterwards they logically dropped the word *Anglo.* It was only natural for the people of the United States to adopt this European usage, which is now confirmed. Historical pedants who nowadays are reviving usage of the awkward phrase *Anglo-Americans,* to distinguish between Americans and other nationals inhabiting North America, such as Mexicans, are guilty of committing a gratuitous solecism. If this anomalous designation could be justly applied to any people, we would suggest the Canadians as more appropriate; but certainly they would not approve.

[2] Van Winter, *op. cit*

Netherlands have been cordial, friendly and unbroken, with little to stress in a history of this scope, an ideal relationship.

The attitude of the United States toward the principles of the Armed Neutrality forms an instructive episode in the diplomacy of the American Revolution. The Czarina did not invite the unrecognized republic to accept those principles, as she had invited the other belligerents. She was anxious to avoid any semblance of recognition, which would have alienated Great Britain from the project of mediation for a general peace that was a part of her diplomatic ambitions.[1] Congress straightway voted into practice the principles of the Armed Neutrality and tried to invite itself into the "League," for that association appeared to be an opportunity to maneuver a great power, perhaps several powers, into recognition of the United States. If the United States might be permitted formally to adhere to the conventions which had set up the Armed Neutrality, the act of ratification with Russia would constitute recognition by that power. Accordingly Congress commissioned a plenipotentiary to St. Petersburg, Francis Dana, with instructions to bring about the adherence of the United States "as an independent nation," if possible to negotiate a treaty of amity and commerce with Russia.[2] It was a fatuous and futile mission. The United States was not even a neutral. Therefore how could it have become a member of the League of Neutrals, even if Catherine had been willing to treat it in any way as a state? The diplomatic representative of the American ally, France, in St. Petersburg, sensing the situation and with instructions from Versailles, refused to support Dana's unsuccessful solicitations. The Empress was determined not to recognize the United States until Great Britain should have done so, and even the signature of preliminaries of peace by the United States, France, Spain and Great Britain was not enough to bring her immediately to this step.

The consummation of American independence in the peace of 1782, to which we shall presently turn, made supererogatory the purpose of Dana's mission. It was no longer necessary to seek recognition anywhere. Congress feared that the agent meanwhile might have engaged the nation to the Armed Neutrality before he could be withdrawn. The Netherlands had not yet concluded their peace with Great Britain and were disappointed at the refusal of that maritime power to accept formally the dicta of 1780. Wishing to perpetuate those maxims as widely

[1] F. A. Golder, "Catherine II and the American Revolution," *Am. Hist. Rev.,* XXI (1915), 92-96.

[2] F. P. Renaut, *La politique de propagande des Américains durant la guerre d' indépendance (1776-1783), Vol. I. Francis Dana à St. Petersbourg* (2 Vols., Paris, 1922).

as possible, the Dutch Government suggested to the United States that it subscribe by treaty to the principles of Catherine, either in particular convention with the Netherlands, or by formal adherence now in time of peace to the Armed Neutrality itself.[1] Congress immediately voted, June 12, 1783, to recall Dana, "as the true interest of these states requires that they should be as little as possible entangled in the politics and controversies of European nations." This wording foreshadows the phraseology of Washington's Farewell Address. Youthful Alexander Hamilton, who is responsible for the literary composition of that Address, was on the committee [2] which brought in this significant resolution.

Formal diplomatic relations with Russia were not established until 1809, when John Quincy Adams, who as a boy of fourteen years had traveled to St. Petersburg with Francis Dana, was received by Alexander I as minister plenipotentiary. Until the great Russian Revolution of 1917 the two countries continued without a break.

[1] E. Albrecht, "Die Stellung der Vereinigten Staaten von Amerika zur bewaffneten Neutralität von 1780," *Zeitschrift für Volkerrecht,* VI (1912), 436-449; and W. S. Carpenter, "The United States and the League of Neutrals of 1780," in *Am. Jour. International Law,* XV (1921), 511-522, discuss this incident capably.

[2] The other members of the committee were James Madison and Oliver Ellsworth.

CHAPTER IV

THE PEACE OF INDEPENDENCE

(1782-1783)

THE peace of 1782 which established American independence and set the boundaries of the new nation has been so potent in consequences for the history of the United States that most Americans overlook the fact that it was a major European peace settlement. It concerned not only the United States and Great Britain, but all the European powers (excepting only Turkey and the Papal States): the belligerents, for their own special interests in all quarters of the globe; the Armed Neutrals for the protection of the principles of 1780, rather weakly contended for; and the mediating neutrals, Austria and Russia. Back of the whole setting of peace lay the European balance of power. All were willing to see British power reasonably checked; none, particularly Austria, wished to see French power too greatly increased.

During the war several attempts, beginning with the Spanish proposals of 1779, were made at mediation among the European belligerents. In each case the mediator expected to advance his own interest by the success of his efforts in the name of peace, and this was the only reason for these efforts. Like the Spanish ultimatum, they rested on the principle of *uti possidetis*—that is, boundaries according to the actual war-map—with some sort of arrangement for the American "Colonies" as a self-governing dominion within the British Empire. Such a status the mediators hoped would be a successful compromise that would satisfy all parties and not be too inconsistent with the obligations of France toward the United States. As a lure to the "Colonies" to enter into a discussion of peace on this basis these projects would have recognized as vaguely as possible their independence *de facto* during and *only during* the negotiations.[1] To meet compunctions against any third party coming between Great Britain and the Colonies, the

[1] This idea, of recognition *de facto* only during the negotiations, came from the official instructions of the British Government to the (Carlisle) peace commission sent to America in 1778, which of course had no intention of recognizing a continuing *de facto* independence, much less a *de jure* independence. If such a procedure had been acceptable to the British themselves in 1778, the mediators assumed it would be acceptable in an international conference.

mediators urged that representatives of Colonies and mother country could talk directly with each other while the general negotiations between the strictly European belligerents were proceeding in the presence of the outside powers; then finally the several peace treaties and arrangements would be signed together and be valid only as a whole, guaranteed by the mediating powers as well as the other signatories. At no time did the American Congress realize the scope or full implication of these projects of mediation and how they could trick the United States out of its complete independence in order to satisfy the interests of some remote European power.

Following the Spanish ultimatum of mediation of 1779, which intended war not peace, Austria and Russia successively made informal proposals of good offices to the European belligerents. Austria had been obliged the previous year by France, supported by Russia, to accept a mediation which frustrated her ambitions in the stalemated war with Prussia over the Bavarian Succession. She now proposed to return mediation for mediation under the guise of good-will and peace, but really for revenge against French intermeddling in 1779.[1] Thus France's designs to abase England too low and consequently herself to rise too high on the continent of Europe would be properly curbed.

At first England, France and Spain all eluded the Austrian offer. Next Russia in 1780 put forth suggestions for mediation. It was Catherine the Great's vainglorious ambition to bring Russia into a dominating position in the councils of western Europe, to magnify her prestige by becoming in effect guarantor of the international structure of the world. The British Ministry suggested that Austria be invited as co-mediator. At St. Petersburg was young Sir James Harris, one of the most able diplomatists in British history, who hoped to sway the Czarina. Austria agreed forthwith to a joint mediation. From Vienna in the summer of 1781 Prince Kaunitz, Austrian Chancellor and dean of European diplomatists, issued in the name of Austria and Russia a formal invitation to the *European* belligerents to meet at that capital to make peace with the assistance of Russia and Austria according to general principles laid down in the invitation. Great Britain already had accepted in principle subject to covert qualifications that the mediators would have nothing to say or do about the American Colonies.[2]

---

[1] We have already seen that in these former negotiations at Teschen the purpose of France was to keep the continent quiet so as to be able to devote her whole forces to the maritime war with Great Britain.

[2] The British Ministry unsuccessfully tried to bribe Catherine II to favor British desires at the proposed conference by offering to Russia the island of Minorca.

France and Spain accepted in principle but eluded in fact: France pending another last campaign in America, Spain in hopes of preparing a successful assault on Gibraltar.

The final campaign in America succeeded, thanks to a happy, improvised combination. Complete victory made peace possible in 1782 without any real assistance from the mistrusted mediators. We now know that if it had not been for the victory of 1781 that Vergennes was prepared to accept, at the hands of the mediators at Vienna, a peace on the basis of the existing war-map,[1] which would have compromised American independence and defaulted on the Franco-American alliance. The devious tissue of mediation diplomacy shows again, like France's alliance with Spain, how the United States had become involved, through its indispensable French alliance, in the complications of European diplomacy. The various proposals for mediation, by Spain, Austria, and Russia, and by Austria and Russia jointly, were also responsible for the formulation by Congress of its own terms of peace.

The first resolutions of the Continental Congress (August 14, 1779) on the terms of peace were drawn up, at the suggestion of France, in the expectation of a peace conference which might follow Spain's proposals for mediation. They were for the governance of John Adams, of Massachusetts, appointed plenipotentiary for the sole purpose of negotiating peace. These instructions pointedly forbade the plenipotentiary to begin any negotiations unless Great Britain should first recognize the United States as sovereign, free and independent. This independence must also be "assured and confirmed by the Treaty or treaties of peace, according to the form and effect of the Treaty of Alliance with his Most Christian Majesty." The required boundary was to be the St. John's River in the east and, roughly, the present northern boundary of New England and New York to the St. Lawrence at 45° north latitude; thence in a straight line to the southern end of Lake Nipissing; from Lake Nipissing straight to the source of the Mississippi (then unknown); on the west the Mississippi River; on the south the line of 31° north latitude from the Mississippi to the Chattahoochee, following that stream to its junction with the Flint, thence straight to the source of the St. Marys and down that river to the Atlantic Ocean.[2] If the line from Lake Nipissing to the source of the Mississippi could

---

[1] Except for New York City and Long Island, which he did not propose to leave in British possession. My *Hussey-Cumberland Mission, op. cit.*, shows the war-map of 1781 in America.

[2] See Map 5.

not be secured, the boundary might be drawn between that lake and the Mississippi anywhere north of 45°. If the designated eastern boundary between Nova Scotia and Massachusetts could not be agreed to, it might as a last recourse be left to a joint commission to determine. "Although it is of the utmost importance to the peace and Commerce of the United States that Canada and Nova Scotia should be ceded, and more particularly that their equal common right to the Fisheries should be guarantied to them, yet a desire of terminating the war hath induced us not to make the acquisition of these objects an ultimatum on the present occasion." With the consent of France, an armistice might be accepted, but only in case "all the forces of the enemy shall be immediately withdrawn from the United States." [1] "In all matters not above mentioned," concluded the instruction, "you are to govern yourself by the Alliance between his Most Christian Majesty and these States, by the advice of our allies, by your knowledge of our Interests, and by your own discretion, in which we repose the fullest confidence." Subsequently (October 18, 1780) Congress modified the instructions to allow of independence by a truce accompanied by evacuation of British troops.

In vain the French Minister at Philadelphia, Gérard, had striven to induce Congress to put its plenipotentiary under the full control of the French Court in the anticipated negotiations. His successor, La Luzerne, was to have better success.

John Adams never acted on his commission as sole plenipotentiary for peace. By the time he reached Europe, Spain's proposal of mediation was a mere matter of history, for that monarchy was already in the war. Adams irritated Vergennes by proposing openly to invite the British, anyway, to discuss peace, hoping thereby to throw on George III the odium of continuing the war. This was the first manifestation of what has since been dubbed "shirtsleeves diplomacy," supposed to be a characteristic of American dealing in foreign relations, i.e., undisguisedly telling the world where one stands in frank and open language and letting the world take it or leave it. Adams also told Vergennes that the United States was as valuable to French policy as France was to the United States. Later, when Vergennes discussed with Adams the possibility of going to a peace conference at Vienna, Adams saw through the network of snares for American independence. He insisted that if the United States attended any such conference it must be only

---

[1] This, presumably, meant the United States according to the boundaries laid down in the instructions.

after preliminary recognition of its full independence by the participating powers. Vergennes saw that he could not control Adams. He therefore sought to have Congress supplant him and even place his successor under the control of the French Minister himself. This became possible when presently it seemed desirable, in the darkest period of the war, to reconsider terms of peace, in anticipation of a formal proposal of mediation by Russia and Austria.

The second French Minister to the United States, La Luzerne, was more successful than Gérard in making Congress do the will of his master. By new instructions (June 15, 1781) Congress grouped John Adams in a Commission of five plenipotentiaries: Adams, Franklin, Jay, Jefferson (who did not reach Europe in time to participate) and Henry Laurens (still in the Tower of London, but released in time to take a feeble part in the peace). They, or a majority of them, or, in case of death or inability of the others to act, any one of them, were to have "liberty to secure the interest of the United States in such manner as circumstances may direct, and as the state of the belligerent and disposition of the mediating powers may require." Except for the one indispensable point of independence, the new instructions placed the American Commission fully under the advice and control of the French Court. Never in history has one people more trustingly and innocently submitted its fate to the disposal of a foreign power. We may well shudder to think what might have happened if it had not been for Yorktown. Should the American Commissioners follow their instructions, Vergennes would be able to modulate the progress of the negotiations among the several belligerents and mediators until the moment came when French interests were fully satisfied, and the interests of France's incompatible allies taken care of only if possible. Perhaps it might now be possible to defer a peace of American independence until Gibraltar were secured for Spain.

The stunning blow of Yorktown enabled the parliamentary opposition in England to overthrow the war government of Lord North and to insist on negotiations for peace. These negotiations began under the new Rockingham Ministry, which was really a shaky coalition of various groups of the opposition. It included Charles James Fox, now appointed Secretary for Foreign Affairs, who advocated outright recognition of American independence and negotiation thereafter of a peace. He believed that thus possessed of their main objective the United States would refuse to fight further for non-American objectives not included in the Franco-American alliance. If such a preliminary recognition were made, by royal proclamation, the negotiation of a peace with the United States, now a foreign nation, would fall within Fox's office. Lord Shelburne, a bitter rival of Fox, was Secretary for Home Affairs, which included what was left of colonial affairs. He was willing to acknowledge independence only as a last resort, and then preferably only in an article of a treaty, not to go into effect until the treaty was ratified. Pending completion of such a treaty, the "Colonies" were still technically under the administration of Shelburne's office. He wished to keep them there and had faint hopes that it was still not too late to patch up some sort of peace within the empire.

It was Shelburne who began the first conversations with the Americans, through an envoy, Richard Oswald, sent to Paris to sound out Benjamin Franklin, following a hint from the latter. It was Fox who began parleys at Paris with the European belligerents, through an accredited envoy of the Foreign Office, Thomas Grenville. Presently Lord Rockingham died. Shelburne became Prime Minister and took over control of the several negotiations. He left the American one resting significantly as the business of the Home Office and its new secretary, Thomas Townshend, and the European ones under the immediate supervision of the Foreign Office and its succeeding secretary Lord Grantham, with Alleyne Fitzherbert as plenipotentiary at Paris. Shelburne it was then upon whom fell the task of salvaging for the British Empire what he could out of the disaster. He soon became persuaded that he would have to yield American independence as the price of peace. It was his aim if possible to defer that recognition until the making of a treaty, and to have it a trading point for various British objects.

Richard Oswald was a former army contractor and slave merchant who had amassed a fortune out of dealing in those sources of human woe. Now an elderly Scot of a philosophic disposition, he had been one of Franklin's many friends and correspondents in England before the Revolution. He had no ambitions for political preferment that would spur him to seek every advantage in a negotiation. Shelburne apparently bethought of him because his supposedly benignant character would commend him to Franklin. The British Ministry was rather abjectly playing up to old Ben Franklin, the man who a few years ago had been reviled and humiliated at the bar of the House of Commons, and of whom throughout the war British diplomatists had spoken as a crafty and artful politician. In desperation they now made particular efforts to appeal to the benevolent humanity of the friendly

philosopher from Philadelphia and to his love for "old England." Doctor Franklin did not reject these subtle advances, but he and Vergennes
made it clear to Oswald and Grenville that Great Britain could expect
no separate peace from either France or the United States, and that
the allies would give nothing for American independence which was
an accomplished fact. Vergennes had by then turned the Anglo-American conversations over to separate discussion between the two parties
concerned. This was best, he said, provided that all negotiations went
hand in hand and that all treaties would depend on each other for validity. The French Minister preferred to do this lest the British be able
to convince the Americans that the presence of France in their discussions was holding up peace for the attainment of non-American objectives like Gibraltar, and thus lead them to desert France for England.
Without participating in the actual parleys between British envoys and
American Commissioners, Vergennes hoped still to control them.

During the confabulations with Oswald, which were of an informal
nature because the British agent still lacked full powers, Franklin confidentially let his old acquaintance know, as a favor, what the United
States expected in the way of peace: some *necessary* terms, and some
desirable terms. Meanwhile Thomas Grenville, Fox's representative,
had given the American diplomatist to understand that Great Britain
was prepared to make a preliminary and unconditional recognition of
the independence of the United States. Franklin's "necessary" terms
included "independence, full and complete in every sense" with evacuation of all troops; a boundary settlement which would confine the
boundaries of Canada at least to what they were before the Quebec
Act (this could be interpreted to limit Canada to the St. Lawrence
Valley); and a freedom of fishing on the Banks of Newfoundland "and
elsewhere." The "desirable" terms, which Franklin thought requisite
for a full and hearty reconciliation, added: about £500,000 or £600,000
by way of indemnification for American towns ruined and burned, with
some sort of official acknowledgment by the British Government of
the error made in distressing the former colonists; American ships and
trade to be received and have the same privileges in Great Britain and
Ireland as British ships, and reciprocally; finally, "giving up every part
of Canada." Immediately Oswald saw that his Government could
agree to the necessary terms. He even thought it not impossible that
Canada might be ceded. Franklin from the first had prepared him for
that as the simplest way of settling the whole business. After these
conversations Franklin quickly perceived that Oswald would make an

ideal negotiator and wrote to Lord Shelburne that he hoped he would
be formally continued and commissioned.

With the beginning of the Shelburne Government, Franklin observed
a tendency not to make the unconditional acknowledgment of the independence of the United States, which he had been led to believe by
Fox's agent would be preliminary to any formal negotiation. He therefore promptly disavowed the terms he had sketched out orally to Oswald,
terms which he had never revealed to Vergennes, nor for that matter
to anybody but Oswald. He now let Oswald know that before he could
make any commitment he must confer with his colleague Mr. Jay, recently arrived from Madrid, but temporarily ill. Presently Oswald
appeared with an advance copy of a formal commission to himself, which
was going through the seals in England, necessary to make it an authentic document. This curious paper empowered him to treat and
conclude with representatives of the "colonies or plantations, or any of
them, or any parts thereof." Far from recognizing the American Commissioners as plenipotentiaries of the United States, it persisted in considering them still in a colonial status, still British subjects. If no
peace of independence should have resulted from negotiations with
Oswald, under such a commission, the British Ministry could have contended very forcibly that it had never recognized the independence of the
United States.

Franklin and Jay sought Vergennes' advice whether to treat under
this commission of Oswald. Vergennes advised them to go ahead. He
said it was all right as long as Oswald treated with them under their
own commissions as plenipotentiaries of the United States. Did not the
King of England still call himself the King of France? asked Vergennes, and observed that even that did not prevent France from treating with British agents. Even Lafayette, now returned to France,
urged the Americans to proceed. This conference of the allied diplomatists at first persuaded Franklin that it was proper enough to go ahead
on this basis with Oswald. Jay demurred. He had become suspicious
of the good faith of the French Minister. He believed Vergennes was
not unwilling to postpone any British recognition of American independence until the formal treaties were agreed upon all around, and the
objectives of France's other ally, Spain, were finally achieved. Documentary evidence now available proves Jay's suspicions pretty well
founded. He succeeded in changing his older colleague's mind. The
two of them informed Oswald that he ought to show a commission
enabling him to treat with the plenipotentiaries of the United States of

America. Apparently they felt that this would be equivalent to an advance recognition of the independence of the United States on which Franklin had at first insisted.

We are now at the dramatic period of the negotiations. To whet Jay's suspicions of the French Court, an English agent put into his hands a translated copy of an intercepted despatch from Barbé-Marbois, French *chargé d'affaires* in the United States, to Vergennes, arguing that France should not support the American claim to a post-war right to participate in the inshore fisheries of British North America. The United States had no right under the terms of the alliance to French support for such a claim, and France did not want the future competition of New Englanders against her share of the North American fisheries; but Jay looked with misgivings on this despatch. At about this same moment came the climax of some informal discussions which Jay had been having with the Spanish Ambassador at Paris, Count de Aranda. Aranda had advanced claims to vast territories on the east bank of the Mississippi, from Florida to Michigan. These claims conflicted with the grants of the old colonial charters cut off since 1763 at the Mississippi by the Peace of Paris and interfered with the boundaries that Congress had mapped out for the United States and had instructed its commissioners to secure, namely, the Mississippi on the west and the line of 31° north latitude as the southern limit. Vergennes acting through his confidential secretary, Rayneval,[1] proposed to Jay a compromise line which would have abandoned the territory north of the Ohio to Great Britain, and would have divided that south of the Ohio and west of the mountains in the following manner: the western part of it (extreme western Tennessee, extreme western Kentucky, Mississippi and a part of Alabama) to be an Indian state under Spanish protection, the eastern part of it for the United States to do with what it wanted.[2]

Jay was astonished at this suggestion emanating from Vergennes. It would almost have done what Franklin later said, would have "cooped us up within the Alleghany Mountains." Jay's mounting suspicions reached the degree of action when he learned the next day that Rayneval had departed on a secret trip to the enemy capital. He leaped to the conclusion that the French agent had gone over to London to connive with Shelburne against the American boundaries, and to talk down the American claims to fisheries. Actually Vergennes had sent

[1] Joseph Mathias Gérard de Rayneval, brother to Conrad Alexandre Gérard, first French Minister to the United States and signer of the alliance.

[2] These conversations are set forth in Jay's reports, published by Wharton, *op. cit.*, and Aranda's *Diary*, published by Yela, *op. cit.* See Map D, p. 55.

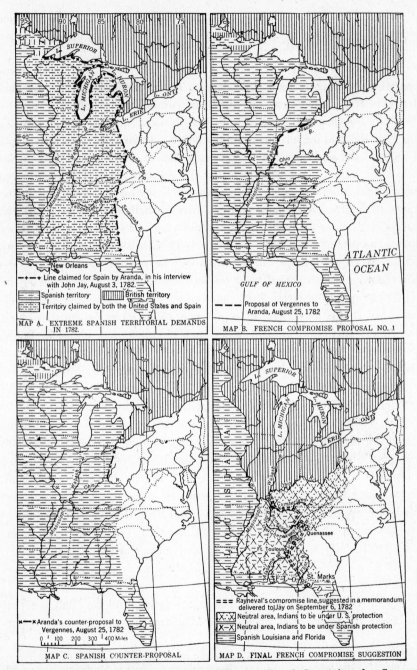

Map 4. Spanish and American Boundary Claims and French Suggestions for Compromise. 1782.

Rayneval to confirm, by a personal interview with Shelburne, some terms of peace which had been ascribed to Shelburne after an interview with him by a returning French admiral, de Grasse, who had just been released as prisoner of war, terms by which Shelburne had been represented as willing to cede Gibraltar.[1] These terms proved to be partially misrepresentations, but the visit established a confidential relationship between the French and British Governments which contributed to the making of the eventual peace. During the first interviews Rayneval did find occasion to deprecate the American claims to fisheries and boundaries. Shelburne gathered from Rayneval that France would not defend American claims, other than insisting on independence. "The point of Independence once settled," wrote Shelburne to the King, "he [Rayneval] appears rather jealous than partial to America upon other points, as well as that of the Fishery."[2] He also suggested to the enemy Prime Minister that the Americans might be put off the trail by keeping them ignorant of what went on between England, France and Spain. This was not a desertion by France of any obligations under the alliance, but it was a betrayal of confidence. We cannot be surprised that the American Commissioners under such circumstances would be loathe to act in full confidence with their French ally during the remainder of the negotiations or to be controlled in the last analysis by Vergennes' advice, as Congress had required of them, or that they, too, might indulge in confidential conversations with the enemy.

Jay on his own responsibility, without telling even his colleague Franklin, sent an English hanger-on, one Benjamin Vaughan, over to tell Lord Shelburne that he had better furnish Oswald with the required commission; that it was to the interest of France, but not of England, to postpone the recognition of independence until the final treaty, that "it hence appeared to be the obvious interest of Britain immediately to cut the cords which tied us to France, for that, though we were determined faithfully to fulfil our treaty and engagements with this court, *yet it was a different thing to be guided by their or our construction of it.*"[3]

Jay did not intend to make a separate peace, and we shall see that such was not done. But Shelburne's Ministry thought it was an oppor-

---

[1] Doniol, *op. cit.*, V, 104-106, 120-145.

[2] The printed *Correspondence of King George the Third from 1760 to December 1783* (6 Vols., London, 1927-1928), VI, 125. Rayneval's own report of his negotiations on this trip to England is printed in *Revue d'histoire diplomatique*, VI (1892), 62-89, and in Doniol's *Histoire*, V, 603-626.

[3] Jay to Livingston, Nov. 17, 1782, Wharton, *Diplomatic Correspondence*, VI, 30.

tunity here to split apart the two allies. The Cabinet had already decided (August 29) that, if indispensable for a peace on the basis of
Franklin's "necessary" terms, it would go as far as to have the King
recommend to Parliament an advance recognition of American independence.[1] It was all the easier now to vote (September 19) Oswald's altered commission in return for such a peace, with the understanding
that independence was to be recognized only in the first article of a
formal treaty. Jay had been alarmed by French activities into construing the new British commission, altered to suit his own taste, as
adequate in lieu of an explicit grant of independence.

As soon as Oswald appeared with his formally altered commission,
empowering him to treat with plenipotentiaries of the United States of
America, negotiations went ahead in earnest between him and Jay,
Franklin having become ill at this stage. By October 5 the two had
agreed on a draft for preliminary articles of peace, not to go into effect,
however, until corresponding preliminary articles were signed between
France and Great Britain. Not until then could there be any cessation of hostilities. The final terms must be envisaged through the articles of this draft, which was in Jay's handwriting, and the changes
which were made in it.

The Jay draft of October 5 contained Franklin's necessary articles,
plus a new article stipulating freedom of navigation by subjects and
citizens of both parties on the Mississippi River, and elsewhere throughout all their dominions, on the terms of nationals. This last was one
of the desirable terms and was not retained in the final treaty. The
boundary corresponded to that laid down by the first instructions of
Congress, of 1779, to John Adams, including on the north what we may
call the "Nipissing" line, and leaving (by a concession appended after
the articles had been first drafted) the northeast boundary subject to
later settlement by a joint commission. We see nothing of the giving
up of all of Canada in this draft, or from now on. Jay had become so
alarmed at the prospect of Spanish acquisition of the left bank of the
Mississippi that he was eager to relinquish any putative chance that the
complaisant Oswald may once have inspired of getting Canada for
the United States. He argued to the British that it would be well for
them to acknowledge the boundaries desired by Congress because the
back lands would fill up with English-speaking settlers who in the future
would form a great consuming market for English manufactures that
could be routed into the new American West by two vestibules of com-

[1] *Correspondence of George III, op. cit.,* VI, 118.

merce, the St. Lawrence-Great Lakes water route on the north, and the Mississippi River on the south from the Gulf of Mexico. He even encouraged the British to seek the return of the Floridas in the final peace, so anxious was he to get Spain out of there and out of the territory north of there. Accordingly a secret article provided that in case Great Britain should retain the Floridas in the definitive peace, then the southern boundary of the United States should be pushed north to the latitude of the mouth of the Yazoo River (present city of Vicksburg, Miss.).

Historians have wondered whether Jay's insistence on an altered commission for Oswald served to hold up the negotiation of preliminary articles so long as to ruin Franklin's design for getting all of Canada. On September 30 news reached London that the Franco-Spanish siege of Gibraltar had been partly relieved, and from then on British tone and demands began to stiffen. There is no evidence that the situation of Gibraltar entered into the discussions in Paris of Oswald and Jay, or of Oswald and his Government before October 5. There is no evidence to show that Lord Shelburne or any other responsible British official (other than Oswald) ever considered giving up Canada, not to mention Nova Scotia. There is plenty of evidence to show that Jay was quite willing to accept the expansive Nipissing boundary (demanded by Congress) without continuing Franklin's efforts to get all of Canada. He would do this in order to protect the territories of the United States against Spanish intrusions. This explains the main outline of the boundary arrangements which were laid down in the final treaty. Jay clinched title to the West, though there was left a legacy of boundary and navigation disputes to be fought out later with Spain.[1]

Oswald initialed the Jay draft only *ad referendum*. When it arrived in London, British hopes were revived by the good news from Gibraltar. The Cabinet resolved to make a stand for the improvement of the Jay draft: by pushing south and west the boundary of Canada as much as possible, by securing compensation for British Loyalists whose property had been confiscated during the war by the United States, by committing the United States to obliging its citizens to pay in sterling money all pre-war debts to British creditors, and by seeking to exclude American fishermen from the territorial waters of remaining British North America. New instructions to this effect went off to Oswald; and Henry

[1] See my article "Canada and the Peace Settlement of 1782-3," in *Canadian Hist. Rev.*, XIV (Sept., 1933), 265-284. This is somewhat revised and extended in my *Diplomacy of the American Revolution, op. cit.*, Ch. XVII.

Strachey, a youthful and energetic Undersecretary of State in the Home Office, was sent over to Paris to assist Oswald with technical data and to strengthen his resistance.

There followed six weeks of give and take. Franklin countered the British demands for compensations for Loyalists with demands for indemnification for property of American citizens wantonly destroyed by British armies, such as the burning of towns. He produced a formidable list of such claims. The British negotiators finally accepted an article protecting Loyalists from *further* confiscations and distresses, and agreeing that Congress should "recommend" to the individual states restitution of confiscated estates, or compensation. They all realized that it was not certain, perhaps not likely, that the states would carry out the recommendation. John Adams, who had now arrived from The Hague, persuaded his colleagues to agree to the payment of private debts, "heretofore" contracted, in sterling money. With Adams a debt was a debt. He said the United States had no desire to cheat anybody. Adams led the Commission's fight for the fisheries, but finally accepted a British wording (which had been subtly introduced in the treaty of Paris of 1763 to define French fishing privileges): instead of insisting on the "right" of American citizens to catch fish within British territorial waters as before the war, he accepted the "liberty" to do such, which implied negation of a right. Even preservation of a liberty to take fish in those waters was a great point won. It is difficult to see how Americans could have any claim at all to fishing within British territorial waters, although lawyers have since argued that they must have retained it out of a "division of empire." On the northern and eastern boundaries the American Commission made some concessions. Strachey was able to advance the northeastern boundary westward from the certain St. John to the cartographically uncertain St. Croix, thus winning a very considerable zone of territory previously claimed by Massachusetts and laying the basis for the later bitter northeast boundary dispute between the United States and Great Britain. At best Strachey was able to secure only minor territorial concessions because—as a Canadian historian, now a professor in an American university, has put it recently—Great Britain was "sick of the war." [1] For a northern boundary the plenipotentiaries of the United States offered the British Government a choice of two lines: the line of 45° from the Connecticut River west to the Mississippi, or the present river-and-lake line. On the last day of the discussions Laurens, who had appeared

[1] Alfred Leroy Burt, *The Old Province of Quebec* (University of Minnesota, 1933).

very belatedly and inexcusably so, succeeded in inserting an article providing for the return to their American owners of slaves who had escaped into British lines during the war. All the British representatives at Paris agreed that this was the best that could be done and urged their Government to accept the treaty.

Shelburne's Cabinet voted to accept. They chose the river-and-lake boundary, on the north, as that was understood from Mitchell's Map, which the negotiators used—the most famous map [1] in the history of American diplomacy. And so the territory of the United States was delimited. And so the Anglo-American peace was shaped. Shelburne hoped that by signing the preliminary articles the United States in effect if not in law would be withdrawn from the war, and that it would now be easier for him to deal with Britain's enemies in Europe.[2] We may agree that Shelburne was right. By these terms he had won a point of vantage, and was able thereby better to salvage other imperial values in Europe, Africa and Asia.

When the time came to sign the preliminary Anglo-American articles, on November 30, 1782, the American Commissioners asked themselves whether they ought first to inform Vergennes of their content and ask him whether they ought to accept. They agreed not to do so. This was not a desertion by the United States of any obligation under the Franco-American alliance. It was a violation of their instructions which they committed at their own risk and triumphantly, for which they were never reproved except by the irritated Livingston who was in such close relationship in Philadelphia with the French Minister, La Luzerne. Congress would have accepted a peace with much less expansive boundaries than Franklin, Jay and Adams had won at Paris; if really necessary it would have taken the line of the Alleghany Mountains! Now that all the confidential archives of the several parties to the peace negotiations have been long since fully ventilated to historical scholarship, we may find no fault with Jay, Franklin, Adams, and Laurens for taking

---

[1] See remarks by Col. Lawrence Martin, printed by Hunter Miller, in *Treaties and Other International Acts of the United States* (Washington, 1931), III, 328-351; and also this eminent geographer's article on John Mitchell in *Dictionary of American Biography*.

[2] American historians have printed a very considerable body of matter trying to prove or disprove that the western conquests of George Rogers Clark had a determining influence in drawing the boundary of 1782. There is no evidence yet discovered to establish this. By the winter of 1781-1782, Clark had been obliged to withdraw his garrisons pretty much to the line of the Ohio, and the Northwest was No Man's Land, so far as military control was concerned. Even if Clark had continued in occupation of the Illinois towns, the British still held at the end of the war the controlling strategic posts of Michilimackinac, Detroit, Niagara and Oswego, all of them south of the boundary which they accepted.

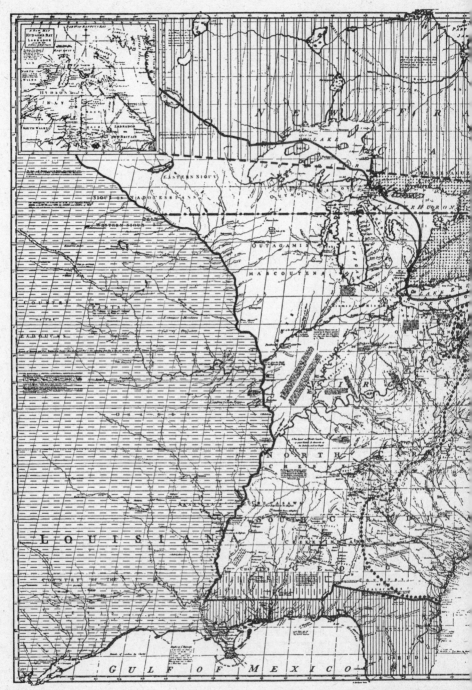

Map 5. Boundary Claims and Settlemen[t]

BOUNDARY CLAIMS AND SETTLEMENT IN THE
ANGLO-AMERICAN NEGOTIATIONS OF 1782
Placed on Mitchell's Map of North America of 1755

(On first impression of the third English edition)

The Negotiators used Mitchell's Map

———— Boundary by the Preliminary Articles of Peace, November 30, 1782.

– – – – Northern line desired, under instructions of the Continental Congress; coincides with "Mr. Oswald's line" of the draft of October 5 (dated October 8 by Wharton) except for the gap left on the northeast for adjustment after the proposed treaty. (The instructions of the Congress allowed this exception.)

–·–·– Alternate acceptable northern line under instructions of the Continental Congress. This was offered by the American Commissioners, as alternate to the river-and-lake line, November 5, 1782

•••• Conjectural minimum boundary acceptable to the Congress, 1782.

"Mr. Oswald's line" would have given this additional territory to the United States.

"Mr. Oswald's line" would have given this territory to Canada (so far as it can be determined by relating modern geographical knowledge to Mitchell's Map)

The Anglo-American preliminary articles of peace allowed this territory to British Florida providing Great Britain retained Florida in the definitive peace (which she did not)

The remainder of British Florida (before 1783)

Spanish Louisiana.

the Anglo-American Negotiations of 1782.

French agreement with Great Britain to become operative. Technically hostilities still continued between Great Britain and the Netherlands. Their preliminary peace was not signed until September 2, 1783. In vain the Dutch held out for restoration of all of their captured colonies and a specific recognition of the principles of the Armed Neutrality of 1780.

The preliminary articles of peace among the various belligerents were in the nature of an armistice agreement, after the conclusion of which it was hoped to work out further details during the indefinite armistice. Actually the tenor of the preliminary treaties was altered only in small details; in the case of the Anglo-American treaty not at all, despite some involved discussions. The preliminary treaties were signed all around as definitive treaties on September 3, 1783. Since ratification was immediate in Europe, and the preliminary articles had already been accepted by the Congress of the United States, the war ended then.

American citizens in their satisfaction over the victory of Franklin, Jay and Adams, must not lose sight of the final terms of the European peace settlement which ended the epochal American war. Aside from the one great blow, the loss of the thirteen colonies, which satisfied the principal war aim of France and of the United States, Great Britain did not suffer heavily in the general peace. In the treaty with France she relinquished all the restrictions that had been imposed on the French naval port of Dunkerque, but otherwise the treaty was pretty much a continuation of the territorial dispositions of the treaty of Paris of 1763, with only minor adjustments in the West Indies (Tobago to France) and Africa (Senegal River to France). France retained only her purely passive trading rôle in India, nothing more. In the Spanish treaty Great Britain ceded the Floridas, without defining their boundaries (thus the secret contingency envisaged by the article of the Anglo-American preliminaries never came into effect), and the island of Minorca in the Mediterranean, which had been captured by French and Spanish forces. It was agreed that British log-cutting settlements on "the Spanish continent" should be restricted within certain stipulated boundaries on the coast of Honduras without any derogation to Spanish sovereignty. George III retained Gibraltar, gateway to the Mediterranean, that old sea-area of civilization soon to become a vestibule of empire to the Orient. In the treaty with the Netherlands,[1] Great

---

[1] The preliminary articles were signed September 2, 1783, the day before the definitive peace of the other belligerents; and the Anglo-Dutch definitive treaty was signed May 20, 1784, ratified in London June 10, and at The Hague, June 15, 1784.

this step. On the contrary they are entitled to high praise.
achieved for their country, in the midst of European self-interest
tured by the experienced arts of eighteenth-century diplomacy,
greatest triumph in the history of American diplomacy. This they
at the beginning of their nation's history.

After the articles were signed without consulting France, it becam
necessary to inform Vergennes what they had done. For this the Commission deputed Franklin. Vergennes did not at first manifest any
astonishment, except at the favorable terms which his ally had extracted contingently from Great Britain. Nor did he refuse the loan
of 6,000,000 additional *livres* which the insatiable Philadelphian asked
in the same breath.

He did not think it wise to deny the Americans at this moment and
perhaps push them into an actual separate peace. Not until the fighting was really ended by the European preliminaries did Vergennes stop
the golden stream of subsidies and loans to the United States. A few
days after Franklin's announcement Vergennes rather belatedly reproved
the venerable doctor. The sagacious old man admitted that he and his
colleagues were guilty of some "impropriety" but urged his French
friend not to let the English get wind of this. This hint was enough.
Vergennes contentedly dropped the matter.

We may guess that Vergennes was relieved at the Anglo-American
preliminary articles because they offered him a means of bringing the
war to a close now that France's main object in breaking up the British
Empire had been achieved. To do this it was necessary to get Spain
to agree to a peace without Gibraltar to which she was entitled by the
convention of Aranjuez. It was now obvious that if the European allies
were to continue hostilities against Great Britain to recover Gibraltar
they could not hope to be assisted by the continuation of the war in
America. After another fortnight of sparring between Spain and Grea
Britain, and some further discussion of adjustments in the East a
West Indies and in Africa, the Spanish Ambassador at Paris, Coun
Aranda, took the responsibility of interpreting his despatches to
peace without Gibraltar.[1] His government accepted this, with
proving or praising him. On January 20, 1783, Spain and Franc
separate preliminary articles with Great Britain, and an arm
mediately went into effect, which automatically included
States, whose preliminary articles of November 30 requi

[1] R. Konetzke, *Die Politik des Grafen Aranda; ein Beitrag zur Gesch*
Englischen Weltgegensatzes im 18. Jahrhundert (Berlin, 1929).

Britain acquired the Dutch trading factory of Negapatam, on the coast of India opposite Ceylon, and presently turned it into a smuggling post for the penetration of the rich Dutch island, itself next to fall into full possession of the British. The Netherlands recognized the right of British subjects to trade and navigate freely among the Dutch East Indies. On the high seas the treaty required Dutch ships to continue to dip their flag to the Union Jack after the old custom. Of the principles of the Armed Neutrality neither the Dutch treaty of peace, nor any of the other treaties, said anything at all. Austria and Russia as mediators were permitted to sign the European peace treaties. It was an empty ceremony, out of deference to their gestures. They really had nothing to do with the negotiations. The mistrustful belligerents trusted each other more than they did the would-be neutral peacemakers.

We have mentioned that between the signature of the preliminary articles and the signature of the definitive articles some further negotiations took place without result. Though it is not worthwhile to say anything here about the European phases of these supplementary but negative discussions, a word is necessary as to the Anglo-American conversations. The British Parliament did not appreciate Shelburne's valuable services to the empire in the negotiation of the preliminary treaties, and turned him out of office. He was succeeded by a coalition, short-lived and anomalous government under Lord North and Charles James Fox, the former an inveterate enemy of American independence, the latter long looked upon as a consistent friend. Fox, as Secretary for Foreign Affairs again, allowed one David Hartley to go over to Paris to talk further with Franklin and see what he could do in negotiating some supplementary commercial articles. Hartley was another philosophical English friend of Franklin. During the war he had kept up a correspondence with the American diplomatist, hoping to persuade him of the desirability of some sort of political reconciliation within the empire. Fox agreed that Hartley might try to erect some sort of close commercial union between Great Britain and the United States which would be an acceptable substitute, a *succedaneum,* they called it, for the old colonial connection. This called for reciprocal trading privileges on the basis of nationals,[1] except that American ships could not carry into British ports other than their own products, and "federal" British-American alliance to be erected on the ruins of the Franco-American

[1] A clause to that effect in the Jay draft of Oct. 5 had run afoul of the British navigation laws, and was omitted from the preliminary articles of Nov. 30. This was a concession to Great Britain, for Jay had intended to balance the free navigation of the Mississippi with freedom of trade to British dominions everywhere.

alliance. The alliance would guarantee the protection of each other's territorial possessions in North America. By it the British navy would defend and protect the United States, and the United States would continue to support and strengthen the British navy with materials and seamen. It does not appear what protection there would have been in such an arrangement for the United States against being reduced to its old colonial status. Nor can we find out from the relevant documents whether American seamen for the British navy were to be secured according to the customary practice of impressment. But the British Government refused to sanction the idea of *fully* reciprocal free trade which the American plenipotentiaries made the basis for any further negotiations, and the Commissioners of the United States would not listen to any of Hartley's fond ideas for a *succedaneum:* a federal union outside the empire to replace the now forever vanished possibility of a federal union within the Empire. Hartley persisted with his proposals after Fox had ordered him to drop them. Finally the Foreign Minister was obliged peremptorily to call him back to London. It was Hartley who signed the definitive treaty for Great Britain.[1]

The United States now stood independent before the world. The exigencies of European diplomacy of the eighteenth century had given the opportunity from which that independence was fashioned. The great question next to face American diplomacy was to preserve independence against a selfish and merciless world of conflicting nations. Happily an event even more world-shaking than the American Revolution was to occur in France in 1789 which would make this possible. Before we turn to the significance of the French Revolution in the diplomatic history of the United States it is well to survey the problems of foreign relations which confronted the first union of the American states from 1783 to 1789.

[1] For more details about the proposed *succedaneum* see *Am. Secs. State and Their Diplomacy, op. cit.,* I, 215-217.

CHAPTER V

THE DIPLOMATIC EFFORTS OF THE CONFEDERATION

(1783-1789)

THE French Minister of Foreign Affairs, Vergennes, had once re-marked, when pressing Spain to recognize the United States and join the Franco-American alliance, that a confederation of republics would be an innocuous territorial neighbor. The republican type of state he considered as necessarily non-aggressive. Certainly the remaining six years of peace that closed the history of the Confederation of the Thirteen United States proved the justice of that remark. The great problem of the Confederation was whether it was strong enough to live at all even under the most serene conditions and with the most peaceable and tractable neighbors. Under the embarrassments of im-perfect union and impotent national government, the task of the Con-federation in the realm of foreign affairs was to fit the new nation safely into the normal world of contentious states and to embark with them upon the functions of commercial life. It was not to prove equal to this task.

The statesmen of independence had exaggerated expectations of the felicities of a trade with all the world unhampered by the restrictions of the old British navigation laws which had obliged most colonial ex-ports and imports to flow through the island of England on their way to and from the markets of other countries. They looked forward eagerly to the profits of a direct intercourse with all foreign nations. Congress immediately charged the commissioners who had made peace to encourage the advances of any commercial nations and to negotiate with them treaties of commerce and amity. Already, immediately after the general preliminaries of peace, Franklin had signed such a treaty with Sweden (April 3, 1783). It was based on the model Plan of 1776 and the French and Dutch commercial treaties, with a new article that permitted each party, both being neutral, to convoy the other's ships in time of war. Sweden was thus the first country with whom we entered into formal commercial relations after the war. This treaty in effect has been revived and elaborated in various later treaties throughout the history of the perfectly peaceful relations between the United States

and Sweden and Norway. In 1784 Congress established a commission
for the express purpose of negotiating treaties of commerce and amity
with other powers. It consisted of Benjamin Franklin, John Adams,
and Thomas Jefferson—the new minister presently to succeed [1] Franklin at the Court of France. The instructions to the new commission
contained some additions to the principles embodied in the Plan of
1776, and are sometimes alluded to as the Plan of 1784: prohibition
of privateering in case of war between the treaty parties; contraband
not to be confiscated but purchased, or at least taken off without bringing in the neutral ship and remaining cargo; application of the formula "imminent danger" to the definition of blockade. There was a
design to supplement the existing treaties with France and the Netherlands and Sweden with such new articles, but this was never done.

Under the new instructions the commissioners negotiated a treaty
with Prussia, in 1785, to which the aged Franklin put his name before
returning home; and in 1787 a delegated agent of Adams and Jefferson signed one with Morocco. Abortive negotiations with other powers,
notably Austria and Denmark, failed because the growing ineptitude
and powerlessness of the Confederation to enforce its treaties against
the thirteen component states convinced foreign nations that the Continental Congress had ceased to be a responsible body and that the
United States itself might soon cease to be a nation. The treaty with
Prussia included some novel articles, idealistic in nature, which had not
previously appeared in European practice. They were partly the result
of Franklin's humanitarian outlook on international affairs. Included
were the new propositions in regard to abolition of privateers in case of
war between the two nations; and the provision for the purchase instead
of confiscation of "articles heretofore deemed contraband." It also included an article that had been written into the Dutch treaty of 1782,
giving a time period of nine months for the retirement of innocent
enemy aliens in case of war between the treaty parties; and a provision
for neutral convoys like that in the Swedish treaty. The article free
ships free goods was excepted from a renewal of this treaty in 1799,
but reincorporated in the new treaty of 1828, as were the other maritime articles of 1785, but not the beneficent one protecting the persons and property of alien enemies in time of war between the two
parties. The Prussian treaties are an example of nations attempting

[1] When Jefferson was first received at the French Court, Louis XVI remarked politely,
"You replace Dr. Franklin, I hear." Jefferson's reply immediately established his good
graces: "I succeed him. Nobody could replace him."

to mitigate the severity of warfare by frank provisions which anticipate even the contingency of war between the parties which signed the treaty. When the United States and Germany became involved in war in 1917 these above-mentioned stipulations of the treaty with Prussia were still in existence, but the practices of the European belligerents had so wiped away the old definitions of contraband that they could no longer be distinguished, and German submarine warfare had destroyed its foundations.

The treaty with Morocco was the one successful negotiation with a piratical Barbary state for the purpose of bringing immunity to American shipping in the Mediterranean from the unblushing depredations of the professional corsairs of northern Africa. Separation from British sovereignty had destroyed the protection which colonial ships formerly enjoyed under the British flag in Mediterranean waters. The treaties of the United States with France and the Netherlands contained hopeful articles by which each of those powers agreed to try to help make favorable treaties with the Barbary states, but this did no good. American shipping was at the mercy of those robbers. The United States must make "arrangements" with them or fight to protect its sailors and ships. The Sultan of Morocco was the least obnoxious of the rascally potentates. Reputed agents of his had been endeavoring to obtain a treaty since 1782, with liberal commissions for themselves. He detained an American ship at Tangier in 1784 in order to show Congress that it would be necessary to make a treaty of amity with him. Congress responded by commissioning Adams and Jefferson to make treaties with all the Barbary states and Turkey. They were successful only in the case of Morocco, where little or no money was required. Largely through the intercession of the Spanish Government, which at that time was engaged in negotiations with the United States by which it hoped to close up the Mississippi, a dignified and favorable treaty was made, without the payment of the tribute usually so necessary. It provided that in future wars captives should be treated as prisoners of war and not enslaved, and set up friendly commercial relations between the two nations. Like later treaties with the Barbary states there was an extra-territorial provision: in case of any disputes between American citizens residing in Morocco, the consul should decide between them and if necessary the United States Government might enforce the consul's decision. The peace confirmed by this treaty was not interrupted by renewed depredations as were the later treaties with Algiers and Tripoli. American relations with Morocco continued peaceful and relatively uneventful until the incorporation of that kingdom under French sovereignty in the twentieth century.

The rulers of Algiers, Tripoli and Tunis in their sinister profession of piracy set in unabashed to make sport of American property and citizens. Unprotected by any navy, the merchant ships were easy prey. American sailors were enslaved with impunity. The Algerians captured two American vessels in 1785 and held their crews and passengers, twenty-one men, for ransom; $6,000 each for the captains, $4,000 for each passenger, $1,400 for each sailor. Adams and Jefferson thought on their own responsibility of offering, through an agent sent to the Coast to negotiate treaties, $200 a man, thinking that the captives might later agree to reimburse Congress; but the Algerian Dey sneered at such derisory tribute. The United States was then poor. Congress could not collect taxes to pay its own expenses or the interest on its loans, to say nothing of ransom for captive citizens. The Bey of Tripoli demanded 30,000 guineas for a thirty-year peace with him, which might be paid in installments; or he would refrain for one year, at 12,500 guineas, from plunder and enslavement. Even if willing to pay—and John Adams wrote home that it would be cheaper than war (to which Jefferson disagreed)—Congress could not raise the money. John Jay, Secretary of Foreign Affairs and advocate of a new national union and government, was grimly familiar with this abject condition. He felt that rather than to try to pay anything it were better to let the humiliation sink into American public opinion. It might at least be a factor in spurring political reform and the establishment of respectable government strong enough to protect its citizens against these avaricious freebooters and slave catchers.[1]

The new commercial treaties with Sweden and Prussia, and the older ones, with France and the Netherlands, established the formal relationship between the United States and Europe for the next decade—until the wars of the French Revolution completely disturbed the European scene. But American trade did not, as hoped, follow these treaties. The great volume of it still went to England, as it had done before the war. The bonds of culture and of custom, not to mention the long-term credit which English merchants were willing and able to advance,

[1] Relations with the Barbary states are handled in great detail in: G. W. Allen, *Our Navy and the Barbary Corsairs* (N. Y., 1905); Emile Dupuy, *Etudes d'histoire d'Amérique; Américains et Barbaresques (1776-1824)* (Paris, 1910); C. O. Paullin, *Diplomatic Negotiations of American Naval Officers, 1778-1883* (Baltimore, 1912); R. W. Irwin, *The Diplomatic Relations of the United States with the Barbary Powers, 1776-1816* (Chapel Hill, N. C., 1931).

still dominated American imports, and exports had largely to follow the same pathway.

During the first months of peace it had seemed possible that a favorable treaty of commerce might be made between Great Britain and the United States. Hartley and the American Commissioners had talked about it before the definitive peace was signed, and Hartley was enthusiastic. Fox listened to the English ship-owners and was unwilling to let American shipping into the carrying trade between the remaining British colonies and England, as before the war. William Pitt, the younger, who as Prime Minister succeeded the Fox-North Coalition in 1784, was sympathetic to a restoration of trade with the United States on terms of entire equality; but pressure from the ship-owning interests, and from the American Loyalists in Canada, who wanted a monopoly of supplying the West Indies with continental products, overcame his liberal tendencies. By act of Parliament and subsequent orders-in-council Great Britain established trade with America on a one-sided basis. American raw materials including naval stores might be brought into England in American ships. These were indispensable to British manufactures and the British navy. No manufactured products could be imported from America to compete with English industries. American ships could not trade with British North America, nor with the British West Indies; what these colonies required from the United States must be brought in British bottoms. In England political and economic thought, at first interested in the liberal theories of Adam Smith, had been captured after the war by the writings of the mercantilist Lord Sheffield, who contended that now that the United States had become independent Great Britain should not concern itself in extending to the former colonies the commercial privileges they had enjoyed under the old empire. There was no danger, Sheffield showed, of the United States being able to retaliate with tariffs or navigation laws of its own against British trade which continued to dominate the American market. The American Confederation was too feeble for this, as helpless as the Diet of Germany. Confidential observers of the Ministry in the United States pointed out that the union was really on the point of dissolution. Accordingly throughout the period of the Confederation, the British Government controlled the American trade according to its own convenience and profit, and contemptuously refused to make any treaty of commerce. Congress lacked any authority to pass laws regulating commerce; and the thirteen states could not unanimously agree to amend the articles to give that power.

Pitt's Government refused even to exchange diplomatic representatives with the United States. John Adams, whom Congress appointed as American Minister to the Court of Great Britain,[1] found himself received unsympathetically and able to do very little in the way of establishing diplomatic relations on a cordial or even effectual basis. He asked to be recalled, but did not leave England until 1788.

Without a treaty of commerce, with no regular diplomatic relations between the two countries, it was impossible to advance the settlement of a number of serious issues which appeared following the peace settlement of 1783. These issues were: the lack of a commercial agreement; the northern frontier posts; pre-war debts; the treatment of returning Loyalists; the question of slaves carried away by British armies evacuating the seaport cities; the northeast boundary. We have already noticed the commercial issue. Each of the others now requires brief mention.[2]

Great Britain had held successfully during the Revolution seven fortified posts south of the river-and-lake boundary between the United States and Canada: Dutchman's Point and Pointe-au-Fer, at the boundary end of Lake Champlain; Oswegatchie, on the New York shore of the St. Lawrence; Oswego, on the southern shore of Lake Ontario, commanding the portage to the Mohawk-Hudson route; Niagara, N. Y.; Detroit; and Michilimackinac, dominating the passages where Lakes Superior, Michigan and Huron join their waters. These fortifications controlled strategically the whole frontier and also the military alliance and fur-trade of the Indian tribes who inhabited the southern drainage shed of the Great Lakes region and even farther south to the Ohio River itself. Despite this military hold on the country, Lord Shelburne, who knew very little about Canada, had accepted the boundary line of 1782. The treaty agreed that all British forces remaining within it should be straightway evacuated "with all convenient speed." This was a surprise to the fur-traders of Montreal and to the British officers in charge of the interior forts. The fur-traders pointed out the disadvantages to their business of the new frontier, which cut off some of their most important interior trade routes, like the Grand Portage between Lake Superior and its upper tributaries. They anxiously importuned the Government to put off

[1] On receiving Adams, George III made some jesting allusion to the American's reputed predilection for France. Adams promptly responded: "I must avow to your Majesty, I have no attachment but to my country." The King quickly replied: "An honest man will have no other."

[2] I have treated these questions in more detail in my *Jay's Treaty: a Study in Commerce and Diplomacy* (N. Y., 1923).

evacuation as long as possible, for at least two or three seasons, in order that they might wind up and readjust their trade with a minimum loss. The commanders of the posts pointed out that if the Indians were suddenly abandoned to the United States they might consider themselves betrayed by their allies—they might even turn and bite the hand that had fed them.[1] Meanwhile the British officers covertly nursed the native affections and continued gifts of food and munitions to which the tribes had grown accustomed during the war. All the interior country still throbbed with memories of the butcheries of Pontiac's Conspiracy twenty years before. These remonstrances from Canada caused the colonial office in London to issue a secret order to the Governor-General of Canada not to evacuate the posts until further instructions. The order was sent out April 8, 1784, the evening before George III proclaimed the treaty of peace to be in effect and enjoined all his subjects to obey its articles. For twelve more years British troops continued to garrison the posts. They forbade the navigation of the Great Lakes by American merchant ships. A British customs officer was stationed at Oswego, N. Y., to shut off American goods from that post and the lakes.[2] Officials of a carefully organized Indian Department did not cease their activities among the tribes far within territory of the United States. Presently the Government of Pitt found in the status of the pre-war debts a convenient pretext to advance as a justification for this occupation.

The treaty of peace had stipulated that creditors on either side should meet with no lawful impediment to the recovery of full value in sterling money of all *bona fide* debts contracted "heretofore." During hostilities some of these debts had been confiscated into the treasuries of various states, mostly southern states. Following the war some of the states refused to let go of such, and put further legal obstacles (stay laws, arbitrary appraisals, paper money) in the way of full recovery. It might be argued that this was done out of irritation at British violation of the treaty in refusing to evacuate the posts, but the plain fact of the matter is that Congress had no authority to prevent the states from doing this, and we may presume they would have done it anyway. There was no supreme court of the entire union to which creditors might appeal for justice under the treaty. There was no executive authority to compel the states to observe the treaty scrupulously. Secretary John Jay, who had no knowledge of the secret British order of April 8, believed

[1] This has been emphasized by A. L. Burt, "A New Approach to the Problem of the Western Posts," in *Canad. Hist. Assoc. Ann. Repts.* (1931), 2-17.
[2] W. E. Stevens, *The Northwest Fur Trade, 1763-1800* (University of Illinois, 1928), 98.

that retention of the posts was not unjustified, under the circumstances.

The British Government also objected to the treatment meted out in some states to returning Loyalists. The treaty stated that there should be no further prosecutions or confiscations on account of parts taken in the war, and that Congress would recommend to the states the restoration of confiscated properties. The states, within their constitutional rights, refused to follow the recommendation when it was faithfully made. This the negotiators had expected. Parliament recognized the propriety of this option by itself appropriating monies for the relief of Loyalists. When a citizen of New York sued a Loyalist for arrears of rents on her property occupied during the war, Alexander Hamilton successfully defended the suit [1] (though the state legislature later overrode the state court). It was eventually recognized that Great Britain had no real case on the point of Loyalists.

The dispute over embarked slaves is not pleasing to the twentieth-century humanitarian mind. The treaty had specifically said that British troops should be evacuated without carrying away any negroes or other property of the American inhabitants. Nevertheless they took away several thousand slaves. The owners had a legal grievance weakened by its very nature in the eyes of the world.[2]

The treaty of peace had indicated the St. Croix River, on Mitchell's Map of 1755, as the northeastern boundary. The physical location of that river was sufficiently uncertain to allow of a dispute, particularly when each party could claim more territory thereby. The United States, espousing the claim of Massachusetts, asserted that the easternmost of two possible streams, the Magaguadavic, was the boundary. The British Government, supporting the claims of frontier colonists of Nova Scotia, contended for the Schoodiac, nine miles to the west. Since the sources of these rivers lay much further even than their mouths to the east and west, respectively, the area in dispute was very considerable. Already the Government of Nova Scotia was making grants of land to Loyalist refugees on the eastern bank of the Schoodiac, and Massachusetts was protesting to Congress against this alleged invasion.[3]

Posts, debts, Loyalists, evacuated slaves, trade, boundaries—none of these issues, except the minor boundary question, need have existed had the United States been a power capable of resolutely defending its rights against all comers. Bereft of active support from the French

[1] In the case of *Rutgers vs. Waddington*.

[2] F. A. Ogg, "Jay's Treaty and the Slavery Interests of the United States," in *Ann. Repts. of the Am. Hist. Assoc.*, 1901, I, 275-298.

[3] J. B. Moore, *International Adjudications* (N. Y., 1929), Vols. I, II.

alliance, and lacking union necessary to confront foreign powers, a nation only in name, with no army, no navy, no executive, no national courts, no control even over national commerce, there was nothing that could be done to oblige the former enemy to comply with the treaty of peace which circumstances of European diplomacy had obliged him to sign in 1783. Affairs remained in this unsatisfactory stage throughout the period of the Confederation. The Governor-General of Canada, aware of the imminent contingency of a break-up of the United States, entered into secret negotiations with a separatist element in Vermont, tempting them with especial trade privileges via the Champlain-St. Lawrence system, which were denied to the thirteen states. It was hoped that when the break-up came, Vermont could be easily attached to Canada, and also the entire territory north of the Ohio River where the handful of actual inhabitants only weakly supported the spineless union of the coastal states. It would then be only a matter of time before British sovereignty would be restored over the lost colonies.

The issues outstanding between Spain and the United States after 1783 were not unlike those with Great Britain on the score of boundaries and relations with the border Indians, except that Spain had a stronger case. In sinister symmetry to the British occupation of the Great Lakes country Spain held the lower southwest, not only occupied it, but claimed it as Spanish territory. What with the hostile activities and territorial pretensions of these two European monarchies the entire western country continued in jeopardy. With Spain there were also the issues of the navigation of the Mississippi, and of commercial relations.[1]

We remember that the preliminaries of peace between the United States and Great Britain had recognized the line of 31°–St. Marys River as the southern boundary, providing by a secret article that in case Florida should remain British at the general peace the line should be moved north to the latitude of the mouth of the Yazoo River (Vicksburg), which had been the boundary of British West Florida since 1764. When the preliminary Anglo-American articles were signed West Florida was in the occupation of victorious Spanish troops, including some of the region between 31° and the Yazoo. In the Anglo-Spanish treaty Spain received the Floridas without any definition of their boundary. There is no evidence yet presented to show that Spain knew anything about the secret

---

[1] A fuller discussion of the various issues with Spain, with further references, can be found in my *Pinckney's Treaty; a Study of America's Advantage from Europe's Distress, 1783-1800* (Baltimore, 1926), and A. P. Whitaker, *The Spanish-American Frontier, 1783-1795; the Westward Movement and the Spanish Retreat in the Mississippi Valley* (Boston and New York, 1927).

contingent article (which never went into effect in the final peace) ; but the Spanish rightly contended that their new conquest could not be bounded by the articles of the Anglo-American treaty. They further claimed by right of conquest against a common enemy territory on the east bank of the Mississippi above Florida as far north as the Ohio. According to whether the disputed boundary should eventually be fixed at the Ohio, or at the Yazoo, or at the line of 31°, then the lower reaches of the Mississippi, that is to say, 1080, or 478, or 312 miles of that river, as the case might be, would flow between Spanish banks. As a consequence, Spain had exclusive control over shipping entering in and out of the river even though the vessels were destined to or came from American territory on the left bank upstream from the boundary. She had just as much right to the exclusive navigation of the lower river as Portugal did over the Tagus, the upper waters of which flow out of Spanish territory to the sea at Lisbon. That the treaty of 1763 had stipulated free navigation of the entire Mississippi for British and for French subjects made no difference, according to Spanish statements: true, Spain had taken over that servitude upon receiving Louisiana from France, but the obligation of the treaty of Paris to Great Britain legally ceased upon the outbreak of war with that power in 1779. Against this solid argument the United States could cite only: (1) the boundary of the Anglo-American treaty (we have noted the weakness of this), (2) the sea-to-sea charters of the old colonies (they had already been cut short at the Mississippi by the treaty of Paris; it was perhaps as reasonable that the Florida part of them should be amputated by the Anglo-Spanish treaty of 1783), (3) that by "natural law" an up-river state ought to have free access to the ocean through down-stream foreign territory (a persuasion not then sanctioned by international law). In 1784 Spanish authorities at New Orleans, acting on express instructions, gave notice that henceforth the river would be closed to American shipping. This cut off the only usable highway, by water, to the markets of the outside world for the newly populating American West. The prosperity of the settlements of Kentucky and Tennessee depended upon the unrestricted navigation of the Mississippi.

Closely related to the boundary question and to the Mississippi question was that of the status of the Indian tribes within the disputed territory: Creek, Cherokee, Chickasaw, Choctaw, inhabiting the present states of Mississippi and Alabama and the contiguous fringes of Tennessee and Georgia. Spain contended they were under her sovereignty and made treaties of defensive and offensive alliance with them, providing subsidies for the chieftains and firewater and munitions for the warriors. Congress made treaties to incorporate them within the United States. The Indians made treaties both ways and sided with the stronger power, which at this time was Spain. The Spanish connection strengthened their border raids and incursions, so deadly to American frontiersmen, so fruitful a cause of intermittent savage warfare. There was a tendency for the Indians acting under Spanish protection to seek an understanding with those acting in the north under British tutelage, and with this a possibility of a widespread rising which might sweep the whole West of its new settlements. It was vital to the territorial integrity of the United States that the western country should be cleared of these twin menaces, that the southwestern boundary be agreed with Spain, that the northern frontier be freed of British occupation and control. It was vital that somehow the Mississippi be opened to the sea for the navigation of the "men of the western waters," as the new frontiersmen delighted to call themselves. But as equivalents for inducing Spain to concede a desirable boundary and free navigation the United States had absolutely nothing to offer.

The remaining issue with Spain was the regularization of commercial intercourse. The trade with Spain constituted only a very small fraction of the total commerce of the United States, but it was at the sufferance of decrees which might be changed at the whim of the Spanish Government at any time, involving loss, perhaps ruin, to commerce embarked under a previous decree. What the United States wanted most of all, and what Spain still refused to allow to any foreign country, was freedom to trade with the colonial dominions of Spanish America. For the neighboring new republic such a commerce was far more inviting, far more expansive in its possibilities than for any other foreign nation. Even so, why should Spain yield it? The United States had nothing to offer in return.

There seemed no reason why Spain should concede to the weak and divided American Confederation valuable boundaries and privileges merely because the latter desired them. Apparently all that she had to fear was that the rapidly populating American West might of itself, with adequate force, descend the Mississippi, occupy the boundaries it claimed, break through any paper trammels upon the navigation of that river, and begin to force a contraband commerce through the frontiers of the rich Spanish provinces to the southwest. This was a very real dread to the responsible officials in New Orleans. We shall see that they set about dispelling the danger by intriguing with separatist elements in the Kentucky country, seeking to attach them to Spanish interests,

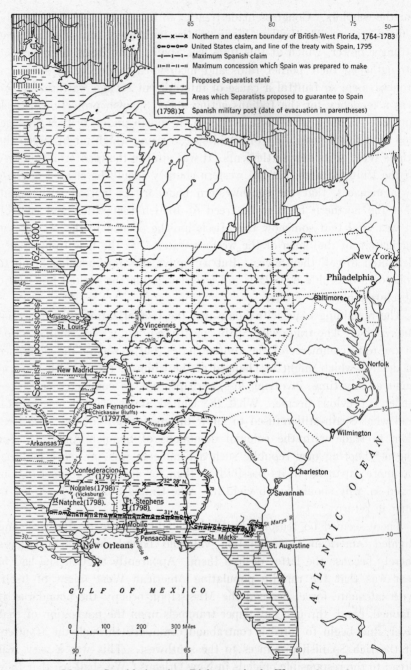

Map 6. Spanish-American Diplomacy in the West, 1783-1798.

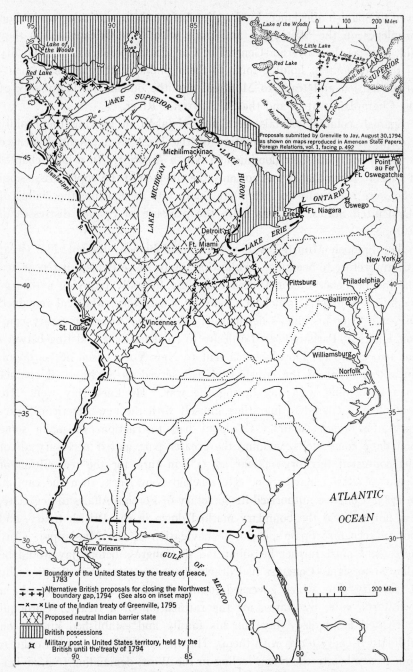

Map 7. British-American Diplomacy in the West, 1783-1796.

even to Spanish allegiance, by dangling before them particular navigation privileges on the Mississippi and trade with New Orleans. This they did, even as the Governor-General of Canada tampered with the loyalty of the Vermonters, holding forth to them similar particular inducements of navigation and trade to Montreal and the outside world by way of the Champlain waters and the St. Lawrence River.

Spanish colonial officials were not mistaken in viewing the rapidly growing and turbulent population of the West as a potential menace to the security of their dominion in North America. In a later chapter it will be shown that it was not only the riflemen of the upper Mississippi who were eventually to intimidate Spain into recognizing the claims of the United States. It was more the pressure of Spain's distresses in Europe.

The Spanish Ministry, still under Floridablanca, did not, like Great Britain, refuse to negotiate. Following the peace settlement it recognized the independence of the United States by formally receiving as *chargé d'affaires* William Carmichael (John Jay's secretary, who had remained in Spain after his chief's departure). When the American treaty commissioners at Paris indicated a desire to treat on issues existing between the two countries, Floridablanca sent to New York Diego de Gardoqui, an able servant of the crown who had served as an informal contact man in dealing with Jay during the war. He knew Jay well. He studiously prepared to ingratiate himself with the new American Secretary of Foreign Affairs. Gardoqui had instructions to make some boundary concessions, yielding the greater part and if necessary all of the contested territory—as far as 31°—in turn for the recognition of Spain's exclusive navigation. He reached New York, then the capital, in 1785. Congress authorized its Secretary of Foreign Affairs to negotiate, but not to yield the boundary marked down in the British treaty, and not to recognize Spain's exclusive navigation of the Mississippi. Any agreement must further be submitted to Congress before Jay would be allowed to sign. Congress had drawn up its Secretary's instructions by a majority vote, which governed routine business, but it would take a two-thirds vote, by states, for the ratification of a treaty. Gardoqui cultivated assiduously Jay and his family and established himself on intimate friendly terms with them. He was anxious to commit Congress to a treaty before the rising feeling in the West, demanding free navigation, should get beyond restraint. After many conversations the two negotiators in 1786 initialed articles of commerce and alliance, which must still await agreement on a further article regulating the Mississippi question and the boundary. This tentative treaty included commercial reciprocity between the United States and peninsular Spain (with the Canary Islands) on the basis of each other's nationals. Each party would guarantee the other's dominions in America, as determined by the treaty, against attack by a third party; and Spain agreed to mediate between the United States and Great Britain for the recovery of the northern posts held by the British, and "to see that they get justice, by force of arms if otherwise it cannot be promptly secured." His Catholic Majesty also undertook to buy for cash specie an unstipulated quantity of hard wood in the United States each year for ship-building.

This was the first of a number of proposals for entangling alliance which were made to the United States between 1782 and 1796. Jay never communicated to Congress the significant articles for alliance, but he did convey the other ones and asked for a modification of his instructions to allow him to sign an article by which the United States would "forbear" to navigate the Mississippi between Spanish banks for a period of thirty years. The Secretary did not consider this an abandonment of any right, rather a practical compromise for a limited period. Like General Washington [1] he thought it sensible to forego exercise of the continuing right until the western country filled up with a large population of fighting men; then Spain could no longer deny it. The eastern and northern states, a bare majority of the thirteen, were willing to change Jay's instructions to allow the compromise. The southern states, with their appanages along the Mississippi and Ohio, considered this as trading away their vital interests in return for commercial privileges valuable only to the ocean-going interests of the northern states. They rose in protest against any such treaty. It became so obvious that two-thirds of the states would not ratify any compromise on the Mississippi that Gardoqui and Jay regretfully suspended their negotiations. A few months later when the delegates to the Philadelphia Convention of 1787 were drawing up the new Constitution the men from the southern states remembered the dangers, so recently presented to them, of any constitution which would allow a bare majority to ratify a treaty, either with a

[1] At Gardoqui's suggestion the King of Spain presented to General Washington a royal gift of two blooded jack-asses to sire mules for Mount Vernon. Gardoqui also "loaned" $5,000 to Washington's friend, Henry Lee, thinking that Lee might influence the General's opinion about the Mississippi. But before this Washington had come to the conclusion that it would be wiser not to try to force the Mississippi at this time, but rather to bind East and West together by a canal and highway route between the Potomac and Ohio For this purpose he had organized in 1785 the Potomac Navigation Company.

foreign nation or with Indian tribes.[1] The Jay-Gardoqui negotiations are responsible for that clause in the Constitution of 1787 which requires a two-thirds majority of senators present for the ratification of any treaty. This provision has been of far-reaching significance in the diplomatic history of the United States, not so much because the Senate has actually rejected many treaties for lack of a two-thirds majority, but because negotiators realize, as Jay and Gardoqui did, that they must so write their treaties as to receive the two-thirds majority.[2] On the whole this provision has served as a salutary check on American negotiators and their foreign colleagues. Occasionally it has been possible for a more experienced foreign negotiator to outwit a shirtsleeves diplomatist of the United States, but it has rarely been possible to overreach the Senate in its unhurried scrutiny of treaties.

When Gardoqui saw there was no hope of getting a Mississippi estoppel through Congress he turned to intrigue with a small group of western adventurers who were willing to ignore Congress and the Confederation to the point of leaving the union and making a separate treaty with Spain. This chapter of American history is mistakenly known as the Spanish Conspiracy.[3] There were several western personalities involved in it, among them John Brown and James White, delegates to Congress from Kentucky and North Carolina, both men of the western waters; and John Sevier and James Robertson, prominent western leaders. They did not all work together, and probably few of them would have gone so far as to accept Spanish sovereignty. The arch conspirator to whom Brown attached himself was General James Wilkinson, a young veteran army officer of the Revolution who had adventured into Kentucky. He took a trading flotilla down the river to New Orleans in 1787. While there he secretly took an oath of allegiance to the King of Spain. In return for special trading licenses, and a pension for himself, Wilkinson became the servant of Carondelet, Spanish Governor of Louisiana, his tool in an intrigue to detach the western district from the Confederation. This never restrained him

[1] The southern states were also anxious lest a majority of states ratify Indian treaties that did not fully satisfy their frontier districts.

[2] No more than seven of the 787 treaties submitted to the Senate, 1788-1928, have failed of ratification because of the two-thirds proviso, according to the studies and tabulations of Royden J. Dangerfield, *In Defense of the Senate; a Study in Treaty Making* (Norman, Okla., 1933). Professor W. S. Holt, *Treaties Defeated by the Senate* (Johns Hopkins Press, 1933), has shown how the two-thirds requirement has lent itself to partisan politics.

[3] T. M. Green, *The Spanish Conspiracy; a Review of Early Spanish Movements in the Southwest* (Cincinnati, 1891). See also Bemis, Whitaker, *op. cit.*, and J. Navarro y F. Solano Costa, *¿Conspiración Española?* (Zaragosa, 1949).

from later holding a commission in the army of the United States. Wilkinson returned to Kentucky and, by promising alluring trading concessions and river navigation from Spain in the event of a separate treaty, sought to induce conventions of Kentucky citizens to set up an independent state. Jay's proposed treaty and the seeming indifference of the dying Continental Congress, after the framing of the new Constitution of 1787, appeared to some excitable persons to be sufficient reasons for separation. Cooler heads looked forward to a stronger national government and the early admission of Kentucky and Tennessee to full statehood in the new union. They carried the day against the separatist conspiracy. It was never able to control the political conventions of Kentucky. Gardoqui retired from Philadelphia just after the new Constitution had gone into effect, still hoping that something might be accomplished for Spain through the western separatists if not through the new national government.

Wilkinson's intrigue, however, had the immediate effect of opening the Mississippi in a limited degree to the commerce of the American West. A royal decree of December 1, 1788, permitted Americans to bring their produce down the river, paying an import duty of 15%, and to sell it at New Orleans; upon payment of an export tax of 6% they could ship it out to any of the ports to which it was legal to trade from Louisiana (French and Spanish West Indies, Spain and France). Westerners attached to Spanish political interests might even get a reduction of the import tax to 6%, particularly if they bore letters of introduction from Wilkinson. In 1793, after the European war began, the import tax was reduced to 6% for everybody coming down the river, and New Orleans was thrown open to the trade of all neutral nations having treaties of commerce with Spain (which did not include the United States). The Mississippi trade, at first a one-way downstream traffic, began a slow but sure increase. The Americans resented paying even these moderate taxes. They craved the entry of their sea-going ships into the Spanish Mississippi, to take away their exports whither they pleased. They further wanted a place of deposit at New Orleans to land their goods pending trans-shipment for overseas destination.[1] This question and the other issues with Spain passed over to President Washington for solution.

The alliance of 1778 had stipulated that France would guarantee the

---

[1] A. P. Whitaker, *The Mississippi Question, 1795-1803; a Study in Trade, Politics and Diplomacy* (N. Y., 1934), describes with diligent, patient and readable scholarship the intricacies of Spanish commercial regulations, and pictures in instructive detail the background of the old Southwest in relation to the Spanish provinces.

independence of the United States and its territory as fixed at the end of the war with England. After the peace France did nothing to help remove the British garrisons from the frontier posts occupied within acknowledged American territory. Jefferson sounded out Vergennes on this point, only to get a noncommittal answer. Congress on its part did not invoke the alliance for this purpose. Since the treaty of alliance had mentioned the territorial possessions of the United States "at the moment of the cessation of their present war with England," and not as fixed by the particular treaty of peace with Great Britain, it could not reasonably have been invoked against Spain, who maintained that the line of 31° had been established only in the irrelevant Anglo-American treaty. The United States had no resource or indeed expectation of help from anyone but itself in the task of redeeming its territorial integrity after 1783, and itself it was powerless to do so because of the creeping paralysis which had assailed its feeble confederation. France was content to see her new client remain in this condition, the normal condition, Vergennes believed, for any confederation of republics. It is true that in this weakness Congress could not collect from the states quotas of taxes to pay interest on the 35,000,000 *livres* ($6,352,500) borrowed from France during the war, not to mention the installments of principal which first fell due in 1785. An involuntary and universally regretted default for the next six years was the result. Though French agents did not fail to remind Congress of the interest and principal due on this honorable and comparatively small debt, Vergennes preferred to see the American Confederation politically too impotent to collect its taxes than strong enough to pay its just debts to France [1] and to defend its rights and interests against all comers. He did not want to see the new republic gravitate outside of the orbit of French diplomatic control.

The great French diplomatist died in 1787 unconscious of any flaw in his system. He had taken skillful advantage at a decisive moment of a great opportunity to cripple the British Empire. Under his guidance France had fought a victorious war to a glorious victory. In the final triumph discordant allies had made a general peace which fully secured French interests. Vergennes did not realize that the financial strain of the American war, of which the loans and subsidies to the United States were only a small feature, would be the final extravagance which would break down the credit of the old regime. We do not say that the French intervention in the American Revolution caused the French Revolution,

[1] For subsequent payment of arrears, remaining principal and full interest, see p. 93

but we do assert that if young Louis XVI had followed the advice of Turgot rather than of Vergennes in 1776 he would not have lost his head as early as 1793. But neither would the United States have been independent in 1783.

France's attitude of self-interested tutelage of the United States is not difficult to understand when one realizes that it was French intervention that clinched American independence. This attitude is exemplified not only in contentment at the political ineptitude of the Confederation and the frontier menace of Great Britain and Spain to the boundaries of 1783. We notice it in the negotiations over the making of a consular convention that occurred during the years 1782-1789. The treaty of amity and commerce of 1778 had provided for the establishment of consuls by each party in the other's dominions, but had not laid down any rules governing their obligations, functions, privileges and immunities. It became necessary to do this after the war, when both governments hoped that a great Franco-American commerce would supplant the traditional trade with England. In 1782 Franklin and Vergennes had drafted a consular convention, nominally reciprocal, which in practice could have been very one-sided in allowing French consuls such intimate privileges and immunities as to be incompatible with American sovereignty, and which had been so drafted as to emphasize the sovereign qualities of the "Thirteen United States of North America" rather than the United States of North America. One feature, providing for consular jurisdiction over disputes between nationals of one party residing in the territory of the other, smacked of extraterritoriality. Another provision, giving full immunity to the persons, houses, papers, *and agents* of consuls, would have made possible an obnoxious political surveillance by foreign consuls over the whole land and its business.

Secretary Jay persuaded Congress to defer ratification of this convention while Jefferson negotiated with Vergennes a new one between France and "The United States of America." [1] This convention, ratified in 1789, was the first treaty to receive the sanction of the Senate under the provisions of the new federal Constitution. It established the normal functions of consular jurisdiction, and was unexceptionable but for one feature that had been in the original draft of 1782: it still provided that in civil cases between nationals residing in the territory of the other party the consul should exercise jurisdiction.

In the critical period of 1783-1789 American diplomacy was at its lowest ebb and power. Internal weakness is ever invitation to foreign

---

[1] *Am. Secs. of State and Their Diplomacy, op. cit.,* I, 250-258.

aggression. This is incontestably the lesson of history. Had the national impotency of this period continued for a few more months it is doubtful whether American independence would have survived the trial. One of the greatest tasks of the new federal government first presided over by President Washington was to redeem the territory of the United States by summoning the real strength of the land and people under a truly national government and feeling. In doing so the first President was to have the assistance of a wholly unexpected event that happened simultaneously with his inauguration, the advent of the French Revolution.

THE ECCLESIASTICAL SEVERANCE

The independence of the United States and the resulting separation of the former British colonies interrupted the ecclesiastical hierarchy of both the Anglican and Roman Catholic churches, which had depended on bishops in England or Quebec for confirmation of the priesthood.

The American Catholics had been in spiritual dependence upon the Vicar-Apostolic of London, under the general authority of the Sacred Congregation of the Propaganda in Rome, which ruled Catholic missionaries. In 1783 the Prefect of the Propaganda instructed the Papal Nuncio at Paris to propose, through the intermediary of the French Government, that Congress approve the appointment of a native American, or if necessary a foreign Catholic (other than English) as Vicar-Apostolic in the United States. Vergennes put the Nuncio in touch with Franklin, who explained that no governmental sanction was necessary. Franklin suggested the appointment of a French bishop as a means of weaning Catholics away from any lingering English influence; but the French Government (conscious of the general feeling in Protestant America against bishops of any kind) wisely declined to interfere. The Church successfully solved the problem by appointing a native American, John Carroll of Maryland, as Vicar-Apostolic in the United States. Carl Russell Fish published "Documents Relative to the Adjustment of the Roman Catholic Organization to the Conditions of National Independence," *Am. Hist. Rev.*, XV (1910), 800-829; but see also Jules A. Baisnée, *France and the Establishment of the American Catholic Hierarchy; the Myth of French Interference (1783-1784)* (Instutut Français de Washington, Johns Hopkins Press, 1935).

In the case of the American adherents to the Church of England there was the difficulty in securing apostolic succession because of the requirement that a bishop must swear allegiance to the English crown in order to obtain consecration. This was solved, in the first instance, in 1784, by Bishop Samuel Seabury of Connecticut accepting consecration from an independent branch of the English Church in Scotland; but in 1787 American bishops were consecrated in England without the oath. Arthur L. Cross has dealt in great detail with this matter in his *The Anglican Episcopate and the American Colonies* (Harvard Historical Series, Cambridge, 1902), 262-272.

CHAPTER VI

GEORGE WASHINGTON AND FOREIGN POLICY

(1789-1797)

GEORGE WASHINGTON was the clear-headed exponent of a new national power. The counter-pullings and cross purposes of the thirteen states during the Revolution, the decay of national strength and morale after the war, had convinced him of the indispensability of a government that would pervade and control the whole country as the several state governments ruled their respective territories and inhabitants. This was essential, first, for domestic life, next, for an united front in the face of foreign nations. The General lent his whole influence and leadership to the framing of a national constitution at Philadelphia in 1787. As it left his hands from the Convention the Constitution was so worded as to be susceptible of construction through vigorous administration into a truly national government. But the restriction of state-sovereignty men, and of theorists like Thomas Jefferson and his convert James Madison, and localism in the ratifying conventions, quickly *federalized* the Constitution by adding to it the first ten amendments, particularly the tenth which reserved to the respective states and to the people all powers not specifically delegated to the federal government. This profoundly altered the Constitution and indeed the history of the United States. Washington however continued to speak of a *national* government, eschewing the word federal. Certainly for the administration of foreign relations that government was a real national authority.

No longer could the states control individually the commerce of the country, making impossible any national commercial policy, paralyzing any attempt at retaliation against nations which discriminated with impunity against American commerce and ships. No longer need the lack of executive power prevent scrupulous execution of treaties, which now became the law of the land. No longer could the law of the land be obstructed by the conflicting decisions of state courts: the Supreme Court offered a refuge against denial of justice under terms of a treaty. The Constitution gave to the United States the requisites for the successful conduct of foreign affairs. It did not guarantee the success of a foreign policy, nor was a foreign policy yet clearly crystallized. Back of

85

the new executive, back of the new paper government, must be a resolute national spirit, true national leadership, and an army and navy capable of adding force to the policy of the chief of state.

Washington gave the required leadership, and he was to achieve marked success in the field of foreign affairs without the prime requisite of military strength. This was because, happily for him and his countrymen, the great powers of the world presently became involved against each other in the long conflicts which followed the outbreak of the French Revolution. Occupied in ardent and deadly struggle in Europe, they had no force to use in America. Europe's distress became America's advantage. Such was the secret of President Washington's success in foreign affairs. Such, again, was the secret of the maintenance of American independence itself in a normally hostile world, and such, finally, served to protect American expansion westward to the Rocky Mountains. Before Washington retired from office the United States had ceased to be a client state and a pawn in the European balance. Before Europe recovered from the Napoleonic Wars the new republic in North America had grown too strong for lightly hazarded imposition or provocation.

The Constitution had not provided for any foreign office, but had implied the existence of cabinet ministers by mentioning heads of departments under the executive power. Henceforth the Secretary of Foreign Affairs ceased to be the creature of Congress. He was transformed into the Secretary of State, responsible to the President alone, although his appointment must be confirmed by a majority of the Senate.[1]

The Senate, a new body in the national structure, was endowed with certain powers ancillary to the executive which touched the conduct of foreign affairs: the confirming power applied to the appointment of ambassadors and ministers; all treaties must henceforth be made by and with the advice and consent of the Senate; specifically they must be ratified by a two-thirds majority of senators present. This power of the Senate has been somewhat constricted by practice: despite some exceptions, Presidents have negotiated without seeking the advice of the Senate step by step or in advance, preferring to submit a finished treaty for approval or rejection; and the confirming power has been weakened by the practice of appointing executive agents with the rank of diplomatic titles but without the confirmation of the Senate, envoys who have been

[1] John Jay in fact went through that very transformation in person: he became Acting-Secretary of State pending the return of Thomas Jefferson from France, when the author of the Declaration of Independence became the first Secretary of State on March 22, 1790.

equally important with fully confirmed plenipotentiaries.[1]   In recent
times even the Senate's power of ratification of treaties has been weakened somewhat by the executive's practice of making "executive agreements" and "gentlemen's agreements" with the executive powers of other
governments. These of course are made at the risk of all executive authorities concerned, and may be ignored by the Senate, if it so desires,
and by Congress; but there is a tendency for a Senate not at odds with
the President to decline to interfere.[2]   It was Washington who set the
precedent of ignoring the advice of the Senate—after one clumsy and
unsuccessful attempt to confer with them in person—and of having resort
to unconfirmed executive agents. It was through such a medium that the
new President immediately attempted to establish friendly relations with
Great Britain.

Washington selected for the first Secretary of State Thomas Jefferson,
the most experienced and best qualified [3] man available for the position.
He did not await Jefferson's arrival from France in order to take up
the gravest foreign problem confronting the new government: Anglo-
American relations. The President instructed an executive agent, Gouverneur Morris, a rather brilliant American political personality then in
France on private business,[4] to cross the Channel and sound out the British
Government as to whether it was willing to enter into formal diplomatic
relations with the new Government of the United States, and to negotiate
a settlement of outstanding issues and disputes. The Ministry at London
was not yet certain whether the new experiment of the American Union
would succeed. Morris had several interviews in 1790 and 1791 with
William Pitt, the Prime Minister (1784-1801; 1804-1806), and Lord
Grenville, Secretary for Foreign Affairs (1791-1801). He asked them
whether they would send a minister to the United States if an American
representative were sent to London. They were non-committal. Only
when the Nootka Sound crisis suddenly appeared likely to involve
Great Britain in war with Spain did Grenville vaguely encourage Morris

[1] Henry Merritt Wriston, *Executive Agents in American Foreign Relations* (Baltimore,
1929), is an encyclopedic treatise on this practice.

[2] The standard edition of treaties of the United States, now in process of publication
under the direction of Dr. Hunter Miller, includes executive agreements, and is significantly entitled *Treaties and Other International Acts of the United States of America*
(Washington, G. P. O., 1931-).

[3] Franklin was too old. Jay had preferred to be Chief Justice. Adams was Vice-
President.

[4] Morris was engaged in contracting with the French tobacco monopoly, the Farmers
General, for the purchase of American tobacco, and also in negotiations looking to the
formation of a syndicate to purchase from France at a profitable discount the debt owed
to it by the United States.

to expect a possible establishment of normal diplomatic relations. In case of war it was to British advantage to preserve friendly relations with the United States.

The Nootka Sound affair was precipitated by the attempt of a British fur-trading expedition in the year 1789 to establish a base on Vancouver Island [1] on the Pacific coast of North America. Spain had never admitted the right of any foreign government or subject to sail or trade within those waters or regions. At very wide intervals British voyages had intruded into Spain's vast claims to monopoly of the Pacific Coast and waters. Spanish authorities in Mexico sent a naval expedition to Nootka Sound, rooted out the new settlement of Englishmen, captured their three ships, and imprisoned their crews. This act afforded Pitt a great opportunity to retrieve British prestige, so lowered by the recent American war. Normally Spain could have counted on the support of France in any such question, and the matter would have remained one of minor importance. But Pitt knew in 1790, when news of the captures reached London, that France was paralyzed by the commotions of her Revolution. After a few weeks of uncompromising negotiation he presented an ultimatum to Spain, demanding restoration of the ships and sailors, indemnity for the latter, and further, recognition of the right of British subjects to trade and make settlements on the unoccupied coasts of America. The Spanish Government capitulated. Pitt won the fruits of a war without firing a gun. He ripped away the last hoary habiliments of the age-old monopoly of Spain. The so-called Nootka Convention, in addition to providing for the restoration with indemnity of the captured ships and crews, recognized the right of British subjects to sail, trade and settle on the northwest coast of North America to the north of the regions already occupied by Spain.[2]

The Nootka controversy, and British maritime actions on the northwest coast that were resumed immediately after it, strengthened British claims to sovereignty in the Oregon country,[3] which were later to come into collision with the United States. The controversy however had a more contemporary interest for American diplomacy. Pitt and Grenville thought that, in case of war between Great Britain and Spain, the United States might profit by the opportunity to take over its northern posts by force at a time when the British garrisons could not be promptly reinforced. They therefore became suddenly more cordial to Morris.

---

[1] It was then still believed to be a part of the mainland.

[2] W. R. Manning has published the standard study of this affair in his "The Nootka Sound Controversy," in *Ann. Repts. Am. Hist. Assoc., 1904,* 279-478.

[3] See Chapter XVI.

At the same time orders went out to the commanders of the frontier forts to avoid all friction. The Ministry also, for a short time, held out a friendly hand to Levi Allen, one of those five remarkable brothers of early Vermont, who was then in London seeking to negotiate a treaty between "independent" Vermont and Great Britain, before the Green Mountain State should be admitted into the American Union.[1] Spain's diplomatic surrender made it unnecessary for Great Britain to follow up these ominous movements.

Washington and his advisers had no idea of forcibly taking the frontier posts in case of an Anglo-Spanish war. On the contrary, when the President heard of the likelihood of such a conflict, he feared that Great Britain might demand permission to march troops from Detroit across the western territory to capture St. Louis and to occupy Spanish Louisiana. In that case she might tighten her constricting military hold on the whole trans-Appalachian territory. Anxiously he asked his advisers what to do in case such a demand were made. Alexander Hamilton, Secretary of the Treasury, who had reasons of state for pursuing friendly relations with Great Britain at almost any cost, favored granting the passage and exploiting neutrality to secure from Great Britain the posts, from Spain the right of American citizens to navigate freely the whole Mississippi River, according to the stipulations of the Anglo-American treaty of 1783. Knox, Secretary of War, vaguely followed Hamilton's views. Jefferson, who had now taken the office of Secretary of State, favored not answering at all. Vice-President Adams favored refusal, but not resistance, to such a passage. The Chief-Justice, John Jay, was also of this opinion. Happily Washington did not have to decide the matter. Nor did the British Government, despite the resourceful contacts of its unofficial observer in America, ever know of this irresolution and division of opinion in Washington's Cabinet.

We have mentioned that, after the peace, the British Ministry had maintained a series of paid agents in this country, to supplement with more extended political information the reports of the consuls. Since 1787 the agent had been Major George Beckwith. When the new Government went into operation Beckwith assiduously cultivated Alexander Hamilton and others of the "British interest," and reported their views to Quebec and to London. Lord Grenville thus came to realize that there was a strong party in the United States friendly to Great Britain and anxious to preserve undisturbed relations. Hamilton, the leader of this party, in effect had told Beckwith that in case the

[1] See my notes in *Am. Hist. Rev.*, XXI (1916), 547-560.

British had any trouble with Jefferson they could get around the Secretary of State to the President through him, the Secretary of the Treasury. Hamilton was pro-British in sentiment, because he realized that the success of the United States Government, under the Constitution of 1787, depended more than anything else on financial credit. The federal government had on Hamilton's advice, and as a part of his system, assumed the war debts of the several states. Money was necessary for the current expenses of government, to pay the interest and sinking fund on the recently funded debt (which included the assumed state debts), and to take up the arrears on the national debt owed abroad. By Hamilton's new taxes the government's principal source of revenue was a tariff on imports and a tax on shipping tonnage. These laws (July 4, and July 20, 1789) had the characteristics of a national navigation law; for they levied a tonnage tax of fifty cents a ton on foreign vessels in American ports and charged 10% higher tariff on goods coming in them.

This advantage to domestic shipping stimulated the transfer of American imports from foreign (particularly British ships, which dominated the trade) to American bottoms, though the additional advantage of the neutral flag, after the outbreak in 1793 of the long European wars, makes it impossible to measure truly the real force of this legislation.

Hamilton was opposed to any further discrimination than this general regulation against all foreign vessels. He was especially opposed to any particular discrimination, directly or indirectly, against British shipping. By far the greatest trade of the United States was still with Great Britain—nine-tenths of all American imports. Over one-half of this came in British ships. Upset political relations with Great Britain, Hamilton believed, and trade would cease. Let trade stop and the nation's revenue would fall off fatally. Credit would be "cut up by the roots." The whole new nationality, so recently salvaged from the chaos of the Confederation, even independence would be endangered. It was for these very real reasons that Hamilton was a champion of Anglo-American tranquillity, despite the irritating disputes that had lain in the background since 1783.

Opposed to Hamilton were Jefferson, Madison, and others who were rapidly coalescing into a party opposition against construing the Constitution any further in a national direction, and who did not believe in turning the other cheek to George III. They felt that the only way to bring the British Government to any willingness to settle the outstanding issues, to make a treaty of commerce and to evacuate the occupied posts, was by taking the resolute and self-respecting step of using the new power over commerce to discriminate sharply in tariff and tonnage rates against British imports and shipping. They put a bill through the House of Representatives lowering tonnage duties for domestic shipping and for the vessels of nations having treaties of commerce with the United States. Hamilton's political friends, the Federalists, controlled the Senate and stopped the bill there. Under Madison's leadership the opposing Republicans (men later called them Jeffersonian Democrats) in the House of Representatives brought forth a national navigation act, similar to the British navigation laws, to prohibit imports from countries that refused to permit the import of American products in American vessels (as did Great Britain in the West Indies and Canada). Hamilton's followers were able to postpone consideration of this bill in the expectation that Great Britain would accept negotiations for a treaty of commerce. Beckwith reported to London that if a minister were not sent to Philadelphia, England might expect the passage of this legislation. Because the United States was England's best single foreign customer Pitt decided to send a minister, George Hammond, who arrived in October, 1791. In return Washington sent Thomas Pinckney, of South Carolina, to the Court of St. James. It was the threat of retaliating tariffs, now possible under the new Constitution, which induced Great Britain to open formal diplomatic relations with the independent United States.

Hammond was so restricted in his powers that his negotiations with Jefferson were wholly ineffective. His superiors hoped that by mere diplomatic palaver he could keep Congress from passing hostile navigation laws like those of England. Therefore they instructed him to *discuss* a treaty of commerce only *ad referendum*. He could agree to evacuation of the northern posts only if payment of the pre-war debts were fully secured, and a neutral Indian barrier state, nominally independent but really under British protection, were set up along the whole northern frontier reaching south to the Ohio. This the Ministry hoped to do under the guise of mediating between the United States Government and its belligerent western Indians. Jefferson sadly worsted Hammond when it came to debating the issues of posts, debts, Loyalists, and boundaries. Even Hamilton himself, with whom Hammond established confidential relations, would not listen to any invasion of American sovereignty in the guise of mediation in the Indian troubles. Hammond successfully blandished Congress for eighteen months, until the more serious issues brought up by American neutrality in 1793 temporarily placed posts and debts in the background. Meanwhile Washington was sending a small army under General Anthony Wayne to retrieve disasters in the Indian campaigns and to pacify those tribes, in the vicinity of the northern posts, with whom the British colonial authorities maintained such sympathetic relations.[1] At this point we may turn to the old issues with Spain.

It was the new Secretary of State, Jefferson, who took up the Spanish problem. His sojourn at the Court of France as American Minister had shown him that Europe was continually on the verge of war, that at any moment it was only a question of a few months before war would break out between the great powers of the Old World. It was natural to assume that in case of war Great Britain and Spain would be on opposite sides, that because of the vulnerability to attack of their possessions in North America, either would pay diplomatic equivalents for American neutrality, that either would fear the possibilities of alliance of the United States with its enemy and would pay and pay well to prevent that. His intention was therefore to argue the issues with Great Britain and with Spain, to pursue a policy of "patience and persuasion" until they should go to war with each other, then to present vigorously to each the demands of the United States, expecting them to be conceded in an effort to retain American friendship and good will. This together with economic coercion represented the diplomatic armory of the pacifist, Thomas Jefferson, both as Secretary of State and later as President. How right he chanced, but only chanced, to be!

At first Jefferson thought the Nootka Sound controversy offered the opportunity to press the frontier issues with Great Britain and Spain. After this passed without war he advised a special mission to be sent to Madrid. Washington accordingly united with the incompetent Carmichael, *chargé* at Madrid, young William Short, then minister to the Netherlands, as joint commissioners plenipotentiary to negotiate a settlement of outstanding issues. The two commissioners found Spain, now under the leadership of Manuel de Godoy, Duke of Alcudia (after 1795 Prince of the Peace), disposed only to argue and procrastinate while Spanish officials at New Orleans and Pensacola pursued their intrigues with the Indians of the Southwest and the separatists of the Kentucky country. By various devices Godoy put off the American commissioners. Instead of being engaged in a war with each other, Spain and Great Britain in 1793 became allies for the next two years in the monarchical

---

[1] *Jay's Treaty, op. cit.*

coalition against republican France. The United States under Jeffersonian strategy seemed able to do nothing with Spain.

While matters continued at a standstill with Spain, as with Great Britain, and while Jefferson practiced patience and persuasion to no avail, one positive and honorable achievement was made, the payment of the war debts of the United States due to France and Spain.[1] Hamilton's prodigious success in transforming almost overnight the credit of the United States from the worst to the best in the world enabled him to take steps in co-operation with the Department of State for paying up the arrears and placing installments of interest and principal on a schedule of prompt payment. With a steady flow of adequate revenue assured as long as peaceful relations with Great Britain continued, Hamilton was able, following permissive acts [2] of Congress, to borrow 34,000,000 *guilders* of new funds from banks in the Netherlands to take up the eight years' arrears owed to France, thenceforth to meet from a sinking fund the established schedule of payments on interest and amortization of all outstanding loans. This unsolicited discharge of a paramount obligation surprised French politicians very pleasantly, particularly at a time when the depleted finances of the revolutionary government were so necessitous. The United States in making these payments did not take advantage of the easy option of doing so in depreciated French paper money (*assignats*) put out by the financiers of the Revolution. It paid its just debts in specie or equivalent equal in value to the original loans. In 1795 an act of Congress made it possible for foreign creditors of the United States to exchange their titles for United States domestic bonds bearing a slightly higher rate of interest. The French Government employed its titles to pay for provisions imported from the United States; and the purchasing agents who thus took payment for the provisions in turn exchanged their paper for the new bonds. So the French debt passed out of history, fully paid, principal and interest, really ingeniously discounted ahead of time to the great benefit of France.[3] Similarly the Dutch bankers traded in much of their credits for United States bonds.[4] Hamilton carefully scrutinized our accounts with Spain. We have noticed how the government of that monarchy, anxious to do nothing which would have implied any recognition of

---

[1] For tabulation of loans and subsidies by France, see above, p. 24.

[2] August 4, 12, 1790.

[3] Aulard, *op. cit.*

[4] J. C. Westermann, *The Netherlands and the United States, Their Relations in the Beginning of the Nineteenth Century* (The Hague, 1935), p. 11. See also another Dutch work, Van Winter, *Amsterdamschen Handel, op. cit.*, II, 399. The last installments on the outstanding Dutch refunding loans were paid in 1809 on schedule.

American independence during the Revolution, took no receipts or obligations for monies or supplies furnished to the insurrectionists. When Hamilton inquired from the Spanish legation how much was owed, they figured up a big bill ($1,640,071.62) including the monies secretly furnished by Charles III *via* Rodrigue Hortalez and Co. in 1776 and other subsidies in kind during the war. Hamilton finally decided, gratuitously, to treat the $174,011, furnished Jay in Spain, as a loan to be paid with accumulated interest, and also to pay the $74,087 supplied from Havana and New Orleans to western military expeditions under Pollock and Willing during the war. In 1793 William Short, who had been the instrument of making the new loans and payments in the Netherlands and France, handed over to the Spanish Treasury $268,033.62, principal and interest on the Jay "loan," and Hamilton paid over to the Spanish legation at Philadelphia $74,087 in acquittal of the other "loans." They could just as well have been considered subsidies.[1] Thus the United States discharged its debts in full, and in exemplary fashion.

The French Revolution was one of the most important events in the diplomatic history of the United States. This was not because of any political influence on American institutions. It had little if any. The importance to the United States of that great upheaval is that it involved Europe in a cataclysm of warfare that profoundly affected the international relations of the republic and its national destiny.

These wars presented a foreign problem out of which the principles of American neutrality were enunciated and enacted.

They so engrossed the powers of Europe as to enable the United States soon to settle its critical frontier issues with Great Britain and Spain, and that without war or much danger. It is difficult if not impossible to see how otherwise they could have been satisfactorily settled.

They crystallized certain tenets of foreign policy and brought an end to the entangling if once life-saving Franco-American alliance of 1778.

The Wars of the French Revolution and Napoleon also precipitated the revolution of the Spanish colonies in North and South America and completed the independence of most of the New World. This was of profound significance to the formulation of American foreign policy in 1823, as well as to the future diplomacy of the United States.

[1] There are some further notes and sources on the Spanish debt in the appendix to my *Pinckney's Treaty, op. cit.*, which I have corrected slightly in figures above.

Finally, these wars absorbed so completely for a generation the contending energies of the principal maritime powers, Great Britain, France and Spain, that the United States enjoyed about thirty years of comparative unmolestation (except for certain maritime questions that helped to bring on the War of 1812). During this fortunate period the new republic, essentially a non-military power, was able to consolidate its newly established nationality, and to expand its territory, resources and potential strength to a degree reasonably consistent with national safety, and to proclaim the Monroe Doctrine at a time when no European power was prepared actively to oppose it.

President Washington was the first to take just profits from this new chapter of European history, not by astute calculation, but by the exercise of sane leadership and unerring judgment in compounding the varying counsel of his principal advisers as the new problems appeared from the European scene.

News of the French declaration of war on Great Britain, February 1, 1793, came to Philadelphia in April as a complete surprise. George III, the recent enemy, ruler of a government which still superciliously refused to make a treaty of amity with the United States, was now engaged in war with France, the old ally of American independence. Despite the economic reasons which had determined Hamilton and the Federalists to a pro-British policy, there was a preponderating popular element, partly disenfranchised, which favored France. This affinity, which dated back to the days when Frenchmen freshened with their blood American soil for the cause of American liberty, was strengthened the more when France went republican and battled for her own liberty against an encircling ring of hostile monarchs. The United States was still the ally of France, pledged to defend the French West Indies in case of war. What should its attitude now be toward that strictly European war? Would the French alliance take the place of the renounced British connection in involving the American people in the perennial wars of the Old World?

Though the President and his Cabinet officers, including Hamilton and Jefferson, were instinctively decided on the maintenance of strict neutrality, none had considered the important political and legal problems so suddenly precipitated, nor their relation to nascent domestic party politics. All agreed on a proclamation of neutrality.[1] Washington signed

[1] At Jefferson's suggestion the word *neutrality* was left out in the hope that Great Britain might make some diplomatic concessions to be absolutely assured of American neutrality. The British Government, however, accepted it as a proclamation of neutrality, and presently in the diplomatic correspondence American officials so referred to it.

such, April 22, 1793, enjoining upon citizens of the United States a friendly and impartial conduct, and warning that those who committed or abetted hostilities against any of the belligerent powers would be "liable to punishment or forfeiture under the law of nations," notably if they carried "articles which are deemed contraband by the *modern usage of nations.*" But what was the law of nations, violation of which was now a crime in each one of the thirteen states, despite the absence of any stipulations on the statute-books? What was contraband according to *modern* usage? These questions the Administration had to face during the ensuing months, as it defined its position on neutral obligations and neutral rights. They bristled with controversies historical and actual.

The question whether to issue a proclamation of neutrality, already decided in Washington's mind and speedily supported by his advisers, was the first of thirteen specific questions which he put to his Cabinet for deliberation. The other twelve concerned the French alliance. Did it continue in effect after the Revolution? Should a minister of the new French Republic be received? How should the obligations of the United States to France be now construed? Hamilton argued that the treaties with France should be suspended pending clarification of the revolution there, and that the new minister should be received with a carefully stated reservation to this effect. He and his followers wished to take advantage of this plausible opportunity to get rid of the treaties of 1778, which might become uncomfortable. Jefferson maintained that the treaties continued in full force—here he was on solid juridical ground—that a minister of the French Republic should be received without qualification, but that the question of interpretation and application of the treaties should be postponed for future decision according to circumstances. Perhaps France might not even invoke the alliance. Washington followed Jefferson's advice. The new French Minister, the Citizen Edmond Genêt, was received without qualification. The treaties were not questioned. France did not choose to demand military aid in defending the West Indies according to the terms of the alliance. Since the United States had no naval force, American neutrality was far more valuable to France, if benevolently interpreted under the maritime articles of the treaty of amity and commerce of 1778. The treaty of amity of 1778 had stipulated that free ships make free goods and that foodstuffs and naval stores are never contraband. It forbade the enemies of one party to outfit privateers within the ports of the other, neutral, or to bring prizes to those ports. If these principles could be made to stand against Great Britain, American vessels could bring in to France through the British navy—as the Dutch would fain have done in 1778— much needed provisions and naval supplies. American neutrality thus seemed more valuable to France than American belligerency, though the history of Dutch neutrality during the last war gave little hope to the informed observer that the British Admiralty would recognize these newer principles of neutral rights.

Genêt was accordingly instructed not to invoke the alliance, but to use neutral American soil as a basis for organizing attacks on British and Spanish colonies and commerce. To finance this he relied on advance payment of the remaining American debt to France, some two and a half million dollars, and the proceeds of the sale of French naval prizes to be sold in American ports, after condemnation by French consular prize courts. Encouraged by tumultuous popular overtures on his arrival in Charleston, S. C., and his triumphant journey overland to the capital, Genêt proceeded to fit out privateers to cruise from American waters against British vessels and to set up the consular prize courts. He contended that since the treaty forbade France's enemies to do this it allowed France to do it. He began to enlist American crews and officers under the French colors of these privateers. He further issued military commissions to American western leaders like George Rogers Clark, who were to organize a legion of frontiersmen to descend the Mississippi and wrest New Orleans from Spain. Finally he planned republican propaganda to stimulate the revolt of British and Spanish colonists in Canada and Louisiana.[1]

Genêt's cool reception by President Washington was in unpleasant contrast to the fervent popular acclaim which had greeted him along the post-roads. Jefferson at first was sympathetic. As Hamilton had kept the British Minister well informed, Jefferson began by giving some friendly political tutelage to the French Minister. But the latter's excesses soon alienated Jefferson. Genêt found Washington's Government determined to enforce the letter of the treaty. The Government forbade

[1] Genêt's first instructions and despatches are printed, edited by the late Professor F. J. Turner, in "Correspondence of the French Ministers to the United States, 1791-1797," in *Ann. Rept. of the Am. Hist. Assoc.* for 1903, Vol. 2, and Professor Turner also edited other documents bearing on the same subject in *ibid., 1896*, Vol. I, 930-1107; *ibid., 1897*, 569-679; *Am. Hist. Rev.*, III (1898), 490-516; and contributed valuable narrations in "The Origin of Genêt's Projected Attack on Louisiana and the Floridas," *Am. Hist. Rev.*, III (1898), 650-671; and "The Policy of France Toward the Mississippi Valley in the Period of Washington and Adams," *ibid.*, X (1905), 249-279. The last two papers are reprinted in the author's *The Significance of Sections in American History* (New York, 1932). Much documentary material bearing on Genêt and other diplomatic problems of the time is published in *American State Papers, Foreign Relations* (Wash. 1832, 6 Vols.)

the outfitting of French privateers in American waters, or the recruiting of crews therein,[1] and promised compensation to Great Britain for damages by such privateers leaving American ports after a stipulated date, when it might reasonably be supposed they were aware of the prohibition. It further refused to recognize French prize courts on American soil. Washington, this time following the advice of Hamilton, refused to advance the payment of installments on the French debt.[2] Genêt's ambitious plans collapsed. In anger and disappointment he had recourse to the last reckless and desperate expedient of a diplomatist: he appealed to the people over the head of their government to support him. This was next to encouraging revolution. It had been done with success by French republican diplomatists in the smaller states of Europe, but it did not succeed in the United States. Washington indignantly requested his recall. A new revolutionary government had come into power in France. It promptly ordered Genêt home.[3] The fallen envoy, afraid of the guillotine, refused to go back to France. Charitably the President let him stay. He lived out the rest of a long life obscurely in the United States.

The activities of Genêt and the incessant complaints of the British Minister against any imminent violation of neutrality led the President to lay down, after study by the Cabinet, a set of Rules Governing Belligerents, to define and govern American neutral obligations, particularly in ports and coastal waters. Announced through instructions by the Secretary of the Treasury to local collectors of the customs, they were not legislation, yet they stood as the law of neutrality by executive interpretation of international law pending decision by the courts.[4] These rules prohibited the original arming or military equipment of belligerent vessels within the ports of the United States; declared legal the equipment of merchant vessels of belligerent flags in the same ports; held lawful all equipments doubtful in nature (i.e., applicable either to peaceful or hostile purposes); and prohibited the recruiting of men by belligerent powers within the United States. They have served ever since as valuable and enlightened precedents for international

[1] A jury failed to convict one Gideon Henfield, an American citizen indicted for violation of the laws of nations by enlisting on a French privateer.

[2] Substantial sums had been advanced to Genêt's predecessor for relief of French sufferers in Santo Domingo. Genêt diverted some of this.

[3] At the same time it requested the recall of the United States Minister, Gouverneur Morris, whose monarchistic proclivities and plottings had made him heartily *persona non grata* in Paris. Washington wisely complied.

[4] The President submitted to the Supreme Court for advisory opinion twenty-nine formal questions concerning belligerent rights and neutral obligations. The justices refused to answer, on constitutional grounds.

law both in this country and abroad. They were important building stones of the law of neutrality. . Genêt's projects in the West had led to presidential proclamations warning against participation in them. These were subsequently confirmed by the prohibitions of our first neutrality law of 1794, which also wrote into law the essence of the Rules Governing Belligerents of 1793.[1] The strict execution by President Washington of neutral obligations commended his government to Great Britain as impartial, and for the time being was accepted without protest by France.

About the historic problem of neutral rights has been gathered a major part of the history of American diplomacy. In these its early stages it called for the most careful handling by President Washington, and involved even more far-reaching possible consequences than did the determination and faithful performance of neutral obligations. The heart of the question was: to what extent should the United States, without a navy, insist that Great Britain, the greatest maritime power in the world, observe those principles of the Plan of 1776 that had been written into the Franco-American treaty of amity and commerce: free ships free goods, freedom of neutrals to trade in innocent goods to or between belligerent ports, and contraband not to include foodstuffs or naval stores? In 1780 France prevailed upon the Netherlands to demand the observance by Great Britain of these dicta, and rather than do so Great Britain declared war. In 1793 George III was not bound by the Franco-American treaty, and Great Britain had consistently maintained that these principles, so increasingly popular among small-navy nations, were not international law. In 1793, moreover, the old Armed Neutrals of 1780 had abandoned them and entered into the coalition against France. The United States alone could not require Great Britain to accept the new interpretation of neutral rights.

At the beginning of the war the British Government made it clear to the United States that it would take enemy property wherever it could find it, even in neutral ships on the high seas. By an order-in-council [2] of June 8, 1793 (the so-called "provision order"), instructions to British naval commanders ordered them to bring in—it proved for pre-emptive purchase—all neutral ships bound for French ports with cargoes of corn, flour or meal. This was designed to starve out the French "armed nation." By a second order-in-council of November 6,

[1] C. M. Thomas, *American Neutrality in 1793; a Study in Cabinet Government* (New York, 1931).

[2] An order-in-council is an executive order under authority of an enabling act of Parliament or of executive prerogative.

1793, they were directed to bring in all ships (including neutrals) laden with goods the produce of any colony belonging to France, or carrying provisions or other supplies for the use of such colonies. This order was not made public until the naval vessels reached the cruising ground of the Caribbean and suddenly captured about 300 American ships trading with the French islands, colonies whose trade and ports had been thrown wide open to American vessels at the beginning of the war. A third order of January 8, 1794, modified the extreme November order into line with the arbitrary Rule of 1756 [1] and the well established right of capture of enemy goods from neutral ships (according to a principle of the *Consolato del mare*) ; furthermore it ordered the capture of all ships laden in whole or in part with military or naval stores (without defining what constituted such contraband) bound for French colonies, and all ships bound for a blockaded colonial port (leaving, tacitly, the definition of blockade to the British Admiralty). British naval policy was thus applied on traditional lines and was this time supported by all the principal powers of Europe (except the Scandinavian states) united against France. Could the United States expect, under these conditions, to enforce against England the dicta of a Franco-American treaty which did not bind England at all?

News of the Caribbean captures reached Philadelphia in March, 1794, simultaneously with a report that the Governor-General of Canada had made a speech to a delegation of hostile Indian tribes from the western territory of the United States which General Wayne's army was preparing to pacify. The maritime spoliations were thus united with the standing sore of frontier relations. A war crisis flared up, at a time when Congress had become convinced that Great Britain had no intention of making a treaty of commerce or of negotiating a settlement of any of the outstanding disputes. Madison's old resolutions for discrimination against British navigation and commerce, once postponed in the hope of a successful negotiation, now found great favor in Congress. Bills appeared for the sequestration of British debts. Even Hamilton advocated raising a federal army and fortifying the principal ports. The public at large, still sympathetic to France, was furious with indignation. Actually none of these bills passed Congress, but an embargo on all American shipping for one month was voted April 25,

---

[1] Already before the war France had allowed American ships to trade with five ports in the West Indies, so that the order of November 6 went beyond the British Rule of 1756 in its reach. For the Rule of 1756, see above, p. 39, n. 3. For text of these orders-in-council see *Am. State Papers, Foreign Relations*, I, 240, 430, 431.

1794, and later renewed for another month. It was a compromise with a proposal for non-intercourse with England. Jefferson had now (December 31, 1793) resigned in disgust against Hamilton's intermeddling in his department. Hamilton, as always, saw in any rupture with England the ruin of American credit and the collapse of the new nationality of 1787. He and Federalist leaders prevailed on Washington to send one of their men, the experienced diplomatist, John Jay, the Chief-Justice, on a special mission to London to see if some sort of settlement short of a break could be arranged with Great Britain.

Jay succeeded in doing this in a treaty signed on November 19, 1794. Pitt proved as eager for peace as Hamilton. His major anxiety was the European war, from the fierce prosecution of which Great Britain must not be unnecessarily diverted. Besides, the United States was England's greatest and most profitable foreign customer. Jay felt that he had obtained the best terms possible; but scholars who have since been able to review the documents, for a long time not open to perusal, now see that Hamilton's intimacy with the British Minister in Philadelphia, Hammond, enabled Lord Grenville to press Jay to the utmost line of concession.[1] The new Secretary of State, Edmund Randolph, had instructed Jay to consult with the Swedish and Danish Ministers at London as to possible common action to be taken diplomatically against British maritime policy. Sweden and Denmark, in fact, did sign in April, 1794, a new armed neutrality, and invited the United States to come in. This invitation arrived after Jay's departure. Washington's Cabinet decided not to accept on the ground that it might be an entangling alliance. Hamilton told this to Hammond, who immediately relayed it to Grenville, who was very nervous about such a possibility. Thus reassured, he made no great concessions to Jay on the score of maritime rights. In addition to Hammond's sources of information from Hamilton, Grenville had a copy of the secret cypher of the Department of State.

Jay's Treaty provided that the United States would guarantee the payment to Great Britain in sterling money of *bona fide* private debts contracted before the peace, the amount of the same to be determined by a mixed commission. Great Britain on her part agreed to evacuate the posts by June 1, 1796, and to pay compensation for spoliations on American shipping made "under color" of the obnoxious orders-in-council, which themselves were not repudiated in principle. The amount of damages was to be fixed by a mixed commission. A mixed boundary

[1] I have reviewed the negotiations in detail in my monograph *Jay's Treaty, op. cit.*

commission was to determine the identity of the true St. Croix River, which had been made a part of the northeastern boundary by the treaty of 1783; [1] and the two governments agreed to concert measures to regulate the northwest boundary, where a gap had been discovered. [2] The navigation of the whole Mississippi was again declared free to the citizens and subjects of both parties. The treaty established commercial relations between the two parties on a non-discriminatory basis, and contained a guaranty against any discriminations by the United States against British trade or sequestration of property of British subjects. American ships henceforth would be admitted into the British East Indies, but not into British North America, and into the British West Indies only under such restrictions that the Senate rejected that article (XII) altogether. [3] On the other hand, overland commerce between the United States and British North America was provided for, on reciprocal terms, each government making tariff charges similar to those levied on goods of its own nationals. Important were those articles which prohibited sequestration of private property, and which recognized the right of the British Government to levy countervailing duties on American goods to balance the discriminations of the American tariff and tonnage laws in favor of domestic shipping. The four mixed commissions [4] set up by the treaty for the regulation of debts, spoliations and disputed boundaries gave a powerful impetus to the principle of arbitration. For adjudicated spoliations citizens of the United States ultimately collected by 1802 $10,345,200 which compares in amount closely to the sums re-

[1] The commission settled on the westernmost Schoodiac as the true boundary, the St. Croix of Mitchell's Map. See Map 8.

[2] The treaty of peace had stipulated that the boundary should run due west from the northwesternmost corner of the Lake of the Woods to the Mississippi River. Mitchell's Map, used by the negotiators, had its northwest corner covered by an inset-map of Hudson's Bay, out from under which the river flowed. It had become evident that the Mississippi rose considerably to the south of any possible treaty-line, thus leaving a considerable gap. Actually it is 151 miles from the latitude of Lake Itasca, the source of the Mississippi, to the latitude of the northwesternmost point of the Lake of the Woods.

No concert of action was taken as to the northwestern boundary, which was not settled until 1818. See pp. 174, 273.

[3] Article XII had allowed American ships of less than 70 tons to trade with the British West Indies, but had contained restrictions designed to prevent any interference in the carrying trade from the islands to England: one was the limitation to ships of small tonnage not adaptable to trans-Atlantic navigation; the other was the absolute prohibition of any exportation from the United States of the principal West Indian products, specifically molasses, sugar, coffee, cocoa, cotton. Whitney's cotton gin was invented in 1793. If the article had been accepted American cotton exports would have been choked off at the start, though the Senate could not have realized the especial significance of this.

[4] See note at end of the chapter for the work of the debts and spoliation commissions

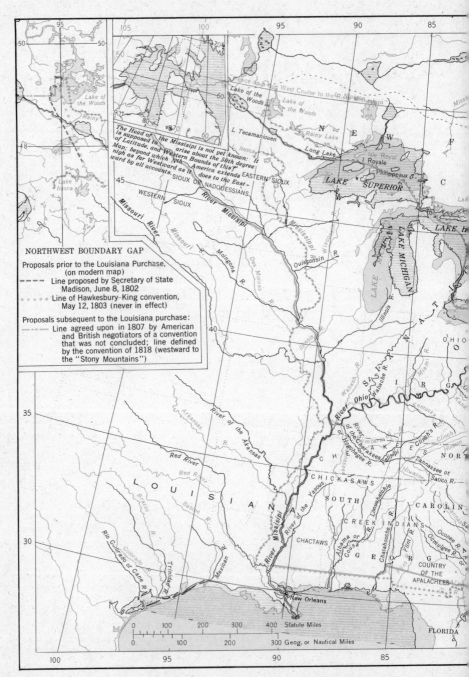

NORTHWEST BOUNDARY GAP

Proposals prior to the Louisiana Purchase,
  (on modern map)
---- Line proposed by Secretary of State
     Madison, June 8, 1802
····· Line of Hawkesbury-King convention,
     May 12, 1803 (never in effect)

Proposals subsequent to the Louisiana purchase:
—·— Line agreed upon in 1807 by American
     and British negotiators of a convention
     that was not concluded; line defined
     by the convention of 1818 (westward to
     the "Stony Mountains")

The Head of the Missisipi is not yet known: It
is supposed to arise about the 50th degree
of Latitude, and Western Bounds of this
Map, beyond which North America extends
nigh as far Westward as it does to the Eastward by all accounts.

Map 8. The Northeast and Northwest
Modern Geography, with a Modern Ins

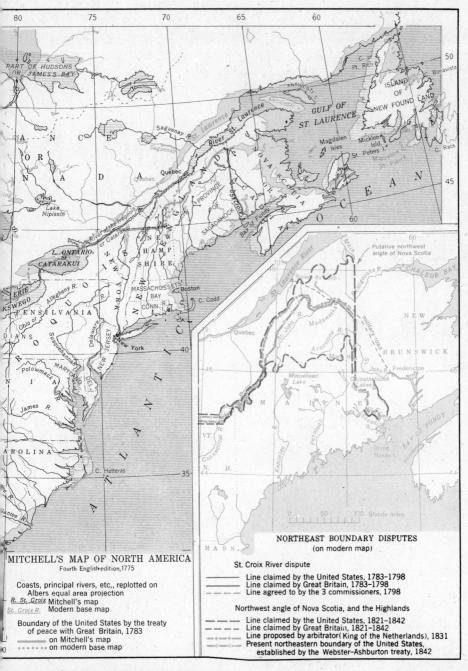

...ary Gaps on Mitchell's Map in Relation to
...of the Northeastern Boundary Controversy.

ceived after the Geneva Arbitration. The United States in 1802 satisfied British private debtors with a lump sum of £600,000.

Nothing was said in the treaty about free ships free goods, or the right of neutrals to trade in non-contraband goods to and between enemy ports. The United States on the contrary allowed taking enemy goods from neutral ships and silently acquiesced in the British Rule of 1756. Naval stores were included as contraband. The treaty said that whenever provisions, and other articles not generally considered contraband, should indeed become contraband, they should be seized and paid for, not confiscated.[1] Blockade was mentioned but not defined, thus leaving open the possibility of paper blockades. These maritime articles were of greatest significance throughout their duration, which was fixed at twelve years. Departures from the Plan of 1776, they were in some sense incompatible with the Franco-American treaty of 1778 but not a violation of it.

To balance against these great concessions to British sea power there was the assurance of continuing commercial prosperity, sound national finances, and the perpetuation of the newly consolidated American nationality. There was also the great achievement of redeeming the territorial integrity of the United States throughout the Northwest, which coincided with General Anthony Wayne's decisive victory over the hostile Indians at the battle of Fallen Timbers (August 20, 1794). But the concessions to England were heavy. They were the price which the Federalists paid for peace, that peace with England so necessary for the maintenance of Hamilton's structure of national credit and with it of the new federal government under the constitution of 1787. It is not an exaggeration to believe that Jay's Treaty, which was really Hamilton's treaty, saved American nationality in an hour of crisis.

The treaty was immensely unpopular. Jay was burned in effigy by turbulent public gatherings. They stoned Hamilton as he spoke in favor of the treaty. The press seethed with arguments for and against it, mostly against. There seems no doubt that at first the people opposed it, after a special session of the Senate by a bare two-thirds majority (20-10) ratified the document (June 22, 1795). Secretary of State Ran-

---

[1] The provision order of June 8, 1793, had been suspended during the negotiation with Jay. It was renewed in effect, April 25, 1795, before the ratification of the treaty, by an unpublished order which ordered cargoes of grain being shipped "on enemy account" to be brought in as *enemy property*. J. T. Newcomb first published it in "New Light on Jay's Treaty." *Am. Jour. International Law*, XXVIII (1934), 685-693.

dolph urged President Washington not to sign it. He had had mysterious conversations with the French Minister, Fauchet, about the Whisky Rebellion, conversations in which money was mentioned. Washington found this out, through French dispatches intercepted by the British.[1] Randolph perforce resigned. The President appointed a Federalist, Timothy Pickering. Washington's Cabinet was fully Federalist during the remainder of his Administration. The President and Hamilton (who remained a power in the Administration despite his retirement from the Treasury) were in harmony of policy. The Republican opposition tried to block the treaty in the House of Representatives by refusing to appropriate the monies to put the several mixed commissions into effect. A historic debate took place. The appropriations passed by three votes, following an eloquent speech by Fisher Ames. It is really possible for the lower house of Congress thus to block a treaty which has been fully ratified by the Senate and President. This possibility has made negotiators more amenable to the House of Representatives, but no treaty has yet been broken down in this way.

While Jay was in England the Anglo-Spanish alliance of 1793 was showing signs of falling apart. The Spanish Minister, Godoy, was preparing to make a separate peace with France. In these circumstances he heard of the signature of Jay's Treaty, and received, early in 1795, from the Spanish Minister at London, the text of the Mississippi article, which suggested a determination of the United States and Great Britain to support each other in forcing Spain to recognize the free navigation of that river. Washington had sent Thomas Pinckney from London to Madrid as a more impressive personage to demand that navigation. He reached Madrid at the psychological moment.

Fearful of British anger at Spain's desertion, Godoy endeavored to bend the United States away from any rapprochement with England. At his insistence the Spanish Council of State decided (July, 1795) to yield on the matter of boundaries and Mississippi navigation. Spain, pressed in Europe, wished to conserve all her strength to defend herself at home and overseas against possible British action. Godoy first tried to get the United States into a triple alliance with France for the common preservation of territories in America; then for an alliance with the United States alone in return for a settlement of boundaries and navigation. Pinckney refused both, and Washington later heartily approved this avoidance of entangling alliances. Soon afterward there

[1] I. Brant pronounces "Edmund Randolph, Not Guilty," in *Wm. and Mary Quar.*, 3d Ser. VII (No. 2, April, 1950), 179-198.

arrived at Madrid a copy of the separate peace signed with France, under Godoy's instructions, at Basle. From a grateful monarch the Spanish favorite received the title of *Principe de la Paz,* Prince of the Peace [1] (of Basle). He now turned to complete the negotiations with Pinckney. There is disagreement among scholars [2] who have studied the Spanish archives as to whether the Prince of the Peace had the whole text of Jay's Treaty before him when he signed with Pinckney at San Lorenzo (October 27, 1795) the treaty, now known as Pinckney's Treaty. No evidence has been cited to prove that he did, although it has been argued that time enough had elapsed since the publication of the text in Philadelphia the previous July 1 for the Spanish legation's despatches of that date to have reached Madrid. If the Prince had the text before him it would have been obvious that Jay's Treaty was not the fearsome alliance with Great Britain that he had imagined possible. On the other hand he may have feared secret articles. At any rate the peace of Basle induced Spain to abandon her sound position on the issues with the United States in order to support herself in Europe and elsewhere. She recognized the boundary of 31° north latitude, and acknowledged the freedom only of citizens of the United States and subjects of Spain [3] to the navigation of the whole

[1] Sometimes too exaltedly translated as Prince of Peace.

[2] See my *Pinckney's Treaty, op. cit.,* where I have suggested that, despite appearances, Godoy did not know the full terms of Jay's Treaty when he signed with Pinckney; and *per contra,* Professor A. P. Whitaker's *Spanish American Frontier, op. cit.* It is Professor Whitaker's thesis that pressure of American frontiersmen rather than European predicaments caused Spain's concessions. In his article "New Light on the Treaty of San Lorenzo," *Miss. Vall. Hist. Rev.,* XV (1929), 435-454, he argues from the known time of transmission of many other despatches, that Godoy "in all human probability" received a despatch of July 2, 1795, with the text of Jay's Treaty before he signed with Pinckney on October 27. In a subsequent article, "Godoy's Knowledge of the Terms of Jay's Treaty," *Am. Hist. Rev.,* XXXV (1930), 804-810, he calls attention to a memoir written in December, 1796, by an undersecretary in Godoy's office, and endorsed by Godoy himself, which explicitly states that Godoy did not know of the content of the articles of Jay's Treaty when he signed with Pinckney (historians agree that Godoy certainly knew about the Mississippi article); but Professor Whitaker himself discredits this confidential and significant statement because, when the memoir was drafted into a note to the French Ambassador at Madrid, the statement was modified to say that the Spanish Government "already knew that the English had signed on November 19, 1794." This does not say that the text was known. No one has ever questioned that the Spanish Government knew that Jay's Treaty had been signed. I have questioned, and still doubt, whether it knew the full text of that treaty, when Godoy signed with Pinckney.

[3] Jay's Treaty of 1794 declared that, according to the terms of the treaty of peace, the navigation of the Mississippi should be free and open to both parties, and that all the posts and places on its eastern shore, to whatever party belonging, could be freely resorted to by both parties. In Pinckney's Treaty of 1795 the King of Spain agreed that the Mississippi should "be free only to his subjects and to the citizens of the United States," thus implying an exclusion of all others, including British subjects for whom the navigation of that river had been declared free by the Anglo-American treaties. In 1795,

length of the river, together with the privilege for American citizens of landing goods for ocean-going transhipment at New Orleans, free of tax for three years. At the end of three years this privilege might run on, or the King of Spain might assign another place on the banks of the lower Mississippi as an *entrepôt*. This *entrepôt* privilege became a few years later the subject of much significance in the diplomacy of the Louisiana purchase. Each side agreed to restrain Indians within its territory from incursions into the territory of the other. This became of great importance in the later negotiations relative to Florida. As to commerce all the treaty said was that it should be regulated according to the advantages of both countries. The maritime articles conformed to the principles of the Plan of 1776, and a mixed commission was set up to adjudicate a comparatively small number of spoliations claims (which Spain promptly paid, $320,095.07)[1] *without* requiring that they should first exhaust the resources of Spanish justice— quite different, in this detail, from the corresponding provision in Jay's Treaty. The Senate ratified Pinckney's Treaty unanimously. With it collapsed the separatist conspiracy in the Kentucky country.[2] The complete opening of the Mississippi to American sea-going commerce made

following General Wayne's pacification of the western Indians (battle of Fallen Timbers, August 20, 1794), the United States also made a treaty with the western Indians (treaty of Greenville, August 3, 1795) by which the tribes ceded their title to territory east and south of a line which ran through the present state of Ohio to the mouth of the Kentucky River, ceded sixteen strategic parcels of land and other specified reserves within the remaining acknowledged Indian territory, provided for the licensing of all traders in the Indian country, and formally accepted the exclusive protection of the United States. Great Britain argued that this Indian treaty was not wholly consistent with the Mississippi article of Jay's Treaty, which among other provisions had guaranteed to the Indians dwelling in Canada and in the United States a right "freely to pass and repass by land or inland navigation" into the respective territories of either party (except within the limits of the Hudson's Bay Company) and to "navigate all the lakes, rivers and waters thereof." Accordingly an "additional article" to Jay's Treaty was signed and ratified in 1796, declaring that "no stipulations in any treaty subsequently [to Jay's Treaty] concluded by either of the contracting parties, with any state or nation, or with any Indian tribe, can be understood to derogate in any manner from the rights of free intercourse and commerce, secured by the aforesaid third article." The ostensible purpose of the additional article—i.e., of reconciling Jay's Treaty with the Indian treaty of Greenville—could have been perfectly satisfied without the use of the phrase "any other state or nation." It was possible for Great Britain at a convenient time to construe these words so as to repudiate any exclusion under Pinckney's Treaty and to reaffirm the British right to the navigation of the Mississippi despite the exclusively worded character of the Spanish-American treaty.

[1] J. B. Moore, *International Adjudications*, V, 64.

[2] Carondelet, Governor of Louisiana, had nursed along the conspiracy, still working for a separatist treaty and the consequent secession of the West. He was in touch with Wilkinson and his henchmen when he received orders to drop the plot. The Spanish posts north of 31° were not evacuated until 1798.

for a prosperous commercial movement in the American West, which the eastern seaboard ports shared; and it had the political effect of making the whole nation "Mississippi-minded." [1] The treaty also speeded peaceful American penetration of Louisiana.

With these twin treaties, Jay's Treaty and Pinckney's Treaty, Washington was able to redeem the territorial integrity [2] of the United States. Truly Europe's distress had been America's advantage.

The first President was less successful in dealing with Algiers, Tripoli and Tunis. In treating with these piratical powers there was no distressing situation weighing on them in Europe which Washington's diplomatists might exploit to compensate for the lack of naval power. For treaties of amity and the ransom of captives, these potentates demanded tribute. Washington and his successor agreed to treaties (Algiers, 1795, Tripoli, 1796, Tunis, 1797) which cost a total of $1,155,949.25 cash, not to mention continuing "presents," treaties observed only a few years by the Corsairs. They cost more than a moderately respectable naval force. But in 1794 upon the President's recommendation Congress had passed an act appropriating money for a small navy to be used against the Barbary states. This was to be the only means by which the Barbary question could be permanently solved in later years.

The French Ministers, Fauchet and his successor Adet, had worked desperately to frustrate the ratification of Jay's Treaty by hook or by crook, in the Senate, by the President, in the House of Representatives, only to fail. They seemed no longer to be able to control the American Government as they had done in Vergennes' time. Fauchet wrote home that it would be well for France to get Louisiana back from Spain in order to have a means of putting pressure on American policy. Adet recommended that the French Directory, on the eve of the presidential election of 1796, give some signal mark of its displeasure with the United States as a warning to the people of the disaster which might follow a re-election of President Washington and a continuance of his confirmed independent policy so injurious to French interests. "Washington must go," said the new French Minister of Foreign Affairs, Delacroix. The Directory decided to suspend diplomatic relations with the United States,

---

[1] To quote an adequate phrase of A. P. Whitaker, *Mississippi Question, op. cit.,* 150-154.

[2] While Jay was negotiating in England in 1794, the small American regular army under General Anthony Wayne was moving against the hostile Indians under British tutelage in the Ohio country. They were crushed in the Battle of Fallen Timbers, 16 miles south of Toledo, Ohio, August 20, 1794. Wayne advanced northward down the Maumee River to a new British fort which had been erected near the present city, but avoided a collision with the British garrison there. The new Maumee Fort was evacuated with the others in 1796.

on the eve of the election. If Washington were kept in power, such was
the intimation, war might follow; if Jefferson, the friend of France, were
elected President, regular relations would be restored, with the hope
that a new French treaty might undo Jay's Treaty with Great Britain.
As the presidential electors were preparing to cast their votes Adet
announced (November 15, 1796) the suspension of diplomatic relations,
in a burning manifesto full of French propaganda. He had already conveyed the decision of the Directory (decree of July 2, 1796) henceforth
to treat American ships precisely as the British did, thus setting aside
the maritime principles of the Franco-American treaty. It was all carefully calculated to influence the electorate to repudiate Washington. It
was a flagrant case of a foreign nation seeking to interfere within the
domestic politics of a sovereign people in order to accomplish its own
interests. It was the only instance where this influence was ever brought
to bear in an American Presidential election.[1]

The Directory had not counted on one contingency: Washington had
already chosen not to run for President in 1796. He had further decided to take advantage of his retirement from public life to deliver a
valedictory of advice to the American people. The purpose of this message, conveyed through the press (September 19, 1796), was an appeal
to rally around the *national* government, to abjure party politics [2] as
offering a medium for foreign intermeddling. It was an appeal for complete independence from subserviency to any foreign power. Too often
the Farewell Address has been considered as urging only a policy
of isolation. Washington's experience with foreign affairs, particularly
with the French alliance, and the experience of the Fathers in general,
had convinced them that it was for the interest of American independence to steer clear of foreign entanglements for which so many opportunities had already presented themselves. He saw in the French alliance a dangerous affinity which might insinuate itself into domestic
politics to the jeopardy of complete independence.[3]

[1] In the election of 1888 the British Minister, Sir Lionel Sackville-West, was trapped
by an electioneering trick into advising an American citizen of British origin to vote for
Cleveland, because a lower tariff would be more favorable to British interests. When the
political tricksters published this ill-considered letter, the United States promptly requested
the imprudent diplomat's recall.

[2] Washington identified party politics with factional opposition. He believed that in
a government of checks and balances, as set up by the Constitution of 1787, that party
politics was not necessary for the preservation of liberty.

[3] See my "Washington's Farewell Address; a Foreign Policy of Independence," in *Am.
Hist. Rev.*, XXXIX (Jan. 1934), 250-268. J. F. Rippy and Angie Debo, "The Historical
Background of the American Policy of Isolation" in *Smith College Studies in History*,
IX (1924), assemble expressions, both private and official, of isolation sentiment and fear
of entangling alliances.

The Address was outlined by Washington and phrased by Hamilton. On the score of foreign affairs, the only relation in which it has been much remembered, it said:

Against the insidious wiles of foreign influence (I conjure you to believe me, fellow-citizens) the jealousy of a free people ought to be *constantly* awake; since history and experience prove that foreign influence is one of the most baneful foes of Republican Government. . . .

The great rule of conduct for us, in regard to foreign nations, is in extending our commercial relations, to have with them as little *political* connection as possible. So far as we have already formed engagements, let them be fulfilled with perfect good faith.—Here let us stop.

Europe has a set of primary interests, which to us have none, or a very remote relation. Hence she must be engaged in frequent controversies, the causes of which are essentially foreign to our concerns. Hence, therefore, it must be unwise in us to implicate ourselves, by artificial ties, in the ordinary vicissitudes of her politics, or the ordinary combinations and collisions of her friendships, or enmities.

Our detached and distant situation invites and enables us to pursue a different course. If we remain one people, under an efficient government, the period is not far off, when we may defy material injury from external annoyance; when we may take such an attitude as will cause the neutrality, we may at any time resolve upon, to be scrupulously respected; when belligerent nations, under the impossibility of making acquisitions upon us, will not lightly hazard the giving us provocation; when we may choose peace or war, as our interest, guided by justice, shall counsel.

Why forego the advantages of so peculiar a situation? Why quit our own to stand upon foreign ground? Why, by interweaving our destiny with that of any part of Europe, entangle our peace and prosperity in the toils of European ambition, rivalship, interest, humour or caprice?

It was these sentiments which by a safe margin of only two [1] electoral votes elected John Adams over Thomas Jefferson as the successor of George Washington and the supporter of his foreign policy. Tolerance of foreign intermeddling was the issue of the election of 1796. Adams realized this. It is just to note however, that Adet, the retiring French Minister, had hoped little from Jefferson. "Jefferson," he wrote to his superiors at Paris, "is an American, and as such he cannot sincerely be our friend. An American is an enemy of all the peoples of Europe."

The foreign policy of the United States was for the first time authentically and clearly defined in 1796. The sage and perfect counsel of

[1] Adams had 71 votes, Jefferson 68, of a total of 138 electors. Since a President could not be elected directly without a majority of the electors, Adams had only two votes to spare, although he had three votes more than Jefferson. If Adams had failed to get a majority and the election had been thrown into the House of Representatives, foreign intrigue would have been brought to bear viciously in the balloting there.

Washington's Farewell Address truly embodied the experience and wisdom of the Fathers. For over a hundred years no responsible American statesman ever seriously gainsaid it.[1]

Thanks to the European wars, Washington's diplomacy had been astonishingly successful. But it had alienated the ancient ally, France. The inflammable French imbroglio was inherited by his successor. Thanks again to Europe's distress it too was to be settled in a perfectly profitable way.

COMMISSIONS ON DEBTS AND SPOLIATIONS UNDER JAY'S TREATY

The debts commission, which met at Philadelphia, was composed of two American and three British commissioners (the fifth one, a British subject, having been chosen by lot). After much wrangling the two American commissioners availed themselves of a provision of the treaty which required the presence of a commissioner of each party to form a board to hear cases, and withdrew. This broke up the commission. In 1802 the United States agreed to pay the British Government the lump sum of £600,000 sterling money in satisfaction of all claims of British subjects for private debts. The United States Government never collected from its own citizens whose pre-war private debts were thus paid; for those individuals separation from the British Empire meant separation from their debts.

The spoliations commission met at London, two British and three American commissioners (the fifth, an American, having been chosen by lot). Its sittings were suspended, when the British Government, in retaliation for American withdrawal from the boards of the debts commission, withdrew its commissioners from the spoliations commission similarly; but sessions were resumed following the debts settlement of 1802, and it wound up its business in 1804, with awards of £2,330,000 ($10,345,200) to American claimants and $143,428 to British claimants, reckoned at $4.44 to the pound.

Subtracting debt settlements from spoliation settlements left a balance of $8,537,772 in favor of the United States after the work of the commissions was entirely liquidated. See J. B. Moore, *History and Digest of International Arbitrations to Which the United States Has Been a Party* (6 Vols., Wash., G. P. O., 1898), I, 343-344; and his *International Adjudications, Modern Series*, IV, 161. I desire to acknowledge at this place a numerical error on p. 320 of my *Jay's Treaty*.

[1] Albert K. Weinberg's logical analysis of "Washington's 'Great Rule' in its Historical Evolution" concludes that "it exhibits . . . a striking correlation with the contemporaneous interests or desires of the American people. . . ." See *Historiography and Urbanization, Essays in American History in Honor of W. Stull Holt* (Johns Hopkins Press, 1940), 109-138. These interests were well served by the traditional interpretation of the "great rule" until 1914.

CHAPTER VII

THE FRENCH IMBROGLIO

(1797-1800)

"So far as we have already formed engagements," said George Washington in his Farewell Address, "let them be fulfilled with perfect good faith. Here let us stop." He had stopped at the line of Jay's Treaty. The quarrel which followed with France was essentially over that treaty. The French revolutionary leaders had desired from the beginning of their war with England a benevolent neutrality useful to their purpose no matter what disaster it might threaten to the American nation. The way Washington handled Genêt disabused the Committee of Public Safety, then the executive power in Paris, on that score. Jay's Treaty, which followed, appeared to the succeeding Directory as proof that the United States would not remain even coldly neutral.

France excoriated that treaty as treasonable to the alliance of 1778, and specifically protested at the acquiescence by the United States in British denial of free ships free goods, British enforcement of the Rule of 1756, British definition of contraband and blockade. All this, it was contended, was a violation of the treaty of amity and commerce of 1778. The United States had not violated that treaty if only because it was not even a belligerent and therefore could not be called upon to observe these rules for the conduct of belligerents as against neutrals. Without pausing to argue this charge, it is sufficient to note here that France, a belligerent since February 1, 1793, and obliged by her American treaty to observe those principles toward the neutral United States, had herself from the beginning been violating the maritime articles of the treaty of 1778. As to contraband and enemy property on neutral American ships, France had been following identically the same practice as England. This the French authorities admitted to themselves, and instructed their representatives in Philadelphia to palliate their conduct in the hope that a friendly ally would understand the desperate situation in which a republican nation was fighting for its life. Really the United States Government did treat the French spoliations, which were in violation of a treaty, more indulgently than the British, which were not. Looking back upon the imbroglio that followed, it seems that Washington made a mistake in not promptly declaring the treaties with France ended because of France's early violation of the treaty of amity. He and his successor were too patient.

When President Washington sent Jay to London he also sent James Monroe to Paris as new Minister of the United States. Monroe was a member of the republican opposition who, as senator from Virginia, had voted against Jay's confirmation and thought his mission mischievous. The President selected him as a republican who would be particularly pleasing to the revolutionary leaders of France. This he certainly was. It also looks as though Washington intended to use Monroe to keep France in good humor while Jay made a treaty of amity and commerce with Great Britain including, perhaps, maritime principles disagreeable to France. Monroe did not know Jay's instructions. He was to tell France that Jay was merely seeking redress for spoliations and evacuation of the occupied northern posts. It was also his task to persuade belligerent France to observe the treaty of 1778 and to withdraw her maritime decrees so far as the neutral United States was concerned.

The French National Convention received Monroe, upon his arrival, in a fervent ceremony in which its president embraced the American Minister with the fraternal *accolade* as symbolizing the affection between the two republican peoples. The envoy replied warmly, using words for which he found permission in his instructions, although it is doubtful whether his principals ever intended that they should be proclaimed so dramatically from such a public tribune. He warmly assured the deputies that French successes as the avengers of liberty would be glorified in the United States and looked upon as successes of the Americans themselves and other friends of liberty. Government and people took him ardently to their hearts as a fellow apostle of the rights of man. He sent to the President of the Assembly an American flag to be hung with that of France on the walls of the hall of the Convention.

Monroe succeeded in persuading the French executive power to repeal the obnoxious maritime decrees, in so far as the United States was affected by them, and to come back to the letter of the treaty of amity and commerce of 1778, also to promise compensation for violations of it. This he did despite the fact that news had just arrived of Jay's having signed a treaty with Great Britain. Its provisions were not yet known. Jay would not reveal the treaty terms to his colleague unless Monroe would agree to keep his knowledge secret. He did send him a sentence, extracted from one of the articles, namely, that nothing in the treaty should be deemed to operate contrary to former and existing public treaties of the parties with other states. Monroe had assured the French Government according to the tenor of his instructions. He now became suspicious of Jay's Treaty and led the French authorities to believe that if it were unfriendly to France it would never be ratified. When it actually was ratified and its text revealed, the Secretary of State instructed the minister to defend it. Monroe perfunctorily did so in his official correspondence. Behind the scenes he disloyally suggested [1] to the French Directory, which had now succeeded the Committee of Public Safety, that the whole question would be taken care of by the defeat of Washington in the approaching Presidential election of 1796. Though Washington never knew this he did begin to suspect the envoy's loyalty to him and his administration and recalled him forthwith.[2]

Monroe's indefensible conduct, as well as the despatches of the French representatives in the United States, had encouraged the Directory to suspend diplomatic relations, to abandon respect for the treaty of 1778, now considered violated by Jay's Treaty, and to proclaim in retaliation that it would treat American shipping precisely as England did. Actually France had already been doing this, as we have noted, up to Monroe's arrival. In vain Washington dispatched to Paris a successor to Monroe, Charles Cotesworth Pinckney [3] of South Carolina, with long instructions, made public as a counterblast to Adet's manifesto,[4] refuting French charges of treachery and of violation of treaty engagements, and defending the exact neutrality of the United States. This state paper,[5] outlined by Hamilton and ably penned by Secretary of State Timothy Pickering, had a very steadying effect on American public opinion, but none in France. The Directory refused even to receive C. C. Pinckney, and took pains to make his sojourn in Paris personally

[1] See my article, "Washington's Farewell Address; a Foreign Policy of Independence," op. cit.

[2] Upon his return Monroe published a review of his mission, with the diplomatic correspondence, A View of the Conduct of the Executive, in the Foreign Affairs of the United States. . . . (Phila., 1797) to show that he had been treacherously treated by Washington; but this becomes less impressive to one who has had the privilege of reading his private communications, unpublished, now in French archives.

[3] Brother to Thomas Pinckney, first minister to Great Britain, who negotiated the treaty of 1795 with Spain, and cousin to Charles Pinckney (who was legally adopted by the father of Charles Cotesworth and Thomas). Charles Pinckney was later minister to Spain, 1801-1805. They were not related to William Pinkney of Maryland, who was joint commissioner to Great Britain with Monroe in 1806.

[4] See above, p. 108.

[5] Am. State Papers, For. Rel., I, 559.

uncomfortable. In contrast the departing Monroe permitted himself to receive a rousing republican send-off.

A new wave of spoliations by French privateers now fell upon innocent American shipping. Since it was left to the irresponsible commanders of these private vessels of war to apply the dicta of British practice to neutral ships, the ensuing captures, insults and persecutions knew no limits. French spoliations, detentions and other illegal treatment of American ships and commerce actually surpassed in amount the arbitrary conduct of Great Britain "under color" of the orders-in-council.

Already in 1796 and 1797 French officials in the West Indies had been authorizing the capture of American ships if merely bound to or from British ports. This went far beyond British practice of taking neutral vessels going to enemy blockaded ports (blockaded even by British definition).

A decree of the Directory of March 2, 1797 (expanding that of July 2, 1796, declaring that neutral shipping would be treated as it allowed itself to be treated by Great Britain) went beyond British practice by declaring that neutral vessels laden in whole or *in part* with enemy property were good prize—this despite the provision of free ships free goods in the Franco-American treaty of 1778. Nevertheless the same treaty was made the pretext for what amounted to a widespread seizure and condemnation of American vessels on the ground that they did not have the precise form of crew's list prescribed in that instrument, a technicality of doubtful validity not hitherto insisted on. Further, all neutrals caught serving on board an enemy ship of war (no distinction was made for impressed seamen) were to be treated as pirates. The Directory's "retaliatory" decree (January 18, 1798) declared all neutral vessels loaded with goods of any kind coming from Great Britain or any of its possessions to be good prize, together with their cargoes. Any vessel which had touched at a British port anywhere was forbidden to enter a French port.

These decrees of 1797-1798 foreshadowed Napoleon's later continental system. Before regular diplomatic relations were restored finally in 1800 there had accumulated 1853 authentic cases of spoliations at the hands of French warships, with a total damage of $7,149,306.10.[1] This total comes

[1] Such was the total finally awarded many years later (1915) by the United States Court of Claims to which fell the duty of determining the damages for payment by the United States Government, after these spoliation claims had been exchanged with France for diplomatic equivalents by the treaty of 1800. Each spoliation claim did not necessarily involve a different ship. There were about three times as many claims as

up to \$12,149,306.10 when we add \$5,000,000 for another class of recognized damages: eventually adjudicated claims for embargoes, seizure of cargoes in French ports, arbitrary purchases, etc., which accumulated between 1793 and 1800.[1] This compares with the total of \$10,345,200 [2] of British spoliations on American ships and commerce before the ratification of Jay's Treaty in 1795.[3]

Crews of the American merchant ships were occasionally treated by their French captors with barbarous indignities and cruelties, such as torture with thumbscrews, to cite one instance. With diplomatic relations ruptured, there was no chance peaceably to protest, to make representations for redress. The nation must defend itself or suffer the consequences.

As Washington had put the questions raised by the outbreak of war between Great Britain and France, so John Adams submitted the French imbroglio for the advice of his Cabinet. The second President's Cabinet was a hold-over of Washington's Federalist Secretaries. They recommended a step similar to that taken by the first President in the issues with Great Britain and with Spain, respectively: a special mission to France as a last desperate diplomatic effort to preserve peace, to offer a new treaty similar in principle to Jay's Treaty with Great Britain. Adams thought of sending Jefferson. This was inadvisable if only because that experienced diplomat was now Vice-President. It was determined to send a joint commission of three members, one of whom would be the rejected Pinckney. The President nominated in addition John Marshall—later Secretary of State, but best known for his subsequent career as the great Chief Justice of the United States—a Federalist like C. C. Pinckney; and Elbridge Gerry of Massachusetts, a personal friend of Adams but a Jeffersonian in politics. The Federalist

ships involved. To date Congress has appropriated only \$3,910,860.61 toward payment of these adjudicated claims. Those not paid include losses of insurance companies (as distinct from losses of individual insurers) holding claims by subrogation. For a summary of the history of the French spoliation claims in the Court of Claims of the United States, and in Congress, see G. A. King, *The French Spoliation Claims*, reprinted from the *American Journal of International Law*, with additions (Wash., G. P. O., 1916) (Sen. doc. 451. 64th Cong. 1st sess.).

[1] These were assumed and paid by the United States Government to the limited amount of 20,000,000 francs, as part payment for Louisiana. See below, p. 135.

[2] The sum paid by Great Britain in execution of the awards made by the mixed claims commission set up under Jay's Treaty, Article VII. Of course the mixed claims commission (three Americans, two British subjects) did not apply precisely the same criteria of damages as the much later U. S. Court of Claims. Therefore we may only roughly compare the damages.

[3] The total American exports for the year 1795, a sample year, were \$47,990,000; imports \$69,760,000.

Senate confirmed the nominations. The three envoys met in Paris in 1797 and announced their mission at the offices of the Directory.

Talleyrand was now Minister of Foreign Affairs. As a political exile he had traveled in America (1794-1796), living on his wits by selling reputed French secrets of state and speculating in western lands. He had returned with a low opinion of the American people and their government and leaders (except Hamilton, who he believed understood Europe). They probably had a low opinion of him too. Talleyrand was now engaged in building French military victories into a series of treaties of peace and making for himself a huge fortune through bribes and speculations on inside information. Characteristically he demanded and sometimes received from those who were negotiating with him huge sums of money for himself and his grafting colleagues. From Portugal, for example, his negotiator had just taken a gratuity of a million francs. Even Pitt, with whose government the Directory was holding peace parleys in 1796 and 1797, was at one moment willing to pay £450,000 provided Talleyrand and the Directors would see that England got peace with what it wanted, namely, some Dutch colonies, Ceylon and the Cape.[1] Under the circumstances it was to be expected that he would demand his cut from the plenipotentiaries of the United States. The avaricious and crafty ex-bishop of Autun refused to receive the American Commissioners officially. Through intermediaries, who later appeared in the envoys' published despatches as Messrs. X, Y, and Z, he demanded $250,000 for himself and associates as well as a loan, under the circumstances really a gift, of several millions of dollars to France as the requisite of any negotiation and treaty. Talleyrand's intermediaries insisted that the United States could evade any violation of neutrality involved in a loan to a belligerent country by buying at par 32,000,000 florins of greatly depreciated bonds of the Batavian Republic (Netherlands) which the conquering French Republic had squeezed out of the Dutch people. The bonds never would have been paid.

The envoys were not so terribly shocked at the suggestion [2] of bribery, but they had no money for that purpose and there was no assurance that they could get what they wanted if they simply paid for a formal reception. It was apparent that it was an unblushing diplomatic hold-up. Marshall wrote, and sent in to Talleyrand, a long memorial stating the American case and arguing for a settlement by conventional diplomatic

---

[1] The obscure ramifications of these intrigues have been ferreted out by Raymond Guyot, *Le Directoire et la paix de l'Europe, des traités de Bâle à la deuxième coalition (1795-1799)* (Paris, 1912).

[2] A. J. Beveridge, *The Life of John Marshall* (4 Vols., Boston, 1916-19), Vol. II.

procedure. It was closely argued and powerful. Talleyrand and the triumphant Directory had no disposition for arguments. Despite the American election of 1796, they believed that a formidable opposition to the Government existed in the United States which would overturn President Adams if his plenipotentiaries came back without a treaty. France was beating down her enemies on the continent one by one, and there seemed a likelihood that even the most inveterate one of all, England, might soon make peace. Why then should they bother with the contemptible and ungrateful United States, which had jilted France (so they had convinced themselves) in Jay's Treaty, if there were not something in it for them personally? In one of the interviews with Talleyrand's contact man, Pinckney hotly cried: "No. No. Not a sixpence!" The two Federalist members of the Commission now left Paris, Pinckney to join his invalid family in the south of France, Marshall to report to President Adams at Philadelphia. The gullible Gerry, Republican member of the joint Commission, allowed the Directory to see that the Commission itself, as well as American opinion, was divided in policy. Gerry considered it to be his duty, contrary to the emphatic advice of his two colleagues, to stay and confabulate with the crooked Talleyrand. The Frenchman had told him that in case he too should depart, war and its horrors would engulf the two republics and their friendly peoples. Talleyrand was able to dally with Gerry until Adams recalled that inexperienced and inexcusable dignitary.

The President was now thoroughly roused. In messages to Congress he flayed French duplicity and urged preparations for war. He declared that he would never send another minister to France without assurances that he would be "received, respected and honored as the representative of a great, free, powerful and independent nation." At first the Jeffersonians could scarcely believe the President's charges. They demanded publication of the correspondence. Adams quickly sent the documents in to Congress. Their publication silenced all effective opposition. Federalist policy now triumphed everywhere. The public reaction to the treatment of the American Commissioners at Paris was to show the French Directory that it had been mistaken in relying so implicitly on a revolutionary republican element in America. Unlike the satellite states of France in Europe, there was in the United States no need for revolution to achieve a liberty already substantially established. Despite their sympathy and predilections for France, the people took Washington's advice to be Americans first. Congress speedily passed a series of laws to place the country on a war footing.

Public armed ships were allowed to capture French *armed* vessels and bring them in for prize court procedure.[1] Commercial intercourse between the United States and France or French possessions was suspended.[2] This of course served the interests of Great Britain, then trying to cut down neutral commerce with France. American merchant ships were permitted to arm themselves defensively and even to make prizes of French *armed* vessels which attacked them.[3] At no time did Congress authorize offensive hostilities or the capture of private property, such as would have ensued in an actual state of war. It declared all treaties (alliance, amity and commerce, consular convention) with France abrogated.[4] Another law provided for the internment of enemy aliens, in case of war, or their licensing or deportation;[5] and the period for completion of naturalization was stepped up from five to fourteen years,[6] lest Frenchmen by origin naturalize themselves to escape the alien act. Riding a wave of righteous popular feeling, the triumphant Federalists capped the legislation with the notorious sedition act providing heavy penalties for conspiracy against the Government or even writing or speaking to bring it into disrepute.[7] Increases to raise the regular army to 13,000 men were authorized.[8] A Navy Department was later created,[9] with appropriations for new war vessels.

At President Adams' request, General Washington agreed to come out of retirement to lead the new American army if necessary, providing Hamilton were second in command. The elevation of Hamilton to this rank emphasized the prestige and power of the Federalists and stressed the prospects of some kind of rapprochement with Great Britain in face of impending war with France. The two governments were now working out a smoother relationship on the problem of neutral rights, based mutually on more generous practice following Jay's Treaty. With Hamilton's man, Pickering, as Secretary of State, the United States no longer insisted in its foreign negotiations on the principle of free ships free goods. The new Prussian treaty of 1799 (instructions for which Pickering wrote to John Quincy Adams in 1797) did not contain that provision nor did it exclude foodstuffs or naval stores from contraband. As if in return for this recognition of the validity of British

---

[1] Acts of May 28, June 28, 1798.

[2] Acts of June 13, 1798, February 27, 1800. By the later act an exception was made in favor of Haiti then in revolt, under the Negro chieftain Toussaint L'Ouverture, against French authority.

[3] Act of June 25, 1798.

[4] Act of July 7, 1798.

[5] Act of July 6, 1798.

[6] Act of June 18, 1798.

[7] Act of July 14, 1798.

[8] Act of July 10, 1798.

[9] Act of March 2, 1799.

contentions, Pitt's government relaxed the severity of its naval practice toward the United States. Under the orders-in-council of January 8, 1794, it had allowed, in effect, a circumnavigation of the Rule of 1756 by permitting the non-contraband produce of French colonies, once imported into the United States, to be re-exported to France provided that meanwhile it had become American property.[1] This, together with special British proclamations opening up an emergency trade in American ships between the United States and the West Indies, made possible a profitable [2] war-time commerce which continued until peace was made in Europe in 1801. Under it American imports, as well as exports, steadily expanded, thereby adding to the tariff revenue and increasing the strength of the national government according to the Hamiltonian policy.

At least a naval co-operation between the United States and Great Britain seemed not unlikely at this time. Hamilton did not believe in an actual alliance. Public opinion would not stand for that, nor was it really necessary because the interests of Great Britain would impel her to common action against France. He thought that a contingent of British warships might be put at the disposal of the United States to equip, man and command. The British were ready to make such a loan, rather than see the United States build a formidable fleet of its own.

At this time Miranda, the South American revolutionist who had been watching opportunities for support of his persistent plottings in the Spanish colonies, became active in London and in Philadelphia. Incomplete documentary collections strongly suggest that Hamilton had in mind a grandiose combination of attack on French and Spanish colonial dominions, under cover of the British navy and with the help of Miranda's insurrectionary constituents. Out of this the United States would

---

[1] This was confirmed by a new order-in-council of January 25, 1798, which extended the same treatment to European neutrals.

[2] The Danish historian, E. F. Heckscher, *The Continental System; an Economic Interpretation* (N. Y., 1922) cites figures of American foreign trade to show the increasing proportion of re-exported colonial products (some of which originated in British islands):

	Exports of the U. S.			Imports of the U. S.	
	Domestic	Foreign		Home	
Year	goods	goods	Total	consumption	Total
1792	$19,000,000	$1,750,000	$20,750,000	$29,750,000	$31,500,000
1794	26,500,000	6,530,000	33,030,000	28,070,000	34,600,000
1796	40,760,000	26,300,000	67,060,000	55,140,000	81,440,000
1801	47,470,000	46,640,000	94,120,000	64,720,000	111,360,000

That is, before the war, re-exported goods were comparatively negligible. The last year of the war they nearly equaled the greatly expanded domestic exportations.

get Louisiana and the Floridas, and Great Britain would take Santo Domingo and other French islands. At any rate Spain's dominions, adjacent to the United States on the Mississippi, and elsewhere in touch of the British fleet, were most vulnerable, because, after Godoy's peace of Basle, Spain had unwisely shifted sides in the European wars. After 1796 she was the exposed ally of France. It is doubtless because of this predicament that the Prince of the Peace now hastened to execute Pinckney's Treaty and thus deprive the United States of any just pretext for war against Spain.[1] As a further blow at France, and in line with the imminent rapprochement with England, the United States extended a *de facto* recognition to the quasi-independent government of Toussaint L'Ouverture, the Negro chieftain who had dispossessed French authority following a fearful Negro insurrection in the island of Santo Domingo. That island was excepted from the non-intercourse law against France.

President Adams had his eye on an effective United States navy rather than any fleet borrowed from Great Britain. He also realized that it was only by the use of naval force that France herself could be reached, and that armed ships were necessary to protect American shipping against the now unbounded depredations. He did everything he could to speed up the construction of the navy, but allowed military preparations on land to go along indifferently despite the complaints of his Federalist advisers and supporters. Fortunately the beginnings of a navy were at hand in the three frigates already launched in 1797, by the act of 1794, for use against the Barbary states.

The legislation of 1798 rapidly created a navy by construction and by the improvisation of combat ships from revenue cutters and purchased vessels. During the hostilities with France between 1798 and 1801, forty-five ships of war of varying power were mobilized and sent cruising against French *armed* vessels, and 365 privately owned vessels were com-

[1] Despite the ratification of Pinckney's Treaty having been completed in 1796, Spain delayed evacuation of the posts left by that treaty within American territory. She had good reasons for doing so. (1) When the text of Jay's Treaty was revealed it proved to have maritime principles which were the opposite of Pinckney's Treaty. After the Franco-Spanish alliance of 1796 Spain tended to take the French point of view on this question. (2) In 1797 Great Britain in imitation of Genêt's western conspiracy covertly conspired with Senator Blount of Tennessee to raise a legion of American frontiersmen to assist a British descent from Canada via the Mississippi against Spanish possessions. (3) In 1796 a supplementary article to Jay's Treaty was ratified which, nominally interpreting the relationship of the United States' treaty of Greenville (1795) with the western Indians (following Anthony Wayne's pacification of the tribes in the battle of Fallen Timbers), threatened to set aside the exclusion, implied by Pinckney's Treaty, of British subjects from the free navigation of the Mississippi.

missioned to be armed and to capture French *armed* vessels.   Other private ships not commissioned were allowed to arm for self-defense; in fact most of them did so.   The small naval force acquitted itself well, though we must remember that France's real fleets during these years were blocked up in European ports by the British navy, if not actually sent to the bottom as Admiral Nelson had done with some of the best of them in the battle of Aboukir Bay in August, 1798.   The United States navy made about 85 prizes of French armed vessels, public and private (only two public), of which 70 valued at $700,000 were condemned.   It made no move against unarmed French merchant ships, as would have been the case in a full-fledged war.   The navy itself cost about $10,000,000, including $6,000,000 for operations.   For the three years 1798-1800 it helped protect a commerce valued at $450,-000,000 (exports and imports for those years), which yielded an import revenue of $22,000,000.[1]   The larger part of this was with England under the terms of Jay's Treaty.

The captures made against the French were not formidable when compared with the total of French spoliations [2] against the ships and property of citizens of the United States (much of which had been in the years 1793-1798).   But they were spirited.   They exhilarated and unified American public opinion, particularly one or two brilliant actions, like that of the *Constellation* versus the *Insurgente*.   In these battles the new warships worsted French public vessels of their own caliber, and showed that the young nation would strike back.   They were thus prophetic, portending increasingly embarrassing trouble with the United States—particularly if that republic should in effect unite with the great enemy England.   They were certainly one of the factors which induced the Directory to reverse its American policy.

There were other factors.   From then till now there always have been pro-French Americans domiciled amid Parisian luxuries—as well as pro-Anglican Americans seated in the lap of London's urbanities —and out of touch with real American feeling.   It had been such persons in France who at first urged the Directory to take firm steps against the Federalist régime in the United States.   In 1798 they were telling the French Government there that its policy was rapidly alienating the Francophils in the United States.   A certain sincere busybody named George Logan, a Quaker pacifist from Philadelphia, went over to France

---

[1] The naval operations are capably summarized by Gardner W. Allen, *Our Naval War with France* (Boston, 1909).

[2] See above, p. 115.

on an unauthorized mission, but equipped with a letter from Vice-President Jefferson (for which later Jefferson lamely disclaimed any official responsibility). Logan talked with the Directors and came back to America saying that they were filled with peaceful intentions. He went to Mount Vernon as an unwelcome guest to argue with General Washington. The well-intentioned Logan might unwittingly have served as a tool of a foreign adversary of his country, for his statements about the benevolence of the Directory weakened the indignation of the American public. Actually his representations do not seem seriously to have interfered with the policy of the nation's chosen President, but they did rouse much resentment elsewhere. Congress quickly passed the celebrated Logan Act (1799), making such missions a crime and punishable by a fine of not more than $5,000 and imprisonment of not more than three years. On several occasions from then till now the Logan Act has had a salutary influence on self-appointed representatives of putative American public opinion who would take it upon themselves to supplement or even correct the representations of the duly elected government of the people.[1]

Not only did this softening influence come from inveterate Francophils on both sides of the Atlantic, but Frenchmen of former experience in subordinate diplomatic positions in America courageously insisted to the Foreign Office that since 1793 it had been antagonizing the friendly United States by a most mistaken policy of appealing to the people over their government. They said this had caused the defeat of Jefferson in 1796 and was now fast driving the United States into the arms of England. One Victor du Pont, formerly a French consul at Charleston, was sent to the United States in 1798 as consul-general. President Adams would not give him an *exequatur,* but du Pont had some confidential conversations with Vice-President Jefferson who convinced him that French violence was throwing the power of America into the balance with England, to the great enhancement of British maritime strength and danger to the remaining French and the Spanish colonies in the New World. DuPont, returning, represented to Talleyrand that Jefferson had suggested that if France should reverse her policy the republicans would triumph in the next elections.[2]

Talleyrand paused. He was at this moment calculating on the re-

---

[1] Charles Warren has ventilated the immediate causes of the Logan Act in his *History of Laws Prohibiting Correspondence with a Foreign Government and Acceptance of a Commission* (Washington, G. P. O., 1917).

[2] J. A. James, "French Opinion as a Factor in Preventing War Between France and the United States, 1795-1800," *Am. Hist. Rev.,* XXX (Oct., 1924), 44-55.

vival of a great French colonial empire in the Mississippi Valley. If the United States should be driven to war New Orleans and Louisiana might be captured from France's vulnerable ally before France could get hold of that province for herself. The American dream of the ex-bishop would have vanished into nothingness. Abruptly the Directory changed front. Talleyrand wrote a letter to the French *chargé* at The Hague, to exhibit to the American Minister there, William Vans Murray, saying that if an envoy were sent to France from the United States he would "undoubtedly be received with the respect due to the representative of a free, independent and powerful nation." Immediately after his accession to power as First Consul, Bonaparte in December, 1799, caused the drastic and obnoxious maritime decree of 1798 to be repealed.

Talleyrand had not made a direct assurance, but Adams sensed the diplomatic situation and saw the opportunity to make a bold stroke for peace. He upset the complacent Federalists by sending in to the Senate a copy of Talleyrand's newest representations, together with the nomination of William Vans Murray as new Minister of the United States to France. The Federalist leaders, including the Secretary of State, Pickering,[1] and Adams' inherited Cabinet, saw their newly-gained popularity endangered by any settlement with France. They sympathized with objections in the Senate to confirming a new minister, but felt obliged to compromise on a joint commission plenipotentiary to settle outstanding difficulties first. Thus there arrived in France, in March, 1800, another commission consisting of Murray; of the Chief Justice of the United States, Oliver Ellsworth; and of William R. Davie, formerly governor of North Carolina. In Paris the envoys were received respectfully. Under Bonaparte's rule nobody asked personal bribes any more. But some delays ensued, owing to the Austrian campaign of the First Consul in northern Italy and to the negotiations for Louisiana which, unknown to the Americans, were then under way.

Talleyrand's purpose now was by a negotiation to keep the United States from confirming any connection with Great Britain and yet to temporize until France could get title to Louisiana from Spain. As the negotiations lagged in France, President Adams considered recommending to the next session of Congress a declaration of war. But by the beginning of autumn Bonaparte for the second time had crippled Austrian power in Italy, in the battle of Marengo, and had successfully

---

[1] Adams dismissed Secretary of War McHenry, May 6, 1800; and the Secretary of State, Pickering, who had tried to frustrate the new negotiation, May 10, 1800. John Marshall served as Secretary of State during the remainder of Adams' Presidency.

pressed Spain to retrocede Louisiana. He was now ready to patch up affairs with the United States as a part of a larger plan for the creation of a new colonial empire in America. In the negotiations the American Commissioners were demanding, according to their instructions, compensation for spoliations since 1793—estimated at $20,000,000 [1]—and the formal annulment of the old treaties, particularly the treaty of alliance. The French negotiators successfully took the position that the United States could claim compensation only on the basis of the old treaties; if at the same time it wished to annul those treaties it must abandon claims based on them. The Commissioners finally accepted a treaty which suspended the old treaties and all claims based by either party on them, pending further negotiation (which never took place). It renewed commercial relations on the most-favored-nation [2] basis, and, what is astonishing, incorporated the maritime provisions of the Plan of 1776, similarly to the old treaty of amity and commerce of 1778 now suspended: free ships free goods, excepting contraband of war; foodstuffs and naval stores not included (but not specifically excluded, as in the first treaty) from the contraband list; and freedom for neutral vessels to trade in non-contraband between port and port of a belligerent. These familiar principles were included at the instance of France rather than of the United States. Bonaparte was even now laying foundations for a resurrection of restrictions by the continental nations against British sea power. He hoped the new American treaty, based on the Freedom of the Seas, might inspire another Armed Neutrality which would be the last blow to his enemy England.[3]

For the United States the treaty at least brought an end to further French spoliations during the European war then in progress, terminated the unwelcome maritime hostilities between the two republics, and clinched the independence of American diplomacy by cutting loose from the entangling French alliance. For Bonaparte it served the purpose

---

[1] Compare with the $7,149,306.10, the total finally awarded by the United States Court of Claims, and the $3,910,860.61 to date appropriated by Congress to pay the awards.

[2] I.e., ". . . the two parties shall enjoy in the ports of each other, in regard to commerce and navigation, the privileges of the most-favored nation." Article VI. This was the ordinary provision of American treaties of commerce.

Talleyrand's original project for a treaty included a provision for perfect free trade between France and the United States, designed to draw American commerce away from Great Britain. It would also have limited contraband strictly to munitions. The American draft threw overboard free ships free goods, which was retrieved by the French and put into the final treaty.

Important documents selected from French archives to portray the history of this negotiation are printed in A. Du Casse, *Histoire des négociations diplomatiques relatives aux traités de Mortefontaine, de Lunéville et d'Amiens* (3 Vols., Paris, 1855), Vol. I.

[3] The Armed Neutrality of 1800 was broken by force by the British navy in 1801.

of reversing without loss of prestige the mistaken policy of his predecessors in dealing with America. The reader instantly asks—and the
negotiators must have been disturbed by the same question—why this
new treaty with the same old maritime provisions did not raise the
same troubles in the face of Jay's Treaty. The reason was that it did
not go into effect completely ratified until after France and Great Britain
had made peace. The first vote of the Senate reflected dying Federalist
opposition. It rejected the treaty, 16 yes, 14 no (20 votes necessary for
two-thirds). Adams resubmitted it shortly before he left the Presidency. This time the Senate accepted the treaty with modifications. It
voted to expunge Article II (which had suspended the former treaties
and all claims connected with them) and to limit the duration of the
treaty to eight years. This left the claims still alive. Bonaparte in turn
ratified the retrenched treaty with this further provision: "that the
two states renounce the respective pretensions which are the object
of the said article." This, if accepted, killed the claims as an international issue. The Senate on December 18, 1801, ratified the treaty with
Bonaparte's proviso accepted. Thus the famous French alliance passed
forever out of American history. Thus, too, the spoliation claims were
abandoned as any claim against France. After over a century of delay
the United States Government itself partially indemnified its own citizens for their property rights which had been relinquished for diplomatic equivalents. Without loss to American honor, President Adams
had prevented the Federalists from rushing the country into war with
France.[1]

---

[1] E. Wilson Lyon has written a basic article on "The Franco-American Convention of
1800," in *Jour. Mod. Hist.*, XII, 305, 333 (September, 1940), 305 to 333.

CHAPTER VIII

THE PROCUREMENT [1] OF LOUISIANA

(1800-1803)

BONAPARTE and Talleyrand had occupied the American Commissioners with the leisurely negotiation of the convention of 1800 while they gathered in title to the expansive province in the valley of the Mississippi. The day after the signature of the Franco-American treaty of September 30—known in French history as the treaty of Mortefontaine —namely, on October 1, 1800, France and Spain signed a secret treaty retroceding Louisiana to France.

The Mississippi Valley had consistently occupied French diplomacy since 1793, when Genêt endeavored to commission a legion of American frontiersmen to descend the river to seize New Orleans from Spain, then France's enemy. Genêt's immediate successors had instructions to try to thwart American efforts to settle the Mississippi question with Spain, particularly to prevent any right of deposit being granted to the United States at the mouth of the river. Early in 1795, Fauchet, the French Minister at Philadelphia, reviving an idea proposed in 1787 by one of his predecessors, de Moustier, urged the Directory to retrieve the province of Louisiana. He argued that it would provide a valuable source of independent supply of provisions for the French sugar islands in the Caribbean, and would be the only way to hold the American Government within the orbit of French policy—French possession of Louisiana would afford an effective means of putting pressure on the United States by menacing the frontier or tampering with the men of the western waters. Following Fauchet's advice, the French executive authorities, in the negotiations with Spain at Basle in 1795, tried in vain to get Louisiana, but actually did secure the remaining Spanish part of the island of Santo Domingo. Fauchet's successor, Adet, in 1796 sent a French General, Collot, on a trip down the Ohio and Mississippi, mapping out the strategical features of that country as if in anticipation

---

[1] The word is Channing's, whose chapters in his general history, Volume IV, have been the most satisfactory summary of Franco-American relations during the period under discussion.

of military operations there. Collot's report said that Louisiana must be enlarged by the western provinces of the United States if it were to be secure. The Directory, still planning somehow to secure Louisiana from Spain, began to study how such additions might be made. At the same time they commenced to intrigue with the Indians in the south-west region of the United States from which Spain had just agreed to retire.

In 1796 and again in 1797 the French Directory urged Spain to cede Louisiana back. They represented that Louisiana in French possession would be a convenient barrier, a rampart of protection against Great Britain and the United States. The Prince of the Peace would have been willing in 1796 to exchange it for Gibraltar, but the Directory, though it could draft such treaties, could not deliver that fortress out of British hands. Possibly at that time the French desired it merely as a territorial trading piece to make over to Great Britain in turn for British diplomatic concessions in Europe during the complicated nego-tiations for peace which went on during those years.[1] After Talley-rand's return to office in 1797 Louisiana was ardently coveted and per-sistently sought. Talleyrand and then Bonaparte himself wanted it as the continental complement of a restored French colonial empire in Amer-ica, the commercial base of which would be the sugar islands of the Caribbean, notably the richest island of them all, Santo Domingo.

After the execution of Pinckney's Treaty of 1795 the Spanish royal house no longer placed great value on the burdensome province of Louisiana, so expensive to govern and so difficult to defend. The Spanish monarchs were willing to exchange the province for political and dynas-tic advantages in Europe. They sent a special mission to France in 1800 discreetly to discover whether a trade might be made of Louisiana by which a kingdom could be created for the son-in-law of Charles IV and his consort Maria-Luisa out of French conquests in Italy. It was easy for Urquijo, the Spanish Foreign Minister, to affect to yield when Bona-parte's diplomatists pressed him to cede Louisiana. Godoy himself, the Prince of the Peace in retirement, approved the cession provided the bargain could be made still more advantageous to Spain.[2] The re-splendent First Consul, flushed with new victories won south of the

---

[1] R. Guyot, *Le directoire et la paix de l'Europe* (Paris, 1912), Ch. XI, describes these negotiations.

[2] A. P. Whitaker, "The Retrocession of Louisiana in Spanish Policy," *Am. Hist. Rev.*, XXXIX (1934), 454-476. In his subsequent volume, *The Mississippi Question, op. cit.*, he shows abundantly how "Louisiana was not only an expensive luxury but a heavy liability."

Alps, readily promised the eagerly desired tinsel kingdom in Italy in exchange for a continental domain across the Atlantic.[1]

These were the terms of the secret treaty of San Ildefonso of October 1, 1800, by which Spain agreed to the retrocession of Louisiana. The French Republic (so it was called) agreed to procure in Italy an enlargement of territory containing at least 1,200,000 inhabitants, for the Prince of Parma, son-in-law of the Spanish monarchs who so earnestly wished a real throne for the young man. The latter was then to become a real king over these domains, with a real crown, to be recognized by the Emperor (Holy Roman) "and all other interested states." In return for this, but not until six months after the full and complete execution of these stipulated equivalents, the King of Spain agreed to retrocede Louisiana "with the same extent that it now has in the hands of Spain, and that it had when France possessed it; and such as it should be after the treaties subsequently entered into between Spain and other states"; also to give six battleships to France. Orders for delivery of both the province and the battleships were to be given as soon as the Duke of Parma were put into possession of his kingdom. By the treaty of retrocession the two parties reaffirmed their alliance of 1796 and agreed to make common cause against any third power which might be provoked by the treaty.[2]

The negotiations for the delivery of Louisiana met some delay, owing to the fact that the new Kingdom of Etruria, constructed for the Duke of Parma, continued to be garrisoned by French troops and Bonaparte could not make the interested states recognize it. Anxious to complete the acquisition of the province, the French Ambassador at Madrid gave soothing assurances as to the "Kingdom" of Etruria. He further solemnly promised (July 22, 1802) in the name of the First Consul never to alienate Louisiana to any third power. The King thereupon agreed that the province should be made over, though orders for the actual delivery were delayed until October 15. Meanwhile (July 14, 1802) royal orders went out to the Spanish Intendant at New Orleans to suspend the right of deposit which had been granted to citizens of the United States by Pinckney's Treaty of 1795. This he did, October 16, 1802, also excluding neutral ships from further trade with Louisiana.[3]

[1] André Fugier, *Napoléon et l'Espagne, 1799-1808* (3 Vols., Paris, 1930), is the latest and most scholarly study. Based on prodigious research it is a worthy sequel to Guyot, *op. cit.*

[2] F. P. Renaut, *La question de la Louisiane, 1796-1806* (Paris, 1918), carries the history of Franco-Spanish diplomacy concerning the province beyond Guyot, *op. cit.*

[3] This did not suspend the free navigation of the river to citizens of the United States

No evidence has been produced to demonstrate that there was collusion between Bonaparte and the Spanish Court for this act, and some has been brought forward to argue that there was not.[1] After a protest by the United States the suspension was revoked (March 1, 1803) by Spain without consulting France, and that just as France was preparing to receive Louisiana. Certainly the suspension of 1802 pleased the French Foreign Office. Certainly the revocation was displeasing. France preferred to take over Louisiana unburdened by the treaty servitude of the right of deposit. Whatever the unknown facts may have been, it looked to the world as though France in the first instance had prompted Spain. As news of the suspension traveled up the American rivers from New Orleans and across the mountains to Washington, it became also generally known on this side of the Atlantic at last that Louisiana had been retroceded to France. People everywhere naturally concluded that there had been collusion. To the historian today, the whole tenor of French diplomacy, from 1793 to 1803, as revealed by archives not then available, suggests strongly, as the late Professor F. J. Turner put it, that Bonaparte was prepared to "intrigue with the Westerners, use the control of navigation to influence them, make of the Indians a barrier, and gradually widen the borders of his province until the Gulf of Mexico should be a French lake, and perhaps the Alleghanies the boundary of the United States."[2]

This presented the most serious menace to the territorial integrity of the United States since its independence had been established. Would distresses in Europe compel the greatest warrior of modern history to relinquish his new position in the interior country of North America, as in 1794 and 1795 such distresses had so compelled Great Britain and Spain to recognize American interests? The man who held to this hope, the man of patience and persuasion, the pacifist who believed in economic coercion as a substitute for warfare, the friend of republican France, was now in the White House. Napoleon Bonaparte became Thomas Jefferson's terrible problem.

[1] See the contributions by A. P. Whitaker, "France and the American Deposit at New Orleans," *Hisp. Am. Hist. Rev.*, XI (1931), 485-502; and in his *Mississippi Question, op. cit.*; and E. W. Lyon, "The Closing of the Port of New Orleans," in *Am. Hist. Rev.*, XXXVII (1932), 280-286.

[2] *Op. cit.* No satisfactory evidence has yet been produced to sustain the thesis that French policy in 1802 was simply the continuation of a series of consistent attempts, commenced by the Bourbons, to get control of Louisiana. This rested on a memoir attributed to Vergennes and first published in 1802, presumably to give this appearance of persistent continuity. Its authenticity has been shattered. For summary of the question, see Mildred Stahl Fletcher, "Louisiana as a Factor in French Diplomacy From 1763 to 1800," *Miss. Vall. Hist. Rev.*, XVII (Dec., 1930), 367-376.

When Jefferson became President in 1801 he did not know of the actual retrocession of Louisiana. He was filled with friendly sentiments for France, particularly now that Adams' new treaty had been ratified, and he glowed with benevolence in putting into execution, in advance of actual exchange of ratifications, the articles of the treaty which called for an end of hostilities. He sent as new minister to France, Robert R. Livingston, a notorious Francophil who in 1781 had owed to French diplomacy his appointment as Secretary of Foreign Affairs. Friendly and unembarrassing relations appeared to be completely restored, and most happily, because France presently signed the peace of Amiens with England. Embarrassing questions of neutral rights now might be expected to vanish in the midst of European peace. Into this prospect, so pleasing to the contemplation of a man like President Jefferson, came disconcerting rumors of the retrocession of Louisiana. These rumors were the more upsetting because it had been Jefferson's fixed belief that in good time the United States would somehow inherit from Spain's weak sovereignty at least the Floridas and Louisiana. The fateful shadow of Bonaparte suddenly had fallen across the Promised Land. It had cast its somber meaning over the whole Mississippi Valley even as the new President was preparing to send Lewis and Clark with a small company of American troops across Louisiana (with Spain's reluctant consent) on an exploring expedition to the Pacific Coast to spy out Canaan.[1] Bonaparte, about to take possession of Louisiana, interrupted Jefferson's whole train of thought.

Reports of the retrocession stimulated Jefferson but strangely enough do not appear greatly to have alarmed him. He and his Secretary of State, James Madison, conceived the idea of trying to offset France's ominous reappearance in the Valley of the Mississippi by purchasing from her West Florida as a substitute outlet for American commerce. That is, purchase it from France if France had acquired it; if not, from Spain, and maybe France would assist such a deal. The new Minister to Spain, Charles Pinckney, was directed to co-operate with Livingston in France to this end. When news of the retrocession was confirmed positively in 1802—Talleyrand at first had denied it to Livingston—Jefferson again turned to the stratagem which had served him so well as Vice-President: to tell France her unwise action would drive the United

[1] It has not been proven that, when Jefferson commissioned Lewis and Clark, he expected immediately to acquire Louisiana west of the Mississippi. Rather his motive was to explore the possibilities of the Indian trade in that region. See R. B. Guinness, "The Purpose of the Lewis and Clark Expedition," in *Miss. Vall. Hist. Rev.*, XX (June, 1933), 90-101.

States into the arms of England. For this message he made use of a
friendly Frenchman.

Pierre S. du Pont de Nemours was a French powder-maker, established in the United States, who was then departing for France on a
visit. Through him Jefferson sent a despatch to Livingston, which
du Pont was allowed to read before sealing. It prophesied that French
possession of New Orleans would drive the United States into an
alliance with the British fleet and nation. Jefferson expected du Pont
to mention the contents of the despatch to influential persons: to Talleyrand, perhaps to Bonaparte himself. He wrote another personal letter
to du Pont, presumably also for display. He thought that his French
friend might be able to impress on the government of France the inevitable consequences of taking possession of Louisiana. "As I here
mention," Jefferson confided, "the cession of New Orleans and the
Floridas to us would be a palliation, yet I believe it would be no more"—
it would some day cost France a war which would annihilate her on
the ocean. The President concluded by saying that *his* administration
felt none but the friendliest sentiments for Talleyrand. Du Pont, as
he set sail, wrote to Jefferson suggesting that he bargain with France
for New Orleans and the Floridas, by offering to guarantee forever
French possession of the west bank of the Mississippi, and to help
France get Canada in her next war with England; maybe he might even
make an offer to buy New Orleans—that would be cheaper than a war
or an armament. While du Pont de Nemours circulated among his
official acquaintances in Paris, Livingston worked tirelessly at the impossible task of persuading Talleyrand and Napoleon to cede New
Orleans, also Louisiana above the Arkansas River, to the United States.
This last was Livingston's own idea. Unwittingly taking a text from
former French notes to Spain, he argued that upper Louisiana in
American possession would be a protecting buffer, against British establishments in Canada, for the remainder of French possessions on the
continent.

So far Jefferson had merely resorted to indirect suggestions to Bonaparte to desist from taking Louisiana. What finally roused him to
sense a great crisis was a menace to the political security of his
administration and his party, even to the Union itself. When news
traveled up the Mississippi of the suspension of the right of deposit, a
cry of indignation swept the western country. The dwindling Federalist
opposition everywhere seized hold of this as a compelling issue. If
Jefferson did nothing immediately to solve the Mississippi question in

its latest form, his hold on power was in great danger. A year later, he said, reviewing the diplomacy of the Louisiana procurement: "I did not expect he [Napoleon] would yield till a war took place between France and England, and my hope was to palliate and endure, if Messrs. Ross, Morris [spokesmen in Congress of the Federalist opposition], &c., did not force a premature rupture, until the event [i.e., a new European war]. I believed the event not very distant, but acknowledge it came on sooner than I had expected." Peace was Jefferson's passion.[1]

The West on the whole at this juncture trusted Jefferson and his party more than it did the Federalists and Hamilton's hand behind them. Notwithstanding exuberant expressions against the Spanish Intendant's proclamation, the men of the western waters were content to let Jefferson deal with their problem in his own way. The increasing stability of settlement and growth of commerce and capital had made them more conservative in recent years and less quick on the trigger. As in 1798, the Federalist attempt to make political profit out of a war crisis was opposed by a President's peace policy. Both parties, it must be said, were playing politics. Jefferson's pacifism was reckless in the extreme for the nation; but war meant the ruin of his party. Thanks to European complications over which he had no control, he was to save his party and unexpectedly to double the territory of his country.

It was the Federalist opposition, then, which forced Jefferson's hand. It was a Frenchman, du Pont de Nemours, who had suggested to him that possibly France might sell New Orleans and that it might be cheaper to pay a good price than to fight a war. In early January, 1803, arrived another letter from du Pont in Paris, repeating the suggestion, and outlining a treaty for the purchase of New Orleans and both Floridas for $6,000,000.[2] Jefferson read it anxiously just as he was trying to think of something to do to quiet the Federalists. At the President's suggestion Congress appropriated $2,000,000 for his use, and Jefferson immediately sent in to the Senate the nomination of James Monroe as a minister extraordinary to France, to be empowered jointly with the regular minister there, to purchase New Orleans and the Floridas.

Monroe was a traditional champion of the navigation of the Mississippi and of western interests. His second mission to France was good domestic politics; it was also another resort to the time-worn, but hitherto successful, American expedient of an impressive special mission as a last resort for peace. The interesting instructions to him and

[1] P. L. Ford, *The Writings of Thomas Jefferson* (10 Vols., N. Y., 1892-99), VIII, 295.

[2] The most complete edition of the *Correspondence of Jefferson and Du Pont de Nemours* is by Gilbert Chinard (Baltimore, 1931).

Livingston attest at once Jefferson's hopes, his uncertainties, his ingenuity, and the influence of du Pont de Nemours. The envoys were
to request France to sell to the United States the Floridas and the
"island" of New Orleans for not over 50,000,000 *livres* (about $10,000,000
at par), and to guarantee the free navigation of the Mississippi to
citizens of both countries (it was already guaranteed to the United States
by the terms of Pinckney's Treaty of 1795). In return for this the
United States would give to French vessels south of the boundary of 31°
equal treatment with American vessels, with a right of deposit, and extend
to France most-favored-nation treatment in the ports of East and West
Florida; and *if necessary* the United States would guarantee forever (as
du Pont had once suggested) the remainder of French Louisiana on the
west bank of the Mississippi (Jefferson thought such a guaranty might
be executed by a subsidy in lieu of military assistance). In case only
a part of the territory desired could be purchased, the Floridas were
to be estimated at one-fourth the value of New Orleans, and East Florida
at one-half the value of West Florida. If France would not cede the
whole "island" of New Orleans, then the Commissioners were to try to
get jurisdiction over a town on the Mississippi for a place of commercial
deposit; if no cession of the Floridas were possible, they should seek
rights of deposit also on the rivers in West Florida. If the French
Government should meditate hostilities against the United States, or
force a war by closing the Mississippi, then Monroe and Livingston
were to cross the Channel and invite Great Britain to a treaty of
alliance in which the two parties would agree to make no separate peace
or truce. In England at this time they were hoping that the United
States would seize New Orleans, as the Federalists demanded, and
accept the issue with Bonaparte.[1] Should France only deny the right
of deposit without otherwise disturbing the navigation of the river, the
envoys were to make no positive engagement but leave it to Congress
to decide between immediate war and further procrastination.

As Monroe set sail again for France (March 8, 1803) there was
nothing, aside from du Pont's mysterious advice, on this side of the
ocean to suggest that Bonaparte would give up his plans of colonial
empire to please President Thomas Jefferson. Never did an envoy sail
forth under less promising circumstances. Three weeks later, as a fast
wind bore him toward the shores of Europe, the whole international

---

[1] Henry Adams in his memorable history has described the varying motives and purposes of England, France and the United States in the rapidly moving international
drama of Louisiana.

situation had suddenly changed. Europe's distress had again become America's advantage. The First Consul, apprised of Monroe's mission, had decided to sell not only New Orleans, but the whole great province of Louisiana, lock, stock and barrel! Historians have tried in vain to unlock the mysteries of the Napoleonic mind so as to learn exactly why he decided to do this and precisely when. Sometime in the early months of 1803 he suddenly made up his mind to get rid of the province, for the following reasons.

The structure of a revived French colonial empire in North America was an inverted pyramid which rested on the island of Santo Domingo. This rich island and the smaller Guadeloupe and Martinique, were expected to furnish a prosperous business in tropical products, which would employ French navigation and, together with the fisheries of Newfoundland, build up sea power. Louisiana would be the necessary continental complement for the islands, an independent source of supply of foodstuffs and lumber; later perhaps the province would be itself immensely wealthy. While uneasy Europe was still at peace Bonaparte had planned to occupy New Orleans. First it was necessary to restore order on the island of Santo Domingo. An army under his brother-in-law, General Leclerc, succeeded in doing this after hard fighting, by the close of 1802, only to be thinned away by yellow fever, a more deadly scourge than the heroic blacks of the betrayed Negro chieftain, Toussaint L'Ouverture. In that one year fifty thousand Frenchmen found their graves on the island, dead from war and fever. This delayed for a decisive year the occupation of Louisiana itself.

Despite the dismaying news from Santo Domingo, notwithstanding the death of Leclerc, the First Consul during the autumn and winter of 1802-3 pushed the assembling of an expedition for the reinforcement of the devastated island and the occupation of New Orleans. Troops and transports under the command of General Victor gathered at Helvoet-Sluis, in Holland, now iced in by early frosts. Had it not been for the untimely heavy cold of that winter which sealed the harbor until spring, this expedition might have embarked in 1802 as planned, and the history of Louisiana, and of the United States,[1] and of Canada, and of Great Britain might have been who knows what. The transports were frozen in until after the appearance of another European crisis. During the winter, events had happened in Europe which induced Napoleon to salvage his whole Louisiana enterprise before any French forces had occupied it.

[1] E. Wilson Lyon, *Louisiana in French Diplomacy, 1795-1804* (Norman, Okla., 1934)

The Peace of Amiens proved to be only an armed truce. After formal hostilities in 1801 had ceased, a bitter commercial warfare continued between France and Great Britain. Other political factors quickly rose to jeopardize the peace. The news of the retrocession of Louisiana and the appearance of Leclerc's forces in the Caribbean so near Jamaica alarmed the English. Furthermore, Bonaparte had begun to upset the European dispositions of the treaty of Amiens by putting himself in controlling power in Holland, in Italy, and in Switzerland. Great Britain in turn postponed restitution of some of her overseas conquests and refused to evacuate Malta as required. The First Consul decided to renew war and to let go the still unoccupied province of Louisiana rather than halt his pace in Europe. In preference to seeing Great Britain capture the province at the outbreak of war he decided to sell it to the United States for 50,000,000 francs and to use the money to launch his military campaigns. To do this it was necessary to work fast while a nominal peace still existed.

Monroe's coach was rumbling towards Paris when Talleyrand astonished Livingston by asking what he would give for all of Louisiana. Sensing another war, Livingston had been assiduously arguing for the cession of New Orleans and upper Louisiana. He tried not to be nonplused at the dazzling offer of the whole, affected some indifference, but did not spurn it. He was unable to nail the bargain then and there as he would have liked for his own political capital and presidential ambitions. He had to await Monroe's arrival, for joint powers. After some haggling with the French Minister of Finance, Barbé-Marbois,[1] the two plenipotentiaries quickly bought the province for 60,000,000 francs [2] plus the assumption by the United States of claims [3] of its citizens not to exceed 20,000,000 francs.

[1] His *Histoire de la Louisiane et de la cession de cette colonie par la France aux Etats-Unis de l'Amérique Septentrionale* (Paris, 1829, Eng. translation, Philadelphia, 1830) though written a quarter century later is one of the important sources for the transaction.

[2] Curiously enough the purchase money was transferred, after the outbreak of the war, through English bankers.

[3] These claims are not to be confused with the spoliation claims wiped out by the Convention of 1800. That convention had provided: (1) restoration of captures made after signature of the treaty; (2) debts owed by the French Government for supplies, mostly provisions, purchased from American citizens, to be paid by France.

Other provisions of the treaty cession: (1) The inhabitants of the ceded territory were to be incorporated in the Union of the United States as soon as possible, meanwhile to be protected in the free enjoyment of their liberty, property and religion. (2) The United States to execute Spain's treaties with the Indians. (3) French and Spanish ships loaded with French and Spanish products, respectively, to be admitted exclusively into legal ports of the ceded territory for 12 years in same manner and charges as American ships similarly freighted. (4) After the 12 years French ships to be treated on a most-favored-nation basis.

Two treaties provided for the cession and for the payment. They were dated April 30, 1803. On May 15 Great Britain declared war on France. Two weeks later, May 27, died the young King of Etruria, for whom the Spanish monarchs had ceded Louisiana to France. His tinsel

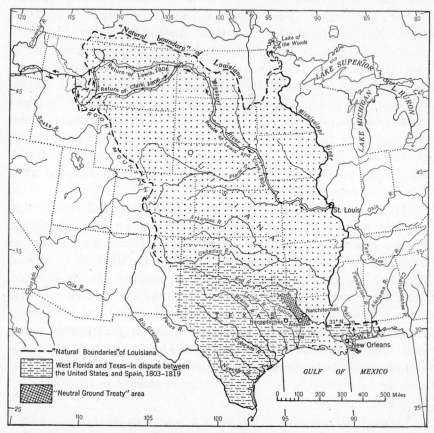

Map 9. Disputed Boundaries of Louisiana.

kingdom speedily disappeared in the swirl of Napoleonic diplomacy and war in Italy.

The American plenipotentiaries purchased in identical words from France what France had recently secured from Spain: "Louisiana with the Same extent that it now has in the hands of Spain, and that it had when France possessed it; and Such as it Should be after the Treaties subsequently entered into between Spain and other States." This was a typical Talleyrandian article full of potential disputation. The significance to the United States of the addition of Louisiana cannot be overestimated. It doubled the territory of the republic, if the most moderate definition of its boundaries be accepted. It presented the federal union with a new domain that was to be a great laboratory for the experiment of democratic nationalism, with all its achievements and problems, including the tragedy of the Civil War. It gave to the nation one of the earth's richest storehouses of foodstuffs, fuel, and power. It impounded within American boundaries the great valley of the Mississippi which some still say will be the terrestrial foundation of English-speaking culture of future centuries. Be that as it may or may not be, Louisiana became the vestibule of American expansion to Florida, Texas, New Mexico, California, Oregon, Alaska. Already in 1805 Lewis and Clark had crossed the suddenly acquired American soil to the Pacific Northwest and placed the flag of the United States at the mouth of the Columbia. There the deep waters of the great ocean beckoned, as they were to beckon throughout the next century and more, a period increasingly freighted with portentous international questions which one day would deny the satisfying name of that vast expanse of sea.

The Louisiana procurement is the most magnificent example of the thesis which we have maintained in this volume: Europe's distresses were America's advantage. The horrible servile insurrection in Santo Domingo, the dreadful yellow fever there, those dire calamities helped the United States to stretch across North America; the stars in their courses were favoring American expansion when the deep frost set in by the harbor of Helvoet-Sluis; but the final turn in American destiny came from another stirring of the hundred years' war between Great Britain and France, now revolutionary France incarnated in the person of the conquering Corsican. That decisive turn was European, not American.

The reader has already divined that the cession of Louisiana by France to the United States at once would raise serious issues with Spain. We must postpone for a couple of chapters a discussion of these while we turn to the reappearance of the "historic problem" of neutral rights brought up again by the renewal of war in 1803 between France and Great Britain.

CHAPTER IX

NEUTRAL RIGHTS AND IMPRESSMENT

(1803-1812)

THE rivalries and wars of European powers had enabled the United States to establish its independence. Separation from British sovereignty straightway had made it possible to escape participation in the next European conflict, the wars of the French Revolution (1793-1801). Neutrality had given to Washington and Adams a free hand to preserve and strengthen American independence, to protect the federal experiment in the years of its infancy, to redeem the territorial integrity of the United States by Jay's Treaty and Pinckney's Treaty, to escape by the treaty of 1800 from the entanglement and patronage of the French alliance of 1778. Europe's distresses, again, had given Jefferson the chance in 1803 by an unparalleled stroke of good fortune to double the territory of the United States with the procurement of Louisiana. The Napoleonic wars (1803-1815) permitted the republic thus strengthened to move ahead unmolested for another decade, only finally to become involved in the world-wide conflict of the warring nations. In 1812 the United States found itself aligned on the side of the autocrat of Europe against Great Britain, the arbitrary defender of such constitutional liberty and representative government as were left in the Old World. The ever-living question of neutral rights, including impressment, combined with the expansionist sentiment of the new American West, took the country into that war. We must therefore analyze the reappearance of the problem of neutral rights, already such a preponderating part of the diplomatic history of the United States; the motives of the belligerents in constructing their opposing maritime systems; the ineligible position of the United States between them; and the curious and complicated history of Jeffersonian policy in dealing with them.

British sea power stood between Napoleon Bonaparte and his ambitions to make himself master of Europe and through Europe of the world. Even by getting together the maritime armaments of subject states like Spain and Holland he could not muster sufficient forces to overthrow Great Britain by naval combat. He tried that early in the war and failed in the campaign that ended with Nelson's great victory at Trafalgar (October 21, 1805). During the rest of the long conflict the Emperor of the French fought without a navy. He was nevertheless resolved to worst England despite her naval supremacy. Napoleon revived and perfected, and made a fundamental principle of his statecraft, an idea that had already been put forward in the earlier wars of the Revolution: Great Britain was mistress of the seas, he would be master of the land, of the continent of Europe. Thus he would be able to seal up the ports of all Europe against British commerce, not only of Europe but the colonies overseas of European countries, for example South America. The great British mercantile fleet, on which the prosperity, the very life, of England rested, from which she drew those opulent revenues that furnished subsidies to continental allies for use against France, that fleet of trading ships, protected by the unconquerable British navy, would be left sailing the seas unmolested but with no ports of trade. With her trading ships thus wandering around the ocean with no place to go, the financial basis of British naval and military power would collapse. This was the essence of the continental system of Napoleon, and the continental system was the basis of his whole policy.

On the other hand, Great Britain relied solely on her navy for her own defense and the protection of her well established trading channels. She clung to her traditional interpretation of international law, lest her enemy by neutral carriage make up for his lack of sea power. Beyond that, in the measures which we are to note, she endeavored to utilize the circumstances of the war to deprive the neutrals from sharing in the shipping formerly possessed by France in time of peace, and to take over that shipping and its profits,[1] thus making the war help to pay for itself. The great struggle between the mistress of the seas and the master of the land was in effect a prodigious trade conflict. Neutral rights went by the board as each powerful belligerent built up a structure of nominally "retaliatory" measures. It is not possible for the scholar at his desk to state precisely who it was who committed the original sin that may have justified a first retaliation. Each bitter adversary was glad of a pretext to draw out and to use his most deadly weapon of war. The contest was a prototype of that between Great Britain and Germany a century later.

When the war began again in 1803 each belligerent took steps to

[1] Professor W. E. Lingelbach has demonstrated this in a notable article written in 1917, "England and Neutral Trade" in *Military Historian and Economist*, II (1917), 153-178, comparing practice in 1914-1917 with what he is convinced to be the more selfish procedure of 1805.

shut off the other's trade. Napoleon controlled Italy and Holland. It was simple for him to close those ports, and those of his trembling ally, Spain. England's most profitable trade on the continent was with the Hanse towns, Bremen, Hamburg, and Lübeck, through which goods filtered into central Europe, into France itself. Napoleon occupied Hanover, a possession of the British royal house. From thence he interfered with the trade of the neutral ports of Hamburg and Bremen, ordering the seizure of all British ships, goods and sailors to be found there. (In 1806 he occupied Lübeck along with Prussia.) The British on their part declared a blockade of the Weser (Bremen) and Elbe (Hamburg) rivers, and in 1804 (August 9) declared all French ports on the Channel and North Sea to be in a state of blockade; this authorized the capture of neutral ships with cargoes, however innocent, which attempted to penetrate the blockade.[1] The French asserted that this blockade was illegal, that it did not conform to the definition of the Armed Neutralities (of 1780 and of 1800), by which a blockade must be maintained with forces sufficiently near to make access to the coast really dangerous. The British denied that the blockade was illegal. They had never agreed, anyway, to the definitions of the Armed Neutralities.

These measures did not greatly interfere with American trade, which had remained on a prosperous basis. That still was regulated, so far as Great Britain was concerned, by the terms of Jay's Treaty; and by the convention of 1800, so far as France was concerned. At the outset (June 24, 1803) a British order-in-council regulated neutral commerce substantially on the same basis as during the last years of the previous war: that is, neutral vessels might trade in non-contraband goods with enemy colonies providing they did not carry produce of enemy colonies *directly* to an enemy home port; they were allowed to import the enemy goods into the neutral homeland,[2] and to re-export these goods, thus neutralized, to the enemy country. This practice of circuitous voyage had been sanctioned by a decision of the British prize courts arising out of the late war, though decided in 1802 during time of peace—the case of the *Polly*. In this case the judge, Sir William Scott (Lord Stowell), did not go into the question of whether a rebate of tariff duty upon re-exportation of the goods nullified the neutralization

---

[1] E. F. Heckscher, *op. cit.*, has sketched instructively the development of these belligerent measures.

[2] The order-in-council of 1803 differed from that of 1798 in that it did not allow neutrals to take enemy colonial produce to an English port. This was reserved for British bottoms.

of them. When war was renewed neutrals took like ducks to water to this lucrative war carriage. In 1805, 1806, and 1807 the total of foreign goods re-exported from the United States was greater than the exports of domestic goods, viz.:

Year	Domestic goods exported	Foreign goods re-exported	Total
1792	$19,000,000	$ 1,750,000	$ 20,750,000
1794	26,500,000	6,530,000	33,030,000
1801	47,470,000	46,640,000	94,120,000
1803	42,210,000	13,590,000	55,800,000
1804	41,470,000	36,230,000	77,700,000
1805	42,390,000	53,180,000	95,570,000
1806	41,250,000	60,280,000	101,540,000
1807	48,700,000	59,640,000	108,340,000

[1808 was embargo year] [1]

It is impossible to tell what proportion of these re-exportations originated in the British or the French West India Islands. In so far as they came from the French islands the neutralized carriage was useful to France, because it afforded for her colonial exports a neutral bridge over the British navy.

This lucrative neutral commerce antagonized the English navigation interests. Responding to public opinion, the Prize Appeal Court of the Privy Council, Sir William Grant presiding, in the celebrated case of the *Essex* (1805) decided that goods could not be neutralized by importation into a neutral country unless they paid a *bona fide* import duty; remission of this duty upon re-exportation of the same goods was a mere subterfuge. To all effects, transit of goods under such circumstances constituted a *continuous voyage* from enemy colony to enemy homeland and was thus a violation of the Rule of 1756.[2] At one stroke this wiped away the neutral carriage by broken voyage that had become established since Jay's Treaty. But British navigation interests were demanding even more. An influential publicist, James Stephen, in 1805, published a famous pamphlet, *War in Disguise, or The Frauds of the Neutral Flags*,[3] attacking any concessions to neutral navigation. According to Stephen, neutrals should be excluded as much as possible from wartime trade in order that British ships might take over that

[1] Statistics from Heckscher, *op. cit.*, 103. See also W. Alison Phillips, *The Napoleonic Period* (Columbia University Press, 1936), Volume III of *Neutrality, Its History, Economics and Law.*

[2] See above, p. 39, n. 3.

[3] The book was reprinted, as a volume of subject matter germane to issues concerning neutral rights, in 1917.

carriage. It was Stephen's idea that the enemy commerce could be made to pass to Europe by way of England, paying import taxes on the way. Neutral ships should be allowed to take it from England to enemy ports (of course a British ship would have been captured immediately it entered an enemy port), providing they received a license to do so, for which a high fee must be paid. Thus should England regulate colonial commerce with the enemy according to her own liking and profit. Thus ought she to make that traffic pay along the way in England a toll that might be used to sustain the war. Stephen's doctrine was presently to be put into effect, in addition to the Rule of 1756 as interpreted in the *Essex* case.

The *Essex* decision, together with other issues soon to be noted in their proper order (British "blockade" of American neutral ports, and impressment), profoundly antagonized American public opinion, though never to the point of war—the profits of neutral wartime carriage were still so great that the maritime states of the Union were willing to tolerate these national wrongs provided they themselves continued to make money; and the inland communities were long apathetic. Announcement of the decision came at a time when Jefferson's Administration was momentarily, if fatuously, aspiring to alliance with Great Britain as a means of forcing Spain, and France, to recognize the claim of the United States to West Florida as a part of Louisiana.[1] The new British policy and the sudden capture of great numbers of American ships engaged in a trade hitherto unmolested showed the President that he could not hope to have England solve his Spanish problems. It forced him to turn to other expedients for settling the question of West Florida, and to seek means of redress for Great Britain's arbitrary Rule of 1756. The result was the non-importation act of 1806.

When the protests of a neutral government are ignored by a highhanded and overbearing belligerent, the neutral may either: (1) submit after protest, with an uncertain expectation that after the war the belligerent will be agreeable to a reasonable settlement including compensation for damages done; or (2) fight in defense of its rights. Jefferson had often thought of war against Spain, weak and helpless. He had expected that sort of war to be carried on under cover of the British navy, also at war with Spain, leaving the Floridas as easy spoil to frontier militiamen. He never thought of making war against Great Britain, resolute and strong. He persisted in a parsimonious policy of reduction of naval defenses when the only means of securing American

[1] See below, p. 184.

rights and preventing national ignominy was at the cannon's mouth. For once his trust in European wars to solve American diplomatic difficulties had failed him. A European war now threatened to drag him into the maelstrom. But the President saw another alternative offering escape from the dilemma of submit or fight: economic coercion. By boycotting a belligerent as the Colonies had done to Great Britain back in 1765, 1767, 1775, to secure redress of imperial grievances, he would force respect for neutral rights.

Successive British ministries had correctly gauged Jeffersonian statecraft. Inveterate dependence upon commercial coercion accompanied by no preparation for war, even by a diminution in naval armament, encouraged them—as well as the rulers of France—to be the more insolent because they were convinced that the United States would not go to war no matter what the provocation. This explains the increasing desperation of American diplomacy in face of the belligerent systems now developing in Europe.

The non-importation act of April 23, 1806, in protest against the *Essex* decision, declared that after the following November 1 the importation of certain British manufactures would be prohibited unless a satisfactory settlement were meanwhile reached between the two countries. At the same time another extraordinary mission—like that of Jay in 1794—was sent to London, consisting of James Monroe, the regular minister at the Court of St. James, and William Pinkney of Maryland, to make a new treaty defining neutral rights. Jefferson was resorting to the Federalist diplomacy which he had so detested twelve years before. Because of the protracted negotiations which followed, the enforcement of the non-importation act was postponed until December 14, 1807.

Monroe and Pinkney had instructions to settle two other issues in addition to the question of neutral carriage: the "blockade" of American neutral ports, and impressment of American citizens. Each of these now requires mention.

Jay's Treaty of 1794, due to expire on October 28, 1807,[1] had given to British warships and privateers with their prizes a freedom of American ports,[2] and provided that their officers should be treated with the

---

[1] Articles I to X, which were concerned with the settlement of the immediate issues of 1794 such as boundaries, posts, debts, Mississippi, etc., were permanent. Articles XI to XXVIII, concerning maritime law and commerce, were limited to 12 years following exchange of ratifications.

[2] Except where contrary to existing treaties. The existing French treaties expired in 1801.

respect due their commissions. The British took advantage of this guaranteed hospitality to make American harbors bases of supply for cruisers hovering off those very ports to capture American shipping alleged to be violating the Rule of 1756 and other British constructions of maritime law, and to impress from their crews alleged British subjects.

Impressment was the most corrosive issue ever existing between Great Britain and the United States. The British Government traditionally had insisted upon the doctrine of inalienable allegiance: once a Britisher always a Britisher. Many European governments still espouse that doctrine today. If unregulated by treaty,[1] it is a source of many disputes concerning subjects who have evaded military or naval service by emigrating within the sovereignty of nations which, like the United States, a nation of immigrants, uphold the right of expatriation.[2] During the wars of the French Revolution and Napoleon, the conditions of service aboard a British man-of-war were so barbarous and inhuman as to discourage decent subjects from enlisting. Consequently the navy had to be recruited by force with press-gangs, operating in seaport towns or boarding British merchant ships. British subjects by the thousands, particularly sailor folk, sought sanctuary in service on American ships. Many of them secured naturalization papers making them full-fledged American citizens. These occasionally included deserters from warships, as well as swarms from British merchant ships. Albert Gallatin estimated in 1807 that the British marine (private and public) was losing annually at least 2500 men by desertion or engagement on vessels flying the American flag.[3] This became a vital problem for the British nation and people then depending on sea power in a battle for life or death. The Admiralty successfully insisted on the right to examine neutral ships in British harbors and on the high seas for British deserters or subjects evading naval duty. It would acknowledge no foreign naturalization of such subjects. It never asserted a *right* to impress American natural-born citizens, but eager "press" captains frequently did so "by mistake" when an American citizen was unfortunate enough to look or speak like an Englishman. A cockney

---

[1] For naturalization treaties of the United States to 1936, see note at end of chapter.

[2] That is the right to forswear allegiance to one nation and accept naturalization in another.

[3] Henry Adams, *History of the United States of America* (9 Vols., New York, 1891-98), III, 94. Despite small errors charged up to him by meticulous writers of more recent monographs, Adams' *History* remains the most notable study of this or any other period of the diplomatic history of the United States.

accent might cost an American months of involuntary servitude or even his life. The British Government tried to make the burden of proof lie on the United States that impressed seamen were really American citizens. When this was proven, after much diplomatic note-writing and official red tape, the seaman was released without indemnity, but the process sometimes took months and even years. The United States went so far as to furnish its mariners with official statements attesting their citizenship; these made no distinction between natural-born and naturalized citizens. Irresponsible sailormen sold these "protections" to British subjects; the established price was about ten dollars. The British refused to recognize a "protection" as proof of citizenship. For Great Britain impressment from neutral ships was a means of procuring indispensably needed man power in time of great national crisis. For the United States it was a threat to its national sovereignty and to the liberty of its own citizens.

The United States, beginning as early as 1791, in vain made repeated attempts to settle the impressment issue. The issue was never settled, although Great Britain has ceased the practice since 1815. Before then it is estimated that a total of at least 10,000 men were forcibly taken from American merchant ships and impressed into British naval service. About one-tenth of these proved to be British subjects. The British Admiralty estimated that during the wars 20,000 British seamen had taken service in American vessels. While the statistics are not precise, it seems that for every ten impressments the British navy retrieved only one real British subject.[1] Many human tragedies are hidden in those figures. The culmination of insults to the American flag and enslavement of its citizens to fight naval battles for England came when in 1807 the United States public ship of war *Chesapeake* was leaving the bay of that name for the Mediterranean station. Not anticipating any hostile action, her deck was encumbered with gear and supplies still to be packed away for the long voyage, articles which cluttered about her guns and made them unworkable. In this helpless condition she was summoned by a British man-of-war, the *Leopard,* to be searched for deserters from certain British ships. The *Leopard* herself had just issued forth from Lynnhaven Bay, where she had been enjoying the hos-

[1] J. F. Zimmerman, *Impressment of American Seamen* (New York, 1925). There is a classic statement of the issue of impressment in A. T. Mahan, *Sea Power in its Relations to the War of 1812* (1st ed., 2 Vols., Boston, 1905), I, 114-128. A more recent and equally perspicuous analysis is in A. L. Burt, *The United States, Great Britain and British North America from the Revolution to the Establishment of Peace after the War of 1812* (Yale Univ. Press, 1940).

pitality of American waters. When Commodore Barron refused to submit, the *Leopard* fired into the *Chesapeake,* killed three and wounded eighteen men, forced submission, and lined up the crew. Four alleged British deserters were taken off and the humiliated commander let go with his ship. One of the four was a genuine British deserter. Him they promptly hanged. The other three were native-born Americans who had escaped from a British warship after being impressed. These were impressed again. After the *Chesapeake* affair, Jefferson ordered all British warships in American waters to get out and stay out. He made the entire abolition of impressment an indispensable part of the satisfaction to be required of the British Government for the incident. Negotiations over this incident, and continuing impressments from American merchant vessels progressively embittered Anglo-American relations for the next five years. Not until 1812, on the eve of war, did Great Britain, when it was too late to preserve peace, make belated amends by formally restoring the two surviving men to the deck of the *Chesapeake,* and providing indemnities for the wounded and for the families of those killed. They were accepted at that last moment without any disclaimer of the "right" of impressment. The failure to obtain a repudiation of impressment was balanced in the public mind by the recent worsting of a British warship in the accidental naval encounter of the *President* and the *Little Belt.* In the popular imagination this atoned the insult on the *Chesapeake* five years before. Really it did not alter the issue.

Submission to impressment marked the nadir of national disgrace in the history of American diplomacy. "However the British Government," wrote Mahan, "might justify in terms the impressment of seamen from American ships, or the delay of atonement for such an insult as that of the *Chesapeake,* the nation which endured the same, content with reams of argument instead of blow for blow, had sunk beneath contempt as an inferior race, to be cowed and handled without gloves by those who felt themselves the masters." The *Chesapeake* affair alone, not promptly redressed, justified war.

Returning to the extraordinary mission of Monroe and Pinkney to England, those envoys signed a treaty, December 31, 1806, with Great Britain, designed to take the place of the expiring Jay's Treaty. It is a commentary on the inconsistency of partisan politics and on the political character of James Monroe that he himself should have signed this instrument so closely resembling the maritime articles of Jay's Treaty which he had once so despised. Monroe and Pinkney's treaty, unlike Jay's, provided for no arbitration of spoliations. The principal other difference—as to maritime articles—was that the proposed new treaty contained a provision by which the neutralization of foreign colonial produce by importation into an American port was to be recognized, and a voyage to an "unblockaded" European port considered broken if a minimum of only 1% import duties were collected, without drawback upon re-exportation. Except for the one word "blockaded" this would have been a great concession by Great Britain, because its practical effect was equal to an abandonment of the Rule of 1756. But Great Britain could declare any port to be "blockaded." If only because the treaty contained no article disavowing impressment Jefferson refused to submit it to the Senate.

During the fruitless negotiations of Monroe and Pinkney, Charles James Fox, who upon the death of Pitt in 1806, had come back into the Foreign Office for a few months, devised an expedient calculated to mollify the United States pending signature of a new treaty, and this without formally repudiating the Rule of 1756 as interpreted by the *Essex* decision. It was an order-in-council, dated May 16, 1806, and known as Fox's Blockade. This curious proclamation declared in existence a blockade of the coast from Brest to the Elbe River, but divided that stretch into two zones. In the inner zone, between the Seine River and the port of Ostend, it would be strictly enforced. In the remaining area, neutral ships would be allowed to trade in non-contraband goods provided they did not come from a hostile port. This meant that ships which broke their voyage by neutralization at an American port, as before the *Essex* decision, might bring cargoes to enemy ports like Rotterdam and Bremen in the outer zones, and of course to all non-blockaded enemy ports such as those south of Brest like Bordeaux. This compromise was proclaimed before news had reached England of the non-importation act passed three weeks before in the United States, and was designed to fend off that proposed legislation. It did not elicit the calculated favorable response. Across the Atlantic they attacked it as an illegal paper blockade and refused to repeal the non-importation act. But presently American objections to the *Essex* decision and to Fox's Blockade were lost sight of on both sides of the ocean by the new issues raised by the drastic decrees of Napoleon in ostensible retaliation against the British maritime system.

In brilliant campaigns in central Europe, Napoleon had defeated (battles of Ulm, Austerlitz, Jena, Friedland) the continental allies, Austria, Prussia and Russia, of the new (third) coalition which British diplomacy and subsidies had raised against him in 1805. Austria was prostrate (1805). Prussia lay at his feet (1806). The King of Prussia and the Czar of Russia made their peace (at Tilsit, July 7-9, 1807) and agreed to support Napoleon's continental policy. The Emperor of the French now controlled the coast of western Europe from the Pyrenees to the Niemen River, the boundary between Prussia and Russia.[1] He could begin to apply to Great Britain his grand project of a continental system. This had already been announced at Berlin (November 21, 1806).

The Berlin Decree began by reciting the arbitrary naval conduct of Great Britain, particularly in the matter of blockade applied to hamper the intercourse of neutral nations with Europe for the purpose of building up British trade and industry on the ruins of other nations. All trade in English goods therefore involved complicity in British lawlessness. The Emperor accordingly decreed, and declared as a fundamental law of his Empire: (1) the British Islands were henceforth to be considered in a state of blockade and all commerce and correspondence with them prohibited; (2) all British subjects in territories occupied by the French were declared to be prisoners of war, and all property belonging to them made good prize; (3) all trade in British goods or goods originating in Great Britain or her colonies was prohibited and the goods declared good prize; (4) every vessel coming directly from the ports of Great Britain or her colonies, or calling at them after the proclamation of the decree, was to be refused access to any port on the continent. Since Napoleon had no navy the blockade was mere paper; but he intended to enforce it by control of the ports of Europe. He obliged the countries allied or subject to France to accept and enforce it. At first there were no captures, even by surviving French privateers, of neutral vessels at sea found to have violated the decree. Later, in 1807, the practice developed of making violation of the decree ground for capture at sea; and it was so interpreted in practice that an enemy destination of a neutral ship was ground for capture. Only the paucity of French armed ships prevented numerous captures at sea. Since Napoleon could not control the sea effectively to prevent neutral goods reaching England, the Berlin Decree was essentially a self-blockade of France and subject countries against British goods brought in neutral vessels, a self-denying ordinance by which he expected to crush England

---

[1] Great Britain anticipated Napoleon's intention to occupy Denmark by herself boldly appropriating the Danish neutral fleet (battle of Copenhagen, September 7, 1807). This arbitrary act threw Denmark into the arms of Napoleon, and that nation became a devout adherent of the continental system.

by breaking down British commerce and industry even though the denial cost France herself much suffering.[1]

Great Britain on her part was now preparing, under the impulsion of James Stephen's philosophy, her system of control and license of neutral trade with the enemy for four objects: (1) to prevent him from receiving contraband goods useful to military operations, (2) to take advantage of the war to wipe out a large measure of normal competitive neutral trade in order to seize it for British profit, (3) to collect revenue by feeding in non-contraband products, including English goods, to Europe by licensed neutral ships, (4) to tax foreign (including enemy) colonial products, thus allowed to go to Europe, sufficiently higher than competing British colonial products. It became the object of the British system to use neutral ships to push goods through Napoleon's self-imposed European blockade and by doing so to raise money to help defeat him in allied military campaigns on the continent of Europe. This was quite in contrast to the policy, attempted in the previous war, of trying to starve the enemy out.[2]

The order-in-council of January 7, 1807, nominally in retaliation against the Berlin Decree, was the first step. This applied a new development of the Rule of 1756 to the subject states of France, by prohibiting neutral trade between all enemy ports (such trade had been perfectly open before the outbreak of war, for example, between French and Spanish ports), and also other ports from which British goods had been excluded by the Berlin Decree. Because the shallow coasting trade was the most difficult to get at, this order did not greatly change the actual situation. In the minds of those who, like the followers of Stephen, were advocating more drastic steps, it did not go far enough. They had their way when late in 1807 another group of orders-in-council, known as the orders of November 11, were issued. They are the ones to which historical writers usually refer when they speak of the British orders-in-council. In summary, they and supporting parliamentary enactments declared that all enemy countries and their colonies as well as all places from which the British flag was excluded were to be considered as if blockaded in the strictest manner, and all trade with them and in their products prohibited. All goods coming from those countries, as well as any vessel trading to them without a special British license, together with its cargo, was to be fair prize. The effect of this

[1] For analyses of French policy see Heckscher, *op. cit.*, and F. E. Melvin, *Napoleon's Navigation System; a Study of Trade Control During the Continental Blockade* (New York, 1919).

[2] See above, p. 99.

order was to leave unmolested American trade with the West India Islands but to compel all exports from parts of the United States to Europe to be subject to British control, license and toll. Before turning to the reaction of the United States toward these measures we must follow the further retaliations and counter-retaliations until the structure of each belligerent policy is complete.

In answer to the orders-in-council Napoleon indignantly launched forth the Milan Decree (December 17, 1807). He had now forced the peace with the Czar of Russia, one of the conditions of which was that Russia would join the continental system, and was busy rearranging affairs in Italy. The new decree stated that all vessels of any nation whatsoever which submitted to examination by an English warship, or undertook a voyage to England, or paid any duty to the English Government were declared denationalized; they were to be considered as having forfeited protection of their own flag, and, as English property, were lawful prize both in port and at sea. The British Islands remained in a state of blockade and all vessels bound to or from English ports or bound to English [1] colonies were good prize. These measures were to continue in force until Great Britain abandoned her illegal practices. The Berlin and Milan decrees of Napoleon, and the British orders-in-council were supplemented and co-ordinated by further proclamations and legislation in the next three years, but with those now mentioned the opposing belligerent systems may be considered as standing complete.[2]

If Napoleon had been able to enforce his decrees on the high seas as well as Great Britain was able to execute the orders-in-council, vessels of the American flag would have been excluded from practically all the ports of the occidental world when the continental system was at its height. Actually they continued to trade with British ports, because Napoleon, landlocked, was for the most part powerless to touch them unless they put in at a port of Europe under his control. Actually, too, neutral American ships with British licenses built up a trade with continental countries in defiance of Napoleon's orders as his control of the continent began to slip and weaken. Spain, for example, and Spanish

---

[1] Napoleon, and the French in general, frequently used the word English as synonymous with British.

[2] In 1809 the British system was put into the form of a paper blockade of all ports and places, from the Ems River southward, under the government of France or Holland or plantations of those governments, and also the northern ports of Italy. This freed the Baltic ports from these restrictions at a time when the enforcement of Napoleon's system was breaking down in that region, and opened up Portuguese and Spanish ports to assist the Spanish rising against Napoleon. See Mahan, *Sea Power and the War of 1812*, I, 200.

colonies were opened up after the revolt of the Spanish people against the French regime. Next came the desertion of Russia and the Scandinavian countries from the continental system. Furthermore, the hardships on France herself of this self-blockade, led Napoleon to mitigate its effects by issuing licenses for exports and gradually to modify it by allowing specified imports over high tariffs.[1] The great duel between the Leviathan of the Sea and the Colossus of the Land was never fought out to as complete a finish as the theorist might desire, because of Spain and Russia. The Spanish revolt gave England a foothold upon the continent; the defection of the Czar from the continental system made in it a fatal breach. If Napoleon's hand could have held the subject countries under his iron discipline, who can say that his continental system would not have overthrown Great Britain and unified Europe into one Empire? Who can deny that it was British sea power that weakened his military grip on that unwilling continent?

The American reply to the illegal systems of the opposing belligerents was a series of prohibitory trade enactments based on the Jeffersonian conception that economic coercion was sufficient to bring these mighty transgressors to a line of proper conduct so far as ships of the United States were concerned. They consisted of the Embargo of 1807, the non-intercourse act of 1809, and what became known as Macon's Bill No. 2, of 1810. These acts were nominally impartial. But any American act which impartially shut off the commerce of the United States to both belligerents actually had the effect of stopping it with Great Britain only, because the British navy already was controlling trade to France and her subject Europe. Because of this the American legislation had the actual effect of supporting and supplementing Napoleon's continental system. The Embargo act (December 22, 1807, with supplementary acts January 9, March 12, April 25, 1808, and January 9, 1809) was added to the non-importation act, which, after repeated suspension in hope of adjustment with Great Britain by diplomatic negotiation, had just gone into effect (December 14, 1807). The Embargo, like the continental system, was "a self-blockade of the purest water,"[2] and, like that, destined to bring adversaries to terms even at the cost of suffering at home. It prohibited the departure of all vessels lying in American harbors and bound for foreign ports.[3] The purpose of this

---

[1] Melvin, *op. cit.*   [2] Heckscher, *op. cit.*, 130.

[3] Foreign vessels were allowed to leave in ballast; coastwise trade was allowed under bond; and later American ships were allowed to leave for foreign ports, in ballast and under bond, to bring home American property. All these modifications were greatly abused.

embargo was to make the belligerents modify their illegal decrees, and to make Great Britain stop impressment by depriving them of much needed American provisions and other raw materials. For reasons already explained it hit England harder than France, and Napoleon should have been quite content with it because it fitted so well into his system. Incidentally it gave him a chance to assume, with predatory logic, that all American ships appearing in French harbors during the Embargo were in reality English ships. He promptly confiscated them (Bayonne Decree, April 17, 1808). Where the Embargo injured England particularly was in the islands of the Caribbean which depended so much on the United States for foodstuffs and supplies. But it hit the United States harder than it did Great Britain. Admiral Mahan has pointed out that this self-imposed blockade of the United States had all the inconvenience of a blockade by an enemy and none of the advantages of actual war, namely, an opportunity to capture British adjoining territory and to make captures of British shipping. Grass grew in the streets of American ports which had so prospered under British arbitrary control of American neutral commerce. The Embargo also failed of its purpose because it could not be enforced. Widespread smuggling went on over the land frontiers, much to the advantage of British maritime towns in Nova Scotia. A few days before Jefferson left office, March 1, 1809, the Embargo was repealed for all countries except Great Britain and France,[1] and the non-intercourse act substituted. This was ingeniously designed to give relief to American commerce and at the same time to continue economic coercion of the belligerents. Its purpose was to play one belligerent off against the other. It interdicted American waters to all public vessels of Great Britain or France,[2] and after the 20th of the following May, prohibited all vessels sailing under the flags of either Great Britain or France, or owned in part by a citizen or subject of either, from entering the waters of the United States, and also prohibited the importation of goods from those countries. In case Great Britain or France should so modify her decrees as to cease to violate American neutral commerce, the President was authorized to declare the same and restore trade with that nation. At the same time the old non-importation act (against Great Britain only) and the Embargo were both repealed, except as they applied to the countries under possession of the belligerent powers, thus allowing American ships to

---

[1] The non-importation act, against Great Britain alone, was repealed at the same time.

[2] The British navy had already interdicted them to French vessels, but itself had been ordered out after the *Chesapeake-Leopard* affair.

trade with the limited portion of mankind that was neutral (which might be a vestibule to belligerent lands).

Thanks to the unauthorized zeal of a British diplomat the non-intercourse act appeared at first to bring immediate results. George Canning, the new British Minister of Foreign Affairs, sent over to the United States a minister plenipotentiary, D. M. Erskine, who had instructions to make an agreement as follows: (1) Great Britain to withdraw her orders-in-council of January and November, 1807, in so far as they touched American shipping, and the United States in turn to repeal contemporaneously all non-importation and non-intercourse acts against Great Britain as well as interdiction of its waters to British ships of war; (2) the non-intercourse act to go into effect immediately against France, and to be enforced by the British navy, which should have a right to capture American ships violating it; (3) the United States to accept the Rule of 1756. Such an arrangement could be coupled with a settlement of the *Chesapeake-Leopard* affair by proper disavowals and reparations. Erskine was authorized to read his instructions *in extenso* to the American Secretary of State. Actually he held back the item about the British navy enforcing the non-intercourse act against France, and, in violation of his instructions, made an agreement without that obnoxious condition; Secretary of State Robert Smith further persuaded him that it was not necessary for the United States expressly to agree to the Rule of 1756. When the resulting Erskine Agreement (April 18, 19, 1809) [1] was signed, President Madison proclaimed that on June 10, 1809, the day on which the orders-in-council were to be withdrawn, the non-intercourse act would cease against Great Britain. When the day came some six hundred American vessels left port with cargoes of raw materials for British consumers. Canning repudiated the agreement as soon as it, and Erskine's [2] unauthorized conduct, was known to him; and the non-intercourse act went back into effect against both powers. The settlement of the *Chesapeake-Leopard* affair, which was a part of it, also fell to the ground. Canning in his irritation unjustly accused President Madison and his Government of "overreaching" the British Minister. The famous Erskine Agreement, instead of being the hoped-for solution, actually embittered Anglo-American relations

---

[1] For the Erskine Agreement, see Charles C. Tansill's sketch of Robert Smith in *Am Secs. State*, III, and A. L. Burt, *op. cit.*, 269-278.

[2] Erskine succeeded the British Minister, Anthony Merry. He in turn was followed by two successive ministers, Francis James Jackson and Augustus J. Foster, neither of whom succeeded in solving the increasingly vexing issues. The American Minister in London, William Pinkney, withdrew February 28, 1811.

still further. The non-intercourse act, which had mothered it, also gave to Napoleon another pretext for confiscating more American vessels; since that act had announced non-intercourse with France, he assumed that all American vessels appearing in French harbors were not American, since that was by American law illegal, but English in disguise. He ordered them seized and sold and the proceeds deposited hopelessly in the *caisse d'amortissement* (decrees of Vienna, August 4, 1809, and Rambouillet, March 23, 1810).

In addition to its failure to bring the desired diplomatic results, the non-intercourse act proved to be too great a strain on American commerce, since it cut off trade with Great Britain and France, which in 1809 and 1810 included much of the western European shore. Another expedient was substituted. Macon's Bill No. 2 (passed May 1, 1810), proved better designed to have results on the European belligerents than its predecessors. It declared that: (1) no British or French armed vessels were to be allowed in American waters except when forced in by distress or bearing despatches; (2) the non-intercourse act repealed and trade reopened with all the world; (3) in case either Great Britain or France should revoke or modify its edicts before March 3, 1811, so that they should cease to affect the neutral commerce of the United States, the President should proclaim this, and if the other nation should not within three months do likewise, then the non-intercourse act would go into effect against that recalcitrant nation. This legislation thus opened up American trade with Great Britain and with France again, subject to the resented control of the British navy. It meant to Napoleon that the United States had deserted his continental system. It was the only piece of American economic legislation which ever had any effect on him at all. To bring back the United States in line with his system he sought to persuade President Madison that the French decrees were withdrawn against it. On August 5, 1810, he caused his Minister of Foreign Affairs, the Duc de Cadore, to state in a note to the American Minister in Paris, General Armstrong, that the Congress of the United States now having revoked its steps (i.e., cessation of non-intercourse against France), "the decrees of Berlin and Milan are revoked, and that after the 1st of November they will cease to have effect; it being understood that, in consequence of this declaration, the English shall revoke their orders in council, and renounce the new principles of blockade. . . . or that the United States . . . shall cause their rights to be respected by the English."[1] The language of this note

[1] *Am. State Papers, For. Rel.*, III, 386-387.

was indeed curious. It was not an express revocation. The decrees, which had been announced as the fundamental law of the Empire, could not be repealed by a mere note from the Minister of Foreign Affairs to the diplomatic representative of a foreign power, any more than the immigration laws of the United States today could be set aside by a note of the Secretary of State to the Minister of Siam. Nor did Napoleon intend that they should be considered generally as repealed. Public documents continued to refer to them as the fundamental law of the Empire. Captures continued to be made under them of neutral vessels, even of American vessels. The British Government quite properly refused to take this diplomatic note as a repeal. But President Madison, envisioning a diplomatic triumph, was eager to believe the decrees repealed as required by the terms of Macon's Bill Number Two. He made public proclamation to that effect, and declared that the non-importation act was in effect against Great Britain. This was confirmed by a new act of Congress, the non-importation act against Great Britain of March 1, 1811. As the historian Henry Adams has put it, Napoleon had "hoodwinked" Madison.

The British Government was hard pressed, particularly in the West Indies, by the revival of non-importation, but loathe to accept Napoleon's trick repeal. It informed the United States that it stood ready to repeal the orders-in-council, however, as soon as the French decrees should be really repealed. Napoleon, hoping for a diplomatic victory over Great Britain, particularly when his continental system was beginning to crumble, played another card. His Foreign Minister, now the Duc de Bassano, delivered a note, May, 1812, to the American chargé, Jonathan Russell, enclosing a hitherto unknown formal decree (the Decree of St. Cloud) dated back to April 28, 1811, stating that the decrees of Berlin and Milan were not to exist for American commerce after the previous November 1 (1810). This inspired revelation of a secret decree was not convincing evidence of good faith, but the British Government was in a desperate position. Whether as a result of American restrictive measures, or of an economic collapse too complicated to diagnose, the Perceval Cabinet (1809-1812) had been overthrown and a new government installed under Lord Liverpool. With the whole-hearted approval of even the opposition, the orders-in-council were immediately revoked on June 23, 1812, so far as they applied to American commerce. It was not known in England, of course, that after another short-lived embargo on June 18 the United States had declared war by a vote of 79 to 49 in the House of Representatives and a vote of 19 to 12 in the

Senate. A proposal made in the Senate also to include France in the war declared against Great Britain failed to pass by only two votes.[1]

It must be said at this place that the question of neutral rights could not alone have caused the War of 1812. The maritime constituencies of the Union voted against it. To the seaboard and commercial communities wartime neutral commerce under British arbitrary control, even with the standing insult of impressment, was preferable to war. But neutral rights and impressment for which President Madison and his Secretary of State, James Monroe, had at length proposed war against Great Britain served as righteous pretexts to those members of Congress who wanted war for other reasons. A study of the debates and vote in Congress shows most of the navigating interests voting nay, and the interior, particularly the whole frontier in a great crescent from Vermont to Georgia, voting aye. Delegates from these regions wanted war for divided reasons. The northwestern frontier saw in it the only way to put an end to British intrigues with the Indians carried on from military posts across the river-and-lake frontier opposite to those evacuated in 1796. As affairs between the United States and Great Britain had become more and more embroiled over the question of neutral rights and impressments, British officials in Canada, anticipating possible war, had developed the more eagerly their contacts with the Indian tribes in the Northwest. Tecumseh's outbreak of 1811 was a result of this. It had set the West aflame against Great Britain. War offered the opportunity of quelling these Indian conspiracies forever and at the same time, so the western "War Hawks" thought, a conquest of Canada. On the other hand, the southern and southwestern states united with the rest of the West for war because they hoped that it would bring to them a conquest of Florida from Great Britain's feeble ally, Spain. The War of 1812, therefore, was finally caused by a western expansionist urge rather than solely by the just grievances of neutral rights and im-

[1] The American spoliation claims against Great Britain and France, arising out of the Napoleonic wars, were never brought to full adjudication.

Any claims for spoliation against Great Britain disappeared in the War of 1812. Claims against France for Napoleonic spoliations were the subject of diplomatic negotiations from 1815 to 1831, when a convention was ratified by which the United States accepted a lump sum of 25,000,000 francs from France in full acquittal of all claims "for unlawful seizures, captures, sequestrations, confiscations or destructions of their vessels, cargoes or other properties." This was paid by France, after some dispute (see below, p. 289) in 1836, and distributed *pro rata* by the United States among the recognized claimants, each of whom received only 59% of his recognized due. The original sum claimed from France for such wrongs was $12,047,286.09 exclusive of interest of which $10,347,961.51 were for claims since 1803. J. B. Moore, *Digest of International Arbitrations*, V, 4447-4485.

pressment.[1] Because of their failure to prevent war, Jefferson's expedients have long since been the laughing-stock of historians. It is only
fair to concede that if an Atlantic cable had existed in 1812 they might

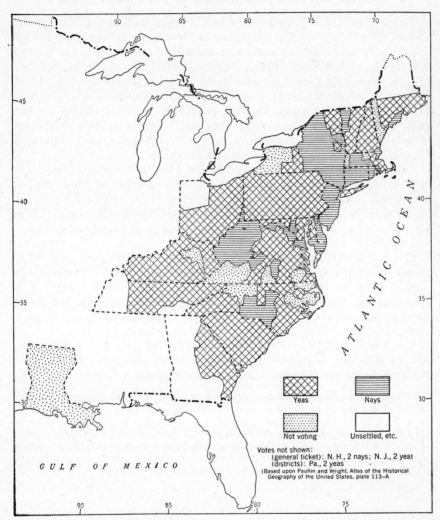

Map 10.   Vote in the House of Representatives on the Declaration of War in 1812.

today be extolled everywhere by amiable and philosophical lovers of
peace as an effective and bloodless remedy for the gravest international
difficulties. The vote in Congress showed only a small majority for war.
It is quite likely that had the impending repeal of the orders-in-council

[1] Julius W. Pratt, *Expansionists of 1812* (New York, 1925).

been known in Washington the declaration of war would not have carried the Senate.[1]

NOTE ON NATURALIZATION TREATIES OF THE UNITED STATES

Today (1942) the United States has in force treaties regulating under various rules the question of naturalization, usually by relinquishing citizenship of naturalized citizens sojourning more than two years in the land of their origin, with Albania (1932), Belgium (1869), Brazil (1910), Bulgaria (1924), Costa Rica (1912), Czechoslovakia (1929), Denmark (1873), Great Britain (1870), Haiti (1904), Honduras (1909), Nicaragua (1912), Norway (1872, 1931), Peru (1909), Portugal (1908), El Salvador (1908), Sweden (1872), and Uruguay (1909). Treaties regulating the military obligations of persons having dual nationality exist with Finland (1939), Lithuania (1937), Sweden (1933), and Switzerland (1937).

The inter-American treaty of 1906 of the Third International Conference of American States (Rio de Janeiro) recognizing the right of naturalization, and regulating status of returning persons after (two years) naturalization, has been ratified by the United States, the Argentine Republic, Brazil, Chile, Colombia, Costa Rica, Ecuador, Honduras, Nicaragua, Panama, and El Salvador.

The multilateral treaty signed at The Hague April 12, 1930, relating to military obligation in certain cases of double nationality, has been signed and ratified by the ten requisite states, including the United States (1932). It is now (1942) in force with Brazil, Great Britain and Northern Ireland, India, Sweden, Australia, South Africa, El Salvador, Cuba, Colombia, and Belgium (listed in order of deposit of ratifications or accessions).

The inter-American treaty of Montevideo on the Nationality of Women, of 1933, is in force (1942) between the United States, Brazil, Chile, Colombia, Ecuador, Guatemala, Honduras, Mexico, and Panama.

---

[1] Warren H. Goodman printed a most valuable historiographical analysis of "The Origins of the War of 1812: A Survey of Changing Interpretations," in *Miss. Vall. Hist. Rev.,* XXVIII (No. 2, September, 1941), 171-186. Alfred L. Burt's later scholarly review of *The United States, Great Britain, and British North America from the Revolution to the Establishment of Peace for the War of 1812* (Yale University Press, 1940) adheres more closely to Mahan's traditional explanation of the War of 1812: i.e., a conflict arising out of the problems of neutral rights and impressment.

CHAPTER X

DIPLOMACY OF THE WAR OF 1812 AND ITS AFTERMATH
(1812-1816)
THE BARBARY STATES
(1801-1816)

THE diplomacy of the War of 1812 was a series of negotiations for peace, negotiations which took place as the Napoleonic wars reached their climax. In these discussions it was strikingly apparent that Great Britain's strains in Europe impelled her to liquidate her minor war with the United States, if necessary by foregoing any profits. Europe's distresses this time proved America's salvation. They made up for the comparative weakness of military and naval power.

The repeal in London of the British orders-in-council five days after the actual declaration of war in Washington removed at a stroke one of the principal causes of hostilities. In England it was felt that this might make possible an early peace without much further parley. The British Admiral Warren, sailing for the American theater of warfare, carried with him proposals for an armistice consequent upon the recent repeal of the orders. President Madison, whose reasons for war were not those of the western War Hawks who had carried the declaration through Congress, was anxious for an early peace that would honor the American contentions as to maritime law and impressment. "At the moment of the declaration of war," wrote Secretary of State Monroe to Jonathan Russell, the American *chargé d'affaires* who remained in London, "the President, regretting the necessity which produced it, looked to its termination, and provided for it." [1] Russell was authorized in instructions, dated eight days after the declaration, to agree on an armistice, looking toward peace negotiations, on two conditions: revocation of the orders-in-council, and abandonment of the practice of impressment. The War Hawks on their part hoped, when it came time to write the peace, they would already have captured either Canada or Florida, or both.

---

[1] F. A. Updyke has described the peace negotiations in methodical detail as registered in successive despatches and instructions, in *The Diplomacy of the War of 1812* (Baltimore, 1915), but the shorter accounts of Mahan, *War of 1812, op. cit.*, and Henry Adams, *op. cit.*, are far more instructive, and are both superbly written. Where not otherwise indicated, quotations of despatches in this chapter are taken from these secondary accounts.

The campaigns of 1812 were a sad disillusionment to these hopes of conquest, and the ambitions of the westerners steadily sank as the war wore on. The occupation in 1814 of an area of Canadian territory opposite Detroit was offset by British occupation of Niagara, the island of Michilimackinac, and a fringe of the seacoast of eastern Maine, and by the crowning humiliation of the burning of the Capitol and White House in Washington. Except for the brilliant triumphs by improvised fleets on Lakes Erie and Champlain, the military and naval operations of the United States during this second war with England offer nothing to boast about, keeping in mind the exuberant expectations with which an unprepared nation embarked upon it. On land the United States barely succeeded in defending its own soil. On the ocean some spectacular victories in heroic individual ship duels fired the national spirit and forced respect from a supercilious enemy. In a strictly strategical sense these victories were unimportant. The British navy successfully blockaded the coast south of New England. It left the New England harbors alone until 1814 only because it hoped thereby to cultivate and detach this Federalist section which had so opposed the war and which toward the end meditated separation from the Union. British fleets, and even British invading armies, were supported in their distant operations against the United States by an unpatriotic and widespread American trading with the enemy, particularly in New England; so much so that Congress voted an embargo in December 1813 that lasted until April of the next year. It was repealed when the collapse of Napoleon opened up a lucrative European commerce. While it lasted it supplemented the efforts of the enemy to seal up American ports by blockade. American privateers proved the most impressive weapon against Great Britain, but an effective convoy system held down their ravages to a tolerable minimum (1,344 prizes, according to Mahan). If it had not been for Great Britain's tenacious and determined engagement in the greater European conflict, the republic would have been conquered, its independence extinguished; in the same thought we must remember that without the European war there would have been no Anglo-American war.

The British Secretary for Foreign Affairs, Castlereagh, refused the American offer of an armistice when it was conveyed by Russell. He made it plain that if Great Britain had revoked the orders-in-council she would not give up her pretension to impressment, the one issue which now stood between the two countries. "The Government could not consent to suspend the exercise of a right," he asserted, "upon which the

naval strength of the empire mainly depends." On the question of impressment, then, either the United States or Great Britain must give way
in the future peace. The United States preferred to fight awhile longer.

Hostilities between the United States and England were inconvenient
to Russia and brought about an offer of mediation by Czar Alexander I.
He had deserted the continental system in 1809 and made peace with
Great Britain in 1812. American and then English ships and goods
began to come into extreme Baltic ports and filter into Europe. Napoleon declared war on Russia, June 22, 1812 (four days after the United
States declared war on England), invaded her vast domains, and captured Moscow, in September, only to be required to retreat amid the
destruction of his grand army of five hundred thousand men. As he
fled back to France to organize another army, another coalition of Russia, Prussia, and Austria rose behind him, in alliance with the inveterate
Great Britain.

The American war not only drained the resources of Russia's British
ally, but it kept the desired American trade out of Russian Baltic ports.
Alexander I also is believed during these years to have had republican
sympathies. On the very day (September 13, 1812) before Napoleon
entered Moscow, the Russian Chancellor asked John Quincy Adams,
American Minister at St. Petersburg, whether an offer of mediation would
be received favorably by the United States. Adams had no instructions
on that point, but wisely said that he believed it would. Straightway
the Czar made a formal offer. President Madison accepted (March 11,
1813) and nominated the Secretary of the Treasury, Albert Gallatin,
and Senator James A. Bayard of Delaware to serve with Adams as commissioners to negotiate peace. The American acceptance of the Czar's
proposal was not known at the distant Russian capital until June 15, 1813,
when Gallatin and Bayard were already approaching Gothenburg,
Sweden, on their way to St. Petersburg. Meanwhile the British Government had rejected the Russian offer, on the ground that issues with the
United States involved the internal government of Great Britain which
was not susceptible to foreign suggestions. Some historians have likened
this to the British attitude during the American Revolution when George
III's advisers refused to brook outside mediation in the differences between himself and his revolted colonists. Of course what the Liverpool
Ministry now referred to as a "problem of internal government" was the
question of impressment; but they also feared Russian mediation because
it might bring into question British interpretations of maritime law.
Russia and the continental countries allied with Russia had traditionally

supported such American conceptions of maritime law as had been in-corporated in the Armed Neutralities, the last of which (1800) had been broken up by British armed force. The United States was sure to bring up these doctrines in any discussion of peace terms, and to rely on Rus-sian support of them. Secretary of State Monroe had not failed to observe, in his instructions to the American Commissioners, that "since 1780, Russia has been the pivot on which all questions of neutral right have essentially turned." [1]

When the American Commissioners reached St. Petersburg the Czar was in Bohemia at the headquarters of the allied armies then engaged in the great campaign that was driving Napoleon back to the Rhine. What proved to be a temporary armistice had just been made. The fortunes of war were by no means certain, and Alexander did not overlook the pos-sibility of having to negotiate with Napoleon under unfavorable military conditions. For reasons not yet wholly clear to scholars, but apparently due to Alexander's sympathetic back glances at France, the opponent of British naval principles, the Czar caused the offer of mediation to be for-mally renewed (September 1, 1813). Again the British Government refused in polite terms, but offered to meet the American Commissioners directly, either at the neutral town of Gothenburg, or in London. The American Commissioners also preferred to deal directly with their one enemy in order to keep their problems disentangled from the highly complicated affairs of Europe, but they had to ask for new powers for any direct negotiation. Madison immediately sent such and added to the Commission Henry Clay, Speaker of the House of Representatives and leader of the western War Hawks, and Jonathan Russell, who had been United States *chargé* at London when the war broke out and who was now appointed as Minister to Sweden.

Gallatin,[2] J. Q. Adams, Henry Clay, James A. Bayard, and Russell constituted as strong a diplomatic mission, in point of combined ability and personality, as the United States has ever sent abroad, equaled only by the famous peace commissions of 1782 and 1919. The first four of them were, along with President Madison and Secretary of State Monroe, who of course remained at home, the leading American states-men of their day. The very strength of the Commission threatened to be a weakness. Distant as they were from home it was necessary for

---

[1] *Am. State. Pap., For. Rel.*, III, 700.

[2] The Senate had refused to confirm Gallatin's nomination to the first commission of three, on the not unexceptionable grounds that he was Secretary of the Treasury. He resigned that office before President Madison nominated him to the second commission of five, and the Senate confirmed him.

these men, under the general instructions, to decide "on their own." The strong-mindedness of the individual plenipotentiaries led to most lively debates in their deliberations. It was the accomplished Gallatin who kept the five in reasonable temper, so that they always presented a united front to the enemy. This was his first appearance in what was to be a long diplomatic career, but he was already an experienced statesman, and, like Franklin before him, a specialist in politics and human nature.

So much time was taken for the various peace proposals to cross and recross the Atlantic and the continent of Europe that it was already August 8, 1814, when the American delegation first met their British opponents at Ghent, a town in the Netherlands and garrisoned by British troops—in fact the British Foreign Office then controlled the diplomacy of the Netherlands as thoroughly as its troops occupied its territory, and from the viewpoint of negotiating on neutral soil the American Commissioners might as well have been in Canterbury. By that midsummer two campaigns had already been fought in North America which had left the military position pretty much what it had been at the declaration of war. But Napoleon had been overthrown in Europe, and exiled to Elba; the Bourbons had been re-established on the throne of France; and two British armies of veteran troops had been dispatched to America, one to invade the United States from Canada via Lake Champlain, the other to create a diversion by harassing the coast and undertaking a movement against New Orleans. After twenty years of incessant warfare (except for the brief peace of Amiens, 1801-1803) against an implacable foe British arms at last were shining in the bright sun of splendid triumph. The outlook was not encouraging for the United States at Ghent.

Compared to the American peace commissioners, the British delegation was of mediocre ability and personality: Lord Gambier, who had the dubious distinction of having commanded the British fleet which bombarded defenseless Copenhagen in 1807; Henry Goulburn, a young and uninspired official, undersecretary in the Ministry of War and Colonies, whose long life led to most respectable higher service but no marked distinction; and William Adams, doctor of civil law and admiralty lawyer. They were really messenger-boys of the Foreign Office, to which they had to refer all important papers and questions for decision. The real opponents of the five Americans were not the mediocre English dignitaries to whom they transmitted their notes and presented their demands, but a group of superlatively able British statesmen, which included Lord Castlereagh, Minister of Foreign Affairs, one of England's greatest diplomats; Lord Bathurst, Secretary for Colonial Affairs and War, an able minister, and the Duke of Wellington, England's greatest soldier. These men were engrossed with the complicated European peace settlement then being worked out at Vienna, but they could exercise a supervisory control over the general trend of the negotiation at Ghent.

Comparison of the original demands of each party with the terms of the final treaty suggests the relative success of each side in the negotiations. The United States insisted, at the outset, on the specific abolition of the practice of impressment as a *sine qua non* of any peace. This was indeed the principal demand. If this were accepted, Madison's Government was willing to go so far as to guarantee to prohibit by appropriate legislation any British subject from taking service on a vessel flying the American flag,[1] and even to provide for the return of deserters from British public and private ships. "If this encroachment of Great Britain is not provided against," wrote Secretary of State James Monroe to the Commissioners, "the United States have appealed to arms in vain. If your efforts to accomplish it should fail, all further negotiations will cease, and you will return home without delay." Gallatin after arriving in Europe counseled omission of the subject altogether. It did not seem to him that the United States was in a position to force Great Britain to yield. Following its pitiful war-making of 1812 and 1813 Madison's Administration finally lowered its tone. In the summer of 1814 the British were landing for the invasion of Maryland and Washington; and another army of Wellington's veterans under General Prevost was in motion to Canada for an invasion by way of Lake Champlain. "You may omit any stipulation on the subject of impressment, if found indispensably necessary to terminate it [the war]," wrote Monroe on June 27, 1814, just before the burning of the American capital. On the question of neutral rights the instructions reflected a traditional American attitude, never successful against British contentions: "no blockade to

---

[1] An act of Congress of March 3, 1813, declared that: "From and after the termination of the war in which the United States are now engaged with Great Britain, it shall not be lawful to employ on board any of the public or private vessels of the United States any person or persons except citizens of the United States, or persons of colour, natives of the United States. . . . No person who shall arrive in the United States, from and after the time when this act shall take effect, shall be admitted to become a citizen of the United States, who shall not for the continued term of five years next preceding his admission as aforesaid have resided within the United States, without being at any time during the said five years, out of the territory of the United States." *The Public Statutes at Large of the United States of America* (Boston, 1845-), II, 809. The last sentence had the effect of prohibiting the enlistment of a foreign seaman who had declared his intention of becoming a citizen, until he had actually become fully naturalized. The act was repealed June 28, 1864.

be legal if not supported by an adequate force"; [1] compensation for spoliations under the orders-in-council; definition explicitly of contraband; repudiation of the Rule of 1756 and an agreed arrangement for neutral trading with enemy colonies. The instructions were silent on free ships free goods, as if it were hopeless to expect Great Britain to bow to that dictum. The British were expected to return Negroes carried off by their armies, or make payment therefor; and compensation should be stipulated for destruction of unfortified towns and private property contrary to the laws and usages of warfare. If possible, the Commissioners should secure the cession of all of Canada; at any event the United States was to be left free to augment its naval forces on the Great Lakes. Mutual restoration of captured territory must be provided for—in case the United States could not acquire any conquests; and in no case could any American territory be yielded south of the old boundary, nor on the Pacific Coast in the neighborhood of the Columbia River. If the question of Florida should come up, the Commissioners were to present the right of the United States to West Florida as a part of the Louisiana cession, to East Florida as compensation for Spanish maritime spoliations still unpaid.

On their part, the British plenipotentiaries were instructed not to yield on the "right" of impressment or any of the questions of British maritime law and naval practice, to insist upon the establishment of a neutral Indian barrier state along the northern frontier of the United States from the Mississippi, perhaps from the Missouri, to Lake Champlain; to seek rectifications of the boundary, (a) by dropping the line down to the navigable portion of the Mississippi in order to give effect to the joint navigation of that river as established by the treaty of 1783, (b) cession of a part of northeastern Maine in order to provide for an all-British route from Montreal and Quebec to St. Johns and Halifax; not to restore the fishery liberty of the treaty of 1783 unless for an acceptable diplomatic equivalent. The Great Lakes were to remain under the military control of Great Britain, and the United States was not to be allowed even to construct fortifications within a stipulated distance of the boundary.

Aside from the proscription of any stipulation in regard to impressment or maritime law, none of the British demands was an indispensable condition precedent of peace. Gambier, Goulburn, and William Adams

---

[1] Monroe was able to take these words out of the mouths of British officials themselves, for they had been so used to define the blockade of Martinique and Guadeloupe in 1803.

at the outset of the negotiations unwisely put forth one of their weakest demands as a *sine qua non*: the establishment of a neutral Indian barrier state. The Americans stood adamant against this old device, which British diplomacy had tried in vain in 1792 and nursed in Canada ever since. The Ministry in London felt obliged to correct its Commissioners on this and to instruct them to accept an article by which each side would engage to make peace with those Indians with whom it might be engaged in hostilities, on the basis of their political status in 1811, provided the Indians would themselves make peace.

The British Commissioners had unskillfully made a demand which neither British opinion nor their superiors was prepared to back up. This allowed their adversaries an initial triumph. Next the British delegates insisted upon a rectification of the boundary on the principle of *uti possidetis* (keep what you hold) and some reciprocal give-and-take concessions: British forces then held Michilimackinac, Niagara, and the coast of Maine east of the Penobscot; the United States held Fort Erie across the outlet of Lake Erie, and Fort Malden opposite Detroit and commanding the western peninsula of Ontario. Gambier and his colleagues proposed to retain Michilimackinac and Niagara (the latter with a territory on a radius of five miles), but would give up Castine and Machias, Maine, if Forts Erie and Malden were relinquished by the United States; they would also relinquish all the territory east of the Penobscot in return for the cession of Maine north of the Aroostook River, and they wanted to drop British territory south to a contact with the navigable waters of the Mississippi. This was more take than give. Gallatin and his companions refused to change the old boundary. The British Commissioners sought delay, hoping that presently more favorable news would come from the new armies sent that summer across the Atlantic. They already had news of the destruction of Washington; they expected a victorious invasion of the Champlain and Hudson valleys by General Prevost's army, and the occupation of New Orleans by further operations of the incendiary, General Ross. They therefore requested the Americans to formulate their demands in a treaty *projet*. This would give abundant opportunity for time-consuming debate.

The expected victories did not materialize. Instead came news of Ross' death in his repulse before Baltimore, and the retreat of Prevost's army following Commodore McDonough's brilliant and decisive naval victory on Lake Champlain. Most serious of all, trouble of a vital nature was brewing in Europe. Following Napoleon's exile to Elba, the victorious allies, having imposed a peace on France, were disputing at

Vienna among themselves about the status of Poland, Saxony, Italy. Division of the allies spelled an opportunity for vanquished France which fretted under the tranquil prostration of defeat. The Napoleonic system and material prosperity for France herself had rested on conquest and plunder. The allies had put a stop to such booty under the régime of the restored Bourbons. In the French capital plottings against the peace of 1814 were fermenting. So dangerous did the situation become that the British Ministry, fearing some attempt on the person of the Duke of Wellington, thought to withdraw him from Paris on the pretext of giving him a command to finish up the American war. But in case of another outbreak in Europe Wellington was more needed there than three thousand miles away across the Atlantic. Nor was the British Parliament willing to vote additional taxes for another year's war in North America to advance the frontiers of Canada. Wellington frankly told the Government that after the battles of Lake Champlain, and the loss of naval control over the lakes, there remained no ground for demanding territorial cessions. He advised a peace on the basis of the *status quo ante bellum*. The Ministry followed his counsel. Anent the American *projet* of a treaty, the Prime Minister, Lord Liverpool, wrote to Castlereagh, November 18, 1814: "I think we have determined, if all other points can be satisfactorily settled, not to continue the war for the purpose of obtaining, or securing, any acquisition of territory. We have been led to this determination *by the consideration of the unsatisfactory state of the negotiations at Vienna, and by that of the alarming situation of the interior of France.* . . . Under such circumstances, it has appeared to us desirable to bring the American war, if possible, to a conclusion." [1] Nothing could state more clearly the advantage to the United States, in getting out of a serious predicament, of the distressed condition of Europe. As soon as peace was signed at Ghent the British Commissioners hurried the news by a special messenger to Lord Castlereagh at Vienna. The treaty which followed was a peace designed "to free Britain's hands for the coming conflict with Napoleonism that was to end on the battlefield of Waterloo." [2]

The abatement of the American demand for abolition of impressment, and the relinquishment of the British demands for the Indian barrier state and rectification of the frontier, made peace now quickly possible.

---

[1] Italics inserted. Goulburn wrote to Bathurst from Ghent, November 25, 1814, expressing his "sincere regret at the alternative which the government feels itself compelled *by the present state of affairs in Europe to adopt with respect to America.*" Italics inserted.

[2] Channing, IV, 557.

Though the American Commission could not insist successfully on their list of maritime articles and other desirabilities, they showed no particular haste to sign the treaty, for they sensed the eagerness of the British to close the war.

With minor additions the Peace of Ghent (signed December 24, 1814) was a simple cessation of hostilities on the basis of the *status quo ante bellum*. It provided for the mutual restoration of all territory, places, and possessions whatsoever [1] which had been taken during the war or after the signing of the treaty; the restoration of prisoners [2] of war; cessation of hostilities of either party with the Indians; the restoration, or compensation therefor, of Negro slaves carried away from their masters by British armed forces; [3] and a pious article, added at the sincere behest of the British Government, by which the contracting parties agreed to use their best endeavors to abolish the traffic in slaves, "so irreconcilable with the principles of humanity and justice." In addition to these articles four mixed commissions [4] were established to settle portions of the old boundary of 1783: to survey and mark the eastern and northern boundary of the United States from the source of the St. Croix to the junction of 45° north latitude and the St. Lawrence; to survey and determine the water boundary from the St. Lawrence to Lake Huron; to settle the disputed possession of the islands in Passamaquoddy Bay and

---

[1] The American plenipotentiaries successfully opposed the subtly worded phraseology advanced by their British opposites: that all territory "belonging to either party and taken by the other" be mutually restored. This would have introduced the possibility of later denial by title of territory alleged not to have *belonged* to one party before the war, Louisiana, for instance. A British expedition was then underway for Louisiana. By resisting this wording the Commissioners saved Louisiana against any British claims in case Pakenham's expedition had been successful, for the treaty restored all territory taken during the war or after the *signing* of the peace. Jackson's victory at New Orleans, January 8, 1815, after the *signing* of the peace, but before it went into effect at ratification, of course removed any shadow of doubt about the status of Louisiana.

[2] The United States contended that the cost of transportation for repatriated prisoners should be paid by the captor government. This caused some delay and led to an unfortunate revolt by American prisoners at Dartmoor Prison, England. Indiscriminate firing to quell the uprising caused a heavy loss of life. There is a very considerable literature on prison life at Dartmoor.

[3] The American Commissioners contended that some of these had been resold into slavery in the West Indies.

[4] The result of the mixed boundary surveys and commissions was as follows:

The commission under Article IV for the islands in Passamaquoddy Bay and Grand Menan Island in the Bay of Fundy awarded, in 1817, Moose Island, Dudley Island, and Frederick Island to the United States, and all the other islands in Passamaquoddy Bay as well as Grand Menan to Great Britain.

As late as 1910 a treaty with Great Britain was ratified to remove uncertainty concerning the boundary line in Passamaquoddy Bay. For the failure of the commission appointed under Article V to determine the northeastern boundary north of the St. Croix, see below, p. 255 ff.

The commission under Article VI for the river-and-lake boundary between the St.

the Island of Grand Menan; to fix and determine the boundary between Lakes Huron and Superior and thence to the most northwestern point of the Lake of the Woods.

Before the treaty of peace had reached Washington, General Andrew Jackson had won a great victory over the British invading army, below New Orleans, January 8, 1815. This occurred during the war, because hostilities did not cease until the Treaty of Ghent was ratified, February 17, 1815. The treaty however stipulated for a restoration of all territories taken from the other during the war [1] or after the *signing* of the peace. Jackson's victory nevertheless inspirited the American people and was a particularly appropriate offset to the ominous spectacle of the Hartford Convention of New England, composed of defeatists and potential nullifiers.[2] The President and Cabinet immediately expressed their approval of the treaty. The Senate ratified the instrument unreservedly (as was required by its text) and unanimously (February 16, 1815).

Had the United States appealed to arms in vain? Peace on the basis of the *status quo ante bellum,* which was the cause of the war, meant that the United States secured nothing for which it went to war, neither a redress of the grievances which were the ostensible, if entirely righteous, justification for making war, nor the hoped-for annexations of Canada and Florida which impelled the War Hawks of the West to vote for the declaration in 1812. Nothing was said on the practice most bitterly resented of all British aggressions, impressment, though it is true that Great Britain, which never had another great maritime war until the United States became a world power, never impressed another American seaman.[3] In a note to the United States in 1841, anent suppression of the slave-trade, the British Government disavowed any right of visit

Lawrence and Lake Huron worked out an agreement on most of the line by 1822. The remainder, between Lake Superior and Rainy Lake, was perfected by an article of the Webster-Ashburton treaty of 1842.

The commission appointed under Article VII (which was the same as for Article VI) failed to locate the boundary between Lake Huron and Lake Superior. This was adjusted by Article II of the Webster-Ashburton treaty.

The proceedings of the commissions are digested in Moore's *Arbitrations, op. cit.,* I. A convenient summary of the survey and marking of the entire boundary between the United States and British North America, as well as other boundaries of the United States, may be found in Edward M. Douglas, *Boundaries, Areas, Geographic Centers, and Altitudes of the United States and the Several States* (Washington, 1932, United States Department of the Interior, Geological Survey Bulletin 817).

[1] See above, note 1, p. 168.

[2] In case the treaty were not ratified by the United States, the British Government proposed to attempt a separate treaty of peace with the New England states, which it believed to be altogether possible. F. A. Updyke, *op. cit.,* 355.

[3] For the impressment issue in the Webster-Ashburton negotiations, see below, p. 266

and search—in time of peace—though clinging to an alleged right to visit a ship to establish the true identity of its flag;[1] but this was no disavowal of impressment. Nor was British attitude in the *Trent* case of 1861 any repudiation of that doctrine. But by the naturalization convention of 1870 Great Britain and the United States recognized each other's naturalized subjects and citizens.[2] This cut the ground out from under the British defense of that practice. Impressment has never been resorted to since 1815. Nothing was said about free ships free goods, illegal blockades or the Rule of 1756. The great powers of Europe in the Declaration of Paris in 1856 accepted the doctrine of free ships free goods; and they defined a blockade by saying that it must be maintained by a sufficient number of ships really to prevent access to the enemy's coast line.[3] This made possible, during the World War, a contention that long-range blockades might prevent access to the enemy's coast line.

One definite advantage was secured by the United States at Ghent. By resisting the British demand for a neutral Indian barrier state, the American delegation was able to break up forever the sinister alliance of Great Britain with the Indians dwelling within the United States. Henceforth there was no serious Indian question in the Old Northwest, and the region was open to rapid and peaceful settlement. Little else tangible had come from the appeal to arms.

Spiritually the outcome of the war was different. Albert Gallatin, himself the elder statesman of Jeffersonian Democracy, the administrative power of the whole political régime from 1801 to 1815, confessed that the war had done much to strengthen the spirit of American nationality. He wrote:

The war has been productive of evil and of good, but I think the good preponderates. Independent of the loss of lives, and of the property of individuals, the war has laid the foundations of permanent taxes and military establishments, which the Republicans [i.e., Jeffersonian Democrats] had deemed unfavorable to the happiness and free institutions of the country. But under our former system we were becoming too selfish, too much attached exclusively to the acquisition of wealth, above all, too much confined in our political feelings to local and state objects. The war has renewed and reinstated the national feelings and character which the Revolution had given, and which were daily lessening. The people have now more general objects of attachment, with which their pride and political opinions are connected.

[1] R. W. Van Alstyne, "British Right of Search and the African Slave Trade," *Jour. Mod. Hist.*, II (March, 1930), 38.

[2] R. L. Morrow, "The Negotiation of the Anglo-American Treaty of 1870," *Am Hist. Rev.*, XXXIX (1934), 663-682.

[3] See below, p. 336.

They are more Americans; they feel and act more as a nation; and I hope that the permanency of the Union is thereby better secured.

This echoes the advice of Washington's Farewell Address *to be Americans first*, to support the national government over the "subdivisions" thereof. The Jeffersonians had become nationalists.

Perhaps Gallatin was thinking of the sorry end of New England separatism.[1] The Hartford Convention had assembled in the winter of 1814-1815 to draw up resolutions of protest against overweening federal authority, and had sent in several proposed amendments to the Constitution calculated to strengthen the sovereignty of the states against military command by the nation. It had repeated the nullification resolves of the Virginia and Kentucky Resolutions of 1798 and 1799. The end of the war brought the utter collapse in national ridicule of the Hartford would-be nullifiers. The war had the effect on national self-respect that an individual experiences when he finally punches out at an inveterate bully. It galvanized American nationality. It swelled a new pride in the Union which was to triumph over the great threat of state rights in the middle of the century. In this sense, we may say that if it had not been for the War of 1812 the Union might not have triumphed in 1865. But here we are digressing to internal questions which are not the subject, strictly speaking, of this history.

The American Commissioners had also been empowered to sign a treaty of commerce with Great Britain. Negotiations for this took place in London between Gallatin and Clay, on the one hand, and Goulburn and Dr. Adams together with a third British representative, Sir F. J. Robinson, in April, 1815. In these discussions Gallatin and Clay tried in vain to weave into a treaty of commerce the maritime principles, including prohibition of impressment, which had been rejected at Ghent. They finally accepted a treaty (ratified 1815) which put into effect for

---

[1] The Governor-General of Canada, Sir James Craig, aware of separatist sentiment existing among some of the Federalist leaders in New England, had employed (1809) an American adventurer and renegade citizen, one John Henry, to report to him on the state of public opinion in the United States "both in regard to their internal politics and the probability of a war with England." Henry visited Vermont and Boston and wrote reports on the Federalist opposition, but got no commitments nor communications. He never was paid for his spying, and, vexed, sold to President Madison his correspondence, for $50,000 secret service money. Madison had it published in 1812 in an effort to discredit the Federalist opposition in New England. See, in addition to the documents officially published by Madison, *Rept. Canadian Archives for 1896* (Ottawa, 1897), 29-75; and documents published by Henry Adams, in *Am. Hist. Rev.*, I (1895-6), 51-69. Much more informative were the reports of another British secret observer, whose activities were unknown at the time, Joseph Howe, made during 1807 and 1808 to Sir George Prevost, Lieutenant-Governor of Nova Scotia. They were printed by W. W Parker in *Am. Hist. Rev.*, XVII (1911-1912), 70-102, 332-354.

four years what amounted to the commercial articles of Jay's old treaty of 1794 (expired in 1807): freedom of commercial intercourse between the United States of America and Great Britain's European (but not North American and West Indian) possessions reciprocally on the same terms as nationals, provision for consuls in each other's dominions, and a prohibition of discriminating duties by either party against the commerce and ships of the other (excepting the colonial dominions of Great Britain). The possibility of such a discrimination by England's most valuable foreign customer had ever been the bugbear of British commercial interests, and was always a matter of concern to British diplomacy. On the other hand, the United States by the act of March 3, 1815, had now embarked on a policy of reciprocal removal of alien discriminations in the direct trade with foreign nations, by particular conventions, as a means of expanding commerce.

Definite renunciation in the peace of Ghent of an aggressive British frontier policy made possible in 1817 the realization of a proposal which had been a favorite ambition of American diplomacy ever since the peace of 1783: the demilitarization of the frontier. John Adams had desired to put some such provision into the treaty of peace and independence; John Jay and Alexander Hamilton hoped in the negotiations undertaken by the former in London in 1794 to provide for the abolition of armed forces on the lakes and the land frontier, and a mutual pledge not to resort to Indian allies in case of future war. Such a pledge the American commissioners at Ghent also proposed. In 1817 an exchange of notes between Richard Rush, Acting-Secretary of State, and Charles Bagot, British Minister at Washington, agreed that neither the United States nor Great Britain should maintain any armed naval forces on the Great Lakes (Superior, Michigan, Huron, Erie, Ontario, Champlain) except stipulated small revenue cutters. The British Ministry was nervous lest this executive agreement might not bind succeeding American administrations; but President Madison submitted it to the Senate which duly ratified it after the procedure of treaties. It was provided in this "arrangement" that either party might annul the agreement upon six months' notice. Secretary Seward gave such notice in 1865 but withdrew it before it went into effect. The Rush-Bagot agreement is still in force.[1] The prohibition of naval armament on the lakes set an example ultimately for disarmament on land as well as water;

---

[1] Both parties agreed by exchanges of notes, June 9-10, 1939, October 30, November 2, 1940, to allow building of warships on the Great Lakes for immediate floating to the seaboard and armament there.

and after 1846 the few fortifications on the eastern portion of the transcontinental boundary fell into decay. We now have the wholesome spectacle of an unfortified frontier, a situation which has come to have the force of an unwritten treaty.

We have already seen that at Ghent the American Commissioners rejected the British proposal to close the northwest boundary gap by running the boundary from the Lake of the Woods down to the navigable waters of the Mississippi. This boundary gap had been a matter of dispute ever since 1792. Jay's Treaty had agreed to "concert measures" to determine the precise line there, but the measures were never concerted. In 1803 Rufus King had signed with Lord Hawkesbury at London a convention which would have taken the boundary along a direct line from the northwesternmost corner of the Lake of the Woods to the source of the Mississippi. This undeniably corresponded as much as could be with the intention of the negotiators of 1782, though it would have been most difficult to survey a line through the then unknown swampy regions which it must needs have traversed. King's convention reached Washington at about the same time as the Louisiana treaty. The Senate judiciously refused to ratify it for fear of prejudicing the northern boundary of the new province just acquired. The addition of Louisiana to the United States raised the larger question of the boundary westward across the continent. Further negotiations in 1807 failed to close the gap.[1] We remember that throughout the later phases of the Napoleonic wars Spain and Great Britain were allies. During the War of 1812 the British planned but failed to occupy New Orleans and detach Louisiana from the United States; perhaps they expected to give part of it back to Spain. In the negotiations for peace in 1814 the British Commissioners would have liked to annul the title of the United States to Louisiana. They eluded any discussion of the boundary west of the Lake of the Woods lest they recognize thereby the American title. After the War of 1812 and after the great European contest was at rest all British opposition disappeared to the possession of Louisiana by the United States. The Rush-Bagot agreement demilitarizing the Lakes was a sufficient indication that Great Britain would not contest American territory along

[1] The United States Commissioners, Monroe and Pinkney, proposed drawing a line north or south from the northwesternmost corner of the Lake of the Woods to 49° N.L. and thence west along that parallel. The British negotiators insisted on adding the words: "as far as the territories of the United States extend in that quarter." Monroe and Pinkney rejected this phraseology because it implied a limitation of American territory anywhere. See J. S. Reeves, *American Diplomacy Under Tyler and Polk* (Baltimore, 1907), 193-201; and Joseph Schafer, "The British Attitude Toward the Oregon Question," *Am. Hist. Rev.*, XVI (1911), 273-299.

the old frontiers, but the western boundary had now become involved in the Oregon Question.[1]

In addition to the boundary west of the Lake of the Woods, there were the two other issues still to be liquidated with Great Britain in 1818: the fisheries, and the navigation of the Mississippi. When no agreement had been reached on the fisheries in 1814 the American plenipotentiaries professed to believe that none was necessary because the fishery "liberty" of the treaty of peace of 1782 had been in the nature of an inalienable right, coming from a division of empire, which could not be extinguished as long as the independence of the inheriting nation, the United States, existed, and must therefore continue. The British on their part concluded that the failure to revive the American fishery liberty, which had been destroyed by the effect of war on former treaties, was their compensation for the loss of the navigation of the Mississippi, which had suffered a like fate. They were correct. Little can be said for the American argument of division of empire, particularly when the word "liberty" instead of "right" had been accepted by John Adams and his colleagues in 1782 as defining American interests.

Lord Castlereagh was anxious to renew the Anglo-American four-year commercial convention of 1815, doubtless because of the provision in it prohibiting discriminatory duties. John Quincy Adams, now Secretary of State, took advantage of this eagerness to present the boundary and fisheries for adjustment. In the discussion in London, which resulted in the convention of 1818, the United States was represented by Richard Rush and Albert Gallatin.[2] They held instructions to yield, if necessary, the American claim to a liberty to the entire inshore fisheries of British North America in exchange for a *permanent right* to fish on certain stipulated coasts—an admission of the weakness of the American claim. The British demanded revival of their right to the navigation of the Mississippi in return for a renewal of fishery liberties, but finally abandoned that demand, and granted a permanent extension of the fishery "liberty" "forever" in common with British subjects on the following coasts: the southern coast of Newfoundland from Cape Ray to the Rameau Islands, and on the western and northern coasts from Cape Ray to the Quirpon Islands; on the shores of the Magdalen Islands, and on the coast of Labrador from Mount Joly northward indefinitely (without prejudice to any of the exclusive rights of the Hudson's Bay Company). Citizens of the

---

[1] See below, p. 273.

[2] Rush was Minister to Great Britain. Gallatin had been appointed as Minister of the United States in France following the peace of Ghent. He served until 1826. Subsequently (1826-1827) he was Minister to Great Britain.

United States were also to enjoy the liberty forever to dry and cure fish on the unsettled shores of Labrador and southern Newfoundland. This was a more extensive stretch of coast line than had been suggested in J. Q. Adams' instructions. In turn the United States formally renounced other liberties previously enjoyed or claimed. This article will come up again in the long series of controversies which took place until the question was finally settled by arbitration before the Hague Court in 1910.

In the negotiations with regard to the boundary line, Gallatin and Rush proposed to extend the boundary from the Lake of the Woods westward to the Pacific Ocean along the line of 49° north latitude. This would have solved without further discussion the incipient Oregon dispute, and solved it almost exactly as it was settled in 1846 after twenty-eight years of controversy. But Great Britain preferred not to abandon its claims to the western slope of the Rocky Mountains south of 49°. Article II of the Convention therefore stipulated that the line of 49° north latitude [1] should be the boundary of the United States and British North America westward from the Lake of the Woods to the "Stony Mountains." Beyond the Rocky Mountains the western territory and rivers claimed by either party were to be free and open for a term of ten years to the vessels, citizens, and subjects of both parties to the treaty without prejudice to the claims of either.

Another article renewed the commercial treaty of 1815 for ten years. A final article dealt with a question which had arisen as to whether, under the treaty of Ghent, the citizens of the United States, owners of slaves carried away by British forces, were entitled to the restitution of the persons of the slaves or compensation therefor in money. It was agreed that this should be referred to the arbitration of some friendly sovereign. [2]

---

[1] Because the western termination of the existing boundary northwesternmost point (arbitrarily located by the commissioners in agreement) of the Lake of the Woods was approximately 21 minutes of latitude, or about 21 geographical miles north of 49°, the boundary had to be dropped that far due south to meet 49°. The line of 49° north latitude was assumed by the negotiators to have been the boundary agreed on between French and British possessions in North America after the treaty of Utrecht of 1713. It was so represented on several maps, but actually it was a cartographical fiction. It was merely proposed during the deliberations of the mixed commission that studied the boundary after Utrecht. See my "Jay's Treaty and the Northwest Boundary Gap," in *Am. Hist. Rev.*, XXVII (1922), 465-484.

[2] The Czar of Russia decided, in 1822, that the United States was entitled to indemnification only for such slaves as had been carried away from territories (including waters) the restitution of which was required by the first article of the Treaty of Ghent (i.e., the article stipulating for mutual restoration of all territories taken during the war). Following this decision the Anglo-American convention of 1822, arranged through Russian mediation, provided for the submission of slave indemnity claims to a com-

The ratification of these treaties and agreements with Great Britain, and the abeyance of maritime questions during the period of profound peace persisting in Europe brought an approach to friendly and sympathetic relationship between the United States and Great Britain. We may say that at least the issues and feelings which had arisen out of the American War for Independence were much softened.

Unsatisfactory relations with the Barbary states continued throughout the Jeffersonian period and the War of 1812. It is as convenient to summarize them at the close of this chapter as anywhere else. According to the first treaties [1] with Morocco, Algiers, Tripoli, and Tunis, the United States continued to make the customary "presents." They were taken there in cash and in kind, sometimes in the form of frigates and naval stores.

The Dey of Algiers inflicted a striking humiliation in 1800 when, under an interpretation of the treaty of 1795, he commandeered the tribute-bearing United States frigate *George Washington,* Captain William Bainbridge, and forced it to take his ambassador to Constantinople. Under such shameful circumstances did the Stars-and-Stripes make its first appearance at the Sublime Porte. The treaties with Algiers, Tripoli, and Tunis were destined to be observed by those potentates only as long as it seemed convenient, because such rulers did not believe such a payer of tribute would be able to do anything about a violation of them. They became truculently exacting in regard to the tribute, and even demanded additional presents to prevent them from declaring war. In 1801, after peace was established with France, an American squadron of four ships, under Captain Dale, was sent to the Mediterranean to convey the agreed tribute for the first time and by a show of force to seek adherence to the exact terms of the several treaties. Before the squadron could arrive the Pasha of Tripoli declared war on the United States by the established custom of chopping down the flagpole of the consulate (May 14, 1801). Dale's force proved ineffective, and a relief squadron was sent out the next year, 1802, under Captain Morris, with instructions for waging war against Tripoli. This was without declaration by Congress,

---

mission composed of one American member, one British member and one arbitrator appointed by each government. The board of commissioners and arbitrators met at Washington in 1823, but broke up in 1825 in disputes. In 1826 Gallatin was commissioned envoy extraordinary and minister plenipotentiary to settle the controversy; and by the convention of November 13, 1826, the United States agreed to accept the lump sum of $1,204,960 to extinguish all claims. In 1827 an American commission was created by act of Congress, which disbursed the money among the claimants, paying the claims in full. J. B. Moore, *Arbitrations, op. cit.,* I, 350-390.

[1] See above, pp. 67-68.

under President Jefferson's interpretation of his constitutional rights to defend the United States. Morris' naval operations proved no more effective than Dale's. Meanwhile the sovereigns of Tunis and Algiers demanded more presents and threatened war. In 1803 Commodore Morris and later Commodore Preble took over command of the squadron in the Mediterranean, now reinforced to six ships by the arrival of new armaments. Preble renewed the desultory and imperfect blockade which his predecessors had established off Tripoli, only to lose his best ship the

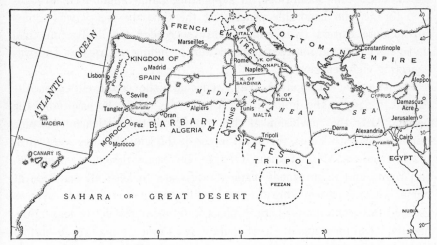

Map 11. The Barbary States in North Africa in Napoleonic Times.

Philadelphia, which was boarded after it had run on a shoal, and its crew of 307 men captured. Later by a spectacular and heroic exploit Lieutenant Stephen Decatur and a small band succeeded in firing and destroying their frigate, under Tripolitan colors, in the harbor of Tripoli. Lord Nelson saw this as "the most bold and daring act of the age." In 1804 Commodore Samuel Barron succeeded to the command, with two additional frigates. A spectacular land campaign was now devised by William Eaton, American Consul in Tunis, to overthrow the Pasha of Tripoli and set up in his place a rival pretender friendly to American desires.

With great ingenuity Eaton organized a mixed expedition of ten Americans, thirty-eight Greeks and some three hundred Arabs, which marched with the pretender against great obstacles across the desert from Egypt and, in conjunction with three American frigates, captured the town of Derne on the east frontier of Tripoli. By this time the Pasha had weakened and offered a peace, one of the articles of which provided for the restoration of Derne. The Pasha had prevailed upon the American naval commander, Barron, to sanction the making of a peace, by threatening, otherwise, to slaughter in cold blood the captured officers and crew of the *Philadelphia*. The treaty of 1805 with Tripoli was a peace without tribute, but nevertheless it provided for a ransom of $60,000 for the surrendered prisoners, together with a provision for presents whenever a new consul should be sent. More heroic resolution on the part of the American naval officers, including the captured Captain Bainbridge, in supporting Eaton might have brought a victorious and honorable peace. At the time the treaty was signed Commodore Rogers (who had recently succeeded the ill Barron) had under his command fourteen ships of war, including six frigates, and was expecting eighteen more vessels.[1]

The so-called "Tripolitan War" reflected little credit either on the American navy or the diplomatic officer, Tobias Lear, who negotiated the peace. After the conclusion of this treaty, and the settlement of some minor issues with Tunis, the naval forces of the United States were withdrawn from the Mediterranean (1807). Increasing difficulties over neutral rights and impressment made it necessary to keep all warships at home. Such American ships in the Mediterranean from 1807 to 1815 as escaped the prohibitions of the Embargo and other restrictive legislation, and the naval measures of Great Britain and France, remained absolutely unprotected. An uncertain peace continued with Tripoli and Tunis, but as soon as the fleet was withdrawn the Dey of Algiers began to capture American vessels and ask for new presents. Actual war with Algiers was, however, avoided until the beginning of war with Great Britain in 1812. During the years 1812-1815 no action was possible by the United States, except a rejected offer of ransom money for the twelve American prisoners in Algiers. "Tell the consul, and the agent of his government, and of the American merchants in Cadiz [who had offered increased ransom money for their unfortunate countrymen]," said the Dey of Algiers, "that my policy and my views are to increase, not to diminish, the number of my American slaves; and that not for a million dollars would I release them."[2]

The Peace of Ghent with Great Britain left the United States free to bring the Algerines to a final and proper accounting. The War of 1812 had developed a national navy and above all a national spirit. Algiers in

[1] Irwin, *op. cit.*

[2] M. M. Noah, *Correspondence and Documents Relative to the Attempt to Negotiate for the Release of the American Captives at Algiers* (Washington, 1816), p. 25.

1815 found herself also at war with several of the smaller maritime states of Europe, who had decided that the time had passed for tolerating shameless piracy. President Madison recommended to Congress a declaration of war against Algiers, and that body responded by the equipping and use of a proper force to bring the pirate state to terms. Two squadrons were equipped for a Mediterranean cruise. One of them, under Commodore Decatur, the hero of the *Philadelphia*, was detailed to carry a peace commissioner to dictate a treaty to Algiers. This display of force brought the Dey to a quick peace (1815). The terms of it provided for no more ransom, no more tribute, by the United States; on the other hand, the Dey was compelled to pay to the United States $10,000 by way of reparation. The Algerian ruler was restive under this defeat, and began to demur as soon as warships left his coast; but later in the year he was injudicious enough to undertake reprisals on Great Britain. A large British and Dutch fleet, under the command of Lord Exmouth, bombarded Algiers and destroyed the corsair fleet. Ever after the events of 1816 the United States has had tolerable relations with the Algerians and all the other states of North Africa, which gradually passed under French dominion, except Tripoli, which was occupied by Italy in 1911.

The Peace of Ghent marked the passing of the first European period of American diplomacy. Following Waterloo, Europe was exhausted for a generation, and, except for England and Spain, not vitally interested in the affairs of the New World. England considered her great objective won with the overthrow of Napoleon and was willing to live and let live in America. The enormous expenditures in blood and treasure which the mighty struggle of the last two decades had involved left the people of that Empire in no mood for aggressive policy. During this period of European repose American diplomacy turned to questions of western expansion and of new relations with the revolted Spanish colonies to the south. The Florida question, the independence of the Latin American states, the pronouncement of the Monroe Doctrine, which are to form the subject of the next two chapters, are essentially American questions settled during these years of European quiescence.

CHAPTER XI

THE FLORIDA QUESTION AND THE TRANSCONTINENTAL TREATY WITH SPAIN

(1803-1823)

"THE colony or province of Louisiana, with the same extent that it now has in the hands of Spain, and that it had when France possessed it; and such as it should be after the treaties subsequently entered into between Spain and other states."

Such were the words describing the extent of Louisiana as ceded to France in 1800. The American negotiators, R. R. Livingston and James Monroe, showed no reluctance in accepting the French draft which used these identical words in ceding Louisiana to the United States.[1] What precisely did this phraseology mean? Nobody really knew. The boundaries had never been marked. On the west, Spanish outposts had thrust themselves well into eastern Texas, as far as the upper waters of the Sabine River, and even across the western boundary of the present State of Louisiana. La Salle's old venture in the seventeenth century had resulted in no French occupation or title in the region of Texas; and though French adventurers and traders in the eighteenth century had crossed from the Mississippi to Santa Fé, there had been no settlement of French Louisiana west of Natchitoches on the Red River. Even more uncertain was the boundary along the northern and northwestern prairie reaches of those rivers which flow into the Mississippi from the west. Really the only reasonable limits which might be argued historically for western and northern Louisiana would be the western and northern watershed of the Mississippi. On the east the boundary as generally understood from 1763 to 1783, at least, was the Mississippi, and the river-bayou known as the Iberville just northeast of New Orleans, which with Lakes Maurepas and Ponchartrain placed water around the "island" of New Orleans.

The American plenipotentiaries had gone to France to buy one or both Floridas and New Orleans. Instead they obtained Louisiana as de-

[1] F. Barbé-Marbois, *Histoire de la Louisiane et de la cession de cette colonie par la France aux Etats-Unis de l'Amérique Septentrionale* (Paris, 1829, Eng. translation, Philadelphia, 1830). For boundaries see Map 9.

scribed in the above-quoted article. During their negotiations they were sure that Florida had not been included in the Spanish cession of 1800.[1] That indeed seemed true. Bonaparte's representative had offered Charles IV still more provinces in Italy for the proposed new kingdom for his son-in-law if only he would throw the two Floridas into the cession, but the Spanish monarch had refused to yield any portion of them. Had French diplomacy endeavored subtly to circumvent that refusal by inserting a treacherous, ambiguous and latitudinous description of boundaries that later under favorable circumstances might be expanded to include at least West Florida, which certainly once (until 1763) had been a portion of Louisiana? There is no evidence that it did. The confidential instructions given to Laussat, the French prefect sent out by Bonaparte's Government in 1803 to take possession of the province, carefully described the boundaries: on the east, the Mississippi and Iberville (including the "island" of New Orleans, but no more on the left bank); on the west the Rio Grande up to 30° north latitude, north of there nothing certain; and no fixed boundary between Louisiana and Canada. We may assume that this is what France at least construed to herself, on the eve of taking possession, as the boundaries of the newly acquired province. These certainly did not include any portion of the Floridas. Whether they would have developed later a more expansive interpretation had France retained Louisiana is another question.

Louisiana under French possession before 1763 did include Florida as far east as the Perdido. This France ceded to Great Britain in the treaty of Paris just before she turned over to Spain, Louisiana west of the Mississippi and the "island" of New Orleans. Spain thus received Louisiana in that year without any portion of Florida east or west. All of Florida became British and remained so from 1763 to 1783. While under that sovereignty it was divided in 1764 at the Apalachicola,[2] into two separate provinces, West Florida and East Florida. These Spain took over by the treaty of peace of 1783.

After the Louisiana treaty with the United States of 1803 Talleyrand asked Bonaparte what the words of the retrocession article meant as to boundary. The First Consul characteristically observed: "If an obscurity did not already exist it would be perhaps good policy to put one there." The American envoys inquired of Talleyrand precisely what they had bought, how France herself would have defined the boundaries.

---

[1] Livingston to the Secretary of State, Paris, May 12, 1803, *Am. State Papers, For. Rel.*, II, 557; Barbé-Marbois, *op. cit.*

[2] This river is considerably to the east of the Perdido which was generally accepted as the boundary before 1763 between French Louisiana and Spanish Florida.

"I do not know," he answered. "Then you mean we shall construe it in our own way?" "You have made a noble bargain for yourselves," replied the Minister, "and I suppose you will make the most of it."

A not unreasonable question could be asked: did the repossession by Spain in 1783 of West Florida and East Florida, that is, all of Florida east of the Iberville, reintegrate the ancient French portion into the original Louisiana now (1763-1803) also in Spain's hands? Studying the language of the retrocession article, Livingston had convinced his colleague of the justice of an interpretation by which West Florida could be included within the purchase on the ground that it had once been a part of French Louisiana. As Henry Adams puts it: "He discovered that France had actually bought West Florida without knowing it, and had sold it to the United States without being paid for it." Livingston would have had a much stronger argument if he could have cited Spanish documents now available to show that West Florida after 1783 actually had been reincorporated into the jurisdiction of Louisiana.[1] These made the claim of the United States much more plausible than Henry Adams and succeeding historians [2] have conceded, but not sound.

At first Spain was not willing to admit the title of the United States to Louisiana, not to mention West Florida. She protested to France against the transfer of the province on the ground that it was a violation of Bonaparte's agreement never to alienate it to any third power. Talleyrand replied glibly that imperious circumstances, and the approaching war with Great Britain, had compelled his master to sell it. He even suggested, with amazing resourcefulness, that it was partly Spain's fault: the suspension of the right of deposit as France was preparing to take over the province, and then the restoration of it at the same place, had created such an unprofitable situation *vis-à-vis* the United States as to impel France to sell.[3] Notwithstanding her protest Spain nevertheless delivered the province to France, well knowing that it was to be handed over immediately to the United States. She also had protested to the United States against the legality of the title, but later categorically

---

[1] Spanish colonial authorities from 1783 to 1803 did consider all of West Florida (except that portion north of 31° which had been recognized by Pinckney's Treaty of 1795 within the United States) as a part of the jurisdiction of Louisiana. See J. Bécker, *História de las relaciones exteriores de España durante el siglo XIX* (2 Vols., Madrid, 1924), I, 75; and W. R. Shepherd, *Guide to the Materials for the History of the United States in Spanish Archives* (Washington, Carnegie Institution, 1907).

[2] H. E. Chambers, *West Florida and its Relation to the Historical Cartography of the United States* (Baltimore, 1898); I. J. Cox, *The West Florida Controversy, 1798-1813* (Baltimore, 1918); H. B. Fuller, *The Purchase of Florida* (Cleveland, 1906).

[3] Whitaker, *Mississippi Question, op. cit.*, 235.

admitted it. Irujo, the Spanish Minister in Philadelphia, had advised his government that if it should contest the American title to Louisiana proper, and delay its delivery to France, the United States not only would forcibly take possession but would also take both Floridas by way of indemnifying itself for the expenses occasioned by the occupation of Louisiana.

Jefferson was determined to have West Florida immediately, East Florida eventually, and in due time even more of Spain's uncontested possessions. At first he thought of trading various claims of American citizens against Spain for a recognition of the contention of the United States that West Florida had been acquired by the Louisiana treaty. Characteristically he thought that as soon as Spain were at war in Europe if he should push this interpretation strongly with one hand, holding out a price (assumption by the United States of the claims) with the other, he would obtain, in good time, both Floridas. At his suggestion Congress passed the Mobile Act (February 24, 1804) directing that the territories ceded to the United States by treaty with France of 1803 "and also all the navigable waters, rivers, creeks, bays, and inlets, lying within the United States, which empty into the Gulf of Mexico, east of the river Mississippi, shall be annexed to the Mississippi district, and shall, together with the same, constitute one district, to be called the 'District of Mississippi' "; and gave the President power when he deemed it expedient to erect a separate customs district there with a port of entry. Jefferson guardedly proclaimed (May 30, 1804) that all these "shores, waters, inlets, creeks, and rivers, *lying within the boundaries of the United States*" to be a customs district, with Fort Stoddert, located above 31° in undisputed American territory, as the port of entry. This careful language, avoiding an explicit occupation of West Florida as included within the Mobile Act, was calculated to meet the furious protest of Irujo. Though willing to recommend the validation of the Louisiana cession, that diplomatist indignantly resisted any claim to West Florida.

Encouraged by Talleyrand's hints in 1803 to Livingston and Monroe to make the best of a "noble bargain," Jefferson soon advanced another step: he now sought to induce Spain to recognize outright the title of the United States to West Florida, and also to cede East Florida in turn for the renunciation by the United States of the pecuniary claims, or for a sum of money. These claims consisted of the following: (1) spoliations by Spanish cruisers on American neutral shipping in violation of the articles of Pinckney's Treaty of 1795, (2) spoliations by French cruisers on American neutral shipping within Spanish territorial waters, for which the United States tried to hold Spain responsible, (3) damages sustained by individuals as a result of the suspension of the right of deposit at New Orleans in 1802 in violation of Pinckney's Treaty.

Spain steadily resisted the last two categories of claims, but in 1802 Charles Pinckney, Minister in Madrid, had signed a convention providing for the adjudication and payment of the first group. The Senate at first rejected but subsequently ratified the convention. When it returned to Spain, the stipulated period for completion of ratification had expired. The King refused, as he had a perfect right to refuse, to ratify the convention. He was not unnaturally outraged by the Mobile Act and the aggressive claim to West Florida as a part of the Louisiana purchase. Pinckney overplayed his hand by threatening war if Spain did not ratify. In 1804 Spain became involved as the ally of France in the war with Great Britain. Jefferson endeavored to take advantage of Spain's predicament as a belligerent, and sent a special plenipotentiary, again James Monroe (who after the Louisiana purchase had become Minister to England), to assist Charles Pinckney in pressing the whole parcel of claims in a diplomatic bargain for the Floridas. Passing through Paris, Monroe, with the assistance of his colleagues there, tried in vain to get the backing of Talleyrand and Napoleon. These two had already promised the Spanish Court diplomatic support in resisting the American claims of all kinds. Far from encouraging the United States to expand the boundaries of Louisiana in a broad interpretation of the "noble bargain" the French leaders were now endeavoring to reconcile Spain to Napoleon's betrayal in alienating Louisiana to the United States and to a whole-hearted participation in France's war against Great Britain.

Monroe was no more successful than Pinckney, though he was authorized to give up American claims to Texas in turn for recognition of the title of the United States to Florida. He returned empty-handed to London. Charles Pinckney was recalled to Washington. Spain, unchecked, continued new spoliations on American neutral shipping, in avowed violation of Thomas Pinckney's Treaty of 1795. The American diplomatic representatives abroad counseled war, and a seizure of all of Florida and occupation of Louisiana up to the Rio Grande. Jefferson and his Cabinet hesitated. They were unprepared for war. He thought again (as he had in the Louisiana affair) of an alliance with England to help the United States against Spain and France; but just at this time came news of the *Essex* decision and the beginning of the long and bitter controversy with Great Britain over neutral rights. Any British alliance was henceforth impossible. Instead of war with or without a British alliance, the President decided to send another minister to Spain and to lend himself to trafficking with Talleyrand. The new minister (Bowdoin) died before this devious maneuver got under way, but the pacifist President persisted in his efforts to make none too respectable a deal with Talleyrand.

Napoleon had refused to be a partner directly to the absorption of West Florida by the United States under the cover of the Louisiana purchase, but Talleyrand caused it to be intimated—in the same indirect and illusive backstairs approach which he had used with Marshall, C. C. Pinckney and Gerry in 1798—that if the United States would pay good money there was a way to have the Floridas.[1] Let the United States ask the good offices of the Emperor in the matter; Spain could be required to pay, in the form of drafts on her South American colonies, that class of spoliation claims which had been recognized by the unratified convention of 1802. The neutral United States with this money in hand would then transmit $7,000,000 directly to Spain for both Floridas. Talleyrand did not have to say to Jefferson that Napoleon would take over this sum in unwilling payment of subsidies from Spain.

Jefferson was willing if not eager to participate in this jobbery. He felt Talleyrand would come down to $5,000,000. He cared no whit who got the money as long as the United States secured the Floridas. After sending in a vigorous public message to Congress loudly recommending military preparation ostensibly against Spain he communicated a secret message requesting $2,000,000 to be appropriated (as it was by the act of February 12, 1806) to assist the progress of negotiations concerning Florida. It was a repetition of his congressional approach to the purchase of Louisiana, but his ground was less sure. Jefferson had already claimed that West Florida had once been bought in 1803 from France and paid for; if this claim were sound, he was now really proposing to buy it again and pay for it a second time, nominally to Spain but really to France. This time the European situation did not play into his hands.

Before this strange negotiation could be put into motion in Paris the political face of Europe altered with dramatic suddenness. In swift and

[1] This was the suggested arrangement. By the terms of her alliance Spain owed France arrears of subsidies. The only way funds could be had to meet these was out of the revenue of the Spanish colonies, with which the British navy cut communication at the outset of the war in 1804. If money could be drawn out of the United States by Spain at some sacrifice to her territory, Napoleon could then manage to lay his hands on the cash. The Floridas could thus be sacrificed to help pay the cost of Napoleon's war against England and her continental allies, just as Louisiana had already served that purpose.

remarkable campaigns against the Third Coalition, Napoleon had crushed
Austria and Prussia in the battles of Ulm, Austerlitz and Jena. He was
in occupation of Prussia and planning to force Russia to a peace which
would assist his mastery of Europe. During these decisive months he
changed his mind about Spain. That country he had now marked for
his own. We hear nothing more about the Florida business. In 1808
Napoleon set aside Charles IV and his heir Ferdinand and put his own
brother Joseph Bonaparte on the throne of that ancient monarchy. The
Spanish people revolted (May 2, *dos de Mayo*). A national *junta* set up
a provisional government and made an alliance with Great Britain. From
1808 to 1814 Spain was the seat of the long and terrible Peninsular War
where Wellington's campaigns in the end proved the downfall of Napoleon I. Already before the revolt Irujo had been recalled at Madison's
request because of an imprudent quarrel with the Secretary of State.
The United States now judiciously and very properly suspended all
formal diplomatic relations with Spain until a stable government there
could be identified. Meanwhile Spanish authority in Florida and elsewhere in the New World weakened to the point of collapse.

From 1808 to 1815 Florida was as much of an Anglo-American problem as an issue in Spanish-American relations. The southern and southwestern elements of the Union looked to the annexation of Florida as
"the manifest course of events," to use Madison's phrase. The northern
states cared little about it, and the West and Northwest cast longing eyes
on Canada. Florida and Canada served as twin magnets for the expansionists of the West and, as we have seen, precipitated the declaration
of war against England in 1812.

A series of revolts assisted by immigrants from the United States in
West Florida and later in East Florida, between 1808 and the outbreak
of the War of 1812 testified to crumbling Spanish power. Following
such an   insurrection in the Baton Rouge district in 1810, President
Madison proclaimed (October 27, 1810) the rightful occupation of the
region between the Iberville and the Perdido rivers, but actually took
over an area only as far east as the Pearl (thus not interfering with
Spanish garrisons still left in Mobile and Pensacola). When Spain's
ally Great Britain protested at this, Congress, in a secret session, passed
at President Madison's request a notable resolution, January 15, 1811,
that the United States "cannot, without serious inquietude, see any
part of the said territory [Florida] pass into the hands of any foreign
power." Like Washington's Farewell Address earlier and the Monroe

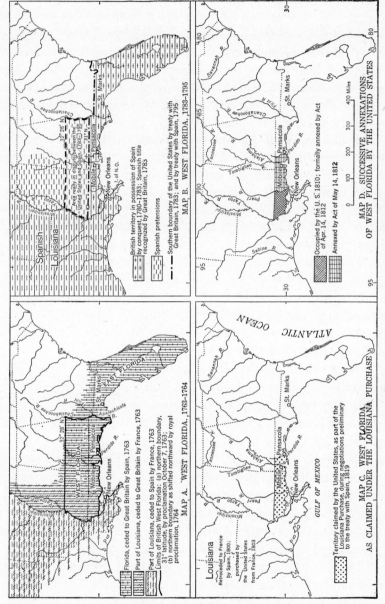

Map 12. The Diplomatic Cartography of West Florida.

Doctrine later this was an historic contribution to the formulation of a distinct American foreign policy. Congress further authorized the President to take custody of East Florida in case it should be in danger of occupation by any foreign power, if possible through a peaceful arrangement with the Spanish authorities there, forcibly if necessary. Madison dallied irresolutely with intrigues for stirring up insurrections looking toward intervention, but aside from an occupation by General Mathews of Amelia Island (1811-1813) in the river on the Georgia border, East Florida was let alone until the War of 1812. A few weeks before war was declared against England, Congress annexed to the state of Louisiana, West Florida west of the Pearl River (April 14, 1812) and a month later added the eastern half to the Territory of Mississippi (May 14, 1812). A week after the declaration of war a bill passed the House secretly authorizing the President to take possession of territory "lying south of the Mississippi Territory [and] of the State of Georgia." But the conflict ended with East Florida still in Spanish sovereignty and possession.

Peace in America and in Europe in 1815 brought a restoration of the Spanish monarchy under Ferdinand VII and the re-establishment of regular diplomatic relations between Spain and the United States. The final settlement of the question of Florida fell to the lot of Luis de Onís,[1] who had been seeking recognition as Minister of Spain since 1809; and John Quincy Adams, Secretary of State.

The West Florida question after 1815 had merged with the western boundary question into a continental problem: the task of adjusting the whole boundary between the United States and the Spanish colonial borderlands in North America from Atlantic to Pacific. In vain Spain had appealed for help to save Florida and recover Louisiana. At the time of the negotiations at Ghent she implored England to that end. At the Congress of Vienna she sought the aid of the other powers as well as Great Britain. Europe, exhausted, and desiring rest and recuperation, was unwilling to come to her assistance, particularly reluctant in the cases of Louisiana where American title had long since been expressly confirmed by Spain, and of the Floridas where the western province had been effectively annexed and occupied and the eastern province was quite prostrate. Once more the distress of Europe left the United States free to take advantage of territorial propinquity.

[1] Monroe would scarcely have received Onís formally as minister in 1816 had he known that in 1811 he had projected a rebellion of slaves in the southern states as a means of frustrating any expected attacks from that quarter on Florida in case of a war

Adams with his long European experience during the Napoleonic wars had a just appreciation of this situation. It was his desire to resist the challenge of foreign powers to the title of his nation to the great western territory, not only Louisiana to the Rio Grande according to France's definition in 1803 of her procurement from Spain, but all the way through to the Pacific Ocean, to secure recognition of title clear across the continent. In his understanding of the broader continental aspects of the Spanish issue Adams showed qualities which entitle him to his premier position as an American diplomatist.

That Spain could not retain the Floridas without the assistance of a European ally was an almost foregone conclusion when Adams began his discussions with Onís late in 1817.[1] There was little difficulty in reaching an understanding by which the various American claims against Spain would be withdrawn in exchange for the two Floridas. The question was just where to draw the western boundary line. Onís at first insisted that the western limit of the United States must be the Mississippi, though he was prepared by instructions to drop back successively to compromise lines, the westernmost of which would be approximately the eastern and northern boundaries of the present state of Texas (except for the "panhandle"). Adams contended that it should be the Rio Grande, or at least the Colorado River (of Texas). Spain stubbornly resisted until it became altogether clear that no European assistance whatever was available. After it was evident that no help would be forthcoming from Great Britain, José Pizarro, Spanish Foreign Secretary, appealed to the British Ministry for a benevolent mediation between the United States and Spain to protect her title to Florida. The British Government half-heartedly offered mediation, but when the United States refused it declined to give Spain military or even diplomatic support. Great Britain had just signalized by the Rush-Bagot agreement her abandonment of any program of resisting American territorial expansion in the Mississippi Valley. She was soon to settle the northern boundary of Louisiana by the treaty of 1818. England at this time wanted peace. Castlereagh wrote (November 11, 1817) to Bagot, British Minister in Washington anent the Spanish request for mediation and help: "The avowed and true policy of Great Britain . . . in the existing state of the world" is "to appease Controversy, . . . and to secure, if possible, for

[1] I wish to acknowledge my indebtedness, in this portion of this chapter, to a doctoral thesis (1933) still in MS., by Dr. Philip C. Brooks, of the University of California, *The Adams-Onís Treaty of 1819 as a Territorial Agreement.* It has now been printed under the title of *Diplomacy and the Borderlands, The Adams-Onís Treaty of 1819* (University of California Press, 1939).

all states a long interval of repose." [1] Spain accordingly must be prepared to purchase peace by the cession of the Floridas, and endeavor
to "secure, on the side of Mexico, the best frontier that Circumstances
will admit of her obtaining in exchange for so serious a concession on her
part." The Spanish Foreign Office instructed Onís (April 25, 1818) to
cede positively and without limitation the Floridas, in return for some
reasonable equivalent west of the Mississippi, and to obtain from the
United States a promise not to assist the revolt of the Spanish colonies
in South America or to recognize their independence. Pizarro instructed
Onís to make his first stand—before retreating—not at the Mississippi,
but at a line corresponding approximately to the present *eastern* boundary
of Texas extended straight north to the Missouri and thence along the
Missouri to its source.

Conclusion of a treaty was interrupted by what Spain considered as an
affront to her sovereignty. General Andrew Jackson invaded [2] the Floridas in 1818 for the purpose of wiping out a base of hostile Indian forays
into American border territory. A focus of infection had existed there
ever since the British forces had withdrawn from that area in 1815.
Jackson broke up the Indian strongholds and caught and executed two
British subjects, Arbuthnot and Ambrister, the former a Scotch merchant
who had been plying a trade in munitions and other articles with the
hostile tribes, the latter an officer who was caught red-handed inciting
the Indians. Protest was prompt from Spain and inquiry from Great
Britain. For a brief time it seemed that Spain perhaps might count on
British resentment and action to relieve her of her predicament. Secretary John Quincy Adams in a notable state paper warmly and thoroughly
defended General Jackson. It was enough for Castlereagh to see the
record of Jackson's courts-martial forwarded from the British Legation.
Even before he received Adams' defense he told the Minister of the
United States in London that the "unfortunate sufferers" had no claim
for interference on their behalf. [3] To Spain, Adams pointed out that it

---

[1] J. Fred Rippy, *Rivalry of the United States and Great Britain over Latin America*
(*1808-1830*) (Baltimore, 1929), 66.

[2] In December 1817, after abortive insurrectionary activities and piratical depredations
in and about Amelia Island, that territory was occupied by United States troops, who
continued in control until the Adams-Onís treaty was signed.

[3] "I have . . . stated to Mr. Rush [Minister of the United States at London]
that . . . as it is impossible not to admit, that the unfortunate sufferers whatever their
intentions, had been engaged in unauthorized practices of such a description as to have
deprived them of any claim on their own Govt. for interference on their behalf, it has
not been deemed fit, under all the circumstances of this case, to instruct you to take
any further step in this case." Castlereagh to Bagot, Jan. 2, 1819; quoted by Brooks,
op. cit.

had been necessary for Jackson to send a body of troops into "western Florida" (i.e., the western part of East Florida) because of Spain's inability to restrain the hostile incursions of Indians (as obliged by Article V of Pinckney's Treaty of 1795), or to cede the province to the United States for a proper pacification. British passivity and Jackson's military movements [1] genuinely alarmed Spain, convinced her rulers of the impossibility of physically holding the province, and greatly strengthened Adams' hand in dealing with Onís.

Negotiations resumed. The two adversaries at Washington accepted the good offices of Hyde de Neuville, French Minister there, in suggesting compromises. Adams finally gave up Texas and accepted the line of the Sabine River to 32° north latitude, thence due north to the Red River. He had championed the claim to all of Texas and he could have secured it to the Colorado River had he insisted,[2] but felt himself overruled by President Monroe and his Cabinet. To this extent he took the line that Pizarro had laid down. But Adams would not agree to extend that line north to and along the Missouri. He insisted that it follow the Red River west to 100° west longitude, north on that line to the Arkansas River and westward up that stream to its source. From the source of the Arkansas Adams pushed on triumphantly in a stroke of real diplomatic genius: he succeeded in drawing the boundary thence north to the 42d parallel of north latitude and westward clear across the remainder of the continent to the Pacific Ocean (along the northern boundaries of the present states of Utah, Nevada and California). North of this line Spain ceded all her territorial claims to the United States; south of it the United States ceded all of its territorial claims to Spain. This greatly reinforced the title of the United States to the Oregon country, where only a few months previously Great Britain had recognized the Republic as an equal occupant.

The United States accepted from the King of Spain as a cession "all the territories which belong to him situated to the eastward of the Mississippi, known by the name of East and West Florida." If this is to be interpreted as an unequivocal cession it means that John Quincy Adams by implication in the treaty of 1819 finally recognized the justice of Spain's title to the two Floridas up to February 22, 1819, and by inference branded Jefferson's claim to and occupation of West Florida as high-

---

[1] The Floridas were evacuated and restored to Spain two weeks before Adams and Onís signed the treaty of 1819.

[2] In the autumn of 1818, Irujo, formerly Minister to the United States, became Secretary of Foreign Affairs. In instructions of October 10, 1818, he authorized Onís to concede the boundary of the Colorado River, if necessary. Brooks, *op. cit.*

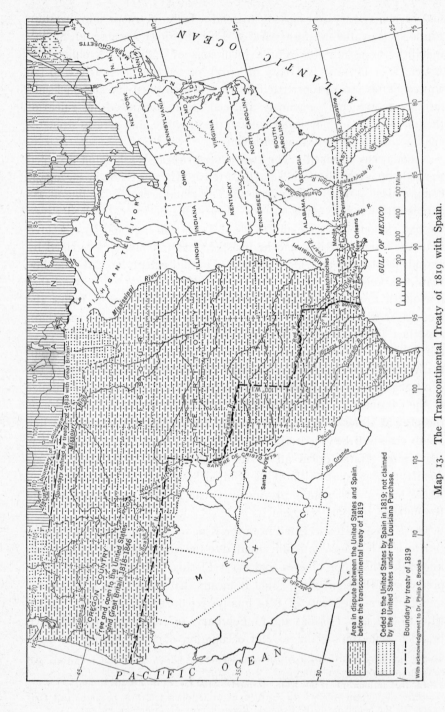

Map 13. The Transcontinental Treaty of 1819 with Spain.

192

handed and outrageous. This was balm to Spain, to have the United States accept a cession. But the wording of the cession is subtle indeed. Whether it was an unequivocal cession all depends on whether there be in the treaty commas to set off the phrase, *which belong to him,* in the portion of the article just quoted. The original manuscript copies of the treaty, in Spanish and in English now in the Department of State, contain no such commas.[1]

Adams succeeded in evading any commitment not to assist or recognize the revolted colonies of Spain, but Congress in 1817 and 1818 strengthened the neutrality laws. Both sides in the final treaty renounced all claims for damages and injuries, though the United States placed a limit of $5,000,000 as its own responsibility toward assuming the relinquished claims of its own citizens.[2] Articles were agreed upon to protect the religious freedom of the inhabitants of the ceded territory and promising to incorporate them into the Union of the United States with full constitutional privileges (as had been the case with the Lousiana treaty). An important detail, which produced immediate wrangling, was the stipulation of Article VIII in regard to Spanish land grants in Florida: all land grants made by his Catholic Majesty, or by his lawful authorities, in the said territories ceded by His Majesty to the United States, before January 24, 1818, were confirmed, and all grants so made after that date were declared null and void. The old treaty of 1795 (Pinckney's Treaty), where not altered by the articles of the Adams-Onís treaty, was confirmed except for the dictum of free ships free goods: in future wars this would be so understood by the two parties only with respect to those powers which also recognized that principle. An important alteration in 1819 in Pinckney's Treaty was the excision of the article in regard to the free navigation of the Mississippi. The War of 1812 had relieved the United States of all obligations of navigation to Great Britain; the new Spanish treaty freed it of all such obligations toward Spain. Henceforth the Father of Waters was to roll untinged by any treaty servitude from its source to the sea.

The Transcontinental Treaty, signed February 22, 1819, was an expan-

---

[1] Nothing in the treaty stipulates which shall be the governing language.

[2] A commission was set up (act of March 3, 1821) to examine and pass upon these claims. It allowed (1824) a total of $5,454,545.13. Each claimant received *pro rata* his share of the $5,000,000 (act of March 24, 1824), thus getting slightly less than the adjudicated amount of his claim. The United States, though abandoning its claims against Spain for the French spoliations committed within Spanish territorial waters, nevertheless insisted on stating formally in the treaty that it had never received from France any payment of these claims and promised to deliver to Spain, for use as she desired, an authenticated list of the cases and amounts of damage claimed. Spain did not push against France these claims, thus purchased by the cession of the Floridas.

sive territorial pendant to the boundary treaty of 1818 with Great Britain, a vast amendment of the Louisiana procurement. The two instruments—the treaties of 1818 and 1819—together notably and profitably advanced American claims to the Oregon country. Well might John Quincy Adams exult in his revealing diary as to the extensions of American territory which were now confirmed beyond that won by his father and colleagues at Versailles in 1783, and by President Jefferson twenty years later. "The acknowledgment of a definite line of boundary to the South Seas forms a great epocha in our history. The first proposal of it in this negotiation was my own, and I trust it is now secured beyond the reach of revocation. It was not even among our claims by the Treaty of Independence with Great Britain. It was not among our pretensions under the purchase of Louisiana—for that gave us only the range of the Mississippi and its waters." Adams' next ambition was to outlaw the further colonial expansion of any European power on this continent. Already when in England in 1816 he had questioned Castlereagh in regard to rumored projects of Great Britain to purchase or otherwise acquire a cession of Spanish territory in America, and had secured a disavowal from that minister (provided the United States did not set the example!).[1]

The final article of the treaty stipulated that it should be ratified "in due form," by the contracting parties, and that the ratifications must be exchanged within six months from date of signature. The Senate of the United States ratified it immediately and unanimously (February 24, 1819). After he had signed the treaty Adams discovered in his recent despatches from Spain that practically all the remaining unappropriated land in Florida had been disposed of by the King of Spain in three great grants to Spanish nobles said to be dated February 6, 1818, that is, a few days too late to be valid under the date line of the treaty. But the Secretary suspected trickery. He did not have the authenticated dates of these grants and therefore insisted on their express renunciation by Spain. It has since been made clear that Adams' caution was abundantly justified: at least two of the big grants had been authorized in a royal order of December 17, 1817. The new minister now going out to Spain, John Forsyth, was instructed to obtain this renunciation at the time of the exchange of ratifications.

The full powers under which Onís had signed the treaty had contained a promise by his Catholic Majesty "on the faith and word of a King, to approve, ratify, and fulfill whatsoever might be stipulated and signed" by his plenipotentiary. This was the customary language of such full

[1] Rippy, *op. cit.*, 67; and Brooks, *op. cit.*

powers; but in 1820 a revolt in Spain forced Ferdinand VII to accept the constitution of 1812 which had required any cession of territory to be approved by the Spanish chamber, the *Cortes*. The demand for the invalidation of the land grants, and the new provision for approval by the *Cortes*, gave pretexts for delaying ratification beyond six months' time limit. The motive for this was Spain's effort thus to coerce the United States into a promise not to assist the revolted South American colonies, nor to recognize their independence. A new Spanish Minister, General Vives, successor to Onís, was sent to Washington to secure such a pledge. John Quincy Adams denied that the United States was violating any of its obligations as a neutral, and added: "As a necessary consequence of the neutrality between Spain and the South American provinces, the United States can contract no engagement, not to form any relations with those provinces." Adams advised the chairman of the Senate Committee on Foreign Relations that the United States could not compel Spain to ratify the treaty as the King had promised, but would be justified in taking over the regions by force and be entitled to indemnity for the expenses of so doing. General Andrew Jackson was for securing the provisions of the treaty "at the mouth of the cannon." The President on May 9, 1820, on Adams' advice, significantly turned the correspondence over to Congress, which adjourned a few days later without taking action. Before it could meet again the *Cortes* had advised the King to ratify the treaty and annul the land grants (October 5, 1820). He did so (October 24). An express annulment of the three grants was made a part of the Spanish instrument of ratification. President Monroe resubmitted the treaty—for the six months' limitation of the original one had expired—to the Senate for ratification, which occurred February 19, 1821. Three days later, exactly two years after Adams and Onís had signed, ratifications were exchanged, and the treaty proclaimed in full force.

Jefferson's desire for the Floridas had been achieved. Europe's distresses, Spain's weakness, the refusal of England, France, or any other European power to help her, had compelled her capitulation to the insistent young Republic of the West. Exhausted by a generation of convulsing warfare, Europe required, as Castlereagh had said, "a period of repose." The period of European repose was the period of American expansion.

CHAPTER XII

THE INDEPENDENCE OF LATIN AMERICA AND THE MONROE DOCTRINE

(1821-1823)

SPAIN had let go the Floridas in despair of any outside help in retaining them. She still hoped for the assistance of the European powers to save her remaining colonies. The overthrow by Napoleon of the Spanish dynasty in 1808 had been the signal for the revolt of all of Spain's colonies on the mainland from the Rio Grande to Cape Horn. Restoration of the "legitimate" Spanish monarchy in Europe in 1814 had brought a temporary return of Spanish authority in the New World, but revolution again flared up in 1817 never to be quieted until the last mainstay of Spanish control on the two continents had disappeared in the battle of Ayacucho (December 9, 1824) in the mountains of Peru. That warfare of liberation was in its most earnest and portentous phases during the four years of Adams' negotiations with Spain that ended in 1821 with the ratification of the treaty of 1819.

One of the first results of the revolution had been to push over completely and forever the stockades of the closed colonial monopoly which had restricted trade with the non-Spanish world. Already foreign smuggling and the exigencies of war had weakened those traditional barriers. A growing commerce between the United States and Cuba had sprung up during and after the War of American Independence, and American consuls under the description of "agents for seamen and commerce" had been stationed there irregularly since 1797.[1] During this period—in fact, ever since he had been Secretary of State (1790-1793)—President Jefferson had looked with roving and jealous eyes on Cuba and other Spanish dominions. During the tension over the Florida question in 1805 Jefferson told the British Minister in Washington that the United States would take Cuba in case of war with Spain, though, as we know, the President shrank from actual war. With Spain's control over her colonies slipping, Jefferson feared that if acquired by France or Great Britain they might

[1] Roy F. Nichols has traced early commercial and consular contacts with Cuba in "Trade Relations and the Establishment of United States Consulates in Spanish America, 1779-1809," *Hisp. Am. Hist. Rev.*, XIII (April, 1933), 289-313.

escape the destiny he desired for them. The Venezuelan Miranda, plotting, with British connivance,[1] for an insurrection in the Spanish colonies,
claimed that he had this support from the Department of State in 1805.
Secretary Madison denied it. Cuban delegates visited the President in
1808 to suggest annexation to the United States in order to save their
island from the expected dominion of Napoleon. Jefferson refused to
encourage them outright, but the Cabinet (October 22, 1808) decided
unanimously on sentiments to be "unauthoritatively expressed by our
agents to influential persons in Cuba and Mexico," *viz:* "If you remain
under the dominion of the kingdom and family of Spain, we are contented; but we should be extremely unwilling to see you pass under the
dominion or ascendancy of France or England. In the latter cases
should you chuse to declare independence, we cannot now commit ourselves by saying we would make common cause with you but must reserve ourselves to act accdg to the then existing circumstances, but in
our proceedings we shall be influenced by friendship to you, by a firm
belief that our interests are intimately connected, and by the strongest
repugnance to see you under subordination to either France or England,
either politically or commercially."

This rather equivocal language foreshadowed the "non-transfer" principle which, as we have observed in the preceding chapter, was molded
into a resolution of Congress in 1811 in regard to Florida, and maintained
since then as a maxim of American foreign policy intimately associated
with the later pronouncement of the Monroe Doctrine.

The early contact of American traders with Cuba and the presence of
our consuls there had already given an advance taste of the profits of
trade with the region of the Spanish colonies. When word came in 1810
of the promise of revolutionary movements in South America, these revolts immediately appeared as further opportunities for extending trade
and navigation into regions hitherto barred by Spain to foreigners—but
now already open to the new ally Great Britain—and of planting political
observers in an interesting part of the world already vastly stimulated
by the example of the independence of the United States. So had the
American Revolution appeared to Spain and to France a generation before. There was moreover in North America a lively public sympathy
for fellow republicans struggling seemingly against a European tyrant,
and little appreciation of the great racial and cultural differences under-

[1] Before the Spanish rising against Napoleon, Great Britain had commenced a campaign
against the Spanish colonies. If it had not been for the new Anglo-Spanish alliance we
may presume that at least a British ascendancy would have been established in South
America.

lying the republican movement in the English-speaking United States and
the regions of "Latin" America, whose people were so heavily endowed
with aboriginal blood and instincts.

An "agent for seamen and commerce in the port of Buenos Ayres,"
Joel R. Poinsett of South Carolina, arrived there in 1810. The purpose
of his mission was to get information and to assure the revolutionists of
the desire of the United States for friendly relations in case of a separation of the province from Spain. Poinsett had a colorful career in the
Argentine and presently in Chile, after he had been appointed Consul-
General (1811) for Buenos Aires, Chile and Peru, a position which did
not prevent him from campaigning personally in the patriot army there.[1]
A new consul, Robert Goddefroy, succeeded Poinsett at Buenos Aires.
These men had instructions from the Department of State similar to the
principles decided in Jefferson's Cabinet in 1808: "The destiny of those
provinces must depend on themselves. Should such a revolution however
take place, it cannot be doubted that our relation with them will be more
intimate, our friendship stronger than it can be while they are colonies
of any European power."[2] From 1811 the United States maintained
consular agents in the principal ports and regions of South America,
though they received no exequaturs until those new nations had been
formally recognized. The opening of the southern continent to the trade
of the outside world was, as had been the case in the British colonies in
North America in 1776, a decisive step in the pathway of independence.

South American agents appeared in the United States in 1811 and thereafter, seeking succors and diplomatic support for their cause, as Silas
Deane and Benjamin Franklin had appeared in France in 1776. They
shipped contraband to their homeland and worked assiduously to fit out
privateers and expeditions hostile to Spanish authority.[3] Unlike France

---

[1] Diego Barros Arana, "El primer cónsul estranjero en Chile, Mr. Joel Poinsett," in his
Obras Completas, XI (16 Vols., Santiago de Chile, 1911). J. Fred Rippy has written the
most recent biography, *Joel R. Poinsett, Versatile American* (Duke University Press,
1935), in which he pays particular attention to Poinsett's part in the initiation of
diplomatic relations with Argentina and Chile.

[2] Secretary of State Robert Smith to Poinsett, April 30, 1811. W. R. Manning,
*Diplomatic Correspondence of the United States Concerning the Independence of the
Latin-American Nations* (3 Vols., New York, 1925), I, 11. F. L. Paxson has described,
from the archives of the Department of State (now published by Manning), relations
with the revolted states in his *The Independence of the South American Republics; a
Study in Recognition and Foreign Policy* (Philadelphia, 1903).

[3] The missions have received much attention from South American historical writers:
Benjamin Vicuña Mackenna, *Ostracismo de los Carreras* (Santiago de Chile, 1857); M.
Varas Velásquez, *Don José Miguel Carrera en los Estados Unidos* (Santiago de Chile,
1912); Alberto Palomeque, *Orijenes de la diplomacia arjentina, misión Aguirre à Norte
América* (2 Vols., Buenos Aires, 1905); F. J. Urrutia, *Los Estados Unidos de América y*

in 1776 the United States did not adopt a policy of secret assistance in addition to watchful diplomatic waiting. Madison and his successor James Monroe were content merely watchfully to wait and meanwhile in rivalry with Great Britain to profit by the new commercial relationship.

President Madison, September 1, 1815, issued a proclamation which amounted to neutrality. Incidentally this was a recognition of the belligerency of the revolted colonies.[1] A commission sent to Buenos Aires in 1817 to investigate the situation of the revolted provinces disagreed as to what it found there. The activities of the South American agents in the United States resulted in widespread violations of neutrality, just how extensive we are not yet able to say for lack of careful historical investigation. This was partly because of the defectiveness of the old neutrality law of 1794 which had not prohibited American citizens from accepting commissions from a foreign prince or state for service *outside* the United States, and which technically did not prevent a citizen of the United States from arming and equipping a vessel within the United States and then *selling* it to a foreigner to be used outside the United States contrary to law. Nor did it provide adequate machinery for executing the law by the seizure of ships suspected of being fitted out for hostilities against a friendly power. New neutrality acts, March 17, 1817, April 20, 1818, only partly remedied this when Adams was engaged in his important negotiations with Onís; but they obliged vessels to give bonds for legal operation and provided for the detention of suspicious vessels.[2] On the other hand they also prohibited unneutral service against a "colony, district or people" as well as against "any foreign prince or State" with whom the United States were at peace. England passed a similar law in 1819.[3]

During the negotiations with Onís over the continental boundary question and the Floridas, John Quincy Adams had walked softly around the

las Repúblicas hispano-Americanas de 1810 á 1830 (Madrid, 1918). Arthur Preston Whitaker has written the latest and best work on *The United States and the Independence of Latin America, 1800-1830* (Johns Hopkins University Press, 1941).

[1] W. S. Robertson, *Hispanic-American Relations with the United States* (New York, 1923). The author has written numerous and enlightening articles in scholarly periodicals on the diplomatic history of this period and subject.

[2] The basic provision of the act was: "Every person, who, within the jurisdiction of the United States, begins or sets on foot, or provides, or prepares the means for, any military expedition or enterprise to be carried on from thence against the territory or domains of any foreign prince or State, or of any colony, district or people, with whom the United States are at peace, shall be deemed guilty of a misdemeanor, and shall be fined not exceeding three thousand dollars and imprisoned not more than three years."

[3] The British law forbade British natural-born subjects from serving henceforth, without royal license, under any conditions anywhere against a country with which Great Britain was not at war.

putative independence of the new republics in South America, whose
agents were in Washington importuning for recognition. He did not
want to frighten off Spain from any treaty containing the great territorial concessions to which he was leading her, and he was not sure
that he would not meet the opposition of European powers, recently organized under the Holy Alliance. We recall that Onís' instructions ordered him to secure a pledge by the United States—in return for the settlement of the Florida question—not to assist the revolted colonies nor to
recognize their independence. The President's proclamation of neutrality
of 1815, and the strengthened neutrality acts of 1817 and 1818 might be
considered as reasonable assurances of policy as to the first point, if not a
pledge; but Adams was unwilling to bind the United States never to
recognize independence. The Secretary's position was made the more
difficult by the vociferous championing of the cause of South American
independence by Henry Clay, who missed no occasion to appeal to
Congress with his powerful and persuasive oratory in favor of recognizing fellow republicans successfully revolting against a European monarchical tyrant after the example of the United States itself. The House
of Representatives in 1820 actually passed a resolution in favor of appropriating funds for the expenses of diplomatic agents in those countries of South America which had already established their independence;
but the Administration studiously ignored it.

The final ratification by Spain in 1821 of the treaty of 1819 freed
Adams' hands to deal with the new states of South America. He had
consistently refused, in the discussions with Spain from 1817 to 1821, to
bind his government not to recognize those republics. By 1821 independence in fact was certainly achieved in the case of the United Provinces of
La Plata (the Argentine), Greater Colombia (present Colombia and
Venezuela), Chile, Mexico and Central America. The following year the
separation of Brazil from any personal union [1] with Portugal was announced, with Dom Pedro as Emperor. With Florida safely annexed, the
President and the State Department could appear to yield to the importunities of Congress. Monroe signed an act of Congress (May 4, 1822)
appropriating $100,000 to defray the expenses of diplomatic missions to

---

[1] The Braganza dynasty, fleeing from Napoleon, took refuge in Brazil in 1807-1808,
and established (1815) an autonomous kingdom, with Rio de Janeiro the capital of all
Portuguese possessions. In 1816 John VI became King of Brazil, and of Portugal.
After a revolution in Portugal in 1820 against a regency that had been set up under
English auspices, John VI departed for Lisbon, to make that city the capital of a
Brazilian-Portuguese Empire, leaving his son Pedro as Regent. Pedro successfully pro-
claimed the independence of Brazil, October 12, 1822, with himself as Constitutional
Emperor.

the "independent nations of the American continent." The President
next formally received the diplomatic representatives of Colombia (June
19, 1822), of Mexico (December 12, 1822), the Empire of Brazil (May
28, 1824), the Central American Confederation (August 4, 1824); and
formal diplomatic agents of the United States were appointed to the
United Provinces of La Plata (January 27, 1823), to Chile (January 27,
1823), and Peru (May 2, 1826).

The United States was thus the first outside nation to recognize the
independence of these fellow-American states. As the revolution of the
English colonies had separated them from the wars and politics of
Europe, so now had the revolution of the Spanish colonies separated
another great part of North America and all of South America [1] from
those wars and those conflicts. Continually Europe's distresses had proved
America's opportunity. On the mainland only British North America
and Russian Alaska were left bound to the political destiny of Europe.

With most of the new states thus recognized, and with later states
which split off from these, treaties of amity and commerce were ratified
between 1824 and 1856.[2] The principal provisions of these typical
treaties of the United States were: most-favored-nation commercial
relations; mutual guaranties against discrimination; religious freedom;
exchange of consuls; and a series of maritime articles setting forth
the duty of one party belligerent toward the other neutral in time of
war.[3] The maritime articles included the traditional American principles: freedom for a neutral to trade in non-contraband goods between port and port of an enemy; free ships free goods except contraband of war;[4] and restriction of contraband to implements of warfare
and articles expressly prepared or formed to make war by sea or land.
These conformed to the model of the Plan of 1776 and the early treaties
of the United States except for one important proviso: that the stipulation free ships free goods should cover the property of neutrals on the
ships of enemies whose governments acknowledge this principle and no
others. John Quincy Adams had introduced this exception into the treaty

[1] Except, of course, the Guianas and British Honduras.
[2] With Colombia (1825), Central American Confederation (1824), Brazil (1828),
Mexico (1831), Chile (1832), Venezuela (1836), Ecuador (1839), New Granada (1846),
Peru-Bolivia (1851), Bolivia (1858).
[3] The treaty with the Argentine (1853) did not contain these maritime articles.
[4] The treaties with Spain, Colombia, Central America, Brazil, Mexico, Chile, Venezuela,
Ecuador, New Granada, and Peru-Bolivia contained the converse rule that when the
neutral flag protected enemy property, the enemy flag made neutral property thereunder
good prize. It is significant that the treaty with Bolivia of 1858 (negotiated after the
Declaration of Paris of 1856 which freed neutral property on enemy ships) omitted this.

of 1819 with Spain, and it was incorporated in the maritime treaties of the United States of the period. The exception was necessary because of the steady refusal of Great Britain and also of France and Russia after the Napoleonic wars, until the Declaration of Paris (1856), to accept the principle as international law. Adams and his successor Henry Clay strove in vain to get these major European powers to recognize what the Latin-American states and some of the smaller European powers like Sweden-Norway (1816), and Prussia (1829) were willing to accept as for themselves in their treaties with the United States.[1] Fortunately no maritime war arose during the century to test again, as they had been tried during the Napoleonic Wars, these traditional dicta of the Plan of 1776. The Crimean War, which resulted in their final acceptance by the Declaration of Paris,[2] did not spread much to the high seas to involve American neutral rights; and none of the above-mentioned treaty parties was a belligerent in that conflict.

Recognition by the United States of the independence of the Latin-American states had been in the face of European and British disapproval. After the overthrow of Napoleon the Czar of Russia, Alexander I, had banded together the continental allies and the restored Bourbon monarchy of France in a Holy Alliance, the purpose of which was to protect the peace of Europe against another eruption of France and further to prevent any subversive or revolutionary movements in their own or other states which might threaten the tranquillity of the "legitimate" and absolute monarchies.[3] Liberal insurrections were promptly crushed in Naples and Piedmont (1821) by Austrian armies under the mandate of the Holy Allies, and in Spain (1823) by a French army with similar authority.[4]

Great Britain refused to be a party to the Holy Alliance and its repressive program. Her great foreign ministers Castlereagh and Canning held that British obligation to continental allies was limited to holding France to observance of the peace settlement of Vienna. They would not help the holy monarchs straitjacket the countries of Europe for absolute divine-right rulers. Besides, they looked skeptically upon the Holy

[1] The Department of State published in 1934 and 1936 a valuable documentary history, compiled by Carlton Savage, of the Policy of the United States Toward Maritime Commerce.

[2] See below, p. 336.

[3] W. A. Phillips, The Confederation of Europe (London, 1920).

[4] These mandates were given at the Congresses of Troppau, 1821 (for Naples and Piedmont), and of Verona, 1822 (for Spain).

Alliance as a scaffolding by which Russia might achieve a military authority over all Europe.[1] It remained British policy to balance European powers in rivalry while Great Britain continued unmolested to consolidate her territorial gains of 1815 and ply the markets and maritime trade of the world. Following this sound policy the British Empire reached its apogee in the nineteenth century under the reign of Queen Victoria.

The intervention of the Holy Allies saved his throne for King Ferdinand VII of Spain in 1823. Might it not save him also his colonies? He appealed to the banded monarchs of Europe to send armies and navies to the New World to put down his rebellious subjects and give him back his rich provinces. The Holy Allies were preparing to meet at another European congress in which this subject might be discussed. Great Britain was disturbed. She feared that any forcible settlement of Spain's colonial affairs by the Holy Alliance might close up the new commerce and give a political tutelage and commercial advantage to some continental power like France. That indeed was the ambition of French diplomacy: to set up in the former Spanish provinces a galaxy of new American monarchies under French Bourbon princes, with close political and commercial ties to France. Here was a remotely possible program of recovery from France's prostration of 1815—an outlet in South America in nominal conjunction with Spain.

Investigation among the confidential archives of European powers by Professor Dexter Perkins [2] reveals that there was not much likelihood of the Holy Allies helping Spain and furthering French ambitions. Though they frowned on independence of the Spanish provinces, neither Prussia, Russia nor Austria, for varying reasons of their own, was sufficiently interested to take forcible steps to prevent it. The only danger was that they might give France a free hand to work out with Spain some settlement. This Great Britain was determined to prevent.

The policy of Great Britain and the United States had had much in common in regard to Latin America. Both desired to continue their new and profitable trade with liberated Spanish colonies. But there was one difference between the two powers. Great Britain had hesitated

[1] Professors C. K. Webster and H. W. V. Temperley have thoroughly discussed British foreign policy in relation to Europe, 1812-1826, notably in the former's two studies, *The Foreign Policy of Castlereagh, 1812-1815* (London, 1931), *The Foreign Policy of Castlereagh, 1815-1822* (London, 1925); and the latter's *The Foreign Policy of Canning, 1822-1827* (London, 1925). For correctives, see Whitaker, *op. cit.*, 199.

[2] *The Monroe Doctrine, 1823-1826* (Cambridge, Mass., 1927). See also his sketch of John Quincy Adams in Volume IV of *The American Secretaries of State and Their Diplomacy, op. cit.*

at actual recognition of independence of the new republics and the Empire of Brazil. Castlereagh had striven to mediate between Britain's ally, Spain, and her colonies, without any sequence of force, on condition that trade should remain open to the outside world. Failing in this, he was preparing for British recognition of the Latin-American states when he died in 1822. If Castlereagh had lived Great Britain might have recognized the new republics and the world might never have heard of the Monroe Doctrine as we have come to know it from the message of 1823.

Spain now appealed to the Holy Alliance. Confronted with the possibility of European intervention, particularly of French intervention, Castlereagh's successor, George Canning, turned to the United States. In a memorable conversation with Richard Rush (August 20, 1823) the famous Secretary for Foreign Affairs laid down the following propositions for an Anglo-American understanding:

1. For ourselves we have no disguise. We conceive the recovery of the Colonies by Spain to be hopeless.

2. We conceive the question of the recognition of them as independent states to be one of time and circumstances.

3. We are, however, by no means disposed to throw any impediment in the way of an arrangement between them and the mother country by amicable negotiation.

4. We aim not at the possession of any portion of them ourselves.

5. We could not see any portion of them transferred to any other Power with indifference.

If these opinions and feelings are, as I firmly believe them to be, common to your government with ours, why should we hesitate mutually to confide them to each other, and to declare them in the face of the world?

Rush on his own responsibility was ready to accept Canning's proposal if he would have altered it to include immediate British recognition of the new states of Latin America; without this, he referred the propositions home for advice. Canning was disappointed. He would not wait for uncertain and conditional American action. Though not wholly averse to recognition at this time, he did not want to have England seem to have been prompted to it by the United States, and he hesitated to take leadership even jointly in a step so disagreeable to his ally Spain. He wanted to use the Latin-American question, and the foreign policy of the United States, as an anvil on which to shatter the Holy Alliance. He decided to act alone, without waiting for an uncertain American cooperation.[1] So he informed (October 9, 1823) the French Ambassador in London, Polignac, that England would recognize the independence of the Spanish colonies if attempt were made to restrict her existing trade with them, or in case any foreign power interfered in

---

[1] William Weed Kaufmann has analyzed, in terms of the balance of power, *British Policy and the Independence of Latin America, 1804-28* (Yale University Press, 1951).

the contest between Spain and them; further, that England would not enter any joint deliberation with the European powers on this question unless the United States were invited to participate.

Canning's Polignac Memorandum was in effect an ultimatum to France and Europe to let Latin America alone. After it there was no substantial danger of European intervention to subdue the independence of the new states of the New World, so recently recognized by the United States, though not yet by Great Britain. This did not mean that there was no likelihood of a British predominance there.

Before we notice the reaction at Washington to Rush's despatches containing the propositions of Canning, we must turn back to John Quincy Adams' interest in western territorial expansion. He was determined to preserve as much of North America as possible for the future sovereignty of his nation. We have already noted how in 1816 he secured a qualified disavowal from Castlereagh of British intentions to purchase or otherwise acquire a cession of Spanish territory in America. We have observed his treaties of 1818 and 1819 securing recognition of American territorial claims to the Oregon country to the north of 42°, claims which he aggressively defended in subsequent months in conversations with the British Minister in Washington.[1] We have not failed to follow the evolution of Jefferson and Madison's policy of opposing the transfer of European colonial possessions from one possessory power to another. This idea Adams embodied in instructions (April 28, 1823) to the minister in Spain. But he was to go further than this in his warnings to European powers. The occasion for vigorous pronouncements by the virile Secretary of State was the progress of Russian expansion from Alaska southward down the Pacific coast.

From its headquarters at Sitka the Russian-American Company (founded 1799) had been extending its activities. It established Fort Ross as a trading-post (1816) at Bodega Bay, in Spanish California just north of San Francisco. The Czar issued an imperial edict, or *ukase,* in 1821, by which he assumed as owner of the coast to exclude all foreigners from trading or fishing within 100 Italian miles of the northwest coast as far south as 51° north latitude. Both Great Britain and the United States protested. At the Court of St. Petersburg in 1809-1810, Minister John Quincy Adams, acting under instructions, had refused to co-operate with Russia to regulate the trade in firearms with the Indians of the northwest coast, because of reluctance to recognize thereby

[1] For Adams' stiff words to Stratford Canning, see his *Diary.*

the Czar's sovereignty there.[1]   Russia's absorption in the distresses
of the Napoleonic wars caused Alexander I's Government to drop the
matter at that time.   Secretary John Quincy Adams in July, 1823, declared to the Russian Minister at Washington, Baron Tuyll, that the
United States would contest the right of Russia, not only to the country
covered by the new decree, but to *any* territorial establishment on this continent, and that "we should assume distinctly the principle that the American continents are no longer subjects for *any* new European colonial
establishments."   Thus had Adams' old anxieties about further extension
of European power—anxieties sharpened by the long-standing closure
of the existing European colonies to American navigation [2]—crystallized
into a dictum which presently he was to have opportunity to write into
a formal pronouncement by the President.   His attempt to contest
Russia's title to *any* territorial establishments in North America was
unsuccessful; but in 1824 the United States and Russia easily agreed in a
practical way to a treaty restricting that empire from any *new* colonial
establishments by accepting the southern boundary of Alaska at 54° 40″.
Great Britain made a similar treaty with Russia in 1825, accepting the
same southern limit and drawing a boundary line from there to the Arctic
Ocean, the present boundary of Alaska.[3]

The new dictum was fresh in Adams' mind and in the councils of
the Government when despatches from Rush arrived in Washington
describing Canning's propositions for a joint Anglo-American pronouncement on the status of the Spanish colonies.   A serious question of
state was thus posed.   President Monroe sought the advice of two
of the elder statesmen, ex-Presidents Jefferson and Madison (but not
ex-President John Adams, father of the Secretary).   These *genro,* who
had grown up with American independence and were experienced with
European diplomatic involvements, who had been anti-British in their
foreign outlook for over half a century—these aged leaders advised
the President to accept Canning's proposal, despite the danger of foreign
entanglements.

[1] John C. Hildt, *Early Diplomatic Relations of the United States with Russia* (Baltimore, 1906).

[2] Westermann, *Netherlands and the United States, op. cit.,* shows how the European
colonial monopolies sharpened Adams' aversion to further colonization.

[3] The relevant state documents concerning the origin and subsequent history of the
Monroe Doctrine are conveniently printed in J. B. Moore, *Digest of International Law*
(8 Vols., Washington, 1906), VI, 368-604.   W. C. Ford has set forth the documents showing John Quincy Adams' part in the evolution of the pronouncement in the *Proceedings
of the Massachusetts Historical Society* for January, 1902, together with a documented
essay, "John Quincy Adams and the Monroe Doctrine," in *Am. Hist. Rev.,* VII (1902),
676-696, VIII (1902), 28-52.

The question of the British overture and Russia's new claims on the northwest coast was the subject of frequent deliberations in the Cabinet during November. Secretary Adams argued against accepting Canning's propositions. He thought the British Minister was trying to ensnare the United States into a public pledge against the future acquisition of any territory still held by Spain in the New World, Cuba for instance. Adams already (July 5, 1820) had instructed the Minister of the United States to Russia, Henry Middleton, to decline, with thanks, a formal invitation from the Czar to join the Holy Alliance. He had used language that recalled Washington's Farewell Address, reminding that "to stand in firm and cautious independence of all entanglements in the European system" had been a "cardinal point of American foreign policy since 1783." He had also said at that time: "For the repose of Europe as well as America, the European as well as the American systems should be kept as separate and distinct from each other as possible." He was none the more disposed to unite with England in 1823. Jefferson's advice to Monroe included this same principle, the principle of a separate American sphere, distinct from that of Europe.[1] If we are to believe Adams' *Diary,* he convinced Monroe and his Cabinet against accepting; and he further urged taking an independent stand against European intervention in the New World. President Monroe decided[2] to embody some such pronouncement in his next annual message. Meanwhile the Cabinet approved a note drafted by Adams to Baron Tuyll for the attention of the Russian Czar: "That the United States of America, and their government, could not see with indifference the forcible interposition of any European power, other than Spain, either to restore the dominion of Spain over the emancipated colonies in America, or to establish monarchical governments in those countries, or to transfer any of the possessions heretofore or yet subject to Spain in the American hemisphere, to any other European power."

[1] T. R. Schellenberg, "Jeffersonian Origins of the Monroe Doctrine," *Hisp. Am. Hist. Rev.,* XIV (February, 1934), 1-32, shows that Jefferson had read with approval de Pradt's *"l'Europe après le Congrès d'Aix la Chapelle, faisant suite au Congrès de Vienne* (Paris, 1819, Philadelphia, English translation, 1820), in which this doctrine was clearly expressed. Adams also had read it.

[2] Governor William A. MacCorkle has made as strong a case as can be made for President Monroe as the author of the doctrine in his *The Personal Genesis of the Monroe Doctrine* (New York, 1923), by showing that it was Monroe who conceived the idea of putting a pronouncement in his approaching message, and that Monroe (like other Americans) had been always against European intervention and in favor of the non-transfer principle.

Canning, with the force of the British navy behind him, in essence already had said this to Polignac. President Monroe and his advisers now put it forward as an independent American policy rooted in the thought and action of the people and government of the United States and in its diplomatic experience.[1]

In his original draft of the momentous message Monroe was in favor of coupling some statement of sympathy for the struggle of the republican Spaniards and Greeks against arbitrary government in Europe while pronouncing against any interference of Europe in the affairs of the new states of the American continents. Prudently this was pruned out, on Adams' advice. As given to the world, through the message of President Monroe to Congress of December 2, 1823, the Monroe Doctrine declared:

(1) It did not comport with the policy of the United States to take any part in the politics or the wars of European powers in matters relating to themselves.

(2) The United States would regard as the manifestation of an unfriendly disposition to itself the effort of any European power to interfere with the political system of the American continents, or to acquire any new territory on these continents.[2]

The Monroe Doctrine was a document rather of the future than of the time of its first utterance. Europe really paid little attention to it. Canning's ultimatum to France settled any possible danger of intervention in South America, and presently the European governments one after another (Great Britain first late in 1824—Spain last in 1836) began to recognize the independence of the new states. South America applauded the Doctrine, and the pecuniary bonds of the new states rose a few points. But the new Latin-American states were not in 1823 "saved" by the pronouncement of the Doctrine.

The significance in 1823 of the Monroe Doctrine is that it served as a capstone to a very positive structure of American foreign policy that had been built up from a half-century of independent dealing with foreign nations. It proclaimed in strong Republican tone an American system for the New World.

Colombia, Brazil, and Mexico successively suggested that the Monroe Doctrine be written into an inter-American alliance. But the Adams

---

[1] E. L. Tatum, Jr., has stressed forcibly the American background in *The United States and Europe, 1815-1823; A Study in the Background of the Monroe Doctrine* (University of California Press, 1936).

[2] The essential portions of the text are reproduced at the end of this chapter.

Administration was careful not to commit the United States to any such agreement. The famous South American Liberator Simón Bolívar called on all the states of the New World to meet the Congress of Panama on October 1, 1825. The United States was invited in the hope of getting it to subscribe to such an alliance. President John Quincy Adams and Secretary Clay were eager to send plenipotentiaries to the Congress, not to cement the Monroe Doctrine into a hemispheric alliance but rather, as a neutral in the war between Spain and the Latin American countries, to commit the new states in multilateral treaties to the Freedom of the Seas and the freedom of commerce without discrimination between the ships, products of citizens of any American state and those of another trading to it. They also wanted to bind the nations of the New World to the doctrine of non-intervention and the principles of "good neighborhood."

The Congress of Panama proved to be a fiasco. Plenipotentiaries from Colombia, Mexico, Peru, and Central America finally met on the Isthmus, June 26-July 15, 1826, and drew up treaties of confederation and alliance, but only Colombia ratified them. Even Bolívar lost his interest in the meeting before it assembled, and turned to a new project, a Confederation of the Andes. A vociferous minority in the United States opposed the appointment of plenipotentiaries because of the danger of foreign entanglements. President Adams insisted, and the Senate rather reluctantly confirmed his nomination of two plenipotentiaries, Richard C. Anderson, Minister to Colombia, and John Sergeant of Philadelphia; and the House of Representatives appropriated the necessary expenses. It was John Quincy Adams's only political success with his Congress. Sergeant delayed setting out until the pestilential summer season was over, and Anderson died at Cartagena on his way to Panama, so the United States was not represented at this first Pan-American Congress.

These were the fundamentals of American foreign policy as crystallized by 1826: (1) Independence, (2) Freedom of the Seas, (3) Freedom of Commerce and Navigation, (4) Isolation, (5) the No-Transfer Principle, (6) Continental Expansion, (7) Self-determination, (8) Noncolonization, (9) Nonintervention, (10) the right of expatriation and the wrong of impressment, (11) Suppression of the African Slave Trade, (12) Good Neighborhood, (13) International Arbitration, (14) Anti-imperialism.[1]

---

[1] Samuel Flagg Bemis, *John Quincy Adams and the Foundations of American Foreign Policy* (Alfred A. Knopf, Inc., New York, 1949), Ch. XXVI.

NOTE

The essential paragraphs of the text of the Monroe Doctrine, taken from the original manuscript of President Monroe's annual message to Congress of December 2, 1823, as now preserved in the archives of the Senate, are *verbatim et literatim:*

At the proposal of the Russian Imperial Government, made through the Minister of the Emperor, residing here, a full power and instructions have been transmitted to the Minister of the United States at St. Petersburg, to arrange by amicable negotiation, the respective rights and interests of the two Nations on the North West Coast of this Continent. A similar proposal has been made by His Imperial Majesty, to the Government of Great Britain, which has likewise been acceded to. The Government of the United States has been desirous by this friendly proceeding, of manifesting the great value which they have invariably attached to the friendship of the Emperor, and their solicitude to cultivate the best understanding with his Government. In the discussions to which this interest has given rise, and in the arrangements by which they may terminate, the occasion has been judged proper, for asserting as a principle in which the rights and interests of the United States are involved, that the American Continents, by the free and independent condition which they have assumed and maintain, are henceforth not to be considered as subjects for future colonization by any European Power. . . .

It was stated at the commencement of the last session, that a great effort was then making in Spain and Portugal, to improve the condition of the people of those countries; and that it appeared to be conducted with extraordinary moderation. It need scarcely be remarked, that the result has been, so far, very different from what was then anticipated. Of events in that quarter of the Globe, with which we have so much intercourse, and from which we derive our origin, we have always been anxious and interested spectators. The Citizens of the United States cherish sentiments the most friendly, in favor of the liberty and happiness of their fellowmen on that side of the Atlantic. In the wars of the European powers, in matters relating to themselves, we have never taken any part, nor does it comport with our policy, so to do. It is only when our rights are invaded, or seriously menaced, that we resent injuries, or make preparation for our defense. With the movements in this Hemisphere we are of necessity more immediately connected, and by causes which must be obvious to all enlightened and impartial observers. The political system of the allied powers, is essentially different in this respect from that of America. This difference proceeds from that, which exists in their respective Governments, and to the defence of our own, which has been atchieved [*sic*] by the loss of so much blood and treasure, and matured by the wisdom of their most enlightened citizens, and under which we have enjoyed unexampled felicity, this whole nation is devoted. We owe it therefore to candor, and to the amicable relations existing between the United States and those powers, to declare that we should consider any attempt on their part to extend their system to any portions of this Hemisphere, as dangerous to our peace and safety. With the existing Colonies or dependencies of any European power, we have not interfered, and shall not interfere. But with the Governments who have declared their Independence, and maintained it, and whose Independence we have, on great consideration, and on just principles, acknowledged, we could not view any interposition for the purpose of oppressing them, or controuling in any other manner, their destiny, by any European power, in any other light, than as the manifestation of an unfriendly disposition towards the United States. In the war between those new governments and Spain, we declared our neutrality, at the time of their recognition, and to this we have adhered, and shall continue to adhere, provided no change shall occur, which in the judgment of the competent authorities of this Government, shall make a corresponding change, on the part of the United States, indispensable to their security.

The late events in Spain and Portugal, show that Europe is still unsettled. Of this important fact, no stronger proof can be adduced, than that the allied powers should have thought it proper, on any principle satisfactory to themselves, to have interposed by force, in the internal concerns of Spain. To what extent, such interposition may be carried, on the same principle, is a question, in which all Independent powers, whose Governments differ from theirs, are interested; even those most remote, and surely none more so than the United States. Our policy in regard to Europe, which was adopted at an early stage of the wars which have so long agitated that quarter of the Globe, nevertheless remains the same, which is, not to interfere in the internal concerns of any of its powers; to consider the Government *de facto;* as the legitimate [*sic*] for us; to cultivate friendly relations with it, and to preserve those relations by a frank, firm and manly policy, meeting in all instances, the just claims of every power; submitting to injuries from none. But, in regard to those continents, circumstances are eminently and conspicuously different. It is impossible that the allied powers, should extend their political systems, to any portion of either continent, without endangering our peace and happiness, nor can anyone believe, that our Southern Brethren, if left to themselves, would adopt it of their own accord. It is equally impossible therefore, that we should behold such interposition in any form with indifference. If we look to the comparative strength and resources of Spain and those new Governments, and their distance from each other, it must be obvious that she can never subdue them. It is still the true policy of the United States, to leave the parties to themselves, in the hope, that other powers will pursue the same course.

PART II

EXPANSION

CHAPTER XIII

MEXICO AND TEXAS

(1823-1845)

For a fortunate century after the overthrow of Napoleon mankind escaped another world war. After 1823 American diplomacy could no longer reap such advantages from the distresses of Europe as before. Thanks to a half-century of conflict, the first republic of the New World, and the other republics following it, had rooted themselves too sturdily in the international soil to be weeded out by the monarchies of Europe. The remaining years of the nineteenth century were to witness throughout the vacant western reaches of this continent a process of self-sustained expansion destined to make the United States a world power fronting on the two great oceans of civilization and ready to control an artificial waterway between them. It was a period of consciously aggressive expansion interrupted by the growing-pains and international risks of the Civil War, and even disguised by decades of digestive tranquillity in the 'seventies and 'eighties, to end in a spectacular climax of expansive force in 1898. Expansion expressed the pent-up forces of the developing national spirit in the United States. It has remained its principal and most successful manifestation. It is embodied in the phrase Manifest Destiny, first coined in 1845, but invoked in spirit, in word and deed, by American statesmen from Jefferson and John Quincy Adams to Seward and Charles Sumner, not to mention the expansionists of 1898, the Mahans, the Lodges and the Roosevelts. Manifest Destiny represented a widespread and swelling popular conviction that it was indeed the manifest destiny of the Republic to expand by peaceful process and by the force of republican example and principles of government over the whole of the continent of North America. It was not based on militarism. Throughout the history of the expansionist movement the United States (except for the interlude of the Civil War) remained a nation with the smallest of armies, without conscription, with a minimum of naval force. Unsympathetically philosophers [1] have analyzed the essential self-interest of

[1] The most conspicuous work is Albert K. Weinberg, *Manifest Destiny, a Study of Nationalist Expansionism in American History* (Johns Hopkins Press, 1935).

215

Manifest Destiny, under its cloak of pious phrases; but we must remember that American expansion across a practically empty continent despoiled no nation unjustly, and that there is no American today who would want to see that expansion undone. Manifest Destiny might much better be described as Manifest Opportunity.

It is our task in the Second Part of this volume to review this process of expansion. The first chapter is Mexico and Texas.

We have observed that during the period between 1803 and 1821, when relations with Spain were strained over the question of the Floridas, the boundary between Louisiana and Spain's frontier provinces had remained unsettled. Texas, to which both the United States and Spain laid claim, was practically unoccupied, though isolated settlements at San Antonio, Los Adaes, Nacogdoches, and La Bahia testified more than did diplomatic documents to the fact of Spanish possession. At most a few hundred Spanish troops defended these outposts on the line of the Sabine River.[1] In any outbreak of war, hostilities would begin on the plains of eastern Texas. When the tension was greatest in 1806, President Jefferson sent a contingent of American soldiers to protect the frontier in this region. They were under the command of General James Wilkinson, who had charge of the western military department which included Louisiana. Wilkinson had a force slightly less in number than the Spanish. It was within his power to provoke a war by some overt act, particularly with the Southwest so eager for it. But he and the Spanish commander prudently agreed on a neutral zone, between the Sabine River and the Arroyo Hondo to the east. Across this ground the two small armies faced each other during 1806. This neutral zone continued to serve as a rough *de facto* boundary until the western limit of the State of Louisiana was fixed at the Sabine River upon the admission of that state into the Union in 1812.

Wilkinson had been plotting with that damaged soul, Aaron Burr, but exactly what no one knows to this day. Some believe they planned secession of the West from the Union and hoped to round out their new state with adjacent Spanish territory: Florida, Texas, and even

[1] There were also a few isolated American settlements at this time in the eastern fringes of the Texas country. Philip Nolan, a frontiersman and correspondent of Jefferson, and of Wilkinson, had made successive expeditions far into Texas to round up wild mustangs. A passport from Spanish authorities did not prevent a party of his from being attacked by Spanish forces on the south fork of the Red River in 1801. Nolan and some of his followers were killed, and the others were imprisoned. After six years' delay one of the prisoners was chosen by lot and executed, by orders from Spain.

more. Some believe [1] it was only a great filibustering enterprise they planned, to be favored perhaps by the outbreak of war with Spain, which certainly seemed imminent in 1805-1806. The researches of historians long afterwards undertaken, in the archives of England and Spain, show that Burr had solicited both the British and Spanish Ministers for funds to aid his enterprise, and had explained it as one of revolution and secession. He did get two or three thousand dollars from Irujo, Spanish Minister in Washington.

Encamped by the Arroyo Hondo, Wilkinson was in a position to make or break Burr. It would have been easy for him to precipitate hostilities and thus set the West on fire, perfecting the scene for the conspirators. But the reader knows how Wilkinson, now in command of the American army, had long since secretly sold himself to the King of Spain and had become a pensioner of his Catholic Majesty. He was a more finished scoundrel than his associate. He resolved to betray Burr. As the American Catiline was floating down the Mississippi, Wilkinson, posing as a patriotic army officer, denounced Burr to President Jefferson, and himself hastened to New Orleans to place the city under martial law against any uprising. He did not forget to apprise the Viceroy of Mexico of his destruction of Burr's schemes and to ask for a reward of $200,000. How much, if any, of this he ever got is still a mystery. [2]

Burr saw the game was up. At Natchez he deserted his followers and fled into the wilderness, to be captured when he emerged at Fort Stoddert, above Mobile.

Jefferson was anxious for Burr's conviction. In the trial [3] for treason at Richmond, Virginia, Chief Justice Marshall, presiding, ruled that conviction, under the Constitution, required two witnesses to an overt act. The Government could not present such testimony, and the jury returned a verdict of not proven. Marshall ordered it to stand as not guilty.

Burr lived to see Sam Houston successful in achieving Texan independence. On that occasion he declared: "There! You see? I was

[1] Henry Adams, in his *History, op. cit.*, is convinced Burr planned to break up the Union, but W. F. McCaleb, *The Aaron Burr Conspiracy* (New York, 1903), concluded that Burr was only a would-be filibuster. Adams appears to have the better grasp of the plot.

[2] V. Salado Álvarez, *La Conjura de Aaron Burr y las primeras tentativas de conquista de México por Americanos del Oeste* (Mexico, 1908); and T. M. Marshall, *A History of the Western Boundary of the Louisiana Purchase, 1819-1841* (Berkeley, Calif., 1914).

[3] With some sympathy for Burr and admiration for Marshall, A. J. Beveridge has told the history of the treason trial in his monumental *Life of John Marshall, op. cit.*

right! I was only thirty years too soon. What was treason in me thirty years ago, is patriotism now!" We need not put too much faith in these words of a proven liar.

After Burr's fiasco other adventurers looked covetously on the disputed plains of Texas so thinly defended by Spain.[1]

Struggles between these filibusters and Spanish troops in Texas denuded the province of most of its few settlers. When Mexico became independent in 1821, the great prairies were still vacant and very thinly garrisoned. There was no longer any motive for organizing filibustering expeditions; from the beginning the new Mexican Government embarked on a policy of attracting settlers into its northern provinces from the United States, by most liberal laws governing immigration and land disposal. In the end this was a sad mistake for Mexico. Despite the good faith and loyalty of the first settlers, Texas filled up speedily with an alien population which soon became a menace to the territorial integrity of the rudely and loosely governed Republic of Mexico. From Mexican policy toward immigrants to Texas, the United States, if it needed to, could learn what it would mean today to stimulate and invite masses of alien, say oriental, populations to settle in California.[2]

Under these favorable laws, about 15,000 American immigrants poured in between 1825 and 1830. Most of them came across an open frontier with practically no inspection or regulation. No adequate Mexican immigration or customs service or patrol existed in Texas. By 1836 the "Anglo-American" population east of the Nueces was approximately 30,000, plus some 5,000 Negro slaves.[3] There were nearly a quarter of a million people in Texas when the first United States census was taken there in 1850. Of these 58,161 were then slaves.

This rapid influx of an alien people, alien in language, alien in culture, alien in religion, and alien in political background caused increasing anxiety among Mexican officials. As early as 1825 one of the *empresarios*, Haden Edwards, revolted and proclaimed near Nacogdoches,

[1] Bernardo de Gutierrez, a Mexican revolutionist, started a filibustering expedition in 1811 with the aid of Augustus Magee, an ex-officer of the United States army. Their movement was wiped out with great slaughter and barbarity in 1813 by Spanish forces, it was said in retaliation for faithless conduct. Gutierrez survived to participate in another unsuccessful expedition, organized in Mississippi and Kentucky in 1819 by James Long of Natchez.

[2] See below Chap. XXXV, for the question of oriental immigration.

[3] Jackson's observer, Morfit, estimated the population of Texas proper in 1836 at 30,000 American settlers, 5,000 Negroes, and 12,000 to 14,000 Indians. Rives, *op. cit.*, I, 391. L. G. Bugbee, "Slavery in Early Texas," *Pol. Sci. Quar.*, XIII (1898), 389-412, 648-668, estimates 1,000 slaves in 1829, with a small proportion continuing till 1843. See also E. C. Barker, in *Miss. Vall. Hist. Rev.*, X, 141-152.

on the Louisiana frontier, an independent republic which he called
Fredonia. Stephen F. Austin, the pioneer *empresario* from the United
States, and his fellow-naturalized Mexicans helped their adopted country put down this insurrection. But there was no question that the
future was full of trouble. Luis Alamán, an able Mexican statesman,
pointed this out in a celebrated report to the Mexican Congress in 1830.
That body then took advantage of conditions which had been attached
to the federal land law and immigration laws of 1824. It passed a law
(1830) forbidding the entrance of foreigners, under any pretext, across
the northern frontier, unless provided with proper Mexican passports.
It prohibited citizens from adjacent countries (of course the only country in question was the United States) from settling in the frontier
states and territories of Mexico; and it declared suspended all unexe-
cuted colonization contracts which conflicted with the new law. Another federal law of 1832 provided for the redistribution to *bona fide*
Mexican citizens of land reverting to the nation by virtue of non-ful-
fillment of colonization contracts. But the door, if shut at all, was
shut too late.

This legislation caused friction with the new immigrants, when an
attempt was made to enforce it. The settlers from the United States
assumed, without justification, that they had legal guaranties against
any modification of the colonization laws. Their assumption had been
fortified by the lack of any enforcement hitherto of the enacted laws.
From 1832 to 1835, when revolution broke out, Texas was in a ferment of expostulation. A majority of the discontented were until 1835
for constitutional adjustments, like the English colonists before 1776,
but after 1835 those in favor of complete separation from Mexico
assumed control, when it became clear that no other solution seemed
possible.[1] Open revolt and war broke out in 1835. On April 21, 1836,
a Texan army, organized and led by General Sam Houston, defeated
decisively an army led by the President of Mexico, General Santa
Anna, at the battle of San Jacinto. From then on Texan independence
existed in fact, if never recognized by Mexico.

The Mexican restrictions on immigration from the United States had
been the more readily forthcoming because of persistent efforts of the
neighboring republic to buy all or parts of Texas. True, the great transcontinental treaty settlement with Spain, ratified in 1821, had fixed the
boundary very exactly; and there was no question but that Mexico inherited those limits from Spain. That could not be challenged. John

[1] E. C. Barker, *Mexico and Texas, 1821-1835* (Dallas, Texas, 1928).

Quincy Adams himself had made the treaty with Onís in 1819. As President (1825-1829), Adams was loathe to confirm the transcontinental boundary with Mexico. He regretted that his own treaty had not taken some or all of Texas, and explained the shortcoming by the advice of Monroe's Cabinet to accept the line of the Sabine. Adams sent Joel R. Poinsett, now back from South America, as the first Minister of the United States to Mexico.[1] Instructions written by Secretary of State Henry Clay in 1825, and again in 1827, bade Poinsett to offer a graduated scale of money compensation for "rectifying" the boundary by moving it as far west as possible: the Brazos River, the Colorado River of Texas, the "Snow Mountains,"[2] or the Rio Grande-Pecos rivers. When Poinsett sounded out the Mexican Minister, Alamán, the latter responded with a readiness to rectify the boundary—by moving it *east* from the Sabine to the Mississippi! Adams finally contented himself with the signature (1828) of a treaty confirming the transcontinental boundary of 1819 and providing for a survey.

Mexico did not promptly ratify the boundary treaty. Then Adams' successor, President Jackson (1829-1837), also bent on buying Texas, discovered a convenient uncertainty as to the precise identity of the Sabine River boundary line. The new Secretary of State, Martin Van Buren, prepared to offer as much as $5,000,000 for the best boundary he could get: the Brazos, the Colorado, the Lavaca-Colorado line, or the divide between the Nueces and the Rio Grande. Poinsett had a penchant for interfering in the domestic politics of the countries to which he was accredited. He had long since become unpopular with the constituted authorities of Mexico. Its government requested his recall. To carry out his plan for the purchase of Texas, Jackson replaced Poinsett with Anthony Butler, who represented the United States in Mexico for the next seven years (1829-1836).

Before Butler revealed the real purpose of his mission—which was nothing essentially different from that of Poinsett's—he signed (1831) a treaty of amity and commerce similar to those which were then being negotiated with the other Latin-American states.[3] Mexico refused to ratify this treaty until the United States ratified the boundary treaty

---

[1] W. R. Manning has described, from the unpublished archives of Mexico as well as of the United States, these early negotiations in his *Early Diplomatic Relations Between the United States and Mexico* (Baltimore, 1916).

[2] Melish's Map of 1820 indicates the "Snow Mountains" corresponding to the present *Sangre de Cristos* and serving as the eastern watershed of the Rio Grande River, with a prominent spur south toward the latitude of El Paso, but splitting above that latitude, into two ranges east and west of the Pecos River.

[3] See above, p. 201.

of 1828. Both treaties were ratified and went into effect April 5, 1832.[1]
Butler's instructions of August, 1835, enabled him to offer _____
millions of dollars for a new transcontinental boundary: the Rio Grande
River to 37° north latitude and thence due west to the Pacific Ocean, or
any other line that would include San Francisco Bay—also coveted by
Jackson—within the United States. The President really was ready to
furnish Butler with a blank check for Mexico to write in if she would
shear off nearly a million square miles [2] of her northern domains, from
Atlantic to Pacific. When Butler wrote home that there did not seem
any way to put through such a big real estate deal except maybe by
indirectly bribing Mexican officials, Jackson wrote on the back of the
despatch: "A. Butler. What a Scamp!" Nevertheless he allowed A.
Butler, the Scamp, to stay in Mexico. But Mexico would not sell
Texas, not to mention California, to the United States, any more than
Jackson would have sold Missouri, not to mention upper Louisiana, to
a foreign power.

Scholars and jurists have much discussed the attitude of the United
States Government, and particularly of President Jackson *vis-à-vis*
the Texan Revolution—whether neutrality was properly observed,
whether Jackson had anything to do with instigating that revolution
which eventually proved to be so profitable for the United States. No
adequate evidence had been presented to show any complicity of Jackson with the Texan revolutionists, though he was in intimate relations
with Sam Houston. In fact, even if Jackson wanted Texas to revolt
against Mexico and establish its independence—with an expectation for
later annexation to the United States—it was not necessary to conspire.
The revolution would have come when it did. Jackson did nothing to
start it or to stop it.[3]

The question of neutrality is another matter. The Mexican Govern-

[1] This did not prevent Jackson from continuing to insist that the Sabine was the
westernmost instead of the easternmost of the two streams which met to flow into
Sabine Lake on the Louisiana frontier. The boundary there was never agreed upon until
settled between the later Republic of Texas and the United States at the easternmost
branch. See Map 14.

[2] Texas to the Rio Grande included 390,000 square miles. From Texas to the Pacific,
between the latitude of El Paso and 42° N. Lat.—the southern boundary of the United
States—constituted 565,000 square miles. This calculation was made for me by the
Topographical Division of the United States Geological Survey.

[3] The subject has been ventilated in J. S. Bassett's *Life of Andrew Jackson* (2 Vols.,
New York, 1916), and E. C. Barker, "President Jackson and the Texan Revolution,"
Am. Hist. Rev., XII (1907), 788-809. More skeptical is R. R. Stenberg, "Jackson,
Anthony Butler and Texas," in *Southwest Social Science Quarterly*, XIII (December,
1932), 264-287; and "The Texas Schemes of Jackson and Houston, 1829-1836," *ibid.*,
XV (December, 1934), 229-251.

ment naturally would have preferred that the United States did not formally recognize the belligerency of Texas. To do so would have given the Texans moral encouragement. But it would also have placed the United States under the obligations of international law to enforce the laws of neutrality. President Jackson issued to the world no proclamation of neutrality, though his orders to the army, and to the district attorneys, to enforce neutrality, speak of neutrality as if in the international sense; and so do the statements to the Mexican Government.[1] It was technically a problem of the enforcement of domestic legislation, of the so-called "neutrality laws" of 1794, 1817, and 1818 that prohibited the departure of hostile expeditions against a friendly state. Sympathy with the Texans was warm and notorious, especially in the southern states from which so many of them had emigrated. Liberal bonuses of land grants to immigrants enlisting in the Texan army attracted thousands across the line. Companies of them bearing all the manifestations of organized and recruited effort descended the Mississippi with bands playing and (United States) flags flying, all bellicose emigrants bound for Texan ports. Others migrated across the unguarded land frontier. The neutrality laws of the United States, even as amended in 1817 and 1818,[2] had nothing in them to prevent *emigration,* nor to prevent military service of an American citizen with a foreign prince or people *outside* the territory of the United States. Nor do they to this day. But the laws of the United States have never sanctioned foreign recruiting within its boundaries. When Great Britain attempted that during the Crimean War, the United States broke it up immediately and insisted on the recall of the British Minister and consuls for their improper activities.[3] Texan recruiting agents more or less openly organized the departure of these "emigrants" in 1836.[4] The Government defended itself against the complaints of the Mexican envoy Gorotiza by stating that every effort was made to enforce the law, and asking

[1] T. M. Marshall, *op. cit.,* reviews some of the documents. See also E. C. Barker's careful article, "The United States and Mexico, 1835-1837," in *Miss. Vall. Hist. Rev.,* I (1914), 3-30. See also the opinion of May 17, 1836, of the Attorney-General (*Official Opinions of the Attorneys-General of the United States* (Washington, 1852-1929), III, 122). The communication to the Mexican Government was ordered in instructions to the *chargé d'affaires* in Mexico, Anthony Butler, Nov. 9, 1835. See also the possibly inspired statement in *Niles Register,* Nov. 14, 1835.

[2] See above, p. 199.

[3] J. B. Brebner, "Joseph Howe and the Crimean War Enlistment Controversy Between Great Britain and the United States," *Canadian Hist. Rev.,* XI (December, 1930), 300-327.

[4] G. L. Rives, *The United States and Mexico, 1821-1848* (2 Vols., New York, 1913), I, 362-388.

for specific evidence of alleged violations. By the time such could be furnished the alleged infraction would be beyond repair.

The Administration also cited the lack of power of the federal authorities. Inadequacy of neutrality laws does not excuse a country from observing to the full its obligations of neutrality. After the Civil War the United States so contended, and successfully, in seeking compensation from the British Government for the *Alabama* and other spoliations. At that time it contended that no sovereign power could "rightfully plead the defects of its own domestic penal statutes as justification or extenuation of an international wrong to another sovereign power." [1] When there was an insurrection in Canada in 1837 American citizens crossed the frontier to participate in it, on a much smaller scale than they did in the case of the Mexican frontier the year before. In this instance a very earnest effort was made to enforce neutrality even though no belligerency of the Canadian rebels was recognized. President Van Buren in a special message to Congress declared that the existing laws, as shown by actual events on the northern frontier as well as experience on the southern border, were inadequate. Congress quickly passed the act of March 10, 1838, which enabled the Government to seize *any* vessel being *prepared* for hostile purposes against a foreign coterminous state and to seize suspicious vessels [2] *or vehicles*, or arms or munitions of war. It is noteworthy that the relatively slight commotions in the adjacent territory of the most powerful empire in the world brought a prompt improvement of hitherto inadequate domestic laws, but that a formidable revolution in the neighboring province of a weak and disorganized Latin-American republic had not brought the necessary amendments. The passage of the act of 1838 (limited to two years) is abundant testimony to the inadequacy of the neutrality of the United States during the Texas Revolution. Admitting the inadequacy of the laws, but considering the widespread sympathy, it is doubtful whether any government of the United States could have been much more strict in 1836 without danger of being forced by public opinion into the war; and European foreign diplomatic observers cast little serious blame on the United States.[3] Meanwhile Van Buren's Administration was insisting on the adjustment of claims of American citizens against Mexico.

[1] Fish to Motley, No. 70, September 25, 1869. Moore, *A Digest of International Law, op. cit.,* VII, 1015.

[2] The act expressly did not interfere with trade in arms and munitions of war "conducted in vessels by sea, with any foreign port of place whatsoever."

[3] Justin H. Smith, *The Annexation of Texas* (New York, 1911), 1-33.

A spectacular act which has received more unqualified censure than the inadequacy of "neutrality" laws was General Gaines' temporary occupation of Nacogdoches with a regiment of United States troops during the revolution (July-November, 1836). It was really less censurable. Gaines had loose instructions from the Secretary of War which he interpreted to allow him, in case a confused situation on the frontier should threaten an Indian outbreak, to cross the "imaginary boundary line." The territory he invaded was at least under dispute between Mexico and the United States; and the treaty of 1832 might be interpreted to justify such a step as Gaines' "invasion" at a moment when Mexican forces were unable forcibly to keep the Indians pacified.[1] Some of the soldiers in this little expedition deserted and took service with Texan troops.

We have already said that there is no evidence to show that the settlement of Texas and its successful revolt against Mexico can be attributed to any intrigues of President Andrew Jackson. Nor can it be explained by putative deliberate machinations of an aggressive southern "slaveocracy" in control of the United States Government.[2] Nevertheless Texas was promising slave territory. Its people were in favor of slavery. Its new constitution entrenched slavery impregnably. Though not all southern leaders wanted Texas, there unquestionably was developing a slave power in the United States. Twenty-four years later it attempted the establishment of a new nation with slavery avowedly its "cornerstone." During the Texan Revolution, Calhoun and some other pro-slavery leaders were advocating the annexation of that new republic. Susceptible of being divided into several future states of the United States, its acquisition would extend the slave power and balance in Congress a covey of free-soil states certain to be hatched in the near future out of the portion of the old Louisiana purchase left north of the compromise line of 1820. Such pro-slavery politicians argued they were only defending their rightful political position.

The slavery-extension element was bitterly opposed by increasingly insistent northern spokesmen determined to block the further advance and political power of that baleful institution. Among these the most eloquent and forceful was the former Secretary of State and President,

[1] For Gaines' occupation of Nacogdoches, see, among others, T. M. Marshall, *op. cit.*; Rives, *op. cit.*, 378-81; and E. C. Barker, *op. cit.*, in *Miss. Vall. Hist. Rev.*, I.

[2] This was the theme of Hermann E. von Holst, in Volume II of his *Constitutional and Political History of the United States* (English edition, 8 Vols., Chicago, 1881-92). But see, *per contra*, C. S. Boucher, "In re that aggressive slaveocracy," *Miss. Vall. Hist. Rev.*, VIII (1921), 13-77.

who so recently had striven to get Texas by diplomacy, first from Spain, then from Mexico. Stopping the onward march of slavery now meant more to John Quincy Adams than expansion to his former goal, the Rio Grande. The issue of slavery in the domestic politics of the United States served to hold off rather than to precipitate annexation.[1] Had it not been for slavery we may think that Texas, its independence once recognized by the world, would have been annexed without delay.

In the first elections under their independent constitution the Texans voted overwhelmingly in favor of annexation to the United States. They sent a diplomatic representative, William H. Wharton, to Washington seeking recognition of their independence and a treaty of annexation,[2] who reported that President Jackson privately encouraged the Texans to expand their boundaries to the Pacific Ocean in order to paralyze the opposition of the North and East to annexation.[3] But an observer whom Jackson had sent to that country to study conditions was not sure that the Texans would be certain to defend their independence against another military effort by Mexico. While nominally leaving to Congress the matter of recognition, the President cautiously advised that body that the best guide of conduct would be a rigid adherence to the principles followed in the contests between Spain and her revolted colonies: "We stood aloof," explained the President, "and waited, not only until the ability of the new States to protect themselves was fully established, but until the danger of their being again subjugated had entirely passed away. Then, and not till then, were they recognized." The Senate resolved on March 1, 1837, that Texan independence was established and ought to be recognized. The House of Representatives the next day appropriated monies for the maintenance of a diplomatic agent in Texas when the President should be satisfied that Texas was an independent power and should deem it expedient to appoint a minister. The action of Congress, if not actually prompted by Jackson, was most acceptable to him. He had begun to fear that, in order to secure recognition of independence by an outside power, the Texans might yield exclusive commercial concessions to Great Britain, and that Texas might entangle her foreign relations so as to render later annexation most difficult.[4] The retiring President immediately

---

[1] This point of view was soundly emphasized by Jesse S. Reeves, *American Diplomacy under Tyler and Polk* (Baltimore, 1907).

[2] His first, informal, interview was with President Jackson, December 20, 1836.

[3] W. C. Binkley, *The Expansionist Movement in Texas, 1836-1850* (Berkeley, Calif, 1925), 28-29.

[4] Smith, *op. cit.*, 60-61.

appointed a minister to Texas (March 3, 1837). The United States had waited seven months after the expulsion of the Spanish armies to recognize the independence of Mexico herself. Not until nearly eleven months after the battle of San Jacinto was the independence of Texas recognized. The act was entirely justified, but Mexico protested, as Spain had protested in 1822.

President Martin Van Buren rejected (August 25, 1837) the Texan suit for annexation. He explained through the Secretary of State, Forsyth, that it was inexpedient under "existing circumstances" to agitate the matter of annexation of an independent state, perhaps an act of doubtful constitutionality; further, that Texas was still at war with Mexico, with which the United States had a treaty of amity. Van Buren, unlike Jackson, had predilections against the expansion of slavery. The Texans formally withdrew their offer. They now turned to a career of independent development with the grand design of pushing through to the Pacific coast and building up another English-speaking trans-continental republic in North America. France recognized the independence of Texas in 1839, and Great Britain, Holland, and Belgium in 1840. For eight years Texas was a full-fledged independent nation, in treaty relationship with the great maritime powers, if not recognized by Mexico. For at least five years after 1837 the Texan issue disappeared from American politics.[1]

It was President Tyler who revived the issue in 1843. He wanted to build up prestige for his discredited political position before the election of 1844. Ex-President Jackson was now urging Tyler to make haste to get Texas before foreign diplomacy blocked annexation. We must have Texas, he said repeatedly, "peaceably if we can, forcibly if we must." Great Britain and France naturally wished to prevent annexation. It meant that much more weight to the United States in the international balance. In addition the British as a national policy were opposed to slavery all over the world, not only for consistent and genuine humanitarian reasons, but because of the competition of continental slave regions with their West Indian colonies where slavery had been abolished as a humanitarian step in 1833. The British particularly wished to bring about abolition in Texas and did demand, as a price of formal diplomatic relations, the ratification (1842) of a treaty for the abolition of the slave-trade with mutual right of visit and search for suspected slavers.

[1] The diplomatic archives of the Republic of Texas have been published in three volumes, edited by Professor George P. Garrison, in the *Annual Reports* of the American Historical Association, for 1907 and 1908.

A major point henceforth of British and of French diplomacy with Texas was to mediate for the Mexican recognition of Texan independence under condition that Texas should not annex itself to the United States.[1] British policy towards Texas, Mexico and slavery was exactly what the policy of the United States twenty years later was toward Cuba, Spain and slavery.[2]

Both Great Britain and France further desired to maintain Texas as a low-tariff or free-trade market for their manufactures, and as a future alternate source of cotton supply for their growing textile industries, a supply independent from the United States.

The Texan diplomats cleverly worked on these possibilities in their negotiations at Washington. An independent Texas had serious implications for the United States. It blocked off further expansion westward. If it were to become a free-soil republic, it would furnish an adjacent asylum for slaves escaping from the southern United States. As a new slave republic it would exert—in the impending conflict over slavery in the United States—a powerful attraction that might pull the southern slave states out of the old United States into a new great confederation stretching from the gulf of Mexico to the gulf of California and the Pacific. Politics or no politics, no President who loved the United States could close his eyes to this situation. With Andrew Jackson pushing hard behind him, John Tyler set in motion a treaty of annexation. Jackson, through President Sam Houston, persuaded the Texans to accept such a negotiation. "Now, my venerated friend," wrote Houston to the aged General, "you will perceive that Texas is presented to the United States as a bride adorned for her espousal. . . . Were she to be spurned she would seek some other friend." Tyler's Secretary of State, Abel P. Upshur, of Virginia, had the negotiation well advanced, when he was accidentally killed by the explosion of a gun on the U. S. S. *Princeton*. John C. Calhoun,[3] an ardent champion of southern rights

---

[1] In 1840 Great Britain signed three treaties with Texas: a treaty of commerce and navigation, a treaty for the abolition of the slave trade with mutual right of visit and search, and a "convention containing Arrangements relative to the Publick Debt," which provided for British mediation between Texas and Mexico; if this resulted in a treaty of peace, Texas would assume one million pounds sterling of the foreign debt contracted by Mexico prior to January 31, 1835. British ratification of these treaties was deferred because of the delay of Texas in ratifying the slave-trade convention. All three treaties were finally ratified by both parties June 28, 1842. E. D. Adams, *British Interests and Activities in Texas, 1838-1846* (Baltimore, 1910), has analyzed British diplomacy with that republic from the unpublished British archives.

[2] See below, Ch. XXIV.

[3] The Texan diplomacy of Upshur and of Calhoun is well depicted in the studies of those men, respectively, by Randolph G. Adams, and St. George L. Sioussat, in *American Secretaries of State and Their Diplomacy*, Vol. V.

and slavery expansion, succeeded as Secretary of State, a man determined to keep European hands out of Texan affairs. It was he who affixed his name to Tyler's treaty, April 12, 1844. The Texans did not sign until Calhoun officially promised them that military and naval forces would be concentrated to meet any emergency "during the pendency of the treaty."

The President sent the treaty in to the Senate April 22, on the eve of the presidential campaigns for the election of 1844. The Whig nominating convention was scheduled to meet in Baltimore, May 1, and the Democratic convention in the same city, May 27. The debate in the Senate took place while the parties were nominating their candidates.[1] The prominent candidates felt compelled to make some statements on it. Henry Clay, who received the Whig nomination, had a deaf political ear to the ground when he wrote a letter from Raleigh, North Carolina, opposing annexation because it would mean war with Mexico. But Clay's letter meant the defeat of the treaty, unless the Whig majority in the Senate wished to repudiate their chosen leader before the people. The Whig platform made no mention of Texas. Meanwhile the Administration, through a reckless step of Calhoun, had placed the annexation of Texas before the country in such a way as to identify it with the defense of slavery and "southern rights."

The preceding August there had been a sympathetic exchange of remarks in the British House of Lords between Lord Brougham, spokesman of British anti-slavery societies, and Lord Aberdeen, the Secretary of State for Foreign Affairs. Brougham said that slavery ought to be abolished in Texas and ultimately in the United States and that he hoped England's efforts were being directed to this end. Secretary Upshur, impressed by reports from unofficial southern informants[2] in England and prompted by Calhoun, if indeed he needed prompting, directed the United States Minister to Great Britain, Edward Everett, to seek explanations from Aberdeen on England's anti-slavery policy. The Foreign Secretary tendered these in a despatch to the Queen's diplomatic representative at Washington, Pakenham, in which he rather mildly stated that "Great Britain desires, and is constantly exerting herself to procure the general abolition of slavery throughout the world" in an open and

---

[1] W. S. Holt, *Treaties Defeated by the Senate* (Baltimore, 1933), 66-75.

[2] These were Ashbel Smith, the Texan diplomatic representative in London, and Duff Green, a Washington newspaper editor from Virginia and Kentucky. Green was a close friend of Calhoun. Tyler and Upshur paid more attention to the reports of these correspondents than to the despatches of the regular minister Edward Everett of Massachusetts. Justin H. Smith, *op. cit.*, 117, suggests that Smith wrote directly to Tyler. Smith and Green were in close relationship.

above-board way, and would rejoice to see it abolished in Texas, particularly as a part of Mexican recognition of Texas (for which Great
Britain was then mediating). Aberdeen disclaimed any intention to
establish a dominant influence in Texas or "to act directly or indirectly
in a political sense on the United States through Texas."

Aggressively Calhoun answered this despatch, a copy of which had
been left with Upshur shortly before his death. The new Secretary of
State, resolute and eloquent champion of the South, declared in a
note to Pakenham that British abolition was the very reason that the
United States had signed a treaty of annexation with Texas—to prevent
abolition there! This was false, but it identified the Texas treaty with
a defense of slavery and was quickly published for that purpose. If
anything more than the repudiation of annexation by the Whig nominee
were needed to defeat the treaty, this was it. The Senate rejected it
(June 8, 1844), 35 votes against, 16 votes for.

Before the Senate's actual vote on the treaty, the Democrats, after
a spirited convention contest (May 27-29, 1844), nominated James K.
Polk of Tennessee for President, rejecting both Tyler, who made the
Texas treaty, and Van Buren, who opposed it. Polk, a political "dark
horse," groomed by the venerable expansionist, ex-President Jackson,
had made his stand on Texas clear: he was for annexation of that country, also all of Oregon.[1] The Democratic platform came out strong for
both. Polk had the support of Tyler, and of Jackson, the strongest
annexationist of all.

The election of 1844 was the only presidential contest in the nineteenth century that depended on an issue of foreign affairs, and one of
three such elections in United States history, the others in 1796 and 1920.
The sentiment for annexation alarmed Clay. He began to wobble, to
equivocate. He declared that he would be glad to see Texas acquired
"without dishonor, without war, with common consent of the Union,
and upon just and fair terms." These were the weasel words of a politician who would rather be President than be right. Polk and the Democrats stood for annexation and expansion, and triumphed by a slender
majority. The election map[2] of the popular vote, however, shows no
sectional division. Henry Clay would have won the election except for
a division of the free-soil votes of New York between him and the
feeble Liberty Party candidate, James G. Birney. Nevertheless the

[1] E. I. McCormac, *James K. Polk: a Political Biography* (Berkeley, Calif., 1922), 226.
[2] C. O. Paullin and J. K. Wright, *Atlas of the Historical Geography of the United
States* (Carnegie Institution of Washington, and Am. Geographical Society of New York,
1932).

election of Polk was taken as a mandate from the people for the annexation of Texas. Since the defeat of his treaty the President had been
urging annexation by a joint resolution of Congress, which would require
only a majority vote of the Senate. On March 1, 1845, he exultantly
signed such a joint resolution, which provided for annexation subject to
arrangements to be completed by the President with the government of
Texas—to be admitted directly into the Union as a state. The boundaries of the new state were left to be adjusted by the United States.

Tyler got his Texas three days before he left office. Polk got the
Presidency. Andrew Jackson died happy (June 8, 1845).

The vote in Congress for annexation was more of a sectional vote
than had been recorded in the Presidential election, which had been
carried by annexationist sentiment for Oregon as well as for Texas.[1]

The Texans in 1845 had an opportunity to choose between annexation
to the United States and acceptance of treaty with Mexico,[2] engineered
by British and French diplomacy, by which Mexico recognized their
independence under the condition that Texas was never to be annexed
to any third power.[3] All but unanimously the Texans rejected independence under these conditions; and all but unanimously the Texans
accepted annexation.[4]

Annexation to the United States cleared Texas of European diplomacy.

[1] The states of Missouri, Arkansas, Louisiana, Tennessee, Mississippi, Alabama,
Georgia, and South Carolina voted solidly for annexation in both houses. New England,
New York and their western "colonists" voted against annexation in the House of
Representatives. In the Senate, both senators from New Hampshire, from New York,
from Pennsylvania, from Ohio, and from Illinois voted for annexation; and one
senator each from Maine and Connecticut. Paullin, op. cit., page 113, plate 114F; and
Rives, op. cit., I, 693.

[2] The Mexican Congress formally voted to accept such a treaty if Texas refused
annexation. The articles left the boundary to be settled by mutual negotiation; but
Cuevas, Minister of Foreign Relations, added that there were "other questions" to be
settled. Rives, I, 704-710.

[3] The British Government thought of arranging a Franco-British guaranty of Texan
independence as a part of the proposed arrangement, reliance being placed on sectional
division in the United States to paralyze the annexation movement; but the French
Government thought it prudent to dissent to any guaranty. Mary K. Chase, Négociations
de la république du Texas en Europe, 1837-1845 (Paris, 1932), has had access to the
British and French archives (the latter not available to J. H. Smith or E. D. Adams).

[4] The process by which annexation was finally consummated is as follows:
March 1, 1845, President Tyler signs the joint resolution of the United States Congress,
    for annexation.
June 21, 1845. The Texan Senate unanimously rejects the Mexican treaty, and Texan
    Congress unanimously approves the United States joint resolution for annexation,
    and calls a convention to draw up a new state constitution.
July 4, 1845. The Texan Convention votes 55-1 for annexation and unanimously signs
    an ordinance for annexation. It also unanimously adopts a state constitution.
October 13, 1845. The Texas state constitution is accepted by a popular referendum

It was followed ultimately (but not immediately) by war between Mexico and the United States. It will be one of our interests in the next chapter to inquire wherein the annexation of Texas caused the ensuing war with Mexico.

and a plebiscite expressly ratifies the acts of annexation. The vote, *viva voce,* seems never to have been made known (Smith, *Annexation*), 460.

December 29, 1845. Resolution of the United States Congress admitting Texas as a state, is approved by President Polk.

February 16, 1846. The new state government of Texas is inaugurated.

CHAPTER XIV

THE MEXICAN WAR; THE ISTHMIAN QUESTION

(1845-1859)

THE United States was not responsible, nation to nation, for the settlement of Texas, nor for the outbreak of the Texan Revolution. That settlement took place and that revolution occurred because of the ill-advised character of Mexican domestic legislation and the weak control by that nation of its vast northern provinces and frontier. If Mexico had a case against the United States for inadequate neutrality laws, she never pressed it. Recognition of Texan independence by the United States was not premature, compared with the recognition of the independence of Mexico herself. Annexation, with overwhelming and enthusiastic approval, freely expressed, of the government and people of Texas was orderly, proper, desired by both peoples. Texas already had a career of nine years as an independent state, during which she had enjoyed recognition by the great maritime powers of the world, bound to several of them by unexceptionable treaty relations. The establishment of Texan independence *de jure* is nowhere more strongly attested than by the willingness of the Mexican Government in 1845 to accept a treaty with Texas providing Texas would agree never to be annexed to the United States.

The Mexican Minister in Washington, Almonte, had declared that he would close his mission, and his government would declare war, if Texas were annexed. The Mexican Government served notice on the United States Minister there that it would "consider equivalent to a declaration of war against the Mexican Republic the passage of an act for the incorporation of Texas with the territory of the United States; the certainty of the fact being sufficient for the immediate proclamation of war."[1] When Congress nevertheless passed such an act the Mexican Government withdrew its minister, and severed official relations with the United States Minister to Mexico.

Confronted by at least this Mexican threat of war—indeed it might, if so desired, have been regarded as a declaration of war—the new President, James K. Polk, sent troops into Texas to protect that republic from attack during the consummation of annexation. He also

---

[1] J. H. Smith, *The War with Mexico*, I, 84.

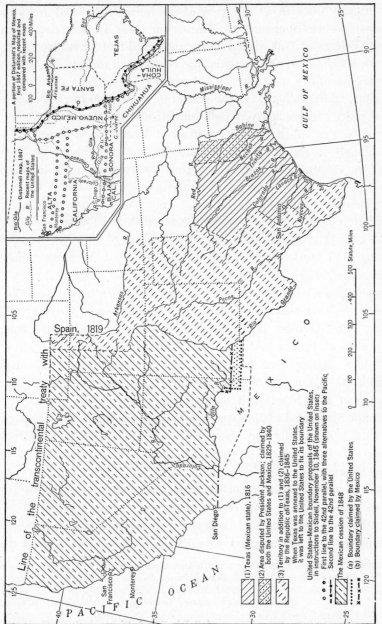

Map 14. Texas and Mexico, 1823-1848.

Line of the transcontinental treaty with Spain, 1819

Spain, 1819

PACIFIC OCEAN

San Francisco
Monterey
San Diego

M E X I C O

GULF OF MEXICO

Mississippi
Sabine R.
Neches R.
Trinity R.
Brazos R.
Colorado R.
Lavaca R.
San Antonio
Nueces R.
Rio Grande
Pecos
Arkansas
Red R.
Colorado R.
Gila R.

(1) Texas (Mexican state), 1816

(2) Area disputed by President Jackson; claimed by
both the United States and Mexico, 1829-1840

(3) Territory in addition to (1) and (2) claimed
by the Republic of Texas, 1836-1845
When Texas was annexed to the United States,
it was left to the United States to fix its boundary

United States-Mexican boundary proposals of the United States,
in instructions to Slidell, November 10, 1845 (shown on inset)
First line to the 42nd parallel, with three alternatives to the Pacific
Second line to the 42nd parallel

The Mexican cession of 1848

(a) Boundary claimed by the United States
(b) Boundary claimed by Mexico

500 Statute Miles
0   100   200   300   400   500

Inset map labels:
A portion of Disturnell's Map of Mexico,
first 1847 edition, reprinted and
compared with recent maps

Rio Gila — Disturnell map, 1847
Gila R. — Recent maps of
the United States

CALIFORNIA
BAJA CAL.
SONORA
NUEVO MÉICO
CHIHUAHUA
COAHUILA
TEJAS
SANTA FE
San Francisco
San Diego
Monterey
Rio Colorado
Gila
Gila R.
Rio Arkansas
Arkansas
Red
Rio Grande
C. Juárez
El Paso

100 200   400 Miles

233

arranged the naval forces of the United States to strategic advantage in
the Gulf of Mexico and off the coast of California, where a squadron had
been cruising since 1842.[1] In view of the formally declared attitude of
Mexico there was abundant justification for these dispositions of armed
forces. Friends of Polk visited Texas and urged that Texan troops move
into the disputed territory between the Nueces and the Rio Grande, thus
renewing hostilities with Mexico before annexation; then the American
President, under authority of the resolution of annexation, could dictate
a final peace and boundary.[2] Polk himself and the Government steered
clear of such complicity. The President of Texas, Anson Jones, did not
lend himself to the stratagem, because he was pledged to the British
chargé to suspend all hostilities during the conclusion, under Anglo-
French mediation, of the proposed treaty between Mexico and Texas.

No hostilities immediately ensued. Polk wanted to restore normal
diplomatic relations on the basis of the accomplished fact of annexation.
At the same time he desired to reach a settlement of all other issues outstanding with Mexico, particularly the boundary of the newly annexed
American territory, and completion of payment of certain already adjudicated American claims. As a part of such settlement he would have
desired to buy from Mexico the territory between Texas and the Pacific
Ocean. Like Jackson, he coveted for his rapidly expanding country
California with its fine harbor of San Francisco Bay. On the same ship
which took Almonte and his family back to Mexico, Polk dispatched
a confidential agent, one William S. Parrott, to sound out the Mexican
Government as to whether it desired to restore friendly relations with
the United States and would be willing to receive a "minister" empowered
to discuss in a friendly and liberal spirit all outstanding issues between
the two countries—except of course the annexation of Texas which had
caused the rupture.

From Mexico, Parrott reported vague and indirect assurances from
persons supposed to be more or less close to the actual Herrera Government, that the President had been heard to say that if a "minister" of
the United States should arrive he would be well received.[3] He had no

---

[1] October 19, 1842, an overzealous naval officer, Commodore T. A. C. Jones, believing
from bellicose expressions of the Mexican Minister Bocanegra, that war was certain,
took time by the forelock and occupied Monterey, California, only to find a state of
profound peace there. He then promptly hauled down his flag, saluted that of Mexico,
and sailed away.

[2] Richard R. Stenberg, "The Failure of Polk's War Intrigue of 1845," *Pacific Hist.
Rev.,* IV (March, 1935), 39-69. J. H. Smith, *Annexation of Texas,* pp. 245-248.

[3] Parrott to Buchanan, Mexico, Aug. 16, 1845, *Despatches, Mexico,* XII, November 10,
1843-April 25, 1845, Department of State Archives.

direct contact with the responsible Mexican authorities. In another letter Parrott said that an "envoy" would be hailed with joy.[1] Polk wanted more explicit assurances. He therefore directed John Black, the consul of the United States in Mexico City, to ask the Minister of Foreign Affairs, Peña y Peña, if the Mexican Government would receive an "envoy from the United States, entrusted with full powers to adjust all the questions between the two governments. Should the answer be in the affirmative, such an envoy will be immediately despatched to Mexico." Peña said that although Mexico was greatly injured and aggrieved by the Texas affair, his Government would be disposed to receive a "commissioner" with full powers to settle the present dispute (*contienda*) in a peaceful, reasonable, and decorous manner, provided the United States would withdraw its naval forces from the vicinity of Vera Cruz. At the consul's suggestion, the squadron sailed away.[2] Parrott brought Black's despatches, with this exchange of notes, to Washington, November 9, 1845. The President immediately sent to Mexico a minister plenipotentiary, John Slidell of Louisiana. Slidell's instructions had been already drawn up when Parrott's first report had arrived stating that Herrera had been "heard say" that Mexico would receive a "minister." [3] They were now formally approved and despatched to him at Pensacola, where he was waiting to be off. Polk probably did not grasp the technical distinction between a regular minister and a special commissioner *ad hoc*.

The instructions to Slidell show that Polk was willing to be reasonable with Mexico. He would have welcomed a war and the conquest of coveted territory, and he was determined to have California, but he certainly gave Mexico every chance for a peaceful settlement, and on terms which stopped short of taking a single square mile of indisputable

---

[1] Same to same, August 26, 1845, *ibid.*

[2] The note and reply, October 13, 1845, is printed by Alberto M. Carreño, *Mexico y los Estados Unidos de América* (Mexico, D. F., 1922), 119, from the *Memoria de la Secretaría de Relaciones Exteriores* for 1846. See also Rives, II, 65. In his "private and confidential" despatch of October 11, 1845, Black reported that Peña had explained that the expressions of aggrievement and injury were for popular consumption. *Consular Letters, Mexico, 1840-1845*, Department of State Archives.

[3] Justin Smith, *op. cit.*, I, 435, quotes Parrott as reporting in his despatch of August 16, 1845: "Herrera has said, 'If a Minister from the United States should arrive, he would be well received.'" What Parrott actually wrote, as revealed in his manuscript despatch in the Department of State Archives, was: "The President, who thus far has received the unanimous vote of the Departments for the high office, is known to be in favor of an amicable arrangement of the effervescences pending with us, and has been *heard* say, that if a minister from the United States should arrive he would be well received; of this, however, I will be better informed before the departure of the British Express about the last of the present month."

Mexican territory. The district of Texas when a part of the Mexican state of Texas and Coahuila had not extended beyond the Nueces River; but the Texans after their Revolution had asserted their boundary to be the Rio Grande—without being able to establish real authority there, particularly on the upper reaches of the river in the region of Santa Fé and Taos. If Mexico would agree to the line of the Rio Grande as the boundary of the United States, the United States would release Mexico from completing the payment of the adjudicated claims of American citizens, which Mexico had quite irresponsibly abandoned after arbitration.[1]

This was the peaceable offer which Polk was prepared to make. If we accept the fact of Texan independence—as Mexico herself was ready to accept it in 1845 under British conditions—it was a fair offer. Beyond these terms, Slidell was to try to buy, but not to present such purchase as *sine qua non*, California and the intervening region north of the latitude of El Paso (approximately the territory ceded in 1848) for as much as $25,000,000; indeed, "money would be no object when compared with the value of the acquisition."[2] If he could not buy that, he was to offer $5,000,000 for New Mexico, which at that time comprised the drainage area of the upper Rio Grande (above El Paso).

Notwithstanding the assurances conveyed to Polk, the Mexican Government refused to receive Slidell. The real reason was that Herrera feared that concession to the United States might afford moral strength

[1] These claims were for supplies of money, arms and other things sold by citizens of the United States to the Mexican Government during the revolution against Spain, and for damages to property and persons of the United States during revolutionary disturbances in Mexico.

A mixed claims commission had made awards of $2,026,139.68 (out of a total of $8,513,752.56 presented). Mexico began payment in agreed installments, in 1843; and stopped payment after April 30, 1843, when only the arrears of interest had been paid. There were other claims amounting to $3,336,837.05 submitted too late for adjudication by this commission; and the two republics had been unable to agree upon a sequent commission for them. See J. B. Moore, *Digest International Arbitrations*, 1209-1359.

Mexico was not the only country against whom the United States had just claims. Claims had been presented against Great Britain, France, Denmark, the Two Sicilies, Portugal, Peru, and in all cases settled by agreements to arbitrate or acceptance of lump sums in lieu thereof. Only with France (see below, p. 290) and Mexico was there any difficulty in securing payment of compensations agreed to be due; and President Jackson was no less resolute in pressing for a settlement by France than were he and his successors in seeking payment by Mexico.

[2] Slidell's instructions, as well as Parrott's and Black's, are printed in J. B. Moore's edition of the *Works of James A. Buchanan* (12 Vols., Philadelphia, 1908-11), VI. Polk notes that he told the Cabinet, which agreed, that he "supposed it [the territory north of 32°] might be had for fifteen or twenty millions, but he was ready to pay forty millions for it, if it could not be had for less." *The Diary of James K. Polk, During his Presidency, 1845-1849*, Milo M. Quaife, ed. (4 Vols., Chicago, 1910), I, 35. Entry for September 16, 1845.

to the Paredes opposition which was then threatening a revolution. When presently the followers of Paredes actually did overthrow Herrera, the new revolutionary government also feared to receive Slidell. There was also belief in Mexico that the United States need not be feared, nor heeded. Mexican diplomatic conjectures miscalculated the possibilities of European assistance, particularly from Great Britain,[1] which had tried to prevent the annexation of Texas, and which was at that moment still engaged in the Oregon controversy with the United States. Despite the failure of Mexico to quell the Texan Revolution there was a considerable body of journalistic opinion, not without influence at the capital, which thought that Mexico could at least hold her own in any war with the abominated United States. Both Mexican régimes, Herrera and the succeeding Paredes government, resorted to the perfectly good pretext that it had been agreed to receive only a "commissioner" empowered to adjust outstanding disputes, not a regular minister plenipotentiary to resume diplomatic relations before everything was settled. Though the reason was valid,[2] the Mexican authorities could have waived this technicality with great advantage to themselves. It was very reckless not to do so. By refusing to receive Slidell they played into Polk's hand. When the President heard that Mexico would not talk peace with Slidell, he disposed the military forces of the United States in a challenging way. Only the fact that the Oregon question was still pending with Great Britain seems to have prevented Polk from sending a war message to Congress immediately upon learning of the failure of Slidell's mission.[3]

But how would Polk have acquired California if Mexico had been so prudent as to negotiate with Slidell and accept the reasonable boundary of the Rio Grande in exchange for a release of obligations for claims? If Mexico had chosen peace and the line of the Rio Grande, Polk was not without resources for California. Already, while the instructions were being drawn up for Slidell, a messenger was on his way to California, bearing instructions for the United States consul at Monterey, Thomas O. Larkin, and letters to Colonel J. C. Frémont then with a company of troops on a topographical reconnaissance of California, in Mexican ter-

---

[1] J. Smith, op. cit., I, 115.

[2] The United States in 1933 received an envoy or commissioner of the Russian Soviet Government, Mr. Litvinoff, to discuss and adjust disputes as a condition precedent to resumption of regular diplomatic relations. Only after a settlement of these had been reached in principle was there an exchange of ambassadors. The analogy is a perfect one and justifies the technical position of the Mexican revolutionary governments in 1845.

[3] McCormac, James K. Polk, op. cit., 405.

ritory. The instructions to Larkin [1] were to watch carefully the situation with a view to prevent California from falling into the hands of
some European power in case of a revolution there which was threatening *à la Texas*. The consul, mindful of impending events, was to assure
the Californians that if they became independent they would be welcomed into the union of the United States. We do not know what messages were taken to Frémont; but on receiving them, that officer immediately took a waiting attitude to the end that he might be able to use
his small force (65 men) in the event of the outbreak of war.[2] Polk
honestly feared [3] that Great Britain or France might acquire California
ahead of the United States. Historical investigation has shown that
while local British and French ministers and consuls in Mexico and
California urged, respectively, their governments to take over California,
neither Great Britain nor France was prepared to accept the responsibilities of such an adventure; but British naval contingents in the Pacific
might have been tempted to extend help to the Mexican authorities in
California if the United States navy had not been on the job at the outbreak of war.[4] As in the case of Texas, they desired that California
should not fall into the possession of the United States. In his annual
message of December 2, 1845, Polk reiterated the Monroe Doctrine "as
our settled policy, that no future European colony or dominion shall,
with our consent, be planted or established on any part of the North
American continent." Three years later, anent a rumor that revolutionists in Yucatan were to transfer dominion over themselves and country
to the United States, or even to Great Britain or Spain, Polk repeated
his declaration in a special message of April 29, 1848, during the war

[1] R. W. Kelsey, "The United States Consulate in California" in *Acad. Pacific Coast History*, Vol. I, No. 5 (June, 1910). For some cogent criticism of this article and other condemnations of Polk's policy, see an excellent analysis by E. C. Barker of "The His-toriography of American Territorial Expansion," in *Trans-Mississippi West* (University of Colorado, Boulder, Colo., 1930).

[2] Josiah Royce's *California, . . . a Study of American Character* (Boston, 1886), shows how Frémont's eagerness precipitated a conflict with Mexican guards near San Francisco Bay (the "Bear Flag Revolt"), frustrated Larkin's efforts to nurse along a revolt that would bring California peacefully into the United States in case of war, and made it necessary to conquer that region during the ensuing war in place of taking it over peaceably.

[3] E. D. Adams, "English Interest in the Annexation of California," *Am. Hist. Rev.*, XIV (1909), 744-763.

[4] E. D. Adams, *op. cit.*, and A. P. Nasatir, "The French Consulate in California, 1843-1856," *Quar. of Calif. Hist. Soc.*, XI (Sept., 1932), 195-223; (Dec., 1932), 339-357; XII (Mar., 1933), 35-64; (June, 1933), 155-172; (Dec., 1933), 331-357. E. A. Wiltsee, "The British Vice Consul in California and the Events of 1846," *ibid.*, X (June, 1931), 99-128.

with Mexico.[1] His invocation of the Monroe Doctrine strengthened that pronouncement as a confirmed principle of American foreign policy. But in displaying that doctrine to hold off non-American intruders from regions which the United States might or might not choose to mark out for itself, Polk revealed new possibilities for the celebrated pronouncement of President Monroe.[2]

Not until Polk heard that Mexico refused to talk peace with Slidell did he order General Taylor to advance from Corpus Christi, at the eastern edge of the disputed territory, to the Rio Grande, at the western edge. The President might have avoided a clash with Mexican troops if he had kept Taylor out of the disputed area; but it is difficult to condemn his move under the circumstances: he had tried to adjust the boundary by peaceful negotiation, and Mexico had availed herself of a diplomatic technicality to evade discussion. This attitude was a rather definite indication that Mexico intended to stand on her early assertion that a state of war existed. According to Mexico's position not only the Nueces-Rio Grande country, but all of Texas, was hers. Under these circumstances Taylor could scarcely sit still and wait for Mexican troops to move into a region so as to have the advantage when hostilities actually started. Taylor already had orders: "Should Mexico assemble a large body of troops on the Rio Grande and cross it with a considerable force, such a movement must be regarded as an invasion of the United States and the commencement of hostilities."[3] So long as Taylor remained at Corpus Christi, no Mexican forces had yet crossed the river into the disputed territory. After the General had reached the Rio Grande (March 28, 1846),[4] Polk waited for news.

For weeks no news came. Could it be that all was quiet along the Rio Grande? The impatient Polk finally called his Cabinet together on the morning of May 9 and proposed a war message to Congress, asking for authorization to use the armed forces of the United States to collect payment for the adjudicated claims. Only the Secretary of the Navy, George Bancroft, demurred, when it was decided to send in such a message. That afternoon however came news that Taylor had been attacked by Mexican forces this side of the Rio Grande. On the previous

[1] Polk's emphasis of North America, instead of the American continents, as defining the scope of the Monroe Doctrine, was unique with him.

[2] "It was the beginning of that historic process by which a principle of non-intervention has been transferred into a principle of intervention." Dexter Perkins, *The Monroe Doctrine, 1826-1867* (Baltimore, 1933).

[3] J. Smith, *op. cit.*, I, 144.

[4] J. M. Callahan, *American Foreign Policy in Mexican Relations* (New York, 1932). 157.

April 23, President Paredes had declared [1] a "defensive war," and two days later a skirmish occurred between General Arista and Taylor's troops. By the time news of this encounter reached Washington, Taylor was already combating Mexican troops on this side of the Rio Grande (Battle of Palo Alto, May 8, 1846). The Cabinet hastily reassembled the evening of May 9,[2] and all now agreed that war existed as an act of Mexico. Congress, after listening to the President's message that Mexico had "proclaimed that hostilities have commenced," declared, May 13, 1846, that "by the act of the Republic of Mexico, a state of war exists between that Government and the United States." [3]

We can barely mention the military history of the war. There were three principal offensive movements by the United States. In the autumn and winter of 1846-7 General Taylor pushed on with an army of 10,000 men into Mexico (Battle of Buena Vista, February 23, 1847) as far as Victoria, capital of Tamaulipas, having by several sharp engagements forced the retreat of Santa Anna's [4] northern army. He then returned along his attenuated communications to remain unmolested at the Rio Grande. Meanwhile a small column of troops under General Stephen W. Kearny had marched overland from Missouri to occupy Santa Fé and press onward across Arizona to California. Already the squadron which had been hovering off that coast (ten thousand miles from a base) had been able, under the command of Commodore Stockton, to take possession of San Francisco and Monterey with the dubious assistance of Frémont. Arriving in California without effective resistance Kearny took command and proclaimed a provisional American government under military rule. The decisive thrust of the American forces was against the capital of Mexico itself. An expedition of 12,000 men landed at Vera Cruz, March 9, 1847, under the command of General Winfield Scott. By September the army was on the plateau before the gates of Mexico City. Santa Anna was facing defeat and surrender of the capital.

Polk himself had renounced uniquely a second term as President; yet he was jealous of military prestige that might make formidable candidates in 1848 of his generals, either Taylor or Scott. If only for this

[1] Callahan, *op. cit.*

[2] Polk's *Diary, op. cit.*

[3] The vote in the House of Representatives, May 11, was 173-14; in the Senate, May 12, 42-2. The bill became law by the President's signature, May 13.

[4] Santa Anna had been an exile since his defeat and capture by the Texans at San Jacinto in 1836. On representations that he would seek to induce Mexico to make an early peace of the kind Polk wanted, he was allowed to land (from Cuba) at Vera Cruz. Far from keeping his bargain he was able to place himself in power again for the duration of the war, the loss of which brought another period of exile for him.

reason he wished to achieve the results of the war with a minimum of fighting and military glory. He designated as an executive agent Nicholas P. Trist, chief clerk of the Department of State, to accompany Scott's army overland in the rôle of a commissioner to negotiate peace. Trist was styled by the President a "commissioner plenipotentiary," and had a letter patent signed by Polk and bearing the great seal of the United States; but he had no regular diplomatic status. He was considered a minor personage who would not be exalted by any diplomatic triumph into a formidable political figure. His success would be Polk's success. His technical status was somewhat like that of the special agents who had negotiated peace with the Barbary states, and, be it said, like that of the commissioners who negotiated the peace with Spain in 1898, like those who represented the United States at the Paris Peace Conference in 1919, and those who signed the separate treaties with Germany, Austria and Hungary in 1921. Such special agents have frequently been more important in American diplomacy than regularly confirmed diplomatic officers.[1] If the Mexican Government refused to accept the project of a treaty which Trist carried with him, or if it insisted on commissioners with full powers, Trist was to report that fact; the President intended in that event to send the Secretary of State, James Buchanan, to Mexico as a formal peace commissioner. Trist's project called for the acceptance of the Rio Grande boundary to El Paso and the cession of all the territory through to the Pacific north of that latitude, for which the United States would assume claims up to a total of $3,000,000, and pay $15,000,000. To add to this the peninsula of Lower California plus right of transit across the "Isthmus" of Tehuantepec in southern Mexico, he might pay as much as $30,000,000. He carried a draft for $3,000,000 to bind the bargain. The *sine qua non* of Polk's minimum terms of peace in 1848 conformed to the maximum that Slidell was to have *tried* for, above his *sine qua non* of 1845, had not Mexico insisted on war.

At first Trist did not get along well with General Scott. The special agent was provided with a sealed despatch for the Mexican Minister of Foreign Relations in which Buchanan pointed out that while an evacuation of Mexican territory would be a surrender of costly gains by the United States, nevertheless a commissioner, "ranking second in the State Department," would attend the army at all times ready to negotiate a

---

[1] For the constitutional rôle of special agents, as distinct from regularly confirmed diplomatic agents, and complete history of special agents, see the encyclopedic work of H. M. Wriston, *Executive Agents, op. cit.*

peace. Though Trist had permission to show Scott his instructions and
the sealed letter to the enemy, he did not do so; and Scott refused to
send the mysterious despatch through the lines. The General and the
agent reached such odds that at one time they were not on speaking
terms. Trist forwarded the despatch to the Mexican authorities through
the medium of the British Legation. The British Minister suggested
it would be necessary to bribe Mexican officials into peace. General
Scott, soon reconciled to Trist, was ready, nothing loath, to help do this
with his secret-service funds. He granted a short armistice, subject to
abrogation at forty-eight hours' notice, at a moment when Santa Anna
was expecting to be forced out of the city and into a peace. The Mexican
leader was willing to make peace on Trist's *sine qua non* (too readily
revealed), and then to employ the money to establish himself in permanent power. Negotiations to this end during the armistice, however,
encountered such a rising protest against alienation of territory that the
anxious Santa Anna did not dare to brook it. The armistice broke down.
Scott occupied Mexico City (September 14). Santa Anna fled the country. By the time a reconstructed Mexican Government was ready to
reopen negotiations for peace it became known to the world that President Polk, dissatisfied with Trist's diplomacy, particularly with the
armistice, had recalled him. The President had decided to make Mexico
sue for peace on the banks of the Potomac. There was rapidly rising
an ominous sentiment for the cession of all of Mexico. Buchanan, Secretary of State, and R. J. Walker, Secretary of the Treasury, shared the
sentiment; but Polk wanted to get the Mexican question out of politics
with éclat to himself.[1]

Trist, deprived of all authority, did a most exceptionable and reckless
thing. At the solicitation of the enemy, and with Scott's advice that
the Senate would ratify a treaty if he took one to Washington bearing
the ratifications of the Mexican Government, he signed on February 2,
1848,[2]—at the village of Guadalupe Hidalgo—a treaty that included
the *sine qua non* of his annulled instructions: the boundary of the Rio
Grande and the cession of the territory[3] between that river and

---

[1] L. M. Sears, "Nicholas P. Trist, a Diplomat with Ideals," *Miss. Vall. Hist. Rev.*, XI
(June, 1924), 85-98. E. G. Bourne, "The United States and Mexico, 1847-1848," in
Am. Hist. Rev., V (April, 1900), 491-502.

[2] During the same week the first gold strike was made in California at Sutter's Mill,
but this was not known in Mexico, of course, nor in the United States until after the
treaty had been ratified.

[3] The treaty line ascended the middle of the Rio Grande, the southern boundary of
New Mexico as shown on Disturnell's Map published at New York in 1847, thence
westerly and then due northerly around the boundary of New Mexico to the intersection

the Pacific Ocean. It took in the present states of California, Nevada, Utah, New Mexico, Arizona, a corner of Wyoming and the west slope of Colorado. For this the United States was to pay $15,000,-000—three million immediately upon ratification by Mexico—and to assume claims of its citizens up to $3,250,000. Trist signed the treaty, contrary to his instructions and without powers, because he feared delay would bring anarchy in Mexico and strengthen the movement at home to take more or all of that country. Further, he was afraid that a larger annexation would cause such protest in the northern states as to lead to their secession and the break-up of the Union.[1]

Trist's disobedience incensed Polk, who promptly dismissed him ignominiously from public employment; but the President could not but like the terms of the treaty, because it secured for the United States what he meant the United States to have, and he wished to clear up the whole Mexican question before the presidential campaign of 1848 should get under way. He sent the treaty to the Senate and the Senate ratified it, 38 yeas, 14 noes (March 10, 1848). Not until 1871 did Trist receive satisfaction through a vote of Congress of his claims for personal expenses and salary.[2] By violating his instructions he had profited his country but heavily damaged himself. True to his determination expressed when accepting nomination in 1844, Polk refused to be a candidate for the presidency in 1848. The Whigs nominated General Zachary Taylor (whose political potentialities Polk had feared, and consequently he had refused to support his military campaign wholeheartedly) as a neglected military hero; and General Zachary Taylor beat Lewis Cass, whom the Democrats nominated after a factional quarrel in New York State.

Polk could have avoided war with Mexico, and that without injury to the vital interests or the national honor of the United States, if he had kept Taylor out of the disputed territory immediately north of the Rio Grande and had pursued a policy of patience and watchful waiting, as Woodrow Wilson did toward Mexico in 1913-1917. James K.

---

of the first branch of the Gila River and down that to the Colorado, thence across the Colorado following the divisional line between Upper and Lower California to the Pacific Ocean. Free navigation of the River Colorado and Gulf of California was stipulated for the United States; and mutually free navigation of the Gila, and of the Rio Grande below the southern boundary of New Mexico.

[1] Sears, *op. cit.* On the other hand there was sound anti-slavery sentiment in favor of the absorption of all Mexico in the belief that it would be geographically and socially hostile to slavery; in fact some pro-slavery leaders, like Calhoun, opposed further annexation for that reason. John D. P. Fuller, "The Slavery Question and the Movement to Acquire Mexico, 1846-1848," *Miss. Vall. Hist. Rev.*, XXI (June, 1934), 31-49.

[2] Sears, *op. cit.*

Polk allowed Mexico to begin the war, and this, too, without any dishonorable action on his part to precipitate it. The war added a vast
domain to the United States, at a total cost of $118,250,000—in addi-
tion to the several thousands of lives on both sides—fifteen millions
for the "purchased" territory, $3,250,000 for the released claims, and
$100,000,000 for the military cost of the war.[1] The acquisition of the
new regions brought to a head the bitter and long dormant controversy
over the status of slavery in the territories of the United States, which
was eased temporarily by the Compromise of 1850, only soon to be upset
—following the election of President Franklin Pierce in the Democratic
triumph of 1852—by the Kansas-Nebraska Act and the tragic train of
events which led directly to the secession of the southern states and
the Civil War. That war cost the United States over a half million
men, untold human suffering, and, if we add the cost of interest on
debt and pensions up to the present time, an amount of money equal
to the total wealth of the country, north and south, at the beginning
of the war in 1861. Notwithstanding all this it would be well-nigh impossible today to find a citizen of the United States who would desire
to undo President Polk's diplomacy, President Polk's war, and the
treaty of Guadalupe Hidalgo negotiated by President Polk's disobedient chief clerk of the Department of State.

Not until the cession of the new territory by Mexico in 1848 did the
executive department of the United States Government turn its attention seriously to the significance of who should control any future
isthmian canal. This was true notwithstanding a persistent general
interest in the possibility of a canal, both in the United States and
abroad, and notwithstanding resolutions of Congress for diplomatic
action.

News of the discovery of gold in California, which came so promptly
after the ratification of the treaty of Guadalupe Hidalgo, and the spectacular rush to the gold fields of the Pacific Coast, emphasized in a
dramatic way the importance of the future waterway between the oceans.
Curiously enough, an American diplomatist, Benjamin A. Bidlack, had
recently negotiated (December 12, 1846) at Bogotá a treaty with New
Granada (Colombia) which became of the greatest importance in the
subsequent diplomacy of the isthmian canal. The article in it, XXXV,
which concerned the future canal, had not been sought by the United
States in any instructions to its minister. Bidlack was trying to adjust

[1] Estimated by Channing, V, 600.

an old controversy concerning differential duties which New Granada had imposed in favor of her own ships bringing goods into her own ports, as against foreign ships engaged in the carrying trade. New Granada feared thinly veiled British ambitions for the control of the Isthmus of Panama, and was thoroughly alarmed at the recently declared British protectorate over the Mosquito shore, which had extended loose territorial claims south into indisputable Granadan territory: to Boca del Toro within the province of Panama. An expedition under the Ecuadorian revolutionary leader, General Flores, then fitting out in London, had further threats for the territory of New Granada. In vain she had tried to secure with Great Britain and France, either singly or jointly, a treaty guaranteeing the neutrality of the isthmus, and the sovereignty of Granadan territory there, a treaty to which the United States and other maritime powers could adhere. Repulsed in England and in France, and highly suspicious of the motives of those powers, particularly of Great Britain, the Granadan Government [1] turned to the United States for outside protection, and offered to yield the point of preferential duties and to cede a right of way across the Isthmus of Panama, in exchange for a guaranty of New Granada's sovereign rights over the transit together with the neutrality of the Isthmus. Incidentally the waiving of differential protective tariffs against ships of the United States as a condition of such a guaranty relieved New Granada of the necessity of waiving them also for other states to whom she was bound by most-favored-nation treaties. The solicitations of the Granadans were very earnest and highly confidential. Still without instructions as to how his government would look upon such a guaranty, Bidlack quickly signed the treaty, *sub spe rati*. It was a far-reaching document. Bidlack was conscious of its character of alliance.

The treaty guaranteed to the United States and its citizens "the right of way or transit across the Isthmus of Panama upon any modes of communication that now exist, or that may be hereafter constructed" for "lawful commerce," with tolls no higher than charged to the citizens of New Granada. It was not an exclusive right. Article XXXV contained the further fateful words:

And, *in order to secure to themselves the tranquil and constant enjoyment of these advantages,* and as an especial compensation for the said advantages, and for the favors they have acquired by the 4th, 5th and 6th articles [re-

[1] The President of New Granada, General Mosquera, gave the impulse to this negotiation which was carried out by the Secretary for Foreign Relations, Manuel M Mallarino.

garding tariff duties] of this treaty, the United States guarantee, positively and efficaciously, to New Granada, by the present stipulation, the perfect neutrality of the before-mentioned isthmus, *with the view that the free transit from the one to the other sea may not be interrupted or embarrassed in any future time* while this treaty exists; and, in consequence, the United States also guarantee, in the same manner, the rights of sovereignty and of property which New Granada has and possesses over the said territory.

Later in this volume we shall see that in 1903-1904 the United States Government argued from the words which have been here italicized for the reader, that this included guaranty of the neutrality of the Isthmus of Panama against domestic revolution. No evidence has yet been presented to show that the negotiators or the ratifying authorities had in mind anything other than a guaranty of neutrality against other states. In the midst of the Mexican War and with his eyes fixed on California, Polk, not without some hesitation, approved the treaty; and the Senate, also not without misgivings at the commitment, ratified it, 29-7 (June 8, 1848), shortly after the peace with Mexico. Polk favored neutrality, not exclusive control by any one nation. He told the Senate he hoped Great Britain and France would make similar treaties. This also was the objective of New Granada's isthmian policy. As to the guaranty of the sovereignty of New Granada, Polk explained to the Senate that it was "a natural consequence of the guaranty of its neutrality, and there does not seem to be any other practicable mode of securing the neutrality of this territory."[1]

The treaty with New Granada was an important diplomatic coup. Unfortunately it could reserve transit rights for the United States over only one principal canal route. The route through Nicaragua was then and long thereafter considered the best of all. A dangerous rivalry developed after the Mexican War between the United States and Great Britain, each seeking by diplomatic arrangements with Central American states to forestall any control by the other of the Nicaraguan route.

The encroachments of British buccaneers on the Spanish Main in

---

[1] Raimundo Rivas, *Relaciones internacionales entre Colombia y los Estados Unidos, 1810-1850* (Bogotá, Imprenta Nacional, 1915), describes these negotiations from the Colombian archives, but not from those of the United States. R. R. MacGregor "The Treaty of 1846 (Seventeen Years of American-Colombian Relations, 1830-1846)" *Clark University Thesis Abstracts, 1929* (Worcester, Mass., 1930), describes them from the archives of the United States, and from Rivas. J. B. Lockey, "A Neglected Aspect of Isthmian Diplomacy," *Am. Hist. Rev.*, XLI (January, 1936), 295-305, has thrown additional light on the Flores episode. See also E. T. Parks, *Colombia and the United States, 1765-1934* (Duke University Press, 1935).

the sixteenth and seventeenth centuries had led to the establishment of unauthorized log-cutting settlements in Belize (the present British Honduras). These settlements were objects of hostilities in the wars between Great Britain and Spain, and of diplomatic controversy in time of peace. We have already seen how the treaty of peace of 1783 agreed that British wood-cutting settlements on the "Spanish Continent" should be restricted between the Belize and Hondo rivers, and that without derogation to Spanish sovereignty there. Later British diplomatists contended that Central America was not the "Spanish Continent" but the "American Continent." Nevertheless by treaty with Spain in 1786 and again in 1815, Great Britain relinquished all claims to sovereignty in Belize. British log-cutters were still nested there when Spain's dominion over that region was supplanted by the Central American Confederation and the later individual sovereign states, who did not admit British sovereignty over Belize. In vain Guatemala appealed to the United States in 1835 for assistance against these British boundary encroachments. Later on, a British resident authority was appointed for Belize and in 1840 English law was proclaimed there. The resident proclaimed Belize to be a crown colony in 1840; but this act was disavowed in London; not until 1862, after the American Civil War had commenced, was it set up as a crown colony. British magistrates from Belize were appointed in 1841 to minister to British settlers on the strategic but unhealthful Bay Islands, commanding the Gulf of Honduras. The history of Belize is a fine example of how successful buccaneering can lead to territorial encroachments, to settlements, to a sphere of influence, to a protectorate with expanding boundaries, and to actual sovereignty.

Another British protectorate had been established by somewhat similar methods along the Atlantic Coast of Central America from Cape Gracias à Dios to Boca del Toro, covering the whole Atlantic approach to any possible canal route. As narrated above, this alarmed New Granada into importuning the United States to make the treaty of 1846. Into this poorly defended and insalubrious coast British interlopers had filtered from Jamaica, in the Spanish days, with contraband goods for the colonies of the hinterland. These clandestine contacts expanded after the revolution of the Spanish Colonies into a protectorate (1820) over the Mosquito Indians of the region. In 1844 a British resident appeared at Bluefields. This was when the United States was engrossed with the Texan question; but after annexation, with the Mexican issue threatening, Polk's reiterations of the Monroe Doctrine

(1845, 1847) might be construed to apply to Central America as well as California. In January, 1848, the Nicaraguan town of San Juan (Greytown) at the mouth of the river of that name, Atlantic terminus of the most plausible of all the canal routes, was occupied by "Mosquitan" forces under British command and the Nicaraguan garrison ejected. Nicaragua appealed to the United States. At that moment the United States was still at war with Mexico, but Polk promptly sent a diplomatic agent, Elijah Hise, to Central America, to inquire into the situation. Shortly after the peace of 1848 Bidlack's treaty of 1846 with New Granada was ratified; that saved a right of way for the United States over any canal through Panama. In June, 1849, Hise signed a treaty with Nicaragua which was a degree stronger than Bidlack's with New Granada. The Hise treaty would have given to the United States the *exclusive* right to construct, fortify, and control a canal or railroad or both, and have established a protectorate over Nicaragua guaranteeing its sovereignty, dominion, peace, neutrality.[1]

The rapid advance of the United States to the Rio Grande in 1845 and to California in 1848, an advance which British diplomacy had so labored to prevent, together with ratification of the treaty of 1846 with New Granada, caused the British Foreign Office to hasten steps to make good a full control over the Nicaraguan route. The American diplomatist, Hise, had been impelled to sign his treaty, without specific instructions, because of the activities of the British Minister, Chatfield, to secure for his nation a control of the canal route. Already an American company had been chartered to dig a canal and was awaiting secure treaty arrangements.

Hise signed the treaty with Nicaragua as a diplomatic agent appointed by President Polk, but after the Whig Administration of General Taylor had come in, and when Hise's successor, Ephraim George Squier, was on his way to Central America. The new Administration did not approve of the policy of guaranty in Hise's treaty. But President Taylor held the document in reserve. Squier signed a treaty with Honduras (September 28, 1849), which ceded, at least temporarily, to the United States Tigre Island, in the Gulf of Fonseca, key to the Pacific terminus of the Nicaraguan route, and provided for a naval base there.[2] Chatfield countered by signing with Costa Rica a British

---

[1] The treaty, and Hise's correspondence, are printed by the Carnegie Endowment for International Peace, *Diplomatic Correspondence of the United States, Inter-American Affairs, 1831-1860*, Vol. III, *Central America, 1831-1850* (Wash., 1933), W. R. Manning, ed.

[2] *Ibid.*

treaty which protected Costa Rica's claims to the north bank of the
San Juan River, thus blanketing any American right-of-way which
Hise might have secured in his treaty. Hise on his part obtained from
Nicaragua a concession for the Pacific Ship Canal Company of New
York to construct the canal. In a new treaty signed by Taylor's agent
the United States agreed to protect the neutrality of the canal route

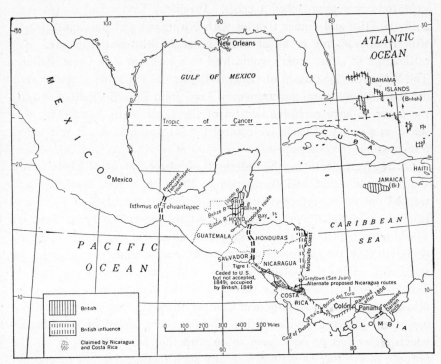

Map 15. The Isthmian Question.

as long as American citizens enjoyed the concession. This treaty recognized the possessions and sovereign rights of Nicaragua in the canal
route, but did not guarantee them, like the Hise treaty; much less did
it give the United States the right to fortify the canal route.[1] At Chatfield's behest, a British naval officer seized Tigre Island, and ran up
the British flag there under the pretext of securing claims against Honduras; but this action was disavowed a few weeks later by the admiral on that station, who knew that the Foreign Minister, Palmerston, was opposed to it. At that very time, in fact, a British plenipotentiary, Sir Henry Bulwer, was leaving England for Washington on a

[1] W. R. Manning, *Diplomatic Correspondence of the United States, Inter-American
Affairs, 1831-1860* (Washington, 1933), III, 360.

special mission to settle the isthmian question. Lord Palmerston preferred to negotiate in Washington, because the new Secretary of State,
John M. Clayton, had told the regular British Minister there, that he
did not hold to the principles of President Monroe with regard to non-
colonization.[1] News of the seizure of Tigre Island, however, caused
much excitement in the United States in the beginning of the year 1850.

Matters now approached a crisis. President Taylor had on his desk
both the Hise and Squier treaties with Nicaragua and the Squier treaty
with Honduras, any or all of which he could send to the Senate. But
ratification of either treaty would lead to a collision with Great Britain.
The Whig Administration of General Taylor did not want a conflict, nor
did the British Liberal government of Lord John Russell. Neither wanted
the other to have exclusive control of the canal route, but neither was
set upon a policy of exclusive control for his own nation. It was therefore possible to compromise.[2]

Both governments in the interests of peace set aside their newly
signed treaties that had threatened to bring them into hostilities and
worked out an imperfect compromise resting on the basis of joint control: the Clayton-Bulwer Treaty, signed by the Secretary of State at
Washington, April 19, 1850. The principal article was the first, which
declared that neither government would ever obtain or maintain for
itself any exclusive control over any ship canal through any part of
Central America; nor fortify the same or the vicinity thereof nor colonize or assume any dominion over Central America; "nor will either make
use of any protection which either affords or may afford, or any alliance
which either has or may have to or with any State or people for the
purpose of erecting or maintaining any such fortifications, or of occupying, fortifying, or colonizing Nicaragua, Costa Rica, the Mosquito coast,
or any part of Central America, or of assuming or exercising dominion
over the same; nor will the United States or Great Britain take advantage of any intimacy, or use any alliance, connection, or influence that
either may possess, with any State or Government through whose territory the said canal may pass, for the purpose of acquiring or holding,
directly or indirectly, for the citizens or subjects of the one any rights
or advantages in regard to commerce or navigation through the said
canal which shall not be offered on the same terms to the citizens or
subjects of the other." Other articles extended the same principle to

---

[1] G. F. Hickson, "Palmerston and the Clayton-Bulwer Treaty," *Cambridge* [England]
Hist. Jour., III (1931), 295-303.

[2] I have followed the account of Professor Mary W. Williams' standard treatise:
Anglo-American Isthmian Diplomacy 1815-1915 (Washington, 1916).

any other canal or railway across the Isthmus connecting North and South America, guaranteed its neutrality, provided that tolls and charges should be equal to citizens and subjects of each party.

After the Senate approved the treaty, but before exchange of ratifications, Bulwer delivered to Secretary Clayton an official note: "Her Majesty's Government do not understand the engagements of that Convention as applying to Her Majesty's settlement at Honduras, or to its dependencies." This obviously withdrew Belize from the purview of the treaty, but did it do more—did it include the Bay Islands, for instance? After consulting with Senator W. R. King, chairman of the Senate Committee on Foreign Relations, Clayton replied that the treaty was not understood by the negotiators "to include the British settlement in Honduras (commonly called British Honduras, as distinct from the State of Honduras) nor the small islands in the neighborhood which may be known as its dependencies." After the exchange of ratifications Bulwer belatedly made a counterstatement: he understood Clayton's answer to his first note to mean that the Secretary of State fully recognized that it was not the intention of the treaty to include the British settlement at Honduras, whatever might be included under this term, nor its dependencies, whatever they might be.[1]

From the beginning this treaty was the subject of much dispute as to its meaning. In the United States it was hailed as a renunciation by Great Britain of her protectorate over the Mosquito Indians. But the British Foreign Office claimed that the studiously worded language of the first article was not a relinquishment of *existing* protectorates, merely an agreement not to use such for any domination of the canal. In 1852, the Bay Islands, under cover of Bulwer's above-mentioned reservation, were declared a British crown colony, much to the indignation of the United States, which understood that group not to be the small islands in the vicinity of British Honduras. Throughout the decade of the 'fifties—a decade in which American diplomacy became much concerned with divers projects of expansion in Cuba and Mexico, and during which the American adventurer William Walker established his short-lived dictatorship in Nicaragua as a hope to slavery-expansionists in the southern states—the question of the Mosquito protectorate remained a

---

[1] There has been controversy regarding the regularity of the delivery of this last note of Bulwer, of July 4, 1850, and Clayton's knowledge of it at the time. The note almost certainly was not delivered at or prior to the exchange of ratifications, but may have been delivered almost immediately thereafter. See M. W. Williams, *Am. Secs. State*, VI, 69; John Bigelow, *Breaches of Anglo-American Treaties* (New York, 1917), 116 *et seq.*, and J. D. Ward, "Sir Henry Bulwer and the United States Archives," in *Cambridge Historical Journal*, III (1931), 304-313.

live issue. After Walker's downfall, negotiations of Great Britain separately with the republics of Nicaragua and Honduras resulted in two treaties in 1859 by which the protectorate was relinquished and the region absorbed within the boundaries of those two states, subject to the condition of a reservation for the Indians and payment to them for a period of ten years of money annuities.[1] The Bay Islands were made over to Honduras. The Foreign Office had been the readier to make these concessions to the United States for fear lest trouble might lead to an interruption of England's cotton supply. On the eve of the Civil War, in December, 1860, President Buchanan declared to Congress that the United States was satisfied with this settlement of the question. It was fortunate that it was out of the way when that war began.

No treaty has been more unpopular, none more violently criticized in the diplomatic history of the United States than the Clayton-Bulwer Treaty, no Secretary of State more savagely scored for a negotiation than Clayton. Surely Clayton was imprudent in telling the British Minister that he did not hold to the non-colonization principle of the Monroe Doctrine. It is certain, too, that Palmerston never conceived he had yielded a jot to that Doctrine. In truth he had not. At best the treaty was a compromise, a compromise to which the United States adhered loyally if uncomfortably during the life of the bargain. In the long run, it proved to be a compromise against the best interests of the United States. We now believe Palmerston if necessary would have relinquished the Mosquito protectorate specifically.[2] But we must remember that in 1850 and for a considerable while thereafter the idea of international control of an isthmian canal, and complete neutrality for such a transit, was the dominating concept in the United States as well as Great Britain. We must remember, too, that this compromise with Great Britain was ratified by the Senate of the United States at a time when the critical domestic question of slavery in the territories was threatening to convulse the country, even to break up the Union. When the treaty was proclaimed by President Taylor, four days before his death on July 9, no one could be certain that the great compromise measures of 1850 would pass Congress. No American administration could then have invited a war with Great Britain over the isthmian or any other question. The Clayton-Bulwer Treaty must be appraised historically in light of that fact.

---

[1] The British Government continued to insist on overseeing the proper execution of the conditions of this treaty, as to reservation boundaries, etc., until 1894, after many expostulations by the United States.

[2] Hickson, *op. cit.*

CHAPTER XV

THE NORTHEAST BOUNDARY AND THE
WEBSTER-ASHBURTON TREATY

(1783-1842)

THE decade of the 'forties witnessed the culmination and settlement of two great boundary controversies with Great Britain that were legacies of the treaty of peace and independence: in the nearer northeast, and in the far northwest.

The northeastern boundary had been described with apparent precision by the treaty. The negotiators used Mitchell's Map of North America of 1755—an excellent map for its time but inaccurate or insufficient in some details—but neglected to annex it to the treaty itself. The American Commissioners, and probably also the British plenipotentiary, marked the entire boundary on copies of Mitchell's Map, but those marked copies disappeared, so there was nothing positive to certify what had been meant. When local authorities tried to trace on the ground the line of the treaty they found that the "St. Croix," described on Mitchell's Map as running into Passamaquoddy Bay, did not correspond incontestably to any one river in that vicinity. Two rivers run into that bay. British officials representing the province of New Brunswick (set apart from Nova Scotia in 1784) contended that the Schoodiac was the St. Croix. The representatives of the border state of Massachusetts maintained that the Magaguadavic, a stream considerably to the east of the Schoodiac, was the real St. Croix. As one ascends these watercourses, respectively, they diverge more and more distant from each other. A glance at Map 8 shows how sovereignty over a large area would depend on whether the international boundary were to be run due north from the source of the easternmost or the westernmost of these two rivers. Only the coastal part of the region was much settled when the treaty was signed; but until the right river should be ascertained and agreed upon, these people could not be sure to which country they belonged.

In the northwest, the treaty had laid down the boundary from the "most northwestern point" of the Lake of the Woods due west to the

Mississippi River. We have already noticed[1] the gap which had been created in that region by a cartographical aberration; that was the beginning of the northwest boundary question which persisted until 1818 and then developed into the larger Oregon Question.

Together with the problem of the southwestern frontier with Spain and Mexico, these boundary disputes with Great Britain constituted one of the gravest and most inveterate diplomatic issues of the United States in the generation following the War of 1812. Because they involved a stronger power, they may be considered more serious than the southwestern issues. As settlers followed fur-traders towards the uncertain parts of the northern boundaries, the issues assumed increasing significance.

Jay's Treaty of 1794 had touched on these boundary difficulties.[2] It provided a mixed commission of three to fix the identity of the St. Croix River and to mark its course. That commission met in 1798 and agreed that the St. Croix corresponded with the western river, the Schoodiac (distinct from the Magaguadavic claimed by the United States). This sanctioned the British pretentions to the territory then in dispute. They placed a monument at its source. Above the St. Croix the line remained unsurveyed through the wilderness: the treaty of 1783 had declared that it should run directly north to the "northwest angle" of Nova Scotia, "viz.: that angle which is formed by a line drawn due north, from the source of the St. Croix River, to the Highlands which divide those Rivers which empty themselves into the River St. Lawrence from those which fall into the Atlantic Ocean." Meanwhile other commissions[3] set up by Jay's Treaty—for the adjudication of pre-war debts and maritime spoliations—got into wrangles that were not cleaned up until 1802. After these had been finally settled, Rufus King, Minister at London, signed with Lord Hawkesbury a convention (May 12, 1803) for closing the northwest boundary gap and for setting up another boundary commission to run the line from the source of the St. Croix to the "north west angle" of Nova Scotia, and thence along the "highlands" to "the northwestern-most head of Connecticut River," all as described by the treaty of 1783. Secretary Madison in King's instructions admitted significantly what President Jefferson announced publicly to Congress,[4] that the commis-

---

[1] See above, pp. 102, 175.

[2] For its unfulfilled stipulations concerning the northwest boundary gap, see above, p. 102.

[3] See above, p. 102.

[4] Moore, *International Arbitrations*, I, 68. Madison was following the loose advice of Sullivan, the American agent before the St. Croix commission.

sioners might depart from the language of the treaty in favor of convenient geographical lines of division, particularly since the "highlands" seemed impossibly described. Rejection by the Senate of the article in the convention of 1803 for the closing of the northwest boundary gap destroyed this attempt at settlement of the northeastern boundary as well, for the amended convention was not ratified. The War of 1812 found these frontier lines still in dispute, and the military events of that conflict resulted in a return to the *status quo ante bellum*.

In the peace negotiations at Ghent the British delegation had tried unsuccessfully to secure a "rectification" of the northeastern boundary of 1783 which would make possible a strategic military road on British soil from Montreal and Quebec to St. John and Halifax, in place of the frozen St. Lawrence, cut off from sea during the long winters, a difficulty abundantly emphasized during the War of 1812. ˋThey also tried to close the northwestern gap by dropping the boundary from the Lake of the Woods to the navigable portion of the Mississippi.[1] Gallatin and his colleagues at Ghent refused to cede any part of the district of Maine or other territory of the United States. The peace of Ghent did set up new boundary commissions[2] intended to mark the whole boundary indubitably from the Atlantic Ocean to the Lake of the Woods, wherever it remained unsettled, including the northeastern boundary from the source of the St. Croix to the source of the Connecticut; but it was silent about the boundary to the west of the Lake of the Woods. To determine the northeastern boundary it provided a joint commission of two to locate and map the line; should they not agree the dispute was to be referred to the arbitration of some friendly sovereign or state.

It was during the attempt in 1821 to survey jointly the northeastern line—that portion running from the source of the St. Croix to the "north west angle" of Nova Scotia—that developed the most significant phase of the boundary controversy. The British Commissioner declared that the "highlands" designated by the treaty were not the height of land that separates the small rivers that fall into the St. Lawrence from the long rivers of Maine that flow into the Atlantic Ocean, but that they were formed by the dividing rise between the upper waters of the St. John (which flows into the Atlantic Ocean at the Bay of Fundy) and the Penobscot, the next large river to the southwest. It is clear that such an interpretation would not have been urged except for strategic considerations; but again the discrepancies between the general indications on Mitchell's Map of 1755 and more recently known topography made

[1] See above, p. 166.   [2] See above, p. 168.

possible arguments and counter-arguments. Upwards of 7,000,000 acres of land, including extensive timber tracts and fertile river valleys, were involved. By a special treaty of 1827, the "points of difference" were submitted to the arbitration of the King of the Netherlands.

The veteran diplomatist and statesman, Albert Gallatin, with William Pitt Preble, represented the United States in this disputation. Gallatin feared, as he put it, that the arbitrator would "split the difference." This happened. Instead of deciding strictly upon the merits of the "points in dispute," the royal arbitrator recommended (1831) a compromise line, which for all practical purposes pretty evenly divided the territory in two.[1] The British Government was willing to accept the compromise. If by disputing arbitrarily a large section of territory one can compromise on half of it containing great strategic value, something is acquired as profit for the ingenuity with which the dispute has been advanced. President Jackson was willing to accept the compromise, too, but the state of Maine objected. Perplexed, Jackson sought the advice of the Senate, which advised against accepting the arbitrator's award, on the perfectly valid ground that he had exceeded his stipulated authority. Great Britain acknowledged in effect that the arbitrator had no authority to lay down a compromise, but was willing to agree on some new treaty line which should follow close to the arbitrator's award. This continued to be the British position to the end of the controversy. Following Jackson, President Van Buren even went so far as to take the advice of Daniel Webster, one of the leaders of the Whig opposition, who was for a conventional line to be worked out in special negotiations, but the persistent opposition of the politically important state of Maine blocked all these efforts at compromise; and in England the aggressive Foreign Minister, Lord Palmerston, would concede nothing which might mar the prestige of his diplomatic successes.

Two other complications had appeared to the boundary commissioners. There was no agreement on the northwesternmost head of the Connecticut River, which involved a hundred thousand acres: on this point of dispute the arbitrator had declared for the British contention. And it had been discovered in 1818 that the northern boundary of 45° N. L. between the Connecticut River and the St. Lawrence had been inaccurately surveyed by the accepted demarcation of 1774: it had arched slightly too far north, by three-fourths of a mile, where it crossed the outlet of Lake Champlain. At that very spot, on Rouse's Point, commanding the outlet,

[1] See Map No. 8, insert.

the United States had recently erected an expensive fort and was still perfecting it. The arbitrator declared for a resurvey of the line, but nevertheless for leaving Rouse's Point with a surrounding radius of territory within the United States. These proposed settlements also collapsed when the award was rejected. The whole northeast boundary thus con-

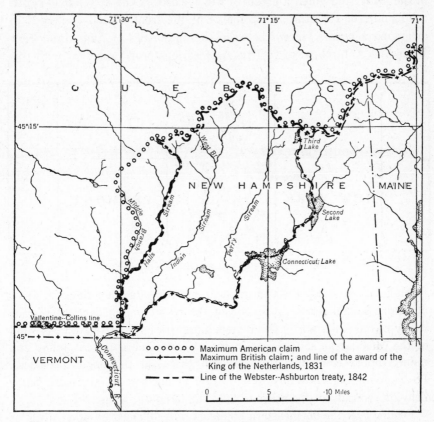

Map 16. Boundary Controversy Concerning the Head of the Connecticut River.

tinued an increasingly vexatious issue. As settlers pushed up from the coast of Maine and New Brunswick into the fertile valley of the Aroostook (which flows into the St. John north of the highlands discovered by the British agent in 1821), the question assumed an even more serious aspect: the diplomatic dispute became exposed to the hazards of local rivalries, local politics, and local personalities.[1] A border strife, traditionally known as the "Restook War" developed in 1838-39. The

[1] Moore, *International Arbitrations*, I, 87.

province of New Brunswick was granting land titles and claiming jurisdiction within the state of Maine. The state of Maine endeavored to
eject British settlers and authorities, armed a civil *posse*, and began to
erect fortifications. Congress passed an act (March 3, 1839) authorizing the President to call out the militia and to enroll 50,000 volunteers
in the army, and voted a credit of $10,000,000. General Winfield Scott,
commander of the army, took charge of the frontier, and succeeded in
arranging a *modus vivendi* between the authorities of Maine and New
Brunswick (March, 1839). Thus a precarious peace was kept with this

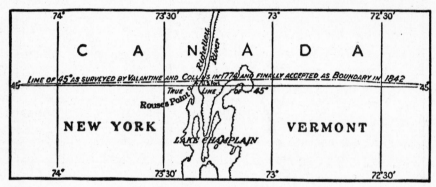

Map 17. Rouse's Point Boundary Controversy.

formula, approved by the two national governments: that the civil *posse*
of Maine should retain possession of the territory it had occupied (the
valley of the Aroostook); the British authorities should retain possession
of the Madawaska settlement (in the valley of the upper St. John) and
uninterrupted communication between that and the upper provinces.
Possession and jurisdiction were to remain unchanged, with each party
denying the right of the other to hold the territory in fact held.[1]

Feeling over the northeastern boundary was inflamed by other disputes
with Great Britain which in their entirety succeeded in exciting violently
all sections of the Republic, north, south, east and west, while in England there was little disposition, so long as the truculent Palmerston
remained Secretary for Foreign Affairs, to make any concessions to a
people of growing power whose manners and polity had been steadily
depicted in an offensive way by English literary travelers.[2] The Oregon
Question will be discussed at length presently; it was at this time not

[1] Miller, *Treaties*, IV, 379.
[2] Mrs. T. A. Trollope, *Domestic Manners of the Americans* (London, 1832); Harriet
Martineau, *Society in America* (3 Vols., London, 1837). Dickens' *American Notes* did not
appear until 1842, but they reflected the same views and opinion.

an acute controversy, though a large and lingering dormant issue. The obstinate refusal of the United States to agree on some mutual right of visit for facilitating the suppression of the slave trade[1] stirred the resentment of British humanitarian opinion, and grated on the Government, which was itself unwilling to repudiate the unjustifiable practice of impressment. British interest in Texas and general support of the principle of abolition roused the suspicions of political leaders of the southern states.[2] More immediate was the case of the *Caroline*, growing out of the Canadian insurrection of 1837, for which there had been widespread sympathy along the entire northern frontier, not dissimilar, but not so acute and uncontrollable as that for Texas in the Southwest. The Canadian rebels had been assisted by sympathizers living in the state of New York. They had engaged an American owned steamship, the *Caroline*, to run men, guns, and supplies to Navy Island, a bit of British territory in the river above Niagara Falls. A group of Canadian volunteers, in defense against the rebellion, had crossed the river and destroyed the *Caroline*, by pushing her out to drift toward the Falls (December 29, 1837). In the fracas one citizen of the United States, named Durfee, was killed on American soil. This was a bold invasion to be justified only by treaty provisions or imperative necessity. Lord Palmerston took the same attitude toward American protests that John Quincy Adams would have taken if this had been a case of Andrew Jackson and Florida, but, unlike Adams, he had no treaty to fall back on, and did not go so far as to say it was a case of imperative necessity. The incident was still a diplomatic question three years later when one Alexander McLeod appeared in the State of New York and was widely believed to be one of the group that destroyed the *Caroline* and that he personally had killed Durfee. He was taken at his word, arrested (November, 1840), and indicted for murder by the authorities of the state. The British Government immediately protested, claiming that McLeod was acting under its orders. It assumed full responsibility for the incident, urgently demanded his release, and held the federal government accountable for him.

The McLeod case now supplanted every other dispute in its immediate importance. Sympathizers with the Canadian insurrectionists vociferated for vengeance on McLeod. Webster feared mob action. He thought that would mean "war within ten days." On the other hand, even McLeod's judicial conviction and execution would have been the signal

[1] See below, p. 330 ff.
[2] See above, p. 224.

for a war [1] in which every effort would have been made by each side to settle the boundaries and other issues by the force of arms. Such a war in 1842 might have seriously jeopardized the later achievements of American expansion under Tyler and Polk.

Fortunately a change of governments took place in both countries. In the national elections of 1840 the Whig party overthrew the Democratic Administration and in March, 1841, the new government took office, with Daniel Webster as President Harrison's, and presently as President Tyler's, Secretary of State. In England the liberal Melbourne Government was supplanted by the Tories over a question of European policy. Peel came in as Prime Minister (September 3, 1841), with Aberdeen as Secretary of State for Foreign Affairs in succession to Palmerston. Whatever the party terminology in either country, each administration was disposed to a friendly adjustment of outstanding difficulties. But first the vexing McLeod case had to be settled.

Like the stand which Maine took on the international issue of the northeastern frontier, the position of New York in the McLeod case —an affair of essentially foreign relations—hampered the efforts of the federal government to keep the peace, even under the guidance of such a sane and conciliatory statesman as Daniel Webster. *Vis-à-vis* foreign powers, it is the federal government which stands responsible, but a federal administration in the United States cannot easily overlook the political consequences of alienating one of its own states. Moreover, the Constitution and the laws passed under it had not then provided, and do not now adequately provide, for the responsibilities of the individual states toward foreign governments. Webster, by his advice conveyed to counsel for the defense, caused the case of McLeod to be taken on a writ of *habeas corpus* to the supreme court of the state of New York, for the discharge of the prisoner. He accepted the British position that McLeod, acting under orders of his government, was not amenable to the civil courts of a foreign country, and held Great Britain rather than her subject responsible for the armed invasion of American territory. The supreme court of New York refused to release McLeod. The trial went on. Governor Seward, however, confidentially informed the Secretary of State that McLeod (despite his boasts) was known to have a good alibi, and that in the remote contingency of a conviction he would be pardoned.[2] The tension eased when a jury acquitted the defendant (Oc-

---

[1] Palmerston so informed the retiring American Minister, Stevenson. Reeves, *Diplomacy of Tyler and Polk*, 19.

[2] C. A. Duniway, in *Am. Secs. State*, V, 16.

tober, 1841). Never has the much abused device of the alibi been put to a more wholesome service. The diplomatic correspondence concerning McLeod's case has made it a *cause célèbre* in international law. It led to the passage by Congress (August 29, 1842) of a law drafted by Webster, providing for the discharge, or the removal from state to federal courts, of any person accused of an unlawful act proved to have been committed under the orders of a foreign sovereign. After McLeod's release there still remained to be settled the question of the violation of American sovereignty by the *Caroline* affair; but the acquittal itself made possible a fresh attempt by two well-disposed governments to settle the long-standing northeastern boundary controversy as well as other existing issues.

Before McLeod's acquittal, Webster had informed the British Minister at Washington that the United States would be willing to consider a new, conventional, northeastern boundary. This was in accord with the opinion he had prepared and expressed to President Van Buren some three years before.[1] It meant a compromise, since a new line was admitted as a subject of discussion; it also meant that Maine must be brought around to accept a surrender of territory claimed under the treaty of 1783, which Maine seemed determined not to do. The federal government had accepted the constitutional argument of the state that its territory could not be ceded without its consent, and commissioners from Maine, as well as from Massachusetts, took a very real part in the negotiations which followed.[2]

One of the first steps of the new administration in England was to send over a special plenipotentiary, Alexander Baring, Lord Ashburton, to negotiate with the American Secretary of State. Ashburton was a man sixty-seven years of age, who had married an American belle and heiress, Anne Bingham of Philadelphia, back in the time of President George Washington. A distinguished British peer, and member of the great financial house of Baring and Company, of London, he was devoted to the preservation of peace and the cultivation of Anglo-American friendship, as was Webster himself, who craved to be appointed Minister of the United States to the Court of St. James's.

Ashburton's instructions held him pretty close on boundary concessions: he was to insist on at least the line of the Columbia River to its intersection with the 49th parallel, in the Pacific Northwest; and on the northeastern frontier he was to labor for territory to cover a strategic road from Quebec to Halifax, and to make no essential concession beyond

[1] Reeves, *op. cit.*, 13.   [2] Miller, *Treaties*, IV, 383-403.

the line of 1831 of the King of the Netherlands. He was permitted to offer monetary compensation to the state of Maine to procure a satisfactory line. He was also instructed to defend the "lamented" invasion of American territory, at the time of the *Caroline* incident, and to hold out for a right of visiting in time of peace vessels suspected of falsely flying the American flag to escape detection by British cruisers of their slaving operations.[1] In Washington, Ashburton had little difficulty in agreeing with Webster on a new compromise boundary. They practically "split the difference" in Maine, and the United States got thereby slightly less than it would have received by the award of the King of the Netherlands eleven years previously. In turn, Great Britain accepted as final the inaccurately surveyed line of 45° as the northern boundary of New York and Vermont, and yielded to the major part of American claims about the head of the Connecticut River. The result was the boundary that now exists. Great Britain's strategic needs for an overland route between Montreal and St. John were satisfied; the United States retained Rouse's Point and the fort commanding the outlet of Lake Champlain. On the Maine frontier 7,697,280 acres had been in dispute; of these 4,489,600 were retained by the United States and 3,207,680 let go to New Brunswick, but Webster felt that the United States had kept hold of those lands which had the greatest intrinsic value. At any rate, both governments were satisfied.[2]

The consent of Maine to the negotiations and the final settlement was won by a most interesting means which had fallen to Webster's hand. Jared Sparks, the historian, had been engaged in researches abroad, during the course of which he examined maps in the archives of the French Foreign Office. He observed there a d'Anville map of 1746, with the boundary of the United States marked thereon in a strong red line. After he had returned, it seemed to Sparks that this map corresponded to the description of Benjamin Franklin in a letter of December 6, 1782, to the Comte de Vergennes, in which he communicated a map with the new boundary of the United States marked on it "with a strong red line." Sparks sketched from memory the French map he had in mind, and informed Webster. The line supported the British claims of 1842 on the northeast. Webster meanwhile had picked up by purchase a copy

[1] The several instructions of Aberdeen to Ashburton are reviewed by E. D. Adams, "Lord Ashburton and the Treaty of Washington," in *Am. Hist. Rev.*, XVII (July, 1912), 764-782. See also C. A. Duniway in *Am. Secs. State*, V, 20-21.

[2] But there was much and lasting opposition in New Brunswick, which is noted in Wm. F. Ganong's valuable and technical "A Monograph of the Evolution of the Boundaries of the Province of New Brunswick," published in *Proceedings and Transactions of the Royal Society of Canada*, 2d series, Vol. VII (1901-1902), Section 2. See Map 8, insert.

of a Mitchell Map—we remember that the negotiations of the boundary of 1782 used a Mitchell—which had a northeastern boundary marked on it corresponding to the British claim, too. It had belonged to General Steuben and had been placed on the market by his legatees. No one knows who marked it thus, or when.

Though Webster, nor Sparks for that matter, was by no means convinced of these maps as unexceptionable evidence for the British claim, the Secretary sent Sparks to Maine on a confidential mission to show the maps to the authorities of that state [1] to persuade them that they had better accept a new compromise line drawn up by him and the British Minister. Ashburton paid £2,998 1s. (about $14,500) for Sparks' "expenses." [1] Maine capitulated to this specious cartographical argument and finally accepted, as did Massachusetts (which had retained property rights in Maine's public lands after the separation of 1820), monetary compensation for the surrendered lands, each state $150,000, payable not by Great Britain as Ashburton's instructions would have permitted, but *by the United States*. In addition the United States agreed to reimburse the states of Maine and Massachusetts for all expenses entailed in defending their territories during the controversy. At the request of the Maine commissioners this stipulation became a part of the treaty. Ashburton even went so far as to protest at this purely domestic obligation being put so anomalously into a treaty and cleared his government of any responsibility for executing that item.

Before signing the treaty as finally worked out, Ashburton was shown the Sparks map and the Webster-Steuben copy of Mitchell's Map which appeared to support the British contention. The British Government had in its own Foreign Office—unknown, however, to Ashburton and presumably to Aberdeen, although Palmerston, of the opposition, was silently aware of it—a copy of Mitchell's Map: the "King George" Map which had the boundary marked thereon as "Mr. Oswald's line." It corresponded perfectly to the American claim. The King George Map was not revealed to the Government of the United States until 1843.[2] We cannot be certain that "Mr. Oswald's line" was marked on it at the time of the treaty of 1783, though it is extremely likely. Sparks' red-line

---

[1] *John Quincy Adams and the Foundations of American Foreign Policy* (N. Y., 1949), Ch. XXIII.

[2] For a convenient summary of the various known editions and impressions of Mitchell's Map, and their relation to the treaty of peace and other diplomatic negotiations, and for other maps relating to the negotiations of 1842, see the notes prepared by Hunter Miller, with the assistance of Lawrence Martin (for Mitchell's Map) in the former's *Treaties*, III, 328-351, and IV, 403-413. Dr. Miller's notes on the Webster-Ashburton treaty are the most voluminous and erudite commentary existing on it and the negotiations.

map had no application whatsoever. In 1933 there was discovered in Madrid a copy of Franklin's red boundary line, traced on a Mitchell for the Spanish Government by its ambassador in France in 1782, the Count de Aranda. It conforms perfectly to the American claim, and to Jay's copy of Mitchell, which was turned up after the Webster-Ashburton negotiations. Had it been known in 1842 there need have been no surrender of territory. But history cannot be written in the past subjunctive: the northeastern boundary was definitely settled in 1842, and the United States under Webster's guidance made a large concession, a compromise, in the interest of peace.

Other articles of this notable document were: the navigation of the River St. John was to be free to citizens and subjects of both parties where it flowed between the territory of both, and citizens of the United States were to have the right to float out products of forest and field from Maine to the mouth of the river in British territory. The Detroit and St. Clair rivers, and Lake St. Clair were declared free to navigation of both parties, together with certain channels in the St. Lawrence River on both sides of the line. Minor disputes [1] in the boundary line between Lake Huron and the Lake of the Woods, which a boundary commission erected under the Treaty of Ghent had been unable to agree upon, were adjusted, in general to the advantage of the United States. The treaty also contained a useful article on extradition. An extradition article in Jay's Treaty had expired with the War of 1812; the Webster-Ashburton Treaty now added to the former list of extraditable crimes. It was further extended in 1889, 1900 and 1905 to include all serious crimes, except offenses of a political character. This shut off an easy refuge for American criminals "gone to Canada." The treaty, with the aid of Webster's spurious maps, was speedily ratified in the Senate by a vote of 39-9.

At the outset of the treaty negotiations, another problem had arisen to bother the diplomatists. An American coastwise slave-trader, the *Creole,* bound with a human cargo from Hampton Roads to New Or-

---

[1] The joint commission of survey set up by the treaty of Ghent of 1815 finished its labors in 1822 without being able to agree on where the boundary should leave Lake Superior and by what route it should arrive at Rainy Lake, the treaty of 1783 not having been clear on this. The American Commissioner claimed a line via Dog Lake, Mille Lacs, and Sturgeon Lake, very considerably to the north of the present boundary; the British Commissioner claimed a line equally far to the south of the present boundary, via Fond du Lac, the St. Louis River, and Vermillion Lake. Both were willing to compromise approximately on the line from Pigeon River via Lakes Seiganagah, Bois Blanc, and La Croix, but the British Commissioner was unwilling to give up the Grand Portage which lies to the south of Pigeon River, around the rapids of that stream. The Webster-Ashburton treaty agreed on Pigeon River and for the remainder of the unsettled bound-

leans, suffered a mutiny of the slaves (November 7, 1841), who after killing one of the owners of the cargo put in at Nassau. British colonial authorities hung the identified murderers, but held the slaves as free when they touched foot on British soil. Naturally little sympathy was shown for the crew and owners. The affair antagonized the southern states. It was one of those distressing features of a hateful traffic which we shall have to notice more in detail in a later chapter. Webster held that international law of hospitality protected persons and property in distress. Ashburton declared that he was without instructions on this matter, which had arisen since his departure. He urged that it be excluded from the treaty and referred to London for settlement. He took the responsibility of declaring that meanwhile there would be "no officious interference with American vessels driven by accident or violence into those ports [of British colonies on the southern borders of the United States]." Webster accepted this, but was not successful in writing into the treaty of 1842 a provision to cover slave mutineers with the formula "mutiny on board ship." [1] By another article of the treaty, the United States engaged with Great Britain to maintain a joint cruising squadron on the coast of Africa,[2] to help suppress the slave trade, but would not agree to any mutual right of visit to ascertain the real identity of a suspected slaver, an arrangement which Great Britain had been writing into treaties with European small-navy states. Webster could hold off on this easily, because Great Britain on her part would not really repudiate the practice of impressment in time of war. In a note to Ashburton, which was merely politely acknowledged, he laid down the American position on impressment: "In every regularly documented American merchant vessel the crew who navigate it will find their protection in the flag which is over them." Ashburton had asked permission from London to include an article against impressment, but Aberdeen sternly refused to accept such a proposal, "tantamount to an absolute and entire renunciation of the indefeasible right inherent in the British Crown to command the allegiance and services of its subjects, wherever

ary followed the compromise previously suggested by the joint commission. Although the area technically in dispute was approximately as great (see Map 21) as that of the northeast boundary controversy, it had not been complicated by the settlement of population there. The possession of the Grand Portage, route of the fur trade to the far Northwest, had been the chief object of contention.

For further details see Paullin and Wright, *Atlas of the Historical Geography of the United States* (New York, 1932), 57, and Plate 91B.

[1] The case of the *Creole* was submitted to the Anglo-American mixed claims commission under the convention of 1853; and the umpire awarded to the United States the sum of $110,330.   [2] See below, p. 332.

found." But Great Britain has never challenged Webster's statement by overt act since 1814.

These exchanges of notes, putting at rest the case of the *Creole*, and the impressment issue, must be considered as indispensable adjuncts [1] of the treaty itself, though the Senate took no official cognizance of them. Another dealt with the affair of the *Caroline*.

Webster declared to Great Britain that it would be for the British Government "to show a necessity of self-defence, instant, overwhelming, leaving no choice of means, and no moment for deliberation." Ashburton replied that it was indeed just that. "Looking back to what passed at this distance of time," he went on to say, "what is, perhaps, most to be regretted is, that some explanation and apology for this occurrence was not immediately made; this, with a frank explanation of the necessity of the case, might, and probably would, have prevented much of the exasperation, and of the subsequent complaints and recriminations to which it gave rise." This was not exactly an apology, but thus the *Caroline* affair was finally and fortunately hushed up.

To the historian looking back over the controversy and having at his side cartographical information unavailable to Webster, unavailable because the American agents Gallatin and Preble had not found it when preparing the American case in 1828, it seems as though Great Britain won a very considerable diplomatic victory in the treaty of 1842. She secured the strategic rectification of frontier for which her diplomats had labored in vain at Ghent in 1814. Later knowledge does not justify condemnation of Webster's concessions under the circumstances. The dispute with Great Britain was full of possibilities of tragedy if it had not been for the sanity of peace-minded administrations in both countries.

[1] Miller, *Treaties*, IV, 457-468.

CHAPTER XVI

OREGON

(1776-1871)

WEBSTER and Ashburton had not been able to reach any settlement of the other great boundary controversy, the Oregon Question. It is now appropriate to review this expansive territorial dispute which presently became an acute issue between the governments that so recently had liquidated such a large measure of their misunderstandings.

The Oregon Question originally involved the claims of four powers, Spain, Great Britain, Russia, the United States, to an indeterminate stretch of coast north of San Francisco Bay; but by 1825 the controversy had narrowed to a dispute between Great Britain and the United States as to the share of sovereignty each should have over the region between 42° N. L. and 54° 40′ N. L. Back from the coast the hinterland stretched to the watershed of the Rocky Mountains.

The Spanish claim rested on the papal bulls of 1493 and the Treaty of Tordesillas of 1494,[1] and on a series of exploratory voyages made north from the Pacific ports of Mexico between 1542 and 1792.[2] Spanish explorers first marked out the coast of California in the middle of the sixteenth century; it was a Spanish captain who first sailed (1774) into the harbor of Nootka Sound of what later proved to be Vancouver Island; a Spanish voyager, Heceta, was the first (1775) to observe the mouth of the great River of the West—later to be named the Columbia; and Spanish navigators vied with British in pushing northward up the coast to Alaska. They sighted Mount St. Elias, above 60° N. L., by 1779, that lofty landmark which Bering had been the first of Europeans to see and name in 1741. Rival powers challenged Spain's sovereign claims on the Pacific coast even as they had done on Atlantic shores. By the Nootka Sound Convention of 1790 Great Britain compelled her rival to admit the right of British subjects to trade and settle on the unoccupied coasts of North America. The northernmost Spanish occupation was San Francisco Bay (1776). This was not a yielding of Spain's entire claims north

---

[1] See above, p. 4.

[2] Henry R. Wagner, *Spanish Voyages to the Northwest Coast in the Sixteenth Century (including those to 1602)* (San Francisco, 1929); and *Spanish Explorations in the Strait of Juan de Fuca* (Santa Anna, Calif., 1933), details the work of the later voyages.

of San Francisco; it was a surrender only of her exclusive monopoly. What remained of her claims north of 42° Spain ceded to the United States in the treaty of 1819 that fixed the first transcontinental frontier.

The claim of Great Britain dates back to 1579 when Sir Francis Drake broke into the Pacific Ocean on his famous voyage around the world. He spent several weeks on the coast of California in the summer of that year, presumably encamped at what is now Drake's Bay, a little north of the Golden Gate, took possession of the region for Queen Elizabeth, and called it New Albion. Drake's landing was antedated by Spanish voyages (Cabrillo, 1542) along the California coast, and was followed up by no English occupation or even visitation. Later the Spanish occupied California (1769-1776). It was exactly two centuries before another Englishman visited the northwest coast of America. Captain Cook, on an official voyage of discovery and exploration, unfurled the Union Jack in those parts in 1778. Cook touched at Nootka Sound, again claimed the northwest coast for the British crown, and skirted the shore of the continent as far north as Mount St. Elias. Thence he put out to sea on the remainder of this notable voyage around the world back home to England.[1] Another official English expedition appeared when Captain Vancouver, who had been a young officer with Cook, was sent out to execute the Nootka Sound Convention, also to map officially and explore. Vancouver's men discovered what is now known as Puget Sound, and penetrated for over a hundred miles the Columbia River (October, 1792), the existence of which Vancouver learned from an American trader, Captain Robert Gray of Boston, who had sailed across the bar and into the estuary the previous spring and had named the river after his ship. After 1792, British, Spanish, and American traders, and even those of some other nations, frequented the northwest coast from the Columbia River north to Alaska, collecting the skins of the sea-otter for the profitable China trade.

British voyages were followed by daring overland expeditions from Canada. The North West Company, a most enterprising group of fur-traders from Montreal, was very active here. One of their pathfinders, Alexander Mackenzie, crossed over the Rockies to the waterways of the Pacific at the mouth of Bella Coola River in 1793, the first white man known to have crossed the continent north of Mexico. Some years later (1806-1808) Simon Fraser also pushed westward through the interior of present British Columbia and down the river which bears his name to its mouth near the site of the present city of Vancouver. A third Nor'wester,

[1] Cook himself was killed during a dispute with natives in the Hawaiian Islands.

David Thompson, penetrated the mountain passes to the source of the
Columbia River and established (1807-1810) a chain of trading posts on
its tributaries, and on the Kootenai. These were all on the western
slope of the Divide and with one exception well south of the later
international boundary of 49°.[1] Thompson had orders to follow the plans
of Mackenzie and Fraser, to erect a chain of trading posts connecting
the mouth of the Columbia with the upper waters of the great prairie
rivers of Canada. By the official voyages of Cook and Vancouver, and by
the exploring and trading expeditions of Mackenzie, Fraser and Thompson, Great Britain had rapidly extended trade into the region north of the
Columbia, as well as the western slope of the Rockies to some distance
east and south of that river, and in that way established a claim to its
basin.

The first Americans to appear on the northwest coast were two sailors
in Captain Cook's crew. One of them, John Ledyard of Connecticut,
spread the news of the profits of the fur-trade between the coast and
China. It was he who originally inspired the interest of Jefferson, then
minister in Paris, in that distant part of the world, a fateful and persistent
interest for later American diplomacy. The first American flags to sail
thither fluttered from the mastheads of two Boston trading craft, the
Columbia, Captain John Kendrick, and the *Lady Washington,* Captain
Robert Gray, in 1788-1789, who traded at Nootka Sound, at Queen Charlotte Island, and along the coast. They witnessed the Spanish seizure of
British ships at Nootka in 1789, which produced the famous diplomatic
controversy between Spain and England. Captain Gray took the
Columbia back to the Oregon coast in 1791-1792. This was the occasion
when (May 11, 1792) he sailed her into the river that since then has
borne her name, only sixty days before the appearance of the first British
trading ship in that river.[2]

There is no evidence that the trader Gray, nor the British trader who
came so soon after him, took formal possession of the Columbia River
country. Years later, when the Oregon Question had assumed international prominence, someone introduced over a caret, in different ink and
handwriting, in the log kept by one of the crew, John Boit, the words

[1] The posts were: Kootenai House near Windemere Lake, B. C.; a temporary post
at Kootenai Falls, near the present town of Libby, in Lincoln County, Montana;
Kullyspell House, on Lake Pend d'Oreille, Idaho; Saleesh House, at Thompson's Prairie,
on Clark's Fork River, Montana; and Spokane House, at the confluence of the Spokane
and Little Spokane Rivers, nine miles from the present city of Spokane, Washington.
See T. C. Elliott, "The Fur Trade in the Columbia River Basin Prior to 1811," *Ore
Hist. Quar.,* XV (Dec., 1914), 241-251. See Map 18.

[2] The schooner *Jenny,* Captain James Baker, of Bristol, England.

"to take possession for the United States." [1]   Boit had merely mentioned that members of the crew had gone on shore.   Apparently Gray never thought of taking possession for the United States.   The later interpolator sought to remedy this inadvertence!   Vancouver honored the

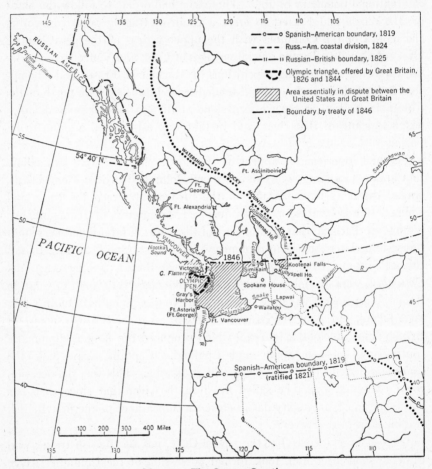

Map 18. The Oregon Question.

American trader Gray by putting on his chart the name Columbia River, and by so doing indubitably recognized the earlier presence of the American flag there.

Russia's claim followed the first visit to Alaska of the Danish mariner, in Russian employ, Vitus Bering, in 1741.   Thereafter adventurous Russians prosecuted a hazardous trade in furs between Siberia and the islands

[1] T. C. Elliott printed the relevant portions of the log, with annotations, in *Ore. Hist Quar.*. XXII (Dec., 1921) ; see p. 310.

of Alaska. The Czar created the Russian-American Company in 1799 and gave it a monopoly of the Alaskan fur trade as far south as 55°. We have noted [1] how the advance of the Russian activities and the Czar's ukase of 1821 provoked the opposition of the United States and was a part of the situation which preceded the pronouncement of the Monroe Doctrine.

The first official expedition of the United States to the disputed territory was that of Captains Lewis and Clark in command of a company of the army, sent across the continent by President Jefferson in 1805. From the contiguous territory of Louisiana, just procured by the United States from France, they descended the western watershed by way of the Clearwater and Snake rivers to the Columbia, and placed the American flag over a fort at its mouth, on the south bank. There they spent the winter of 1805-1806, formally taking possession of the territory which Vancouver had also claimed twelve years previously for the King of Great Britain. Lewis and Clark did not penetrate any of the region north of the Columbia, as Vancouver's men had done, in Puget Sound, nor any of that territory east of the Columbia and north of the Snake and Clearwater subsequently explored by David Thompson. Six years later (March, 1811), after one attempt by the American, C. W. Winship, had failed (1810) to establish a trading post at the mouth of the Columbia, a company controlled by John Jacob Astor of New York City forestalled David Thompson and the North West Company by founding the post of Astoria, near the site of Lewis and Clark's old fort, with three branch trading posts up-river. This was the first American settlement. Alarmed by the outbreak of war, the owners soon sold out (1813) to the North West Company, but the American flag continued to fly over Fort George (as Astoria was renamed) until it was captured during the War of 1812 by a British cruiser in 1813. By the terms of the treaty of Ghent all territory taken by either party during the war was to be restored. Belatedly but loyally, in 1818, the British lowered their own flag there and saluted the Stars and Stripes; [2] but the trading post continued to be owned by the North West Company, until merged in 1821 with the larger and older Hudson's Bay Company, the most powerful fur-trading organization of all Canadian history. That company now (1821) received a special license conferring on it new privileges—beyond those of its ancient charter for trading in the lands drained by the waters entering into Hudson's Bay—in-

[1] See above, p. 205.

[2] T. C. Elliott, "The Surrender at Astoria in 1818," *Ore. Hist. Quar.*, XIX (1918), 271-282.

cluding the exclusive right to trade in the region northward and westward
of the territory of the United States not incorporated in any British province or belonging to any other country. This language included the Oregon
country according to the British point of view, but in that region this
monopoly excluded only British subjects. The act of Parliament conveying the license expressly gave to the company the right to administer
justice to British subjects in the regions of its activities, applying the
laws of Upper Canada with appeal to Canadian courts. Thus did British
law enter the Oregon country. The Hudson's Bay Company, at the
suggestion of Canning, removed its headquarters from Astoria and established its principal factory and trading counter at Fort Vancouver, a
strategic spot on the north bank of the river just above the mouth of the
Willamette and below Point Vancouver, which had been so named by
Broughton in Vancouver's visit of 1792. Here for the next twenty
years it ruled over the handful of white inhabitants in the valley and
kept the peace with the Indians, under the beneficent rule of the now venerated chief factor, Doctor John McLoughlin. Its trappers and traders
further explored, and even named, the mountains and valleys from Mount
Shasta in California and Mount Hood in Oregon to the rugged Fraser
River region of British Columbia. During this period there arrived small
bands of Protestant [1] missionaries to the Indians, Jason Lee and associates in the Willamette Valley, and Doctor Marcus Whitman [2] and associates in the Walla Walla, Spokane and Nez Percé countries; also individual pioneers like Erving Young from California; and roving "mountain men" from the trapping grounds of the Rockies; all ardent Americans; later and most important of all, as hereafter related, the large
emigrant population in covered wagons over the Oregon Trail. The
policy of the Hudson's Bay Company was, in line with instructions from
Canning at the British Foreign Office, to treat all these people kindly, and
to trade with them, but to see that they established themselves south and
east of the Columbia River.[3] Chief Factor McLoughlin did this with
marvelous tact and generosity. The attempt of rival American fur trad-

[1] There were also Catholic missions in the Willamette and Umatilla Valleys, and
with the Blackfoot tribes of the region of present Idaho and Montana; but, of course,
without families or proclivities for land owning; they did not consequently become foci
of settlements.

[2] There is no official record or reference to the missionaries as an influence or factor
in the diplomacy of the Oregon Question.

[3] Not until 1844-1845 did the American settlers begin to make their way in small
numbers into the Nisqually, Cowlitz and Olympia districts north of the Columbia,
against the wishes but without the resistance of the Hudson's Bay Company's officials.

ers, Nathaniel Wyeth from Boston, and to an extent Captain Bonneville, to gather furs in the Columbia Basin was also firmly and judiciously overcome. In fact the Company tried to "trap out" the furs to the south and east of the river in order to create a sterile belt of territory uninviting to American trappers.[1]

The treaty of 1818 between Great Britain and the United States, which agreed on the line of 49° from the Lake of the Woods to the Rocky Mountains, was a pendant to the negotiations of John Quincy Adams who was then striving to bring Spain to cede her claims to territory north of a determined transcontinental boundary. Great Britain would not agree, as Spain did in 1819, to extend her boundary through to the Pacific Coast. This would have given the United States a well-nigh (except for possible Russian claims not extinguished until 1824) perfect sovereignty inside definitely agreed boundaries on the shores of the South Sea (Pacific). The treaty of 1818, strictly speaking, did not provide a "joint" occupation, as so many historical writers have assumed. It did state that any territory claimed by Great Britain or the United States to the west of the Rocky Mountains, as well as the rivers and harbors of that region, should be for ten years "free and open . . . to the citizens and subjects of the two powers" without prejudice to the claims of any power to any part of that territory. There was nothing in the treaty which need have prevented the United States on its part from chartering a trading company like the Hudson's Bay Company to establish another post at the mouth of the Columbia, or itself to establish a military post there (as President Monroe recommended to Congress in 1824), or a line of fortified stockades between the upper waters of the Missouri or other tributaries of the Mississippi and those of the Columbia, or the providing of American law and courts for citizens in Oregon. As interest in the Oregon country developed, such proposals were actually made in Congress, but uniformly voted down. American expansion was still limited to the cis-Rocky Mountain region. The object of the treaty of 1818 had been to prevent disputes and differences between the United States and Great Britain, and Congress still hesitated to take steps in that remote region which might cause such trouble. The predominance of the Hudson's Bay Company remained unchallenged for two decades.

The Russian ukase of 1821 led to a discussion with the Czar's Government which finally resulted in the treaty of 1824. At first the United

[1] Frederick Merk, "The Snake River Expedition, 1824-1825; an Episode of Fur Trade and Empire," *Miss. Vall. Hist. Rev.*, XXI (1934), 49-62.

States proposed to Great Britain joint negotiations with Russia, for the purpose of partitioning the Oregon country: to the United States all as far north as 51° N. L., to Great Britain the region between 51° and 54°, and to Russia all north of 54°. George Canning, the British Foreign Minister, who regretted the restoration of Fort George, and who refused anyhow to acknowledge the dictum of the Monroe Doctrine that the American continents were not a field for further European expansion, rejected the invitation. By treaty (1824) with the United States, Russia agreed not to allow any establishment by its subjects south of 54° 40', and the United States agreed not to permit its citizens to make establishments north of that latitude. The next year, 1825, Great Britain made a similar treaty with Russia, setting at approximately 54° 40' the boundary between them on the Pacific coast; and also designating the eastern boundary of Russian territory from there to the Arctic Ocean. This line, too vaguely described, was later taken over by the United States when it purchased Alaska, and became ultimately involved in the Alaska boundary dispute with Great Britain at the close of the century.[1] By these two treaties, Russia withdrew from any contest of territory south of 54° 40' and abandoned her claim to exclusive sovereignty over any of the high seas on the Pacific Ocean off that shore. Spain having withdrawn in 1819 by making over all her claims to the United States, the contest for the territory between 42° and 54° 40' narrowed to the two contestants, the United States and Great Britain. By actual exploration the United States had the better claim to the region south of the line of the Columbia, and Great Britain similarly had the better claim to the lands and waters to the north of that river.

The British claim, however, was weakened by the fact that the United States by the treaty of 1819 had inherited Spain's claim, though this was not fully exploited in the later negotiations. Great Britain claimed to have established previously a share in Spain's claim by the Nootka Sound Convention of 1790. The United States contended that the Nootka Sound Convention had been wiped out by the outbreak of war between Great Britain and Spain in 1796.[2]

---

[1] See below, Ch. XXIII.

[2] There was another Anglo-Spanish convention, of 1794, never officially printed in English, supplementing the convention of 1790. It provided, among other things, that the subjects of both nations might "frequent occasionally" the port of Nootka, construct temporary buildings, etc., and further that "neither the one nor the other of the two parties shall make any permanent establishment in the said port or claim there any right of sovereignty or territorial dominion to the exclusion of the other." (Manning, *op. cit.*, prints a translation.) Though this convention was printed in Spanish in 1842, it was never made use of in the final diplomatic discussions over the Oregon Ques-

The United States and Great Britain were unable to agree in negotiations between 1824 and 1826. Canning was willing to take as a "compromise" the line of 49° westward only to its intersection with the Kootenai, thence down that river to the Columbia and down the Columbia to its mouth, with free navigation to the citizens and subjects of both powers. He finally went so far as to offer to the United States an area of territory north of the Columbia: the Olympic Peninsula north of a line from Hood's Canal west to the ocean. This was the first British recession from the line of the Columbia. The United States offered to accept as a "compromise" the line of 49° extended from the crest of the Rocky Mountains straight through to the Pacific Ocean, with the free navigation of the Columbia to and from British territory north of the line.[1] Discounting the exaggerated claims of each party, the real area of dispute was the triangle of territory comprising the northwestern two-thirds of the present state of Washington including Puget Sound: to wit, that region between the Columbia River and the 49th parallel of latitude.

Failing to agree on a boundary, the two powers ratified a new convention (1827) extending indefinitely the stipulations of the treaty of 1818, but providing that it might be abrogated by either party after one year's advance notice. The Oregon Question then remained dormant until the negotiations of Webster and Ashburton in 1842. President Tyler was an ardent annexationist, if not so determined as his successor Polk. In addition to his desire to annex Texas, he thought he saw a way of combining a settlement of the Oregon Question with the acquisition of northern California, including San Francisco, by a voluntary cession by Mexico to the United States. Ashburton recommended this to Aberdeen as good policy; but the negotiators felt that to bring in the question of Oregon might jeopardize the removal of their more immediate anxiety, the northeast boundary dispute, so they shelved Oregon for the time being. Webster may have hesitated because of a report in June, 1842, by Lieutenant Charles Wilkes, U. S. N., who had returned from a voyage of reconnaissance to the Oregon country, that it was desirable to advance the boundary line north of 49° so as to include Vancouver Island, the

---

tion. If the convention of 1790 was still in force during the Oregon negotiations, as the British maintained, so then was the supplementary one of 1794, which made the American claim inherited from Spanish sources equally good with the British. If the supplementary convention of 1794 were not in force, then neither was the Nootka Convention of 1790, and thus also would have preserved the American claim of equality inherited from Spain. Dr. Hunter Miller drew my attention to this important point.

[1] Joseph Schafer, "The British Attitude Toward the Oregon Question, 1815-1846," *Am. Hist. Rev.*, XVI (1911), 291.

mouth of the Fraser River and Puget Sound, for strategic purposes.[1] As the British Government had complicated the northeastern boundary by demands for a strategic rectification, so at least this American naval officer opposed the line of 49° as inadequate.

In the atmosphere of good will that followed the ratification of the treaty of 1842 both governments were desirous of proceeding to a settlement of the northwestern boundary. It was then that Tyler and Webster concerted to pursue the President's pet project. The Secretary of State privately suggested to Edward Everett, American Minister in London, that the United States would concede a large portion of the territory north of the Columbia if Great Britain would join in putting diplomatic pressure on Mexico to cede California north of 36° for a substantial sum of money, to be agreed upon, out of which Mexico would then pay British and American creditors. The territorial concession that Tyler and Webster had in mind to make to Great Britain was the region north of the Columbia and east of a line dropped from the head of Admiralty Inlet on Puget Sound straight south to that river. This would have retained for the United States the Olympic Peninsula and the land to the south of it, and harbors on Puget Sound. Webster informed the British Minister at Washington that a special mission would be sent to England [2] to settle the Oregon Question by a tripartite agreement among the United States, Great Britain and Mexico which would include a cession of California, with San Francisco for the United States. Webster expected to go to London himself to work out such a diplomatic combination, but after confidential consultation by the President with the Committee of Foreign Affairs of the House of Representatives, that committee reported against any appropriation to defray the expenses of such a mission. After Webster's resignation, Tyler became engrossed with Texas treaty negotiations. The proposed Tyler-Webster combination contrasts vividly with the staunch stand of every other American diplomatist at the line of 49°.[3] Unlike Canning's embarrassing concession offering a settlement which would have left the Olympic Peninsula to the United States, this project of the President and the Secretary of State does not appear to

[1] This report was printed in the *Congressional Record* for July 15, 1911 (Vol. XLVII, 2977 *et seq.*). A former mission of investigation, under William A. Slacum, a purser in the navy, had made an informing report on conditions in Oregon in 1837.

[2] The mission was suggested by the British Minister, Fox, acting on instructions. I am indebted for this point to an unpublished thesis by Mr. Jarves O. McCabe of Glasgow, Scotland, who perused the records of the British Foreign Office and the private papers of Lord Aberdeen.

[3] Reviews of this proposal are in C. H. Carey's *History of Oregon* (Chicago and Portland, 1922), and C. A. Duniway, in *Am. Secs State,* V, 57-60.

have gone any further than informal discussion with Ashburton. Canning's proposal, on the other hand, remained a matter of formal diplomatic record for all to see.

Both governments expressed desire to settle the Oregon Question after 1842: the British on the line of the Columbia, the United States on the line of 49°. Secretary Calhoun, however, perceived that a policy of "masterly inactivity" would work more to the advantage of the United States than of Great Britain. He refused an offer of arbitration.

What awakened the Oregon Question and made a political issue of it, and hence an international issue, was the increasing weight of American immigration which had set in beginning 1841, and the interest of the western states in protecting these emigrants. Postponement of a definitive settlement of the boundary had been of great advantage to the United States because it had allowed time for overland migration. In the "great emigration of 1843" over 800 pioneers crossed the plains and mountains in covered wagons and settled in the Willamette Valley. Oregon by 1843 had become a burning political issue in Congress. There was a movement for the abrogation, in due form, of the convention of 1827, and organization of an American Territory of Oregon, to extend as far north as 54° 40'. The Democrats sensed popular sentiment running strongly, particularly in the western states, for the annexation of all of Texas and all of Oregon. They epitomized the demand in the alliterative slogan "fifty-four forty or fight." We remember that the Democrats won the election of 1844, in which the issue of expansion had been vociferously championed. With one war now imminent with Mexico, would the new expansionist President, James K. Polk, want also to fight Great Britain for fifty-four forty, supposing that Great Britain were determined not to yield?

Despite the fire and heat of campaign oratory, Polk preferred not to fight for fifty-four forty, if he could avoid it. The American public had been impressed by debates in Parliament, following the President's inaugural address, which showed unanimity of British opinion in support of the Government's determination not to be pushed out of Oregon by words. The new President found a way to retreat from extremes. His Secretary of State, James Buchanan, stated (July 12, 1845) to Pakenham, the British Minister at Washington, that the President was willing to retire from the demand for fifty-four forty because he "found himself embarrassed, if not committed by the acts of his predecessors." Buchanan offered to divide the territory by the 49th parallel extended across Vancouver Island to the Pacific Ocean, with free ports for Great Britain on that island south of the line. Pakenham, feeling strengthened, no doubt, by the echo of the recent debates in Parliament, abruptly refused this offer without even first referring it home. At the express direction of the President,[1] Secretary Buchanan reluctantly but formally withdrew the offer, and the President pronounced for fifty-four forty. Somewhat disingenuously [2] in his annual message Polk was able to place on Great Britain the responsibility for failure to adjust the issue peaceably. He invoked the Monroe Doctrine to forbid the extension of any European colonization or dominion on the continent of North America—undoubtedly he had in mind Oregon and California; and he advocated a resolution by Congress in favor of giving the one year's notice required for abrogation of the treaty of 1827. "The only way to treat John Bull is to look him straight in the eye," he confided to his diary, which was never intended for publication. The President's eye wavered when presently he heard of British preparations for war.[3]

If Polk was cautious, Peel's Government was even more so. During the American election campaign Aberdeen had made up his mind to concede the line of 49° carried to the sea, if the United States would not arbitrate the question.[4] Acceptance by the local authorities of the Hudson's Bay Company in 1845 of the jurisdiction of the provisional government organized by American settlers in the Oregon country, the corporation's change of its western base from the Columbia River to Vancouver Island in the same year, and its apathy thenceforth for the valley of the Columbia and its depleted fur reserves, confirmed Peel in Aberdeen's policy of concession.[5] The Government began to prepare public opinion [6] to accept a reversal of long-standing policy.[7] Aberdeen had privately writ-

---

[1] *Diary* of James K. Polk, Aug. 26-30, 1845.

[2] Polk had already heard from Louis McLane, Minister to London, that Aberdeen was in favor of accepting the line of 49° if Great Britain could retain all of Vancouver Island, and continue certain rights of the Hudson's Bay Company. He knew this, in fact, when he withdrew the offer of 49° which Pakenham had rejected. Miller, *Treaties*, V.

[3] J. W. Pratt, *Canadian Hist. Rev.* (Dec., 1943), 241-49.

[4] The significant letters of Aberdeen to Peel, used by historians on this point, have been published by R. C. Clark, in *Ore. Hist. Quar.*, XXXIV (1933), 236-240.

[5] Frederick Merk, "The Oregon Pioneers and the Boundary," *Am. Hist. Rev.*, XXIX (July, 1924), 681-699.

[6] Frederick Merk, "British Government Propaganda and the Oregon Treaty," *Am. Hist. Rev.*, XL (October, 1934), 38-63.

[7] This decision was fortified by reports from special inquiries made in the Pacific Northwest: one by a military mission (Lieutenants Warré and Vavasour) sent overland from Canada (whose report arrived too late to serve in any decision); and another under Captain Gordon, brother to Aberdeen, and Lieutenant William Peel, son of the Prime Minister, who visited Puget Sound early in 1846 on a British frigate, *America*.

ten Pakenham (April 18, 1845) that if Buchanan should offer the line of 49° to the sea it might prove to be not unacceptable.[1] He reproved the minister for peremptorily rejecting Buchanan's offer of that line carried across Vancouver Island, and he directed him again to propose arbitration. Polk's Cabinet persistently rejected arbitration. They decided to prepare for war, not to put forth the offer of 49° again (as Pakenham now suggested); but if the British Minister would offer on his part the line of 49° as far as Fuca Strait, the President at least would take the Senate's advice on acceptance. Despatches from the American Minister at London had made it clear that the British Government would put forward such an offer, as it prepared new armaments. Soundings of representative senators made reasonably certain that the Senate would accept. This disposition was allowed to become known to the British Foreign Office.[2] At the same time Polk recommended to Congress increased naval and military forces for protecting emigrants to Oregon. With the mandate of a joint resolution of Congress (April 26, 1846) he courteously transmitted the required year's notice for the termination of the treaty, expressing the hope that this would hasten a friendly adjustment.

It did. The British Government saw the United States meant business at least up to 49° and that Polk was backed strongly by public opinion, particularly in the West.[3] Oregon was vital to American expansion; at best it was a distant outpost for the British colonial empire. The Peel Ministry was addicted to the prevailing political philosophy in England that colonies were becoming liabilities rather than assets. Neither the weakening Peel Cabinet, nor Russell and Palmerston, the leaders of the Liberal opposition, nor the English people, wanted to fight for faraway Oregon any more than they did for Texas or for California; but the United States chose to deal with the reasonable Aberdeen in preference to the redoubtable Palmerston who was likely to succeed him at any moment because of the precarious condition of English party politics. The disposition of Peel, with his new free-trade policy, to keep on friendly terms with an American administration which had embarked on a low-tariff policy, also had a soothing influence. Nor must one overlook the fact that the British navy in 1845 and 1846 was entangled in an embarras-

[1] St. George L. Sioussat, in *Am. Secs. State*, V, 395.

[2] R. L. Schuyler, "Polk and the Oregon Compromise of 1846," *Pol. Sci. Quar.*, XXVI (1911), 443-461.

[3] D. W. Howe has analyzed the mounting demand of the West for all of Oregon in "The Misssisippi Valley in the Movement for Fifty-four Forty or Fight," in *Miss. Vall. Hist. Assoc. Proc.*, V (1911-1912), 99-116.

sing intervention with France in the La Plata River region.[1] After reaching an understanding with the Opposition [2] on the line of 49°, and knowing that it would be acceptable in Washington, Aberdeen sent over a draft treaty embodying that boundary to the Straits of Fuca, providing for the free navigation of the Columbia River for the Hudson's Bay Company,[3] and confirming the possessory rights of that company and its subsidiary, the Puget Sound Agricultural Company. This proposal, which Polk had good reason to expect before he sent in his war message on Mexico, reached the United States after the declaration of that war. Polk could not have been displeased to read it. He immediately (June 10, 1846) submitted the draft, intact, to the Senate for its advice. That body quickly voted (June 12), 37-12, in favor of such a treaty. Straightway Buchanan and Pakenham signed it (June 15), word for word as it had been drafted at Downing Street, and the Senate formally ratified it, by a vote of 41 to 14, three days later. They were in a hurry now. War had broken out between the United States and Mexico. Peel's Government might any day fall from power in England and ruin a chance of immediate settlement.

Thus President Polk had won a major diplomatic victory with the greatest power in the world, and the United States was left perfectly free to pursue by war its affair with Mexico. Even before news had reached England of the actual settlement of the Oregon boundary, Lord Aberdeen had sent word to Mexico declining to interfere in her

[1] R. C. Clark, "British and American Tariff Policies and Their Influence on the Oregon Boundary Treaty," *Proc. of the Pacific Coast Branch of the Am. Hist. Assoc.*, 1926, 32-50. T. P. Martin, "Free Trade and the Oregon Question, 1842-1846," in the Gay Memorial volume, *Facts and Factors in Economic History* (Cambridge, Mass., 1932), states that the imminent repeal of the British corn laws, with consequent advantage to western wheat exporters, broke the force of the extremist demand for 54° 40'. Henry Commager published a thoughtful analysis of British motives for concession, "England and the Oregon Treaty of 1846," *Ore. Hist. Quar.*, XXVIII (1927), 18-38. A most important article by Frederick Merk, "The British Corn Crisis and the Oregon Treaty," *Agricultural History*, VIII (July, 1934), 95-123, completely destroys the thesis that Great Britain was impelled to concessions because of her requirements for uninterrupted importations of foodstuffs from the United States.

[2] Frederick Merk, "British Party Politics and the Oregon Treaty," *Am. Hist. Rev.*, XXXVII (1932), 653-677.

[3] Secretary Buchanan, two days before signing the treaty, instructed McLane to state to the British Government the Senate's "conviction" that the right of the Hudson's Bay Company would expire May 30, 1859 (i.e., the Hudson's Bay Company's license to trade with the Indians in those regions). In reply to this Aberdeen instructed Pakenham (July 1, 1846) to insist that the negotiators of the treaty fully understood that the right to navigate the Columbia would not be limited by time. Aberdeen also made the same clear to McLane, American Minister in London. Miller, *Treaties*, V.

In the argument before the arbitration of 1868, relative to the possessory rights of the Hudson's Bay Company, the counsel for the United States publicly admitted the right of navigation "exactly as laid down in the 2d article."

war with the United States.[1] "Just to see, Mr. Minister, how events un-
roll in this country," wrote the disinterested Minister of France in Washington, "one would say that there is something providential in the success that crowns the enterprises of the young republic, for it seems to act
more by the instinct of its destiny than by serious reflection on its
power."[2] Historians have dwelt much on the then current expression
of "manifest destiny,"[3] a manifest destiny to expand pacifically so as to
include the whole continent under the American flag, which certainly
captured the imagination of the people and their more virile leaders.
James K. Polk never espoused the more extravagant expressions of this
popular idea, but there is no gainsaying the courage and success, not to
mention the nerve and good fortune, with which he guided American
diplomacy during the greatest years of territorial expansion.

The Oregon Question was not cleared up fully and finally until after
two international arbitrations, at least one of which, the water boundary,
might have been avoided if Polk at the last minute had not been eager to
accept *verbatim* the British draft of the treaty of 1846. One was to determine the precise value of the possessory rights of the two British companies, and to extinguish them by purchase. A joint commission, set up
by a convention of 1863, awarded (1869) a total of $650,000 gold. The
treaty of 1846 stipulated that from the point where the 49th parallel
reaches the coast line the international boundary should proceed along
the middle of the channel which separates the continent from Vancouver
Island to the Straits of Fuca and out to sea. Again the lack of a map and
precise descriptions of boundary caused trouble. The question arose
which was that channel, the Canal de Haro, claimed by the United States,
or the Strait of Rosario, claimed by Great Britain. The answer involved
the possession of the San Juan Islands, which were beginning to be

[1] Channing, *Hist. U. S.*, V, 561-562. In sending the draft treaty for Pakenham to
present, Aberdeen gave him full discretion to postpone the delivery of it, in case "some
state of things may have arisen in the United States, which, in your judgment would render it desirable to withhold our proposals from being made to the government." Pakenham correctly interpreted Aberdeen's thought that this did not mean the outbreak of war
between the United States and Mexico. We may guess that Aberdeen had in mind a
collision and local hostilities in the Oregon country. Hunter Miller, in his voluminous
notes to Volume V of his *Treaties* has given an extended treatise on the negotiation of
the Oregon Treaty, reprinting relevant documents, and printing for the first time many
important American and British despatches and instructions.

[2] Quoted in the digest of correspondence published by George Verne Blue, "France
and the Oregon Question," *Ore. Hist. Quar.*, XXXIV (March and June, 1933), 39-59,
144-163.

[3] In addition to the many historical passages on this idea, see J. C. Parish, *The
Emergence of the Idea of Manifest Destiny*, a lecture printed by the University of
California Press (1932), and Julius W. Pratt, "John L. O'Sullivan and Manifest Destiny,"
in *New York History*, XIV (July, 1933), 213-234.

settled in 1853. More important than that was the question of the
strategical defense of Vancouver Island, considered to be menaced by any
American island only seven miles away, if the Haro Channel were accepted. This strategic factor, rather than refinements of treaty interpretation, or cartographical argument, was the principal British concern.

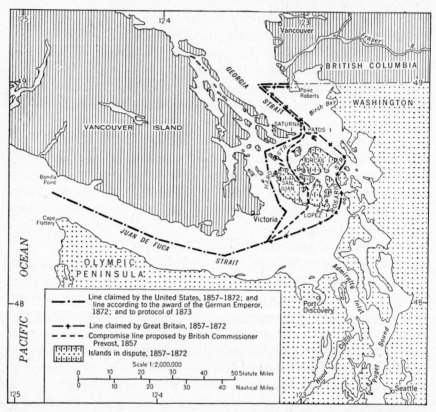

Map 19. Controversy and Settlement of the Water Boundary from the 49th Parallel
out to the Pacific Ocean.

The San Juan Islands were also (and are more so today in the age of
aerial navigation) of great importance to the United States in commanding the entrance to Puget Sound. A mixed commission of two, created
by the two governments in 1856 to determine the proper channel,
disagreed.

The controversy assumed more significance when the Fraser River gold
strike was announced in 1858. Local conflicts in the islands brought to
the defense of nationals the military and naval forces of both powers,
but their commanders wisely abstained from conflict. Not until the

treaty of Washington of 1871 was this question put in the way of settlement, by reference to the arbitration of the German Emperor. During the negotiations for a convention of arbitration Great Britain had sought to empower the arbitrator to draw a compromise line if he should see fit to do so. It was hoped that such a possibility might save at least the strategically valuable island of San Juan. Any compromise at all would have had to award that island to Great Britain, for it adjoined the Haro Channel and was nearest to Vancouver Island. The Senate refused to ratify a convention (signed January 16, 1869) which would have permitted a compromise. In the treaty of Washington the American negotiators successfully resisted any possibility of allowing a compromise award: the arbitrator was obliged to decide which channel the treaty of 1846 really meant, Haro or Rosario. He decided in favor of the Canal de Haro (October 21, 1872), thus placing the whole San Juan archipelago, with its pleasing sites for summer homes, within the acknowledged possession of the United States. Today the ocean liners take the Haro Channel from the Straits of Fuca to the port of Vancouver on the mainland, thus confirming in a practical way the arbitrator's judgment that this is the main channel.

We can balance against each other the two major boundary settlements with Great Britain. In the northeast the title of the United States which Great Britain had challenged was perfectly good—recent investigations into historical cartography prove that beyond a doubt.[1] In the northwest the title of Great Britain against which the United States had contended was much better than that of the Republic. No fair-minded student of the Oregon controversy can maintain that the American claim to the region north of the Columbia River was as strong as that of Great Britain. Webster sanely compromised in 1842, for the sake of peace, where compromise represented really a retreat, as we see it now. Aberdeen wisely compromised in 1846, for the sake of peace, where compromise was essentially surrender, surrender of territory to which his government certainly had the better claim, and to which preceding governments had clung with unyielding tenacity. Really neither settlement was a compromise. The new northeastern boundary was a British diplomatic victory. The new northwestern boundary was an American diplomatic victory. Both were victories for peace.

[1] Even before the discovery of the Aranda transcript of Franklin's Red Line Map, such acute Canadian historians as W. F. Ganong, *op. cit.;* James White, in *Canada and Its Provinces,* Adam Shortt and A. G. Doughty, eds. (23 Vols., Toronto, 1914-17), VIII, 824-825; and E. Dudley Mills, in *United Empire Magazine* for October, 1911, had made this clear. See L. Martin and S. F. Bemis, *N. E. Hist. Quar.,* X (Mar., 1937), 105-111

CHAPTER XVII

CLAIMS AND COMMERCE

(1815-1861)

THE most prominent chapters of the diplomatic history of the United States in the period between the Peace of Ghent and the outbreak of the Civil War concerned the defense and extension of its political frontiers. This should not obscure from our vision certain other more prosaic developments of national growth. During this half-century of expansion from Atlantic to Pacific in which the territorial basis of the federal republic was secured, the overseas commerce of the nation was steadily growing, the American merchant marine was establishing itself as the largest, and the formal diplomatic relations of the government, hitherto confined to the maritime fringe of western Europe and the Baltic, were extending throughout the rest of the civilized world. The expanding sphere of foreign relations across the seas brought up for solution an array of new subjects, distinct from continental expansion and policy. Among them, it is appropriate at this point to review the subject of international claims, and questions connected with the regulation of foreign commerce.

A rather careless assumption by certain historical writers is that the United States has always kept a quiverful of pecuniary claims to exchange for coveted territory. Providing the claims are just there would be nothing reprehensible about their satisfaction in that way. Possibly the cancellation of claims by two of the greater powers, France and Spain, as partial payment for Louisiana and Florida, has been the basis for this unwarranted suggestion. The fact is that the United States, in contradistinction to European powers, has never issued a full-fledged ultimatum over an international monetary claim; this may be why American citizens have sacrificed so many billions of dollars to foreign countries, particularly in recent years. Far from being the manifestation of a predatory process, the presentation and liquidation of claims of this sort constitute a proud and enduring record of peace.

The international claims which formed such an active chapter of American diplomacy during the period under discussion were principally of two categories: those arising out of spoliations during the great European wars of 1793-1815; and those originating from irresponsible damages to

American citizens or their property during the revolutionary disturbances which had swept over Hispanic America. Because during this period the United States had been at peace with all the world except England in 1812-1814, undisturbed by revolutionary violence, and blessed with a constitution admirably suited, during that period of its history, to secure the equality of all classes and persons, national and alien, before the law, there were very few claims against itself by foreign powers. The War of 1812 had wiped out spoliation claims against Great Britain. A claims convention of 1853 settled "with complete and even felicitous success"—to use Seward's later reference—all the miscellaneous claims then accumulated between the two countries.[1] The United States assumed claims against Spain for spoliations, and other reasons, as a part of the bargain for the Floridas struck in 1819. Another group of Spanish claims was for illegal captures (1821-23) made during the war against her revolted colonies. These were settled for a lump sum by the so-called Van Ness convention of 1834. The early claims against France for spoliations had been liquidated by the convention of 1800 and the Louisiana purchase of 1803; but another group, for spoliations committed in the wars between 1803 and 1815, remained a solicitude of American diplomacy. There were also spoliation claims against Russia, Denmark, Portugal, the Netherlands, and the Two Sicilies, all [2] arising out of the maritime operations of the Napoleonic wars. Despite continued importunities, little was accomplished with these until President Jackson's time.

Except with France, the claims presented no serious difficulties. After tedious discussions Russia and Portugal [3] accepted them and paid, the arrangements being made by executive agreements. This was a precedent for an expanding list of executive agreements for the settlement of such questions which has steadily encroached on the treaty-making power of the Senate, so far with no bad results. The issues with Denmark, Sweden, the Two Sicilies, and the Netherlands were more involved. Claims against those countries were for confiscation of American neutral shipping by execution of Napoleon's arbitrary decrees which the Emperor had obliged those smaller kingdoms to enforce.

[1] Moore, *International Arbitrations, op. cit.*, I, 391-425. The total awarded to American claimants was $329,734.16, to British claimants, $277,102.88.

[2] One item of the Russian claims was for damages resulting from expulsion of the Brig *Pearl* from waters of the northwest coast in 1823.

[3] The claims settled with Portugal by the executive agreement of 1832 were for damages for detention of three American ships during an irregular blockade of Terceira, in the Azores, in 1829-30, in a civil war of succession to the Portuguese crown. Not until 1851 was the long-standing spoliation claim of the *General Armstrong*, arising out of the Napoleonic wars, submitted to arbitration (and lost) by a special convention.

The Danish Government did not attempt to elude its responsibility. It resisted the claims by refusing to admit that the decisions of its prize courts—which were conducted on an unusually high plane of justice—could be subjected to review in discussions with any foreign power. Henry Wheaton, an able international lawyer, went to Copenhagen as *chargé d'affaires* and argued that prize courts, instead of exempting the sovereign of the belligerent state from responsibility, were designed to fix that responsibility; until a prize court had confirmed the acts of captors the neutral could not complain, but if the sentence was unjust the neutral could then hold the belligerent sovereign responsible; this was what the United States was doing. The Danish Government offered a lump sum of $650,000 for release from all claims.[1] This the United States accepted (convention of 1830).

Sweden in 1825 compounded for a lump sum of $60,000 with American claimants on account of the so-called Stralsund claims [2] for property sequestered in Swedish Pomerania during the Napoleonic wars. These claims had long been supported by the Department of State.

The claims against the Government of the Two Sicilies were on account of seizures of American neutral ships in Neapolitan waters in execution of Napoleonic decrees during the reign there of Napoleon's brother-in-law, Joachim Murat. In a long-drawn-out controversy, the Neapolitan Government had refused to pay them on the ground that Murat had been an interloping sovereign, never recognized by the legitimate Bourbons who were restored after Napoleon's downfall and Murat's execution. The United States held the Kingdom of the Two Sicilies responsible nation to nation, and persistently pursued the matter. In 1832 the monarchy offered to compromise by paying a lump sum. After considerable haggling, John Nelson, Andrew Jackson's minister sent to Naples for the purpose, accepted $2,119,230 [3] in full satisfaction. He believed that the friendly visit of a small squadron of American warships had assisted him in securing agreement to a convention. Another factor in his favor was that the French Government had just agreed to payment of a lump sum for spoliations in France, many of them under these same decrees.[4]

[1] The whole number of captures or seizures had been 160, of which 42 were condemned. The total claims against Denmark, as presented by the claimants, had aggregated $2,662,280.36 in 1827. Moore, *International Arbitrations*, V, 4549-4573.

[2] K. E. Carlson, *Relations of the United States with Sweden* (Allentown, Pa., 1921), 45-71.

[3] This represented 2,115,000 ducats payable in 10 annual installments with interest at 4% from date of ratification of the convention.

[4] Paul C. Perrotta, O. P., has described the settlement of the Neapolitan claims, from the American sources, in *The Claims of the United States Against the Kingdom of Naples* (Washington, D. C., 1926).

The United States in 1820, under Secretary John Quincy Adams' direction, abandoned its efforts to collect from the Kingdom of the Netherlands for similar spoliations during the usurping French régime there. The technical distinction made between such captures in the Netherlands under French decrees, and similar captures in Denmark and Naples, was that the Netherlands had been actually annexed to the French Empire in 1810; liability for those spoliations was therefore attached to France, and they were ultimately paid off from the French indemnity.[1]

The French spoliations claims, 1803-1815, presented the most spectacular dispute, not in securing admission of liability, but in getting them actually paid. These were, of course, the largest group of claims outstanding from the Napoleonic wars. As presented by the claimants, without deflation by judicial scrutiny, they totaled over $12,000,000 without interest. They included cases of appropriations and condemnations of property in violation of the Convention of 1800, irregular condemnations or confiscations, retroactive condemnations, condemnations under the "retaliatory" Berlin and Milan decrees, both before and after their pretended revocation on November 1, 1810, and other arbitrary procedures. The tremendous task of digesting these complicated technical cases and presenting them for redress was assigned to the able diplomatist Albert Gallatin, Minister to France, 1816 to 1823. The French Ministry was not disposed to deny the justice of many of them. They told Gallatin that there were similar claims held by other powers, too, that although a large part of these had been abandoned, the remainder, which France had agreed to settle, were so great that France could not contract to pay. A "silent postponement" until better times was suggested.

Gallatin departed from France without an adjustment. The technicalities of the controversy were becoming blurred by the passage of time, and the lack of national feeling made it difficult for Presidents Monroe or Adams to present them forcefully. General Jackson, when he came into the White House in 1829, personified the rising national consciousness more than even the veteran diplomats who had been his predecessors in office. In the first message to Congress he based his foreign policy on an announced purpose "to ask nothing that is not clearly right and to submit to nothing that is wrong." The claims against France he apparently thought clearly right, and not to pay them clearly

---

[1] Peter Hoekstra, *Thirty-seven Years of Holland-American Relations, 1803-1840* (Grand Rapids, Mich., 1916). The payment to claimants, *pro rata* 59.8% of their awards, out of the French indemnity totaled $536,907.01. Moore, *International Arbitrations*, V, 4468-4475; and *International Adjudications*, V, 350-403.

wrong. Jackson sent over to Paris the forceful William C. Rives, who
now found the French Government disposed at least to talk about a
final settlement. By way of set-offs it brought up the claims of Beaumarchais' heirs for money alleged to have been due him for supplies
furnished by him to Congress during the American Revolution; and
other claims, for misconstruction, so it was contended, of the most-
favored-nation commercial provisions of the Louisiana treaty of 1803:
Great Britain and other nations, in turn for certain equivalents rendered
by them, had received commercial privileges in all American ports (including those of Louisiana) which France did not enjoy.

The claim of Beaumarchais' heirs raised the old question of whether
the fictitious house of Rodrigue Hortalez and Company, which had
served as a commercial pipe-line from French neutral arsenals to the
American insurrectionists, really should receive payment, despite the
form of a contract by which Congress had agreed to pay. The real
intent for payment had long been questioned by succeeding Congresses
of the United States. The second group of claims advanced by France
brought up the interesting and far-reaching question whether the most-
favored-nation principle should automatically apply, after the prevailing
European practice, to include concessions made to other foreign nations
in return for particular equivalents rendered by special agreements. The
United States took the position that most-favored-nation advantages
included only those enjoyed by other nations without particular bargain
therefor. It had inserted in most of its commercial treaties an article
to this effect, really of French origin,[1] which had first appeared in the
first treaty of the United States, that with France in 1778; the two
parties "engage mutually not to grant any particular Favour to other
Nations in respect of Commerce and Navigation, which shall not immediately become common to the other Party, who shall enjoy the same
Favour, freely, if the Concession was freely made, or on allowing the
same Compensation, if the Concession was Conditional." The Convention of 1800, which succeeded this treaty and continued most-favored-
nation arrangements, omitted the conditional reservation, and the treaty
ceding Louisiana in 1803 stipulated that the ships of France and of
Spain should "forever" be treated "upon the footing of the most favored
nation" in the ports of the ceded territory. With Great Britain (1815)
and with Brazil (1828) the United States had negotiated treaties allow-

---

[1] Vernon G. Setser pointed out the French origin of this article: "Did Americans
Originate the Conditional Most-favored-nation Clause," *Jour. Modern History*, V
(1933), 319-323.

ing, reciprocally, to vessels of the signatory parties, the same treatment accorded to national vessels. This applied of course to all the territory of the United States, including Louisiana; France contended that her ships therefore should be treated in Louisiana ports the same as British ships. Perhaps through oversight [1] the French treaty of 1803 had attached no conditions whatsoever to most-favored-nation treatment. The resulting controversy counseled greater wariness in putting the conditional clause into later most-favored-nation treaties.

After patient negotiation, interrupted by the July Revolution of 1830, Rives accepted in a convention of 1831 a write-off of the American claims against France in return for a lump sum of 25,000,000 francs,[2] payable in six annual installments, the money to be distributed *pro rata* to the claimants by the United States Government. Out of this 25,-000,000 francs was first to be taken 1,500,000 francs in satisfaction of all French claims against the United States (without enumerating them). In the same convention the French construction of the most-favored-nation article of 1803 was abandoned in turn for a reduction of import charges on French wines for a period of ten years.

The new constitution of France of 1830, like that of the United States, gave to the national legislature the control of the nation's purse-strings. Before an appropriation for the agreed reparation had actually been made by the French Chamber, the United States Treasury, upon the occasion of the first installment falling due under the terms of the convention, negotiated through the Bank of the United States a draft on the French Treasury. Now ensued a curious controversy, interesting because it raises the question of what the Congress of the United States itself would do under similar circumstances.[3] The French Minister of Foreign Affairs complained of this prompt action by the United States. He said that the French executive could not pay out money without an appropriation any more than could the President of the United States.

[1] The reason, presumably, had been that neither the Convention of 1800, nor that of 1803 for the transfer of Louisiana, had been treaties of commerce. Consequently they had not contained the usual conditional article.

[2] The sum accepted by the United States was less than half the principal of the original total of claims presented, without allowance for interest; but when the claims were later examined by an American commission which distributed the money they were scaled down from the first total of $12,047,286.09 to $9,362,193.27. Each claimant ultimately received *pro rata* out of the French indemnity 59.8% of his award.

[3] On a number of occasions, but notably in the debates on Jay's Treaty of 1794, on the "Gadsden Purchase" of 1853, and on the Alaska Treaty with Russia of 1867, vigorous objection has been made in the United States House of Representatives to making the appropriations necessary to carry into effect a treaty ratified by the Senate and proclaimed by the President. In no case has the opposition been successful; thus an international issue on such a point has never been precipitated.

The executive would make every effort to carry out the treaty, but it must await the necessary appropriation. The United States held strictly to the terms of the treaty, and maintained that it bound all departments of the French Government to prompt and faithful execution. The Chamber of Deputies repeatedly rejected (1833-1834) the Government's bill for the necessary appropriations. A French Minister of Finances resigned as a consequence.

Jackson now sent to France as minister no less a person than Edward Livingston, recently his Secretary of State, an able lawyer thoroughly familiar with the French language and the background of French law. The King received him cordially and declared that France would honor the convention, though circumstances prevented executing it imme-diately; but the Government's bill for the necessary appropriations again failed, by eight votes, to pass the Chamber (April 2, 1834). Liv-ingston advised Jackson that only energetic measures would save the claims from being lost. Jackson himself was personally responsible for the words written into his annual message of 1834 which expressed doubt of the intention of the French Government, in all its branches, to carry the convention into effect, and asked for the passage of a law authoriz-ing reprisals upon French property in case the Chamber should not provide for payment. Further negotiation, he declared, was out of the question. The Senate, inspired by Whig opposition, refused to back up the President in the matter of reprisals; the House of Representa-tives made a declaration of support; but of course any retaliatory legis-lation required the vote of both houses.

Possibly encouraged by this lack of a united front at Washington, the French Government proceeded to take umbrage at the tone of the President's message and to break off diplomatic relations. At the same time it appropriated the money to pay the debt, but only when a satis-factory explanation should be given of the remarks in the President's message. Before he left Paris, Livingston explained that this was merely a communication between two branches of the American Govern-ment, and that the President had explicitly disavowed any intention of influencing France by a menace. The newly established Orleanist monarchy could not have stood the strain of a conflict. It caused it to be intimated through the friendly offices of Great Britain that an appropriate sentence in the next Presidential message would clear the air. Though Jackson refused to make any explanation direct to France, in his next annual message (1835) he declared to his own nation's Con-gress that the conception that he had intended "to menace or insult

the Government of France was as unfounded as the attempt to extort
from the fears of that nation what her sense of justice might deny
would be vain and ridiculous." The American public was not aware
that this was an apology to a foreign nation, and indeed it was not;
but the French Government was pleased to find in it the satisfaction
it sought and went ahead and paid off the indemnity cordially and
promptly. It had saved its face and honor, and Jackson had submitted
to "nothing that was wrong." [1] Both nations at the last moment had
agreed to accept British mediation for the settlement of their dispute—
Lord Palmerston was eager to mediate so that Great Britain might have
the undistracted support of France in whatever measures might be
necessary against Russia in the Near East. Formal mediation, however, became unnecessary.[2]

Claims against several Hispanic-American nations arose from damages
to American citizens in the war against Spain and in subsequent revolutionary disturbances in various of the new republics. Whether by executive agreements, as in the case of Colombia (1825, 1829), Brazil
(1829), or by actual treaties as with Mexico (1840, 1843), Brazil
(1849), New Granada (1857), they were all adjusted by cash sums, except for the Mexican treaty of 1840. This, as we have seen in another
connection,[3] provided for adjudication of claims by a mixed commission, and the treaty of 1843 arranged for payment of the awards by
a schedule of instalments.

The peaceful settlement of these numerous claims against nations in
both hemispheres, for wrongs done to American citizens, enhanced the
prestige of the United States by demonstrating that it was not a nation
whose rights could be sported away or trifled with. They were the first
of a steady stream of claims both for and against the nation which have
since become an accepted and peaceable, though sometimes an uncomfortable, routine of American diplomacy. In a volume of this scope we
may in the future note only exceptionally significant claims, like the
Alabama claims, the claims against Mexico of 1910-1934, and the claims
arising out of the World War of 1914-1918. In no case have monetary
claims led the United States into war.

[1] The history of the claims against France is set forth in Moore's *International
Adjudications*, V, 311-442. R. A. McLemore has thrown some fresh light in "The
French Spoliation Claims, 1816-1836; a Study in Jacksonian Diplomacy," a pamphlet
published by Vanderbilt University, 1933.
[2] C. K. Webster, "British Mediation Between France and the United States in 1834-
1836," *English Hist. Rev.*, XLII (1927), 58-78.
[3] See above, p. 236.

One of the expectations of American independence was freedom to trade unshackled by British navigation laws with all the nations and ports of the globe. We have seen that the new nation was disappointed in the large expectations which it had nursed in this direction. Independence brought it face to face with the commercial restrictions of the nations of Europe, including their colonial empires. The treaty policy of the new republic, resting on the Plan of 1776, had been to negotiate treaties of commerce and amity with as many nations as possible based on as great a freedom of trade as possible. By freedom of trade one does not mean "free trade" without tariffs—though the United States remained for a long time a very low-tariff country —but freedom from discriminatory duties levied by nations in favor of their own shipping or commerce. The countries with which the United States enjoyed, reciprocally, most-favored-nation privileges were free, as was the United States itself, to levy prohibitions, restrictions, tariffs, and shipping dues and charges on foreign vessels and commerce providing they were no higher on American ships and products than on any other foreign goods. This was the meaning of that "reciprocity" which was such a fundamental of American trade policy: really reciprocity meant equality.

The United States was a growing nation with no colonies but possessed of a virile merchant marine and a large share of natural resources for export; in turn it offered a growing market for manufactures. The founders of the nation were eager to offer a relatively easy access to the growing American market in return for the removal of unequal restrictions and discriminations on their own ships and their own products in the outside world, particularly the prohibitions of foreign trade with the colonies in America of the great maritime powers of Europe, Great Britain, France and Spain, which were so characteristic of the navigation laws of the eighteenth century.

Reciprocity of commercial equality appeared in various treaties of commerce in the period before the War of 1812: with France (1778-1800), Great Britain (1794-1807), the Netherlands, Sweden, Prussia. In other treaties, with Spain, and France after 1800, trade relations were on the basis of mutual convenience for the interests of both parties. Except for the treaty of commerce with France which was in effect from 1778-1800, and allowed a restricted commerce in American vessels with designated ports in the French West Indies during those years, these treaties secured no privileges for ships of the United States to trade with colonial ports of the great maritime powers in America. But again Europe's distresses came to America's aid. The European Wars of 1793 to 1815 brought about an opening into colonial ports in America which no American diplomatist had been able to write expressly into a treaty. French colonial ports were thrown open to neutral shipping by decree, after 1793. Great Britain opened her West India ports by local emergency proclamations to American ships and products during the period of the war from 1795 on. So likewise did Spain in her American colonies. American neutral navigation from 1793 to the Embargo days of 1808 throve and reaped huge profits, despite the restrictions of the European belligerents on neutral rights, those restrictions which were one of the factors that ultimately involved the United States in the same conflict.

The American Revolution, by destroying the British trade walls around thirteen colonies, made the first great breach in the system of colonial monopoly. The French Revolution by the exigencies of war itself made the second breach. The Revolution of the Spanish-American colonies made the third breach. Of these adventitious circumstances in international affairs the United States took the fullest advantage.

After the Napoleonic wars the maritime powers promptly clamped the restrictive devices again upon their American colonies. A spectacular slump in the trade of the United States with those regions immediately took place. Eager to remove discriminations, prohibitions or restrictions, Congress passed the act of March 3, 1815, providing for the repeal of extra, alien duties assessed by the acts of 1789 on foreign ships and goods, in American ports, of such nations as should, on their part, abolish discriminating or countervailing duties operating to the disadvantage of American shipping in their ports.

It became the object of American diplomacy in the following decades to extend as greatly as possible the equal treatment and freedom of American commerce all over the world. So far as the Spanish colonies were concerned, these were opened relatively soon by their independence. For the remaining colonies of Cuba and Puerto Rico, Spain opened their commerce to foreigners in 1823 by a belated reform calculated to help win back the others. We have seen how typical American commercial treaties were negotiated with the new Hispanic-American republics, between 1823 and 1860. They embodied the "small-navy" principles of neutral rights and the most-favored-nation clauses for navigation and commerce. Trade with Hispanic America was steady and growing—averaging about 14% of the total trade of the United States,

1790-1860;[1] and these treaties laid the friendly foundations for the development of what later was to prove a most expansive and profitable field.

It was not so easy to secure with British colonies in the New World a reciprocal equality of trade and navigation. Great Britain by Jay's Treaty and by the commercial convention of 1815 had opened the direct trade of her East Indian colonies to American ships and goods, but she insisted that British North America and the British islands of the West Indies receive the exclusive protection of the imperial navigation system. Trade overland with Canada or by the interior lakes and rivers, continued open after the War of 1812, subject to regulation by either side without treaty provisions; but American ships were excluded from British maritime ports there, as from the West Indies, and so also were competing American products in both colonial regions. In these important areas the old colonial monopoly persisted, fenced in by the characteristic British navigation laws, after that system had begun to break down elsewhere in the colonial world. The benefits of this to the Empire were considered to be as follows: (1) reservation to British ships of the carrying business, (a) between colonies and the British Isles, (b) between the colonies themselves (for example, Nova Scotia and the British West Indies), (c) between the colonies and foreign countries (for example, between the United States and the British West Indies, or Nova Scotia or other maritime provinces); (2) a regulated reservation to British continental colonies of the British West Indian market for foodstuffs and lumber; (3) a help to British navigation in the commerce between England and the United States, through development of the triangular traffic[2] with the continent of North America and the West Indies. The maritime trade between the United States and the British Colonies in North America and the Caribbean was therefore excluded from any regulation by the treaty of commerce of 1815 and its renewals in 1818 and 1827.

The commercial treaty of 1815[3] with Great Britain was the first

[1] See tabulation at end of chapter.

[2] Commerce between England and the United States usually comprised light cargoes of manufactured articles going west and heavy, bulky cargoes of raw materials going east. Frequently American ships went home in ballast. Because British vessels were also loaded with additional cargo for the West Indies, they could freight with a shipment for a port of call in the United States *en route,* and could underbid American freighters accordingly; or, if not having a full cargo on sailing from the West Indies, they could make a short run to a southern port of the United States for a full load at a cheaper rate.

[3] See above, p. 171.

fruitage of the new American policy which we have mentioned as having been laid down in the act of 1815. It wiped out discriminating rates on imports in vessels of the two countries, exclusive of Great Britain's colonial possessions. Goods imported in American vessels were to pay the same rate as those coming to the United States in British vessels, and *vice versa* for imports into the British Isles, with equality of tonnage duties for the ships of both nations. But this treaty did not apply to British colonies in North America or the West Indies. British statesmen saw no reason why the benefits of the imperial navigation system should be extended to the United States unless there were some advantage for Great Britain or its colonies in so doing. Nor can the American historian today see any such reason, particularly when conscious of the fact that foreign ships are excluded from the traffic between the United States and its overseas territories and possessions.

However natural it might be to expect that the larger purposes of commercial regulation within the British Empire, and the stimulation of British navigation might argue for the exclusion of American ships from the British West Indies, however beneficial it might be to Canadian producers to have rival American products excluded from the British Caribbean islands even if brought in British ships, there were powerful motives operating against such exclusion. These came from the British island plantations. Their proprietors were absolutely dependent on the importation of provisions for the feeding of their labor, slave and free, and lumber for the boxing and barreling of their exports; and the British continental maritime provinces, although they could supply an adequate quantity of salt fish, could not furnish enough of the indispensable other provisions, and lumber, to keep the prices within the sphere of profitable plantation management. One of the principal factors leading to the decline of the prosperity of the British sugar islands, and the consequent fall of the planter class there,[1] was the exclusion of American ships for so many years. The planters, and their English affiliates, clamored for the direct entry of American vessels with their cheaper cargoes of provisions and lumber. The lumber and fishing industries of British North America, on the other hand, pled for the continuance of the restriction. This division of interests within the Empire, particularly the sad plight of the West India planters, with their dependence on American foodstuffs, ultimately led to the breakdown of certain parts of the monopoly of colonial navigation.

[1] Lowell Joseph Ragatz, *The Fall of the Planter Class in the British Caribbean, 1763-1833* (New York, 1928).

To John Quincy Adams while he was Secretary of State and later President, during the years 1817 to 1829, fell the task of dealing with the "West Indian Question." He realized of course the dependence of the West India Islands on American products and their cheaper importation in American ships. Resolved to use this weapon to the utmost for the furtherance of reciprocal trade equality with the British colonies, he ultimately overreached himself. Here he made the one great diplomatic mistake of his career. Under Adams' impulsion Congress passed successive acts (1817, 1818, 1820) retaliating with discriminations against British shipping engaged in the colonial trade with the United States. By 1820 this legislation had gone so far as to refuse entry to British ships coming from British colonies in the New World and to prohibit the importation of their products unless coming *directly* from the colony in which they were grown (this last to prevent an indirect importation in British ships around through Canada). It dealt a sharp blow both to the island planters and to the British carrying trade via Canada. It also injured severely southern agriculture in the United States by cutting off the whole West Indian market in an effort to coerce Great Britain to open the colonial ports to American shipping, which was concentrated in the northern and eastern seaboard states.

Thus appeared a division of interest on sectional lines to weaken the stand of the United States in this trade war, just as it had appeared within the British Empire to give pause to imperial policy. It became a race whether Parliament would yield to the plaints of the island planters before Congress bowed to the remonstrances of agrarian interests in the United States. Parliament yielded first. By an act of 1822 it opened a stipulated number of British colonial ports to American ships, on the same terms as enjoyed by British ships, bringing a limited number of American products (enumerated so as to compete the least possible with British North American products), and the exportation of enumerated island products *directly* in American ships to the United States. The act depended on like privileges being extended to British ships in American ports. At the same time it tacitly reserved freedom to levy preferential tariff rates on the same imports when they should come from British North America in British ships. President Monroe thereupon by contingent but temporary powers vested in him by the act of Congress of 1820, opened, until the next session of Congress, American ports to British ships coming *directly* from the colonies, but did not exempt those vessels from the discriminatory alien tonnage and tariff (10% higher) duties imposed on all foreign vessels entering the United States without treaty exemption from such. This last served to keep alive the controversy.

Diplomatic discussions failed to remove these discriminations. It was Adams' contention that British preferential duties on imperial products (some of which were of American origin) imported into the islands solely in British ships from British North-American ports, more than balanced the favors given to American ships by the imposition of the alien tariff and tonnage duties in the United States. He refused to see that Great Britain had the unchallengeable right to regulate to her own advantage navigation exclusively between her own colonies. At Adams' advice Congress passed the act of 1823 allowing the admission of British ships engaged in the limited colonial trade that had been authorized by the act of Parliament of 1822, but making the removal of the alien duties in the United States contingent upon Great Britain's renouncement of preferential duties on similar goods imported into British colonies from "elsewhere" than the United States, i.e., to the British West Indies from British North American ports in British ships. An act of Parliament made certain, conditional concessions in 1825. It extended most broadly the hitherto restricted enumeration of permissible articles of colonial trade with the United States in British or in American ships, on equal terms, but it established the system of preferential duties on imperial products and vessels. Most important, it made the continued admission of American ships into the colonies contingent upon the removal of the American alien duties on British vessels engaged in the same trade.

Congress refused to remove the alien duties. There was a breach in diplomatic discussions for adjustment of the question. Too late, President Adams came to see that he had demanded too much. Not until 1828 did his Secretary of State, Henry Clay, authorize Albert Gallatin, then Minister in London, to concede an entire and reciprocal abolition of all alien and discriminating duties, without insisting on the removal of preferential duties in the British inter-colonial trade. Before Gallatin could make overtures the British Government had closed the colonies again to American ships. Great Britain did this with all the more equanimity because during the interval in which the colonial trade had been open to American ships even on a restricted basis, those vessels had quickly taken over nine-tenths of the carrying trade between the West India islands and the United States. Thus, by British or by American legislation, the direct maritime trade between the United States and British colonies in America (including the West Indies and

South America) was now absolutely closed. To use a word so dear to journalists and professors, the West India Question had reached a perfect *impasse.*

The loss of the regained West Indian commerce became one of the issues in the presidential campaign of 1828. It at least helped to defeat Adams. The election of Andrew Jackson brought a quick solution of the problem. Jackson offered to restore the trade on the basis of the act of Parliament of 1825, stating that the American people had repudiated the policy of Adams. The British Government refused to make a move until the United States by positive legislation had made good Jackson's proposals. Accordingly the President in 1830 secured from Congress an act empowering him, between sessions, to open the ports of the United States to British vessels from the colonies in case he received satisfactory evidence that Great Britain would open its colonial ports to American ships on the terms of the act of 1825. This assurance was presently forthcoming. By the end of the year the trade with the British West Indies and the other colonies in America was completely opened on terms of full reciprocity to British and to American ships, without discriminating duties against the vessels of either nation or their cargoes.[1]

Jackson's "Reciprocity of 1830," essentially a compromise between the extreme positions that had been taken during the controversy, signalized the end of the traditional British system of colonial monopoly, already collapsed in 1822. Soon Great Britain was to become essentially a free-trade country, with the ports of the British Isles and of British colonies all over the world for a long period open on equal terms to foreign and to British ships. This is one of the great achievements of British statesmanship. It has helped powerfully to retain the growing colonies and commonwealths in loyal cohesion within the Empire. After settlement of the colonial trade with the United States on this reciprocal basis, Parliament immediately passed legislation extending preferential tariff treatment to British goods trading with the colonies. That preference is the precedent for the system of inter-imperial preferences which is such an inveterate feature of the British Empire in our own day, and such a valuable economic cement for its structure. Successive American treaties of commerce with Great Britain, as with most countries, have been ever since on a basis of reciprocal treatment

[1] F. Lee Benns has lucidly described the complicated features of *The American Struggle for the British West India Carrying-trade* (Indiana University, Bloomington, March, 1923). (Ind. Univ. Studies, X.)

of ships and cargoes on the same terms as national ships and cargoes, without prejudice to the right of each party to regulate commerce and navigation between its own dominions.

Settlement of the West India Question still left another problem for Anglo-American commercial regulation: the overland commerce with the provinces of North America. This overland commerce, and that by interior navigation, had already been established by domestic legislation on either side of the boundary line, without discrimination, despite the expiration of treaty arrangements.[1] It became of increasing significance in the period between the West India reciprocity of 1830 and the full development of the American railroad system. Upper Canada was developing a closer trade relationship with the neighbors south of the lakes than with fellow Britishers across the ocean. Chafing at the imperial ties and restrictions on self-government, inland Canada became an area of discontent, which led to the easily suppressed armed outbreak of December, 1837. Sympathy with Canadian strivings for independence was quite general in the United States, whose people felt that there was a natural tendency for all the inhabitants of this continent to divorce themselves from European sovereignties, even ultimately to cluster together under the Stars and Stripes. The leaders of the revolt, escaping across the boundary to New York, received enthusiastic welcome. Popular meetings in the larger towns of northern New York and Vermont raised money and supplies for the insurrectionists, who began to enlist volunteers. Quick action by British colonial authorities at Navy Island, and in the affair of the *Caroline,* rather than the resolute vigilance of federal authorities along the frontier, was responsible for breaking up this movement; but it is fair to note that Congress, in contrast to its attitude toward then recent events on the Texas frontier, promptly passed amendments to block up holes in the neutrality law of 1818, and that the Government took more energetic steps to prevent recurrence of such happenings on the northern frontier.

In Canada a pervasive sentiment for annexation to the United States appeared in the 'forties. Support came from conservative elements who feared political domination by a combination of French Canadians and the liberal portion of the English-speaking population, from those who opposed the subordination of Canada (until 1847) to the British navigation laws, and from commercial elements which had been grievously injured by the disappearance of preferential duties for Canadian goods when England began to go free-trade in 1846. "Canadian protests

---

[1] D. R. Moore, *Canada and the United States, 1815-1830* (Chicago, 1910), 99-123.

against the new British policy were unavailing, and to many observers separation from the mother country and union with the United States, whose tariff wall was one of the chief obstacles to Canadian prosperity, seemed inevitable."[1] Until 1850 even responsible British statesmen showed surprising complaisance to the possibilities of Canadian independence, which was widely regarded as only the first step toward annexation by the United States. It is needless to say that public opinion regarded such a tendency with equanimity. It was in 1845 that the phrase Manifest Destiny crystallized a sweeping popular enthusiasm for the ultimate Americanization of the entire continent. In the direction of Mexico this national psychology supported war, but Manifest Destiny was essentially a peaceful phrase—that was the peculiar thing about it. Its seers and its prophets preached no military preparedness. They relied on the spearhead of peaceful penetration and the driving force of political principles.

Out of this tension in Canada came a demand for the leveling of tariff barriers by some sort of reciprocal agreement with the United States. The great majority of the Canadian leaders, who were for preserving the imperial connection, saw in a tariff reciprocity a salutary alternative to annexation, and an arrangement which would prosper Canadian export trade. This appealed to the British Government, in which was vested the power for making treaties, and which was becoming conscious of the political significance, to the Empire, of Canadian economic depression. Lord Elgin, the far-seeing Governor-General of Canada, in 1849 urged on the British Government free navigation and reciprocal low tariffs for trade with the United States as indispensable to prevent convulsion or annexation. In the United States there was little disposition to keep the tariff up as a means of inducing Canadian annexation as a means of avoiding the high tariff. There was sentiment in the northern states in favor of a reciprocal free trade across the boundary in goods the produce or growth of either country, in the belief that it would expand trade and divert an increasing proportion of Canadian raw materials to export from American ports by way of the American rivers, canals, and railroads from the Great Lakes. But sectional rivalries prevented the passage of legislation appropriate to such a reciprocity, despite the eagerness of the Canadian legislature, supported by the British Government, to do its part.

The British Government now sought to accomplish the same result through a treaty. Five years of negotiation were necessary. The United

---

[1] H. L. Keenleyside, *Canada and the United States* (New York, 1929), 122.

States Government refused to consider any reciprocity arrangement which did not also include the British maritime provinces, and desired Great Britain to open all the territorial waters of those provinces to American fishermen beyond the limited coasts available by the treaty of 1818, and also to grant the free navigation of the St. Lawrence River. These demands were acceptable, subject to permission for the importation of British fish into the United States duty free.

The gaining of these equivalents eased the way for the treaty of June 4, 1854. The final negotiations were conducted in Washington by Secretary Marcy and Lord Elgin, the Governor-General of Canada. The historian cannot overlook the fact that Elgin's lavish and liquid hospitality helped greatly to achieve a two-thirds majority in the Senate for the success of the treaty; nor can he be blind to the very considerable and less worthy expenditures of an American agent sent to the maritime provinces to "facilitate" their assent to the fishery article.[1] What really clinched ratification by the Senate was the desire of southern senators to do something to help prevent the possibility of annexation of free-soil Canada,[2] which if it occurred would destroy the political supremacy of their section. The treaty as ratified provided for extension of the fishing "liberties" of the treaty of 1818 to all the coasts, and gave reciprocal privileges to British subjects to fish within American territorial waters on the Atlantic coast as far south as 36° N. L. Great Britain acknowledged the free navigation of the St. Lawrence River by American citizens on equal terms with British ships and subjects; and the United States admitted British subjects and ships to the free navigation of Lake Michigan. A schedule of articles the product and growth of both countries was written into the treaty as free from payment of import duties in either country. It did not include manufactured articles.

The reciprocity treaty of 1854 is the first agreement of the kind in American history for free trade in enumerated products, and one of the very few ever negotiated by the United States.[3] It served to increase the trade of the United States and Canada during the decade of its lifetime; and it allayed Canadian economic and political discontent by giving to the King's subjects nearly all of the advantages of belonging to the American Union, so far as commercial privileges were concerned, at the same time leaving them free to set up a tariff against

[1] Charles C. Tansill, *The Canadian Reciprocity Treaty of 1854* (Baltimore, 1922).

[2] C. D. Allin and G. M. Jones, *Annexation, Preferential Trade and Reciprocity* (Toronto, 1912).

[3] For later experiments with reciprocity treaties, see below, Ch. XXXVIII.

the influx of manufactured goods from the United States.[1] The treaty supplemented the West Indian "Reciprocity of 1830," and, combined with the Anglo-American commercial convention of 1815 (renewed in 1818 and extended indefinitely in 1827), it placed British-American commerce—the most important category of all American foreign commerce—on a most liberal basis. It was hoped that Canadian reciprocity might be the model for other limited free-trade arrangements with more countries, particularly those of the North American continent. A reciprocity treaty was actually negotiated with Mexico in 1859, but its combination with certain expansionist features, and the sectional opposition of Buchanan's foreign policy, laid it to rest in the Senate. After the Civil War the policy of tariff protection seized a firm hold on the United States, as it did on the rest of the world. The Marcy-Elgin Treaty was not renewed, much to the disadvantage of Canada and the United States.[2] Unfortunately efforts to accomplish a similar dispensation by mutual legislation, during the administration of President Taft in 1911, failed largely because of political reasons: Theodore Roosevelt, aggressively attacking Taft and seeking the Presidency for himself again, unblushingly bared the ghost of the old annexation bugaboo to defeat his opponent; and the Canadian Parliament, alarmed, refused to match the contingent tariff reductions of the United States. Since 1866 Canada and the other British provinces in North America have remained on an equality with other nations outside the American tariff wall, while since 1897 a system of imperial preferences to British trade with Canada, over similar trade with the United States, has arisen.

There remained the question of entrance for American vessels into the other European colonies in the New World. The Netherlands persistently refused to admit vessels of the United States into its American colonies until 1852,[3] when a treaty allowed them and their cargoes to come in on the same terms applying to ships flying the Dutch flag— except, of course, for the closed carriage between the Dutch colonies and their home country. The treaty with Sweden-Norway of 1816 admitted

---

[1] Keenleyside, op. cit., 116-137, 294-300, presents an instructive analysis of the economic and political effects of the Marcy-Elgin Treaty. See also J. Laurence Laughlin and H. Parker Willis, Reciprocity (New York, 1903), 30-69.

[2] It ran on by its own force, after the expiration of its ten year term, for two years more, until denounced in due form by the United States.

[3] A reciprocity of equal treatment of Dutch and American nationals and ships was established by legislation in both countries by 1818, for the trade between the United States and the Netherlands in Europe, but this was soon transgressed by the Dutch law of 1822, which allowed a 10% drawback of tariff charges on goods imported in Dutch vessels. Westermann, Netherlands and the United States, op. cit., examines with great detail the question of Dutch-American reciprocity.

American ships on a basis of equality with Swedish-Norwegian ships to the ports of all the dominions of Sweden-Norway; and in 1827 this was extended even to allow American ships to participate on equal terms with Swedish-Norwegian vessels in the carrying trade between the tiny West Indian colony of Saint Bartholomew's Island and Sweden-Norway itself. This was an exception to the general rule of the imperial countries to keep exclusively to themselves the navigation with their own colonies or dominions overseas; when in 1898 the United States became an imperialistic nation it followed the general practice. Neither France (Martinique and Guadaloupe), nor Russia (Alaska) would make treaties acknowledging entrance of American vessels into their colonies —to say nothing of the direct carriage between colonies and mother countries—but the French navigation laws admitted them to French colonies after 1866. Alaska, of course, was purchased outright by the United States in 1867 and immediately came under the latter's monopoly of coastwise navigation.

Another diplomatic problem of commercial relations was the subject of discriminating duties in favor of national shipping. In different countries these assume varying forms: a discrimination for national ships by charging lower tonnage than for foreign ships; the granting of lower tariffs for goods imported or exported in national ships rather than foreign bottoms; and various discriminations in favor of national ships as against foreign ships engaged in the carrying trade from other countries than their own. Following the Peace of Ghent, the United States, by a series of enabling acts, empowered the Executive with means to combat the international practice of such discriminations. Whether by reciprocal legislation or by actual treaty these discriminations in the direct trade, with minor exceptions, and in a large volume of the indirect trade, disappeared by 1850.[1] It is difficult to say whether the increase in American commerce and navigation which followed the abolition of discriminatory duties was due to their removal or to the expanding territory and resources and the growing population of the United States.

The commercial treaties negotiated by the United States during the period 1815-1861 in general followed the model of the earlier treaties, and rested on the *conditional* most-favored-nation basis. For example, the treaties of 1822 and 1831 with France contained special tariff rates exchanged by each side; these, being conditional on special bargains, did

---

[1] L. W. Maxwell, *Discriminating Duties and the American Merchant Marine* (New York, 1926).

not extend *ipso facto* to most-favored nations. Special schedules of tariff charges were incorporated in the treaties made with the nations of the Far East (Siam, China, Japan), and with the Ottoman Empire. The field of regular diplomatic contacts and of treaty relations had expanded by 1860 to include all the nations of the civilized world.[1]

The years under review, 1816-1860, constituted a distinct epoch in the history of American foreign commerce.[2] It was the youth-time of the Republic, when the foreign trade was still characteristically that of an agricultural people. For the first three years after peace, foreign trade swelled to abnormal proportions after all wartime prohibitions had been abolished, only to be followed by a violent reaction and depression beginning in 1818. The great re-export commerce in West Indian commodities, which had been such a profitable portion of the American neutral carrying trade during the long European wars, disappeared almost completely. It was not until 1835 that the total volume of foreign trade of the United States passed the peak that had been reached in 1807 during the Napoleonic wars, the year before Jefferson's Embargo. Jackson's panic of 1837 depressed it again below that peak, until 1846. That year marked the beginning of a lower tariff policy in the United States and of a free-trade policy in Great Britain. From then until 1861, assisted by the Marcy-Elgin Treaty of 1854, foreign commerce expanded with rapidity. The accompanying chart [3] gives a comprehensive statistical glance at the rise of American trade and navigation throughout the years 1790 (when national statistics first began) to 1860. It is not possible to indicate in any but the most general terms the reasons for the fluctuations and the gradual rise of foreign commerce during those years, but certain truths stand out. (1) The wars of the French Revolution and of Napoleon made the United States the principal carrier of the world until it in turn was involved in the conflict and blockaded by its own Embargo and subsequently by the British navy. (2) The period of 1815 to 1836 is a period of burdens on commerce by the international practice of discriminating

---

[1] From 1848 to 1868 there was a United States legation at the Vatican. It was discontinued after the fall of the temporal power of the Pope. Professor L. F. Stock has published *United States Ministers to the Papal States: Instructions and Despatches, 1848-1868* (Catholic University Press, 1933), with an instructive introduction.

[2] E. R. Johnson *et alii, History of Domestic and Foreign Commerce of the United States* (Carnegie Institution of Washington, 1915), II, 5-53; John H. Frederick, *The Development of American Commerce* (New York, 1932).

[3] This chart is on p. 58 of J. H. Frederick, *The Development of American Commerce* (New York, 1932), "from U. S. Shipping Board." Acknowledgment is made to D. Appleton-Century Co. in reproducing it here.

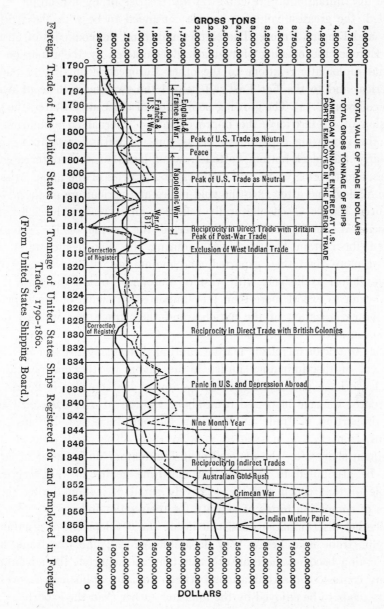

GROSS TONS

------- TOTAL VALUE OF TRADE IN DOLLARS

——— TOTAL GROSS TONNAGE OF SHIPS

— · — · — AMERICAN TONNAGE ENTERED AT U.S. PORTS, EMPLOYED IN THE FOREIGN TRADE

England & France at War

France & U.S. at War

Napoleonic War

War of 1812

Peak of U.S. Trade as Neutral

Peace

Peak of U.S. Trade as Neutral

Reciprocity in Direct Trade with Britain
Peak of Post-War Trade

Exclusion of West Indian Trade

Correction of Register

Correction of Register

Reciprocity in Direct Trade with British Colonies

Panic in U.S. and Depression Abroad

Nine Month Year

Reciprocity in Indirect Trades

Australian Gold-Rush

Crimean War

Indian Mutiny Panic

DOLLARS

Foreign Trade of the United States and Tonnage of United States Ships Registered for and Employed in Foreign Trade, 1790–1860.

(From United States Shipping Board.)

305

duties and by the remaining shackles of the European system of colonial monopoly—it is noticeable that foreign trade increased perceptibly as these discriminations were cut away by treaties or by legislation. (3) Though the greatest volume of trade continued to be with the British Isles and Empire, France, The Netherlands, and the countries of northern Europe, the opening of regularized commerce by the extension of formal diplomatic relations to the other European countries, to South America, and to the Far East, all helped the swelling volume of overseas commerce. (4) The growing population of the United States, the expansion of its territory, the improvement of internal communications, and the increasing exploitation of its unusual natural resources—particularly the black-bottom cotton-growing lands of the southern gulf states, and the rich wheat and cattle-raising prairies of the upper Mississippi Valley, and after 1850 the gold mines and agriculture of the newly acquired Pacific Coast—naturally reflected an increasing foreign commerce. At the beginning of the period the people of the country, except for certain abnormal years during the Napoleonic wars, imported more than they exported, and maintained their overseas commerce almost exclusively with western Europe. Toward the close they had begun to export more than they imported—a signal of the impending industrialization of the nation,—and their trade was webbed over the seven seas.

The American merchant marine continued a steady expansion. The removal of discriminatory duties in its favor, by the understandings which we have noted, did not depress it; on the contrary it flourished the more: tonnage increased from about 250,000 to over 6,000,000, and the proportion of trade in American bottoms increased, by ups and downs, from 23.6% in 1789 to 71% in 1860. The persistence of this dominant share after the removal of discriminatory duties must in large part be attributed to the inherent maritime genius of the American people of that epoch and the relatively small attraction during those years of competing forms of activity for their sailor folk.

Whether discriminations assist or injure the development of a nation's carrying trade is at best a very debatable subject, like free trade, but as a nation becomes more an exporter than an importer, the advantage in any contest of discriminations between equally sophisticated governments tends to be enjoyed by the importer rather than the exporter.

An analysis of the foreign trade of the United States, 1790-1860,[1] shows it to be that of an agrarian nation. In the decade before the

[1] For commerce and diplomacy, 1860-1936, see below, Chap. XXXVIII.

Civil War manufactured articles constituted, as they had through the bulk of the period, only slightly above 10% of the total exports, but this proportion almost doubled in the last years of that decade, indicating that the country was on the eve of the great economic revolution which was to transform it from an agricultural to an industrial nation. As this period closed, nearly one-half of the foreign trade of the United States was with the British Empire; about one-fourth with continental Europe, and about 15% with Latin America.

NOTE

The following tabulation compiled under direction of the author, gives an idea of the foreign trade of the United States during this period, 1780-1860:

COMMERCE OF THE UNITED STATES,[a] IN MERCHANDISE AND GOLD AND SILVER, WITH THE LEADING COUNTRIES AND REGIONS OF THE WORLD FROM:

1789-1860 [b]

	Imports [c]	%	Exports	%	Total Imports and Exports [d]	%
World:	8,641,876,196		7,925,992,146		16,567,868,342	
United Kingdom:	3,229,926,281	37.37	3,296,517,436	41.59	6,526,443,717	39.39
Continental Europe, exclusive of France:	783,995,778	9.07	1,323,293,135	16.69	2,107,288,913	12.72
France:	932,105,822	10.78	955,110,566	12.05	1,887,216,388	11.39
Latin America:	1,422,294,470	16.45	1,109,508,997	13.99	2,531,803,467	15.28
China: [e]	336,279,735	3.89	124,087,792	1.56	460,367,527	2.77
Japan: [f]	78,734	.0009	142,774	.0018	221,508	.0013
Africa:	39,267,744	.45	58,427,475	.74	97,695,219	.58
Other regions:	1,897,927,632 [g]	21.96	1,058,903,971	13.35	2,956,831,603 [g]	17.84
British Empire (1790-1860):	3,732,256,869	43.18	4,051,193,795	51.11	7,783,450,664	46.97
Cuba (1821-1860): [h]	522,283,855	8.30	265,241,842	4.34	787,525,697	6.35
Mexico (1825-1860): [h]	142,659,293	2.38	124,555,844	2.14	267,215,137	2.26
% of Exports which are manufactures [i] (1803-1860):			782,815,445	10.77		

1851-1860 [b]

	Imports	%	Exports	%	Total Imports and Exports	%
World:	2,922,257,539		2,983,986,417		5,906,243,956	
United Kingdom:	1,180,864,020	40.41	1,533,056,182	51.37	2,713,920,202	45.95
Continental Europe, exclusive of France:	288,741,524	9.88	366,186,742	12.27	654,928,266	11.08
France:	375,074,391	12.83	363,838,457	12.19	738,912,848	12.51

(See notes at end of chapter.)

	Imports	%	Exports	%	Total Imports and Exports	%
Latin America, exclusive of Cuba and Mexico:	356,998,118	12.21	181,449,847	6.08	538,447,965	9.11
Cuba:	254,224,432	8.69	97,702,935	3.27	351,927,367	5.95
Mexico:	39,275,839	1.34	32,463,715	1.09	71,739,554	1.21
Canada:	118,445,871	4.05	151,938,466	5.07	270,384,337	4.57
China: e	103,527,731	3.54	40,687,008	1.36	144,214,739	2.44
Japan: f	78,734	.0026	142,774	.0047	221,508	.0037
Africa:	21,519,547	.73	23,310,610	.78	44,830,157	.76
Other regions:	183,507,332	6.27	193,209,681	6.47	376,717,013	6.37
British Empire:	1,430,222,705	48.94	1,858,365,508	62.27	3,288,588,213	55.68
% of Exports which are manufactures i			386,757,001	12.97		

1860 b

	Imports	%	Exports	%	Total Imports and Exports	%
World:	362,166,254		400,122,296		762,288,550	
United Kingdom:	138,596,484	38.26	171,494,531	42.86	310,091,015	40.67
Continental Europe, exclusive of France:	34,991,522	9.66	45,537,447	11.38	80,528,969	10.56
France:	43,219,549	11.93	62,206,278	15.54	105,425,827	13.83
Latin America, exclusive of Cuba and Mexico:	43,573,912	12.03	21,837,935	5.45	65,411,847	8.58
Cuba:	34,032,276	9.39	12,382,869	3.09	46,415,145	6.09
Mexico:	6,935,872	1.91	5,354,073	1.33	12,289,945	1.61
Canada:	18,861,673	5.21	14,083,114	3.52	32,944,787	4.32
China: e	13,566,587	3.74	8,906,118	2.22	22,472,705	2.94
Japan:	55,091	.01	138,774	.03	193,865	.02
Africa:	3,746,693	1.03	3,186,618	.79	6,933,311	.91
Other regions:	24,586,595	6.78	54,994,539	13.74	79,581,134	10.44
British Empire:	177,913,585	49.12	238,887,117	59.70	416,800,702	57.37
% of Exports which are manufactures i			91,829,275	22.95		

a Compiled for the author from *American State Papers, Commerce and Navigation,* official reports of the United States Bureau of Statistics, and *The Foreign Commerce and Navigation of the U. S.*

b Fiscal years.

c Computed from the early import records, which are complete for world totals, but are incomplete for specific countries prior to 1821. The resulting figures and percentages in this column are therefore proportionally reduced.

d The figures are proportionally smaller than they would be if complete figures for imports were available for the early years.

e Includes Hongkong.

f Trade with Japan did not actually begin until after 1854.

g These figures also include the amounts which are deficient in the above imports (see "c").

h Percentages based on years indicated.

i Includes manufactured foodstuffs. Percentages figured on the basis of total exports, domestic and foreign.

CHAPTER XVIII

THE WHIG INTERLUDE

(1849-1853)

BEFORE 1848 the diplomacy of American expansion controlled politics. After 1848 domestic politics tended more and more to dominate diplomacy. The Whig triumph and the passing of President Polk were reactions to the great expansionist achievements of the preceding four years. Under the Whigs, whose statesmen Clay and Webster had opposed aggressive expansion, the nation struggled to adjust the slavery problem to the newly acquired domains; meanwhile it observed a cautious foreign policy—exemplified by the Clayton-Bulwer Treaty of 1850 with Great Britain. The men of the Whig Interlude, with Daniel Webster as Secretary of State again, succeeded at his death by his friend Edward Everett, tried to keep slavery out of sight in international affairs and to nerve the national pride at home in an effort to make people north and south forget talk about disunion and stand firmly on the political Compromise of 1850. They were unsuccessful. Both parties in 1852 stood for the finality of the Compromise, and there was no essential difference between their published platforms; but the Democrats were able to support their candidates with unreserved unity, while some leading Whigs faltered or were silent. The Democrats were accordingly returned to power only to betray the Compromise they had pledged themselves to defend. These were the years when northern presidents held the stirrup for the South to mount to the saddle. To occupy the White House both Pierce and Buchanan (1853-1857 and 1857-1861) had to seek a balance of power between the sections; to do this they had to reconcile their party to the demands of the southern politicians for expansion further into areas attractive to slave labor, as a means of increasing and perpetuating their power in national politics and thus protecting the established institution of slavery. Though Manifest Destiny continued to inspire some northern expansionists, there was in the 'fifties a steady tendency for expansion to become more and more of a sectional demand. This in turn antagonized the North so as effectively to paralyze the foreign policy of the neo-Democrats.

While the triumphant expansion of the United States had been march-ing westward to the Pacific Coast, revolutionary liberalism was sweeping Europe with political ideals of representative government. When the American people turned from their violent territorial growth to observe the interesting events in Europe the new liberalism seemed a victory for the ideals and principles on which their own nation had been founded (if the picture of slavery had been ignored). They responded with eager and sympathetic interest to the struggling republican movement in Ger-many and Hungary, even as they had formed their democratic clubs and rung their church bells when the French Revolution shook Europe at the close of the previous century. But fundamentally they were no more anxious in 1848-1850 than in 1793 to desert counsels and instincts against involvement in European strife.

A safe opportunity to exalt the national spirit over sectional feeling in his own country and to appeal to the new consciousness of national importance presented itself to Webster at the outset of his brief second secretaryship. The famous note to Hülsemann illustrates how in a democratic government responsible political leaders, even statesmen of Webster's stature, are tempted to take advantage of the domestic pre-dicaments of friendly foreign powers to curry popular favor and serve their own political purposes.

The Austrian Government, through its *chargé d'affaires ad interim,* the Chevalier Hülsemann, complained to the United States about its having sent an emissary to the revolted province of Hungary, to watch, "in impatience for the downfall of the Austrian monarchy" for a "favor-able moment to recognize Hungarian independence." This was per-fectly true; the Austrian Government had got hold of the instructions of the agent, A. Dudley Mann, probably through the American consul at Vienna, one Schwarz, who was an Austrian subject.[1] The mission had come to naught, because before Mann arrived in Hungary the revolt had been crushed, with the help of Russian troops. Hülsemann had complained privately to Secretary Clayton about his proceeding, but took no step for formal remonstrance until President Taylor had given expression publicly to sympathy for the Hungarian cause, in his annual message of December, 1849, and had published (March 28, 1850) the papers relating to Mann's mission, including the instructions. Hülse-

---

[1] Such is the surmise of Merle C. Curti, the authority for "Austria and the United States, 1848-1852," in *Smith College Studies in History,* XI, No. 3 (Northampton, Mass., April, 1926). This is a good illustration of the inexpediency of allowing foreign subjects to serve as American consuls, prohibited by law since 1855.

mann asked Webster what the United States would have done if Austria had sent such an agent to South Carolina in 1832? There was no possibility of war with Austria over this incident. Webster decided on a play for popular support by making the American eagle scream. "If you say that my Hülsemann letter is boastful and rough, I shall own the soft impeachment," he wrote to a friend. "My excuse is twofold: 1. I thought it well enough to speak out, and tell the people of Europe who and what we are, and awaken them to a just sense of the unparalleled growth of this country. 2. I wished to write a paper which should touch the national pride, and make a man feel *sheepish* and look *silly* who should speak of disunion."

In reply to Hülsemann's complaint, Webster not only defended the Mann mission, but took occasion also to expand on the proud position of the United States as a successful example of free government: "True, indeed, it is, that the prevalence on the other continent of sentiments favorable to republican liberty is the result of the reaction of America upon Europe; and the source and centre of the reaction has doubtless been, and now is, in these United States." That European sovereigns had on occasion denied the lawfulness of the origin of the government of the United States did not disturb the latter, which covered a rich and fertile region, "in comparison with which the possessions of the House of Hapsburg are but as a patch on the earth's surface." As to implied threats of retaliation, "the government and people of the United States are quite willing to take their chances and abide their destiny." [1] The quickly published note flattered the national pride of the American people in both parties. Even Webster, who had opposed Polk's policy of expansion, had now spoken in glowing comparisons of the great territorial possessions of the United States. The Austrian Government felt about this as the United States would feel today if similarly addressed by the Union of Socialist Soviet Republics. It squirmed in indignation, but could do nothing.

Encouraged by the swelling popular approval of his note to Hülsemann, and conscious of his own candidacy for the Whig nomination for the Presidency in 1852, Webster made one more play to the gallery for political capital at the expense of the Hapsburgs of Austria. Kossuth, the famous Hungarian patriot, was an exile in Turkey. President Fillmore (March 3, 1851) signed a joint resolution of Congress which had been passed in harmony with the new national elation: "for the relief

[1] Webster to Hülsemann, December 21, 1850. The affair is conveniently summed up by Duniway, in *Am. Secs. State*, VI, 85-94.

of Louis Kossuth and his associates, exiles from Hungary." An American naval vessel was detailed from a Mediterranean cruise to fetch them to the United States, though Kossuth rather ungraciously got off at Gibraltar to make a visit to England. When he finally reached Washington, Congress gave him a banquet. Webster was the principal speaker. The Secretary of State, who later explained to Austria that he was speaking only as a private citizen—he could hardly have uttered words in a more public manner—made a political speech extolling Hungarian liberty: "Hungarian independence, Hungarian self-government, Hungarian control of Hungarian destinies." Again the public applauded him, but he lost the nomination because of the opposition of the northern Whigs to the stand he had so resolutely taken for compromise with the slavery question in the interests of union in 1850. Hülsemann after this speech withdrew from the capital in order to avoid contact with the obnoxious Secretary of State, who refused to take back his words. After Webster's death (October 24, 1852) the Austrian Government declared that all causes of complaint for the Hülsemann note or the banquet speech "had been buried in the grave of that great statesman." [1]

Aside from the empire of the Archduke Maximilian in Mexico, there was only one other incident before the outbreak of the World War in the next century to disturb the harmony of friendly relations between the autocratic empire of the Hapsburgs and the unique republic of the West. That was the case, in 1853, of Martin Koszta, another Hungarian refugee, who had reached the United States and taken the required oath for announcing his intention to become an American citizen, abjuring allegiance to any other sovereign power. Twenty-three months later he went back to Turkey. While at Smyrna he was abducted by a lawless gang and put in irons on board an Austrian brig-of-war. An American naval officer, lying opportunely in that harbor with a sloop-of-war, investigated Koszta's predicament, and at the cannon's mouth forced the Austrian warship to surrender him. He was placed in the French consulate pending decision of what was to be done. The Austrian Government demanded of the United States his delivery, punishment of Captain David A. Ingraham, the American officer, and reparations. Secretary of State Marcy backed up the naval officer, and refused to give up Koszta. He successfully held that the man was protected by his first papers for citizenship, according to Turkish practice of treating such foreigners. He astutely avoided the questionable ground of invul-

[1] Curti, *op. cit.*

nerable national protection for a person whose naturalization was not even complete. This successful diplomatic parry, like Webster's thrusts, met with enthusiastic popular approbation at home, and did not seriously disturb international relations.

Cuba had always been an island of seductive interest to the United States, particularly since the acquisition of Florida. Consistently the Government, irrespective of the party in power, maintained one attitude, which it had previously assumed *vis-à-vis* Florida: that the United States was content to see Cuba remain in the possession of Spain, but would resist by force, if necessary, its transfer to any other European or even American power.[1] The reason for this was that Spain's position in the New World as in Europe was weak and every year more feeble. Any other power coming into possession of the island would be stronger and so much the more an inconvenient neighbor. It was also because the United States meant to have Cuba for itself in case Spain should relinquish sovereignty over it to anybody. Jefferson had looked forward to ultimate possession of that island, indeed the whole continent of North America, as the natural order of things in the New World; he was the first apostle of Manifest Destiny, a philosophical apostle. When the elder statesmen studied the doctrine to be pronounced by President Monroe in 1823, Cuba was in the back of their minds: they did not want to commit themselves against ever acquiring it; they did not want to acknowledge any European, other than Spanish, interest in the island. Until Polk's time no effort, no *démarche* of any kind was made to acquire Cuba. At the close of the Mexican War Polk offered to buy the island from Spain. He was afraid that Great Britain or France might seize it as security for huge Spanish debts. Taking advantage of chaos in Cuba and political confusion in Spain, he was ready to offer up to $100,000,000 for the Pearl of the Antilles. If Spain had been willing to part with this, the principal relic of her past great empire in America, public opinion in the United States would doubtless have supported the acquisition in 1848—the full slavery question had not then been precipitated, and the strategic importance of the island, particularly in relation to the Isthmus of Panama, was rather irresistible. But Spain would not sell Cuba any more than the United States would have sold Long Island. The Spanish Minister for Foreign Affairs told the American Minister that "it was more than any minister dare to entertain such a

[1] F. E. Chadwick, *The Relations of the United States and Spain: Diplomacy* (New York, 1909), 178-223.

proposition; that he believed such to be the feeling of the country, that, sooner than see the island transferred to any power, they would prefer seeing it sunk in the ocean." [1]

The less aggressive Whig diplomatists naturally did not pursue the subject after this rebuff to Polk—they reverted to the traditional policy of contentment with Spanish possession, opposition to any transfer of sovereignty, and refusal to commit the United States before the world to any self-denial for the future of Cuba. But the pro-slavery expansionists of the southern states did not give up their ambitions to acquire Cuba as another slave state. Of a population of 1,200,000 on the island in 1850, one half were whites of Spanish origin, 450,000 were slaves. Its human material presented a good sort of population for a slave state. Politically things seemed propitious. Discontent with Spanish rule, operating through the arbitrary authority of the Captain-General, was widespread. During the insurrections of the other, continental colonies the example for fomenting successful revolutions against Spain had been repeatedly, and sometimes successfully, set by adventurous English filibusters, before the British foreign-enlistment act of 1819. The idea occurred to southern slavery expansionists: might not a successful revolution, and independence, be the first step for ultimate annexation *à la* Texas? With the rousing spirit of Manifest Destiny abroad in the land, the pro-slavery leaders could count on a certain volume of northern expansionist support which would have been greater if it had not been for increasing opposition to the further spread of slavery. In Cuba a growing white element began to favor annexation to the United States as a lesser evil to Spanish misrule or to a régime of abolition which might be expected from any British protectorate. Slave-owners feared Spain might emancipate the slaves as a war measure (as Lincoln later did in the Civil War in the United States) in case of any revolution against Spanish authority; and indeed the Captain-General in 1849 had proposed just that, if worse came to worst. For those who remembered the terrible spectacle of the slave insurrection in the neighboring island of Santo Domingo a half century before, this dreadful sort of emancipation was to be avoided at all costs; in fact the social and political economy of the island was so based on slavery that the creole element opposed emancipation of any degree or kind. They thought slavery would be safer if Cuba were joined to the great slave-holding republic to the north.

[1] Moore, *Digest International Law*, I, 588.

Patriotic Cubans turned to this annexationist sentiment as a means of achieving ultimate independence. Once separation from Spain were won by some insurrectionary endeavor, they believed the sectional issue over slavery in the United States would prevent the admission of Cuba into the Union, and would leave the island dangling in an independent condition. To this group belonged Narciso Lopez, an adventurous Venezuelan of the type of Miranda, who had once held high office in Spain and then in Cuba, and who seems himself to have been inspired by patriotic motives.[1] He became the instrument of revolt in Cuba and the tool of the slavery expansionists in the United States.

Unsuccessful in first insurrectionary efforts in Cuba, Lopez and other Cubans went to New York in 1849. At first he sought to get an experienced American military figure to take first command of an expedition. Jefferson Davis declined, when approached, but suggested Robert E. Lee. After some deliberation Lee decided it was incompatible with his commission in the United States Army. Lopez continued conferences with Southern leaders, like Senators Calhoun, Jefferson Davis, and Foote of Mississippi. One of the interviews took place in the gloomy Hall of Columns far down beneath the great dome of the Capitol building at Washington, as if such unworthy conversations should be shrouded with the furtive shadows of the sandstone pillars in that sepulchral chamber.

The activities of the Cuban filibusters became notorious. President Taylor issued a proclamation warning all citizens against violating the neutrality act of 1818 by participating in any such expedition, notifying them that they would forfeit all protection of their government. Federal authorities broke up the first attempt, organized at New York for a rendezvous at Round Island near New Orleans. Lopez went south, where public sentiment was more favorable. The Government again upset his plans at Savannah. At New Orleans he succeeded. With the help of General Quitman, Governor of Mississippi, and other prominent southerners, he got together an expedition of 750 men, mostly veterans of the Mexican War, who cleared from New Orleans (April, 1850) ostensibly bound for the Isthmus of Panama and the new gold fields of California. At Yucatan they embarked for Cuba, disembarked at Cardenas, and proclaimed revolt. The populace refused to join them. They fled back to Key West, where the filibusters were allowed to disperse, though their

---

[1] Herminio Portell-Vilá, *Narciso López y su Época* (Havana, 1930), has in his first volume carried Lopez's career and the annexationist movement only to 1849. R. G. Caldwell, *The Lopez Expeditions to Cuba, 1848-1851* (Princeton University Press, 1915), is inclined to look upon the filibusters in an heroic way. He sees the expedition of 1851 the first step in the breakdown of the Compromise of 1850.

ship was confiscated.[1] Lopez and fifteen other leaders were arrested, and indicted, at New Orleans, but the Government could not convince local juries that the filibusters had violated the neutrality of the United States.

Even while under indictment the filibusters renewed their preparations. In August, 1851, Lopez left New Orleans with 450 men, mostly Americans, organized in companies. Second in command was Colonel W. L. Crittenden, nephew of the Attorney-General of the United States. They landed this time some sixty miles from Havana. Again the reckless leader miscalculated the unity of insurrectionary leadership and the willingness of the people to risk their lives in open revolt. Spanish forces broke up his band. They garroted Lopez in a great public ceremony at Havana. Crittenden and forty-nine others who had attempted to escape in small boats they caught and summarily shot. One hundred and thirty-five more were imprisoned in Spain but eventually released after the intercession of the American Minister there, in 1852. President Fillmore excoriated the expedition in strongest terms, and it is in justice to the Whig Administration to say that its earnest efforts to break it up had been circumvented by widespread and enthusiastic local sympathy which commanded the support of leading citizens. This, of course, did not justify the departure of the filibusters in the eyes of a foreign power.

After the well-deserved executions at Havana rioters in New Orleans wrecked the Spanish consulate there and destroyed property of other Spanish residents of that city. Webster condemned the outrage and promised reparation for the consul; but he reserved himself as to damages to ordinary Spanish subjects. In view of later claims of American citizens for damages by riot in foreign countries, notably Mexico, Webster's statement to the Spanish Minister in Washington is noteworthy: "The rights of the Spanish consul, a public officer residing here under the protection of the United States Government, are quite different from those of the Spanish subjects who have come into the country to mingle with our own citizens, and here to pursue their private business and objects. The former may claim special indemnity; the latter are entitled to such protection as is afforded our own citizens." [2] A special salute was ordered to the Spanish flag at New Orleans. Congress later, after

---

[1] Spanish naval authorities meanwhile had broken up the remnants of the expedition on the island of Contoy, in Mexican waters. The United States Government protested at the seizure of its citizens outside of Spanish territorial waters, and they were released or pardoned.

[2] Chadwick, *United States and Spain, op. cit.*, 224-250.

hearing of the pardon of the American filibusters imprisoned in Spain, appropriated $25,000 to repair damages to Spanish subjects in New Orleans.[1]

If it had not been for the straightforward attitude of the Whig Administration to take forthright measures for the repression of filibustering expeditions, the Lopez adventurers, and the efforts of the Cuban council of revolutionists established in New York, might have had much more success.   Lopez's attempts however were enough to alarm the governments of France and Great Britain as to the possibilities of Cuban separation and annexation to the United States.   Texas and California were only recent memories.   Pressed by Spain to do something to save Cuba which she feared herself powerless to protect, the two powers went so far as to serve notice on Secretary Webster that a naval force had been sent to the Caribbean "to prevent by force any adventurers of any nation from landing with hostile intent on the island of Cuba" (September 27, October 18, 1851).   Webster let it be known that any such surveillance of the activities of American citizens on the high seas could never be tolerated.   He informed the French Minister that the Department of State viewed the situation with much gravity.   Great Britain and France, acting (April 23, 1852) upon the "anxious desire" of Spain, then suggested a tripartite agreement declaring that they "severally and collectively disclaim, now and for hereafter, all intention to obtain possession of the island of Cuba; and they respectively bind themselves to discountenance all attempt to that effect on the part of any power or individuals whatever" or to "obtain or maintain for themselves, or for any one of themselves, any exclusive control over the said island, nor assume nor exercise any dominion over the same."   The British Minister, Crampton, believed that even if such an agreement were not adopted, the mere proposal of it would take away from the annexationists in the United States the chief argument by which they hoped to create a general feeling in favor of the measure: the fear that Great Britain intended to get it for herself.   This reasoning proved sound.

[1] When in 1891 a mob of several thousand citizens in New Orleans lynched eleven persons widely believed to have been guilty of murder and unpunished because of legal subterfuge and lack of enforcement of law (resulting, so it was alleged, from the machinations of the secret and criminal Mafia society), the United States Government assumed responsibility for the deaths of three Italian subjects among the eleven deceased, Italians who by treaty were guaranteed "most constant protection for the security of their persons and property."   The federal Government paid an indemnity of 125,000 francs for the families of the victims; and the Italian Government accepted this as closing the affair.   J. Alexander Karlin discussed "Some Repercussions of the New Orleans Mafia Incident of 1891" in *Research Studies of State College of Washington*, XI, No. 4 (Dec., 1943).   See also *Social Sci. Quar.*, XXV, 235-246 (March, 1945).

Webster made a cautious preliminary answer. He and President Fillmore really had a mind to go ahead with such an agreement—the President was willing to include Hawaii [1]—but they feared that any discussion of it might be jeopardized by the presidential campaign then under
way; they therefore persuaded the French and British representatives
to put off the business until after the election. Webster died before the
election; and in November the Democratic Party, with its strong "Young
America" sentiment for expansion, triumphed at the polls. Fillmore was
the only person left in the American Government who knew about the
earlier confidential and sympathetic conversations on the tripartite proposal. He did not choose to recall them,[2] when the proposal was promptly
renewed. It fell to the lot of Webster's successor in office, Edward
Everett, to reply, in an outstanding state paper directed to the British
Minister, a document which shows that there was more than slavery
ambition involved in the interest of the United States in Cuba. The
Whigs had been opposed to the filibusters, and to annexation; but it was
unreasonable for any administration, particularly one defeated and going
out of office, to attempt to bind the nation forever against exercising
dominion over Cuba. On the grounds of traditional American policy
averse to political alliances with European powers, the last Whig Secretary of State eloquently declined the invitation, disclaiming for his Government any coveting of Cuba, but wording his statement so as to make
an appeal to all sections north and south:

The United States . . . would . . . disable themselves from making an
acquisition which might take place without any disturbance of existing foreign
relations, and in the natural order of things. The island of Cuba lies at our
doors. It commands the approach to the Gulf of Mexico, which washes the
shores of five of our States. It bars the entrance of that great river which
drains half the North American continent, and with its tributaries forms the
largest system of internal water-communication in the world. It keeps watch
at the doorway of our intercourse with California by the Isthmus route.
If an island like Cuba, belonging to the Spanish Crown, guarded the entrance
of the Thames and the Seine, and the United States should propose a convention like this to France and England, those powers would assuredly feel
that the disability assumed by ourselves was far less serious than that which
we asked them to assume. . . . The history of the past—of the recent past—
affords no assurance that twenty years hence France or England will even
wish that Spain should retain Cuba. . . . Even now the President cannot
doubt that both France and England would prefer any change in the condition

[1] Van Alstyne, *loc. cit.*, see below, p. 349.
[2] A. A. Ettinger, "The Proposed Anglo-Franco-American Treaty of 1852 to Guarantee
Cuba to Spain," *Transactions of the Royal Hist. Soc.*, 4th Series, XIII (1930), 149-185.

of Cuba to that which is most to be apprehended, viz: An internal convulsion which should renew the horrors and the fate of Santo Domingo.

The two powers presently let the matter drop. Everett's note not only fitted into the pattern of policy of Washington and Monroe: it also defined the relations of the United States toward Cuba so clearly and so permanently that President McKinley in 1898 was impelled to argue from it that he had made no departure from traditional policy. Like Webster, and equally harmlessly, Everett had played up to the pervading sentiment for a still greater territorial future.

CHAPTER XIX

SLAVERY AND DIPLOMACY

(1853-1861)

BOTH Whigs and Democrats the country over had applauded the virile tone of Everett's note on Cuba, but it did not go far enough for the new Democratic Administration: they wanted Cuba, and wanted it primarily for another slave state. "The policy of my Administration will not be controlled by any timid forebodings of evil from expansion," President Pierce declared boldly in his inaugural address. "Indeed, it is not to be disguised that our attitude as a nation and our position on the globe render the acquisition of certain possessions not within our jurisdiction eminently important for our protection." Straightway he sent ardent expansionists to the most important diplomatic posts. To England went James Buchanan, a man whose ambitions for the Presidency had been dampened by the election of 1852, who wanted to keep slavery out of politics, but, if impossible to do so, would defend southern "rights." John Y. Mason of Virginia took the legation in France. Senator Pierre Soulé became Minister to Spain. Soulé was a fiery French republican émigré of Louisiana, who had extolled the members of the Lopez expedition as heroes. The new Minister to Portugal was none other than John L. O'Sullivan, a Democratic editor from New York State, who had coined the thaumaturgical phrase, Manifest Destiny, and had consorted with Lopez and the Cuban filibusters.[1] The post in Mexico was filled by James Gadsden, a prominent South Carolinian who was personally interested in the project for a southern railway route to California through territory still left in northern Mexico. In the Cabinet at Washington sat Jefferson Davis of Mississippi, as Secretary of War, a dominant power in the Administration, who had helped Pierce make his appointments; Caleb Cushing, a one-time Whig, of Massachusetts, now an ardent Democratic expansionist and northern exponent of southern "rights" as to slavery; and William L. Marcy of New York, Secretary of State, who was to prove a methodical and able diplomatist and who possessed the outlook on slavery shared by those other two northern

[1] Julius W. Pratt, "John L. O'Sullivan and Manifest Destiny," *N. Y. History*, XIV (July, 1933), 213-234.

Democrats, Pierce and Buchanan. For this group foreign affairs focused on Cuba.

The Southern element were determined to get Cuba, if not by purchase, then in some other way, and their importance in domestic politics gave them influence over Marcy and President Pierce. Irritating incidents involving American ships and property before the unjust Spanish law in the island, like the arbitrary detention and fining of the innocent packet-vessel *Black Warrior*,[1] they used to enforce their arguments that Cuba even in Spanish possession was becoming a menace to the national safety of the United States. Marcy confidentially instructed Soulé to try to buy the island, but if Spain would not sell for a reasonable sum—the United States would go as high as $130,000,000—then Soulé was to direct his efforts to the "next most desirable object," which was "to detach that island from the Spanish domination and from all dependence on any European power." The Secretary of State hoped that some movement for independence might develop in Cuba to which the United States might somehow lend a hand, under just what circumstances he could not state. Lacking sufficient knowledge of such possibilities, no special instructions could be given to the minister for his action in such a contingency. The inference was that Soulé would use his own judgment and devices. Marcy mentioned reports (some from the United States consul at Havana) that Spain was preparing to introduce in Cuba an agricultural apprentice-labor system. "You are furnished in your instructions with the President's views on the apprentice system [Soulé's *written* instructions do not reveal these]. If it should be gone into extensively and carried out in good faith it would inevitably Africanize the island."[2] From these words Soulé constructed a policy, which, somewhat qualified by his colleagues in Europe, appeared presently in the "Ostend Manifesto": the danger of emancipating slaves in Cuba might justify wresting that possession from Spain to prevent the incendiary sparks of human freedom from taking flame and spreading to the United States, Africanizing the southern states.

Spain would not sell. Soulé's diplomatic conduct in that country was

[1] This vessel was a packet-ship plying between New York and Mobile, calling at Havana. The practice had grown up of exempting the vessel from declaring a manifest of its through cargo. On its eighteenth voyage the Cuban port authorities suddenly made a demand for production of a complete manifest, and allowed no time for it; as a result they seized the ship for violation of customs regulations, later released it after energetic protest of the United States, but fined it $6,000. In due course of time Spain made proper amends.

[2] Marcy to Soulé, July 25, 1853, and April 3, 1854, Archives of the Department of State, *Instructions, Spain*, Vol. XV.

a progression of blunders and intemperate conduct, involving an unwarranted ultimatum to the Spanish Government over the *Black Warrior* affair, indiscreet connection with Spanish revolutionists, and a duel with the French Ambassador. Because of Soulé's failures, Pierce and Marcy had thoughts of sending a special commission to Spain, but this gave way to the idea of a conference in Europe of American diplomatists to canvass the Cuban question—in Washington they had information from Buchanan that British and other holders of Spanish bonds might be quite content to see the Spanish treasury relieved by the sale of Cuba. The result was the notorious "Ostend Manifesto," drawn up by Buchanan, Mason and Soulé at Aix-la-Chapelle, later published to an astonished world. Said these three pro-slavery annexationists:

(1) The United States ought to try to buy Cuba, for not over $130,-000,000.

(2) "Our past history forbids that we should acquire the Island of Cuba without the consent of Spain, unless justified by the great law of self-preservation. . . . After we shall have offered Spain a price for Cuba, far beyond its present value, and this shall have been refused, *it will then be time to consider* the question, does Cuba, in the possession of Spain seriously endanger our internal peace and the existence of our cherished Union. Should this question be answered in the affirmative, then, by every law human and Divine, we shall be justified in wresting it from Spain, if we possess the power; and this upon the very same principle that would justify an individual in tearing down the burning house of his neighbor, if there were no other means of preventing the flames from destroying his own home. Under such circumstances, we ought neither to count the cost, nor regard the odds which Spain might enlist against us." [1]

That is, they asseverated that if Spain would not sell Cuba then it might be considered whether it would be expedient for the United States to go to war and take it. This contingent and qualified character of the manifesto—in which the cautious Buchanan toned down the more ardent views of Soulé—weakened the force of the document; [2] but the publicity given to the declaration shocked the world, and Secretary Marcy was forced by indignant public opinion at home and abroad to repudiate the manifesto. Though not so positively worded as the world took it to be, it was a most equivocal and compromising document, a naked exhibition of the union of slavery and diplomacy; but it is significant that it was rejected, just as it is significant that the whole un-

[1] Italics inserted.

[2] Roy F. Nichols, *Franklin Pierce* (Philadelphia, 1931).

blushing program of the pro-slavery politicians came to naught before the rising forces of human freedom.[1]

The Democratic platform of 1856 advocated the annexation of Cuba. It nominated the Pennsylvanian Buchanan, the real author of the Ostend Manifesto, a document which made him particularly acceptable to the South—a man who had the advantage of having been abroad during the recent embarrassing disputes at home over slavery in the territories. The party won the election of that year by an appeal to the voters not to endanger the Union by a sectional struggle that would be precipitated by the election of a Republican candidate pledged against the extension of slavery in the territories. As late as 1860 both divisions of the ruined party persisted in declaring in favor of the annexation of Cuba on terms "honorable to us and just to Spain." But Cuba as another slave state had proved more than the whole country could stomach. Meanwhile other fields had appeared to tempt the slavery expansionists: more of Mexico, and the possibility of filibusters upsetting republics in Central America and the Caribbean and annexing them to the United States. An agent of the Pierce Administration, William L. Cazneau, drafted in Santo Domingo a treaty for the cession of the harbor of Samaná Bay to the United States; but French and British opposition induced the island republic to repudiate the project.[2] For many years thereafter Cazneau frequented Santo Domingo as an advance agent of American annexation. Through the United States Commissioner to Hawaii, Marcy also negotiated (1854) an abortive treaty for the annexation of those islands, but he appears to have been outwitted by British advice to the Hawaiians to insist on a clause for statehood. In that critical year of American domestic politics this clause would have defeated the treaty. Pierce did not submit it to the Senate, and the island government eluded further negotiations.[3]

The execution of the treaty of peace of Guadalupe Hidalgo of 1848 opened up to the Democratic slavery-expansionists possibilities of aggressive diplomacy which the Whigs had been unwilling to pursue. The treaty had stipulated that the southern boundary of the United States should run westwardly from the Rio Grande River "along the whole southern boundary of New Mexico (which runs north of the town called

---

[1] For the Ostend Manifesto, and attendant diplomacy, see, in addition to Nichols, op. cit., H. B. Learned, in Am. Secs. State, VI, 183-216, and the voluminous study of A. A. Ettinger, The Mission to Spain of Pierre Soulé, 1853-1855, a Study in the Cuban Diplomacy of the United States (Yale University Press, 1932).

[2] Perkins, Monroe Doctrine, 1826-1867, op. cit., 268-271.

[3] See below, p. 349.

Paso) to its western termination," as those boundaries were laid down on Disturnell's Map published at New York in 1847. It said nothing about longitude and latitude. When the joint survey met in 1851 to mark the line, it found the latitude and longitude of towns and lines on Disturnell's Map inaccurate, especially as to the location of the town of El Paso and the course of the Rio Grande. The American Commissioner Bartlett wanted to correct the map by making it conform to the observed latitude and longitude of the landmarks; the Mexican Commissioner Condé went strictly by the treaty map. They finally compromised on a line that President Fillmore would have been willing to accept had he remained in office. Upwards of 3,000,000 acres in the Mesilla Valley near El Paso were involved between the extremes at first claimed by each side. This region by 1853 contained a population of about 3,000 persons, Mexicans and Americans. Then of little value agriculturally (though now an irrigated country supporting about 25,000 people), it was important as a gateway for a southern transcontinental railroad across the United States, a project then of tremendous significance in domestic politics. The pro-slavery element in Congress was struggling to get the railroad built through southern territory in order to hamper the settlement along the northern routes of free-soil farmers who would hatch out free states there to overbalance the South politically. For this reason it opposed bills for free homesteads to settlers, as well as any charter for a railroad along the northern prairies through the homestead country. Jefferson Davis, Secretary of War, was in charge of the surveys then in progress to ascertain the best railway route to the Pacific Coast, and he was determined that the southern route, so advantageous politically to his section, should be selected. The diplomatic compromise reached by the Bartlett-Condé boundary survey blocked the route in the Mesilla Valley. Farther west, the best route lay south of the Gila River, in unchallengeable Mexican territory. President Pierce promptly repudiated the compromise.

Article XI of the treaty had obliged the United States to restrain the Indians dwelling within the ceded territory from making incursions across the boundary, and, when that could not be prevented, to punish them with the same diligence as if their incursions had been meditated or committed on its own citizens within its own territory. Along that rough and difficult terrain of wild and extensive frontier this was proving a most expensive duty and the Government was anxious to get out of the obligation by rendering some diplomatic equivalent. There were also various claims of American citizens against Mexico which had arisen since the peace, some of them very exaggerated, and a heavy claim by Mexico against the United States for alleged inadequate control of the Indians. Pierce desired to make a general treaty settlement with Mexico which would include another big cession. He and his advisers believed that the disorganized political condition of Mexico, and the necessity of money to keep Mexican administrations in power, would induce one of them to sell more territory. He sent to Mexico General James Gadsden, a prominent South Carolinian who, we have observed, was himself interested in a southern railway route, to attempt to secure the cession of the peninsula of Lower California (on which no railroad has been built to this day) and a huge area of Mexico that would include the southern watershed of the Rio Grande. For this he was authorized to pay up to $50,000,000, and proportionately less for alternate lines involving various areas which would include an outlet on the Gulf of California: as a last recourse he might sign a treaty rectifying the frontier only sufficiently to take care of the proposed southern railway route.

Gadsden found Santa Anna re-established for a brief period in control of the Mexican Government and pressed for money to keep himself in power, ready to sell a minimum amount of his country's territory to get cash. He succeeded in making a treaty settling definitively the southern boundary, with the inclusion of El Paso in the United States, and the addition of the triangle of territory (19,000,000 acres of desert land, south of the Gila River) since known as the "Gadsden Purchase," for $10,000,000; an abrogation of Article XI and release of the United States from all claims thereunder (without mention of claims against Mexico by citizens of the United States) ; [1] free passage for citizens of the United States through the River Colorado and the Gulf of California, and the Rio Grande (Bravo) below the new international boundary; and a right of transit for the United States Government, and its citizens, across the

---

[1] By a claims convention of July 4, 1868, all claims of citizens of either republic against the other, "which yet remain unsettled" were submitted to a mixed claims commission. Mexico presented over $31,000,000 worth of claims arising out of Indian depredations unrestrained by the United States by its obligations under the treaty of Guadalupe Hidalgo. The English umpire of the commission threw out these claims on the ground that the United States had been released from them by the Gadsden Treaty. The commission awarded, of other claims, the following sums to citizens of the United States (compared with a total of $470,126,613.40 originally presented): $402,942.04 United States currency (greenbacks), $426,624.98 United States gold dollars, and $3,296,055.18 Mexican gold dollars. To Mexican claimants it awarded (of original total claimed of $86,661,891.15) $89,410.17 United States currency, $10,569.67 United States gold dollars, and $50,528.57 Mexican gold dollars. The Mexican gold dollar was reckoned, in payments, at 98.39 U. S. gold cents. By terms of the original treaty the debt balance of the one party to the other, after adjudication, was paid off in installments at the rate of $300,000 a year. Moore, *International Arbitrations*, II, 1287-1359.

Isthmus of Tehuantepec, to which the United States might extend its protection.[1] The latter (cancelled by treaty, 1937) was not forbidden by the Clayton-Bulwer Treaty, which applied only to the Isthmus of Central America. In a certain way it was a reply to the British contentions that their *existing* protectorate on the Mosquito Coast was not relinquished by the treaty.[2] No use was ever made of it.

After the war of 1846-1848 Mexico suffered a decade of political and administrative breakdown, followed by foreign invasion again. The fortresses were dismantled, the frontiers destitute of any protection,[3] the treasury bankrupt, the army disorganized and demoralized. The country was wide open to intrigue and aggression. Nor was it easy for the United States Government, on its side of the new boundary, to police the frontier to stop the numerous filibustering expeditions that were being fitted out to subvert Mexican authority, nor to defend its own territory from retaliatory raids. Santa Anna had inserted into the original text of the Gadsden Treaty an article for the suppression of filibusters; but the Senate significantly threw it out, and the treaty was ratified by both parties without it. The Whig Administration had made conscientious efforts to restrain the filibustering expeditions organizing in Texas and California, but found it difficult to secure convictions from local juries, or indeed to prevent the departure of some of the expeditions. In the Pierce Administration that followed, Jefferson Davis as Secretary of War made only perfunctory efforts to stop the filibusters. Until the outbreak of the American Civil War involved all the energies of the United States, and the contemporary French invasion of Mexico distracted all the resources of that republic, the border was a scene of chronic turbulence, filibustering, raiding, robbing and shooting.

After the conclusion of the treaty of 1853, which had been practically rewritten by the Senate, Gadsden and other succeeding representatives in Mexico of the Pierce and Buchanan Administrations aggressively continued their efforts to secure more Mexican territory: Lower California, and a bite off the top of the Mexican cornucopia which would take in

[1] The negotiations are described in great detail by Paul N. Garber, *The Gadsden Treaty* (Univ. of Penna. Press, 1923).

[2] Above, p. 251.

[3] The Mexican Government (if one may call by such the bewildering series of ephemeral ministries and changing presidents and dictators which characterized these years) tried out the idea of establishing on the frontier of Sonora buffer settlements of French colonists recruited from footloose French immigrants and adventurers in San Francisco. One or two abortive attempts proved that such colonists were scarcely more reliable than filibusters themselves. See Rippy, *U. S. and Mexico, op. cit.*, and R. K. Wyllys, "The French of California and Sonora," *Pacific Hist. Rev.*, I (Sept., 1932) 337-359.

most of the northwestern state of Sonora. The chaos in that country, the increasing accumulation of claims of American citizens for damages, and the imminence of European intervention professedly to protect foreign owners of bonds and other property, gave cause for real anxiety to President Buchanan, as well as affording pretexts for his unscrupulous annexationist ambitions. He failed, however, in his efforts to get most of Mexico by diplomacy. In his annual message to Congress of 1858 (December 6) Buchanan asked in vain for powers to assume a "temporary protectorate" over northern Chihuahua and Sonora; and again in 1859 (December 19) he requested authority to employ military force to enter Mexico for the purpose of obtaining indemnity for the past and security for the future. If the United States did not step right in and take full charge, he said, "it would not be surprising should some other nation undertake the task, and thus force us to interfere at last, under circumstances of increased difficulty, for the maintenance of our established policy." The events of the next few years were to emphasize the force of this statement; but the crowding vehemence of sectional politics in the United States broke down the expansionist program of the Democratic Party by splitting it on sectional lines and throwing the South out of the saddle. All that the pro-slavery expansionists really accomplished before they lost the support of the northern wing of the party was the Gadsden Treaty.[1]

One of the filibusters whose incursions into Mexico from California had given concern to both governments in 1853-1854 was William Walker. He got away from San Francisco on a filibustering expedition to Nicaragua in 1855. Like Cortez in the conquest of Mexico, Walker was able to take advantage of the internal dissensions of the people he desired to master. He succeeded in establishing himself as dictator of that republic, 1855-1857. Walker's expedition was not a plot of the pro-slavery leaders, although many of them sympathized with it and expected annexation to flow from it, and he himself was a Southerner. It was rather the crime of a reckless and unscrupulous soldier of fortune who wished to possess himself of all Central America and Cuba, and after its inception it was partly financed by the Accessory Transit Company, a group of American capitalists who were operating a land and water transit business across the Isthmus there. The shameful enterprise brought nothing but death and desolation to the suffering populace

---

[1] This period of Mexican-American relations has been covered in great detail by J. F. Rippy, *op. cit.*, Paul N. Garber, *op. cit.*, J. M. Callahan, *op. cit.*, and in a shorter compass by Lewis Einstein, in *Am. Secs. State*, VI, 324-368.

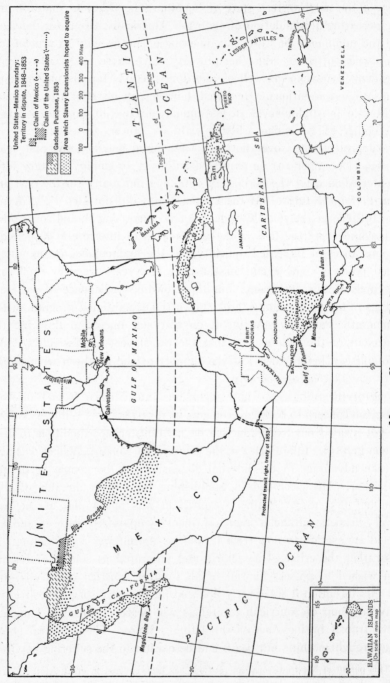

Map 20. Slavery and Diplomacy.

of Nicaragua and to most of Walker's following. Secretary Marcy was opposed to Walker's schemes, but they elicited much sympathy, not only in the southern states but among expansionists and vociferators of Manifest Destiny everywhere. The adventurer made the most of this feeling to bolster his precarious position. After conferring with Pierre Soulé, who visited the intruder president, he set on foot plans for the reintroduction of slavery in Nicaragua and the reopening of the African slave trade.

President Pierce was not as uncompromising as Marcy in his condemnation of Walker's usurpations and violation of the neutrality laws by the recruiting of "colonists" in the United States, who turned out to be soldiers in Walker's forces when they reached Nicaragua. The enterprise in a way served as a countercheck to Great Britain's aggressive interpretation of the Clayton-Bulwer Treaty.[1] On its part the British Government suspected the United States was lending countenance to the subjection of a state which would become its puppet for power in the Isthmus, forbidden under that treaty. When Costa Rica, and presently the other Central American states, declared war on Walker both Great Britain and France strengthened their naval contingents in the neighborhood of the Isthmus, despite the exigencies of the Crimean War. The British Government furnished Costa Rica with 2,000 muskets and other munitions from its own arsenals. Pierce had hitherto hesitated to recognize Walker's government. He now did so immediately, on the ground that the United States could not remain entirely inactive and see Great Britain obtain complete ascendency in all the states of Central America.[2] It was incidentally the eve of the Democratic national convention, and politicians within that organization, including the President, were angling for the support of Manifest Destiny north and south, as well as for that of southern radicals who hoped for slavery extension out of Walker's activities. The party platform of 1856 extolled Walker in veiled terms and looked forward to the "regeneration" of Nicaragua along the canal route. But the filibuster's régime there suddenly collapsed, just after President Buchanan came into office in Washington, and Walker himself, after two more attempts in Central America, finally met his just deserts before a firing-squad in Honduras.[3] After the second fiasco,

[1] See above, p. 251.

[2] M. W. Williams, *Anglo-American Isthmian Diplomacy, op. cit.,* 210-214.

[3] Walker was defeated in Nicaragua in 1857. His life and the lives of his surviving followers were saved by an act of mediation by a United States naval officer, who brought them back to the United States. He immediately organized another expedition, and successfully departed. It was broken up in Nicaraguan waters, by an unauthorized intervention of Captain Hiram Paulding, U. S. N., who was censured and removed from

in 1858, President Buchanan piously reprobated such filibusters but continued to talk of peaceful penetration of Central America, a protectorate over northern Mexico, and the purchase of Cuba. In 1859 Great Britain arranged the treaties with Honduras and Nicaragua by which she withdrew her protectorate from the Mosquito Coast. These treaties were not put into execution until Walker was out of the way. The Isthmian Question then quieted down on the eve of the American Civil War. The downfall of the Democratic Party, and the annihilation of slavery during that war, wrote a sudden end to this aggressive phase of American diplomacy.

We cannot finally dismiss the main subject of this chapter without mention of the diplomacy of the abolition of the African slave trade. The United States had abolished that trade contemporaneously with Great Britain (1807-1808), and in 1820 declared it piracy, punishable by death, for its own citizens by its own law; but it had consistently refused to co-operate with British diplomacy for the suppression of the illegal traffic by a treaty—similar to those between Great Britain and other powers [1]—for mutual right of visit and search in time of peace of vessels flying the British or American flag and suspected of being slavers, and the trial of accused before mixed international tribunals. The reason for this was the sensitiveness to visit and search because of the old grievance of impressment. Only in case Great Britain would expressly abandon the practice of impressment could any government in Washington agree to a mutual right of visit and search even to suppress the slave trade. Moreover, the practical application of visit and search by British officers was not always too scrupulous of the rights of competing

his command by President Buchanan for so doing. Walker, who had been placed under arrest by Paulding and brought back, was eventually indicted for violating the act of 1818, but a New Orleans jury failed to convict him. In the South he was received and fêted more like a conquering hero than a fallen filibuster. He was able to organize and depart with a third expedition, which was broken up by the British navy on the shores of Honduras. It is significant that the British navy stepped in and stopped a proceeding which American naval officers were forbidden to do after Paulding's act. Walker surrendered to Captain Salmon, R. N., who turned him promptly over to the Hondurans. They executed him, September 12, 1860. The standard work on Walker's career is W. O. Scroggs, *Filibusters and Financiers* (New York, 1916).

[1] Great Britain had negotiated treaties for mutual right of visit and search of slave-traders, and mixed tribunals to try them, with Spain, Portugal (north of the Equator only), Brazil, the Netherlands, France, Haiti, Uruguay, Venezuela, Bolivia, Argentina, Mexico, Texas, Denmark, and the Hanse Towns. Supplemental treaties with France and Spain enabled seizure if vessels were proven to have on board equipment for prosecuting the slave trade, even though no Negroes were found. Soulsby, *post cit.* The practical effect of the aloofness of the United States, together with its denial of the practice of visit and search, was to leave the American flag the only subterfuge immune from scrutiny, except by American naval vessels.

merchant vessels: the presence on board of what a naval captain, not oblivious to prize money, might choose to call "equipment" for slave-trading would sometimes be sufficient for the condemnation of a vessel, even though it contained no Negroes. There were many complaints, too, that American ships engaged in innocent commerce were overhauled, delayed, and sometimes unjustly seized. On the other hand, it is clear that the flag of the United States was fraudulently employed by foreign traders seeking to elude visit and search, and consequent capture, when carrying Negroes, particularly to Cuba and Brazil, the most profitable markets. Nor can it be denied that American citizens were among the criminals participating in the nefarious traffic, though few Negroes were actually smuggled into the United States.[1]

After elaborate and vigorous diplomatic discussion the British Government explicitly disavowed any right of visit *and* search in time of peace, but continued to insist that it was not improper to visit a ship suspected of flying illegally the American flag, that it was necessary to do this in order to verify the status of the vessel, otherwise a slaver of another nationality could cover himself with that flag with comparative impunity, and the hateful traffic, condemned by Christian nations, would continue. This of course rather assumed that the United States was not doing its part to prevent its own flag from such desecrations, and the assumption was not wholly unjustified, although American cruisers had fitfully patrolled the African coast since 1820. The United States consistently maintained that ships illegally flying its flag might be searched, even captured and punished— what was done to foreign vessels was none of its own concern; but there must be no mistake made in molesting any real American vessel. To do so would give rise to serious claim for satisfaction. That reparation in such cases would be proper was admitted at Downing Street. The British Government did not pretend to interfere with genuine American vessels, even if flagrantly prosecuting the slave-trade, but it did persist in a claim at least to identify real non-American slavers. This last was actually the contemporary practice of the American navy itself; and in rejecting it the United States Government was denying to another power what it assumed to practise itself.[2]

The most [3] that any American administration could be brought to, in co-

[1] St. George L. Sioussat, *Duff Green's "England and the United States"; with an Introductory Study of American Opposition to the Quintuple Treaty of 1841* (Am. Antiquarian Society, Worcester, 1931).

[2] Soulsby, *post cit.*, 23, 73.

[3] Following a resolution of the House of Representatives, Secretary John Quincy

operation with the British objective of suppression of the trade, was to
accept the articles of the Webster-Ashburton Treaty of 1842 which provided for joint remonstrance against any power allowing the traffic to
exist within its dominions, and agreed to maintain separate cruising
squadrons for the destruction of the condemned commerce, each government according to the laws of its own country, without any mutual right
of visit and search. The question remained quiescent for fifteen years
afterward, with no further British visitations of American vessels. The
provisions of this treaty were not enthusiastically or even effectively
carried out by succeeding Democratic administrations, particularly after
the British statement of a desire to see slavery abolished in Texas as
elsewhere throughout the world. After the Crimean War in 1857, the
articles of the Webster-Ashburton Treaty of 1842 having become mostly
a dead-letter, the British revived the visitation of suspected vessels
flying the Stars and Stripes. Secretary Cass, in Buchanan's Administration, could hardly be expected to co-operate for the execution of these
articles. When minister in France he had protested to Secretary Webster
against these provisions of the treaty (and Buchanan had attacked them
in the Senate); and in 1842, acting on his own responsibility, he had at
least helped to persuade the French Government against ratification of a
quintuple treaty (Great Britain, France, Russia, Prussia, Austria) of
Anglo-French origin agreeing to the mutual right of visit and search
and intended to make it the common policy of the principal powers of
Europe.[1]

Anxious for the support of the South to secure the nomination for
the presidency in 1856, Cass had roundly applauded Walker's filibus-

Adams had negotiated with Great Britain in 1824 a convention declaring the slave
trade piracy. If ratified this *ipso facto* would have allowed a belligerent right of
searching suspected ships of either nation for pirates, the enemies of mankind, who
were to be tried however in the courts of their own country. This convention guarded
against the possibility of impressment by a provision that "no person shall be taken
out of the said visited or captured merchant vessel of either nation by the commanding
officer of the visiting vessel or under his order." Great Britain after promptly ratifying
this treaty, and passing an act of Parliament making the slave trade piracy, refused
to accept the Senate's amendments, particularly one excluding the American coasts from
the scope of the treaty. Ten years later the British Government offered to accept a
treaty with this amendment, but the United States refused. Such a treaty would have
settled the whole question; but by then the slavery question in the United States had
become too strong to admit it. Compare the treaty finally ratified in 1862, which
restricted the patrol to certain areas and did not contain the clause designed to protect
against impressment.

[1] Had this been ratified the position of the United States would have been increasingly
isolated in Christendom on this great moral issue. As it was, France by a new convention with Great Britain in 1845 substituted for the mutual right of visit and search,
Webster's principle of independent but co-operating cruising squadrons.

tering activities in Nicaragua—that Walker who had planned to re-establish slavery there and reopen the slave trade. With the renewal of the British visitations, some of them in the Gulf of Mexico, Buchanan's Government became rigid in its resistance. A critical tension speedily developed between the two countries, exacerbated by the recent recruiting controversy. In 1858 the British Government abandoned even the claim to visit any vessel which flew the American flag, and placed in the course of reparation those cases where American vessels had been interfered with on suspicion of being slave-traders of other nationality. At the same time it appealed to the United States to work out some arrangement to verify the nationality of a vessel suspected of flying false colors. Cass promised merely to carry out the provisions of the Webster-Ashburton Treaty. The patrol was increased and the two governments were able to agree upon a set of identical instructions to their respective squadrons, but the Secretary obstinately evaded every constructive proposal for international action. Despite the maintenance of American cruising squadrons off the coasts of Africa and Cuba, the African slave trade was more virulent than ever in 1860. Nothing but an American cruiser could now challenge any vessel, however suspicious, once it hoisted the flag of the United States.

The Civil War ended this unsavory situation. A slave-trader was hanged, the first in the United States for this crime, in February, 1862. To attract the sympathy and moral support of the European powers, Secretary Seward immediately began negotiations and at length in 1862 signed (April 7) a convention with Great Britain providing for mutual right of visit and search in specified waters off the coasts of Africa and Cuba,[1] with mixed courts at New York, Cape Town, and Sierra Leone, composed of an equal number of judges of each party, to try offenders. With the southern states temporarily absent from the Union, the Senate unanimously ratified the convention.[2] No longer were British motives for the suppression of the trade questioned. The United States stepped into the great humanitarian procession. No invasion of American rights was noticed. It is clear enough that once the slave power was removed from national politics all opposition disappeared to co-operation against the atrocious trans-Atlantic traffic in black human beings. So

---

[1] Extended in 1863 to specified areas off the coasts of Madagascar, Puerto Rico, and Santo Domingo.

[2] A recent luminous and critical survey of the controversy is Hugh G. Soulsby, *The Right of Search and the Slave Trade in Anglo-American Relations, 1814-1862* (Johns Hopkins University Studies in Historical and Political Science, Series LI, No. 2, 1933). See also the short note by R. W. Van Alstyne, "The British Right of Search and the African Slave Trade," *Jour. Mod. Hist.*, II (March, 1930), 37-47.

also vanished objection to the homestead act for the free disposal of western land to actual settlers, and to the act chartering a transcontinental railroad by the northern route. The settlement of the Far West and the binding of coast to coast with spans of steel rail depressed the importance of the Isthmian Question, which had been such an aid to the ambitions of slavery expansionists before the Civil War. The first Republican Secretary of State, William H. Seward, was a great expansionist as well as anti-slavery leader. On the eve of the Civil War he looked forward to the day when the United States might acquire Cuba and Puerto Rico by "just and lawful means, with the consent of their sovereign." [1] But Seward's projects for the annexation of the Danish West Indies and Santo Domingo, the latter ardently backed later by President Grant, could not get through the Senate or Congress. All attempts at southern expansion beyond the national boundaries after the war failed for a generation. All motive had disappeared.

During the Democratic régime of 1853-1861 a number of special diplomatic problems presented themselves, unrelated to the question of slavery directly or indirectly. These were in addition to the broad and active field of commercial negotiations, noted in a recent chapter. The Crimean War produced two prominent questions: recruitment of foreign troops on American soil; and the old American objective of freedom of the seas.

The early military disasters of the autumn of 1854 staggered the British public and created an urgent demand for man power to mend the broken army in the Crimea. Instead of a conscription law Parliament passed an act (December 23, 1854) authorizing the enlistment and commissioning of a foreign legion in the British army, to be employed chiefly outside the realm. The British Minister in Washington, John F. T. Crampton, and under him the consuls, directed agents in leading American cities in assembling men and arranging for their transportation to Halifax, where they were formally sworn into the Queen's service. The cost of transportation was paid for them or, in some cases, by previous understanding, it was deducted from their enlistment bounty. The agents openly advertised for recruits. Quite in contrast to its complaisance toward the generally similar inducement of men to go to neighboring American republics like Texas and Nicaragua, the federal authorities moved quickly and effectively against the recruitment of Americans to fight British battles on the shores of the distant

---

[1] Moore's *Digest of International Law,* I, 589.

Euxine. Alarmed by indictment of some of the agents, and by protests through the United States Minister in London, the British Government gave unpublished orders to cease all recruiting in the United States. After some delay it was stopped, but not before a British consul at Cincinnati had been arrested and indicted (the President later ordered the case dismissed), and one of the agents actually convicted. During the trial abundant evidence implicated the Minister Crampton and three of the consuls. No satisfaction having followed American protests, Secretary Marcy requested the withdrawal of the minister, and the consuls at Philadelphia, Cincinnati and New York. This the British Government refused to do. President Pierce then formally dismissed them. Intelligent British opinion supported the American position; and the fact that the Government did not in turn dismiss the American Minister in London suggests that its own inner sense of justice was favorable to the United States. It is worth noting in connection with this affair that only a few years later the United States drew large numbers of immigrants into its armies during the Civil War. Some of them were attracted from Europe by bounties on enlistment: if there was no recruiting abroad, the American consul-general at Paris, John Bigelow, without authority from Washington, advertised for immigrants in the leading continental journals. "You have *usurped* with discretion and with wisdom," Secretary Seward later wrote to him,[1] far from disapproving. In contrast to British recruiting in the United States in 1855, Lincoln's representatives abroad were more skillful and successful in keeping within the law.

After the close of the Crimean War the principal powers [2] of Europe endeavored to write a definition of freedom of the seas into international law. They agreed on articles which, with the exception of the first, established principles that the United States had contended for from the beginning: from the drafting of the Plan of 1776 through all the struggles over neutral rights during the wars of the French Revolution and Napoleon, principles which it had sought in vain to write into the Peace of Ghent of 1814. The other powers were invited to adhere, and all except the United States, Spain, and Mexico have adhered. These principles were:

---

[1] The late Henry Barrett Learned published a scholarly summary of the recruitment controversy in his sketch of Marcy in *Am. Secs. State*, VI, 237-262; and J. H. Bartlet Brebner has supplemented it by an account of the activities of the most important agent: "Joseph Howe and the Crimean War Enlistment Controversy Between Great Britain and the United States," *Canad. Hist. Rev.*, XI (Dec., 1930), 300-327.

[2] Great Britain, Austria, France, Prussia, Russia, Sardinia, Turkey.

1. Privateering is and remains abolished.

2. The neutral flag covers enemy's goods, with the exception of contraband of war.

3. Neutral goods, with the exception of contraband of war, are not liable to capture under enemy's flag.

4. Blockades, in order to be binding, must be effective; that is to say, maintained by a force sufficient really to prevent access to the coast of the enemy.

The reason why the United States did not adhere to these articles was because it seemed too much of a sacrifice for a weak naval power to give up privateering unless the great maritime powers would abolish the capture of private property, excepting contraband, under all conditions. Marcy, in the name of the President, refused to adhere to the Declaration unless Article I should be amended by adding the words: "And that the private property of subjects or citizens of a belligerent on the high seas shall be exempted from seizure by public armed vessels of the other belligerent, except it be contraband." [1] Thus was lost an admirable opportunity to join with the other nations of the world in codifying a large measure of essentially American principles into the law of nations. That the United States did not formally adhere to the Declaration did not mean that these became less essentially American principles. In fact it has observed all of them ever since. We shall meet with the question of privateering and this Declaration of Paris presently, early in the diplomacy of the Civil War.

Diplomatic achievements of the neo-Democrats of the Pierce-Buchanan régime were the opening of the South American River La Plata,[2] with its principal tributaries to the merchant vessels of all nations by a treaty of 1853 with the Argentine Republic; and the compounding of Danish Sound dues four years later. For four centuries Denmark had levied duties on ships passing from the North to the Baltic seas, a public nuisance in the eyes of the maritime powers, particularly those bordering on those seas, and sanctioned rather by custom than international law. Previous American diplomatists had ques-

---

[1] Carlton Savage, *Policy of the United States Towards Maritime Commerce in War*, Vol. I, 1776-1914 (Wash., Gov. Print. Off., 1934), 63-73.

[2] Efforts to open the Amazon by a similar treaty with Brazil were unavailing; but in 1867, following the exploration of the Amazon by the distinguished American naturalist, Professor Agassiz, and the gracious hospitality extended to his party, the Brazilian Government proclaimed the freedom of navigation of that river and its principal tributaries, within Brazilian borders, to the merchant vessels of all nations. This was completed by a similar decree of Peru in 1868. See Lawrence F. Hill's notable work on the *Diplomatic Relations Between the United States and Brazil* (Duke University Press, 1932).

tioned these levies. Marcy brought the matter to head by threatening to abrograte, according to its provisions for so doing, the treaty of commerce of 1826 with Denmark, unless that power would consider some way of discontinuing the levies. The Danish Government called an international conference for the purpose of capitalizing the dues and making some political arrangement satisfactory to all concerned. Marcy refused to participate in such a conference, because: (1) it avoided the question of the right to levy the dues, and (2) such a conference might involve the United States in political arrangements of Europe out of accord with traditional American policy. Nevertheless delegates from the various European countries met at intervals in Copenhagen in 1856 and 1857 and arranged a general treaty capitalizing the dues into a fixed sum payable then and forever, calculated by the amount necessary to provide a proper service, buoys and other fixtures of channel navigation. By a special treaty with Denmark the United States paid as its share $393,011. American initiative, at least, had contributed to the freedom of the seas in this detail,[1] even though the United States passed purposefully by the larger opportunity of the Declaration of Paris, and had failed to give a decent measure of cooperation in the abolition of that gangrenescent curse of the seas, the African slave trade.

More than by any of the major subjects of diplomacy with which this chapter has been concerned, the average American reader remembers Secretary Marcy by the somber detail of his famous dress circular of 1853, prescribing the sartorial habiliments for American diplomats at European courts. Loyal democratic citizens, like Senator Charles Sumner, traveling abroad, had been shocked by the representatives of the United States conforming to European etiquette and rigging themselves up with court breeches, silk stockings over the diplomatic calves, buckles and all the regalia prescribed by the social tradition of the Old World. Marcy took it upon himself to put an end to this. In a general circular to the service he gave his opinion that official representatives of the United States ought to wear the "simple dress of an American citizen," in accordance with early practice (like that of Benjamin Franklin). Though the circular left much freedom and discretion to the individual diplomat, it came to mean ordinary dress clothes, which meant on formal occasions a full dress suit, sometimes even in the glare of the noonday sun. At first this brought embarrass-

---

[1] The late Professor Charles E. Hill exhausted the subject in his standard work, *The Danish Sound Dues and the Command of the Baltic* (Duke University Press, 1926).

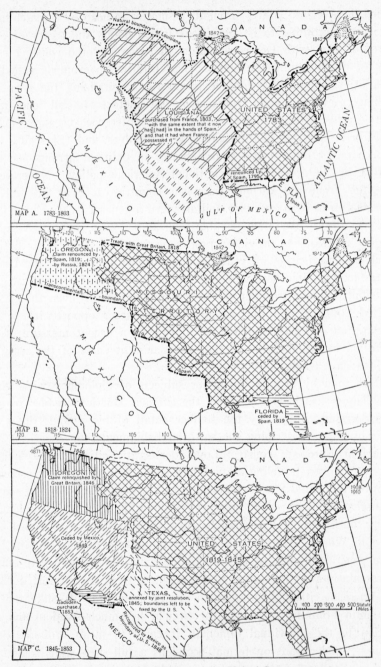

Map 21.   Territorial Acquisition of the United States, 1783-1853.

ment and some snubbing, and American diplomatists even ran a danger of being confused with entertainers or perhaps undertakers. It was difficult to establish the order as a dignified rigueur, fitting for the representatives of people who had thrown away all the trappings of European monarchies. Charles Francis Adams, Minister to Great Britain during the Civil War, went back to the old costume, breeches, buckles, silk stockings, and all. "I am thankful we shall have no more American funerals," Queen Victoria is reported to have remarked to him at a court reception.[1] State Department instructions of 1866 allowed diplomats who had been volunteer officers during the Civil War to appear in military dress uniforms. But in the twentieth century civilian ambassadors and other representatives again began to depart from simple democratic garb. After the First World War, Ambassador George Harvey, apostle of the "return to normalcy," appeared before the King of England and Ireland and Dominions beyond the Seas, Defender of the Faith, Emperor of India, in knee breeches! An executive order of President F. D. Roosevelt (February 2, 1937) stopped this folderol: "No person in the diplomatic service shall wear any uniform or official costume not previously authorized by Congress."

A more general and sweeping reform was directed to the diplomatic service by an act of Congress of 1856, repealed within a twelvemonth: it graded the whole service, fixed salaries and fees, and provided for a system of apprenticeship to mitigate the prevailing custom of political appointments. This proved more than the democratic body politic could suffer, but it was an interesting symptom. No legislation for systematic organization of the diplomatic and consular service making possible a career for young men, safe from the stress of political turnovers, took place until the acts of 1915, 1924, and 1946. But it was fortunate that no civil tenure existed when the Civil War began in 1861 and unbending loyalty to the Union became necessary for its very preservation. Before we proceed to the critical diplomacy which accompanied that conflict, it is appropriate to turn to the first contacts of the United States with the peoples of the Pacific Ocean, the Far East and the Near East.

[1] *The Journal of Benjamin Moran,* edited by Sarah Agnes Wallace and Frances Elma Gillespie (University of Chicago Press, 1949), has many descriptions of court regalia. See particularly Vol. II, 828, 907.

CHAPTER XX

THE NEAR EAST, THE PACIFIC, AND THE FAR EAST

(1783-1868)

WHILE the continental domain of the present United States as a world power was being established by the events narrated in the previous chapters, and diplomatic intercourse was being extended to the capitals of the occidental world, the allurements of commerce had attracted American traders to both fringes of Asia, the Near East, and the Far East. Approach to the Near East was a sequel to the chapter of relations, at first so humiliating, with the Barbary states of North Africa. First contacts with the Far East were trading voyages to Canton in the earliest years of the nation's existence. It would be several generations, of course, before the Far East would be more than a remote exotic region to the United States, before these peoples and governments would present, as they do now in the twentieth century, the most vital of the foreign problems of our own times. It is in order at this point to review the beginnings of diplomatic relations with the countries of Asia.

Sporadic voyages of American trading vessels to the eastern Mediterranean date back as far as 1785. An appreciable commerce, unprotected by any treaty guaranties, began to run the gauntlet of the Barbary corsairs to the Turkish port of Smyrna. The first American official to visit Constantinople had been Captain William Bainbridge, tribute-bearer to Algiers in 1800. The Dey of that principality, under a gratuitous interpretation of the English translation of his treaty (of 1795) with the United States—or perhaps merely as an arbitrary act—forced Bainbridge and his ship, which bore no other name than *George Washington,* to carry an Algerian envoy to the Sultan of Turkey, shadowy sovereign of the Barbary states.[1] Despite the inglorious circumstances

---

[1] The contemporary English translation, which was ratified equally with the Turkish text, of Article XIV of the treaty of 1795, reads, in part: "Shou'd the Dey want to freight any American Vessel that may be in the Regency or Turkey said Vessel not being engaged, in consequence of the friendship subsisting between the two Nations he expects to have the preference given him on his paying the Same freight offered by any other Nation." A careful translation made in 1930, for the authentic Miller edition of the treaties of the United States, did not reveal any counterpart of this sentence.

under which the American flag first appeared in the Dardanelles, Bainbridge was received in a friendly manner at the Ottoman capital, where he learned of a desire to welcome a minister from the United States. An American consul was formally recognized at Smyrna (1824), but several more years passed before successive diplomatic missions [1] finally culminated in the ratification (1831) of the first treaty. It provided reciprocally most-favored-nation arrangements for commerce, permitted American merchant ships to pass through the Bosporus into the Black Sea, and, in the English copy (not in the Turkish original text [2]), provided for extraterritorial juridical status of American citizens in Turkey.

Notwithstanding disputes over extraterritoriality, relations with Turkey enjoyed a comparatively undisturbed tranquillity—despite the temporary alienation of American public opinion by the Armenian massacres during the latter years of the century—until the entrance of the United States into the World War in 1917. The United States never hankered after Turkish territory, as did the major European powers. On the contrary, humanitarian impulses poured out toward that strategic land which dominated the overland path of Europe to the trading wealth of the Orient. Missionaries, proselyting educators, (Robert College, founded 1863) and hospitalizers were welcomed, and they prospered in their pious and disinterested endeavors.[3] After the Balkan states (Greece, 1829, Roumania,[4] 1881, Serbia, 1881, Bulgaria,[5] 1908) won their independence from the Turks, the United States proceeded to establish ordinary diplomatic intercourse with them—without capitulations—relations devoid of any especial significance until the World War of the twentieth century.

First Americans in eastern Asia sailed there on the trading ship *Empress of China* out of New York around Cape Horn direct to Canton in 1785. The modest profits of this voyage excited emulation. Other ports and merchants, particularly in New England, took up the trade to China, and also to Manila, Java, Batavia, India, Arabia and even to

---

[1] C. O. Paullin describes them in his *Diplomacy of American Naval Officers, op. cit.*, 122-153. See also Wriston's *Executive Agents, op. cit.*, 319-334.

[2] Miller, *Treaties*, III, 554.

[3] L. J. Gordon, *American Relations with Turkey, 1830-1930, an Economic Interpretation* (University of Pennsylvania, 1932).

[4] By a letter of August 15, 1878, of the President to the Prince of Roumania, that state was recognized soon after the Treaty of Berlin, which constituted it an independent principality. A diplomatic agent and consul-general were commissioned to Roumania, June 11, 1880.

[5] No American diplomatic agent reached Bulgaria until June 5, 1903, although one was commissioned April 24, 1901. Bulgaria did not reach full independence until 1908.

the eastern coast of Africa. The commerce was persistent, but irregular in volume, and suffered grievous interruption by the Embargo and the War of 1812, but it soon surpassed in value the traffic to the Near East by way of the Mediterranean. On these private trading voyages the Stars and Stripes sailed up and down the western coast of the two Americas and was temporarily raised on many an islet in the South Seas. The Far Eastern trade came to center at Canton, the only port to which foreign goods were permitted to come to China. Its first prosperity was connected with the rich fur preserves of the western hemisphere: the fur seals of the South Atlantic, and the sea otters of the northwest coast of America. From eastern Asia came back marketable shiploads of nankeens, spices, tea, and novel oriental products and articles. We have already observed the significance of the fur trade to China in the development of the Oregon Question. Compared with other nations trading to Canton from Europe, the American commerce was greater than that of any except Great Britain, whose trade was about five times that of the United States.

Some American ships left Atlantic ports by the other route, eastward to Asia, carrying specie, ginseng, furs collected in the United States, and more usual cargoes for ports of call in Europe and colonial ports in Africa and the Indian Ocean. After the War of 1812 the China trade steadily increased, though at no time was it more than three per cent of the total foreign trade of the United States. After the exhaustion of the fur trade there developed the ordinary traffic in agricultural and extractive products—principally the latter—of the growing United States, competing with that of England, France and the other nations of Europe.

The first tariff act (July 4, 1789) of the United States gave substantial preferences to goods imported from China and India in American ships, as compared with foreign, but otherwise the Government followed only languidly the initiative of the maritime traders. Underpaid consuls or agents for seamen were appointed: at Calcutta, 1784, Canton, 1787, Isle de France, 1794, Batavia, 1807, Manila, 1819, Honolulu, 1820. Captain Thomas Ap Catesby Jones commanded a naval cruise to the Pacific in 1826 in the course of which he negotiated articles with the native rulers of Tahiti, the Society Islands, and Hawaii for the friendly reception and treatment of American ships and traders. Jones regarded the articles as provisional agreements operative only until the President's pleasure could be known. The President's pleasure never was made known.[1] In contrast to the restrictions placed by Great Britain and Spain on American trade with their American colonies, their Far Eastern colonial ports were open with little or no discrimination;[2] and French ports like the Isle de France (Mauritius) were also open, as were the French colonies in the West Indies.

In the competition for the China trade at Canton the American traders were at an apparent disadvantage. The European powers had approached the Far East by way of their colonies *en route*, in Africa, India or Malaysia—colonies where they had established naval bases, and from which they could easily summon force for the protection of their nationals and the advancement of their commercial and political interests. The Americans, on the other hand, were absolutely without military or naval support, except for an occasional weak naval-training cruise—the nearest naval base of the United States was on the Atlantic coast, the other side of the world. The United States Government paid very little attention to the activities or interests of its citizens adventuring in the commerce of Asia and was not in a position to help them there in case of trouble. The Chinese, theoretically, did not distinguish between different nationals in their narrowly restricted commercial contact with the western world; in Chinese eyes all foreigners, particularly foreigners wandering for mercenary purposes so far from the tombs of their ancestors, were coarse barbarians.[3] A spirit of cooperation and joint protection, a united front, was natural among the merchants and navigators of all nations in the Whampoa anchorage below Canton—indeed it has always been more natural for occidental individuals, including diplomatic agents in the Orient, to co-operate in dealing with Asiatic monarchs than it has been for their governments at home; but when this came to the test of force the Americans stepped aside. With no force of their own to bring up, of necessity they adopted a policy of respect for Chinese sovereignty, and conciliation, and propitiation of the Chinese authorities on whose sufferance their trade and their fortune depended. Relations between the Chinese and the American traders were therefore friendly, and on the whole not unsuccess-

---

[1] Miller attributes to the articles sufficient character to include them in his rigidly edited *Treaties and Other International Acts of the United States of America.*

[2] Jay's Treaty of 1794, Article XIII, admitted American ships and commerce to a direct trade between the United States and British East Indian ports, and by local licenses this was frequently extended, during European wars, to permit Americans to carry Indian produce to other Asiatic ports. Dennett, *post cit.*, 27.

[3] Kenneth S. Latourette has given a careful description of American relations with China in the pre-treaty days, in *The History of Early Relations Between the United States and China, 1784-1844* (Yale University Press, 1917).

ful, though there were exceptions. The policy of the American traders at Canton became later the policy of the United States: to respect and preserve the territorial and administrative integrity of the Chinese Empire, and to demand for its citizens an opportunity for trade equal to what the other occidental powers, at one time or another, by armed force obliged China to grant. Foreign territorial concessions would have meant exclusion of American trade. On the other hand, if the Chinese officials arbitrarily stopped the trade of Great Britain or France, they were likely to get into trouble; warships were not too far away.

The first diplomatic mission to Asia was in the person of Edmund Roberts, once an early American trader to the region of the Indian Ocean, later an official in the United States consular service. His importunities, and those of the American consul at Batavia, the fact that Great Britain had recently made a treaty with Siam (1826), together with the plundering of an American ship by natives off the coast of Sumatra, roused the Government of President Andrew Jackson. Roberts received a commission to make treaties with Cochin-China, Siam, Muscat, and Japan. He went out with the lowly title of "secretary to the commander" of a squadron of three small warships. The ruler of Cochin-China refused to treat with him except after the preliminary *kowtow*—a gesture of prostration in obeisance—which, of course, Roberts refused to give. The agent proceeded to Siam, where he signed a treaty (1833) similar to the British one, and then to Muscat, where he concluded a treaty with the Sultan of that principality, who was also the potentate of Zanzibar on the east coast of Africa. He made a return trip to the East in 1835 to exchange ratifications of the treaties, during which he was urged by the Secretary of State to proceed to Japan. Roberts put off his trip to Japan as his last, instead of his principal, duty on this mission, and died at Macao *en route* to the island kingdom. For the success of any negotiation with Japan it is just as well that Roberts did not reach there: the Shogunate was not yet ready to open the door to the outside world. Roberts' treaties with Muscat and Siam opened those realms to American trade on most-favored-nation terms, with fixed minimum tariff charges. Since that time relations with Siam were unexceptionable until 1942, when Siam declared war on the United States.

The first treaty with China rose out of the circumstances of the Anglo-Chinese War of 1839-1842. All the occidental traders to Canton —with extremely rare individual exceptions in principle—were purveyors of opium, including the Americans, but most of all the British, who were able to supply it most profitably from India. The Chinese Emperor attempted to root out the traffic in that drug, both on moral grounds and from dislike of the foreign barbarians. The Americans were willing to comply. The British refused and found their trade cut off. While the opium question was the occasion for the war that followed, the essential cause was the desire of the British merchants for favorable treaty guaranties for their trade. They withdrew their trading ships from Whampoa. British naval forces blocked the river. It was evident that the resulting war would force the Chinese to accept British demands, and that the British, if victorious, would open up a number of ports to their commerce, perhaps exclusively. The American traders petitioned their government to protect their interests against any such possible exclusion. President Tyler sent out a plenipotentiary, Caleb Cushing, a member of the Committee of Foreign Affairs of the House of Representatives.[1] News had reached Washington of the treaty of Nanking (1842) which Great Britain had forced on China at the end of hostilities. Cushing had instructions "to secure the entry of American ships and cargoes into these ports [Kwang-chow (Canton), Amoy, Ningpo, Foochow, and Shanghai] on terms as favorable as those which are enjoyed by English merchants." He did not have instructions to protect the opium traffic, or to secure a cession of territory like Hong Kong which had been made over to the British in their treaty.

The task of Cushing was the easier because the Chinese themselves had insisted, in the treaty of Nanking, that the nationals of other European powers should be allowed to come to the new treaty ports "for the purposes of trade, to which the English were not to make any objections." China herself it was, thus, who first laid down the principles out of which the Open Door doctrine later sprouted and expanded. This position seems to have been prompted by an American naval commander, Commodore Kearny, and his squadron. He had reached a *modus vivendi* for the trade of all foreign nations, including the United States, on the basis of entire equality in the newly opened treaty ports.

Cushing's treaty of Wanghia (1844), the negotiation of which was not unaccompanied by veiled threats, provided for full trading privileges of American citizens and vessels in the treaty ports with scheduled tariff and tonnage charges and most-favored-nation guaranties. Consuls might be established in those ports, and American citizens might reside there

[1] C. M. Fuess, *The Life of Caleb Cushing* (2 Vols., New York, 1923); T. Kearny, "The Tsiang Documents." *Chinese Soc. and Pol. Sci. Rev.*, XVI (1932), 75-104.

and hire land for residential and business buildings, also for hospitals, churches, and cemeteries. They were at liberty to engage Chinese teachers, interpreters, and servants. The British treaty had strongly implied certain extraterritorial rights, but Great Britain depended more for the protection of her subjects on a naval base at the newly ceded island of Hong Kong. The United States, without any naval base, relied on a diplomatic substitute in the shape of explicit extraterritorial articles; but it agreed not to extend its protection to smugglers or the opium traffic. It should be said that the smugglers preferred this to the article of the British treaty which had held the British Government responsible for the policing of its own subjects violating customs laws and treaty regulations. Treaties similar to that with the United States were straightway negotiated between China and France, and also Belgium and Sweden-Norway.[1] By operation of most-favored-nation clauses in her previous treaties, Great Britain *ipso facto* received all the advantages accorded to the United States in the treaty of Wanghia, notably the extraterritorial rights now so positively defined. In fact, this first American treaty became the legal matrix of China's international relations for the next decade, until the treaties of Tientsin (1858).

Thus was extended, upon China's original initiative as a means of protection against exclusive exploitation by any one power like Great Britain, the open door of equal commercial opportunity for all foreign powers in the Chinese Empire. "It became a device by which every nation thereafter could secure for itself any privilege which had been extorted by some other Power from China by force, or tricked from her by fraud, without having to assume the moral responsibility for the method by which the concession had been obtained. Usually in after years when China took a hand in the international game she must play alone, against the entire and united company of Powers, a trick taken by her most unscrupulous opponent counted equally for the benefit of all."[2] Nevertheless the principle of equality became a device of protection against exclusive exploitation, if not against appropriation of territory, and to some extent it enabled China to play the rival powers against each other.

The onrush of expansive forces which ushered in the decade of the 'fifties in the United States brought the Orient much closer to America, particularly the new Chinese treaty port of Shanghai. The Oregon

[1] Henri Cordier, *Histoire générale de la Chine et de ses rélations avec les pays étrangers depuis les temps les plus anciens jusqu' à la chute de la dynastie mandchoue* (4 Vols., Paris, 1920), IV, 26.

[2] Tyler Dennett, *Americans in Eastern Asia* (New York, 1922), 111.

treaty of 1846, the Isthmian treaty with New Granada of the same year, the Mexican conquest of 1846-1848, and the California gold rush of 1849, were preludes to the speedy settlement of the newly won Pacific Coast. The introduction of the clipper ship, the construction of an Isthmian railroad, and later the application of steam navigation to the trans-Pacific trade, multiplied oriental contacts in the decade before the Civil War. The new events and developments emphasized the importance of eastern Asia in future American commerce and policy. Great Britain, with fortified naval bases in India and Hong Kong, became the dominating power in the Orient, the one serious trade rival. In rivalry with British policy on that side of the world the United States had to rely on a diplomatic substitute unsanctioned by force. This was the policy of the former traders to Canton as elaborated in the treaty of Wanghia, the policy of conciliation and of moral support to the integrity of China, as contrasted with the European policy of intimidation and partition. With this was mixed a sentimental sympathy for China in her developing contest with the European powers, a sympathy which sprang from preponderant American Protestant missionary endeavor.[1] This support of the integrity of China, this studied and necessary conservation of the friendship of the Chinese, enabled the United States successfully to claim always its nominally equal share in the commercial concessions, *never the territorial concessions,* forced by the aggressions of the European powers.[2]

The approach to Asia had steadily emphasized and increased the strategic importance of the Hawaiian Islands. Hawaii at first was a lonely outpost of refreshment for China traders making the long voyages by way of Cape Horn and the North West Coast, next a base for the whaling cruises in the North Pacific, still later a commercial stepping-stone to Japan, the opening of which by American diplomacy will be described presently; and finally the appearance of steam navigation made the islands the logical site for an indispensable coaling station. The archi-

---

[1] Of the 150 Protestant missionaries who arrived in China by 1851, 15 came from continental Europe, 47 from England, 88 from the United States. Dennett, *op. cit.*, 181.

[2] The new treaty régime allowed foreign consuls and other residents to establish themselves in the five treaty ports. At Shanghai the British consul leased tracts over which he later claimed full control as to sub-lease from the inhabitants. The United States consul, who had a previous understanding to rent there, successfully protested against this control; so did later the American Commissioner, and in 1863 the American Minister, Anson Burlingame. Thus at the outset American initiative opposed the establishment of exclusive foreign concessions in the treaty ports, which could easily and quickly develop into spheres and protectorates. Instead an international settlement, under a municipal code, developed under acknowledged Chinese sovereignty.

pelago is nearer to the American mainland than to the dominions of any other power; its possession by the United States would threaten the territory of no other nation, but in the possession of some other power it might easily be a menace to the homeland of the United States. A naval base self-sufficing for provisions at least, it controls at the very cross-roads of the ocean the trans-Pacific trade. Given the remoteness of effective American naval forces it is extraordinary that some European government with Pacific interests—particularly Great Britain, Russia, France or Spain—had not picked up the islands before the United States became a Pacific power. Certainly there was no lack of activity on the part of naval officers of those nations who visited Hawaii.

Though the islands had been discovered by Captain Cook in 1778, and had been a way station for all navigators since then, American influence predominated from the earliest years. Traders were there from the end of the eighteenth century. Missionaries from the United States established themselves at Honolulu in 1820 and softened the harsh contact between the mild-mannered natives and the wayward navigators of all the maritime nations of the distant Occident. Some of them became political advisers to the native kings. Following Captain Jones' agreement with the King of Hawaii in 1826—the binding force of which was very doubtful—a British officer made a treaty in 1836, and a French naval commander in 1839. These were the forerunners of other treaties by which the powers recognized the independence of Hawaii without real extraterritorial provisions. This European interest in the islands led President Tyler, with the advice of Secretary of State Webster, to declare in 1842 that the United States while itself having no designs on Hawaiian independence would be "dissatisfied" to see any other power threaten to take possession of the islands, colonize them, or subvert the native government. Such a threat occurred in 1843 when a British officer seized them. Commodore Kearny, then on his return voyage from China, protested vigorously, as did the Department of State. Great Britain quickly disavowed the seizure. An Anglo-French declaration, prompted by Lord Aberdeen (1843), engaged to observe the complete independence of the Hawaiian Islands. The United States declined an invitation to join in such an engagement. The first American diplomatic (as distinguished from consular) agent went out to Hawaii in 1843 as commissioner. The acquisition of Oregon and California vastly emphasized the importance of the islands to the United States now fronting on the Pacific Ocean. After the Mexican War, Secretary Buchanan (August

28, 1848) instructed the American Commissioner, sent to Honolulu to negotiate a treaty, that: "It would be highly injurious to our interests, if tempted by their weakness, they [the islands] should be seized by Great Britain or France; more especially so since our recent acquisitions from Mexico on the Pacific Ocean." When France temporarily seized Honolulu in 1849, Secretary Clayton declared that the United States "could never with indifference allow them to pass under the dominion or exclusive control of any other power. We do not ourselves covet sovereignty over them." France let go.

Four thousand miles east of the Hawaiian Islands, and a half-century earlier, both Federalists and Jeffersonians had taken toward Florida and Louisiana the same attitude that Whigs and Democrats now took toward Hawaii. Similarly, but belatedly, this policy was to lead to annexation. The first treaty (1849) was limited to amity, commerce, navigation, and extradition. In 1851 the King, alarmed at the possibilities of French aggression, tried to cede his domains to the United States. Consistently with Whig policy, Secretary Webster (again in office) rejected the offer. He repeated that, though the purpose of the United States was to observe scrupulously the independence of Hawaii, it could never consent to see the islands pass into the possession of any great European power. The Whigs applied to Hawaii the same policy that they attached to Cuba. President Fillmore would have been willing, had he continued in office, to enter with England and France into a tripartite self-denial ordinance concerning Hawaii as well as Cuba; but the election of 1852 stopped that.[1] After Perry's treaty of 1854 with Japan, a plenipotentiary of President Pierce, a chief executive who had publicly declared that he would have "no timid forebodings of expansion," negotiated a treaty of annexation (1854). After a sharp protest by Great Britain, Pierce rejected the treaty on the ground that it had unwisely provided for admission of the islands as a state in the Union. There is reason to believe that the Hawaiians, coached by the British Minister Resident at Honolulu, incorporated this provision in the treaty which made it certain to fail. A reciprocity treaty failed of ratification by the Senate in 1855, and again in 1867 when it was regarded as a step toward annexation at a time when popular opinion was set against expansion.[2] Despite reluctance to assume responsibilities of sovereignty, the United States remained determined to

[1] R. W. Van Alstyne, "Great Britain, the United States, and Hawaiian Independence," *Pacific Historical Review*, IV (March, 1935), 15-24.

[2] Holt, *Defeated Treaties, op. cit.*, 102-106, explains that the defeat of the treaty was due to this rather than to jealousy of sugar growers.

prevent any other nation from taking over the islands.[1] President Grant stated that "we desire no additional similar outposts [like Bermuda] in the hands of those who may at some future time use them to our disadvantage." This fixed policy was embodied in the treaty of commercial reciprocity finally ratified in 1875 which provided that none of the territory of the Hawaiian Islands should be leased or disposed of to any third power, and none of the privileges granted by the treaty should be conferred on any other nation.

At this point we must turn back to China. In the internal disturbances which overwhelmed that vast country during the middle of the century, the United States lent its moral support to the maintenance of the integrity of the Empire and to the supremacy of the imperial throne. Russia, France and Great Britain took advantage of the situation to extract further concessions. France and Great Britain fought a joint war against China (1857-1858) this time to ensure the cheerful execution of the treaties of 1842, to secure access to all the country, and to establish legations at Peking, so that the representations of their governments might secure ready and proper attention. The four separate treaties of Tientsin (1858) negotiated simultaneously by the two belligerents, and by Russia and the United States, opened up eleven more treaty ports to foreign trade and residence. From them, protected by extraterritoriality, foreigners might travel and trade through all China. The British treaty further stipulated the right of a diplomatic representative to appear at Peking,[2] and the toleration of the Christian religion, missionaries and converts. Supplementary tariff agreements fixed import charges at a general level of 5%—with collection by foreign officials under Chinese sovereignty—and legalized the traffic in opium. Great Britain, whose envoy, Lord Elgin,[3] had forced on China the major concessions in the treaties of Tientsin, remained throughout the century the dominant power in the Far East. Her treaty of 1858 set the mold for the

[1] See also "Report upon the official relations of the United States with the Hawaiian Islands from the first appointment of a consular officer there by this government," Feb. 15, 1893. *Sen. Ex. Doc. No. 77, 52d Congress, 2d sess.* Hawaiian policy is more briefly calendared by John Bassett Moore, in his *Digest of International Law*, I, 475-509.

[2] Before then it had been the effort of the Chinese Court to restrict all diplomatic approaches to contact with subordinate officials, preferably at Canton. By holding the foreigners at arm's length the Imperial Government held also foreign claims, grievances and demands at arm's length. Tribute-bearing envoys were permitted to visit Peking, thus sustaining the popular illusion that the Chinese sovereign was the mightiest in the world.

[3] The same who had negotiated in Washington so recently the Marcy-Elgin reciprocity treaty of 1854.

relations of the other powers and fixed the international relations of China for four decades. France, her ally, and Russia, only a nominal [1] neutral; and the United States, a real neutral; included in their new treaties with China the usual most-favored-nation articles which permitted them to indulge in all the privileges secured by Great Britain. The smaller powers followed suit.[2]

The United States had formally refused to ally itself [3] with Great Britain and France to take advantage of China's difficulties; but it did not decline, indeed proved eager to accept, in its treaty of 1858, equality of treatment [4] in the wake of the new foreign privileges which flowed from the territorial aggressions of the European powers. Further friction induced the allied powers to resort to additional military action (the so-called second Anglo-French War, 1859-1860) to enforce those articles of the treaty which prepared for the establishment of the legations at Peking. They occupied the Manchu capital. In the peace which brought these renewed hostilities to a close, Great Britain forced the cession of Kowloon Point, the tongue of land that juts from the mainland into Hong Kong Bay, dominating the British island; [5] and both powers forced China to pay the expenses of these later military operations. Russia opportunely took advantage of the situation to secure from China recognition of Russian sovereignty over the maritime provinces. France, aware of China's increasing weakness, made war on her vassal states in Indo-China, securing for herself (1862-1867) the provinces of Cochin-China, and a protectorate over Annam and Tonkin (1882) at the cost of another war with China. Great Britain in 1885 added Burma, hitherto a vassal state of China, to India, and extended a protectorate over Nepal and Bhutan, farther north. China was thus stripped of her loosely attached outer layer of territory. The great core lay exposed.

[1] We say Russia was a nominal neutral. She had already taken advantage of the preoccupation of China with civil and foreign wars to secure in the treaty of Aigun (1858) the surrender by China of the vast territory north of the Amur River, and to leave for future settlement the maritime provinces beyond the Ussuri. Russia profited far more than the actual belligerents: she got territory.

[2] H. B. Morse, *The International Relations of the Chinese Empire* (3 Vols., New York, 1910), I, 512-570.

[3] The abortive negotiations by Great Britain, proposing in Washington such an alliance for joint action against China, are described by Dennett, *op. cit.*, 300-303. It was to be preliminary to similar action against Japan.

[4] The American plenipotentiary, William B. Reed, negotiated a separate claims agreement allowing $735,288 for satisfaction of American claims against China growing out of violation of the treaty of 1844. An American commission parceled out the money among the claimants, adjudicating their claims, to the total of $489,694.78. An act of Congress of 1885 returned to China the balance, with accumulated interest, totaling $453,400.

[5] The ceded area of Kowloon was enlarged in 1898.

The first American Minister to reside in Peking was Anson Burlingame, who arrived in 1861. Like all American envoys to China, Burlingame was anxious to co-operate with the European representatives to secure

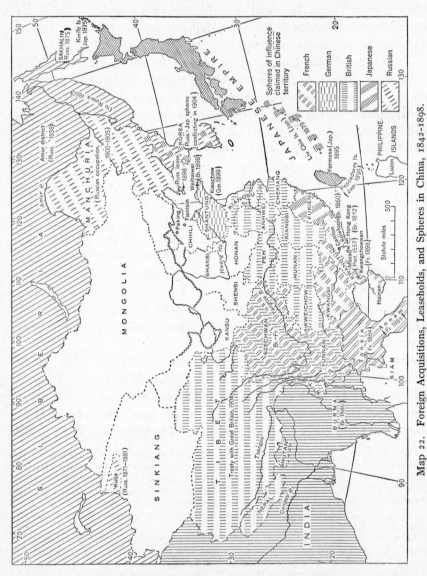

Map 22. Foreign Acquisitions, Leaseholds, and Spheres in China, 1842–1898.

the enforcement of the treaty regime, but, as always, American co-operation could go no farther than peaceful suasion. This was all the more a fact when the Civil War monopolized all the energies of the United States. Burlingame by his personal magnetism and force of character established such a moral ascendancy at Peking that he was actually commissioned by China as her first plenipotentiary to the outside world. After his resignation as American Minister in 1867 he became an envoy of the Empire to all the western powers. As the most conspicuous member of a joint Chinese mission of three, he negotiated with Secretary Seward, at Washington, eight additional articles to the American treaty of Tientsin. One of these gave to China the privileges of the most-favored nation in regard to visit, travel and residence in the United States, thus opening up the country to Chinese immigrants. In London Burlingame succeeded in softening British policy toward China. He died in St. Petersburg (1870) while on a diplomatic tour of the European capitals. The Chinese archives [1] show that Burlingame was not the chief of the mission, as he represented himself to be. He had two Chinese colleagues. But his peculiar appointment bears testimony to the great trust which China put in him and in the friendly policy of his own country.

Before the acquisition of California, American diplomatic interest in Japan was, as in the cases of Siam and Muscat, incidental to China. Following the intrusion of Christian missionaries in the sixteenth century and the wiping out of Christianity by a great persecution, Japan had shut herself to western traders, western civilization, and western warships. Only through one portal entered any glimmer from the occidental world—that was through the trading factory at Nagasaki of the Dutch East India Company, which enjoyed an exclusive concession. Even this factory was isolated in the harbor, like a pesthouse, on the rocky islet of Deshima. For two hundred years Nagasaki was the lock, Deshima the keyhole, to the closed realm of Japan. Except for a few alert individual traders, Americans were little interested in this sealed kingdom. The only necessity for a treaty was to safeguard occasional shipwrecked sailors, who, falling into the hands of the Japanese, found it difficult—because of Japan's immurement from the western world—to get back home; and to make possible the return to Japan of occasional seamen picked up at sea or even across the Pacific from disabled sailing junks. Shipwrecked American mariners were known occasionally to have been cruelly treated in Japan in those distant days. Commissions to negotiate a treaty with Japan were sent to several American plenipotentiaries [2] who were engaged in Eastern Asia, but none of these actually

[1] K. Biggerstaff, "The Burlingame Mission," *Am. Hist. Rev.*, XLI (July, 1936), 652-682.
[2] To Edmund Roberts, who negotiated the treaties with Siam and Muscat, in 1832-1835; to Caleb Cushing, who negotiated the Chinese treaty of Whanghia, 1844; to Alexander Everett, 1844, who delegated his powers to Commodore Biddle.

visited Japan, and there was no public disappointment or even notice of the fact. In 1846 Commodore Biddle, who exchanged ratifications of the treaty with China, entered the Bay of Yedo (at the head of which stands the city of Tokyo) with two frigates and inquired whether Japan would like to make a treaty and open its ports to the United States. The Japanese said no. They acquired a mean opinion of Americans because Biddle, anxious not to provoke hostilities, did not avenge an insult by a Japanese soldier who struck or pushed him. It became evident that any negotiation with Japan to be impressive must be carried on, not only with a display of magnanimity, but with a show also of force and convincing readiness to use it.

Soon after Biddle's visit to Japan, the question of a treaty of friendship and commerce assumed increasing significance. The growing trade with the new Chinese treaty port of Shanghai and the advent of steam navigation to the Pacific seemed to indicate the necessity of Japan as a port-of-call where the indispensable coal might be bunkered. The development of the whale fisheries in the north Pacific brought many American ships closer to Japanese waters, with increasing numbers of wrecks there. The sudden settlement of California and Oregon pointed to a great future trade with all the countries of Asia. Japan was now only three or four weeks from San Francisco, much nearer than Europe. In the eastern United States, manufacturers, particularly of textiles, were hopeful of sharing that expanding commerce of the future, thanks to the construction of an isthmian railroad and the prospect of a canal some day. It was a representative of one of the trading concerns [1] to the Far East who induced Secretary Clayton, in Fillmore's Administration, to consider a treaty with Japan on the model of that of 1844 with China.

It was at this period, the middle of the nineteenth century, that the European powers were encroaching on Chinese territory: Great Britain from the south, Russia from the north. Warships of those powers began to appear in Japanese harbors. The defenseless islanders were alarmed lest they suffer the fate of China. The Dutch agents at Nagasaki kept the Japanese fairly well advised as to what was happening in the world outside. It was known, for example, that the United States had recently defeated Mexico in a war and annexed large portions of her territory on the Pacific coast. Through the keyhole of Deshima the revealing light of western science and military craft had begun to filter. As the occidental powers seemed to converge on Japan, Japan herself was

[1] A. H. Palmer, of the American and Foreign Agency, commission merchants.

ripening fast for that miraculous revolution which soon was to take her from feudalism to modernism, from isolation to a career of continental conquest, finally back in crashing defeat to her own islands.

Such was the impending turn of affairs when President Fillmore dispatched Commodore Matthew Calbraith Perry to Japan in 1852. Secretary of State Webster, Clayton's successor, had drafted instructions a year before, authorizing some naval officer to make a coaling treaty, with trading articles similar to those with Siam, Muscat and China—"friendly commercial intercourse and nothing more." During the illness which preceded Webster's death, the acting Secretary of State, C. M. Conrad, redrafted these instructions, in line with suggestions by Commodore Perry himself, who had been appointed to command a squadron of five steamers and six sailing vessels to take him to Japan as plenipotentiary. The final instructions stressed the duty of protecting American navigators in those seas and the significance of the recent settlement of the Pacific Coast:

Recent events—the navigation of the ocean by steam, the acquisition and rapid settlement by this country of a vast territory on the Pacific, the discovery of gold in that region, the rapid communication established across the Isthmus which separates the two oceans—have practically brought the countries of the east in closer proximity to our own; although the consequences of these events have scarcely begun to be felt, the intercourse between them has already greatly increased and no limits can be assigned to its future extension.[1]

The fleet was an "imposing persuader" to back Perry's negotiations. Although the commander and plenipotentiary possessed large discretionary powers, his instructions emphasized the pacific character of the mission. They enjoined him not to resort to force except in self-defense in the protection of the vessels and crews under his command, or in resenting an act of personal violence[2] offered to himself or to one of his officers. The President, he was reminded, had no power to declare war. It is not improper to remark that there could have been no danger of an insult to Perry or his officers, which might require forcible requital, except in Japanese waters to which the squadron was destined. The Commodore carried with him an appropriate ceremonial letter from the President to the Emperor, and a considerable array of presents, particularly new mechanical devices, including a telegraph set and a miniature steam locomotive with cars and rails.

[1] Dennett, *op. cit.*, 262.
[2] Compare the insult to Biddle in 1846 and its interpretation by the Japanese.

The squadron, including only two steam warships, as compared with the larger force originally planned, put in at Yedo Bay, July 8, 1853, decks cleared for action. Perry refused to comply with the Japanese order immediately to retire to Nagasaki with his ships, but he steamed away from Japan after leaving the President's letter with two high princes, counselors of the Emperor. He gave notice that he would return in the spring with a larger force. If by that time the President's letter had not been received by the Emperor and properly replied to, he "would not hold himself responsible for the consequences." The Japanese at that time were impressed. In his absence from Japan, Perry took possession of some of the Bonin Islands, 500 miles southeast of the Japanese archipelago (later one of Japan's principal naval bases), and laid down a coaling base on Okinawa Island in the Lew Chews (that string of islands which lies between Japan and Formosa). He made a treaty with the ruler of that group.[1] It was Perry's grand design to lay hold of the Bonins, Okinawa (Grand Lew Chew Island) and Formosa, as the beginning of American territorial footholds in the Far East in order to sustain what he called American "maritime rights" in that part of the world after the fashion of the European powers and in rivalry with them. Thanks to his Government's [2] rejection of his proposals, such departures were postponed for half a century.

Returning to Japan, Perry found the Japanese authorities disposed to a policy of conciliation. In most skilful negotiations the American naval officer mingled a bold display of dignity with vague threats, that if Japan refused a treaty similar to the treaty with China the

[1] The Senate ratified the treaty (signed July 11, 1854), which provided for the protection of shipwrecked sailors and the opening of Napa for trade and procurement of naval supplies. Japan re-established her sovereignty there in 1872 and assumed responsibility for the maintenance of American treaty rights, with the cordial acquiescence of the United States.

[2] There is no evidence to justify the assumption that Perry's proposals would have been approved by the Whig Government had it remained in power. This assumption, and the general further assumption that the Federalist-Whigs were more aggressive expansionists than the Democrats (see Charles A. Beard, *The Idea of National Interest*, New York, 1934), will not hold water for the period before the Civil War. The Jeffersonians wanted to conquer Canada as well as Florida, in 1812, and the urge for the annexation of Canada in Jackson's time was as much Democratic as Whiggish. It was the Whigs who opposed the program of the slavery filibusters and the annexation of Cuba. It was a Democratic Administration which tried to annex Hawaii in Pierce's time. Perry's instructions were for a treaty similar to that negotiated by Jackson's Administration with distant Siam and Muscat, no more. Except for Pierce's proposal in regard to Hawaii, no administration was for the annexation of distant islands in the period before the Civil War, or before 1893, when Harrison wanted to annex Hawaii; and it must be remembered that Hawaii is closer to the United States than to any other country.

United States might send back more ships and more stringent instructions to their commander. He secured (March 31, 1854) a treaty of friendship with very restricted trading concessions. American ships and citizens were permitted to enter two of the smaller and unimportant ports of Japan, Hakodate, on the large northern Island of Hokkaido, and Shimoda, on the main island of Honshu near the Bay of Yedo, with a consul for Shimoda but no provision for permanent residence of Americans. All trade was to be for cash under strict government supervision. "In fact the treaty was hardly more than a shipwreck convention, the necessities of distressed mariners being amply provided for. It bore no resemblance to and could stand no comparison with the Treaty of Whanghia."[1] It had no provisions for coaling, no extraterritorial articles; but it did have a most-favored-nation article by which the United States could receive any further concessions which might be granted to other powers in the future.[2]

Perry's Treaty, rather an incidental occurrence in the contemporary diplomatic history of the United States, was a momentous event in the history of Japan, and ultimately in that of the modern world and of the United States. It was the signal for the making of similar treaties by Japan with other occidental powers, and eventually for the adoption of their industrial, military, and diplomatic technique by a highly cultured, socially homogeneous and warlike people, who, once started on their career, became determined to out-occidentalize the West in these achievements, at the same time to retain and cherish the essential character and spirit of their ancestors. No one then could see that Perry's Treaty meant the opening of a new epoch in the history of Asia, the force of which was not to be realized fully until the next century.

In each of the new treaties with other powers, Japan granted additional concessions which *ipso facto* accrued to the United States. Admiral Sir James Sterling, commanding a British squadron, concluded one for Great Britain (1854) with a most-favored-nation article and a trace of extraterritoriality. In 1856 a British naval force at Hong Kong ostentatiously prepared to proceed to Japan to widen the bounds of this treaty. The Netherlands in two treaties (1855 and 1856) established

---

[1] Dennett, *op. cit.*, 269.

[2] Perry's mission, and his negotiation, are described from the official American point of view, in Francis L. Hawks, *Narrative of the Expedition of an American Squadron to the China Seas and Japan, Performed in the Years 1852, 1853, and 1854 under the Command of Commodore M. C. Perry, United States Navy, by Order of the Government of the United States* (3 Vols., Washington, 1856). Compiled from the original notes and journals of Commodore Perry and his officers. A recent work is Arthur Walworth, *Black Ships Off Japan* (New York, 1947).

extraterritoriality and the right to freedom of religion. Count Putiatin, commander of a Russian squadron, who had been unable to persuade Perry to act jointly with him in 1854, signed a treaty of commerce, navigation and delimitation (determining sovereignty of the two countries in Sakhalin Island and the northern Kurile group), stipulating reciprocal extraterritoriality and opening the three ports of Nagasaki, Shimoda, and Hakodate for trade and the residence of consuls. It remained for an able American diplomat to take advantage of a situation which was impelling the Japanese to open further the doors until so recently closed to foreign intercourse. Townsend Harris appeared at Shimoda in 1856 as the first American consul (after 1859 the first American Minister).[1] He came at a critical juncture when the Japanese were thoroughly alarmed at the Russian advance from the north and the British advance from the south. He signed a treaty (1857) which stipulated in writing the privileges which already had accrued to the United States by the operation of the most-favored-nation article of the Perry Treaty, as to extraterritoriality, trade and consuls. In 1858 he perfected a convention which became the basis for Japan's commercial relations with foreign powers for the remainder of the century, as the British treaty of Tientsin was for China. It provided for a Japanese Minister and consuls in the United States and a diplomatic representative of the United States to reside at Yedo (Tokyo) the Shogun's capital. American consuls could reside at the open ports (six[2] in number), and could travel freely about Japan. Within the treaty ports American citizens might reside permanently, lease land and erect dwellings and warehouses thereon, and freely practice any religion therein. A fixed tariff was stipulated, low on staples, which comprised the bulk of imports from America, and high on wines and luxuries which came principally from Great Britain and Europe. The treaty invited Japan to study naval construction and buy ships of war and peace in the United States. The President agreed to act as mediator between Japan and foreign powers whenever requested by Japan. Ships of war of the United States, and American consuls, were to extend friendly assistance everywhere, within the obligations of neutrality. The Netherlands, Russia, Great Britain and France immediately secured similar treaties (1858) slightly lowering some of the duties; the concessions of these treaties *ipso facto* extended to all the other treaty powers.

[1] M. E. Cosenza, *The Complete Journal of Townsend Harris, First American Consul General and Minister to Japan* (Garden City, N. Y., 1930).

[2] Shimoda (until 1860), Hakodate, Kanagawa, Nagasaki, Niigata, Hiogo.

Harris, unaccompanied by force,[1] secured this treaty by pointing out emphatically to the Japanese: (1) that the Government of the United States prohibited the acquisition of territory in the Far East—it would not even admit into the Union countries, like Hawaii, which had requested admission; (2) that Great Britain and Russia, converging on Asia south and north might soon fight another war [2] in which one of them might seize Japanese territory as a base of operations; (3) that Japan might best protect her menaced homeland by "going western" and training herself under American tutelage to meet the European powers in their own manner; she should therefore give up the policy of exclusion, admit all foreigners freely to her trade, and preserve her own independence and integrity by playing off their rivalries against each other. Harris was able to point to events in China, where the powers had just secured the privileges of the treaties of Tientsin at the cannon's mouth. The English Governor of Hong Kong, he stated, was preparing to come to Japan with a fleet of fifty warships, for a treaty. It were better, he said, to open foreign intercourse with all nations by honorable treaty terms modeled on one to be signed peaceably with the United States.

"I have come to Japan as a representative of the United States," he declared, "not with any intention of disregarding the inconvenience which I may cause you, or of creating disorder. The things the President has ordered me to obtain will benefit Japan, but we have no intention of procuring them against your will and by force. You should bear in mind, however, the calamities which will inevitably arrive if you reject these proposals. These dangers will not come from the United States but from other countries. . . . If you accept the treaty I now offer you, no other country will demand anything more. If I display

---

[1] "Understand fully that there is no danger of the United States and Japan becoming enemies," Harris stated to the Japanese negotiator, Lord Hotta. "Whether you grant what I desire or do not grant it at all, the President will hold you no ill-will. Be assured of this. There will be no alienation if you reject the treaty if you only do so understandingly."

The Japanese Commissioners during their conversations with Harris kept a full verbatim record, through secretaries, of everything that was said. The original official documents have been destroyed by fire, but copies were kept by Lord Hotta, who allowed the Imperial University of Tokyo to publish them in the series *Bakumatsu Gaiko Kankei Bunsho* [Foreign Relations of Japan During the Later Years of the Shogunate] (Tokyo, 1910-1933, 24 Vols., in progress). Mr. Eugene H. Dooman of the Division of Far Eastern Affairs of the Department of State allowed me to read his translations of these documents. A few of them, including the passage quoted above, were printed in translation (by Dr. David Murray, interpreter to the American Legation in Japan) in *Foreign Relations of the United States, 1879*, 620-636.

[2] The Crimean War, 1854-1856, had occupied these two powers in the Near East, to the advantage of peaceful American diplomacy in the Far East.

this treaty to the Europeans, they will desire to conclude identical treaties, and the matter will be settled by the mere sending over of a minister." [1] From the Dutch the Japanese already had heard exaggerated reports of bellicose British plans and the destructive nature of their war in China. They now took Harris at his word.

The policy of Townsend Harris fitted perfectly the expanding commercial interests of the United States,[2] as they were then understood— to conserve the independence and territorial integrity of eastern nations so that they might not fall under the exclusive exploitation of any one European power or group of powers. It was a policy of peaceable and profitable diplomatic equipoise. It suited also perfectly the interests of Japan, conserving and developing her natural strength until she were strong enough to upset that balance and to begin to assert her own hegemony in Asia. "If you accept my proposals," Harris had predicted, "Japan will become the England of the Orient." [3]

In presenting the policy of the new foreign treaties to the Emperor's court at Kyoto, Lord Hotta, the Shogun's Prime Minister, argued in flattering and subtle terms that "among the rulers of the world at present, there is none so noble or illustrious as to command universal vassalage, or who can make his virtuous influence felt throughout the length and breadth of the whole world. To have such a Ruler over the whole world is doubtless in conformity with the Will of Heaven." To create such a world empire a first step must be treaties of amity or alliance, and a study of foreign affairs, and "in establishing relations with foreign countries, the object should always be kept in view of laying a foundation for securing the hegemony over all nations." The statement continued:

"When our power and national standing have come to be recognized, we should take the lead in punishing the nation which may act contrary to the principle of international interests; and in so doing, we should join hands with the nations whose principles may be found identical with those of our country. An alliance thus formed should also be directed towards protecting harmless but powerless nations. Such a policy could be nothing else but the enforcement of the power and authority deputed (to us) by the Spirit of Heaven. Our national prestige and position thus ensured, the nations

[1] Minutes of conversation with the American envoy at the Bansho Shirabejo on the 14th day of the 12th month (January 28, 1858) with Inouye Shinano-no-kami and Iwase Higo-no-kami. Dooman translations, *op. cit.*

[2] The beginnings of Japanese-American trade were very meager. Total exports and imports of the United States to and from Japan, 1855-1860, were $212,272, i.e., .0053 of the total American commerce.

[3] Conversation with the American envoy Harris at the Bansho Shirabejo on the 19th day of the 12th month (February 2, 1858) with Inouye Shinano-no-kami and Iwase Higo-no-kami. Dooman translations, *op. cit.*

of the world will come to look up to our Emperor as the Great Ruler of all
the nations, and they will come to follow our policy and submit themselves
to our judgment." In conclusion the statement urged that "now is the
opportune moment offered us by the changed condition of the world to
throw off the traditional policy three centuries old, and make a united
national effort to seize the opportunity for realizing the great destiny awaiting our country, as stated above. For this purpose, speedy permission is
respectfully and humbly solicited for opening intercourse with foreign
countries." [1]

Nevertheless, the treaties were signed without the consent of the
Mikado.

On the eve of the American Civil War, when the first Japanese diplomatic delegation visited the United States (May, 1860), treaties and
formal diplomatic relations had been established with all the independent civilized nations of the globe, and the Republic fortunately was enjoying peace with every one of them. During that war the first step
was taken toward a policy of active co-operation with European powers
in the Far East. The Japanese treaties of 1858 with the foreign powers
had been made in the name of "His Majesty the Ty-coon" (Shogun).
When Perry arrived in Japan few Japanese would have doubted the
authority of the Shogun for such sovereign acts. The Shogun's Court at
Yedo had developed from a sort of major-domo office which in previous
centuries had gradually taken over the rule of the Empire, the Mikado remaining in Kyoto almost a mythical figure. Things were now changing
rapidly. Japanese nobles or *daimyos* capitalized popular hostility to the
foreigners as a means of overthrowing the Shogun and setting up another
régime under the Mikado. They compelled the retirement and restriction of Lord Hotta, despite the reverence of that statesman for the
Mikado. They assassinated Lord Ii, the strongest minister at Yedo and
champion of the foreign treaties. Outbreaks against foreigners ensued,
with frequent assassinations, including that of an interpreter to the
American legation, Heuksen, in 1861. Such incidents as these the Japanese Government had feared when negotiating with Harris in 1857-
1858, if the country were opened too suddenly.[2] Next the British, and

[1] Quoted by Payson J. Treat, *Diplomatic Relations Between the United States and
Japan, op. cit.*, I, 67. I have relied much on this standard work for Japanese-American
relations of this period. Treat takes this document from Satoh's *Life of Lord Hotta.*

[2] "We were not indulging in idle argumentation when we told you that the government is greatly concerned over the feelings of the public." Conversations of Inouye
Shinano-no-kami and Iwase Higo-no-kami with the American envoy Harris at the Bansho
Shirabejo on the 18th day of the 12th month (Feb. 1, 1858), Dooman translations,
op. cit.

then the American, legation was burned (1863). The foreign nationals, nominally protected by treaty, suffered insults, brutality, and murder, amidst the civil commotion. The anti-foreign element fired on French, Dutch, and American ships.

It was evident that to maintain the new treaties in Japan the foreign powers must retaliate. The U.S.S. *Wyoming* destroyed two craft of hostile *daimyos* who opened fire on her in Japanese waters. British naval forces bombarded and destroyed the city of Kagoshima and some ships there. Secretary Seward permitted a small American (chartered) armed ship to participate with nine British, four Dutch, and three French warships in a punitive bombardment of Shimoneseki, in the fief of the hostile *daimyo,* Choshiu (August, 1864). This international punitive expedition had the tacit sanction of the Shogun's Court. The United States received its share in the indemnity of $3,000,000 required from Japan. In 1883 an act of Congress returned the money, which was accepted "as a strong manifestation of that spirit of justice and equity which has always animated the United States in its relations with Japan," [1] and set aside for the building of a new American legation.

The affair at Shimoneseki stopped at the beginning the anti-foreign movement. The powers now (1865) secured the ratification of their treaties by the Emperor, together with a new convention (1866) lowering the tariff toward a 5% level like that of China. The recalcitrant *daimyos* became convinced that Japan could not resist the foreigners except by adopting their own technique. They overthrew the Shogun, made the Emperor unchallenged on his throne (1868), reversed their policy of opposition to foreign contact, and made Japan a modern nation in the course of one generation, the era of Meiji, advancing from feudalism to world power—the most remarkable national achievement in the history of the modern world. On the eve of Japan's first great victory, the Sino-Japanese War of 1895, the unequal tariff and extraterritorial burdens were thrown off in a general revision of the treaties (1894-1899) abolishing (by 1911) all servitudes, and freely opened the Empire to full foreign contact on the western model. Until then the treaty of Townsend Harris remained the basis of Japan's international relations, as did Lord Elgin's British treaty of 1858 for China. Thanks to the United States, and to two remarkable and sympathetic American diplomatists, Townsend Harris, and his successor Robert H. Pruyn, Japan had opened her gates without occupation of her territory, and without humiliation.

[1] John W. Foster, *American Diplomacy in the Orient* (New York, 1903), 194.

There is, of course, an historical connection between American policy in China and Japan at the middle of the nineteenth century, and the later crystallization of the Open Door policy, insofar as the Open Door was limited, as it was for a brief time at the very first, to the formula of equal opportunity for the trade of all nations in China, including treaty ports or areas. That is a logical development of the most-favored-nation principle for commerce, the basis of early American policy in the Far East, but it is not likely that the Open Door would have been presented to the world as a major American policy if the United States had not stepped into the Philippines. Before 1899 the most-favored-nation treaty formula was *with China alone*. After 1899 the United States, as we shall see in Chapter XXVII, widened that precept into an attempt to secure from the *powers other than China* an agreement to observe the Open Door and the integrity of China. This was a much larger order of diplomacy, and a radical departure. It has often been thought that Seward's diplomacy in the Far East also set the policy to which the United States came back at the time of the Boxer Rebellion, in 1900: co-operation with the European powers for the guaranty of the structure of treaty rights in China. We cannot say this so securely. American participation in the Shimoneseki expedition was an isolated break in policy. Presumably it would not have happened except for Seward's eagerness to cultivate the good will of foreign governments during the American Civil War, to the diplomatic history of which we must now turn our attention.

CHAPTER XXI

THE CIVIL WAR

(1861-1867)

DOMESTIC strife invites foreign difficulties. This is an axiom of diplomacy. The Civil War constitutes a unique period in the diplomatic
history of the United States because it was the only occasion since the
crystallization of American nationality in 1789 when the Republic's hands
were really tied at home by internal convulsion. What liabilities had
its foreign policy meanwhile incurred which might press upon it in the
hour of trial?

The country was in a comparatively favorable position to indulge in
a civil war. It had no vital interests overseas to be taken from it while
its power of resistance was paralyzed. It had no weak frontiers to be
invaded by strong and unscrupulous neighbors taking advantage of opportunity, such as was customary in Europe. In case of critical difficulties over neutral rights with Great Britain, weakly defended Canada
gave pause to any British thought of hostility. The chief anxiety was
the obvious one, to prevent the break-up of the nation, which would have
been so agreeable to the great powers of the world. Aside from the primary problem of maintaining the Union intact against any foreign recognition of the southern Confederacy, there were two hostages outstanding
to fortune: the American merchant marine, then one of the greatest
on the seas, which might be endangered if the Confederacy could build
a navy in benevolently neutral foreign countries; and the policy of the
Monroe Doctrine, which was reduced to a mere phrase once civil war
broke out in the United States. The subjects of principal interest to
the student of the history of American diplomacy become, during these
years: the question of foreign recognition of the belligerency, perhaps
even the independence, of the South; the problems of neutral rights and
neutral duties, principally in regard to Great Britain; and the defense
of the Monroe Doctrine. The first two of these will form the content
of this chapter. They involve, of course, the general attitude of Europe
toward the United States.

The example of successful republican government in the United States,
and the advent of democracy there, did not commend themselves to the

ruling authorities of European states when the Civil War broke out as
the first great test whether any nation so conceived and so dedicated
could long endure. Great Britain, though long since committed to representative government, was far from manhood suffrage. The ruling
classes of all the great powers were eager to believe that democracy across
the Atlantic was riding for a fall. The aggressive diplomacy of the
neo-Democrats, American opposition to the abolition of the slave trade,
the exuberant expressions of Manifest Destiny, and the depredations of
the filibusters had aroused exasperation and apprehension. The past two
decades of Anglo-American relations particularly had been full of provocative issues, always with the possibility in the background of unprofitable war with a bothersome enemy. British public opinion was
not displeased at the trials which democracy had now encountered in
America.

British complacence at the impending breakdown of the American
democratic republic rested on more than political philosophy and sentiment. Southern independence would divide the one formidable power
in the New World and remove a barrier for the advancement of Britain's
interests in that hemisphere. It would throw down a large portion
of the tariff wall of the United States which had protected in Southern
markets the competing manufactures of the northern states. It would
free a source of cotton supply from the political leverage of the Washington Government—four million persons in England depended directly
or indirectly on the cotton textile industry. Except for fortification of
the aspirations of liberals struggling to widen the suffrage and strengthen
faith in democracy, and the hopes of anti-slavery humanitarians, there
was nothing to impel the Mother Country to wish well for the Union
cause. Even English humanitarian vision was somewhat obscured at the
beginning of the war by President Lincoln's statement—designed to hold
in the Union the wavering border states—that he did not propose to
interfere with slavery within a state.

France, after a second experiment with liberal democracy, had succumbed to another Emperor Napoleon. Though discerning observers
may have seen his power slipping when the conflict began in America,
he was still apparently at his apogee. Greedy for "glory" and prestige
to distract the public from the strivings of uneasy republican remnants,
he had developed an adventurous foreign policy, recently victorious
in the Crimean and Austro-Italian wars. The new Emperor had turned
to America with revived plans for a colonial empire built up through
the guise of protectorates. Political chaos in Mexico seemed to offer

the opportunity of setting up a puppet state there as a pedestal for the further spread of French influence and power. The Civil War played into his hands at an opportune moment by devitalizing the Monroe Doctrine, which stood in his way. He was therefore anxious to see the United States break into halves hateful to each other, and to make a treaty with the South to suit his own purposes, but he dared make no decisive move of recognition except in conjunction with Great Britain: interference meant war. French textiles also depended on American cotton. Six hundred thousand Frenchmen won their bread directly or indirectly from them. A shortage, and unemployment, offered good pretexts for advancing the Emperor's political designs in America. The greater weight of articulate French public opinion [1] supported imperial policy, but submerged democrats of the working classes of both France and Great Britain showed a steady sympathy for the North.

Spain shared the official feelings of France and Great Britain. Spanish diplomacy had reason for no gratitude toward the United States, and Spain during the war attempted the reconquest of Santo Domingo. Austria, which furnished the puppet archduke for Napoleon III's enterprise in Mexico, was solicitous of that venture, and content to see a spread of monarchical Catholic influence in Latin America. The smaller powers of Europe were not unsympathetic to the North, but generally indifferent. This sympathy was more widespread, possibly, in the German states than elsewhere; the investing public there took up heavy blocks of United States bonds, purchasable at attractive prices because of the weakness of exchange against United States currency. Since interest and principal were paid off in gold these proved to be superlatively good investments. The German states were not quite yet an appreciable factor in trans-Atlantic politics.[2] Russia stood distant from the scene, but desirous of seeing the United States continue a balance against British power and anxious to keep on good terms with the North in order to make use of its ports as bases for preparing the Russian fleet for cruising against British commerce in Atlantic and Pacific in case of war over the disturbing Polish question.[3] It may be said that in the

[1] W. Reed West, *Contemporary French Opinion on the American Civil War* (Johns Hopkins Studies in History and Political Science, XLII, No. 1, Baltimore, 1924).

[2] Otto Graf zu Stolberg-Wernigerode, *Deutschland und die Vereinigten Staaten von Amerika im Zeitalter Bismarcks* (Berlin and Leipzig, 1933), 55-76.

[3] A Russian fleet visited New York and San Francisco harbors in 1863. It was hailed as a friendly gesture from the Czar Alexander II, who had just abolished serfdom in Russia, to a nation which had just abolished slavery. This explanation was accepted by historians until 1915 when the late Professor F. A. Golder, after examining the Russian archives, published his article on "The Russian Fleet and the Civil War," *Am*

desperate struggle to save a mighty nation from falling apart, Lincoln's new government could look nowhere for help or active sympathy. The student of the history of diplomacy may remember that no nation laments the dissolution of a great power unless some dangerous rival power becomes greater thereby.

The advent of William H. Seward, considered to be the most prominent leader in the Republican Party, to the office of Secretary of State, worried the foreign statesmen, particularly the British. Seward was a political leader of high intellectual power, though not so adamant for logical principle as Abraham Lincoln. He was an avowed expansionist, a Republican apostle of Manifest Destiny. Rather than face the terrible prospect of civil war as the consequence of the triumph of his party, Seward preferred to pick a quarrel with some power or powers in an effort to unite the country by a common struggle against a foreign foe. "If the Lord would only give the United States an excuse for a war with England, France or Spain," he told the Minister of the Hanseatic Cities, "that would be the best means of re-establishing internal peace." [1] His sentiments were well known to the diplomatic corps before he took office. The new Secretary indited his first despatches with an aggressive tone, as if paving the way for war. Three weeks after inauguration, he proposed to the President his famous "foreign-war panacea," in an astonishing memorandum entitled "Some Thoughts for the President's Consideration":

I would demand explanations from Spain and France [as to intentions in Mexico and Santo Domingo], categorically, at once.

I would seek explanations from Great Britain and Russia, and send agents into Canada, Mexico, and Central America, to rouse a vigorous continental spirit of independence on this continent against European intervention.

And, if satisfactory explanations are not received from Spain and France, Would convene Congress and declare war against them. [2]

Hist. Rev., XX (1915), 801-812. This showed that the cruises were made in anticipation of possible war with Great Britain over the Polish question, and with a view of getting the fleet out of the Baltic to distant seas where it could damage the British merchant marine. See also his article "The American Civil War Through the Eyes of a Russian Diplomat," *ibid.*, XXVI (1921), 454-463; and E. A. Adamov, "Russia and the United States at the Time of the Civil War," *Jour. Mod. Hist.*, II (1930), 586-602.

[1] The most important work on Anglo-American affairs at this time is E. D. Adams, *Great Britain and the American Civil War* (2 Vols., New York, 1925). The standard general histories by Rhodes (1899), Channing (1925), and McMaster (1927), devote much space to foreign relations during the Civil War. Of these Rhodes stresses Anglo-American relations, and has stable judgments; but much research has been done since then, a great deal of which (up to the year of his publication) will be found embodied in Channing's shorter but very acute analysis.

[2] J. G. Nicolay and John Hay, *Abraham Lincoln, A History* (10 Vols., New York, 1890), III, 445-447.

Seward proposed to take over the real leadership of the Government
for conducting such a war. Lincoln quietly pigeonholed the document,
for historians to bring to light long afterward. The Secretary presently
settled down under the President's leadership and throughout the rest
of the Civil War he conducted the foreign affairs of the United States
on the basis of peace, and with greatest ability, despite his lack of previous experience in that department of government. Peace, that is,
providing no foreign power intervened to aid the South: such would have
meant a war to which the Administration would have responded promptly
and undivided, with the support of the people.

The first preoccupation of the new Government, in its conduct of
foreign affairs, was to prevent recognition of the southern Confederacy.
There is no question but that secession and revolt had created real war
on a large scale, though Seward hoped to persuade foreign powers it
was a mere insurrection which did not evoke the laws of war between
nations and their consequences on neutrality. Three days after the
firing on Fort Sumter by Southern batteries, President Lincoln (April 15,
1861) issued a call for volunteers for the purpose of "repossessing"
federal forts seized by the South. This was followed (April 17) by a
proclamation by Jefferson Davis, President of the southern Confederacy,
offering letters of marque for commissioning privateers. Lincoln promptly
responded (April 19) by proposing to seal up Southern ports against any
such activity, and to cut off their commerce and resources for importing
military and other supplies. He set on foot a blockade of the coast of
the seceded states and declared that any Confederate authority molesting
a vessel flying the flag of the United States would be treated as a pirate.
This was an attempt to circumscribe the rebellion as a purely domestic
matter not affected by the laws of war. It was supplemented by eager
but unsuccessful efforts to adhere unconditionally to the Declaration of
Paris which the previous administration had refused as it stood, and
which prohibited privateering. Under the lead of Great Britain the
powers presently rejected such unconditional adherence, unless limited
to the period following the war; but they were willing to accept it for
the period of the war, with the exception of the first article which
abolished privateering. This was because the South, informally approached,[1] had signified its willingness to accept all but the first article.

[1] This was done through the British consul, at Charleston, Robert Bunch. The
French consul there had similar instructions. Bunch gave an irregular passport to a
British merchant, who had taken out his first naturalization papers, to carry despatches
to England. This person was arrested when about to embark from New York and
found to be carrying over 100 private letters to Confederate agents and sympathizers

Privateering, however, proved of no use to the Confederates. The foreign powers closed their ports to privateers and prizes, and the Union navy quickly ran down the half-dozen privateers that were fitted out early in the war. In 1863 Congress passed an act authorizing the President to issue letters of marque, but this was a diplomatic threat against Great Britain, issued when war seemed not unlikely over the construction of Confederate ironclads in English ports. It was never used.

Simply calling the Confederates pirates did not dismiss the juridical responsibilities of a state of war as defined by international law. The existence of a blockade involved the visit and search of foreign vessels, and there can be no right of visit and search on the high seas except in time of war—this was an established American principle and an in-disputable tenet of the law of nations. The European powers were quite correct in declaring neutrality once these facts were known, thus recognizing the belligerency of the South and giving it *de facto* the status of a nation for the purpose alone of prosecuting war. Recognition of independence, a more definitive matter, would depend on policy and the success of Confederate arms. The British Government, nevertheless, proclaimed its neutrality somewhat eagerly and precipitately, and thereby wounded the feelings of the United States at the outset. It issued the proclamation even before official news had been received of the blockade, and just as the new American Minister, Charles Francis Adams, was arriving in London—before he could be received. So speedily however did the facts conform to the situation that Adams could not protest effectively. With European neutrality a fact, and the rebellion undoubtedly a war, the United States Government abandoned the legal fiction of an insurrection and proceeded to apply the rules of international law to define the rights of neutrals and their obligations.

It now became a struggle to prevent the recognition of the independence of the South by any foreign state. Events on the fields of battle rather than diplomatic maneuvers really were to decide this vital contest, as is usually the case in war; but the Confederate Government made every effort to assist its cause by diplomacy. It sent abroad able

abroad. One letter mentioned that Bunch had stated that his mission was a first step in British recognition of the Confederacy. The State Department delivered the despatch bag unopened to British authorities, and promptly revoked Consul Bunch's exequatur. The French consul, more discreet, did not get into trouble. E. D. Adams, *op. cit.*, I, 184-198; Milledge L. Bonham, *The British Consuls in the Confederacy* (Columbia University Studies in History, Economics and Public Law, 1911).

agents to importune for recognition, to float loans, to purchase cruisers, and to spread propaganda. The most notable of these men were James M. Mason of Virginia, and John Slidell of Louisiana, veteran diplomat of Polk's time. Destined for London and Paris, respectively, they successfully ran the blockade to Havana. There they took passage on the British mail packet *Trent* bound immediately for the neutral port of St. Thomas in the Danish West Indies, where they expected to embark again for England. Captain Charles Wilkes of the U.S.S. *San Jacinto* was then bringing his vessel back from an extended cruise on the African station. In the West Indies he heard of the presence of the Confederate Commissioners on board the *Trent*. Without instructions he straightway intercepted that vessel on the high seas, forcibly took off the two envoys (November 8, 1861) and sent them as prisoners to Boston. The British proclamation of neutrality itself would have sanctioned taking in the ship to a prize court for carrying enemy despatches (which Wilkes overlooked), but the captain made the mistake of taking off the rebellious American citizens, seemingly *impressing*[1] them, although not into naval service, instead of bringing in the ship for adjudication. When news of this capture reached the North a disappointed nation was yearning for military successes which had not materialized. People welcomed the spectacular act with hysterical and unthinking acclaim. Congress immediately voted Wilkes a gold medal of honor, with little thought of the historical import of the seizure or of its effect on foreign affairs at a vitally critical time.

In England the Ministry had already considered what it would do if the Confederate Commissioners were taken from a British ship by a federal cruiser, having in mind the presence of an American warship recently at Southampton. The Prime Minister had told Adams that seizure of despatches or the agents might raise serious questions. Adams had replied that no such incident would occur off a British harbor. In anticipation of such an incident the law officers of the Crown had delivered an opinion stating that "the United States' ship of war may put a prize crew on board the West India steamer, and carry her off to a port of the United States for adjudication by a Prize Court there;

---

[1] Of course there was a legal distinction here. The United States maintained that they were rebellious citizens, just as Great Britain had once maintained that her sailors taking service on American merchant vessels were disobedient subjects, but actually by practice the United States had treated rebellious citizens as belligerents, and the world had extended belligerent recognition to them. This gave them *de facto* the rights of enemy aliens. On the other hand before the War of 1812 naturalization in many cases of impressment (in the eyes of American law) had made aliens of alleged British subjects.

but she would have no right to remove Messrs. Mason and Slidell, and carry them off as prisoners, leaving the ship to pursue her voyage." When news reached England a fortnight later of the seizure in this very manner of the envoys in West Indian waters, public opinion was lashed to a fury of indignation, which would perhaps have been equally as great even if the *Trent* had been taken into prize court in the way the law officers of the Crown had hypothetically opined to be legal. Whatever the violence of public opinion or the extent of official sympathy for the South, the British Government stood perfectly within its rights in maintaining that the seizure of the men, who were not military persons, or recognized diplomatic agents, was illegal and that the *Trent* should have been sent in to prize court. The minister at Washington was instructed to demand the immediate return of Mason and Slidell and a suitable apology for the aggression, and to close his legation and come home at once if his demand were not acceded to within seven days. The Admiralty rushed preparations for war; eight thousand troops were straightway dispatched for the defense of Canada; and a royal proclamation prohibited, for the time being, the further export of arms and ammunition.

In Washington a majority of the Cabinet shared the popular jubilation. Lincoln was more cautious. Before the British ultimatum arrived Seward came to see that a mistake had been made. He instructed Adams to inform Palmerston, confidentially, that Wilkes had acted without instructions, but he let pass the splendid opportunity immediately to restore the men to British protection on the ground that traditional American interpretation of international law had never sanctioned taking one nation's subjects or alleged subjects from the vessels of another on the high seas. Nothing was done about the outrage till the British ultimatum arrived. Then Lincoln's Government was forced by the righteousness of the British position and the necessities of the situation to restore the captured Confederate agents. Seward announced that Wilkes was justified in seizing the men as "personal contraband," even though they were destined to a neutral state; he had erred only in not bringing the ship and passengers into prize court for judicial decision. Therefore Mason and Slidell would be returned. This ridiculous definition of contraband, not yet sanctioned by American practice nor by international law, detracted from the affirmation, in reply to the British ultimatum, that England was at last adopting American principles and now demanding of the United States what once she had refused to yield. The Secretary expressed satisfaction that "a question is finally and rightly settled . . . which heretofore, exhausting not only all forms of peaceful discussion but also the arbitrament of war itself, for more than half a century alienated the two countries from each other, and perplexed with fears and apprehensions all other nations." This soothed public opinion at home; in England they were then concerned principally with the delivery of the men and the disappearance of a war crisis.[1]

First and foremost the South relied on "King Cotton" to dictate diplomatic success. Southern statesmen were firmly convinced that the dependence of French and English textile industries on their plantations for 80% of their requirements of raw cotton would force those nations to intervene to put a stop to any prolonged conflict. For this reason the South at first welcomed the blockade and actually supplemented it, in one way, by threatening a domestic embargo on the export of cotton during the first year of the war.

King Cotton proved a feeble monarch because of his very opulence. Recent years had yielded bumper crops; that of 1860 was already exported when hostilities broke out and the blockade commenced. Instead of the normal one year's supply on hand in foreign warehouses, enough cotton was stored away to supply needs for two and a half years. The jobbers were delighted at the blockade which relieved a glut and rocketed the price of the raw material; they naturally wished no early cessation of the war. When the supply began to dwindle in the latter part of 1862, alternate sources had opened up in Egypt and India, thanks to high prices. Thousands of spindles stopped, and great distress from unemployment appeared, particularly in England, but by then the military situation, so favorable to the South during the first eighteen months, had begun to veer away from prospects of victory for secession. The unemployed textile operatives in England instinctively sympathized with Lincoln's Government, particularly after they became convinced that the end of slavery was in sight. Those who suffered most from the economic situation thus offset the inclinations of the ruling classes and the assiduous propaganda of Southern

[1] The *Trent* affair has produced a prodigious amount of printing and of historical investigation, which has been capably examined by Rhodes, E. D. Adams, Channing, and H. W. Temple (*Am. Secs. State,* VI), all of whom have written their passages since the appearance of the monograph on *The Trent Affair* by T. L. Harris in 1896, and the last three of whom have had the benefit of the several articles by Charles Francis Adams, Jr., son of the minister. Professor J. P. Baxter 3rd published the opinions of the law officers of the Crown, of November 12 and November 28, 1861, in *Am. Hist. Rev.,* XXXIV, 84-87 (October, 1928).

spokesmen. Then, too, old King Cotton, impotent on his throne, had somewhat of a rival in healthy young King Corn. Intervention by Great Britain to end the war and lift the blockade would mean war with the United States and the cutting off, for a while, of imports not only of cotton, but of wheat during bad harvests in Europe and elsewhere.[1] There were also the mounting profits of a lucrative trade in supplying both sides with the necessities of war, the South through a leaky blockade, the North by an open commerce. More economic factors in England worked against intervention than for it.

Such intervention was urged by the Emperor Napoleon. He proposed that France, Great Britain and Russia jointly offer their mediation to end the war, on the basis of a six months' armistice for peace negotiations, the blockade to be lifted meanwhile. This would have been a decisive step towards the recognition of Southern independence. Already the British Cabinet had considered such a move. The Foreign Minister, Lord Russell, had favored it, and at first the Prime Minister also, but Palmerston hesitated when he heard of Lee's defeat at Antietam (September 16-18, 1862). This news caused the Cabinet to decide against mediation. When the French Emperor made his formal proposal (November 1, 1862) both Great Britain and Russia were prepared to reject it. Later Napoleon alone proposed mediation, without stating terms, to the two belligerents, in February, 1863, after the Union defeat at the battle of Fredericksburg (December 13, 1862). Lincoln's Government politely declined. The British leaders continued to toy with the idea, but never was the military situation in the United States sufficiently favorable, and there was always the weak British flank of Canada exposed in case of a break with the North. Attempts of Southern sympathizers in the British Parliament to revive the project of mediation failed thereafter. News of the Union victories of Gettysburg and Vicksburg (July 4, 1863) completely destroyed any chance of foreign recognition of Southern independence.

As the eventual military defeat of the South seemed certain, and the real significance of the Emancipation Proclamation came to be realized in England, the force of Southern propaganda rapidly wilted, thanks also to the efforts of native English publicists and humanitarians, to the counter-propaganda of the United States in the islands, and to the moral value of the Northern cause. So strong was this revulsion of feeling at the time of Lincoln's assassination that it amounted to a

[1] See note at end of chapter.

national recantation.[1] With defeat staring it in the face, the Confederate Government in 1865 sent a special commissioner to Europe, Dun-
can F. Kenner, to try to win recognition of independence by treaties
committing the Confederacy to the gradual abolition of slavery. This
mission was a confession of the moral defeat of Southern diplomacy.
Kenner reached Europe too late. His proposal would have had much
greater chances of success in 1861. The campaign to win recognition
of independence, whether outright or through the form of mediation,
was defeated, first by the military events of the war, and secondly by
the moral weakness of the Southern cause so tainted as it was with
slavery. The efforts of the South to exploit British neutrality were to
be more successful. This leads us again to the historic problems of neutral
rights and neutral duties.

We recall that the United States before 1861 had consistently espoused
the "small-navy" conception of neutral rights: that is, in the great controversies over the Rule of 1756, the nature of contraband, the status of
enemy property on neutral ships, it had advocated and practiced those
principles most advantageous to a belligerent or to a neutral possessed
only of a small navy to protect its rights or interests. Thus it had
opposed the Rule of 1756, had stood for an enumerated list of contraband strictly limited to implements of warfare, had championed the immunity of enemy property (excepting contraband) on neutral ships—
the rule of free ships free goods; and had contended for the reality of
blockades, that is, they must be maintained by a sufficient number of
warships to make entrance to the blockaded port really dangerous. The
Declaration of Paris—to which the United States was never a party—
had codified the principles of free ships free goods, and the definition
of blockade; and the United States, following the failure of Seward's
efforts to adhere unconditionally to that code, followed it in practice (reserving the article against privateering—this too was followed). We
may therefore accept the definition of blockade in the Declaration of
Paris of 1856 as international law from the point of view of the United
States: "Blockades, in order to be binding, must be effective; that is to

---

[1] Owsley, *post cit.*, describes in detail the remarkable efforts of the agents of Southern
propaganda in England and France. E. D. Adams, *op. cit.*, is also of the greatest value
in assessing the battle of propaganda. Donaldson Jordan and E. J. Pratt have presented
an elaborate and extremely readable survey of British and European public opinion in
their *Europe and the American Civil War* (New York, 1931). L. F. Stock describes
the unsuccessful efforts of Southern diplomacy to secure recognition at the Papal
Court, in the introduction to his *United States Ministers to the Papal States; Instructions and Despatches, 1848-1868* (Am. Catholic Historical Assoc., Documents: Vol. I
Catholic University Press, 1933).

say, maintained by a force sufficient really to prevent access to the coast of the enemy."

During the Civil War the United States ultimately appeared in a new rôle, as a belligerent with "big-navy" interests. Its practice adapted itself in moderate measure to this new situation. When the war began, the navy was widely dispersed and not at all adequate for prompt and effective enforcement of a blockade of all the Southern ports. Lincoln's proclamation of April 19, 1861, cautiously declared that he "deemed it advisable to set on foot a blockade" of the ports of the Southern states of South Carolina, Georgia, Alabama, Florida, Louisiana, and Texas, "in pursuance of the laws of the United States and of the law of nations in such cases provided." On April 27 this was extended to Virginia and North Carolina. It was left to naval commanders on the coast to apply the blockade thus set on foot. To avoid all possibilities of a mere paper blockade, no vessel was to be captured for violation until after it had once been warned away. This last is most important in establishing the reality of a *bona fide* blockade. Blockading the entire South *ipso facto* greatly diminished the significance of the question of contraband [1] during the war except by way of land frontiers, for it shut out all trade with the Southern ports (except those reconquered) whether in contraband or non-contraband.

The legal sufficiency of the blockade has been a matter of much discussion from then until now; but, despite all that has been written and said, we are without precise enough data for a categorical judgment. As months went by the blockade became more and more effective, but the immense coast line and numerous shallows and indentations made possible a form of blockade-running in ships especially constructed for the business, lying low in the water, small and speedy, with shallow draft.[2] These kept up some form of intercourse all through the war;

---

[1] A definition of contraband, however, appears in the form of instructions to collectors of customs (May 23, 1862) forbidding the export from ports of the United States to the three ports of Beaufort, Port Royal, and New Orleans, which had been occupied by forces of the federal government. It included the old-fashioned enumeration of implements of warfare and explosives, plus naval stores, military persons in the service of the enemy, despatches of the enemy "and articles of like character with those specially enumerated." Savage, *op. cit.*, I, 446. This was, however, a domestic regulation rather than a professed execution of international law. Nevertheless, it applied to foreign ships (interdicted from the coastwise trade) leaving those ports, because it was stated therein that foreign ships could not be placed on a more favorable footing in this respect than American ships. It is noteworthy for adding naval stores and military persons and despatches. On April 29, 1865, President Johnson proclaimed a similar domestic contraband list that included "articles from which ammunition is manufactured." *U. S. Statute: at Large*, XIII (1866), 776-777.

[2] J. R. Soley, *The Blockade and the Cruisers* (New York, 1883).

in fact they supplied the Confederate armies with a minimum of munitions and vital necessities.[1] Few will deny, however, that the blockade was one of the great factors in the defeat of the Confederate cause. "The outcome was, in fact, the result of the naval superiority of the North and the acquiescence of England and France, although with reluctance, in the greatest commercial blockade that had ever been undertaken—a blockade which seriously disturbed their trade and industry." [2]

If England and France were as complacent, at least, as we have stated, about the breakup of the American Union, why then did they stand by so readily and accept the legality of this faulty blockade? The recent researches of Professor Baxter [3] have answered this. The whole question depended on Great Britain, the traditional champion, out of vital necessity and interests, of a wide measure of belligerent restriction of neutral commerce. If Great Britain accepted the blockade as sufficient, we could scarcely expect France to challenge it. Great Britain accepted it, as documentary evidence now available abundantly testifies, because it was to her interest to encourage such a precedent by the United States. The time might come, so the British Admiralty thought, when Great Britain itself might want to make use of a loose interpretation of the sufficiency of blockade, and it would be well if the United States (likely to be a large trading neutral then) by its own example had set the precedent. That time did come during the World War when Great Britain—despite some details of altered circumstances —cited in general the precedents of 1861-1865 with telling effect. Never was a policy formulated with a shrewder and more far-seeing grasp of vital interests than British acquiescence in the blockade of the Southern ports.

[1] Owsley, *post cit*. Professor Owsley contends, pp. 25-291, that during the first year of the war the blockade was almost non-existent and that during the other years it was never able to stop more than one vessel out of four; and that the average of captures for the period of the war was one out of six. He estimates by calculations characterized for their ingenuity rather than the completeness of statistical data (impossible now to assemble) that, since 1500 vessels were actually captured during the war, there must have been at least 7500 which got through the blockade safely. The reader should constantly bear in mind that most of the vessels getting through were very small craft, and that, according to the first instructions of May 1, 1861, neutral vessels were not captured until after first having been warned away. This provision does not appear in the recapitulation of instructions of August 18, 1862.

[2] J. H. Latané, *A History of American Foreign Policy* (New York, 1927), 361.

[3] James P. Baxter, 3rd, "The British Government and Neutral Rights, 1861-1865," *Am. Hist. Rev.*, XXXIV (1928), 9-29, 77-91; and "Some British Opinions as to Neutral Rights, 1861 to 1865," *Am. Jour. Internat. Law*, XXIII (1929), 517-537. The same author in an erudite study has demonstrated the significance to naval and diplomatic history of *The Introduction of the Ironclad Warship* (Harvard University Press, 1933).

During the Napoleonic wars the British Admiralty Courts had constructed the doctrine of "continuous voyage" to prevent circumnavigation of the arbitrary Rule of 1756. The United States had accepted neither the Rule of 1756 nor the doctrine of continuous voyage which supported it, although both governments had been willing to enter into a practical compromise by treaty arrangements which were never ratified because of other issues. The naval instructions of August 18, 1862,[1] ordered that neutral vessels be allowed to continue on their voyage to a neutral port if found to be "in good faith and without contraband." The existence of contraband on board implied ultimate enemy destination of the cargo justifying bringing the ship in to prize court for violation of blockade even though bound for a neutral port. The prize courts, sustained by three notable decisions (*Bermuda, Springbok, Peterhoff*) of the Supreme Court at the end of the war, applied the doctrine of continuous voyage so as to prevent circumnavigation of a blockade by ostensible voyages between neutral ports as the first leg of a real maritime transit to ultimate enemy destination. In the First World War,[2] Great Britain and her allies perfected this doctrine and condemned all goods going in neutral ships to neutral ports if the ultimate destination by sea or *by land* of the cargoes, contraband or non-contraband, was enemy territory.[3] The Civil War practice of the United States was a useful pedestal for taking this last step.

Unable to make a go of privateering because of the blockade and the closure of foreign ports to privateers, with no provisions at home for the building of ships of war, the South turned to neutral ports for the building of cruisers. The actual construction of warships for a belligerent power was contrary to international law, and to the British neutrality law, although some British opinion advanced the customary argument that it is no more a violation of neutrality to sell warships than munitions. Captain James D. Bulloch, formerly a lieutenant in the United States Navy, was the Confederate agent sent to Europe to contract for the building of cruisers.[4] He sought the advice of an English lawyer who pointed out a way to get around the neutrality laws, as embodied in the foreign enlistment act of 1819. The gist of this

---

[1] Savage, *op. cit.*, I, 450.

[2] Julius W. Pratt has published a fine analysis of these cases, in relation to British practice during the World War, "The British Blockade and American Precedent," in *U. S. Naval Institute Proceedings*, XLVI (Nov., 1920), 1789-1802.

[3] See below, p. 596.

[4] J. D. Bulloch, *The Secret Service of the Confederate States in Europe, or, How the Confederate Cruisers Were Equipped* (New York, 1884, 2 Vols.).

legal circumambulation was: a ship had to be both built *and* equipped in British dominion for hostile operations against a friendly power to constitute a violation of the law. A vessel might be legally built but not equipped—later to be equipped outside Great Britain even by equipment sent from British territory itself, providing the builder did not send the equipment. Observing these technicalities, Bulloch contracted for the construction of two cruisers subsequently known as the *Florida* and the *Alabama*—this as a starter.

Since the peace negotiations of 1782 no such vitally important task had devolved on an American diplomat abroad as fell to the duty of Charles Francis Adams, Minister to the Court of St. James. His work it was to prevent the creation in British shipyards of a Confederate navy which would sweep the American merchant marine off the seas, open the blockade and win the Southern War for Independence. His agents promptly brought information of the real character of the ships under construction. He vigorously protested to Russell. The *Florida* (under name of "Oreto") got away under British registry in March, 1862, ostensibly for a neutral port. At Nassau the American consul in vain instituted legal proceedings against her. At a desert islet sixty miles from that port she took on armament sent out from England on a separate ship, and raised the Confederate flag. The second cruiser, known as "No. 290" and the "Enrica," was the famous *Alabama*. As she was getting ready for sea, Adams reiterated his protests. He submitted to Russell an opinion of an eminent Queen's Counsel, R. P. Collier, that the evidence showed conclusively that the "290" was destined for the Confederate naval forces, that if the vessel were allowed to escape, the neutrality act "would be little better than a dead letter." Russell for the first time now appeared concerned. The collectors of the customs had refused to act against the "290" for lack of evidence, despite the fact that they had been provided with a copy of Collier's opinion. Russell submitted Adams' evidence and other relevant papers to the law officers of the Crown for an opinion (July 23-July 26, 1862). These papers lay for five days at the house of the senior law officer, the Queen's Advocate, while the last preparations went briskly forward on the suspected vessel. The delay was due to his illness, in fact he went insane. Not until July 28 did the other law officers, the Attorney-General and Solicitor-General, get hold of the papers. The next day they promptly recommended the immediate seizure of the ship. She was already out to sea, off the English coast. Even then vigorous action on the part of the Admiralty might conceivably have detained her. It made no effort. In the Azores the *Alabama,* as she was now christened, took on armament in a manner similar to the equipment of the *Florida,* and was likewise commissioned a Confederate cruiser. The British Ministry had not connived at her escape, as was widely believed at the time in the United States if only because of the advantage of her depredations to a rival merchant marine; but tergiversation, negligence, hesitation and delay of what Dickens once dubbed the "circumlocution office" had allowed the vessel to get out.

Adams' immediate anxiety was not ultimate responsibility for this grave damage, a question to be settled at some later date, but to save his nation by preventing the departure from British ports of any more warships for the Confederacy. Elated at the success of the cruisers, the resourceful Captain Bulloch prepared for the construction of more warships: a gunboat, the *Alexandra,* and two iron-clad rams intended to sink the wooden navy of the Union and open the blockade. On Adams' instance, the Government seized the *Alexandra,* but the courts released her (June 23, 1863) on the ground that neutral English subjects had a right to build and sell warships to a belligerent. She took to sea. The decision proved that Great Britain had no adequate legislation on her statute books, just as the United States had no adequate legislation on its statute books during the Texan war of 1836. Lacking the adequate legislation, should the British executive idly limit itself to the letter of the insufficient law as President Jackson had done?

The Ministry had been slower to realize the implications for Great Britain's own interests of the building of belligerent warships within its neutral ports than the Admiralty had been to see the significance of acquiescing in the imperfect Union blockade. The question now began to dawn on Palmerston, Russell and their colleagues: suppose Great Britain should be involved in a war with a small-navy power like Russia or Japan, and the enemy were allowed to fit out in the United States, after British example, a fleet of *Alabamas* to prey on British commerce in both hemispheres? The first of the Confederate iron-clads—built by Laird and Co.—was launched on July 4, 1863. Adams told Russell (July 11), that if the rams escaped, Great Britain would be a participant in the war. The American Minister received news of Gettysburg and Vicksburg on July 16. In foreign eyes that meant the turn of the military tide and the ultimate defeat of the South. Adams continued to deluge the Foreign Office with evidence and protests against the rams. On September 3, having heard from Russell that the Government had legal advice to the effect that it could not interfere with the vessels, he sent in a last protest. Russell replied that the subject was "under serious and anxious consideration." At the moment the foreign office was at least considering precautions against any repetition of the *Alabama* incident. At this juncture Adams received information that one of the rams was about to put to sea. The next day (September 5, 1863) he made his celebrated declaration to Russell: "It would be superfluous to point out to your Lordship that this is war." This clinched the desired result. The authorities seized the rams.[1]

Despite the real vigilance of the British authorities from 1863 on, other ships got away from Great Britain for hostile cruises against a friendly power. The *Alexandra,* which had been liberated by the Courts, was seized later at Nassau, in December, 1864, and condemned there for violation of the foreign enlistment act. Confederate agents covertly purchased a steamer, which successfully got to sea, was equipped at sea from English sources, and began an ineffective cruise as the C.S.S. *Georgiana.* Fortunately the United States navy was able to destroy this warship before it did any tangible damage. Another such cruiser, the *Georgia* (April, 1864), proved unseaworthy, returned to England, was sold to a neutral owner, and subsequently captured and condemned. In October, 1864, similarly, they purchased another steamer, and equipped it at sea from English sources. As the C.S.S. *Shenandoah* this warship rivaled the depredations of the *Alabama* on a notable 58,000 mile cruise around the world. After the war was over her captain surrendered her to British authorities at Liverpool.[2] Confederate orders had also been placed in France for the building of ships of war. Napoleon III secretly approved, but the protests of the American Minister, Dayton, and the work of the vigilant consul-general, John Bigelow, broke up the project.

For the North these cruisers built in England and equipped from England became scourges of the seas. Responsibility of Great Britain was further increased by unneutral hospitality furnished them in colonial ports in the way of supplies and recruits. They, and prizes and tenders which they fitted out as small cruisers, captured a great number of merchant vessels flying the Stars and Stripes, burning many at sea without the formality of judgment—there was no prize court outside the blockade to which prizes could be sent or taken. The damage to national inter-

[1] *The Journal of Benjamin Moran* (Univ. of Chicago Press, 1949), II, 1218-19.
[2] For enumeration of the cruisers, their careers, and prizes, see J. T. Scharf, *History of the Confederate Navy* (New York, 1887), 782-818.

ests was greater than the actual depredations. Insurance rates leaped up and the American merchant marine scurried by sale to the cover of neutral flags, much of it to the British flag,[1] the government of which had been responsible for the destruction. The Civil War witnessed the final step in the decline of the once dominant American merchant marine. In 1860, 2,379,396 tons of private shipping engaged in the foreign commerce of the United States, of which American ships carried 66.5%; in 1865 of a total of 1,518,350 tons, they carried only 27.7%.[2]

After diplomatic danger for the Union had disappeared in England, and hence in Europe, the aspect of affairs on the Canadian frontier became in turn alarming to Great Britain. Confederate agents, reversing the rôle of 1837 when Canadian insurrectionists had endeavored to use the United States as a base for the support of rebellion in Canada, organized raids south across the line. One of these shot up and rather gently pillaged the sleepy Vermont village of St. Albans (October 19, 1864), the raiders escaping back across the boundary line. The leaders, apprehended by colonial authorities, pleaded personal irresponsibility and showed they were acting under orders of the Confederate Government. A Canadian judge released them. The incident caused a division of federal troops to be diverted to the protection of the northern frontier, induced Lincoln to give notice of the abrogation of the Rush-Bagot disarmament agreement of 1817 (a notice presently withdrawn when things quieted down), and led to the imposition of a few months' régime of strict passport requirements, hitherto unnecessary, for all visitors from Canada. On the whole, British officials in Canada showed more enthusiasm and alacrity to prevent the recurrence of such a provocation than had federal authorities after the *Caroline* affair of 1837. A victorious Union army might easily be turned northward. Queen Victoria noted in her diary, February 12, 1865:

Talked of America and the danger, which seems approaching, of our having a war with her as soon as she makes peace; of the impossibility of our being able to hold Canada, but we must struggle for it; and far the best would be to let it go as an independent kingdom under an English prince! [3]

---

[1] The President of the British Board of Trade stated January 20, 1864, that for the year 1863-1864 the number of clearances of British ships had increased to 14,000,000 tons as against 7,000,000 tons for all foreign tonnage, and gave the decrease in American tonnage between Great Britain and the United States at about 47%. Transfers of American shipping to the British flag were in 1861, 71,673 tons; 1862, 64,578; 1863, 252,579; 1864, 92,052. Hill, *American Treaties, op. cit.,* 283.

[2] W. L. Marvin, *The American Merchant Marine* (New York, 1902), 284, 353.

[3] George E. Buckle, ed., *Letters of Queen Victoria,* Second series (3 Vols., London, 1926-28), 250.

It would not have been difficult for Lincoln's Government, nor that of his successor in its first months, to turn against Great Britain with terrible effect the warm indignation stirred up in American hearts by the escape of the Confederate cruisers from English shipyards, indignation fanned by the lingering ambitions of Manifest Destiny, supported by a host of bayonets now without employment. Ardent expansionist as he was, Seward took no advantage of this opportunity for revenge. The United States sought first the channels of friendly arbitration with the Mother Country for adjustment of the *Alabama* claims. President Johnson's Administration took prompt action to co-operate with Canadian authorities for the breakup of the invasion of Canada projected by the Fenians, a society of Irish-Americans hateful of Great Britain and working for the independence of Ireland. For this the President received the "warmest acknowledgments" of the British Government. The net result of the whole affair of the Confederate raids from Canada was the abrogation of the Marcy-Elgin reciprocity treaty of 1854, by proper notice under its provisions. It was believed in Congress, and the thought was doubtless shared by Seward, that the resulting dislocation of Canadian commerce might quicken natural impulses for voluntary annexation.[1] These impulses existed, but they were quieted forever by the successful British experiment in nation-building,[2] the creation of the Dominion of Canada in 1867.

American diplomacy really lost only the prosperity of the American merchant marine during the Civil War, despite the desperate nature of the conflict and the singlehanded fight it had to wage. The nation's safety and the perpetuation of the Union, however, were not assured entirely by the faithful efforts of high-minded and able diplomatists like Charles Francis Adams. That the North had the greater moral weight on its side was not enough. Victory was won on the field of battle by millions of young men who were ready to lay down their lives that the nation might live undivided. Only when individuals are ready to make this sacrifice can great causes triumph. Only this way can worthy nations live.

[1] Joe Patterson Smith has privately published an instructive study of Canadian-American relations, 1864-1867, *The Republican Expansionists of the Early Reconstruction Era* (distributed by the University of Chicago Libraries, 1933).

[2] R. G. Trotter, *Canadian Federation, Its Origins and Achievement: A Study in Nation Building* (London, 1924).

WHEAT *versus* COTTON

The influence of wheat *versus* cotton has not been precisely established. In 1859 Great Britain imported 99,000 "quarters" of "wheat and flour" from the United States; in 1860 over 2,000,000 quarters; in 1861 over 3,500,000; in 1862 over 5,000,000; in 1863 approximately 3,000,000. See E. D. Fite, "The Agricultural Development of the West During the Civil War," *Quar. Jour. Economics*, XX (Feb., 1906), 259-278, and L. B. Schmidt, "The influence of Wheat and Cotton on Anglo-American Relations During the Civil War," *Iowa Jour. History and Politics*, XVI (July, 1918), 400-439. Professor F. L. Owsley in his voluminous and informing study of *King Cotton Diplomacy; Foreign Relations of the Confederate States of America* (Univ. of Chicago Press, 1931), notes that "no mention has been found in official or private correspondence of these [British political] men which would indicate that a wheat famine would accompany a war with the United States." (E. D. Adams, however, notes a speech of Forster on this point.) Owsley attributes the idea to Union propaganda in England. He explains abnormal British importations of wheat from the United States in 1860, 1861, 1862, and 1863 as due to the convenience of British trade in accepting payment that way for munitions, and notes that when demand for munitions fell off (after Northern manufacturers caught up) so did wheat imports. This does not explain the abnormal imports for 1860 and 1861, at least, nor why British trade found it convenient to accept wheat rather than something else, nor are there as many statistics presented in regard to the munitions industry as we would like to support the thesis.

CHAPTER XXII

THE MONROE DOCTRINE; EXPANSION AFTER
THE CIVIL WAR

(1823-1872)

WHILE the United States was torn by the Civil War the main task of American diplomacy was to supplement the military efforts that were being made on land and sea to save the Union and the nation, that is, to prevent the intervention of foreign powers within the Republic itself. Foreign policies hitherto fixed had to be left, so to speak, to drift for themselves. What were these fixed policies? They were the Monroe Doctrine, continental expansion, the freedom of the seas. They did not constitute, as has been said before, immediately vital hostages to fortune. The Monroe Doctrine was trampled on by France and Spain in Mexico and Santo Domingo, but it could be redeemed by a nation with a million victorious bayonets. The process of continental expansion was interrupted—slavery, which had given it such an impetus toward the southwest, disappeared—but the process could be resumed if desired. The American blockade qualified the freedom of the seas by a precedent highly convenient to the mistress of the seas, but the latter's careless attitude toward the Confederate cruisers created a precedent as dangerous to herself as it was presently to be advantageous to American diplomacy. After the war Seward had to pick up the traditional policies qualified and tempered by that great national experience, and to face foreign issues which were aftermaths of the civil conflict. Contemporaneously reappeared lingering manifestations of the interrupted expansionist urge, which now lacked popular support, but which had behind it the force of this vigorous and far-sighted statesman. It will be simplest to consider in this chapter first the French adventure in America, then Seward's expansionist program. The settlement of the so-called *Alabama* claims will be deferred to the following chapter on Anglo-American arbitrations.

The intervention of Napoleon III in Mexico in 1861-1867 was the climax of French ambitions in America that had been incubating ever since the revolution of the Spanish colonies, designs that certainly ran counter to the warnings of President Monroe.

Monroe's pronouncement in 1823 had said that the extension of Euro-

pean colonies in America, or European interference with the free destiny
of any American nation, would be regarded as the "manifestation of an
unfriendly disposition" toward the United States. Did this mean that
the United States would take arms to defend any American nation anywhere in the New World against such an unfriendly disposition? We
recall that President John Quincy Adams repeatedly refused to discuss
alliances with the Latin-American nations and avoided the possibility of
commitments when preparing for the abortive Panama Congress of
1826. Was Monroe's pronouncement a youthful bravado safely trum-
peted to the world from behind the wooden walls of the British navy?

The first real challenges to the Doctrine came in the most distant
parts of South America. Great Britain in 1833, over the protests of
the Argentine Confederation, occupied the strategically located Falkland
Islands, commanding the South Atlantic approaches to the Pacific Ocean.
President Jackson's Government avoided an issue by considering this to
be merely a reassertion of a previous occupation which had been since
in suspense.[1] A more clear-cut case occurred during the regime of the
French Orléanist monarchy (1830-1848). It is remembered that the
United States had been the first to recognize the independence of the
Latin-American states. This fact, compared with the hesitations of
Great Britain, and the public pronouncement of the Monroe Doctrine
had served at first to establish all over Latin America a preponderance
of good will for the sister republic of North America. Great Britain
countered, under the leadership of George Canning, and promptly recognized (1824) the independence of Spain's former colonies and negotiated
treaties of commerce with them.[2] These treaties ignored the features
of freedom of the seas which were a conspicuous part of the contemporary treaties of the United States with Latin America. Some of
them, like that with the Argentine (1825), gave particular dispensations
to British subjects, and placed British merchants on a basis of commercial equality with local citizens. British prestige soon triumphed
in the Plata region, where the United States [3] never enjoyed any treaty
relations until 1853.

[1] Julius L. Goebel, *The Struggle for the Falkland Islands; a Study in Legal and
Diplomatic History* (New York, 1927), argues powerfully that the Argentine title to the
islands was good.

[2] H. W. V. Temperley, "The Later American Policy of George Canning," *Am. Hist.
Rev.*, XI (1906), 779-797. J. F. Rippy, *Rivalry of the United States and Great Britain
over Latin America (1808-1830)* (Johns Hopkins University, 1929).

[3] Jackson's Government became embroiled in a dispute with the Argentine Government
over some seizures of American ships and property at the Falkland Islands prior to the
British reoccupation. This greatly delayed the establishment of satisfactory relations.

Canning's successes were at the expense of France as well as the United States. France had no treaties with the new states of the southern continent because the restored Bourbons, obstinately espousing the sacred principle of legitimacy, had refused to have anything to do with nations born out of revolutions against a monarchical sovereign. The overthrow of legitimacy in France herself in 1830 resulted in a speedy recognition by the new revolutionary king, Louis Philippe, of the independence of the former Spanish and Portuguese colonies. South America, particularly the Plata region, continued to offer an attractive field for the restlessness of a convalescent warlike power whose premature exertions the watchful Dr. Canning had restrained in 1823 with his distasteful prescription of the Polignac memorandum.[1] In 1838-1839 a French consul at Buenos Aires became involved in disputes with the Argentine dictator, Rosas, who refused to extend to French citizens the treaty rights enjoyed by British subjects. In an effort to establish French prestige in South America, the government of Louis Philippe took hold of this issue and of a lesser one with Mexico. A French fleet enforced the claims of nationals against Mexico by blockading Vera Cruz (1838) and bombarding the fortress of San Juan de Ulloa. At this time in the United States the House of Representatives invoked the Monroe Doctrine in a resolution suggesting explanations from France and the President's mediation. Though President Van Buren had already indicated his willingness to mediate, France and Mexico signed a claims convention at Vera Cruz under the mediation of the British Minister.[2] The resolution of Congress alluded also and similarly to events in the Plata region. There the hearty Rosas was proving to be a more difficult problem. French diplomacy and military and naval forces organized the dictator's enemies against him in Uruguay and the up-river provinces, blockaded Buenos Aires and the Argentine bank of the Plata River, sent warships and marines up the Paraná River—the Ohio of South America—and occupied the island of Martin García at the mouth of the Plata. Great Britain from the first opposed the French policy, and in the Argentine and the Banda Oriental[3] the forces of patriotism rallied round the dictator. Unsuccessful, France withdrew with damaged prestige from this first adventure in 1840. Britain's ascendency remained complete in those parts.

The downfall of the Whig Government in England in 1841 retired

---

[1] See above, p. 205.
[2] Dexter Perkins, *The Monroe Doctrine, 1826-1867, op. cit.,* 40-49.
[3] The eastern bank of the La Plata and Uruguay rivers.

Lord Palmerston from the Foreign Office and brought in the pacific Aberdeen under whose direction so many of the troublesome Anglo-American issues were settled between 1841 and 1846. Anxious to establish and strengthen an entente with France and thus to fortify the peace of Europe, but at the same time jealous of France's policy in South America, Aberdeen drew the French into a joint intervention in the Plata country for the purpose of strengthening foreign rights there, particularly those of British mercantile and banking interests. The two powers blockaded the Argentine coast again, 1845-1849, a "peaceful blockade" which Palmerston later denounced as piracy and "equivalent to stopping neutral vessels on the high seas and making them pay blackmail."[1] They again seized the island of Martin García in the estuary of the great river, and once more a foreign fleet ascended the Paraná, bombarding forts on the way. As a spearhead against the powerful Rosas, who had chased his own political enemies into Uruguay, the European allies sanctioned a foreign legion of French immigrants for the defense of Montevideo and the elimination of Rosas' influence in the Banda Oriental. France armed and subsidized these legionnaires. There was a not inconsiderable volume of public opinion in France which demanded the landing of troops in Montevideo, as French agents on the ground urged repeatedly. There is plenty of reason to believe that Great Britain never would have tolerated this move. The activity of the dictator proved too much for the halfway measures of the allied powers, not really able to invade the Argentine in force, divided in policy between themselves and co-operating only with the greatest difficulty. Palmerston, after he returned to office in 1846, was glad to liquidate the whole intervention, under most embarrassing circumstances, and to warn France to do the same. In 1848 another revolution in France paralyzed the last manifestations of her adventure in South America. Louis Napoleon came to the Presidency of the Second Republic and presently (1852) to the throne of the Second Empire. Before undertaking further adventures in South America he desired to establish himself solidly in France, and France more strongly in Europe.

The foreign intervention in the Plata country was a direct violation of the Monroe Doctrine as proclaimed in 1823. The intervention was unsuccessful, thanks to the rough resistance of Rosas, and to the dissension between the allies, but not thanks to the Monroe Doctrine.

---

[1] John F. Cady, from whom this passage is quoted, has contributed a history of *Foreign Intervention in the Rio de la Plata, 1838-50* (Philadelphia, 1929), which clearly establishes the relationship between that event and Polk's restriction of the Monroe Doctrine to North America.

Whatever danger there may have been—and there was danger—of French territorial lodgment there, was blocked by British diplomacy again, as in 1823. The United States stood aside. It was too much occupied with diplomatic problems of the first dimension on the northeast frontier, in Texas, in Oregon, and finally with the Mexican War and the Isthmian Question. In fact it proved of great advantage that Great Britain, particularly, was entangled in the distant Argentine between 1845 and 1848. Southern South America was then too far away to be of vital interest to the United States. President Polk informed the allies that he would not oppose their intervention. Even if it had led to territorial acquisition there, we may believe that the President, occupied with his own problems of expansion on the continent of North America, would have acquiesced. In his notable messages to Congress of 1845, 1847, 1848, reaffirming the Monroe Doctrine, messages evoked by the questions of Oregon, California, Yucatan, and the Isthmus, Polk went out of his way to limit the application of the Doctrine to North America.

There was a continuity of inhibited French desire in Latin America from 1823 to the Mexican adventure of 1861-1867. Before 1859 France's position in Europe was too insecure to oppose effectively Great Britain, not to mention the United States, in the New World. But by that year, at the close of the Austro-Italian War, Napoleon III seemed to have restored French primacy in Europe; in 1861 the American Civil War began, and emasculated the Monroe Doctrine in the one remaining continent to which Polk had applied it.[1] At last the opportunity was at hand to checkmate the United States and to make French influence paramount in Latin America. "The American war has made it impossible for the United States to interfere," the Emperor was quick to note.[2]

The political chaos in Mexico, which from 1857 to 1861 had invited the intervention of President Buchanan's expansionist policy, presented an equal opportunity to France, where it was remembered that in 1838 Mexico had proved more easy to handle than the Argentine. Mexico was in civil war between the conservative clerical party, which looked towards monarchy, and the republican party under the aboriginal leader, Juárez. The Buchanan Administration recognized and supported the Juárez régime, hoping for a territorial cession in return for protection of Mexico against European intervention. Such a development was in

[1] Cady, op. cit., Ch. VI; Perkins, op. cit., Ch. III, and Polk's Diary.
[2] Napoleon III to the Comte de Flahaut, October 9, 1861, quoted in fuller form by Perkins, op. cit., 365.

fact estopped by the growing sectional opposition in the United States; but, genuinely alarmed, conservatives in Mexico turned to Europe, particularly to France: Mexico could be saved from absorption by the United States only through European intervention, they said; and they were willing to accept a French protectorate for that purpose. Incidentally this would appeal to French clericals as the preservation of a Catholic kingdom against the encroachments of aggressive Protestantism from the north. At first they talked of a monarchy under French protection with a Spanish Bourbon prince for king. The Mexican clerical, José de Hidalgo, was the person through whom these proposals reached the ears of Napoleon III and his young empress Eugénie,[1] herself of Spanish birth. In Paris high in office speculators in repudiated Mexican bonds pushed along the project for intervention, to their great personal profit.[2] In the summer of 1861 anarchy was still rife in Mexico. The foreign governments had abundant grievances for the continuous plundering of their citizens, even their legations (in the case of Great Britain). The Juárez Government (July 17) specifically suspended its international obligations as defined in the conventions previously negotiated. Shortly afterward the British vice-consul at Tasco was murdered. This made Great Britain more inclined to some sort of international co-operation with the eager French Emperor and the willing Spain. The three powers agreed in the London Convention of October 30, 1861, to use their joint forces "on the coasts of Mexico" and "for other operations," to enforce their contractual rights against Mexico, but not to seek for themselves "any acquisition of territory or special advantage and not to exercise in the internal affairs of Mexico any influence of a nature to prejudice the right of the Mexican nation to choose and to constitute freely its form of government." At Great Britain's suggestion

---

[1] Egon Caesar, Count Corti, has given the background of these approaches and of Napoleon's connection with and abandonment of the unfortunate Maximilian in his notable biographical study *Maximilian and Charlotte of Mexico* (New York, 1928, 2 Vols., translated from the German edition of 1924).

[2] A Swiss banker, Jecker, in 1859 had loaned 3,375,000 francs to the Miramón government (preceding Juárez), covered by Mexican bonds of a nominal value of 75,000,-000 francs. Juárez stopped payment on the bonds. Jecker's bank failed in 1860. In January, 1861, the Duc de Morny, half-brother of Napoleon III and President of the *Corps Législatif,* acquired from Jecker, whom he caused to be naturalized as a French citizen, a 30% interest in any profits that might be made from collection of the bonds. French diplomacy championed these bonds, at first at face value, later (1864) accepting from Maximilian a scale-down to 30% of the par value thereof. In 1865 Jecker actually collected 12,660,000 francs. Perkins, *op. cit.,* 382; Corti, *op. cit.* (see index under Jecker).

Excluding accumulated interest the amount collected afforded a profit of 9,285,000 francs, of which 30% (Morny's share) would have been 2,785,500 francs. Morny himself died before the money was collected. So did thousands of French soldiers in Mexico, and many more thousand Mexicans.

an article provided for the accession of the United States. This article was a gesture, an empty formality; the powers agreed to proceed toward their end without waiting for such accession.[1] Great Britain desired (in addition to equal satisfaction of the claims of her nationals) to keep the other powers from aggressive occupation of territory; she also had exposed the weak flank of Canada—a factor continually to ·be borne in mind in Anglo-American relations of this decade. Her not unsympathetic attitude toward the progress of French designs in Mexico was however later revealed by her prompt recognition of the new Emperor of Mexico.

Spain was less reserved in her attitude, but became distracted by her interest in the occupation of Santo Domingo, to be noted presently, and less eager to follow up the intervention jointly with France when it was revealed that an Austrian rather than a Spanish prince was destined for the new Catholic throne of Mexico. Napoleon III was altogether deceitful. Already three weeks before agreeing in the Convention of London not to interfere within the domestic affairs of Mexico, he was planning to put forward as the new ruler the name of Archduke Maximilian, brother of the Austrian Emperor, Francis Joseph.[2]

The allied forces occupied Vera Cruz and seized the customs, but the country did not rise in their favor. Nor did Juárez yield. The French decided to push on to the capital; and eventually 28,000 men, plus a small foreign legion of 8,000 Belgians and Austrians, under Marshal Forey, and later Marshal Bazaine, occupied the country. The British immediately withdrew from the prospect of such a war. The Spanish felt the undertaking beyond their resources, and departed for Santo Domingo, bent on restoring that island to their sovereignty while the United States was fully occupied at home. In Mexico City the French commander brought together a hand-picked Council of Notables who declared (1863) for a monarchy, and invited Maximilian to take the throne. After signing a convention with France, the former Archduke and his youthful wife Carlotta, daughter of the King of the Belgians, Leopold I, and granddaughter of Louis Philippe, left for their new tropical empire. The convention of Miramar (April 10, 1864) provided that "as soon as possible" the French army in Mexico should

---

[1] Text of the convention in E. Schmit Ritter von Tavera, *Geschichte der Regierung des Kaisers Maximilian I. und die Französische Intervention in Mexiko,* 1861-1867, 2 Vols (Wien und Leipzig, 1903), I, 12-13.

[2] Perkins, *op. cit.,* 359.

be reduced to 25,000 men, but a secret supplement to the convention promised that "however events in Europe may turn out, the assistance of France shall never fail the new Empire." For the present, by this supplementary instrument, the army in Mexico, including the foreign legion, should be reduced to 28,000 in 1865, 25,000 in 1866, and 20,000 in 1867. Maximilian agreed to reimburse France 270,000,000 francs for the expenses of the army of intervention to July 1, 1864, with 3% interest from that date, and to pay 1,000 francs per annum for every French soldier in Mexico after that date. Annual installments of 25,-000,000 francs cash were to start immediately in payment to France. The new Emperor, before he even saw his realm, decreed the issue of a loan of 201,000,000 francs, at 6%, issued at 63. Of this he got immediately 8,000,000; the French treasury got 66,000,000 as a portion of monies due it.[1] Other sums were set aside to take care of the interest on a £10,200,000 (nominal value) English loan of 1851. A London banking house floated the loan, which offered an unexpected opportunity for satisfying in part dubious claims of British subjects; the unfortunate subscribers were mostly French.

Thus at the beginning, and with no consultation of the Mexican people or nation, the new régime was saddled with heavy financial obligations to France (in addition to the exorbitant claims which had accompanied the original intervention) which could be made the lever for ascending political concessions in the future. Maximilian at this time successfully resisted a French article giving Napoleon's Government the right to exploit all the mines of Sonora and to maintain troops there for their protection.[2] This was an earnest of what French influence in Maximilian's puppet state meant for the future. Maximilian on his side had dreams of absorbing all of Central America, the Isthmus and northern South America,[3] and extending his influence to Brazil by arranging a marriage of one of his brothers to a daughter

[1] Corti, op. cit., I, 325-327. The text of the convention and accompanying decrees are printed in E. Schmit von Tavera, op. cit., I, 235-240. A second 6% loan of 250,000,000 francs was floated at 68 in Paris in 1865. Of this only 70,000,000 were placed at the disposal of the new Mexican Empire.

[2] The McLane-Ocampo treaty, negotiated by the Buchanan Administration in 1859, was a document of this nature which was rejected by the United States Senate (27 nay, 18 aye). By it Mexico was to receive a loan of $4,000,000, and the United States a perpetual right of way across the Isthmus of Tehuantepec, with two railroad routes across northern Mexico to the Gulf of California, free ports at their termini, the right to protect the transit with troops, and to intervene, in cases of extreme danger, without even the consent of Mexico. According to Perkins, the first article of the treaty further would have given the United States a general power of police protection over all of Mexico.

[3] See map 23.

of the Emperor of Brazil. France, Austria, Spain, Great Britain, Portugal, Belgium, Prussia, Italy, and Sweden quickly recognized the new Mexican Empire. This was more recognition than Texas ever had. Was it not an auspicious beginning, as Maximilian surveyed the beauties of his new realm from the delectable mountain retreat of Cuernavaca?

It was soon evident that the safety of the puppet Emperor's crown and person depended on the continuing presence of the French troops.

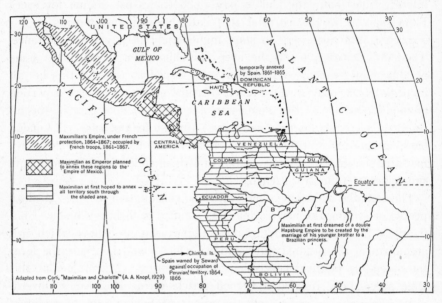

Map 23. Threats to the Monroe Doctrine during the American Civil War.

Every month made more certain the triumph of the Northern armies in the United States, brigades soon to be liberated to assist, if necessary, the Juárez patriots to put the French out. Events in France and in Europe were conspiring meanwhile to force withdrawal if the United States should not compel it. From the beginning the Mexican adventure had incurred the ill will of the Liberals in the French Chamber. The scandalous Jecker claims gave tone and color to the attacks of the opposition. This increased as the difficulties and expenses of the enterprise accumulated. Profound events were shaping across the Rhine. Napoleon had been outwitted by Bismarck in 1865 to remain neutral as Prussia prepared to fall on Austria in preparation for the consolidation of a new German Empire. Continued occupation of Mexico meant more money and more men when both were needed at home. Already the extravagance of this ill-timed intervention had compelled economies which curtailed the forces in France herself in order to maintain these thousands of troops in North America. The Prussian victory of Sadowa, by which Bismarck crushed Austria in the summer of 1866 and forged the North German Confederation, was soon to stun thoughtful Frenchmen. Napoleon's mistakes in every quarter were ominously mounting against his country.

Amidst this combination of difficulties had appeared a rapidly rising tone of protest from the United States. Until the end of the war Secretary Seward had been compelled to adopt a policy of neutrality between the contenders for Mexican sovereignty, and of professed confidence in France's good faith.[1] He had restrained himself with only warnings and caveats against any permanent occupation of Mexican territory. The protesting resolutions of Congress had been empty of action. General Lee's surrender at Appomattox made it possible for the Secretary of State to insist where previously he had suggested. His despatches to the Minister of the United States at Paris, designed to be read by the Emperor's advisers, became successively more emphatic. November 6, 1865, he stated that "the presence and operations of a French army in Mexico, and its maintenance of an authority there, resting upon force and not the free will of the people of Mexico" was "cause of serious concern to the United States." President Johnson's annual message (December 4, 1865), which bears the verbal markings of Seward's handiwork, declared: "We should regard it as a great calamity to ourselves, to the cause of good government, and to the peace of the world should any European power challenge the American people, as it were, to the defense of republicanism against foreign interference." Seward made this more pointed in a despatch (December 16, 1865) stating that the French design of establishing a foreign monarchy upon the ruins of an American republican government would inevitably imperil the friendly relations of France and the United States. Finally, February 12, 1866, he demanded that a time limit be set for French evacuation. Already Napoleon, mindful of increasing domestic and European difficulties, as well as the unchallangeable force of the restored American Union and its veteran armies, had decided to "cut the painter" and to leave Maximilian to his own fate. Seward's information from Bigelow, the American Minister, had made him aware of this;[2] in fact the Secretary found himself under the necessity of restraining

---

[1] J. M. Callahan, *American Foreign Policy in Mexican Relations, op. cit.*, 278-340.

[2] C. A. Duniway, "Reasons for the Withdrawal of the French from Mexico," *Am Hist. Assoc. Annual Report for 1902*, I (1903), 313-328.

opinion in the United States, particularly among higher army officers like General Grant, who wanted to drive the French out of Mexico with Civil War veterans.[1] He preferred to extract a diplomatic victory from the plain necessities of France. The unpleasant demands of the United States, backed by the presence of 50,000 troops in Texas under General Sheridan, ready to seek touch with Juárez's forces across the Rio Grande, allowed of no more hesitation or equivocation. A desperate mission of the young Empress Carlotta to the Court of Napoleon, and to the Pope, was of no avail; and under the strain of her solicitations her reason collapsed. Napoleon, who had sworn to protect Maximilian no matter what happened in Europe, deserted him. A vigorous protest of the United States to Austria, together with the necessities of the Austro-Prussian War, prevented the recruitment of a division of volunteers there for the support of the tottering throne in Mexico. The last of the French troops embarked for home in the spring of 1867. Now fell on the House of Hapsburg the first of a long series of tragedies: Maximilian courageously met his fate before a native firing-squad at Querétaro (June 19, 1867). Scarcely three years later the collapse of the Second Empire in the Franco-Prussian War swept Napoleon III from his throne. He died in exile in England in 1873. The Mexican misadventure, never popular with his subjects, at least contributed to his downfall. How the world changed during the lifetimes of the two sad widows left by the two Emperors, of France and of Mexico! They survived the First World War and the break-up of the Hapsburg Empire in middle Europe.

In dealing with Napoleon III, Seward was careful not to mention the Monroe Doctrine by name. He referred to the established policy by which the United States was opposed to the interference of European powers for the purpose of setting up monarchial institutions on the ruins of American republican governments. This made it possible to take time to analyze the purpose of France as long as the domestic situation at home had compelled him to go slow. In the end he made the most of his opportunity without coming to a pointed ultimatum. When the French got out of Mexico it seemed to be at the demand of the United States. The Maximilian affair tremendously strengthened the stamina of the Monroe Doctrine and gathered for it immense popular approval. The nation became conscious, by vivid illustration, that European powers

---

[1] General Schofield had been given leave of absence by General Grant for the purpose of assisting the organization of the armies of the Juárez régime, perhaps with American veterans. Seward astutely diverted him from this purpose by sending him on a private mission to Paris to advise Napoleon of the robust attitude of American opinion.

were eager to take advantage of any opportunity to overthrow the prohibitions of President Monroe. Other threats to the Monroe Doctrine
during the American Civil War were to strengthen that Doctrine as a
national policy after the victorious conclusion of the conflict.

We have stated that Spain was more occupied with Santo Domingo
than with Mexico. That eastern half of the island had revolted against
Haitian sovereignty in 1844.[1] Precarious peace and independence
in the face of the Negro dominance in the island impelled the white
element successively to make overtures to Great Britain, France, the
United States, and Spain to extend protection, over their state, even
to annex it; but the jealousies of the powers of each other prevented
any action. The interlude of the Second Republic and then the European policies of the succeeding early years of Napoleon III distracted
French attention; but Spain waited watchfully for an opportunity.
When the American Civil War broke out she maneuvered a "spontaneous" declaration by the actual Dominican President of annexation
to Spain. Promptly Spain declared the island annexed (May 19, 1861)
and sent troops there. Seward got first news of these proceedings during March, 1861, when he was seriously recommending a foreign war
to swallow up American civil dissension. We must interpret in that
light his communication to the Spanish Minister, Tassara, stating that
if the Spanish Government should sanction the step of annexation it
would be regarded as manifesting an unfriendly spirit towards the
United States, which would "meet the further prosecution of enterprises of that kind in regard to either the Dominican Republic or any
part of the American Continent or islands with a prompt, persistent,
and, if possible, effective resistance." This gave Spain no pause. She
made the most of her opportunity and Lincoln rejected his Secretary of
State's foreign-war panacea. Seward had to swallow his words and bide
his time. Fortunately for the United States, Spain's military efforts in
Santo Domingo completely collapsed early in 1865, despite the 28,000
troops which she sent to the island. This challenge to the Monroe Doc-

---

[1] The United States, because of the race question and its implication for domestic politics, was unwilling to recognize the Negro republic of Haiti fully until 1862. The Pierce
Administration concluded in 1854 a treaty with the Dominican Republic, for the cession
of Samaná Bay as a naval base. It contained, however, an article which by implication
would have discriminated against citizens of the Dominican Republic if they desired to
travel or trade in the Southern states of the American Union. French and British representatives, who had recognized the republic without such racial discrimination, were
quick to point this out and to persuade the Dominican Government not to ratify the
treaty except with amendments. These amendments were distasteful to the American
Government and the treaty was not sent to the Senate. The accrediting of a plenipotentiary in 1854 was an aborted recognition.

trine broke down of its own weight before the United States was free to accept it.[1]

Spain in 1864 took advantage of the American Civil War also to make war on Peru (the independence of which state she had never recognized), and thereby she presently became involved in war too with Chile, Bolivia and Ecuador (1865-1868). Seward instructed (May 19, 1864) the Minister of the United States in Madrid to inform the Spanish Government "that the United States cannot yield their assent to the positions thus assumed in the name of Spain, or regard with indifference an attempt to reduce Peru by conquest and reannex its territory to the kingdom of Spain." Spain disclaimed any such intention, but she later seized the Chincha Islands as a gauge of war. To this Seward prepared a statement (July, 1866) to be conveyed by the American Minister, that if Spain persisted she could not expect the United States "to remain in their present attitude of neutrality between Spain and the Spanish-American republics." It was enough to exhibit this confidentially to the Spanish Minister in Washington; it was never necessary formally to deliver the warning. Impressed by the firming attitude of the United States against French troops in Mexico, Spain did not choose actively to continue the war under the circumstances of recovery of the United States from the Civil War; though it proved impossible to arrange a formal armistice until 1871.[2]

President Andrew Johnson left his Secretary of State in entire and responsible control of the conduct of foreign affairs. So seated, the able Seward endeavored to carry forward the process of expansion that had been so interrupted by the Civil War.[3] We have already spotted him as a free-soil Republican apostle of Manifest Destiny.[4] He desired to take advantage of the new spirit of national confidence and the sudden increase of military and naval strength to expand American power beyond the contiguous continental domain, to acquire strategic islands in the Caribbean. He had looked forward to the peaceful acquisition of Cuba and Puerto Rico some day from Spain. Imbued with these expansionist projects in the Atlantic and Pacific, he made sure of a

---

[1] Mary Treudley, "The United States and Santo Domingo, 1789-1866," *Jour. Race Development*, VII (July, 1916), 83-274; Perkins, *op. cit.*, 253-317.

[2] J. B. Moore, *Digest International Law, op. cit.*, VI, 508.

[3] T. C. Smith printed a cogent analysis of "Expansion After the Civil War, 1865-1871" in *Political Science Quarterly*, XVI (1901), 412-436.

[4] The most exuberant expression of Seward's views of the Manifest Destiny of the United States is in his famous speech at St. Paul, Minnesota, September 18, 1860, envisioning the peaceful expansion of the United States over the whole continent of North America, with the future capital "not far" from where he then stood (perhaps Minneapolis?).

transit right in any canal route across Nicaragua (treaty of 1867), the United States in turn guaranteeing the neutrality of the canal but not the territory of Nicaragua as had been the case with New Granada in the treaty of 1846. He wanted to annex the Hawaiian Islands. He had a lively interest in the affairs of the Far East. He availed himself of a unique opportunity to purchase Alaska from Russia. Turning his back on redeemed Mexico only for the time being, he hoped for the ultimate annexation of Canada. A dramatic and successful leadership of an old and powerful expansionist movement conceivably might place him in popular political favor at a time when the President had lost all such support.

For Alaska—as it is now called—there was no public demand. Except for a few individuals, no one had ever had the remotest idea of purchasing that territory from Russia. In San Francisco and in the new settlement on Puget Sound at Seattle a handful of persons were interested in obtaining fishing or fur-trading concessions in southern Alaskan waters, but these people did not think of Alaska's ever coming under American sovereignty. It was from Russia that came the offer to sell. The Russian-American Company, a quasi-governmental corporation which had administered Alaska since 1799, was in bad straits financially. The territory was too distant to be defended. During the Crimean War an agreement between the Hudson's Bay Company and the Russian-America Company had removed each other's concessions from the theater of hostilities, but it was evident that in case of another maritime war [1] Alaska would be easily captured. Senator Gwin of California had a scheme of empire in the Pacific to include Alaska, and claims he first tried to persuade the Russian Minister in Washington. Later in 1860, President Buchanan, in a round-about way behind the back of Secretary of State Cass, caused the suggestion to be repeated through Senator Gwin, and mentioned $5,000,000 as a purchase price. Between the Crimean War and the Civil War the imperial authorities weighed the value of Alaska in their councils [2] and came to the conclusion that it was better to sell before such a possible occurrence, and to sell it to

[1] Russia's next maritime war was not until the Russo-Japanese War.

[2] F. A. Golder was the first to examine the Russian archives on this subject. He found that Stoeckl's despatches reveal conversations with Senator Gwin of California, Secretary Marcy, and (in 1859) Assistant-Secretary of State Appleton (but not the Secretary, Cass) in which these officials are represented to have revealed willingness to buy. "The Purchase of Alaska," *Am. Hist. Rev.*, XXV (April, 1920), 411-425. See also B. P. Thomas, *Russo-American Relations, 1815-1867,* in Johns Hopkins Univ. Studies in Historical and Political Science, XLVIII (1930); and H. M. McPherson, "The Interest of William McKendree Gwin in the Purchase of Alaska, 1854-1861," *Pac. Hist. Rev.*, III (1934), 28-38.

the United States, a territorial as well as a maritime rival of England, and thus to introduce a buffer of American territory between British and Russian possessions. The Civil War interrupted Russian plans to dispose of the region. There is no evidence to show that Seward thought of buying Alaska earlier than March, 1867, when Baron de Stoeckl (if we believe his account), the Minister of Russia at Washington, acting upon instructions, maneuvered Seward into inquiring whether Russia would sell the territory. Stoeckl said yes. Seward was one of the few individuals who at least had thought that some day Alaska—as well as British North America to which so many of his countrymen looked forward—might peaceably, by its manifest destiny, gravitate within the American Union. He jumped at the chance to buy.[1] The Cabinet approved. A treaty of cession for $7,200,000 was quickly drafted and signed (March 30, 1867).

This lucky chance, comparable only to Louisiana, was the only fruit of Seward's multifarious projects for expansion. He immediately submitted the treaty to the Senate. He had the powerful support of Charles Sumner, Chairman of the Committee on Foreign Relations, who was present when the treaty was signed, and who looked on it as a step toward the ultimate annexation of Canada. Within ten days, before the country could really wake up to what was going on, the Senate ratified the treaty (April 9, 1867) by a vote of 37 to 2. Before the House of Representatives had actually appropriated the purchase money Russia transferred the territory (October 18, 1867). A great debate arose in the House of Representatives, where some unscrupulous and interested members had espoused the cause of certain persons who possessed invalid claims against the Russian Government for supplies alleged to have been delivered during the Crimean War.[2] But the spirit of Manifest Destiny, a warm feeling toward Russia engendered by the belief in her particular friendship for the Northern cause during the Civil War, and the active propaganda of Stoeckl and Seward won the day: the necessary appropriation carried by a vote of 113-43 (July 14, 1868). Ignatius Donnelly from Minnesota said this was but one step in an inevitable movement to extend the beneficent American system of government over all of North Amer-

---

[1] Victor J. Farrar, *The Purchase of Alaska* (Washington, 1934, revised edition, 1935). This writer has discussed the background of interest in Alaska in several articles in the *Washington Historical Quarterly*, in 1920, 1921, 1922, 1923.

[2] For the Perkins claims see Golder, *op. cit.*, and W. A. Dunning, "Paying for Alaska," *Pol. Sci. Quar.*, XXVII (Sept., 1912), 385-398. T. A. Bailey has analyzed motives for voting, both in the Senate and the House, in "Why the United States Purchased Alaska," *Pacific Historical Review*, III (March, 1934), 39-50.

ica, from the Isthmus of Panama to the extremest limits of human habi-
tation under the frozen constellations of the north. Said a Mr. Mungen,
a member from Hancock County, Ohio: "We cage the British lion on the
Pacific coast; we cripple that great and grasping monopoly, the Hudson's
Bay Company."

Mr. Mungen was short-sighted. Seward regarded Alaska as a naval
outpost toward Asia. On September 30, 1867, the United States took
possession of the uninhabited Midway Islands, west of Hawaii,
and Seward urged annexation of the Hawaiian group.[1] But Congress
would not follow him beyond Alaska. Nobody then, not even Seward,
measured the full future political consequences of this territorial leap
toward Asia. Alaska lies within sight of Siberia. The Aleutian Islands,
stretching across the North Pacific toward Kamchatka, point a finger
also at the Japanese archipelago. In 1875 a Japanese-Russian agreement recognized Japanese sovereignty over the Kurile group in return
for Russian sovereignty over Sakhalin. Few Americans then realized how
the northernmost Japanese islands and the westernmost American islands
stand almost face to face amidst the bleak fogs of the North Pacific
Ocean. This is a profound factor in twentieth-century aerial and naval
strategy. Today as never before Americans appreciate how Alaska, that
fabulous storehouse of natural resources, that Arctic realm which
has returned Seward's purchasing millions more than one hundred to
one, has become even more important as a bastion of American defense
in the twentieth century.

There was no public demand for Alaska, thus acquired by Seward's
quick and astounding coup. Inconsistently the Senate refused to ratify
a reciprocity treaty with Hawaii (September 21, 1867), which some
regarded as a first step toward annexation, though Seward thought it
did not go far enough. It rejected the treaty, little realizing that the
Hawaiian Islands are closely related to the defense of Alaska. Nor did
the Senate act on a treaty with Samoa, later presented to it by the
President in 1872, which would have given to the United States an exclusive naval base in Pago Pago, one of the finest harbors in the Pacific,
located at the cross-roads of the southern half of that ocean.[2] Nor
was there any public demand for the islands in the Caribbean, for the
acquisition of which Secretary Seward was negotiating in 1865-1868
with Denmark, Spain, Sweden, and the republic of Santo Domingo.

Seward had hardly disposed of the Maximilian affair when he made

[1] Dennett, *Eastern Asia, op. cit.*, 416.
[2] For Hawaii, see above, pp. 347-350. For Samoa, see below, pp. 454-459.

a sudden cruise "for his health" to St. Thomas, in the Danish West Indies, and to Santo Domingo (January, 1866), Haiti and Cuba. These islands and the intervening island of Puerto Rico control the principal passages from the Atlantic into the Caribbean—the Windward passage and the Mona passage. The naval exigencies of the Civil War, and the foreign interventions in Mexico and Santo Domingo had convinced the Government [1] of the desirability of adequate naval bases in the Caribbean to prevent such intrusions in the future and to cover the approaches to the isthmian transit which held an important relationship to Seward's expectations of expanding trade and navigation in the Pacific and Far East.

The cruise to the West Indies was a part of Seward's project of purchasing the Danish West Indies from their sovereign, and of securing from Santo Domingo, so recently evacuated by Spain, the cession of the capacious harbor of Samaná Bay. He had already suggested (January, 1865) to the Danish Minister in Washington the purchase of the islands in the Virgin group; and in Santo Domingo, Wm. L. Cazneau, who had been an American agent in that still unrecognized republic at various occasions since 1854, was urging a treaty for a naval base, even a protectorate. Negotiations for Samaná Bay, and of the Virgin Islands, went on contemporaneously in 1867 with Santo Domingo and with Denmark. Harassed by the omnipresent possibility of revolution, or of invasion from the black republic of Haiti, successive Dominican presidents offered to lease Samaná, even to sell it outright, or to accept a protectorate over the entire Dominican Republic. Seward signed a treaty with Denmark (October 24, 1867) for the purchase of two of the Danish islands of St. Thomas and St. John,[2] subject to a plebiscite of the inhabitants, for the sum of $7,500,000. The opposition developing in the House of Representatives to appropriations for the purchase of Alaska, plus the dormant opposition now waking in the Senate Committee of Foreign Relations to the Danish Treaty, caused him to pause when agreement of the terms of purchase of Samaná Bay was within reach with Santo Domingo.

This hesitation only increased the eagerness of the Báez Government in that island, which now pressed the United States to take over the

[1] Welles, Secretary of the Navy, favored St. Thomas rather than a base in Santo Domingo.

[2] Denmark considered it necessary because of a previous obligation to secure the consent of France for the transfer of the remaining island of Santa Cruz. Later, in 1868, she explained that this consent had been secured and that supplementary articles could be negotiated for the cession of Santa Cruz.

unstable republic outright; they even offered to declare themselves annexed, trusting for an American protectorate until the details of annexation could be worked out by the United States. Seward responded that annexation was a matter for Congress. He secured President Johnson's approval. In his annual message of December 9, 1868, the President declared: "It can not be long before it will become necessary for this Government to lend some effective aid to the solution of the political and social problems which are continually kept before the world by *the two* Republics of the island of St. Domingo, and which are now disclosing themselves more distinctly than heretofore *in the island of Cuba.* The subject is commended to your consideration with all the more earnestness because I am satisfied that the time has arrived when even so direct a proceeding as a proposition for an annexation of *the two Republics* of the island of St. Domingo would not only receive the consent of the people interested, but would also give satisfaction to all other foreign nations." The italics here introduced show how quickly susceptible was Seward's mind to large and expansive ideas. The government of Haiti had made no suggestion of annexation, though its President, Salnave, had offered the harbor of Môle St. Nicholas if the United States would assume the debt of Haiti to France.[1]

There was no movement for annexation in Cuba, where a revolution against Spanish authority was taking shape. At this time Seward had also approached Sweden for the possible purchase of St. Bartholomew's Island, and was preparing to ask Spain to sell the islets of Culebra and Culebrita off the coast of Puerto Rico.[2] Secretary of the Navy Welles' *Diary* records that in a Cabinet meeting of December 11, 1868, no action was taken on Seward's proposal for a Dominican

[1] I am indebted to Professor Charles C. Tansill for the profitable perusal of portions of his work on the United States and Santo Domingo, when it was still in manuscript; and for his instructive volume, *The Purchase of the Danish West Indies* (Johns Hopkins University Press, 1932), on which I have relied for relevant paragraphs of this chapter.

[2] George Bancroft, *en route* to his post in Germany, was instructed to discuss this project with J. P. Hale, American Minister in Spain. The latter advised that the time was inopportune to make such a suggestion to the Spanish Government. None was made.

The Swedish Government, which had offered in 1818-1819, to sell St. Bartholomew's to the United States for $200,000, and again in 1825 for $500,000 (K. E. Carlson, *op. cit.*, 68), proved amenable in Seward's time to the cession of that island, but the discussions were discontinued after the signature of the Danish treaty. In 1878 Sweden transferred St. Bartholomew's Island to France, obviously a violation of the non-transfer principle so closely associated with the Monroe Doctrine. The island was so insignificant that the United States did not choose to challenge the transfer. It is the only clearcut example of such a violation of the Monroe Doctrine.

protectorate. The House of Representatives defeated 36-126 (January 13, 1869) a resolution introduced by Nathaniel P. Banks, chairman of the Committee on Foreign Affairs, authorizing the President to extend a protectorate over Santo Domingo and Haiti. A resolution of Orth of Indiana, looking to the annexation of Santo Domingo and its incorporation into the Union, was also decisively defeated, 63-110 (February 1, 1869). Seward explained the defeat of the Orth resolution by resentment in the House at the refusal to submit to it all of the confidential correspondence with the Dominican authorities, and to the "present juncture of political affairs." One may question his assertion that the resolutions were nevertheless in harmony with the general sentiments and expectations of the people and government of the United States.[1]

Seward had used the parallel negotiations to stimulate each other; particularly did he display the possibility of acquiring Samaná as a means of hastening the deliberate Danes, whose principal object was to get as high a price as possible for these unprofitable and (for Denmark) indefensible islands. Denmark quickly ratified the treaty. The inhabitants of the islands, looking to a renewal of drooping prosperity by the establishment of a naval base, promptly and almost unanimously voted in favor of annexation. In the United States the treaty was doomed from the beginning. A month after its signature, the House of Representatives resolved, by a vote of 93-43: "That in the present financial condition of the country, any further purchases of territory

---

[1] By an act of Congress of August 18, 1856, it was provided that any American citizen might take peaceable possession in the name of the United States of uninhabited islands, containing guano deposits (in demand for fertilizer), and not in the possession or occupation of any other government. This led to the occupation by 1880 of some 70 small islands, or groups of islets. The location of some of these islands bonded under the guano act was inaccurately reported, and such cannot be identified with any islands now known. The guano deposits having been practically exhausted, many of the islands have been since abandoned. Among them was the island of Alta Vela, 15 miles south of the coast of Santo Domingo, from which the American exploiters were ejected on the eve of Spanish re-occupation. The proprietors engaged as consul Jeremiah S. Black, formerly Secretary of State, who resigned as President Johnson's defense counsel for the impeachment of 1868 when the latter would not order Secretary Seward to approve the Alta Vela claim.

The occupation of guano islands led to other small controversies, e.g., Marcus Island (with Japan), the Lobos Islands (with Peru), Navassa Island (with Haiti), Aves Island (with Venezuela). In fact the first step in the acquisition of overseas possessions by the United States came through the occupation of guano islands. Among the more important of the islands thus occupied are: Baker's (0°-15'-00" N. Lat., 173°-30'-00" W. Long.), Christmas (1°-58'-00" N. Lat., 157°-10'-00" W. Long.), Howland's (0°-52'-00" N. Lat., 176°-52'-00" W. Long.), and Jarvis (0°-22'-30" S. Lat., and 160°-01'-00" W. Long.). See J. B. Moore, *Digest International Law*, I, 567-569; Roy F. Nichols, "Navassa: A Forgotten Acquisition," *Am. Hist. Rev.*, XXXVIII (April, 1933), 505-510, and "Latin-American Guano Diplomacy" in *Modern Hispanic America* (George Washington University, 1933), a symposium of summer-school lectures; E. M. Douglas, *Boundaries, op. cit*

are inexpedient, and this House will hold itself under no obligation to vote money to pay for any such purchase unless there is greater present necessity for the same than now exists." Congress was notoriously hostile to the President. In 1868 it impeached him. A disastrous hurricane harassed St. Thomas. A terrible earthquake shook it. A tremendous tidal wave flooded it. These phenomena inopportunely strengthened the popular reaction to annexations which had set in so speedily after the ratification of the Alaska purchase, and added to the avalanche of objections.

The Senate showed no enthusiasm, and the proponents of the treaty preferred to let it go over to the new Grant Administration. So anxious was the Danish Government now for the fate of its good bargain that it was ready to add the remaining island of Santa Cruz at a nominal price. In vain its agent, General Raasloff, employed publicists to win popular favor for the purchase in the United States. In 1870 the Senate Committee on Foreign Relations recommended the rejection of the treaty. No vote was ever taken on it in the Senate before the time for ratification, repeatedly extended, finally expired.[1] Despite the article which made ratification contingent upon the action of the Senate of the United States, the rejection of the treaty by the Senate, and by the Grant Administration, aroused much criticism at home as well as abroad. The Danish Cabinet, which had trusted to acceptance of the treaty after the plebiscite had been held, resigned.[2]

President Grant's attitude was the more cogently taken to account because of the ardent efforts he was now making to carry into execution another plan of Seward's, the annexation of Santo Domingo. General Orville E. Babcock, Grant's private secretary, went to Santo Domingo in July, 1869, and signed an agreement with authorized agents of the republic containing bases for definitive treaties. The Dominicans stated that they would transfer their country to the United States for $1,500,000 to pay the national debt of Santo Domingo. There was a further provision to the effect that in case annexation was not desired the Dominican Government would sell Samaná Bay to the United States for $2,000,000. These "treaty bases" contained a curious article which specified that "his excellency General Grant, President of the United States" would promise privately to use all his influence in order that the idea of annexing the Dominican Republic to the United States might acquire such a degree of popularity among members of Congress

[1] For the negotiations of 1899-1900, and 1916-1917, see below, p. 521.
[2] Tansill, *op. cit.*

as would be necessary for its accomplishment. The Cabinet, with the possible exception of Fish, was dumbfounded. By accepting Grant's Dominican policy, Secretary Fish got a freer hand to deal with the important issue of the *Alabama* claims with Great Britain and with the related Cuban question. Babcock went back to Santo Domingo and signed (December 3, 1869) two treaties: one for the lease of Samaná Bay, the other for the annexation of the entire republic. Grant agreed during the pendency of the treaty to guarantee the Dominican Republic against all foreign intervention—just as Tyler had agreed with Texas. During 1870 the presence of a squadron of American warships in Dominican waters supported President Báez, the treaty signer, against revolutionary opposition.

Grant carried out vigorously his promise to do everything in his power to get annexation ratified. He even called on Senator Sumner, chairman of the Senate Committee on Foreign Relations, and mistakenly assumed he had secured a pledge to support the treaty. He worked on other senators. The Senate however rejected the treaty of annexation by a vote of 28-28. The other treaty did not come to a vote. Sumner had favored the annexation of Alaska, and wanted Canada too, but he was dead set against admitting Caribbean populations into the American Union. He was now using his tremendous prestige and his intimacy with his friend Motley, United States Minister to London, to block the settlement of the *Alabama* claims unless Great Britain should withdraw from North America altogether. Infuriated at Sumner for having opposed the Dominican treaty, the President took advantage of the senator's interference in the Administration's British diplomacy and dismissed the former's friend as Minister to London, then succeeded in putting party pressure sufficiently on the Senate to remove Sumner from the chairmanship of the Committee on Foreign Relations, which he had occupied with great renown since 1861. Grant's subsequent efforts failed to push through annexation—by the device of joint resolution.

In the wave of reaction that followed the purchase of Alaska, Congress was opposed, and the public was opposed, to further territorial expansion. The American nation proved to have been surfeited with territory. It was now engrossed with the new political problems of reconstruction, with the settlement and exploitation of the Far West, with the booming impulses of the industrial revolution which had the eastern part of the country in its dynamic grasp. The net result of Seward's vast vision of expansion was Alaska and the Midway Islands.

CHAPTER XXIII

THE GREAT ANGLO-AMERICAN ARBITRATIONS

(1870-1914)

THE United States has had more diplomatic controversies, and more serious ones, with Great Britain than with any other nation. Since 1815 they have all been peaceably settled. Except for two issues adjusted by diplomacy (the Isthmian Question, and the Panama Canal tolls controversy) the appeasement of Anglo-American controversies following the Civil War took effect through the medium of arbitration. The diplomacy of the two kindred peoples, whose defense in certain areas of the world is now so increasingly dependent on their close cooperation, is a sensible example of the possibilities of this means of conciliation. Such common sense rests on the pervading fact that it has been well for these nations to put aside their own quarrels in the face of greater menaces. The nature of these menaces, which in this period were principally for Great Britain, will appear as we now proceed to the remarkable series of arbitrations which successively narrowed and finally dissipated the subjects of controversy: the Geneva arbitration, the fur seals of Bering Sea, the Venezuelan boundary, the Alaskan boundary, the North Atlantic fisheries. It will give us occasion also to observe the construction of the American pediment of international peace through general treaties of arbitration, to note the two Hague Conferences, and the London Naval Conference. In this convenient grouping of Anglo-American relations we shall have to carry ahead chronologically our narrative beyond the time when we shall resume it in the next chapter.

Immediately after the Civil War the general international situation threatened to involve Great Britain in another maritime war. In the Far East difficulties with Japan arising out of the execution of the recent treaty with that power, in Europe complications connected with the continental wars and many diplomatic repercussions attending the consolidation of the German Empire, and the Eastern Question made peace problematical. Thoughtful Englishmen soon began to realize what a blunder the Palmerston (Liberal) Government had made in handling American affairs during the Civil War: in nursing and exhibiting a not unnatural unfriendliness to the Union cause, in creating a precedent for the fitting out of warships by Britain's enemies in neutral ports, in haughtily refusing after the war to arbitrate the claims of the United States for damages for the depredations of the *Alabama* and ships of her class. In future wars a power like Germany, Russia, or Japan, even though it might have no fleet, would be free by Great Britain's own pronouncements of policy to build cruisers in time of war in American neutral harbors on both the Atlantic and Pacific oceans. The seas would swarm with new *Alabamas* to destroy British commerce everywhere or drive it back under cover of the neutral American flag. The House of Representatives in July, 1866, unanimously approved a bill to remove the prohibition of American neutrality laws against selling ships of war to foreign citizens or governments at peace with the United States. The threat was obvious and avowed.[1]

A change in government in England in 1866 made it possible for the new Conservative Ministry to reverse the stand of Palmerston and Russell, and to intimate a willingness to adjust the claims, though not to consider any indemnity for the alleged premature recognition of the belligerency of the Confederate States. Seward negotiated claims conventions with Great Britain in 1868 and 1869. They proved abortive because they contained no special provision for the *Alabama* claims (as this group was called). In the new Grant Administration, Senator Charles Sumner, chairman of the Committee on Foreign Relations in the Senate, was, next to the President, the most prominent man in public life. In a powerful speech in April, 1869, he administered the last rites to the rejection (1-54) of the second of these conventions (the Johnson-Clarendon convention), which Seward had placed before the Senate in the last days of the expiring Johnson Presidency. He pointed out that it did not contain one word of regret or even of recognition of the "massive grievance under which our country [has] suffered for years." He implied that not only the depredations of the cruisers ($15,000,000), the cost of chasing them down (as yet unestimated), the ruin of the American merchant marine ($110,000,000), but in addition half the cost of a $4,000,000,000 war, should justly be charged up to Great Britain. Ex-

---

[1] For diplomacy of the Treaty of Washington see: Charles Francis Adams, Jr., *Before and After the Treaty of Washington: the American Civil War and the War in the Transvaal* (New York, printed for the N. Y. Hist. Soc., 1902); Rhodes, VI, 355-376; J. B. Moore, *Arbitrations, op. cit.*, I, 495-753. C. E. Hill, *Treaties, op. cit.*, has a useful chapter on the Treaty of Washington and the Geneva arbitration, based on this material. See also Baxter, *post cit.* The latest work is Lester B. Shippee, *Canadian-American Relations 1849-1874* (Carnegie Endowment for International Peace, New York, 1939).

cept for the cruisers, he argued, the war would have ended much earlier. The purpose of this speech was to sink into the popular mind in both the United States and England a claim so big that it could be satisfied only by the cession of Canada to the United States. The Fenian raids, and the obvious attempts of the United States to dragoon Canada by terminating the reciprocity treaty were great factors in killing much of the annexationist sentiment which had existed in Canada. The fact was that the Canadians did not wish to be annexed to the United States. If only because of that, no British Government could embrace such a solution.

If ever there were an adjacent country to tempt aggression, it was Canada in 1866. To the peoples of the New World the relations between Canada and the United States ought to be a convincing demonstration of the essentially peaceful character of Manifest Destiny. Nothing could have stopped annexation at this time had the United States wished to do so by force.

The new President, General Grant, who had not yet quarreled with Sumner over Santo Domingo, supported the eminent senator's thesis, and so, at first, did the new Secretary of State, Hamilton Fish. Fish looked forward to the ultimate independence of Canada and final absorption by the United States, but he saw the futility of any such consequential claims, not to mention the impossibility of a settlement of them by the cession of Canada. He abandoned the unattainable and asked "merely an expression of regret on the part of Great Britain, an acceptable declaration of principles of international law and payment of claims." That the British Government was turning to such acceptable principles was indicated by the passage of an act of Parliament in the summer of 1870 designed to prevent the building, fitting out, arming or recruiting for, of ships like the *Alabama*. But the final reason that impelled the British Government to settle with the United States was the ominous European situation: the Franco-Prussian War and Russia's denunciation, October 31, 1870, of those articles of the Treaty of Paris that neutralized the Black Sea. In a Russian war Britain could not be sure of American neutrality; at least Russia would build *Alabamas* in United States shipyards.[1]

Informal negotiations took place between Fish and Sir John Rose, a Scotsman who had already achieved a successful career in Canada, and who was tactfully deputed by the Foreign Office in 1871

[1] James Phinney Baxter, 3rd., "The British High Commissioners at Washington, in 1871," *Proc. Mass. Hist. Soc.*, LXV (1937-1939), 334-357.

for such "unofficial discussions." [1]   Meanwhile, at Fish's impulse, the
President in his annual message (December 5, 1870) professed to despair
of a settlement and recommended that a domestic commission be established to authenticate the individual claims, that Congress pay them,
thus giving to the United States the possession of them for prosecution
with any *other* national claims.   This suggestion had had its effect by
the time Rose returned from England in January, 1871, for his second
conversations with Fish.   It was now quickly agreed that all the outstanding issues should be submitted to a joint commission which should
propose a settlement in terms of a treaty.   The San Juan Islands dispute, too, had awaited an adjustment of the *Alabama* claims and the
fisheries question.

A Joint High Commission, consisting of five American representatives
and of five British representatives,[2] convened in Washington in the spring
of 1871 (February 27-May 8).   With an eye to the strategy of American neutrality in the future, the British Commissioners were not unwilling to admit, in principle, liability for the *Alabama* claims in the
form of agreed definitions of international law which would reduce the
arbitration to a question of fact-finding.   It remained to content Canada
about claims for damages alleged to be due to Fenian raids from the
United States, to reach a solution for the vexing fisheries problem and
if possible to arrange a renewal of Canadian-American reciprocity.

It is remembered that by the reciprocity treaty of 1854 the United
States had reacquired for a period the inshore fisheries of British North
America lost by the War of 1812 (which put an end to the relevant

---

[1] Rose had been a member of the mixed commission which had arbitrated the claims
of the Hudson's Bay Company and its subsidiary Puget Sound Agricultural Company,
recognized by the Oregon Treaty of 1846.   He enjoyed in this capacity most friendly
relations with the American counsel, Caleb Cushing, who had brought him in touch
with Fish for the initiation of these discussions.   From 1869 to 1880 Rose served as an
informal Canadian commissioner in London, an office which became formalized in 1880
in the person of Sir A. Galt.   Morden H. Long has described his remarkable career
and services in "Sir John Rose and the Informal Beginnings of the Canadian High
Commissionership," in *Canadian Hist. Rev.*, XII (March, 1931), 23-43.

[2] The membership of the Commission admirably represented the various political and
sectional interests both within the United States and the British Empire.   The American
members were: Secretary Fish, Mr. Justice Samuel Nelson, of the Supreme Court of the
United States; Judge Ebenezer R. Hoar, who had been Attorney-General in Grant's
Administration; General Robert Schenck, the newly appointed Minister to Great Britain,
and Senator George H. Williams of Oregon.   The British members were: the Earl de
Grey and Ripon, a member of Gladstone's Cabinet (a new Liberal Government which
had now again succeeded the Conservatives), Mountague Bernard, Professor of International Law at Oxford, Sir Edward Thornton, British Minister at Washington, Sir
Stafford Northcote, Governor of the Hudson's Bay Company and a prominent member
of the Conservative opposition, and Sir John A. Macdonald, Prime Minister of the
newly created Dominion of Canada.

article of the treaty of 1783, and which were revived only on specified coasts by the treaty of 1818); in return British subjects had received a reciprocal concession to fish within the territorial waters of the United States on the Atlantic coast as far south as the 36th parallel. The reciprocal fishing privileges expired with the treaty (March 17, 1866). At Washington in 1871 the New England fishing interests wanted to get back their full privileges beyond the stipulated coasts of the treaty of 1818 without reciprocal liberties for British subjects, but, even more, they wanted to exclude the free entry of Canadian fish and fish products. The Ohio Valley and the Great Lakes also wanted the free navigation of the St. Lawrence River and its appurtenant canals. This nexus of issues had to be adjusted along with the *Alabama* claims, and the Commission must construct something which the United States Senate would ratify. Doubtless recalling the success of Lord Elgin's useful hospitality in 1854, the British members entertained lavishly to float the treaty through the Senate on a tide of champagne; and London paid all the expenses of the Canadian Prime Minister at Washington, lest some of his constituents find a pretext for attacking the treaty because of the expense. The Commission finally agreed on a treaty containing:

(1) An expression of regret "for the escape, under whatever circumstances, of the *Alabama* and other vessels from British ports, and for the depredations committed by those vessels." There followed a definition of rules to which the British Government agreed for the purpose of governing the coming arbitration. The British representatives succeeded in recording the view of Her Majesty's Government that these rules of "due diligence" were not international law at the time the cruisers escaped, but were consented to for this particular purpose and for the future merely for the purpose of strengthening friendly relations. These now famous rules were:

That a neutral Government is bound—
First, to use due diligence to prevent the fitting out, arming, or equipping, within its jurisdiction, of any vessel which it has reasonable ground to believe is intended to cruise or to carry on war against a Power with which it is at peace; and also use like diligence to prevent the departure from its jurisdiction of any vessel intended to cruise or carry on war as above, such vessel having been specially adapted, in whole or in part, within such jurisdiction, to warlike use,
Secondly, not to permit or suffer either belligerent to make use of its ports or waters as the base of naval operations against the other, or for the purpose of the renewal or augmentation of military supplies or arms, or the recruitment of men.

Thirdly, to exercise due diligence in its own ports and waters, and as to all persons within its jurisdiction, to prevent any violation of the foregoing obligations and duties.

The two high contracting parties further agreed "to observe these rules as between themselves in future, and to bring them to the knowledge of other maritime Powers, and to invite them to accede to them."

Acceptance of these rules meant that the British Government characteristically had built a defense against a dangerous precedent without yielding its original contention that the rules were not international law at the time of the events to which they were now applied. By implication it also disposed of Canadian complaints about Fenian raids, for the British Government, after its previous expressions of gratulation,[1] could not seriously accuse the United States of not having used due diligence to prevent those. It meant further that the *Alabama* claims were won in advance, in principle. The United States fully expected that these rules would presently be embodied in a neutral code.[2] Later Great Britain resisted this. Not until [3] the second Hague Conference (1907) were the rules, in a still more drastic form, accepted fully as international law as a part of Convention Number XIII governing neutral rights and duties in maritime warfare.[4]

(2) To submit all other claims of British subjects and American citizens to a mixed commission for adjudication and payment.

(3) For a minimum [5] period of ten years to readmit citizens of the United States to inshore fishing privileges in British North America, in return for which the United States agreed to admit free of duty Canadian fish and fish oil and to open coastal fisheries of the United States north of 39°. A special mixed commission was to sit at Halifax

---

[1] See above, p. 382.

[2] Moore, *International Arbitrations,* I, 666-670.

[3] The Institute of International Law in its session at Geneva in 1874 voted that the rules were only "declaratory" of the law of nations.

[4] "Art. VI. The supply, in any manner, directly or indirectly, by a neutral Power to a belligerent Power, of war-ships, ammunition, or war material of any kind whatever is forbidden. Art. VII. A neutral Power is not bound to prevent the export or transit, for the use of either belligerent, of arms, ammunitions, or, in general, of anything which could be of use to an army or fleet. Art. VIII. A neutral Government is bound to employ the means at its disposal to prevent the fitting out or arming of any vessel within its jurisdiction which it has reason to believe is intended to cruise, or engage in hostile operations, against a Power with which that Government is at peace. It is also bound to display the same vigilance to prevent the departure from its jurisdiction of any vessel intended to cruise, or engage in hostile operations, which had been adapted entirely or partly within the said jurisdiction for use in war."

[5] The privilege should continue thereafter until abrogated after two years' notice by either party. This article expired in 1885, after notice given in 1883 by the United States.

to determine the amount in money of any additional compensation that might be awarded to Great Britain for this revived inshore fishing privilege.

(4) To submit to the arbitration of the German Emperor the San Juan Island maritime boundary dispute.[1]

(5) Free navigation forever, for citizens of the United States, of the British St. Lawrence north of the northern boundary of New York to the sea; free navigation forever for British subjects of the American portions of the Yukon, Porcupine and Stikine rivers, which flow out of British territory to the sea through Alaska; free navigation to British subjects for a minimum of ten years of the American Lake Michigan;[2] recommendations by each party to the appropriate American states and to the Dominion of Canada for the reciprocal use of local canals connecting with the Great Lakes-St. Lawrence system along the international boundary.[3]

(6) Reciprocal transit in bond of goods across each other's territories, for a minimum period of ten years;[4] and no export duty on American timber and lumber floated down the St. John River through British territory.[5]

This comprehensive treaty, of a preamble and forty-three articles, together with the separate naturalization treaty of 1870[6] (already ratified) placed in the way of adjustment all disputes then existing between the United States and Great Britain. It was a magnificent triumph of conciliation. Thanks to careful preparation and adequate attention on the part of the Commission to the Senate, that body ratified the treaty promptly (May 24, 1871) by a vote of 50 to 12. Sumner, who at first had refused to co-operate in any settlement which did not include the withdrawal of the British flag from all of North America, had as a result lost his chairmanship of the Committee of Foreign Relations.[7] He did not oppose the treaty. He actually cast his vote for it.

---

[1] See above, p. 283.

[2] This depended on and expired with the fishery article in 1885. It was renewed by the water boundary treaty of 1909, which set up the International Joint Commission.

[3] These were carried out on both sides, and generally observed by the local authorities.

[4] This depended on and expired with the fisheries article in 1885.

[5] According to the limited free navigation provided by the Webster-Ashburton Treaty.

[6] See above, p. 170.

[7] J. C. B. Davis, *Mr. Sumner, the Alabama Claims, and Their Settlement,* a letter to the N. Y. *Herald* (New York, 1878), contends that Grant's removal of Motley, Sumner's friend, Minister at London, and of Sumner from his chairmanship, was not the result of any political intrigue or vindictiveness about Santo Domingo, but a wise and necessary measure to secure the success of the Treaty of Washington. C. F. Adams, Jr., *op. cit.*,

The Treaty of Washington had not expressly set aside the indirect or consequential claims arising from the depredations of the Confederate cruisers. In the great arbitration at Geneva [1] the American agent, J. C. Bancroft Davis, assiduously pressed the consequential claims. This caused the greatest indignation in England. Disraeli, leader of the opposition, declared that the American case demanded an indemnity larger than could be imposed by a conquest of the island. Resurrection of the indirect claims threatened to wreck the arbitration, but conciliatory efforts in both governments, assisted by the anxiety of eminent individuals on both sides of the Atlantic, saved the day. An extra-judicial agreement by Charles Francis Adams, the American Commissioner, and Sir Alexander Cockburn, the British Commissioner, excluded the consequential claims; this was proclaimed in a statement of the whole court. The final award was the lump sum of $15,500,000 [2] in gold for the depredations of the *Alabama* and *Florida,* and their consorts, and of the *Shenandoah* after she left Melbourne harbor. Sir Alexander Cockburn angrily dissented from the award. He did not exhibit that good sportsmanship so precious to the British character. His government and countrymen, however, supported the award cheerfully. The sum was much more than enough to compensate the individual American claimants. [3] The general claims commission, sitting for other claims of British

strengthens the case, but is rebutted by D. H. Chamberlain, *Charles Sumner and the Treaty of Washington* (Cambridge, Mass., 1902). Certainly Sumner's opposition to Grant's Dominican policy made it easier for Grant to insist on these removals.

[1] The treaty provided for arbitration of the *Alabama* claims before a tribunal of five jurists: one to be chosen by the United States (Charles Francis Adams was thus appointed), one by Great Britain (Sir Alexander Cockburn, Lord Chief Justice of England, thus appointed), one by the President of Switzerland (Justice Jacques Staempfli, thus appointed), one by the Emperor of Brazil (Viscount d'Itajubá, thus appointed). The fifth member of the tribunal was Count Frederic Sclopis, of Italy, who was president of the tribunal. The agent for the United States was J. C. Bancroft Davis, for Great Britain, Lord Tenterden. As counsel for the United States appeared Caleb Cushing, William M. Evarts, and Morrison R. Waite; as counsel for Great Britain, Sir Roundell Palmer, assisted by Mountague Bernard and Mr. Cohen, two experts. Caleb Cushing, who served as counsel to the American agent, published an account, *The Treaty of Washington: Its Negotiation, Execution, and the Discussions Relating Thereto* (New York, 1873), which, among other interesting data, has some notes on the personalities of the arbitration; as does also the American secretary, Frank W. Hackett, in *Reminiscences of the Geneva Tribunal of Arbitration, 1872, the Alabama Claims* (New York, 1911).

[2] This included interest but no damages covered by insurance; and no premiums for insurance written except where an insurance company could show that its war losses in the premises exceeded its premiums.

[3] A special domestic judicial court awarded a total of $9,316,125.25. It completed its labors in 1876. The balance was distributed *pro rata* by a second special court (1876-1885) among claimants who had not been recognized by the rulings of the Geneva arbitration, including claims for damages by cruisers exculpated at Geneva, and insurance premiums. Moore, *Digest of International Arbitrations,* V, 4639-4685.

or of American citizens, awarded $1,929,819 to British claimants, and dismissed all the American claims presented. The Halifax Commission awarded $5,500,000 gold as additional compensation to Great Britain for the fisheries concession. The United States agent filed a reservation against the validity of this award, but his government recognized it and paid it. Balancing up the account of the arbitrations of the Treaty of Washington, the United States received $15,500,000, Great Britain $7,429,819. The balance of $8,070,181 was one of the most excellent investments the British Empire ever made. It bore rich dividends in international accord and in strengthening the maritime defenses of the British Empire. At a cost equal to no more than what would be then required to build a few cruisers, Great Britain had stopped forever the possibility of small naval enemies building fleets in neutral territory in future wars. During the Boer War she reaped her reward for her wise policy at Washington in 1871, just as during the World War she profited beyond measure by her far-sighted decision not to protest the blockade during the Civil War in the United States.

The second great Anglo-American arbitration of this period involved a dispute which appeared after the Treaty of Washington: jurisdiction over fur seals in Bering Sea. Despite the mountainous volume of diplomatic correspondence and judicial documents which it entailed, we must dismiss it briefly.

Amphibious is the fur seal, ubiquitous and carnivorous, uniparous, gregarious and withal polygamous. The herds roam the seas but come back every year to home islands to bear young and to breed. During this time the females widely range the adjacent waters for food to sustain them whilst they support their pups. The male seals, living off their accumulated fat, remain basking on the island and interesting themselves with the activities and problems of their harems. At this season hunters can easily surround the males and club them to death. In the water male and female are indistinguishable and can be netted as they swim through the narrow passes of the seas on their way to the annual rendezvous. The females can be shot as they cruise off their islands during the homing season along with their young.

So valuable is the fur, and so easily do the habits of these sleek mammals of the sea make them the prey of marine hunters, that by the last quarter of the nineteenth century the great herds had practically disappeared in all but the North Pacific, about the islands of Bering Sea, notably the Pribilof group, north of the Aleutian chain, and belonging to the United States since the purchase of Alaska. When Con-

gress extended territorial government over Alaska it introduced certain
game laws to preserve the wild life of that region and of the "waters
thereof" and "adjacent thereto." It limited the annual killing of fur
seals on the Pribilofs to a certain number of males, and leased the exploitation of the industry exclusively to one corporation. It forbade the
killing of females and of young seals. These well intended measures
did not prevent an alarming diminution of the seal herd, because foreign

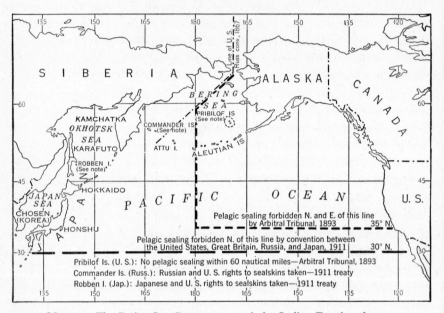

Map 24. The Bering Sea Controversy, and the Sealing Treaties of 1911.

hunters took the animals indiscriminately on the high seas, which meant
nearly always the death of the female, along with the solitary young one
which accompanied her. Could the United States Government, which
traditionally had resisted all forms of visit and search on the high seas
in time of peace, now step in and police the North Pacific to prevent ex-
termination by non-Americans of a form of life highly interesting and
valuable to all mankind? This question, prompted by British protests at American seizures of Canadian sealing vessels in Bering Sea,
was the subject of the arbitration agreed to by the convention of February 29, 1892.

The American agent, John W. Foster, recently Secretary of State
under President Harrison, resorted to the argument that Bering Sea,
because of rights and customs inherited from Russian sovereignty, was
mare clausum under exclusive American jurisdiction. He also argued

that the seals were not *ferae naturae* but domestic animals wandering out of bounds, and hence subject to domestic regulation even beyond territorial waters. The tribunal gave a very clear-cut decision against the United States. American practice had been too definitely against *mare clausum* in Bering Sea,[1] too consistently against the right of visit and search in time of peace on the high seas, to support the case of the United States.

Having rejected the contention of the United States, the arbitrators, under the terms of the treaty, prescribed certain regulations which were duly put into effect by the two governments.[2] This did not suffice to save the seals, because of continuing depredations of other than British or American nationals. In 1911 Russia and Japan joined the United States and Great Britain in signing a wholesome quadruple convention, meant to regulate definitively the whole sealing industry of the North Pacific, and sharing profits by a definite scale of division. Since then the animals have increased ten-fold. The agreement applied also to sea otters, now nearly extinct.[3] Alas, in 1940 Japan abrogated the convention.

A much graver controversy suddenly flared up in 1895 concerning the disputed boundary of Venezuela and British Guiana. When in 1835 British settlers at Belize had encroached upon the limits of Guatemala that republic in vain solicited the mediation of the United States under the Monroe Doctrine.[4] No great immediate harm to the Doctrine came from this neglect, although the passive attitude of the United States at that time doubtless encouraged the activities of Great Britain on the Mosquito Coast which became such a challenge to the Monroe Doctrine in 1848-1850. The Guatemala incident had been an example of how a little aggression, unrebuked, may lead to others more serious. The Venezuela boundary affair was similar.

The frontier between Venezuela and British Guiana had never been agreed on between the two sovereigns. The roots of the controversy reached far back into colonial history, and the area concerned was a

---

[1] For example, the protest against the Czar's ukase of 1821; and the terms of the Russian-American treaty of 1824, which stipulated that the citizens and subjects of high contracting parties should be neither disturbed nor restrained either in navigation or fishing in *any part* of the Pacific Ocean.

[2] As a result of a separate arbitration (agreed to by treaty February 8, 1896), the United States paid $473,151.28 as reparation for the seizure of the Canadian sealers.

[3] For a history of the fur seal controversy and its adjustment, see J. B. Moore, *International Arbitrations*, I, 755-961, summarized in his *The Principles of American Diplomacy* (New York, 1905, 1918); John W. Foster, *Diplomatic Memoirs* (2 Vols., New York, 1919); T. A. Bailey, "The North Pacific Sealing Convention of 1911," *Pacific Historical Review*, IV (March, 1935), 1-14.

[4] See above, p. 247.

pestilential hinterland at first of little value. In 1840 Robert Schomburgk surveyed the boundary for Great Britain. Great Britain put forth his survey as "merely a preliminary measure, open to further discussion between the Governments of Great Britain and Venezuela." It threatened Venezuela's control of the Orinoco River. Venezuela would not take it, even when Lord Aberdeen offered (1844) deviations away from the Orinoco which left Great Britain an equivalent amount of territory in the interior. Civil commotion in the South American state made impossible any negotiations before 1876. Venezuela in 1884 offered to accept Lord Aberdeen's proposed line, but Great Britain now rejected it. Prospectors had discovered gold fields in the back lands of both countries. Great Britain expanded her claims westward to take in gold fields in Venezuela and the Venezuelans countered by pushing their claims extravagantly eastward to the Essequibo River, to include the Guiana gold fields. Venezuela had no force to defend her claims, while Great Britain was the most powerful empire in the world. The Venezuelan Government since 1876 had invoked, without tangible result, the good offices of the United States. It next offered to arbitrate the whole area in dispute, i.e., the expanded claims of both countries. The United States expressed to England sympathy with this proposal, but the British Government refused to arbitrate unless Venezuela would first give up all the region east of the Schomburgk line. Venezuela broke off diplomatic relations with Great Britain (1887). President Cleveland, during his first Administration, offered to Great Britain the good offices of the United States for arranging an arbitration, but without success.

A case had now arisen in which a first-class power still possessing colonies on one of the American continents, might, by advancing boundary claims and refusing to arbitrate them, arbitrarily expand its territory in violation of that dictum of the Monroe Doctrine which interdicted further colonization of the American continents. The statistics in the British official yearbook, *The Colonial Office List,* had suddenly increased the area of British Guiana by about 40% between 1885 and 1886. Cleveland, during his second term, in 1894, recommended arbitration to Great Britain. Congress supported him by a vigorous joint resolution. The President had been further nettled at Great Britain's seizing the Nicaraguan customs in April to force payment of a claim, as well as by her persistent refusal to arbitrate the Venezuela controversy. Secretary of State Gresham was loath to make an issue of the Venezuela boundary; but after his death his successor, Richard Olney, at Cleveland's suggestion, presented, in the form of a despatch

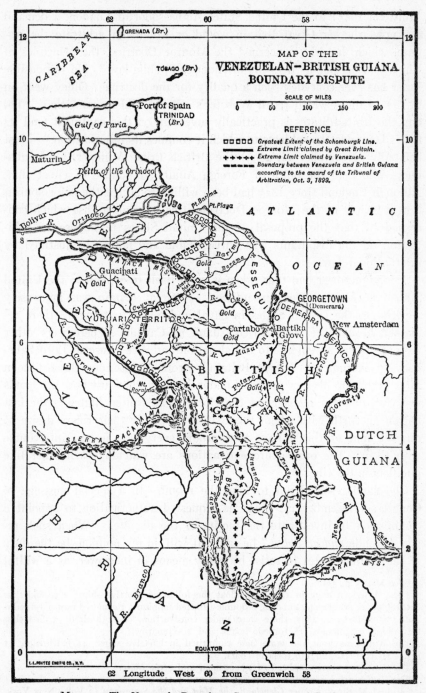

Map 25. The Venezuela Boundary Controversy and Settlement.

(July 20, 1895) to the United States Ambassador at London, a demand
to know whether Great Britain would or would not arbitrate the dispute, which, he said, concerned the Monroe Doctrine, the principles of
which had become a "doctrine of American public law." No responsible
jurist has ever conceded such a quality for the doctrine. Olney went on
to say in tones which recall Webster's note to Hülsemann [1] that: "Today the United States is practically sovereign on this continent, and its
fiat is law upon the subjects to which it confines its interposition." Most
belatedly (November 26, 1895) the British Prime Minister, Lord Salisbury, who held the office of Foreign Affairs, responded in effect that,
although England since 1823 had been willing to accept the non-colonization principle of the Monroe Doctrine, this was not a case which concerned it, that the proposal of the United States to impose an arbitration on the disputants was unreasonable and not to be justified by
international law.

A foreign power had thus taken it upon itself to explain to the United
States the Monroe Doctrine *ad hoc*. If Great Britain was immensely
superior to the United States in naval and military strength,[2] there remained always the weak British flank of Canada. There were other
factors present to enter into the situation and give pause to Lord Salisbury's Government. "Great Britain," wrote Ambassador Bayard, soon
after taking up his new post at London in 1893, "has just now her hands
very full in other quarters of the globe. The United States is the last
nation on earth with whom the British people or their rulers desire to
quarrel, and of this I have new proofs every day in my intercourse
with them. The other European nations are watching each other like
pugilists in the ring." [3]

Cleveland resolved not to take the rebuff. In a special message to
Congress (December 17, 1895) he requested authorization to appoint a
commission to investigate the merits of the dispute. "When such report is made *and accepted*," he said, "it will, in my opinion, be the duty
of the United States to resist by every means in its power, as a willful

---

[1] See above, p. 311.

[2] The American navy in 1896 had afloat the following effective ships: 2 second-class
battleships, 12 cruisers, 9 gunboats, 6 double-turreted monitors, 1 armored ram, 1 torpedo-
boat. On March 4, 1897, there were under construction, or authorized: 5 first-class
battleships, 9 gunboats, 18 torpedo-boats, and 1 submarine.

The British navy at the same time comprised in effective ships: 44 battleships, 41
first-class cruisers, and 136 torpedo-boats.

The American army consisted of 25,000 men and 2,160 officers.

The British army consisted of 147,959 men and 7,496 officers.

[3] Robert McElroy, *Grover Cleveland, the Man and the Statesman* (2 Vols., New York,
1923), II, 178.

aggression upon its rights and interests, the appropriation by Great Britain of any lands or the exercise of governmental jurisdiction over any territory which *after investigation* we have determined of right belongs to Venezuela. In making these recommendations I am fully alive to the responsibility incurred and keenly realize all the consequences that may follow." Congress speedily created the fact-finding commission.

The qualified character of Cleveland's statement, indicated by the italics introduced above, left the President plenty of room to back out if the people did not rally nationally to stand behind him on this new foreign issue. His correspondence, now printed, suggests more anxiety about the radical political situation within the United States than the safety of the Monroe Doctrine. Cleveland's whole career in the White House was so forbearing on matters of foreign policy that some have been led to suspect that in this spectacular exception he was resorting to the time-honored device of beating the big drum on a foreign issue in order to deafen the country to political dissidents at home a few months before the nominating conventions of 1896. In the West the Populists were rapidly gathering strength and threatening to capture the leadership of the Democratic Party. In private and public utterances, at the time and since,[1] Cleveland has explained his stand solely on the issue of the Monroe Doctrine and his confidence that Great Britain would really arbitrate. The standard biographies of Olney (H. James) and Cleveland (A. Nevins) have accepted this explanation. The fact that Olney's famous despatch, which Cleveland called a "twenty-inch gun," was not published until the message of the President to Congress confirms Cleveland's explanations.[2] The country as a whole—despite the chagrin of intellectuals[3]—rallied behind the President. Events in distant parts of the world were conspiring to afford him—as they did

[1] See Cleveland's long letter of Dec. 29, 1895, to Bayard, Ambassador to Great Britain, Nevins, *Letters of Grover Cleveland, 1850-1908* (New York, 1933); and Cleveland's *The Venezuelan Boundary Dispute* (New York, 1901). C. C. Tansill's recent study of *The Foreign Policy of Thomas F. Bayard* (Fordham Univ. Press, 1940) is severely critical of Cleveland.

[2] A letter to Olney by Thomas Paschall, a former Democratic member of Congress from Texas, suggested that the Venezuela question was a sure cure for the country's internal ills (printed in C. A. Beard, *The Open Door at Home* (New York, 1934), p. 100. The Paschall letter was dated October 10, 1895. Olney seems to have made no reply. There is no indication that Paschall, who was at home in Texas hoping for a federal appointment, had seen Olney's note of July 20, which was not published until December 17. More impressive is Nelson M. Blake's analysis of "The Background of Cleveland's Venezuelan Policy," *Am. Hist. Rev.,* XLVIII (No. 4, January 1942), 259-277.

[3] Andrew Carnegie, the Scotch-American philanthropist, naturally deplored the message. John Bassett Moore, then Assistant Secretary of State, earnestly urged the President

Seward in 1867—the opportunity for a striking diplomatic victory. In South Africa a crisis was rapidly heading up over the question of the Transvaal. Kaiser Wilhelm II of Germany, having dropped Bismarck, was addressing himself energetically to the development of naval power and to colonial expansion. On January 2, 1896, occurred Jameson's raid, in which a handful of British subjects invaded the Transvaal for the purpose of stirring up a rising of the "outlanders" against the Boer State. It collapsed miserably. The next morning the German Kaiser deliberately published a telegram to Kruger, the Boer President: "I express to you my sincere congratulations that without appealing to the help of friendly powers you and your people have succeeded in re-pelling with your own forces the armed bands which had broken into your country and in maintaining the independence of your country against foreign aggression." The effect on England of Cleveland's Vene-zuela message was mild compared with the shock to the British Empire that followed the publication of the Kaiser's message,[1] which Langer [2] terms one of the greatest blunders in the history of modern diplomacy. In the London music halls the crowd now cheered *Yankee Doodle* and booed *The Watch on the Rhine*.[3] The trend of future German policy revealed itself as under a flash of lightning. At that moment Great Britain in "splendid isolation" stood before the world without allies, without friends among the great powers, on the verge of a war crisis with the United States over the paltry issue of the jungle boundary of Guiana, involving a principle which meant so much to the American mind, so little to the British Empire. Joseph Chamberlain, Secretary for Colonial Affairs, urged the Prime Minister (January 4, 1896) to make a naval demonstration against Germany coupled with a declara-tion against interference in South Africa, and "to make a serious effort to come to terms with America. . . ." [4]

From that time British foreign policy took a different direction, toward conciliating disputants and building up allies and friends against a new menace, that of a German colonial and naval power which might

against making an issue of the Venezuela affair. On the other hand Professor Woodrow Wilson lauded the President's stand, and Henry Cabot Lodge, for whom Cleveland had a great dislike, vigorously applauded. So did Theodore Roosevelt, whom Cleveland thanked.

[1] "There has been a welcome and unmistakable difference observable, in the manner in which the possibilities of conflict with the United States—and with Germany— were discussed and treated in this country." Bayard to Olney, London, January 15, 1896. Henry James, *Richard Olney and His Public Service* (New York, 1923), 231.

[2] W. L. Langer, *The Diplomacy of Imperialism* (2 Vols., New York, 1935), I, 234-254

[3] J. L. Garvin, *The Life of Joseph Chamberlain*, III (London. 1934), 96.

[4] Garvin, *op. cit.*, p. 96.

combine with England's rivals on the Continent to upset the British Empire. It would have been the height of folly to add to that hostile group the United States, with whom so recently all diplomatic issues had been liquidated. From the day of the Kruger telegram Great Britain's American policy has clung steadily to the path of conciliation, of friendship, of possible alliance. Since then she has left to the United States the American sphere. The old order of affairs had passed forever. A new alignment of European powers and alliances was ushering into the twentieth century another mighty conflict of the nations similar to the wars of the French Revolution and Napoleon. A century before, Europe's distresses had redounded to the advantage of the United States in achieving its independence, in consolidating its nationality, in laying the territorial basis for its future. Now an analogous situation was taking shape, soon to turn to America's advantage as she stepped into the position of a world power.

Overnight the Anglo-American crisis disappeared when Chamberlain, in a memorable speech at Birmingham (January 25, 1896), stated: "We do not covet one single inch of American territory. War between the two nations [England and the United States] would be an absurdity as well as a crime. . . . The two nations are allied and more closely allied in sentiment and in interest than any other nations on the face of the earth. While I should look with horror upon anything in the nature of a fratricidal strife, I should look forward with pleasure to the possibility of the Stars and Stripes and the Union Jack floating together in defence of a common cause sanctioned by humanity and justice." Lord Salisbury publicly declared in the House of Lords: "I do think the bringing in of the Monroe Doctrine was controversially quite unnecessary for the United States. Considering the position of Venezuela in the Caribbean Sea it was no more unnatural that the United States should take an interest in it than that we should feel an interest in Holland and Belgium." Within a few weeks Venezuela and Great Britain had agreed in principle to arbitrate, after long negotiation as to detail, during which Joseph Chamberlain made a flying visit to the United States.[1] They concluded at Washington (February 2, 1897), in close understanding with the United States, a treaty prescribing the conditions. The tribunal consisted of two justices of the Supreme Court of the United States, two English jurists, and an umpire chosen by the four, the Russian jurist, F. F. de Martens. It brought in an award

---

[1] Garvin, *Chamberlain, op. cit.,* 159-166.

(October 3, 1899) roughly conforming to Lord Aberdeen's proffered modifications of 1844 of Schomburgk's line.[1]

Great Britain's new foreign policy, developed by her predicaments in Europe, Asia, and Africa, greatly strengthened the position of the United States in dealing with the Cuban crisis [2] and readjusting the international situation of the Isthmus,[3] also, as we shall presently see, in settling a new and serious dispute with the Dominion of Canada over the Alaskan boundary.

The Venezuelan controversy at first appeared to help consecrate the general principle of international arbitration. In the correspondence which followed the celebrated message of December 17, 1895, Secretary Olney had suggested a convention which might provide for settlement by arbitration of all future controversies between the United States and Great Britain, including the Venezuelan boundary, and which, as to the latter, would give due recognition to long-continued occupation by Venezuelans or by British subjects. Lord Salisbury, too, desired to sweep the Venezuelan question into some broad arrangement for arbitration. Though this had to give way to the conclusion of a treaty between Venezuela and Great Britain, worked out under Anglo-American discussions, both governments were now eager to follow up the idea, then novel, of a general arbitration treaty. They signed such a convention at Washington (Olney-Pauncefote Convention, January 11, 1897). By its terms important issues, such as questions of territorial claims or national rights, could be presented to a tribunal of six arbitrators, three from each side, with a majority of five necessary for a binding award. In case of no award, there would not be recourse to hostile measures of any description until the mediation of one or more friendly powers had been invited by one or both disputants. A separate tribunal was to settle minor issues by simple majority vote. Parliament promptly ratified this, but the United States Senate withheld its consent, principally because it feared being thus deprived of its authority to pass on the matter of allowing arbitration of particular disputes as they came up. This senatorial insistence really marked the setting of brakes on the American policy of arbitration.[4]

---

[1] General accounts of the Venezuela controversy are to be found in Rhodes, *Hist. U. S.*, VIII, and in Montgomery Schuyler Jr.'s sketch of Richard Olney, *Am. Secs. State*, VIII, 291-319. They lean heavily on H. James' *Olney* and Cleveland's own account, and can be supplemented with A. Nevins' *Cleveland*, and Tansill's *Bayaru*.

[2] Lord Salisbury told Henry White, secretary at the London Embassy, in June, 1896, that it would be a matter of indifference to Great Britain whether the United States annexed Cuba or not. H. James, *Richard Olney, op. cit.*, 244.

[3] See below, p. 509.   [4] W. S. Holt, *op. cit.*, 154-163.

Despite the reaction to the Olney-Pauncefote Anglo-American convention of arbitration, the United States signed and ratified, without any reservation by the Senate, the three conventions agreed on at the first Hague Conference in 1899, the first[1] of which set up machinery for the pacific settlement of international disputes, in the form of the Hague Permanent Court of Arbitration, to which disputants might, if both voluntarily desired, agree to have recourse, under judges of their own choice selected from an international panel. This convention provided that the powers resorting to the tribunal should sign in each instance a "special act" or "*compromis,*" clearly defining the subject of dispute as well as the extent of the arbitrators' powers. The United States delegation signed under the express reservation that "nothing contained in this convention shall be so construed as to require the United States of America to depart from its traditional policy of not intruding upon, interfering with, or entangling itself in the political questions of policy or internal administration of any foreign state; nor shall anything contained in the said convention be construed to imply a relinquishment by the United States of America of its traditional attitude toward purely American questions." The Senate, in ratifying the treaty, without further reservation, apparently overlooked the possibility (blocked up by an appropriate reservation in ratifying the convention when it was renewed and procedurally amended at the second Hague Conference of 1907) that the executive might arrange a *compromis* or protocol of arbitration which it would not be called upon to ratify. The first case to go before the Permanent Court of International Arbitration, the Pious Fund controversy between the United States and Mexico in 1902, went there by executive agreement. So did the Venezuelan preferential claims case[2] in 1903. These cases involved, however, only claims of the United State *against* other powers; and it had been customary to arrange arbitrations of such claims by mere executive agreement when they did not involve claims against the United States. When a vitally important dispute came to a head, the Alaskan boundary controversy, President Theodore Roosevelt did not attempt to submit that to the Hague Permanent Court by an executive agreement with Great Britain.

Russia had ceded Alaska to the United States in 1867 with its existing boundaries which had been described in the treaty of 1825 between Great Britain and Russia as follows: from the head of Portland Canal northward to 141 west longitude "along the summit of the mountains

---

[1] The other two related to the customs of land and naval warfare.
[2] See below, p. 522-525.

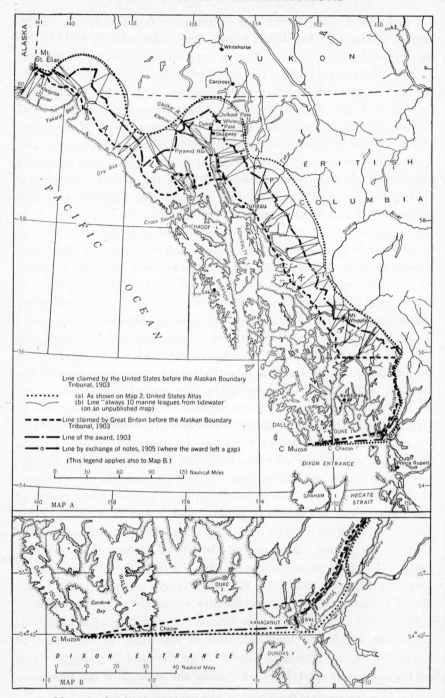

Map 26. Southeastern Alaska Boundary Controversy and Settlement.

situated parallel to the coast"; but where the line "shall prove to be at the distance of more than ten marine leagues from the ocean, the limit between the British possessions and the line of coast which is to belong to Russia as above mentioned shall be formed by a line parallel to the winding of the coast, and which shall never exceed the distance of ten marine leagues therefrom."

It is inconceivable that, in retaining for herself the strip of coast line (*lisière*) south to the latitude of 54° 40', Russia would have agreed to a line which would have given her only the tips of the promontories leaving the arms of the bays and indentations within British territory. Neither Russia nor Great Britain, of course, had any such idea. Despite minor disputes of jurisdiction, until 1898 British authorities in the Dominion of Canada recognized without question the sovereignty of Russia and her successor the United States along the whole coast, and admitted without protest the jurisdiction of American courts over British subjects there, never contending British soil ran down to salt water at any place. In the inaccessible and mountainous terrain of that wild country no actual boundary had been surveyed. Not until after the discovery of gold in the Klondike did Canada claim,[1] in June 1898, during the Spanish-American War, that the line of 1825 cut across the deep Alaskan fjords on that jagged coast so as to leave within British territory, north of 54° 40', Pacific harbors and control of important water passes to the gold country of the interior It was a ridiculous and preposterous claim, just as weak as it could be. The British maps before then showed these waters as Russian or as American, according to the date of the map.

The claim derived its only strength from the fact that a great government was willing to espouse it, and to insist on its arbitration: if Great Britain should lose the arbitral award, there would be no loss of a real possession; if the decision were not altogether in favor of the United States it would mean something gained for the Canadians for having raised the extravagant claim. President Cleveland's dramatic insistence on arbitration in other directions, however, gave good support in principle to the British demand for the arbitration of this artificial Alaskan boundary controversy. Great Britain offered to arrange all other matters in discussion with the United States if only it would

---

[1] The claim was made during the discussions of a joint "high commission" which had met at Quebec to consider twelve subjects of difference between the United States and Canada. Except for the Alaska boundary these were mostly minor frontier and navigation questions.

agree to arbitrate the Alaskan boundary. The United States confidentially offered,[1] through the joint high commission then sitting at Quebec, to submit the boundary to a commission of six jurists, three from each side and a majority vote to determine the issue. This overture was not immediately welcomed. The Canadians preferred to arbitrate the whole issue before a mixed tribunal with a neutral umpire, but insisted that whatever the decision, Pyramid Harbor, that is a corridor bisecting southern Alaska, must go to Canada.[2] Secretary of State John Hay succeeded in adjusting the Isthmian Question during the South African War without any bargain on Alaska. The Alaskan boundary question was allowed to drift under a *modus vivendi* until 1902.

President Theodore Roosevelt at first refused to arbitrate. He strengthened military garrisons in the Alaskan panhandle. If the Canadian claim were as ridiculous as he believed it—and certainly it was—there was no justification for arbitrating it. The United States could have defended its territory in that quarter of the world. Roosevelt was determined to do so. As a friendly act to Great Britain, as a means of allowing that government to withdraw gracefully from a difficult and impossible situation, the President, however, consented to the form of an arbitration: by a convention' (January 23, 1903) the boundary was submitted to the kind of settlement suggested by John Hay in 1899: a commission of six "impartial jurists," three from each country, a majority of four necessary for an award. This meant that no award was possible unless one member should judge against his own country's claim. The Canadian Prime Minister, Sir Wilfrid Laurier, realized the weak position of his Government on this issue, and was glad to co-operate with the British Ministry to get out of it through the channel of ostensible arbitration.[3]

Roosevelt saw to it that the personnel of the American representatives made it impossible to judge against the United States—indeed it would have been difficult to find any eminent American who would not have a fixed opinion on this question before it was argued. He appointed ex-Senator George Turner, of the State of Washington, geographically nearest to Alaska Territory; Senator Henry Cabot Lodge,

[1] A. L. P. Dennis, *Adventures in American Diplomacy, 1896-1906* (New York, 1928), 134-155.

[2] Tyler Dennett, *John Hay, from Poetry to Politics* (New York, 1934), 229 *et passim*.

[3] A. L. P. Dennis, *op. cit.*, 143-147; Allan Nevins, *Henry White, Thirty Years of American Diplomacy* (New York, 1930), 192-197; Dennett, *John Hay, op. cit.*, 224-239, 350-363.

of Massachusetts, whose early years were strongly tinged with Anglo-
phobia, close friend and political confidant of the President; and Elihu
Root, Secretary of War, a trusted member of the President's Cabinet,
under whose supervision the garrisons had recently been strengthened.
No one would now deny that Root possessed the qualities of an eminent
jurist, but certainly the two senators did not. Their instructions made
it clear what was expected: "You will, of course, impartially judge the
questions that come before you for decision, . . ." the President laid
down to them; "in the principle involved there will, of course, be no
compromise." The principle, that was the boundary as interpreted by
the United States. The British representatives included two Canadians
who could present no better claims to be impartial jurists than the
three Americans: Louis A. Jetté, Lieutenant-Governor of the Province
of Quebec, and A. B. Aylesworth, a Toronto lawyer; but the third member was Lord Alverstone, the Chief Justice of England. Roosevelt wrote
strong "confidential" letters to individuals, Henry White, first secretary
at the American Embassy at London, and Mr. Justice Oliver Wendell
Holmes, then vacationing in England, which those gentlemen were
expected to show to the Prime Minister, Arthur Balfour, and to the
Colonial Secretary, Joseph Chamberlain. Roosevelt made it abundantly
clear that, if the tribunal did not agree, there would be no more attempt
at arbitration; the President would run the line and defend it.

To the bitter chagrin of many Canadians, Alverstone joined the three
American "impartial jurists" and adjudged the case in favor of the
United States. "If when any kind of arbitration is set up they don't
want a decision based on the law and the evidence, they must not put
a British judge on the commission," he sturdily declared in answer to
the storm of criticisms [1] from Canada. Lord Alverstone's feelings
are greatly to be contrasted to those of Sir Alexander Cockburn in the
Geneva arbitration. The two Canadian members of the tribunal refused to sign this part of the award, like Cockburn at Geneva, and to
a less degree like the American Commissioner who protested at the Halifax award. The Commission unanimously awarded to Canada two of
the four disputed and uninhabited islands in the southern part of the
"panhandle" chain, concerning which Roosevelt in his "confidential"
letters had said there was room for argument. Canadian historians [2]

[1] George W. Smalley, *Anglo-American Memories* (New York, 1911), 270-271.

[2] D. A. MacArthur, "British Diplomacy and Canada: II. The Alaska Boundary
Award," *University Magazine*, VI (1907), 412-426.

Hugh L. Keenleyside, *Canada and the United States; Some Aspects of the History of
the Republic and the Dominion* (New York, 1929), 210-229.

have since appraised the award much more objectively than their countrymen did at the time, just as American historians consider the feeble
legal arguments of the United States in the case of the fur seals and
Bering Sea.   The so-called Alaskan boundary arbitration, by which
Great Britain availed herself of President Roosevelt's device for stepping
with honor and dignity out of an indefensible position, was really a
diplomatic arrangement.

Roosevelt wrote to his anglophile friend Captain Mahan: "The settlement of the Alaskan boundary settled the last serious trouble between the British Empire and ourselves as everything else could be
arbitrated. . . . I feel very differently towards England from the way
I feel towards Germany." [1]   Another attempt was made in 1904, by Secretary of State John Hay, to set up between the two countries a general treaty of arbitration, which might serve also as a model for similar
treaties of the United States with other nations.   It agreed in advance
to arbitrate all differences, not settled by diplomacy, which were "of a
legal nature or relating to the interpretation of treaties," but excepted
from this restricted category all questions affecting the "vital interests,"
the "honor," the "independence" of either party, or "the interests of
third powers."   Who was to decide, in the United States Government,
what constituted such a question?   The Senate, jealous of its function
in the conduct of foreign relations, amended the signed treaty by requiring that the "special agreement" defining the particular arbitration,
that is the *compromis,* must in every instance receive its advice and
consent.   Dissatisfied, President Roosevelt withdrew from the Senate
this treaty; but later he accepted such an amendment for similar treaties
which Secretary of State Elihu Root negotiated in 1908 with twenty-
five nations for five-year terms (which were extended by periodical renewals in most cases through a period of twenty years, until supplanted
by the recent Kellogg type of arbitration treaties).[2]   To friends of
arbitration who regret the "emasculation" of arbitration treaties by
anchoring in them these constitutional powers of the Senate, it must
be observed that in the American system of government it is quite possible for a President on his own responsibility to submit a vital national
interest to arbitration without the consent of a Congress entirely of
another political party than the President.   The definition of vital interests, national honor, independence, or the interest of third powers,
of course, afforded a number of blankets any one of which could be used
to cover an issue from arbitration.

[1] Rhodes, *McKinley and Roosevelt, op. cit.,* 260.   [2] See below, p. 731.

The Root arbitration treaty with Great Britain led to the last great Anglo-American arbitration, which took place, however, not under a special tribunal, but under the provisions of the Hague Convention of 1907 which continued, with procedural amendments, the Permanent Court of Arbitration set up in 1899. This was the historic North Atlantic fisheries question. Since the expiration of the treaty of 1871 the fishing "rights" of the United States within British territorial waters in North America had reverted to the provisions of the treaty of 1818, which granted the "liberties" on stipulated coasts and not elsewhere in British territorial waters. The governments of the maritime provinces and Newfoundland, however, had hedged about the American fishermen there with numerous restrictions designed to put them at a disadvantage with British subjects fishing the same waters: the Americans were harassed with local police regulations, refused bait, supplies, transshipment of their catch, and finally were excluded from some of the great bays, which the United States had considered parts of the high seas, notwithstanding its own successful contention that Delaware Bay and Chesapeake Bay had always been a part of its own territorial waters. After much controversy, and unpleasant incidents of seizures and protests, the whole dispute went to the arbitration of the Hague Court by the convention of 1909. The proceedings, published in twelve voluminous tomes, afford a textbook for the student of international law. The Court decided on all of the seven specific questions put before it, and thus regulated the various local questions which had caused such persistent irritation. Through its award it put into effect the provisions of the unratified Bayard-Chamberlain treaty of 1888 for the definition of territorial bays, specifying some of them as exclusively British, and for the others accepting the rule that a territorial bay must be less than ten miles across from headland to headland.

When Woodrow Wilson became President in the new Democratic Administration, in 1913, Secretary William Jennings Bryan set about the negotiation of his conciliation conventions with the principal powers. Technically styled "Treaties for the Advancement of Peace," these bilateral conventions were negotiated and ratified with twenty-one nations. Great Britain responded readily to such an arrangement (1914). The Bryan treaties in each case provided for a special standing commission of five members,[1] to which for investigation and report the two treaty

[1] One member chosen from each of the two countries by the government thereof; one member chosen by each government from the nationals of a third country; the fifth member chosen by common agreement between the two governments, it being understood that he should not be a citizen of either government.

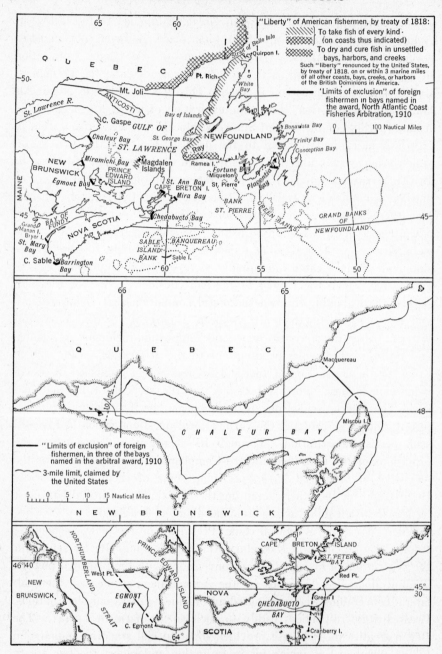

Map 27. The North Atlantic Fisheries.

parties agreed in advance to submit all disputes which were not arbitrable and which they should have failed to settle by diplomacy. The investigation and report must be made within one year; and the two parties to the treaty, in each instance, agreed not to go to war or resort to hostilities pending the investigation and report. These treaties are usually referred to as the Bryan "cooling-off" treaties, because in theory they provide for a year's cooling-off period during which excitement and provocation may die down. In no instance has a Bryan treaty been invoked. It remains to be seen whether the year would cool down or indeed heat up national issues and passions during a vital dispute. During the next fifteen years in many instances the Bryan treaties fell into desuetude because of the dying out of the personnel of the numerous commissions, or neglect to appoint them. In 1928 they were revived by Secretary Kellogg's peace program.[1]

On the eve of the World War in 1914 only one Anglo-American difference of opinion, latent but potent, remained unsettled: the Freedom of the Seas. The Hague Conference of 1907 had endeavored to solve this by resolving in favor of an international prize court, but had been unable to create such a novel and exalted tribunal because of lack of agreement on a code of neutral rights. This question the delegates referred to a naval conference at London in 1909, which agreed on a code, elaborating the provisions of the Declaration of Paris, themselves corresponding to historical American definitions, defining and classifying contraband and refining the doctrine of continuous voyage. The United States Senate approved the London Naval Convention but President Taft withheld final exchange of ratification after the British House of Lords, inveterately clinging to traditional British interpretations of maritime law, refused to ratify. We shall return to this subject later.

The record of arbitration with Great Britain, with which the United States had most of its serious international controversies during the period after its Civil War, is the proud and peaceful record of two great peoples whose vital interests make it much more profitable to agree than to quarrel. If no longer kindred in blood they were henceforth kindred in peace—and in war. In discussing these Anglo-American arbitrations from the Civil War to the World War we have drifted far ahead of the chronological moorings of the chapters of this volume. We must now go back to the Cuban question and the war with Spain.

[1] See below, p. 731.

CHAPTER XXIV

THE CUBAN QUESTION AND THE WAR WITH SPAIN

(1868-1898)

"OUR relations with foreign nations today [1889] fill but a slight place in American politics, and excite generally only a languid interest. We have separated ourselves so completely from the affairs of other people that it is difficult to realize how large a place they occupied when the government was founded." So wrote young Henry Cabot Lodge in opening a chapter on foreign affairs in his life of George Washington. Little could this author then have realized that in his political generation foreign affairs would again occupy the center of the national stage.

After the diplomatic settlements which had marked the aftermath of the Civil War and the subsidence of the expansionist urge, the attention of the American people engrossed itself with the great economic and political activities connected with the settlement of the West, and sociological problems germane thereto—with the building of the transcontinental railroads, with the exploitation of the natural resources of newly won continental domain, with the development of mighty industrial functions summoned to life to supply the vast home market, free from tariff barriers, which was now the good fortune of citizens of the United States. A satiated nation, with a territory sufficient to occupy its activities for a century to come, provided it were prudently tilled by proper national policy; a people without a dangerous frontier; such a nation of happy beings seemed to have little concern for foreign affairs. The Isthmian Question had lapsed into relative quietude when steel rails first spanned the continent. The friction with Canada over the fisheries and the fur seals was a petty local annoyance such as beset a busy farmer who had to stop and patch up temporary fences separating a neighbor's land which some day by the natural course of things he expected to be joined peaceably to his own. The Congo Free State, Liberia,[1] Samoa, the Hawaiian Islands,[2] Brazil, Chile,[3] these with foreign

[1] For these African questions, see Ch. XXXI.
[2] See Ch. XXV.
[3] For Latin-American and Pan-American questions, see Ch. XXXIX.

commerce were technical problems to be left to the Department of State to be worked out somehow; they were not paramount national issues. The Cuban Question was a chronic nuisance, but even it had subsided for a time by 1878, and, with slavery abolished and a distressing race problem persisting in the political reconstruction of the South, no one at that time wanted to annex more land inhabited chiefly by peoples who would bring more race problems. Chinese immigration was an issue only in California, and national party politicians were glad enough to stop it in expectation of local political support or for the gratitude of the numerous voters within the newly organized labor associations; China was a long way off and incapable of being a compelling factor in the local situation. All these questions were then of such minor importance that they can best be considered, in a history of this scope, with other developments of foreign relations later in the twentieth century—all except the Cuban Question.

The Cuban Question became critical at the close of the nineteenth century, at the end of an unique epoch of American history. It coincided with the completed settlement of a continent, with the disappearance of the American frontier, with the turning of national imagination to other fields of interest.[1] It came to a climax when the people had suddenly been made conscious of their adolescent world power, of their approaching maturity. President Cleveland's bugle call for the support of the Monroe Doctrine in 1895 had awakened them to this new feeling. The railways were built, the continent settled, the frontier gone, the home market seemed approaching satiation, the now populous Pacific Coast was indicated for future naval protection and communications. The need of an isthmian canal suddenly faced the nation.

If the United States had been looking for a pretext for vengeful and aggressive hostilities with Spain and the separation of Cuba from Spanish sovereignty, it could easily have found one in the years immediately following the end of the American Civil War when the military and naval forces of the country were unchallengeable in North America and its adjacent seas. The pretext could have been found in the annoyances of Cuban insurrectionary warfare, just as Spain had found a similar pretext for her intervention in Mexico and Santo Domingo.

The persistence of slavery in Cuba and the military and absolute government of the Spanish Captain-General there, excluding the natives

---

[1] It perhaps is noteworthy that the creation of the rank of ambassador in 1893 occurred at the time ascribed by historians to the disappearance of the frontier.

from all participation and from all enjoyment of the fruits of administration, was responsible for the outbreak of revolution in the island in
1868 with the object of independence. A parallel chapter of violence
and revolution in Spain prolonged the insurrection and chaos in Cuba
for ten years. The hostilities of 1868-1878 were more sanguinary and
exhausting than the warfare of 1895-1898, and the general annoyance
was equally exasperating, but there was a great difference in American
attitude during the two insurrections. The Cuban insurrection of 1868-
1878 came at a period of revulsion in the United States to further territorial expansion or further projection of national influence, when the
American people had turned their faces inland. The insurrection of
1895-1898 took place in a different generation, when the American people
had become fed up with stay-at-home activities, when shrewd young
expansionists were demanding a larger national policy, when the energies
and imagination of the nation conscious of its strength were expectant
for new and adventurous activities, emotions and experiences, when the
people had come to turn their faces outward from the continent.

The proximity of Cuba made the long and sanguinary insurrection
of 1868-1878 excessively vexing to the United States because of the
effect of the suppressive measures on American naturalized citizens with
Cuban names and insurrectionary habits, and because of the expense
of policing American territorial waters for ten long years to prevent the
departure of hostile expeditions against a friendly power. In 1869 President Grant, through Secretary of State Fish, offered the good offices of
the United States to Spain for settling the contest in Cuba on the
basis of abolition of slavery, and Cuban independence, in exchange for
an indemnity to Spain, the payment of which was to be guaranteed by
the United States. Spain refused to talk of peace unless the insurgents
first surrendered.[1] Despite the anomalous character of these bothersome naturalized Americans, Spain nevertheless felt constrained to
recognize their status and their right to full protection, under the old
Pinckney Treaty of 1795, against arbitrary military tribunals, unless
caught with arms in their hands (protocol of January 12, 1877). She
also agreed (1871) to adjudicate claims of American citizens before a
mixed claims tribunal.[2] Fish wisely prevented President Grant from
following the lead of Congress to recognize the belligerency of the

---

[1] A. Nevins, *Hamilton Fish* (New York, 1936).

[2] Spain paid $1,293,450.55 of these awards, and in 1896 an additional claim of
$1,500,000 for the Mora claim not settled under the claims convention of 1871. For the
claims, J. B. Moore, *International Arbitrations, op. cit.*, II, 1050-1053.

Cubans.[1] Such a recognition would have given gratuitous moral encouragement to the Cuban rebels, would have stultified Fish's contemporaneous objection to precipitate British recognition of Southern belligerency in 1861, and would have given to Spain the right to visit and search American vessels on the high seas, suspected of carrying contraband, and to bring them in to prize courts. The fact that Cuban belligerency had not been recognized gave to the United States a strong position when in 1873 the Spanish Government seized on the high seas a filibustering ship, the *Virginius*, fraudulently (so it later proved) flying the American flag, and summarily (after a nominal court-martial) executed 53 of its passengers and crew. After a pointed ultimatum by the United States, Spain restored the ship and paid an indemnity of $80,000 to be distributed to the families of the men killed. A salute to the American flag was dispensed with when it was ascertained by the United States that the *Virginius* really had no right to fly the American flag. Promises to punish the Spanish officers involved in the outrage were never carried out. Spain also paid an indemnity to Great Britain for nineteen British subjects slaughtered in the same executions.

The significance of the *Virginius* [2] case is that it afforded abundant pretext for war, but that no one in the United States Government wanted to take advantage of it. Public opinion might have supported war—mass meetings in New York and other eastern cities protested violently against the executions and abused Secretary Fish—but there was no yellow journalism to whip up hysteria, no real demand for war. This was when a small war might have helped to pull the country out of the industrial depression of 1873, when little effective resistance could have been expected from Spain, paralyzed as it was by civil war at home in the peninsula, and when no European power would have lifted a finger of protest.

The rebellion in Cuba continued to try the long-suffering and exemplary patience of President Grant's Administration. The cases of embargo and confiscation, of arbitrary arrests and punishments of American citizens continued, and the officials responsible for the *Virginius* killings remained unreprobated. Fish was unwilling to intervene in Cuba without at least an implied mandate from the European powers. All issues between the United States and Great Britain were now cleared

---

[1] Grant's message of June 13, 1870 (J. B. Moore, *Digest International Law*, I, 194-196), explaining that the Cuban insurrection did not justify a recognition of belligerency, has remained a classic exposition of the juridical conception of belligerency.

[2] For the correspondence see Chadwick, *op. cit.*, Bécker, *op. cit.*, and J. B. Moore's *Digest of International Law, op. cit.*

away. Would it not be appropriate to take England into partnership for imposing peace in Cuba with the approval of all Europe? Such would indeed show the disinterestedness of the United States. Fish dispatched (November 5, 1875) a long note to be read by Minister Caleb Cushing to the Spanish Minister of Foreign Affairs, expressing the determination of the President that ways and means be found to bring about peace in Cuba on the basis of emancipation and self-government. He directed the American Minister at London to suggest that it would be agreeable to the United States if the British Government would support by its influence the position assumed by the United States Government. It was also intimated to the other governments (France, Germany, Italy, Russia, Austria) that the United States would be glad to have them urge on Spain the necessity for abandoning or terminating the contest in Cuba.[1] Fish at the time, and since, was sharply criticized for proposing something that jeopardized the Monroe Doctrine by inviting European co-operation to solve an American question—and such an overture has not been made before[2] nor since. In noting this curious proposal, one thinks of Bismarck's partnership with Austria for determining the status of Holstein, and how easily it led to friction (as intended) and war. Fortunately the European powers had been sufficiently alarmed on their own continent that summer over the possibilities of another Franco-German war,[3] or Russo-Turkish war, to have time to bother with Cuba, though Germany, Russia and Italy said they had instructed their representatives at Madrid to urge the wisdom of restoring peace in Cuba. Lord Derby, British Foreign Minister, declared that "if Mr. Fish's proposal contemplated nothing beyond an amicable interposition having peace for its object, the time was ill-chosen and the move premature." Fish in 1876 suggested to Spain peace based on gradual abolition and the establishment of a reform government in Cuba.

Peace came suddenly. The "contest in Cuba" ended in 1878, when the end of the Civil War in Spain by the accession of Alfonso XII released forces sufficient to pacify for twenty years the exhausted islanders. Slavery was abolished (1886) after gradual emancipation, and a form of

---

[1] J. B. Moore, *Digest of International Law,* VI, 99-105 prints the relevant documents. See also Chadwick, Bécker, Latané, Callahan, and Nevins, *op. cit.*

[2] John Quincy Adams in 1826 suggested to Russia that she urge Spain to make peace with her former colonies; but that was after the independence of those colonies had been recognized, and after Adams had expressly refused to concert with Great Britain, a circumstance which was responsible for the declaration of the Monroe Doctrine.

[3] Joseph V. Fuller's sketch of Fish in *Am. Secs. State,* VII; and W. L. Langer, *European Alliances and Alignments, 1871-1890* (New York, 1931), 31-55, 59-86.

representation of Cubans in the Spanish *Cortes* was introduced. The Cuban Question dropped out of sight for seventeen years.

A recrudescence of the insurrection came in 1895 when the Cubans had recovered sufficiently from the exhaustion of the previous generation to be able to make, more determinedly than ever, another effort to end the continuing arbitrary powers of the Captain-General and the Spanish exploitation of the island. Added now to the grievances against misrule were the hardships of an economic crisis bringing widespread idleness and destitution from which to recruit the ranks of revolt. Sugar constituted four-fifths of Cuba's wealth. The executive agreement [1] with Spain of 1884 by removing a 10% extra ad-valorem duty on products of Cuba and Puerto Rico, had given a favored market made free by the McKinley tariff of 1890, which terminated suddenly with the passage of the Wilson tariff law of 1894. Hard times in the United States also cut down sugar imports. Far from pushing the United States to interfere in Cuba to protect plantations in the events of 1895-1898—a legend once eagerly accepted in academic circles—American capital interested in Cuban sugar was powerless to prevent Congress from threatening its ruin by the termination of reciprocity; moreover it preferred Spanish to Cuban rule. Actually business interests in the United States were to the last opposed to any war with Spain.[2]

The island was again aflame with revolt. The Cuban revolutionists resolved to break the power of their oppressors by methodically destroying the sugar plantations and cattle ranches, "determined to unfurl triumphantly, even over ruin and ashes, the flag of the republic of Cuba," if necessary to raze and wreck the island so that it would be valueless to Spain. As before, they drew their funds from *juntas* of compatriots organized in the United States and in other countries; and as before these groups tried to run out hostile expeditions from the waters of the United States in violation of domestic "neutrality" laws. Spain, on her part, determinedly met this stratagem of frightfulness and devastation by a "thorough" policy of ruthless suppression, entrusted to General Weyler in 1896, who proceeded to the military reconcentration of civilian population, treating all outside the concentration camps as rebels. In those days of no real sanitation the starving civilian *reconcentrados* of the tropical camps, men, women, and children, died like flies. Considering, however, the savage and inhuman character of warfare pursued by

---

[1] See below, p. 743, n. 1.

[2] Julius W. Pratt, "American Business and the Spanish-American War," *Hispanic American Historical Review*, XIV (May, 1934), 163-201; J. F. Rhodes, *The McKinley and Roosevelt Administrations, op. cit.*, 55.

the insurrectionists themselves, it is difficult to see how any other effective military steps could cope with it. It certainly was not in violation
of the laws of civilized warfare. The candid student must recall that
other civilized nations have been impelled to similar measures; the
British in South Africa, and the United States in the Philippines, in both
instances at near this same time. The Cubans themselves were more to
blame than the Spaniards for the character of the hostilities. The responsibility of Spain was in not being able properly to care for the civilians
whose concentration was thus compelled, in not delaying the step until
civilian supplies and sanitation were available.

All of this procedure interfered arbitrarily with the property and
persons of American citizens, naturalized or otherwise, domiciled in the
island. The same problem with which President Grant and his Secretary
of State had struggled for many years so forbearingly, now suddenly
became the concern of President Cleveland in the last years of his
second administration. The policy of Cleveland and Olney was in fact
a repetition in a general way of that of Grant and Fish: uncompromising
protection of treaty rights of all American citizens, and importunity to
Spain to accept American mediation to end the contest, lest it continue
for another ten years to harass Spanish-American relations.

Fortified now by experience, by greater financial resources, by more
popular support and sympathy, the activities of the *juntas* presented a
bigger police problem than ever before. Practically the whole Atlantic
forces of the revenue service, reinforced by naval units, had to be pressed
into service to prevent the departure of resourceful filibusters and gun-
runners,[1] resorting to all kinds of subterfuges along the 5470 miles of
indented sea coast from Long Island to the Rio Grande, near enough to
Cuba for tugboat voyages. The Spanish Government relied almost altogether on the United States for prevention of such departures from its
territory, rather than the expense, vigilance, and action of its own forces
to stop them in Cuban waters. Of the 71 expeditions known to have
been attempted, Spanish forces stopped 5 on the coast of Cuba; the
United States broke up 33, Great Britain 2; storms frustrated 4, and
27 were successful.[2] That most of those expeditions put out from the
United States, rather than from England or continental Europe as the

[1] H. S. Rubens, in *Liberty, the Story of Cuba* (New York, 1932), is a romantic reminis-
cence of his youthful association with the *juntas* and their filibustering activities.
[2] Marqués de Olivart, "Le différend entre l'Espagne et les Etats-Unis, au sujet de la
question cubaine," *Révue générale du droit international public*, IV (1897), 577-620, V
(1898), 358-422, 499-555; VII (1900), 541-629; IX (1902), 161-202.

Spanish Carlists did during the revolutions in Spain, was because the
United States was nearer and cheaper for the purposes of the *juntas,*
not because its government failed to exercise due diligence against them
even without obligation in the sense of the international law of neutrality,
in lack of a recognized state of war. While saying this, it must be
acknowledged that early decisions of the lower federal courts in 1896
gave some leeway to filibusters before the law was tightened up by later
decisions of the Supreme Court.[1]

In Congress there was a mounting tide of sentiment for the Cubans,
in favor even of downright intervention by the United States to free
them. The two houses passed a concurrent (not joint) resolution (April
6, 1896) in favor of recognizing belligerency, and urged the President to
offer Spain the good offices of the United States for a peace of Cuban
independence. This last is just what President Grant had proposed in
1869, while refusing, thanks to Secretary of State Fish, to recognize
Cuban belligerency. Cleveland contented himself with quietly proposing to co-operate with Spain to bring peace to Cuba on the basis of
home-rule. He coupled this offer with assurances against any design
on Spanish sovereignty, which, he went out of his way to say, was necessary for the stability of Cuba.[2] After some hesitation and debate among
themselves, the Spanish Cabinet politely declined the offer. They feared
the United States wanted to detach Cuba in order to get control of it for
itself. Well they might so fear, for Cleveland's domination of American
domestic politics was slipping. In the Senate youthful warhawks like
Henry Cabot Lodge were declaring that God would curse the American
people if they waited for Cuban independence until the island should be
desolated by fire and sword. The Spanish Secretary of State, in declining
Cleveland's honest offer, told the President that his government might
the better help pacify Cuba by adopting more effective means to prevent
the departure of unlawful expeditions of filibusters. Disappointed, Secretary of State Olney warned the Spanish Minister to the United States,

---

[1] One cannot draw a parallel between the outfitting in *neutral* England of *belligerent*
Confederate cruisers and the contraband shipment of men and munitions from the
United States to *insurrectionary* but not belligerent Cuba. Obligations of friendliness
and dictation of policy were responsible for the application of the municipal laws of the
United States to prohibit the departure of military expeditions for operations in Cuba.

For a review of the court cases, and other problems of international law, see E. J.
Benton, *International Law and Diplomacy of the Spanish-American War* (Baltimore,
1908), who criticizes early decisions of the lower federal courts which gave some leeway to
filibusters before the law was tightened up by decisions of the Supreme Court.

[2] Secretary of State Olney, to the Spanish Minister at Washington, Dupuy de Lome,
April 4, 1896, *Papers Relating to the Foreign Relations of the United States* (1897), p.
540-544.

in the summer of 1896, that if a new administration should come it might not be able to curb the forces hostile to Spain.

Under the inspiration of Senator Lodge the Republican Party soon declared, in the convention of 1896, for the independence of Cuba, American control of Hawaii, and ownership and operation of a Nicaraguan canal. In his last annual message to Congress, after the defeat of his party in the elections of 1896, President Cleveland, after a dispassionate review of the Cuban Question, declared that a situation conceivably could arise "in which our obligations to the sovereignty of Spain will be superseded by higher obligations, which we can hardly hesitate to recognize and discharge." A man of massive conscience, Grover Cleveland had dealt without gloves with a strong power, Great Britain, but had used infinite patience and persuasion with a weak power, Spain. At the same time he had fully protected American citizens and property in the enjoyment of their treaty rights, despite the questionable associations of some of the naturalized citizens.[1] Then he turned over to his newly elected successor the developing situation. Within a year it was out of hand.

There was at first little change in policy with the change of administration. Cleveland had endeavored to be a leader of public opinion. McKinley was a follower. The momentum of Cleveland's sanity and courage had its effect on the country and on the new President for several months, until dramatic untoward incidents inflamed to the bursting point a public and its politicians that were already saturated with a genuine sentiment of sympathy for Cuban revolution. McKinley had a fleeting thought of buying Cuba, but soundings made through the Spanish Embassy in London fully discouraged him.[2] After all, it would not have been politic to buy a first-class insurrection, even if Spain would have sold it. Like Grant and Cleveland, if in more urgent terms, McKinley once more offered (September 23, 1897, through the new minister at Madrid, W. L. Woodford) the good offices of the United States to Spain. Recklessly Spain again declined them. The Spanish Government replied (October 23, 1897) that it would continue unflaggingly, but in humanitarian forms, its military efforts, accompanying them with measures of reform looking toward autonomy under "immutable Spanish sovereignty." Again it said that the United States might co-operate most efficiently for peace in Cuba by stronger enforcement, even by amend-

---

[1] Nevins, *Cleveland, op. cit.,* has some luminous pages on the President's Cuban policy.
[2] L. B. Shippee and R. B. Way's sketch of William Rufus Day in *Am. Secs. State,* IX, 44.

ment of its municipal laws to prevent the departure of filibusters, and also by disbanding the Cuban *juntas*.[1]

The new Liberal Government in Spain this time made good its professions for reform by proclamations of the Queen Regent (November 25, 1897) extending to the Antilles all rights enjoyed by peninsular Spaniards, by establishing in Cuba the electoral laws of Spain, and by launching (subject always to ratification by the *Cortes*) a series of measures going far toward autonomy if the Cubans would cease fighting and accept them. There is no doubt of the good intentions of the Sagasta Government to set up in Cuba home-rule like that of Canada, but its measures were opposed in Cuba both by the Spanish elements in and about Havana, who would have been swamped by autonomy, and by the Cuban revolutionists, who would accept nothing now but independence.

We recall how in 1778 Great Britain was willing to repeal all the obnoxious legislation since 1763 against which her colonists had taken arms in America, and to grant some sort of home-rule within the Empire, thus to bring about reconciliation on the brink of French intervention. So in 1897 Spain was willing to offer the same to the Cubans, who had risen against conditions far more oppressive than those which had caused the American Revolution. Like the English colonists in 1775, the Cubans would have accepted in 1894 the program which three years later Sagasta offered, but in 1897 they refused it, not without hopes of American intervention. Nevertheless the prompt reform measures, and the removal from command of General Weyler, caused McKinley to declare, in his first annual message to Congress, in December, 1897, that before taking the next step, whether of recognition of belligerency, of independence, or of downright intervention—though never of annexation, that would be immorally aggressive—the United States should stand by, and allow time to test the sincerity and efficacy of the new Spanish program. He stated that no American citizen was known to be illegally detained in Cuba. To Spain shortly afterwards he read a lecture on the laborious and now wholly effective efforts of the United States revenue service and navy—the latter largely mobilized in Gulf waters—in enforcing the municipal neutrality laws.

[1] It recalled the alacrity with which the United States had amended its insufficient legislation in 1838 at the time of the Canadian insurrection, and how President Taylor had withdrawn all protection from American citizens engaged in filibustering—a perfectly apposite reminder, so far as the expeditions were concerned, but the United States has never undertaken to break up on its soil alien political organizations with foreign political programs, whether in the case of Cubans, or Hungarians, or Canadians, or Irish.

The new year began with considerable surface improvement of Spanish-American affairs,[1] but in an atmosphere heavily charged with emotional feeling before the persistent spectacle of human suffering so close to American shores. It was a spectacle continually presented in horrid and lurid colors and spectacular headlines and illustrations by the recently created yellow press, at a time when political leaders were looking for new issues to distract the public mind and bring achievements to their party. We have pointed out that the country was ready, economically and psychologically, for a glamorous foreign policy.

Irresponsible and self-interested journalism must bear its large burden of responsibility for the Spanish-American War, but who has ever been able to get satisfaction by showing the character of irresponsible journalism? Quickest to do damage, it is also quickest utterly to escape responsibility. It is not an adequate justification to say that it gave the people what they wanted. It made the people want it, and making the people want it they made Congress want it. Conditions in Cuba were bad enough, without exaggeration; they cost 200,000 lives before American intervention took place to prevent this in 1898; but sober historical scrutiny today shows that the Cubans were more inhumane in their warfare than the Spaniards. "It is generally conceded that a large part of the American newspaper ferocity toward Spain was due to the accidental circumstance that Mr. Hearst [owner of the New York *Journal*] and Mr. Pulitzer [owner of the New York *World*] were at the time locked in their famous struggle for supremacy in the field of sensational journalism in New York. It was a battle of gigantic proportions, in which the sufferings of Cuba merely chanced to furnish some of the most convenient ammunition. Whenever one side sprang a sensation the normal reply was of course for the other to spring a better one." [2]

The popular frenzy whipped up by the yellow press, and the eagerness of politicians to find personal prominence supporting new and safe

[1] *Spanish Diplomatic Correspondence and Documents, 1896-1900, Presented to the Cortes by the Minister of State* [translation] (Washington, G.P.O., 1905).

[2] Walter Millis, *The Martial Spirit; a Study of Our War with Spain* (Boston, Mass., 1931), 68. This author has ably portrayed the national psychology of the Spanish-American War, embodied in the title. J. K. Winkler, in his work, *W. R. Hearst, an American Phenomenon* (New York, 1928), has shown the lengths to which the leading "yellow journalist" of his generation was willing to go. He sent the popular artist Frederic Remington down to Cuba to draw pictures of Spanish atrocities. After a short time, says Winkler, Remington sent this telegram from Havana: "W. R. Hearst, New York *Journal*, N. Y.: Everything is quiet. There is no trouble here. There will be no war. I wish to return." Hearst is said by Winkler to have replied: "Remington, Havana: Please remain. You furnish the pictures and I'll furnish the war." Reming-

issues of foreign affairs, overrode the reluctance of business men and played into the hands of a little group of young Republicans who took advantage of the situation to further their "large" policy: to acquire for the United States strategical command of the Caribbean and the approaches from both oceans to the future isthmian canal, the necessity for which was becoming daily more prominent. The control of Cuba was the keystone to this policy. The leaders of this group were Senator Henry Cabot Lodge of Massachusetts, and Theodore Roosevelt, Assistant Secretary of the Navy. Their philosophical mentor was Captain A. T. Mahan, the eminent historical expositor of the significance of sea power in history, who since 1890 had been stressing in periodical articles [1] the importance of Samoa, the Hawaiian Islands and the Caribbean for the protection of a naval communication by the isthmian canal, which one day would be vital to the defenses of the two American coasts and the domination of the Pacific Ocean. Their more popular apostle was the learned Dr. Albert Shaw, editor of the *Review of Reviews*.[2] Vigorous students and martial philosophers of American history, these expansionists of 1898 incarnated, in a bellicose way, the old spirit of Manifest Destiny.[3] They expected the eventual domination of the entire continent of North America, with the canal and island outposts of defense in both oceans. Lodge and Roosevelt looked beyond that, *usque ad Indos*—they had their eyes on the distant Philippines as a vestibule for the trade of the Orient. Such is the background against which we see the critical events of the early months of that portentous year 1898.

It is a remarkable mystery precisely who caused the battleship *Maine* to be sent to Havana, ostensibly under bettered conditions, to resume the friendly visits of American naval ships to that port. The consul-general there, Fitzhugh Lee, himself reputed to be an interventionist, at first

ton's picture falsely representing Spanish officers searching a naked American girl is reproduced from the New York *Journal* in Millis, *op. cit.*, p. 68. The New York *Sun* was another paper which led the clamor for war.

Joseph E. Wisan has printed a voluminous analysis of *The Cuban Crisis as Reflected in the New York Press (1895-1898)* (Columbia University Studies in History, Economics and Public Law, No. 403, New York, 1934).

Herminio Portell Vilá's sensational *Historia de Cuba en sus relaciones con los Estados Unidos y España* (4 Vols., Habana, 1938-1941) sweeps together all evidence to show a century-long plot for the annexation of Cuba without adequately explaining the factors in United States history which prevented this.

[1] Reprinted in *The Interest of America in Sea Power, Present and Future* (Boston, 1897).

[2] The editor until the review's demise in 1937.

[3] Julius W. Pratt, "The 'Large Policy' of 1898," *Miss. Vall. Hist. Rev.*, XIX (Sept., 1932), 219-242.

favoring this, finally advised against such a measure, because of the emotional intensity of anti-American feeling among the dominant Spanish element in the city. He counseled rather the stationing of warships within summons at Key West. The *Maine* dropped anchor at Havana January 25, 1898. There were also other foreign warships there on friendly sojourns, notably two German craft. As a gesture of dignity the Spanish battleship *Vizcaya* detoured for a visit to New York harbor *en route* to Cuba. While the *Maine* was swinging at its hawsers in Havana harbor, the New York *Journal* published, February 9, 1898, a private letter of Mr. Dupuy de Lome, the Spanish Minister to the United States, written to a friend in Cuba, and procured from the Cuban *junta*.[1] It contained frank appreciations of President McKinley, which, if true, it would have been diplomatic to have left to the utterance of the President's own countrymen. The letter further reflected a lack of sincerity in the Spanish program of autonomy for Cuba, and expressed preference for a military settlement. The most offensive passage was the appraisal of McKinley as "weak and a bidder for the admiration of the crowd, besides being a would-be politician who tries to leave a door open behind himself while keeping on good terms with the jingoes of his party." It said nothing about McKinley's kindly qualities and the wellsprings of human sympathy which were his most lovable characteristics.[2] The publication made Dupuy's position immediately untenable. He resigned before his government could accede to the request for his recall. The unfortunate episode served to aggravate public feeling. A few days later, on the evening of February 15, 1898, the *Maine* blew up in Havana harbor, no one surely knows how, with a tragic loss of 260 men.

Spain immediately conveyed sincere condolences and proposed a joint investigation to determine responsibility. In Havana the obsequies of the unfortunate sailors received every dignity from the government and inhabitants of the city. It is impossible to believe that the Spanish Government was in any way responsible, though some irresponsible individual, or possibly a plotting Cuban, may have touched off a mine.

---

[1] Rubens, *op. cit.*, 287-292, explains how a friend of the secretary to Mr. Canalejas (de Lome's correspondent) stole the letter from his desk in Havana, and gave it to the Cubans.

[2] On the day before Christmas, 1897, the President caused an appeal to be issued through the Department of State to the public for contributions to a Cuban relief fund, which to the amount of $200,000 was expended in Cuba by the Red Cross. The Spanish Government co-operated in facilitating the importation and distribution of these supplies, although the action by the United States must be considered as intrusive, even though in a kindly way.

It is difficult to believe that the explosion was a mere accidental co-incidence. The United States refused to participate in any joint investigation. An investigation by Spanish naval officers attributed the catastrophe to some internal cause. An inquiry by a court of American naval officers, who included Captain F. E. Chadwick, later a most dispassionate historian of the war, reported (March 21, 1898) that the vessel's bottom plates were radically thrust up and in, indicating explosion from the outside, by a submarine mine, possibly with secondary internal explosions.[1]

Whipped on by unscrupulous journalists, the public hastily held Spain responsible for the vengeful destruction of an American warship. The Administration took no immediate step. Meanwhile the *Maine* affair rapidly melted into the general Cuban Question, heating it greatly. At the instigation of President McKinley,[2] Congress without a dissenting vote appropriated (March 9, 1898) $50,000,000 "for national defense and each and every purpose connected therewith." While the *Maine* inquiries were underway Senator Proctor of Vermont, a temperate man who had recently visited Cuba, made in the Senate (March 17) a terrific indictment of Spain's responsibility for the appalling state of affairs in the island. The American report on the destruction of the *Maine* was next made public (March 28). The Administration made no demands on Spain for reparation, leaving it to that government to make offers. The diplomatic exchanges between the two governments concerning Cuba were now reaching a climax.

At the last moment Spain proved willing to accept substantially all the American demands as they were so far embodied in the cabled

---

[1] *Message from the President of the United States, transmitting the Report of the Naval Court of Inquiry upon the Destruction of the United States Battleship Maine . . .* (Washington, G.P.O., 1898). See also Chadwick, *op. cit.*, 561, n. 1.

In 1911 the *Maine* was uncovered by coffer-dam operations. This revealed that the entire forward part of the ship had been destroyed, with decks and sides blown up and out. This is where the magazines and boiler-rooms were. In this part of the ship about one-half of the bottom was in place, mainly on the starboard side. Wisely the report of 1911 did not attempt to fix the cause of the explosion, and under equally wise instructions the engineers towed the hulk out to sea and sank it where inquisitive historians cannot get at it. The reader can make up his own mind from the technical language, reduced to common phraseology above, but it seems to me to suggest an outside explosion against the bottom of the port side forward, with prodigious explosions from the inside in the region of the magazines and boilers. See *Final Report on Removing Wreck of Battleship "Maine" from Harbor of Habana, Cuba*, 63d Congress, 2d Session, House of Representatives Document, No. 480. The condition of the wreck is described on pages 26 to 28.

An official summary of the Spanish report of 1898 is printed in *Spanish Diplomatic Correspondence, op. cit.*, 102.

[2] Millis, *op. cit.*, 116.

despatch of Assistant Secretary of State Day,[1] March 27, 1898, to Woodford, the minister at Madrid:

Believed the *Maine* report will be held in Congress for a short time without action. A feeling of deliberation prevails in both houses of Congress. See if the following can be done:

First. Armistice until October 1. Negotiations meantime looking for peace between Spain and insurgents through friendly offices of President United States.

Second. Immediate revocation of *reconcentrado* order so as to permit people to return to their farms, and the needy to be relieved with provisions and supplies from United States co-operating with authorities so as to afford full relief.

Add if possible:

Third. If terms of peace not satisfactorily settled by October 1, President of the United States to be final arbiter between Spain and insurgents.

If Spain agrees, President will use friendly offices to get insurgents to accept plan. Prompt action desirable.

This was not an ultimatum. The President was moving toward a peace of Cuban independence, and Spain was slowly dropping back toward that, but resisting at every step.

Spain revoked the *reconcentrado* order on March 30. The same day she formally offered to arbitrate all differences arising from the *Maine* affair. Anxiously Woodford cabled to ask if the President would sustain the Queen and prevent hostile action by Congress if she should proclaim unconditional suspension of hostilities as soon as accepted by the insurgents. McKinley replied he could only transmit the whole matter to Congress. It was now quite possible that Congress might declare war over his head.[2] April 9, at the last moment, and on the advice of the Pope as well as the representatives in Madrid of the European powers, the Queen gave orders to Blanco, Captain-General in Cuba, "to grant a suspension of hostilities for such time as he might think prudent to prepare and facilitate peace negotiations." Though the duration of the suspension was left to the discretion of the Captain-General, this action went far toward meeting the essential American

[1] McKinley had appointed the superannuated Senator John Sherman as Secretary of State in order to make possible the appointment by the Governor of Ohio of the President's friend and backer, Mark Hanna, as Senator for the remainder of Sherman's term. W. R. Day, who as Assistant Secretary handled the important business under Sherman, succeeded him as Secretary, April 28, 1898. Sherman's lament was: "They deprived me of the high office of Senator by the temporary appointment of Secretary of State." Quoted by Rhodes, *McKinley and Roosevelt Administrations, op. cit.,* 32. Sherman's infirmity made it necessary to replace him with Day.

[2] C. S. Olcott, *The Life of William McKinley* (2 Vols., Boston and New York, 1916), II, 27.

demands.[1] Further than this the Spanish Government would not go, for fear of a reaction which might overthrow the dynasty. The watchful Republican and Carlist oppositions would have made the most of any surrender of Cuba, and it required a courageous statesman to brook them. The lack of a clear-cut ultimatum, however, still confused the situation. Woodford cabled that he was confident that during the armistice a peace of Cuban independence could be worked out. Would the Cubans themselves, with their goal of independence so close, voluntarily agree to an armistice on their part, without an express and unconditional grant of independence? This was hardly likely. At any rate, the United States never waited to see.

The last moment this time was too late for Spain. Public opinion had already overwhelmed the reluctance of the President. He had decided as early as April 5 to submit the Cuban Question to Congress, which meant war. He wrote his message but held it up to give the consul-general at Havana time to evacuate American citizens. Meanwhile the European powers presented peaceful importunities, both at Washington and at Madrid.

As usual Spain had appealed to European powers to help her save her territory in the New World. It is now known, since the publication of the German series of diplomatic correspondence, *Die Grosse Politik der Europäischen Kabinette,* that the proffered mediation of the Pope, on the principle of independence for Cuba, was urged at Rome by the German Foreign Office, which was anxious to prevent any war between Spain and the United States because it might interfere with a German project for purchasing the Spanish islands in the Pacific, including the Philippines.[2] Germany suggested at Madrid the Spanish sacrifice of Cuba for peace. She also worked at Washington to prevent war, and for the same reasons, although very gingerly and circumspectly. But German diplomacy would not, as Spain requested, lead

---

[1] The text of General Blanco's actual suspension was: "Article first. From the day following the receipt of this proclamation in each locality hostilities are declared to be suspended in the territory of the island of Cuba.

"Article second. The details for the execution of the above article shall be the subject of special instructions that will be communicated to the different commanders in chief of the army corps for the most prompt and easy execution, according to the situation and circumstances of each." In the copy printed in *Foreign Relations, 1898,* p. 750, this is dated April 7, but the announcement was made at Madrid on April 9. The text was handed to Assistant Secretary of State Day on the 11th, presumably after McKinley's message had been sent to Congress, because the message does not mention it.

[2] L. B. Shippee, "Germany and the Spanish-American War," *Am. Hist. Rev.,* XXX (July, 1925), 754-777.

in organizing a joint representation at Washington by the great powers against American intervention in Cuba. This fell on the shoulders of Germany's European ally, Austria-Hungary, whose Foreign Minister secured the approval of each of the six great powers, Great Britain, Germany, France, Italy, Austria, and Russia, to a joint note, which their ambassadors presented on April 7 to President McKinley at the White House, stating that they hoped for humanity's sake that the Cuban Question could be solved peaceably. Great Britain had consented to this only after inquiring about it beforehand from the American Government. Apprized of what to expect, McKinley promptly and appropriately told the Ambassadors that he too hoped so, but that if the United States were obliged to intervene it would indeed be for humanity's sake.[1] This was the first time that the European powers, even including Great Britain, had ventured to do what they would not go so far as to do back in the days of the Holy Alliance: to take a joint step to help Spain in her colonial troubles in America. It was a feeble, faltering step. It amounted only to the expression of a pious hope for peace. The fact was that with the Far Eastern situation so uncertain—with China on the brink of partition—none of the great powers desired to involve itself in difficulties with the United States. Once more, then, Europe's rivalries were America's advantage.

News of the Queen's order arrived at Washington April 10, after McKinley's message was completely prepared, but before it had gone to Congress. On April 11 he delivered the message. After reviewing the Cuban situation and the *Maine* affair, noting the Spanish offer of arbitration, he recommended that he be authorized to use the armed forces of the United States as might be necessary for enforcing a pacification of Cuba. In two new paragraphs at the end he referred to the recent order of the Queen directing General Blanco to grant a suspension of hostilities, "the duration and details of which have not yet been

---

[1] A response of the Spanish Minister in Washington, later, to an identical copy of the same note, stating that the Queen had given orders for the suspension of hostilities in Cuba, impelled the foreign representatives to meet again and draft, under the hand of Sir Julian Pauncefote, the British Ambassador and dean of the diplomatic corps, another joint note deprecating intervention as unjustifiable. This note was never delivered. The ambassadors referred it back to their respective governments who could not agree to this second step. Alfred Vagts, *Deutschland und die Vereinigten Staaten in der Weltpolitik* (London, 1935), II, 1259-1307, suggests plausibly that Pauncefote's willingness for a second note may have come directly from Queen Victoria, to whom Maria Christina had appealed personally. Victoria was much distressed at the plight of Spain. Nevertheless Downing Street repudiated the suggestion of the British Ambassador. See Dennis, 72, Shippee, Garvin, *op. cit.;* and O. Ferrara, *Last Spanish War* (New York, 1937).

communicated to me." [1] "This fact, with every other pertinent consideration, will, I am sure, have your just and careful attention in the solemn deliberations upon which you are about to enter. If this measure attains a successful result, then our aspirations as a Christian, peace-loving people will be realized. If it fails, it will be only another justification for our *contemplated action.*" [2]

Congress did not wait to see what would happen following the Queen's orders. It promptly gave the President the requested powers. After a preamble stating the abhorrent conditions which prevailed in Cuba, "culminating, as they have, in the destruction of an United States battleship," Congress passed a joint resolution (April 19, 1898) which declared: (1) Cuba to be independent, (2) demanded that Spain withdraw from the island, (3) directed and empowered the President to use the entire forces of the army and navy, and the militia of the several states, to put the resolutions into effect, (4) disclaimed any "disposition or intention to exercise sovereignty, jurisdiction, or control over said Island, except for the pacification thereof, and asserted its determination, when that is accomplished to leave the government and control of the Island to its people." This last provision, the famous Teller Amendment, had been added to the original resolutions after they came to the Senate from the Committee on Foreign Relations. A noble self-denial, it was adopted without a dissenting voice. The resolutions passed the Senate by a vote of 68 to 21, and the House, after some conference, by 311 to 6. That the war was not a party measure is shown by the fact that nineteen Republicans and two Democrats formed the vote against the measure in the Senate. It was a nation-wide popular measure.

The President signed the joint resolutions, April 20, 1898. The same day he despatched a formal ultimatum to Spain, conveying a copy of the resolutions, and instructing the Minister of the United States, that if at noon of April 23, 1898, the Spanish Government should not give a complete and satisfactory response to the demands expressed in such terms as to assure peace in Cuba, the President would proceed without further notice to use the powers conferred upon him to the extent necessary to give effect to the resolutions. Spain still had time to capitulate with a clean-cut recognition of Cuban independence and withdrawal from the island. Rather than do this at the point of an ultimatum, her Government preferred war to peace, disaster to dishonor. Spain not having answered the ultimatum, Congress on April

---

[1] See note 1, p. 447.   [2] Italics inserted.

25, 1898, declared a state of war to have been in existence since and including April 21. On April 22 the President had proclaimed a blockade of the north coast of Cuba and the port of Santiago.

The American people wanted war and got it. Spain by its procrastination had run a fatal risk. She must assume thereby her share of responsibility before the bar of history. A frank and prompt welcome of Cleveland's irenic offers, or even of McKinley's first proposal in 1897, would have had much chance of solving the Cuban Question without war. Even when nothing but independence was any longer a solution, the Spanish Government shrank from the necessary steps. "The hour of great decision had come," writes the historian of Spanish diplomacy in the nineteenth century, "but the Government was afraid, afraid of unpopularity, because one part of public opinion, led along by the press, and deceived as it was, unaware of the enormous disproportion of forces between the two nations, showed itself bellicose; afraid of a revolutionary movement on the part of the Carlists. If a great statesman should at that moment have appeared at the head of the Government, he would have had the courage to tell the truth to the country: that we had no navy, and that since we had no navy the United States could compel the army in Cuba to surrender without striking a blow, by hunger alone; and he would have faced the consequences and have sacrificed himself to save Spain from catastrophe. Cuba was irretrievably lost, and that being the case, we, while protesting any violence, should have renounced our sovereignty, thus saving the rest of our colonial empire."[1]

American historians are today agreed that the war with Spain could have been avoided with honor, if McKinley had been resolute enough to exercise a little more patience with Spain and defy Congress. Writers like Flack,[2] Benton,[3] and Rhodes[4] see very flimsy justification for the war, even on humanitarian grounds (there was no mandate from the other powers). The question, that these men have not answered, is: If McKinley had been adamant would not Congress have declared war on its own account, overridden his veto, and left him a newly elected but early repudiated President?

We must now turn to the astonishing and partially unexpected results of the war, as signalized in the treaty of peace and in the events which in the Pacific Ocean had been leading up to it.

---

[1] Jeronimo Bécker, *Relaçiones exteriores de España, op. cit.*, III, 875.
[2] *Spanish-American Diplomatic Relations Preceding the War of 1898* (Johns Hopkins University, Studies in Historical and Political Science, XXIV, Nos. 1, 2).
[3] *Op. cit.*   [4] *Op. cit.*

CHAPTER XXV

THE ISLANDS OF THE MID-PACIFIC

(1875-1899)

THE Spanish-American War brought to a head and unexpectedly projected a process of American expansion in the islands of the Pacific which had been quietly under way for half a century. Before describing in the next chapter the peace settlement of 1898 at Paris, and the acquisition of the Philippine Islands, it is proper here to review the expanding interest of the United States in strategic Pacific island crossways of navigation. The American people, engrossed with their own continental problems and activities, were slow in becoming Pacificminded. It was not until 1898 (except for Alaska) that Congress was willing at last to sanction explicitly the steps which successive Republican Presidents had been advocating for expansion including the acquisition of the Hawaiian Islands and Samoa.

We recall that in 1875 the Senate finally ratified a reciprocity treaty with Hawaii, which contained a political article conferring unique privileges upon the United States, placing those islands definitely under an American sphere of influence. The widespread opposition to further expansion which had set in after the Civil War caused Grant's Administration to compromise with the foes of annexation by an article which provided only that none of the ports or territory of the Hawaiian Islands should be leased or otherwise disposed of to any third power and that none of the special privileges enjoyed by the United States should be conferred on any other nation. In this way President Grant was able to fend off the possibilities of British or of French control pending the time when the public mind should be ripe for a move of annexation. It would have been grossly careless to allow those islands, so intimately bound up with the defenses of the United States, to pass under the possession of any other maritime power and become a potential jumping-off place for enemy attacks on the Pacific Coast or Alaska.

Successive Republican administrations continued this policy of anticipated annexation. The Hawaiian reciprocity treaty was renewed eventually in 1884,[1] with an important additional clause, which gave

[1] For seven years at least and thereafter until abrogated by either party after 12 months' notice. This had been the case also with the original treaty of 1875.

the United States the exclusive right to a fortified naval base at Pearl Harbor (hard by Honolulu), the matchless haven of the mid-Pacific. Great Britain and France in 1887, when the United States was favoring a tripartite protection of Samoan independence, proposed a joint declaration guaranteeing the independence and neutrality of the Hawaiian Islands, but Secretary Bayard, in Cleveland's first Administration, eluded the overture. No American government had ever gone so far as to pledge the United States never to acquire Cuba or Hawaii—although President Fillmore came near to doing this for both in 1852. In Garfield's time, Secretary of State Blaine declared against the transfer of the Hawaiian Islands to any other power, and proclaimed them a part of the "American system," to which the Monroe Doctrine was applicable. He placed his Government on record as believing "that the position of the Hawaiian Islands as the key to the dominion of the American Pacific demands their neutrality, to which end it will earnestly co-operate with the native government. If, through any cause, the maintenance of such a position of neutrality should be found by Hawaii to be impracticable, this [United States] government would then unhesitatingly meet the altered situation by seeking an *avowedly American solution* for the grave issues presented." [1]

The reciprocity treaty, which nearly approached a free-trade arrangement, opened an era of unprecedented prosperity for Hawaii, particularly for sugar-growing which had now supplanted the former chief activity of the islanders in furnishing an emporium successively for fur-traders, sandalwood-buyers, whalers, and trans-Pacific steam navigators. It enriched the American colony, many of them descendants of missionaries and early traders, men who had developed on modern lines the cultivation of the succulent cane. On the native inhabitants, as on the American Indians, the impact of western civilization had a fatal effect. By 1860 less than one-third remained of the aboriginal population of upwards of 200,000 at the beginning of the century; by 1890 only 34,436 were left, by then miscegenating rapidly with the immigrants from East and West. For labor, the sugar planters turned to Chinese, to Portuguese, and to Japanese. The oriental immigrant proved the most satisfactory and easy and cheap. Like Mexico in the settlement of Texas, the sugar-planters of Hawaii made the egregious mistake of actually encouraging the inundation of the islands with a wave of alien

---

[1] Italics inserted. Mrs. Alice Felt Tyler has sketched Republican policy toward Hawaii in *The Foreign Policy of James G. Blaine* (University of Minnesota Press, 1927), 191-217.

population. Within a few decades the Chinese and Japanese, eventually the Japanese alone, would constitute the majority of the entire population. By 1890 Hawaii was rapidly becoming an archipelago ruled by white planters and traders on a basis of immigrant oriental labor. The dominating element was the residents of American origin, first or second generation. In the middle of the century they had furnished the principal ministers and advisers [1] to the native kings; now they controlled the elected legislature which in turn controlled the ministry after parliamentary forms that American advisers had persuaded the kings to adopt.

The Samoan, once called the Navigators' Islands, are to the south Pacific what the Hawaiian group is to the north. They are closer to New Zealand and Australia than to any other civilized country. As the British Bermudas and Bahamas cover strategically the Atlantic approaches to the United States, so do the Samoan Islands, and the Fiji and Tonga archipelagoes, control the naval approaches from the northern and eastern Pacific to Great Britain's antipodal Dominions. The harbor of Pago Pago, in the Samoan island of Tutuila, is surpassed in capacious safety and strategic importance among Pacific island groups only by Pearl Harbor and Manila Bay. Like Hawaii, the Samoan Islands lingered late into the nineteenth century under native rule. In the third decade came British missionaries, at the same time occasional American whalers and Captain Wilkes, the American naval explorer (1839), who worked out with native chieftains on Tutuila Island a code of regulations for treatment of commerce and shipwrecks; finally, in the middle of the century, German traders and settlers pursuing commerce in copra and buying up tribal lands from the chiefs for firearms and firewater.[2] Of all the foreign element in Samoa, the Germans, concentrated at Apia on Upolu Island, were the most numerous and domineering. They were less interested than the British missionaries in

---

[1] H. W. Bradley, "The American Frontier in Hawaii," *Proc. Pacific Coast Branch Am. Hist. Assoc., 1930,* 135-150, gives details of the personnel and influence of American advisers and officials.

[2] Sylvia Masterman has paid particular attention to British evangelical and political interests in *The Origins of International Rivalry in Samoa, 1845-1884* (Stanford University Press, 1934), written from the British archives alone. It was written in apparent ignorance of George H. Ryden's *The Foreign Policy of the United States in Relation to Samoa* (Yale University Press, 1933), a longer study which relied on the American archives. Neither used Count Stolberg's *Deutschland und die Vereinigten Staaten, op. cit.,* based on American and German official archives. Stolberg regarded England as the key to any understanding of German-American relations, but the British archives are closed after 1885. Vagts, *Weltpolitik,* 1935, I, 638-938, and Tansill, *Foreign Policy of T. F. Bayard* (1940), are the latest treatments.

the welfare of the natives, looking as they did, mostly to the commercial profit of the trading house of Goddefroy and Son of Hamburg.[1]
The local German element would fain have seen the new German Empire
annex the islands but was really content with any power's sovereignty
there if it could be assured of profitable exploitation of the natives and
their lands. Bismarck was willing to subsidize the German company,
though the Reichstag refused the necessary [2] appropriation; but before
1884 he refused to embark upon any policy of colonial expansion. New
Zealand, nervous at the increasing strength of the Germans at Apia,
and knowing of their desire for German rule, pleaded with the Mother
Country to take over the islands. This was during the time when British
governments were still apathetic about more colonies; not until 1874,
when the neighboring Fiji Islands were annexed, did Great Britain
rise from its satiated colonial torpor and begin another period of colonial
expansion; even then its interests were primarily fixed in the Near
East and Africa. Despite the anxiety of New Zealand, Britain's policy
toward Samoa remained one merely of preventing the islands from passing under the control of any other maritime power.

The economic contacts of the United States with Samoa were less
than those of either Great Britain or Germany, very small indeed. The
first political interest developed from the activities of William H. Webb
of New York, a promoter of steam navigation who had applied to Congress for a subsidy for a line of steamships between San Francisco and
New Zealand and Australia. President Grant favored such assistance,
but Congress refused it. New Zealand, however, gave Webb what his
own country denied, and he began operations in 1869, with Samoa as
a port of call.[3] Webb had sent an agent, one Captain Wakeman, to
visit the islands and make a report to him. Wakeman's report, em-
phasizing the desirability of Pago Pago harbor, which Wilkes had
praised thirty years before, found its way through Webb to President
Grant and the Departments of Navy and State. Thereafter various
Secretaries of the Navy stressed in their annual reports an ever-recurring
concern for a base at Samoa to protect the contemplated isthmian canal

[1] Established in Samoa, 1847, reorganized, after financial troubles due to bad investments in Europe in 1880 into the *Deutsche Handels- und Plantagengesellschaft für
Südseeinseln zu Hamburg.*

[2] Miss Masterman shows, *op. cit.*, 161, that the defeat of the bill in the Reichstag was
due not so much to opposition to a colonial policy as to support of a private firm.

[3] The line discontinued operations in 1872. Also interested in the expansion of
American interest in Samoa, and proponents of an American protectorate there, were a
group of California land speculators, the Polynesian Land Company. They seem to
have had little influence on the Government.

and the navigation routes, present and future, to the South Pacific.

Without troubling to consult the administration, Commander R. W. Meade in 1872 negotiated a treaty with chieftains on the island of Tutuila, giving the United States an exclusive naval station at Pago Pago and taking the natives under its protection. President Grant urged the Senate to ratify this treaty, but that body, though not advising against it, took no action. After his experience with Santo Domingo, Grant did not dare to press the matter further, fearing to kill it altogether. He nevertheless used all the influence of his Administration to sustain by executive action the political primacy of the United States in Samoa, pending the time when hostile public opinion might become converted. The Samoans meanwhile seemed genuinely ready for such a union. A special agent of Grant, Colonel A. B. Steinberger, a self-interested adventurer and soldier of fortune, established a personal ascendancy over the natives in Samoa, united the tribes, organized with remarkable effectiveness a government with himself as prime minister, then resigned as special agent. The natives at first looked on him as an American governor. Without committing the United States, he did his best to strengthen the impression that an American protectorate was being extended. Steinberger's anomalous position, the fact that the United States disavowed any official relationship with him, and the natural jealousy of the British and German consuls, indeed of the American consul too, resulted in his downfall and his deportation on a British cruiser. Pressed by the aggression of the local German representative, Consul Theodor Weber, who was also the director of the Hamburg trading company, the ductile Samoans appealed now to the United States, now to Great Britain—but never to Germany—for annexation or at least a protectorate. Neither government was prepared, all things considered, to assume that responsibility, but neither wanted to see the islands pass under the control of any third power—no more did Germany. The Samoans sent a Polynesian plenipotentiary, La Mamea, to Washington, who succeeded (1878) in negotiating with Secretary of State William M. Evarts their first foreign treaty. Not inappropriately the negotiations were handled by Frederick W. Seward, Assistant Secretary of State, son of the great Republican expansionist. It was a treaty of amity, most-favored-nation commerce, extraterritoriality, and quasi-protection. It provided for a naval station, not exclusive, of the United States at Pago Pago;[1] and stipulated that in case of differences between the Samoan Government

---

[1] No naval station was established there until after the partition in 1899; but a cargo of coal was sent out in 1880, to testify to the treaty rights.

and any other government, the United States would "employ its good offices for the purpose of adjusting these differences upon a satisfactory and solid foundation." Young Seward explained to La Mamea that the change in public opinion on the extension of national boundaries made it impossible to go further than this.[1] Notwithstanding some objection in the Senate against the carefully drafted article for good offices, the treaty was ratified. It was a slight gain for executive ambition for Pacific naval bases. Henceforth the treaty of 1878 became the cornerstone of American policy in Samoa—a policy which aimed at preventing the archipelago from slipping under the control of any other maritime power before the United States itself might be ready to take it. There is no question but that the Senate and the legislative branch had acted as a powerful brake on the executive's desire to extend dominion over these distant islands and their aboriginal inhabitants. In the first years of the 'seventies, though not after 1874, this could have been done without serious objection by either Germany or Great Britain.

After the American treaty Germany and Great Britain speedily made generally similar treaties (1879) with Samoa, but with significant additions. The German treaty secured rights to an exclusive naval base at Saluafata, near Apia, confirmed extensive German land claims, and paved the way for a later protectorate, if desirable, by an extraterritorial article that said that the Germans in Samoa were "to observe such laws and regulations as may be, in the future, agreed upon between the two Governments." The British treaty, however, placed a bar in the way of any such later German designs, and also of American ambitions, by engaging the Samoan Government not to grant to any other sovereign or state "any rights, privileges, authority, or predominance in Samoa in excess of such as are or may be accorded to Her Britannic Majesty." It also allowed Great Britain the right to establish a naval station anywhere in Samoan harbors except in Saluafata (German) or in the portion of Pago Pago which the United States might select. The rival powers were thus balanced.

After the signature of the British treaty the United States instructed its consul in Samoa to co-operate with the other consuls in securing, amidst the shifting native regimes, a stable government. The American, German, and British consuls then worked out a three-headed control (1879) for the municipality of Apia, the principal foreign settlement, which after written agreement with the native government was ex-

[1] F. W. Seward, *Reminiscences of a War-Time Statesman and Diplomat, 1830-1915* (New York, 1916), 438.

tended (1880) into substantially a joint protectorate over all the islands, with King Malietoa as native potentate. Knowing that this agreement would never be ratified by the Senate, succeeding Republican administrations in the United States were content to observe it informally as only an executive agreement.

Prince Bismarck before 1884 had not considered colonies worth the bones of a single Pomeranian grenadier. In that year, yielding to increasing commercial pressure, Germany joined under Bismarck's leadership the scramble for such remaining colonies as might be secured in Africa, Malaysia and the islands of the Pacific. The Germans intervened aggressively in native Samoan politics, and in November, 1884, forced King Malietoa Laupepa to sign a treaty, anticipated by the phraseology of the first German treaty of 1879, which set up a régime that amounted to a German protectorate. Directly after signing the agreement, Malietoa and 48 chiefs appealed to Great Britain to annex the islands in order to prevent "other governments" from taking Samoa. The Germans then stirred up an insurrection under a pretender, Tamesese, declared war against Malietoa, and raised the German flag at the seat of the native government near Apia. Secretary of State Bayard, in Cleveland's first Administration (Democratic), protested to Germany (June 19, 1885) against this disturbance of the *status quo* in Samoa. He asserted that the United States had a "moral right" to expect that no change in native rule should extinguish the independence of the islands. As the imbroglio thickened, Bayard became wary. He caused it to be declared that the United States was unwilling itself to assume any protectorate, "either for itself alone, or under any joint arrangement whereby the native autonomy of Samoa would be replaced by a *permanent* [1] tri-partite Government of the powers." At the same time he called for a conference of the three treaty powers in Washington to adjust the situation. Germany agreed to suspend hostilities meanwhile and to observe the old *status quo*. Before the conference assembled in 1887, Great Britain and Germany came to an agreement *à deux* in regard to colonies in the Pacific and Africa, by one detail of which Great Britain agreed to support at Washington the proposition of a German mandate for the administration of Samoa. Great Britain needed German support for her policy in Egypt and the Near East. Thus, when the diplomats assembled to consult and discuss, the United States met a united Anglo-German front prearranged by a settlement in which little attention had been given to American interests. Bayard stoutly resisted the proposition for a

---

[1] Italics inserted.

German mandate, and the conference adjourned without any decision. Immediately Germany set up a new regime in Samoa, under the chieftain Tamasese, with a German officer, one Brandeis, as prime minister, supported by the German navy and German marines.[1] The new régime favored the interests of the German trading company and discriminated heavily against British and American residents at Apia, in matters of land titles, taxes, and local improvement. Again Bayard protested, not on the ground of the unratified tripartite control of 1879, but on the basis of American good offices incorporated in the treaty of 1878. At first there was no yielding by Germany. Impatient at the drift of the whole affair, President Cleveland characteristically submitted it to Congress in January, 1889. Bismarck, seeing the possibility of serious friction with the United States, suggested a reassembly of the adjourned Washington conference, to meet at Berlin. At the same time he suspended hostilities in Samoa against Mataafa, a redoubtable defender of native rights who had sprung up against the Brandeis-Tamasese régime following the German deportation of Malietoa. Bayard accepted this proposal and the new Republican Administration of President Harrison carried it through under the guidance of Blaine, again back in office at the Department of State.

In the Berlin conference of 1889 it was evident that the only way the United States could prevent the islands from passing under a German protectorate with British acquiescence was to accept reluctantly the idea of a tripartite protectorate. Under the presiding office of Count Herbert Bismarck, son of the Chancellor, and German Minister of Foreign Affairs, the three treaty powers worked out an elaborate scheme for a joint protectorate, in which the principal officials at Samoa were to be, not the three consuls, but two neutral officers: a chief justice and a president of the elected municipal council of Apia. The independence and neutrality of the islands, under an imposed foreign tripartite condominium, was the anomalous principle of this treaty. It was something manifestly incompatible with the traditions of American diplomacy. It was a manger of potential international dispute, as are all condominiums, but it was something into which the United States was forced, rather than see Pago Pago pass under the exclusive dominion of any other power. The Republican Senate ratified this triple partner-

---

[1] During his last years, at Apia, Robert Louis Stevenson described the German intervention, including the disastrous landing affray at Fangali, and the great hurricane of 1889, in his well-known *Footnote to History; Eight Years of Trouble in Samoa*, published in the many editions of his works.

ship, which forever afterward suffered increasing attack as an entangling alliance. For a few years the condominium brought hitherto unknown peace and stability in the archipelago, with King Malietoa restored as the tribal potentate. There was some altercation between the consuls and the treaty officials, and the rivalries among the consuls did not fail to reappear; still the new régime worked better than any previous government in Samoa. President Cleveland, coming back to power in 1893, and his second Secretary of State, W. Q. Gresham, expressed themselves repeatedly against the international partnership as full of embarrassment, entanglement, and liabilities for the United States. The President was opposed to American imperialism anywhere, in any form, at any time, even in Hawaii.

The Hawaiian reciprocity of 1875 had tightened relations with the United States by renewing and greatly increasing the prosperity of those islands and making them dependent upon the interested continental neighbor. Advisers of American origin had mostly disappeared from the councils of the king, but in the legislature American influence was predominant, and it controlled agriculture and business. Meanwhile the aboriginal stock was dwindling rapidly; the royal line of Kamehameha died out in 1872. Queen Liliuokalani, who came to the throne in 1891 as second ruler of a new native dynasty, was a champion of native pride. She had believed that the naval base at Pearl Harbor should not have been ceded to the United States.[1] Sympathetic to Hawaii for the Hawaiians, she threw all her influence against constitutional limitations of her power, determined as she was to prevent the outlander pro-American legislature from controlling her government. This was the signal for the revolt (January 17, 1893) on the part of the outlanders—Hawaiians of European and American origin, the Americans predominating—which reminds one of the Texans in 1836, except that it was bloodless. Like the Texans' revolt it was with the object of annexation to the United States—in the case of Hawaii, openly avowed —and was precipitated by arbitrary constitutional changes. Unlike the Texan revolt it was connived at by the United States Government.[2] The substance of the plan was known in Washington by the Secretary

[1] See the photograph of her diary in Ralph S. Kuykendall's *History of Hawaii* (New York, 1926), 259. The same eminent Hawaiian-born scholar published a more detailed history, *The Hawaiian Kingdom, 1788-1854* (University of Hawaii, 1938).

[2] Julius W. Pratt, "The Hawaiian Revolution, a New Interpretation," *Pacific Historical Review*, I (1932), 273-294, shows that the cause of the revolution was not to avoid the undermining of reciprocity by the sugar bounties of the McKinley tariff act of 1890, but a widespread desire to set up a stable white government.

of State, who left a wide range of discretion to the American Minister there, John L. Stevens, an advocate of annexation. It had long since been customary to leave a warship stationed in Hawaiian waters most of the time. At Stevens' direction marines landed and protected the local committee of public safety in its occupation of the public buildings of Honolulu. Stevens ran up the American flag in protection of the new *de facto* régime. "The Hawaiian pear is now fully ripe," he wrote to the Department of State, "and this is the golden hour for the United States to pluck it." [1] The Queen surrendered her authority under protest and appealed to the President of the United States for a restoration of her rights. A committee of Honolulu business men, under the presiding direction of Judge Sanford B. Dole, formed a provisional government "to exist until terms of union with the United States of America have been negotiated and agreed upon." They sent a diplomatic commission immediately to Washington. Within a month of the Honolulu revolution, they signed (February 14, 1893) with Secretary Foster a treaty of annexation.

President Harrison was unable to rush the Hawaiian treaty through the Senate before he went out of office. President Cleveland suspended judgment, withdrew the treaty from the Senate, and sent a special commissioner, James H. Blount—an avowed small-navy anti-imperialist—to the islands to pull down the American flag and to uncover the relationship of Stevens to the revolution; next the President proceeded to ventilate the whole diplomatic correspondence relating to Hawaii.[2] Convinced of the existence of a sinister plot, he sent out a new minister, Albert S. Willis, to undo the outlanders' revolution and restore the Queen to her throne, on condition that she grant amnesty to the revolutionists. This the Queen found it difficult to accept; she wanted to chop off the heads of the leaders and confiscate their property. The provisional government on its part would not accept any return to "native" rule. When the treaty failed they set up a republic under a constitution which contained an article expressly authorizing the president to conclude whenever possible a treaty of commercial or political union with the United States. Embarrassed by this turn of affairs, President Cleveland turned the whole matter over to Congress, which did nothing. Cleveland then recognized the new republic, as did the other powers. Obviously the new Hawaiian Government intended to

---

[1] Nevins, *op. cit.*, 549-562.

[2] *Affairs in Hawaii*, Appendix II to *Foreign Relations of the United States, 1894*, House Ex. Doc. 1, 53d Congress, 3d Session (Washington, G.P.O., 1895).

wait for annexation until Cleveland passed out of office, and public opinion in the United States tacitly supported this waiting attitude.

The revolution in Hawaii seemed a providential opportunity for expansionists like Captain Mahan and Senator Henry Cabot Lodge, who [1] justly appreciated the significance of the islands to the naval defenses of the United States, particularly in anticipation of an isthmian canal. They might also have stressed the defense of Alaska. The facts of geography were plain enough: there stood those islands, closer to the American continent than to any other, more a part of the "American system" than of any other "system," a strategic archipelago which in the possession of any great naval power would be a certain menace to the United States, but which in the possession of the United States need be a menace to no one. The danger of the annexationist sentiment, which the Republican opposition immediately championed, was that it might not stop at Hawaii.

President McKinley after his inauguration immediately turned his attention to Hawaii, negotiated a new treaty of annexation, and sent it in to the Senate on the same day of its signature (June 16, 1897). At this time the Hawaiian Government had become alarmed at the significant volume of Japanese immigrants and had just turned back about a thousand of them. Japan had protested against this as a violation of her treaty of 1886 with Hawaii. When Harrison's treaty of annexation had been signed in 1893 Japan cheerfully acquiesced. Since then she had defeated China in the spectacular war of 1895, and now felt that she was a power to be reckoned with in the settlement of any Pacific question. She protested to the United States against the McKinley treaty of annexation, on the ground that it might further jeopardize the treaty rights of Japanese residents in Hawaii. There were by then 25,000 Japanese in the islands, equal to the combined total of Europeans and Americans. After some correspondence, and the settlement with the Hawaiian Republic of a small indemnity for the immigration episode, Japan withdrew her protest, being assured that the United States would protect her treaty rights. The Japanese action had nerved McKinley to speed on annexation.[2] In the Senate there were enough reluctant Democrats and anti-imperialist Republicans to endanger a two-thirds

---

[1] See A. T. Mahan's notable article, "Hawaii and Our Future Sea-Power," in the *Forum*, XV (March, 1893), 1-11, reprinted in *The Interest of America in Sea Power, Present and Future, op. cit.*, and Henry Cabot Lodge, "Our Blundering Foreign Policy," *Forum*, XIX (March, 1895), 8-17.

[2] T. A. Bailey has an instructive analysis in his article on "Japan's Protest Against the Annexation of Hawaii," *Jour. Mod. Hist.*, III (March, 1931), 46-61.

majority for the treaty. While the treaty lagged there the President in March, 1898, resorting to the precedent of Texas, urged annexation by a joint resolution of Congress, which required only a majority vote in the Senate. Thus, before the outbreak of the war with Spain, the issue of outright imperialism had been raised in the Pacific, raised on an issue of naval strategy. Even the joint resolution introduced in Congress for the Administration languished until after the beginning of the war with Spain. The Hawaiian Government committed itself to every kind of help to the United States within its power to give after the war began, thus strengthening sentiment for annexation.[1] Impelled by the rushing events of the war—particularly American military action in the Philippine Islands—Congress at last caught up with the executive pace on the historical road of American expansion in the Pacific. On July 7, 1898, the anxious McKinley was able to sign a resolution of annexation. The islands were formally transferred to the United States on August 12, 1898. United States forces *en route* to the Philippines occupied vacant Wake Island, 2,305 miles west of Honolulu, and the Spanish island of Guam, 1,535 miles west of Wake and 1,595 miles east of Manila. Wake was formally annexed to the United States, January 17, 1899, and Guam by the treaty of peace with Spain (ratified by the Senate on February 6, 1899). Guam was taken for a possible naval base and cable station, though it has not been much developed for the navy. Wake Island, with the Midways (annexed 1867), the southern islet of Palmyra in the Hawaiian group, together with the guano islands of the mid-Pacific, Jarvis (1857), Baker's (1857), and Howland's (1858) are now of importance as landing places for aerial navigation west and south of the Hawaiian group.

The advance into the regions of the Pacific Ocean—Alaska and the Aleutian Islands, and the Midways; Hawaii; Samoa; and the small islets of the mid-Pacific; was a most significant feature of the diplomatic history of the United States during the tranquil period between the Civil War and the Spanish-American War. We are now ready to turn to the events of that war which closed the century of American expansion, to the epoch-making decision of policy which it precipitated, the sudden acquisition of another archipelago on the other side of the world.

---

[1] T. A. Bailey, "The United States and Hawaii During the Spanish-American War," *Am. Hist. Rev.*, XXXVI (April, 1931), 552-560, makes a good case to show that there was such opposition both to the treaty and to the joint resolution that, except for the war, annexation might not have come for many years, if ever.

CHAPTER XXVI

THE GREAT ABERRATION OF 1898

WITH the three months' warfare which began in April, 1898, collapsed the final remnants of Spanish power in the Indies, West and East, almost the last bits of that great empire sanctioned by the treaty of Tordesillas of 1494, with which we began this history. For this decisive conflict the military preparedness of the United States was woefully disproportionate to the martial spirit, but the new navy proved to be in fighting trim, and it was sea power which decided the issue. There was a small Spanish squadron in the Philippines; this was almost immediately destroyed in the battle of Manila Bay (May 1, 1898) by a superior American force which had been carefully prepared and stationed in Far Eastern waters under the command of Commodore George Dewey. From the remaining naval forces of Spain in Europe a fleet under Admiral Cervera steamed to the Caribbean and took refuge, by bad strategy, in the bottleneck harbor of Santiago de Cuba, where it was immediately blockaded by the American fleet under Admiral Sampson. A valorous but ill-trained expeditionary force of 16,000 troops commanded by Major-General Shafter, including a volunteer regiment of "Rough Riders" under Colonel Leonard Wood and Lieutenant-Colonel Theodore Roosevelt, who had just resigned as Assistant Secretary of the Navy, and not excluding a large company of enthusiastic war correspondents, landed in the environs of Santiago and besieged the city. Cervera's ships filed out of the bottleneck in an heroic effort to battle their way through the American fleet, only to meet swift and complete destruction (July 3, 1898). Santiago then was surrendered. Meanwhile a small expeditionary force had been sufficient to take possession of the Spanish island of Puerto Rico. The fighting was over. War had quickly ended the horrors and destitution of chronic insurrectionary hostilities and saved thereby the lives of hundreds of thousands, not only of Spanish soldiers, but of Cuban *insurrectos* and civilian population, men, women, and children. It was in this sense a merciful war.

The decisive military events convinced the Spanish Government and people that to fight further was hopeless. Through the intermediary of the French Republic, and its ambassador in Washington, Spain asked for an armistice, which was signed August 12, under terms dictated by the victor. Spain relinquished all claim of sovereignty over the island of Cuba, and agreed to cede to the United States, Puerto Rico and one island of the Ladrone group in the west Pacific to be selected by the United States, and immediately to evacuate Cuba and Puerto Rico and all Spanish islands in the West Indies. The status of the Philippines was left to the peace conference which was called to meet in Paris not later than October 1. The armistice stated that meanwhile the United States would "occupy and hold the city, bay and harbor of Manila pending the conclusion of a treaty of peace which shall determine the control, disposition, and government of the Philippines." [1]

Before we consider the fateful decision which the United States had to make, it is best to notice the circumstances of Dewey's presence in the islands before and after his victory, and his relations with the native insurrectionary leaders and with foreign powers, notably Germany. Dewey's station in command of an American squadron in the Far East, in readiness for offensive operations in case of war with Spain, was due to the foresight of the young and alert Assistant Secretary of the Navy, Theodore Roosevelt. He had successfully pulled wires to get Dewey appointed to command of the Pacific squadron and had seen that his ships were well prepared for the contemplated action. Before sailing from Hong Kong for the historic naval action at Manila Bay, Commodore Dewey got in touch with certain Filipino insurrectionists, led by Emilio Aguinaldo, who had been exiled from the islands. The Commodore saw that they might be useful in undermining Spanish authority in the islands. After the destruction of the Spanish squadron, he called Aguinaldo and some of his comrades to Manila and planted them in the island of Luzon. They immediately organized an insurrection, assisted by American arms and ammunition. At no time did any American official make any specific agreement with them that the independence of the Philippines would be established in case Spain should be defeated, but there seems little question that Aguinaldo honestly so understood, and enthusiastically he rallied the natives to the American cause. His troops invested Manila from the land while the American fleet blockaded it from the sea.

During the summer various neutral warships appeared as observers at Manila: on June 17 a German fleet of five vessels under Vice Admiral

---

[1] News of the armistice did not reach the Philippines until the 16th. On the 13th the Americans had occupied Manila. Since the armistice had delivered the city over to American control, it was not necessary to restore the conquest of the 13th.

von Diederichs, at least equal in weight and guns to Dewey's force; a few days later came three British ships under Captain Chichester; there was also a French and a Japanese warship there.

We know from the German diplomatic correspondence published since the World War that the German squadron had been sent to Manila Bay to lend its watchful presence to the hope that Germany might somehow, some day, be able to take over part or all of the Philippines in case the United States did not keep them. "His Majesty, the Emperor," wrote Foreign Minister von Bülow to the Ambassador at Washington, July 1, 1898, "deems it a principal object of German policy to leave unused no opportunity which may arise from the Spanish-American War to obtain naval *fulcra* in East Asia." [1] Germany endeavored to bring about the neutralization of the islands pending a time when events might be propitious for procuring a partition; [2] but she could not get the co-operation of Great Britain for such a step. At Manila, the German Admiral annoyed Dewey excessively by violating the blockade in various ways, by making a gesture against Aguinaldo's forces, and by opening up communication with the Spanish authorities—he was listening to proposals by the Governor that some neutral power take over the islands in deposit for the duration of the war. The culminating incident of this officious and intrusive conduct occurred on August 13, when, after arrival of an expeditionary force from San Francisco, Dewey took position to shell the Spanish shore batteries, in support of an attack on the defenses of Manila by General Merritt's troops. One of the legends of American history is that on the day of the bombardment Captain Chichester of the British fleet conspicuously moved his vessels in between the Germans and Dewey, as if to serve notice that if Diederich opened fire on Dewey the British men-of-war would come to the American Commodore's defense. [3] After the surrender of Manila (August 13, 1898) the German squadron departed suddenly, to be seen there no more. Germany abandoned hopes of getting anything out of the Philippines in the near future in defiance of the United States and perhaps of England.

[1] Von Bülow to von Holleben July 1, 1898, *Die Grosse Politik der Europäischen Kabinette, 1871-1914* (Berlin, 1924), XV, 44-45. Professor Lester B. Shippee utilized this new material, when first published, in his enlightening article, "Germany and the Spanish-American War," *op. cit.,* superseding all earlier accounts.

[2] During the war the American Ambassador at Berlin, Andrew D. White, had given the German Foreign Office to understand that the United States would not object to Germany's having a naval base in the Philippines or in the other Spanish islands in the East, an assurance for which he was reproved by his own Government. The German Ambassador at Washington corrected this mistaken impression.

[3] Professor T. A. Bailey is preparing an article on this.

The appearance of the German squadron in Manila Bay and its un-friendly attitude there lent marked emphasis to the rivalry in imperialism between two new world powers, which was sharpened in the Vene-zuela affair of 1902,[1] and by the eagerness of the German Admiralty to secure naval bases or maritime *fulcra* in the Caribbean region. German and American naval officers began to measure themselves and their navies against each other. Back of the new rivalry in imperialism lay a mutual popular resentment in each country against the other's high protective tariff system.[2]

The archives are not yet unlocked which will reveal fully the secrets of British foreign policy in 1898 and the inner history of British action at Manila Bay, including Captain Chichester's instructions, if he had any, but this much seems clear: since the Kruger telegram of 1896 Great Britain had changed her outlook and was seeking possible allies to end her increasingly dangerous isolation. It was also to her interest to encourage the United States to take a place physically in the Far Eastern arena where it might support British policy to keep China open to the trade of the Occident, which was predominantly a British commerce.

Anglo-American relations now became more harmonious than at any time since the Revolution. We have already observed how this resulted in the arbitration of outstanding issues, and in later chapters we shall see how it led to the temporary equipoise of the question of China, to the readjustment of the Isthmian Question in line with American desires, and to the cordial reciprocation of the United States toward Great Britain during the Boer War. The foundations for this revived Anglo-American amity were laid in 1896-1898. On her part, Germany for her own obvious interests, worked without success to break down this new Anglo-American cordiality.[3]

After the signature of the Spanish-American armistice, Germany entered into a secret agreement with Spain (September 10, 1898), dependent upon the results of the war with the United States, for the purchase of the islands of Kusaie, Ponape, and Yap, in the Caro-line group. This was followed up (treaties of December 10, 1898, and February 12, 1899) by the actual purchase for $5,000,000 (ptas. 25,000,000) without objection by the United States,[4] of the Carolines,

---

[1] See below, pp. 522-525.

[2] Alfred Vagts, *Deutschland und die Vereinigten Staaten in der Weltpolitik* (2 vols., London, 1935), Vol. I, *passim*, and Vol. II, 1275-1635.

[3] *Grosse Politik*, XV, 49.

[4] The southward-lying Sulu Islands went to the United States as a part of the Philip-pine group. Germany took the position that, after Spain, she had the best claims

the Pellews, and the Ladrones, except for Guam Island which had been occupied during the war and ceded by the treaty of peace to the United States. They were the last of the Spanish islands left in the Pacific. Germany held them until the World War, when they were conquered by the Japanese. They went to Japanese mandate during Japan's membership in the League of Nations, and remained there in nominal mandate, unchallenged, after Japan's resignation from the League. Of small importance otherwise, they have the greatest strategical value as roosting-places for airplanes and naval bases for submarines, located across the communications from North America to the Philippines. Japan had shown an active interest in the Philippines in 1898. In a note of September 8 to the United States, the Japanese Government, while fully recognizing that the decision of the future of the islands rested with the United States, suggested that if it should feel disinclined to undertake alone the administration of the Philippines, Japan "would be willing to join with the United States, either singly or in conjunction with another Power having identical interests, in the endeavor to form, subject to proper conditions, a suitable government for the territory in question under the joint or tripartite protection of the guaranteeing powers." This offer was politely declined, and not made public.[1] Great Britain too was interested in buying the islands if the United States did not heed British urgings to keep them. It was obvious if the United States stepped out some other power than Spain would step in, perhaps more than one power would jostle each other to get in first. However insufficient, this was one of the reasons which impelled the Administration to continue in control.

After his victory at Manila Bay, Dewey could have sailed right along home, and it is a pity that he did not. Instead of that he continued to hold Manila Bay and to blockade the city. He suggested that if five thousand troops could be sent he could occupy Manila. Eleven thousand were sent and the city occupied August 13, with only a prearranged

to these (possibly because of proximity of her colonies in New Guinea), but offered to make no objection to American acquisition if the United States would place no obstacle in the way of Germany's acquisition of the other Spanish islands not ceded to the United States. (Shippee, *op. cit.*, 776-777.) At the very moment of acquiring the Philippines the United States acquiesced to a threat to its naval communications with them. Germany had made a treaty with Great Britain (August 30, 1898) dividing the Portuguese colonies of Angola and Mozambique into spheres of influence in anticipation of Portugal becoming insolvent and selling or mortgaging the colonies. Mary E. Townsend, *The Rise and Fall of Germany's Colonial Empire, 1884-1918* (New York, 1930), Ch. VII.

[1] A. L. P. Dennis first made it known in 1929 in his sketch of John Hay in *American Secretaries of State and Their Diplomacy*, IX, 126.

sham resistance by the Spanish garrison, which then concerted with the Americans to keep out the Filipino forces, who had helped to beleaguer Manila, and who already controlled most of the remaining parts of the islands. General Merritt had instructions to insure order in the Philippines as long as the United States should hold them, and to avoid any joint occupation with the native insurrectionists. Aguinaldo, feeling that he had been betrayed, organized the formidable two years' insurrection against the American occupants.[1] By the irony of fate, the United States, which fought a war with Spain to end an insurrection in Cuba nearby, soon found itself with an insurrection on its own hands in distant islands on the other side of the globe. The suppression of the insurrection was not without shameful and unnecessary cases of brutality and atrocity which reflect no honor on the individuals concerned, much as they have been condemned by enlightened American public opinion.[2]

In the peace negotiations at Paris there were two essential questions remaining to be settled: the Cuban debt, and the final disposition of the Philippines. Spain had given up Cuba and Puerto Rico already in the armistice of August 12, and was now willing to cede the island of Guam to the United States. She resisted unsuccessfully the American demand that she should assume the debt of Cuba existing in the shape of about $400,000,000 of Spanish bonds, a debt accumulated largely for the political purpose of subjecting the island. The great question therefore remaining before President McKinley and his advisers was whether to keep any or all of the Philippines. They were confronted squarely with the issue of outright and undisguised imperialism. This was the most important question in foreign policy which the nation had been called upon to decide since its independence. An absolutely new question, it had to be decided promptly in the fever-time of exuberant war feeling. President Washington a century before had warned his countrymen not to involve themselves in European political questions. The Monroe Doctrine had laid down such abstention as a fundamental principle of American foreign policy. Should the United States now involve itself at once in both European and Asiatic political questions, as it must needs do if it took over the Philippines, assuming vast liabili-

[1] James A. Leroy has minutely described these negotiations and operations in his *The Americans in the Philippines; a History of the Conquest and First Years of Occupation* (2 Vols., Boston, 1914).

[2] One cannot resist the simple and powerful indictment of American policy in the Philippines in 1898 and after, as set forth with documentary support by Moorfield Storey and M. P. Lichauco, *The Conquest of the Philippine Islands, 1898-1925* (New York, 1925).

ties in a part of the world where its interests were not vital, treading a political labyrinth where its step was least secure and its vision least luminous? Should it choose the perilous path of imperialism in the Far East, amid lands and peoples so distant from the American system and so alien to it?

Before the war there had not been the slightest demand for the acquisition of the Philippine Islands. The average American citizen could not have told you whether Filipinos were Far Eastern aborigines or a species of tropical nuts. The American people had no more interest in the islands than they have today in Madagascar. At the time of Dewey's victory, President McKinley himself had to look them up on the globe; he could not have told their locality, he said, within two thousand miles. But the expansionists of 1898, the new imperialists, the Roosevelts, the Lodges, the Mahans, the exponents of a "large" policy, knew where the Philippines were and they soon wanted them for the United States, wanted them as a valorous young swain yearns for the immediate object of his feelings, knowing only the passion of the present and seeing only the more appealing allurements of the hour. They inspired the vociferous desires of lesser leaders, and finally the President himself was seduced. Not long after the battle of Manila Bay, Colonel Roosevelt was writing his friend Lodge repeatedly opposing any peace "until we get Puerto Rico, while Cuba is made independent and the Philippines at any rate taken from the Spaniards."[1] Captain Mahan was seeing the problem of Asia as one which must be solved by the tutelage of the Teuton nations, including among them the United States with its own base in the Philippines. In his annual message of 1897 President McKinley had stated, anent Cuba, that forcible annexation was unthinkable,—"that, by our code of morality, would be criminal aggression." This did not prevent him from thinking of annexation of other islands once the war began. "While we are conducting war and until its conclusion," he noted, "we must keep all we get; when the war is over we must keep what we want."[2] What did the country want?

With the victories of American arms, imperialist sentiment had flared up and spread like wildfire, fanned by the psychology and self-esteem that accompanied a victorious war. The press, at first only speculative, became soon fascinated by the precipitate intrusion of American arms into the Far East and began to conjure the possibilities of American

---

[1] May 25, 1898. *Selections from the Correspondence of Theodore Roosevelt and Henry Cabot Lodge, 1884-1918* (2 Vols., New York, 1925), I, 299, 301.

[2] C. S. Olcott, *Life of William McKinley, op. cit.*, II, 165.

dominion over the Philippines. By the end of the summer a strong tone had set in for retaining them.[1] Business leaders, who had opposed the war with Spain, now began to see vistas of trade expansion from it.[2]

Rapidly moving events on the continent of Asia contributed to the quick development of this sentiment. After the Sino-Japanese War of 1895, the powers of Europe intervened, first to stay Japan's foothold on the Liaotung Peninsula, and next (1897-1898) to acquire for themselves fortified naval bases and spheres of territorial interest over China. Germany forced a lease of Tsingtao and fixed her sphere in Shantung. This precipitated action by Russia to secure a lease of Port Arthur and the Liaotung Peninsula and to fasten her influence on Manchuria. Great Britain leased Weihaiwei on the north coast of Shantung,[3] extended her holdings at Kowloon, opposite the British island of Hong Kong, and established her sphere in the Yangtze valley. France obtained a lease of Kwang-chou Bay, and set up a sphere over the island of Hainan and the three southern Chinese provinces (Yunnan, and Kwangsi, and Kwangtung) bordering on French Cochin-China; and Japan, after having been ousted from southern Manchuria by Russia, Germany, and France, extended her sphere over the province of Fukien, opposite the recently conquered island of Formosa. In each instance China was obliged to agree not to sell, lease, hypothecate, or otherwise alienate to any third power any port or territory within the designated sphere.

The normal expectation was that these spheres would soon become protectorates maintained from the naval bases, that their extension and transformation into actual dominion would be only a question of time. In that case all equality of trade would disappear in favor of the partitioning powers in each instance, and (so it was feared) the United States, whose merchants and navigators had long enjoyed most-favored-nation commercial privileges by treaties with China made in the wake of western wars against that Empire, would finally be left out in the cold. Let it be said, too, that each of the European powers, notably Great Britain, was more or less impelled to establish its sphere for fear that a rival would dominate China exclusively.

[1] According to a poll of 192 answering newspaper editors, made by the *Literary Digest* (September 10, 1898), 84 favored American possession of the whole archipelago, 63 wanted a naval base there, 14 an American protectorate, 6 favored getting out altogether, none advocated giving up the islands to Spain.

[2] Julius W. Pratt, "American Business and the Spanish-American War," *op. cit.*, 165-201.

[3] Pending the duration of the Russian leasehold.

With China thus on the brink of partition the Spanish-American War fortuitously and coincidently placed the American navy in control of Manila Bay and with it the whole Philippine archipelago. To the expansionists of 1898 here was the miraculous opportunity to keep step in the East with the powers of Europe and with Japan and prevent exclusion from the commerce of Asia. The Philippines would be the Hong Kong, the Kiaochow, the Port Arthur of the United States in the Far East, with a string of island bases and cable stations communicating with them from the Pacific Coast. From the new possession could be pursued the traditional American policy of conserving the independence and territorial integrity of China. It never occurred to these hasty thinkers that trade with a partitioned China might be greater and richer than trade with a preserved China. There was a widespread belief that the American home market for manufactures and native products had become saturated, and their minds played on this. Few could foresee how the tremendous internal development and transformation of the United States within the next generation would multiply the capacity of its people to consume. It seemed then that the markets of the East were the great vents of the future for a competitive industrial society based on capitalistic nationalism. The Philippines would be the American vestibule to the fabulous trade of the Orient. It appears never to have dawned on these adventurers into eastern imperialism that it would be difficult if not impossible to defend those distant islands, there on the other side of the globe, in case the balance of diplomatic power in the Far East should be upset by the complete dominance of any one naval power. They did not glimpse the future collapse of the Occident and the coincident rise of Japan.

Against these champions of a new adventure arose an opposition, dominated by New England intellectuals and organized into the Anti-Imperialist League. They argued on grounds of policy and morality against territorial expansion in the East and the dominion over alien peoples in distant islands in a way never envisaged by the Fathers of the American nation. Their most eloquent spokesman was Senator George F. Hoar, of Worcester, Massachusetts.

In the last analysis it is President McKinley who must bear the responsibility of the acquisition of the Philippines, as well as of the war with Spain, for it is he who commanded the army and navy, and who dictated the instructions to the American plenipotentiaries at Paris. When the peace Commission left the United States its instructions were indecisive as to the Philippines: a pledge to civilization, duty, humanity, a new opening for trade, and general morality, said the President, made it impossible to accept less than the cession in full right and sovereignty of the island of Luzon.

At Paris the Commissioners were perplexed and divided among themselves how much more to take. They held hearings of army officers and other persons (excluding any Filipinos), who had special knowledge of the Philippines and the East. General Merritt, who had commanded the first expeditionary force, pointed out that it would be easier to hold all the islands than one. It was apparent that other powers would step in where the United States left a foothold. Obviously from the strategical point of view, which was an important one, it was a question of taking the whole archipelago or nothing. Senator Gray, the Democratic member of the peace Commission and a steadfast opponent of imperialism, was opposed to taking anything. Judge Day, recently Secretary of State, favored retention of three islands: Luzon, Mindoro, and Palawan, which he thought would afford a sufficient naval base. A majority of the Commission, Senator Frye, Senator Davis, and Mr. Whitelaw Reid, opposed divided control of any kind and wanted the whole archipelago. The President was puzzled what to do. He has left an explanation of how the decision came to him, a statement made to a delegation of clergymen who visited him in Washington a year or so afterward.

"I walked the floor of the White House night after night until midnight," he said, "and I am not ashamed to tell you, gentlemen, that I went down on my knees and prayed Almighty God for light and guidance more than one night. And one night late it came to me this way—I don't know how it was, but it came: (1) That we could not give them back to Spain—that would be cowardly and dishonorable; (2) that we could not turn them over to France [sic] or Germany—our commercial rivals in the Orient— that would be bad business and discreditable; (3) that we could not leave them to themselves—they were unfit for self-government—and they would soon have anarchy and misrule over there worse than Spain's was; and (4) that there was nothing left for us to do but to take them all, and to educate the Filipinos, and uplift and civilize and Christianize them, and by God's grace do the very best we could by them, as our fellowmen for whom Christ also died. And then I went to bed, and to sleep, and slept soundly. . . ." [1]

So the President directed the peace Commission to demand the cession of the whole archipelago. Strangely, the Spanish resisted, and, finally,

---

[1] C. S. Olcott, *McKinley, op. cit.*, II, 108-111, quoting from the *Christian Advocate* of Jan. 22, 1903.

to smooth the matter over, the American plenipotentiaries actually offered a compensation of $20,000,000. Spain had already agreed to sell out her other Pacific islands to Germany; she now quickly accepted the twenty millions and got out of the East with alacrity.

Peace had come, bringing with it a protectorate over Cuba, and the possession of Puerto Rico, Guam, and the Philippines, in addition to the Hawaiian Islands annexed during the war. Over and above the $20,-000,000 paid for this liability in Eastern Asia, the Spanish-American War cost 2910 lives,[1] $250,000,000 war costs,[2] plus the costs of suppressing a two years' native insurrection against American dominion in the Philippines (1000 lives and $170,000,000). It has cost since then to date $919,369,440.38 [3] in pensions, but that cost is due to domestic folly, not war itself. A balance sheet in 1929 of material profits and losses on the account of the Filipinos with the people of the United States since the occupation of the islands, showed only losses for the Americans, profits for the Filipinos.[4] There was also the long accumulation of ill-will against American sovereignty, despite its good works.

The Senate of the United States ratified the treaty by the narrow margin of two votes: 57-27 (February 6, 1899). After the final vote on ratification, it rejected a resolution promising ultimate independence to the Philippines. This resolution met defeat by the casting vote of the Vice President, who thus won himself a remembered place in history: Garret A. Hobart is the name. Meanwhile Aguinaldo and his heroic followers had determined to fight it out to the end against the American occupants. President McKinley and his party leaders, and the Republican newspapers, had appealed successfully in the Congressional elections of 1898 to return Republicans to Congress so that the task of the peace Commissioners in dealing with Spain would be the easier. In the Senate, Senator Lodge, leader of the imperialists, said that to reject the treaty would be to repudiate the President and humiliate the country in the eyes of the civilized world. The President in fact had proclaimed

[1] Deaths from all causes in the army May 1 to Sept. 30, 1898, according to a report to the Secretary of War. This does not count deaths before complete demobilization. Dulles, *op. cit.*, estimates the total at 5642.

[2] C. A. Conant, "Cost and Finances of the Spanish War," *American Review of Reviews,* XVIII (1898), 314-320.

[3] To February 28, 1935. This is the total for pensions paid to veterans and dependents of deceased veterans of the Spanish-American War, the Philippine Insurrection, and the Boxer Rebellion. The Boxer Rebellion constitutes only a small fraction thereof, but has never been segregated in costs.

[4] Rufus S. Tucker drew up such "A Balance Sheet of the Philippines," in *Harvard Business Review,* VIII (1929), 10-23.

sovereignty over the islands already (December 21, 1898) before the Senate voted on the treaty. Nevertheless there was enough opposition to defeat the treaty until William Jennings Bryan, anti-imperialist and titular leader of the Democratic Party, went to Washington and advised senators of his party to vote for the treaty in order to end the war. He wanted to subordinate the issue of imperialism to that of free-silver in the next presidential election.[1] For imagined political advantages the Democrats sacrificed their principle. The issue of imperialism, like that of the League of Nations twenty years later, showed how foreign affairs are frequently made the football of party politics in the United States.

The Spanish-American War precipitated a final settlement of the Samoan Question. In the United States there had been steady discontent at participation in an "entangling" condominium. In Germany there persisted an ambition to own the islands. Great Britain had colonial liabilities on every hand, particularly in South Africa, where the Boer War was preparing; except to content New Zealand she was indifferent as to Samoa. The end of the condominium came not because of the breakdown of its government, which on the whole had functioned successfully, but because of the now ripened desire of the two new world powers—Germany and the United States—to partition the islands, and the acquiescence of Great Britain. The death of Chief Malietoa Laupepa was the signal for new native disturbances, and these in turn gave the pretext for partition. By the treaty of December 2, 1899, Germany received the two largest islands of Upolu and Savaii and all east of 171° W. L.; the United States received Tutuila with the harbor of Pago Pago and all the islets east of that longitude. Great Britain received from Germany compensation in the shape of the Tongas and a part of the Solomon Islands, and certain adjustments in West Africa. At the outbreak of the World War in 1914, the German holdings in Samoa were promptly snapped up by New Zealand forces—which considered them almost in the light of irredentist territory—and today they are held by that British Dominion under the mandate of the League of Nations.

Between Guam and Hawaii lie the tiny uninhabited Wake Islands. They were unclaimed by any power when the United States annexed them in 1899, principally for the purpose of a trans-Pacific cable station. Little did the expansionists of 1898 realize how useful this string of

[1] Merle E. Curti has introduced convincing evidence to show that, contrary to generally accepted explanations, Bryan did not urge ratification for the first purpose of making imperialism one paramount political issue in 1900. See his *Bryan and World Peace* (Smith College Studies, XVI, nos. 3-4, April-July, 1931), 128-129.

islands, Hawaii-Midway-Wake-Guam-Philippines, and the other little
islands between Hawaii and Samoa, would become for the aerial navigation of the Pacific in the present day.

The American people entered into the war with Spain without counting
in advance the costs in men and treasure, and they made peace with little
heed to the commitments it involved or the possibility of further wars
and expenditures much greater in size, which those commitments might
bring in another generation. The chief advantages of the victory were
the control of the Caribbean and of the ocean approaches to the future
isthmian canal; but it is doubtful whether an aggressive billion-and-a-
half-dollar war was necessary to obtain these. Today few citizens of the
United States would wish to undo the results of the Spanish-American
War so far as the Caribbean is concerned, but most of them fervently
regret the results of that war in the Far East. Not so did men think in
1900. In that year McKinley and his party were re-elected. Looking
back on those years of adolescent irresponsibility we can now see the
acquisition of the Philippines, the climax of American expansion, as a
great national aberration.[1]

The Philippine Islands under the sovereignty of the United States
became a monument to American good works and good will, a model for
colonial dominion and administration in the world. They also became a
military and a diplomatic liability. They were the Achilles' heel of
American defense, a hostage to Japan for American foreign policy in the
Far East. In the chapters that follow we shall see how time and again
Theodore Roosevelt and other American diplomatists had to make concessions to Japanese aggression on the Continent of Asia in return for
Japanese disavowal, either explicit or implicit, of aggressive intentions
toward the Philippines. The principal concern of the United States in
the Islands became that of liquidating decently and honorably an uncomfortable imperialism there, leaving them able to sustain their independence in a sea of sharks. In the Second World War they served
as a battle ground for a magnificent rear-guard action that may have
held up the Japanese juggernaut just long enough to make all the difference between final defeat or victory for the United Nations in that
conflict. But it wasn't planned that way in 1898.

[1] See below, p. 821, for preparation for American withdrawal from the Philippines.

PART III

THE TWENTIETH CENTURY

CHAPTER XXVII

THE OPEN DOOR AND THE FAR EAST

(1899-1914)

THREE new world powers made their appearance in the years 1870-1905. They were: Germany, 1871; the United States, 1898; Japan, 1905. By world powers we mean powers which have to be taken into consideration in most major international questions. Three new world powers multiplied the complications of diplomacy. They were all of them, after 1884, Pacific powers. The United States had been potentially a Pacific power since 1805, actually since 1846, emphatically after 1867. Germany became such when she embarked on her colonial career in 1884; Japan was a Pacific power native to the Asiatic fringe, but she, like the United States, would not come decisively into the arena until the eve of the twentieth century. The sudden appearance in the international firmament of these three new constellations upset the calculations of the diplomatic astrologers and produced new signs and portents of great significance in matters of daily welfare, indeed of life and death, to hundreds of millions of human beings on this earth. It boded a century of perturbations and wars, of vast territorial changes, of epoch-making political, economic and social upheavals. In these great cycles first the Atlantic countries, then the Pacific countries, would be the scene of world-shaking political happenings following the birth of these new world powers.

The United States as a world power since 1898 has been involved in the whirlpool of these terrific events and tendencies. In the third part of this volume our narrative lends itself most conveniently to consider at the outset the developments of Far Eastern affairs that followed the acquisition of the Philippines, to turn next to the activities of American policy in the Caribbean and the Isthmus and their borderlands, then to the diplomacy of the United States preceding and during the First World War, and between the two world wars, with a final focus on the world crisis of mid-century.

Before we observe the new diplomatic setting in the Pacific which was ushered in by the year 1898, we must at this point catch up briefly, if belatedly, the diplomatic contacts of the United States in the Far East from where we last left them in 1865 following the ratification of the new treaties of the western powers with Japan, their enforcement, and the ensuing revolution of enlightenment in that island empire.

After the fixation of the treaty relations of the powers with China and Japan, as we recall from Chapter XX, the United States remained till the close of the nineteenth century on the whole a passive spectator. The aim of American diplomacy was to preserve the integrity of the nations of the East, notably China, Japan, and Korea, in order to preserve an equality of opportunity for trade with them. This was also the principal object of British diplomacy, with this difference: Great Britain had ensconced herself in a fortified position (Hong Kong) in Eastern Asia, and was willing if necessary to do battle for her commercial interests, actually had done so; and Great Britain was ready if there were no other choice to join in a further scramble of the powers for Chinese territory in order to prevent any one of them or combination of them from encroaching on China to Britain's disadvantage. In the competitive imperialism of national capitalism China had become "the backyard of European politics." [1] Before 1898 the United States kept out of that wretched backyard territorially but desired that no special gates should be cut through the Chinese fence which would not be equally open to its missionaries and traders. The European powers and Japan meanwhile sought to make their gates and widen them by interpretation and manipulation of their treaty privileges. In China a hostility to all things foreign continued and smoldered among the people who sensed that treaties and foreigners encroached inevitably upon their territory and their independence. During this continuance of feeble interest by the United States in Asiatic affairs, two diplomatic questions stand out: the issue of oriental immigration (which is best considered in a later chapter), and Korea.

Rather casually an American expedition under Admiral John Rodgers was sent in 1870 to escort the American Minister to China, F. F. Low, to open up treaty relations with Korea, under a show of force, as Perry had done with Japan in 1854. The Koreans, who still kept their strategic peninsular kingdom closed to the western world, fired on Rodgers' ships in the Salee River below Seoul, the capital. Rodgers fired back, and destroyed five forts (May, 1871), but had not authority to involve the United States in further hostilities. He retired without a treaty, and the Koreans jubilantly felt they had successfully repulsed a

[1] Dennett, *Eastern Asia, op. cit.,* 472.

western power. In 1880 Commodore Shufeldt [1] attempted to approach Korea through Japan, but the Japanese endeavored to manipulate the negotiations so as to make Korea appear to be a Japanese protectorate. Exasperated, Shufeldt then sought the good offices of China to obtain a treaty with Korea, only to find the Chinese, on their part, seeking to show Korea as a Chinese protectorate. Shufeldt this time signed a treaty (May 22, 1882, ratified February 13, 1883) generally similar to the sum of the two previous American treaties with Japan, which avoided any reference to Korea as a dependent state of China.[2] Straightway the other principal powers (except Russia) made treaties with Korea, treaties which would have been much more one-sided had it not been for the American model. Japan already (1876) had made a commercial treaty with Korea which had described that kingdom as an independent state, and the presence of Japanese forces at the Korean capital in 1882 was responsible for Shufeldt's successful avoidance of an article acknowledging Korea's dependence on China. In the background was Russia with far-reaching designs of her own to make Korea an outlet for Russian expansion southward from Siberia across Chinese Manchuria.

In opening Korea to western commerce and western political rivalry, the United States had unwittingly stepped on the very touchstone of Far Eastern diplomacy. For three hundred years China and Japan had contested for a protectorate over that "hermit kingdom," a buffer among three powers, Russia, Japan, and China. Japan was now resorting to a policy of recognition of the nominal independence of Korea as a means of cutting it loose from any traces of Chinese sovereignty. Once independent Korea would be weak enough, and close enough to Japan, to pass eventually under the latter's control, if Russia should not intervene. By making a treaty with Korea as an independent state, the United States, followed by the other powers, really played into the first designs of Japanese expansionists. China, resenting this turn of affairs, began to contest Korea's independent status. The result was the disastrous war with Japan of 1894-1895, in which the victor took (Treaty of Shimonoseki, 1895) Formosa, the Pescadores Islands, and the Liaotung Peninsula, and occupied Weihaiwei as security for the payment of an indemnity of 200,000,000 *taels* ($145,800,000 at par). It was at this

---

[1] Shufeldt had already commanded an unsuccessful expedition in 1867 to investigate the destruction, with her crew, by Koreans of an American schooner, the *General Sherman*.

[2] C. O. Paullin has described these naval diplomatic missions to Korea in his *Diplomacy of American Naval Officers, op. cit.*, 282-328.

point that Russia (by previous understanding with China), France, and Germany stepped in to make Japan give up the Liaotung Peninsula— outlet of Manchuria to warm water—and then took over for themselves a portion of Japan's spoils. France unwisely supported Russia's advance in Manchuria in return for Russia's alliance with France in Europe. Germany encouraged it as a lightning-rod to draw Russian energies away from the tension of Western Europe (as similarly she had encouraged French colonial adventures in Indo-China and North Africa). Great Britain had not joined the three powers to take from Japan her plunder, but anxiously she joined the scramble for concessions in 1898, lest the door be closed against her growing trade in China. Never was a more fateful mistake made than by this application of Europe's international rivalries to the "backyard" of Asia. It nerved the Japanese to prepare for the expulsion first of Russian, then of German, finally of all European or occidental influence from eastern Asia. Little could the desperate Japanese then realize how events in Europe and America within the next generation would conspire for their success, as the convulsions of Europe of the period 1763-1823 had conspired for the success of an independent, continental United States of America.

The acquisition of the Philippines, we have suggested, was the greatest blunder of American diplomacy; it led rapidly to involvement in the politics of Asia and through them of Europe, and to a long row of further diplomatic blunders. The second great blunder in the East was the pronouncement, after British prompting, of the Open Door Doctrine.

China in 1898 on the brink of dissolution presented to Great Britain a problem much like South America in 1823: if the vast area of independence and free trade should be partitioned British trade would be shut out or discriminated against in favor of the partitioners. Great Britain was eager to sustain the principle of equal opportunity of trade for all nations because on the basis of even competition at that period she could dominate the market with her goods and her ships; moreover, she then controlled the sea from Gibraltar to Hong Kong, and in a war she could close to her enemy ocean trade routes from Europe to the East, and keep them open to herself. The Open Door in China was a British even more emphatically than an American policy, for Great Britain was willing to take positive action to keep it open. The events of 1898 and 1899, with partition every day more imminent, meant that Great Britain must either: (1) stand by and see China partitioned; (2) join the partitioners; (3) take action alone to stop it, which meant war with one or more powers; or (4) secure some international sanction for the integrity of China. The British Government naturally inclined to the last; and it was during this period 1898-1902 that it was shopping for allies. We must remember constantly that Great Britain was at this time involved in intense rivalry with France in Africa (until 1904), with Russia in the Near East (until 1907), with Germany in commercial and naval problems, and engaged with the Boers in open warfare in South Africa (1899-1902). With the United States now present in force in the Far East, and Great Britain withdrawn in force and in policy from the Caribbean, the kindred American republic seemed the most redoubtable as well as the most compatible of possible allies; but there were also Germany and Japan as offsets against Russia and France, then the potential enemies of Great Britain.

In March, 1898, the British Government, aware of the trend of rapidly developing events in China, confidentially invited the United States to co-operate in opposing any action by foreign powers which might violate the Open Door in China.[1] At this time the British proposed Open Door meant more than equality of trade rights throughout China; it meant equality of rights for economic concessions and privileges, the territorial integrity of China against further cessions. The overture reminds one in a striking way of George Canning's proposal to Richard Rush, in 1823, for a joint stand against European interference in South America; the motives were the same. Great Britain wanted to call in the United States to redress the European balance of power in Britain's favor, this time in the Far East. President McKinley, engrossed with the Cuban Question and the impending war with Spain, instructed Secretary Sherman to decline the invitation. He minimized the danger to the Open Door and, further, saw no reason for departing from the traditional policy respecting foreign alliances. The Open Door to Chinese trade was of no such vital interest to the United States as the independence and integrity of the American continents had been since 1823—there were strategic and defensive interests in America which were not at stake in China. The sudden acquisition of the Philippines changed the shadings of the Eastern picture, and more complete information showed the danger of partition to be very real. The paramount motive for acquiring the distant archipelago had been the trade of the East. Should China be partitioned, so it was feared, that prospect of commerce would vanish behind the restrictions of the partitioners.

[1] Dennis, *Adventures, op. cit.,* Ch. VII.

John Hay, now Secretary of State, recently Ambassador in London, knew well the attitude of the British Government. He realized that Great Britain might leave the United States a free hand in the New World and wanted in return a joint hand in Eastern Asia. He was taking advantage of this change in British policy in his efforts to secure a revision of the Clayton-Bulwer Treaty and the control of the future isthmian canal. He felt that the Open Door fitted into American policy as well as into British, if not so vitally. John Hay knew that American public opinion was set against anything resembling a foreign alliance, and that the "unspeakable Senate" would not ratify any formal treaty. He had as an adviser on Far Eastern affairs Mr. W. W. Rockhill, who had served briefly in the American diplomatic service in China and who was a close student. Rockhill represented to Hay that the policy best suited to American interests was not a British one, for England had been as great an offender in China as Russia herself. Hay accepted the advice [1] of Rockhill to take an independent step for the preservation of China—and with it of American trade through an open door there—by an appeal to the jealous powers to guarantee to all nations equality of opportunity within their special spheres. Since 1928 it has been known [2] that Mr. Alfred E. Hippisley, a British subject formerly in the Chinese customs service, who arrived in the United States in 1899, had a strong hand in formulating the basis of the Open Door notes—previously attributed to Rockhill—and persuading Hay to issue them.[3] More recently it has been established that a small pressure group of American exporters to North China (Manchuria) organized a powerful propaganda which seems to have had its effect on the Department of State.[4] The Hay notes, to Great Britain, Russia, Germany, France, and Japan, dated September 6-November 17, 1899, stated:

The principles which this Government is particularly desirous of seeing formally declared . . . by all the great powers interested in China, and which will be eminently beneficial to the commercial interests of the whole world, are:

[1] Rockhill's memorandum was called forth by the lectures, conferences and publications of Lord Charles Beresford, a quasi-official British propagandist who circled the globe in 1899 urging a joint Anglo-American policy in the Orient.

[2] Dennis, *Adventures, op. cit.,* 186, and Dennett, *John Hay, op. cit.,* Ch. XXIV.

[3] It would be interesting to know if Mr. Hippisley had any connection, direct or indirect, with the British Embassy, in Washington, or with the Foreign Office. The *British Documents on the Origin of the War, 1898-1914* omit the documents relating to the Open Door notes, though copious selections of documents relating to other Far Eastern affairs of that time are printed.

[4] Charles S. Campbell, Jr., "American Business Interests and the Open Door in China," *Far Eastern Quarterly,* I (November, 1941), 43-58.

First. The recognition that no power will in any way interfere with any treaty port or any vested interest within any leased territory or within any so-called "sphere of interest" it may have in China.

Second. That the Chinese treaty tariff of the time being shall apply to all merchandise landed or shipped to all such ports as are within said "sphere of interest" (unless they be "free ports"), no matter to what nationality it may belong, and that duties so leviable shall be collected by the Chinese Government.

Third. That it [each power] will levy no higher harbor dues on vessels of another nationality frequenting any port in such "sphere" than shall be levied on vessels of its own nationality, and no higher railroad charges over lines built, controlled, or operated within its "sphere" on merchandise belonging to citizens or subjects of other nationalities transported through such "sphere" than shall be levied on similar merchandise belonging to its own nationals transported over equal distances.

That the United States was now a power established with military and naval forces in the Philippines, that its policy, if independent, accorded with that of Great Britain—as also with that of Japan in 1899—made Germany, France, and Russia more attentive to Hay's proposals. Great Britain adopted them conditionally, and in language which reserved Hongkong and Kowloon. Germany accepted on condition that the other powers would; so did France, Japan, and Italy (which had failed to establish a sphere), but Russia equivocated. Hay, by what then passed for a skillful coup, replied in identical language to all the powers, severally, that all having complied with the proposals of the United States, the latter (in each case) would consider the assent given to the principles as "final and definitive."

The notes were extremely gratifying to England,[1] and undoubtedly helped Hay in adjusting the Isthmian Question and the Alaska boundary dispute, although there is no evidence of a specific diplomatic bargain. As the leading authority on this phase of American diplomatic history has put it, the net result was that Great Britain got out of the Caribbean and the United States got into Asia.[2] It should be noted that the Open Door, an international understanding of doubtful[3] binding power, was then limited in its application to tariff, railroad charges, and port dues. It did not open the door to equal opportunity of investment or of industry. It did not, in 1899, attempt to preserve the territorial integrity,

[1] Nevins, *Henry White, op. cit.*, 167.

[2] Tyler Dennett, "The Open Door," in *Empire in the East*, ed. by Joseph Barnes (Garden City, New York, 1934), 280.

[3] Each power made its acceptance conditional upon the full acceptance by all the other powers. Since Russia did not accept, and Great Britain excluded the leasehold of Kowloon, this left everything much qualified, indeed.

the administrative entity, or the independence of China, as the British Government had suggested in March, 1898.

Was Hay's policy a wise one? As a temporary expedient, perhaps yes, it was good as long as the diplomatic equipoise should last in the Far East. As a far-sighted permanent policy to stick to and defend like the Monroe Doctrine, no. The Open Door would not stay open should the territory of China or its administration pass under the full control of any other power, that is should China's independence be threatened. The fate of Korea was soon to be a complete example of this truth. In the ensuing years, to keep the Open Door in China the Government of the United States was drawn further and further into the diplomatic entanglements of the Far East by expanding the doctrine so as to include the territorial and administrative integrity and the independence of China. This was assuming responsibilities of policy compensated by no corresponding advantages to the United States. The structure of the Open Door would be threatened as soon as any one power in the Far East should become paramount. Then the United States would have to fight for the Open Door or retreat in the face of the world from its declared principles. At no time have the American people been willing to fight for the Open Door in any part of Asia, or indeed in any other land. Again, it cannot be shown that, even if China had been partitioned and its territory placed under other sovereignties, the opportunity of American trade would have been smaller instead of greater. One may notice how American trade with the sovereign Japanese Empire, one of the putative partitioners, increased while that with China, unpartitioned further (until 1931), relatively languished. So, at least it can be argued, the Open Door may have been a second blunder of American diplomacy in the Far East.

The Open Door notes did not prevent an explosion in China on the part of patriotic groups resentful of foreign exploitation and of the imperial Manchu Government which had succumbed to it. The Boxers, a patriotic society in North China, stirred up the people to end the encroachments by wiping out the hated barbarians and their Christian converts. The Dowager Empress encouraged the movement, which pillaged and murdered foreign missionaries and other residents in the provinces, and finally attacked and besieged the legations in Peking, after killing the secretary to the Japanese legation, and the German Minister. A total of 231 [1] (mostly missionaries and their families) were

---

[1] Exclusive of the Marine guards (76 killed, 179 wounded) defending the legations during the siege, and, of course, of military casualties during the ensuing intervention.

massacred between June 24 and July 24, 1900, including 53 children. The Manchu authorities, caught between native resentment and foreign punitive measures, managed to prevent a general slaughter. For a month Peking was totally cut off from the outside world, which assumed that the 920 foreigners penned in the legations had perished. Intervention seemed imperative, but would it stop short of war and partition? The western powers and Japan hastily brought up from their naval bases and ships an aggregate of approximately 19,000 troops, and, after some sharp engagements, relieved the legations (August 14, 1900, after a seven weeks' siege), opened up communications with Tientsin and the sea, and occupied Peking and Chili province. Other contingents of troops reinforced the occupation after the taking of Peking. The United States had finally a total of 5,000 troops in China. The international settlement at Shanghai was also reinforced. After prolonged negotiations the powers imposed punishment and reparations on China.

During the Boxer crisis Secretary Hay successfully strove to prevent an actual war (although China had declared one when the foreign troops came), to limit intervention to the protection of foreign nationals, to withdraw troops promptly, to stop the jealous, avaricious powers from vengeful extensions of their existing leaseholds and spheres, and to keep down the total of reparations to be demanded from China. This was also the policy of Great Britain, then engaged in the Boer War in South Africa. Hay issued a circular (July 3, 1900): "The policy of the Government of the United States is to seek a solution which may bring about permanent safety and peace to China, *preserve Chinese territorial and administrative entity*,[1] protect all rights guaranteed to friendly powers by treaty and international law, and safeguard for the world the principle of equal and impartial trade with all parts of the Chinese Empire." It was the capstone of American policy in the Far East.

Only Great Britain, France and Germany responded favorably to this principle; nevertheless its application softened the terms imposed on China. Unfortunately Hay contradicted himself by asking the Japanese Government if they would have any objection to the United States establishing a naval coaling station at Samsah Bay, Fukien Province (within the recently established Japanese sphere of influence). Japan replied that she would indeed have objection: "The Imperial Government harbor no territorial designs on China; their policy, on the contrary, is directed to the maintenance of her territorial integrity; and they have noted with entire satisfaction the declaration made on several occasions

---

[1] Italics inserted.

by the Secretary of State that the United States were also anxious to preserve the territorial entity of that empire." [1]

The protocol [2] of September 7, 1901, stipulated for the punishment by death or exile enumerated Chinese officials implicated in the outbreak, the erection of expiatory monuments where foreigners had been killed or outraged, or tombs defiled, protection of foreign communications between Peking and the sea, and the payment of 450,000,000 *taels* ($333,000,000) reparations. Of this the United States had claimed only $25,000,000. This proved more than adequate to indemnify the claims of nationals, and in 1907 $10,785,286 was returned to the Chinese Government. This generous act ingratiated the United States further in Chinese estimation, as had been the case with Japan and the Shimoneseki indemnity. The Chinese Government placed the money in a trust fund for the education of Chinese youths in China and in the United States. The rest of the balance due ($6,137,552.90) was remitted by the United States in 1924. [3]

The American policy of the Open Door now rapidly floriated into the preservation of all China in full sovereignty against foreign encroachments. During the occupation of Peking, Russia had occupied Manchuria, and despite subsequent promises refused to get out unless the Chinese consented to place Manchuria under Russian protection. Secretary John Hay made successive protests against Russian advances on Chinese sovereignty. He protested (February 1, 1902) against the granting to Russia of any exclusive mining or railroad privileges as wrecking the policy of "absolute equality of treatment of all nations in regard to trade, navigation, and commerce within the confines of the Empire," and against any commercial monopoly as a violation of the Open Door "accepted by all the treaty powers having commercial interests in that Empire." He protested (April 25, 1903) against a proposed Russo-Chinese convention then being pressed on China which would have prohibited treaty ports and foreign consuls in Manchuria, and would have excluded all foreigners except Russians from Chinese public service in North China; and in the Chinese-American treaty of commerce (October 8, 1903) the Open Door Doctrine was asserted in treaty form, accompanied by the opening of Mukden and Antung in

[1] *Foreign Relations, 1915*, 115, note.
[2] Not a treaty ratified by the Senate.
[3] During the war of 1917-1918, payment was by agreement of the Entente allies suspended for five years. Germany had renounced hers by the peace of 1919 (also returning artistic and scientific treasures plundered from Peking in 1900), and the Soviet Government renounced its remaining share in 1920.

Manchuria to foreign trade, thus thwarting Russian attempts to close it. At the outset of the Russo-Japanese War the United States appealed (February 10, 1904) to both belligerents to limit as much as possible their military operations in order to preserve the neutrality and "administrative entity" of China (with no mention of Korea); and joined the neutral powers in a disclaimer of compensation for themselves with Chinese territory. At this time the war was being fought in Chinese territory. Hay then stated (January 13, 1905) the broad policy of the United States to maintain "the integrity of China and the 'Open Door' in the Orient."[1] Hay had advanced from a policy of a limited Open Door to a policy of preserving the sovereignty and territorial and administrative entity of all of China's vast empire. At the very time he was writing these fine words, Russia and Japan were engaging in a duel, at first in peace, and then in war, ultimately to possess themselves of large portions of Chinese territory. Under the guidance of Hay, American policy in Eastern Asia was rapidly assuming responsibilities far greater than any advantage promised or interests involved.

We have said that the success of the Open Door policy—not to mention now its floriations—depended on a complete equipoise in the Far East, that it could not be maintained if one power should upset the balance. That power began to emerge to a position of challenge very soon. It was Japan.

In the situation heading up in Asia, Japan, like Great Britain, needed an ally. Great Britain, engaged in the Boer War, at odds with France in Europe and Africa, and with Russia in the Near East and Asia, and desiring to preserve the territorial integrity of the remainder of China and the Open Door there, unable to make friends with Russia, had deserted her traditional policy of "magnificent isolation." She had looked first hopefully to the United States, glanced distrustfully at Germany, and then turned again to her traditional adversary Russia,[2] as possible allies. None would commit itself. Japan was now confronted with Russia, established in the Liaotung Peninsula and building with French loans a railroad south across Manchuria to a naval base at Port Arthur. This was the concession which China had secretly promised to Russia in return for getting the three powers to thrust Japan out of her conquests in 1895. After the Sino-Japanese War Japan considered nominally independent Korea as her preserve and looked be-

[1] M. J. Bau, *The Open Door Doctrine in Relation to China* (New York, 1923).
[2] W. L. Langer, *The Diplomacy of Imperialism, op. cit.*, II, 711-786, describes in detail these negotiations with Germany, Russia and Japan.

yond it toward Manchuria. Russia considered Manchuria as her preserve and looked beyond it toward Korea. In back of the immediate
ambitions of both rival powers in Korea and Manchuria lay their larger
ambitions and rivalry for the ultimate domination of all China. Japan
prepared for another war, but wished to make sure that Russia would
have to stand alone, without allies. The result was the Anglo-Japanese
alliance of January 30, 1902. The contracting powers declared themselves to be actuated solely by a desire to maintain the *status quo*
and general peace in the Far East, being moreover specially interested
in maintaining the independence and territorial integrity of the Empire
of China and the Empire of Korea, and in securing equal opportunities
in these countries for the commerce and industry of all nations. Disavowing aggressive tendencies in China and Korea, they recognized the
right of either ally to take such measures as might be necessary to
safeguard its existing interests; and in case either should become involved in war with a third power in defense of those interests, the
other party would remain neutral, but would come to the defense of
its ally in case the enemy were joined by another power. The treaty
was to remain in force for at least five years.

Before the first five years had elapsed Great Britain had pacified
South Africa, and in the face of the German advance, had liquidated
her historic issues with France in Morocco, Egypt, and other parts of
the world by the Entente of 1904, and Japan was engaged in the war
with Russia. The early Japanese victories at Port Arthur and on the
plains of Manchuria, Britain's concern to protect the northwestern
frontiers of India against future Russian expansion, and the continuing
menace to England of the rising German navy made it possible for
Japan to reframe the alliance in 1905 during her peace negotiations
with Russia. The object of the alliance, renewed for ten years, was
now (August 12, 1905) stated to be: "(a) The consolidation and maintenance of the general peace in the regions of Eastern Asia and of India.
(b) The preservation of the common interests of all powers in China,
by insuring the independence and integrity of the Chinese Empire and
the principle of equal opportunities for the commerce and industry of
all nations in China. (c) The maintenance of the territorial rights of
the high contracting parties in the regions of eastern Asia and of India,
and the defense of their special interests in the said regions." Great
Britain agreed to go to Japan's assistance in case, during the existing
war, Russia should be joined by a third power. Further, if by reason

of unprovoked or aggressive action *wherever arising*,[1] on the part of any other power or powers, either party should be involved in war in defense of its territorial rights in "the regions of Eastern Asia and of India," the other party would at once come to the assistance of its ally. As for the future, Great Britain explicitly recognized a free hand for Japan in Korea, subject to the maintenance of the Open Door there, and Japan implicitly and tacitly gave to Great Britain a free hand to sap Chinese suzerainty in Tibet, which had been penetrated by British forces in 1904. The new alliance enabled Japan to clinch its hold on Korea in the coming treaty of peace with Russia, and it made it possible for Great Britain to concentrate her sea power in European waters. At the same time Japan pledged herself to observe the Open Door in Korea, and in China the Open Door and "the independence and integrity" of that Empire.

The peace negotiations had opened meanwhile at Portsmouth, New Hampshire. To understand the background of President Roosevelt's proffer of good offices to the belligerents in 1905, we must bear constantly in mind the relationship of the "backyard" of European diplomacy in Asia to its frontyard in Europe. With Russia "mired" in Manchuria after the Japanese victory at Mukden (March 10, 1905) the German Kaiser and his advisers determined to reap the diplomatic profits arising in Europe, from their inveiglement of Russia into Asiatic adventure: (1) by breaking the new Anglo-French entente on the anvil of Morocco, (2) by nullifying the Franco-Russian alliance through attaching a salvaged Russia to Germany in a defensive alliance against France. As the first move the Kaiser disembarked at Tangier (March 31, 1905) to greet the Sultan of Morocco in his position as an independent sovereign. This German challenge to the dual entente for an open door in Morocco precipitated a major European diplomatic crisis. We shall see in a later chapter,[2] how the exuberant Roosevelt went out of his way unnecessarily to participate in the first Moroccan crisis— the first of a series that led to the outbreak of the World War in 1914.

---

[1] Under this phrase the aggressive action might arise in Europe or in America. In 1911 the alliance was renewed for ten years from date, to continue thereafter until abrogated by either party at one year's notice. It contained a modification intended to remove the United States from its scope: "Should either high contracting party conclude a treaty of general arbitration with a third power, it is agreed that nothing in this agreement shall entail upon such contracting party an obligation to go to war with the power with whom such treaty of arbitration is in force." Great Britain was then negotiating a general treaty of arbitration of justiciable questions with the United States, but it was never ratified.

[2] For the first Moroccan crisis, see below, p. 581.

He also went out of his way to play unnecessarily a part in the Asiatic sphere of world policy.

During the first Moroccan crisis, France's embarrassment at the paralysis of her Russian ally inspired her to suggest to Japan her willingness to be a peace-maker. The Japanese Government suspected French disinterestedness. It was nevertheless eager for a peace which would preserve its victories against the danger of exhaustion by a long war of attrition in northern Manchuria. It ceased major military movements and intimated to President Roosevelt a preference and readiness for his good offices. Germany, whose policy had been to push Russia along diplomatically into the Manchurian quagmire in order to paralyze France's ally in Europe, was now content with the predicament of Russia, and somewhat alarmed at the possibility of revolutionary disorder in European Russia, which might infect Germany and endanger the monarchical principle there. The Kaiser therefore supported the move for peace, through Roosevelt. He also was planning a secret treaty with weakened Russia (Björkö, July 25, 1905) which would detach her from the Franco-Russian alliance, and he desired to win Roosevelt's support for that. Roosevelt [1] had let the Japanese know that he thought that they deserved to have Korea, and Secretary Hay's [2] note on the Open Door had ignored that expiring kingdom. The President now attached one condition for his services to bring about a peace: that Japan pledge herself to the doctrine of the Open Door in Manchuria. Having secured from the Czar—after the destruction of the Russian fleet at Tsushima Straits—an agreement to meet the Japanese, Roosevelt made to both parties a formal offer of good offices (June 8, 1905). The belligerents accepted and successfully worked out indirect negotia-

---

[1] Dennett, *Russo-Japanese War, op. cit.*, p. 2, quotes an authentic letter of Theodore Roosevelt to the British diplomatist, Sir Cecil Spring-Rice, dated July 24, 1905, in which he said: "As soon as the war broke out, I notified Germany and France in the most polite and discreet fashion that in the event of a combination against Japan to do what Russia, Germany and France did to her in 1894 [*sic*], I should promptly side with Japan and proceed to whatever length was necessary on her behalf. I, of course, knew that your government would act in the same way, and I thought it best that I should have no consultation with your people before announcing my own purpose."

The Anglo-Japanese alliance itself had never promised more than this, and (so far as we know) Great Britain had never served such notice. That Roosevelt really did do precisely this is doubtful, like his now disproven "ultimatum" to Venezuela of 1902-3. Vagts, *Weltpolitik, op. cit.*, p. 1178, could find no trace of it in the archives of the State Department, the German Foreign Office, or in the personal papers left by Roosevelt or John Hay.

[2] Secretary Hay was now ill and on leave. He died July 1, 1905. Roosevelt meanwhile had taken over the administration of foreign affairs, leaving Secretary of War Taft in nominal control of the Department of State. Taft presently was sent on a mission to the Philippines via Japan.

tions without the presence of a formal mediator, the peace of Portsmouth, New Hampshire (signed, September 5, 1905).

While the Japanese envoys were *en route* to the peace conference, President Roosevelt confirmed the bargain with Japan concerning Korea and the Philippines: the secret [1] Taft-Katsura memorandum (July 29, 1905). This avowedly had no constitutional force binding upon the United States; but President Roosevelt, speaking in the most non-committal way through Secretary of War William H. Taft, then in Tokyo on a mission to Manila, approved a free hand for Japan in Korea, and Count Katsura, the Premier of Japan, disavowed "any aggressive designs whatever on the Philippines."

The Treaty of Portsmouth, a landmark in the diplomatic history of the modern world, contained these terms: (1) Russia recognized that Japan had "predominant political, military, and economic interests in Korea," and agreed not to interfere with them in any way. (2) Both countries agreed "to completely and simultaneously evacuate Manchuria" and to restore it to "the exclusive administration of China," excepting always the Russian leasehold with all concessions in Liaotung, which was transferred completely to Japan. Russia declared she had no "territorial advantages or preferential or exclusive concessions in Manchuria of such a nature as to impair the sovereignty of China or which are incompatible with the principle of equal opportunity." [2] Both parties mutually pledged themselves not to place obstacles in the way of general measures, applying equally to all nations, which China might adopt for the development of commerce and industry in Manchuria. Russia transferred to Japan her mining and railroad concessions in southern Manchuria, south of Changchun. Both countries reserved the (arbitrary) right to maintain railway guards to a maximum of fifteen per kilometer. (3) Russia ceded to Japan the southern half of Sakhalin Island. This treaty was a striking triumph for Japan, definitely establishing her position as a world power, an epoch-making step for that nation on the continent of Asia.

[1] The text, without mention of Taft's name, is printed in Dennett's distinguished study of *Roosevelt and the Russo-Japanese War* (New York, 1925). P. C. Jessup, *Elihu Root* (N. Y., 1938), II, 5, makes out that Taft did this on his own initiative. "Your conversation with Count Katsura absolutely correct in every respect," Roosevelt cabled to Taft, July 29, 1905. "Wish you would state to Katsura that I confirm every word you have said." Henry F. Pringle, *Theodore Roosevelt, a Biography* (New York, 1931), 384. Great Britain informed Roosevelt of the substance of the alliance during its negotiation. He did not object. Gelber, *Anglo-American Friendship*, 216-250.

[2] Note that this was not a disavowal of territorial advantages or exclusive concessions. In fact, the Russian reply of itself was sufficiently equivocal to nullify any general binding agreement.

President Roosevelt thought the peace just to Russia and Japan and also good for England and the United States. It is difficult to see how the President's diplomacy in this instance benefited the United States. The Open Door was not really strengthened by the substitution of Japan for Russia in southern Manchuria, as Mr. Roosevelt came presently to realize. In Japan a disappointed populace raged at the failure to secure an indemnity and the whole of Sakhalin Island, and attached, unreasonably, the odium for this to the United States where the treaty had been signed. From this time begins a steadily mounting feeling of enmity in Japan against the United States, hitherto her best and most disinterested friend. The feeling was sharpened by the immigration policy of the United States, and, more and more, by the Open Door policy, which stood in the way of Japanese expansion on the continent of Asia, for which the way had been prepared by the winning of the war against Russia. President Roosevelt received the Nobel peace prize and the plaudits of the world for his conspicuous diplomacy, but really it did some harm and no good to the United States; therefore it was another blunder, the third blunder of American policy in the Far East, part and parcel of the growing Open Door policy which had been the immediate sequel to the fateful aberration of 1898. It is to be noted that Great Britain, whose interests in China surpassed those of all other powers, kept clear of all these peace negotiations, except to confirm and reshape her alliance with Japan, as above noted, recognizing the new Japanese position in Korea.

During the decade after Portsmouth, American diplomacy in the Far East is featured on the one hand by continuing efforts to hold the door open in China including, after Roosevelt's departure from office, Manchuria, and to preserve its territorial and administrative integrity and independence, and on the other hand by the appearance of new issues between the United States and Japan arising out of domestic legislation within the United States on matters of immigration and alien land-holding. We must reserve the last of these questions for special consideration later.[1]

Japan had stepped into a continental foothold and a policy of expansion which must necessarily envisage Korea, China, or Russian Siberia, in the long run all of them. Over Korea she established a protectorate during the war (1904), which rapidly, and despite disclaimers of any intention to annex, developed into outright possession (1910). In China, Japan confronted the concessionaire powers and the doctrine

[1] See Chapters XXXV and XXXVI.

of the Open Door blossoming into the preservation of that country. Siberia was not of immediate importance, and the account was already squared with Russia for that generation. As to China, until the World War and the preoccupation of the western powers with other problems it was necessary to speak softly and go slow. Japan therefore did lip service to the Open Door and its expanding principles which really stood in the way of her "manifest destiny," and concentrated her diplomacy on establishing a special position in that part of China known as Manchuria. She quickly secured from China (treaty of Peking, 1905) an acquiescence in the transfer of the Russian leasehold and attendant railway concessions and a secret statement[1] that China would not allow any parallel or branch railways prejudicial to the interests of the South Manchuria Railway. She then started a development of the railway and ancillary concessions directed toward the economic and, eventually, the political control of Manchuria. The first step was to work quietly for treaties with individual powers, which, while recognizing in a general way the principle of the Open Door and the integrity of China, would nevertheless confirm—in return for equivalent recognitions by Japan in other spheres—Japanese special interests and the network of particular treaty rights regarding Manchuria. Japan signed such treaties[2] with both France and Russia in the summer of 1907, and considered the negotiation of one with the United States, but the time was then unpropitious for this last because of the serious tension between the two nations arising from the California immigration question. After the temporary adjustment of that issue, and the acceptance by the United States of Japan's invitation for the American fleet to visit her ports on the famous cruise around the world, there was worked out the Root-Takahira executive agreement, November 30, 1908; not a treaty to be sure, but an understanding of the first importance, binding at least on the Roosevelt Administration.

In this exchange of notes—which followed the spectacular American naval demonstration in the Pacific—the United States and Japan declared themselves to be: (1) uninfluenced by any aggressive tendencies

---

[1] The Lytton Report of 1932 (see below, p. 816) showed that this was not an agreement, but merely a statement in the minutes of the discussion between the representatives of the two governments.

[2] For English text of the treaties, and of all other treaties revealed before 1919, see the standard compilation by J. V. A. MacMurray, *Treaties and Agreements with and Concerning China, 1894-1919* (2 Vols., New York, 1921), I, 640, 657.

The French treaty (June 10, 1907) recognized the "independence and integrity of China." The Russian treaty (July 30, 1907) recognized "the independence and territorial integrity of the Empire of China."

in their policy to maintain the "existing *status quo*" in the "region of the Pacific Ocean," (2) resolved to respect the territorial possessions belonging to each other in that region, and (3) "determined to preserve the common interests of all powers in China by supporting by all pacific means at their disposal the independence and integrity of China and the principle of equal opportunity for commerce and industry of all nations in that Empire." "Should any event occur threatening the *status quo* as above described or the principle of equal opportunity as above defined, it remains for the two Governments to communicate with each other in order to arrive at an understanding as to what measures they may consider it useful to take."

The Root-Takahira understanding, so studiously phrased, was another executive adventure of Roosevelt—unsustained by the Senate. It supplemented the earlier Taft-Katsura "agreed memorandum." It appears to have been calculated to recognize indirectly Japan's increasing interests in Manchuria. One should note: (1) that there is a distinction between the region of the Pacific Ocean (where lie the Philippines and Formosa) and China; (2) that only "peaceful means" are mentioned; (3) that the phrase "integrity of China" is not preceded by the qualifying word "territorial." It suggests that Roosevelt was preparing to give to Japan a free hand in Manchuria as he had done already in Korea.

He had already come to feel that the Philippines—for the conquest of which he had been so ardent in 1898—were the "Achilles heel" of the United States, and that the United States could not fight Japan over Manchuria. His executive agreements reflect this conviction, the greatest anxiety of his Eastern policy.

If the Root-Takahira agreement might be construed to make, tacitly but realistically, some concessions to Japan's ambitions in Manchuria, at the expense of China's complete territorial integrity, the policy of President Taft ignored such an interpretation. He endeavored to push the door still wider open by a highly legalistic reliance on the construction of the Open Door and the territorial integrity of all China, including Manchuria. Taft was a constitutional lawyer; so was his Secretary of State, Philander C. Knox.

Taft and Knox saw that the territorial integrity and political independence of China in Manchuria were being menaced by the railway concessions to Japan and Russia, and were convinced that this was contrary to the spirit and letter of the Open Door and ought to be stopped. Secretary Knox believed that if these special railway concessions—to gain which it is remembered the two nations had gone to the point of war, and to war itself—could be done away with, the Open Door and China's sovereign rights would be protected. To achieve this he relied on paper and ink, a memorandum (December 14, 1909), the principle of which the British Government had agreed to support diplomatically, which he presented to the Governments of China, Japan, France, Russia and Germany, proposing a joint loan to enable China to buy up all the railways, including those in Manchuria, in her territory which were then under foreign lease or hypothecation; or, alternately, to construct south to north through Manchuria from Chinchow to Aigun another railway under neutral administration—a scheme of "commercial neutralization." Thus would the Open Door be guaranteed by neutral administration throughout Manchuria and all other parts of China, and thus would China eventually throw off the trammels which the railway concessions had established upon her sovereignty.

This, said Secretary Knox, was "perhaps the most effective way to preserve the undisturbed enjoyment by China of all political rights in Manchuria and to promote the development of those Provinces under a practical application of the policy of the open door and equal commercial opportunity." Neither Russia, who had never agreed with the United States to the Open Door, nor Japan, who found it irksome, desired any practical application of that doctrine in Manchuria, particularly after they had reached understandings with some of the powers (including the Root-Takahira agreement) which appeared to confirm their special interests there. The Knox neutralization proposal was the fourth blunder of American diplomacy in the Far East. Despite the willingness, in principle, of China, Great Britain and Germany, to accede to it, the ill-considered proposal had no chance of success [1] with the three other powers opposed. Its only result was to impel Japan and Russia to delimit and agree to defend their respective special interests in Manchuria and also the adjacent area of Eastern Inner Mongolia (treaties of July 4, 1910,[2] and June 25, 1912). It undid Roosevelt's

---

[1] France, true to the spirit of her Japanese treaty of 1907, declined the proposal unless it was acceptable to Russia and Japan.

[2] Ironically, this treaty reaffirmed attachment to the principles of the previous convention of July 30, 1907, in which the two powers had recognized the "independence and territorial integrity of China and the principle of equal opportunity" and agreed to defend the *status quo* and respect for this principle by all pacific means within their reach. The *status quo* and the principle were of course incompatible.

policy of give-and-take with Japan. It did not help keep the door open in Manchuria and it brought resentment from both powers, particularly Japan, against the government which had initiated the proposal. Japan proceeded to construct feeder lines to the South Manchuria Railway, particularly for the exploitation of the rich coal fields, and to connect with a trunk line through Korea to its southern tip. Along the new railroad trackage Japan extended her military guards and developing political jurisdiction over the loosely defined railway zones.[1] In northern Manchuria, Russia likewise expanded her political influence.

After the failure of the neutralization proposal, Taft and Knox desired a share for American corporations henceforth in China's foreign loans and big construction contracts. The service of these loans had demanded the pledging of various classes of internal revenues, and even Chinese employment of designated foreign subjects for the collection and administration of the hypothecated revenues. Hence there was grave danger of eventual political control by the powers so eagerly competing to be China's creditors. As in 1898 the powers strove for geographical spheres of political influence, so now the rivalry was for political control, or to prevent unique political control through the supervised service of the loans. In 1910 French, German, British and American banking groups, with the support of their respective governments, signed an agreement for joint action and participation in foreign loans to China. Into this consortium, further perfected in 1913, were admitted Russia and Japan in 1912.[2]

The consortium loaned to the Chinese Government a total of only

---

[1] The original contract of September 8, 1896, granting to the Russo-Chinese Bank the right to construct a railroad, under the organization of the Chinese Eastern Railway Company, stated that the company might hold "the lands actually necessary for the construction, operation and protection of the line"; and that "the company will have the absolute and exclusive right of administration of its lands." Russia and Japan used this clause to justify political control of the railway zones including administration of cities, within their respective spheres, and to guard the road with troops. It has been noticed already that both powers incorporated this into the treaty of Portsmouth. Japan's right to do so was confirmed by an interpretative additional agreement to the treaty of Peking of 1905. See the three volumes by C. Walter Young: *Japan's Special Position in Manchuria; the International Legal Status of the Kwang-Tung Leased Area;* and *Japanese Jurisdiction in the South Manchuria Railway* (Johns Hopkins University Press, 1931).

[2] Space forbids any more detailed analysis of the political and economic aspects of these loans. We refer the reader to Stanley K. Hornbeck, *Contemporary Politics in the Far East* (New York, 1916); W. W. Willoughby, *Foreign Rights and Interests in China* (Johns Hopkins Press, 1927); H. B. Morse and H. F. MacNair, *Far Eastern International Relations* (N. Y., 1931); and more particularly to C. F. Remer, *Foreign Investments in China* (New York, 1933); and Edward H. Zabriskie, *American-Russian Rivalry in the Far East* (Univ. of Penna. Press, 1946).

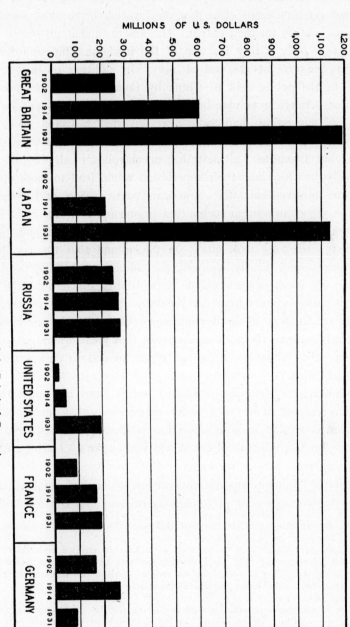

MILLIONS OF U.S. DOLLARS

Total Investments in China of the Principal Countries.

From C. F. Remer, *Foreign Investments in China*, p. 75. (Acknowledgments to the Macmillan Company.)

£27,000,000. American bankers furnished but $7,299,000 [1] of this. It has not yet been made clear how the favored corporations secured government support for their entrée. The American share of the consortium loans were only a tiny fraction of the immense Chinese foreign debt of $835,000,000 [2] at the end of 1913. In addition to this $7,299,000 share of the public debt of China by favored American banking corporations, American private business of one kind or another—merchants, shippers, navigation—had $42,000,000 invested in China in 1914, plus mission property of $10,000,000. The whole stake was very small indeed,[3] but President Taft felt that uncontrolled rivalry by the powers for loans to China and their supervision would lead to bankruptcy and political intervention, that American participation and co-operation were necessary to prevent such a catastrophe and to preserve the integrity of the nation.[4] President Wilson promptly reversed this policy (March 18, 1913) when he took office, on the ground that the conditions of such loans very nearly touched the administrative independence of China. He would not accept the responsibility which would be implied in requesting bankers to undertake loans "which might conceivably go the length in some unhappy contingency of forcible interference in the financial and even the political affairs of that great oriental state." The Wilson policy (abandoned in 1917) put an end to American banking loans to China.

Following the exit of the United States from the consortium, the powers resumed their rivalry for supervision of Chinese loans and finances, a rivalry in which the European governments gave way to Japan after the outbreak of the World War in 1914. During these years of international contest for loans and public works the Chinese revolted against the Manchu imperial government which had led them into the increasing entanglement of foreign concessions and control, and set up

---

[1] This was their share in the so-called Hukuang railway loan of £6,000,000. Remer, *op. cit.*, 268-272.

[2] Of this $174,600,000 was on account of a loan to pay off indemnity to Japan after the Sino-Japanese War; and $309,200,000 was outstanding on account of the Boxer indemnity. That is, obligations on account of these two indemnities then constituted 57.9% of China's total foreign indebtedness.

[3] Remer, *op. cit.*, 125-130, 272-274.

[4] "I have an intense personal interest in making the use of American capital in the development of China an instrument for the promotion of the welfare of China, and an increase in her material prosperity without entanglements or creating embarrassments affecting the growth of her independent political power and the preservation of her territorial integrity." President Taft to the Prince Regent of China, July 15, 1909. *For. Rel., U. S., 1909*, 178. There is no reason to believe that Taft had other than the interest of China at heart.

(1911) a republic, out of which it was hoped would develop a strong national government able to cope successfully, like the Japanese, with foreign nations. The United States, with over-optimistic expectations, eagerly welcomed the new government into the family of nations.

Throughout this period of 1898-1914 American policy had endeavored by diplomacy to support the independence and integrity of China in order to share with the world an open door to the foreign trade and investments of that crumbling Empire. The diagram on page 499 shows the actual American (all *privately owned*) stake in China as compared with other foreign nations. It shows that Great Britain and Japan by 1914 were, as they still were in 1939, the principal capitalistic [1] and indeed political rivals in China—next came Russia, Germany and France. The United States had committed itself before the world to a policy of obligingly helping to hold open a door used far more by Great Britain, Japan, Russia, France and Germany than by itself, to defending at least by peaceful means the independence and integrity of a distant, vast and uncertain country where its interests were less than those of any other great power and not in any sense vital.[2] Until 1914 this had been possible because of the diplomatic equipoise in the Far East which sustained the Open Door and its floriation. The World War was to upset that balance in favor of Japan. After that the Open Door remained only a verbal and paper challenge to Japanese ambitions of expansion and hegemony in eastern Asia, spiritedly backed by bayonets and battleships strategically placed. If the expansionists of 1898 could have read the future as we can read the past, or if they had even taken the pains to study a few statistics of trade and investment demonstrative of the small stake which the United States had in the Far East compared with other parts of the world, or the problems of strategy involved, we are constrained to believe that they would not have embarked so precipitately upon the conspicuous but unprofitable and foolhardy venture into the world politics of Asia, so alien to American continental traditions and interests, so dangerous to the welfare

[1] As regards exports and imports, the United States stood third, after Great Britain (including British dominions and colonies); in 1932 and 1933 American trade with China surpassed Japan's, presumably because of Chinese boycotts. Commercial tabulations of China's trade with the principal countries may be found in Field, *op. cit.*, 424-425.

[2] The exports of the United States to China in 1914 were less than 1% of the total exports; the imports from China to the United States only 2% of the total imports into the United States. The investments of the United States in China in 1914, $42,000,000 (exclusive of $10,000,000 mission property) were 2.8% of the total American investments abroad.

of the United States.   Perhaps they would have applied logically to Asia that dictum of the Monroe Doctrine which opposed American participation in the entanglements of Europe.   It is significant that, except for the Treaty of Paris of 1898, the whole unsound structure of American foreign policy in the Far East from 1898 to 1914 rested on executive act and executive agreements and not on the expressed sanction of the Senate or of the Congress.

CHAPTER XXVIII

CUBA AND PANAMA

(1899-1939)

THE Cuban-Spanish-American War signalized the predominance of the United States over the future isthmian canal. The primary concern of American foreign policy in the years between the Peace of Paris of 1898 and the World War was to consolidate the newly established position in the Caribbean and Central America, to make the necessary diplomatic arrangements for the construction and control of the canal, and to assure the protection of the approaches from both coasts of the United States. After the World War the exhaustion of Europe, comparable only to its exhaustion a century before, following the Napoleonic wars, and the consequent strengthening of the position of the United States on this side of the Atlantic diminished the danger of intervention and diluted the established measures of control. This and the following chapter will bridge the period of the World War and will witness the rise of American imperialism in the Caribbean and Central America, and in turn some indications of its decline. A third sequent chapter will deal with Mexico; further on, after we have covered the diplomacy of the First World War, the peace settlement, and its aftermath, we shall touch on general Pan-American relationships and problems.

The Teller Amendment at the beginning of the Spanish-American War had pledged the restoration of Cuba to the Cubans—Cuba, that island so close to the United States, so important to the strategy of the Caribbean which was in turn to be the strategy of Panama, the strategy of American naval defense. At the close of the war the Senate had refused by the casting vote of the Vice-President to pledge the country to restore the Philippines to the Filipinos, those Philippines and those Filipinos on the other side of the globe, those islands and people where the United States had no vital interests. Who can penetrate the mysterious inconsistencies of such expressions of policy?

The reconstruction of Cuba by the American army authorities, during the military occupation of 1898-1902, the sanitation of the island, the start of the Cubans on the road to self-government at first so promising,[1] all these Samaritan achievements in Cuba, as in the Philippines, are outside the scope of this history, which must stick closely to American diplomacy. The United States kept the pledge of the Teller Amendment, though the expansionists of 1898 regretted this hasty expression. An amendment to the army appropriation act of March 3, 1899 (the Foraker Amendment) provided:

That no property, franchises, or concessions of any kind whatever shall be granted by the United States, or by any military or other authority whatever, in the island of Cuba during the occupation thereof by the United States.

It was Elihu Root, Secretary of War, who formulated the future relationship of Cuba to the United States, the same notable jurist who was responsible for the structure of government in the Philippines, the island of Puerto Rico and the other overseas possessions. Root was determined that the United States should not be placed after the war with Spain in a worse position in regard to its vital interests in Cuba than it had been while the island was in Spanish possession. He wished to make it certain that no foreign power other than the United States should interfere with the destiny of Cuba—and this meant a protectorate. Root submitted to the Cuban constitutional convention the proposals which soon afterward were embodied in the Platt Amendment (to the army appropriation bill passed by the Congress of the United States, March 2, 1901), but the Cubans rejected the provisions, which gave the United States a right to intervene in order to maintain a stable government in Cuba and to have naval bases there. The Platt Amendment provided that the United States would leave the government and control of the island of Cuba to its people as soon as they would imbed in their constitution the following terms:

1. Cuba not to enter into any treaty or other compact with a foreign power which would impair its independence, nor permit colonization for military or naval lodgment of control.

2. Cuba not to contract any public debt beyond its resources reasonably considered.

3. The United States to have a right to intervene "for the preserva-

---

[1] Charles E. Chapman has told with penetrating understanding the history of the formation of the Cuban Government and its subsequent shortcomings in his *History of the Cuban Republic, a Study in Hispanic American Politics* (New York, 1927). A very serviceable review of Cuban-American relations is Russell H. Fitzgibbon, *Cuba and the United States, 1900-1935* (Menasha, Wis., 1935).

tion of Cuban independence, the maintenance of a government adequate for the protection of life, property, and individual liberty," and for discharging the obligations assumed by the Treaty of Paris.

4. Ratification of all the acts of the United States during the military occupancy.

5. Execution by Cuba of the sanitary arrangements already undertaken by the United States, thereby assuring protection against infectious diseases "to the people and commerce of Cuba, as well as to the commerce of the southern ports of the United States and the people residing therein."

6. The title to the Isle of Pines to be left for future adjustment.[1]

7. The United States, for its defense as well as that of Cuba, to have the right of purchase or lease of two naval stations.

8. These provisions to be embodied in a permanent treaty with the United States.

The fact that the Platt Amendment was the indispensable condition precedent of American evacuation overcame the Cuban objections to the right of intervention and the naval stations, particularly after Secretary Root had explained, for the President, that the Amendment was "not synonymous with intermeddling or interference with the affairs of the Cuban Government, but the formal action of the Government of the United States, based upon just and substantial grounds, for the preservation of Cuban independence and the maintenance of a government adequate for the protection of life, property, and individual liberty, and adequate for discharging the obligations with respect to Cuba imposed by the Treaty of Paris on the United States."[2] The terms were embodied both in a treaty (May 22, 1903) and in the Cuban constitution itself. General Leonard Wood, the military governor—intimate of President Roosevelt, the leading expansionist of 1898—privately thought that the Platt Amendment would practically annex Cuba,[3] and many Cubans feared so; but American public opinion steadily

---

[1] This island contains 1180 square miles and is located 35 miles off the southwest coast of Cuba. A Cuban-American treaty signed March 4, 1904, recognized Cuba's sovereignty over the island, but was not ratified by the United States until 1925. The delay was due to the influence of the American colonists who had gone there in the belief that they were settling under the American flag.

[2] Article XVI, Treaty of Paris of December 10, 1898: "It is understood that the obligations assumed in this treaty by the United States with respect to Cuba are limited to the time of its occupancy thereof; but it will, upon the termination of such occupancy, advise any Government established in the island to assume the same obligations."

[3] Professor Herminio Portell-Vilá, of the University of Havana, brought this out in a paper read before the American Historical Association at Urbana, Ill., in 1933, citing a letter of General Wood to President Roosevelt, October 29, 1901.

moved in a different direction particularly after the First World War.
Trusteeship of Cuban independence thus assumed and maintained by
the United States compatibly with its own vital strategical interests
in the Caribbean has stood as a notable example to the powers.

The Cuban protectorate brought its problems for the United States.
One problem since 1902 has been to resist the importunities of Cuban
political parties to place or maintain them in power during inveterately
recurring political disorder. Another has been to arrange beneficent
commercial treaties with Cuba which should not be too painful for
sugar-growers in the United States. Finally, in a safer age, there has
been the problem of modifying or dissolving the Platt Amendment.
During the lifetime of the Platt Amendment, however, the principal
problem was the maintenance, with a minimum of intervention, of peace
and stable government in the island. With great reluctance the United
States intervened, and set up a provisional régime, 1906-1909, after the
second Cuban national election had paralyzed the island's government.
The people, who had not submitted to 200,000 Spanish troops in 1898,
made no resistance to a handful of soldiers in the second American intervention because they had confidence in its righteousness. The action
conferred a benefit by stiffening for a time the stability of the government. Since then the United States has followed a preventative policy
of seeking by diplomatic methods to avoid intervention. In 1911 on the
occasion of a Negro revolt, and again during the war with Germany, a few
companies of marines were stationed in Cuba, mostly at the United
States naval base at Guantanamo, to lend aid in case the established
government should not be able to ward off anarchy; and from time to
time various American missions have been sent to the island to un-
tangle electoral difficulties or straighten out financial troubles.[1] A
reciprocity treaty, ratified early in 1903, was the basis of Cuban-American commercial relations until it was superseded by the agreement of
1934. It gave special reductions, of 20% under the general tariff line of
the United States, to Cuban products, and of 20 to 40% upon importations
into Cuba from the United States. Under it Cuba enjoyed a rousing
economic prosperity based on sugar, until after the First World War.

Despite persistent Cuban dissatisfaction with the protective status
imposed by the Platt Amendment, the entrance of the United States into
the First World War furnished a test of that relationship. Cuba de-

---

[1] Dana G. Munro has summarized Cuban-American relations after digesting the
voluminous literature, both Spanish and English, in *The United States and the Caribbean Area* (World Peace Foundation, Boston, 1934). See also Fitzgibbon, *op. cit.*

clared war on Germany the day following the resolution of Congress
that a state of war existed between the United States and Germany.
The island republic, instead of finding an opportunity to press for readjustment of the protectorate, manifested a sentiment of complete
solidarity and loyal co-operation with the United States.[1] Cuba's principal contribution to the war proved to be her economic undoing, immensely profitable as it was at first: the stimulation of sugar production under high price control. In the months of unexampled prosperity
that followed, both the Cuban Government and Cuban business, in
many instances representing American capital, were able to borrow
huge sums within the Platt Amendment. Cuba's principal export crop
of sugar expanded far beyond its normal base of the preferential market
of the United States. Its collapse at the end of 1921 brought widespread
bankruptcy in its wake, though a mission from the United States under
General E. H. Crowder succeeded in restoring order to the finances of
the Government.

Economic conditions ameliorated, but collapsed again with the Great
Depression that plunged the world into misery in 1929. Cuban politics
went from bad to worse. A revolution began to smolder in 1932 against
the repressive administration of President Gerado Machado. Determined to smother it, he resorted to a veritable reign of terror, with
excesses which, in the case of individuals, rivaled those of the Spanish
régime. The Cuban revolutionists importuned the United States to intervene. Intellectuals in the United States meanwhile urged a revision
of the Platt Amendment, echoing the propaganda of Cuban liberals. The
economic collapse added to the distresses of the island. The result was,
in the second year of the Administration of President Franklin D. Roosevelt, a radical revision of Cuban-American relationship. Machado was
eased out of office, what with the pressure of the revolutionists, without military intervention of the United States; and after a period of
diplomatic uncertainty, because of succeeding provisional governments,
the United States recognized a new but none-too-stable régime and ratified a treaty "of general relations" (1934), and signed an executive
agreement (under authority of the act of Congress of June 12, 1934),
putting into effect reciprocal preferential tariffs, suspending, during the
existence of the new agreement, the old reciprocity treaty of 1903. The
new treaty abolished the Platt Amendment and the protectorate, retaining the naval station at Guantanamo.

[1] Percy Alvin Martin, *Latin America and the War* (Johns Hopkins Press, 1925),
107-172.

Cuban politics continued to be highly volatile, with the "outs" continually importuning the United States to put them in power, and the "ins" persistently asking for intervention to repress the insubordination of the "outs." The abandonment of the protectorate and the right of intervention, coupled with ratification by the United States of the Pan-American treaty of the rights and duties of states, which renounced the right of intervention, meant that henceforth the United States would not intervene in Cuban politics no matter how unsavory they might become. To use a vulgar phrase, Cuba, like all other Caribbean and Central American states, must now stew in its own juice, except should a non-American power attempt to season the dish; then the United States might be expected to say hands off, under the Monroe Doctrine. It is still too early, and the domestic situation in the United States is too uncertain economically and politically, for us to know how the new tariff relationships will work out for both countries, but it can be said that great and sympathetic effort was exerted in its negotiation really to benefit Cuba as well as the United States. The United States in its present system of unconditional most-favored-nation treatment [1] for nations enjoying treaties of commerce, has uniformly reserved a privilege of special preferential tariffs with Cuba.

Puerto Rico never presented any diplomatic problem after its outright annexation in 1899. Since 1917 Puerto Ricans have become American citizens, and the island enjoys a territorial form of government in all but name.

Contemporaneously with this installation of the Cuban protectorate, the State Department, under Secretary John Hay, had been negotiating with Great Britain for a modification of the Clayton-Bulwer Treaty of 1850, which had internationalized and neutralized the status of any isthmian canal under the joint control of Great Britain and the United States and any other nations which might adhere to the instrument. Repeated attempts by corporations, both American and French, to build a canal had demonstrated that it was beyond the resources of private capital. If any government should construct the waterway it was incompatible with American interests that this should be any other than the United States. If the United States should build a canal under the Clayton-Bulwer Treaty it would assume all the risks and expenses, with Great Britain equally in control of the canal and all the world sharing its facilities equally. The United States could not even fortify it. For

[1] See below, p. 755.

half a century this treaty had barred the way to any "American canal on American soil for the American people."

After the West had filled up, the people of the United States had turned their attention back to the canal. The naval operations of the war with Spain—including the long and dramatic voyage of the U. S. S. *Oregon* from the Pacific Coast to the Caribbean around South America— had vividly emphasized the necessity of full national control over the future waterway; in fact the underlying motive of the expansionists of 1898 was to clear the way for the control of the canal, the future nodal point of American naval defense from ocean to ocean. Political parties and successive governments were increasingly annoyed at the persistence of the Clayton-Bulwer Treaty estoppel. Immediately after the war an act of Congress (approved March 3, 1899) authorized an investigation into all possible isthmian routes, with a view of digging the canal as a government enterprise.

Hay's task of modifying the Clayton-Bulwer Treaty was eased by Great Britain's new decision to strengthen her position by withdrawing from any contest for predominance in America and by cultivating the United States as a possible ally in Asia. From the Venezuela boundary arbitration in 1896 to the signature of the Anglo-Japanese alliance of 1902 it was the effort of Great Britain to seal an Anglo-American alliance in preference to some other. Hay was personally not averse to an alliance, but he knew that the Senate was dead set against it; he therefore made, as he thought, the best of the situation by arranging a new canal treaty, and, subsequently, a settlement of the Alaska boundary dispute. British diplomacy tried to couple the two questions, but the outbreak of the Boer War weakened this attempt to secure compensations in Alaska for concessions in the Isthmus.

The terms of the first Hay-Pauncefote treaty, signed on February 5, 1900, but never ratified, modified the continuing Clayton-Bulwer Treaty to permit the construction of a canal anywhere across the Isthmus under the auspices of the United States, to be maintained by the United States; but the United States could not fortify it, nor blockade it; it was to be open in time of peace and in time of war to the vessels of peace and of war of all nations, on terms of entire equality, under rules of neutralization substantially similar to the international convention for the regulation of the Suez Canal. That is, the United States could go to the expense of constructing the canal and maintaining it, but could have no special advantage of any kind, even in case it were engaged in war; in time of war an enemy might sail its fleet right through the canal to attack San

Francisco or Savannah. As Governor Theodore Roosevelt objected to his friend, Hay, the proposed canal under such conditions would fetter the navy rather than assist it: "Our fleet would have to watch it, and therefore do the work which a fort should do; and which it could do much better."

The first Hay-Pauncefote treaty would have thrown away the real victory of the Spanish-American War. The refusal of the Senate to ratify it as it stood is at least one striking example of the advantages of the Constitution in requiring the advice and consent of the Senate for the ratification of treaties. The three amendments attached to the treaty by that body, as a condition of its consent, were: (1) The Clayton-Bulwer Treaty is superseded; (2) the United States might take measures "for securing by its own forces the defenses of the United States and the maintenance of public order;" (3) other nations might not adhere to the treaty.[1] Great Britain refused to accept these changes. Hay resigned in disgust, but President McKinley, who had not lifted a finger to help his Secretary's treaty through the Senate, persuaded him to stay and try again with Great Britain. The multifarious exigencies of Great Britain in other parts of the world made her amenable to further negotiation.

The second Hay-Pauncefote Treaty (signed November 18, 1901, ratified February 21, 1902, after a Senate vote of 72-6) was a compromise between the first treaty and the Senate amendments. The text stated that it "superseded" the Clayton-Bulwer Treaty.[2] In the preamble it declared its purpose to remove any objection that might arise under that treaty to the construction of the canal under the auspices of the Government of the United States, without impairing the "general principle" of neutralization established in Article VIII of that convention. It incorporated "substantially" the rules of neutralization for the regulation

[1] The Senate adopted unanimously the first and third of these amendments, the second by a vote of 65-17; it then advised and consented to ratification by a vote of 55-18. This time party politics had little to do with the vote, except in the sense that an endorsement of Hay's treaty as it stood would have jeopardized any party in power in the coming national elections. Holt, *Rejected Treaties, op. cit.*, has a sharp eye for all possible political implications of the treaty.

[2] President Roosevelt carefully stated in his annual message of December 3, 1901, that the Clayton-Bulwer treaty "is abrogated"; and the British Government in its note of November 14, 1912, declared it was "superseded." It was the rules incorporated in the Hay-Pauncefote Treaty rather than the Clayton-Bulwer Treaty on which Great Britain chose to rest her successful protest against the act of August 24, 1912, which exempted from tolls American coastwise vessels using the Panama Canal. Rule 1 stated: "The canal shall be free and open to the vessels of commerce and of war of all nations observing these Rules, on terms of entire equality, so that there shall be no discrimination against any such nation, or its citizens or subjects, in respect of the conditions

of the Suez Canal as in the convention of Constantinople of 1888, but rewritten here with certain small changes from the text of the first Hay-Pauncefote treaty and with this vitally important difference: the omission of any article prohibiting fortification of the canal by the United States. It was further agreed that no change in the territorial sovereignty of the canal would alter the obligation of the parties to the treaty. There was no provision for other nations to adhere.

In the interim between the two negotiations Theodore Roosevelt had become President. He vigorously supported the new treaty. By the implication of silence, as compared with the first, rejected treaty, it would appear that the second Hay-Pauncefote Treaty gave the United States the right to fortify the canal and defend it against enemies in time of war. Academicians argued that omission of prohibition did not give consent to fortification, particularly in view of the rules for neutralization which expressly prohibit the exercise of any act of war within the canal; but all these academic arguments have no significance because during the negotiation of the second Hay-Pauncefote Treaty, Great Britain, the only other party to the treaty, admitted the right of the United States to fortify and defend the canal against enemies.[1] These fortifications have long been a vital factor in American naval defense and a fundamental factor in the foreign policy of the United States.

Within a few years after this treaty Great Britain reduced her permanent garrisons in the West Indies and withdrew her principal naval forces from that area. She rather definitely acquiesced in the predominance of the United States in that part of the world, so vital to its own interests.

The way was now clear for the diplomatic arrangements with the Central American state through which the canal must run. There had been much debate, and still is, among engineers and in public opinion which was the better route, Nicaragua or Panama. The United States

or charges of traffic, or otherwise. Such conditions and charges of traffic shall be just and equitable."

President Wilson induced Congress to repeal the articles omitting coastwise shipping from the same burden of tolls; but Congress in the repeal declared its right to do so if it wished. Many students of the tolls question believed that the United States abandoned a perfectly good legal case for arbitration. Wilson's recommendation was the result of his personal connections, and of a tacit diplomatic bargain by which he received British support for his contemporary Mexican policy. The details reveal themselves in Charles Seymour's edition of *The Intimate Papers of Colonel House, loc. cit.*, I, 191-206.

[1] Memorandum of Lord Lansdowne, Aug. 3, 1901. Moore, *Digest International Law,* III, 212-216.

had secured transit rights—but not construction rights—from both Colombia (treaty of 1846) and Nicaragua (treaty of 1867) : in the former case guaranteeing "positively and efficaciously" both the neutrality of the canal route and the sovereignty of Colombia, in the latter case recognizing the sovereignty of Nicaragua over the canal route and guaranteeing only its neutrality. An official engineering commission in 1876 favored the Nicaraguan route. An American corporation, the Maritime Canal Company, working under a charter from Congress and a concession from Nicaragua, failed after three years (1890-1893) of initial construction labors there. On the Isthmus of Panama a French company, organized by DeLesseps, the engineer of the Suez Canal, already had gone bankrupt after spending nearly $300,000,000 (1881-1887) and digging less than a third of the way. Immediately after the Spanish American War, and while Hay was negotiating his canal treaties with Great Britain, another official American commission investigated the merits of the rival routes and their abandoned works. These engineers, the Walker Commission, pronounced just after the signature of the second Hay-Pauncefote Treaty, in favor of Nicaragua. The cost of a river-and-lake canal there it estimated at $189,864,062. It would cost only $144,233,358 to complete the Panama Canal—according to the estimates of this commission, which fell far short of realities—but to this must be added $109,141,500 which the bankrupt French Panama Company demanded for its concession and property rights.

The House of Representatives quickly passed a bill for the construction of a Nicaraguan canal. If enacted this bill meant that the stockholders of the ruined French company would get nothing. From now on the ring of men who controlled the rusting remains of this bankrupt French corporation succeeded in manipulating the destiny of the canal route and the political and international and moral factors bound up with it. The French company now quickly offered to sell for $40,000,000. Forthwith, at the suggestion of President Roosevelt, the Isthmian Canal Commission reversed its decision and pronounced for the Panama route. The United States Senate, under a powerful lobby of representatives of the Panama Company, adopted the amendment of Senator Spooner to the House canal bill, switching the site to Panama under condition that the French concession and property could be purchased for $40,-000,000 or less. If Colombia should refuse to accept this reasonable offer, the President was authorized to go ahead with the Nicaraguan route, making the necessary diplomatic arrangements with that state, and with Costa Rica, which had claims of sovereignty over the San Juan River. The law passed Congress in this form.

The act gave to the President a strategic position in dealing with the rival canal countries. After nine months of negotiations the Secretary of State signed with the Colombian Minister the famous Hay-Herrán treaty (January 22, 1903). This treaty authorized the New Panama Canal Company (the reorganized French company) to sell its properties to the United States, and granted to the United States full control over a strip across the Isthmus covering the canal site, six miles wide. For this the United States promised to pay to Colombia $10,000,000 cash, and, beginning nine years after the exchange of ratifications, an annuity of $250,000 gold. The money was the least of the great benefits to Colombia; the real value of the treaty was that it would bring suddenly to Colombia, particularly to the Colombian state of Panama, the inestimable advantage of a highly prosperous seat at the crossroads of one of the two greatest waterways of the world. Like the Hay-Pauncefote treaties, and all treaties signed by plenipotentiaries of the United States, this treaty was to come into effect when ratified according to the laws of the respective countries, which meant, in this instance, by the Senate of the United States and by the Senate of Colombia.

The Colombian Senate threw away this priceless advantage by failing to ratify the treaty. Those small-minded senators thought they might get more money both from the United States and from the Panama Company. Their conduct exasperated President Roosevelt greatly, but we must remember, we must remember most emphatically, that Colombia had a perfect sovereign right to refuse to ratify the treaty, just as the United States had a perfect right to refuse to ratify without amendments the first Hay-Pauncefote treaty, the early treaties for the purchase of the Danish West Indies, or the Treaty of Versailles, to mention only a few of those where the Senate has exercised its constitutional prerogative. That Colombia, for whatever motives, according to its constitutional forms, allowed for in the treaty itself, rejected the treaty, did not give the United States a right to interfere within the internal affairs of that nation. Nor did the old treaty of 1846 give the United States any such right beyond that of guaranteeing the neutrality of the canal route; more especially, it expressly guaranteed the sovereignty of New Granada (the earlier name for Colombia) over the Isthmus.

The President was at first undecided what step to take after the Colombian Senate's rejection: whether to take up Nicaragua, or "in some shape or way to interfere when it becomes necessary so as to secure the

Panama route without further dealing with the foolish and homicidal corruptionists of Bogotá."[1] A trusted adviser presented a confidential memorandum to this effect: that if Colombia should reject the Hay-Herrán treaty, then the old treaty of 1846—the one which had guaranteed so "positively and efficaciously" the sovereignty of New Granada—could be interpreted to cover intervention in Panama to prevent interruption of the transit by domestic disturbances, as well as to protect Colombian sovereignty and the neutrality of the canal route against attack by an outside power. He pointed out that the United States had repeatedly landed troops to protect the canal route against riots and insurrectionary disturbances (he did not cite instances where the United States had intervened to the advantage of insurrectionists and secessionists). "Once on the ground and duly installed," this memorandum stated, "this government would find no difficulty in meeting questions as they arose."[2] In the first draft of his proposed annual message to Congress, Roosevelt recommended that the United States should purchase all the rights of the French Panama Company, and, without any further parley with Colombia, enter upon the completion of the canal which the French company had begun.[3] The message was never delivered in this form.

Again the New Panama Canal Company stepped into the situation. Mr. Philippe Bunau-Varilla, who once had been the chief engineer of the company on the Isthmus, hurried from Paris to the United States. He and a New York lawyer who was counsel for the French company, organized a revolution in the state of Panama, working through the employees of the Panama Railroad Company, a subsidiary. Bunau-Varilla also had conferences with Professor John Bassett Moore, Secretary Hay and President Roosevelt, who became well aware of the imminence of a revolution for the independence of Panama. No evidence has been presented to show that these high officials of the United States directly conspired with the plotters, but they certainly did nothing to discourage a movement which presented itself for their convenience. The President ordered the Department of the Navy to hold warships within striking distance of the Panama transit, on both sides. On November 2, orders went out to the commanders of these vessels to

---

[1] Joseph Bucklin Bishop, *Theodore Roosevelt and His Times, op. cit.,* I, 278.

[2] The memorandum, initialed "J. B. M." (presumably John Bassett Moore), is printed in the appendix to Helen Dwight Reid's *International Servitudes in Law and Practice* (University of Chicago Press, 1932). Mr. Moore was then professor of international law at Columbia University, but previously had long been an assistant secretary of state.

[3] H. C. Hill, *post cit.,* 59.

proceed to Panama and to "maintain free and uninterrupted transit," even to the extent of using armed force to occupy the route and to prevent Colombian troops being landed. Bunau-Varilla and his fellow conspirators, including Doctor Amador, the agent of the Panamanians in New York and Washington, guessed that the United States would use its naval forces to prevent Colombian troops from being landed to put down the insurrection and prevent the secession of Panama.[1] This is exactly what happened when the revolution occurred, as planned, on November 3, 1903. It was the formal statement of the United States Government to Colombia (November 11, 1903), that it would oppose the landing of Colombian troops to suppress the insurrection, which is the touchstone of the whole affair. That guaranteed the success of the insurrection; in effect it completed it. The United States had promptly recognized the *de facto* government, November 6, and on November 18 signed a treaty with the plenipotentiary of the Republic of Panama, none other than the Frenchman Bunau-Varilla. *Ipso facto* the treaty acknowledged the independence of Panama. The European powers also quickly recognized the new state. The Latin-American republics (except Colombia) followed promptly (March, 1904) in greeting the full-fledged independence of a new sister republic.

The treaty conferred upon the United States the right to build the canal, fortify it, and to possess the canal zone, ten miles wide from Colon to Panama, "as if it were sovereign." For this Panama received $10,000,000 in gold coin, plus an annuity of $250,000 "in like gold coin,"[2] beginning nine years after ratification. The first article of the treaty stated: "The United States guarantees and will maintain the

---

[1] Philippe Bunau-Varilla, *Panama, the Creation, Destruction and Resurrection* (New York, 1914).

Dr. Amador wrote to his son, Lt. Raoul Amador, a surgeon in the United States Army at Fort Revere, Mass., October 18, 1903, that he had spoken to Bunau-Varilla about him: "He said that if all turns out well, you shall have a good place on the medical commission, which is the first that will begin work; that my name is in Hay's office and that certainly nothing will be refused you. The plan seems to me good. A portion of the Isthmus declares itself independent and that portion the United States will not allow any Colombian forces to attack. An assembly is called and this given authority to a minister to be appointed by the new Government in order to make a treaty without need of ratification by that assembly." *The Story of Panama* (Hearings on the Rainey Resolution before the Committee on Foreign Affairs of the House of Representatives) (Washington, G.P.O., 1913), 371.

Raoul Amador became a Panamanian diplomat and died, March 24, 1934, as President of the Council of the League of Nations!

[2] The treaty did not specify the weight and fineness of this gold coin. After the devaluation of the United States gold dollar in 1934 to 59.06% of its former value, Panama paid coupons on her dollar bonds in the devalued currency, but insisted on collecting her annuities from the United States in the old standard dollars. The treaty

independence of the Republic of Panama." Other articles gave to the
United States the use, occupation and control (subject to indemnification
for private owners) of any other lands and waters necessary and convenient for the construction and maintenance of the canal, the right

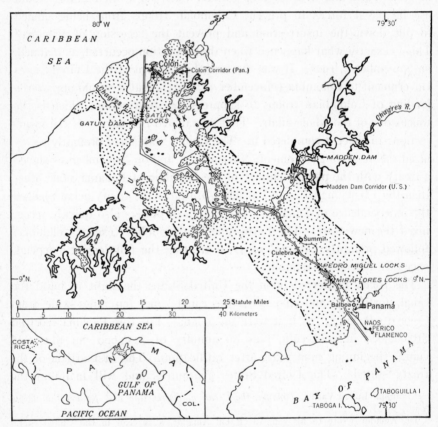

Map 28. The Panama Canal Zone.

to intervene for its maintenance and protection, and the right of eminent
domain within the limits of the cities of Panama and Colon and adjacent
territories and waters. This, of course, made Panama a protectorate.[1]

President Roosevelt immediately set in motion the work of construc-

signed on March 2, 1936 (below, p. 518), provided that Panama was to be paid in her
own currency, *balboas* 430,000 per annum, slightly more than the equivalent of $250,000
of the old standard.

[1] The scope of this volume does not permit any history of treaty relationships and
negotiations between Panama and the United States since 1903, other than mention at
the end of this chapter of the new treaty signed in 1936, ratified in 1939, which ended
the protectorate. Munro, *Caribbean Area, op. cit.*, gives a good summary.

tion and fortification of the canal. It opened its locks to the commerce and the warships of the world on terms of entire equality (so long as the United States remained a neutral) in 1914. In office and out of office, Theodore Roosevelt throughout the remainder of his life defended his intervention in Panama. The verdict of history must be summed up in his own frank words: "I took Panama." [1] With patience, diplomacy could have secured control of a canal route in a more creditable way without the use of force. The episode antagonized Latin America. Public opinion there began to brand the sponsor-nation of the Monroe Doctrine with the accusation of conquest in that part of the world which it professed to have liberated from European interference. It has taken much diplomacy and a generation of time to soften away this stigma.[2]

Despite the confidence of the President in the rectitude of his proceeding, the United States later pursued with Colombia a sort of conscience-stricken diplomacy. Even during President Roosevelt's Administration, Secretary of State Root arranged three companion treaties intended to satisfy Colombian grievances: a treaty between Colombia and Panama which recognized the independence of that republic and agreed to a boundary, with certain privileges in the use of the proposed canal; a treaty between the United States and Colombia which transferred to Colombia the first ten installments of Panama's annuity; and a treaty between the United States and Panama which sanctioned these changes and started the annuity five years earlier than required by the treaty of 1903. Popular opposition in Colombia led to the rejection of this settlement. Negotiations continued. Under Woodrow Wilson's Administration Secretary of State Bryan signed a treaty with Colombia (April 6, 1914) by which the United States expressed "sincere regret that anything should have occurred to interrupt or mar the relations of cordial friendship that had so long subsisted between the two governments." It also agreed to pay $25,000,000 indemnity, and to allow to Colombia and her citizens the same treatment as the United States and its citizens in the use of the canal; Colombia in turn recognized the independence of Panama, with a specified boundary. The opposition of ex-President Roosevelt, who vigorously denounced it as a "blackmail treaty," was

---

[1] *Autobiography.* At the University of California, March 11, 1911, he declared: "I took the Canal Zone."

[2] Four useful reviews of the diplomacy of the Panama Canal and United States intervention are: H. C. Hill, *Roosevelt and the Caribbean Area* (Univ. Chicago Press, 1927); Pringle, *Theodore Roosevelt, op. cit.;* D. C. Miner, *The Fight for the Panama Route* (Columbia University Press, 1940), and an unpublished doctoral thesis by William G. Fletcher, 1940, in Yale University Library.

sufficient to prevent its ratification by the Senate during his lifetime. After he died, his friend Senator Henry Cabot Lodge, chairman of the Committee on Foreign Relations, supported a treaty (ratified 1921 by a vote of 69-19) which paid the indemnity but omitted the apology. Colombian threats to refuse petroleum concessions to American capitalists seem to have been a decisive influence on Senator Lodge and his colleagues who previously had opposed paying any indemnity. This settlement closed the affair but it took time to wipe out the rankle.

A recent, and important, adjustment in the relations between the United States and Panama is the treaty signed March 2, 1936, and finally ratified July 25, 1939. It ended the protectorate and the right of land takings by the United States in Panama by eminent domain, and substituted therefor a pledge of joint co-operation for the furtherance of common interests. Article X reads:

In case of an international conflagration or the existence of any threat of aggression which would endanger the security of the Republic of Panama or the neutrality or the security of the Panama Canal the Governments of the United States of America and the Republic of Panama will take such measures for prevention and defense as they may consider necessary for the protection of their common interests. Any measures essential to one Government to take, and which may affect the territory under the jurisdiction of the other Government, will be the subject of consultation between the two Governments.

The Senate did not advise and consent to ratification of this treaty until it was made clear by a final exchange of notes [1] that in case of great emergency the United States could act first and consult with Panama afterward; that the treaty permits expansion and new construction for the canal; and that it does not prohibit military maneuvers in Panama's territory.

The new treaty is in line with the liquidation of imperialism which began after the First World War, and the Doctrine of Non-Intervention which President Franklin D. Roosevelt accepted as a part of his Good Neighbor Policy.

During the Second World War consultations between the United States and Panama resulted in the expansion of canal defenses throughout the Isthmian Republic's territory, particularly air bases. The two governments signed a new treaty (May 18, 1942) providing for the lease during the war and for one year thereafter of these new bases and areas already occupied as a result of the previous consultations.

[1] *Senate Ex. Rept.* No. 5, 1st Sess., June 21 (legislative day, June 19), 1939.

CHAPTER XXIX

DEVELOPMENT OF THE PANAMA POLICY IN THE CARIBBEAN AND CENTRAL AMERICA

(1902-1936)

WE have said that the prospective Panama Canal had become a fundamental factor in the foreign policy of the United States. The conscious development of a policy based on this truth began contemporaneously with the negotiation of the canal treaties, and the Cuban protectorate in the first years of the twentieth century, and rapidly built up a structure of comparatively benevolent imperialism and tutelage in the Caribbean and Central America. What generally is referred to as the Caribbean policy of the United States more appropriately might be called the Panama Policy.

Inescapably the canal is open to some danger of terrestrial accident that might close it, particularly an earthquake. With that waterway a prime factor in the naval defenses of the United States, American policy could not tolerate the risk of any political disturbance or intervention that would block it. The danger that some non-American power might welcome a pretext for effecting a lodgment within this wide strategical diameter was continually a possibility to be reckoned with alertly before the World War. President Theodore Roosevelt was acutely conscious of this and promptly took steps to avoid it.

There were several ways to proceed. First there was the traditional Monroe Doctrine; Roosevelt resorted to this in 1902 in the Venezuelan debts controversy, and the Senate invoked it in 1912 in the Magdalena Bay episode.[1] Secondly there was the expedient of buying Caribbean islands, belonging to small powers, which otherwise might be acquired by larger naval powers contrary to the non-transfer principle historically associated with the Monroe Doctrine; such was the eventual purchase of the Danish West Indies. The third way was to assume a sort of vicarious responsibility for foreign nationals and property within those republics where law and order might collapse, intervening by force to make them behave lest good reasons be presented for intervention by some other power less vitally interested in the strategy of the Caribbean.

[1] For the Lodge Resolution, see below, p. 535.

Theodore Roosevelt and Woodrow Wilson did this when they imposed temporary protectorates over the Dominican Republic and Haiti. Journalists unfortunately dubbed it the policy of the "big stick"; and more responsible writers have called it the "Roosevelt corollary" of the Monroe Doctrine, an infelicitous formula lately repudiated. The fourth means, applied to Central America, was an active diplomacy aimed at stiffening the independence of those states and strengthening their economic and political stability in order to remove pretexts or justifications for foreign intervention. Taken together with the possession of Puerto Rico and the already established protectorates over Cuba and Panama, this self-interested benevolence might be said to constitute the Panama Policy of the United States from 1898 to 1934.

Publicists in both Americas, Europe and Asia have accused the United States of intervention in the Caribbean area for motives of economic profit. It is true that trade and investments have followed the flag, but we have already seen that although American investments in Cuba under the Spanish régime had become quite considerable, "big business" was opposed to the Spanish-American War. That breaks down this economic interpretation of the war. In all the other states where the United States has intervened—Panama, Santo Domingo, Haiti, Nicaragua—those republics have been the regions where the least American capital,[1] or foreign capital of any kind, had been invested, and which were the least promising for economic development. Only in the Philippines—from which the United States has since withdrawn, after costs of over $1 billion since V-J Day alone—the initial motive seems to have been economic; even there it was the politician who led on the businessman, not the businessman who pushed the politician into the Far East.

The interventions in Central America and in the Caribbean were the result of the developing Panama Policy following the Spanish-American War. That fundamental strategical requirement of foreign policy becomes all the stronger when international agreements impose a limitation of naval armament, as they did between 1922 and 1936. The naval limitations of those years were, of course, adjusted to the strategic advantages and possibilities of the finished canal. Having described in the previous chapter the intervention in Cuba and the episode of the creation of the Republic of Panama and its sequent problems, we may now review [2] the rapidly developing diplomacy of the United

[1] Max Winkler, *Investments of United States Capital in Latin America* (World Peace Foundation, Boston, 1928) tabulates comparative statistics.

[2] There is, of course, a voluminous literature on this subject, little of which can be cited here. For some detailed classified bibliography, with a modicum of critical com-

States in other portions of this interesting region of the New World.

Ever since the Senate's rejection of the Danish treaty in Grant's Administration the executive branch of the Government had been apprehensive at recurring rumors that Denmark was preparing to sell or exchange her West Indian islands to Germany or France, particularly Germany. Denmark had been eager to dispose of them to the United States, but successive Presidents had hesitated to sign another treaty for fear that the Senate might again reject it. Sentiment for acquisition increased as an American canal became more likely. The expansionists of 1898 favored the purchase and committed the Republican Party to it. The movement gained headway after the turn of the century from rumors that Germany was seeking to acquire the islands for a naval base in the Caribbean. Researches [1] in the German archives have revealed that Admiral von Tirpitz wanted such a base in the Danish West Indies, and he was also actively interested in the Galápagos Islands, belonging to Ecuador, on the Pacific side of the Isthmus, 640 miles at sea from Panama, and in the possibilities of naval *fulcra* along the coast of Costa Rica, Colombia, and Venezuela, within touch of the Canal; but the Foreign Office hesitated to challenge the Monroe Doctrine for these demands of the Admiralty.

Much discussion, formal and informal, finally resulted in the signature of a Danish-American treaty (January 24, 1902) for the purchase of the islands for $5,000,000. This time the Senate readily ratified the treaty, but the upper house of the Danish Parliament rejected it by one vote. It was not until 1917 that both governments were able to exchange ratifications of a treaty of purchase; by then, in the atmosphere of war, the price had gone up to the exorbitant figure of $25,000,000. Though Denmark had held the islands at a budgetary loss for decades, it was all made up, with a handsome profit, by this lucrative sale.[2] The poverty-stricken Virgin Islands, as they are now called in the possession of the United States, have proved to be a worth-while insurance policy against

ment, see Bemis and Griffin, *Guide to the Diplomatic History of the United States, 1775-1921* (Library of Congress, G.P.O., 1935). The best summary by an American authority is Dana G. Munro, *The United States and the Caribbean Area, op. cit.* Raúl de Cárdenas y Echarte, *La Política de los Estados Unidos en el continente Americano* (Havana, 1921), is one of the most temperate Latin-American reviews, and Manuel Ugarte, *The Destiny of a Continent* (New York, 1925, translated from Madrid edition of 1923), is the most passionate Latin-American polemic against the policy of the United States.

[1] Alfred Vagts, *Weltpolitik, op. cit.*, II, 1410-1524.

[2] The Danish Parliament did not ratify until after a national plebiscite had voted overwhelmingly in favor of the change in sovereignty.

the violation of the non-transfer principle of the Monroe Doctrine.[1]

An international incident in Venezuela made American opinion fear, in 1902, that the new isthmian diplomacy of the United States might be frustrated by the lodgment of Germany within striking distance of the future canal. The dictator Castro had played fast and loose with foreign creditors and bondholders, who had also played fast and loose with the risky credit of Venezuela. Citizens and corporations of Great Britain, Germany, Italy, France, Belgium, Mexico, the Netherlands, Spain, Sweden and Norway, and also of the United States, had claims against the Venezuelan Government for default on contracts. Castro treated these claims quite frivolously. Diplomatic soundings at Washington had given the German Government the impression that a chastisement of Venezuela would meet with no objection on the ground of the Monroe Doctrine provided action led to no "lasting" occupation of Venezuelan territory. So reported the German Ambassador Holleben, after conversations with President Roosevelt and Secretary John Hay.[2] Under this impression Germany resolved to use force and to occupy one or more Venezuelan harbors, and perhaps the customs, as security for the flouted credits of German nationals. When this intention became known Great Britain proposed a joint intervention. The precise reasons [3] for this will remain unknown until British confidential archives are unlocked. A good guess is that the British Government, feeling that the United States was not going to object to, and would not join a non-American intervention, was loath to see Germany take steps alone and perhaps set up a régime similar to that of Egypt. We also recall Great Britain's joining with France in the Plata region in the 1830's and 1840's under somewhat analogous conditions.[4] As the intervention ripened, Germany's nominal ally Italy was allowed to join. The three powers blockaded [5] the Venezuelan ports, in December, 1902, bombarded two forts and seized several Venezuelan gunboats.

Despite the aggressiveness of Great Britain in handling the Venezuelan question and the joint responsibility which she had assumed, the De-

[1] Charles C. Tansill in his detailed study of *The Purchase of the Danish West Indies, op. cit.*, was unable to find, in searches made for him in the Danish and German archives, any evidence of German pressure being responsible for Denmark's rejection of the treaty of 1902. Vagts, *op. cit.*, in a more detailed personal search does not seem to have found any.

[2] Vagts, *Weltpolitik, op. cit.*, II, 1540. Italy participated only in the blockade.

[3] Vagts guesses it may have been a feeler of England toward a more permanent German alliance. These were the months when England was seeking everywhere a serviceable ally, presently first found in Japan.

[4] Above, p. 386 ff.

[5] The German Government maintained that this was a "pacific blockade." The

partment of State was much more apprehensive about the real intentions and designs of Germany; British intention to relax in the Caribbean became plain with the Hay-Pauncefote Treaty. German policy on the other hand, though never venturing, in the existing naval strength of the Empire, to challenge the Monroe Doctrine outright, had consistently resented it, the more strongly after the United States in 1898 had seemed to wander into the Far East contrary to the original isolationist dogma of that Doctrine. German leaders felt that if the United States had deserted the Doctrine to this extent, for its own advantage, it was unfair to cling to the rest of it in the Caribbean and in South America. They secretly nursed the ambition some day to break it down, particularly in southern Brazil, where German immigrants were strongly concentrated (though exasperatingly lukewarm toward *Deutschtum*), also in the Caribbean, near the approaches to the future canal.[1]

During the development of the Venezuelan crisis the powers had notified the United States of their intention to use force against Venezuela if their claims were not requited. Germany stated that under no circumstances did she in her proceedings intend the acquisition or the "permanent occupation" of Venezuelan territory, but did not exclude a "temporary occupation" and collection of customs duties to pay the debts. In answer Secretary Hay invoked the Monroe Doctrine, but was careful to quote President Roosevelt's recent exposition of it: "We do not guarantee any state against punishment if it misconducts itself, provided that punishment does not take the form of the acquisition of territory by any non-American power." [2] He professed to believe that Germany would not undertake any "occupation." [3] The British Secretary for Foreign Affairs, Lord Lansdowne, declared in the House of Lords three

British Prime Minister, Arthur Balfour, declared in the House of Lords that "there can be no such thing as a pacific blockade," but that "evidently a blockade does not involve a state of war." The reader will remember that when Lincoln in 1861 declared the Southern ports blockaded, Great Britain considered that tantamount to a declaration of war which justified the British proclamation of neutrality, without consultation with the United States Government.

[1] Alfred Vagts, *Weltpolitik, op. cit.*, has dissected German policy, and German-American naval and imperialistic rivalry after a close examination of German and American archives. For the Monroe Doctrine, see particularly pp. 1452-1814.

[2] Annual message, December 3, 1901. Note that this is not qualified by the adjective *permanent,* as Holleben had reported in his earlier despatches.

[3] The insincerity of the German professions is demonstrated by the instructions to Prince Henry during his visit, as quoted by Dennis out of the *Grosse Politik:* ". . . should the Americans manifest concern about German ideas of acquisition or of influence as regards Central and South America, that should be disclaimed as an absurd fantasy by pointing to the pacific character of His Majesty's policy and to the many problems we have to solve elsewhere in the world, without, however, imparting the character of a solemn declaration to such a rather ironical denial."

days after the bombardment that there was no intention to land a British force "and still less to occupy Venezuelan territory." Germany made similar professions.

Roosevelt had informed both Great Britain and Germany, as the crisis approached, that he hoped a peaceful solution could be worked out, such as the American claimants were trying to do in Venezuela. Castro paid no attention to the threatening powers until they presented their ultimata; then he ran under cover of the Monroe Doctrine by requesting the United States to transmit to Great Britain and Germany his proposal that their claims be arbitrated by the United States Minister to Venezuela. Great Britain promptly agreed to arbitrate certain classes of the claims, and urged Germany to do so. Germany hesitated but soon acquiesced, as American public opinion presaged a collision with the Monroe Doctrine. Admiral Dewey's fleet had been mobilized in the Caribbean off Puerto Rico,[1] a natural wintering place, but there seem to have been no formal or informal demands by President Roosevelt on the intervening powers. Italy, of course, followed along with the other two blockading powers. We may regard the Venezuelan incident of 1902 as a feeler by Germany to see to what extent the United States would really defend the Monroe Doctrine.

The claims of all the creditor powers were adjudicated by a group of mixed commissions sitting at Caracas, all except certain reserved claims of Great Britain and Germany which were settled by diplomatic conversations through the good offices of the United States at Washington. The question then arose whether the blockading powers should receive preferential treatment in payment of their claims. This went to the Hague Permanent Court of Arbitration. The tribunal in its decision put a premium on the use of force for the collection of contract debts by giving the belligerent powers a prior right of payment.

Despite this discouraging decision, the Venezuelan debts question led to the outlawry of force for the collection of contract debts if debtor powers agree to arbitrate. During the dispute Mr. Luis M. Drago,

---

[1] Theodore Roosevelt some years later in a celebrated letter of August 21, 1916 (during the World War) to one of his biographers, W. R. Thayer, described how he notified the German Ambassador that he would send the fleet to Venezuela if the Kaiser would not arbitrate. Historians have not been able to discover any evidence of this in the German correspondence printed in the *Grosse Politik*. Hill, *Roosevelt and the Caribbean, op. cit.*, dismisses this as a vainglorious boast *ex post facto,* but Dennis, *Adventures, op. cit.*, and Pringle, *Theodore Roosevelt,* introduce bits of contemporary evidence to confirm the impression of a suggested and informal warning. Vagts's and Perkins's subsequent thorough researches in German and American archives revealed no additional support for Roosevelt's later dramatic statement. But see S. W. Livermore's recent naval study in *Am. Hist. Rev.*, LI (April, 1946), 452-471.

the Minister of Foreign Relations of the Argentine Republic, submitted to the United States a note embodying a proposition that has since been associated with his name. He proposed "that the public debt can not occasion armed intervention nor even the actual occupation of the territory of American nations by a European power." [1] In reply Hay referred to "the general position" of his Government, as expressed in President Roosevelt's recent message (December 3, 1901). Convention II adopted at the Hague Conference of 1907 finally made international law of a modified form of the Drago Doctrine: [2]

> The Contracting Powers agree not to have recourse to armed force for the recovery of contract debts claimed from the government of one country by the government of another country as being due to its nationals.
> This undertaking is, however, not applicable when the debtor State refuses or neglects to reply to an offer of arbitration, or, after accepting the offer, prevents any "Compromis" from being agreed on, or, after the arbitration, fails to submit to the award.

The Drago Doctrine supplemented the Monroe Doctrine by an international convention; and in turn it foreshadowed the Pact of Paris of 1928 by which all the nations agreed not to have recourse to war as "an instrument of national policy." American diplomacy played a decisive part in the adoption of both these great formulas of peace.

Between Cuba and Puerto Rico the island of Hispaniola bridges the approaches to the Caribbean and the canal from the North Atlantic. It had long been a matter of strategic interest to American diplomacy. That interest received additional emphasis as the United States turned to the construction of the canal. The two native republics, the Dominican Republic in the eastern half of the island, and Haiti in the western half, had been the scene of perennial revolution, war, confusion and intermittent dictatorial tyranny ever since their independence. Injuries to the citizens and property of European powers had frequently threatened intervention. We have seen how Spain took advantage of the American Civil War to attempt to re-establish her sovereignty in the island, only to fail rather ignobly. The default on bonds and other obligations of the Dominican Republic threatened in 1904 to bring about another

---

[1] Moore, *Digest*, VI, 593.

[2] Not to be confused with the "Calvo clause" which denies the right of a foreigner to appeal to his own government for enforcement of contracts. It is the custom of Latin-American governments to introduce into the contract of a concession to a foreign national a so-called Calvo clause by which the concessionaire formally renounces his right of appeal to the protection of his own government for the execution of the contract Whether the foreigner can of his own act sign away his right is a question.

situation similar to that of Venezuela a few months before. The public debt was about $32,000,000, of which European creditors claimed title to $22,000,000. The distressed government had hypothecated various port revenues to Belgian, French, German, Italian and Spanish bond-holders. In October, 1904, after an arbitration, the Dominican President turned over to an American agent the collection of customs at Puerto Plata, to satisfy the debts to a New York corporation, the Santo Domingo Improvement Company, which had transferred its property to the government. This was over the protests of the other foreign creditors.

The Dominican President looked to the United States as an alternative to imminent European intervention. Reluctantly, Roosevelt, as a means of preventing a repetition of the Venezuela incident, decided to accept the protecting responsibility of a collection of the Dominican customs and an arrangement with all creditors. With the assistance of a naval officer, who served as special commissioner, the American Minister to the Dominican Republic drafted the protocol of an agreement (February 7, 1905) which provided for the installation, and protection by the United States, of a collector of customs who would apply 45 per cent of the revenue to the current needs of the Dominican Government and turn the rest over *pro rata* to the creditors on an equal basis. The original, rejected protocol contained a guaranty of the territorial integrity of Santo Domingo. The way in which the negotiations were carried on suggests that the President had not planned to submit this to the Senate for advice and consent, but to let it stand as an executive agreement; at the last moment, however, it was deemed the better part of wisdom to insert an article requiring the consent of the Senate, lest that body accept a challenge of its constitutional powers, and to sub-stitute for the territorial guaranty a pledge to respect the sovereignty of the Dominican Republic.[1]

The Senate adjourned its session without a vote on the treaty, and for two years it refused its advice and consent. Meanwhile American agents collected and administered the customs of the republic according to an executive *modus vivendi* under the protecting presence of warships, which refrained from intervening in local political strife. The conse-quent increase in revenue was quite astonishing. Arrangements with the foreign creditors scaled down the outside debt to $12,407,000, mutually acknowledged, so that the total national debt, with arrears of interest, stood at $17,000,000, which the republic could handle quite solvently

---

[1] Holt, *Defeated Treaties, op. cit.*, 212-229.

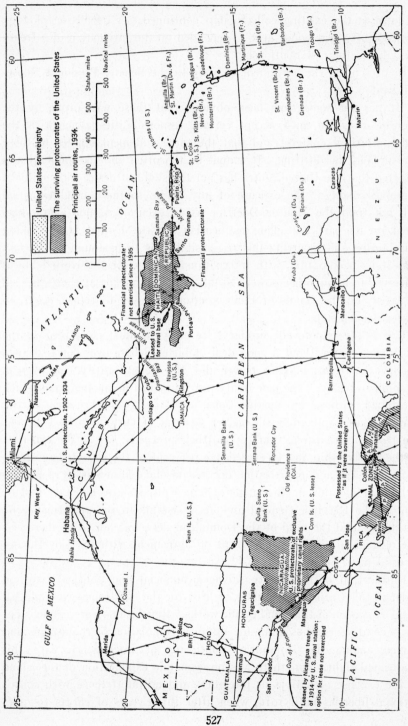

Map 29. The Caribbean and Central America as of 1934.

527

so long as the existing collectorship continued. A new issue of $20,-
000,000, fifty-year bonds at 5%, depended on the ratification of a treaty
formalizing the new relationship.

In presenting the agreement of 1905 to the Senate, President Roosevelt said:

"It has for some time been obvious that those who profit by the
Monroe Doctrine must accept certain responsibilities along with the
rights which it confers; and that the same statement applies to those
who uphold the doctrine. It cannot be too often and too emphatically
asserted that the United States has not the slightest desire for territorial
aggrandizement at the expense of any of its southern neighbors, and
will not treat the Monroe Doctrine as an excuse for such aggrandizement on its part. . . . The justification for the United States taking
this burden and incurring this responsibility is to be found in the fact
that it is incompatible with international equity for the United States
to refuse to allow other powers to take the only means at their disposal
of satisfying the claims of their creditors and yet to refuse, itself, to
take any such steps."

This is the "Roosevelt corollary," recently repudiated, to the Monroe
Doctrine. Not without a good deal of bitter debate over constitutional
residues of treaty-making power did the Senate ratify, in 1907, a
Dominican treaty. The new treaty put into effect an arrangement which
continued, with certain modifications, until 1941. The President of the
United States appointed a Receiver General of customs, who collected
the Dominican customs and applied their proceeds: (1) to the expenses
of the receivership, not to exceed five per cent of the collected revenue;
(2) to interest and amortization on the consolidated new issue of bonds;
(3) to the Dominican Government. The United States had the right to
protect the Receiver General and his assistants in the performance of
his duties, and the total of the Dominican debt was not to be increased
nor customs duties changed except on agreement with the Government
of the United States.

Ratification of this treaty salvaged financial and political law and
order in this Caribbean republic, at least for the next four years, and led
to an expansion of trade and public works. Revolutions were non-existent
for several years, thus damming up an accumulation of resentment and
hatred among the Dominican politicians at interference with this
traditional right. But there was no economic exploitation of the island
at the expense of natives or foreigners and no interference with constitutional liberties until 1916, when after three years of efforts to quiet

by diplomatic means revolutionary disturbances chronic since 1911, President Wilson finally resorted to an armed intervention which lasted until 1924. A new constitution was adopted under American tutelage, elections under it took place under American policing, and a program of public works, sanitation and education marched rapidly ahead. The United States permitted new Dominican bond issues to care for this. The terms of evacuation, written into a second treaty in 1924 by which the military government ended, validated all the acts of the intervention, including the new bond issues, and provided that the terms of the treaty of 1907 should continue during the lifetime of the bonds (they were paid off before 1950), with a new provision for arbitration of any disputes arising under it.[1] The "financial protectorate" over the Dominican Republic looked very positively toward a termination. A third treaty in 1941 ended the protectorate and receivership.

Events in Haiti paralleled those in Santo Domingo a few years later in time. Germany was just about to land marines there when the World War began. A state of complete anarchy appeared the following year when an enraged populace in Port-au-Prince cut into small pieces the body of President Guillaume Sam after he had arbitrarily slaughtered 167 political hostages. With promises of no designs on the political or territorial integrity of Haiti, President Wilson ordered the intervention of American naval forces in July, 1915. Haiti continued under the supervision of American marines and political, economic and educational advisers until 1934. A twenty-year treaty imposed at the beginning of the intervention set up a régime similar to that in the Dominican Republic, but more extended: it added provisions for the establishment of a Financial Adviser as well as a Receiver General, of a native constabulary under American control, and for the co-operation of the United States in the sanitation and public improvements on the islands. A degree of protection, much stronger than that of the Dominican treaties, is visible in the following provisions which resemble the Platt Amendment:

Article XI. The Government of Haiti agrees not to surrender any of the territory of the Republic of Haiti by sale, lease, or otherwise, or jurisdiction over such territory, to any foreign government or power, nor to enter into any treaty or contract with any foreign power or powers that will impair or tend to impair the independence of Haiti.

Article XIV. The high contracting parties shall have authority to take such steps as may be necessary to insure the complete attainment of any of

[1] Carl Kelsey wrote for the American Academy of Political and Social Sciences an objective survey of *The American Intervention in Haiti and the Dominican Republic* (Philadelphia, 1922). There is of course a voluminous controversial literature.

the objects comprehended in this treaty; and, should the necessity occur, the United States will lend an efficient aid for the preservation of Haitian Independence and the maintenance of a government adequate for the protection of life, property and individual liberty.

The intervention took place not without some severe fighting; notably the "Caco Revolt" of 1918 marked by isolated atrocities which years later (after the World War) excited justified popular indignation in the United States; but it should be emphasized that these were rare exceptions, and the constitution, approved in Washington, scrupulously avoided any particular advantages for economic exploitation by citizens of the United States as compared with other foreign nationals. The treaty provided for the arbitration of all foreign claims, and their payment by new bonds. This took place in 1919, through a new issue of $40,000,000, thirty-year bonds, of which $16,000,000 was issued in 1923, and only small amounts of the remainder in later years. A protocol supplementary to the treaty of 1915 extended American "control and allocation" of the hypothecated revenues through a twenty-five-year period (that is, to May 3, 1941). The extensive treaty service, involving a widespread control over internal affairs in the island, continued until 1934, with remarkable benefit to the people. Public opinion in the United States, however, had grown increasingly restive about this measure of intervention, until President Hoover initiated in 1931 a policy for the gradual Haitianization of the treaty service, which was written into a new "accord," in the form of an executive agreement, negotiated by the Administration of President Franklin D. Roosevelt in 1933. Under the terms of this, American military forces withdrew from Haiti in 1934. The receivership of the customs was discontinued in July, 1935, and the revenues are now collected by the Haitian government-owned national bank, in which outsiders representing the foreign bondholders' interests have a measure of control. As in the case of the Dominican Republic, the "financial protectorate" over Haiti[1] was limited in time; in fact it was not exercised after 1935. The treaty of 1915, which expired in 1936, contained article XI, above quoted, by which Haiti agreed "not to surrender any of the territory of the Republic of Haiti by sale, lease, or otherwise, or jurisdiction over such territory, to any foreign government or power, nor to enter into any

[1] One may single out of the plethora of relevant literature Arthur C. Millspaugh, *Haiti under American Control, 1915-1930* (Boston, World Peace Foundation, 1931). The author was an American professor who after an experience as financial adviser to the Persian Government, was Financial Adviser and Receiver General of Haiti, in 1927-1929.

treaty or contract with any foreign power or powers that will impair or tend to impair the independence of Haiti."

Central America had remained since the break-up of its Confederation in 1838 a backward area, divided into five sovereign and independent states continually torn by revolutions which brought local international wars in their wake.[1] External loans to European bankers went intc default there, too. Nicaragua alone attracted much attention: it was the seat of Anglo-American rivalry before the Clayton-Bulwer Treaty, and was the field of the later operations of the notorious filibuster, William Walker; the canal route and the trans-isthmian lake-and-railway transit gave it continuing importance. Nicaragua abrogated, according to its provisions for so doing, Seward's transit treaty of 1867, shortly before the United States made its canal treaty with Panama in 1903. The new Panama Policy made the United States immediately interested in promoting the tranquillity and stability of these five governments. A rival canal route lay through Nicaragua, and the collapse of law and order in any one state might mean the danger of European intervention on the Isthmus. It was contemporaneously with the installation of the protectorate in Santo Domingo that the United States took steps in 1906 by friendly good offices and tutelage to establish stability in Central America by promoting local treaties which would do away with the scourge of revolution and internecine warfare and thus remove the danger to foreign nationals and property.

The Washington Government united its good offices with Mexico in 1906 to bring about a truce between Guatemala and El Salvador, which had become involved in hostilities when the Salvadorian Minister of War supported a revolution against the President of Guatemala. Following this a general Central American peace conference met at San José, Costa Rica, and adopted a series of treaties looking toward federation. They included one for the judicial arbitration of international disputes among them, and another by which each state pledged itself not to support revolutions against the government of another, and not to harbor revolutionists against its sister states. When notwithstanding this a new war broke out presently between Honduras and Nicaragua, President Zelaya, dictator of Nicaragua, blocked all peace machinery and succeeded in putting into power in Honduras a new revolutionary

[1] The leading American authority on the history of the diplomacy of the United States in Central America and the Caribbean is Dana G. Munro. I wish to make special acknowledgment to his two books: *The Five Republics of Central America; Their Political and Economic Development and Their Relations With the United States* (New York, 1918), and *The United States and the Caribbean Area, op. cit.*

government. He threatened later to upset the government of El Salvador and put his man in there, too. It was at this stage that the
United States and Mexico persuaded the Central American states to
participate in a conference at Washington, in 1907, from which they
emerged parties to a number of treaties which set up a new international framework in Central America, a miniature league of nations.
The United States was the tutelary sponsor of this political structure
but not party to the treaties, nor was Mexico. They provided for
the compulsory settlement of all international disputes among the Central American nations before a Central American Court of International
Justice. They neutralized the central state of Honduras, across whose
territory the other states often had to go to make war on each other.
They covenanted not to harbor revolutionary leaders or movements
against each other. They agreed not to recognize new governments set
up by revolutionary process, pending the reorganization of the government through a free election. They recommended the creation of a
number of cultural institutions, such as a pedagogical institute, and
technical schools allied thereto, and a Bureau of Central American
Republics.

These treaties proved more than the Central American states could
live up to. The United States as a consulting and advising party to
the Washington treaties of 1907 was continually called upon by one
or the other of the signatories to exert itself for their enforcement.
Most of the complaints were directed against Zelaya, the contumacious
dictator of Nicaragua. When a revolution broke out in Nicaragua
against Zelaya in 1909 the United States gave its moral and physical [1]
support to the revolutionists, who set up a new régime.

The collapse of Nicaraguan finances during these disturbances and
the pressure of foreign creditors for adjustment resulted in the signature of the Knox-Castrillo convention (June 6, 1911) similar to the
Dominican treaty of 1907, with this difference: the bankers of the new
consolidated loan, for the refunding of Nicaragua's indebtedness, were
to present a list of names from which the President of the United States
was to nominate the Receiver General of the customs, who was to be
protected by the United States in the performance of his duties. The
Senate, which at first had opposed the Dominican treaty, refused now
to ratify this Nicaraguan protectorate and a similar one which Secre-

[1] American cruisers prohibited the bombardment, by opposing Nicaraguans, of the
revolutionary forces in the port of Bluefields, on the ground that it might injure the
lives and property of American citizens.

tary Knox negotiated with Honduras. President Taft gave to these proposed treaties and to his contemporary diplomacy in China the unhappy description of "dollar diplomacy," and public opinion, which did not distinguish between American policy in China and in Central America, turned against it.[1]

The New York bankers who had been willing to underwrite the proposed new bonds, contingent upon ratification of the treaty, made a series of short-time loans under arrangements of their own with Nicaragua and Honduras, thus allowing them the means of satisfying their creditors. These arrangements, which included receiver generals of customs appointed by the local governments from nominees of the bankers, were based on consultation with the Department of State and its approval, without any guaranty of anything by the United States. Nicaragua meanwhile, like some of her sister states, agreed at the instance of American diplomacy to set up mixed commissions which adjudicated other claims of foreigners. The abortive Knox treaties and contemplated dollar diplomacy also spurred other Central American states to make satisfactory arrangements with their foreign creditors, European and American.

An agreement between factions in Nicaragua on a compromise president did not bring political peace even when extended under the good offices of the United States. At the request of a succeeding President, Adolfo Diaz, the United States in 1912 intervened to end the sanguinary political turbulence and thus strengthen the local international treaty régime. A legation guard of about 100 marines continued on in Nicaragua until 1925, during which time the intervening power labored to bring political tranquillity to that distracted country.

President Wilson repudiated dollar diplomacy only in name—except in China, where he later returned to it. Secretary Bryan signed a treaty with Platt-Amendment articles which granted to the United States an exclusive proprietary concession to build any canal through Nicaraguan territory—waiving always any proven rights of the neighboring states of El Salvador and Costa Rica over the route.[2] The treaty

[1] See Scott Nearing and Joseph Freeman, *Dollar Diplomacy; a Study in American Imperialism* (New York, 1925), for the classic polemic and excoriation.

[2] El Salvador and Honduras claimed sovereign rights in the Gulf of Fonseca, and Costa Rica sovereign rights over the San Juan River. The Senate ratified the treaty only with the reservation that nothing in it was intended in any way to affect any existing right of Costa Rica, El Salvador or Honduras. Notwithstanding this careful provision Costa Rica and El Salvador (but not Honduras) sued Nicaragua before the Central American Court of Justice for conveying their rights to the United States, and secured a judgment in their favor. Nicaragua refused to admit the jurisdiction of the

included a lease of Great Corn and Little Corn islands [1] off the eastern coast of the canal route; and a ninety-nine-year (renewable) lease of a naval base (never established) under American "sovereign authority" on Nicaraguan territory in the Gulf of Fonseca, into which any probable Nicaraguan canal would lead on the Pacific side; the Gulf of Fonseca is also strategically located between California and Panama. In return, by the terms of this Bryan-Chamorro Treaty (August 5, 1914), the United States agreed to pay Nicaragua $3,000,000, to be spent under American supervision for the reduction of the foreign debt and any other agreed purposes. In ratifying this treaty the Senate cut out the Platt-Amendment articles.

The Bryan-Chamorro Treaty nevertheless made Nicaragua a protectorate, though diluted in comparison with the Cuban protectorate of 1902-1934. Article II, the article leasing the naval base, states that it is in order "to enable the Government of the United States to protect the Panama Canal and the proprietary rights [to any Nicaraguan canal] granted to the United States by the foregoing article, and also to enable the United States to take any measure necessary to the ends contemplated herein." This language reflects the Panama Policy. Under it the United States has exercised a larger measure of tutelage and intervention than in Cuba. The State Department sanctioned the adoption of agreements between the bankers and foreign bondholders and Nicaragua embodying a plan for the reorganization of the country's finances by which a Financial High Commission was set up by Nicaragua in 1917 to supervise the expenditures of certain portions of the revenues.[2] Under this plan, modified in 1920, the debts for advances by American bankers were paid off by 1924, and the service of the foreign (British) bonds taken care of. During the Great Depression, Nicaragua, ravaged again by revolution, suspended amortization payments on its debt as did other Caribbean and Central American governments, not to mention European governments.

It was during the revolutionary disturbances in Central America and

---

Court. Already weakened by the political character of its judges, the Court suffered by this action a final blow, and expired in 1918, to be resurrected by the later Washington treaties of 1923. The United States has not yet been able to quiet the easements of Costa Rica and El Salvador.

[1] So far the United States has taken up only a sufficient part of Little Corn Island to establish a lighthouse.

[2] One member of the commission was appointed by the President of Nicaragua, one by the Secretary of State of the United States, and, when necessary, an umpire appointed also by the Secretary of State.

Roscoe R. Hill, formerly one of the commissioners, has written an authoritative history of *Fiscal Intervention in Nicaragua* (New York, 1933).

in Mexico, that a circumstance occurred which brought forth a formal application of the Monroe Doctrine to any "non-American" power, as well as to any European power which the Doctrine hitherto had envisaged in all its expressions. Rumors, whether exaggerated or not, had announced that a Japanese fishing company was about to lease from the Government of Mexico an extensive tract of land on the shore of Magdalena Bay, in Lower California, a situation admirably located for a naval base to intercept the communications between the Pacific Coast of the United States and the Panama Canal. This promptly evoked the adoption by the Senate of the resolution presented by Senator Lodge, member of the Committee on Foreign Relations, in 1912:

. . . when any harbor or other place in the American continents is so situated that the occupation thereof for naval or military purposes might threaten the communications or the safety of the United States, the Government of the United States could not see without grave concern the possession of such harbor or other place by any corporation or association which has such a relation to another Government, not American, as to give that Government practical power of control for national purposes.

The Lodge Resolution is thus part and parcel of the Monroe Doctrine, and a logical adaptation of it to twentieth-century conditions and particularly to the Panama Policy.

The first intervention in Nicaragua had back of it the general policy of the United States, manifest since 1907, of smothering out revolutionary strife and stimulating constitutional union among the Central American states. The weakening force of the Washington treaties of 1907 and the ominous strength of chronic revolutionary symptoms and outbreaks had led, after another abortive attempt at union in 1921,[1] to the acceptance by the five states, of an invitation by the United States to a second general conference at Washington, which took place in 1922-1923. Again they adopted treaties which repeated and strengthened the provisions of the conventions of 1907. New features were: a reformation of the failing Central American Court of Justice by providing that its tribunals should be drawn from a panel of jurists instead of from political appointments; a provision for international commissions of inquiry on the model of the Bryan "cooling-off" conciliation treaties then in effect between the United States and most countries; and an

---

[1] The history of the movement for federation in Central America is presented, in a careful factual manner, by Laudelino Moreno, *História de las relaciones interestatuales de Centro-América* (Madrid, 1928).

agreement not to recognize the legal existence of governments installed by revolution. The United States was a party to only the conciliation treaty, but during the lifetime of the quintuple treaty of peace and amity, namely, until January, 1934, it considered itself morally bound not to recognize revolutionary governments in Central America. To implement this policy—not only in Central America but elsewhere—Congress empowered the President to embargo the shipments from the United States to revolutionists, of arms, ammunition and implements of war. The resolution of January 21, 1922 (extending one of March 14, 1912) declared:

That whenever the President finds that in any American country, or in any country in which the United States exercises extraterritorial jurisdiction, conditions of domestic violence exist, which are or may be promoted by the use of arms or munitions of war procured from the United States, and makes proclamation thereof, it shall be unlawful to export, except under such limitations and exceptions as the President prescribes, any arms or munitions of war from any place in the United States to such country until otherwise ordered by the President or by Congress.

President Coolidge put this into effect in respect of Honduras (March 22, 1924), and in respect of Nicaragua (September 15, 1926), and President Roosevelt in respect of Cuba (June 29, 1934). On October 10, 1935, the Secretary of State, acting under authority delegated by the President, announced that the exportation of arms, ammunition and implements of war [1] to Cuba, Honduras, and Nicaragua would be licensed only when the Department of State had been informed by the respective legations of those countries in Washington, that it was the desire of the government concerned to have the exportation authorized.[2]

The Panama Policy of the United States has built up, through the Washington Conferences of the Central American nations, in 1907 and 1923, a special treatment of these nations in the effort to bring about union and political stability and tranquillity. The great project of federation has so far failed, but there is no question that the preventative features of the Panama Policy as applied to Central America, as well as the Caribbean, brought comparative prosperity and peace to that portion of the western world. The assistance by American commissions, under the general supervision of the State Department, in the regeneration of

[1] As defined by the proclamation of that date putting into effect the neutrality legislation of August 31, 1935 (see below, p. 667).

[2] This regulation also applied to China.

International Traffic in Arms; Laws and Regulations Administered by the Secretary of State Governing the International Traffic in Arms, Ammunition, and Implements of War (Washington, Department of State, 1935).

broken-down finances,[1] in the settlement of boundary disputes,[2] and in the reference of international controversies to peaceful means of settlement has also lessened the ravages of war, international and civil. The motive of it has been the security of the Panama Canal.

Nicaragua continued to be a source of disturbance and of danger to the peace of Central America.

The presence of the legation guard of 100 marines from 1912-1924 gave passive assistance to the efforts of American diplomacy to steady Nicaraguan politics by supervising elections. The persistent voicing of popular opposition in the United States to "imperialism" in Nicaragua and Hispaniola led to a withdrawal of the handful of marines remaining there in 1925. Nicaragua immediately reverted to its traditional revolutionary anarchy, and in a few months revolutions undid much of the healthful salvage work that had been accomplished since 1912. The marines returned almost immediately, and during a second intervention American diplomacy laboriously repeated its prophylactic labors to clean up new revolutions and prevent further ones. This time the forces stayed in Nicaragua until January 1, 1933. President Coolidge explained to a Congress and to a puzzled public at home that the intervention was due to the necessary implications of Nicaraguan disturbances as they affected the Panama Canal and to the confirmed policy of the United States to protect the lives, property and interests of its citizens and of the government itself. President Coolidge expressed the Panama Policy of the United States in its most brusque form, a form from which his successors have retreated. He sent Colonel Henry L. Stimson, formerly Secretary of War, to Nicaragua in 1927 who assisted the existing government in the reform of electoral machinery and the supervision of a fair election under the policing of American forces, which in 1928 amounted to over 5,000 men. Elections were supervised again in 1930 and 1932. The Administration of President Hoover followed a policy of tapering off the military forces and turning over responsibility as fast as possible to the existing local government. Despite the persistence of guerilla insurrectionary warfare under a native leader, Sandino (killed by Nicaraguan forces in 1934), the American marines were withdrawn altogether at the beginning of 1933.

It was Colonel Stimson himself, Secretary of State under President

[1] In Honduras, El Salvador and Guatemala, without treaty contracts. The State Department was not involved in Costa Rica's successful refunding of her foreign bonds in 1911.

[2] The United States has mediated to secure the arbitration of boundary disputes between Honduras and Guatemala, and between Costa Rica and Panama.

Hoover, who reversed the Coolidge policy, when in 1931 he said that the Government would refuse to send more marines to Nicaragua, following the cold-blooded murder by Sandino forces of eight American citizens.[1] The United States would not assume general protection of American nationals throughout the territory of Nicaragua: "To do so would lead to difficulties and commitments which this Government does not propose to undertake." He warned all American citizens who did not feel secure to withdraw from the country or at least to the coast towns from which they could be easily evacuated.

This warning—similar to warnings by the Wilson Administration to citizens sojourning in revolutionary Mexico—foreshadowed the later policy by which the "Roosevelt corollary" of the Monroe Doctrine has been completely repudiated, and the preventative features of the Panama Policy largely discarded. The time had come when Europe did not appear to challenge the United States by intervening in the strategic area of the isthmian canal. The Department of State published officially in 1930 an exegesis of the Monroe Doctrine, the so-called Clark Memorandum, which had the effect of pruning the "Roosevelt Corollary" from the historical structure of the Doctrine and suggesting that the United States would no longer guarantee that the American republics must behave responsibly toward foreigners or suffer the "big stick." The prohibitions against non-American intervention still exist, but not the "corollary."

The Panama Policy has thus been brought back to the pristine Monroe Doctrine, plus the possession and protection of the Canal Zone, plus an optional canal route in Nicaragua. The Panama protectorate, the Cuban protectorate and the two protectorates in Hispaniola have been liquidated. More than that, the United States has ratified (1935, 1937) a treaty abjuring the right of intervention, directly or indirectly or for whatever reason, within the internal or external affairs of any other American state.[2]

It remains to be seen whether this benevolence will stand the tests of time and tropics.

[1] This occurred after a fearful earthquake which destroyed the city of Managua, when the marines already at that capital were engaged in relief activities and the normal forces of the local government were completely paralyzed.

[2] "The High Contracting Parties declare inadmissible the intervention of *any one* of them directly or indirectly, and for whatever reason, in the internal or external affairs of any other of the Parties." Article 1 of Additional Protocol Relating to Non-Intervention, of Buenos Aires, 1936, supplementing the Montevideo Treaty on the Rights and Duties of States of 1933. See below, p. 777. (Italics inserted.)

CHAPTER XXX

MEXICO

(1867-1950)

It has been the habit of a certain school of publicists to cite the relations between the United States and Mexico as exhibiting a shameful aggression which serves historically as a sorry model for other nations to vex the peace of the world today. Nothing could be more false, even if we go back a hundred years in history. Texas, recognized as an independent state by the world for nearly a decade, and later annexed by its own choice to the United States by what was tantamount to a national plebiscite, was certainly no Manchuria. Those who have studied carefully the diplomatic history preceding the outbreak of the war of 1846-1848 must be convinced that the war, which resulted in the purchase of those vast but almost vacant domains of northern Mexico, was as much the fault of Mexico as of the United States. When the student turns to the history of Mexico in the last hundred years he must see in the United States the great example of the peaceful disposition, patience, complaisance and self-sacrifice of a powerful people, and their friendliness, largely unrequited, for an unfortunate and helpless neighbor burdened with tragic domestic problems. It is true that there have been individuals and groups within the United States who advocated intervention during the revolutionary disturbances of 1910-1925, and there have been a few persons who would have willingly annexed more Mexican territory; they can scarcely be said, however, to be leaders of American thought. Nor have the heavy investments in Mexico of American capital, the spokesmen of which advocated military intervention, had any enduring or decisive influence on the policy of the United States. With one of the richest storehouses of natural resources at its very door, where abundant provocation and justifications for intervention and control have existed, the United States has exhibited, at great cost of life and property to its citizens, almost a Galilean forbearance. The ideals of Woodrow Wilson largely explain this. Where else in the world is there such another example? Certainly not in Africa. Assuredly not in Asia. The history of Mexican-American relations, too, is a gauge of the essentially defensive character of

539

the Monroe Doctrine and of the Panama Policy. The United States has warned non-American nations to keep hands off Mexico, in 1867 and again in 1912, but itself has not, since 1848, laid its own hands on Mexico except for brief punitive actions following extreme provocations —actions which themselves exhibit rare self-restraint.

Mexican-American relations between the enforced French evacuation in 1867 and the outbreak of the Mexican Revolution in 1910 were of a routine nature,[1] but not devoid of a significant development which was to create a major problem when that Revolution occurred—the permeation of Mexico by foreign, particularly by American capital. Mexico during this period was under the dictatorship of Porfirio Diaz, who smothered the hitherto chronic revolutionary strife at the price of stifling individual liberty and the continuation of a benighted peonage, akin to serfdom, for the masses of the people. The United States during these same years was occupied by the settlement and exploitation of the new West, by the rising crescendo of the industrial revolution, and by the new foreign problems ushered in by the Spanish-American War. As the republic approached its climax of expansion without ambitions for further continental territory to the south, those who governed Mexico, heartened by the events of 1867, became less and less fearsome of their northern neighbor. Diaz, wishing to advance the material progress of his impoverished country, without equal regard for the elevation of human values, invited foreign capital, under broad and frequently lavish concessions, to exploit its natural resources and to organize its economic life. Two billion dollars poured in from abroad—one-half of it from the United States—by the year 1912, for the development of Mexican mines, petroleum, power, railroads, agriculture.[2]

These funds flowed into Mexico in good faith, as similarly foreign capital went into Canada during the same years, and as it had been

---

[1] A general claims commission was provided in the treaty of 1868. It adjudicated all claims accumulated on either side since 1848. It awarded a total of $4,125,622.20 on a total of claims of citizens of the United States originally entered at an aggregate sum of $470,126,613.40, and a total of $150,498.41 of a total of 998 claims of citizens of Mexico originally filed at an aggregate of $86,661,891.15. J. B. Moore, *International Arbitrations, op. cit.*, II, 1314-1320.

For the later, separate settlement of the Pious Fund case by arbitration before the Hague Permanent Court, see above, p. 423.

Numerous conventions and agreements took place during this period for the settlement or arbitration of minor boundary disputes (including the unsuccessful and still unsettled controversy over the Chamizal tract, near El Paso, Texas, and Ciudad Rodriguez, Chihuahua); for regulation of frontier water courses, notably on the Rio Grande and Colorado rivers; and for mutual trans-frontier pursuit of hostile Indians.

[2] J. Fred Rippy, *United States and Mexico, op. cit.*, discusses this inflow of capital and its results.

invested in the United States itself during a previous generation. The foreign investors took the constitution and laws of Mexico at their face value, which was valid so long as Diaz held power, and they did not inquire into, nor were they interested in, the deeper implications of Porfirianism for the history of the Mexican nation, nor the appropriateness of those policies for the people of that land. The concessions to foreigners aroused a smoldering popular hostility not altogether dissimilar to that which animated the Boxer movement in China. This directed itself most strongly against the United States, nearest of the foreign exploiting nations. Diaz kept it down, but under unsettled conditions it could flame into great intensity and express itself in horrible atrocities.

The economic invasion of Mexico was not so formidable as the contemporary flow of foreign including American capital into Canada in the north; but Mexico had a different historical heritage than Canada, a heritage which combined with these new economic forces in the most explosive way.

The English colonies, from which the United States and the Dominion of Canada have risen to nationhood and expanded across a practically empty continent to inter-oceanic domains, had a fundamental difference from the Spanish colonies out of which came Mexico: they were settled by home-makers and state-builders alive with English ideas of self-government; Mexico was conquered by Spanish adventurers who wanted to go home with their plunder. Their women did not come in large numbers to Mexico. The conquerors imposed in feudal forms the forces of Spanish absolutism, in state and church, on the masses of Mexican aborigines. The Spaniards who stayed there mixed frequently with the aboriginal stock. Throughout the Spanish colonial period, throughout the history of independent and nominally republican Mexico during the nineteenth century, the Creole element kept in power. The native Indians and the mestizos, constituting nine-tenths of the population, dwelt in poverty, ignorance, superstition, and disease. No significant middle class developed, capable of advancing self-government.[1]

The policies of Porfirianism organized many of the economic resources of Mexico but the mass of the benighted people remained as badly off as before. The profits of the foreign concessions paid the fees of a small group of Mexican lawyers, bureaucrats, and politicians who lived in Mexico City, provided the salaries of young foreign engineers, swelled the estates of foreign residents, or flowed abroad as dividends to stock-

---

[1] Ernest Gruening has made this abundantly clear, with philosophical insight supported by a plethora of reality in his *Mexico and Its Heritage* (New York, 1928).

holders. There was practically no progress in education, in sanitation, in public welfare, in social improvement. In Canada during this period and in the United States earlier, the forces of human freedom, enlightenment and self-government—the heritage from England as compared with the heritage from Spain—prospered under a similar flow of foreign capital and were able to make it useful to themselves while generally protecting it for the investors. This could not be so in Mexico.

The Revolution which broke out in 1910 continued in movements of action and reaction throughout the next ten years—a decade which witnessed also the World War. Like all violent revolutions it went through successive phases. It began as a revolt, under Francisco I. Madero, for the restoration of constitutional liberties ruthlessly suppressed by the dictator Diaz. It ended with the completion of a revolution under the leadership of General Alvaro Obregón and finally Plutarco Calles for the social regeneration of the destitute masses of the Mexican people, a revolution which included the bridling of foreign concessions to Mexican sovereign control. During these gruesome years of civil warfare there were chaos and anarchy, banditry and plunder, robbery and cold-blooded butchery, with short intervals of promised order as successive revolutionary leaders came for brief times on the scene.

A comparatively orderly type of warfare such as prevailed in the United States during the Civil War was impossible in a country with Mexico's historical heritage, which included an accumulated hostility to foreigners. The history of the Revolution has not yet been written, nor has any complete census been compiled of the casualties and deprivations of foreign nationals, to say nothing of the loss of native life. The best estimate [1] for American citizens, from 1910 to 1920, is:

American citizens (civilians) killed in Mexico............. 397
United States soldiers killed in Mexico................... 64
American citizens killed along the border, in the United States 58
United States soldiers killed along the border, in the United
   States 68
American citizens (civilians) outraged or wounded in Mexico 32
American soldiers outraged or wounded in Mexico......... 29
American citizens (civilians) wounded on the border, in the
   United States 90
United States soldiers wounded on the border, in the United
   States 47

[1] The names are given in the "Partial Report" of the Fall sub-committee of the Senate Committee on Foreign Relations, Sen. Rept. No. 645, 66th Cong., 2d Sess., pp. 77-90.

In many instances the slaughter and outrages were not inescapable results of a revolutionary disorder; they were perpetrated on the victims simply because they were citizens of the United States. A rough estimate of actual property damages is $170,400,000 (Mex.),[1] much of which, of course, shared the companion fate of similar Mexican property, without recourse; but other portions suffered by violence to American citizens alone. Forty to fifty thousand American citizens abandoned their property and left the country, either on their own impulse or under the reiterated advice of the Department of State to do so. Only judicial inquiry—which has proved impossible—could determine how many of these violent deaths were casualties of the Revolution, shared by native and foreigner alike, and beyond the control, and thus beyond the responsibility of the existing Mexican governments. It should also be remembered, as Secretary of State Lansing did justly note in 1915, that 92 Mexicans were reported killed in American territory during the years 1913, 1914, and 1915, victims of the incomparably high ordinary homicide rate which the people of the United States permit themselves in so-called times of peace and for which the Government of the United States assumes no responsibility toward foreign governments unless the foreign nationals are murdered because of their nationality. This compares with 47 Americans who lost their lives in Mexico during the first three years, 1910-1912 inclusive, of the Revolution, and 76 during the three years 1913, 1914, 1915. Incomplete estimates of the number of other foreign nationals killed in Mexico during the Revolution are 927,[2] their property destroyed $134,900,000 (Mex.).[3]

The greater part of this violence took place after the outbreak of the World War in Europe in 1914, when the European powers were in no position to take steps to protect their nationals. Even before the World War, Great Britain, after some hesitation, decided to co-operate with President Wilson's Mexican policy of "watchful waiting" and the other powers followed suit. They did not again challenge the Monroe

---

[1] Based not on the Fall Committee's estimate of $505,002,434, but on Turlington's calculation of one-tenth the amount of claims later presented.

[2] Chinese, 471 (303 of whom perished in the Torreón massacre).

Spanish,	209	Italian,	16
Arabs,	111	French,	14
British,	38	Japanese,	10
	Miscellaneous,	58	

See Report of Secretary of State Robert Lansing to President Wilson of December 3, 1919, transmitted to the Senate by the President December 5, 1919. Sen. Doc. 165, 66th Cong., 2d Sess.

[3] Turlington, *Mexico and Her Foreign Creditors, post cit.*, presents the following estimates of property damages to foreign nationals, based in large part on one-tenth

Doctrine in Mexico; but had it not been for the protecting circumstances of the European War during the later and more bitter phases of the Mexican Revolution, the United States might have been forced by the pressure of foreign powers to an intervention in Mexico.

In order to understand the diplomatic issues which emerged during and after this confused decade of Mexican history, we must carry in mind the several movements through which the Revolution passed.

1. The revolt of Francisco I. Madero, 1910-1913. Madero's democratic revolt rested on an appeal for the restoration of constitutional liberties which had been suppressed by the dictator Diaz. It was purely political. Installed in power, he allowed to his political foes complete use of the new liberties. They soon overwhelmed him, by a treacherous *golpe de cuartel*, and murdered him and the Vice-President, Suárez (February 23, 1913).

2. The reactionary régime of Victoriano Huerta, February, 1913–July, 1914. Huerta represented a counter-revolution back towards Porfirianism. His success would have restored a dictatorship and, presumably, law and order until the pent-up forces of Mexican misery found a chance to explode. The refusal of President Wilson to recognize him brought about his downfall (July 15, 1914) and released the radical forces.

3. A period of confusion, April, 1914–October, 1915, and of strife between various Mexican military leaders for control of the nation, in which they introduced promises of radical social reform [1] now in line with half-articulate public opinion. This lasted from the downfall of Huerta to the recognition by the United States of the *de facto* government of Carranza October 19, 1915.

of the amount of claims subsequently presented to mixed commissions, and justifying this calculation by the general history of international awards:

United States	$170,400,000 (Mex.)
Spain	68,800,000 "
Great Britain	35,100,000 "
France	19,200,000 "
Germany	6,800,000 "
Netherlands	1,600,000 "
Belgium	1,800,000 "
Switzerland	1,600,000 "
Total	$305,300,000 "

Adjudication by the mixed claims commissions suggested that an estimate of 3% is closer than 10%.

[1] Frank Tannenbaum has made much simpler the intricate question of Mexican national and regional sociology in *The Mexican Agrarian Revolution* (Washington, Brookings Institution, 1930).

4. The régime of Carranza, October, 1915, to April, 1920.

Carranza, after his election, was recognized *de jure* by the United States, April 17, 1917. The new Mexican Constitution of 1917 was adopted, embodying the political, agrarian and other economic and social reforms of the Revolution. Carranza proved more ready to proclaim the revolutionary reforms than to execute them with integrity, and was high-handed, ruthless and not incorrupt. He in turn was overthrown, and murdered, in 1920, by a new uprising led by General Alvaro Obregón.

5. The régime of orderly government, from 1920, which ended the Revolution and began to consolidate its reforms in detailed legislation.

The principal diplomatic problems brought forth by the revolutionary disturbances were: recognition of new Mexican governments, protection of American citizens and property and of foreign nationals, and the honorable chastisement of provocative insults and attacks. These in turn involved the grave decision of policy, whether it would be necessary to intervene by force in Mexican affairs to achieve this protection.

President Taft was inclined to look on the Madero revolution through conventional legal eyes. He immediately recognized the new government, and, fortified by the resolution of Congress of March 14, 1912,[1] he embargoed shipments of arms destined to Madero's subversive opponents. As Madero's authority weakened, Taft and Secretary of State Knox became alarmed lest he be unable sufficiently to protect American citizens and their property according to their existing legal rights. On the advice of the American Ambassador to Mexico, Henry Lane Wilson, Secretary Knox sent a stiff note to the Madero Government, enumerating a number of grievances of American citizens (they were so few at that time that they could be enumerated) and demanding that the administration of Mexico actively and competently bestir itself "to fulfill its international duties toward American citizens and their interests," or else the United States might have to abandon its policy of friendliness.[2] The answer to this was an able refutation of the specified charges, an allusion to contemporary attacks on Mexican citizens in the United States, a willingness to do complete justice, with an expression of the

[1] "That whenever the President shall find that in any American country conditions of domestic violence exist which are promoted by the use of arms or munitions of war purchased from the United States, and shall make proclamation thereof, it shall be unlawful to export except under such limitations and exceptions as the President shall prescribe any arms or munitions of war from any place in the United States to such country until otherwise ordered by the President or by Congress."

[2] The correspondence is printed in *Foreign Relations of the United States* for 1912 and 1913.

difficulties involved by domestic turbulence. Ambassador Wilson recommended to Washington vigorous and drastic action. "These Latin-American countries," he wrote, "should be dealt with justly and calmly but severely and undeviatingly." To act otherwise would "bring disaster and forfeit to us, in the estimation of these peoples, the respect and awe with which they have been taught to regard us." On his part, in Mexico City, he used his influence to weaken Madero, and even to organize a demand on the part of the diplomatic corps that Madero resign.

President Taft had ordered the mobilization of 100,000 troops in Texas to enforce neutrality, and the Secretary of State intimated that, if Mexico did not succeed in protecting "American interests," the President might open the sluiceways of munitions across the frontier to Madero's insurrectionary foes; but he shrank from any policy of intervention. Such was the situation when Huerta came into power following the *coup d'état* of February 9, 1913, less than a month before the end of the Taft Administration.

Henry Lane Wilson at once congratulated Huerta upon his seizure of the presidency. He urged President Taft to recognize the new government *de facto*. Had his advice been followed by Taft or by Woodrow Wilson it is possible that another epoch of Porfirianism, safe for foreigners, might have followed for years. But Taft was too shocked at Madero's brutal death to recognize in any way the régime of his murderers. He left the Mexican question to President Wilson.

Woodrow Wilson viewed the Mexican problem in a new light. A reformer himself, he was sympathetic to the reform movement in Mexico, particularly to the Madero program, and to the revealing necessity of agrarian reforms. Henry Lane Wilson, the ambassador of the Taft Administration, pressed the Department of State to recognize Huerta *de facto* and to hasten arrangements with him, as the other governments were doing, for the satisfaction of all claims. The President ignored this advice and gave expression to a new policy of recognition of Latin-American governments: the United States would not recognize those which were not constitutionally right. Judging by the past, during which so many Latin-American governments had established themselves as durably by revolution as by constitutional procedure, and in a congeries of states where so many different constitutions existed, this novel policy would require a wide and penetrating scrutiny into the internal affairs of the governments involved. It nevertheless rested on lofty motives.

"We hold," said the President a week after his inauguration, ". . . that just government rests always upon the consent of the governed, and that there can be no freedom without order based upon law and upon the public conscience and approval. . . . We shall lend our influence of every kind to the realization of these principles . . . knowing that disorder, personal intrigue and defiance of constitutional rights weaken and discredit government and injure none so much as the people who are unfortunate enough to have their common life and their common affairs so tainted and disturbed. We can have no sympathy with those who seek to seize the power of government to advance their own personal interests or ambitions."

Later, in a public address at Mobile, Alabama (October 27, 1913) Woodrow Wilson, after first declaring that the United States would never again seek to add additional territory by conquest, opposed by implication the policy of the European powers which had recognized Huerta *de facto* with the hope of securing the vested interests of their citizens by choking off further revolutionary disturbances with another dictatorship: "We have seen material interests threaten constitutional freedom in the United States. Therefore we will know how to sympathize with those in the rest of America who have to contend with such powers, not only within their borders but from outside their borders also."

President Wilson, determined not to recognize "the unspeakable Huerta" in any way, endeavored by his counsel peaceably to direct the Mexican situation into some constitutional channel. He accepted the resignation of Ambassador Henry Lane Wilson—who thenceforth became a confirmed but powerless advocate of forcible intervention in Mexico and an American protectorate there—and dispatched a personal representative, ex-Governor John Lind (of Minnesota), in a vain attempt to bring the leaders of the revolution to an agreement which would eliminate Huerta, set up a provisional president, and proceed to fair elections of a clean government and president by constitutional methods. Lind was authorized to say that if the Huerta government acted favorably, and at once, on these suggestions, the President would inform American bankers that the United States approved the extension of an immediate loan sufficient to cover the temporary demands of those holding possession of the government in Mexico.[1] This was a curious overture from an opponent of "dollar diplomacy." Huerta would not step down. Lind reported that the Mexicans respected only force, and he too urged a military occupation of the capital. Wilson persisted in

[1] George M. Stephenson, *John Lind of Minnesota* (University of Minn. Press, 1935)

his peaceful endeavors to get Huerta out. He made the tacit diplomatic bargain by which Great Britain ceased to oppose American policy in Mexico and the President secured from Congress a repeal of the exemption from tolls of coastwise vessels of the United States using the Panama Canal.[1] Armed with this the Secretary of State explained to the diplomatic corps at Washington (November 24, 1913) that such usurpers as Huerta "put the lives and fortunes of citizens and foreigners alike in constant jeopardy. . . . It is the purpose of the United States therefore to discredit and defeat such usurpations whenever they occur. The present policy . . . is to isolate General Huerta entirely; to cut him off from foreign sympathy and aid and from domestic credit, whether moral or material, and to force him out. It hopes and believes that isolation will accomplish this end and shall await the results without irritation or impatience. If General Huerta does not retire by force of circumstances it will become the duty of the United States to use less peaceful means to put him out. . . . Beyond this fixed purpose the Government of the United States will not go. It will not permit itself to seek any special or exclusive advantages in Mexico or elsewhere for its own citizens but will seek, here as elsewhere, to show itself the consistent champion of the open door."

To Congress in his annual message (December, 1913) the President disclaimed any intention of intervention. The foreign powers accepted this policy. Under British leadership their diplomatists in Mexico City formally advised Huerta to accept the demands of the United States. This the usurper refused to do. The United States now offered to act as an intermediary for foreign powers in cases needing the protection of their citizens. Wilson removed the embargo on shipments of arms and munitions to Mexico, thus replenishing Huerta's armed opponents, and stationed naval vessels off Vera Cruz to make sure that the dictator did not get shipments from Europe, where he was making a desperate loan for such purchases.

The presence of American warships in Mexican waters, and the anti-American feeling rapidly mounting among Huerta's followers, produced a provocative incident, which at the disposition of a less patient and humanitarian President of the United States might have led to prolonged intervention. A party of uniformed American sailors went on shore with a launch at the port of Tampico to buy gasoline. Local military officials summarily arrested them and took them from the boat flying the American flag to headquarters, where they were quickly re-

[1] See above, pp. 510-511.

leased. Admiral Mayo, commander of the naval forces, demanded a salute of the American flag by way of reparation.

Huerta saw a possible chance, by provoking the United States into forceful action, to strengthen his position by rallying opposing Mexican factions behind him. He refused the salute. President Wilson backed up the Admiral. He informed Huerta that if the salute were not given he would turn the question over to Congress. When a President of the United States resorts to such a statement he usually is sure that Congress will support forcible action. Huerta still adamant, Wilson informed Congress that Tampico was only one spectacular incident in a series of events which showed contempt for American rights. Disclaiming aggression or purpose of intervention, he asked for authority to use force if necessary to bring about a proper respect for the flag of the United States. Congress supported this request overwhelmingly and immediately; [1] but the President had to act before the resolution passed the Senate. Just as the German merchant ship *Ypiranga,* was about to land a cargo of arms at Vera Cruz, Admiral Mayo's forces shelled the defenses there (April 21, 1914) and, after some sharp fighting, took the customs house and the entire city, and seized the ship. There followed a proclamation prohibiting the importation of arms into Mexico. This incident caused a complete cessation of all relations between the two governments. The American *chargé d'affaires,* who had remained in Mexico in informal and personally friendly contact with Huerta, now left the country. The President strengthened garrisons on the frontier and restored the embargo on shipments of munitions to Mexico; and the Department of State advised American citizens to leave Mexico at once. Huerta sought in vain to rally all armed Mexicans to a united resistance of the "invader." The "constitutional" opposition, under Carranza and other leaders, looked with increasing disfavor upon the American occupation of Vera Cruz, "a violation of the national sovereignty," as Carranza notified the Department of State, but, with success so imminent, they would not rally to Huerta.

President Wilson's position at Vera Cruz was as unwelcome to himself as it was to his opponent. He accepted with alacrity an invitation of the diplomatic representatives of the Argentine, Brazil and Chile in Washington to mediate.[2] This cleared him from the imputation

---

[1] The vote in the House of Representatives was 323-19 (April 20); in the Senate, 72-13 (April 22, 1914).

[2] Rippy, *United States and Mexico, op. cit.,* has some interpretative chapters summarizing the non-interventionist Mexican policies of Presidents Taft, Wilson, Harding and Coolidge.

of any contradiction of his declared policy of non-intervention, and molded good will for the United States over all South America. It was the point of departure also for a new Latin-American policy, suggested to the President by his intimate adviser, Colonel E. M. House —that of Pan-Americanizing the Monroe Doctrine by an inter-American pact mutually to guarantee the territorial integrity and political independence of each contracting state.[1] From then on, the President, favoring this policy, was scrupulous not to stultify it by the exhibition of any aggression by the United States toward Mexico. His Mexican policy added to the moral force of his diplomacy of war and peace in Europe in 1917-1919.

Huerta, isolated at home and abroad, was obliged to accept the advice of the ABC powers. The *Carranzistas* also accepted an invitation to send a delegate. In Mexico, the "constitutional" forces under Carranza were rapidly gaining in the field when the ABC mediation conference met at Niagara Falls, Ontario. The mediators proposed the following settlement: elimination of Huerta; the installation of a provisional government "actually, avowedly and sincerely in favor of the agrarian and political reforms" advanced by the revolutionists; a commission to arrange settlement with the new provisional government of foreign claims for indemnity; agreement of the mediating powers to recognize the provisional Mexican Government on this basis; no indemnity for the United States for the expenses of occupation. This the delegates of the United States accepted, under reservation of not recognizing in any way the government of Huerta.[2] The *Carranzistas* would not sign. When the terms of the protocol were read at Mexico City the Huerta Government collapsed, and the General left for Europe. The government of Mexico fell among rival armed factions, temporarily to the *Carranzistas* who at all times denied the right of foreign powers to mediate in any settlement of Mexican affairs. Huerta eliminated, but Mexico still in ferment, American forces evacuated Vera Cruz (November 23, 1914).[3]

The elimination of Huerta did not bring peace to Mexico. Rival revolutionary armies, under Zapata in the southwest and the bandit

---

[1] Seymour, *Intimate Papers of Colonel House, op. cit.,* I, 207-234. See Ch. XXXIX.
[2] Chapter XII in J. M. Callahan's *American Foreign Policy in Mexican Relations* gives us a time-table of these happenings, a *précis* in effect, of the correspondence published in the official series *Foreign Relations.*
[3] Ray Stannard Baker's review of the Mexican crisis, to the evacuation of Vera Cruz, in the fourth volume of his *Woodrow Wilson, Life and Letters* (8 vols., New York, 1927-1939), is most sympathetic to Wilson's idealistic policy.

Villa in the north among others, ravaged the country. Wilson's task now was to get placed in authority a group which could command the support of the people of Mexico as a provisional government that could receive the sanction of later free elections, a government from which satisfactory guaranties could then be had for the protection of American and other foreign life and property in Mexico. The *Carranzistas*, despite their unsympathetic response to Wilson's attitude, seemed to offer the best chance of such a government.

Confusion worse confounded, murder and pillage, swept Mexico. Anxious to hasten the establishment of order, President Wilson summoned a conference of diplomatic representatives of six Latin-American powers—the Argentine Republic, Brazil, Chile, Guatemala, Bolivia and Uruguay—at Washington (August, 1915) to advise on which warring faction to recognize and support as the government *de facto* of Mexico.

The conference invited representatives of the Mexican groups to participate. Despite the fact that Carranza refused the invitation and consistently denied the right of outside parties to give advice to Mexico, the conferees announced their decision that the *Carranzista* party was "the only party possessing the essentials of recognition as the *de facto* government of Mexico." This was an anxious response to the desire to see somebody in authority in Mexico whom foreign powers could support and with whom they might expect to make conventions for the settlement of claims and the protection of lives and property of their nationals. The United States then promptly (October 19, 1915) recognized *de facto* Carranza's authority, followed by similar action by the six Latin-American conferee powers. "We will aid and befriend Mexico," President Wilson explained to Congress,[1] "but we will not coerce her."

The *de facto* recognition of Carranza proved premature. He was unable to control the ravaging chieftains who refused to accept his leadership. The most notorious and bloodthirsty of these, Pancho Villa, operating in the northern states, deliberately attempted, by a series of sanguinary incidents, to provoke an armed intervention of the United States which might enable him to supplant Carranza in public estimation as a leader of a patriotic revolutionary Mexico to repel the hoped-for invasion. Carranza had invited American mine owners, who had abandoned their properties on advice of their government, to return and operate the mines. A group of fifteen graduate engineers promptly entered the State of Chihuahua for this purpose. Villa's forces took

---

[1] Annual message of December, 1915.

the young men from a railroad train and murdered them in cold blood at Santa Ysabel (January 10, 1916). In the Congress of the United States resolutions for armed intervention were introduced, but Wilson accepted, this time, the promise of Carranza to punish the perpetrators of the massacre. To this day they have gone unpunished. Next Villa led a hostile raid on American soil, "shooting up" the town of Columbus, New Mexico, with the loss of seventeen American lives—innocent citizens killed within their own country, in their own home town (March 9, 1916).

President Wilson with the quick approval of Congress immediately sent a punitive expedition of 15,000 men under General Pershing in hot but ineffective pursuit of Villa's band across the Chihuahua desert. The President mobilized 150,000 militia on the southern frontier against further contingencies, to supplement the regular army, a military episode which exhibited to the world such a lamentable unpreparedness for war that it encouraged Mexicans of all groups, including Carranza, to re-sist American demands, however reasonable. The untamed Villa perpetrated new raids into Texas (affairs of Glen Springs and Boquilla, May 5, 1916), which happened at the time of the *Sussex* crisis with Germany.

From now on the increasing uncertainty of American neutrality *vis-à-vis* the war in Europe exerted its influence on the benevolent "watch-ful waiting" of the exasperated President Wilson. Carranza refused to accept American requests for co-operative action for the suppression of Villa with American troops on Mexican soil. Another column of 8,000 crossed the frontier over the rising protests of Carranza. The Department of State again publicly advised all American citizens remaining in Mexico to leave. The American President was sincere in his explanations that these punitive expeditions were necessary to prevent further and general intervention, for which public opinion within the United States began to clamor, led by Theodore Roosevelt, and backed of course by those people whose legitimate investments in Mexico were being wiped out. The second pursuit of *Villistas* led to a collision with Carranza's forces at Carrizal. Other smaller attacks on American naval or land forces on the ports and frontiers of Mexico showed the eager enmity of Carranza's Government. General hostilities seemed to have been averted only by a hair's breadth by Carranza's prudence in accepting Wilson's demand (June 25, 1916) for the immediate release of 17 American troopers who had been cut off and made prisoners at Carrizal.

A series of futile conferences (at New London, Atlantic City, Phila-

delphia and New York) between commissioners of the United States
and of the *de facto* Mexican Government, endeavored in vain to agree
on bases for evacuation of Pershing's regiments, based on a right to intervene again when necessary and sufficient promises of protection by
the Carranza forces. Only when the crisis of approaching war with
Germany developed, in January, 1917, did Wilson order the withdrawal
of the troops, without adequate guaranties. The Mexican Congress,
acting as an electoral college, elected Carranza as President, March 11,
1917, and adopted a new constitution, embodying the reforms of the
Revolution. Wilson now hastily recognized the new government *de jure*.
When Henry P. Fletcher, the new Ambassador of the United States,
entered the Chamber of Deputies, the members received him with
hisses, in shameful contrast to the applause which greeted the German
Ambassador, whose proposal to Mexico the British secret service and
Washington Government had just ventilated to the world: a war alliance, to include Japan, for the purpose of conquering back from the
United States "the lost territory" in the states of Texas, New Mexico
and Arizona.

It was a spectacular victory for Carranza, who maintained his authority successfully—though not faithfully to the principles of the Revolution—in Mexico during the remainder of the World War, in which the
United States was now involved.

Despite his loss of respect in Mexico for the time being, Wilson had
gained the good will of Latin America in general and had prevented the
United States from becoming involved in a war with Mexico on the eve
of its entrance into the World War. The settlement of Mexican-American affairs and the liquidation of the claims of the foreign nationals
now had to await the settlement of the far greater issues of the World
War.

We have seen that, after the Civil War, the United States with a million
men under arms did not take advantage of its power to march into
Canada, despite provocations. It was the same after the World War
in regard to Mexico although the provocation was unspeakably greater.
The demand for it, too, particularly on the part of the despoiled investors,
was great. In Washington in the upper house Senator Albert B. Fall
of New Mexico, spokesman for the Doheny oil interests,[1] presided over

---

[1] Senator Fall was later convicted of betraying public trust, in connection with the
award to Doheny interests of the Elk Hill oil leases on United States public lands
while he was Secretary of the Interior during the Harding Administration. Doheny
"loaned" Fall $100,000 and destroyed the latter's note, at the time of passing the leases.
Fall spent a year in a federal prison. The public utterances of this person in regard to

a sub-committee of the Committee on Foreign Relations, which diligently collected evidence concerning the multitude of outrages. These were embodied in a "Preliminary Report and Hearings" of 3,000 printed pages, parts of which were widely distributed in 1919 as fuel for warming public opinion to demand a more positive Mexican policy. This protest was gathering volume when suddenly the end of the Revolution in the spring of 1920 vindicated Wilson's policy. The radical party, under the leadership of General Alvaro Obregón, overthrew the corrupting Carranza Government. Obregón was then elected President by national suffrage (September, 1920). The Fall Committee limited its recommendations to: diplomatic pressure for the security of American property and citizens in Mexico; no recognition of Obregón without a specific agreement to that effect and a settlement of all claims for damages; only in case of failure ought intervention to be considered.

Both political parties in their platforms of 1920 expressed unwillingness to recognize the new Obregón Government without a specific understanding for the adjudication and payment of American claims and the protection of American nationals and property. This was the policy of the Wilson Administration in its closing days and of the new Republican Administrations of Presidents Harding and Coolidge. Did it mean that such an agreement must be written into a formal treaty as the price of recognition, a treaty which would be binding on the Mexican nation, or merely a diplomatic agreement which would not bind any other than the Mexican Government at that time in power? Bainbridge Colby, Wilson's last Secretary of State, seemed to mean a treaty.

The legacy of issues [1] between the United States and Mexico which had come down from the decade of revolution was intricate and confusing. We are straining for simplicity when we summarize them as follows: claims for damages to American citizens suffered since the last mixed commission of 1868; claims for damages of American citizens and their property by violence or arbitrary decrees during the Revolution; claims for damages for the appropriation of lands, owned in good legal title by American citizens, for the restoration by the new reforms

Mexico must be always suspect. President Wilson must have realized this when he remarked to his private secretary (as quoted by Joseph Tumulty, *Woodrow Wilson as I Knew Him* (New York, 1922), p. 146): "I have to pause and remind myself that I am President of the United States and not of a small group of Americans with vested interests in Mexico."

[1] F. S. Dunn, *The Diplomatic Protection of Americans in Mexico,* prepared for the Columbia University Council for Research in the Social Sciences (Columbia University Press, 1933), has a succinct account of the technical points involved in these issues.

of communal holdings or *ejidos* for the agrarian population of Mexico;
damages to American citizens by virtue of the nationalization of subsoil deposits according to the provisions of Article 27 of the new Mexican Constitution of 1917; claims based on the non-payment of interest
or principal of Mexican Government bonds. A brief description of each
category is in order.

The so-called general claims since 1868 were routine claims under international law and treaty provisions; the tranquillity of the Porfirian
régime had kept these within normal limits. The special claims for
damages arising from the events of the Revolution were various and
multitudinous: they included deaths, mutilations and other injuries to
persons, damage or confiscation of property, inadequate police protection, denial of justice, to mention only the more prominent.

The claims for *ejido* land takings arose out of the most fundamental
reform of the Revolution, the effort to restore to the agrarian population
the communal land holdings, the custom of which dates back to aboriginal history, of lands of which they had been despoiled during the century of Mexican independence. In the great agrarian states of Mexico
over 90% of the population was landless and in a system of peonage no better than slavery; their misery was profoundly pitiful, worse
than the Negro slave in the United States before the Civil War, and
it had been growing steadily worse decade by decade; because of this
Mexico herself, once a country self-sufficient for foodstuffs, had decreased in production and depended, in the last years of the Diaz régime, on imports of foodstuffs.[1] The redistribution of the colossal private
land holdings accumulated largely by fraud and graft under legal forms,
some of them held by foreign citizens, innocent investors, was the greatest problem of the Revolution, a problem not solved today. One
factor in it was the historic custom among these native peoples of
holding and working their land in common, in the environs of their village communities. The redistribution of land under Article 27 of the
new Constitution, and earlier decrees and subsequent legislation, was
adapted to this custom. Article 27 of the Constitution of 1917 declared
the ownership of all lands and waters, and of the mineral deposits under
them, to be vested in the nation, which might then prescribe the conditions under which private property might be held in the public
interest. At the same time it stated that private property so defined
should not be expropriated except for reasons of public utility and by

---

[1] For a sympathetic and luminous description of the agrarian population, and its
fundamental relation to the Mexican Revolution, see Gruening, *op. cit.*

means of indemnification. Under this principle the land which was re-distributed in the agrarian reforms for the re-establishment or creation of *ejidos* was not confiscated from the *hacendados,* or proprietors; the Government took it by eminent domain at appraised valuation, with payment in national bonds which had no live value, and gave it over to native agrarian communal holdings. Protests arose over the appraisals and the method of payment. The Mexican Government contended that foreigners received no worse treatment than Mexican proprietors in this respect, and that, as to payment in bonds, it was a recognition and a promise, and the only way during a great and vital emergency to execute a reform indispensably necessary for the restoration of peace and public tranquillity.

Another fundamental principle of the Mexican Revolution was "Mexico for the Mexicans": the liquidation of foreign economic dominion, particularly of natural resources which constituted the material patrimony of the nation. Before the Revolution the mineral subsoil products, *excepting carboniferous minerals including petroleum,* had been separated by law from the surface ownership and vested in the state, which licensed their exploitation under regulatory laws and decrees. On the basis of this exception the extensive petroleum industry had rested upon private ownership, almost altogether foreign, predominantly American owners who had bought vast tracts of land (including subsoil petroleum) for this purpose under good title according to the existing legal system. Some of this land was held in reserve for future exploitation.

The new Constitution of 1917 in Article 27 now brought subsoil petroleum deposits also under the ownership of the state. A series of provisional decrees, pending the enactment in 1925 of an organic national petroleum law, laid down the new conditions under which petroleum operators, hitherto owners outright, now might continue to exploit their holdings, for terms of not more than fifty years, under license and confirmatory concessions, which must be registered within two years under pain of total lapse of all title. The new registration required: new taxation, Mexicanization of corporations, and of a controlling fraction of their stock; limitation of existing titles of foreign individuals to one life after which the holdings must be liquidated to Mexican citizens or corporations; exploitation by some "positive act" of all land held; agreement by foreign concessionaires not to call upon their governments for support of their titles against the Mexican Government (the so-called "Calvo clause" increasingly in usage in contracts of

Latin-American states with foreign nationals), and prohibition of concessions to foreign citizens or corporations in coastal or frontier zones.

The foreign holders of petroleum lands saw their titles suddenly converted into fifty-year leaseholds under increasingly complex conditions and growing tax burdens. It looked to them as though the Mexican Government was deliberately trapping the funds and ability which they had been invited to invest under constitutional guarantees. The United States Government took the position, in the diplomatic disputes which followed, that, while not denying the right of the nation to reform its constitution and legislation in its own way, such reforms could not (as the new Mexican Constitution itself said they could not) be applied *ex post facto* to property rights already secured by foreign nationals in contracts in good faith under earlier constitutions and laws. This legalistic position, at least debatable, paid no attention to the circumstances, propriety, or morality, under which such a former legal system had existed. The United States also contended that a foreign national could not, without the consent of his government and solely by his own will, sign away any right to protection by his government.

The issue of defaulted interest on loans abroad, either by the Mexican Government, or by railroads or states guaranteed by Mexico, was, due to the impoverished condition and political insufficiency of the country, a large but simple question of adjustment between debtor and creditor, although complex in its details. The Revolution bankrupted the country and brought about a suspension of interest and amortization on its bonded public debt, nearly all of which was held by foreign nationals, mostly in the form of Mexican external bonds contracted in foreign currencies. As suspension continued for two decades, arrears of interest rapidly added to the total indebtedness. French citizens held the largest share of this direct foreign debt, next British, next Americans, with smaller shares for German, Dutch, Belgian, Swiss and Spanish nationals. Foreign governments by international law had the right to interpose their authority for the settlement of the portion of the external debt contracted with their nationals; but, since the Second Hague Convention of 1907, they had no right to use force for the recovery of such contract debts unless Mexico should refuse to arbitrate or, having arbitrated, refuse to pay the adjudicated awards. We shall see that the warring foreign governments did not officially interpose for the settlement of these debts. They left the negotiations to representatives of the bondholders under the leadership of American bankers.

President Obregón, seeking full recognition of his government, offered his personal assurances for the security of American property and citizens in Mexico and the ownership of lands acquired by American citizens before the adoption of the new Constitution on May 1, 1917. He would shape his policy, he said, "according to the dictates of law and morality." These ambiguous promises bound only Obregón and his actual government; similar promises from one man and one administration previously in the case of Carranza had been worth nothing. Apparently, too, there was a loophole left for the alienation of title to the subsoil products of such lands on which no "positive act" of exploitation had taken place before 1917. Secretary of State Charles E. Hughes, in the new Republican Administration of President Harding, insisted that recognition must be contingent upon a treaty which would explicitly bind the Mexican nation itself to adequate guaranties. Obregón refused this. Eventually Hughes gave way and accepted, instead of a treaty, a statement of agreement written into a protocol of informal conferences in Mexico City—the so-called Bucareli Conferences—of a commission composed of delegates from the two countries.

In these Bucareli Conferences the American spokesmen were willing to accept in general the position of the Mexican Government that it had an unquestioned right to regulate the oil industry according to the new reforms providing they did not apply to property acquired under other conditions before the new Constitution went into effect; and they denied the necessity of having performed *before May 1, 1917,* "a positive act" of exploitation in order to validate continuing title to petroleum lands acquired before that date. Such a necessity, laid down in principle in a then recent case of the Supreme Court of Mexico involving the Texas Corporation, they held to be *ex post facto.* The Mexican representatives set forth a definition of a "positive act" which they said "has constituted and will constitute in the future the policy of the Mexican Government." This definition, while clinging steadfastly to the theory of the necessity of such an act before 1917, nevertheless was so phrased that the merest trace or wisp of action, such as payment for the lands of a higher price than their surface value alone would justify, or even manifestation of intent to exploit, would suffice for the indispensable "positive act." [1] This new statement seemed to mean that such lands and their subsoil products were excluded from the nationalization pro-

---

[1] Such as "drilling, leasing, entering into any contract relative to the subsoil, making investments of capital in lands for the purpose of obtaining the oil in the subsoil, carrying out works of exploitation or exploration of the subsoil, and in cases where from the contract relative to the subsoil it appears that the grantors fixed and received a price higher than would have been paid for the surface of the land because it was purchased

gram of Article 27. In the cases of owners who had not, indeed, performed such a positive act, they would have preferential rights, to the exclusion of third parties, for the exploitation of the subsoil. In answer the American delegates on behalf of their government said that they reserved all the rights of citizens of the United States in respect to the subsoil of lands in Mexico owned by citizens of the United States, or in which they had an interest in whatever form owned or held, under the laws and constitution of Mexico in force prior to the promulgation of the new Constitution, May 1, 1917, and under the principles of international law and equity.

At the same conference the representatives of the United States accepted a statement of the Mexican representatives of the principles that takings of land for *ejidos, for existing villages,* could be paid for in bonds, up to 1,755 *hectares;* all taking of acreage above that figure was to be compensated in cash; and the former owner might appeal to a general mixed claims commission (to be mentioned directly) the appraised valuations. The payment in bonds of this limited class of agrarian claims was not to constitute a precedent for any future expropriations; and other types of existing, disputed agrarian claims were to be settled by the general claims commission. This settlement in principle was an acceptance of the Mexican argument that the emergency nature of the appropriations justified in some cases the particular form of payment, the only form immediately possible.

Finally, in the Bucareli Conferences, the Mexican spokesmen agreed that their government, when recognized, would negotiate two claims conventions for the settlement of all outstanding claims between the two governments: one, a general claims commission for claims accumulating since the last liquidation by the mixed commission of 1868; the other, a special claims convention for claims arising out of the Revolution, 1910-1920. The separation of the claims into two classes implied that they were susceptible of separate treatment.

On the basis of this understanding the United States formally recognized (August 31, 1923) the Government of Mexico, *de jure,* under the presidency of General Obregón.

The claims conventions were quickly negotiated and ratified. British, French and other foreign recognition followed. The other powers made

for the purpose of looking for oil and exploiting same if found; and, in general, performing or doing any other positive act, or manifesting an intention of a character similar to those heretofore described." The exchanges are printed in *Proceedings of the United States-Mexican Commission Convened at Mexico City, May 14, 1923* (Washington, G.P.O., 1925), 47.

similar claims conventions with Mexico. When a revolution broke out in the north against the established Mexican Government, the United States saved it by selling, on deferred payment, munitions to the constituted authorities.

The long years of controversy between the United States and Mexico appeared, thanks to the inveterate forbearance and persistent patience of the stronger nation, at last well on the way to a satisfactory settlement. But when in 1925 the Mexican Congress enacted permanent legislation for the application of the petroleum and agrarian reforms of the Constitution of 1917, hitherto embodied only in temporary decrees, further controversy immediately ensued. Secretary of State Frank B. Kellogg, in the Administration of President Coolidge, saw in these laws a violation of the Bucareli understandings. The Secretary made it clear in a public manner, as this legislation impended, that the United States would continue to support the Mexican Government against revolutionary movements only so long as it protected American lives and American rights and complied with its international engagements and duties. When the laws were passed he made public an *aide-memoire* to the Mexican Ambassador (November 17, 1925) in which he referred to clouds gathering on the horizon of friendship. It was a few months after this that Mexico interfered in American policy in Nicaragua by shipping munitions to the insurrectionists there.[1]

The new Mexican laws [2] violated the Bucareli understandings and emphasized the wisdom of Secretary Hughes' original preference for treaty guaranties. They required, under pain of forfeiture, all foreign owners of petroleum lands on which positive acts of exploitation had taken place before 1917, to confirm their holdings by fifty-year licenses to exploit, renewable upon expiration provided the licensee had observed the terms of the concession. They defined the "positive act" much more narrowly than the Bucareli definition. They omitted reference to previous owners who had not performed a positive act. They seemed to apply only to individual foreign nationals, and not to corporations at all. They required a "Calvo clause" for all licenses.

To the protests which followed, the newly elected (1924) Calles Government, which had succeeded Obregón by orderly constitutional process, replied that the promises made in the Bucareli Conferences were not binding on the Mexican Congress—exactly what Secretary Hughes had

[1] See above, p. 537.
[2] C. W. Hackett prints an English translation of these laws in the appendix to his pamphlet on *The Mexican Revolution and the United States, 1910-1926* (World Peace Foundation Pamphlets, IX, No. 5, Boston, 1926).

feared. The diplomatic discussions came to a deadlock. Most of the American oil corporations meanwhile had refrained from applying for concessions under these conditions, and were, consequently, in danger of having their properties utterly lost by the contingencies of the protested laws. The Mexican Government made no step, however, to execute the annulments, which would have taken effect January 1, 1927; and in November of that year the Supreme Court of Mexico declared unconstitutional the provisions of the act which limited to a period of years the confirmed titles of subsoil rights in lands acquired before 1917 on which a positive act of exploitation had taken place before that date. President Calles thereupon recommended to Congress amendments to the oil legislation, in conformity to this decision, which were duly enacted in January, 1928. The new amendments removed one issue. New regulations for the administration of the oil laws defined a "positive act," now in language identical with that of the Bucareli protocols, dropped the requirement for the Calvo clause, and recognized the position of foreign corporations as well as individuals.[1] These new interpretations and changes satisfied the Government of the United States, and the Department of State issued (March 28, 1928) a statement that, with this basis, future questions could be adjusted through the Mexican administrative departments and the Mexican courts.

In the compromise which thus set at rest the tangled issue both governments had achieved in substantial degree their practical aims: the United States had secured the substance for which it contended, but the Government of Mexico had succeeded in protecting the full integrity of its constitutional and legislative independence; it did so only by refraining from exercising them in an unreasonable way.

Instrumental in achieving the administrative features of this compromise was Ambassador Dwight W. Morrow, a personal friend whom President Coolidge sent to Mexico in October, 1927, after the Senate had passed (January 25, 1927) unanimously a resolution for the arbitration, if necessary, of the outstanding issues with Mexico. Morrow succeeded in restoring an abundant measure of good will between the estranged peoples and governments. He showed a sympathetic understanding of Mexico's heavy problems, which President Coolidge shared, and he was resourceful in his manner of turning public opinion to friendly appreciation. One of the spectacular devices thus promoted

[1] In one respect these new laws and regulations left unfilled one of the Bucareli promises: they reserved no preferential rights for owners of petroleum lands who had made no positive act of exploitation before May 1, 1917.

was the exchange of non-stop aerial flights between the two capitals by American and by Mexican aviators. The American hero of the air, Charles A. Lindbergh, led off in this pleasing gesture, and, as every schoolgirl in both countries then knew, ended up by marrying one of Mr. Morrow's talented daughters.

The portion of controversy which had been shelved for settlement by the mixed claims commission had an even more labored history.

The general mixed claims commission met in 1924, composed of one Mexican commissioner, one U. S. commissioner, and a neutral umpire. After repeated extensions of its conventional lifetime it lapsed in 1931, after having adjudicated only 148 claims out of a total of 3,617 filed by both governments,[1] to be renewed again in 1932, subject to the exclusion from it of all agrarian claims.

The administration of President Franklin D. Roosevelt made an executive agreement (April 24, 1934), which created new machinery for expediting the adjudication of the remaining claims within two years, by commissioners, respectively, of the two governments; in case of disagreement of the two commissioners meeting together later to compare their decisions, the disagreed cases were to be finally settled by a special convention still later to be negotiated by both governments. This could dispose of the disputed claims (together with the agreed awards) *en bloc,* or refer them to an umpire under terms to be fixed in the future convention. Certain agrarian claims which it had been agreed previously to submit to this commission were reserved for further discussion. Thus the two governments speeded up the grinding of the general claims mill without definitely agreeing upon a means of payment of the final awards.

The special (revolutionary) claims commission met first in Mexico City in 1924. At the proposal of the United States as a gesture of good will the two governments chose a Latin-American umpire for the third commissioner. The commission's labors were contentious and consequently slow, and its lifetime was repeatedly extended by mutual agreement until it expired in 1931. Only two groups of claims went before this commission in its seven years' history: the Santa Ysabel massacre claims, and one other individual death claim, selected because of their flagrant nature. In both instances the umpire threw out the claims on the ground that the

---

[1] The claims filed before 1931 were:

	Number	Amount
United States against Mexico	2,781	$513,649,267.17
Mexico against the United States	836	245,158,395.32

Dunn, *op. cit.,* 404.

United States could not show that the Mexican Government had not taken reasonable steps to suppress Villa (who was later granted amnesty and pardon by the Carranza Government). It seems to have been a mistake to suggest a Latin-American national for such an umpire, in view of implications of such claims for countries in which revolutions are frequent: if the cases had been presented to a tribunal of the Hague Court presumably they would have been acted on with more celerity and different interpretations of justice.

After the failure of the commissions to pass on the mass of claims, a settlement in this manner was no longer expedient.

It had been only an executive agreement which had expedited the final settlement of the general claims, a part of which were of Mexican citizens against the United States. A formal treaty, signed the same day (ratified, 1935), arranged a settlement *en bloc* of the special (revolutionary) claims, all of which were of the citizens of the United States against Mexico. That government now agreed to pay to the United States, in total quittance of all this class of unsettled claims, a sum of money equal to the proportion of the total in money of final awards to the total in money of original claims as decided by all the other mixed claims commissions then at work with Mexico adjudicating the claims of European governments (Belgium, Great Britain, Italy and Spain). Mexico agreed to pay for the American claims in installments of $500,000 per annum, beginning January 1, 1935, until paid.[1] The expenses to the United States for its share of the maintenance of the two mixed claims commissions were $350,000 a year from 1927 to 1932: total, 1925-1932, $2,574,730.[2] In this very general way, after much negotiation and much patience, the United States secured for its nationals a treatment approximately equal to that of the nationals of European claimant governments; and payment began in small and insufficient annual driblets.[3] Considering the obligations of Mexico also to other governments and its foreign bonded debt, this was perhaps all that could be expected. It was generous and fair to Mexico, and exemplary.

[1] The first and second installments of $500,000 were paid promptly in January, 1935, and January, 1936.

[2] A. H. Feller has presented a thorough analysis of the history and procedure of all these mixed claims commissions, including the two Mexican-American ones, in *The Mexican Claims Commissions, 1923-1934, a Study in the Law and Procedure of International Commissions* (New York, 1935).

[3] If the lump sum proves to be one-tenth of the total claimed, or $42,130,000, it would take over 81 years to pay off at $500,000 per year, exclusive of interest. The awards of the mixed commissions of Mexico with other foreign nations indicate, however, an average of about 3% of the amount claimed.

The United States Government kept its hands off the question of Mexico's bonded indebtedness to foreign nationals, including American citizens. Representatives of the foreign bondholders, organized through an international committee of bankers, treated directly with the Mexican treasury. The total foreign debt of Mexico (including certain internal bonds mostly held by foreigners, and railroad bonds guaranteed by the Mexican Government, but exclusive of obligations for claims) was in 1922 about 1,000,000,000 *pesos* [1] bonded in various foreign currencies. Arrears of interest added 40 per cent. Repeated attempts to reach agreements to refund proved abortive. Between 1922 and 1928, however, the Mexican Government remitted $43,000,000, then stopped. In 1943 it began to make current interest payments on the direct debt, after an offer to discharge back interest with a token payment and pay off the principal in *pesos* for dollars by 1968, including future interest in *pesos* at 4.35 per cent. A somewhat similar offer was made in 1946 (and eventually accepted) to holders of Mexican railroad bonds under a schedule to extend to 1974. The hands-off policy enabled the Mexican Government to re-establish itself financially at the expense of American bondholders.

Because the policy of the United States has been not to support diplomatically the collection of contract debts due to its nationals by defaulted foreign states, Mexico's vast defaults thus have been excluded from the area of diplomatic controversy. Therefore we can say that by December, 1936, Mexican-American relations had been adjusted, except for the claims arising from expropriations of agrarian lands owned by citizens of the United States. Even on this score the Mexican Government had slowed down its program of land takings. It was in December, 1936, that the United States signed at Buenos Aires, at the special inter-American Conference for the Maintenance of Peace, the Additional Protocol Relative to Non-Intervention (additional to the Montevideo multilateral Treaty on the Rights and Duties of States, of 1933): "The High Contracting Parties declare inadmissible the intervention of any one of them, directly or indirectly, and for whatever reason, in the internal or external affairs of any other of the Parties."

Just as soon as this Protocol had been ratified by the two nations, the newly elected (1934) radical government of President Lázaro Cárdenas launched a thoroughgoing expropriation of agricultural and grazing properties remaining in the possession of United States nationals. There was no longer even a pretense of paying for these new takings for com-

---

[1] Throughout 1941 a *peso* equaled about 20 U. S. cents. When the bonds were issued it was near par, approximately 50 cents. In 1950 it was worth about 11.50 cents.

munal agrarian reform—the *ejido* system [1]—and the older expropriations, since 1927, remained uncompensated.

Resting for political support on the aggressively organized labor organizations of Mexico, the Cárdenas Government next passed labor laws that bore down destructively on the operations of foreign corporations. Tacitly it encouraged the labor unions to strike against the foreign-owned concerns for heavy increases in pay, shorter hours, double pay for overtime, automobiles and chauffeurs for labor leaders, labor halls for union meetings, holidays, vacations and vacation travel for employees and families (numerously construed), and an increasing control over books and management. These demands abruptly drove up the costs of the foreign corporations, particularly the petroleum companies (American, British, and Dutch) which had been operating under the guaranties of 1928, which said nothing about labor.

One suspects that the purpose of the labor demands was not only a rapid rise in the standard of living for the Mexican workers (such of them as were lucky enough to be employed by the foreigners, who notoriously afforded higher pay and better working conditions than most Mexican employers), but also to make it financially impossible for the foreign oil companies—and after them foreign mining and other properties—to operate, so that the Mexican Government might then take them over by default.

New legislation had opened the way for this program. A federal expropriation law of November 13, 1936, had provided for the expropriation of private property of public utility "to satisfy collective necessities in case of war or interior upheaval." To make sure that the courts would interpret the new laws to suit his purpose, President Cárdenas put through Congress a law reducing the life tenure of the judges of the Supreme Court to the tenure of the President who appointed them.

The judges now became creatures of the executive, and the executive, if only because of the Buenos Aires Protocol, no longer had any reason to fear intervention by the United States, direct or indirect, or for whatever reason, to protect its nationals against denials of justice in American republics. All that the United States could resort to was diplomatic expostulation. There were some Latin Americans who claimed that even this was "indirect intervention"! There were, of course, various domestic resources of economic retaliation against Mexico, but this was not much

---

[1] Eyler N. Simpson published a highly sympathetic, and not unbiased, study of *The Ejido, Mexico's Way Out* (University of North Carolina, 1937), with a commendatory introduction by Mexico's principal diplomatic dialectician, Ramón Beteta.

to be feared because economically the United States depended on Mexico more than Mexico depended on the United States. It would also have been politically dangerous to hold Mexico too categorically to account, because organized labor in the United States—on which the New Deal depended heavily for its political existence—sympathized with the demands of organized labor in Mexico as championed by the Cárdenas Government. Mexican and American labor organizations and leaders fraternized conspicuously in the capitals of both countries. Labor had now become a factor to be reckoned with in American diplomacy.

The expropriation issue came to a head when President Cárdenas ordered (March 18, 1938) properties of the foreign-owned petroleum corporations to be taken over by the state after they had failed to accept the award of a Mexican labor board, confirmed by the Supreme Court of Mexico following a strike of the petroleum workers. The award called not only for drastic increases in pay retroactive to the beginning of the strike, 26,000,000 *pesos,* and the radical easement of work—terms which the Mexican Government itself proved unable to meet when it took over operation of the properties. It also enjoined a degree of control by the union over books and management. The companies proved not unwilling to accept the other terms, but stuck at the intrusion of labor unions into management. The properties thus expropriated were valued by the owners at approximately $450,000,000 of which $200,000,000 was American-owned. Mexico contended they were worth a total of $262,000,000, and advanced various ingenious devaluations and set-offs to bring American properties down to less than $50,000,000.[1]

The United States never contended that the Mexican or any other government had no right to expropriate property, including foreign property, for purposes of internal reform. What it objected to was expropriation without compensation. That meant confiscation. In a series

---

[1] There is an enormous literature, documentary and secondary, on this controversy. The American companies have published the memoranda stating their grievances with appendices of official documents, in the following publications: *Mexico Labor Controversy, 1936-1938* (no place or date of publication); *Mexico, Expropriation of Foreign-Owned Oil Properties,* 1938, Huasteca Petroleum Co., "printed in the U. S. A.," preface dated, 1938; *The Reply to Mexico* (Standard Oil Co. [N. J.], New York, 1940); *Present Status of the Mexican Oil "Expropriations,"* 1940 (Standard Oil Co. [N. J.], New York, 1940). *Donald R. Richberg's Story, The Mexican Oil Seizures* (*circa* 1939) digests these data of the oil companies into an appeal to public opinion for justice to the expropriated owners. Richberg was formerly NRA administrator and Co-ordinator in the Roosevelt Administration whom the companies employed as counsel. Roscoe B. Gaither, not a representative in any way of the companies, has published a revealing account of the legal injustice of *Expropriation in Mexico: The Facts and the Law* (New York, 1940). Josef L. Kunz has an objective analysis, in international law of *The Mexican Expropriations,* New York University School of Law, Contemporary Pamphlets, 1940, Series 5, No. 1.

of protests,[1] Secretary Hull insisted that "recognized rules of law and equity require the prompt payment of just compensation for property that may be expropriated." But the Department of State was quicker to insist on settlement for the agrarian takings, "farms," from individual United States citizens than for the expropriation of petroleum property from United States nationals in the form of corporations. The word "farm" was politically popular among the electorate in the United States at this time; the word "corporation" was politically hateful.

Mexico agreed in 1938 to pay for the expropriated agrarian properties, estimated by the owners as worth a total of approximately $10,000,000, after their value had been fixed before June 1, 1939, by a mixed commission composed of one representative of each government. In cases where the commission disagreed, an umpire, to be designated by the permanent commission established by the Gondra Conciliation Convention, was to decide within two months after his intervention had been requested. Meanwhile the Mexican Government agreed to pay $1,000,000 (U. S.) in May, 1939; after that at least $1,000,000 (U. S.) on each June 30 until the awards had been paid off. In agreeing to this settlement, the Mexican Government asserted that it should not constitute a precedent "in any case, nor for any reason." That is, it agreed to adjudicate and pay the agrarian claims, nothing else.

The United States Government did not abandon the petroleum claims, but it did not press them decisively until after the Presidential elections of 1940 in the United States and in Mexico. In the United States President Roosevelt was re-elected for a third consecutive term; in Mexico a middle-of-the-road government under President Avila Camacho came into power. Meanwhile World War II had broken out and the neutrality of the United States had collapsed. A treaty between the United States and Mexico, signed April 1, 1941 (ratifications exchanged April 25, 1941), provided for the reciprocal passage, refueling, and supplying "for the duration of the present state of possible threats of armed aggression against either of them" of military airplanes and seaplanes in the territory of each party, a great advantage for the United States in communications with Panama. This testified to the cordiality existing between the two governments in the face of dangers from the Old World. On November 19, 1941, less than a month before the Japanese attack on Pearl Harbor, the Department of State announced "with deep satisfac-

---

[1] *Compensation for American-Owned Lands Expropriated in Mexico: Full Text of Official Notes, July 21, 1938, to November 12, 1938.* In English with Spanish translation. Department of State Publication 288, Inter-American Series 16.

tion" that a comprehensive agreement had been reached with the Mexican Government on various matters,[1] including the expropriated petroleum properties.

As to the expropriated petroleum properties, an exchange of notes of that date provided for a mixed commission of experts, one from each government, to determine the just compensation to be paid the American owners for their properties and rights and interests. Simultaneously with the exchange of notes the Mexican Government made a cash deposit of $9,000,000 on account of the compensation to be paid to the affected American companies. If the American and Mexican experts agreed on the amount to be paid, they were to render a joint report to their two governments within five months. They promptly agreed. Their joint report, April 17, 1942, stated:

Expropriation, and the exercise of the right of eminent domain, under the respective constitutions and laws of Mexico and the United States, are a recognized feature of the sovereignty of all states.

Accordingly they awarded the sum of $23,995,991 (U. S.) covering all elements of tangible and intangible value.[2] They "recommended" that the balance due by the Mexican Government for the payment of the sum awarded be paid as follows: one third on July 1, 1942, and the balance in five equal annual installments, the debt to carry 3 per cent interest.

By a claims convention of the same date, November 19, 1941 (ratifications exchanged April 2, 1942), the Mexican Government agreed to pay to the United States the sum of $40,000,000 (U. S.) in full settlement of other outstanding property claims, including the hitherto unsettled general claims, and the agrarian claims on which $3,000,000 had been paid to date on claims arising between August 30, 1927, and October 7, 1940. Payments were to be made as follows: $3,000,000 on account at the exchange of ratifications of the convention (paid on April 2, 1942), the balance of $34,000,000 to be liquidated in annual payments of $2,500,000 beginning in 1942.[3]

The dangerous status of American negotiations with Japan impelled Secretary of State Cordell Hull to hasten this general settlement with Mexico.[4] Any sacrifice of just interests of the property owners was

---

[1] Multigraphed *Press Release* No. 555 (November 19, 1941) of the Department of State, with the text of exchange of notes of November 19, 1941, for settlement of expropriated petroleum properties.

[2] Department of State *Press Release,* No. 165 (April 18, 1942).

[3] The eighth installment was regularly paid in November, 1949.

[4] *Memoirs of Cordell Hull,* 2 vols. (New York, 1948), p. 1141.

therefore for the benefit of the United States and its people at large.

Coincidentally the two Governments announced their decision to negotiate a reciprocal trade agreement; the United States Treasury Department agreed to co-operate with the Mexican Government and Bank of Mexico to help stabilize the *peso* by purchases with dollars, and announced its "willingness" to purchase newly mined Mexican silver on a basis similar to that under which purchases were made prior to 1938. Finally, the official Export-Import Bank of the United States opened a credit to the Mexican Government by purchase of "certain" highway bonds of the Mexican Government as a means of expediting construction work in Mexico which incidentally would advance toward ultimate completion the projected Inter-American Highway. The official bank took up these bonds which no privately owned bank would think of buying, after Mexico's wholesale repudiation of her obligations. The Export-Import Bank even announced its readiness to consider sympathetically other requests for credits, to be guaranteed by the Mexican Government, for development in Mexico.

Such was the design for Mexican-American harmony at the end of 1941. After Pearl Harbor, Mexico established a joint defense commission with the United States, and declared war on Germany, Japan and Italy in the darkest days of the Second World War, June 1, 1942. Mexico welcomed the declaration known as the Act of Chapultepec for reciprocal assistance and American solidarity during the war, signed in her capital (March 6, 1945), and was one of the first to ratify the inter-American treaty, the Pact of Rio de Janeiro (September 2, 1947), for the future defense of the Western Hemisphere.[1]

During the Second World War Mexico experienced the golden flood of lend-lease ($38,639,450.63 to Mexico out of $491,456,432.64 to all Latin America during hostilities)[2] and the rising tide of inflation that bathed all Latin America, and greatly profited from the prodigious purchases of belligerent requirements. The United States Government extended loans on easy terms to Mexico, through the Export-Import Bank totaling $18,900,000 for the development of Mexican resources and to ease adjustments to war economy; and since the war a total of $73,000,000[3] plus post-V–J Day lend-lease of $600,000 and outright gifts: $7,500,000 "grants-in-aid" from the United States Office of Inter-American Affairs

[1] See below, Ch. XXXIX.

[2] *Twenty-fifth Report to Congress on Lend-Lease Operations* (State Department Publication 3064, Washington, 1948).

[3] To end of fiscal year, June 1, 1948. See *Fuel Investigation, Mexican Petroleum*, 80th Cong. H. Rept. 2470 (Washington, G.P.O., 1949), p. 86.

during the War, and \$4,800,000 since—for food supply, health and sanitation, and education; and \$45,000,000 (to April 1, 1949) to help stamp out the hoof-and-mouth disease (Mexico contributed about \$2,000,000) before it spread to American herds north of the border. These government loans and gifts poured forth lavishly to the neighbor south of the Rio Grande whose defaults on her foreign debt to private American citizens and corporations and wholesale expropriations (with meager compensation) of their private property trapped in Mexico, had made it difficult for that Republic any more to borrow in the money markets of the world. Such is the new "dollar diplomacy"!

Mexico successfully negotiated a water-treaty (signed February 3, 1944, ratifications exchanged November 18, 1945) securing an equitable share, to say the least, of water flowing down from the United States in international rivers (Rio Grande, Colorado, Tiajuana) to water the arid regions of her northern states. This important treaty, supplementing earlier conventions of 1889 and 1905, placed the common waterways and waterworks under the regulation and administration of an International Boundary Commission, United States and Mexico, but without any independent arbitral function.

At the mid-century mark no serious issue existed between the United States and Mexico. The only dispute remaining unsettled was the long-standing legal question of sovereignty over the Chamizal area left uncertain by the meandering of the Rio Grande River.[1] By ratifying the United Nations Charter and the International Court of Justice both nations have bound themselves, along with the obligations of the inter-American peace pacts, to the peaceful settlement of their disputes, including international adjudication of all legal questions.[2]

---

[1] Involving a tract of 600 acres of land near El Paso, Texas, left in dispute by the sudden shift of the Rio Grande boundary river. The United States refused to accept an arbitral award of 1910 which "split the difference" instead of awarding the whole tract to Mexico or to the United States, as required by the Arbitration Treaty.

[2] Both the United States and Mexico have accepted as compulsory ipso facto the obligation to submit any legal question to the decision of the International Court of Justice, but both have reserved therefrom any dispute which in their opinion involve questions of domestic jurisdiction.

CHAPTER XXXI

AFRICA AND EUROPE

(1884-1914)

In the period of the twentieth century, before 1914, American foreign policy tended to follow the geographical distinctions emphasized by Captain Mahan: predominance in the Caribbean and its periphery; "co-operation," that is, participation in the politics of the Far East; abstention from European political questions. Excluding non-American and non-Asiatic questions, one is impressed by the routine character of American diplomatic contacts with the European countries. As long as the question of neutral rights remained asleep the United States could keep profitably aloof from all European politics and generally did so. Aside from those affairs of the Pacific and the Far East, and of Latin America, described in the previous four chapters—and with the one exception of Morocco and the Algeciras Conference, 1905-1906—the diplomacy of the United States in Europe was limited to the maintenance of friendly commercial and cultural contact, the technical problems of citizenship and immigration,[1] and participation in multilateral international conferences of a humanitarian rather than a political nature.

This type of international conference came into existence during the last half of the nineteenth century. The growing complexity of civilization rapidly increased their number until now there is some sort of international gathering at work almost any day of the year. The United States began the practice of attending such conferences in 1875, when it signed and ratified an international convention for regulation of weights and measures. In 1882 it formally adhered to the Geneva Convention of 1864 for bettering the condition of the wounded in time of war. The Senate between 1883 and 1898 ratified five multilateral treaties signed in European international conferences by representatives of the United States: they dealt with protection of industrial property, submarine cables, exchange of official publications, repression of the African slave trade, and the publication of customs tariffs. After the Spanish-American War these contacts and engagements multiplied. We have already noticed the two Hague Conferences and the London Naval

[1] See above, p. 158.

571

Conference of 1909; a long series of Pan-American conferences will receive attention in another chapter. There was a great increase in non-political conferences in the period 1898-1914, sixteen in all, producing treaties signed and ratified by the United States, a multifarious nexus: sanitation, traffic in white women, hospitals, institute of agriculture, amelioration of wounded in the field in time of war, public health, importation of spirituous liquor into Africa, pharmacopoeial formulas. The First World War interrupted the program; since then these gatherings have taken place very largely under the auspices of the League of Nations, with the United States sitting in *ad hoc,* and the United Nations, with the United States an active, leading member. These conferences were non-political. The unnecessary contact of the United States with opposing systems of European political alliances came through its Far Eastern diplomacy and its touch with the Moroccan Question.

Mention of Morocco brings up the subject of Africa. The American people had manifested a passive interest, mostly of a humanitarian and scientific nature, in the opening of that continent to civilization and commerce, but had assumed no political responsibility in the European partitions of its vast domains and had engaged in no participation in the imperialistic rivalries of the powers for dominion there.

The origin of American interest in Africa was the establishment by the American Colonization Society, with the assistance of the United States navy, of a colony of freed Negroes in Liberia, on the coast of Guinea in 1821. All told about 15,000 Negroes were transported thither by 1870. This is the only overseas colony which the United States ever has begotten. It continued to be a receiving station for free American Negro immigrants sent out by the Society and of captured Africans who had been liberated from condemned slavers by the United States courts. Theoretically the Colonization Society and the United States Government had distinct functions, the one tutelary, the other mildly protective, but actually agents of each worked together and frequently were one and the same person. The colonial government occupied an anomalous position in Africa; it was not itself a sovereign state nor would the United States assume a formal protectorate over it. It continued to be a convenient distant dumping-place for American free Negroes and liberated Africans. European authorities in adjacent areas, like the British in Sierra Leone, would not respect the colonial officials; to secure a more regular place in the society of nations a republic declared itself in Liberia in 1847, and was recognized as such soon afterward by the principal European states but not by the United States, its parent. Though the United States expressed "sympathy and solicitude" for Liberia, the slavery question in American politics prevented any recognition of Negro republics until 1862 after the southern states had seceded from the Union; then diplomatic relations were established with Liberia, as with Haiti (1864), and the Dominican Republic (1866).

American Negro emigration to that African shore slackened with the passing of the sailing ship. The "scramble for Africa" in 1884 made the rival powers cast covetous eyes on Liberia. Though they at least respected its independence, Great Britain from the west and France from the east and north picked boundary disputes, and by settling them through aggressive diplomacy successively cut down the area of the black republic into a small coastal enclave. If the United States had unwisely desired to plunge into the scramble for Africa, a Liberian protectorate—eagerly solicited—would have offered a jumping-off place.

Though no protectorate was ever admitted to exist, the United States repeatedly has manifested a benevolent and active interest in the perpetuation of Liberian independence. In 1880 the Department of State was disposed to maintain that "peculiar relations" existed between Liberia and the United States, which was "prepared to take every proper step to maintain them"; and Secretary Hay declared in 1899, that "our position in reference to the citizens of Liberia is such that we could not be justified in regarding with indifference any attempt to oppress them or deprive them of their independence." [1] When Germany threatened to interfere in Liberia, Hay stated the "grave concern" which the United States would have at any threat to the liberty or the independence of the African republic. He was also prepared, in the same year, 1899, to say the same to France, if possible to say it in co-operation with Great Britain; and he endeavored to prevent the granting by Liberia of any monopolistic concessions to foreign powers.[2] But at no time would the United States acknowledge legitimate paternity of this foundling which it had left on Africa's doorstep.

The Liberian Government, fearful of its remaining territory being absorbed by Great Britain and France, in 1908 sent a commission to the United States to seek a treaty which would guarantee the independence and territorial integrity of the republic. Incompetent policing and management of finances were inviting foreign intervention. President Roosevelt dispatched a commission of investigation. It recom-

[1] Moore, *Digest, op. cit.*, V, 762-768.
[2] Dennis, *Adventures, op. cit.*, 437-441.

mended [1] a protectorate similar to that previously established over the Dominican Republic, and over Haiti. With proper prudence, the United States declined a protectorate; with the rueful exception of the Philippine Islands, American imperialism had not yet ventured, even for philanthropic purposes, into regions in which the Republic has no vital interests and which it could not defend, whether in Liberia or Turkish Armenia.[2] Instead the United States co-operated with an international commission which helped to straighten out the financial affairs of Liberia and to strengthen her internal condition, with an American citizen as financial adviser. The fact that Liberia has been able to claim the United States as a god-parent, and that the United States has appealed to the world to lend a friendly sympathy to that infirm and dubious little state, undoubtedly helped to sustain its shaky independence.

Serious charges of slave traffic in native Negroes within Liberia (founded by liberated slaves!) within recent years have supported impressive arguments for European intervention.[3]

Southeastwardly from Liberia, around the bight of Guinea, lie the vast regions of equatorial Africa, drained to the westward by the mighty river Congo. An Anglo-American journalist-explorer, H. M. Stanley, who in 1870 set out under the auspices of the New York *Herald* to the relief of the celebrated English missionary-explorer, David Livingstone, had been the first person to make known to the world (1874-1878) the true nature of the Congo Basin. At that time most of the "dark continent"

[1] Roland P. Falkner, chairman of the commission, wrote an informative summary of the relations of "The United States and Liberia," *Am. Jour. International Law,* IV (1910), 529-545. The commission's report is in Senate Doc. 457, 61st Cong., 2d Session, March 25, 1910.

[2] The shocking and widespread massacre of thousands of Armenian men, women, and children by the Turks, in 1894 and 1895, elicited expansive sympathy in the United States and Great Britain, coupled with demands from humanitarian groups and leaders to intervene. Secretary Olney, speaking for the Cleveland Administration in answer to a British request whether it would join in any action with regard to Turkey, said that "if England should now seriously set about putting the Armenian charnel-house in order, there can be little doubt that the United States would consider the moment opportune for vigorous exertion on behalf of American citizens and interests in Turkey . . . its attitude would morally and materially strengthen the hands of England." (Dennis, *Adventures,* 450). This was too vague an assurance to engage Great Britain in intervention. The Cuban crisis soon crowded Armenia out of American attention, and the Boer War and succeeding international complications monopolized British concern. As the prospect of intervention disappeared the revolutionary plottings of the Armenians subsided and the bloody Turkish reprisals abated.

American diplomacy was active from 1900 to 1914 in securing equal rights and treatment among foreigners, for missionaries, schools, traveling nationals in the Ottoman Empire, the collection of small claims, and the protection of neutral interests during the Balkan Wars, but wisely steered clear of any political commitments in the Near East

[3] See note at end of chapter.

was still unpartitioned—only four European powers claimed any dominion: Great Britain in the Cape Colony region, and on the west coast at Gambia, Sierra Leone, the Gold Coast and Lagos—old coastal stations for the abolished maritime slave trade; France in Algeria, and on the west coast at the Senegal and Gabon rivers, also old slaving coasts; Spain opposite Gibraltar, with bits of shore along the west coast of Morocco, and trading stations along the Gold Coast; and Portugal, at Angola and Mozambique as well as her ineffective claims from the Congo River south along the Atlantic shoreline shadowing away from old trading posts on that coast. The remainder of Africa had remained unclaimed by any power. Not until 1881 did France take Tunis, and, 1882, did Great Britain occupy Egypt.

King Leopold II of Belgium saw in the newly discovered regions of the Congo an opportunity for building up a great personal fortune and ultimately a colonial empire for Belgium. Capitalizing the world-wide interest aroused by the exploits of Livingstone and Stanley he organized the International African Association in 1876 with branches in all the principal countries of Europe and America, to discuss ways and means of opening equatorial Africa to civilization. Out of this quickly developed the International Association of the Congo. The Association engaged explorers, among them Stanley, to establish a line of stations to help open the country, to assist in abolishing the slave trade, and to make treaties with the native chieftains. The treaties placed the natives under the patronage and protection of the Association, but jurists debated its power to assume sovereignty without some sort of international mandate or agreement. Stimulated by these activities Portugal, Great Britain and France [1] began advancing claims from the borders of the Congo Basin toward the river.

The territorial claims of the organization were facing extinction when (April 22, 1884), the United States Government recognized the flag of the Association as "that of a friendly Government," and negotiated a treaty of friendship and commerce. The preservation of the Association offered the least possibility of discrimination against American trade.[2] France and Germany followed suit. We are now in a feverish and decisive year in the history of Africa. Germany, viewing the vacant places of the earth as about to pass under sovereignty of one or another

---

[1] The French Committee of the International African Association sent out an explorer, de Brazza, who in 1880 made treaties with chieftains not in the name of the Association, but of France. Thus France established claims to the north bank of the Congo far into the interior.

[2] Stolberg, *Deutschland u. Vereinigten Staaten, op. cit.*, 223-231.

power, had suddenly become a competitor for colonial empire, and thus precipitated the European scramble for Africa in which the powers quickly appropriated the remaining empty portions. Bismarck, fearing some one or more powers might lay hold of the Congo country to the exclusion of German trade, invited them (October, 1884) to a conference at Berlin to agree on the following principles: 1. Freedom of commerce in the basin and mouths of the Congo. 2. Freedom of navigation of the Congo and Niger rivers. 3. Definition of the formalities to be observed in order that new occupations on the coast of Africa might be considered effective.

By this announcement and by occupation of coastal districts in Togoland, Kamerun, and also in East Africa and Southwest Africa, did Germany proclaim to the world her determination to be considered in any partition of the remaining unappropriated parts of the continent. The powers, including the United States, accepted the invitation to the conference at Berlin. Secretary Frelinghuysen directed the United States Minister to Germany, John A. Kasson, to accept the invitation with the understanding that the discussion be strictly limited to the three heads mentioned, without assuming to decide any territorial claims, and that all arrangements reached be *ad referendum* so far as the United States was concerned. This caution was due to an unwillingness to depart from the traditional policy of non-interference in European questions; yet in the same instructions the Secretary indicated his preference for a neutralization of the Congo Basin, to be held in trust for the benefit of all peoples. Is this not the germ of the idea of international mandate for backward areas? Ironically enough, this great basin of equatorial Africa, Belgian after 1908, escaped any proposal of international mandate in 1919.

The Berlin Conference adopted a General Act which established freedom of commerce and navigation for all nations in the Congo Basin, both in time of war and of peace, outlawed the overland slave trade,[1] established freedom of religion and of proselyting for all faiths, defined freedom of navigation of the Niger River, drew up rules for *future* new coastal occupation of African territory (the coast had by now been nearly all occupied), and established an international commission (one delegate from each signatory) to execute the provisions of the Act. The commission had power to call upon warships of the signatory powers to enforce its execution, unless the commanders were instructed to the contrary, and to negotiate a loan for improvement of navigation. It is

---

[1] The maritime slave trade had long since been declared piracy.

desirable to mention this commission, even though it never came into existence because of the refusal of any of the powers to assume any

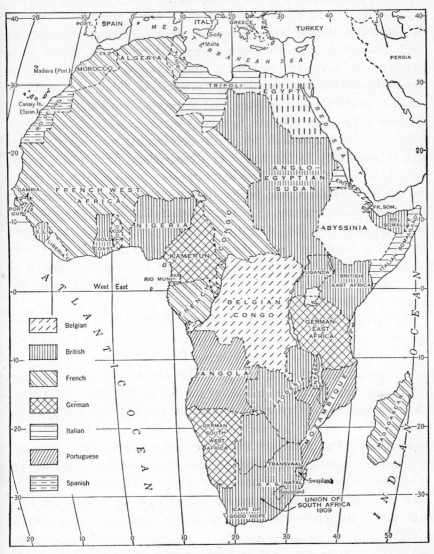

Map 30. Africa, 1914.

responsibility for guaranteeing its acts, because it displays the degree of international involvement contemplated by the Act.

The Conference ended by recognizing the International Association of the Congo as a sovereign state, thus giving it powers to exercise the rights as well as the obligations conferred on it by the Act, including that of a rather elaborately qualified neutrality.[1] Thus did an artificial new state, just welcomed by the United States, emerge full-fledged in the heart of Africa,[2] filling up a vacuum there which might have brought the powers of Europe into conflict. A series of bilateral treaties, in-cluding treaties between European powers with conflicting African terri-torial limits, fixed its frontiers. King Leopold, organizer of the Association which was now a state, proclaimed (May 29, 1885) the existence of the Congo Free State, and he became its separate sovereign, thus constituting an absolute monarchy under a personal union with Belgium, a vast appanage which the self-created monarch began to exploit, eventually to the horror of Christendom, for his own profit. Leopold devised the Congo Free State to go to Belgium after his death. As sovereign of the Congo he had become debtor for loans advanced from the Belgian treasury. The maladministration of the Congo, stimu-lating demands from the old treaty powers for another general conference, hastened reforms and also hastened annexation in 1908 after long negotiations between the two states. Europe eventually acquiesced in the transformation of Leopold's wretched political monstrosity, the Congo Free State,[3] into a Belgian colony.

The United States had never ratified the Berlin Act, as did the other powers, although it continued in treaty relations with the Congo Free State until its absorption by Belgium. President Cleveland had come into office immediately after the conclusion (February 26, 1885) of the Conference, and he refused to submit the Act to the Senate for advice. He reminded the country in his first annual message that the delegates of the United States had attended the Berlin Conference under the understanding that their part should be merely deliberative. Notwith-standing this specific reservation they had signed the Act, "thus making the United States appear, without reserve or qualification, as signatories to a joint international engagement imposing on the signers the con-servation of the territorial integrity of distant regions where we have no

[1] The signatory powers engaged themselves to respect the neutrality of the territories, and parts of territories, belonging to the various powers *in the conventional area* as long as the duties of neutrality were observed. The conventional area, in which free trade applied no matter under what sovereignty, was much larger than the Congo Basin— a belt from coast to coast approximately the width of the most extreme latitudes of the Basin.

[2] Jesse S. Reeves has carefully described the establishment of the new state in *The International Beginnings of the Congo Free State* (Johns Hopkins University Studies, 12th Series, Nos. XI-XII, Baltimore, 1894).

[3] A. B. Keith, *The Belgian Congo and the Berlin Act* (Oxford, 1919).

established interests or control." [1] Cleveland's abstention from an "alliance" to enforce the European balance of power in Africa was a well-justified caution in line with the clear-cut definitions of American foreign policy. The President refused to sanction such a departure as twenty years later was to be made by executive action in Asia after the expansionists of 1898 had entangled the United States in the European balance of power in that distant continent. When Belgium annexed the Congo in 1908 the United States was free to recognize the new régime, as it was in the case of Korea in 1910. It had assumed no such policy of preservation of the Open Door and territorial integrity as later were to become so embarrassing in China and Manchuria.

Another danger spot in Africa was Morocco. A "white man's land" nearest to Europe of any part of Africa, it was a region of small immediate but great future importance for European expansion. Only the fact that three powers had been rivals for its control had preserved the independence of that backward country under the corrupt, weak, and semi-barbarous rule of the native Sultan, "his Sherifian Majesty." Great Britain was determined not to allow any power to ensconce itself in Morocco, lest a naval base might offset Gibraltar, and for fear that foreign political control might erect discriminations against the preponderant British trading interests (two-thirds of the small Moroccan trade by 1880). The hostile incursion of turbulent Moroccan tribesmen across the unnatural Algerian frontier continually invited French intervention, and the fact that France had marked out Morocco for colonial expansion made her insistent that no other power should block her ambition in that direction. Spain also desired to keep foreign hands off Morocco: she did not care to be hemmed in by two French frontiers, north and south; she did not want Gibraltar supported by a British hinterland across the straits; she esteemed herself to have a "mission" in Morocco, by history, culture, tradition and geography destined with Portugal and Gibraltar to pass eventually under Spanish sovereignty. So the Sultan of Morocco sat on his trembling throne and still commanded with diminishing authority an independent but wretchedly misruled nation.

The sharpening of European imperialism in the late 'seventies made the *status quo* more difficult to maintain in all North Africa, from the Red Sea to the Atlantic. The rivalry of the three powers and a drift of internal affairs toward anarchy brought Morocco to the threshold of foreign intervention in 1880.

[1] J. B. Moore, *Digest, op. cit.*, I, 117-119.

We must remember constantly that the atrocious government of the country abundantly justified extraterritorial protection for foreigners sojourning there. But Morocco is an impressive example of how abuse of the rights of extraterritoriality can undermine the sovereignty and independence of a weak state on which powerful neighbors cast covetous eyes. Foreign nationals were able to take increasing numbers of natives under their extraterritorial protection. The American consul at Tangier was no exception to this, although no one accused his country of political ambitions in northwest Africa. To end the threat of this practice to Moroccan independence, British diplomacy, which favored for reasons of policy the integrity of the Sherifian Empire, and Spanish diplomacy, which supported it also during the period of Spain's recovery from the prostration of her civil wars, called the Conference of Madrid in 1880. It was proposed to reach some agreement even by the adjustment of previous treaties which would end the abuse of extraterritorial protection to native Moroccans attached in loose ways or pretenses to foreign officials or merchants. France refused to make any concessions of treaty rights sufficient to permit this. Germany, anxious to draw French national energies away from Alsace-Lorraine toward colonial adventure, supported France. Though the powers agreed to a treaty at Madrid, it was inadequate to the purpose. The abuse of protection continued. Presently France took under her protection one of the potential pretenders to the throne of Morocco. Each of the powers with interests in the country now strove not to be outdone by rivals in the number and importance of protégés. The Sultan ceased to have control over thousands of his subjects, much to their comfort and satisfaction. The Madrid Conference nevertheless had served to bring the Moroccan Question within the purview of the European concert of powers; any attempt in the future by one or two powers to upset the *status quo* in Morocco could be a cause of legitimate grievance to the other conference powers, should any of them desire to make an issue of it.[1]

The United States, which was the only non-European government (aside from that of Morocco) to participate in the conference, ratified the Convention of Madrid without reservation.[2] Since it contained merely a definition of extraterritorial protection, and no provisions for international sanction, there was a minimum of political involvement therein,

---

[1] Earl Fee Cruickshank has examined with great detail and multiarchival research the early phases of the Moroccan Question in his *Morocco at the Parting of the Ways; the Story of Native Protection to 1885* (University of Pennsylvania Press, 1935).

[2] The United States also ratified in 1865 a multilateral convention for the maintenance under Moorish sovereignty, of a lighthouse on Cape Spartel.

as contrasted with, say, the later Berlin Act of 1885 for the regulation of the Congo Basin. American political interests in Morocco were nil; commercial interests were as small as they could be. There was little likelihood of entanglement, so it would seem, in this treaty. But the fact that the United States had sat in with the European concert gave it a voice in Moroccan affairs; in a later day of world power an American President was persuaded to use this voice to speak in major European affairs.

In Theodore Roosevelt's Administration the Moroccan Question came up again, as an aftermath of the Anglo-French *entente* of 1904. In the general liquidation of colonial rivalry by which France and Great Britain drew together in the face of rising German power, Great Britain gave France a free hand to do whatever she wished in Morocco in return for a free hand similarly for Great Britain in Egypt. By secret articles Great Britain agreed to a partition of Morocco between France and Spain—this was in turn specified in a secret Franco-Spanish treaty which left to Spain, in any future partition, the narrow Rif strip opposite Gibraltar, most of the rest to France. By agreeing (1902) to future Italian control of Tripoli, France already had pledged Italy to the new trend of affairs in Morocco. The other treaty powers were not consulted about these arrangements. Germany had meanwhile built up an appreciable commercial interest in Morocco, and certainly had a right, as did the United States or Denmark, to be consulted in any modification of the treaty regulation of the Sherifian Empire. To the United States or Denmark it made little difference who controlled Morocco—the country in fact would be a better place to live in under the domination of almost any European power. To Germany Morocco came to be a *Machtfrage*, a question of power. To stand aside while that country was being arranged for partition would mean for Germany a loss of power and prestige in Europe. One of the putative advantages of the imperial system of government in Germany was its supposedly more effective control and conduct of foreign affairs. The Liberals in that Empire were now pointing out derisively that the diplomatists of the democratic countries, France and Great Britain, were outwitting the Wilhelmstrasse.[1] Prince von Bülow, the Chancellor, and his inherited adviser, Baron von Holstein, men who at first had reacted rather complacently to the new dispensation in Morocco, now resolved to make it a test of German power in Europe.

In her efforts to scotch the newly formed Anglo-French *entente*

[1] Alfred Vagts, *Weltpolitik, op. cit.*, II, 1841-1913, has presented the most detailed account of American-German relations during the first Moroccan crisis.

cordiale Germany succeeded in enticing the United States unprofitably into European affairs for Germany's purpose, but not, as calculated, to her ultimate advantage. Morocco afforded the opportunity. The United States was a signatory to the Madrid convention and quite recently had intervened at Tangier in a spectacular way to release one Jon Perdicaris, an alleged American citizen, from bandits. On the eve of the Republican nominating convention in the summer of 1904, the notorious Riffian bandit Raisuli had kidnaped Perdicaris and his stepson, a British subject, from their villa three miles from Tangier. The Department of State made most vigorous representations to the Sherifian Government. American and British warships were rushed to Tangier. Three or four American marines were actually landed to protect the consulate and to guard Perdicaris' home. He was released on ransom (eventually repaid by the Moorish Government, with $4,000 additional for American expenses) just as Secretary Hay was dispatching a celebrated telegram, indited after conference with the President: "We want Perdicaris alive or Raisuli dead" (but also instructing not to land marines, though this was not published). The Chicago convention roared its patriotic applause, and the press echoed. It remained for historians later to discover that Roosevelt knew when he authorized the message that the American citizenship of Perdicaris was questionable.

Doubtless the abduction for ransom of Perdicaris had been encouraged by the successful kidnaping in Turkish European territory, by Macedonian political bandits in 1901 of Miss Stone, an American missionary. With wide publicity in the following months a ransom of $65,000 was collected by public subscription in the United States from pious folk. Quite shockingly, the Department of State had allowed this to be paid to the kidnapers, and the lady was released. No government or person was held to account for the outrage.

The Perdicaris affair seemed to indicate a possible active American interest in Morocco. Furthermore, the exuberant temperament of the robust Roosevelt, who personified the appearance of the United States as a world power, and who was already busying himself in Far Eastern affairs, invited contacts. Early in 1905 the German Foreign Office, feeling irked by Liberal derision, determined to do something in Morocco. It sounded President Roosevelt whether it would not be worth while for Germany and the United States separately to take a stand against any one-sided disposition of Moroccan sovereignty, which was now being threatened by new French demands shaping toward a protectorate, demands which the Sultan was resisting by referring them to an assembly of notables. Despite the President's non-committal language, it was believed that he had given some encouragement. As we have already observed, the paralysis of Russia in Manchuria presented a favorable juncture for Germany to make an issue of the Open Door in Morocco in the spring of 1905. Somewhat against the Emperor's will, Prince von Bülow, the Chancellor, and Holstein, *die graue Eminenz* of the German Foreign Office, persuaded the Kaiser to disembark from his yacht at Tangier (March 31, 1905), and make an ostentatious official call on the Sultan. "I hope," the Kaiser declared, "that under the sovereignty of the Sultan a free Morocco will remain, open to the peaceful rivalry of all nations without monopoly or annexation, on the basis of absolute equality. The object of my visit to Tangier is to make known that I am determined to do all in my power to safeguard efficaciously the interests of Germany in Morocco, for I look upon the Sultan as an absolutely independent sovereign."

Germany thus proclaimed to the world her determination to be consulted in any settlement of the Moroccan Question. On the face of it, this was to support the Open Door, like the United States in China. Under German suggestion the Sultan called for a conference of the powers to propose reforms instead of adopting the French demands for a reorganization of his army and police by French instructors, control by France of his finances, and a treaty excluding the political influence of all other nations except France in Morocco. The French Foreign Minister, Théophile Delcassé, who had built up the *entente* with England, opposed a conference. The British Government backed him, but Delcassé could not command his own Cabinet, which feared war with Germany and knew that even if Great Britain should support France with force it would be difficult to withstand Germany on the land frontier. Accordingly, with the connivance of Germany, the French Government dropped its own Foreign Minister (June 6, 1905) to make way for compromise. This was a humiliation for France, a triumph for Germany. It was even then difficult to find a formula for a conference which if agreed upon would relieve the tension. Germany ardently desired a diplomatic victory, and was not wholly unwilling to go to war. The Kaiser appealed to Roosevelt to urge France to accept a conference and to advise Great Britain against lending military support to France. His most effective argument was that the destruction of the German navy in any war would leave Great Britain and France free to partition China, and would endanger the President's peace maneuvers between Russia and Japan. Whatever decision the President would consider the most fair and practical, the Kaiser said he would accept and support. Roosevelt told France he would not urge a Moroccan conference unless France wanted it, but strongly advised her to accept, intimating that he would support the French position in a conference. The French Government agreed and a conference was called to meet at Algeciras, in southern Spain, January 16, 1906.

As the powers prepared for the conference, the Kaiser persisted with his efforts to wean a weakened Russia away from the French alliance and to attach her to Germany. In a meeting on their yachts at Björkö (July 24, 1905) in the northern Baltic, the two Emperors signed with solemn vows under heaven a secret treaty unknown to the Czar's most intimate advisers, by which they agreed to lend each other mutual help in case either were attacked in Europe by a third power, and to ask France to be a co-signatory. This "reinsurance" treaty was to come into effect immediately upon the conclusion of peace between Russia and Japan. Though nominally defensive it was incompatible with Russia's obligations to France. The jubilant Kaiser was bitterly disappointed when Nicholas II, upon advice of his Foreign Minister, backed out of the agreement (October, 1905).[1] Had this secret treaty held, Germany would have been in a position to make radical demands at the Algeciras Conference.

The powers at Algeciras [2] presented a cleavage foreshadowing the opposing belligerents in 1914. France would have preferred a mandate for Morocco south of the Rif, but failing that wished to staff the Sultan's army and police with French, or, at least, French and Spanish officers, and to have charge of an international bank to salvage Moroccan finances; this would have turned Morocco into a French sphere of influence. Germany preferred to see several powers, including herself, put in charge of police in particular ports, thus implying a future partition; failing this, that the Sultan be free to select such foreign officers as he chose, with an evenly balanced international control of the finances.

[1] The voluminous literature on the personal negotiations between Kaiser and Czar in 1904-1905, including Herman Bernstein's publication of *The Willy-Nicky Correspondence, Being the Secret and Intimate Telegrams Exchanged Between the Kaiser and the Tsar* (New York, 1918), is thoroughly digested by Sidney B. Fay in the chapter on the Moroccan crisis of 1905 in his *The Origins of the World War* (2 Vols., New York, 1928).

[2] Eugene N. Anderson has published a detailed study of the intricate diplomacy of Morocco, *The First Moroccan Crisis, 1904-1906* (University of Chicago Press, 1930), in which he was able to utilize the correspondence published in the German and British series of diplomatic correspondence preceding the First World War, but not the French, which series was not then printed for those years.

As the greatest concession Germany would accept the officering of the Sultan's police and army with soldiers from some small minor power without political interests in Morocco, like Switzerland or Denmark. England supported the French position, but hesitated about pledging certain military support in case of war, although Sir Edward Grey, the new British Secretary for Foreign Affairs, told the German Ambassador in London (January, 1906) that "in the event of an attack upon France by Germany arising out of our Moroccan agreement, public feeling in England would be so strong that no British Government could remain neutral." Italy favored France, following her secret treaty of 1902, exchanging a free hand in Morocco for one in Tripoli. Spain in her feeble way clung to the bargain she had made with France. Austria-Hungary supported Germany. Russia could support France in word only.

At Algeciras the United States was represented by the experienced diplomatist Henry White, then Ambassador to Italy, and Samuel Gummeré, Consul-General to Morocco. White followed Roosevelt's instructions to "keep friendly with all" but "to help France get what she ought to have." In the end Roosevelt suggested a compromise which in effect the powers adopted. The Act of Algeciras, signed April 7, 1906, by the plenipotentiaries of the United States and the other powers assembled there provided: (1) recognition of the "triple principle of the sovereignty and independence of His Majesty the Sultan, the integrity of his domains, and economic liberty without any inequality"; (2) organization of the police under Spanish and French officers; (3) a state bank divided into 14 equal shares of which one share was allotted to each of the 12 signatory powers and the other two to French banks. Though France and Spain in this way became the mandatories of the conference powers, they also received a privileged position, and France more so than Spain. Germany triumphed in her insistence on a conference; France won the conference. If one could justify President Roosevelt's diplomatic interference at all, one would recognize the skill and adroitness with which he had brought the powers to a peaceful compromise. What is more, both sides were pleased with the result, in contradistinction to Portsmouth the year before. It was risky business, and the United States had nothing to gain by it. That Roosevelt prevented a European war is to be doubted; the crisis had passed when Delcassé resigned in June, 1905. The collapse of the Björkö treaty insured against a second crisis in 1906. The President derived enormous satisfaction from his perilous but successful rôle as world statesman, for which the Kaiser had really given him the cue.[1]

The Senate considered the Algeciras Convention more soberly and objectively. It prudently embodied in its resolution of advice and consent to ratification a statement and reservation that the participation of the United States in the conference and the general act "was with the sole purpose of preserving and increasing its commerce in Morocco, the protection as to life, liberty, and property of its citizens residing or traveling therein, and of aiding by its friendly offices and efforts, in removing friction and controversy which seemed to menace the peace between powers signatory with the United States to the treaty of 1880, all of which are on terms of amity with this Government; and without purpose to depart from the traditional American foreign policy which forbids participation by the United States in the settlement of political questions which are entirely European in their scope." Had the Senate realized the extent to which President Roosevelt had concerned himself with a critical and purely European question, in which the United States had no vital or even substantial interest, we may well doubt whether it would have ratified the act at all. This wise reservation relieved the United States from any responsibility in Morocco when in 1911 another crisis between France and Germany, between the Triple Alliance and the Triple Entente, again strained the peace of Europe. In great contrast to Roosevelt, President Taft kept out of the Agadir affair, which signalized the second Moroccan crisis.[2] From 1899 on the Senate cautiously has attached such a reservation to all multilateral treaties which had the slightest political implication, even Hague Conventions and the unratified Declaration of London with its code for naval warfare.

Morocco was made a French protectorate by the Franco-Spanish convention of November 27, 1912. The United States recognized it in 1914.

The repeated European crises—first Moroccan crisis of 1905-6, the first Balkan crisis of 1908, the second Moroccan crisis of 1911, the second Balkan crisis of 1913—betokened to informed observers that European diplomatists were lighting their cigarettes over an enormous powder-bin.

---

[1] Joseph Bucklin Bishop published in his *Theodore Roosevelt and His Time, op. cit.*, selected letters from Roosevelt's papers illustrating his participation in the Moroccan crisis. Dennis, *Adventures, op. cit.*, Nevins, *Henry White, Thirty Years of American Diplomacy* (New York, 1930), and Henry F. Pringle, *Theodore Roosevelt, op. cit.*, have reviewed the subject more critically with fuller information.

[2] By a convention between France and Germany, November 4, 1911, Germany yielded to France an implied protectorate *de facto* in Morocco, in return for the cession to Germany in the French Congo of two prongs of territory to bring the German Kamerun into contact with the Ubangi and Congo rivers, respectively.

Of the precarious nature of European peace the American public knew little and cared less. Only a few individuals, and these outside the general diplomatic personnel, had any imaginative penetration into the critical balance of power between the opposing European alliances, the Triple Alliance and the Triple Entente, and into the bases of this international imperialistic rivalry and fear which pointed toward war: the contest for control of the backward regions of the world and their enormous potentials for trade and the supply of raw materials for modern industry, a contest which approached a climax as the German navy pushed toward parity with Great Britain; the latent French desire for the return of Alsace-Lorraine; and the complications of nationalism in the Balkans and within the Austro-Hungarian Empire.

The mind of President Wilson, when the new Democratic Administration came into power in 1913, was occupied almost exclusively with domestic questions. His chief adviser in domestic policy and in political strategy was Colonel E. M. House, of Texas, with whom the President formed one of the strangest friendships in history. Without consultation of the Department of State, over which William Jennings Bryan now presided, House envisaged the unsteady European situation, and directly after the triumph of the Democrats in the election of 1912 he set his mind to play on it. To President Wilson he proposed a roving mission for himself to the capitals of Europe to suggest by tête-à-tête conversations with the ruling personalities some new arrangement which would tranquillize European diplomacy and stabilize peace. He had in mind, rather vaguely as to precise details, an understanding among the United States, Great Britain, Germany and France, by which Germany might be promised a greater activity in overseas regions (including South America), and in return for which she might be willing to check her naval building. He felt that this might lead to some general agreement for the peaceful development by the capitalistic powers of the economically and politically backward regions of the world, notably the tropics, and to progressive limitation of armaments and the dissipation of fear.[1] Wilson permitted the inexperienced House to undertake this unprecedented personal mission without precise instructions, and gave to it his affectionate personal blessing.[2]

---

[1] The mission is described and essential documents are printed in Professor Charles Seymour's publication of *The Intimate Papers of Colonel House* (New York, 1926-1928, 4 Vols.), I, 235-275.

[2] "In short," says Wilson's biographer, "this is the first demonstration of the working of that strange and unclear relationship which was to becloud American foreign policy and exasperate European diplomats until, in the end, a revelation of the real disparities

These were as bold ideas as even Theodore Roosevelt ever played with: bringing in discussion of South America [1] suggested sacrifices by the United States for the peace of Europe; but House felt that the peace of Europe might mean the peace of the world, and he romantically thought of his peripatetic mission as the Great Adventure. In the spring of 1914 he had conversations with the German Kaiser and then with the leaders of the British Government. They listened politely to the softly challenging Texan, because they knew he represented the President in an intimate way, and they made non-committal statements of amenity and willingness to talk to his points. In bitter post-war days these men thought back to House and his idealistic proposals and attached more significance to his ideas than they did in 1914. Whether House could have brought Germany and Great Britain to a friendly arrangement, basking in French and Russian countenance, is highly problematical, but before his suggestions had made any real headway war suddenly engulfed Europe.

NOTE ON THE PROBLEMS OF LIBERIA

An international inquiry into the slave traffic in 1930, initiated by the United States in response to discussions in the anti-slavery commission of the League of Nations, reported in essence that the attempt to establish an independent civilized Negro state in West Africa had nearly failed. Technically the inquiry was set up by the Liberian Government, with one representative of the United States, one of the League of Nations, and one of Liberia. The report is printed in Department of State, Publication 147 (Washington, G.P.O., 1931), or League of Nations official publication Nos.: C. 658. M. 272. 1930. vi.

In 1926 an American corporation, the Firestone Tire and Rubber Company, entered into a contract with the Government of Liberia for the rental of 1,000,000 acres for a rubber plantation, and (through subsidiaries) for a 7% loan, to be floated at 90, to refund Liberia's outstanding foreign indebtedness and commence a program of public works, including dock facilities, under supervision of the American financial adviser to the Liberian Government and an increased staff of expert assistants. The Great Depression, and eventual default by Liberia on the new loan cut short this program. The United States suspended formal diplomatic relations with

led to serious difficulties. On Wilson's part it seemed always to have been a relationship of faith without complete understanding, of trust without actual commitment—wholly creditable to neither, and deplorable in some of its results. But it was one of those 'necessary friendships' which throughout his life so often influenced, and sometimes warped, Wilson's clear-running judgment." Ray Stannard Baker, *Life and Letters of Woodrow Wilson* (New York, 1935), V, 50.

[1] Roosevelt had suggested to a German agent in 1903 the establishment of an independent state by Germans in Brazil, *Grosse Politik, op. cit.*, XVII, No. 5151, cited by Dennis, *Adventures, op. cit.*, 296.

Liberia, 1930-1935, and co-operated with the Council of the League of Nations in long and complicated negotiations to place the Government of Liberia under a Chief Adviser responsible ultimately to the Council, with a salvage of the outstanding Firestone investments (most of which had so far gone to pay off the older European loans) in co-operation with that capitalist. This seemed to be working toward a species of mandate for the Council over Liberia, when the plan was rejected by Liberia in 1934.

In 1935 Premier Hertzog of the South African Union made the unpopular suggestion that Liberia—as well as former German Southwest Africa—be placed under mandate to Germany in case that power should re-enter the League of Nations. It was very soon after this that the Department of State announced formal recognition of a new Liberian Government, of President **Edwin Barclay**, who agreed to a program of adjustment of the Firestone contract debts which allowed a reduction in interest charges from 7% to 5%. The devaluation of the American dollar meanwhile had already cut the principal and the interest burden 40%. Contemporary announcements foreshadowed the withdrawal of the American financial adviser.

Two eminent scholars have sharply criticized the Firestone contracts and the policy of the United States: R. L. Buell, in *New Republic*, LXXVI, 17-19 (August 16, 1933), and W. E. B. DuBois, "Liberia, The League and the United States," *Foreign Affairs*, XI (July, 1933), 682-695.

For a Liberian scholar's analysis, see N. Asikiwe, *Liberia in World Politics* (London, 1934).

More justificatory is Charles Morrow Wilson's study of the sociology and economy of *Liberia* (New York, 1947).

Located 750 miles south of Dakar, so close to the "Atlantic Narrows," opposite the easternmost bulge of Brazil, Liberia occupied an important strategic position during the Second World War. The historically friendly non-imperialistic affinity between the United States and the little African republic bore good fruit. Liberia placed herself under the protection of the United States for the duration of the war (executive agreement of March 31, 1942); became a member of the United Nations by adhering to the Declaration of January 1, 1942, and also the Atlantic Charter; enjoyed lend-lease and other assistance from the United States; declared war on Germany and Japan (January 27, 1944); and served as a valuable military base for the transport of American personnel and supplies by air and by sea to the North African, European, and Asiatic fronts (executive agreements of June 8 and December 31, 1943). President Roosevelt visited President Barclay at Monrovia on his way back from Casablanca in January, 1943, and President Barclay returned the visit as a guest at the White House in Washington in May of the same year. See Documents on *American Foreign Relations* (World Peace Foundation, 1944-1945), V, 600-604, VI, 213-214, 222; and *Dept. State Bulletin* VIII (No. 207, June 12, 1943), 515-517.

CHAPTER XXXII

NEUTRALITY AGAIN

(1914-1917)

The World War that broke out in August, 1914, was caused by the dislocation in the European international system accompanying the development of the German Empire. Amidst all the conflicting opinion about the immediate circumstances that precipitated that conflict, one thing is historically certain: the United States was the only great power completely disassociated from the controversies which led to the outbreak of the war. Neither the people of the United States nor the persons whom they had placed in governance knew very well what it was all about. This included the diplomatists, several of them literary personages, most of the others political appointees, newly installed in the principal capitals of Europe by the incoming Wilson Administration. At home, all leaders of American life were in favor of neutrality, when the President promptly proclaimed it.

President Wilson at the outset offered the good offices of his government for peace. Both groups of belligerents politely declined them. The President enjoined his countrymen to be neutral in thought and feeling as well as in outward act. To be neutral in thought and feeling proved eventually impossible even for the President himself, to say nothing of his ambassadors [1] and ministers abroad. Even before the engines of belligerent propaganda had begun to function in the United States the great majority of the people were immediately sympathetic to the "Allied," that is, to the Entente side, which contained the two great democracies of Great Britain and France. This feeling was confirmed by the tone of the American foreign press service which filtered through British channels, at least at the beginning of the war.[2] The

---

[1] Walter Hines Page, Ambassador in London, quickly developed into an avowed Anglophil and interventionist. His remarkable letters to President Wilson, supplementing his official despatches (printed in *Foreign Relations*), are interesting principally for his urging of England's cause. Burton J. Hendrick printed them in *The Life and Letters of Walter Hines Page* (3 Vols., New York, 1922-1926).

[2] Walter Millis has emphasized this in his *Road to War; America, 1914-1917* (New York, 1935), an historical study of national psychology which must be used with greatest

violation of Belgian neutrality gave to the Allied cause at the outset a potent moral instrument of propaganda, powerful because of its awful validity. As the weeks wore on, British and Allied propaganda [1]—some of it most unscrupulous—steadily reinforced American sympathies. It was difficult for Germany to reply in kind to this sort of stuff: first, because of her own conduct, but also because of limited understanding of American history, character, thought and institutions, which were historically more associated with Great Britain and France; and, later, because of American public indignation at the sabotage covertly practiced by German and Austrian authority in American munitions factories filling orders for the Allies,[2] as they had a right to do by existing international law.

Behind the neutrality of the Government there was more than a cultural attachment to the Allied cause. Loans to the Allied governments by American banks, which set in motion during the second year of the war, created an economic tie-up.

Under the leadership of J. P. Morgan and Company, purchasing

caution by the experienced reader, and which because of its captivating style is as effective a persuasion for the average reader as was the Allied propaganda which the author excoriates. Millis does not discuss for example the moral and political implications of Belgian neutrality, nor does he seek for the least validity in any of the Allied propaganda, although he suggests much validity in German counter-propaganda. This book, undocumented, reflects conspicuously the labors of research embodied in the earlier, carefully documented work, of similar tendency, by C. Hartley Grattan, *Why We Fought* (New York, 1929).

Charles Seymour, *American Diplomacy During the World War* (Johns Hopkins Press, 1934), was the first and most objective analysis of American problems of neutrality. He has further discussed disputed problems in his *American Neutrality 1914-1917* (Yale University Press, 1935). By far the best of the controversial works is Charles C. Tansill, *America Goes to War* (Boston, 1938).

[1] J. Duane Squires has described the machinery of *British Propaganda at Home and in the United States from 1914 to 1917* (Harvard University Press, 1935).

[2] It was because of their connection with this sabotage, revealed by the British secret service, that the United States requested the recall of the German military and naval *attachés,* Captains von Papen and Boy-Ed, and the Austrian Ambassador, Konstantin Dumba.

In previous wars Germany and Austria-Hungary as neutrals had allowed their subjects to export munitions and other contraband to belligerents without regard to the special circumstances of the belligerents. As the reader recalls, there is nothing in international law to prohibit this, although the belligerent may capture neutral ships taking contraband to the enemy. During the World War of 1914-1918 British sea power, as in some previous wars, prevented the Central Powers from access to American markets. They therefore requested that the United States in its neutrality maintain an attitude of "strict parity with respect to both belligerent parties." In a notable state paper directed to the Austro-Hungarian Government (August 12, 1915) Secretary of State Lansing said, in effect, that it would not be consonant with strict neutrality to change the rules while the game was in progress.

International law does not forbid a neutral to prohibit the export of munitions or other contraband; this would be a matter of policy. See below, p. 667.

agent [1] for Great Britain and France, prominent banking firms under-
wrote loans for popular subscription, in the autumn of 1915, after Secretary of the Treasury McAdoo and Secretary of State Lansing persuaded
the President to alter former Secretary Bryan's policy of officially frown-
ing on private loans to belligerent governments as inconsistent with the
spirit of neutrality.[2] During the remaining period of neutrality a total
of $1,900,000,000 in loans was extended privately in the United States
to Allied governments, compared with only $27,000,000 to Germany.[3]
American trade, because of British control of the seas, became increasingly identified with Great Britain and France, and with it the national
prosperity which early in 1914 had been declining in a serious way. This
new business included the lucrative manufacture and sale of munitions
of war. It is now known that, following technical defaults on rifle contracts, the British Government, anxious to keep up deliveries of desired
weapons, felt obliged to take over control, but not ownership, of some
leading American arms factories.[4]

These emotional, cultural and economic factors predisposed the
people of the United States in favor of Great Britain, Canada and the
other Dominions, and France and Belgium, *but not to fight for them*. As
the able German Ambassador, Count von Bernstorff, recognized, the
United States, though predisposed in favor of the Allied cause, was a
profoundly pacifistic nation and people, under a peace-loving President,
anxious to keep out of war.[5] The obvious fact is that to April 6, 1917,
the United States did not join the war, notwithstanding the exhortations of ex-President Roosevelt and other minority leaders. It went
to war in 1917 because Germany had announced a renewal of her un-

---

[1] Mr. J. P. Morgan testified that during the period of American neutrality his firm
ordered in the United States about $3,000,000,000 of materials of different sorts, receiving
therefor a commission of roughly one per cent, or $30,000,000. New York *Times,*
January 8, 1936.

[2] For this policy of disapproval of such loans and its reversal see *Foreign Relations,
1914, Supplement,* xii, 580; *1915, Supplement,* 820; and Ray Stannard Baker, *Life and
Letters of Woodrow Wilson,* V (New York, 1935), 175-177, 381-383; and particularly
the testimony before the Senate Munitions Investigation Committee, January 7-11, 1936,
as published contemporaneously in the New York *Times.*

In previous wars, notably the Russo-Japanese, neutral bankers, including German,
French, English and American, loaned to either or both belligerent governments.

[3] The figures for the Allies are computed from the estimates of foreign loans, 1914-
1919, in a letter of the Secretary of the Treasury to the President of the Senate, January
27, 1920. 66th Cong., 2d Sess. Sen. Doc. 191. The estimate of loans to Germany
is from Grattan, *op. cit.,* 159. R. W. Van Alstyne digests press comment in "Private
American Loans to the Allies, 1914-1916," *Pacific Hist. Rev.,* II (1933), 180-193.

[4] *Report* of the Senate Munitions Investigation Committee, Sen. Rept. No. 944, Part V,
74th Cong. 2d Sess., pp. 88-97, *et passim.*

[5] J. C. von Bernstorff, *My Three Years in America* (New York, 1920).

restricted submarine warfare. If it had not been for that great mistake in German policy the United States would not have intervened, despite the overwhelming sympathy for the Allies in all but German-American and Irish-American constituencies. In that case the war would have ended much differently. In any diplomatic history of the United States, therefore, the obvious fundamental for the years 1914-1917 is the intricate and unwelcome question of neutral rights, that historic question which has necessarily occupied already such a large proportion of this volume.

The erection of opposing belligerent maritime systems and their effect on the rights of neutrals, in so far as those rights were securely defined in international law, was a repetition of the great struggle between England and Napoleon: the off-shore blockade versus the continental system. To adapt himself to the twentieth-century struggle the historian need but substitute Imperial Germany and her allies for Napoleonic France and her allies, submarine warfare for the continental system. During the Napoleonic period the opposing belligerents professed to be resorting to admittedly illegal conduct against neutral shipping only because driven in desperation to retaliation and reprisal by the enemy's disregard for international law. So it was in the world wars of the twentieth century. Each mighty belligerent was eager to draw forth and to use mercilessly his most deadly weapon of war: economic strangulation and starvation. With Great Britain that weapon was the blockade, which raised at least moot points of international law. With Germany it was the unrestricted use of the submarine for the destruction on the high seas of merchant ships, enemy or neutral, coming to the British Islands, destroying them without examination or warning; this was clearly contrary to established law.

There was some delay by both Great Britain and Germany in forging and using these deadly weapons.

Great Britain had to feel her way carefully because too confirmed an opposition by the United States to interference with neutral rights might produce a general embargo and deprive the Allies of an indispensable source of raw materials and munitions, without which they could not equip armies to survive the onslaughts of Germany on the continent.[1]

[1] Sir Edward Grey, the British Secretary for Foreign Affairs, later stated this very clearly in his memoirs after the war.

"After Paris had been saved by the battle of the Marne, the Allies could do no more than hold their own against Germany; sometimes they did not even do that. Germany and Austria were self-supporting in the huge supply of munitions. The Allies soon became dependent for an adequate supply on the United States. If we quarreled with the

It is clear that in an embargo, at least on munitions of war, if neces-sary on other commodities, applied equally to all belligerents, the United States had available an unexceptionable weapon by which peaceably to force Great Britain to an observance of American definitions of inter-national law. It is also certain that an embargo would have brought an abrupt and calamitous decline of trade, as in Jeffersonian times; it would have precipitated the United States, which was sliding at the outset of the war toward an industrial depression, into a real economic tailspin which might have thrown the Democratic Party out of its seat. Such an economic catastrophe would have been calamitous, but by no means as calamitous as war. Great Britain astutely deferred her blockade measures until the developing war trade of the Allies had stayed the United States from the brink of an imminent depression and made its swelling prosperity contingent upon acquiescence, under protest, in the British maritime measures, which after all were in large degree moot.

Germany delayed her maritime system: first, because she hoped to end the war by a quick campaign on land before her great pile of mili-tary stores, man power and foodstuffs could run low; this expectation was ruined by the Battle of the Marne and the ensuing stalemate in the trenches. Secondly, her fleet of 28 sea-going submarines at the beginning of the war did not seem certainly adequate to the task of starving out England by unrestricted operations against merchant ships. Thirdly, Germany feared to some extent the effect of such measures, in the face of international law, on the United States. German councils were di-vided however on this last point. The naval advisers believed that, given the submission to British sea power, the United States could not be in a much more unfriendly position as to Germany, even in case of war. No one then dreamed that two million American troops would or could be sent to France.

The existence of this compelling weapon of the embargo has led one school of historical writers to argue that the United States could have avoided the Great War if only it had used this legitimate weapon of policy to make Great Britain conform to American interpretations of international law, that the unwillingness to use it was due to the effect which it would have had on economic conditions in the United States

United States we could not get that supply. It was better therefore to carry on the war without blockade, if need be, than to incur a break with the United States about contraband and thereby deprive the Allies of the resources necessary to carry on the war at all or with any chance of success. The object of diplomacy, therefore, was to secure the maximum of blockade that could be enforced without a rupture with the United States." *Twenty-five Years, 1892-1916* (2 Vols., New York, 1925), II, 107.

and consequently upon the fate of the Democratic Party.[1] This thesis assumes that if Great Britain had conformed, Germany, deprived of pretexts for retaliation, would have conformed too, there would have been no unrestricted submarine warfare on merchant ships, and American neutral rights would have been safe. The argument is very plausible; for one thing it is based on the correct assumption that it was the issue of submarine warfare which finally brought the United States into the war. But it assumes further that Germany would not have found some other pretext for unrestricted submarine warfare, or that she would not have resorted to it anyway without pretext, as she violated Belgian neutrality, on the principle that self-preservation knows no law. Nevertheless there is no question but that the Wilson Administration willfully refused to raise up this effective weapon of an embargo on all shipments of munitions to belligerents, a weapon so feared by British diplomacy.[2] The historian must be very suspicious of political motives for not using an embargo at the outset of the controversy over neutral rights.

With these fundamental factors in mind we may now turn to the development of the opposing maritime systems of the belligerents and the relation of the neutral United States thereto.

International maritime law was to a large degree in an uncertain state when war broke out in 1914, even as it is now. There had been no great maritime war for a hundred years. The important developments in law had been the Declaration of Paris of 1856 (following the Crimean War) and the accepted Civil War practice of the United States. The Declaration of Paris, we remember, had stated in 1856 that: "Blockades, in order to be binding, must be effective; that is to say, maintained by a force sufficient really to prevent access to the coast of the enemy." It did not say precisely where the ships must be stationed. Since 1856

---

[1] The leader of this school was the late Joseph V. Fuller. This serious scholar died before his thesis could be developed fully, but see his (anonymous) sketch of W. J. Bryan's diplomacy, in *Am. Secs. State*, X, 22-44; and his article, "The Genesis of the Munitions Traffic," *Jour. Mod. Hist.*, VI (Sept., 1934), 280-293.

[2] An important group of Democratic members of Congress, headed by no less a person than the majority leader of the House, Claude Kitchin, and the Speaker, Champ Clark, urged the President to threaten such an embargo, and in February, 1916, Kitchin advocated an actual embargo, and believed that Congress would pass one, except for the opposition of the President; it was this same group that believed, as Secretary Bryan had urged, that the United States should warn its citizens against traveling on the armed vessels of the belligerent powers and disclaim responsibility for those who insisted on so doing.

Professor A. M. Arnett read at the Chattanooga meeting of the American Historical Association, December 27, 1935, an enlightening paper, based on Kitchin's personal papers, on *Claude Kitchin and the Wilson War Policies* (Boston, 1937).

the powers had not been able to agree to any further definitions of blockade. The United States, however, in the Civil War invoked the doctrine of continuous voyage to extend a blockade to the interception of neutral cargoes bound to a neutral port on the first leg of a voyage *en route* to the enemy by a sequent short *maritime* leg. Great Britain had been careful to make no objection to that step; because later she might want to do the same,[1] and take another step in addition: that is, to stop neutral cargoes continuously *en route* to a blockaded belligerent where the second leg of the voyage lay *overland* via contiguous neutral countries.

In addition to the definition of blockade in the Declaration of Paris, one recalls that it protected neutral property on enemy ships as well as enemy property on neutral ships (free ships free goods) except contraband of war. But what was contraband? There was no universal agreement on that. The spreading relationship to the conduct of war of previously innocent articles made contraband much more difficult to define in the twentieth century than a hundred years before.

Attempts at the Hague Conferences of 1899 and 1907 and at the London Naval Conference of 1909 to codify rules for maritime and for land warfare had met with meager success because of failure of complete ratification.

The Senate of the United States advised and consented to ratification of the Declaration of London which among other things validated, in effect, the American Civil War practice as to continuous voyage; but protected neutral commerce in conditional contraband when bound to neutral countries. The German Government embodied it intact in its prize law. It was favorable to German strategy because it protected such a large degree of neutral trade; and in a future maritime war Germany could draw on adjacent neutrals for supplies. In Great Britain the House of Lords blocked ratification for the same reason which impelled the German Admiralty to accept it: it was too favorable to neutral commerce. When Great Britain rejected the Declaration, the President of the United States withheld final ratification. So did the other governments. So the Declaration of London, *qua* Declaration, never became international law, although most of its articles represented a consensus of international juridical opinion on the existing law of the sea, together with some innovations as to precise classification of contraband and a revised definition of blockade.

What was "existing law"? In view of the lack of explicit agreements

---

[1] See above, p. 276

by the nations, this was difficult to state with all security. According to a recent and careful study of this question, an international lawyer might advise a neutral client in regard to maritime law in war in 1914, as follows:

1. "Paper" blockades are illegal. A blockade to be binding must be effectively maintained by an "adequate" naval force.
2. Even enemy goods are safe on a neutral ship, *if* they are not contraband and *if* they are not destined for a blockaded port: "Free ships make free goods."
3. Neutral goods are safe even on an enemy ship, *if* they are not contraband and *if* they are not destined for a blockaded port.
4. *A fortiori,* neutral goods are safe on a neutral ship *but* only if they are not contraband and if they are not destined for a blockaded port.
5. Contraband goods are divided into two categories: absolute and conditional.
6. Absolute contraband consists of goods exclusively used for war and destined for an enemy country, even if passing through a neutral country en route; the rule of "continuous voyage" applies.
7. Conditional contraband consists of goods which may have a peaceful use but which are also susceptible of use in war and which are destined for the armed forces or a government department of a belligerent state; the rule of "continuous voyage" does not apply.[1]

Immediately the war began Great Britain declared that Germany was violating international law by planting mines "of the prohibited class" in the open waters of the North Sea, and doing it with cruisers disguised with neutral flags. Having stated this, the British Government reserved full freedom to take retaliatory measures. Germany denied that she had been laying mines illegally, and pointed out that the Hague Convention on mines was not binding because not ratified by all belligerents.

Here is the starting point for retaliation from which the opposing belligerents so eagerly reached for their deadliest weapons. Belligerent use of the neutral flag had always been a legitimate *ruse de guerre*—as the British Government was soon to argue to the United States on another issue; but who can now tell or could then tell whether the mines were "legitimate" or not? In acknowledging this notice the United States tolerantly stated that hostile measures on the high seas should not increase the hazards of neutral shipping, "so far as the exigencies of the war permit." Encouraged by this non-committal response, the British Government notified (October 2, 1914) the neutral world of

[1] Philip C. Jessup, in Preface to Vol. III, *The World War Period,* by Edgar Turlington, of *Neutrality, Its History, Economics and Law* (Columbia University Press, 1936, 4 Vols.).

retaliatory measures: in consequence of the German policy of mine laying, combined with their submarine activities, the British navy would
now itself take counter-measures and lay mines in "designated areas" or
"zones," through which it would be dangerous for neutrals to pass. Subsequently (November 3, 1914) Great Britain declared the whole of the
North Sea to be a "military area" into which neutrals would go at
their own risk except in accordance with Admiralty instructions. The
risk, of course, was from mine fields.

There was no settled international law of "military areas" on the high
seas. The United States did not protest:[1] but in 1917—after its rupture with Germany over unrestricted submarine warfare—it made a
statement reserving "all its rights in the premises."[2]

Uncommitted to the Declaration of London, Great Britain and her
allies proceeded in 1914 and after to define contraband to suit themselves, being cautious at first not to include even as conditional[3] contraband commodities like cotton and tobacco, resin and turpentine
which might antagonize too large a section of American opinion and
thereby possibly raise in the Congress of the United States the menace
of an embargo. Foodstuffs were treated from the beginning as conditional contraband and after the German Government extended its con-

[1] "You may inform the Minister for Foreign Affairs that this Government does not
see its way at the present time to joining other governments in protesting to the British
Government against their announcement that ships entering the North Sea after November 5 do so at their own peril." Secretary of State W. J. Bryan to United States
Minister in Norway, November 10, 1914. *Foreign Relations, Supplement, 1914,* 466.

"As the question of appropriating certain portions of the high seas for military operations, to the exclusion of the use of the hostile area as a common highway of commerce, has not become a settled principle of international law assented to by the
family of nations, it will be recognized that the Government of the United States must,
and hereby does, for the protection of American interest, reserve generally all of its
rights in the premises, including the right not only to question the validity of these
measures, but to present demands and claims in relation to any American interests
which may be unlawfully affected, directly or indirectly, by virtue of the enforcement
of these measures." Secretary Lansing to the British Ambassador, February 19, 1917.
Ibid., 1917, Supplement I, 519.

The voluminous correspondence with foreign governments, belligerent and neutral, in
regard to neutral rights, is fully printed in the Supplements to this official series, for
1914, 1915, 1916, 1917.

[2] American participation later as a belligerent in laying the anti-submarine mine barrage across the northern entrance to the North Sea stultified the earlier caveat to Great
Britain on this score. On some other questions of neutral rights—blockade measures,
diversion for search, mails, etc., the United States carefully refrained from any belligerent
conduct which would be irreconcilable with its earlier neutral protests to Great Britain.
American belligerent definitions of contraband were very sweeping. Savage, *op. cit.,*
II, 151.

[3] A customary definition of contraband, in the unratified Declaration of London,
which comprised articles that were used generally by civilian populations as well as by
armies; only where destined for army use were such to be treated as contraband.

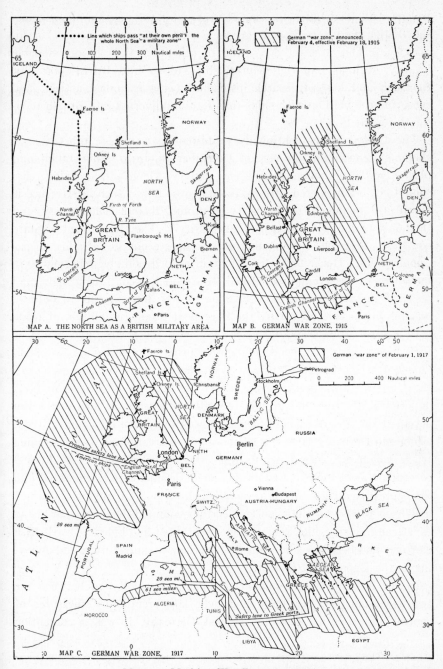

Map 31. Maritime War Zones, 1914-1917.

trol over all foodstuffs (January 26, 1915) for the purpose of rationing, the British navy seized such cargoes bound to Germany directly or indirectly.[1] The Admiralty resorted to other practices of questionable legality, such as requiring neutral ships to go into British ports for thorough and leisurely search instead of being examined at sea; and censoring the mail on such ships thus forcibly diverted into British territorial jurisdiction.[2]

The United States continually protested against these practices. A classic statement was the note of December 26, 1914. This stated complacently: "The commerce between countries which are not belligerents should not be interfered with by those at war unless such interference is manifestly an imperative necessity to protect their national safety, and then only to the extent that it is a necessity." The Department of State contended that the objectionable practices were not so necessary to national safety. Henceforth Great Britain argued politely that they were indeed so necessary, and continued to extend her contraband lists, and resorted to other practices, obnoxious indeed, but difficult to outlaw: placing on the neutral carrier the burden of proof, prohibition of trade with neutral firms suspected of trading with the enemy, and denial of fuel to ships carrying goods of neutral firms enumerated on a British "black list," suspected of trading with the enemy. In these exchanges the United States, in effect, challenged the legality of British practice and reserved claims for adjudication after the war. It also informally accepted the British arrangements agreed to by neutral countries contiguous to Germany or to the Baltic Sea: the creation of private trading trusts which guaranteed not to allow the re-exportation of conditional contraband, which Great Britain thereupon permitted to be imported into the neutral countries. In return Great Britain relaxed an embargo which had been placed on the export of certain commodities indispensable to American industry, like wool, manganese, rubber and hides. This British embargo had been most injurious to American manufacturers, and annoying to the Department of State.

In the arguments and counter-arguments that followed between the two governments, over these and over later retaliatory measures of control and eventual blockade against Germany, it was a contention

[1] The seizure of foodstuffs went into effect for ships leaving home ports after January 26, 1915. These regulations were swallowed up by the more inclusive blockade measures of the "effective cordon," which went into effect March 11, 1915.

[2] Edgar Turlington has described in great detail these and other devices, and their effect on neutrals, in Volume III, *The World War Period* (Columbia University Press, 1936) of the series *Neutrality, Its History, Economics and Law*.

of the United States that such practices had not only the effect of restraining neutral commerce with the enemy but also of delivering that commerce over to British firms who shipped it to the enemy by neutral routings. That Great Britain was to some measure guilty of the old abuses of the Napoleonic wars, the use of war and sea power to destroy neutral commerce for commercial profit instead of employing the navy solely for purposes of war, legitimate or illegitimate, has been emphasized by British writers since the war.[1]

These earlier disputations over neutral rights with Great Britain resemble the preliminary controversies between President Jefferson and the British Government, before the announcement of the Berlin Decree by which Napoleon without a navy declared the British Islands in a state of blockade and prohibited neutral commerce with them. As in Napoleonic times, the earlier belligerent practice now soon was overshadowed by the extraordinary range of sweeping retaliatory measures on both sides.

Germany, having decided that her small[2] submarine flotilla—then 27 in number—was sufficient at least greatly to harass England's importations, announced on her part (February 4, 1915) a retaliatory war zone around the British Islands into which neutral shipping would enter at its own peril because of the impossibility always of identifying it given the British practice of disguising belligerent ships with neutral flags.[3] The pretext for retaliation was the British war zones and the British practice in regard to contraband, particularly foodstuffs, both moot points in law. It was now the avowed intention of Germany to torpedo merchant ships making for ports of the British Islands, without stopping them for examination to see whether they were really belligerent or neutral. This presented not a possibly moot point, but an unquestionable violation of international law.

Age-long practice of surface navigation had confirmed the right of visit and search precisely to verify, no matter what flag it had been flying, that the accosted ship was really a belligerent and not a neutral vessel, and also to make sure that the examining cruiser provided for the safety of the crew and passengers and the ship's papers, in case

---

[1] For example, Montagu Consett, *The Triumph of Unarmed Forces (1914-1918)* (London, 1923).

[2] Complete statistics are given by Andreas Michelsen, *Der U-Bootskrieg, 1914-1918* (Leipzig, 1925), on which I have relied for numbers of submarines at various epochs. Only one-third of the U-boats could be kept continually in the cruising waters.

[3] Great Britain ordered the use of neutral flags as a *ruse de guerre,* when necessary to protect merchant shipping (January 31, 1915). The *Lusitania* hoisted the Stars and Stripes as it neared the English coast, February 5, 1915.

destruction were justified. Only in case Germany could win the war could she force recognition of her new and deadly practice, deadly to neutrals on the common high seas as well as to the enemy in his own domain. She had resolved to try that chance, convinced that the unrestricted use of the submarine would help her win the war, persuaded that the United States would interpose no fatal objection.

To the German announcement the United States quickly and fatefully replied (February 10, 1915) that it would hold Germany to "strict accountability" for any American lives or property thus injured or destroyed. What did this "strict accountability" mean? Immediate coercion, or accountability later on in dollars and cents, by some adjudication? President Wilson, who edited the note, had not decided what the phrase did mean.

Germany's announcement of a submarine war zone gave Great Britain and her allies the ideal pretext for retaliation with their deadliest weapon, the long-range "blockade," effective under modern naval propulsion, and, as the British Government stated, operable without risk to neutral ships or neutral life. The Allies announced that they would "hold themselves free to detain and take into port ships carrying goods of presumed enemy destination, ownership, or origin. It is not intended to confiscate such vessels or cargoes unless they would otherwise be liable to condemnation." [1] The formal announcement eschewed the word blockade; later descriptions referred to it as an "effective cordon"; but even official correspondence soon lapsed into usage of "blockade." The British made no effort to justify the new procedure by law, except through the right of retaliation, a retaliation humane to neutrals, destructive to the enemy. In Paris, Winston Churchill, First Lord of the British Admiralty, declared in an interview: "Germany is like a man throttled with a heavy gag. You know the effect of such a gag. . . . The effort wears out the heart, and Germany knows it. This pressure shall not be relaxed until she gives in unconditionally." [2] It was not.

The new practice, elaborated by successive orders-in-council, was converted into a real blockade, in effect if not in name, in February, 1917, after the United States and Germany had ruptured relations. Great Britain then frankly returned to her practice of a century before: prohibition under pain of confiscation of ship and cargo of all trade to enemy destination, or carriage of enemy property, unless with British or allied license, or unless the neutral ship had voluntarily stopped at a British

[1] Carried into effect by the order-in-council of March 11, 1915.
[2] New York *Times*, February 3, 1915.

or allied port for examination.[1] But the British Government no longer sold licenses for revenue, as in Napoleonic days.

To the neutral and innocent United States these rival retaliations meant the facing of grave issues, graver with Germany than with Great Britain. The Department of State endeavored to avoid them by good offices, suggesting to the opposing belligerents a *modus vivendi* which would bring them back to general principles of international law, somewhat improved: that Germany give up mine laying and submarine attacks on merchant vessels in return for British restriction of the use of neutral flags and permission of neutral transport of foodstuffs, subject to safeguards under American supervision to guarantee *bona fide* destination to only civilian population. The real motive of the belligerents is clear from their unsatisfactory replies, in this instance, as well as in a later instance—in May following—when the proposal was repeated informally, with the added condition of German renunciation of the use of poison gas. Great Britain and her allies refused to consider such a proposal on the ground that Germany could not be trusted. Germany refused unless *raw materials* were added to foodstuffs—raw materials as defined in the German reply included materials that could enter into the equipment of armies in the field. The German replies to this sane American suggestion must puncture in the mind of every careful student the later lament against the British "hunger-blockade," which had such a strong appeal to neutral opinion.

Thus the two opposing systems assumed their ominous shapes notwithstanding the anxious desire of the United States to avoid them.

Submarine warfare, so terrifying to England, so nearly the cause of her downfall, was actually a great blessing to her, finally her salvation. By taking 223 neutral American lives on the high seas [2] (28 on American ships, one on a neutral Norwegian ship, 183 on British, one on French, and 10 on Italian belligerent merchant ships), German prac-

---

[1] The American protests at these measures denied the right of a belligerent to injure a neutral by retaliating on the illegal conduct of an enemy; and they assailed the blockade measures as illegal because they did not apply equally to all nations since they did not block Scandinavian ships from entering German Baltic ports, while preventing other neutral vessels from so doing. They also denied the application of the blockade to neutral ships bound for neutral ports (adjacent to Germany) with conditional contraband or non-contraband; in this the British were going one step ahead of the advance in continuous voyage made by the United States in its Civil War blockade. See the United States note of October 21, 1915, to Great Britain. *Foreign Relations, 1915, Supplement,* 578-602.

[2] Prof. E. M. Borchard and Mr. W. P. Lage have adjusted for me the official figures presented in Savage, *op. cit.,* II, 85, 506, by adding the Norwegian and French ships and excluding the foreigners lost on American ships. See tables in their *Neutrality for the United States* (Yale University Press, 1937).

tice softened by contrast the interference of the Allies with neutral commerce. "We looked forward," states Winston Churchill in his memorable
history of the war, writing of the effect on the United States of submarine
warfare, "to a sensible abatement of the pressure which the American
Government was putting upon us to relax our system of blockade, and we
received a whole armoury of practical arguments with which to reinforce
our side of the contention." [1] By returning finally in 1917 to unrestricted
submarine warfare, after the suspension which we are about to note,
Germany caused her own downfall, and the triumph of her enemies, by
bringing the United States into the war.

The full meaning of the new German policy first fell on the United
States with dramatic horror in the torpedoing without warning of the
great British unarmed passenger liner *Lusitania,* May 7, 1915, off the
southern coast of Ireland, with a loss of 1,198 lives, including 128
Americans, of whom 37 were women and 21 children.[2] Of 129 children
on board, of all nationalities, 94 were suffocated, including 35 babies.
The outrage raised a cry for war among a virile and vociferous minority,
which at first included the President's intimate counselor on foreign
affairs, Colonel House, then in England; but the President stayed the
clamor, and, it proved, with general popular support. In a public address
he directed to the crisis with Germany the idealism which he had applied
so far without success to Mexico: "There is such a thing as a man being
too proud to fight. There is such a thing as a nation being so right that
it does not need to convince others by force that it is right." This was
the language of the Sermon on the Mount, to which neither Mexican
bandits would pay heed, nor European belligerents at their death grips.
Turning to the German Government the President resorted to a not
impatient diplomatic debate, in which he finally had this last but not
conclusive word:

The United States understood the German Government "to accept as
established beyond question the principle that the lives of non-combatants
can not lawfully or rightfully be put in jeopardy by the capture or destruction of an unresisting merchantman, and to recognize the obligation to
take sufficient precaution to ascertain whether a suspected merchantman is
in fact of belligerent nationality or is in fact carrying contraband of war
under a neutral flag. The Government of the United States therefore deems
it reasonable to expect that the imperial German Government will adopt the
measures necessary to put these principles into practice in respect of the

[1] *The World Crisis* (London, 1927), II, 283.
[2] For status of *Lusitania,* see note at end of chapter.

safeguarding of American lives and American ships, and asks for assurance that this will be done."

The United States elected to protect citizens traveling under a foreign belligerent flag, even on an armed merchant ship. Once this position had been assumed, of protecting American citizens against violations of international law on the high seas, even though those violations were directed against a foreign, even a foreign belligerent flag, it proved impossible to recede from when later the position was challenged by force before the world. This caused Bryan's resignation, his succession by Lansing.[1] Bryan felt that Great Britain should be held to equal accountability and that in both cases the final reckoning should be deferred. He had recommended requesting Americans to keep off belligerent ships. Lansing was an able legal technician, a subordinate by training and by temperament. Like Wilson he favored the Allied cause, but he was a political funambulator, walking the unsteady tightwire of neutrality to the end, leaving the decision to others. But he deliberately submerged in argumentative verbosity issues with Great Britain over property rights so as to leave the United States free to act if it should desire to enter the war against Germany on the side of the Allies against military autocracy.[2] From 1915 on Wilson became more and more his own Secretary of State.

Germany still hesitated. In June, 1915, she had only 40 U-boats, though she was building faster now. There was still the question in the minds of the high civilian officials and the Kaiser whether the promise of submarine warfare was worth the possibility of a break with the United States. The issue was finally presented for immediate decision when the British liner *Arabic* was torpedoed without warning, August 19, 1915, with the loss of two American citizens. Without waiting for reports from the Admiralty, the German Foreign Office assured the American Ambassador that the ship must have struck a mine because instructions had been issued (secretly, it proved, on June 5 and August 27) to naval officers not to torpedo passenger ships. "What instructions?" asked Ambassador Gerard. Finally (September 1, 4, 1915) the new Secretary of State got from the German Ambassador in Washington,

---

[1] Baker, *Wilson, op. cit.*, V, 323-360, narrates fully the issues which impelled Bryan to resign.

[2] In his *War Memoirs*, written shortly before his death in 1928 (published, New York and Indianapolis, 1935, posthumously) Lansing pictured himself as a statesman who was consistently in favor of military intervention by the United States if necessary to prevent the defeat of the Allies. In 1939, the Department of State published the voluminous *Lansing Papers* (2 Vols., Washington, G.P.O.), which show him consistently clinging to neutrality until 1917.

Count von Bernstorff, a statement that German submarines would not attack unarmed [1] "liners" which did not themselves attack German vessels nor try to escape when summoned to surrender. He disavowed the act and offered reparation.

The Central Powers played two more cards before they exhausted their hand on this trick. On November 7 the Italian passenger liner *Ancona* was torpedoed, not without warning, with a loss of American lives. Demands on Germany elicited the information that this must have been an Austrian submarine (it was really a German). American protests now belabored Austria, and obtained similar equivocal assurances. On December 30, 1915, the armed British passenger liner *Persia* was torpedoed in the Mediterranean with the loss of an American consul; this time Germany and Austria-Hungary denied any part in it; Turkey was perhaps responsible, though she denied it. Protests were inconclusive, because nobody could then identify the nationality of the guilty submarine. Nevertheless the German flotilla had suspended its unrestricted operations against unarmed passenger liners, although it formally declared (February 10, 1916) that enemy merchant vessels armed with cannon could not be considered as peaceable vessels of commerce, and after March 1 would be treated as war vessels by German submarines.

It was increasingly difficult for the President to keep his country out of war if he should insist, as he had insisted, on the right of American neutrals to travel on belligerent merchant ships on the high seas. To

[1] *Note on armed merchant ships.* At the beginning of the war the United States treated as merchant ships British merchant ships armed solely for defensive purposes against converted German raiders, and issued a circular, September 19, 1914, setting forth criteria to test the defensive character of armaments. By an informal understanding, British armed merchant ships kept out of American waters from September 19 until after the proclamation of the "retaliatory" German submarine campaign, February 4, 1915. Then Secretary Lansing believed that the changed character of the war should cause armed merchantmen to be treated as warships. With President Wilson's approval, he tried to solve the problem by submitting to Great Britain and her allies (January 8, 1916) the following *modus vivendi:* (1) Great Britain not to arm merchantmen, (2) Germany not to attack merchantmen without visit and search and provision for the safety of the crew and passengers. At the same time, *pour encourager les Anglais,* he suggested to the Central Powers that they proclaim their intention to treat all armed merchantmen as ships of war. Germany accordingly announced (February 10, 1916) that she would treat all armed merchantmen as ships of war. Great Britain rejected the *modus* on the ground that Germany could not be trusted to observe the rules. The United States did not then insist on treating the armed merchantmen as warships, as Lansing had threatened, but went back to the old policy of September 19, 1914, in a new announcement of March 25, 1916. It would appear that President Wilson reversed Lansing's démarche because it threatened to abort the House-Grey understanding (see p. 613) *Foreign Relations, Supplements, 1914, 1915, 1916,* sections "armed merchant ships," and *Lansing Papers* (Washington, 1939), I, 330-331.

forego such a right, voluntarily, out of policy, announced in time of peace in anticipation of war, as the United States later did in 1935, is one thing; but in the midst of a situation and at the point of a torpedo to accept orders to give up rights is another thing: dishonorable and pusillanimous. "Once accept a single abatement of right," wrote President Wilson to Senator Stone (February 24, 1916) "and many other humiliations would certainly follow." The stand earlier taken in the "strict accountability" note, and in the *Lusitania* case, made it now too late to abate the right claimed so solemnly.

As one looks back upon the First World War it becomes increasingly clear that it was Woodrow Wilson's *choice* of neutral policy that brought his country into war. All within the realm of neutrality, he could have claimed protection of American citizens against violations of international law directed against a foreign flag, or he could have told them originally that they must run the risks of the flag under which they traveled. Actually Woodrow Wilson thought that the United States would probably have to go in on the side of the Allies *if peace did not come in Europe*. "He said he had never been sure that we ought not to take part in the conflict and if it seemed evident that Germany and her militaristic ideas were to win, the obligation upon us was greater than ever." [1] Under this persuasion he authorized the eager Colonel House to initiate a correspondence with Sir Edward Grey, supplemented by another trip of House to Europe. This resulted in this proposal by House, as the President's personal representative, to the British Government: the United States, in previous agreement with Great Britain and the Allies, would invite the belligerents to a peace conference under American mediation, which would endeavor to secure peace terms not unfavorable to the Allies; if Germany refused to come, the United States would probably enter the war on the side of the Allies; if the conference met and failed because of the unreasonableness of Germany, the United States would [probably] join the war on the side of the Allies. President Wilson from the first had insisted on the contingent word *probably* before the proposal was finally sanctioned and sent back to London (February, 1916). Both contingencies must be probable because of the necessity for Congress to vote any declaration of war. At that very time the President was engaged in a test of control of Congress in his demand—it was to prove successful—for the defeat of the McLemore resolution forbidding the issuance of passports

[1] "One evening, in September, 1915," *Intimate Papers of Colonel House, op. cit.,* II, 84.

to American citizens traveling on [1] armed belligerent merchant ships.

Here was an opportunity for the Allies to get the United States into the war and to tap its treasure chest and man power, if Germany would not make a peace roughly conforming to the terms which the Allies had forged among themselves by secret treaties made *after* the declaration of war in 1914, and then not precisely known by the Government of the United States. The British Government did not, however, accept Wilson's offer. They were not yet ready to throw up the sponge, nor did they wish to weaken the resolution of their allies by any mention of an American mediation; besides, was it not possible that German submarine policy might soon drive the United States into war anyway? The imminence of a rupture between the United States and Germany was vividly emphasized by the torpedoing (March 24, 1916) without warning, and with heavy loss of life, of the unarmed French cross-channel passenger packet *Sussex*, and the resulting injury of several American citizens.[2] Nothing could be more flagrantly violative of German pledges to the United States. Again a series of notes between the United States and Germany. This time the United States finally demanded (April 18, 1916):

"Unless the Imperial Government should now immediately declare and effect an abandonment of its present methods of submarine warfare against passenger and freight-carrying vessels, the Government of the United States can have no choice but to sever diplomatic relations with the German Empire altogether."

There were in April, 1916, 52 U-boats, of which a relay of no more than 18 could keep cruising. The German Government, still unpersuaded that unrestricted submarine warfare would be unquestionably conclusive with the inadequate flotilla then available, temporarily capitulated, until more submarines could be launched. It promised (May 4, 1916): "In accordance with the general principles of visit and search and destruction of merchant vessels recognized by international law, such vessels, both within and without the area declared as a naval war zone, shall not be sunk without warning and without saving human lives, unless these ships attempt to escape or to offer resistance." But this treatment was to be conditional upon insistence by the United States that Great Britain "shall forthwith observe the rules of international law universally recognized before the war" and laid down by the United States itself in

---

[1] For Colonel House's conversations and letters, and the text of the House-Grey memorandum, see *Intimate Papers of Colonel House, op. cit.,* II, 166-204.

[2] No American citizen was killed.

protests to England. Again President Wilson had the last word (May 8, 1916). "Responsibility in such matters," he told Germany, "is single, not joint; absolute, not relative."

The *Sussex* suggested to the Allies that it was only a matter of time before Germany would again resort to unrestricted submarine warfare; then the final test of the great war would come, but then the United States, with its man power and treasure would probably be driven into it by Germany. The United States had failed to control the problem, first by delay, then by giving away its hand in the House-Grey memorandum. Following the Allies' rebuff, the President turned back to an inveterately neutral policy. In the campaign of 1916 he permitted his supporters to appeal successfully to the electorate on the issue "He kept us out of war"; at the same time he weakened the aggressive Republican opposition by advocating rapid military preparedness, for all contingencies; particularly did he urge that the United States navy be built up to be the most powerful on the oceans.

The House-Grey memorandum was now dead. If, without German resort to unrestricted submarine warfare, the Allies should later have faced defeat and Sir Edward Grey or his successor Arthur Balfour should have turned back in desperation to the Wilson-House proposal, we may believe it could not have been resurrected.

In the autumn of 1916 the great offensive and counter-offensive (Verdun and the Somme) of the opposing armies on the western front had reached a deadlock over a million graves, with little promise of either side being able in the near future to push through the enemy's lines. Germany held Belgium and northern France, and the Central Powers had occupied Serbia and were pushing into Roumania (occupied by December). In the eastern theater they held an advantageous line for negotiations—they did not, of course, then glimpse that the coming Russian Revolution would open up that frontier completely to them. The war map was highly favorable, but German man power and materials could no longer be securely replenished against a continuing war of attrition. The only way to victory seemed to be by immediate negotiation, or by ending the war with the unrestricted submarine. The U-boats now were 103 in number.[1] The German high staff argued by statistics that the unrestricted use of submarines then available could cut British carrying space 39% in five months, and meanwhile the terror

---

[1] The maximum of 140 was reached in October, 1917. At the end of the war they were reduced to 121, thanks to British, and (after April, 1917) American counter-offensive measures. During the war Germany lost a total of 178 submarines. Michelsen, *op. cit.* 194.

of their operations would keep neutral vessels in home ports. It was the hope for an economic paralysis of England, rather than the mere stoppage of the flow of munitions from America, that led the German Government to look again to the terror of the submarine.[1] There was of course the certainty—at least so Ambassador Bernstorff pointed out from Washington—that this would bring the United States into the war. The German Government therefore decided first to invite direct negotiations for peace; if this failed, then to lash out with unrestricted submarine warfare.

In the United States, President Wilson recognized the precarious situation after the *Sussex* correspondence. The possibility of war with Mexico also had to be reckoned with, as a result of the punitive expeditions of 1916. He had resolved if re-elected to invite the belligerents to a peace conference. Germany asked for American good offices. After election, questionable submarine incidents and German deportations of Belgian civilians caused him to pause.[2] Germany was impatiently asking for action. When the President hesitated, Germany anticipated him, and issued, through the United States, an invitation (December 12, 1916) to the enemy to open direct negotiations. The German terms, not then divulged but indicated confidentially to Washington a few weeks later, were: "Germany to give up Belgium but retaining so-called guaranties such as railroads, forts, a garrison, ports, commercial control, etc.; a slice of France through rectification of frontier; will only give back a small part of Serbia, and Bulgaria can do as she likes with Roumania and everybody must pay indemnities to Germany, etc."; colonies for Germany "adequate to her population and economic interest"; and "the freedom of the seas."[3]

Great Britain and her allies refused negotiations when Germany would not state her terms in advance. Britain's designs for peace, as embodied in a confidential memorandum of the new Foreign Secretary, Arthur Balfour, not made public until long afterwards, were:[4] "diminishing the area from which the Central Powers can draw the men and money

[1] Charles Seymour has stressed this with convincing effect, from the German sources, in his *American Neutrality, op. cit.*

[2] At least so Secretary Lansing told the German Ambassador. *War Memoirs, op. cit.*, p. 178.

[3] These terms were conveyed to the United States coincidentally with the notification of resumption of unrestricted submarine warfare. See confidential letter of Bernstorff to Colonel House, January 31, 1917, and a telegram of Gerard to the Secretary of State, February 4, 1917. *Foreign Relations, 1917, Supplement* I, 35, 37, 114.

[4] *War Memoirs of David Lloyd George* (4 Vols., Boston, 1933-34), II, 300-308. The Balfour memorandum did not discuss colonial dispositions.

required for a policy of aggression" by Balkanizing Central Europe on the principle of nationality; Alsace-Lorraine for France; Constantinople for Russia; some sort of autonomy under Russian sovereignty for a Poland to include the German and Austrian provinces; and reparations for German submarine sinkings, and the damage done in Belgium, northern France, and Serbia.

The belligerents were still far apart. Discouraged, President Wilson (December 18, 1916) suggested that they state their war aims to see if approximations might be revealed which would lead to peace discussions. Germany answered, with her allies, that she would be glad to do so but only in a peace conference. The Prime Minister of Great Britain, Lloyd George, publicly summarized the allied peace terms in the House of Commons (December 19, 1916): "complete restitution, full reparation, and effectual guarantees" for the future.[1]

It was obvious to Germany that no peace of victory by negotiation was possible at the existing stage of the war. The German Emperor, in a conference of military, naval and civil officials [2] (January 9, 1917), decided in favor of a prompt resumption of unrestricted submarine warfare on the first of February, and instructions were sent to Ambassador von Bernstorff to notify the United States accordingly but not until the last day of January. Unaware of this, and still more profoundly discouraged by the belligerents' refusal to talk peace, President Wilson, in a notable address to the Senate, January 22, 1917, lamented their recalcitrance and stated with prophetic insight, which the world could not then appreciate, that there could be no peace with victory. He still hoped he might bring them together for a compromise peace. The depleted finances of the Allies might have made them willing to reconsider, if Germany had held off her submarines.

But a few days later the thunderbolt dropped. Count von Bernstorff delivered to the Department of State the German note:

Germany will meet the illegal measures of her enemies by forcibly preventing after February 1, 1917, in a zone around Great Britain, France,

---

[1] These were set forth more in detail in the note of the French Government, January 10, 1917. See *Foreign Relations, 1917, Supplement* I, 6.

[2] The formulation of German policy, at successive epochs of the war, is revealed in the published memoirs of Admiral von Tirpitz, Chancellor von Bethmann-Hollweg, Field Marshal von Hindenburg, Generals Ludendorff and Falkenhayn, Ambassador von Bernstorff, and in the stenographic minutes of testimony in the Reports of the First and Second Subcommittees of the Committees appointed by the National Constituent Assembly to inquire into the responsibility for the war, translated into English and published by the Carnegie Endowment for International Peace: *Official German Documents Relating to the World War* (2 Vols., New York, 1923).

Italy, and in the eastern Mediterranean all navigation, that of neutrals included, from and to England and from and to France, etc., etc. All ships met within that zone will be sunk.

The Imperial Government is confident that this measure will result in a speedy termination of the war.

As a special concession to the United States, the note offered to permit one American passenger ship a week to go to and from Falmouth, England, without contraband, if marked with "3 vertical stripes 1 meter wide each to be painted alternately white and red," and the display at each masthead of "a large flag checkered white and red," fully illuminated by night.

The President immediately announced the rupture of diplomatic relations with Germany, according to the warning of the *Sussex* ultimatum. Did this mean war? To the press, to Congress, to the country at large, yes; to the President, no. He tried desperately but unsuccessfully to induce Austria-Hungary to desert Germany on promises of the integrity of that Empire. The United States even notified Great Britain (February 17, 1917) that it reserved the right to enter claims for any damages to American citizens resulting from British proclamation of war zones, concerning which the principles of international law were still "unsettled."[1] Wilson still hoped that Germany would not in fact resort to an "overt act." Such soon occurred, in a succession of sinkings, including American as well as enemy ships. The President then turned with despairing hope to "armed neutrality" including the arming of merchant ships by the Government under authority of an ancient statute of 1797.[2]

It was while the President's policy was still undecided, and while the Senate was inconclusively debating a resolution to arm American merchant ships, that the British Government made a carefully timed delivery to the Department of State (February 24, 1917) of a message which had come to the German Embassy in Washington more than a month previously over the Department of State's wires on January 17. It was a telegram from the German Minister of Foreign Affairs, Zimmermann, to the Embassy in Washington, with instructions to be sent to the German Minister in Mexico. These instructions Bernstorff had relayed promptly to Mexico City, on January 19, 1917. The telegraphic messages had been sent from the Foreign Office in Berlin in cypher

---

[1] See above, p. 598.

[2] A filibuster by Senator Robert M. LaFollette of Wisconsin, and a "little group of willful men," brought an adjournment of the Senate on March 4, 1917, without passage of a specific enabling statute; it was after this that the old law of 1797 was brought out.

through the hospitality of the American Embassy there and of the Department of State, after Bernstorff had complained of the difficulty he had in communicating confidentially with his government on the peace overtures of President Wilson. The United States, whose hospitality was thus abused against itself, had required no key to the cypher, and had not attempted to read the letters entrusted to its courtesy.[1] By a double irony, the British secret service had intercepted the diplomatic communications between the American Embassy in Berlin and the United States Government in Washington, had extracted from it the German cypher messages, and with formidable resourcefulness had decyphered them. It then turned over to the United States the results of this particular espionage of American diplomatic communications, and the United States, under the circumstances, could do nothing but return thanks. The content of the telegrams was astounding. After informing the German Minister in Mexico that Germany would resume unrestricted warfare on February 1, it instructed him, *in case the United States should not remain neutral,* to propose to Mexico an alliance with the object of reconquering the "lost territory" in Texas, New Mexico, and Arizona, an alliance to which Mexico might invite immediate Japanese adherence. Once war existed between the United States and Germany, this was certainly not an abnormal measure to propose. One may even guess that Germany may have expected that the United States would decypher it and read it, and that its contents would give pause to a decision for war.

President Wilson gave the Zimmermann note to the press on March 1. It galvanized American opinion against Germany, and against the eleven filibustering senators who were striving to prevent the arming of American merchant ships. It was the unexpected Revolution in Russia on March 12, 1917, which crystallized the American decision for war. The welcome with which the United States first greeted the Revolution is witnessed by its prompt recognition (March 22, 1917) of the provisional government as the "Government of Russia"—a promptness which contrasts with the sixteen years of delay in recognizing the Soviet Government following the second revolution in November, 1917. If the Russian Revolution had occurred three or even two months earlier, Germany, with the promise of victory and relief on the eastern front, would not have played the "last card" of unrestricted submarine warfare, the United States would not have entered the war and Germany would

---

[1] Lansing, *War Memoirs, op. cit.,* 227.

have won,[1] or there would have been a compromise peace which would have kept Germany astride the war-map. Coming just when it did, the Revolution was not only thus a decisive event in the history of the World War, and, it was to prove, in the history of the twentieth century; it also had, in this its first phase, a decisive effect on American policy at a psychological moment, particularly on President Wilson, still struggling to keep his country out of actual war. "If our entering the war," he declared, "would hasten and fix the movements in Russia and Germany it would be a marked gain to the world and would tend to give additional justification for the whole struggle."[2] It made it seem truer that the Allies were fighting the battle of democracy against autocracy, as Secretary Lansing had reiterated to the President—far-away Japan counted little at that time of forced decision on European policy.

The President now concluded that armed neutrality would not be an adequate defense of the Freedom of the Seas against the unleashed submarine. Following an insistent public opinion, he went over to the cause itself of the Allies. He appeared before a special session of Congress, April 2, 1917, and recommended that a state of war, thrust on the United States by the acts of Germany, be formally recognized. Congress responded overwhelmingly; the resolution for war passed the House of Representatives by a vote of 373-50, the Senate by a vote of 82-6, April 6, 1917. A declaration followed belatedly against Austria-Hungary, December 7, 1917, delayed in the chance that power might be moved to seek a general peace to preserve intact the territorial integrity of its empire. The United States did not declare war against the other two allies of Germany: with Turkey it severed diplomatic relations, but with Bulgaria it remained quietly in formal diplomatic relations throughout the war. Turkey and Bulgaria were more likely to drift from their moorings in Central Europe in case of the worst weather; Bulgaria, in fact, became the first to sue for peace.

[1] Churchill, op. cit., III, 212-215. "The beginning of 1917 was marked by three stupendous events: the German declaration of unlimited U-boat warfare, the intervention of the United States, and the Russian Revolution. Taken together these events constitute the second great climax of the war. The order in which they were placed was decisive. If the Russian Revolution had occurred in January instead of March, or if, alternatively, the Germans had waited to declare unlimited U-boat war until the summer, there would have been no unlimited U-boat war and consequently no intervention of the United States. If the Allies had been left to face the collapse of Russia without being sustained by the intervention of the United States, it seems certain that France could not have survived the year, and the war would have ended in a Peace by negotiation or, in other words, a German victory."

[2] David F. Houston, Eight Years with Wilson's Cabinet, 1913-1920; with a Personal Estimate of the President (2 Vols., New York, 1926), I, 244.

Germany's resumption of unrestricted submarine warfare it was which forced the United States into the World War. The chemist in his analysis adds to the test-tube one reagent after another. At last there may be a precipitation. This does not necessarily mean that it is the final reagent alone which is the precipitant. It means that, in the order of additions, precipitation followed the last addition. So it may be with the historian's analysis of American neutrality.[1] The existing combination in 1917 contained the following ingredients: the natural predisposition by cultural and political affinity of the American people for the democracies of the British Empire, and of France, deepened by Allied propaganda, much of it unscrupulous, some of it awfully valid; the economic tie-up, fostered by private loans, between American business and Allied war orders, which seized hold of American domestic politics and led the Wilson Administration to ignore the compelling diplomatic weapon of the embargo. The submarine was the last reagent necessary to precipitate war, although the reaction was not clear until after the Russian Revolution.

In his war message President Wilson baptized American intervention with the moral attributes of the Allied cause. He epitomized it all, not unjustly though history was to prove mistakenly, with the words: "The world must be made safe for democracy,"—by the crushing out of militarism and the creation of an international organization for the enforcement of world peace. To the people it became a crusade. It seemed a war to end wars. For this ideal many a gallant American was to lay down his young life on European soil.

THE LUSITANIA

The commander of the German submarine did not know what ship it was when he fired the torpedo. Only as the vessel was sinking, with her bow in the air, did he discern the name *Lusitania*.

The captain of the *Lusitania* was in possession of the general orders of the British Admiralty, to commanders of British merchant vessels, to attempt to ram submarines if they showed up off the bows "with obvious hostile intent." It has been argued, particularly by Germany, that this made it impossible for the commanders of submarines to give warning safely, or to hail for visit and search. So it did; but we must remember that (before the Admiralty orders) Germany had announced her intention to proceed against belligerent merchant ships in the war zone without warning.

Germany also laid stress on a general warning, published over the name of the German Embassy, in New York newspapers, before the sailing of the *Lusitania*, warning American citizens not to take passage on belligerent

[1] I have borrowed the figure from Charles A. Beard.

merchant vessels bound for the war zone. The answer to this is that the German Embassy had no authority to communicate with American citizens through a newspaper advertisement, nor in any other way than to the United States Government through the regular diplomatic channels. American citizens had a self-respecting and legal right to ignore statements made to them by the German Embassy through newspaper advertisements.

The existence of the 4,200 cases of cartridges and some fuses and shrapnel in the cargo of the *Lusitania* did not absolve the German authorities from the necessity of visit and search. Incidentally, these cartridges were not explosive *en masse*, and not so regarded as explosives by United States port laws for passenger ships. The ship was unarmed and carried no troops.

An extraordinary fact is that absolutely no convoy or protection was furnished for the *Lusitania* in the war zone by the British Admiralty, and that the captain ignored the general instructions of the Admiralty to proceed at full speed with a zigzag course on an irregular route when in the war zone. The captain exposed his ship on the regular track of shipping in the fullest possible way, even to the extent of slowing down. He did this despite receiving wireless messages apprising him of the activities of submarines in the vicinity.

Previous to the sinking of the *Lusitania* the Admiralty had on occasion convoyed merchant ships loaded with horses.

One might well wonder whether the British Government purposely exposed to attack the *Lusitania* and other British passenger vessels carrying American citizens, in order to lead the Germans on to a rash act which might bring the United States into the war. King George remarked to Colonel House, as the *Lusitania* was nearing her fate, "Suppose they should sink the *Lusitania* with American passengers on board." (*Intimate Papers, op. cit.*, II, 432.)

The same exposure, possibly deliberate, was true in the case of the unarmed cross-channel passenger steamer, *Sussex*, the torpedoing of which caused the German-American crisis of April, 1916. It was lumbering along, without escort, through a sea littered with the wreckage of recently torpedoed vessels.

The truth probably never will be known whether the British and French Governments deliberately exposed these ships for high diplomatic stakes.

Thomas A. Bailey discusses the facts and law concerning "The Sinking of the *Lusitania*," in *Am. Hist. Rev.*, XLI (October, 1935), 26-54, although not with all the facts and suggestions in this note.

CHAPTER XXXIII

THE FIRST WORLD WAR AND THE PEACE SETTLEMENT

(1917-1921)

THE United States in 1917 went over to the Allied cause unconditionally, wholeheartedly, overwhelmingly.

It is the unconditional feature of that decisive intervention which most concerns the historian of American diplomacy.

That the intervention was decisive we are told by British and French historians. They say that it marked the turning-point of the war. They declare that, without this intervention, which followed the collapse of Russia, Germany would have won the war. We may believe this.[1]

This is not the place to say much about military participation in the last eighteen months of the World War: the immediate joining of the American and British fleets; the bridling of the submarine with mine barrages and destroyer convoys; the industrial and financial mobilization of the nation; the conscription and training, behind the protection of secure sea power, of a civilian army of 4,000,000 men; the transport of 2,000,000 American troops to transfuse the bleeding man power of France and the British Empire; the collapse of the Central Powers in the autumn of 1918 before these freshened odds. It is rather the diplomatic history of the United States during this terrible world war which concerns us here: (1) the relations with the nations associated in the war against Germany and Austria-Hungary, (2) the evolution of the American peace program, (3) the pre-Armistice negotiations, (4) the negotiation of peace at Paris, (5) the rejection by the United States Senate of the League of Nations and with it of the Treaty of Versailles, (6) the separate peace with the enemy, (7) the aftermath issues of neutral rights and the freedom of the seas.

The declarations of war against Germany and Austria-Hungary did not in themselves signalize departure from the traditional policy of the Fathers, from the Farewell Address and the Monroe Doctrine. The United States was careful to avoid any alliance with the partners in war. Pres-

[1] See, for example, Churchill, *World Crisis, op. cit.*, III, 212, 215 *et passim;* and Pierre Renouvin, *Grande Guerre, post cit.*, p. 420 *et passim.*

ident Wilson studiously referred to them as "associates." He spoke of the "Allied and Associated Powers." Other associates rather than allies, like the United States, were, of course, those Latin-American nations which followed the call of the United States to declare war against Germany, namely: Brazil, Cuba, Costa Rica, Guatemala, Haiti, Honduras, Nicaragua, and Panama.[1] In the Far East, another associate, China, declared war in order to be able to defend her interests at the peace negotiations. Fighting by the side of the Allies, the United States studiously refrained from those infringements on neutral rights against which it had complained to Great Britain and to Germany. It is true that the United States helped to lay the barrage of mines across the northern entrance to the North Sea, thus aiding to shut German submarines out of the Atlantic, but we must remember that the caveat (rather than protest) filed against Great Britain on mined war zones in February, 1917, had acknowledged that this subject was "unsettled" in international law. The United States co-operated with the Allied blockade not by the use of naval force but rather by domestic embargoes, allocation of bunker fuel, and the wide extension of contraband, without distinction of conditional contraband. There were no naval captures of neutral ships and cargoes, no prize court decisions.[2]

The first question to come up between the Allies and the United States concerning the conduct of the war was the command of the American troops at the front. In their desperate need for man power to stem the final offensive of the Germans on the western front the British and French requested that American troops, as they arrived, be brigaded into the British armies. There was of course something reasonable to be said for this: time seemed of the essence in the general strategical situation, with Russia now out of the war and Germany preparing for a knock-out offensive before an American army could appear in force; the British commanders had more experience; and the English language would make the command easily possible. Insuperable and highly proper reasons forbade the use of American troops to fill the British ranks. National pride alone made it impossible—there were the old historical issues dating back to before impressment; further, to have accepted a British command would have destroyed the national identity of the American army and have greatly diminished American influence in the making of the final peace. So President Wilson insisted that, ex-

---

[1] Peru, Bolivia, Uruguay, Ecuador, and the Dominican Republic severed relations with Germany. The Latin-American nations which remained neutral were: Argentina, Chile, Colombia, Mexico, El Salvador, Venezuela, Paraguay.

[2] T. A. Bailey, *Policy of U. S. toward Neutrals, 1917-1918.*

cept for a few diversions in emergencies, the troops of the United States moved to the front as an army under the command of an American General, subject later, of course, like the British armies and those of the Allies, to the Generalissimo of the Allied and Associated forces, Marshal Foch. For this unity of command, indispensable to victory, the United States was an unswerving advocate.[1]

It would have been quite possible, and honorable, for the United States to have restricted itself to the maritime sphere, to defending the freedom of the seas, the violation of which had brought the Republic into the war. Toward the fighting on the continent of Europe it could have remained in only a state of war, like Brazil and Cuba, without sending an army to Europe or raising from its citizens huge loans for support of the Allies. At least this full endeavor could have been with-held until there was some sort of agreement upon the terms of a victorious peace which would be won now only by full American co-operation. That an explicit understanding of such a nature was not made a prerequisite by the Government of the United States showed diplomatic ineptitude. It meant that the United States gave without stint of its treasure and its manhood, of its power and its soul, with no guaranty that its ideals or its interests would be written into the peace of victory. That the Allies were prepared to expect some such demand as a reasonable condition of full American participation is indicated by the British mission led by Arthur Balfour which came to Washington in April, 1917, and the French mission which immediately followed. Balfour had full details about the secret treaties which the European Allies had made among themselves marking out the share which each was to have in the final victory.

These treaties were generally unknown in the United States when it entered the war although American diplomatic advisers like Colonel House [2] knew the general nature of the contents of at least the European ones—they were published in the press in November—and had apprised the President; and Secretary of State Lansing knew at least of the Anglo-Japanese accord of 1915 with regard to the conquered German islands in the Pacific. These treaties,[3] which molded the final peace, were not so bad as some publicists have painted them. It is instructive to note that where they were followed there was no sore point left in the sub-

[1] The question of command is to be followed in *Intimate Papers, op. cit.;* T. C. Lonergan, *It Might Have Been Lost* (New York, 1929); General J. J. Pershing, *My Experiences in the World War* (2 Vols., New York, 1931).
[2] *Intimate Papers, op. cit.,* I, 462; III, 40-41.
[3] Seymour, *American Diplomacy During the World War, op. cit.,* 266.

sequent peace settlement. Students of the war have excoriated the treaties as proof of the naked imperialistic designs of the Allies as contrasted with the hypocrisy of their professions of fighting for the defense of democracy and the rights of small nations. That the treaties were tinctured with imperialism and selfishness is without question; but many commentators do not notice the obvious fact that these treaties were not the cause of the European War; they were negotiated *after* the war had already commenced. This holds true at least for the Allied powers which went to war in 1914. No spoils treaty antedated the war. In the cases of Italy and Roumania, the secret treaties by which they entered the conflict represented what the Allies had to promise to them in advance in order to bring them over.

There were five of these treaties or understandings, or groups of such, made to solidify the enthusiasm of the original Allies and to bring new ones into the circle.

(1) Russia secured her claims by a treaty with Great Britain and France made in March, 1915, at the beginning of the Allied attack on the Dardanelles. By this the two western Allies agreed that Russia might annex Constantinople and the Asiatic shore of the Bosporus and the Dardanelles, leaving free transit of the straits for the merchant ships of all nations. Russia on her part agreed to the separation of the Caliphate from Turkey and to sharing with France and Great Britain an influence over other portions of the Turkish Empire, reserving to England particular influence in the neighborhood of the Suez Canal and the Gulf of Persia—the British buffer of influence in Persia also was to be extended. These partitions of the Turkish Empire were marked out with more precision—conformable to the later mandates to France and Great Britain—in supplementary understandings (the Sykes-Picot agreement of May 16, 1916, and the agreement at St. Jean de Maurienne, April 17, 1917), reserving for Italy (in conformance with the Treaty of London) a share in the region of Adalia (which the entrance of Greece into the war later stopped her from taking, after the European peace). Thus did the Allies imperturbably dispose of the territory of Germany's Turkish ally, that vigorous "sick man of Europe" near whose bedside the European powers for a century had been waiting either so anxiously or so eagerly.

(2) Italy's claim to expansion had been recognized in principle by the Treaty of London (April 26, 1915) which brought, or bought, that nation into the war. The Central Powers had been willing to promise a redemption of Italy's irredentist population at the end of the war,

but not to deliver immediate occupation of the territory concerned. Ardent to weaken their enemy, the Allies promised the irredentist territory with strategical control of the Adriatic and of the Alpine passage into Austria, specifying a line which delivered over to Italy a Slavic and an Austrian *irredentum* at the head of the Adriatic and on its eastern shores.

Italy was also to have the strategic part of Albania, unchallenged government of the Dodecanese Islands in the Eastern Mediterranean, and a share in the partition of the Turkish Empire.

(3) Roumania was in a most favorable position for bargaining: the Central Powers offered her the irredentist province of Bessarabia, Russian; but the Entente Allies offered her the larger and more populous irredentist part of Hungarian Transylvania and even the Banat of Temesvár, where there was a numerous Serb population. After much wavering Roumania accepted the Allies' offer (Treaty of Bucharest, August 8, 1916), and entered on their side, only to be speedily crushed and occupied during the remainder of the war by German, Austro-Hungarian, and Bulgarian troops. Her separate treaty of peace in 1918 abrogated the obligations of the Allies.

(4) In the Far East, Japan and Great Britain by mutual understanding had divided up the conquered German islands in the Pacific: at the outset of the war British forces occupied those islands south of the Equator; Japan took over those north of that line. When it became apparent that the United States might enter the war Japan reached an understanding (February-March, 1917) with Great Britain, France, Italy and Russia, sanctioning her claim to the transfer of all German rights in the Chinese province of Shantung, and, of course, to the islands north of the Equator.

(5) Finally there was the arrangement between France and Russia, also made (March 11, 1917) after the United States had broken relations with Germany, just on the eve of the first Russian Revolution. Each gave the other a free hand in arranging its frontier on the side of Germany—this meant at least Alsace-Lorraine for France and the Polish provinces for Russia.

Such were the famous secret agreements which Arthur Balfour presumably had in his portfolio, with their boundaries drawn on a large map, when he hurried to Washington in April, 1917, to secure full American participation in the war on the continent of Europe. To his surprise he found the United States enthusiastic for winning the war first and talking peace only afterward. Congress was appropriating

(April 24, 1917) $7,000,000,000, of which $3,000,000,000 was to be loaned to Allied governments, the first great credit of a total which rapidly amounted to $7,077,144,750 before the armistice of November 11, 1918, and $2,170,200,000 more after it.

The President felt it would be a pity to let Balfour go home without a thorough discussion of the peace terms of the Allies. Colonel House thought it would be inadvisable at that time to have a general discussion with *all* the Allies: "If the Allies begin to discuss terms among themselves," he wrote to the President, "they will soon hate one another worse than they do Germany and a situation will arise similar to that in the Balkan States after the Turkish War. It seems to me that the only thing to be considered at present is how to beat Germany in the quickest way." Balfour easily concurred in House's sentiments. During the Balfour mission peace terms were nevertheless canvassed in long conferences. To Colonel House Balfour showed his map with the territorial lines of the secret treaties drawn on it. With the President and House, he went over the same ground. Russia had now collapsed, and the British spokesman did not defend her claims in Washington: Constantinople might be a free city, and Poland a resurrected state, though it would be a problem to find an outlet for that state to the sea. Roumania could have Bessarabia (Russian). As to the surviving Allies, the British Secretary insisted on keeping the bargains made with them.[1] There appears to have been no mention of the freedom of the seas.

Upon House's request, Balfour promised to furnish copies [2] of the secret treaties and agreements, but he returned to London without any new American demands. With the sequent French, Belgian and Italian missions which had hurried to the United States, there was no discussion of peace terms, so far as we know.

President Wilson had agreed with his confidential adviser that it would not be well to disturb Allied unity before the enemy with any discussion of peace terms. He seems to have felt that his defense of immutable principles, together with American military and financial power, would be so unchallengeable at the final peace conference that he could brush aside these secret agreements by the force of his prestige and that of his country. In this he was sadly mistaken. Having neglected the opportunity presented by the Balfour mission, at a time when it would have been a fatal mistake for the Allies to have cooled the

---

[1] House recorded the substance of these conferences, and it is printed in *Intimate Papers, op. cit.*, III, 29-63.

[2] We do not know when these were delivered.

military ardor of America, the President's crystallizing American peace terms began to conform more and more to the obligations to each other of the surviving Allies—objectives which themselves were of no mean service to the principle of nationality—and more and more he was forced to fall back on the unexceptionable principle of a League of Nations as the protected refuge for his peace policy and the sanctuary of his hopes for the future.

There was no longer any doubt that the United States would use all of its resources to help win the war. The Allies had found an ideal Associate, better than a real ally who would have extracted an equivalent for his sacrifices. A national conscription act passed Congress, May 18, 1917. A few weeks later the President promised Arthur Balfour a million and a half American troops on the western front by the end of 1918. The diplomats settled down now to the difficult task of gearing American resources to the military requirements of the Allies.[1] In August the President rejected as impossible the Pope's proposal to the belligerents for a peace without victory on the basis of mutual restoration, disarmament, organization for future arbitration, indemnity for civilian damages, general condonement, "community" of the seas, with a negotiated settlement of territorial questions like Alsace-Lorraine and the Trentino. These would have been ideal Wilsonian terms the previous January.

We recall again that during the American Revolution, following the Declaration of Independence and the signature of the French alliance, the United States refused the British terms of home-rule within the Empire, terms with which they would have been so content as colonies of Britain before July 4, 1776. So now in 1917 President Wilson, launched on the war without stint or condition, insisted on a peace with victory where six months previously he had declared there could be no peace with victory.

A peace of victory, would it be really possible? The military situation had steadily blackened. The near collapse of Italy after the Austrian victory of Caporetto, in the autumn of 1917, eased the Central Powers on that flank. American troops could not appear in force be-

---

[1] Charles Seymour, *American Diplomacy During the World War, op. cit.,* 212-252, is the only satisfactory account of the diplomatic labors of co-ordinating Allied requirements to American resources in shipping, food-supply, credits, munitions and questions of military and naval administration; and the creation of the inter-allied Supreme War Council with which the United States co-operated without political commitment. Colonel House was the chief American spokesman in arranging these difficult but vital matters to a point where technical men could work out the details.

fore the summer of 1918. The collapse of Russia was made complete and definitive by the Bolshevik Revolution of November, 1917. Straightway the Russian revolutionists began the negotiation of a separate peace (signed at Brest Litovsk, March 3, 1918) which assured the Central Powers a free hand in regulating and expanding their eastern frontiers for future penetration beyond, and complete liberty to concentrate their whole war efforts on the western front of battle.[1] The Bolsheviki in December, 1917, tore open the archives of the Czar and published to the world the secret treaties by which the Allies after the beginning of the war had pre-arranged a territorial settlement of Europe and the Near East. It was an appeal to the laboring masses of the Allied countries to repudiate a war for what the revolutionists now branded as imperialistic ambitions hitherto masked by moral professions. In France mutiny was brewing among the weary patriotic troops. In Flanders the German high staff, nervous at popular restiveness, and disappointed by the Allies' checking of the submarine campaign, were preparing for a last mighty offensive to break through into France before their man power should give out in face of the American reinforcement.

It was in this black winter of the war that the Allies looked desperately for some moral impetus to their cause which would hold their peoples fighting together against complete military disaster. It was then that President Wilson made his notable pronouncement to the Congress (January 8, 1918) of Fourteen Points for a peace acceptable to the United States. The Fourteen Points were formulated by the President and Colonel House, after the latter had become convinced that the President must take a hand himself in a liberal crystallization of Allied war aims, if the Russians were to be kept in the war, and the morale shoved up of the Allied peoples. House had studied carefully the previous expressions of the Allies' terms of peace, as they had been conveyed to him in his contact with Sir Edward Grey and Arthur Balfour, and as they had been proclaimed by Great Britain and France in January, 1917. If we bear in mind the new Russian situation, the Fourteen Points did not conflict seriously with the secret treaties which Balfour had discussed in the White House.[2] They proposed if possible to remake Europe along boundaries of nationality which perhaps would break up the Austro-Hungarian Empire and destroy the military strength

[1] H. W. V. Temperley, A History of the Peace Conference of Paris (6 Vols., London, 1920-1921), I, 1-14.

[2] This is seen by a comparison with the British Prime Minister's statement to the British Trades Unions Congress of Allied peace terms, January 5, 1918, the very day that the Wilson address was finally drafted.

of the Central Powers. The American emphasis came in a demand for the freedom of the seas and insistence on a League of Nations to organize peace after the war with a general guaranty thereafter of political independence and territorial integrity to great and small states alike. The authors of the Fourteen Points carefully phrased them so as to be useful under any of the three following conditions: (1) complete victory, (2) a stalemate war and a peace of compromise, (3) defeat. Witness the use of the words *must* and *should* which we have italicized:

"The program of the world's peace, therefore, is our program, and that program, the only possible program, as we see it, is this:

1. Open covenants of peace, openly arrived at, after which there shall be no private international understandings of any kind, but diplomacy shall proceed always frankly and in the public view.

2. Absolute freedom of navigation upon the seas, outside territorial waters, alike in peace and in war, except as the seas may be closed in whole or in part by international action for the enforcement of international covenants.

3. The removal, so far as possible, of all economic barriers and the establishment of an equality of trade conditions among all the nations consenting to the peace and associating themselves for its maintenance.

4. Adequate guarantees given and taken that national armaments will be reduced to the lowest point consistent with domestic safety.

5. A free, open-minded, and absolutely impartial adjustment of all colonial claims, based upon a strict observance of the principle that in determining all such questions of sovereignty the interests of the populations concerned *must* have equal weight with the equitable claims of the government whose title is to be determined.

6. The evacuation of all Russian territory and such a settlement of all questions affecting Russia as will secure the best and freest cooperation of the other nations of the world in obtaining for her an unhampered and unembarrassed opportunity for the independent determination of her own political development and national policy and assure her of a sincere welcome into the society of free nations under institutions of her own choosing; and, more than a welcome, assistance also of every kind that she may need and may herself desire. The treatment accorded Russia by her sister nations in the months to come will be the acid test of their good will, of their comprehension of her needs as distinguished from their own interests, and of their intelligent and unselfish sympathy.

7. Belgium, the whole world will agree, *must* be evacuated and restored, without any attempt to limit the sovereignty which she enjoys in common with all other free nations. No other single act will serve as this will serve to restore confidence among the nations in the laws which they have themselves set and determined for the government of their relations with one another. Without this healing act the whole structure and validity of international law is forever impaired.

8. All French territory *should* be freed and the invaded portions restored, and the wrong done to France by Prussia in 1871 in the matter of Alsace-Lorraine, which has unsettled the peace of the world for nearly fifty years, *should* be righted, in order that peace may once more be made secure in the interest of all.

9. A readjustment of the frontiers of Italy *should* be effected along clearly recognizable lines of nationality.

10. The peoples of Austria-Hungary, whose place among the nations we wish to see safeguarded and assured, *should* be accorded the freest opportunity of autonomous development.

11. Rumania, Serbia, and Montenegro *should* be evacuated; occupied territories restored; Serbia accorded free and secure access to the sea; and the relations of the several Balkan states to one another determined by friendly counsel along historically established lines of allegiance and nationality; and international guarantees of the political and economic independence and territorial integrity of the several Balkan states *should* be entered into.

12. The Turkish portions of the present Ottoman Empire *should* be assured a secure sovereignty, but the other nationalities which are now under Turkish rule *should* be assured an undoubted security of life and an absolutely unmolested opportunity of autonomous development, and the Dardanelles *should* be permanently opened as a free passage to the ships and commerce of all nations under international guarantees.

13. An independent Polish state *should* be erected, which *should* include the territories inhabited by indisputably Polish populations, which *should* be assured a free and secure access to the sea, and whose political and economic independence and territorial integrity *should* be guaranteed by international covenant.

14. A general association of nations *must* be formed under specific covenants for the purpose of affording mutual guarantees of political independence and territorial integrity to great and small states alike."

The President and Colonel House studiously went over the whole document after they had first drafted it, qualifying it with their *musts* and *shoulds*.

The Fourteen Points, it proved, were to be interpreted under conditions of complete victory and solely by the Allied and Associated Powers, with the defeated enemy reaching desperately to the Wilsonian principles in the hope to save at least something. In these circumstances it was easy for the victors to interpret *should* to mean *must*.

The final German offensive in the west failed in July, 1918. The Turkish, Bulgarian and Austrian allies began to crack all along their respective fronts and at home. With the victory now surely in sight, the Allies themselves were reeling with exhaustion. During 1918 there took place a series of long-distance exchanges of peace views in the shape of pronouncements from the rostrums of the different governments.[1] These varied in their force according to the military situation. At no time were the Allies driven to accepting a "peace by compromise and negotiation" which the Central Powers offered. Meanwhile President Wilson in public addresses had piled the Fourteen Points with further general principles of durable peace which included: the destruction or at least reduction of arbitrary power capable of upsetting the peace of the world, satisfaction of "well-defined national aspirations," prohibition of especial leagues or embargoes within the proposed League of Nations, no secret treaties, self-determination for peoples and territories whose sovereignty was in question, and, finally, "impartial justice." [2]

The end of the war suddenly appeared when Bulgaria signed an armistice of military surrender and occupation, September 29, 1918. Already Austria-Hungary (September 16, 1918) had proposed to the enemy a discussion of peace by all belligerents. Facing complete collapse, and in panic at the furious and general advance of the Allies and Associates all along the western front, General Ludendorff and the Field Marshal von Hindenburg, the German Chief of Staff, urgently advised the Government to sue for peace and to try to salvage something by an appeal to the Wilsonian principles. On October 6, Germany, and on October 7, Austria-Hungary, transmitted to the United States (instead of to the Allies) a request for an armistice. With victorious

---

[1] They are printed by the Carnegie Endowment for International Peace, Division of International Law. Pamphlet No. 11 (Washington, 1921).

[2] Since these points became a part of the discussions for an armistice, and were actually embodied in the German armistice, they should be added to the Fourteen Points. Note the more imperative tone, which we have stressed by italics, in the note at the end of the chapter.

troops exultantly pushing through on all fronts the President made the most of his advantage, and kept control of the preliminary moves for peace. He used in a masterly way the strategy of delay. In a correspondence with Germany he insisted that he must know that he was treating with a government that really had the support of the people; to Austria he replied that the recent recognition of the belligerency of Czechoslovakia by the United States had modified Point X, which stressed "autonomy" for the peoples of Austria-Hungary: now it was the Czechoslovaks themselves, and also the Jugoslavs, who must themselves judge of their own rights and destiny.

Before the discussion with the United States could be completed the crumbling and vanishing Austro-Hungarian Empire signed (November 3, 1918) an armistice with the Italians, technically with the Allied and Associated Powers. The Wilsonian principles, therefore, were not made a certain condition of peace in the Austro-Hungarian surrender. The historic but volatile empire had suddenly exploded before it could securely seize hold of them. Turkey had accepted a controlling British armistice, October 31, 1918, before its appeal to Wilsonianism could be heard and transmitted to the Allies.

A frantic constitutional reformation of the German Government did not prevent the proclamation of a socialist republic in Berlin, but it induced President Wilson at least to transmit to the triumphing Allies the German request for an armistice, making it first well understood to Germany that it must be an armistice of complete surrender. The Kaiser abdicated (November 9, 1918), fleeing ignominiously to Holland. The Central Powers, who had almost grasped the fringe of victory's robes in the spring of 1918, were now at the mercy of their enemies.

Germany had appealed to the United States for peace on the basis of President Wilson's pronouncements, particularly the Fourteen Points. The President had leisurely consented to transmit the appeal to the Allies. He had left it unreservedly to the commanding generals in the field, notably to Marshal Foch, the Generalissimo of the Allied and Associated armies, whether the military situation justified an armistice. Foch replied yes, if Germany agreed to an effectual disarmament he was ready to sign. In view of obstinate public ignorance it is necessary to emphasize what British and French historians and statesmen have repeatedly pointed out [1]; that President Wilson did not interfere with the

---

[1] *The Memoirs of Marshal Foch* (translated by Colonel T. Bentley Mott, N. Y., 1931), p. 463; B. H. Liddell Hart, *The Real War, 1914-1918* (London, 1930), 409; Pierre Renouvin, *La Crise Européenne et la Grande Guerre (1904-1918)* (Paris, 1934), 596.

command in the field and force them to agree to an armistice without further invasion and the complete pulverization of Germany. It was Marshal Foch who dictated the military terms of the armistice and was completely content with it, as were the other commanders, except Pershing. The French General said: "One makes war only to get results." In the military and naval surrender of Germany and her allies the results would be obtained, so far as they could be had by war.

It was for the Allies to decide among themselves what political conditions they would attach to the military surrender. Could they all agree to the Fourteen Points and later pronouncements of President Wilson as the fundamental basis of peace, to be interpreted to suit themselves in the condition of complete victory, then to be dictated to Germany? Were there any other conditions to attach to the Fourteen Points before accepting a German surrender?

In the important pre-Armistice negotiations between the United States and the Allies, conducted by Colonel House as the personal representative of the President, Great Britain reserved her interpretation of Point 2, the freedom of the seas, the historic American principle. Prime Minister Lloyd George said he could not give up control of a means which had enabled the Allies to win the war, notably by transporting American troops to France. Premier Clemenceau of France agreed to this; and on his part insisted on specifying broadly for "reparation for damages." He insisted that there must be compensation by Germany, "for all damages done to the civilian population of the Allies and their property by the aggression of Germany by land, by sea and from the air." House, and Wilson behind him, contented themselves with a general understanding that Point 2 might be made the subject of future discussion with the Allies. With these, two essential modifications, the significant emasculation of the freedom of the seas, and the sweeping provision for reparation, the Fourteen Points and the subsequent pronouncements of the President became by the terms of the Armistice of November 11, 1918, the agreed basis of the peace to be negotiated between the Allied and Associated Powers and Germany.

The negotiation of the Armistice had taken place while the American congressional elections of 1918 were approaching. Republicans and Democrats during the war had put away their political opposition in common patriotic endeavor. It had been the Republican spokesmen who had been more aggressive in demands on Germany than the Administration, more forward for war. During the war they had at least equaled their old political adversaries in their demand for the utmost national exertions. Including the two ex-Presidents, Roosevelt and Taft, they had demanded, during the autumnal political campaign, the election in November, 1918, of a Republican Congress to push through the war and control a peace of unconditional surrender by the enemy. Roosevelt in particular contemned the Fourteen Points as "soft."

President Wilson feared that if the Republicans should secure control of Congress they would sweep away his program for peace. He was nervous about reports of large sums of money being spent by his political opponents to carry the elections, notably in Michigan. A friend asked him, in a long conversation in the White House (September 13, 1918), what he would do in case he should lose the elections. Would he resign the Presidency, following his well-known convictions about responsible government? It was recalled to him that he had planned to resign that high office in case Mr. Hughes, the Republican candidate for the Presidency, had been elected in November, 1916, thus allowing the President-elect to come into office immediately without waiting until March 4. "I cannot do it," Woodrow Wilson now said, "on account of the world-wide situation, in which American influence is very important and may be decisive. It happens to be a case where, even if defeated by the people, I shall have to try to obtain the objects for which we went to war." [1]

It was this fear which led the President into what has been generally regarded as a strategical misstep. But for this mistake he might have kept his position as the leader of a politically undivided nation. He could have appealed to the voters to return senators and representatives, of whatever party, who would support him in finishing the war and settling the peace. With the end of the war in sight, he issued a public appeal for the election of a Democratic majority in both houses of Congress in order that he might be wholly unhampered in the approaching negotiations. It is true that President McKinley issued a similar call, successfully, in 1898. But it was unnecessary for President Wilson and unwise. Some of his political advisers counseled against it. The appeal invoked a partisan issue where previously there had been little for the public to discern between the two parties united in war. The country was normally Republican—Wilson had come to power and stayed in power only because of the division of his Republican opponents; now, with the war over, they united to meet his challenge.

The elections resulted in a clear Republican majority for the new

[1] Statement to the author by the friend in question, the late Professor William E. Dodd, who recorded the conversation at the time.

Senate (and House too) which would meet after March 4, 1919, to consider the treaties of peace. Ex-President Roosevelt, presuming to speak for a reunited and victorious Republican Party, declared to the world after the election: "Our allies and our enemies, and Mr. Wilson himself, should all understand that Mr. Wilson has no authority whatever to speak for the American people at this time. His leadership has just been emphatically repudiated by them. . . ."

The world cried for peace. The overturn of three great empires, Germany, Austria-Hungary, and Russia, and their satellites, displayed throughout the eastern half of Europe a panorama of confusion, anarchy and chaos. The question of the hour was how to shape the machinery of procedure directly, and efficaciously, to dictate peace quickly on the terms of the Allied and Associated Powers, terms couched as yet in the very general Wilsonian principles. France had suggested to the United States, in a memorandum to Washington of November 29, 1918, that the five great victors (the United States, Great Britain, France, Italy, Japan) should sweep the table clear of all previous special agreements arrived at by some of the Allies only, and straightway agree among themselves on the principal bases of peace. The small belligerents, the neutral states, and the new states in formation could be called in for consultation as their special interests were touched on one by one. In subsequent conferences, after a preliminary peace had been dictated, garnished with the invocation of moral principles, all the nations could meet in a congress to work out the permanent organization of world peace in a League of Nations. Colonel House and Secretary Lansing were inclined to favor some such procedure. President Wilson did not even answer the French proposal. He had his mind first on a League of Nations. He was determined that it should be interwoven with the peace treaties, and that he himself would take the American delegation to Paris to make sure that this was done; otherwise the peoples of the embattled nations might be overreached by the more sophisticated spokesmen of their governments. He did not realize that actually the peoples could be more uncompromising than their spokesmen.

If repudiated by the electorate of his own homeland, it was at the apogee of his prestige in the world that Woodrow Wilson surveyed the European shore from the bridge of the *George Washington*. He arrived in Europe as a true friend of mankind, closer to the principles of Christian charity and justice than any statesman in history. The new great ideal seemed really possible. If only he could bring Europe to agree to a peace of justice resting on the foundations of a league of democratic nations which would execute and regulate the treaties of peace, he was convinced that the opposition of Congress at home would have to yield to the force of public opinion. By the gospel of his principles he would overbear the Republican politicians in the Senate, as abroad he expected to sweep aside whatever obstacles the Allies' secret treaties presented to the application of his Fourteen Points.

The American peace Commission consisted of executive agents appointed without the advice and consent of the Senate, a custom which had been engrafted by practice to the American constitutional system by virtue of the President's control over diplomatic negotiations.[1] In the language of the treaties which he later signed, the President was "acting in his own name and by his own proper authority." Very unwisely he did not include in the Commission, according to traditional practice, representatives from both parties in that Senate which would be called upon to ratify his treaties. He was also criticized, even by his own Secretary of State,[2] for jeopardizing his dominant position in the world by descending into a conference with the foreign statesmen in Europe. One of the real advantages of the American diplomatic system has been the reserve power which the President, back home across the ocean, has had to stiffen the demands of his plenipotentiaries in the give and take of negotiation; and back of this, and despite the shocking abuse of it by party politics, lies the still greater reserve power of the Senate in the right to advise and consent, by a two-thirds majority, to the ratification of any treaty. These advantages the President, in his convictions, threw away by going to Paris at the head of a personal executive delegation. The other members were: Secretary of State Robert Lansing; Colonel Edward M. House, the President's constant political mentor; General Tasker H. Bliss; and Mr. Henry White, veteran career diplomatist of pale Republican allegiance, who had never made any public statement hostile to the President. The latter was the only Republican on the Commission, and through him Senator Lodge, leader of the Republican Senate and chairman of the Committee on Foreign Relations, unsuccessfully tried to speak to the Allies behind the back of the President.[3]

A shipload of officials of the State Department, intelligence officers, specialists and secretaries accompanied the Commission. The "ex-

[1] Henry M. Wriston has traced with a wealth of detail the growth of this practice in his *Executive Agents in American Foreign Relations, op. cit.*

[2] Robert Lansing, *The Peace Negotiations, a Personal Narrative* (New York, 1921).

[3] Nevins, *Henry White, op. cit.,* 353.

perts" had been recruited quietly from academic and other walks of life under the direction of Colonel House. Organized unostentatiously under the name of The Inquiry, after the immemorial habit of professors everywhere they had diligently assembled during the previous twelve months a mass of facts and information of a special nature for the advice of the diplomatists who were to discuss the intricate political, territorial and economic questions of several continents. These specialists played an important part in drafting the non-debatable articles of the peace treaties and in fortifying the plenipotentiaries in the diplomatic disputations.

At the Peace Conference at Paris, which opened January 12, 1919, met the plenipotentiaries of twenty-seven nations, enemies of Germany or of her allies, or nations, like five of the Latin-American states, who had severed relations with Germany. There had never been such a diplomatic gathering in history. Even the Congress of Vienna, once consecrated to the principle of Legitimacy as the Paris Conference was now consecrated to the principle of Nationality, could not approach its vast importance. It was the focus of seething national rivalries, resentments, despairs, ambitions, triumphs. President Wilson, it must be generally conceded, was the only statesman of the great powers who had no selfish national interest to serve, no particular necessitous war bargain to fulfill. Each of the other war-weary nations, except for those like the South American Republics which had been only nominally at war, had some special right or attachment to protect, some vital or profitable interest to secure. Among the actual fighting belligerents only Canada stood in the American relationship, but she had her responsibilities to the British Empire. How can we blame the plenipotentiaries for not having made a perfect peace? The marvel is that they agreed to any peace at all.

Able participants, conscious of the historic importance of the occasion, have pictured the highlights of the momentous gathering and its vivid personalities: Clemenceau, who presided, the dauntless Premier of France, acclaimed by his compatriots as the Father of Victory, seventy-eight years old, ancient, wrinkled, with his black skull cap, his gray-gloved and imperturbably folded hands, his fringe of white hair, a tiger statesman, frank exponent of the balance of power, fighting first and always to sustain his rescued France; Lloyd George, Prime Minister of Great Britain, crystal of perspicacity, indomitable dynamo of human energy, the parliamentary chiefs of the daughter Dominions arrayed at his side, a prime minister conspicuously serving the interests of the British Empire but a sincere striver for permanent reconciliation with the enemy—providing no fleet were left him; Orlando, the Italian Premier, virile, ardent, eloquent, little concerned with anything but the questions which affected Italy; Saionji, aged Elder Statesman of Japan, who as a lad had fought in feudal wars with bow and arrow—quiet, inscrutable, intervening only to protect Japan's winnings and to make sure her position as an equal among the Great Powers; finally, Woodrow Wilson, President of the United States of America now come to Europe, his eager academic countenance alive with success, the crusader for organized world peace.

It had been the President's first thought that all the Allied and Associated Nations, great and small, should meet together at the conference to interpret and apply the Fourteen Points. The small nations would welcome the League more unconditionally. For all the powers, big and little, to meet equally to dispose of issues, proved impossible. The Big Five (the United States, Great Britain, France, Italy, and Japan) therefore agreed that their chiefs of state and foreign ministers should meet in a Council of Ten, settle things, and prescribe articles to be ratified at the plenary sessions of the Conference. Smaller powers would be consulted as their interests were touched. In reality this Council of Ten was an *alter ego* of the Supreme Allied War Council which had developed in recent months to deal with inter-allied war interests. The Council of Ten appointed representative commissions, fifty-two in number, to study and report on particular questions. The meetings of the Council of Ten, always attended by a numerous entourage of advisers, interpreters and experts, proved too cumbersome, and too public, for frank and expeditious settlement of delicate subjects. Eventually a Council of Four:[1] Wilson, Lloyd George, Clemenceau and Orlando, began to meet confidentially together with only one secretary—sometimes none—to keep their records. Here the main points of the peace were settled. These meetings were really continuing the method instituted at the time of the conferences on the impending armistice, when Clemenceau, Lloyd George, Orlando and House had settled essential points before they were treated in the Supreme War Council. Orlando quit the Four, when later in disposing of Austria-Hungary they would not award Fiume to Italy, so the last weeks of the conference were under the diplomatic tribunal of the Triumvirate of the chiefs of state of the United States, Great Britain and France. Thus it was the prin-

---

[1] Japan did not choose to sit in on discussions of debatable occidental political and territorial subjects.

The Big Four at Paris, 1918

(Left to right: Orlando, Lloyd George, Clemenceau, Wilson.)

cipal powers which arranged the peace, as France had proposed after the armistice; but it was only after Wilson had persuaded them to agree on the League; on the other hand there had been no sweeping aside of the secret treaties as France at first was willing to suggest.

The history of the Conference can be divided into three stages. The first extended from January 12 to February 14, 1919, on which date President Wilson left Paris for a visit to the United States to attend to his constitutional duties at the close of the Congress. During these weeks Wilson's insistence forged the first draft of the League of Nations, setting aside, until the great Convenant could be agreed upon, the final decision of the crucial territorial and political questions that were being examined by the commissions. The second stage was the interval of the President's absence, a month, during most of which Lloyd George was in England to attend to pressing duties at home, and Clemenceau lay stricken by the attack of an anarchist. It had been agreed that during the President's absence discussion should proceed on the territorial and political questions. During this period much important work was done by the special commissions appointed to consider territorial, economic and other technical questions. The third and final stage was from March 14, when the President returned to Paris, until the signature of the Treaty of Versailles. This was the period in which the Four, and then the Three, made the most important decisions on the great issues among the victorious Allies and Associates.[1]

When Wilson returned to Paris on March 14 these paramount questions, though clarified by discussion, still remained to be settled. In the intimate discussions which followed among the Four, with Japan included where she so desired, it boiled down to this, from the American point of view: President Wilson, in his endeavor to mold the peace settlement to the matrix of the principles of his pronouncements as interpreted by the American delegation under his leadership, found himself obliged to make compromises with the special demands of the great Allies and their commitments to each other. He reached this point not only through the necessity of bargaining with the Allies but also after the conclusions of his own advisers that his principles were inapplicable in their entirety.

Great Britain and the Dominions wished to keep the colonies they had conquered from Germany in Africa and on the Pacific. A Dominion

---

[1] Robert C. Binkley has made a notable and critical analysis, from records then available, of the procedural history of the conference in relation to the great issues, in his "New Light on the Paris Peace Conference," *Pol. Sci. Quar.*, XLVI (September and December, 1931), 335-361, 509-547.

spokesman, General Smuts of South Africa, had proposed the system of mandates for the regions detached by the war from the Ottoman Empire, but he did not apply that also to Africa and the islands of the Pacific. Nobody on that side of the Atlantic thought of returning to Germany any of these conquests, despite Point 5, "a free, open-minded and absolutely impartial adjustment of colonial claims." This, in victory, was interpreted by all the victors to mean the claims only of the victors to the colonial spoil. To adjust the colonial question, Wilson acceded to the compromise suggestion of a graded mandate system for all the conquered colonies, as well as for Asia Minor and Mesopotamia. The appointed mandatory under the direction of the League of Nations, in each instance, proved to be either the conqueror, or the beneficiary of a secret treaty. Men have sneered at this as an hypocritical disguise of annexation; at least it was an appeal to an international control of backward peoples and colonial areas, stakes of imperialistic contention. The efficacy of the system would depend on the strength of the League of Nations.

France required a demilitarized buffer Rhineland state to protect her from dreaded German attacks in the future; and she insisted on repayment of separation allowances and military pensions to civilian relatives and survivors of soldiers. Here were the most difficult issues. They were settled by France agreeing to content herself with Alsace-Lorraine and her old frontiers, back of a military occupation for fifteen years [1] of the left bank of the Rhine and its bridgeheads, and a demilitarized zone in Germany for a depth of 50 kilometers east of the Rhine; in return France was to possess the Saar Valley, with its rich coal mines, subject to a determining plebiscite in 1935 (as a result of which the district was finally returned to Germany). Clemenceau, against the advice of Marshal Foch, agreed to this only when Lloyd George and Wilson signed a tripartite alliance pledging their countries to come to the aid of France if attacked in the future by Germany. It was strictly and significantly stated that the alliance would not apply unless ratified by all three parties, according to their respective constitutional requirements. Great Britain and France ratified. The United States Senate, as President Wilson probably knew it would and as Premier Clemenceau must have suspected it would, refused to consider the proposed pact, so radically contrary to George Washington's historic advice against "permanent alliances." The President made no great battle for this

[1] With provisions for evacuation of successive zones by 5-year periods in case Germany fulfilled the treaty loyally.

treaty in the Senate. It was a way the diplomatists had to get around a difficult corner. The President and the Prime Minister readily agreed to Clemenceau's demand that the dubious allowances for military separation and pensions be added to the German debt of reparations under category of "civilian damages" sanctioned by the Armistice. Computations of this kind could double the already astronomical character of calculating reparations debits—projecting their reckoning even unto the outer spaces of the ether drift beyond the great Magellanic Cloud.

In the case of Italy, the President assented to the strategical frontier of the Treaty of London, with some modifications, but not including the city of Fiume. The treaty of peace with Austria gave Italy possession of the Alpine passes into Austria, creating an Austria *irredenta* in the Tyrol of some 250,000 souls, in place of the old *Italia irredenta*. It remained to fix the boundary between Italy and the new state of Jugoslavia at the head of the Adriatic and along the Dalmatian littoral. President Wilson sought to apply Point 9 of the Fourteen Points to temper the extreme Italian claims, but it is uncertain whether Italy was explicitly bound by the Fourteen Points in the armistice with Austria-Hungary. Wilson, Lloyd George and Clemenceau were willing to make generous strategic concessions to Italy beyond the line of the Treaty of London, but not to give to Italy the half-Slavic city of Fiume, necessary for a usable outlet for Jugoslavia to the sea, a city of mixed population with an entirely Slavic hinterland. The peace conference ended without this intricate question being settled.[1]

Japan insisted on two things: an explicit recognition in the Covenant of the League of Nations of the principle of equality of all races, and title to her conquests from Germany in the Chinese province of Shantung as well as control of the conquered former German islands north of the Equator. She was willing to accept a mandate for the islands, a mandate of the class which administered them as integral parts of the mandatory state, except for prohibiting fortification; and she even made the promise ultimately to get out of Shantung in her own way, a promise subsequently fulfilled. Unfortunately the Council did not agree to the principle of racial equality. If also it had refused to transfer to Japan the German holdings in Shantung, Japan undoubtedly would have left

---

[1] In 1920, by the Treaty of Rapallo, Italy and Jugoslavia agreed on a frontier, and created a nominally independent city state of Fiume with a finger of territory stretching along the Adriatic to Italy; and giving Italy possession of the strategic islands of the Dalmatian shore, where there were heavy, if spotty, Italian populations. By a treaty of 1924 between Italy and Jugoslavia after Mussolini's capture of the Italian state, Fiume was annexed by Italy. This final settlement left a rankling *Jugoslavia irredenta* of over half a million people.

the Conference and refused the treaty; with European powers still on the mainland of Asia, she was determined not to have dictated to her, after 1895, another relinquishment of the fruits of victory. To secure Japanese assent to the treaty and hence to the League, President Wilson reluctantly accepted the Japanese position in Shantung, contrary as it was to the gospel of self-determination. China then refused to sign the Treaty of Versailles, but became a member of the League of Nations by ratifying the Treaty of St. Germain with Austria, which cost her none of her own territory, though it also violated in Central Europe the consecrated principles of self-determination and nationality.

All these major concessions in principle the President made in order to secure the consent of all the great victor powers to the League of Nations as an integral part of the treaty. He believed that the regrettable compromises in each case justified the great end in view.

The other provisions of the treaties with Germany, Austria, and Hungary involved no essential difficulty, although there was intense disputation in regard to the regulation of the status of the Saar Valley before the plebiscite postponed until 1935, and concerning the establishment of the Free City of Danzig at the mouth of the Polish corridor. They contained, among the countless routine articles: creation of the special commission to calculate and to charge up to Germany the total sum due for reparations, with no indemnity for war expenses by the Allies; the shaping of the nine new remnant and succession states in Central Europe—Austria, Hungary, Czechoslovakia, Jugoslavia, Poland, Lithuania, Latvia, Estonia, Finland; the Polish corridor; the marking off of patches of German peripheral territory for determination of sovereignty by plebiscites; the regulation of the Kiel Canal and the rivers within enemy territory; the effectual disarmament of Germany and her allies on land, on sea, and in the air "in order to render possible the initiation of a general limitation of the armaments of all nations"; and the one hundred and one incidental details of so vast a settlement of peace.[1] The Principal Allied and Associated Powers

[1] R. C. Binkley appraises the authorities for the peace conference in "Ten Years of Peace Conference History," *Jour. Mod. Hist.*, I (December, 1929), 607-629, and "New Light on the Paris Peace Conference," *Pol. Sci. Quar.*, XLVI (1931), 335-361, 509-547, to which Paul Birdsall's article serves as a sequel: "The Second Decade of Peace Conference History," *Jour. Mod. Hist.*, XV (Sept., 1939), 362-378. The standard account is Temperley, *Peace Conference of Paris, op. cit.*, a co-operative work by specialists, British and American. Shorter and more general are: C. H. Haskins and Robert H. Lord, *Some Problems of the Peace Conference* (Harvard University Press, 1920) by two specialists from the American delegation; and Edward M. House and Charles Seymour, *What Really Happened at Paris; the Story of the Peace Conference, 1918-1919, by American Delegates* (New York, 1921), a series of chapters by members of and advisers

were easily agreed on the famous Article 231 and its sweeping provisions: "The Allied and Associated Governments affirm and Germany accepts the responsibility of Germany and her allies for causing all the loss and damage to which the Allied and Associated Governments and their nationals have been subjected as a consequence of the war imposed upon them by the aggression of Germany and her allies."

Strictly speaking, this article required Germany to accept responsibility for damages done by the war, rather than "war guilt"; but it has been denounced on many occasions as an unjust branding of that nation as solely responsible for the war itself.

Only the Russian enigma remained unsettled. At the signing of the peace treaties Allied and Associated forces still remained on Russian territory, in the bleak and distantly separated sectors of Archangel and Vladivostok, whither they had been sent during the war to stay the dizzy collapse of Russia's resistance to the Central Powers.[1]

As for Germany and Austria and Hungary, they were permitted to show cause why the dictated terms should be altered. In a few details only, like that of the boundary of Silesia, did the victors condescend to change the drafted treaty. Perforce they accepted, they the

to the American Peace Commission. Ray Stannard Baker's *Woodrow Wilson and World Settlement* (3 Vols., New York, 1922) is informing but premature and one-sided, and his later biography of Wilson does not cover the peace conference. Harold Nicolson's *Peace Making, 1919* (N. Y., 1939) is a glancing literary essay of a disillusioned middle-aged man who participated in the conference in his youth. A better-balanced account of the fate of Wilsonian principles at Paris is Paul Birdsall, *Versailles Twenty Years After* (New York, 1941). The most valuable source for American diplomacy at Paris is *The Paris Peace Conference, 1919* in *Foreign Relations of the United States* (11 vols., 1942-1947).

[1] See below, p. 687, for Siberian expedition.

In May, 1917, the United States sent to Russia a special diplomatic mission under Elihu Root to institute ways and means of counteracting Germany's efforts to bring Russia to a separate peace. The net result of the Root Mission was to open up for the Provisional Government credits to the extent ultimately of $325,500,000 for the purchase of military supplies in America, of which $187,729,750 had been advanced in cash before the withdrawal of credit after the Bolshevik *coup* of November 7, 1917.

Another commission of railroad experts was sent to Russia under the command of John F. Stevens, with the rank of minister, to facilitate the transport of war material, particularly across Siberia from Vladivostok.

Point 6 of President Wilson's Fourteen Points, it is remembered, demanded the evacuation of all Russian territory, and unembarrassed self-determination for the people of Russia. "The treatment accorded Russia by her sister nations in the months to come will be the acid test of their good will. . . ." Within a few months, however, the sister nations had intervened in Russia. At Paris in 1919 Clemenceau and Orlando successfully opposed the efforts of Wilson and Lloyd George to invite representatives of all the contending Russian parties to the Peace Conference. They finally agreed to sound out the Russian groups about sending delegates to a special conference with representatives of the Allies at Prinkipo Island, in the Sea of Marmara; but the failure of all the opposing factions to agree to send delegates resulted in the default of this proposed conference. The Bolsheviki on their part were willing to send representatives.

vanquished. Obscure German plenipotentiaries signed the Treaty of Versailles, June 28, 1919, in the Hall of Mirrors, in the historic palace of Versailles, where in 1871 after the prostration of France the German princes in arms had proclaimed, amidst a mass of military glory, King William I of Prussia to be German Emperor.

In all this dictation of peace one great factor stands out. It was an imperfect but not a Carthaginian peace. If it did violence in certain regions to the Wilsonian principle of self-determination, it is also true that more millions of peoples enjoyed self-determination and national identity after the peace than before it. It did not undo the legitimate part of Bismarck's work, crowned in this same Hall of Mirrors forty-eight years before. It disarmed Germany. It took away her great navy. It dismantled her air force. It stripped her of her colonies. It levied an unfairly excessive amount of reparations, by including separation allowances and military pensions. It pared her of territory inhabited by conquered alien populations. But it did not destroy the Reich. It left a united nation. That vital fact is often ignored. The living core remained to rise again.

The Treaty of Versailles of the twenty-seven nations with Germany filled a stout volume, with smaller supplementary volumes for the Treaty of St. Germain with Austria (signed, September 10, 1919), and the Treaty of the Trianon with Hungary (signed, June 4, 1920).

There were two other treaties of peace, with Bulgaria (signed at Neuilly, November 27, 1919) and with Turkey (signed at Sèvres, August 10, 1920). The Bulgarian treaty, settling the present boundaries of the Balkan state, and fixing a staggering total of reparations for that small country, does not concern American diplomacy. The treaty with Turkey registered the dismemberment of the Ottoman Empire. This treaty did not stand. Before it could be executed a revolution of Turkish nationalists under the leadership of the redoubtable Mustafa Kemal, still master of that new republic, cast off the victor's bridle, drove out foreign forces from Anatolia, redeemed Constantinople, did away with extraterritoriality and the capitulations, fixed boundaries along the lines of nationality, and made no mention of indemnities or reparations. The United States at the same time signed (1923) a separate treaty with Turkey, of amity and commerce, also abolishing the capitulations, and re-establishing relations between the two republics, important to the United States because of the heavy interest of American philanthropic, religious and educational endeavor there. This treaty failed to pass the Senate, because of opposition aroused against any treaty with the "red-handed" Kemal régime, which many expected to fall. But the Kemal Government proved permanent. A short, new treaty (signed, 1931, ratified, 1933) finally fixed relations of establishment and sojourn of nationals, on a most-favored-nation basis, between the two countries. With all nations except Russia normal diplomatic relations had been now established in Europe.

President Wilson and his plenipotentiaries signed the treaties of peace in 1919. How would the new Republican Senate in Washington look upon his diplomatic handiwork?

THE FOUR SUPPLEMENTARY POINTS OF PRESIDENT WILSON OF FEBRUARY 11, 1918; THE FOUR ADDITIONAL POINTS OF JULY 4, 1918; AND THE FIVE ADDITIONAL POINTS OF SEPTEMBER 27, 1918.[1]

Address to Congress, February 11, 1918:

"First, that each part of the final settlement *must* be based upon the essential justice of that particular case and upon such adjustments as are most likely to bring a peace that will be permanent;

"Second, that peoples and provinces *are not* to be bartered about from sovereignty to sovereignty as if they were mere chattels and pawns in a game, even the great game, now forever discredited, of the balance of power; but that

"Third, every territorial settlement involved in this war *must* be made in the interest and for the benefit of the populations concerned, and not as a part of any mere adjustment or compromise of claims amongst rival States; and

"Fourth, that all well defined national aspirations *shall be* accorded the utmost satisfaction that can be accorded them without introducing new or perpetuating old elements of discord and antagonism that would be likely in time to break the peace of Europe and consequently of the world."

Address at Mount Vernon, July 4, 1918:

"I. The destruction of every arbitrary power anywhere that can separately, secretly, and of its single choice disturb the peace of the world; or, if it can not be presently destroyed, at the least its reduction to virtual impotence.

"II. The settlement of every question, whether of territory, of sovereignty, of economic arrangement, or of political relationship, upon the basis of the free acceptance of that settlement by the people immediately concerned, and not upon the basis of the material interest or advantage of any other nation or people which may desire a different settlement for the sake of its own exterior influence or mastery.

"III. The consent of all nations to be governed in their conduct towards each other by the same principles of honor and of respect for the common law of civilized society that govern the individual citizens of all modern

[1] Italics inserted.

States in their relations with one another; to the end that all promises and covenants may be sacredly observed, no private plots or conspiracies hatched, no selfish injuries wrought with impunity, and a mutual trust established upon the handsome foundation of a mutual respect for right.

"IV. The establishment of an organization of peace which *shall make* it certain that the combined power of free nations will check every invasion of right and serve to make peace and justice the more secure by affording a definite tribunal of opinion to which all *must* submit and by which every international readjustment that can not be amicably agreed upon by the peoples directly concerned *shall* be sanctioned."

Address in opening the Fourth Liberty Loan Campaign, September 27, 1918:

"First, the impartial justice meted out *must* involve no discrimination between those to whom we wish to be just and those to whom we do not wish to be just. It *must be* a justice that plays no favorites and knows no standard but the equal rights of the several peoples concerned;

"Second, no special or separate interest of any single nation or any group of nations *can be* made the basis of any part of the settlement which is not consistent with the common interest of all;

"Third, there *can be no* leagues or alliances or special covenants and understandings within the general and common family of the League of Nations;

"Fourth, and more specifically, there *can be no* special, selfish economic combinations within the League and no employment of any form of economic boycott or exclusion except as the power of economic penalty by exclusion from the markets of the world may be vested in the League of Nations itself as a means of discipline and control;

"Fifth, all international agreements and treaties of every kind *must* be made known in their entirety to the rest of the world."

CHAPTER XXXIV

THE GREAT DEBATE AND THE SEPARATE PEACE

(1919-1936)

WOODROW WILSON was the true founder of the League of Nations, but of course it was not his original idea. Philosophers and publicists had invoked for centuries the concept of a league or confederation of the nations for peace, but only in the twentieth century had statesmen begun to urge it as a practical measure. In the United States, ex-President Theodore Roosevelt had been a vigorous advocate since 1910, when he declared, in accepting the Nobel peace prize: "It would be a master stroke if those great Powers honestly bent on peace would form a League of Peace, not only to keep the peace among themselves, but to prevent, by force if necessary, its being broken by others." [1] He repeatedly urged, during the earlier years of the World War, such a "solemn agreement in a great world league for the peace of righteousness," a "solemn covenant." The elder statesmen of both parties were for it: Roosevelt, Taft, Bryan, Elihu Root, Lodge, and finally Wilson, although Lodge was to desert the idea when Wilson later coupled it with a proposed peace without victory. No one took exception to the proposal of a league of nations before 1917, and then, among the prominent leaders, only Lodge. As the war continued, and American neutrality became more and more uncertain, enlightened public interest in a league of nations became more pronounced. The interest crystallized in the formation in June, 1915, of the non-partisan civic League to Enforce Peace,[2] a propagandist organization for a league of peace at the

---

[1] Quoted by Denna F. Fleming, *The United States and the League of Nations, 1919-1920* (New York, 1932). This excellent historical tract is full of disconcerting *tu quoque* quotations for the later Republican opponents of the League, among whom Roosevelt cannot be classed. He died, January 6, 1919, before the first draft of the Covenant was formulated at the Paris Conference. We can only guess what his views would have been on the Covenant, remembering the intense partisan that he was, his intimate friendship with Lodge, and that he probably would have been the Republican nominee for the Presidency in 1920.

[2] Its statement of principles was summarized as follows:

(1) Submission of all justiciable questions to an international court of justice "both upon the merits and upon any issue as to its jurisdiction of the question."

(2) Submission of all other questions to a council of conciliation for hearing, consideration, and recommendation.

(3) Agreement "to jointly use forthwith both their economic and military forces" to

end of the war, in which over a thousand distinguished citizens, including Senator Lodge, took part.

Only when the movement, like the demand for military preparedness, had gained a large volume of public support, and when it seemed that the United States might at any time become involved in the war, namely, after the *Sussex* exchange of notes with Germany, did the President publicly champion a league of nations, as he also advocated military and naval preparedness. His first utterance was to the League to Enforce Peace, in May, 1916, and, it so happened, speaking from the same platform with Lodge.

In England, and to a less degree in other countries, similar organizations and advocates urged such a league to accompany the peace settlement. Under the horror of war the idea was taking hold of a thoughtful mankind. Various plans for the constitution of a league of nations appeared during 1918 in Great Britain, France and the United States. A committee of British specialists, acting under the chairmanship of the jurist, Lord Phillimore, drew up the first actual draft (March 20, 1918). It was mild and juridical. It called for only voluntary arbitration of international disputes, and avoided political or territorial guaranties. It limited membership to selected allied and associated powers and a few neutrals. A French official plan (June 8, 1918) provided for a similarly restricted membership, a tribunal of arbitration, an international political council which would have power if need be to carry out its decisions with economic, military and naval force, and an international police force recruited *pro-rata* from the members. This was characteristic of all French thought on a league: an international force to maintain the *status quo* established by the victor powers, which meant of course the protection of triumphant France against the future recovery of an aggressive or revengeful Germany.

The American plans came from Colonel House and President Wilson. House worked out a plan (July 16, 1918) in collaboration with Mr. David Hunter Miller, later one of the legal advisers to the American Peace Commission. It contained provision for guaranties of territorial integrity and political independence of members of the league, subject to changes pursuant to the principle of self-determination if approved

coerce any member committing acts of hostility against another before submitting to arbitration or conciliation.

(4) Periodic conferences to formulate and codify international law.

Except for the vital novelty of coercion this program was closely in line with the practice of American diplomacy hitherto. The exception, of course, was a tremendous one, contrary to the traditions of the Republic's policy since Washington and Monroe.

by the delegates of two-thirds of the members. The House plan also provided a secretariat and a permanent court, with compulsory arbitration. It provided for economic sanctions against outlaw states. President Wilson himself worked out a draft in the late summer of 1918 in which he borrowed the prominent features of the House draft, and added military and naval sanctions when necessary, with a provision (later Article XI of the League) expressing not only "concern" (as House's plan did) but providing for consultation and possible action in case of any threat to the peace of the world. Force against outlaw nations was characteristic of President Wilson's ideas of a league, as it had been of the late Theodore Roosevelt's. Yet his first draft for a league of nations called for "the reduction of national armaments to the lowest point consistent with *domestic* [1] safety."

General Smuts of South Africa drafted a plan (December 16, 1918), accompanied by a lengthy exposition, which urged, among many other things, the abolition of conscription, the nationalization of the munitions trade with international inspection, a council of the great powers, and a system of mandates for the separated portions of the Ottoman Empire (but not for the conquered German colonies in Africa and in the Pacific), and *ipso facto* war against covenant-breakers.

At Paris President Wilson formulated two more drafts, in which he incorporated ideas from the Smuts plan and from a memorandum by Mr. Miller and by Mr. James Brown Scott, legal advisers to the American Commission. At the same time Lord Robert Cecil had drawn up a draft which became the official British suggestion. The last Wilson draft and the recent Cecil draft were referred to Mr. Miller and Sir Cecil Hurst, British legal adviser, and worked into a draft which President Wilson accepted and presented to the first meeting (February 3, 1919) of the special commission of the Peace Conference for the formulation of a league of nations. The commission deliberated almost continually for the next ten days and reported the first conference draft of the League of Nations, proposed to be incorporated as the first chapter of the treaty of peace with Germany. The plan naturally contained many features and much phraseology of the basic Miller-Hurst preliminary draft, to which the earlier British and American drafts had in turn made their contributions. The Conference published it to the world on February 14, when President Wilson left Paris for a trip to the United States to attend to his constitutional duties associated

[1] Italics inserted.

with the ending of the Congress, and to introduce the proposed covenant
to the people of the United States.[1]

In the present expanded edition of this Diplomatic History we have
no place to include the text of the Covenant of the League of Nations, and
the amendments made between the two world wars of the twentieth
century, which documents were printed in parallel columns as an appendix to the first edition.

Well-wishers to the Covenant criticized the President, and hostile
partisans blamed him bitterly, for not having taken the document
directly to the Senate, then in session, to ask for its advice. He could
then have known in advance the indispensable amendments which would
satisfy that body. Instead he discussed the document first in public
addresses, and after this met informally the Committee on Foreign
Relations of the Senate jointly with the Committee on Foreign Affairs
of the House in an unsatisfactory dinner conference at the White House.
This may have been another strategical mistake in handling the Senate;
but if the other powers in Paris had realized that there were certain
formulated amendments which the President must have in order to
secure the consent of the Senate they could have held him up for further
diplomatic equivalents at Paris. Nations do not concede favors
gratuitously.

This proposal for the League, now formulated into actual articles and
presented to the world, elicited a widespread sympathy and approval in
both Europe and the United States. William Howard Taft, the only
living ex-President, hailed it as a partnership with the world not incompatible with the sovereignty of the United States "regulated by
international law and morality and consistent with the same sovereignty
as other countries." He pleaded publicly for the Senate's unanimous
support of the document. Academic and religious leaders acclaimed it
as a bright new dispensation for harassed mankind. Presently more
cautious heads began to discern difficulties and to qualify their support.
Even the proponents of the League feared it might be impossible to
live up to such serious limitations on the sovereign rights of the United

---

[1] Historians will always be grateful to David Hunter Miller, as they have been to
James Madison for his notes on the Federal Convention at Philadelphia in 1787. Mr.
Miller has published the preliminary drafts of plans for a League of Nations, the
minutes of the special commission on the League at the Paris Peace Conference, with
ancillary documents, together with his own valuable commentary: *The Drafting of the
League of Nations* (2 Vols., New York, 1928). He had interpreted these data in a popular lecture in 1921, "The Making of the League," published in House and Seymour, *op. cit.*

In his history, *The Society of Nations, Its Origin and Constitutional Development*
(Washington, 1932, Brookings Institution), Felix Morley traces its origin in great detail

States. The partisan opposition, of course, stressed these vigorously, and brought up all other conceivable objections.

Cutting through a great medley of expression of opinion, both in the Senate and out of it, one may say that a responsible public demand for a certain minimum of amendments to the proposed Covenant was apparent in the United States. In noting these objections to the text as it then stood, we give the gist of President Wilson's responses to them, either then or later.

First and foremost there was a demand for an explicit recognition of the Monroe Doctrine as a reserved policy for the United States quite beyond the touch of the League. Wilson declared that Article X had now made a world doctrine of the principles of Monroe. Article X was the one which guaranteed "the territorial integrity and political independence" of all members of the League. Then there was a demand for an explicit reservation that no sanctions could be shared by the United States in the enforcement of Article X or any other article of the League without an express vote of Congress. The President had declared that there was nothing in the document legally to oblige such sanctions, though he would not deny a moral obligation. There was much objection to Article X, itself, particularly by Mr. Elihu Root, voiced later. To the President this was the "heart of the covenant." It was, as we have seen already, the keystone of the proposed pact of 1916 to Pan-Americanize the Monroe Doctrine. He had now given it a global concept. It was indeed his principal contribution to the great constitution. He would not change it.

With the tariff and oriental immigration particularly in mind, cautious students insisted that all subjects of domestic legislation should be excluded from the League's purview. The President explained that the League could take cognizance of no dispute without unanimity of the Council powers (one of which would always be the United States). even though one or more of them be involved in the dispute and obliged to withdraw from sitting in judgment on its own case when later the Council by unanimous vote might take the dispute under examination. This was only an interpretation of what at best was not clearly defined in the Covenant; it would remain for future practice to confirm or reject it. There was a strong demand for an explicit statement about unanimity. There was also a desire for a provision for withdrawal from the League, although Mr. Wilson implied that such was not necessary if a power wanted to withdraw.

Friends to the League suggested amendments to cover these objections. One or more of these suggested amendments had the support of statesmen like Elihu Root and William Jennings Bryan, and of public leaders like A. Lawrence Lowell and Charles Evans Hughes, and many other eminent citizens. Their supporters felt that such changes would secure the loyal membership of their country, that they were necessary to overcome the opposition of a strong partisan group of Republican Senators. There were other men, particularly in the Senate, who were opposed to any League in any shape or form. They would vote for amendments when the time came, but frankly they would not, in the final decision, vote for the treaty even with their amendments. During the great debate in the Senate, these Senators were known as the "irreconcilables." The irreconcilables joined with other Republican Senators not opposed to a League in principle to demand that the whole idea be separated from the negotiations at Paris; that a peace be first made with the enemy, and the League taken up later. Under the leadership of Senator Lodge, whose precise attitude toward the League may never be known, thirty-nine Republican Senators or Senators-elect, declared, as Congress was closing, March 4, 1919, that it was the sense of the Senate that peace terms should first be negotiated with Germany, "and that the proposal for a League of Nations to insure the permanent peace of the world should be then taken up *for careful consideration*." [1] This was not a resolution of the Senate, but it was a clear-cut ultimatum from more than one-third of the membership of the next Senate in which a two-thirds majority would be necessary for the ratification of any treaty.

President Wilson met this challenge by declaring in a parting public address, in New York City, the eve of his return to France, that the Covenant would be made a part of the treaty, "not only in it, but so many threads of the treaty tied to the covenant that you cannot dissect the covenant from the treaty without destroying the whole vital structure." Speaking from the same platform ex-President Taft declared that the Covenant ought to be a part of the treaty and urged the President to make it so.

It was evident that if the President did not at least secure some of the generally supported amendments that the otherwise sympathetic Republican senators would join with the irreconcilables to defeat the whole thing.

After the President's departure Taft became alarmed at the rising tide of criticism and opposition and cabled to him in Paris that to carry

---

[1] Italics inserted.

the treaty and League in the Senate it would be advisable to secure reservations in regard to the Monroe Doctrine, domestic legislation, unanimity of Council voting, and withdrawal from the League.

Taft cabled to Wilson (March 18, 1919): "If you bring back the treaty with the League of Nations in it make more specific reservation of the Monroe Doctrine, fix a term for the duration of the League, and the limit of armament, require expressly unanimity of action of Executive Council and body of Delegates, and add to Article XV a provision that where the Executive Council of the Body of Delegates finds the difference to grow out of an exclusively domestic policy, it shall recommend no settlement, the ground will be completely cut from under the opponents of the League in the Senate. Addition to Article XV will answer objections as to Japanese immigration, as well as tariffs under Article XXI. Reservation of the Monroe Doctrine might be as follows:

'Any American State or States may protect the integrity of American territory and the independence of the Government whose territory it is, whether a member of the League or not, and may, in the interests of American peace, object to and prevent the further transfer of American territory or sovereignty to any power outside the Western Hemisphere.'

"Monroe Doctrine reservation alone would probably carry the treaty, but others would make it certain."

A second telegram (April 13), from Taft and A. Lawrence Lowell, President of Harvard University, added:

"Friends of the covenant are seriously alarmed over report that no amendment will be made more specifically safeguarding Monroe Doctrine. At full meeting of Executive Committee of League to Enforce Peace, with thirty members from eighteen States present, unanimous opinion that without such amendment Republican Senators will certainly defeat ratification of treaty, because public opinion will sustain them. With such amendment, treaty will be promptly ratified." [1]

Once a draft of the Covenant had been agreed upon it was not easy to secure amendments. Once the door to revision was opened other governments proposed amendments, too, or opposed them as their political exigencies dictated. French and British representatives in the commission on the league of nations opposed the President's desire for an amendment on the Monroe Doctrine. The British withdrew their

[1] Fleming, *op. cit.*, 183-187.

objections after a private understanding that the President would agree to a future limitation of naval armaments.[1] Wilson then arranged a personal bargain with Clemenceau, regarding the disposition of the Saar Valley, in order to secure French approval in the commission for a curiously qualified exemption for the Monroe Doctrine, in the shape of a new article, XXI: "Nothing in this covenant shall be deemed to affect the validity of international engagements, such as treaties of arbitration, or regional understandings like the Monroe Doctrine, for securing the maintenance of peace." This gave to the Monroe Doctrine a puzzling international recognition. What is a regional understanding (*entente régionale*, in the equally official French text) like the Monroe Doctrine? This question is very difficult for even most learned jurists to answer precisely. There was also another amendment in the final text of the Covenant, as incorporated in the Treaty of Versailles, permitting states to withdraw, after having fulfilled their obligations, upon two years' notice. There were many small changes in the wording and arrangement of the final Covenant.[2] At the final session of the commission the Japanese delegates labored for an amendment, as important for them, and be it said to the world, as the Monroe Doctrine was for the United States: "the endorsement of the principle of equality of nations and just treatment of their nationals." With his eyes downcast on the table, Lord Robert Cecil, the British delegate, said that under instructions from his government he refused the amendment.

At the close of the regular session of Congress, on March 4, 1919, a Republican filibuster had defeated appropriation bills with the design of forcing the President to call a special session of Congress before the end of the fiscal year June 30, while the treaty was still in negotiation.[3] The special session of the new Congress, with its Republican majority in both houses, convened May 19, 1919. Senator Lodge now declared, in June, that the amended Covenant would not do. His friend on the Peace Commission, Henry White, had confidentially cabled him to send over the texts of the amendments that in Lodge's opinion would satisfy the Republican Senate. This the senator had refused to do. His refusal of White's invitation to agree on amendments suggests that Senator Lodge's real motive was to load the Covenant and the treaty with such amendments as to make it unacceptable to the President and his sup-

[1] *Intimate Papers, op. cit.,* IV, 416-417; Miller, *Drafting of the Covenant, op, cit.,* I, 338, 419-427.
[2] Miller, *op. cit.,* gives complete minutes of the commission and its discussion of amendments.
[3] Fleming, *op. cit.,* 212.

porters in the Senate.[1] He acknowledged that public opinion over-whelmingly favored the League. The man in the street did not know what it was all about, he said, but "the preachers of sermons," and the university teachers, and generally the newspaper editors favored it as it stood.[2]

It was by way of delay, by interminable hearings, by slow formulation of amendments and reservations that the Committee on Foreign Relations, with a majority of its members hostile to the League, at least as it stood, proceeded to consider the treaty. In Paris, the President and his advisers had felt, that with the Monroe Doctrine amendment, the Republican opposition had no chance of defeating the League or the treaty—such a repudiation of the President before the world, followed by a separate peace with the enemy, seemed unthinkable. Senator Lodge once had said something like this to the Senate.

He had declared: "Suppose we reject the treaty; what follows? Let us look at it practically. We continue the state of war, and every sensible man in the country, every business interest, desires the re-establishment of peace in law as well as in fact. At the same time we repudiate the President and his action before the whole world, and the repudiation of the President in such a matter as this is, to my mind, the humiliation of the United States in the eyes of civilized mankind and brands us as a people incapable of great affairs or of taking rank where we belong, as one of the great world powers." [3]

But this declaration was in 1899 when he was advocating the ratification of a treaty negotiated by a Republican President, a treaty which acquired the Philippines and entangled the United States in the international politics of Asia where it had no vital interests. Now it was a Democratic President, whose success with the treaty and the League

[1] That is the testimony of his daughter, who was apparently unusually intimate with his political activity; but his grandson states that he really wanted the League with reservations. Fleming, op. cit., 476. Lodge's own apologia, The Senate and the League of Nations (New York, 1925), does not reveal whether he really wanted the treaty and League even with his reservations.

[2] "I said to Senator Borah" (one of the irreconcilables, a member of the Committee on Foreign Relations), "it seemed perfectly obvious to me that any attempt to defeat the treaty of Versailles by a straight vote in the Senate, if taken immediately, would be hopeless, even if it were desirable." Believing that "the interests and safety of the United States might be so protected by amendments or reservations that a large majority of Republicans could vote for it, I told him that in any event there was only one thing to do and that was to proceed in the discussion of the treaty by way of amendment and reservation." Lodge, Senate and League, op. cit., 147. It would have been very easy for the Senator mistakenly to have believed, in his remembrance of the conversation, that he had used the phrase "even if it were desirable."

[3] Congressional Record, January 24, 1899.

might make the Democratic Party, instead of the Republican Party, the normal party in power in the United States.

Woodrow Wilson, too, as a younger man had appreciated the force of this argument, when in his treatise on *Congressional Government*, he had pointed out that the President, with his control over negotiation, could so commit the country in the eyes of the world that it would be most difficult, if not impossible, for the Senate to use its constitutional power to repudiate him.

It became apparent after Wilson's return from Paris that with the strategy of delay the opposition was making considerable headway with public opinion. It had raised a fund for speakers and writers against the League, "the evil thing with a holy name." [1]

Contrary to custom, the hearings of the Committee on Foreign Relations were in public. [2] "Pitiless publicity" was turned against the President. There was appearing an increasing conviction that the Covenant had not been sufficiently amended. A natural reaction, "the slump in idealism," had set in, in the United States, and all over the world, weary as the peoples were of war and international politics. The President, resorting to his most effective political weapon, started on a speaking tour of the country, to rally public opinion to his support and to that of an unamended treaty. His plea was for the League of Nations as the hope of the world, against a separate treaty as a shameful desertion of the associates in war. In the midst of this tour the overworked statesman collapsed, September 26, 1919. He was never to recover his health. The cause had lost its most eloquent champion.

The Committee on Foreign Relations at last submitted its report to the Senate, September 10. It recommended forty-five amendments to the treaty, and four reservations. Most of these amendments [3] were to separate the United States from any responsibility in executing the political and economic provisions of the treaty in Europe. The reservations were to protect, in every conceivable way, American sovereignty

---

[1] The principal contributors to the fund were Henry C. Frick and Andrew W. Mellon, industrialist millionaires of Pennsylvania. Mellon became the Secretary of the Treasury under subsequent Republican administrations.

[2] The hearings were promptly published for public consumption, *Hearings Before the Committee on Foreign Relations of the United States on the Treaty of Peace with Germany Signed at Versailles, on June 28, 1919* (66th Congress, 1st Session, Senate Document No. 106, Washington, G.P.O., 1919). This publication is a rich mine of source material.

[3] There were only two amendments recommended for the Covenant, both designed to insure equality of voting between the United States and the whole British Empire, regardless of Dominions.

from the League of Nations. A minority report, from six Democratic members of the Committee, recommended the ratification of the treaty as it was signed. The Senate proceeded first to vote on the proposed amendments and reservations. These it could accept or reject by majority vote, before the final vote on the treaty itself, which required a two-thirds majority. By the time the treaty had advanced to a vote on advice and consent, fourteen reservations had been added, the so-called Lodge reservations:

(1) Reservation to the United States in case of its withdrawal from the League of sole judgment whether it had fulfilled its international obligations under the Covenant.

(2) Disavowal of any obligation to preserve the territorial integrity or political independence of any other country, or to interfere in controversies between nations, under Article X, or any other article of the entire treaty, or to employ the military or naval forces of the United States for any purpose except by act of Congress.

(3) No mandate to be accepted by the United States without vote of Congress.

(4) Exclusion of domestic questions from the consideration of the Council or of the Assembly of the League.

(5) Declaration that the Monroe Doctrine was "wholly outside the jurisdiction of the League of Nations" and entirely unaffected by any provision of the treaty.

(6) Withholding assent of the United States to the Shantung settlement, and reserving complete liberty of action.

(7) Reservation to Congress of the right to enact law for the appointment of representatives of the United States to the League.

(8) That the Reparations Commission should have no right to interfere with trade between the United States and Germany, without the approbation of Congress.

(9) Necessity of an act of Congress for appropriation of expenses of the United States in the League.

(10) Right to increase armaments of the United States, under any League plan of disarmament, in case the United States is threatened with invasion or engaged in war.

(11) Right to allow nationals of covenant-breaking states, residing in the United States, to continue their normal relations.

(12) Freedom to regulate private debts, property, rights and interests of citizens of the United States.

(13) Withholding assent to the section of the treaty setting up an international labor organization, until Congress should have voted approval.

(14) Protecting the United States against any unequal vote, in the League, of the entire British Empire, notwithstanding the votes of self-governing Dominions or Colonies.

As we look back on the Lodge reservations today, they do not appear to be so exorbitant as they did in 1919. President Wilson opposed them, and advised his senatorial supporters to oppose them; they would nullify the treaty, he said, not ratify it. The assertion failed to persuade his opponents.

The Senate voted three times on the Treaty of Versailles on November 19, 1919. Two votes were for the treaty with the Lodge reservations. The Democrats, loyal to Wilson's desires, joined the irreconcilables to vote it down: first vote 39 for, 55 against; second vote 41 for, 51 against. Senator Hitchcock, Democratic leader, asked for reconsideration of the defeated treaty with only five reservations attached: the right of Congress to authorize or forbid the use of American forces for League sanctions; the Monroe Doctrine; equality of voting power of the United States with the British Empire, including each Dominion; the right of withdrawal; exemption of domestic questions from the League's jurisdiction. The Senate rejected Hitchcock's plea: 41 for, 51 against. But it allowed itself to vote once more on the treaty, without reservations. Again the reservationists joined with the irreconcilables: 38 for, 53 against.[1]

The rejection of the treaty provoked a widespread popular demand for still another vote. The Senate reconsidered and voted again, March 19, 1920. This time the President told his followers he would not object to mild interpretative reservations. But the Senate again attached the fourteen Lodge reservations, and added a fifteenth, expressing sympathy with Ireland's struggle for independence. For the last time the Senate voted down the treaty with the Lodge reservations: 49 votes for, 35 against. Some League defeatists voted for Ireland, confident the treaty would not get a two-thirds majority. In his successful attempt to get the League of Nations written into the treaty, Woodrow Wilson had made great concessions from his principles to the national interests of Great Britain, France, Italy and Japan. Now he would not make necessary concessions to his political opponents at home. He rejected the sage counsel of his friend Colonel House, to leave to the Senate, this second time, full responsibility on the treaty.[2] Now a shadow fell be-

---

[1] For best analysis of the Great Debate, see T. A. Bailey, *Woodrow Wilson and the Great Betrayal* (New York, 1945).

[2] "Practically every one who is in close touch with the situation admits that the Treaty cannot be ratified without substantial reservations. You must not be a party to those reservations. You stood for the Treaty as it was made in Paris, but if the Senate refuses to ratify without reservations, under the circumstances, I would let the Allies determine whether or not they will accept them. . . . If you take the stand indicated, it will

tween the two men, darkening one of the strangest friendships in history.[1]

There is good reason to believe, from the brief mission of Viscount Grey,[2] as Ambassador to the United States in the winter of 1919-1920, that the Allies would have accepted whatever reservations the Senate might have voted, as Colonel House had advised the President they would probably do. Ostensibly on account of his desperate illness, Wilson refused to receive the new British Ambassador, and he retired after a brief mission of three months.

It has been bitterly and rather generally remarked that if Woodrow Wilson had been a Republican President, presenting the same treaty to the same Senate, he would have secured its ratification according to his heart's desire. That is probably true. The vice of partisan politics explains the rejection.[3] Partisan politics, nevertheless, is a part of the American system of constitutional government, on which Woodrow Wilson was an authority. In this case the opposition stood on secure constitutional ground with an elected majority behind them. One must feel that the Democratic President would have had less trouble with the Senate if he had appointed the plenipotentiaries to the Paris Peace Conference with due deference to its new Republican leadership, and with the Senate's confirmation. As it was, he could have had the treaty ratified with the Lodge reservations, at the very worst.

Passionately interested students and commentators have debated the question: Who was responsible for the defeat of the treaty and the League in the United States? The answer is easy, very obvious: both Lodge and Wilson. In effect these personal enemies united, for opposite motives, to kill the treaty. Lodge was content. Wilson died broken and bitterly disappointed. It will be for the historian of the future to decide whether the succession of academic and political defeats which opened and closed the career of Woodrow Wilson transcend the political victories which fell to Henry Cabot Lodge.

There is one more chapter to the great debate. Before the last vote on the treaty, the President had announced that if it were rejected, he would take the issue to the people in a "great and solemn referendum," making it the outstanding issue between the two parties in the approach-

aid rather than hinder those working for mild reservations. It will absolutely ensure the passage of the Treaty and probably in a form acceptable to both you and the Allies." Seymour, *Intimate Papers, op. cit.*, IV, 510-511.

[1] George Sylvester Viereck, *The Strangest Friendship in History; Woodrow Wilson and Colonel House* (New York, 1932).

[2] As Sir Edward Grey he had been the former British Secretary for Foreign Affairs.

[3] Holt, *Rejected Treaties, op. cit.*, has the most acute analysis of the political struggle. See also Fleming, *op. cit.*, and H. B. Learned's chapter in the sixth volume of Temperley, *Paris Peace Conference, op. cit.*

ing national election of 1920. Success here was presumably his hope when he opposed uncompromisingly the Lodge reservations and rejected the advice of Colonel House.

In that election it did not prove to be a clear-cut issue for the voters. The Democratic platform came out for the League, "without reservations which would impair its essential integrity"; but did not oppose the acceptance of any reservations making clearer or more specific the obligations of the United States to the League associates. The Republican Party stood "for agreement among the nations to preserve the peace of the world." It continued with ambiguous and latitudinarian phrases: "such an international association must be based upon international justice, and must provide methods which shall maintain the rule of public right by the development of law and the decision of impartial courts, and which shall secure instant and general international conference whenever peace shall be threatened by political action, so that the nations pledged to do and insist upon what is just and fair may exercise their influence and power for the prevention of war." The Republicans would not take a stand clearly against the League. The Democrats would not oppose reservations.

The Democratic candidate, Governor Cox, advocated the League and lost. The Republican candidate, Senator Harding, who had voted for the League twice with the Lodge reservations, declared that he was for "an association of nations." He allowed his party followers to believe what they pleased from that. The irreconcilables said this meant that he was against the League. Republicans who wanted the League asserted that "association" meant *the* League. Thirty-one eminent Republicans (including Elihu Root, Charles Evans Hughes, Herbert Hoover, A. Lawrence Lowell, Nicholas M. Butler, John Grier Hibben, and several other presidents of the leading universities) signed a statement assuring the American people that this meant the League. No one knows how many people thought they were voting for the League, with the reservations of course, when they voted for the Republican ticket. Harding and Coolidge were elected by an overwhelming landslide.

The election was not a referendum, nor was it even solemn. On the League there was no clear issue. Nor was there much on any other subject. The Republican campaign leaders plastered the country with huge billboards, bearing flattering likenesses of the candidates framed in red, white and blue, with the ridiculous and meaningless slogan: "Let us be done with wiggle and wobble." It is easy to see that the Republican platform wiggled and wobbled more than the Democratic statement on the League.

Inaugurated, President Harding declared that "the Administration which came into power in March, 1921, definitely and decisively put aside all thoughts of entering the League of Nations. It doesn't propose to enter now, by the side door, back door, or cellar door."[1] Before he made this announcement the most eminent two of his cabinet members, who had signed the assurance of the Thirty-One that "association" meant really the League, had accepted office under his Administration.[2]

Congress interpreted the election to be a mandate from the people against joining the League. If there be question what the people meant in 1920, and certainly there must be question, there is no question what they later felt. If there were a majority sentiment discernible for it, the politicians would have been quick to put a League plank in a party platform; from 1920 to 1940 no political party in the United States dared to come out for the League.

"To many of us who lived through those war years and who ardently hoped for a better world to follow the tragedy of the nations, it seemed as though the partisans of 1919, on both sides, in the great debate on the League of Nations, joined in folly to defeat the League, each group for opposite reasons: the irreconcilables because they wanted no League at all; the Wilsonians because they would have no essential reservations. It seemed, too, as though the election of 1920 was a joke on the people, so far as any great and solemn referendum was concerned. It seemed in short as though the United States foolishly threw away the victory it had won at war. Those of us who have lived on into two decades after must now see things in a different light. The League of Nations has been a disappointing failure as a promise to keep the peace of the world or to make wars less likely. It has been a failure, not because the United States did not join it; but because the great powers have been unwilling to apply sanctions except where it suited their individual national interests to do so, and because Democracy, on which the original concepts of the League rested for support, has collapsed over half the world. If the United States had been a party, these same selfish national interests would have been at play, and American diplomacy would have been obliged to contend with them. Amidst a world studded with dictators, the European powers, unwilling to join in sacrifices to enforce peace, would have urged the United States to do the sanctioning

[1] Fleming, *op. cit.*, 472.
[2] Charles E. Hughes, Secretary of State, and Herbert Hoover, Secretary of Commerce

in regions where, in turn, it had no vital national interests. Before the great powers can join in sacrifices of blood and treasure to keep the peace in regions where they have no real interests, a great transformation of will must take place among the peoples of the nations. I am afraid there must be much more suffering in the world before that transformation takes place. But in the end the idea of the League will prevail or civilization as we know it today in Europe and America may collapse. Woodrow Wilson's steadfastness to that ideal may then transfigure his political mistakes."

The above paragraph was written in the first edition of this history, when the League was breaking down, in Manchuria, Ethiopia, and in Europe, because the powers shrank from the sacrifices necessary to make it work, even though the United States gave notice that it would cooperate with League sanctions at least to the extent of not opposing them. Now, in 1950, the time of suffering has come to transform will and to teach the United Nations the sacrifices necessary for the commonwealth of mankind in any future peace of victory.

The defeat of the Treaty of Versailles, both in the Senate, and (so the Republican Party immediately proceeded to construe it) in the national election of 1920, meant a separate peace with the enemy. Hostilities had ceased to exist since the armistice of November 11, 1918, and trade with Germany had already set in following the European peace. In the United States the technical state of war terminated with a resolution of Congress, July 2, 1921, which declared the war with Germany to be at an end, reserving to the United States all rights which would have accrued to it by benefit of the Treaty of Versailles, or by the European treaties of peace with the remnants of the Austro-Hungarian Empire. During the war the Government had sequestered German and other enemy private property within the United States as pawn for American claims against Germany and Austria-Hungary.[1] The resolution ending the war retained custody of this property pending separate treaties by the United States which would satisfy claims over a wide field. The act of one belligerent, of course, cannot terminate a war unless the other parties to the war acquiesce. There was no question but what the former enemy acquiesced, but it remained to make treaties settling outstanding uncertainties. In a short treaty of August 25, 1921, Germany confirmed to the United States all the rights, privileges, in-

[1] This was in violation of the treaty of 1828 with Prussia, reviving Article XXIII of the treaty of 1799, but that treaty had long since been thrown overboard by German naval practices.

demnities, reparations, or other advantages which had been set forth in the resolution of Congress, including also "all the rights and advantages stipulated for the benefit of the United States" in the Treaty of Versailles. A similar treaty was signed (August 24, 1921) with Austria, in reference to the Treaty of St. Germain; and with Hungary (August 29, 1921), in regard to the Trianon Treaty.[1] Both were ratified promptly. The United States thus secured from the enemy all the advantages of the treaties made by the Allies, and none of their obligations, and, let it be added, none of the hatreds left in their wake. A series of treaties established normal diplomatic relations and amity with the seven new European succession states, and with Turkey.[2]

It remained to settle the claims against Germany and Austria-Hungary arising out of protested acts during the period of neutrality, notably the submarine cases, and to wind up the war claims of nationals on both sides. This was done not by a treaty, but by executive agreements of extraordinary significance for the treaty-making power.

The Mixed Claims Commission the United States and Germany, set up by the agreement of August 10, 1922; and the Tripartite Mixed Claims Commission the United States, Austria, and Hungary, set up under the agreement of November 26, 1924; and the American arbiter provided by the War Claims Act of March 10, 1928, for the settlement of American, German, Austrian, and Hungarian claims, involved property on both sides of hundreds of millions of dollars, by far the greatest amount ever submitted to adjudication in the history of arbitration. The total of actual awards by the two commissions and the arbiter was more than ten times greater than the total awards of the tribunals set up under Jay's Treaty of 1794 with Great Britain, and under the Treaty of Washington of 1871 with Great Britain, including the Geneva Arbitration. The Commission with Germany consisted of one commissioner from each side and an umpire (whose decision was final) chosen by agreement of the two governments. It was at the suggestion of Germany that the umpire was appointed by the President of the United States. The Tripartite Commission was limited to one sole commissioner to be agreed upon by the three governments (he proved at first to be the same person [3]) who also

[1] C. C. Hyde in *Am. Secs. State,* X, 225-230, 253-256, briefly describes the technical questions involved.

[2] For Turkey, see above, p. 640.

[3] Hon. Edwin B. Parker, who died October 30, 1929, before he could complete the umpire's work of the Mixed Claims Commission, United States and Germany. He was succeeded by the Hon. Roland Boyden, who died in 1931, and was in turn succeeded by Mr. Justice Owen J. Roberts of the United States Supreme Court, who carried the work forward.

acted as umpire of the Mixed Claims Commission the United States and Germany, and later as the American war claims arbiter.

In addition to the claims of American nationals against Germany, Austria, and Hungary that went before the respective arbitral commissions, there were large claims of German nationals and relatively much smaller claims of Austrian, and of Hungarian nationals against the United States, that were adjudicated by the American arbiter. Most of these involved the seizure, after the outbreak of the war, of German merchant ships which had been interned in American harbors during the period of neutrality, and of patents and a radio station. The War Settlements Act of 1928, passed by the Congress of the United States, provided for the adjudication of these claims by an American arbiter appointed by the President, and for the payment of all awards by the arbiter for German, Austrian, and Hungarian claims; and by the Mixed Claims Commission for claims of nationals of the United States. This legislation proved acceptable to both the foreign and the American claimants.

A tabulation of the intricate work of these arbitral settlements—which occupied the greater part of two decades—and of the partial payment of the awards achieved before the collapse of German reparations in 1932, is given on p. 661.

We observe here that payment has not been completed of the total awards of either the American claimants or the German. Approximately $92,665,000 as of January 1, 1941, on which interest is accumulating at the rate of five per cent, is still owing to citizens of the United States; and $100,275,000 as of September 30, 1940, on which interest is accumulating at five per cent, is still owing to German claimants in whose favor the Commission made awards.

The Settlement of War Claims Act of 1928 provided for the complicated pay-off of the awards to the claimants of all nations concerned in these arbitrations, by creating a pool or special German deposit fund in the Treasury of the United States, made up of: appropriations by the United States Government; 20 per cent of the proceeds of German enemy property sequestered during the war (after all properties under $10,000 had been unconditionally released) plus accumulated interest on the whole of it while in sequestration; and moneys received and to be received from Germany on account of reparations (after certain sums had been set aside on account of the satisfaction of occupation costs of the United States army in the Rhineland).[1]

[1] See note at end of chapter.

AUSTRIA AND HUNGARY

	Principal	With interest[1] accumulated to January 1, 1928, in accordance with the Settlement of War Claims Act of 1928	With arrears of interest accumulated on unpaid principal to September 30, 1940	Amount paid or in process of payment by April 7, 1941
Awards of the Mixed Claims Commission, United States and Germany, to nationals of the United States and to the United States Government				
Total awarded to nationals of the United States:	$139,316,214.04	$201,507,975.18	$254,274,158.89	$161,608,544.66[2]
Total awarded to the Government of the United States:	42,034,791.41	61,244,119.63	100,274,695.87	
Awards of the Tripartite Mixed Claims Commission, United States, Austria, and Hungary:	*Principal and Interest to date of award:*			
Against Hungary	$172,619.70			Substantially paid [3]
Against Austria	370,032.14			Substantially paid [3]
Awards of the American Arbitrator	*Principal and Interest to December 31, 1928, in accordance with Settlement of War Claims Act of 1928*			
To German nationals:	$86,738,320.83		$116,901,476.57	$43,368,899.61
To Austrian nationals:	912,687.94			Substantially paid [3]
To Hungarian nationals:	53,799.56			Substantially paid [3]

1 Interest allowed on awards for property damage during neutrality, from date of spoliation at 5%. Interest allowed on awards for property damage during belligerency, from November 11, 1918, at 5%. Interest allowed on death or personal injury awards from date of award, at 5%.

2 This includes approximately $23,600,000 paid in January, 1941, on account of the sabotage awards entered October 30, 1939, plus approximately $2,222,000, being a 5 per cent dividend on account of Class III awards in process of payment in April, 1941. Payment on account of the sabotage awards, which stated as of January 10, 1941, amounted to approximately $52,000,000, was delayed for over a year due to litigation instituted in the Federal Courts by certain holders of prior awards in an endeavor to have the sabotage awards set aside by the Courts. The decision of the Court of Appeals of the District of Columbia (114 Fed. (2d) 464) dismissing the bill of complaint was affirmed in a decision of the Supreme Court of the United States handed down January 6, 1941 (311 U. S. 470).

3 These payments had not been completed because of the failure of claimants to file applications required by law.

Thus approximately $199,300,000—of which Congress appropriated approximately $86,700,000—was made immediately available pursuant to the Settlement of War Claims Act for the satisfaction of these awards on both sides; the remaining unpaid part of awards was to be taken care of by the proceeds of German bonds deposited under a Debt Agreement that would replenish the pool in future years until all financial obligations were satisfied.

American claimants possessing awards for injury or loss of life, or for other claims under $100,000, were to be paid in full; those with awards over $100,000, and for other than death or personal injury, were to receive in cash preferential *pro rata* payments on account of their awards until such time as the total payments to American nationals equalled 80 per cent of the total awards to such nationals; the balance of these awards was to be paid in installments. German claimants with awards from the arbiter were to be paid 50 per cent in cash and 50 per cent in installments, and the 20 per cent of temporarily withheld alien property funds, plus the unallocated interest fund, was to be paid back eventually out of the pool. The comparatively small sums of the awards to American, Austrian and Hungarian claimants by the Tripartite Commission and the American arbiter were to be paid in cash out of the Austrian and Hungarian special deposit accounts provided for in the act.

The United States Government under the Settlement of War Claims Act had to wait for the payment of its awards by the Mixed Claims Commission until all claims of American and German nationals were fully satisfied. No provision was made in the act for the satisfaction of the army of occupation costs of $247,865,645. This, however, was fully provided for in the Debt Funding Agreement of June 23, 1930.

Summing up the whole schedule, it may be said that 20 per cent of individual awards to American nationals, 100 per cent of the awards to the United States in its own right, 50 per cent of German awards, and 20 per cent of the liquidated German enemy property plus the unallocated interest fund, depended on the continuation of the German stream of reparation payments in future years as provided for in the Debt Funding Agreement of 1930; for the pool was not big enough to pay all awards outright. Meanwhile 80 per cent of the liquidated German alien property was immediately released, including earnings and profits thereon accruing since the passage of the Winslow Act on March 4, 1923. The owners thus lost only a portion of their interest, namely, that prior to March 4, 1923, which was eventually to be returned, and had to wait along with the American nationals for 20 per cent of their principal, and also suffered the losses inherent in a forced liquidation in time of war of the sequestered property. All in all, however, they were satisfied; because these funds in America had been kept relatively intact for them, whereas if they had been previously transferred to Germany they would have disappeared in the disastrous inflation of German currency. The treatment measured out to former enemy claimants and property holders was nearly as good as that secured by the victorious government for its own nationals. The whole settlement contrasts brightly with the loss of private property by German aliens in the European [1] Allied countries, where enemy property was sequestered and totally credited after the war to the huge reparations bill charged up to Germany; this amounted to confiscation in all but name.

Arrangements for the German reparation payments, part of which was to flow into the pool for the payment of awards on both sides, and part of which was set aside for the satisfaction of army occupation costs, were made under a series of three executive agreements with several powers concerned. The Wadsworth Agreement of May 25, 1923, regulated the amounts and payments by installments for army occupation costs only. The other two agreements, the Paris Agreement of January 14, 1925, with the Allies, and the German-American Debt Agreement of June 23, 1930,[2] accommodated all German payments to the United States to the readjustments of the general reparation problem effected by the Allies through the Dawes Plan (1925) and by the Young Plan (1929) which was expected to supersede the Dawes Plan.

The collapse of German reparations payments in 1932 upset the remaining payments to German claimants; and to American claimants (for installments, on awards over $100,000, of the 20 per cent which remained to be paid to them). In 1932 Germany postponed indefinitely payment of the coupons on the occupation bonds, though some interest was paid (part of it in marks deposited or "blocked" in Germany)

---

[1] Japan returned all of the German enemy property seized within the territorial limits of the Japanese Islands.

[2] The effect of the last of these agreements was to spread German payments to the United States, separately on claims and on army occupation costs, over a long period of years. To cover these payments Germany deposited with the Secretary of the Treasury of the United States two series of non-interest bearing bonds: one series totaling RM. 1,048,100,000 (approximately $250,000,000) to satisfy original army occupation costs by installments over a spread of 36 years; and another series of RM. 2,121,600,000 (approximately $505,000,000) to satisfy obligations on account of awards of the Mixed Claims Commission, payable by installments through the next fifty years, or as long as might be necessary short of fifty years to complete the awards. This was the stream expected to flow into the pool above referred to.

on account of the postponed coupons. Of the total occupation costs of $247,865,645 Germany had paid by 1932 $65,998,512.13. Germany also suspended payments on the second series of bonds for the obligations of the awards of the Mixed Claims Commission, according to an announcement of the President of the United States on March 2, 1935.[1] The payment of the remainder of the awards due the creditor claimants on both sides was thus indefinitely held up.[2] Having repudiated this obligation in 1932, Germany, under the Hitler régime, directed money (which otherwise might pay reparations, at least in part) to rearming on land, on sea or in the air. There was no way for the victors of 1918 to stop this, except to go to war again. This they were still unwilling to do.

None of the treaties with the former enemy states, and none of the executive agreements, said anything about settling the principles of submarine warfare which caused all the trouble. Three later multilateral international conventions, to none of which Germany was an original signatory, defined the law of submarine warfare: the unratified treaty of 1922 among the United States, the British Empire, France, Italy and Japan, signed during the Washington Conference; the treaty of 1930 among the United States, Great Britain and Japan, signed at the London Conference for the limitation of naval armaments; and the Pan-American treaty of 1928.

The attempt to regulate submarine warfare in 1922, an attempt which failed because France did not ratify the treaty, stipulated:

The Signatory Powers recognize the practical impossibility of using submarines as commerce destroyers without violating, as they were violated in the recent war of 1914-1918, the requirements universally accepted by civilized nations for the protection of the lives of neutrals and noncombatants, and to the end that the prohibition of the use of submarines as commerce destroyers shall be universally accepted as a part of the law of nations they now accept that prohibition as henceforth binding as between themselves and they invite all other nations to adhere thereto.

[1] For summary of the work of the mixed claims commissions, see: *Report [1934] of Robert W. Bonynge, Agent of the United States before the Mixed Claims Commission, United States and Germany* (Washington, G.P.O., 1935); and *Report of Robert Bonynge, Agent of the United States Before the Tripartite Claims Commission, United States, Austria, and Hungary* (Washington, G.P.O., 1930).

In this summary of claims and awards and payments, I am indebted to an unpublished memorandum of October 24, 1935, prepared by Mr. H. H. Martin, counsel to the United States agency before the Mixed Claims Commission of the United States and Germany.

[2] The comparatively equal amount due to claimants on each side (approximately $40,000,000 each) made possible the consideration of reciprocal assumption by the governments concerned, at least to that amount. This would have greatly simplified the final solution.

This convention, if ratified, also would have outlawed the use of poison gas among the signatory powers.

The Pan-American convention of maritime neutrality of 1928 laid down rules of visit and search for the purpose of identifying the real nationality, cargo and destination of a ship, and added:

If the merchant ship does not heed the signal to stop, it may be pursued by the warship and stopped by force; outside of such a case the ship cannot be attacked unless, after being hailed, it fails to observe the instructions given it.

The ship shall not be rendered incapable of navigation before the crew and passengers have been placed in safety.

Belligerent submarines are subject to the foregoing rules. If the submarine cannot capture the ship while observing these rules, it shall not have the right to continue to attack or destroy the ship.

This convention by September, 1935, had been ratified by the United States and four small Caribbean states, protectorates of the United States, none of which has a navy, Dominican Republic, Haiti, Nicaragua and Panama; and by the land-locked South American state of Bolivia.

Finally, the London naval treaty of 1930 among the United States, the British Commonwealth of Nations and Japan stipulated that the following are accepted as established rules of international law:

(1) In their action with regard to merchant ships, submarines must conform to the rules of International Law to which surface vessels are subject.

(2) In particular, except in the case of persistent refusal to stop on being duly summoned, or of active resistance to visit or search, a warship, whether surface vessel or submarine, may not sink or render incapable of navigation a merchant vessel without having first placed passengers, crew and ship's papers in a place of safety. For this purpose the ship's boats are not regarded as a place of safety unless the safety of the passengers and crew is assured, in the existing sea and weather conditions, by the proximity of land, or the presence of another vessel which is in a position to take them on board.

The United States, Great Britain and Japan ratified the treaty. The naval treaty of London expired by its own limitation on December 31, 1936. Before then, on November 6, 1936, the United States, Great Britain, France, Italy and Japan signed a special protocol renewing indefinitely these articles for the regulation of submarine warfare. They invited other powers to adhere. Germany adhered, November 23, 1936, and Russia on February 19, 1937. Though codification of existing law is not necessary to make it law, nevertheless the formal acceptance of these principles by all of the great submarine powers confirms their binding character. It was on the basis of such principles of international law that the United States chose to defend its citizens, to the extent of going to war with Germany, even when those citizens were traveling under a foreign, even a belligerent flag. Their validity is not contested.

The controverted issues of neutrality between the United States and Great Britain were brought to an end without arbitration. The entrance of the United States into the war against Germany weakened the moral if not the technical force of the American neutral protests and caveats before 1917. In 1926 an examiner of the Department of State, acting in collaboration with a British opposite, eliminated all but 95 of 2,658 American neutral claims against Great Britain, and found that only 11 had conspicuous merit. "We are one of the principal naval forces of the world," he reported, "and should we become involved in another war it would be to our interest to have our naval forces free to operate in any way which would make them most effective against the enemy." [1]

Under this persuasion the United States then made with Great Britain the notable War Claims Agreement of May 19, 1927. It agreed reciprocally not to claim any damages or demand arbitration of damages to its nationals growing out of the "war measures" of Great Britain. Each government retained its right to maintain in the future such position as it might deem appropriate with respect to the legality or illegality under international law of measures such as those giving rise to the claims which it had agreed in this instance not to present. The American claimants were left mostly to the judgment of the British prize courts to be held in England.

Thus did the historic question of neutral rights emerge uncertainly from the diplomatic aftermath of the war. We cannot dismiss the subject without referring to the crystallization of public opinion and legislation in the meditative years since then.

The United States as a champion of neutral rights found that the defense of those rights led not to neutrality but to war, when violation touched American lives rather than American property. Reflective opinion slowly began to ask whether legal neutral rights, the defense of which spells war rather than neutrality, were after all the best sort of rights. An inquiry by Congress in 1934 and 1935 into the munitions industry and traffic recalled the war profits of this enterprise in 1914-1917,

[1] *The Foreign Relations of the United States,* 1926 (Washington, Government Printing Office, 1926), II, 287.

and the economic tie-up between the United States and the Allies. Publicists [1] appealed to a public realization of the horrors of war by stressing this economic relationship with the Allies, without pausing to remember that this would not have brought war except for Germany's unrestricted submarine warfare. These reflections and the persisting uncertainty of the law of contraband and of blockade, and the status of armed merchant ships, gave rise to much searching of mind among students of international law and of American diplomacy.[2] Increasing precariousness of world peace in recent years suggested the recurrence of a neutrality which might mean another war for the United States, as in 1917. The threat to the general peace of Europe caused by the Italo-Ethiopian crisis precipitated the passage by Congress of the neutrality legislation of 1935, amended in 1936 and 1937. This legislation provided for the prohibition, in time of war between foreign states, or of foreign "civil strife," of the export from the United States of arms, ammunition, or implements of war, as defined by the President's proclamation, "to any port of such belligerent state, or to any neutral port for transshipment to, or for the use of, a belligerent country," with an exception [3] in favor of an American republic at war with a non-American state. Loans or credits, or dealing in such, by an American national, with the same exception,[3] were also prohibited. This much was mandatory on the President, though it was left to him to define the existence of a war. The act of 1937 gave the President discretionary power (for two years) to forbid export on American ships to belligerent countries of articles or materials other than arms, ammunition or implements of war, and to forbid the export of any American property in such articles or materials on foreign ships. The neutrality law provided for the control of the munitions industry in time of peace as well as in time of war. It required the licensing, with full publicity, of the exports of arms, ammunition and implements of war, during times of peace. This was in response to a persuasion, which had taken such a hold on public opinion as to be of influence on Congress, that munitions-makers were "merchants of death" and conspired wars for their own profit. The law specifically forbade any vessel, domestic or foreign, in time of war, to take out from American ports "men, or fuel, arms, ammunition, implements of war, or other supplies" to bel-

[1] C. H. Grattan, *Why We Fought* (1929), and Millis, *Road to War* (1935), *op. cit.*
[2] Charles Warren published the most effective of these inquiries, "Troubles of a Neutral," *Foreign Affairs,* XII (April, 1934), 377-394.
[3] The law of May 1, 1937, states: "This Act shall not apply to an American republic or republics engaged in war against a non-American state or states, provided the American republic is not co-operating with a non-American state or states in such a war."

ligerent warships or tenders. It empowered the President to forbid to belligerent submarines or armed merchant ships the use of American neutral ports. It made it unlawful for American citizens to travel under a belligerent flag, except as prescribed by the President. It forbade the arming of American merchant ships trading to belligerent countries.

The neutrality legislation of 1935-1937 showed prevailing conviction not only of inadequacy of previous legislation in regard to neutral rights, but also of the unsatisfactory status of acknowledged neutral rights, subject to encroachment by belligerents' retaliations against each other. Incidentally it set up a neutral definition of contraband,[1] and supported the doctrine of continuous voyage to ultimate destination, the British practice of the First World War. The most significant feature of the new legislation was expression of the policy that it was not worth while to go to war for rights which were undoubtedly legal in 1914-1917. It abandoned Wilson's policy of protecting neutral American citizens against violations of international law even when those violations were directed against a belligerent ship and flag, even a belligerent armed ship and flag. A most significant sequent announcement was the statement of President F. D. Roosevelt (October 5, 1935), when applying (October 5, 1935, to June 20, 1936) the law to the Italo-Ethiopian War, that "in the specific circumstances all transactions" of American citizens with belligerent countries would be at the risk of those citizens. Here was a formula for co-operating with the League of Nations' sanctions to the extent of not insisting upon neutral rights for the carriage of goods to belligerents when the League intervened. It meant that in the face of the League of Nations the United States was willing to abandon the traditional policy of the Freedom of the Seas. It was the existence of the League of Nations which had made possible such a radical change in neutral policy.

The cost, direct and indirect, of the First World War to the belligerents in lives and property will never be precisely measured. An estimate of the Carnegie Endowment for International Peace is 10,000,000 lives and 6,300,000 seriously wounded; and approximately $200,000,000,000 of direct costs.[2] It cost the United States 223 neutral lives lost on the

---

[1] Proclamations of September 25, 1935, and May 5, 1937, enumerated a list of arms, ammunition and implements of warfare. It included among these: tanks, military armored vehicles and armored trains, vessels of war of all kinds, aircraft assembled or dismounted, and equipment for same, flame-throwers and poison gas.

[2] The indirect cost of the First World War—loss of earning power, care of crippled, economic wastage, etc.—was estimated in 1919 at $170,000,000,000. E. L. Bogart, *Direct and Indirect Costs of the Great World War* (New York, 1919), prepared for the

high seas, without mentioning those neutral passengers injured but not killed; 47,949 soldiers and 2,307 sailors killed in battle or died of wounds, and 83,390 severely wounded; and $35,000,000,000, without counting interest on moneys borrowed, which in the end would double the cost. To this direct cost must be added payments to veterans in the shape of "adjusted" compensation (bonus) by states and federal government, hospitalization, and other expenses, including those of administration, totaling by June 30, 1935, in the case of the federal government alone, $7,754,422,529.06.[1] Here was only a small part of this heavy continuing item. The economic dislocation wrought by the war exacerbated the inevitable Great Depression by wearing down the machines of national and international finance. The loss in men fortunately was small [2] for the United States; the loss in money certainly was great but not necessarily vitally grievous (unless combined with domestic folly). It was diplomatic ineptitude which caused the greatest losses, that ineptitude which neglected the embargo weapon, and which extended unstinted war effort *unconditionally* at the side of the Allies. The blunders of diplomacy were balanced, on the other hand, by the largest measure of idealism that a nation has ever brought into a world conflict, personified in Woodrow Wilson and his gallant, if imperfect, fight for the League of Nations. Unfortunately it did not make the world safe for democracy. The rise of the dictators completely upset the basis of Wilson's hope for world peace: a league of *democratic* nations.

What the United States really gained from the war was the overthrow for a generation of the military German Empire, which, victorious, would have been in a position for an inevitable Japanese alliance that would have caught the nations of the New World in the jaws of a crushing vice of Occidental and Oriental military and naval power. The price of temporary immunity, while high, was hardly excessive.

NOTE ON THE WAR CLAIMS ACT OF 1928

A more detailed analysis of the increments making up the special deposit fund of the War Claims Act of 1928 indicates:

Carnegie Endowment for International Peace; and J. M. Clark, *The Costs of the World War to the American People* (Yale University Press, 1931), also prepared for the same Endowment.

[1] Of this $1,043,846,740 was disbursed from insurance premiums, allotments and vocational rehabilitation gift fund.

[2] Compare the annual loss, in 1934, of 36,000 men, women and children killed by automobiles in the United States; and 954,000 injured, of which 105,000 were disabled (statistics from American Automobile Association). These deaths and mutilations are fully as horrible as those of war, many being burned to death, *and much easier to prevent than war.*

(a) The unallocated interest fund (approximately $21,750,000), being the earnings and profits on German enemy property held by the Alien Property Custodian and accruing prior to March 4, 1923, the date of the passage of the Winslow Act (releasing amounts under $10,000).

(b) 20% of the proceeds (approximately $32,950,000) of the liquidation of the German enemy property seized by the United States during the war and held by the Alien Property Custodian—the remaining 80% (that is, 80% of approximately $165,000,000) of the German enemy property was to be immediately returned to the former owners.

(c) The moneys received by the United States (approximately $32,200,-000) as its share under the Paris Agreement of January 14, 1925, of the annuities paid by Germany under the so-called Dawes Plan; in addition to these payments the United States likewise received under this Agreement the sum of approximately $39,200,000 on account of the costs of the army of occupation. These payments represented the percentages of German reparation payments which the Allies were willing to have diverted to the United States. There had already been received by the United States from Germany under the Wadsworth Agreement of May 25, 1923, the sum of approximately $14,700,000 on account of army occupation costs.

(d) Proceeds of German bonds (approximately $19,500,000) deposited under the Debt Funding Agreement of June 23, 1930; in addition there has been received by the United States under this same Debt Agreement the sum of approximately $12,000,000 on account of army occupation costs.

(e) The appropriation by the Congress (approximately $86,700,000) as provided for in the Settlement of War Claims Act to satisfy the awards of the arbiter for German ships, German patents used by the United States, and for the German radio station at Sayville, Long Island. 50 per cent of this appropriation was to be paid immediately to German nationals. The remaining 50 per cent was to be used toward the satisfaction of awards of the Commission.

Among the former German ships that were paid for by the United States under the provisions of the Settlement of War Claims Act were seven, with a total gross tonnage of 62,888, that were sunk by German submarines during the war. These seven ships had a total valuation as found by the arbiter of $7,379,000, including interest to December 31, 1928. The former German owners of these vessels have consequently already been paid 50 per cent of this valuation. These seven vessels included the former Hamburg-American S.S. *Cincinnati* that became the U.S.S. *Covington*, and the former S.S. *President Lincoln* of the same line, that continued to be called the [U.S.S.] *President Lincoln*.

(f) In addition to these amounts there was also placed in the pool the amount of approximately $8,200,000, representing earnings and profits on investments of funds by the Secretary of the Treasury and interest on German bonds, payment of which was postponed in accordance with the provisions of the Debt Funding Agreement of June 23, 1930.

CHAPTER XXXV

ORIENTAL IMMIGRATION

(1850-1914)

AND THE PROBLEM OF THE PACIFIC

(1914-1921)

THE principal focus of American diplomacy in the years immediately after the First World War and the separate peace settlement was the Far East. Across the Pacific a serious issue was rapidly developing with Japan. The gravest difficulties of Japanese-American affairs were involved in the relation of American policy in the Far East to Japanese ambitions on the continent of Asia, but the main issue was aggravated by the feeling that had arisen in Japan because of legislation in the United States concerning oriental immigration and alien land ownership. Before passing presently to the larger aspects of the Problem of the Pacific it is appropriate at this time to review the question of oriental immigration and attendant subjects.

Oriental immigration to the United States began with the American settlement of the Pacific Coast after the acquisition of California. The comparatively higher wages (low for California) proved a lure for Chinese workmen, generally imported by labor contractors. By 1852 there were 25,000 Chinese [1] there, mostly in California, approximately one-tenth of the population at that time; by 1867, 50,000. The treaty negotiated by the plenipotentiary of China, Anson Burlingame, in 1868 at Washington was really a cheap-labor treaty signed readily by Secretary Seward when labor was greatly in demand for completing the Union Pacific Railroad. It guaranteed to Chinese subjects "visiting or residing" in the United States, "the same privileges, immunities, and exemptions in respect to travel and residence as may there be enjoyed by the citizens or subjects of the most favored nation," except for the right of naturalization—from the first appearance of oriental immigration the United States has refused to extend naturalization to Orientals.[2] It may have been a mistake in policy for the United States ever to have

[1] The Census of 1850 showed for California a total population of 92,597, of whom 660 were listed as foreign-born Chinese; the figures in 1860 were total 379,994, Chinese 34,935; in 1870, total 560,247, Chinese 49,277.
[2] States were not forbidden to do so until 1882.

671

introduced into treaty obligations any reference to the sovereign right of regulation of a domestic subject like immigration, but in doing so in the Chinese treaty it was simply following the practice of previous treaties with the European nations. The influx of Chinese, so much desired at first, soon created a serious racial, economic and political problem.[1] China yielded to American representations and signed the treaty of 1880, which recognized the right of the United States to "regulate, limit or suspend" but not to prohibit the immigration of Chinese laborers, and guaranteed most-favored-nation treatment for Chinese already established in the United States—a contemporary treaty stringently prohibited American citizens from engaging in the Chinese opium trade. Congress in 1882 suspended immigration of Chinese laborers for ten years, and later renewed the restriction. After over a decade of painful diplomatic negotiations and unedifying domestic legislation, a new immigration treaty was ratified with China in 1894 which prohibited for ten years the entry of laborers. Teachers, students, merchants, travelers and officials were exempted. When this treaty expired in 1904 Congress re-enacted all existing laws without term. After the annexation of Hawaii and the Philippines the Chinese exclusion laws had been extended to those possessions, too. Following exclusion, the Chinese population within the United States decreased to an insignificant number.[2]

The Japanese replaced the Chinese as a factor in the problem of Oriental immigration at the turn of the century.[3] At the beginning the Japanese Government followed the policy of discouraging undesired labor emigration to the United States, though in later decades it actively encouraged it to countries where Japanese laborers have been welcome, like some countries of Latin America. The treaty of 1894 between Japan and the United States allowed, reciprocally, free entry regardless of purpose, but reserved for domestic control the regulation of immigrant laborers, as well as trade or public security. The Japanese Government fended off statutory exclusion by itself withholding

[1] "South China had a superabundant population; California was sparsely settled and yielded large returns not merely in its mines but in its agriculture to the plodding, indefatigable labor of the Oriental. If natural laws were permitted, unchecked, to assert themselves it was only a question of time when the Chinese, with lower standards of living and lower wage standards, would be able to displace the whites. The condition in the southern states after the emancipation of the slaves was ever before the citizens of California, so many of whom had come from the South." Dennett, *Americans in Eastern Asia, op. cit.,* 539.

[2] 77,504 by the census of 1940, including 40,262 American citizens born of Chinese parents. Chinese population was at its maximum in 1882, at 132,300.

[3] Raymond Leslie Buell has a convenient summary of *Japanese Immigration,* World Peace Foundation Pamphlets, VII, Nos. 5-6 (Boston, 1924).

passports, after August, 1900, to labor immigrants going to the mainland of the United States, but not to those destined for Hawaii.[1] Coolie immigrants fell off by 50 per cent thereafter, although the Japanese restriction was imperfectly administered. There were also vestibules of Japanese immigration via Hawaii (to which passports continued to be issued by Japan) and via Canada and via Mexico.

DISTRIBUTION OF ADULTS AND MINORS BY RACE IN HAWAII AFTER

CENSUS OF 1940

	Native Born		Foreign Born				
Racial Origin	Adults	Minors	Natural-ized Adults	Alien Adults	Un-known	Minors	Totals
Total	180,608	190,109	5,417	46,608	16	572	423,330
Hawaiian	9,051	5,324	....	....	..	....	14,375
Part-Hawaiian	17,405	32,503	14	10	..	3	49,935
Caucasian	61,235	34,605	5,013	2,757	4	177	103,791
Chinese	11,347	12,583	193	4,535	2	114	28,774
Filipino	36,318	16,251	....	....	..	....	52,569
Japanese	39,888	80,664	147	36,932	10	264	157,905
Korean	1,213	3,248	37	2,342	..	11	6,851
Puerto Rican	3,694	4,602	....	....	..	....	8,296
Negro and other	457	329	13	32	..	3	834

In the Kingdom of Hawaii oriental immigration, once actually contracted for by the Hawaiian Government, had taken root. There were 12,000 Japanese there in 1890 and 15,000 Chinese, out of a total population in the islands of 90,000, and Japan was insisting on the same rights of citizenship and office-holding for Japanese immigrants as for native-born Hawaiians. At the same time Japanese law rigorously maintained (until 1924) that an emigrant or even an emigrant's son could not divest himself of allegiance to the Emperor until he had done military service in Japan. A Japanese warship appeared at Honolulu to lend its presence to these demands, based on treaty. Until the annexation

[1] This has been sometimes referred to as the First Gentlemen's Agreement.

of the islands by the United States, Japan successfully opposed Hawaiian plans to exclude Oriental immigrants. Japan's very positive attitude in Hawaii, indeed, was one of the factors which hastened the Hawaiians toward American annexation in 1898. The immigration of Japanese into Hawaii continued after annexation so that by 1940 the population of Japanese extraction composed 37.3% of the population.

Because every person born in Hawaii since annexation is a citizen of the United States, it was only a question of a relatively short time before American citizens of Japanese extraction would be a majority of the voting population.

Agitation against the admission of Japanese immigrants developed on the Pacific Coast; and in October, 1906, the San Francisco school board ordered that all Japanese school children [1] attend a school in which Oriental children were segregated. Japan, flushed with national pride after her recent great victory over Russia, quickly protested this act as a violation of most-favored-nation treatment to which her people in the United States enjoyed treaty guaranties. President Theodore Roosevelt recognized the justice of this protest. With difficulty he persuaded the school board to rescind its action on the understanding that he would somehow bring about a cessation of further Japanese immigration. The school board capitulated only when a hasty amendment to the immigration act of February 20, 1907, opened the way for this. It authorized the President to refuse entrance to the continental United States to immigrants with passports "to any other country than the United States." President Roosevelt promptly applied this to Japanese coming from Hawaii and Mexico, but not from Japan directly. This last was effected under an understanding—the so-called "Gentlemen's Agreement" of 1907—that Japan would not object to this restriction of Japanese coming to the mainland of the United States from adjacent countries or from Hawaii; and that Japan herself would not issue passports to laborers wishing to emigrate to the continental United States, excepting returning immigrants, and excepting also parents, wives, and children under twenty years of age of emigrants already established there. Though not by the terms of this unwritten understanding, Japan also in practice cut down passports to Hawaii.[2] In return the United States did not exclude Japanese immigrants. Exclusion was accom-

[1] A few were very mature boys whose presence among young school children of both sexes created at least the apprehension of a social problem.

[2] See annual reports of the United States *Commission of Immigration*, 1909, 1910, in *Department of Commerce and Labor* reports for those years, 219 (for 1909) and 279 (for 1910).

plished, in fact, by Japan. It was the year after the Gentlemen's Agreement, and in consequence of it, that President Roosevelt, who felt that his sympathetic handling of the problem of Japanese immigration was regarded by Japan as due to fear on his part and that of his countrymen, sent the American battleship fleet on a cruise around the world,[1] really as a naval demonstration that the United States was not only willing to negotiate a settlement like that of 1907 but resolute and ready to defend a just position, if necessary, in the future. At Japanese invitation the fleet visited Yokohama and was most cordially entertained there. The cruise proved of great potency for peace, at least in the then immediate future.

After the Gentleman's Agreement of 1907 had come into operation the United States ratified a treaty, in 1911, with Japan, which omitted the clause of the treaty of 1894, reserving the question of domestic legislation for the regulation of immigration; but the United States Senate, in the resolution of advice and consent to ratification, made the reservation that the treaty should not be deemed to repeal or affect any of the provisions of the immigration act of February 20, 1907.[2] This treaty granted, reciprocally, the free entry, residence, and privilege of owning or leasing houses, shops, and land *for the purpose of residence and trade,* but not regardless of purpose as had been provided by the treaty of 1894 (subject to the latter treaty's reservations concerning domestic legislation for the regulation of immigrant laborers).

The unwritten Gentlemen's Agreement solved fairly well the problem of Japanese immigration until 1924.

In the fifteen years during which the Agreement was in operation a total of 8,681 more Japanese arrived in the continental United States than departed; the net gain of Japanese residents in Hawaii was 7,415. The Japanese population in California nevertheless continued to increase more rapidly than the occidental population because the birthrate of Japanese women, a relatively young group, was three times[3] that of occidental women and because Japanese men brought in women as wives,

---

[1] See above, p. 495. Thomas A. Bailey has described the relation of the fleet's trip around the world to Japanese-American affairs in *Theodore Roosevelt and the Japanese-American Crises; an Account of the International Complications Arising from the Race Problem on the Pacific Coast* (Stanford University Press, 1934). For additional details and documents on the Gentlemen's Agreement, see Jessup's *Root, op. cit.*

[2] This act did not exclude Japanese coming directly to the mainland of the United States from Japan.

[3] It should be remembered that these Japanese women immigrants were then nearly all of childbearing age, as compared with average life groups of indigenous occidental women.

selected by picture postcards and married by proxy in Japan.[1] This was eventually to lead to a renewal of demands on the Western Coast for exclusion by federal law.

The Gentlemen's Agreement did not solve the social and economic problem of Japanese already in the United States. The Japanese proved superior workers and savers. They quickly established a dominance in certain agricultural industries and localities. Of a different race, they found impediments as well as difficulties in assimilating themselves to American society,[2] and they tended (more than occidental immigrants) to stick together and set up their own schools and churches. Meanwhile, even those born in the United States (and consequently American citizens) continued by Japanese law to owe allegiance to the Emperor until after they had done military service for him.

It was the economic and social aspects of Japanese immigration, rather than these legal anomalies, which provoked the legislation of western states that created another diplomatic issue. These laws, beginning with the California land law of 1913,[3] denied to alien residents ineligible for citizenship (*i.e.*, oriental aliens) the right to own, and even to lease land, directly, or indirectly *for agricultural purposes*, though sometimes expressly observing all treaty rights (which included the right to own or lease land "incident to or necessary for trade").[4] These laws hit. the oriental agricultural land-owner and lease-holders in California, Arizona, Arkansas, Delaware, Idaho, Kansas, Missouri, Montana, New Mexico, Texas and Washington. Japan protested against such state laws, but ineffectually because technically they did not violate a treaty. This indirect discrimination by the states—which applied

---

[1] The growth of Japanese population in the continental United States by decennial censuses has been:

Year	Number	Native born.
1870	55	
1880	148	
1890	2,039	
1900	24,326	269
1910	72,157	4,502
1920	111,010	29,672
1930	138,834	68,357
1940	126,947	79,642

Compilation from Ichihashi, *post cit.*, p. 64, plus census of 1930 and 1940.

[2] For a careful study of the social as well as economic position of Japanese immigrants, including the second generation, citizens of the United States, see Y. Ichihashi, *Japanese in the United States; a Critical Study of the Problems of the Japanese Immigrants and Their Children* (Stanford University Press, 1932).

[3] Thomas A. Bailey, "California, Japan, and the Alien Land Legislation of 1913," *Pacific Hist. Rev.*, I (1932), 36-59.

[4] California, Kansas and Missouri have clauses protecting treaty rights of alien landholders.

principally to Japanese aliens, and was so intended—coupled with the naturalization laws of the United States which withheld citizenship from Orientals—rankled the spirit of a proud people; [1] but Japan herself had argued before the Hague Permanent Court of Arbitration (in the Japanese house tax case) that a sovereign power possesses the right to make all reservations concerning the land situated within its territory; and she herself then had laws which prohibited the owning or leasing of land by foreigners for agricultural purposes. As long as the principal problem of immigration was delicately handled by the Gentlemen's Agreement, and treaty rights were not overtly violated, these questions remained subordinated to the routine of diplomacy. Once the Gentlemen's Agreement of 1907 should be discontinued Japan would fall back on her new treaty of 1911 to argue against discrimination in exclusion.[2]

The reader of Part I of this work has noted how, during the years of the foundation of American foreign policy and the beginning of expansion westward through the continent, Europe's distresses were America's advantage. Similarly in the twentieth century the distresses of the Occident have made for the advantage of Japan in the pursuit of her vast objectives on the continent of Asia. The parallel would be more striking if Japan, like the United States, had started a career of expansion through an empty continent obstructed by no foreign barriers in force. Japan, however, had to confront and to saddle the teeming continent of Asia, to throw down old kingdoms, and to do this in a region where the imperialistic powers of Europe had ensconced themselves in possessions of territory, of military and naval posts, fortified also by diplomatic influence over China, in such a way as to be able to stop the advance of Japanese imperialism as long as their own continent of Europe remained quiet behind them. British opposition, for example, had prevented Japan from intervening in the Manchurian provinces of China as late as 1911, the year in which the Anglo-Japanese alliance was renewed for the last time. The American doctrine of the Open Door, to which had been added the principle of the administrative and territorial integrity of China, was also at least a principle, to which Japan herself had subscribed, which stood in the way of both occidental and oriental imperialism in China.

[1] Iichiro Tokutomi, in *Japanese-American Relations* (New York, 1922, translated from the Japanese) presents, *suaviter in modo fortiter in re,* the Japanese case against exclusion laws.

[2] For the United States immigration act of 1924 in effect excluding Japanese laborers and thus terminating the Gentlemen's Agreement of 1907, see below, p. 708.

When the First World War convulsed Europe, there appeared the prospect of comparatively secure freedom for Japan to pursue her ambitions for the domination of China and of Eastern Asia and its littoral, the necessary step toward her goal of the greatest of world powers and the most powerful of imperial peoples. Thanks to the convulsed and confused condition of the Occident since 1914, particularly since 1917, Japan in three astonishing decades was able to take giant strides toward what her rulers beheld as her manifest destiny and her manifest opportunity.

When the war broke out in Europe the United States proposed to the belligerents that they limit the area of hostilities in the Far East, so as to preserve the *status quo*. Both Great Britain and Germany were anxious to do this, though Germany apparently had reservations as to what she might wish to do as to Russian forces there; but Japan delivered an ultimatum to Germany, requiring immediate surrender of her bases in that region and withdrawal from the East, and delivered it without fully consulting her ally. All circumstances considered, the British Government deemed it judicious to announce to the world that the two governments had agreed to take action against Germany in the Far East under their alliance of 1911, "keeping specially in view the independence and integrity of China as provided for in that agreement." Japan then signed the London pact of September 5, 1914, by which Great Britain, France and Russia agreed to make peace only in common. By the Anglo-Japanese Alliance she had not, of course, been bound to such a general obligation.[1]

The first step for Japan was to capture the German naval base at Tsingtao, in Kiaochow Bay, together with the German concessions in Shantung which had been forced from China in 1899. The Japanese quickly blockaded the place from the sea, and marched an army of 20,000 from the northern shore of Shantung across that Chinese province—a distance as long as from New Haven to Cambridge—to invest it from land. This they did without the slightest regard for Chinese neutrality. Great Britain ignored this offense to Chinese sovereignty by her ally and even participated, without enthusiasm of the Japanese, in the naval and military operations, though not passing her

[1] A detailed survey of the diplomatic history of the Far East is contained in H. B. Morse and H. F. MacNair, *Far Eastern International Relations* (New York, 1931). A shorter account, more sympathetic to Japanese policy, is Payson J. Treat, *The Far East; A Political and Diplomatic History* (New York, 1928, 2d. ed., 1935). See also the selected documents in *British Documents on the Origins of the War*, XI (London, 1926), Documents Nos. 499, 534, 549, 571, 641.

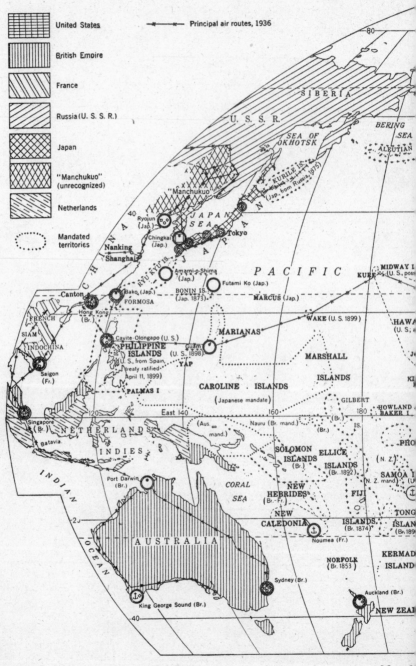

United States

British Empire

France

Russia (U. S. S. R.)

Japan

"Manchukuo" (unrecognized)

Netherlands

Mandated territories

Principal air routes, 1936

SIBERIA

U. S. S. R.

BERING SEA

SEA OF OKHOTSK

ALEUTIAN

KURILE IS. (Jap. from Russia 1875)

"Manchukuo"

J A P A N

40

Ryojun (Jap.)

JAPAN SEA

Chingkai (Jap.)

Tokyo

Nanking

RYU KYU IS.

Shanghai

Amami-o-Shima (Jap.)

Futami Ko (Jap.)

PACIFIC

MIDWAY I. (U. S. poss.)

KURE

Canton

Bako (Jap.)

BONIN IS. (Jap. 1873)

MARCUS (Jap.)

FORMOSA

Hong Kong (Br.)

WAKE (U. S. 1899)

HAWA (U. S.)

FRENCH

SIAM

INDOCHINA

Cavite-Olongapo (U. S.)

PHILIPPINE ISLANDS (U. S. 1898)

MARIANAS

Guam (U. S. 1898)

MARSHALL

Saigon (Fr.)

U. S. from Spain, treaty ratified April 11, 1899

YAP

ISLANDS

KI

PALMAS I

CAROLINE ISLANDS

(Japanese mandate)

GILBERT

HOWLAND BAKER I.

East 140

160

180

Singapore (Br.)

NETHERLANDS

120

(Aus. mand.)

Nauru (Br. mand.)

(Br.)

IS.

PHO

Batavia

INDIES

SOLOMON ISLANDS (Br.)

ELLICE ISLANDS (Br. 1892)

(N. Z.)

SAMOA I (U

Port Darwin (Br.)

CORAL SEA

NEW HEBRIDES (Br.-Fr.)

FIJI

(N. Z. mand.)

TONG

NEW CALEDONIA

ISLANDS (Br. 1874)

ISLAN (Br. 189

20

AUSTRALIA

NEW

Noumea (Fr.)

NORFOLK (Br. 1853)

KERMAD ISLAND

INDIAN OCEAN

Sydney (Br.)

King George Sound (Br.)

40

Auckland (Br.)

NEW ZEAL

Map 3.

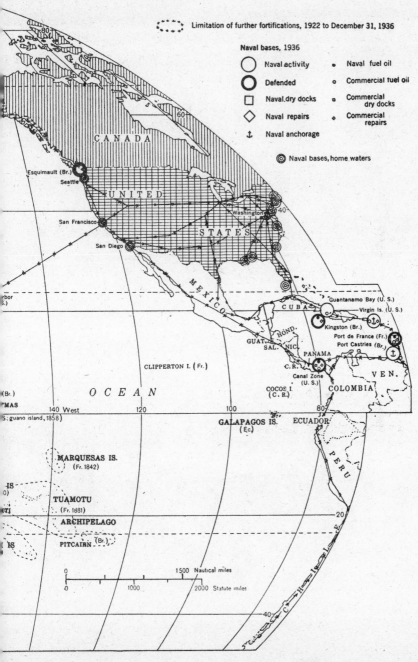

Limitation of further fortifications, 1922 to December 31, 1936

Naval bases, 1936

○ Naval activity   • Naval fuel oil

◎ Defended   ○ Commercial fuel oil

□ Naval dry docks   ▫ Commercial dry docks

◇ Naval repairs   ◈ Commercial repairs

⚓ Naval anchorage

◉ Naval bases, home waters

CANADA

Esquimault (Br.)

Seattle

UNITED

San Francisco

STATES

San Diego

Washington

MEXICO

CUBA

Guantanamo Bay (U. S.)

Virgin Is. (U. S.)

Kingston (Br.)

Port de France (Fr.)

Port Castries (Br.)

GUAT. HOND.

SAL. NIC.

PANAMA

CLIPPERTON I. (Fr.)

C. R.

VEN.

Canal Zone (U. S.)

COCOS I. (C. R.)

COLOMBIA

OCEAN

140 West   120   100   80

GALAPAGOS IS. (Ec.)   ECUADOR

S.; guano island, 1858)

MARQUESAS IS. (Fr. 1842)

PERU

IS

TUAMOTU (Fr. 1881)

ARCHIPELAGO

20

PITCAIRN (Br.)

0   1500 Nautical miles

0   1000   2000 Statute miles

40

Area.

own troops outside the German leasehold.[1] Hopelessly overpowered, the German garrison surrendered (November 7, 1914).

While the operations against Tsingtao were under way, British naval contingents from Australia and New Zealand had made a sweep of the German colonial possessions in Micronesia and Polynesia from New Guinea to Samoa. In addition to German islands south of the Equator, an Australian contingent had proclaimed occupation (September 12, 1914) of the Solomon, Marshall, Caroline, and Mariana Islands which Germany had acquired from Spain in 1899. A few weeks later a Japanese squadron took possession of several of the islands in these groups; this notwithstanding the fact that the British announcement of Japanese operations under the Alliance had declared to the world that "it is understood that the action of Japan will not extend to the Pacific Ocean beyond the China Seas, except in so far as it may be necessary to protect Japanese shipping lines in the Pacific, nor beyond Asiatic waters westward of the China Seas, nor to any foreign territory except territory in German occupation on the continent of eastern Asia." [2]   In a few weeks Japan had established by conquest her claim to the German concessions and leaseholds in China and to the German islands north of the Equator, a string of nesting places for submarines and roosting places for airplanes that would thrust future Japanese naval and aerial power far out eastward into the Pacific, across the communications between Hawaii and the Philippines. These had later powerful strategic value notwithstanding the fact that the condition of the later mandate of the League of Nations prohibited any fortification. It remained for Japan in the peace settlement to clinch her title to these advantages.

In the ultimatum to Germany, Japan had demanded unconditional withdrawal from the leased territory at Tsingtao "with a view to eventual restoration of the same to China." Japanese policy was eventually to return to China nominal possession of Shantung but before

[1] The Japanese did not even ask the consent of China to march across Shantung, and did it over Chinese protest. After the Japanese landing the Chinese proclaimed a war zone, to which the Japanese paid little attention. Japan let it be understood by China that she would be opposed to China's declaring war on Germany to get back Kiaochow for herself. See Morse and McNair, *op. cit.*, who differ widely from Treat, *op. cit.*

The case of Belgian neutrality is, of course, quite different from either that of China (or of Greece) and far more heinous: Belgian neutrality was guaranteed by solemn international covenant to which Germany, the ravishing power, was a party. Chinese neutrality had never been guaranteed, though the lack of guaranty gives no right to violate.

[2] *Foreign Relations, 1914, Supplement,* p. 171. Charles Roger Hicks has probed *Japan's Entry into the War, 1914* (University of Nevada Press, 1944).

then to have reduced all China itself to a Japanese sphere of influence as a first step to the establishment of a protectorate over the entire country. It is easy to let go an arm if one has a strangle hold on the whole body. This was revealed very suddenly to the world by Japan's presentation of an ultimatum (May 7, 1915) embodying drastic demands on China. As originally put forth they consisted of Twenty-One Demands, in five groups. Despite Japanese insistence on secrecy, the President of China, Yuan Shih-kai, dared to let them leak out. At first the Japanese Government denied them, then admitted part of them. In a note to the United States the text of the Twenty-One Demands was conveyed, with an explanation that some of them were not really demands—they were only requests. Nevertheless in the negotiations with China the Japanese representative insisted for a long time that a request was just as important as a demand. The demands were lengthy and detailed, every word of them packed with anaesthesia for Chinese sovereignty. In their entirety they amounted to a protectorate over China.[1] That vast region, since 1910 an enfeebled republic, was, it seemed, about to become, very suddenly, Japan's India.

Actually the position of the United States caused Japan to hesitate with the result that her mastery of China was postponed for at least twenty years. This partial frustration by American diplomacy of Japan's principal national ambition was the cause of the chronic tension between the United States and Japan during those two decades, a tension which was to be strained further by American immigration policy, the alien land legislation of various states in the American Union, and the strategically vulnerable position of the Philippine Islands *vis-à-vis* Japan.

In appraising the effect, from this point on, of the United States on Japanese policy in Asia we must keep in mind the varying force of American diplomacy in 1915-1917, when the Republic was unprepared for war and under the governance of pacifist statesmen, and in 1917-1921, when it had effectively expanded its forces on land and sea to a position second to none.

When the Twenty-One Demands became known to the world in 1915 the United States was in no position to enforce single-handed against Japan—even if it cared to do so, which it did not—its traditional policy of the Open Door, expanded in the Root-Takahira Agreement of 1908 to a formula for preserving the common interest of all powers in China

[1] Thomas Edward LaFargue, *China and the World War* (Stanford University Press, 1937).

by supporting by all *pacific* means at their disposal the independence and integrity of China as well as the principle of equal opportunity for commerce and industry of all nations in that Empire.

The Root-Takahira Agreement[1] of 1908, one recalls, had stipulated (among other things) that: "Should any event occur threatening the *status quo* as above described or the principle of equal opportunity as above defined, it remains for the two Governments to communicate with each other in order to arrive at an understanding as to what measures they may consider useful to take." It was on the basis of this article that Secretary Bryan directed a note (March 13, 1915) to the Japanese Ambassador in Washington, the content of which he also communicated by cable to China, while the Twenty-One Demands were under discussion between Japan and China. He stated that while the demands might be argued not to infringe on the territorial integrity of China (as Japan had pointed out when communicating to the United States on February 8 an abridged version of them) it was difficult to reconcile them with the maintenance of the unimpaired sovereignty of China "which Japan, together with the United States and the Great Powers of Europe, has reaffirmed from time to time during the past decade and a half in formal declarations, treaties and exchanges of diplomatic notes." The United States, therefore, "could not regard with indifference the assumption of political, military, or economic domination over China by a foreign Power." This note was tempered by a significant passage declaring that the activity of Americans in China had never been "political," and a frank recognition that in regard to Shantung, South Manchuria, and Eastern Inner Mongolia, "territorial contiguity creates special relations between Japan and these districts." The note closed with a very tactfully couched hope that Japan would find it consonant with her interests "to refrain from pressing upon China an acceptance of proposals which would, if accepted, exclude Americans from equal participation in the economic and industrial development of China and would limit the political independence of that country," and would thus create a situation which it was confidently believed that Japan did not desire.

During the discussions between Japan and China over the original Twenty-One Demands, they were considerably modified, coincidentally with friendly expostulations of the United States, and finally presented (May 7, 1915) as an ultimatum to China to be accepted within forty-eight hours. China accepted. Immediately the Chinese acceptance became known by telegraph in Washington, Secretary Bryan cabled (May

[1] See above, p. 495.

11, 1915, while the *Lusitania*[1] crisis was at its height) to Japan and China the following caveat:

In view of the circumstances of the negotiations which have taken place and which are now pending between the Government of Japan and the Government of China, and of the agreements which have been reached as a result thereof, the Government of the United States has the honor to notify the Imperial Japanese Government [Republic of China] that it cannot recognize any agreement or undertaking which has been entered into or which may be entered into between the Governments of Japan and China, impairing the treaty rights of the United States and its citizens in China, the political or territorial integrity of the Republic of China, or the international policy relative to China commonly known as the open door policy.[2]

Chinese acceptance of the Japanese demands was embodied in two treaties of May 25, 1915, and certain contemporary exchanges of notes. Group V of the Demands, the most serious of all for Chinese sovereignty, was "postponed for later negotiations."

It remained now for Japan to solidify diplomatically her position in China, as won by these Demands of 1915. The European War played admirably into her purposes. While Russia was so fully occupied with the other Allies against the Central Powers, Japan secured her acceptance of a treaty which openly pledged the two governments to unite their efforts for the maintenance of a "permanent peace in the Far East"—a phrase which decorates many an Asiatic agreement; and secretly the contracting parties agreed to "enter into open-hearted dealings" to "safeguard" China from the political domination of "any third power whatever, having hostile designs against Russia or Japan." Presumably these words meant the United States.[3] Thus was distressed Russia brought

---

[1] There was no relation between the sinking of the *Lusitania* and the delivery of the Japanese ultimatum (which had already arrived in Peking as early as May 6), although both occurred on the same day, May 7. Of course, the Japanese Government could not have been unaware of the possibility of difficulties between Germany and the United States over submarine warfare, particularly after Wilson's "strict accountability" note of February 10, 1915.

[2] For the notes, and the diplomatic correspondence of the Department of State, relating to the Twenty-One Demands, in so far as that correspondence has been published, see *Foreign Relations, 1915*, 146.

[3] Morse and McNair, *op. cit.*, 589, marshal the following reasons for believing that this "third power" could have been only the United States: (1) the well-known policy of the United States of the Open Door, and its attitude toward the Twenty-One Demands; (2) the United States was still a neutral in 1916; (3) it could not have been Germany because if Germany were defeated in the war there would be nothing to fear from her, while if she were victorious the Russo-Japanese alliance would be useless [and, we may add, the Anglo-Japanese alliance, too]; (4) there was no reason to keep secret a pact against Germany; (5) the Bolshevists published it from the Russian archives in 1918 under the title: "Secret Treaty between Russia and Japan, with reference to a possibility of their armed conflict together against America and Great Britain in the Far East before the summer of 1921."

in line with Japanese policy. The desperate situation of the other Allies following the resumption by Germany of unrestricted submarine warfare on February 1, 1917, next gave Japan her opportunity to secure pledges from them on the eve of the entry of the United States into the war. In return for the assistance of Japanese convoys in the Mediterranean—thus releasing Allied naval forces for work in critical fighting areas—Great Britain agreed (February 16, 1917) to support at the peace conference Japan's claims to Shantung and to retention of the German islands north of the Equator. France similarly agreed (March 1, 1917) to support Japan's claims, in return for Japan's obtaining from China a rupture of diplomatic relations with Germany (which among other advantages would make available for the Allies the German ships interned in Chinese ports). Russia (March 5, 1917) and later Italy also pledged themselves to support the Japanese claims at the end of the war.

The entrance of the United States into the war seemed an immediate advantage and possibly an ultimate disadvantage to Japan's policy of expansion in Eastern Asia. It meant that in the near future all American energies would be occupied by the war in Europe and on the Atlantic; it also meant the arming of the United States on land and sea to a formidable strength which might give renewed emphasis after the war to the traditional American policy for the integrity and independence of China. It was the objective of Japanese diplomacy therefore to commit the United States to the new program in China while it was still fully occupied in the war against Germany. This was the real object of the special mission to Washington of Viscount Ishii, announced in June, 1917, as a natural sequel to the other Allied missions which had visited the United States to arrange effective military and financial coöperation.

When the United States severed diplomatic relations with Germany, it had invited the neutral powers, including China, to do the same. The Chinese Parliament so declared, March 9, 1917. Then followed a confused domestic situation in that hapless republic, the seat of contest among President, Parliament, and Premier, and among the military provincial governors. Japanese policy encouraged this confusion by loans to the rival groups of shifting control, in return for economic concessions. It was the old story of *divide et impera*. Many Japanese leaders dreaded the economic, moral and military energy of a united China independent of their control, and for that reason resisted the entrance of China into the war. Nevertheless the Chinese Government momentarily united sufficiently to declare war on Germany (August 14, 1917). Thus it insured itself a place at the peace conference where it could claim Shantung. Japan, on her part, now strove to bring under her management the military efforts of a divided China, meanwhile avoiding encouragement of Chinese unity. During the period of confusion between the rupture by China of diplomatic relations with Germany and her declaration of war, the United States invited (June 4, 1917) Great Britain, France and Japan to co-operate for the restoration of Chinese national unity and internal peace as of first importance to itself and to the world, and to relegate the question of China and the World War to a second place. The failure of these powers to unite in any common policy here rendered useless this move for stiffening the integrity of China.

It was the effort of Viscount Ishii, appearing in Washington in the critical period of the First World War, to get from Lansing a recognition of Japan's "paramount interests" or at least "special influence" in China. Lansing on the other hand desired a reaffirmation of the Open Door and was willing to admit no closer "special relations" than Bryan had conceded two years previously. Ishii introduced the ominously suggestive statement, delicately but significantly put, that the German Government had three times sought to persuade Japan to withdraw from the Allies and to remain neutral, but that in every case his government had firmly rejected the suggestion.[1] The special Japanese envoy also mentioned a conversation which he had had in London in 1915 with Sir Edward Grey in which he had told the British Foreign Secretary that although Japan intended to restore Shantung to China at the end of the war, she was determined to keep the German islands north of the Equator; and that Grey "practically consented" to a division of the islands on the line of the Equator. Lansing would make no comment on such an agreement. Ishii did not mention the formal Anglo-Japanese agreement of February 16, 1917.

The result of this diplomatic logomachy was the cautiously phrased Lansing-Ishii Agreement[2] embodied in a public exchange of notes of November 2, 1917, by which the two co-belligerents in the war against Germany shelved their China issue with an ambiguous formula. Each

[1] Robert Lansing, *War Memoirs* (New York, 1935), 293. K. Ishii, *Diplomatic Commentaries* (Johns Hopkins University Press, 1936). This English translation is somewhat abridged.

[2] The negotiations are described by Julius W. Pratt, *Am. Secs. State*, X, 126-139, who had access to Lansing's papers which the former Secretary used in his *War Memoirs*, *op. cit.*, published posthumously in 1935.

party made nominal concessions to the other's position but sought cover for its own policy in studiously worded language. The agreement read:

The governments of the United States and Japan recognize that territorial propinquity creates special relations between countries, and, consequently, the government of the United States recognizes that Japan has special interests in China, particularly in the part to which her possessions are contiguous.

The territorial sovereignty of China, nevertheless, remains unimpaired, and the government of the United States has every confidence in the repeated assurances of the Imperial Japanese Government that while geographical position gives Japan such special interests they have no desire to discriminate against the trade of other nations or to disregard the commercial rights heretofore granted by China in treaties with other powers.

The governments of the United States and Japan deny that they have any purpose to infringe in any way the independence or territorial integrity of China, and they declare, furthermore, that they always adhere to the principle of the so-called "open door" or equal opportunity for commerce and industry in China.

Moreover, they mutually declare that they are opposed to the acquisition by any government of any special rights or privileges which would affect the independence or territorial integrity of China or that would deny to the subjects or citizens of any country the full enjoyment of equal opportunity in the commerce and industry of China.[1]

During the negotiations with Ishii, Secretary Lansing desired to include the following agreed statement: "They [the Governments of the United States and Japan] will not take advantage of the present conditions to seek special rights or privileges in China which would abridge the rights of the subjects or citizens of other friendly states." Ishii objected to putting this in the published exchange of notes. So a secret protocol, signed by Lansing and Ishii, accompanied the published exchange of notes that constituted the Lansing-Ishii Agreement. It stated: "It was, however, well understood that the principle enunciated in the clause *which was thus suppressed* was in perfect accord with the declared policy of the two Governments in regard to China." This secret ambiguity made the ambiguity of the public clauses of the Agreement doubly ambiguous. Though considered by the United States Government as an inseparable part of the Lansing-Ishii Agreement, it was not

[1] A convenient text of the note, with superficial information about the mission of Ishii, appears in Publication No. 15 of the Carnegie Endowment for International Peace, *The Imperial Japanese Mission, 1917* . . . (Washington, D. C., 1918). The publication significantly publishes together the texts of the Root-Takahira Agreement of 1908 and the new Lansing-Ishii Agreement of 1917.

published until long after the Lansing-Ishii Agreement had been super-seded by the Nine-Power Treaty of Washington of 1922.[1]

Ishii was content with this agreement, which in Tokyo was regarded as a diplomatic victory. He believed the time would come when Japan could interpret it to her own satisfaction. Japan translated the docu-ment into Chinese in words that meant "paramount interests." Lansing told the disheartened Chinese—and later the American Senate—that the Agreement recognized only the "special interests" of an economic nature created by geographical propinquity—"an axiom and nothing more." He was convinced that it had resulted in commitments by Japan more far-reaching and vital to the preservation of China's sovereignty than the Root-Takahira Agreement of 1908, and that the "special interests" which in return the United States had ratified were only the natural economic interests of geographical propinquity, not political interests. Ishii continued to believe and to declare in his country that it was essen-tially a political rather than an economic agreement which he had signed with Lansing.[2]

Before the First World War ended, Japan, in co-operation with her allies and associates, had made another significant intervention on the continent of Asia—this time in Siberia, where Russian control col-lapsed after the Bolshevist Revolution. Japan was eager to make ad-vantage of the confusion and take charge of that region. Great Britain and France, anxious to marshal anti-Bolshevik forces against the Rus-sian communists, in order to keep Russia in the war, urged the United States to agree to a Japanese occupation of Siberia along the railroad clear to the Urals. All major factions of the Russian people feared Japanese intervention as a danger to their future sovereignty. The United States persistently opposed such a step, even a joint occupation, on the ground that it would antagonize Russia and throw her into the arms of Germany; and stood obstinately in favor of letting the Russian people work out their destiny unembarrassed. But after the German-Russian peace of Brest-Litovsk in the spring of 1918 the situation in Siberia became so involved and volatile that Japanese intervention was imminent. After this peace a legion of 50,000 Czechoslovaks, prisoners

---

[1] *Foreign Relations of the United States. The Lansing Papers, 1914-1920.* Vol. II (De-partment of State Publication No. 1421. Washington, G.P.O., 1940), 450-451. Italics inserted.

[2] Both diplomatists have left on record their recollections of these conversations and negotiations, and their significance, records apparently based on contemporary diaries: Lansing in his *War Memoirs, op. cit.,* and Ishii in his *Gaiko Yoroku* (Tokyo, 1930), published in an abridged English edition, William R. Langdon translator, under the title of *Diplomatic Commentaries* (Johns Hopkins Press, 1936).

of war organized by Russia to fight against the Central Powers, started on a desperate anabasis across Siberia to Vladivostok. They were striving to reach the western front in Europe, via America, to fight for the liberation of their newly revolted nation and homeland. There was danger that these heroic troops might be cut off and destroyed by Bolshevist and other forces, and that the depot of munitions of the former Czarist Government at Vladivostok might become available to the Germans. Japan was opposed to the re-establishment of any kind of stable Russian Government in eastern Siberia, whether Czech, Bolshevist, or Cossack. The looseness of the situation, and its danger to the Allied cause in Europe, presented an admirable opportunity for intervention, even with the applause of the European Allies. A step in this direction was the Sino-Japanese military convention of May 16, 1918, which Japan secured from China in return for loans to the Anfu faction then in control of the Chinese Government at Peking. This pact put China in Japanese lead-strings so far as military activity during the war was concerned; further, it provided for "joint" military operations in the Siberian provinces of Transbaikalia and the Amur "to assist Czechoslovak forces and to drive out German and Austrian forces and such as may be rendering assistance to them." [1]

The Japanese move led to a joint occupation by the Allies and the United States, in the summer of 1918, of the strategic port of Vladivostok and its hinterland. To forestall an exclusive Japanese occupation and control of eastern Siberia, the Government of the United States proposed a Japanese-American expedition of a "few thousand men" to Vladivostok, to protect the rear of the eastward-moving Czechoslovak legion. Japan (with the other powers) in agreeing to this reaffirmed her "avowed policy of respecting the territorial integrity of Russia and of abstaining from all interference in her internal politics." She further declared that upon the realization of the objects above indicated (the relief of the Czechoslovak legion) she would immediately withdraw all Japanese troops from Russian territory.[2] In the discussions accompanying the framing of these statements of intention, Viscount Ishii again suggested the words "special interests," this time to describe Japan's relationship to Siberia. Acting Secretary of State F. L. Polk opposed the inclusion of any such declaration in the Japanese or American explanation of action and purpose. The American expeditionary force

---

[1] Morse and McNair, op. cit., 649-668.
[2] Statement of the Japanese Ambassador to the Acting Secretary of State, August 2, 1918. Foreign Relations, 1918, Supplement, Russia, II, 325.

was limited to 7,500 troops and less than a thousand additional civilian workers; and British, French, Italian, Roumanian and Serbian contingents were well below that limit; but Japan soon had 72,000 soldiers in Siberia.

In Siberia, more friction [1] than co-operation developed between the United States and Japan, for it was apparent that the American insistence on a joint, if any, intervention, had grouped Japan's opportunity. It was the object of American diplomacy to bring the joint intervention to steady the efforts of the Russians for self-government while protecting the ammunition stores at Vladivostok and the retreating Czechoslovaks, thus to remove the necessity for further intervention. It was the purpose of the Allies to bolster their position by building another front against Germany in the east. It was the aim of Japanese diplomacy to take advantage of this desire of the Allies for intervention, but to keep the Siberian situation confused in order to prolong intervention, by Japan alone when the other powers should step out.[2] One point at issue, outside of Siberia, was control of the Chinese Eastern Railway, running east and west across Manchuria to Vladivostok, a road formerly under Russian control. Japan was impelled by the joint intervention in Siberia to consent that it should be placed under the temporary control of an Inter-Allied Railway Commission. After the defeat of Germany, the foreign forces, with the exception of the Japanese, were withdrawn from Siberia by April, 1920.[3] But Japanese troops remained in Eastern Siberia. They were there when the Washington Conference assembled in November of 1921. Other Japanese forces were still in occupation of Shantung.

[1] William S. Graves, *America's Siberian Adventure, 1918-1920* (New York, 1931).

[2] The Department of State has published a voluminous record of the diplomatic correspondence, and relevant documents, relating to the Siberian intervention, in *Foreign Relations, 1918, Russia* (3 Vols., Washington, G.P.O., 1932). For Siberia see Vol. II, 1-467. It was the documents therein published which later induced Russia to waive all claims to damages on account of American participation in the Siberian intervention.

[3] The United States also participated with 4,500 troops in 1918-1919 in the joint intervention of Allied and Associated forces (British, 6,000, French, 1,500 men, with small contingents from other Allied nations) in the Murmansk region of northern Russia in Europe. At first with the co-operation of the Bolsheviki these troops occupied that region for the purpose of preventing that depot of ammunition and supplies from falling into the hands of Germany after the German-Russian peace of Brest-Litovsk. The United States did not participate in the interventions of France and Great Britain in Russia from the Black Sea after the Armistice in Europe. For the Murmansk intervention, see *Foreign Relations of the United States, 1918, Russia* (Washington, G.P.O., 1932), Vol. II, 468-577. Leonid I. Strakhovsky in a paper, "The Origins of American Intervention in North Russia, 1918," read at the American Historical Association at Chattanooga, Tennessee, December 27, 1935, showed the co-operation of Bolshevik authorities with this intervention, later protested by Russia. Russia nevertheless has not yet waived claims to damages for American participation.

We recall, at the Peace Conference at Paris, President Wilson acquiesced to the agreements by which Japan had secured the support of the European Allies to her conquest of the German concessions in Shantung and of the German islands in the Pacific north of the Equator. He had felt obliged to make this concession in order to secure Japan's signature to the treaty and to the League of Nations. In the discussions at Paris about the mandated islands the President had entered an oral reservation as to the status of the island of Yap, in the Carolines, nodal point for American cables running between the United States and the Far East. Japan after the peace settlement refused to recognize this reservation, and an issue arose between the two countries concerning the status of the tiny island, which aggravated the other complications of the Far East and the question of the Pacific.

At the Peace Conference, it is further recalled, neither Great Britain nor the United States, unfortunately, would recognize the demand of Japan for recognition in the League of Nations of the principle of racial equality. This was, and remained, a sore spot with the Japanese. But Japan had emerged from the First World War in a triumphant position, with an equality in power and prestige, her feet well planted in new regions on the continent of Asia, in Shantung and in Siberia, grasping tenaciously a network of treaties thrown over China with the design of reducing that country to Japanese protection. She was also in occupation of the Russian half of the island of Sakhalin (northernmost island of the Japanese group) which Japan had seized as security for a satisfactory settlement for the slaughter by Bolshevik forces of the Japanese garrison of 640 men in a collision at Nikolaevsk across the strait in Siberia in March, 1920. Far out in the Pacific she had hold of the former German islands north of the Equator. It was the rapid rise of Japanese power in the First World War which brought to a head the vast diplomatic problem of the Pacific Ocean and the Far East.

CHAPTER XXXVI

THE WASHINGTON AND LONDON NAVAL TREATIES

(1921-1936)

THE First World War ended with the Allied and Associated Powers of the Occident in a strong bond of friendship and military strength despite their varying interests. After their defeat of Germany they were in a position to look with less preoccupation upon the problems of the Far East and the Pacific and their continuing interests there. It was evident that a serious situation was shaping itself between the United States and Japan, who now regarded her old friend as an inimical power whose diplomacy had repeatedly stood in the way of her expansionist ambitions, first and continually in China, and now in Siberia; and whose laws as to citizenship and state land-ownership seemed incompatible with the spirit of the Gentlemen's Agreement of 1907. The United States in particular had emerged from the war in a position of great military strength, in fact promising soon to be the greatest naval power once the building of the program of 1916 should be completed. Great Britain and Japan were anxious to see that naval power limited in line with their own resources. If Japan were to gainsay the American policy for the independence and integrity of China, and now for the same in Siberia, naval force was imperative. The way the naval programs of the three powers were then progressing, the most favorable relationship of Japanese naval power to that of the United States would seem to be likely in the year 1923: after that Japan might steadily fall behind in the race for naval armament. The year 1923 loomed ahead as a possible date for war.

The shadow of a coming Japanese-American crisis that might precipitate a war of the Pacific sobered the British Dominions, bordering on that ocean, which also had their problems of excluding oriental immigration. What would be the relation of the Dominions, particularly Canada, to such a war, presuming the still unfettered scope of the Anglo-Japanese Alliance? That alliance had been renewed for ten years in 1911, to continue after the decade subject to abrogation by either side at one year's notice.

The alliance had stipulated that in case the interests of either party in the regions of the Far East should become endangered as a result of "an unprovoked or aggressive act wherever arising,"[1] they should fight such a war together. When the treaty was renewed in 1911 it contained a clause to the effect that it should not apply to powers with which either party had a general treaty of arbitration. In 1911 President Taft had been engaged in negotiating a general arbitration treaty with Great Britain. The Senate did not ratify his treaty. Hence the United States was not immune from the touch of the Anglo-Japanese Alliance.[2] In case of a Japanese-American war Canada might be called upon to take sides against her southern neighbor and greatest friend, almost relative. This possibility was uppermost in the minds of Canadian leaders when they met with the other statesmen of the Empire in the Imperial Conference at London in the summer of 1921. In March, on the eve of that significant gathering, the Crown Prince of Japan, Hirohito—the present Emperor—made a visit of state on a Japanese battleship to the capital of the British Empire. It seemed, particularly to Canadian statesmen, backed emphatically by Canadian public opinion, that Britain must now choose between the United States and Japan.

The insistence of Canada, under her vigorous Prime Minister, Arthur Meighen, in guarding against any renewal of the Anglo-Japanese Alliance such as might involve her in a break either with the United States, or with the new British Commonwealth of Nations, brought to focus the whole group of issues in regard to Anglo-American and Anglo-

[1] Conceivably it might arise in the United States, over an incident of immigration or land ownership, which might be made the pretext for a war of larger issues.

[2] In 1914 Great Britain seems to have made a secret statement to the Japanese Government that it would regard the Bryan conciliation treaty with the United States—the so-called "cooling-off" treaty—as an arbitration treaty in the sense of the Anglo-Japanese Alliance. The statement was not made public until 1921. Japan does not appear on her part ever to have accepted the interpretation.

Great Britain persuaded Japan to make a joint statement to the League of Nations, July 8, 1920, that the alliance, "though in harmony with the spirit of the Covenant," was not entirely consistent with its "letter," and that they recognized that, if renewed, it must be put in a form consistent with that Covenant. On July 13, 1921, six days before the ten-year term of the Alliance would have expired (though it continued unless denounced), the two allies notified the League of Nations that pending further action they were agreed that, "if any situation arises whilst the agreement [i.e., the Anglo-Japanese Alliance] remains in force in which the procedure described by the terms of the agreement is inconsistent with the procedure prescribed by the terms of the Covenant of the League, then the procedure prescribed by the said Covenant shall be adopted and shall prevail over that prescribed by the Agreement."

This did not remove the United States from the scope of the Alliance, because the United States had rejected the Covenant of the League of Nations. See Buell, *Washington Conference, op. cit.*, 113, 133. Note that the statement was made during the Imperial Conference of 1921 when Canada was protesting against any renewal of the Alliance.

Japanese policy, the status of the Far East, the question of the Pacific, and post-war rivalry of naval armaments. The British Government was on the point of proposing to the interested powers a conference to settle these issues when it learned of the intention of the United States to do so and yielded the initiative to President Harding.

The President's call for a conference was based on the prime necessity of an understanding on naval armaments, but he proposed a discussion at the same time of Pacific and Far Eastern problems, a solution of which, he said, was of "unquestionable importance." He directed the invitations first to the Principal Allied and Associated Powers (except Russia, which had dropped out of the group after the Bolshevist Revolution) during the war against Germany and her Allies.[1] All accepted, Japan after some hesitation about the vague scope of the agenda. Later it was agreed to include in the Conference the Netherlands, which had large colonial holdings in the East Indies; Portugal, which possessed the settlement of Macao, near Canton; Belgium, which had an interest in Chinese railways and a concession at Tienstin; and China herself, the principal patient for the diplomatic doctors at Washington. Bolshevist Russia, the other patient, was in no condition to come to the clinic. For her only absent treatment could be indicated. Germany already had been operated on, and her convalescence was not disturbed. Austria-Hungary was deceased.

Back of the whole complex of issues, which were turning the face of the United States from the Atlantic to the Pacific, lay the fact that American diplomacy, though traditionally involved, was not vitally interested in the independence and integrity of China, to say nothing of Siberia. American leaders realized that their people would not then fight for these principles in Asia and that Congress could not be counted on for continuing big naval appropriations, notwithstanding rejection of the League of Nations Covenant. Under these circumstances Secretary Hughes was anxious for a diplomatic settlement. In the British Empire, in the United States and in Japan the situation made for peace as well as for war.

President Harding's advisers profited by the recent experience of the Wilson Administration in dealing with the Senate. As in the case of the delegates to the Peace Conference at Paris, the American representatives were executive agents, with the rank of ambassador, except for

[1] Of these five powers, Great Britain, Japan and France had territory in eastern Asia. Italy and Belgium had small concessions in Tientsin, and Belgian capital was interested in some of the Chinese railways.

the Secretary of State, who headed the delegation with his own title. Even though Congress was in session when the conference was called the President did not nominate the ambassadors to the Senate;[1] but he was careful to select his agents with regard to the Senate's power over treaties (he already had the advantage of a Republican Congress). In addition to Secretary of State Charles E. Hughes, there were Senator Henry Cabot Lodge, Republican leader in the Senate and Chairman of the Committee on Foreign Relations; Senator Oscar Underwood, ranking Democratic member of that committee; and former Secretary of State Elihu Root, an ex-senator.

Secretary Hughes opened the negotiations with the trump card of high naval strength, actual and potential, backed by undoubted support of the Republican Senate. Quite to the astonishment of the delegates, and perhaps with not perfect success, he played his trump at the first meeting. He proposed that "preparations for offensive war stop now." He then offered an itemized plan for the reduction of armaments according to an agreed ratio finally fixed at 5—5—3—1.7—1.7 (or 10—10—6—3.4—3.4),[2] corresponding generally to the existing ratio before the conference, which involved the sinking or scrapping of designated ships, built or building, of the three great naval powers, and a naval holiday in the construction of capital ships for ten years, with only limited replacements of superannuated ships thereafter until 1936. For Great Britain and Japan this program meant the scrapping mostly of old battleships and ships under construction, but including the new monster Japanese battleship, *Mutsu*, already launched and over 90% finished; for the United States it meant the scrapping of old battleships, of two new battleships already launched but not quite finished, plus seven battleships and six heavy cruisers on the ways. The delegates accepted in principle Mr. Hughes' startling proposal and the committees of experts proceeded to discuss it in detail as the Conference went into the consideration of the broad political subjects of the agenda. It was obvious that no naval agreement could be ratified at that time unless the political questions of the Far East and the Pacific also could be adjusted. The Hughes proposal emerged from the Conference fairly intact in treaty form, although modifications had to be made because of the refusal of Japan to scrap the *Mutsu;* but balanced by the acceptance

---

[1] The Senate voiced no word of criticism at this procedure. "This appears to indicate that a tacit agreement has been reached to the effect that executive agents are not officers" [that is, in the sense of the Constitution, requiring nomination to the Senate and confirmation]. Wriston, *Executive Agents, op. cit.*, 311-312.

[2] Great Britain, 5; the United States, 5; Japan, 3; France, 1.7; Italy, 1.7.

of a proposal by Japan limiting fortification of certain of the islands of the Pacific, including the Philippines and Aleutian but not the Hawaiian Islands.

The following principal limitations of fortification were established by Chapter I, Article XIX, of the naval treaty:

"The United States, the British Empire and Japan agree that the status quo at the time of the signing of the present Treaty, with regard to fortifications and naval bases, shall be maintained in their respective territories and possessions specified hereunder:

"(1) The insular possessions which the United States now holds or may hereafter acquire in the Pacific Ocean, except (a) those adjacent to the coast of the United States, Alaska and the Panama Canal Zone, not including the Aleutian Islands, and (b) the Hawaiian Islands;

"(2) Hongkong and the insular possessions which the British Empire now holds or may hereafter acquire in the Pacific Ocean, east of the meridian of 110° east longitude, except (a) those adjacent to the coast of Canada, (b) the Commonwealth of Australia and its Territories, and (c) New Zealand;

"(3) The following insular territories and possessions of Japan in the Pacific Ocean, to wit: the Kurile Islands, the Bonin Islands, Amami-Oshima, the Loochoo Islands, Formosa and the Pescadores, and any insular territories or possessions in the Pacific Ocean which Japan may hereafter acquire.

"The maintenance of the status quo under the foregoing provisions implies that no new fortifications or naval bases shall be established in the territories and possessions specified; that no measures shall be taken to increase the existing naval facilities for the repair and maintenance of naval forces, and that no increase shall be made in the coast defenses of the territories and possessions above specified. This restriction, however, does not preclude such repair and replacement of worn-out weapons and equipment as is customary in naval and military establishments in time of peace."

The treaty left the United States and Great Britain each 15 capital ships of 525,000 tons total; Japan 9 of 272,070 tons; and France and Italy free to build up to a maximum of 175,000 tons each. The United States and Great Britain might have each 135,000 tons additional of aircraft carriers; Japan, 81,000 tons; and France and Italy each 60,000 tons. Roughly this kept to the ratio of 5—5—3—1.7—1.7. The real effect of the naval agreement, including the ancillary part on fortified areas, was to make it impossible for any one of the three navies alone to fight an offensive war against one of the others in the Pacific. To forestall two of the navies suddenly leaguing against the third was the purpose of a new ten-year quadruple consultative pact for preserving the *status quo* of the Pacific which replaced the Anglo-Japanese Alliance. In case the rights of any party in the region of the Pacific Ocean were threatened by the aggressive action of any power, the four treaty powers (the United States, France, Great Britain and Japan) agreed "to communicate with each other as to the most efficient measures to be taken, jointly or singly, to meet the exigencies of the particular situation." Thus Japan protected her own islands against any likely attack from Pacific waters, and established an irresistible dominance of her power in Eastern Asia. For a recognition of this position the other powers demanded, and received from Japan, certain pledges, which in form of a nine-power treaty were made binding on all, for the observance of the Open Door, the administrative and territorial integrity of China, and the abstention by all powers from seeking special privileges in China. Japan announced that she would now totally abandon Group V of the Demands of 1915, which she had hitherto reserved for future consideration. With the ratification by Japan and the United States of the Nine-Power Treaty for the conservation of the integrity of China, the public part of the Lansing-Ishii Agreement of 1917 was formally annulled by an exchange of notes, April 14, 1923.

The secret protocol [1] of the Lansing-Ishii Agreement had become the first part of paragraph 4 of Article I of the Nine-Power Treaty, by which the contracting powers other than China agreed "to refrain from taking advantage of conditions in China in order to seek special rights or privileges which would abridge the rights of subjects or citizens of friendly states, *and from countenancing action inimical to the security of those states.*" The last, italicized words were new, not in the secret protocol of 1917. Their significance has never been sufficiently noticed. What powers other than Japan could feel their *security* endangered by special foreign rights and privileges in China?

Japan during the Conference made a separate treaty with the United States recognizing American cable rights on Yap Island, and a separate treaty with China for the speedy return of Shantung (subject to the inviolability of private contracts, multifarious in number and character, procured during the Japanese occupation) and the purchase by China, in installments, of the former German railway there for *yen* 61,000,000.

[1] See above, p. 685.

As to Siberia, Japan successfully protested against any disposition of that subject by the assembled powers, but on her own responsibility pledged herself to withdraw. The pledge was spread on the minutes of the Conference. Japan evacuated Siberia in October, 1922. Not until 1925 did she restore the northern half of Sakhalin to Russian sovereignty, after securing exclusive concessions for the exploitation of oil and coal fields in that region, and further concessions for the lease of fisheries and the working of other national resources in Siberia.

The Washington treaties did not much undo the special privileges and concessions which had been forced from China by the imperialistic powers in the past: they were merely a general self-denial ordinance for the future. Nevertheless a series of formal resolutions opened the way, at least, for tariff autonomy for China, the removal of foreign post-offices and radio stations, and the anticipation if not the consummation of the abolition of extraterritoriality.[1]

The Washington Conference amounted to a face-saving retreat of the United States from active diplomacy in the Far East under the cover of a multilateral international agreement for the observance of the traditional American policies for the Open Door and the administrative, political and territorial integrity of China. In case of any future violation of these solemn pledges, which was not anticipated, redress of the wrong would as much concern, at least juridically, the nine powers parties to the treaties and resolutions in regard to China as it would the United States. After 1921 the United States was no longer sole proprietor of these policies, nor, because of the naval limitations, able to rely on anything stronger than peaceful means for co-operation.

The Washington naval treaty of 1922 limited only capital ships—over 10,000 tons displacement;[2] it said nothing about auxiliary craft: Class A cruisers (carrying 8″ guns), Class B cruisers (carrying 6″ guns), destroyers, submarines. For three years the United States did not lay down a keel of any kind, and for three years more a very small number of new ships were begun;[3] but in 1928, after the other powers, first of all

---

[1] W. W. Willoughby, who served as adviser to the Chinese Government before and during the Conference, has published expert analyses of China's problems in diplomacy in *Foreign Rights and Interests in China* (Johns Hopkins Press, revised edition, 1927, 2 Vols.) and *China at the Conference, a Report* (Johns Hopkins Press, 1922).

[2] None could be built over 35,000.

[3] In 1925, 1 submarine.

In 1926, 1 Class A cruiser and 6 river gunboats, and 2 submarines.

In 1927, 1 Class A cruiser and 2 submarines.

In 1928, 6 Class A cruisers.

In 1929, none.

Japan, had engaged in a formidable program of armaments in cruisers, destroyers and submarines; six more Class A cruisers were laid down, and, in 1930, three more, in a belated effort to catch up with the new rivalry. During these years the United States had pressed for further limitations, in the auxiliary categories to which competition had transferred itself after 1922. It took the initiative for a preliminary conference under the auspices of the League of Nations at Geneva in 1927, which failed. Meanwhile all projects of the nations for a limitation of land armaments and armies also failed.[1]

The advent in the United States in 1929 of the Republican Hoover Administration, and in England of the new Labor Government, and a personal conference of the Prime Minister, Ramsay MacDonald, with President Hoover at Washington, and Rapidan, Virginia, laid the basis for another naval conference, of the five great naval powers, the United States, the British Commonwealth of Nations (as it had now come to be known), Japan, France and Italy. The London Treaty of 1930 postponed until 1936 the replacements in capital ships allowable under the Washington Treaty after 1931, and extended limitations to the auxiliary ships (subject to certain allowable replacement), limitations which were to be worked up or down to by December 31, 1936, after which all surplus tonnage in the stipulated categories must be disposed of according to a fixed schedule. The new limitations were vigorously opposed by naval authorities in the United States, Great Britain and Japan (France and Italy did not subscribe to the principal limitations, and finally did not ratify the treaty at all), which seems fairly good evidence that the treaty contained a reasonable compromise; but the three powers ratified the agreement, good until December 31, 1936, and providing for a third naval conference in December, 1935, one year before the expiration of the treaty.[2] On the following page is represented a tabulation of the fleets, ratios and tonnage, with which the powers emerged from the London Treaty.[3] An "escalator clause" permitted any contracting party to step up out of the limitations in case a non-contracting party should modify seriously the existing situation of naval construction.[4] It proved to be of utmost importance when the time came,

---

[1] The United States with its small standing army of 165,000 could not be a great factor in these efforts.

[2] Benjamin H. Williams has published a very summary and wishful history of *The United States and Disarmament* (New York, 1931).

[3] For a more detailed statement, see note at end of this chapter, "A Birdseye View of the Washington and London Naval Treaties." The treaty, an intricate document, must be carefully studied.

[4] Great Britain invoked it, May, 1936, and April, 1938.

NAVAL LIMITATION OF THE LONDON TREATY OF 1930 TO BE REACHED ON DECEMBER 31, 1936

Categories	United States		British Commonwealth of Nations		Japan	
	No. Ships	Total Tonnage	No. Ships	Total Tonnage	No. Ships	Total Tonnage
Capital Ships	15	464,300	15	474,750	9	272,070
Aircraft Carriers		135,000		135,000 (with 70,350 replacements)		81,000 (with 7,470 replacements)
Cruisers, Class A (8″ guns)	18	(No more than 10,000 tons each)	15	(No more than 10,000 tons each)	12	(No more than 10,000 tons each)
Cruisers, Class B (6″ guns)		143,500		192,200		100,450 (Replacement 1 ship in 1935)
Destroyers		150,000		150,000		105,500
Submarines		52,700		52,700		52,700 (with 31,200 anticipated replacement)

December 31, 1936, to begin disposing of the surplus tonnage, over and above the stipulations of the limited categories. By then the naval race had begun again, due to Japan's break-off on the one hand, and the European situation on the other. The United States, therefore, did not scrap all its First World War decommissioned destroyers. Looking back on this situation after the critical days of 1940 we could be glad that these precious ships were not junked.

Notwithstanding the warnings of American naval experts that the London limitations were not safe for the secure defense of the United States and its territorial possessions, despite the ominous trend of international relations in Europe and in Asia since 1930, the United States (and to a small extent, Great Britain) underbuilt its navy beneath the treaty limits. Japan, on the other hand, built snugly up to the treaty line. Consequently in the last treaty year, the United States found itself particularly weak in under-age warships, notably in cruisers, destroyers and submarines. Japan surpassed the United States in effective Class B cruisers, destroyers,[1] and submarines; and crept perilously close in new tonnage of air-craft carriers and Class A cruisers.[2] With warships, as with automobiles, victory is likely to go to the new models. Under her right as a party to the Washington Treaty, Japan in December, 1934, gave formal notice of the cessation of any continuation of that agreement after its lifetime ending December 31, 1936,[3] when the London Treaty also expired. Great Britain, alarmed in 1936 for the security of her Mediterranean route to India and for her African Empire, by the Italo-Ethiopian War, prepared for vigorous additions to her naval armament.

Under these unpromising conditions the treaty powers assembled for another naval conference in London in December, 1935, as provided by the terms of the London Treaty, only to prove themselves unable to agree on any effective limitations. The naval *status quo* of 1936, thanks to underbuilding by the United States during 1931-1936, was, as the reader will observe by the tables at the end of this chapter, much more favorable to Japan than was the *status quo* of 1931. These figures

---

[1] This superiority in these categories of new tonnage was increased by the construction by Japan of an unknown number of small torpedo boats, under 600 tons. There were no treaty restrictions on this size of warship.

[2] For detailed tables of tonnage and ratios in 1922, 1930, and 1935, see note at end of this chapter.

[3] Without such notice registered by one of the parties the treaty by its terms would have continued for two additional years.

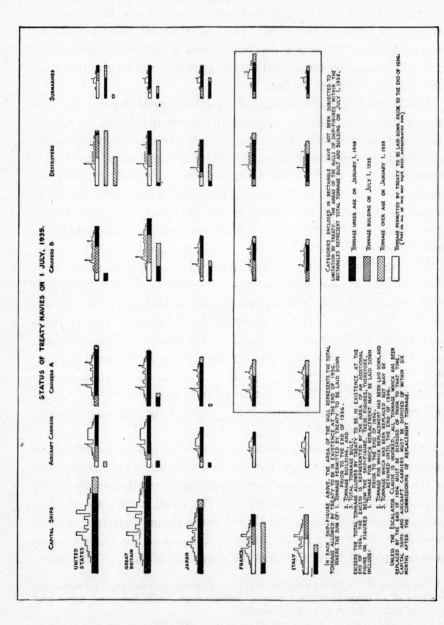

Pictorial Diagram of Treaty Navies.

show that on July 1, 1935—the year in which the Washington period of naval truce came to an end—these were the *de facto* ratios of the five principal navies:

TOTAL TONNAGE OF UNDER-AGE SHIPS OF ALL CATEGORIES

United States	*Great Britain*	*Japan*	*France*	*Italy*
7.46	10	6.62	3.78	3.01

In under-age tonnage in the categories of light cruisers, destroyers and submarines, Japan by 1935 had already forged ahead of the United States under the treaty regime of 1922-1936. By secret encroachments on the treaty limits, revealed by the Second World War, she brought her actual fighting ratio even higher than the above *de facto* figures show.

The statesmen of the great powers left Washington in 1922 with the certainty that the tension had been relaxed and that a breathing spell was at hand, for at least fifteen years, for the development of peace and prosperity in the Pacific. Good will had taken the place of fear and suspicion. That happy atmosphere was suddenly vexed by the passage of the American immigration law of 1924, which superseded the "Gentlemen's Agreement," under which the immigration of Japanese to the United States had been regulated since 1907 without discrimination directly or indirectly against the Japanese. Over the opposition of the President and of the Secretary of State, Congress declared that "aliens not eligible for citizenship," which by existing law meant all Orientals born outside of the United States, were excluded from admission into the United States and its territories, except for certain exempted classes of individuals. This really was intended for Japanese, since other Orientals, including Chinese, had been excluded by previous legislation. The exempted classes were: government officials, those coming to the United States as tourists, travelers, seamen, former residents returning from temporary absences, professors, ministers of religion, students, and those who entered solely to carry on trade in pursuance of existing treaty provisions. President Coolidge felt obliged to sign the act in order to have the advantages of the general regulation of immigration which it placed on the statute-books, in the face of a menacing deluge of postwar European immigrants. To Japan it was a bitter blow: not the exclusion—Japan had accepted that in fact, and was willing to help block up any holes in the previous arrangements—but the essential discrimination. When the bill was being debated in Congress, and seemed likely to pass, the Japanese Ambassador, Mr. Hanihara, lodged with the Department of State a note of protest which stated that "grave consequences" were likely to ensue if it were enacted. There is reason to believe that this note was prepared in collaboration between the Japanese Embassy and the Department of State for the purpose of staying the hand of Congress. When Secretary of State Hughes transmitted a copy of it to Congress it was taken as a threat of war. Probably there was enough sentiment in the Senate to have carried Japanese exclusion by a narrow margin anyway, but Mr. Hanihara's veiled threat turned the vote in Congress into a veritable landslide for exclusion.[1]

Toward the end of this History we shall return to Japan's program in Asia, her conquest of China in defiance of the principles so solemnly agreed to in the Nine-Power Treaty, the patient caveats and protests of the United States, and Japan's treacherous attack on the Hawaiian Islands and the Philippines in the momentous war that began on Sunday morning, December 7, 1941.

[1] Rodman W. Paul wrote an undergraduate essay on *The Abrogation of the Gentlemen's Agreement* (Harvard Phi Beta Kappa Prize Essay for 1936, Cambridge, 1936) worthy of a doctoral dissertation.

COMPARATIVE NAVAL STRENGTH OF TREATY POWERS IN JULY, 1935, AS COMPARED WITH TREATY ALLOWANCES OF 1922 AND 1930

(SEE ALSO "BIRDSEYE VIEW OF WASHINGTON AND LONDON NAVAL TREATIES" FOLLOWING THIS TABLE.)

COUNTRY	WASHINGTON TREATY ALLOWANCE 1922 — TONS	RATIO (US·GB·JAP·FR·ITAL)	LONDON TREATY (mods. eff. Dec. 31, 1936) No.	TONS	RATIO 1935 (US·GB·JAP·FR·ITAL)	TOTAL TONNAGE BUILT 1935 No.	TONS	RATIO (US·GB·JAP·FR·ITAL)	UNDER-AGE SHIPS 1935 No.	TONS	RATIO (US·GB·JAP·FR·ITAL)	BUILDING 1935 No.	TONS	APPROP. 1935 No.	TONS	ADDITIONAL TONS
UNITED STATES																
CAPITAL SHIPS	525,000	10·10·6·3.333·3.333				15	464,300	9.78·10·5.7·3.7·1.83	12	384,200	9.08·10·5.11·1.41·1.35					
AIRCRAFT CARRIERS	135,000	10·10·6·4.444·4.444				4	92,000	8·10·5.91·1.91·0	3	80,500	7.04·10·5.91·1.91·0	2	40,000	1	14,500	
CRUISERS -A-			18	(18 ships not over 10,000 tons each)	10·8.33·6.66	16	149,775	8.19·10·6.77·5.79·5.68	15	142,425	8.2·10·6.12·4.92·4.92	3	30,000			
CRUISERS -B-				143,500	7.5·10·5.2	10	70,500	4.21·10·7.40·3.07·4.21	10	70,500	7.39·10·8.43·4.06·6.15	7	70,000	2	20,000	
DESTROYERS				150,000	10·10·7	211	238,315	10·7.98·5.16·5.16·3.4			8.33·6.66·8.09·10·5.47	40	63,500	15	23,550	51,765
SUBMARINES				52,700	10·10·10	84	70,020	9.15·10·6.09·4.83·3.37	43	45,600	7.18·7.03·9.68·10·5.93	10	13,200	6	8,400	19,160
TOTALS						340	1,084,910					62	216,700	24	66,450	70,925
BRITISH EMPIRE																
CAPITAL SHIPS	525,000					15	474,750		15	474,750						
AIRCRAFT CARRIERS	135,000					6	115,350		6	115,350		1	15,000			19,100
CRUISERS -A-			15	(15 ships not over 10,000 tons each)		19	183,396		18	173,400						
CRUISERS -B-				150,000		33	166,210		17	96,390		12	86,800	3	27,000	28,160
DESTROYERS				150,000		163	189,669		54	72,694		25	34,185	9	12,200	39,382
SUBMARINES				52,700		56	56,209		36	44,954		7	7,240	3	3,665	4,081
TOTALS						292	1,185,584		146	977,538		45	143,225	15	42,865	90,723
JAPAN																
CAPITAL SHIPS	315,000					9	272,070		8	242,740						
AIRCRAFT CARRIERS	81,000					4	68,370		4	68,370		1	10,050	1	10,000	
CRUISERS -A-			12	(12 ships not over 10,000 tons each) 100,450		14	123,520		12	107,800						50
CRUISERS -B-				105,500		20	93,375		17	81,455		5	42,500	1	8,500	500
DESTROYERS				105,500		102	123,313		63	86,213		8	10,944	12	18,013	1,500
SUBMARINES				52,700		57	68,349		49	61,837		12	17,000	2	700	1,550
TOTALS						206	748,997		153	648,415		26	80,494		37,213	
FRANCE																
CAPITAL SHIPS	175,000					9	185,925		3	66,567		2	53,000	1	35,000	52,000
AIRCRAFT CARRIERS	60,000					1	22,146		1	22,146						37,859
CRUISERS -A-				NOT LIMITED		10	105,923		7	70,000						NOT LIMITED
CRUISERS -B-				NOT LIMITED		8	51,814		6	38,902		6	45,600			NOT LIMITED
DESTROYERS				NOT LIMITED		80	123,219		56	105,431		16	17,035			NOT LIMITED
SUBMARINES				NOT LIMITED		97	83,890		69	64,183		14	14,556			NOT LIMITED
TOTALS						205	572,917		142	367,229		38	130,191			
ITALY																
CAPITAL SHIPS	175,000					4	86,532		3	64,714				2	70,000	105,000
AIRCRAFT CARRIERS	60,000															60,000
CRUISERS -A-				NOT LIMITED		11	103,641		7	70,000		2	70,000			NOT LIMITED
CRUISERS -B-				NOT LIMITED		16	71,183		12	59,067		3	22,539			NOT LIMITED
DESTROYERS				NOT LIMITED		88	91,488		55	63,475		6	7,087			NOT LIMITED
SUBMARINES				NOT LIMITED		69	45,720		48	37,550		10	8,778	2	830	1,830
TOTALS						188	398,564		125	294,806		21	108,404			

(1) This Table is compiled from detailed information in "Comparative Strength of Treaty Navies (Parties to the Washington Conference) July, 1935," printed for use of the Committee on Naval Affairs, 74th Congress, 1st Session, Committee Print (Washington G.P.O., 1935) and from Report of Secretary of Navy for fiscal year ending June 30th, 1935.

CHAPTER XXXVII

THE UNITED STATES AND EUROPE

(1921-1937)

IN a previous chapter we have described the peace settlement of 1919-1921 and the liquidation of those questions of neutral rights that were such an intricate legacy of the First World War. The first fifteen years of diplomatic relations between the United States and Europe in the interval between the two world wars concerned largely certain other issues arising from the aftermath of the first war and its train of revolution: reparations, inter-governmental war debts, the organization of peace, recognition of Soviet Russia, disarmament. Historians hardly realized that as soon as they had placed these issues in their proper perspective they would have to deal with another world war.

The policy which the United States pursued toward Europe after the separate peace with Germany, Austria, and Hungary, following the rejection of the League of Nations, may be compared to that of Great Britain after the Napoleonic wars and the peace settlement of 1815. Great Britain refused to make of the Quadruple Alliance, in which the great powers had united to overthrow Napoleon, a pedestal for the Holy Alliance, which was to mold Europe in the principles of absolute monarchy invoked at Vienna under the mantle of Legitimacy. Unchallenged in her absolute control of the sea, and thus safe behind the English Channel, she preferred to stand aloof from the issues of continental politics as long as no one upset the balance of power. Similarly a century later the United States, safe behind the Atlantic, rejected Woodrow Wilson's ideal of internationalism and stepped back from Europe to its own continent after the defeat of Germany. It refused any direct participation in the succeeding conferences,[1] after Versailles, that met to execute and adjust the peace settlement of 1919 which straitjacketed Europe again, this time under the principle of Nationality. It refused membership in the League of Nations, which Wilson had founded to enforce the peace henceforth all over the globe by guaranteeing the existing political independence and territorial integrity of its members.

[1] London, San Remo, Hythe, Lympne, and Spa, in 1920; Cannes, London, and Genoa, in 1922; London, 1924; Locarno, 1925; Genoa, 1926.

Its Senate even rejected membership in the Court of International Justice, the judicial organ of the League, set up by separate statute so that a nation might belong to it without necessarily being a member of the League. Only in numerous humanitarian, cultural, economic and technical international conferences held under the aegis of the League did the United States take a full part; and in membership in the separately organized International Labor Office, for the co-ordination, by separate sovereign legislation, of national labor legislation throughout the world.[1]

For more than a decade after 1921, this policy of "isolation" encountered a steady, vigorous and highly articulate opposition on the part of the intellectuals, speaking through the pulpit, the public forum, the textbooks and the universities; but following the appearance of the European dictatorships, and the clanging appeals to force for the rearrangement of political and economic frontiers in Europe, Asia and Africa, it became obvious that Woodrow Wilson's conception of a league of *democratic* nations to enforce world peace was only delicately viable under new stresses.

Default by the European Allies[2] of their so-called "war debts" to the United States, and the tangled question of reparations, rooted in the Versailles Treaty, had been at least a minor factor in this revulsion of opinion in the United States from the League of Nations. Before we turn to the American peace policy, as manifested in the network of treaties for voluntary arbitration and conciliation, and the pledges against war as an instrument of national policy, and against intervention in the foreign or domestic affairs of any foreign state, it is necessary to set forth these sore and chafing issues of "war debts" and reparations, legally separate yet actually joined, theoretically unconnected yet really related.

Entering the First World War, the United States opened its credit unstintedly to the Associated Governments, at the moment when they were hardest pressed for money, even as it raised its armies and finally hurled them against the enemy on the continent of Europe. The Allies were desperate to borrow, in the hour of their darkest need; and the United States, intent on winning the war, was eager to lend to sustain the fighting strength of its Associates while American man power was being

---

[1] Denys P. Myers has traced the history of these multifarious activities in the *Handbook of the League of Nations* (World Peace Foundation, Boston, 1935).

[2] In using the word Allies, reference is made to the European Entente Allies allied among themselves. They were Associates of China, the United States, and the belligerents of the New World.

drilled to take its place in battle at the European front. The United States lent without stint and later it fought without condition. Before the armistice of November 11, 1918, it had loaned to the Allies a total of $7,077,114,750.00 in cash, nine-tenths of which was spent in the United States for supplies useful in prosecuting the war, not only munitions but also many kinds of materials for war-busy populations.

These sums thus loaned before the armistice, and hence during the hostilities of the war, may properly be called *war debts*. There was some difference of opinion expressed in the debates in Congress as to whether they might in the end be treated as subsidies or loans; but there was no misunderstanding concerning the terms on which they were furnished to the Allied Governments. They were loaned on promises to pay, backed by the national faith of the borrowing governments, the terms of repayment to be agreed upon later, interest at 5% to be charged meanwhile. The United States Government in turn secured the money by its own credit from its own citizens by the sale of bonds, the "liberty bonds," on which the Government promised to pay back principal and interest, usually 4¼%, in dollars of the weight and fineness of gold which existed at the time of issue of the loan, and according to a schedule stipulated in the bonds. So if the Allies should not pay their debts, for these moneys borrowed in the hour of direst distress to help them save their very lives, then the burden of their indebtedness, principal and interest, would rest upon the people of the United States, on the lenders instead of the borrowers. That burden did so rest, as a matter of fact, upon the American people immediately after the war, when interest payments were suspended,[1] at least until the day should arrive for the funding of the payment of these sums.

After the armistice of November 11, 1918, the United States loaned in addition to the sums above mentioned, the sum of $2,533,288,825.45 cash, and $740,075,499.25 war supplies and relief supplies—total $3,-273,364,324.70. This was not used for fighting, but for relief of civilian populations, rehabilitation of credit of the Allied nations, big and little, old and new, and sustenance of the new remnant and succession states of Europe while they were staggering to their feet amid the ruins from which they rose: Poland, Czechoslovakia, Roumania, Serbia, Estonia, Lithuania, Latvia, Finland, even Austria and Hungary.[2] These were

---

[1] Interest payments in most cases were kept up by the debtors during the war, for the compelling reason that they might not be able to borrow more if they did not pay interest on the previous loans.

[2] As noted in the tabulation below, this included a loan of $10,000,000 to Cuba, $431,849.14 to Nicaragua, and $26,000 to Liberia.

really *peace debts,* incurred after Germany and her allies had surrendered, some of them borrowed by the former enemy. The United States Government, however, made no distinction between these war debts established before the armistice and the peace debts created after November 11, 1918. Nor was any such distinction ever made in the later funding of the debts (except in the case of Belgium) nor during the few years in which the debtor nations paid on their debts according to the agreed schedule.

The following statement [1] shows the total principal of these original debts to the United States, $10,350,479,074.70, as separated into pre-armistice and post-armistice indebtedness.

Country	Pre-armistice Cash Loans	Post-armistice Cash Loans	War Supplies and Relief Supplies	Total Indebtedness
Armenia			$ 11,959,917.49	$ 11,959,917.49
Austria			24,055,708.92	24,055,708.92
Belgium	$ 171,780,000	$ 177,434,467.89	29,872,732.54	379,087,200.43
Cuba	10,000,000			10,000,000.00
Czechoslovakia		61,974,041.10	29,905,629.93	91,879,671.03
Estonia			13,999,145.60	13,999,145.60
Finland			8,281,926.17	8,281,926.17
France	1,970,000,000	1,027,477,800.00	407,341,145.01	3,404,818,945.01
Great Britain	3,696,000,000	581,000,000.00		4,277,000,000.00
Greece		27,167,000.00		27,167,000.00
Hungary			1,685,835.61	1,685,835.61
Italy	1,031,000,000	617,034,050.90		1,648,034,050.90
Latvia			5,132,287.14	5,132,287.14
Liberia		26,000.00		26,000.00
Lithuania			4,981,628.03	4,981,628.03
Nicaragua			431,849.14	431,849.14
Poland			159,666,972.39	159,666,972.39
Rumania		25,000,000.00	12,911,152.92	37,911,152.92
Russia	187,729,750		4,871,547.37	192,601,297.37
Yugoslavia	10,605,000	16,175,465.56	24,978,020.99	51,758,486.55
	$7,077,114,750	$2,533,288,825.45	$740,075,499.25	$10,350,479,074.70

In addition to these loans of the United States Government, the people of the United States contributed, through the Red Cross and other agencies, over a billion dollars for the relief of war-stricken populations between 1914 and 1921.[2]

[1] From mimeographed "Memorandum Covering the Indebtedness of Foreign Governments to the United States and Showing the Total Amounts Paid by Germany under the Dawes and Young Plans," Treasury Department, Office of Commissioner of Accounts and Deposits, revised March 1, 1935 (Washington, D. C.), 16.

[2] See statement of Senator S. P. Spencer, *Congressional Record,* March 4, 1921. Through the Red Cross was contributed $978,512,225; by Congressional appropriations for European relief, $100,000,000. Spencer's report estimates $490,000,000 (one-half the Red Cross total) contributed through other channels.

In the Peace Conference at Paris the French and British spokesmen desired to make some all-round agreement for the settlement of inter-Allied indebtedness in relation to the reparations which were to be demanded from Germany on account of her damages to civilian populations on land, at sea, and from the air, as interpreted by the victorious Allies. In 1923 Great Britain was a creditor for $10,447,761,000 lent to Allied nations outside the Empire ($4,321,976,000 of it to Russia), and a debtor for $6,489,492,000 of which $4,277,000,000 was to the United States. Assuming that revolutionary Russia would never pay the Czar's war debts, Great Britain would come out more than even in any general cancellation. She was therefore not unwilling, in fact she was ready to agree to collect no more than she had to pay. France was a creditor for $3,463,744,000 ($1,165,720,000 of this to Russia) and a debtor for $7,020,616,000 ($3,-404,818,945 to the United States); Italy was a creditor for $389,988,000 and a debtor for $4,747,527,000 ($1,648,034,050 to the United States); these two nations were naturally eager for a general cancellation.[1] If each power could have canceled off its debits against its credits, and made the payment of any surplus debits left over dependent and contingent upon its receipts from German reparations—leaving the immediate cash to be raised from a bonded loan from America secured by anticipated proceeds of German reparations—the burden of the war debts could then be paid partly by the people of the defeated nation, Germany, and partly by the people of the United States. Then if unforeseen contingencies should in future interrupt the flow of reparations from Germany, it need disturb only the holders of the German reparation bonds which, it was often thought, could be sold to people in the United States. The ally which failed to collect its German reparations would stop contingent payment on its own war debts.

The United States had loaned vast sums, and borrowed none. Therefore proposals of this nature would have made the payment of the uncanceled portion of the debts of its Associates depend upon the collection of German reparations, a problem of European political complexities and entanglements. Incidentally such an arrangement would have made the United States interested in the inter-Allied machinery for the enforcement and collection of reparations against Germany, just as the creditors of the thirteen original states once were made interested, by Alexander Hamilton's fiscal device of federal assumption of state debts,

---

[1] H. E. Fisk, *The Inter-Ally Debts; an Analysis of War and Post-war Public Finance, 1914-1923* (New York, 1924), 348-349; and Treasury "Memorandum Covering the Indebtedness," *op. cit.*

in the success of the new federal government of the United States after 1789. Woodrow Wilson and his colleagues successfully resisted all suggestions of melting together at Paris the debts to the United States and the reparations to be extracted from Germany.[1]

The peace-makers at Paris could not agree on any sum of total reparations to be required of Germany, so vast were the damages alleged to civilians from Germany and her allies, so astronomical were the implications of the interpretation [2] placed by the victorious powers on civilian damages to include war pensions and separation allowances. Article 231 of the treaty of Versailles stated:

The Allied and Associated Governments affirm and Germany accepts the responsibility of Germany and her allies for causing all the loss and damage to which the Allied and Associated Governments and their nationals have been subjected as a consequence of the war imposed upon them by the aggression of Germany and her allies.

This responsibility for civilian damages (as so interpreted by the victors) to Allied and Associated nationals was limited to the period of the belligerency of nations in the war. Such guaranteed little to the United States, whose claims for damages, as is recalled, were mostly for outrages against American neutral lives and property in violation of international law, before the period of American belligerency.[3] The treaty required 20,000,000,000 gold marks to be paid by Germany on account during the two years while reparations were being figured up, together with a schedule of payments in kind. The final calculation was referred to a special Reparations Commission, created by the treaty, to report before May 1, 1921, the total demanded from Germany, to arrange a schedule of payments, and to supervise its execution. The Commission was also empowered by the treaties with Austria and Hungary to fix and supervise the payments of reparations due from them. The Commission duly announced the colossal sum of 132,000,000,000 gold marks, or approximately 33,000,000,000 gold dollars in the currency of that time. As if in its inner wisdom the Reparations Commission doubted the

[1] They presented to the French and Italian commissioners the following statement from the Treasury of the United States, March 8, 1919: "The Treasury . . . will not assent to any discussion at the Peace Conference or elsewhere of any plan or arrangement for the release, consolidation, or reapportionment of the obligations of foreign governments held by the United States." Thomas W. Lamont, in House and Seymour, *What Really Happened at Paris, op. cit.,* 289.

[2] See above, p. 637.

[3] After the separate peace with Germany these claims for spoliations on neutrals were adjudicated by the Mixed Claims Commission United States and Germany. See above, p. 659.

capacity of Germany to pay the 132,000,000,000 gold marks even over a long time, it divided the sum into three categories; established the order of priority of each; and ordained a schedule of payment for each, in the form of three classes of bonds, with dated coupons for interest and amortization. Germany was called upon first to assume the service by payments partly in cash and partly in kind, of the Class A bonds totaling 12,000,000,000 gold marks and the Class B bonds, totaling 38,000,-000,000 gold marks bearing 6% coupons, representing 5% interest and 1% amortization. The Class C bonds, 82,000,000,000 gold marks, held in abeyance without interest, were never actually issued.

Needless to remind the reader, Germany never paid any more than a few years' installments toward serving the Class A and B obligations. While doing this, and making huge payments in kind, she depleted her currency and went through a catastrophic cycle of inflation. When she failed to pay more, France occupied (1923) the Ruhr Basin, Germany's principal industrial region, a coercive step allowed by the treaty; and Great Britain deducted 26 per cent from the payments by her nationals for current imports from Germany, applying the proceeds to reparations account. These coercive measures proved ineffective as a means of adequate collection, though not as a means of coercion. The only way to try to collect all was to use further force, and this was too costly, even if force could overcome passive resistance. Germany on her part was still helpless after military defeat and inflation. Alarmed by the occupation, she was willing to agree to a new compromise schedule. At the indirect suggestion of the Secretary of State of the United States, Charles E. Hughes, the Reparations Commission invited American financial experts, General Charles G. Dawes, and Mr. Owen D. Young, to head successive international commissions to devise a receivership for a bankrupt, helpless, and, it must also be said, unwilling, conquered debtor nation. First by the Dawes Plan (in operation, 1924 to 1929), and then by the Young Plan (which dated from 1929) successively lighter schedules of payments were prescribed and accepted.

The Young Plan (agreed upon December 22, 1928) stepped German reparations down to an annual burden that was possible for the Third Reich to bear. It laid down a new schedule of a "final and definitive settlement" based on a revised total liability stretching over 59 years. During this period Germany was to make unconditional payments of 612,000,000 gold marks per year (approximately $153,000,000 pre-devalued gold dollars). Conditional payments (contingent on German prosperity) might rise above the unconditional annuities to a total of

RM.1,641,600,000 ($410,000,000) per annum to RM.2,352,700,000 ($588,-175,000) in 1965, and descending to less than a billion marks ($250,000,-000) for the last three years of the long term. The unconditional annuities represented an amount almost precisely equal to what the Allies had agreed, meanwhile, to remit per annum to pay their funded debts to the United States. A part of the unconditional annuities was pledged for another immediate "mobilization loan" of a $200,000,000 bond issue to commute into ready cash for the creditors that much of Germany's revised obligations. In return for a German pledge to pay these new annuities all established controls and coercions were abandoned by the Allies. Contemporaneously they agreed to evacuate all occupied zones of German territory (held since the armistice) by 1930.

Defeated Germany no longer had any great domestic war debt (it had been withered up by the catastrophe of inflation and deflation), and her small army and navy were strictly limited by the treaty of Versailles. The reparations debt was now no more of a burden to Germany than were their war debts to the victorious powers (where the burden of war debts in many cases had also been alleviated by inflation and devaluation); but the Allies had to spend huge sums on armies and navies necessary, in the background, to hold Germany down to these terms of defeat. And Germany under Adolf Hitler was able *within five years*, 1934-1939, to spend upwards of 90,000,000,000 reichmarks [1] (re-established German currency) at first secretly then openly on rearmament for the purpose of tearing up the treaty obligations of Versailles and conquering the victors of 1918! This sum should be compared to the original total reparations bill to be paid over a stretch of sixty years. The additional military expenses spent by Germany after the beginning of the Second World War quickly equaled and surpassed the *total* original reparations bill of 132,000,000,000 gold marks (of which 82,000,000,000 was never bonded).

While the Allies were saddling on Germany the terms of reparations the United States was patiently awaiting a settlement of the debts due to it, interest on which had been suspended by the debtors at the end of the war. An act of Congress (February 9, 1922) had created a World War Debts Funding Commission, appointed by the President, by and with the advice and consent of the Senate, with the Secretary of the Treasury as chairman. The law authorized the Commission to fund anew the foreign debts into bonds bearing 4.25% interest, to be

---

[1] See Hitler's Reichstag speech of September 1, 1939, in collection of Adolf Hitler's speeches in English translation, entitled *My New Order* (New York, 1941), p. 689.

completely paid off, principal and interest, by 1947. This corresponded generally to the obligations of the United States for the payment of its own bonds from which had come the money that was loaned to the Associates in war and in peace. The funding agreements, made by the Commission with the different debtor nations between 1923 and 1930, were much more lenient than these terms allowable by the statute, because of radical cuts in interest and lengthening of terms of payment; but Congress by separate acts ratified each revision. The tabulation [1] on the following page shows the terms on which the total debts were funded, without distinction between war debts and peace debts, and excluding the unfunded debts of Armenia, Nicaragua and Russia.

Calculating on the basis of an original obligation to pay 5% interest, these funding agreements represented a cancellation of approximately 51.3 per cent of the *then value* of the total indebtedness, ranging from a minimum of 30.1 per cent cancellation allowed to Great Britain to 80.2 per cent cancellation allowed to Italy. On a 4.25% interest basis (corresponding to domestic liberty-loan rates) this cancellation would be 43.1 per cent of the whole, ranging from 19.7 per cent of the British to 75.4 per cent of the Italian.

Though the sums were large, some thought impossible, the terms were generous. The Allies pledged their faith and started to pay to the United States. Meanwhile they made among themselves other funding agreements for the settlement of inter-Allied war indebtedness.[2] There was no legal connection between the inflow of German reparations and the service on inter-Allied war debts with the obligated remittances to the United States; but actually the Allies intended to pay no more to their creditors, including the United States, than they collected in the end from German reparations. Great Britain, for example, in the average of years would take in from her debtors slightly more than she paid out to the United States; and debtors to Great Britain, like France, relied on Germany. So, in reality, the payment of war debts was made to rest upon the payment by Germany of reparations. And, in reality again, Germany's payments rested on her capacity to borrow from private foreign capital, over a third of it American.

The United States, which had refused to allow war debts to be coupled with reparations, was not unwilling to couple them with disarmament.

---

[1] From Treasury *Memorandum Covering Indebtedness of Foreign Governments, op. cit.*, p. 22.

[2] In dealing with this tremendous and intricate subject the author has relied heavily on Harold G. Moulton and Leo Pasvolsky, *War Debts and World Prosperity*, published by the Brookings Institution (New York, 1932).

STATEMENT SHOWING PRINCIPAL AND INTEREST COMPUTED AT THE RATES SPECIFIED IN DEBT AGREEMENTS ON INDEBTEDNESS OF FOREIGN GOVERNMENTS TO THE UNITED STATES AT TIME OF FUNDING, CREDIT ALLOWANCES, THE CASH PAYMENTS ON EXECUTION OF AGREEMENTS, AND THE TOTAL DEBT AS FUNDED.

Country	Indebtedness at Time of Funding			Credit Allowances and Cash Payments on Execution of Agreements		Funded Debt
	Principal	Interest	Total	Applied on Principal	Applied on Interest	
Austria	$ 24,055,708.92	559,176.08	$ 24,614,885.00	....	....	$ 24,614,885
Belgium	377,029,570.06	40,767,664.60	417,797,234.66	....	$ 17,234.66	417,780,000
Czechoslovakia	91,879,671.03	25,978,742.91	117,858,413.94	....	2,858,413.94 [1]	115,000,000
Estonia	13,999,145.60	1,765,219.73	15,764,365.33	$1,933,923.45 [2]	1,441.88	13,830,000
Finland	8,281,926.17	727,389.10	9,009,315.27	....	9,315.27	9,000,000
France	3,340,516,043.72	684,870,643.17	4,025,386,686.89	386,686.89	....	4,025,000,000
Great Britain	4,074,818,358.44	529,309,727.30	4,604,128,085.74	....	4,128,085.74	4,600,000,000
Greece	27,167,000.00 [3]	3,127,922.67	30,294,922.67	2,922.67	....	30,292,000
Hungary	1,685,835.61	253,917.43	1,939,753.04	....	753.04	1,939,000
Italy	1,647,869,197.96	394,330,268.38	2,042,199,466.34	199,466.34	....	2,042,000,000
Latvia	5,132,287.14	647,275.62	5,779,562.76	....	4,562.76	5,775,000
Lithuania	4,981,628.03	1,049,918.94	6,031,546.97	....	1,546.97	6,030,000
Poland	159,666,972.39	18,898,053.60	178,565,025.99	....	5,025.99	178,560,000
Rumania	36,116,972.44	8,477,479.10	44,594,451.54	4,451.54	....	44,590,000
Yugoslavia	51,037,886.39	11,819,226.00	62,857,112.39	7,112.39	....	62,850,000
	$9,864,238,203.90	$1,722,582,624.63	$11,586,820,828.53	$2,533,563.28	$7,026,380.25	$11,577,260,885
Cash received upon execution of agreements	600,639.83	4,167,966.31	4,768,606.14			
Credit allowances	1,933,923.45 [2]	2,858,413.94 [1]	4,791,337.39			
	$2,533,563.28	$7,026,380.25	$9,559,943.53			
Amount funded	$9,861,704,640.62	$1,715,556,244.38	$11,577,260,885.00			

[1] Amount of interest written off in compromise settlement with Czechoslovakia.
[2] Allowance for total loss of cargo of S. S. *John Russ* sunk by a mine in Baltic Sea.
[3] Includes 4% twenty-year loan of $12,167,000 authorized by Act of February 14, 1929.

In discussions of possible further cancellation—that is, of *transfer* of the burden from European taxpayers to American taxpayers—it was always observable that the European debtors, who asserted that the burden was becoming impossible to bear, were expending vast sums on increased armaments, greater than before the war; France was even loaning money to Poland and Czechoslovakia for new armaments in defense against a possible German eruption. It was just as illogical to couple further cancellation with disarmament as with reparations; but President Hoover intimated that the United States might be willing to make additional concessions in exchange for real relief everywhere, by international agreements, from the staggering and mounting burden of increased armament cost. No disarmament, beyond the naval agreements of 1921 and 1930, proved possible in a European world ruled by fear. This was particularly galling to disarmed Germany. The victors of 1918, never really trusting her, feared she would be able some day to tear up the treaty of Versailles, which had suggested that German disarmament was the first step of general disarmament.

Contemporary with the funding of the Allied debts and the inauguration of the Dawes Plan, a flood of foreign money, mostly American, poured into Germany and Europe, in the form of bonded loans to municipalities and corporations. It was these funds, filtering through the German state, which really paid such reparations as were remitted.

As long as private loans [1] continued, they freshened the bloodstream of German national economy sufficiently to support the payments under the Young Plan. But in 1931, in the second year of the Great Depression, private investors became nervous and ceased to loan to Germany. In the summer of that year a political factor of international character helped precipitate a financial panic in Austria and Germany: French credit to Austrian banks was withdrawn following the attempt to set up a German-Austrian customs-union as a step toward a political union (*Anschluss*). This caused the failure of the leading Austrian commercial bank, the *Creditanstalt*, which already was in a straitened condition. In turn this threatened the leading German private banks and insurance companies, and started a renewed flight of capital from Germany. The German budget became unbalanced. American private credits to Germany, held by banks in the United States, were endangered. If the impending collapse could not be prevented, the second bankruptcy of

---

[1] Much of the borrowed money was used for permanent, private or public, improvements, which must remain in Germany, embedded in steel and concrete, no matter what the fate of the loans.

Germany threatened widespread bank failures in foreign countries, particularly in the United States. To fend this off, President Hoover, June 20, 1931, proposed [1] to the foreign governments a one year's standstill agreement on the payment of all inter-governmental debts, the year's arrears to be postponed and spread over the next ten years.

The passing months brought no certainty that payments would be resumed all around when the year's moratorium should expire. With difficulty the principal central banks (including the Federal Reserve Bank of New York) sustained the German financial institutions against collapse by short-time loans totaling $100,000,000. In September, 1931, the increasing intricacy of the financial situation forced Great Britain off the gold standard, and with it those dependencies and European countries which in times past had linked their currencies, by exchange, with that of England. Meanwhile the debtor governments, eager to rid themselves of the burden of indebtedness, anxiously considered what should be done at the end of the year's standstill. Could a belated all-round cancellation of war debts and reparations clean up the whole mess?

This general clean-up would be at the expense of the United States. The European Allies easily agreed that the service charges on their "war debts" to America were so heavy as not to be possible to pay out of their own resources in gold or cash without stripping the currency reserves of the debtor governments and bringing on economic chaos, damaging to creditor and debtor alike. The annual payments could be remitted only in bills of exchange; bills of exchange could be purchased only from firms having money due them for goods sold to American customers; —that is, payment of "war debts" depended upon the United States being willing to accept an increasing volume of imports from the debtor countries. Economists in the debtor states argued that the American tariff walls kept out the foreign goods and thus made impossible payment of such huge debts. American economists overwhelmingly agreed with this: that a creditor country, as the United States was believed to be since the war, could not successfully remain a high tariff country. It is nevertheless instructive to note that in 1934 and 1935 Great Britain, France and Belgium exported to the United States, without stripping their currency cover or seriously injuring it, several times more gold

[1] The President had to make this proposal contingent upon approval of Congress. He hurriedly sounded out a sufficient number of members to pledge approval once Congress should assemble in December. The "Hoover Moratorium" was promptly approved by Congress, when it convened.

(privately owned) than was necessary to pay public debt installments for those years.[1] This gold was seeking refuge in the United States. In the case of Italy, organized for war, all private export of gold was prohibited, but the phenomenon shows that the debtors could have paid during those years if they preferred to, without upsetting their currency.[2]

For the debtor countries any program of general cancellation of war debts and reparations, at the end of the "Hoover year" of relief, depended on what the United States would do.

The European governments promptly took the initiative. In a conference meeting at Lausanne (June-July, 1932) they wrote off, contingently, 90 per cent of German reparations due under the Young Plan, lumping the total into one easily-supportable principal bonded 5% debt of RM.3,000,000,000 ($750,000,000) to be redeemed by a 1% per annum sinking fund. In addition Germany would pay off by regular schedule the loans received in the Dawes Plan and Young Plan, totaling $400,-000,000. The Lausanne Agreement, which thus canceled nine-tenths of Germany's surviving obligations for reparations, and reduced her payments on that account to only $43,000,000 a year (plus the service on the Dawes Plan and Young Plan loans), was not to go into effect until ratified by Belgium, France, Great Britain, Italy and Japan, as well as Germany. The creditor powers signed among themselves a memorandum embodying a "gentlemen's agreement" that they, on their part, would not ratify until a "satisfactory settlement is obtained between them and

---

[1] The following shows the amount due by the principal debtor countries in the years of default 1934 and 1935, and the amount of gold exported by those countries in those years to the United States:

		Defaulted Installment of "War Debt" Due to U. S.	Private Gold Export to U. S.
Great Britain	1934	$182,780,000	$510,161,190
	1935	181,660,000	316,092,897
France	1934	75,000,000	290,530,897
	1935	80,000,000	934,301,508
Italy	1934	15,075,500	898,783
	1935	15,459,750	4,310
Belgium	1934	6,150,000	12,968,055
	1935	6,650,000	3,257

In the cases of Great Britain, France and Belgium these huge exports of gold were made without any great fluctuation of exchange, and with no damage to currency cover. The transfer was not for the purpose, principally, of settling commercial accounts. It was capital seeking a safe refuge. If to seek refuge this transfer could be made without injuring currency cover, the question arises, could not the debt installments have been safely made?

[2] The governments could have purchased enough of this exportable gold from their nationals for shipment on their own government accounts.

their own creditors." In case of no ratification, the *legal* status of the reparations question would continue to be the same as before the Hoover year, namely, the Young Plan.

The Hoover year expired as the United States was in the midst of a national electoral campaign. Neither party dared to pledge itself to scale down war debts proportionately to the proposed Lausanne schedule. There was widespread feeling among voters of both parties that the debtors had pervertedly spent money on armaments which might have been paid on account of the "war debts" already eased by the generous funding agreements. No proposals of further concessions were tolerated unless the European powers were willing to pare down their armament burdens. In Europe such disarmament was impossible because of the rise of the dictators in Italy and Germany, leaders who preferred war to peace, because war might undo the restrictions on expansion imposed by the treaty of Versailles. The Hoover Administration went out and the Roosevelt Administration came in without any essential change in the corrosive questions of war debts, reparations and increasing armaments.

Before giving up office, the Hoover Administration did agree to send representatives to a general economic conference to be held at London in the spring of 1933 to consider some international agreement on these vital economic problems: (1) monetary and credit policy; (2) prices; (3) resumption of the movement of capital; (4) restrictions on international trade; (5) tariff and trade policy; (6) organization of production and trade. Debts were not included in the agenda, but credits were, which might mean the same thing. Following the example of the British Prime Minister, Ramsay MacDonald, the French and Italian Governments sent distinguished statesmen to Washington, to try to reach some agreement with the incoming Roosevelt Administration for a workable program (presumably on international debts) at the approaching conference, which public opinion hailed as one of the most significant of contemporary history. Little seems to have been accomplished in these preliminary conversations. President-elect Roosevelt and his advisers were preoccupied with the rapidly approaching débâcle of American credit which had made its ominous appearance in December, 1932, and January, 1933, as the incoming Administration came closer to power. The ensuing conference at London was a fiasco. Before it met, the United States had gone off the gold standard, deliberately, as a means of raising prices at home, and meeting foreign competition abroad. The new President suddenly refused, in a telegram to the American delegation, to agree to any program of stabilization which would "peg" the dollar in international exchange. Aside from agreement on a program of silver-purchasing, the delegates left London with no real accomplishment.

Germany never paid any more reparations after the Hoover year (though she kept up, in case of certain favored nationals,[1] the service on the Dawes Plan and Young Plan loans). Most of the debtor governments then stopped payment on their installments to the United States, and to each other. Great Britain, Italy, Latvia, Lithuania, and Yugoslavia made "token payments" toward interest, throughout 1933, hoping that some general scale-down, proportionate to the reparations scale-down, might be possible with the new Roosevelt Administration. Then they stopped. Only Finland adhered to her bonded word, in full and without question.

It was bitterly disillusioning for American bondholders and taxpayers to read the net results of:

Reparation Payments and Debt Payments Compared in Relation to Foreign Loans to Germany (at time of stoppage of payments in 1931):

Total private capital borrowed by Germany [2]
    In U.S.A. (estimated) $2,475,000,000
    In other countries (estimated) 3,809,000,000
                                              ─────────────
    Total $6,284,000,000

Total cash reparations paid by Germany... $4,470,000,000.00
Total war debts paid by Allies to U.S.A.... 2,606,340,987.52

This meant that:

(1) Germany really paid her cash reparations out of long-term loans from the gullible victors and had $1,814,000,000 left over, which she devoted to rearmament for another war.

(2) The Allies paid to the United States on account of war debts an amount approximately equal to the American share (39.37 per cent) of the private capital thus loaned to Germany and its nationals.[3]

---

[1] In 1934 the German consulate at New York announced willingness of Germany to pay Dawes Plan currency loan coupons, 50 per cent in foreign exchange, and 50 per cent in German marks blocked against export from Germany; and to pay to nationals of certain countries only (Great Britain, France, Switzerland, Holland, Belgium, Sweden and Italy), who held Young Plan bonds, their coupons in foreign exchange. American holders, however, had to take 5/6 in blocked *Reichsmarks*. *Foreign Bondholders Protective Councils, Inc., Annual Report for 1934* (New York), 90-92.

[2] Estimates summarized from the Wiggin-Layton figures of the Report of the Committee appointed upon the recommendation of the London Conference, 1931. See Royal Institute of International Affairs Information Department, *Memorandum on Foreign Short-term Loans in Germany, 1919-1932* (London, 1933), p. 49. This statement includes also the long-term loans.

I have converted dollars into marks at four marks to the dollar.

[3] Of the total of American private loans to Germany, a major portion was repatriated by German purchase of low-priced defaulted bonds, but more precise statistics for this have not been available.

As the years passed, defaulted reparations and war debts receded farther and farther into history. Every party to them but the United States wanted to forget about them, because every one but the United States was a debtor. A disgusted Congress in 1934 passed the Johnson Act forbidding the making of loans within the jurisdiction of the United States to any foreign government which had defaulted on its debts to the United States. But during the Second World War, Congress passed legislation (March 11, 1941) permitting the President to lend, lease, *or otherwise dispose of* property of the United States to nations defending themselves against aggression and thereby helping to defend the United States. The neutrality laws of 1935-1939 prohibited making loans to belligerent governments but were amended, February 21, 1942, so as not to apply when the United States is at war, with the Johnson Act left standing. Under this Lend-Lease Act of 1941 over $50,000,000,000— five times the war loans of 1917-1919—were extended to allies all over the world with little expectation of repayment. This is a good example of how politics controls economics in diplomacy, rather than economics controlling politics—as is sometimes maintained.

Only eleven years before the nations became engulfed in the Second World War, they had made a solemn agreement, entered into upon the initiative of the United States and France, known as the Pact of Paris, or the Briand-Kellogg Pact, after the two ministers of foreign affairs who drafted it:

Article I. The High Contracting Parties solemnly declare in the names of their respective peoples that they condemn recourse to war for the solution of international controversies, and renounce it as an instrument of national policy in their relations with one another.

Article II. The High Contracting Parties agree that the settlement or solution of all disputes or conflicts of whatever nature or of whatever origin they may be, which may arise among them, shall never be sought except by pacific means.

The treaty is perpetual. The preamble expresses enigmatically the conviction that a resort to war *denies to a Power the benefits furnished by the treaty*. Did these words mean that neutrality could no longer exist when a power resorted to war as an instrument of national policy? That where in violation of the treaty it waged aggressive war it subjected itself to all the sanctions which the use of force could impose? The Nuremberg trials of 1946-1947 and the trials of the major Japanese war criminals of 1946-1948 were to answer these questions with an awful affirmative.[1]

This agreement arose from an informal suggestion made by the French Minister of Foreign Affairs, Mr. Aristide Briand, in 1927, that the United States and France, who were then facing a renewal of a general treaty of arbitration which was due to expire in 1928, should pledge themselves in a treaty of perpetual friendship never to go to war with each other under any circumstances. Though possibly not intentionally so, this was tantamount to an agreement that either party, France or the United States, would remain neutral in case the other were involved in war with a third party. This, one recalls, was a feature of many an alliance, for example the Anglo-Japanese alliance of 1902. Secretary Kellogg eluded the implications of this proposal by consenting to agree to such a treaty if it were general in its membership. Consequently the two governments formulated the above articles and the United States, by pre-concerted arrangement with France, invited fourteen other nations to sign jointly: Great Britain, and the several self-governing Dominions, Belgium, Czechoslovakia, France, Germany, Italy, Japan and Poland. After considerable interchange of observations, all fifteen nations signed the above-quoted Pact of Paris (August 27, 1928). The other nations [2] of the world, invited by the United States to join the Pact, speedily adhered. Sixty-three nations are now members. Only seven [3] nations have failed to adhere.

The United States Senate, in ratifying the treaty, this time attached no reservation, after Secretary Kellogg had included in the diplomatic record a statement explaining that the pact did not preclude a war of self-defense, and after the Committee of Foreign Relations had reported that "the United States regards the Monroe Doctrine as a part of its national security and self-defense." The other powers accepted the pledge only after Secretary Kellogg had made assurances, in the record of the negotiations leading to the pact, that each power was the sole judge of what constituted self-defense, and that the proposed treaty could not be construed to impair existing treaty obligations, like the European

---

[1] See below, Ch. XLVI.

[2] France it was who conveyed the invitation to Russia, with which nation the United States was not then in diplomatic relations.

[3] On May 15, 1949, those nations which had not adhered were: the Argentine Republic, Bolivia, El Salvador, Israel, Lebanon, Syria, and Yemen. New states arising out of the British Commonwealth and Empire are presumed to have inherited the obligations of the Pact of Paris.

Locarno treaties and the League of Nations (which might require war as an instrument of international policy). The French Government, for example, which had stood out for limiting its anti-war agreement to a pledge not to fight a war of "aggression," was not willing to accept the formula of the multilateral treaty until it was clear that it alone could construe its own necessities of self-defense. It was professedly as an act of self-defense that Japan had since sent large armies into China, and had detached great areas of her territory, and that Italy had conquered Ethiopia. In neither case had a formal war been declared. Such a *declared* war would be illegal!

The British reservation to the Kellogg Pact was very far-reaching:

. . . there are certain regions of the world [unspecified] the welfare and integrity of which constitute a special and vital interest for our peace and safety. His Majesty's Government have been at pains to make it clear in the past that interference with these regions cannot be suffered. Their protection against attack is to the British Empire a measure of self-defense. It must be clearly understood that His Majesty's Government in Great Britain accept the new treaty upon the distinct understanding that it does not prejudice their freedom of action in this respect.

The Russian Government, of the Union of Soviet Socialist Republics, in accepting the pact, lamented that it did not unequivocally forbid any kind of aggression or armed conflict short of war, or provide for disarmament, and noted with emphasis the sweeping nature of the British reservations, which it refused to accept as binding upon itself inasmuch as they had not been communicated officially to Russia.

Following the adoption of the Pact of Paris,[1] the United States, under the direction of Secretary Kellogg, negotiated with most of the non-American [2] nations a new series of bilateral treaties. They adjusted the old Root arbitration treaties to the new resources of arbitration and con-

---

[1] Several American commentators have written on the Kellogg Pact. Professor James T. Shotwell, who stimulated public opinion following Mr. Briand's original suggestion by presenting academic propositions for an anti-war treaty, describes the negotiations, and as an advocate of peace analyzes the document in his *War As an Instrument of National Policy and its Renunciation in the Pact of Paris* (New York, 1929). Hunter Miller interprets juridically this unique treaty in *The Peace Pact of Paris; a Study of the Briand-Kellogg Treaty* (New York, 1928), with a documentary appendix. See also Denys P. Myers, *Origin and Conclusion of the Paris Pact; the Renunciation of War as an Instrument of National Policy* (World Peace Foundation Pamphlets, XII, No. 2, Boston, 1929).

[2] In the case of the nations of the New World the Root-Bryan conciliation treaties have given way to a multilateral inter-American conciliation treaty (on a Bryan chassis), the so-called Gondra Convention; and the Root arbitration treaties to a multilateral inter-American treaty of arbitration (on a Kellogg chassis). See Chapter XXXIX, below.

ciliation presented by the League of Nations, to which the non-American partners to the treaties were now pledged. The Root treaties had been for short periods of time, generally five years, requiring repeated renewals to keep them alive. The formula adopted in the new Kellogg arbitration treaties called for the arbitration by the Hague Permanent Court of Arbitration, or *any other competent tribunal,* of all justiciable disputes which could not be settled by diplomacy or by the Bryan devices of conciliation through inquiry.[1] The Root treaties, it is recalled, had excluded from the purview of arbitration all disputes involving national honor, independence or vital interests; and the Senate had reserved its right to pass upon the *compromis* which in each case would define the subject and scope of a particular arbitration. In ratifying the Kellogg treaties, the Senate made similar reservations to pass upon the *compromis.* The twenty-eight[2] new Kellogg treaties excluded from the scope of arbitration any dispute which:

(a) is within the domestic jurisdiction of either of the high contracting parties,

(b) involves the interest of third parties,

(c) depends upon or involves the maintenance of the traditional attitude of the United States concerning American questions, commonly described as the Monroe Doctrine,

(d) depends upon or involves the observance of the obligations of [the other non-American treaty party] in accordance with the Covenant of the League of Nations.

Significant abstentions from Kellogg arbitration treaties with the United States were Great Britain, Japan, Russia and Spain.

Contemporaneously with the new arbitration treaties, Secretary Kellogg set on foot negotiations for treaties of conciliation on the Bryan model with non-American states which had not yet entered into such with the United States. There were in January, 1942, thirty-five of these Bryan "cooling-off" treaties in effect. The most notable exception was Japan, which had neither conciliation nor arbitration treaty with the United States. Both nations, however, had pledged themselves to the Pact of Paris.

The provision in the new Kellogg treaties, for arbitration before *any other competent tribunal,* doubtless envisaged the accession of the United

---

[1] For the Bryan conciliation treaties, see above, p. 429.

[2] The United States on May 15, 1949 was a party to Kellogg bilateral arbitration treaties with the following twenty-eight countries: Albania, Belgium, Bulgaria, China, Czechoslovakia, Denmark, Egypt, Estonia, Ethiopia, Finland, France, Germany, Greece, Hungary, Iceland, Italy, Latvia, Liberia, Lithuania, Luxemburg, Netherlands, Norway, Poland, Portugal, Roumania, Sweden, Switzerland, and Yugoslavia.

States to the protocol embodying a statute for the establishment of a Court of International Justice, which had been set up under the patronage of the League of Nations, as anticipated in the League of Nations Covenant. Though technically this Court, established in 1921, was an organ of the League of Nations, non-League members could join it without being parties to the League, or might without being statutory members of the Court avail themselves of its judicial facilities. The purpose of this court, the so-called World Court, was to decide on the basis of law rather than arbitration cases brought before it, and to give advisory decisions when requested by the League of Nations. In part, therefore, the Court fitted in with the traditional American aspirations for a truly international court of justice to make international law a regnant concept in the voluntary settlement of disputes and to build up by a series of judicial rather than arbitral decisions an expanding body of law.

The distinguished American jurist and elder statesman, Elihu Root, was one of the principal formulators of the original statute. Another most eminent American international lawyer and *genro,* John Bassett Moore, was selected at the outset (1922-1928) as judge of the Court, and, after his resignation, the former Secretaries of State, Charles E. Hughes (1928-1930) and Frank B. Kellogg[1] (1930-1935) served in the Court. American Presidents since 1923 without exception recommended to the Senate the adoption, with reservations, of the protocol which would make the United States a supporting member, but the Senate steadily refused to accept the Court until after the Second World War and the ratification of the covenant of a new league of nations: the Charter of the United Nations.[2]

We have already observed in a former chapter how normal relations were restored by the United States after the First World War with all but one great nation, Russia, and its 168,000,000 people in Europe and Asia. Following the failure of the Peace Conference at Paris in 1919 to devise any solution of the problem of Soviet Russia, the United States during sixteen years refused to extend recognition to that republic. The fundamental reason for this was the irreconcilability of the revolutionary communistic theory and practice of government with the theory and practice of American democracy and capitalism. The Soviet Government strengthened this determination of the United States Government by its

[1] In 1936 Professor Manley O. Hudson, of the Harvard Law School, an unquenchable protagonist of American entry into the League of Nations as well as the Court of International Justice, was chosen judge.

[2] See below, Ch. XLVI.

refusal to sanction the loans and contracts made by previous Russian governments with the United States and its nationals, and by its refusal to extend to American citizens in Russia the type of protection customarily extended to aliens in the other countries of Europe. Further, the ardor of revolutionary propaganda, not technically from the Soviet Government in Moscow, but from its international image, the *Third Internationale,* or international communistic revolutionary society, militated against American recognition. So long as a foreign community permitted its nationals to propagate seditious activities within the United States and to seek to overthrow by revolution the existing government and Constitution of the United States, it was not difficult to understand why that government should shrink so inveterately from extending its own recognition to the source of the subversive activities. The passage of time, however, tended to smooth down the hitherto insuperable asperities and difficulties and incompatibilities between the two peoples. One by one the great powers of Europe had recognized Russia; and in 1934 Russia took its place in the League of Nations. Even without recognition a very considerable volume of trade, more indeed than existed after recognition, sprang up between the two republics. Their citizens visited each other even without directly visaed passports. The more radical features of Russian government gave way to a slightly less rigorous state communism. To keep in friendly relations with the states of the capitalistic world, the Russians temporarily abated their revolutionary ambitions and made agreements not to excite propaganda in foreign states. Above all, the increasing tension of Far Eastern politics, where the interests of Russia and the United States supported each other more than they did Japanese policy, impelled the two nations, so different in their constitutional structure and social organization, to close up the gap of diplomatic irreconcilability.

The opportunity for attempting normal relations with Russia came in the autumn of 1933, when President Franklin D. Roosevelt, unembarrassed by recent party commitments on Russian policy, invited the President of the All Union Central Executive Committee to send a representative to the United States to discuss ways and means of effecting a re-establishment of regular relations between the two peoples. The Soviet Government immediately sent to Washington its Minister for Foreign Affairs, Mr. Maxim Litvinoff. On November 16, 1933, regular relations were resumed, after a lapse of sixteen years, on conditions which were laid down in a series of notes exchanged between President Roosevelt and Mr. Litvinoff:

1. Direct assurances by the Russian Government scrupulously to respect a policy of non-interference with life and affairs within the jurisdiction of the United States.

2. Pledge by the Russian Government to refrain from, and to restrain all persons and organizations directly or indirectly under its control—or receiving money from it (without indicating by name the *Third Internationale*)—from agitation or propaganda within the United States or its territories, or from violation of the territorial integrity of the United States or its possessions.

3. Pledge by the Russian Government not to permit formation or residence within Russian jurisdiction of any organization or group revolutionary to the United States, or to lend its support to such.

4. Reasonable expectations (but not guaranties) given by the Russian Government to the United States to secure freedom of conscience and religious liberty for American citizens residing temporarily or permanently within Russian jurisdiction.[1]

5. Promise of a consular convention to be negotiated with most-favored-nation provisions, including right of fair trial for American citizens accused of crimes in Russia.

6. Existing claims between the two countries to be adjusted by negotiations to be undertaken after resumption of regular relations, the Russian Government waiving all claims on account of United States intervention in eastern Siberia (but not in northern Russia) ; [2] the Russian Government meanwhile to respect the previous and future acts of the United States and its courts regulating the property of the Russian Government or its nationals.

The complicated negotiations for an adjustment of the outstanding claims of both governments, including war debts of the former Czarist government and the provisional revolutionary government of 1917, have not yet been settled, although ambassadors were duly exchanged in 1934. With the re-establishment of formal diplomatic relations with Russia the circle of normal contacts of American diplomacy, interrupted by the First World War, was complete at last even though the promises of Soviet Russia in the Roosevelt-Litvinoff agreement proved to be no settlement of the questions broached in it.

[1] This may be said to have adjusted an issue with the Czarist Government, arising over exclusion of Jews who were naturalized American citizens, which caused American abrogation, in 1913, according to form, of the Russian-American treaty of commerce of 1832.

[2] See above, pp. 639, 688, n. 3.

CHAPTER XXXVIII

ECONOMICS AND DIPLOMACY

(1860-1950)

THE United States in 1860 was already over the threshold of the persistently expanding industrial revolution which since then has so profoundly modified American life, running successively and quickly from steam and rail to electricity, the internal combustion engine, concrete highway, automotive transportation, general instantaneous communication, automatic machinery and great technology. President Lincoln freed the black human slaves, and the American people acquired new mechanical slaves on farm and in factory, speechless, nerveless slaves who could work day and night, with the power of thousands of horses, expanding and transforming production, competing for the markets of the world with other oily slaves of steel and copper toiling for corporate masters in the industrial countries across both oceans.

The Civil War marked a turning point in American economic history, as well as in the political evolution of the United States. The demands of the armies furnished quick and powerful impetus to manufacturing. War-time tariff primarily for revenue gave way after the return of peace to protective tariffs quietly legislated into being amid the noisy domestic politics of the reconstruction era,[1] to become a protean part of the American national system. For a generation after the war agriculture, grazing and mining, thanks to the expanding frontier and the settlement of the Far West, held their predominant place in the face of the new industrial forces for which they created a growing home market. By 1900 manufactured products [2] constituted, nevertheless, 35.38 per cent of the total exports of merchandise from the United States, as compared with 15.32 per cent in 1860. During the next decade the character of exports showed a radical change. The frontier had disappeared by 1890, although it took a few years for the effect of this to be felt clearly in foreign trade. The West was filling up. Population was rapidly agglomerating in new cities and towns west and east. The continuing industrial

---

[1] H. K. Beale, *The Critical Year; a Study of Andrew Johnson and Reconstruction* (New York, 1930), dissects the motives of business protection in the politics of the reconstruction era.

[2] Not counting manufactured foodstuffs, which were 23.32 per cent.

726

revolution entered a phase of scientific intensification. The United States became in our times primarily an industrial nation. By 1913, before the First World War, manufactured articles [1] accounted for approximately one-half the total exports of the United States. The war slowed up this tendency to proportionate increase of manufactured exports, because of the great demands for raw materials, particularly foodstuffs. After the war the exports of finished manufactures surpassed those of the extractive industries. As manufactured goods assumed increased weight in exports, the total of imports showed a heavier share of raw materials and lighter receipts of foreign manufactures,[2] at least until the Great Depression. As the shift took place in imports toward raw materials, non-European countries slowly began to contribute a larger share of the total imports. For a long while it was protectionist policy to raise the tariff on manufactures and to keep raw materials on the free list—this increased the imports from the countries of simple economy notably in the New World, Asia and Africa. There was, it seemed, a healthy equilibrium for a complex economy in the United States. Foreign capital poured into the Republic. The United States remained a debtor nation (we speak of course of private debts), serving its debts with an excess of exports over imports, with a surplus left over debt charges to pay for foreign freightage, tourist expenditures abroad, immigrant remittances and foreign insurance premiums.

These new conditions of a complex national economy [3] cannot be ignored by any historian of American diplomacy. In previous chapters we have noted some of their effects. At first they served the apostles of sea power to stimulate by false reasoning an imperialistic expansion in the Far East. Later they united with the politics of American neutrality to cause the Wilson Administration to keep its hands off the irresistible weapon of the embargo. Today they meet in a greater crisis of economy and thought which remains to be solved. With these thoughts in mind we may observe the development of American policy to secure freedom of commerce and navigation from national discriminations.

Until the close of the nineteenth century American commerce con-

---

[1] Not including manufactured foodstuffs.

[2] G. G. Huebner, "The Foreign Trade of the United States Since 1789," in *History of Domestic and Foreign Commerce of the United States* (2 Vols., Carnegie Institution of Washington, 1915), II, 69 (citing the *U. S. Bureau of Statistics*); and John H. Frederick, *The Development of American Commerce* (New York, 1932).

[3] John Donaldson has presented a lucid analysis of the evolving character of American national economy, in its reference to foreign policy, in "Fundamentals of the Foreign Economic Processes and Policy of the United States," in *Weltwirtschaftliches Archiv*, XXX (Juli, 1929), 4-77.

tinued to flow pretty much in the old channels of trade, with increases most marked in commerce to the prosperous industrial nations of the world. Canada became an increasingly important factor in American foreign commerce, as it filled up with an English-speaking population. The doubling of the volume of trade with British North America in the period 1865-1900 counterbalanced a depression in the commerce with other portions of the New World, notably Central America and the West Indies. It was not until the twentieth century that the channels of foreign commerce began to change notably.

In the first half of the national period of American history it had been one of the main objects of foreign policy to clear away the barriers of European colonial monopolies, particularly in the New World, which restricted the entrance of American ships and goods.[1] This was accomplished by the beginning of the period under review in this chapter. With a growing export of manufactures searching for markets abroad the resources of American diplomacy turned next to the objective of securing, wherever possible, at least equal or even special advantages for American trade and incorporating them in treaties. The United States generally adhered throughout the century to the *conditional* type of most-favored-nation clause [2] in its treaties of commerce, in order to protect itself against general and unrequited diffusion to most-favored nations of particular trade privileges bargained for corresponding equivalents. This ran counter to the desire of most of the great trading nations of Europe, who preferred the unconditional interpretation of a most-favored-nation clause. It was to the advantage, so the opinion ran, of the greater trading nations to keep down the general level of tariffs throughout the world. They preferred therefore the unconditional most-favored-nation formula, by which a tariff concession or privilege of nation A to nation B, must also be extended to nations X, Y and Z if the latter had unconditional most-favored-nation articles in their treaties with A; that is, it must be extended no matter what unique equivalents B had paid to A for the privilege.[3]

Commercial bargains by give-and-take, written into reciprocity treaties, became the objective of the Department of State in its negotiations for

[1] See above, Chapter XVII.

[2] See above, p. 303. Exceptions were Switzerland (1850), Orange Free State (1871), Serbia (1881). Only one of these nations, Switzerland, ever protested tariff rates on the basis of the clause, and the United States recognized the validity of the protest, but presently (with due notice) abrogated the treaty.

[3] Benjamin H. Williams has analyzed, with an historical background, the various factors and implications of the most-favored-nation formula, and its relation to commercial reciprocity, in his *Economic Foreign Policy of the United States* (New York, 1929).

treaties with foreign nations. Such treaties would purchase, on each side, particular privileges in return for particular concessions, and would be protected by a *conditional* most-favored-nation article against possible extension automatically to conventional most-favored nations. Such was the objective of the Department of State, it is true, but the objective met two obstacles: many greater trading nations, for reasons explained, were unwilling during the nineteenth century to negotiate reciprocity treaties except when coupled with an unconditional most-favored-nation article; and the Senate, imbued with the philosophy of protection, would not ratify reciprocity treaties which lowered the tariff through the treaty-making power, even when tariff acts authorized the President to make such changes (subject, of course, to ratification in regular treaty form). The net result was only two reciprocity treaties—following the termination of the Marcy-Elgin Canadian reciprocity treaty of 1854-1866—with Hawaii (1875) and with Cuba (1902). In each of these cases there was an obvious political and strategical interest which made the Senate willing to accept them.

It should be remembered that during the half-century after the Civil War the Government of the United States was under the control of political parties which either espoused outright the political economy of protection, as did the Republican Party, or secretly accepted it, publicly preaching against protection but actually tolerating it when in power, as did the Democratic Party. That this assisted the one-sided industrial development of the United States at the expense of agriculture, few thoughtful historians today would deny. When we speak, then, of domestic tariffs, we do not mean protective taxes on imports that were based on any scientific calculation. There was little thought to approach the question from a balance sheet of commercial needs adapted to the best economy of the nation and people as a whole. Tariff schedules contained largely what representatives of powerful industrial interests, to which both parties responded, persuaded Congress was necessary for the prosperity of, first, those industries, and next, the people dependent upon them.[1] The negotiation of a treaty of commercial reciprocity was less susceptible to lobbying, but after signature it must secure an approval of two-thirds of the Senate.

It was the agrarian nations, relatively untouched by industrial revolution or the political economy of protection, like Canada and the nations

---

[1] There is a stimulative rush of thought, not without historical *ex-parte* argument, on this in Charles A. Beard's two notable books, *The Idea of National Interest, op. cit.* and *The Open Door at Home, op. cit.*

of Latin America, which seemed most inviting for reciprocity treaties. But Canada competed, more than the tropical or subtropical countries, with the raw materials of the United States, lumber, fish, and agriculture. Hence it could not be such good bargaining ground as the Latin-American nations. Great Britain made repeated proposals for a renewal of commercial reciprocity with Canada: in 1869, 1874, 1888, 1889. They all failed. A system of imperial preferences inaugurated in 1897 tended to improve the Canadian market for British manufactures. Meanwhile Canada herself entered the infant industry stage, and the new native manufactures blunted her desire for reciprocity with a competitor so close at hand.

The Latin-American countries offered the greatest hopes for reciprocity without any essential undermining of the American protective system. The United States, under proper treaty arrangements, could admit most of their raw materials, some of them exotic, cheaply or altogether freely, and with advantage to its own economy; they in turn could profitably lower their tariffs to American manufactures. Widespread reciprocity with the nations of Latin America meant, indeed, the capture, in the face of European competition, of those growing markets for the increasing manufactures of the United States. It was one of the factors which led to the Pan-American movement—conceived by Secretary of State James G. Blaine as a device for getting himself out of some embarrassing diplomatic predicaments relative to Peru and Chile.

But the Arthur Administration abruptly displaced Blaine at President Garfield's death, and turned its attention from the channels of Pan-American trade negotiations to individual treaties of commercial reciprocity. A treaty was quickly negotiated in Washington (January, 1883) with Mexico. It granted free entry for twenty-eight products of Mexico, including tobacco and sugar, at a sacrifice of less than $90,000 annual duty hitherto collected. Mexico in turn agreed to let in duty-free seventy-three American articles, many of them manufactured, upon which previously a high tariff had been collected. It was a most advantageous treaty for the United States; but protectionist influences in the Senate delayed action on it for a year. Finally advice and consent to ratification were made dependent upon the passage by Congress of legislation to allow to Mexico the lowered tariffs fixed by the treaty. Under these conditions the President withheld final ratification. Similar reciprocity treaties signed with the Dominican Republic, and with Spain for her West India Islands (Cuba, Puerto Rico) encountered much delay in the Senate. When these treaties appeared likely to be consummated the British Government saw disaster for its sugar planters in the West Indies if they should not secure at least similar tariff reductions in the markets of the United States. With some alacrity it opened reciprocity negotiations for the trade of those islands, to which the Arthur Government eagerly responded; but failure of the United States to agree to an unconditional most-favored-nation article (to which Great Britain then stood committed in her treaties with other nations) resulted in the collapse of these discussions.[1] When President Cleveland came into office he withdrew from the Senate the pending treaties with Spain and the Dominican Republic.[2] The Democratic Party, which now took over the government for the first time since 1861, professed belief in a general lower tariff by legislation, rather than by treaties; and Cleveland made unsuccessful efforts to accomplish this in Congress.

Reciprocity reappeared as an objective of American diplomacy when the Republicans came back under the Harrison Administration in 1889, with Blaine again Secretary of State. It offered a means of consoling that element of opinion which could not brook immitigable high protection. Blaine was now able to go ahead with his ambitious project of a Pan-American Congress, for the promotion of peace by arbitration and the removal of barriers to inter-American trade, a project which President Arthur, under the influence of partisan politics,[3] had quashed after President Garfield's death and Blaine's resignation. In fact, invitations to an inter-American conference at Washington had already been sent out by Bayard, Cleveland's Secretary of State, in response to an act of Congress (1888) for inviting a conference of the Latin-American governments with that of the United States in Washington for settling a plan of arbitration and for considering questions relating to the improvement of business intercourse, communications, and commercial relations. It

---

[1] By an executive agreement of January 2, 1884, between Spain and the United States (negotiated pursuant to the old law which authorized the President to add or remove extra duties) in reference to nations discriminating against the United States, the United States removed a previously imposed extra duty of ten per cent on products and articles coming in from Cuba and Puerto Rico. In return Spain removed all discriminating duties on American ships and products in Cuba and Puerto Rico.

[2] George Frederick Howe, *Chester A. Arthur, a Quarter-Century of Machine Politics* (New York, 1934), 267-271.

[3] Blaine was the most dynamic personality in the Republican Party and a continual possibility for Presidential nomination (he became the defeated candidate of the party in 1884). He was also the leader of a faction which in Garfield's Administration, and previously, had opposed the Republican machine in Arthur's state of New York, a machine to which Arthur owed his nomination for the Vice-Presidency in 1880, and hence his position as President. It is easy therefore to understand why Arthur did not follow along with Blaine, who was his principal rival for the nomination for President in 1884.

was fitting that Blaine should preside over this conference when it assembled at Washington in October, 1889. It is noteworthy that a powerful motive for the conference was the expansion of the commerce of the United States.[1] The very first activity on the program was a grand official excursion by the delegates throughout the industrial United States with inspection of factories.[2] The main purpose Blaine veiled in oratorical expressions of friendship, arbitration and peace, and the promotion of the general welfare of the American nations of the New World.[3] Then the delegation of the United States brought forth the proposal for a Pan-American customs union—commercial reciprocity approaching free trade on a vast scale. It would have given the United States preference over European nations in the markets of Latin America, in return for free imports of articles many of which were already on the free list of the United States. The project failed before the opposition of the Latin-American delegates. Spurred on by European diplomacy, they were unwilling to damage their established trade with Europe for the advantage of American manufacturers, and some of them feared the political effects of a customs union.[4] The Conference shelved the proposed customs union with a resolution declaring in favor of bilateral reciprocity treaties. The achievements of the first Inter-American Conference were most meager, but they led to the establishment of a permanent secretariat at Washington, which developed into the Pan-American Union, housed (after 1910) in a beautiful building the gift of Andrew Carnegie, one of the delegates of the United States to that Pan-American Conference. Out of

[1] The agenda included in the act of Congress was: first, measures to preserve and promote the prosperity of American states; second, an American customs union; third, transportation and communication; fourth, uniform custom and port regulations; fifth, uniform weights and measures and uniform laws of copyrights and patents and extradition of criminals; sixth, adoption of a common silver coin; seventh, a plan for the arbitration of all disputes; eighth, any other subjects relating to the welfare of the several states that might be represented.

[2] Described, with illustrations, by C. A. O'Rourke, *Congreso Internacional Americano* (New York, 1890).

[3] Alice Felt Tyler, *The Foreign Policy of James G. Blaine, op. cit.*, 177. Joseph B. Lockey has a good summary of the significance of the First Inter-American Conference in his sketch of Blaine in *Am. Secs. State*, VIII, 164-181.

[4] "It is easy to foresee the squirmings of Europe," remarked Mr. Peña, an Argentine delegate, "when she should feel the effects of a continental blockade, maintained, it is true, not by warships but by belligerent tariffs. It would not be countries bound together by political bonds that would enter into compacts inspired by a national sentiment. It would be the war of one continent against another, eighteen sovereignties allied to exclude from the life of commerce that same Europe which extends to us her hand, sends us her strong arms, and complements our economic existence, after having apportioned us her civilization and her culture, her sciences and her arts, industries and customs that have completed our sociologic evolutions." Williams, *op. cit.*, quoting proceedings of *International American Conference* (Wash., G.P.O., 1890), I, 124.

this grew the notable Pan-American movement and the present Organ-ization of American States, described in the next chapter.[1]

In his striving toward freer trade with the American nations Blaine was impressed with the fact that the United States in 1889 imported from the Latin-American republics $142,000,000 worth of goods in excess of exports; that 87 per cent of commodities imported from these countries came in free of duty, compared with only ten per cent of products of the United States entering free. Having failed to adjust this unbalance by the Pan-American Conference, the Secretary next tried to do so through a series of reciprocity treaties. To give him advantage in negotiation he urged Congress, then debating the McKinley tariff bill, not to take off the duties on sugar and coffee. The McKinley Act as passed placed sugar, tea, coffee, hides and molasses on the free list but authorized the President to impose duties on the "tropical list" when, in his opinion, a nation failed to extend similar tariff favors to the United States, or treated its products in a "reciprocally unequal or unreasonable manner." It was therefore by a series of executive agreements, made under threat of the penalties of the McKinley Act of 1890, that Blaine secured tariff concessions from ten countries: Austria-Hungary; Brazil; Dominican Republic; Spain for Cuba and Puerto Rico; Salvador; the German Em-pire; Great Britain for Barbados, Trinidad, Leeward Islands, Windward Islands, and British Guiana; Nicaragua; Honduras; and Guatemala. Each of these countries granted lower tariffs on imports from the United States in order to avoid the penalty duties otherwise to be encountered on tea, coffee, hides, sugar and molasses. Most of these agreements re-sulted in increased trade during their brief lifetimes, and suggest the manifold advantages that might have been general in a Pan-American customs union. The Democratic tariff act of 1894, however, placed a duty on sugar and other commodities, free in 1890, and thus put an end to these agreements which depended on legislative provisions rather than treaty guaranties, legislative provisions that were subject to political caprice or party overturns.

The Republican Dingley tariff act of 1897 renewed provisions for tariff bargaining similar to those of the McKinley Act of 1890, with a "tropical list" of somewhat different variety (not including sugar). It led to only

[1] The governments represented at the Conference did not act to give effect to this resolution nor to the plan of arbitration which was recommended; but they adopted a resolution expressing the principle of illegality of conquest, in defiance of arbitration, similar to that later invoked by the world in refusing to recognize conquests or mutilations of territorial sovereignty in violation of the Pact of Paris (notably in Man-churia and South America).

one Latin-American agreement, with Brazil (1904-1922). There was another bargain list (the "argol list" [1]) designed for European countries. Using this leverage, a series of executive agreements (the "argol agreements") were negotiated with France, Germany, Spain, Portugal and Bulgaria, and to a minor degree with Italy, Great Britain and the Netherlands. These were terminated by the new Payne-Aldrich tariff act of 1909. The Dingley Act also authorized the President—as if, forsooth, such authorization were necessary—to negotiate treaties of commercial reciprocity, limited in time, in which the tariff rates of the United States might be reduced not over 20 per cent, with transfer of dutiable articles to the free list when they were not produced in the United States—all such treaties to be ratified by the Senate (as the Constitution required anyway). Several reciprocity treaties were signed between 1890 and 1899. Under "McKinleyism" reciprocity went hand in hand with a high protective tariff.[2] The Government of the United States, in fixing reciprocal tariff concessions, never proposed to lower duties on any major category of manufactured products. When the treaties came to the Senate it was evident that there was no willingness to lower the tariff—even in bargains—for *any* articles which could reasonably be produced in the United States. The Senate refused to ratify the treaties.[3] Reciprocity as a general policy was abandoned in 1903, not to be taken up again (except for Canada) until 1933.[4] For expansion of commerce the country turned confidently to the new colonial markets created by the Cuban protectorate (with its singular reciprocity treaty of 1902), and by the acquisition of the Philippines, Puerto Rico and Hawaii. The two latter were incorporated into the United States and

[1] The list ran "argols, or crude tartar, or wine lees, crude; brandies," etc., etc.—hence the name "argol agreements."

[2] The standard work by J. Laurence Laughlin and H. Parker Willis, *Reciprocity* (New York, 1903) constitutes an argument for reciprocity with *unconditional* most-favored-nation policy.

[3] These unratified treaties (the so-called "Kasson treaties") were: Great Britain for Newfoundland (1890); Great Britain for Barbados, British Guiana, Turks and Caicos Islands, Jamaica and Bermuda (1899); Denmark for the Danish West Indies (1899); Dominican Republic (1899); Nicaragua (1899); Ecuador (1899); the Argentine (1899); France (1899). United States Tariff Commission, *Summary of the Report on Reciprocity and Commercial Treaties* (Washington, G.P.O., 1919).

[4] President Wilson made no use of the supererogatory provision of the Underwood tariff act of 1913 (on the whole lowering tariff schedules) enabling him to negotiate trade agreements subject to final approval by Congress.

Percy W. Bidwell has an unusually helpful review of *Tariff Policy of the United States; a Study of Recent Experience,* in his Report to the Second International Studies Conference on the State and Economic Life, London, May 29 to June 2, 1933, prepared for the American committee appointed by the Council on Foreign Relations (New York, 1933).

assimilated into its tariff structure. With the Philippines a system of preferential tariffs was built up—in general larger than those within the British Empire—to fasten the islands economically to the United States.

An exception to the new apathy toward reciprocity was Canada, next to Great Britain the biggest single foreign customer of the United States. The Payne-Aldrich Tariff of 1909, which repealed the bargaining features of the Dingley Act of 1897, introduced a two-column schedule of tariff rates—minimum rates for imports from all countries which did not discriminate against imports from the United States, and maximum rates, 25% higher, for all others. Since Canada had applied similar maximum rates against the United States, the new penalties of the Payne-Aldrich Act logically envisaged that Dominion. To avoid this and the disruption of trade which was likely to follow, President Taft negotiated an agreement with Canada arranging for reciprocal reductions on tariffs to be accomplished by legislation in each country. It provided for a free admission of nearly all the important products of Canada in return for lowered rates on American manufactures.

The appropriate law passed the American Congress; but political considerations, which had undoubtedly helped to pass the bill in Congress, wrought its defeat in the Canadian Parliament. In the midst of the debate in Congress, Champ Clark, Speaker of the House of Representatives, had declared: "I am for it [the bill] because I hope to see the day when the American flag will float over every square foot of British North American possessions clear to the North Pole." This indiscreet utterance provided ammunition for the Canadian nationalists and protectionists.[1] The issue of reciprocity became in the parliamentary elections an issue of annexation. The Liberal Government of Sir Wilfrid Laurier suffered defeat, and with it, for twenty-five years, Canadian-American reciprocity. The penalties of maximum rates of the Payne-Aldrich tariff (and of later American tariffs) were never applied to Canada, nor indeed to any other country. Meanwhile foreign tariff systems developed the technique of restriction by ingeniously devised quotas of imports, administrative restrictions, exchange controls and special bilateral agreements from the benefit of which the United States was excluded. They generally avoided specific discrimination in name but accomplished it in fact.

We have noted that before the First World War the industrialization

---

[1] W. G. Swartz analyzed the opposition to reciprocity of various economic groups in both countries, in "The proposed Canadian-American Reciprocity of 1911," *Journal of Economic and Business History*, III (1930-1931), 118-147.

of the United States had proceeded to the point where one-half of the total exports consisted of manufactured articles. That great war opened a phenomenal demand for manufactures at the very moment when American industrial production seemed, at least for the moment, to have geared up beyond the markets in reach. The demand for munitions alone produced an unheard-of commerce, the effects of which on the diplomacy of neutrality we have been obliged to analyze in a previous chapter. The demand spread to ordinary manufactures. Europe was no longer able to supply its overseas markets—or even its own home markets—and the United States quickly and easily supplanted its competitors in the New World, and even elsewhere. Before the war (for the year 1913) the United States supplied 25.03% of the imports of the Latin-American states and took 30.78% of their exports. At the close of the war (for the year 1919) it supplied 48.79% and took 44.49%.[1] American credit, too, largely displaced—to its misfortune—European credit and European banks in South America.

The demand for American goods and credit, although dislocated temporarily by the advent of peace, continued after the war for a decade in industrial products, but not in foodstuffs, which went back to pre-war levels, throwing agriculture into a prolonged distress. The war-torn European countries needed replacements of peace-time goods, and they were able to pay for these with loans tapped by their governments and corporations from surplus American industrial profits, through the sale of bond issues underwritten by American banks. In South America, which needed no war replacement of goods, governments found it was possible to borrow, without much examination of their credit, for ambitious projects of public works for which politicians are always so delighted to make contracts and disbursements. Agents of American banks, eager to collect commissions for these loans, urged them on the financially irresponsible republics. In the United States the banks easily resold the bonds to American investors, without being further responsible to them.

The phenomenal demand for American produce during and after the war seemed to extinguish altogether any lingering ideas of reciprocity agreements and treaties. With the world crying for American goods (and paying for them with American credits thrust on foreign governments and corporations) there seemed no need for reciprocity to sustain American commerce. The State Department became concerned

---

[1] *Latin American Foreign Trade in 1914, 1920, 1933.* Foreign Trade Series, Pan-American Union.

with two major problems of foreign trade and investment: (a) to prevent the United States from being excluded or discriminated against in
competitive regions of the world like the concessions and spheres in
China, and the Class A and Class B mandates set up by the treaty of
Versailles; [1] and (b) to prevent discrimination in tariffs within national
territories. To solve the last problem the Government resorted in 1923
to a fundamental change of policy in its formula of commercial treaties.
In the new treaties made in 1923 and thereafter, the Government of the
United States, whether in Republican or Democratic administrations
(Secretary Hughes in the Harding Republican Administration was, however, responsible for the change in policy) inserted the *unconditional*
most-favored-nation formula, in sharp contrast to the traditional *conditional* formula. Thus it adopted the policy and practice of the European nations before the war, the theory being that, by a network of
unconditional most-favored-nation articles in treaties of commerce, discriminations would be done away with and the tariff walls lowered to a
level consistent with the fundamental protectionist desires of each sovereign nation applied to commodities rather than to the source of origin.
But after the First World War, European practice reversed itself in large
measure. By quotas and bargain tariffs the nations embarked upon a new
mercantilism [2] which aimed at autarchy, or building up, by national
planning, among other things, as great as possible economic and military
self-sufficiency, against war, or against the economic strife of peace, or
even against the possibility of economic sanctions by the League of
Nations. Consequently the reform in American commercial policy, so
desired by some specialists [3] at the turn of the new century, and even
after the First World War, came too late. To the extent [4] that

---

[1] Secretary Bainbridge Colby, in the Wilson Administration, and Secretary Hughes in
the Harding Administration, were successful in securing equal treatment in these mandates
(not administered as an integral part of the mandatory like Class C) on the ground that
the United States as one of the principal Allied and Associated Powers had helped win
the war and make the mandates possible.

[2] Ferdinand Fried [Friedrich Zimmermann] noted this most impressively in his two
works *Autarkie* (Jena, 1932) and *Die Zukunft des Aussenhandels durch inners Marktord-
nung zur Aussenhandels Freiheit* (Jena, 1934).

[3] Laughlin and Willis, *op. cit.*

[4] These treaties, with year of possible termination, were with: Austria (at one year's
notice), Germany (terminated 1935), China (no date of termination), Estonia (1936),
Honduras (1938), Hungary (1936), Latvia (1938), Morocco (at one year's notice),
Muscat and Zanzibar (no date), Norway (one year's notice), Poland (six months'
notice), Danzig (six months' notice), El Salvador (1940), Siam (one year's notice), Turkey (one year's notice), Yugoslavia (one year's notice).

In addition, there were unconditional most-favored-nation provisions in executive agreements which could be terminated at short notice (ranging from 15 days to 6 weeks), or by
conflicting legislation: with Albania, Belgo-Luxemburg economic union, Bulgaria, Chile,

it negotiated unconditional most-favored-nation treaties of commerce, the United States, best endowed in resources for a strife of autarchy, sacrificed one of its best bargaining assets for the negotiation of reciprocity treaties or agreement in the future. As we shall presently see, in a time of paralyzed international trade, the Republic was again to turn to reciprocity.

The United States had changed from the position of biggest debtor nation before the war supposedly to that of biggest creditor nation. But what were the credits, and what were they worth? First, there were the moneys loaned to the military Associates before the armistice for war purposes, and after the armistice for reconstruction, relief, and the maintenance of credit. The money was borrowed from American taxpayers who took United States government bonds, which were to be paid with interest in gold dollars of the same weight and fineness of gold as loaned. We recall how the debts were leisurely funded, at great concessions, according to the "capacity to pay" of each of the debtor Associates, transferring a large part of the interest burden to the American people; and how, after a few years, in 1932, the Associates suspended payment altogether, leaving the whole burden of their debts on the shoulders of the same American people. And we remember how the United States in 1934, after the debtors ceased payment, itself repudiated approximately 40 per cent of its own bonds and outstanding interest by devaluing the dollar notwithstanding the covenant of the bond. Such was the value of one class of these foreign credits, that owed to the United States Government by the countries where the American crusaders in arms had been so fervently and anxiously welcomed in 1917 and 1918.

The United States rapidly slid back toward its old position of a debtor nation. One reason for this was that some debtor nations were able to suspend payment of interest on their official dollar debts, and at the same time find money to buy back large quantities of bonds thus debased in value of principal. Others were able to provide huge sums for increased armaments amidst the hot rivalry of European nationalism. Finally European investors, frightened at the explosive nature of the politics of the Old World, sent their savings to the United States for the purchase of securities, apparently believing that an American promise to pay was (despite devaluation of the dollar in 1934) better than a European promise to pay. These investments, at long or short terms—mostly short terms—were owed to the foreign investors, and were subject to

Czechoslovakia, Dominican Republic, Egypt, Finland, Greece, Guatemala, Haiti, Iran (Persia), Lithuania, Nicaragua, Roumania, Saudi-Arabia, Spain, Sweden.

withdrawal according to their terms, or to liquidation and quick removal, whilst most of the credits of the United States and its citizens abroad, when solvent at all, were long-term investments. Under such conditions the foreign creditor could remove his money from the United States on much shorter notice than the United States creditor could remove his money, if at all, from abroad. Until the breakdown of American neutrality in 1941 the United States made no move to impound or sequester this rich horde of foreign private wealth within its gates as security for payment of defaulted foreign public debts. In 1940 and 1941, for obvious war reasons, it "froze" the property and funds of nationals and governments of some European and Asiatic countries; and after the outbreak of war sequestered enemy alien property.

The lesson of all this was that hard-pressed nations like individuals will pay for armaments to continue their security and what they conceive to be their vital national interests, even at the abandonment of debts for moneys which helped save their lives in crises happily passed. The credits of some of the Latin-American governments proved to be equally untrustworthy, after the general financial collapse of 1929. All except Argentina suspended payment on their dollar bonds, and even there full service on foreign loans contracted by some of the provinces was suspended. In Europe, even before the war of 1939, other government debtors, notably Germany, defaulted on their dollar [1] bonds (also Bulgaria, Greece, Hungary, Roumania, Russia, Jugoslavia, Czechoslovakia [provinces]).

Under the illusion of payments through first portions of the proceeds of loans flowing back to the United States, American industry—but not agriculture—had continued at its high level of production and export until the collapse of foreign credit in 1929-1932 and the precipitation of the Great Depression in the United States, with all its sociological and political consequences both in the Old World and the New.

The colossal defaults of government and private debtors brought about a collapse of the creditor position of the United States from nearly nineteen billions in 1929 to only half a billion in 1940,[2] while the huge defaulted private loans to Germany assisted in the recovery of her aggressive military might. By the outbreak of the Second World War the United States had practically ceased to be a creditor nation. In the new conflict it poured forth of its remaining wealth to the United

[1] For German defaults on foreign obligations in other currencies, see Chap. XXXVII above.
[2] For tabulations establishing the debtor-creditor balance of American economy with the outside world, see previous editions of this History, pp. 752-753.

Nations in amounts many times the loans of the First World War, this time as contributions for the cause of freedom and liberation without thought of repayment except in terms of victory and principles of universal justice: the net total of "lend-lease" aid sent abroad 1941-1946 was $42,872,787,000,[1] a sum larger than the total national debt of the United States at the close of the First World War. The total lend-lease aid was $50,243,996,158.79; but against this was balanced generous estimates of $7,819,322,790.89 "reverse lend-lease," received by the United States from the aided nations.[2]

These enormous grants helped to place the United States after the Second World War more deeply than ever in the status of a debtor nation in the balance of international debits and credits. Even after these national war credits of the United States Government were written off in lend-lease settlements with some of the Allies after the war, or ignored by others like the USSR, the debtor-creditor position of American economy was as follows in 1946:

American-owned assets in foreign countries....$20,900,000,000
Foreign-owned assets in the United States (including gold reserves of $14,681,000,000)....$28,681,000,000 [3]

Taking into consideration the foreign assets and liabilities of the United States and its citizens in 1947 and the balance of international credits and debts, it can be said that the Republic ended up the Second World War as a *debtor nation* to the outside world of $7,781,000,000 and loaded with a national domestic debt of $252,000,000,000 as of 1949.

Demoralization of world commerce by the Great Depression, and cuts in American exports due to restrictive import systems of competing industrial, and even competing agricultural nations, wrought a reversion in American commercial policy, back to reciprocity. Amid the unprecedented depression in American agriculture which set in after 1921 and became worse after 1929, and the later crippling volume of industrial unemployment, the Democratic Administration of President Franklin D. Roosevelt frankly abandoned traditional tenets of Jeffersonian democracy, states' rights, and tariff for revenue only. In both

---

[1] *Docs. Am. Foreign Relations*, VIII, 126-158; *Twenty-Third Report to Congress on Lend-Lease Operations, for the Period Ending September 30, 1946* (Department of State Publication No. 2707), p. 27.

[2] Edward R. Stettinius, Jr. described the stream of *Lend-Lease, Weapon for Victory* (New York, 1944). See tabulation at end of this chapter.

[3] *Foreign Assets and Liabilities of the United States and Its Balance of International Transactions* (80th Cong., 1st Sess., Sen. Finance Committee print, Wash., 1948).

of these directions the new Administration out-Hamiltoned Alexander Hamilton himself. It passed no lower tariff law. To placate low-tariff constituents, the new government embarked, as had the Republicans in the regime of McKinleyism, upon a program of three-year [1] reciprocity agreements for mutual lowering of tariffs (within a range of 50 per cent, increased another 50 per cent by the extension act of 1945) [2] on agreed articles, but with this far-reaching feature: the act of Congress of June 12, 1934 (successively extended to 1952) put into the new law the policy of extending gratuitously to all nations—unless, perhaps, they discriminated against the United States [3]—every advantage purchased by any [4] particular reciprocal trade bargain. The President was not obliged to except—and as a matter of fact excepted only Germany, and temporarily Australia—even the discriminatory nations from the benefit of the lowered tariff which thus spread out generally to all nations (whether or no they had made reciprocal argreements with the United States or even whether or no they had general commercial treaty commitments of either conditional or unconditional most-favored-nation nature with the United States) from the individual "reciprocity" arrangements.[5]

---

[1] Continuing thereafter as terminable at six months' notice.

[2] The extension act of 1948, passed by the Republican Congress, removed the Tariff Commission from the inter-departmental organization set up to advise and assist the President in formulating trade agreements and required the Commission to hold independent hearings and report to the President: (1) the point beyond which tariff concession could not be made without imperiling domestic industries; (2) what, if any, additional duties or import restrictions were required to prevent such injury. The Democratic Congress repealed these safeguards in the extension act of 1949.

[3] " . . . the President may suspend the application [of the new duties from a reciprocity agreement] to articles the growth, produce, or manufacture of any country because of its discriminatory treatment of American commerce or because of other acts or policies which in his opinion tend to defeat the purposes set forth in this section."

These very wide powers to the President enable him to except any recalcitrant nation from the advantages of the new duties; to date (1950) they have not been utilized in time of peace except in regard to Germany, and very briefly as to Australia.

The President also had power under the tariff act of 1930 (continued in this respect from the act of 1922) to levy retaliatory increases up to 50 per cent or new tariffs, against states discriminating against American commerce; and even to prohibit imports, in case discrimination continued. This was also applied to Germany (after June 4, 1936).

[4] Unique preferential tariff treatment was specifically reserved for Cuba.

[5] In negotiations under this act there was an effort to mitigate the descending bargaining power of American diplomacy, signalized by general extension of concessions in each successive agreement, by limiting the agreement to key products which more or less singularly dominated the trade of the two parties concerned; thus, coffee with Brazil, pulp with Canada, guava jelly with Honduras, etc.; but this device weakened as soon as negotiations were completed with a great industrial country. There was also in some of the agreements, i.e., that of Belgium, the ingenious clause which provided that if imports of specified commodities increased unduly from third countries, the general extension by the United States of the concessions would be withdrawn.

In addition to the new policy of general extension of reciprocity bargain concessions there was another striking difference between the reciprocity policy of McKinleyism and the new reciprocity policy sponsored by Secretary of State Cordell Hull. The reciprocity arrangements made in a half-hearted manner in the 1890's had required ratification by the Senate, if they were in the form of treaties, approval by Congress if they were in the form of executive agreements for mutually lowered rates. The reciprocity agreements to be worked out under the act of Congress of 1934 were ratified in advance by Congress, and were independent of competition with any national tariff law.

The advantages of the Hull policy of trade agreements were that it made possible the lowering of tariff with less pressure from a lobby of special interests, and according to the requirements of the national economy as measured by the Department of State and other official agencies. Of course, only a start had been made in measuring and planning for the national economy as a whole and adjusting tariff and trade agreements to it, when the Second World War occurred and deranged all international trade. The Hull policy thus marched in the direction of freer trade while the Democratic Party amidst a sea of unemployment did not dare to lower the tariff by domestic legislation. Opponents of the policy—that is, opponents for other than political reasons—argued plausibly that because the world was moving in the direction of higher tariffs and multiple special restrictions through the ingenious devices of the new mercantilism, it was hopeless to advance far with reciprocity agreements when they were accompanied by a gratuitous generalization of the advantages thus traded for; for one reason the shrewdest bargainer would hold out to the last before negotiating, until he garnered the greatest possible volume of concessions without having to bargain for such favors by the granting of particular concessions to the United States. And the major industrial nations were reluctant to make reciprocity agreements which undid the protection, or endangered the self-sufficiency, enjoyed by their own industry or agriculture. Critics also pointed out that the United States, being best endowed with natural resources and well advanced in technical industry, had a natural advantage in economic bargaining which in the age of the new mercantilism took up an increasing proportion of the activities of diplomacy. They contended that it was folly, like disarmament by example, to weaken this advantage by the generalization, gratuitously, of reciprocal concessions. They asserted that the increasing tendency toward state control of foreign trade, where the state rather than the individual merchant, firm or even trust buys and sells its commodities on the basis of a planned economy, had radically altered the old liberalistic tendency toward free trade. It had also contracted the flow of international trade and finance. Because of the derangement of normal trade by the Second World War, its antecedents and aftermath, it is difficult to determine how much, if any, the reciprocal trade agreements have improved the foreign commerce of the United States. For several years immediately after the Second World War the labor costs of American manufacturing had mounted to such a level, and the demand for foreign products was so avid that wherever available they could have come in over almost any tariff wall.

Secretary Hull's reciprocal trade agreement program was only one feature of his determined attack on the new mercantilism, and all of its discriminations. In this larger sense we may refer to the Hull policy as the New Reciprocity. When the United States became a full belligerent in the Second World War the New Reciprocity was one of the first peace aims to crystallize as a cornerstone of American foreign economic policy. It became a condition of all the lend-lease agreements that were signed with the various co-belligerents following the Declaration of United Nations, that in the final settlement of accounts the respective signatories, together with all like-minded nations, would strive "in the light of governing economic conditions" for the elimination of all forms of discrimination in international commerce, and for the reduction of tariffs and other trade barriers.[1] That is, the recipients

[1] The standard formula was taken from Article VII of the Mutual Aid Agreement between the United States and Great Britain of February 23, 1942, as follows:

"In the final determination of the benefits to be provided to the United States of America by the Government of the United Kingdom in return for aid furnished under the [Lend-Lease] Act of Congress of March 11, 1941, the terms and conditions thereof shall be such as not to burden commerce between the two countries, but to promote mutually advantageous economic relations between them and the betterment of world-wide relations. To that end, they shall include provision for agreed action by the United States of America and the United Kingdom, open to participation by all other countries of like mind, directed to the expansion, by appropriate international and domestic measures, of production, employment, and the exchange and consumption of goods, which are the material foundations of the liberty and welfare of all peoples; to the elimination of all forms of discriminatory treatment in international commerce, and to the reduction of tariffs and other trade barriers; and, in general, to the attainment of all the economic objectives set forth in the Joint Declaration made on August 12, 1941, by the President of the United States of America and the Prime Minister of the United Kingdom.

"At an early convenient date, conversations shall be begun between the two Governments with a view to determining, in the light of governing economic conditions, the best means of attaining the above-stated objectives by their own agreed action and of seeking the agreed action of the other like-minded Governments." Department of State *Bulletin*, VI, No. 140 (February 28, 1942), p. 192.

of lend-lease agreed to pay the United States not in money or kind, but in principles of the New Reciprocity.[1]

The lend-lease settlements undoubtedly contributed to increasing the number of nations with which the United States had negotiated reciprocal trade agreements from twenty-three in 1942, to a total of forty-one as of December 1, 1949, including all the major countries excepting Germany, Japan, Spain, and the Soviet Union and its satellites (but not Czechoslovakia, which was party to a reciprocal trade agreement with the United States). The phrase "governing economic conditions" introduced a wide area of bargaining reservation on the part of those countries who resorted to state control of trading to repair their war-ravaged economies following the Second World War. This bargaining took place both in bilateral reciprocal trade agreements with the United States, and in drafting the charter of an International Trade Organization which the United States proposed to the Economic and Social Council of the United Nations Organization.

President Truman considered the New Reciprocity to be "an integral part of our foreign policy," one of the three main objectives: "peace, freedom, and world trade." [2] It remained for his Administration to make it an international policy and objective.

Preliminary conversations with the Governments of the United Kingdom and Canada during the negotiation of a 50-year 2 per cent rehabilitation loan of $3,750,000,000 to Great Britain secured the limited cooperation of these two countries for such a world policy. The Economic and Social Council then invited nineteen countries,[3] including Soviet Russia, estimated to share among them two-thirds of the world's trade, to take part in a Preparatory Committee meeting at Geneva, in April, 1947, to draw up the charter of an International Trade Organization, on the basis of a draft proposed by the United States. All except Russia accepted. The Preparatory Committee elaborated a new draft to be submitted to a plenary International Conference on Trade and Em-

---

[1] Notwithstanding her solemn agreements with the United States against discrimination, made in return for cancellation of lend-lease, the Anglo-American loan of 1947, and other huge rescue grants for British economy and defense, Great Britain, over the initial protest but later reluctant acquiescence of the United States, entered into a special bilateral trade treaty with Argentina, 1949, discriminating in favor of Britain's commerce and diverting much American trade from the Argentine.

[2] See statement of President Harry S. Truman, February 25, 1947, in Department of State *Bulletin,* XVI, No. 401 (March 9, 1947), 438; and his speech at Baylor University, Waco, Texas, March 6, 1947, in *ibid.,* XVI, No. 402 (March 16, 1947), 481.

[3] Australia, Belgium, Brazil, Canada, Chile, China, Cuba, Czechoslovakia, France, India, Lebanon, Luxemburg, the Netherlands, New Zealand, Norway, South Africa, the United Kingdom, the USSR, and the USA.

ployment [1] at Havana (December, 1947-March, 1948). While at Geneva the delegates also drew up a General Agreement on Tariffs and Trade, signed originally by twenty-three nations, as a sort of provisional code of fair competition in foreign trade practices,[2] as well as numerous bilateral trade agreements among themselves agreeing to tariff concessions covering nearly half the world's national imports.

At Annecy, France, in 1949, ten more countries [3] applied for accession to the General Agreement of Geneva and negotiated bilaterally new tariff schedules with twenty-one of the twenty-three original contracting parties, including the United States which generalized its own Annecy concessions into one schedule applying to all countries. Each country's accession and reciprocally lowered tariff rates are to become binding when two thirds of the parties have signed at Lake Success, N. Y., in respect to that party, the Annecy Protocol. Accession was to become effective from January 1 to May 30, 1950. The twenty-three original parties contracting at Geneva, plus the ten new ones acceding at Annecy, carried on among them four fifths of all world trade.[4] Meanwhile the Truman Administration announced that it would participate in negotiations with additional countries wishing to accede to the Geneva Agreement. The Annecy Agreement and the new tariff concessions to be expected would bring the United States tariff wall, already reduced approximately one half, still lower.

The Havana Conference of delegates from fifty-four countries [5] signed (March 24, 1948) a much modified Charter for an International Trade Organization. In its final form the Charter differed considerably from the original proposals of the United States for consideration by the peoples of the world. It represented a compromise between statism and non-discrimination, between the New Mercantilism and the New Reciprocity. It was a statement of guiding principles with wide reservations, more

[1] In addition to the eighteen states members of the Preparatory Committee, the following states signed: Burma, Ceylon, Pakistan, Southern Rhodesia, Syria. *U.S. and World Affairs, 1947-48,* pp. 244-246.

[2] All the signatories to the final Act of Geneva which contained the General Agreement on Tariffs and Trade gave the Agreement provisional application subject to denunciation on short notice.

[3] The ten additional countries were: Denmark, Dominican Republic, Finland, Greece, Haiti, Italy, Liberia, Nicaragua, Sweden, and Uruguay. The United States had entered previously into bilateral agreements with Finland (1936), Haiti (1935), Nicaragua (1936), Sweden (1935), and Uruguay (1942).

[4] *General Agreement on Tariffs and Trade: the Annecy Protocol of Terms of Accession and the Annecy Schedules of Tariff Concessions* (State Department Publication 3664, Commercial Policy Series 121, Washington, October, 1949).

[5] The USSR abstained from attending. Argentina and Poland did not sign.

than of compulsory obligations. Through the long, complicated and difficult Charter runs the theme of the New Reciprocity, American plan.

Any advantage, favor, privilege, or immunity, granted by any Member to any product shall be accorded immediately and unconditionally to the like product originating or destined for all other Member countries.

Reservations, exceptions, and qualifying language to the numerous articles of the Charter attached at Havana greatly weighed down and hampered this fundamental principle of American foreign policy. For example, exceptions had to be made for important *existing* preferential systems, like the preferences within the British Empire and Commonwealth of Nations, and those (always cited by persons who argue for such preferences) between the United States and Cuba. Other exceptions gave leeway for quantitative restrictions to remedy current shortages of goods, and special situations. During difficulties in making balance of payments, some discriminatory quantitative restrictions could be permitted. But at least the Members agreed *not to increase* any existing preferences, and not to create any new preferential arrangements without permission of the Organization by majority vote of Members present in Conference—one-half the membership necessary for a binding quorum. The Members undertook at least to "negotiate" with each other for substantial reduction of the general level of tariffs; in principle they abandoned the quota system as a protective device; they agreed to work for simplification and easing of customs formalities, and for bridling of private cartel activities. And they engaged to settle their economic disputes by peaceful means either within the machinery of the Organization or by the International Court of Justice.

The ITO was a bark designed by Mr. Hull's architects of economic amelioration and hopefully launched at Lake Geneva with a pretty name and fair sails, which descending to the open oceans of international trade got heavy-bottomed with barnacles of preferential nationalistic reservations picked up in Cuban waters. So encrusted, it was capable of slow progress even though most urgent winds might blow. And it could not even set forth from the port of Havana on its world voyage until a majority of the Charter parties signatory to the ship's articles had deposited "instruments of acceptance" with the Secretary General of the United Nations. Many of the signatories did not trust their future too confidently to this ship; otherwise they would not have built into it so many escape hatches. The period for ratification ended (September 30, 1949) without any of the signatories—not even its principal sponsor, the United States—having accepted it.[1] Meanwhile Washington itself had taken steps in the direction of statism. The United States Senate ratified (June 13, 1949) a multilateral treaty (USSR and satellites not parties thereto) fixing export quotas and prices of wheat for the next four years; and agreeing in the Anglo-Canadian-American financial conversations of September, 1949, to further discriminations by Great Britain, with the help even of the Marshall plan, against the United States, in order to bolster British economy and power to face the impending world crisis. Nevertheless, thoughtful Americans wished well to the ITO. It was freighted with hopes for a better world.

During the war (Bretton Woods [N. H.] Conference, July 1-22, 1944) American policy had sponsored and underwritten the establishment of an International Monetary Fund of $8,046,500,000 (American quota, $2,-750,000,000) to facilitate the expansion and balanced growth of international trade, and to promote exchange stability; and an International Bank for Reconstruction and Development, authorized capitalization $10,000,000,000 (American share, $3,175,000,000). The International Monetary Fund and the International Bank proved to be more than many of the subscribers could afford unless with loans from the United States. Nevertheless, the two institutions were set up to care for an economically creaking world.[2] A measure of the International Monetary Fund, during the momentous Anglo-Canadian-American financial discussions in Washington in September, 1949, was its recommendation to

---

[1] If a majority of the Charter signatories should not have accepted within one year after signature (March 24, 1948) then it was to enter into force sixty days after twenty Charter signatories should have accepted. If the Charter should not thus have entered into force by September 30, 1949, then the Secretary General of the United Nations was empowered to invite those Governments which had deposited "instruments of acceptance" to enter into a consultation to determine whether and on what conditions they desired to bring the Charter into force.

The most thoughtful analysis (and sympathetic appraisal) of the ITO Charter and the general agreements on tariff and trade is by William Adams Brown, Jr., *The United States and the Restoration of World Trade* (Brookings Institution, Washington, 1950).

[2] The ratifying members of the United Nations Monetary and Financial Conference (Bretton Woods) were the following signatories: Australia, Belgium, Bolivia, Brazil, Canada, Chile, China, Colombia, Costa Rica, Cuba, Czechoslovakia, Dominican Republic, Ecuador, Egypt, El Salvador, Ethiopia, France, Greece, Guatemala, Honduras, Iceland, India, Iran, Iraq, Luxemburg, Mexico, Netherlands, Nicaragua, Norway, Panama, Paraguay, Peru, Philippine Commonwealth, Poland, Union of South Africa, United Kingdom, USA, Uruguay, Venezuela, and Yugoslavia. Haiti, Liberia, New Zealand, and the USSR attended but did not sign. *United Nations Monetary and Financial Conference, Bretton Woods, New Hampshire, July 1 to July 22, 1944. Final Act and Related Documents* (Department of State Publication 2187, Washington, G.P.O., 1944), pp. 25-27. Haiti and Liberia have since applied for admission to the Bank and Fund Agreements. By January 1, 1950, the following states not signatories had been admitted: Austria, Denmark, Finland, Italy, Lebanon, Thailand, and Turkey.

countries whose exchange was strained for dollars that they devalue their currencies accordingly. The dramatic devaluation of the British pound and the currencies of the "sterling block" followed almost immediately, accompanied by far-reaching economic indulgences of the United States to Britain and Canada.

Neither the Fund, nor the Bank, nor the New Reciprocity magnified into the International Trade Organization, nor all the king's horses and all the king's men, proved sufficient to bring Europe together again, quick enough. Amid the stresses and strains, political and ideological as well as economic, that followed in wake of the Second World War, including the abstinence of Soviet Russia and its satellites, too little time has passed to measure the healing efficacy of these international institutions.[1] One thing seemed certain: their success in mending the economic disruption of the world depended upon the success of the United Nations; and the success of the United Nations depended upon the attitude of the Soviet Union. So far the USSR had refused to help man the economic machinery of the United Nations. As a powerful and permanent member of the Security Council it had braked and blocked the peace machinery too.

To hasten the recovery of Europe against the rising tide of communist revolution spearheaded by the USSR, the United States in 1947 took the astonishing step of initiating and underwriting to the amount of $20,000,000,000 a five-year European Recovery Program. Open to all the states of Europe, it was designed to bring their economies to a level of well-being 25 per cent above pre-war conditions. The USSR refused to participate in this unprecedented enterprise or to allow its satellite states to do so. It set up a plan of its own for them. The Soviet Union's attitude signalized a heading conflict between free economies and controlled economies, between free peoples and controlled peoples, in short between freedom and power in the world, a crisis in thought and action with which we close our final chapters.

---

[1] The USSR participated in the Bretton Woods Conference, but has had nothing to do since then either with the Fund or the Bank.

LEND-LEASE AND REVERSE LEND-LEASE

1941-1947 (June 30)

Recipient	Lend-Lease	Reverse Lend-Lease to U. S. A.
American republics:		
Bolivia............................ $	5,523,113.77	
Brazil.............................	372,018,982.63	
Chile..............................	21,603,647.88	
Colombia..........................	8,264,954.63	
Costa Rica........................	156,330.15	
Cuba..............................	6,550,610.38	
Dominican Republic................	1,617,315.60	
Ecuador...........................	7,794,178.09	
El Salvador	878,275.90	
Guatemala.........................	2,598,045.84	
Haiti..............................	1,423,658.75	
Honduras..........................	368,364.24	
Mexico............................	39,238,971.45	
Nicaragua.........................	887,199.28	
Panama............................	667.33	
Paraguay..........................	1,956,128.55	
Peru..............................	18,925,731.36	
Uruguay...........................	7,129,488.01	
Venezuela.........................	4,523,680.08	
Total—American republics......... $	501,459,343.92	
Other governments:		
Belgium........................... $	159,464,430.26	$ 191,215,983.35
British Empire.....................	31,384,810,121.25	6,752,073,165.40
China.............................	1,626,998,524.86	3,672,000.00
Czechoslovakia....................	641,839.17	
Egypt.............................	2,319,691.15	
Ethiopia..........................	5,251,480.09	
France and possessions.............	3,223,891,229.32	867,781,244.70
Greece............................	81,521,726.17	
Iceland...........................	4,371,496.03	
Iran..............................	5,303,624.18	
Iraq..............................	891,469.57	
Liberia...........................	11,554,901.20	
Netherlands and possessions.........	251,137,540.95	2,367,699.64
Norway............................	47,000,522.22	
Poland............................	12,475,376.00	
USSR.............................	10,982,088,888.95	2,212,697.81
Saudi Arabia......................	18,984,227.45	
Turkey............................	42,876,877.88	
Yugoslavia........................	32,192,067.91	
Total—other governments..........	$47,893,776,034.61	

Total—charged to foreign governments $48,395,235,378.53

(Table continued on p. 750.)

1941-1947 (June 30)

Recipient	Lend-Lease	Reverse Lend-Lease to U. S. A.
Not distributed by foreign governments:		
Transfers to Federal agencies.........	$ 725,589,141.95	
Losses on inventories and facilities.....	31,072,272.57	
Production facilities.................	720,641,686.66	
Miscellaneous charges...............	332,200,098.31	
Administrative expenses.............	39,257,580.77	
Total—not distributed by foreign governments...................	$ 1,848,760,780.26	
Grand total........................	$50,243,996,158.79	$7,819,322,790.90

Total Lend-Lease.................	$50,243,996,158.79
Total Reverse Lend-Lease.........	7,819,322,790.90
Net Lend-Lease.................	$42,424,673,367.89 [a]

[a] *Twenty-Fifth Report by the President to Congress on Lend-Lease Operations. Lend-Lease Fiscal Operations March 11, 1941, through June 30, 1947.*

CHAPTER XXXIX

THE UNITED STATES AND LATIN AMERICA

(1889-1950)

THERE have been a few small wars between the nations of the New World in the twentieth century, but compared to the Old World of Europe, Asia and Africa, their general lot has been one of relative peace and serenity in international affairs. This is because the European political system has been fenced away (except in the case of Canada) by the American Revolution, by the successful revolutions from Spanish sovereignty of the Latin-American nations, by the defensive exertions of the South American states themselves unaided, and, more recently, by the Monroe Doctrine. We remember that the Monroe Doctrine did not in itself at first "save" Latin America from the re-imposition of Spanish authority at the hands of the Holy Alliance.[1] Nevertheless the United States speedily grew up to the stature of defending the Monroe Doctrine. Its attitude toward French or Spanish aggressions in Mexico, the Dominican Republic, and Peru, and British boundary policy in Venezuela; and Great Britain, Germany and Italy later in Venezuela; gave pause to adventures of those monarchies across the Atlantic. One has only to compare the maps of Asia and Africa, recording as they do the advances of European and Japanese imperialism, with the map of South America and the persistence there of sovereign independence.[2]

In this chapter we shall treat of South America, as distinct from the Caribbean fringe, the Isthmus, and Central America, that nearer field of the Panama Policy of the United States, where a mild imperialism—now fully liquidated—was built up in an area from which European intervention had been held aside by the Monroe Doctrine. Before the days of aerial navigation the nations of Hispanic America, south of the Caribbean fringe, were quite as distant from the United States as from Europe. Indeed, from the geophysical point of view, Asia and Africa are more closely connected to Europe than is South America to North America. The United States had less contact with these South American states, before the First World War, than with Europe. During the nine-

---

[1] Above, Ch. XII.
[2] See Map 33, between pp. 752 and 753.

751

teenth century the noteworthy features of the history of the diplomacy of the United States with South America were: the extension of good offices on several occasions to end strife between South American nations; Blaine's attempt to freshen commerce by a system of reciprocity to be erected through the First Inter-American Conference, at Washington in 1889, and the resulting feeble beginnings of the Pan-American movement;[1] the *Baltimore* affair with Chile in 1891; and the sympathetic reaction of the United States in 1893 to the republican government in Brazil when it was threatened by a naval insurrection intent on restoring the old empire.

It has been a consistent policy of the United States to encourage peace in South America through the extension of good offices and proposals of mediation. One motive for this has been to enhance its good will at the expense of Europe; but the policy has by no means necessarily opposed similar good offices and mediations by European nations; the Monroe Doctrine has never been invoked to exclude peace at European hands from the American continents. It was under American[2] good offices, for example, that Spain's war with the Pacific coast republics of South America (1864-1871)—Ecuador, Peru, Bolivia and Chile—came to a legal end long after actual hostilities had ceased. It was the United States which, after much discouraging diplomacy, eventually helped to end the Tacna-Arica controversy, which alienated Chile and Peru from the end of the War of the Pacific (1879-1883) until the treaty of Santiago (1929).[3] President Hayes served as arbitrator of a disputed boundary between the Argentine Republic and Paraguay, by a treaty between those two countries in 1876. His decision in favor of Paraguay was accepted by the disputants. President Cleveland, in 1895, acted successfully as arbitrator for the settlement of another boundary dispute in the same general region, that between Brazil and Argentina, the Misiones arbitration. The American Minister to Argentina, W. I. Buchanan, served as umpire in a mixed Chilean-Argentine boundary commission, successfully bringing to a settlement a standing dispute over their long mountainous boundary line. These are noteworthy examples in a long list of good offices for the peaceful settlement of Latin America's numerous and vexing boundary disputes.

[1] Above, p. 732.

[2] For my justification for the use of this adjective for the United States, see above, p. 43.

[3] An adequate monograph is W. J. Dennis' *Tacna and Arica; an Account of the Chile-Peru Boundary Dispute and of the Arbitrations by the United States* (Yale University Press, 1931).

[Adapted from maps publish

Map 33. The New World with the Mo

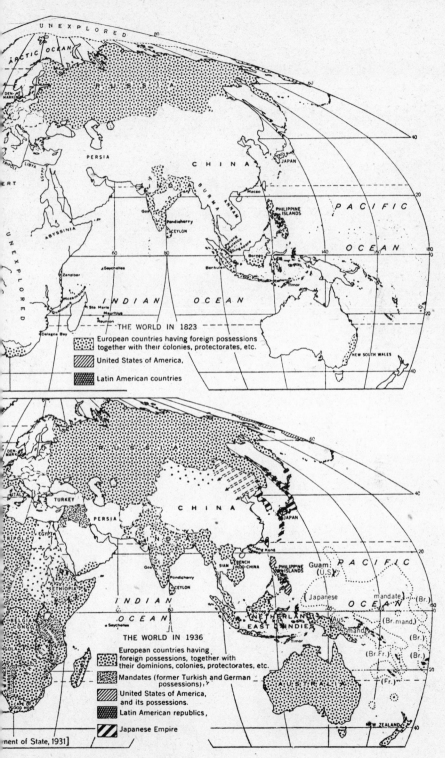

THE WORLD IN 1823

European countries having foreign possessions together with their colonies, protectorates, etc.

United States of America,

Latin American countries

THE WORLD IN 1936

European countries having foreign possessions, together with their dominions, colonies, protectorates, etc.

Mandates (former Turkish and German possessions),

United States of America, and its possessions.

Latin American republics,

Japanese Empire

ment of State, 1931]

nd the Old World Without it 1823-1936.

The nearest the United States ever came to any actual conflict with a South American nation was with Chile. A revolution in that distant republic against the praetorian practices of President Balmaceda broke

Map 34. Latin America, 1940.

out in 1891. The American Minister, Patrick Egan, of Irish birth, appeared to the Congressionalists to sympathize overmuch with the *Balmacedistas,* disfavored by British interests in Chile. The revolutionists sent a ship to San Diego, California, to buy a cargo of rifles and other military supplies. It was doubtful whether this was in violation of American domestic neutrality laws, but the vessel, the *Itata,* was detained on suspicions at that port and a United States marshal placed on board. The captain put out to sea notwithstanding, temporarily shanghaied the marshal, took on the military cargo at Catalina Island, and steamed away for Chile, followed by two American warships. At the port of Iquique, held by the Congressionalists, the revolutionary authorities complied with the request of the American naval officer for the surrender of the ship and cargo to be sent back to the United States for trial—where eventually it was acquitted of any violation of the neutrality laws. The Congressionalists nevertheless triumphed, with arms imported successfully from Germany.

Egan gave customary asylum in his legation to fleeing *Balmacedistas.* This, and the sentiments previously attributed to him, created bitter popular feeling against the United States. In such an atmosphere a mob of Chileans in the port of Valparaiso attacked (October 15, 1891) a party of 116 sailors on shore leave from the U.S.S. *Baltimore,* killed two, and seriously wounded several others. The new government made no efforts either to protect the visitors or to punish the assailants. It offered no apology or explanation; rather the contrary. Despite a wave of indignation in the United States, Secretary Blaine did not allow the Harrison Administration to be precipitated into a rupture. The *Baltimore* was called home, and an unhurried investigation of the incident took place. Then after due consideration Blaine despatched an ultimatum to Chile, demanding, under the alternative of a rupture of diplomatic relations, a suitable apology for the attack on sailors of the United States wearing the American uniform, and adequate reparation. At the same time President Harrison laid the whole matter significantly before Congress for ultimate decision. In Chile the personnel of the new government had meanwhile changed. A sincere expression of regret was promptly forthcoming, and the United States accepted a sum of $75,000 by way of reparation for the families of the victims. Since then relations between Chile and the United States have been of the most friendly nature.[1]

The United States was the first (outside of Latin America) to recognize the new republican government in Brazil, when that empire was overthrown by the bloodless revolution of 1889. A counter-revolution followed in 1893 by the monarchists, who secured control of the Brazilian navy. President Cleveland declined to recognize the belligerency of the

[1] H. C. Evans, *Chile and Its Relations with the United States* (Duke University Press, 1927) and W. R. Sherman, *The Diplomatic and Commercial Relations of the United States and Chile, 1820-1914* (Boston, 1926).

monarchists. An American squadron hastened to Rio de Janeiro, where
warships from the European powers also appeared. At the cannon's
mouth, the American admiral refused to permit the anti-republican warships to enforce a blockade on American vessels carrying alleged contraband into Rio. The insurrection had the sympathy of the European
monarchical powers, which, particularly Germany, hoped for its success.
There was a considerable concentration (300,000) of sturdy German
immigrants in southern Brazil, for whom Pan-German enthusiasts had
higher hopes than really could be justified because of the rapid Brazil-
ianization of the majority of these people. The Kaiser secretly applauded
the monarchical strivings. There was even a chance that Prince August
von Coburg, a nephew of the late Dom Pedro, might be the new monarch:
"Then we shall be the big people there," declared Wilhelm II. Germany
was also jealous of the good will which the United States had created for
itself in Brazil by its open sympathies for the republican government,
and feared the intrusion and future competition of American trade there,
as elsewhere in South America, under the impetus of a Pan-American
movement for which the Brazilian republicans had shown enthusiasm
(Brazilian-American reciprocity agreement, 1891-1894).

The attitude of the United States gave the European monarchical
powers pause in their desire to recognize the belligerency of the monarchists. England refused to antagonize the United States by such a
step. Count Caprivi, Bismarck's successor, considered that the Brazilian
revolutionists were of more promise to Germany than the established
republican government, because of their opposition to Pan Americanism
and because of possible favors to be expected to German colonization, but
he opposed any single-handed recognition of their belligerency and the
consequent legality of their blockade, because of its injury to German
trade, including the munitions trade.[1] The successful suppression of the
monarchists by the established republican authorities meant the triumph
in Brazil of this form of government. The policy of the United States
at that decisive hour of trial was an earnest to Brazil of the real feelings
of the American people and laid the foundations for a persistent cordiality
between the two republics ever since.[2]

The United States bought from the group of South American countries
far more than it sold to them, though there have been notable exceptions
in the case of individual countries, like Argentina; Europe sold more
than it bought. It was Secretary Blaine's effort to make use of an inter-

[1] Alfred Vagts, *Weltpolitik*, *op. cit.*, II, 1673-1700, has a full analysis of German policy.
[2] Lawrence F. Hill, *United States and Brazil*, *op. cit.*, is the best account.

American Conference (that of 1889) for the purpose of furthering reciprocal trade arrangements between the increasingly industrial United
States and the agrarian republics of South America which would overcome this unprofitable disparity. We have seen that he failed; [1] but the
Pan-American movement which followed "Blaine's Conference" has always had a reciprocity tinge,[2] and if only for this reason has been opposed
by European diplomacy, particularly German.[3] European industrial nations feared that political amenities of the United States with South
America would eat into the commercial predominance which they enjoyed
down to the outbreak of the First World War, and which they endeavored
to retrieve in the interlude of peace after 1919. They welcomed the
appearance of counter-movements, so far of no treaty or even diplomatic structure, like Pan Hispanism and Pan Iberianism, by which South
American Yankeephobes tried to rally public sentiment about a common
Latin culture, and with it to keep trade in European channels, and even
to hope for political followings.[4]

The second inter-American Conference, at Mexico in 1901-1902, did
not take place until after the Cuban-Spanish-American War, which had
made some of the Latin-American nations suspicious of the platonic
intentions of the United States. The Conference accomplished very little,
except to put in motion a train of such conferences which have assembled
more or less regularly (except for the interruption of the two World
Wars) ever since. At first fruitful only of feeble accomplishments, the
Pan-American movement, as represented by these conferences, has come
in our own times to be an impressive vehicle for the organization of peace
in the New World, with most elaborate machinery. Particularly with
ultra-Caribbean nations of South America are the diplomatic relations
of the United States now contained in the formula of Pan Americanism.

What is Pan Americanism? Is it a policy or is it a tendency? It is
both. It may be described as a tendency, more or less pronounced, of
the republics of the New World to associate together in a neighborly
way for mutual understanding of common aspirations and interests and

[1] Above, p. 732.
[2] A European conception of this appears in Jens Jessen, "Die ökonomische Grundlage
der panamerikanischen Idee," *Schmollers Jahrbuch*, LII, No. 5 (1928), 79-111.
[3] Vagts, *Weltpolitik, op. cit.*, I, 72-75; II, 1637-1814.
[4] For example, the *Ibero-Amerikanisches Institut* had its headquarters in Germany. An
expression of this German patronage appeared in the Argentine historian, Ernesto
Quesada's *Die Wirtschaftsbeziehungen zwichen Latein-Amerika und den Vereinigten
Staaten* (Leipzig, 1931). Santiago Magariño presented the case for Pan Hispanism in
his *Panhispanismo, su trascendencia histórica, política y social; obra premiada en el
concurso hispano antillano de 1925* (Barcelona, 1926).

their realization. The greatest of these common aspirations is peace. It is a policy of the United States to encourage this tendency in order to cause the American nations not to look to Europe or to depend on Europe for leadership, because (as past and present history suggests) Europe might possibly exploit such tutelage for the selfish interests of particular European powers. This in turn might lead to the exercise of political influence or even sovereignty of a non-American power in the American world, which would be possibly a menace to the common American republican form of government and perhaps a threat to independence itself. Rather let the American republics look to themselves and their common counsel for such leadership. In this sense Pan Americanism may be considered as a complement to the Monroe Doctrine.

It has been called a "twin policy" to the Monroe Doctrine.[1] At first, 1888-1936, it was a movement, sponsored by the United States, toward *moral union* of the American republics under the protection of the Monroe Doctrine. Later, 1936-1950, it developed into a political regional arrangement of the republics of the New World in formal alliance—all for one and one for all—to protect the peace and security of the Western Hemisphere against attack or menace of aggression, from without or within.

Before the First World War the accomplishments of the Pan-American movement were meager. The intervention of the United States to clinch the secession of Panama, and the installation of the protectorates in the Caribbean and Central America, had provoked a vigorous skepticism of the good faith of the "Colossus of the North," a skepticism which over-weighed the protection from European imperialism which had been secured by the Monroe Doctrine. The inarticulation of cultural backgrounds between the United States and Latin America made it difficult for the people of the southern republics to think and feel like their "Anglo-Saxon" neighbors north of the Rio Grande. This cultural incompatibility lent itself to a literary Yankeephobia among South American publicists [2] which frequently displayed (at least so it appeared to the North American mind) more emotion than common sense. North American imperialism in the Caribbean gave fuel for the flames of these burn-

[1] G. H. Blakeslee, *The Recent Foreign Policy of the United States; Problems in American Cooperation with Other Powers* (New York, 1925), p. 129.

[2] J. Fred Rippy has an analysis of South American opinion in his introduction to the English edition of Ugarte, *The Destiny of a Continent* (New York, 1925); and a further survey in his "Literary Yankeephobia in Hispanic America," *Jour. of International Relations*, XII (Jan., 1922), 350-371, 524-538. One of the best analyses of opinion at a later time is C. H. Haring, *South America Looks at the United States* (New York, 1928).

ing critics; and there was generally little consideration of the strategic necessities which had thrust up the Panama Policy of the United States in the Caribbean and in Central America. Successive inter-American conferences that followed Mexico City before 1914 (Rio de Janeiro, 1906, and Buenos Aires, 1910) really accomplished very little of vital importance. Their principal achievement was the abatement, by treaties, of trade nuisances: they provided for the international regulation of such common conveniences as bills of lading, trade-marks, copyrights, patents, publicity of customs dues, sanitary precautions, etc. Ancillary to these diplomatic conferences were held special Pan-American conferences of professional, scientific, and humanitarian representatives of the different American republics, meetings initiated by the diplomatic conferences themselves or organized by the Pan American Union from its headquarters in Washington: conferences of bankers, journalists, railroads, motor-roads, advocates of the advancement of women's rights, educators, historians, geographers, and so on. These conferences did much to bridge the cultural gap and to tone down discordances among the leaders of thought.

For several reasons it was difficult to achieve multilateral political conventions. The South American states suspected that the United States would like to impose a political tutelage over them even while it would prevent non-American powers from doing so. They suspected the Monroe Doctrine of such import, and desired to pan-Americanize it. They resented the shadow of the Washington Monument falling across, so to speak, the Pan American Union in the capital of the United States. This shadow appeared in the persistent presiding over the Union by a citizen of the United States, either as chairman of the group of diplomatic representatives from the several American republics accredited to Washington, which chair according to the rules of the Union until 1923 was held *ex officio* by the Secretary of State of the United States; or as Director General of the Pan American Union, which office was held until 1947 by a citizen of the United States. Until 1923 only a recognized diplomatic representative at Washington could sit in the Pan American Union; hence the rupture of diplomatic relations, for whatever reason, with the United States, would deprive a republic of its seat.[1] In short, there lingered a general distrust which it has been a task of the Pan-

[1] The Sixth (Havana) Inter-American Conference adopted a convention controlling the organization of the Pan American Union, already reformed at Santiago de Chile in 1923. This adjusted these questions with this treaty article: "The government of the Pan American Union shall be vested in a Governing Board composed of the representatives

American policy of the United States to overcome. Nascent nationalism in South America itself, and racial differences in the midst of a common Hispanic heritage, also prevented Pan-American political agreements, like treaties for the limitation of armaments and the lowering of tariff walls. Nevertheless the Pan-American nations did agree, before the First World War, to the convention establishing the Hague Court of Arbitration which had been set up in 1899 by a conference in which they did not sit; to the Root arbitration treaties with the United States, and in many instances also to Bryan conciliation treaties.

It was one of the principal objects of Woodrow Wilson's foreign policy to wipe out this distrust and to reach a common understanding about the Monroe Doctrine as an instrument of protection, this with acceptance of the accomplished fact of a benevolent North American imperialism in the Caribbean and in Central America as evidenced by the protectorates in Cuba, Panama, the Dominican Republic, Nicaragua and Haiti. In a notable speech at Mobile, Alabama, in the first year of his administration (October 27, 1913) on the eve of the opening of the Panama Canal, he took occasion to say that "the United States will never again seek one additional foot of territory by conquest." This assurance, the treaty of reparation negotiated with Colombia (not ratified however till 1921), and Wilson's sympathetic policy toward Mexico did much to win the confidence of the sister republics all over the southern continent and Central America. Particularly ingratiating, as evidence of the sincerity of Wilson's remarks, was his ready acceptance of the mediation of the joint ABC and other republics of South and Central America for the solution of Mexican peace.

Wilson's adviser, Colonel E. M. House, urged that this good will be capitalized, during the First World War, in the cementing of an inter-American pact which in effect would pan-Americanize the Monroe Doctrine by a common guaranty of the existing political independence and territorial integrity of every republic of the New World. In November, 1915, House and Wilson formulated the following articles:

that the American governments may appoint. The appointment may [not must] devolve upon the diplomatic representatives of the respective countries in Washington."

"The Board shall elect its Chairman and Vice-Chairman annually."

This convention does not go into effect until ratified by *all* the member states of the Union. The United States has ratified; but to January 1, 1949, ratifications were missing from: Argentina, Colombia, El Salvador, Honduras, Paraguay. The Charter of the Organization of American States, signed at the Ninth International Conference of American States, March 30-May 2, 1948, may be said to have superseded previous attempts to formulate the organization in treaty form. It required ratification by only two-thirds of the signatories, and went immediately into provisional effect by resolution. See below, pp. 780-783.

"Article I. That the high contracting parties to this solemn covenant and agreement hereby join one another in a common and mutual guaranty of territorial integrity and of political independence under republican forms of government.

"Article II. To give definitive application to the guaranty set forth in Article I, the high contracting parties severally covenant to endeavor forthwith to reach a settlement of all disputes as to boundaries or territory now pending between them by amicable agreement or by means of international arbitration." [1]

When he broached the subject of such a broad pact, President Wilson encountered hesitations from Peru and Chile, arising out of the then unsettled Tacna-Arica dispute. Peru would not enter into any guaranty of the territorial *status quo,* so grievous to her; and Chile was not willing to assume a general obligation to submit boundary disputes to arbitration. Before negotiations for the consummation of such a Pan-American treaty could be pursued further, the rupture of diplomatic relations with Germany and the entrance of the United States into the First World War drew the President's attention from this pact and engrossed his energies with even larger affairs. It is emphatically noteworthy that during the period of belligerency of the United States the sympathy of the Latin-American republics, with the possible exception of Argentina, was with the great republic of the north. We recall that eight of the Latin-American republics declared war against Germany, at the invitation of the United States, and that five others broke off diplomatic relations. [2] In the Peace Conference at Paris Woodrow Wilson wrote into the Covenant of the League of Nations the principles of his proposed Pan-American pact, notably Article X, to him the most vital article in the Covenant. He believed that by this article he was globalizing the Monroe Doctrine, whereas previously he would have merely panAmericanized it. At the instance of those who feared the defeat of the treaty without an article reserving the Monroe Doctrine specifically from the purview of the League, he secured the adoption of the equivocal Article XXI for that purpose. [3]

. Republican administrations following Wilson did much toward prun-

[1] Seymour, *Intimate Papers, op. cit.,* I, 207-234.
[2] Above, p. 618.
[3] Above, p. 650.
Article XXI of the Covenant: "Nothing in this Covenant shall be deemed to affect the validity of international engagements, such as treaties of arbitration or regional understandings like the Monroe Doctrine, for securing the maintenance of peace."

ing off the "Roosevelt Corollary" of the Monroe Doctrine, which an earlier Republican President had invoked to justify intervention by the United States in the Dominican Republic in 1905. The United States ratified in 1924 the so-called Gondra Convention, signed at the Fifth Inter-American Conference at Santiago in 1923, which has replaced, by a multilateral treaty among the Pan-American states, the series of Bryan conciliation treaties, previously in effect bilaterally in each case with the United States. The Pan-American nations, including of course the United States, at the Havana Inter-American Conference of 1928 adopted a resolution outlawing aggression as an international crime against the human species (without defining aggression), and another for the obligatory arbitration of all justiciable disputes, the minimum exceptions to justiciable questions to be worked out by a special conference on arbitration and conciliation appointed to meet at Washington the following year. The delegates at Havana signed a number of treaties, since ratified in less or greater degree, of a distinct political nature: they concerned the status of aliens,[1] asylum, civil strife,[1] aviation,[1] consular rights,[1] maritime neutrality,[1] alteration of the Pan American Union,[1] private international law, and rules governing treaties. Both at Santiago in 1923 and at Havana in 1928 the majority of the Latin-American countries displayed an antagonistic feeling toward the United States—because of American interventions then established in the Caribbean and Central America—a feeling which restricted the possibilities of still wider accomplishment. Notwithstanding the fact that the intervention of the United States then underway in Nicaragua, and the presence of American marines still in Haiti, served to prolong hesitations among the Latin-American delegations, the Havana Inter-American Conference of 1928 gave real impetus to the Pan-American movement, a headway which has since continued unchecked as it became increasingly evident that American policy toward intervention was undergoing a change.

At Havana, in a speech outside the Conference to the American Chamber of Commerce in that city, one of the delegates of the United States, ex-Secretary of State Charles E. Hughes, declared that the "pillars of Pan Americanism" were independence, and political stability to secure independence, together with good will and co-operation. He said that the interventions of the United States then in evidence were only for the purpose of ensuring stability as a means of securing independence. "We have no desire to stay. We entered to meet an imperative but temporary

[1] Since ratified by the United States.

emergency, and we shall retire as soon as possible." This may be considered as the last statement of the policy of intervention for prevention of political or economic disorder, the policy of the "Roosevelt corollary" of the Monroe Doctrine.

As if to clarify the relation of the Panama Policy to the Monroe Doctrine, the Department of State prepared, after the Havana Conference, the "Clark Memorandum on the Monroe Doctrine," dated December 17, 1928, and later made public in 1930 under the imprimatur of the Department and over the name and title of the Undersecretary of State. Its principal purpose appears to have been to repudiate, by historical exegesis, the "Roosevelt Corollary" as an unwarranted interpretation of the Monroe Doctrine. Public addresses of Secretary of State Henry L. Stimson (February 6, 1931), and of the new Undersecretary of State, W. R. Castle (July 4, 1931), corroborated this irenic interpretation. Said Mr. Stimson: "The Monroe Doctrine was a declaration of the United States versus Europe—not of the United States versus Latin America." Mr. Castle declared that the Monroe Doctrine "confers no superior position on the United States," and said that it had been wrongly credited with giving the United States a right to interfere in the internal affairs of other nations. The next step of assurance to the nations of the New World that the United States was not going to interpret the Monroe Doctrine in an imperialistic way was signature of the two treaties worked out by the special Washington conference of 1929, the General Convention of Inter-American Conciliation, and the General Treaty of Inter-American Arbitration. The new conciliation convention empowered the commission of inquiry, provided by the Gondra Convention of 1923, to investigate into and report upon disputes not settled by diplomacy or arbitration, with function also of proposing modes of conciliating (as well as reporting). The arbitration convention of 1929 condemned war as an instrument of national policy and adopted obligatory arbitration as the means for the settlement of international differences of a juridical character between or among the contracting parties, when it has proven impossible to adjust them by diplomacy, viz.:

"There shall be considered as included among the questions of juridical character:

"(a) The interpretation of a treaty;

"(b) Any question of international law;

"(c) The existence of any fact which, if established, would constitute a breach of an international obligation;

"(d) The nature and extent of the reparation to be made for the breach of an international obligation." [1]

"There are excepted from the stipulations of this treaty the following controversies:

"(a) Those which are within the domestic jurisdiction of any of the Parties to the dispute and are not controlled by international law; and

"(b) Those which affect the interest or refer to the action of a State not a Party to this treaty."

Both treaties remain in force indefinitely, but may be denounced by any party on one year's previous notice.

In signing the arbitration treaty the delegates of several states (Venezuela, Chile, Bolivia, Honduras, Guatemala, Ecuador, Colombia, El Salvador) made a reservation (among others) that the obligation to arbitrate should not involve old disputes, and in some cases treaties, antedating the arbitration treaty. The Senate of the United States in advising and consenting to ratification attached the usual reservation stating that the special agreement (*compromis*) for any particular arbitration must be the subject of a special treaty negotiated by the President and ratified by the Senate; and that the general treaty should not be applicable to past or pending controversies or treaties. To date 18 nations [2] (including the United States) have ratified the conciliation convention, and 16 nations [3] (including the United States) the treaty of arbitration.

President Franklin D. Roosevelt, upon taking office in 1933, hit upon the happy phrase "the good neighbor" to characterize his foreign policy. In regard to Pan America, he continued, under the benevolent impulse of Secretary of State Cordell Hull, the trend which had been pursued by his Republican predecessors: to bring American policy back toward the pristine dicta of the Monroe Doctrine: for non-American nations, hands off the New World; for the United States also, hands off Latin America— accepting, of course, the accomplished fact of the Canal treaties. In the new order of naval security that followed the victory of the First World War, it seemed no longer necessary to pursue a policy which might provoke a challenge by a non-American power to the Monroe Doctrine. That

[1] This definition of justiciable questions is that of Article 36 of the Statute of the Permanent Court of International Justice.

[2] The conciliation convention had been ratified (on January 1, 1949) by: Brazil, Colombia, Cuba, Chile, Ecuador, El Salvador, United States, Guatemala, Haiti, Honduras, Mexico, Nicaragua, Panama, Paraguay, Peru, Dominican Republic, Uruguay, Venezuela; all except Argentina, Bolivia, and Costa Rica.

[3] The arbitration treaty had been ratified (on January 1, 1949) by: Brazil, Cuba, Chile, Colombia, Ecuador, El Salvador, United States, Guatemala, Haiti, Honduras, Mexico, Nicaragua, Panama, Peru, Dominican Republic, Venezuela; all except Argentina, Bolivia, Costa Rica, Paraguay, and Uruguay.

Doctrine alone, without any corollary of vicarious responsibility, seemed sufficient to protect the independence of the republics of the New World and the naval communications of the United States via the Isthmus of Central America. No more interventions would be necessary, unless for the immediate protection of the legitimate rights of American citizens generally recognizable and acceptable under international law and international conventions. This banned future political interventions. Accompanying this was a process of liquidation of the Caribbean protectorates, the result of past interventions.

The Good Neighbor Policy, at first greeted as a mere phrase, bore rich and friendly fruit at the Seventh Inter-American Conference at Montevideo in 1933. The old feelings of suspicion and resentment vanished before the proven sincerity of the Good Neighbor of the North. The delegates there assembled proceeded to the signature of a number of treaties which marked great advance in Pan Americanism, particularly in regard to the organization of peace, in the preservation of which the nations of the New World had a common vital interest. They adopted no less than 114 resolves and recommendations for the furtherance of worthy projects of inter-American life, enterprises of social, economic, and cultural value, which vastly extended the ancillary functions already increasingly developed through Pan-American channels. Since many of these projects required negotiation of treaties and conventions, and subsequent ratification, or at least a community of uniform national legislation, this part of the work of the Conference was a program and a tribute rather than an accomplishment. One of these resolves, for the removal of trade barriers, including high tariff walls, was very significant. It was the treaties which were most important. In addition to treaties defining the nationality of women, the requirements for naturalization in general, political asylum, the teaching of history [1]—treaties which have a long road to ratification by sufficient countries to make them important—the Conference adopted an additional protocol to the general convention of inter-American conciliation [2] and a convention henceforth to define the rights and duties of states, which had been drawn up by a special commission of American jurists appointed after the Sixth (Havana) Inter-American Conference of 1928. It was the last-

[1] "To revise the text books adopted for instruction in their respective countries, with the object of eliminating from them whatever might tend to arouse in the immature mind of youth aversion to any American country," and to found an "Institute for the Teaching of History" at Buenos Aires.

[2] In this the parties to the Gondra Convention of 1923 agreed to negotiate among themselves bilateral conventions setting up as between themselves particular commissions of investigation and conciliation.

named convention that was of fundamental importance as a capstone of the new Pan-American policy of the United States and of the Pan-American structure of peace. Ratified by the United States (June 29, 1934), it contained among other articles:

"Article 2. The federal state shall constitute a sole person in the eyes of international law.

"Article 8. No state has the right to intervene in the internal or external affairs of another.

"Article 9. The jurisdiction of states within the limits of national territory applies to all the inhabitants.

"Nationals and foreigners are under the same protection of the laws and the national authorities and the foreigners may not claim rights other or more extensive than those of the nationals.

"Article 10. The primary interest of states is the conservation of peace. Differences of any nature which arise between them should be settled by recognized pacific methods.

"Article 11. The contracting states definitely establish as the rule of their conduct the precise obligation not to recognize territorial acquisitions or special advantages which have been obtained by force, whether this consists in the employment of arms, in threatening diplomatic representations, or in any other effective coercive measure. The territory of a state is inviolable and may not be the object of military occupation nor of other measures of force imposed by another state directly or indirectly or for any motive whatever even temporarily."

The first of these quoted articles, Article 2, settles a long-standing question: whether a federal government is responsible for the acts of its states or provinces.

Article 8 was the most significant of all. It was a self-denial of the right of intervention in the internal or external affairs of any other state. It would make impossible political interventions. It was a disclaimer for the future, in the case of the United States, of such interventions as Cuba, Panama, the Dominican Republic, Nicaragua, Haiti, insofar as those interventions involved more than the protection of the rights of American citizens under international law and treaties. It was therefore a repudiation of the "Roosevelt Corollary." In signing this treaty Secretary Hull appended a lengthy reservation, repeated by the Senate in ratifying, by which the United States, in cases of difference of opinion or of interpretation as to its provisions, declared that it would follow "the law of nations as generally recognized and understood."

Article 11 resembles the "Stimson Doctrine" already adopted as a resolution of the League of Nations,[1] which doctrine is really of inter-American origin conceived in essence in 1889. It had been reaffirmed, a few months after the "Stimson Doctrine," by an important Pan-American Declaration of August 3, 1932: the nineteen neutral American republics declared to Bolivia and Paraguay, engaged in the Chaco War, that they would "not recognize any territorial arrangement of this controversy which has not been obtained by peaceful means nor the validity of territorial acquisitions which may be obtained through occupation or conquest by force of arms." Article 11 of the Rights and Duties of States was designed to implement by moral and juridical force not only this Declaration, but also the outlawry of wars of aggression (undefined) by the Sixth (Havana) International Conference of American States, and the renunciation of war as an instrument of national policy by the Pact of Paris and by the Inter-American Arbitration Treaty (Washington, 1929).

. At Montevideo the delegates resolved to call upon their respective governments for the speedy ratification by all of them of the multilateral peace treaties which remained unratified by many of the signatories. The United States had accepted the inter-American convention for conciliation promptly in 1929, and in 1935 it ratified the inter-American convention for arbitration. It also signed and ratified (July 6, 1934) the Saavedra-Lamas Anti-War Pact, of Argentine initiative, originally signed October 10, 1933, by the Argentine Republic, Brazil, Chile, Mexico, Paraguay and Uruguay. The pact condemned wars of aggression and territorial acquisitions secured by armed conquest, and declared that the signatories would recognize no territorial arrangement not obtained through pacific means, nor the validity of an occupation brought about by armed force.[2] It pledged neutrals to undertake in common "the political, juridical or economic means authorized by international law"—including the machinery of commissions of conciliation but not diplomatic or armed intervention—to restore peace between parties violating the pact. It prohibited intervention. In ratifying it, the United States reserved all rights under international law and existing treaties.

Before these treaties had been ratified by all principal American republics other than the United States, a special Inter-American Conference for the Maintenance of Peace assembled in December, 1936, at Buenos Aires, at the initiative of President Franklin D. Roosevelt, to

[1] Below, p. 814.
[2] This treaty was open to any nation which wished to adhere.

add further blocks to the Pan-American peace structure. It adopted an Additional Protocol Relative to Non-Intervention which removed any reservations about rights of intervention even under international law, by stating: "The High Contracting Parties declare inadmissible the intervention of *any one*[1] of them, directly or indirectly, and for whatever reason, in the internal or external affairs of any other of the Parties." Any question concerning the interpretation of the Additional Protocol, not settled by diplomacy, was to be submitted to conciliation, arbitration, or judicial settlement.

A Convention for the Maintenance, Preservation and Re-Establishment of Peace provided for consultation of the parties "for the purpose of finding and adopting methods of peaceful co-operation," when peace among the American republics is threatened, "or in the event of an international war outside America which might menace the peace of the American Republics,"—with the possibility of co-operation "in some action tending to preserve the peace of the American Continent." There was at least the conception here of pan-Americanizing the Monroe Doctrine. A Treaty on the Prevention of Controversies provided for a series of bilateral mixed commissions, between the various pairs of American republics, to devise ways and means of eliminating the causes of future difficulties or controversies. An Inter-American Treaty on Good Offices and Mediation provided rules for mediation between disputants by some eminent citizen of a third American republic. A Convention to Co-ordinate, Extend and Assure the Fulfillment of Existing Treaties between the American States pledged the signatories "to take counsel together, with full recognition of their juridical equality, as sovereign and independent states, and of their general right to individual action, when an emergency arises which affects their common interest in the maintenance of peace." In case, despite all the peace machinery, a war should break out between or among American republics, the non-belligerent parties pledged themselves "through consultation, immediately [to] endeavor to adopt in their character as neutrals a common and solidary attitude, in order to discourage or prevent the spread or prolongation of hostilities" —including such means as restrictions or prohibitions on the sale and shipment of arms, munitions and implements of war, loans or other financial help to the states in conflict,[2] "in accordance with the municipal

---

[1] Italics inserted.

[2] Before the assembly of this special Inter-American Peace Conference, the United States Congress had made a significant amendment to the neutrality act of August 31, 1935, which was later extended by acts of February 29, 1936, and May 1, 1937: it excepted from embargo of arms, ammunition and loans to belligerents, those American re-

legislation of the High Contracting Parties"—but nothing in the treaty was to affect the rights and duties of parties members at the same time of the League of Nations.[1]

In addition to the treaties for the maintenance of peace, the nations signed at Buenos Aires a Convention for the Promotion of Cultural Relations, proposed by the United States. It provided for the exchange of professors and students. This is a perfection of the traditional striving of the Pan-American movement to bridge the gap between differing cultures as a help to political solidarity.

The United States ratified these treaties and the Additional Protocol without reservation, June 29, 1937.

One of the sixty-four declarations, resolutions, tributes, recommendations and pious wishes signed at Buenos Aires was a Declaration (No. XXVII) of Principles of Inter-American Solidarity and Cooperation, to stand in the face of future wars in the Old World. Because these principles were to become the basis of collaboration in critical years to follow, we beg the reader's leave to quote the entire document as an approved definition of Pan Americanism and of continental solidarity. Note particularly the paragraph which we have italicized.

The Governments of the American Republics, having considered:
That they have a common likeness in their democratic form of government and their common ideals of peace and justice, manifested in the several Treaties and Conventions which they have signed for the purpose of constituting a purely American system tending towards the preservation of peace, the proscription of war, the harmonious development of their commerce and of their cultural aspirations in the various fields of political, economic, social, scientific, and artistic activities;
That the existence of continental interest obliges them to maintain solidarity of principles as the basis of the life of the relations of each to every other American nation;
That Pan Americanism, as a principle of American International Law, by which is understood a moral union of all of the American Republics in defence of their common interest based upon the most perfect equality and reciprocal respect for their rights of autonomy, independence and free development, requires the proclamation of principles of American International Law; and
That it is necessary to consecrate the principle of American solidarity in all non-continental conflicts, especially since those limited to the American

publics which might be at war with a non-American power, the United States being neutral. This was a sign to the world that the United States might not be as coldly neutral in such an instance as it could be toward other wars.

[1] Space is lacking to detail the other conventions and resolutions adopted at the Buenos Aires Conference.

Continent should find a peaceful solution by the means established by the
Treaties and Conventions now in force or in the instruments hereafter to
be executed,

The Inter-American Conference for the Maintenance of Peace
DECLARES:

1. That the American Nations, true to their republican institutions, proclaim their absolute juridical liberty, their unqualified respect for their
respective sovereignties and the existence of a common democracy throughout America;

2. That every act susceptible of disturbing the peace of America affects
each and every one of them, and justifies the initiation of the procedure of
consultation provided for in the Convention for the Maintenance, Preservation and Reestablishment of Peace, signed at this Conference; and

3. That the following principles are accepted by the American community
of Nations:

(a) Proscription of territorial conquest and that, in consequence, no
acquisition made through violence shall be recognized;

(b) Intervention by one State in the internal or external affairs of another State is condemned;

(c) Forcible collection of pecuniary debts is illegal; and

(d) Any difference or dispute between the American nations, whatever
its nature or origin, shall be settled by the methods of conciliation, or unrestricted arbitration, or through operation of international justice.

To be sure, this was not a treaty, but the United States, along with all
the other American republics, subscribed to it in good faith as an agreed
declaration of principles.

The Pan-American policy of the United States was thus brought into
line with the real tendencies of Pan Americanism. It is indeed exemplary
and ideal. It may not be easy to live up to in a crisis. In pledging
itself against resort to war as an instrument of national policy, and
against intervention in the internal or external affairs of any other state,
the United States was uninfluenced by the existence of $1,188,665,400 of
South American dollar bonds defaulted as to interest, out of a total of
$1,564,116,860 borrowed in the United States.[1] Huge expropriations of
property owned by nationals of the United States, in Mexico,[2] and in
Bolivia,[3] and confiscatory taxes on property in Ecuador under the
Enriquez *de facto* government following acceptance in Washington of
the Doctrine of Non-Intervention, presented denials of justice which

---

[1] See tabulations printed at end of this chapter.

One may wonder whether the debtor countries have been uninfluenced in debt policy
by the self-denial ordinances to which the United States has subscribed.

[2] See above, p. 566.

[3] In 1937 a *de facto* government in Bolivia outrageously confiscated, on the flimsiest
pretexts, property belonging to a Bolivian subsidiary owned by the Standard Oil Com-

taxed the Good Neighbor's rights and patience, but these questions have now been adjusted.

Pan Americanism in no way impeded the membership of American republics in the League of Nations and their full co-operation with it. Nor did the Pan-American peace structure, or the policy of the United States under it, brace itself against peace efforts in South America by the League of Nations, or by non-American powers. After some hesitation, the United States ungrudgingly welcomed the settlement by the League of Nations of the distressing Leticia dispute between Peru and Colombia; and the League efforts to stop the Chaco War between Bolivia and Paraguay. It co-operated with the League's embargo on arms and ammunition to the Chaco belligerents by the passage of an act of Congress (May 28, 1934) empowering the President to prohibit the sale of arms and munitions to those countries. This the President promptly did.[1] Nor has the United States stood in the way of arbitrations between an American republic and a non-American state; for example, the award in 1932 by the King of Italy to France, of Clipperton Island, about 1,300 miles west of the Panama Canal, in dispute between Mexico and that European power—not wholly dissimilar in principle to the arbitration between Venezuela and Great Britain in 1896 of their boundary.

As the European situation "deteriorated"—to use a gloomily current word of the diplomats in London and Washington—the tendency of the American republics to firm in their solidarity became more and more pronounced, with one possible exception: Argentina. Militarization of the Rhineland by Germany in March, 1936, which gave the Nazi power the lead in Europe, had introduced a note of anxiety in Pan-American relations as early as the Buenos Aires Conference. We have mentioned how the signatories to the Convention for the Maintenance of Peace agreed to consult in the event of the peace of the American republics being menaced from either inside or outside the New World. We have just quoted the Buenos Aires Declaration of December 21, 1936, of Prin-

---

pany of New Jersey and then packed the courts, and stirred up public opinion so as to deny justice to the claimants in the tribunals of the country.

In 1942 the company accepted from the Bolivian Government $1,500,000 for property valued by the claimants at $17,000,000. The petroleum formerly exploited by the company was later diverted to Argentina by means of a state-owned Argentine company.

[1] Congress, however, would not go so far as to empower the President to embargo only one belligerent, Paraguay, as the League recommended, a step resented by Latin-American nations generally. Elton Atwater has published an authoritative history of *American Regulation of Arms Export* (Carnegie Endowment for International Peace, Washington, 1941). See 193-203 for the Chaco Embargo.

ciples of Inter-American Solidarity and Cooperation *vis-à-vis* all non-continental conflicts. The forcible annexation of Austria by Germany in March, 1937, was a signal to the world of the growing might of Nazi Germany; Hitler's triumph at Munich made that unquestionable. With increasing alarm the American republics looked across the Atlantic. When the Eighth Inter-American Conference of States met at Lima in December, 1938, war in Europe seemed inevitable before the passing of another twelve months, providing Great Britain and France dared to resist the next German *Machtfrage.*

The Eighth Pan-American Conference met at Lima in December, 1938, three months after Munich, with the nations of the New World determined by a solidary neutral front to keep out of the approaching conflagration. The Lima Conference was more noteworthy for statements than for treaties. There were 112 resolutions, declarations, recommendations, tributes, etc. —a whole bookful of whereases and desires, but not a single treaty or convention requiring further ratification at home. Number 110 was a Declaration of American Principles, eight in number, introduced by Secretary of State Cordell Hull of the United States: (1) the doctrine of absolute nonintervention, (2) peaceful settlement of all international differences, (3) proscription of the use of force, (4) rule of international law, (5) respect for treaties, (6) peaceful collaboration and intellectual interchange, (7) economic reconstruction for international welfare, and (8) international co-operation. Henceforth these were to be guiding principles of the foreign policy not only of the United States but also of all the republics of the Western Hemisphere.

The Declaration of Lima, No. 109, was more than an enumeration of idealistic principles of inter-American relations. Not itself a treaty, it presumed to "improve" the process of consultation set up in the Buenos Aires treaties of 1936. Technically it was no more binding in force than any of the 111 other declarations, but in weight of content it had more force. It reaffirmed and elaborated the Declaration of the Principles of Inter-American Solidarity of Buenos Aires of 1936, quoted above. At Lima the twenty-one republics declared that, always acting independently in their individual capacities, they would consult in meetings of their Foreign Ministers, at the initiative of any one republic, for defense of their "peace, security, or territorial integrity."

This resolution gave further support to the program of solidarity which the United States had been advocating ever since Buenos Aires: consultation among the assembled Foreign Ministers whenever their common interests should require it. At Buenos Aires in 1936 the United

States proposed, but Argentina had succeeded in defeating, a treaty that would have set up a Permanent Inter-American Consultative Committee of Foreign Ministers, to meet and consult "whenever emergencies arise which affect their common interests." Now a step toward this was taken by the Declaration of Lima, a resolution which was called on to do the work of a treaty. It is not likely that the Declaration of Lima would have been ratified by all the states, particularly Argentina, had it been signed as a treaty. As a declaration no state has objected to it.

From Lima on, Pan-American diplomacy, after the fashion of United States diplomacy, began more and more to resort to resolutions and declarations which are at most multilateral executive agreements, but do not require ratification by the constitutional processes that characterize the treaty-making power in most of the republics: ratification by one or more branches of the legislative body. The growth, strength, prestige and binding force of executive agreements present an interesting study not only of constitutional history in individual states like the United States but also of inter-American relations; in fact, a multilateral executive agreement was the basis of the 1942 alliance of the United Nations in the Second World War. No sooner did consultations of Foreign Ministers begin to take place, under the provisions of the Buenos Aires treaties and the Declaration of Lima, than documents emanating from them commenced to refer to the "agreements" of Buenos Aires *and* Lima. Such official language helped exalt the power of a declaration to that of an agreement. These declarations or multilateral executive agreements have been taken over without demur by governments succeeding those which made them. Thus doth current custom speedily snatch away from senates their ancient treaty-making powers. We shall see that these consultations of Foreign Ministers soon came to have the importance, and indeed the character, features, procedure, and dignity, of full International Conferences of American States, like the periodic Pan-American Conferences (I to IX) with which we have become familiar for the years 1889-1948.[1]

The First Meeting of the Foreign Ministers was at Panama, September 23 to October 3, 1939, called for by that republic immediately after the outbreak of war in Europe. At the same time occurred in

---

[1] The Carnegie Endowment for International Peace has published all the treaties, conventions, resolutions, declarations, and other expressions of Inter-American Conferences and Meetings since the first Pan-American Conference of 1889-1890 down to and including the Havana Consultation of 1940: *The International Conferences of American States, 1889-1921* (Washington, 1931), and *Ibid., First Supplement, 1933-1940* (Washington, 1940). The latter volume also contains an enumeration of special technical con-

Washington a special session of the Congress of the United States summoned by President Franklin D. Roosevelt to revise the neutrality legislation of the United States so as to remove the embargo on the shipment to belligerents, in ships not flying the flag of the United States, of arms, ammunition and implements of warfare. The purpose of this law, of course, was to permit France and Great Britain, who controlled the seas, to get arms to defend themselves in their struggle for existence against the might of German aggression. It was the first deviation in a series of acts, to be reviewed in later chapters, that brought collapse of the neutrality of the United States by the end of 1941 under pressure of German conquests in Europe and Japanese conquests in Asia.

By impressive coincidence the Meeting at Panama took place simultaneously with the special session of Congress that revised the neutrality laws of the United States by the Neutrality Act of 1939. The purpose of the meeting on the Isthmus was to shape the neutrality policy of the American republics in a common front, with an "unanimous intention not to become involved in the European conflict." The effort of the United States was to mould that neutrality as much as possible after the policy of the United States: increasing benevolence toward Great Britain and France. The result was the Act of Panama. It was in effect a multilateral executive agreement, consisting of resolutions, declarations, and recommendations, but using very binding language, and frequently employing the imperative auxiliary *shall*, and the not uncertain word *will*.

If an inter-American declaration can modify an inter-American treaty, then the Act of Panama released the five states (United States,[1] Bolivia, Haiti, Nicaragua, and the Dominican Republic) which had ratified the Maritime Neutrality Convention signed at Havana in 1928, from the obligation to treat armed merchant ships as ships of war, and the implied obligation to allow to submarines the same rights of hospitality in neutral waters as enjoyed by surface warships. This made it possible for all the American republics to open their ports to armed merchant ships and close them to submarines, an obvious advantage to Great Britain and France over the situation which had prevailed at the outbreak of the war. President Roosevelt promptly put this into effect for the United States (November 4, 1939).

A Declaration of Panama, already almost forgotten, proclaimed as a

ferences, with synopses of their proceedings, and bibliography, and a list, with synopses, of permanent inter-American commissions and other bodies.

[1] The United States was not bound by the article on armed merchant ships, because it had attached a reservation to that when ratifying the treaty in 1932.

"measure of continental self-protection" a neutrality belt for several hundred miles out to sea from the shores of the neutral American republics and forbade any hostile act therein by any non-American belligerent nation. But the belligerents paid no more attention to the neutrality belt than the tides of the sea did to the commands of King Canute not to rise on his shores. This so-called Declaration of Panama remains only an interesting specimen in the historical museum of neutrality, armed or unarmed. More important still was another declaration of continental solidarity, and a joint suggestion for a second meeting of Foreign Ministers at Havana, October 1, 1940, or earlier, and the creation—by resolutions—for the duration of the war of an Inter-American Neutrality Committee of seven experts in international law, and an Inter-American Financial and Economic Advisory Committee.

The outstanding achievement of the Panama Meeting was a Resolution on the Transfer of Sovereignty of Geographic Regions of the Americas Held by Non-American States. We have seen that at Buenos Aires the American republics in effect had pan-Americanized one part of the Monroe Doctrine by the arrangements for consultation for common defense in case the peace of the Americas should be threatened from either inside *or outside* the New World. The resolution on the transfer of sovereignty pan-Americanized the remainder of the Doctrine, namely the Non-Transfer Principle, a principle older than the Monroe Doctrine, and generally regarded as an integral part of it since 1870.[1] Said this Declaration of Panama: "In case any geographic region of America subject to the jurisdiction of a non-American state should be obliged to change its sovereignty and there should result therefrom a danger to the security of the American continent, a consultative meeting such as the one now being held will be convoked with the urgency that the case may require."[2] This is a hemispheric landmark in the history of the Monroe Doctrine and of the foreign policy of the United States. Congress reaffirmed the principle, in a joint resolution of June 18, 1940, when the German occupation of Denmark, Norway, the Low Countries and France made the danger seem very real:

(1) That the United States would not recognize any transfer, and would not acquiesce in any attempt to transfer, any geographic region of this

[1] Dexter Perkins, *The Monroe Doctrine, 1867-1907* (Johns Hopkins University Press, 1937), 1-64.

[2] At the instance of Argentina, who claimed the Falkland Islands, occupied by Great Britain since 1832, an article was added: "It is understood that this resolution shall not apply to a change of status resulting from the settlement of questions now pending between non-American states and states of the Continent."

hemisphere from one non-American power to another non-American power; and

(2) That if such transfer or attempt to transfer should appear likely, the United States shall in addition to other measures, immediately consult with the other American republics to determine upon the steps which should be taken to safeguard their common interests.

The German conquests of European colonial powers with holdings in the New World hastened the assembly of the Second Meeting of Foreign Ministers that had been scheduled for October, 1940. It met at Havana in July. Again the American republics confirmed the "non-transfer" principle of the Monroe Doctrine. In the first place they signed a resolution which declared that whoever committed an act of aggression against one of them committed an act of aggression against all of them, in which case they would consult again at the request of any one party to negotiate measures of common defense. In the second place, they signed a declaration, the Act of Havana, which declared that if necessary they would step in and take over any colonial possession of a non-American power in the New World which might be threatened by a non-American power. They also signed a convention settling details.

The Act of Havana provided for an emergency committee, composed of one representative of each American republic, to administer the territories thus taken over, for the two-fold purpose of contributing to the security and defense of the Continent, and to the economic, political, and social progress of such regions, until the reasons requiring the provisional administration should cease to exist. Then the territories should be either organized as autonomous states under the principle of self-determination, or restored to their previous status, "whichever of these alternatives should appear to be the more practicable and just." The convention was to go into effect as soon as ratified by two-thirds of the signatories, that is, fourteen states. Fourteen states ratified by January 8, 1942.[1] The Act further stated that in case of urgent emergency, any one or more of the signatories might act first and consult later,

---

[1] The first fourteen states to ratify were, in this order: United States, Dominican Republic, Costa Rica, Brazil, Peru, Panama, El Salvador, Haiti, Guatemala, Argentina, Venezuela, Colombia, Ecuador, Honduras. The Havana Convention was one of seven Pan-American treaties and conventions, out of ninety, which Argentina had ratified to January 1, 1949. Like the Non-Transfer Declaration, of Panama, it contained a paragraph excluding application to territories or possessions which are subject of dispute or claims between European powers and one or more of the Republics of the Americas. In ratifying the treaty Argentina attached a reservation stating its understanding that the Malvinas (Falkland) Islands were a part of Argentine territory "as was stated at the Panama meeting . . . and also with reference to other southern Argentine regions." Perhaps it is not too cynical to suppose that Argentina ratified the treaty with this

either before or after the treaty went into effect. This last provision was really a Pan-American mandate to the United States by itself alone to enforce the Non-Transfer Principle if urgently necessary. It was a striking act of confidence in the Good Neighbor Policy of the United States and in the Monroe Doctrine, pruned since 1930 of the Corollary of Theodore Roosevelt.

The climax of the Pan-American movement, and with it the great test of the reformed Latin-American policy of the United States, came with Japan's attack without warning upon the Hawaiian Islands and the Philippines, December 7, 1941, and the subsequent declarations of war on the United States by Japan, Germany, Italy, et alii. Immediately the United States, and several of the other American republics, called for a consultation of the Foreign Ministers, which took place at Rio de Janeiro, January 15-28, 1942, to determine what should be done now that an act of aggression had been committed against all the Republics by an attack on one of them.

Before the Foreign Ministers assembled in the capital of Brazil for their third consultation, Cuba, Haiti, the Dominican Republic, Panama, Costa Rica, Nicaragua, Honduras, El Salvador, and Guatemala had already declared war on Japan, Germany, and Italy. Mexico, Colombia, and Venezuela had severed diplomatic relations with those three powers. As a result of the consultation five Latin-American republics—Brazil, Ecuador, Paraguay, Peru, Uruguay—broke off diplomatic relations with the Axis powers. In June, 1942, Mexico declared war. Only two Latin-American countries, Argentina and Chile, resisted the general desire, and even those two states [1] joined in a general resolution of the Foreign Ministers "recommending" the break by all, and signed the other significant resolutions and recommendations for the co-operation of all the republics in measures for common defense. These called for severance of economic and financial as well as diplomatic relations with the enemies of the United States; general economic mobilization for war and post-war purposes, including establishment of an international stabilization fund for currencies; hemispheric purging of Axis spies, saboteurs and

reservation, fancying that it gave some sort of Pan-American support to her century-old claim against Great Britain.

The six other Pan-American treaties ratified by Argentina are: the Argentine Anti-War Pact of 1933 (not at first a Pan-American treaty), two postal conventions, two sanitary conventions and a naturalization treaty. See the semi-annual tabulations by the Pan-American Union of the *Status of Treaties and Conventions Signed at the International Conferences of American States and Other Pan-American Conferences.*

[1] They refused to recognize the American republics at war as belligerents.

fifth-columnists, and co-ordination of censorship; and unification of defense measures to be pointed up in a projected meeting immediately at Washington of military and naval technicians representing the twenty-one republics.[1] Straightway the United States concluded a series of bilateral lend-lease agreements with the American Republics, those who had declared war and those who had broken off relations, opening to them such supplies as could be afforded, and delivered, from the Arsenal of Democracy. In short, the Rio Meeting made plans for a non-shooting war against the Axis powers by the Latin-American states, belligerent or nonbelligerent, with the United States in effect the dynamic co-ordinator and economic and military supporter of all. Final success of the Good Neighbor Policy, in principle as well as in practice, was testified by a Rio resolution extolling it as a "norm of American international law."

Facing the heaviest threats of all their independent history, the American republics and their peoples huddled together instinctively under the military wings of the Good Neighbor of the North. They made exclusively available to the United Nations vitally important war materials. They afforded to the United States highly important and useful temporary[2] naval and air bases for controlling strategic coastal waters. This made possible a "corridor of victory" for the flight across the South Atlantic of American men and arms to the African, European, and Asiatic fronts. In return the fighting Republic made available to the Latin-American belligerents and allies (all except recalcitrant Argentina) a golden flood of $500,000,000 ($10,000,000 of which was distributed *after hostilities were over*) in lend-lease for military equipment and economic support of the war,[3] not to mention gigantic purchases ($2,500,000,000) of raw materials for war purposes, and $431,116,968 (net) loans by the United States Government, 1940-1947, after defaults by Latin-American governments (excepting Argentina) on external dollar bonds had dried up their private credit abroad.[4] In addition the

---

[1] The first meeting of the Inter-American Defense Board convened in Washington, March 30, 1942.

[2] All bases were returned to their respective sovereigns after the war. In the case of Ecuador the United States tried to purchase continuing rights to bases in the Galapagos Islands. Failing to do so, it returned both the Galapagos base, and the Salinas base on the mainland under arrangements permitting United States troops to remain there for the purpose of training Ecuadoreans in the use of the installations.

[3] See tabulations in *Twenty-Fifth Report to Congress on Lend-Lease Operations* (Department of State Publication 3064, Washington, 1948).

[4] See Charts of Status of External Dollar Bonds of Latin-American Governments, and of United States Government Credits to Latin-American Governments, at end of this chapter.

United States Government contributed as actual gifts a total of nearly $80,000,000 to all and sundry republics of Latin America.[1]

Before the war ended all of the nations of the New World (including even unfriendly Argentina at the last moment) declared war on the enemies of the United States.[2]   Brazil, in addition to extensive naval patrols, sent a division of troops to the Mediterranean; they engaged in heroic combat on the Italian front, and captured an entire German division.   Before the Pacific war was over Mexico sent an air-squadron to the Far East.   Mexican and Cuban navies helped to clear the Gulf of Mexico of German submarines.

Argentina, ruled by a military dictatorship aping those of Europe, held aloof until the fag-end of the war, hoping for and expecting a victory of the Axis powers.   Only when the jig was manifestly up for Hitler's Germany did the Argentine Government scramble to get in on good neighborhood in the Western Hemisphere, begrudging even then the military and moral ascendancy of the United States, a nation "alien" to Latin-American culture and politics.   The Argentine Government safely if unheroically declared war on Germany and Japan (March 27, 1945).   Even then her Government furnished aid and comfort to the enemy.[3]   Argentina was allowed to sign (April 4, 1945) the Act of Chapultepec, already signed by the other American republics in Mexico City, March 3, 1945, a declaration (not a treaty needing ratification) [4] for temporary alliance during the remaining days of the war.

At San Francisco, on June 26, 1945, all the American republics became charter members of the United Nations Organization.

It remained to forge inter-American solidarity of war into a pact for future defense of the Western Hemisphere: one for all and all for one. Acting under Article 51 of the United Nations Charter,[5] nineteen of the

[1] *Foreign Assets and Liabilities of the United States,* Committee Print for Committee on Finance, House of Representatives, 80th Cong., 1st Sess. (Washington, 1948), p. 36.

[2] *The Memoirs of Cordell Hull* (New York, 1948), II, 1377-1409, describe American diplomacy with Argentina, "The Bad Neighbor."

[3] As established in the United States "bluebook" issued on the eve of the Argentine national election in February, 1946: *Consultation among the American Republics with Respect to the Argentine Situation* (Department of State Publication No. 2473, Washington, 1946).

[4] Argentina had not ratified any of the inter-American treaties for inter-American peace and solidarity, except the Saavedra-Lamas Anti-War Pact of 1933.

[5] "Nothing in the present Charter shall impair the inherent right of individual or collective self-defense if an armed attack occurs against a Member of the United Nations, until the Security Council has taken the measures necessary to maintain international peace and security. . . ."

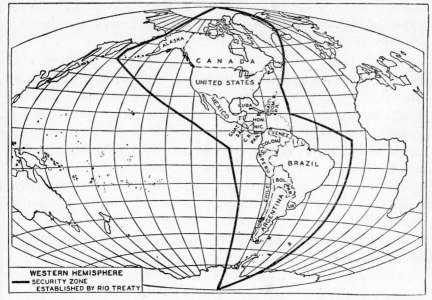

Map 35. Regional Security Zone of Western Hemisphere as Defined by Treaty of
Rio de Janeiro, 1947.[1]

American republics (all except Nicaragua[2] and Ecuador) met in a
special Inter-American Conference for the Maintenance of Continental
Peace and Security, and concluded an Inter-American Treaty of Reciprocal Assistance—the Pact of Rio—signed at the Brazilian capital
September 2, 1947 (effective December 3, 1948, following required
ratification by two-thirds of the signatories). The essential articles of
this epoch-making alliance are the first and second:

1. The High Contracting Parties agree that an armed attack by any state
against an American State shall be construed as an armed attack against all
the American States, and consequently, each one of the said Contracting
Parties undertakes to assist in meeting the attack in the exercise of the inherent right of individual or collective self-defense recognized by Article 51
of the Charter of the United Nations.

2. On the request of the State or States directly attacked and until the
decision of the Organ of Consultation of the Inter-American System, each
one of the Contracting Parties may determine the immediate measures which
it may individually adopt in fulfilment of the obligation contained in the
preceding paragraph and in accordance with the principle of continental

[1] Reproduced from *Major Problems of United States Foreign Policy, 1949-1950,* p. 263,
with permission of Brookings Institution.
[2] Nicaragua later signed and ratified the treaty.

solidarity. The Organ of Consultation [1] shall meet without delay for the purpose of examining those measures and agreeing upon the measures of a collective character that should be adopted.

Thus the treaty left it to each of the signatories to determine what measures it would adopt pending decision as to future joint measures by a two-thirds majority of the Members of the Pact. No more could one state, like Argentina, paralyze joint and solid action by holding out against the wishes of the majority.

How about another equally great danger not constituting immediate armed attack by another state: such as a communist revolution, like those which had occurred in Greece and China after the Second World War, inspired and abetted by an outside power? In that case the parties agree to meet immediately in special consultation and decide what to do.

The Pact of Rio of 1947 became a prototype for the North Atlantic Alliance of 1949. [2]

The most recent efforts in inter-American organization for peace and solidarity in the World of Columbus that this History can record, were the treaties signed at the Ninth International Conference of American States at Bogotá in 1948 under tragic circumstances (an attempted revolution in the capital of Colombia that caused considerable loss of life and great damage to the city).

First was a Charter for the Organization of American States, placing Pan Americanism at last on a treaty basis, within the framework of the United Nations. [3] Under the Charter the old Pan-American Union at Washington is the central and permanent organ and general secretariat of the Organization. Its governing Council consists of a representative from each one of the member republics, who does not need to be the diplomatic representative of that government to the United States. The Director of the Union [4] becomes Secretary General of the Organization, elected by the Council for a ten-year term, not re-eligible or to be succeeded by a person of the same nationality. The Charter specifies the nature and purposes of the Inter-American Organization; its

[1] I.e., a special meeting of the Foreign Ministers of the American Republics, to be called by the Pan American Union at the request of any one of the American Republics.

[2] See below, p. 926.

[3] M. Margaret Ball in a scholarly dissertation analyzed *The Problem of Inter-American Organization* as it had developed up to 1944 (Stanford University Press, 1944). Manuel S. Canyes has described the relationship of the Charter of the Organization of American States to that of the United Nations (Pan American Union, Washington, 1949).

[4] Mr. Alberto Lleras of Colombia was elected March 11, 1947, by the Governing Council of the Union, for a term of ten years, to succeed Dr. Leo S. Rowe, deceased.

ORGANIZATION OF AMERICAN STATES

The International Organization of the 21 American Republics established by the Charter signed at the Ninth International Conference of American States, Bogotá, Colombia, 1948.

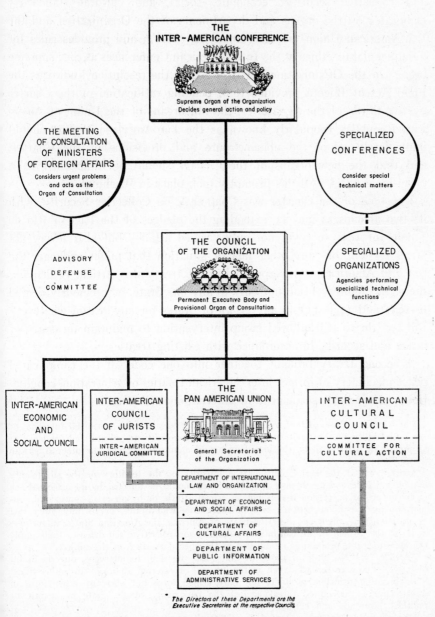

THE INTER-AMERICAN CONFERENCE

Supreme Organ of the Organization
Decides general action and policy

THE MEETING OF CONSULTATION OF MINISTERS OF FOREIGN AFFAIRS

Considers urgent problems and acts as the Organ of Consultation

SPECIALIZED CONFERENCES

Consider special technical matters

ADVISORY DEFENSE COMMITTEE

THE COUNCIL OF THE ORGANIZATION

Permanent Executive Body and Provisional Organ of Consultation

SPECIALIZED ORGANIZATIONS

Agencies performing specialized technical functions

INTER-AMERICAN ECONOMIC AND SOCIAL COUNCIL

INTER-AMERICAN COUNCIL OF JURISTS

INTER-AMERICAN JURIDICAL COMMITTEE

THE PAN AMERICAN UNION

General Secretariat of the Organization

DEPARTMENT OF INTERNATIONAL LAW AND ORGANIZATION

DEPARTMENT OF ECONOMIC AND SOCIAL AFFAIRS

DEPARTMENT OF CULTURAL AFFAIRS

DEPARTMENT OF PUBLIC INFORMATION

DEPARTMENT OF ADMINISTRATIVE SERVICES

INTER-AMERICAN CULTURAL COUNCIL

COMMITTEE FOR CULTURAL ACTION

The Directors of these Departments are the Executive Secretaries of the respective Councils

Courtesy of Mr. Alberto Lleras, Secretary General

781

principles; the fundamental rights and duties of states; the duty of pacific settlement of international disputes; inter-American solidarity and collective security; economic, social, and cultural standards; elaborates on the organs and departments of the Organization and the Pan American Union (see accompanying chart); and provides rules for quinquennial meetings of the Inter-American Conferences as the "supreme organ" of the Organization. Article XL of the resolution known as the Final Act of Bogotá provided that, pending ratification of the Charter by two-thirds of the signatories, the old organs of the Union of American Republics (popularly known as the Pan American Union) should immediately adopt the nomenclature and provisions of the Charter, and that the new organs of the Charter should be established on a provisional basis. All this promptly took place in Washington.

Keystone of the Charter was Chapter V on Collective Security, with its two articles 24 and 25, extending the pledges of the Pact of Rio de Janeiro of 1947 to cover not only "armed attack" but also "every act of aggression" or "any other fact or situation that might endanger the peace of America."[1] Incorporated in the treaty was Article 15 denying the right of intervention not only to any *one* State, as previously denied in 1933 and 1936, but to any *group* of States for any reason whatever.[2] But Article 19 still allowed group intervention to maintain measures of peace and security in accordance with existing treaties.[3]

A second treaty brought together into one code all the complicated peace machinery of former inter-American treaties of arbitration, conciliation, and judicial settlement of international disputes.

[1] Article 24: "Every act of aggression by a State against the territorial integrity or the inviolability of the territory or against the sovereignty or political independence of an American State shall be considered an act of aggression against the other American States."

Article 25: "If the inviolability or the integrity of the territory or the sovereignty or political independence of any American State should be affected by an armed attack or by an act of aggression that is not an armed attack, or by an extra-continental conflict, or by a conflict between two or more American States, or by any other fact or situation that might endanger the peace of America, the American States, in furtherance of the principles of continental solidarity or collective self-defense, shall apply the measures and procedures established in the special treaties on the subject."

[2] Article 15: "No State or group of States has the right to intervene, directly or indirectly, for any reason whatever, in the internal or external affairs of any other State. The foregoing principle prohibits not only armed force but also any other form of interference or attempted threat against the personality of the State or against its political, economic and cultural elements."

[3] Article 19: "Measures adopted for the maintenance of peace and security in accordance with existing treaties do not constitute a violation of the principles set forth in articles 15 and 17."

Article 17 stipulates that the territory of a State is "inviolable."

A third lengthy treaty stipulated, within the framework of the United Nations Charter, principles of economic co-operation for the well-being of all the American republics.

There were also two conventions on the rights of women, political and civil.[1]

These treaties, epoch-making for the inter-American regional movement, adjusted to the United Nations, await (1950) ratification by two-thirds of the signatories, to enter into effect.

Nothing was more hopeful, in disheartening post-Potsdam years of disillusion and world crisis, than the peaceful structure of inter-American organization and solidarity based on equal sovereignty, juridical equality, non-intervention, territorial inviolability, co-operation for the general welfare, peaceful settlement of inter-American disputes, and consultation for common defense on the agreed premise that an attack on one is an attack on all.

[1] The United States did not sign the last-named convention on civil rights for women, that subject not being constitutionally a power of the Federal Government.

PUBLICLY OFFERED DOLLAR BONDS ISSUED OR GUARANTEED BY LATIN-AMERICAN GOVERNMENTS OR POLITICAL SUBDIVISIONS THEREOF AS OF DECEMBER 31, 1934[1]

Country	National Governments Outstanding	National Governments In Default as to Interest	States, Provinces, Depts. Outstanding	States, Provinces, Depts. In Default as to Interest	Municipalities Outstanding	Municipalities In Default as to Interest	Government Guaranteed Corporate Issues[2] Outstanding	Government Guaranteed Corporate Issues[2] In Default as to Interest	Totals Outstanding	Totals In Default as to Interest[5]	Default as to Sinking Fund Only
Argentina	250,904,500	......	87,424,900	81,725,900	22,960,000	10,329,500	......	......	361,289,400	92,055,400	4,222,500
Bolivia	59,422,000	59,422,000	......	......	......	......	......	......	59,422,000	59,422,000	......
Brazil	144,672,500[3]	144,672,500	142,558,800	119,296,800	66,944,000	66,944,000	......	......	354,175,300	330,913,300	23,262,000
Chile	175,404,000	175,404,000	......	......	20,459,500	20,459,500	68,745,000	68,745,000	264,608,500	264,608,500	......
Colombia	51,223,500	51,223,500	59,989,500	59,989,500	22,145,900	22,145,900	10,296,500	10,296,500	143,655,400	143,655,400	......
Costa Rica	8,781,000[3]	8,781,000	......	......	......	......	......	......	8,781,000	8,781,000	......
Cuba	91,878,100	40,000,000	......	......	......	......	......	......	91,878,100	40,000,000	51,878,100
Dominican Republic	16,292,000	......	......	......	......	......	......	......	16,292,000	......	16,292,500[4]
El Salvador	12,619,300	12,619,300	......	......	......	......	......	......	12,619,300	12,619,300	......
Guatemala	2,214,000	2,214,000	......	......	......	......	......	......	2,214,000	2,214,000	......
Haiti	10,511,360	......	......	......	......	......	......	......	10,511,360	......	......
Mexico	62,037,500	62,037,500	3,252,000	3,252,000	......	......	......	......	65,289,500	65,289,500	......
Panama	15,214,000	11,356,000	......	......	416,000	......	3,097,500	3,097,500	18,727,500	14,453,500	416,000
Peru	87,210,000	87,210,000	1,189,000	1,189,000	2,887,000	2,887,000	......	......	91,286,000	91,286,000	......
Uruguay	52,947,500	52,947,500	......	......	10,420,000	10,420,000	......	......	63,367,500	63,367,500	......
TOTAL	$1,041,331,260	707,887,300	294,414,200	265,453,200	146,232,400	133,185,900	82,139,000	83,139,000	1,564,116,860	1,188,665,400	96,071,100

[1] "Latin-American Dollar Debts," *Commercial Pan America*, No. 37 (Pan American Union, January, 1935).
[2] Includes only direct guarantees.
[3] Exclusive of bonds issued to fund interest.
[4] The Dominican Republic has made a proposal to bondholders concerning readjustment of the sinking fund which has been approved by the Foreign Bondholders Protective Council, Inc.
[5] Includes defaults in interest and in interest and sinking fund

STATUS OF SERVICE (INTEREST, SINKING FUND, AND PRINCIPAL) ON LATIN-AMERICAN DOLLAR BONDS (PUBLICLY OFFERED) ISSUED OR GUARANTEED BY GOVERNMENTS OR POLITICAL SUBDIVISIONS THEREOF, AS OF DECEMBER 31, 1949.

Country	Issued	Outstanding	Receiving Full Service Int. and S.F.	Adjusted Service Available	In Default as to Int. and S.F.	In Default as to Principal	Maturities Extended
Argentina	Retired	....	....	....	....	....	....
Bolivia	68,400,000	59,422,000	....	....	59,422,000	23,368,000	28,667,550 c
Brazil	391,013,145	162,252,455	....	162,252,455	....	3,457,800 b	11,958,000 c
Chile	296,592,000	119,547,000	....	119,547,000	....	645,000 b	14,457,300 c
Colombia	169,289,960	78,480,400 a	....	78,480,400	....	14,293,800 b	....
Costa Rica	11,853,668	8,103,951	....	....	8,103,951	1,589,000	....
Cuba	93,506,100	74,219,700	5,443,900	68,468,800	307,000 d	307,000 d	39,910,000 c
Dominican Republic	Retired	....	....	....	....	....	....
Ecuador	14,437,800	12,262,700	....	....	12,262,700	12,262,700	....
El Salvador	18,515,400	7,463,800	....	7,463,800	....	241,500 b	1,262,000
Guatemala	1,749,000	478,000	478,000	....	....	....	....
Haiti	Retired	....	....	....	....	....	....
Mexico	381,782,429 e	240,199,716 e	....	24,358,746	215,840,970	60,188,609	....
Panama	16,941,600	15,099,350	3,789,850	11,309,500	....	....	....
Peru	95,079,600	71,428,100	....	68,541,100	2,887,000	386,500 b	640,500
Uruguay	67,757,000	44,480,300	....	44,480,300	....	242,000 b	4,847,500
TOTAL	1,626,917,702	893,437,472	9,711,750	584,902,101	298,823,621	116,980,909	101,742,850

This table includes outstanding funding bonds, but excludes outstanding convertible scrip.

a Includes $3,456,000 principal amount, equivalent to 75 per cent (less unconverted scrip) of the old nonguaranteed corporate bank bonds of Colombia which have been exchanged for a National issue in accordance with the June 25, 1942, debt plan, without adjustment for retirements.

b In these countries debt plans are currently in effect, and bonds in default as to principal may have their maturities extended, if assented to the plans.

c In these cases it has not been possible, from the data available, to exclude those new bonds which were issued in exchange for formerly matured bonds in default as to principal, and which have been retired in accordance with the terms of the exchange plan, since they have been included along with a number of other issues exchanged for a single new issue of bonds; hence the acceptances to a particular debt plan without adjustments for retirements have been used.

d The Exchange Agent reports that $217,000 of these bonds have been exchanged (in Havana, Cuba) since the close of the debt plan of 1937 on June 30, 1941; these bonds are shown as uncanceled and outstanding on the records of the New York Fiscal Agent.

e Includes railways expropriated in 1937.

Source: Foreign Bondholders Protective Council, Inc. Report 1946 through 1949.

LOANS (IN DOLLARS) BY THE UNITED STATES GOVERNMENT (EXCLUSIVE OF LEND LEASE, $501,459,343.92) TO THE AMERICAN REPUBLICS, JULY 1, 1940, THROUGH JUNE 30, 1947

(EIB = Export-Import Bank. RFC = Reconstruction Finance Corporation. ODS = Office Defense Supplies. State = Department of State. Treas. = Treasury Department.)

	Commitments				Utilizations			Collections		Outstanding
	Gross	Cancellations and expirations	Net	Unutilized	Total	Direct	By agent banks	Principal	Interest and commissions	
American Republics	1,085,411,260	409,222,418	676,188,842	245,071,874	431,116,968	247,234,087	183,882,881	183,039,948	27,186,149	248,077,020
EIB	1,082,100,160	408,758,735	673,341,425	245,071,874	428,269,551	244,386,670	183,882,881	181,387,605	27,168,722	246,881,946
ODS	924,627	463,683	460,944	.....	460,944	460,944	.....	377,242	17,427	83,702
USCC	2,138,441	.....	2,138,441	.....	2,138,441	2,138,441	.....	1,071,134	.....	1,067,307
State	248,032	.....	248,032	.....	248,032	248,032	.....	203,967	.....	44,065
Argentina (EIB)	93,690,000	93,090,000	600,000	210,000	390,000	390,000	.....	390,000	28,376	.....
Bolivia	23,080,643	48,250	23,032,393	9,935,000	13,097,393	13,097,393	.....	3,499,577	201,116	9,597,816
EIB	20,678,004	48,250	20,629,754	9,935,000	10,694,754	10,694,754	.....	2,129,754	201,116	8,565,000
ODS	300,000	.....	300,000	.....	300,000	300,000	.....	300,000	.....	.....
USCC	2,102,639	.....	2,102,639	.....	2,102,639	2,102,639	.....	1,069,823	.....	1,032,816
Brazil	270,463,827	86,663,717	183,800,110	47,615,705	136,184,405	70,767,328	65,417,077	46,516,503	7,484,890	89,667,902
EIB	270,433,215	86,663,717	183,769,498	47,615,705	136,153,793	70,736,716	65,417,077	46,516,503	7,484,890	89,637,290
USCC	30,612	.....	30,612	.....	30,612	30,612	.....	.....	.....	30,612
Chile (EIB)	89,756,008	6,991,378	82,764,630	47,538,294	35,226,336	7,525,228	27,701,108	17,061,865	2,021,825	18,164,471
Colombia (EIB)	50,243,456	907,154	49,336,302	14,864,714	34,471,588	10,947,974	23,523,614	15,459,320	2,462,611	19,012,268
Costa Rica (EIB)	8,823,000	1,463,393	7,359,607	100,000	7,259,607	7,259,607	.....	456,632	1,178,482	6,802,975
Cuba (EIB)	90,306,535	26,888,062	63,418,473	7,310,000	56,108,473	30,070,973	26,037,500	43,887,348	1,044,467	12,221,125
Dominican Republic (EIB)	3,300,000	16,068	3,283,932	.....	3,283,932	3,000,000	283,932	1,652,979	447,013	1,630,953
Ecuador	18,194,817	559,513	17,635,304	10,230,000	7,405,304	7,405,304	.....	1,011,645	760,348	6,393,659
EIB	17,565,000	95,830	17,469,170	10,230,000	7,239,170	7,239,170	.....	933,092	742,921	6,306,078
ODS	624,627	463,683	160,944	.....	160,944	160,944	.....	77,242	17,427	83,702
USCC	5,190	.....	5,190	.....	5,190	5,190	.....	1,311	.....	3,879
Haiti (EIB)	13,350,000	2,670,000	10,680,000	.....	10,680,000	10,680,000	.....	3,449,000	1,985,050	7,231,000
Honduras (EIB)	2,700,000	1,700,000	1,000,000	.....	1,000,000	.....	1,000,000	422,750	30,320	577,250
Mexico	154,287,315	5,993,309	148,294,006	79,701,623	68,592,383	48,714,046	19,878,337	14,392,105	2,468,919	54,200,278
EIB	154,069,446	5,993,309	148,076,137	79,701,623	68,374,514	48,496,177	19,878,337	14,205,117	2,468,919	54,169,397
State	217,869	.....	217,869	.....	217,869	217,869	.....	186,988	.....	30,881
Nicaragua (EIB)	5,235,000	585,000	4,650,000	.....	4,650,000	4,000,000	650,000	2,360,500	701,857	2,289,500
Panama (EIB)	4,500,000	2,012,296	2,487,704	.....	2,487,704	2,487,704	.....	2,487,704	207,791	.....
Paraguay (EIB)	7,800,000	1,600,000	6,200,000	.....	6,200,000	6,000,000	200,000	1,298,550	926,386	4,901,450
Peru (EIB)	37,450,000	37,000,000	450,000	73,494	376,506	376,506	.....	28,238	7,231	348,268
Salvador (EIB)	1,726,000	250,000	1,476,000	.....	1,476,000	1,476,000	.....	218,628	167,285	1,257,372
Uruguay	43,615,163	29,211,125	14,404,038	2,593,044	11,810,994	109,038	11,701,956	227,726	702,258	11,583,268
EIB	43,585,000	29,211,125	14,373,875	2,593,044	11,780,831	78,875	11,701,956	210,747	702,258	11,570,084
State	30,163	.....	30,163	.....	30,163	30,163	.....	16,979	.....	13,184
Venezuela (EIB)	42,551,000	36,806,922	5,744,078	.....	5,744,078	3,045,900	2,698,178	3,715,578	581,236	2,028,500
Unclassified	124,378,496	74,766,231	49,612,265	25,000,000	24,612,265	20,044,815	4,567,450	24,451,400	3,757,794	160,865

CHAPTER XL

CANADA THE COUPLING PIN OF ANGLO-AMERICAN RELATIONS

(1914-1950)

STRICTLY speaking, the Dominion of Canada is not a republic like the other American nations. It is a democratic kingdom which has the same king, today George VI, as Great Britain, Australia, New Zealand, and South Africa, and is an independent member of the British Commonwealth of Nations. But by history, culture, religion, economy, and general ways of life it has been more closely associated with the United States than with any other foreign nation. So unrestricted and so natural have been the freedom of movement and interplay of populations,[1] that Canadians and Americans do not think of themselves as foreign to each other; rather they consider themselves independent of each other.

The United States has always scrupulously respected Canada's independence. At various periods in North American history, always coinciding with economic depressions, there has developed a strong—but progressively weaker—minority in Canada which has desired annexation or at least commercial union with the United States. And before the First World War there was always an influential minority in the United States —surviving apostles of Manifest Destiny—who had been prophets and advocates of the peaceful and mutually voluntary union of the two countries. We have seen that they included such men as William Henry Seward, Charles Sumner, Hamilton Fish, Ulysses S. Grant, Henry Cabot Lodge, Theodore Roosevelt. Even so, it is doubtful whether at any time an appeal by Canada for annexation would have been accepted by a majority of the United States Congress. Certainly not before the Civil War, because the southern states feared being overwhelmed by anti-slavery territory; they wanted Cuba instead, where, reciprocally, they were opposed by the northern states who feared the growing power of slavery. Remember that in 1866 when the United States had a million veteran bayonets and a first-class navy, no step toward Canada was made; on the contrary, the army and navy were demobilized.

---

[1] See the late Marcus Lee Hansen's *The Mingling of the Canadian and American Peoples* (Canadian-American Series, Carnegie Endowment for International Peace, Yale University Press, 1940).

President Grant and Secretary Fish hoped that Canada, deprived of reciprocity after 1866, would seek and secure independence, and afterwards seek and secure annexation. British statesmanship by the North American Act of 1867, creating the self-governing Dominion within the then British Empire, contented Canada [1] just as British statesmanship in 1774, by the Quebec Act, had kept Canada out of the American Revolution. Recurring periods of prosperity lifted Canada's economic head above water handsomely, assisted from time to time by imperial commercial preferences.[2] As time went on, both nations became addicted to high protective tariffs: the United States under the long reign of the Republican Party; Canada under the continuing control of the Liberal Party. By 1910 high tariffs and other forces of domestic discontent in both countries threatened the parties in power. President Taft turned to Canadian reciprocity—in the form of an executive agreement to be made good by agreed legislation in both countries—as a means of offsetting tariff reform sentiment in the United States and propitiating the press (by duty-free newsprint paper) in favor of himself and his party. Prime Minister Laurier accepted it as a means of restoring personal and party prestige by getting free entry into the United States market for important Canadian exports. Imprudent political bombast in both countries camouflaged reciprocity with the issue, the bogey, of annexation: reciprocity would be a step toward ultimate organic union. The issue ruined both the Republicans in the United States and the Liberals in Canada. After 1911 Canada became a confirmed protectionist nation.[3]

So strong have been the forces of tariff protection in the United States and the jealousy of sections, that it is extremely doubtful whether any enthusiastic minority, even since the Civil War, could have got a treaty of annexation through the Senate, had Great Britain been willing to negotiate one; or a joint resolution through Congress, if the Canadian Parliament had voted annexation on its part. Since the First World War annexation has had no political following in Canada. The Canadians do not want it. Neither do their neighbors to the south.

Canada established a legation at Washington in 1927, setting up direct diplomatic relations independent of Great Britain.[4] As such she con-

[1] Above, p. 382.

[2] Donald Frederick Warner, *The Movement for the Annexation of Canada to the United States, 1849-1893* (unprinted doctoral dissertation, 1940, Yale University Library).

[3] L. Ethan Ellis, *Reciprocity, 1911: a Study in Canadian-American Relations* (Canadian-American Series, Carnegie Endowment for International Peace, Yale University Press, 1939).

[4] Other former parts of the British Empire to set up independent legations or embassies at Washington were: Irish Free State, 1924; Union of South Africa, 1929;

tinued the historic role which she had played as a part of the British Empire. As a member of the British Commonwealth of Nations (confirmed by the Statute of Westminster, 1931) she has continued her work for peace between the United States and Great Britain, as illustrated by the last hundred years of Anglo-American relations.

During the nineteenth century the British navy was the greatest power in international politics, in both the Old World and the New. It not only carried an army of invasion to Washington and New Orleans in 1814; it also stood in the way of any conceivable intervention of Europe to restore Spain's sovereignty over her revolted colonies in 1823. But it was not principally the British navy that preserved the independence and territorial integrity of the Latin-American states in that really happy century of British maritime power. Remember the interventions in Argentina and Uruguay, and in Central America; remember also that the British navy helped at least to escort Napoleon III's army to Mexico, and did nothing to stop French intervention in that republic nor Spanish intervention in Santo Domingo, in 1861-1865. If any nations, other than the Latin-American states themselves, can be credited with preserving the republican liberties of the New World, certainly in North America since 1823, and later in South America too, they are the United States and Canada: the United States because of the Monroe Doctrine and in our times the Good Neighbor Policy; Canada because she has always been in effect a hostage for the benevolent conduct of the British navy toward the United States and the Monroe Doctrine.

At no time during the nineteenth century could the United States have withstood a challenge of the British navy on the seas; but at no time since, say 1850, certainly since 1866, could Great Britain have defended Canada against an overland movement by the United States on the long exposed flank of her Empire. Great Britain was cautious about forcing mediation during the Civil War of 1861-1865, because of the military strength of the United States and the consequent danger to Canada in case of war. War between the United States and Great Britain at any time since 1866 not only would have been genuinely "unthinkable," but also would have meant the loss of Canada to the Empire, either by conquest or by secession. Canada's successful pressure on British foreign policy on the eve of the Washington Conference to abandon the Anglo-

Australia, 1940; New Zealand, 1943; India, 1946; Pakistan, 1947; Burma, 1947; Ceylon, 1948.

Japanese Alliance, to choose the United States instead of Japan as a friend, shows how she read her own vital interests in that crisis.[1]

Canada has always been instinctively conscious of this position of hostage for the good conduct of Great Britain toward the United States. She has been aware of her terrible alternatives in case of any Anglo-American conflict. If only for this reason—among many other pleasanter ones—she has become the natural link of friendship, geographically, politically, economically, and culturally, between the two great English-speaking powers.[2] No nation has ever had a more pacific, a more praise-worthy, or a more easily successful role. Let it be understood in speaking of the historic role of Canada as the lynch-pin, or coupling-pin, of Anglo-American amity, that the Great Dominion under the control of any other imperialistic power of the Old World, say Germany or Russia, would have been not a shield of peace but rather a base for the invasion of the Continental Republic.

The Monroe Doctrine has always applied to Canada in spirit if not in word. Even in word it has covered Canada through the Non-Transfer principle. From the very nature of North American security Canada as a part of the British Empire, or later as a member of the British Commonwealth of Nations, could be fairly certain that she would have the ulti-mate military protection of the United States in any war which she en-tered, as soon as that war came to threaten her own homeland. Such a threat would be a menace to the security of the United States, too. Thus Canada and, through Canada, Great Britain ineluctably have had a cer-tain control over the foreign policy of the United States. And because the security of the Latin-American republics rests in the last analysis on the United States, Canada and her relative nations have an ultimate influence on the destiny of the whole New World, as illustrated by the World Wars of the twentieth century. So does the Dominion of Canada bind together the international politics of Europe and the Western World.

From this analysis it seems that Canada is as important to the diplo-macy of the United States as all the Latin-American republics put to-gether. The reader of this History may realize that Canadian-American

---

[1] See above, p. 691.

Professor J. Bartlett Brebner has explained the problem of "Canada, the Anglo-Japanese Alliance, and the Washington Conference," in *Pol. Sci. Quar.*, L (March, 1935), 45-58.

[2] F. H. Soward, J. F. Parkinson, N. A. M. Mackensie, and T. W. L. MacDermot have analysed the position of *Canada in World Affairs, the Pre-War Years* (Canadian Institute of International Affairs, Toronto, 1941).

relations [1] have occupied almost as much space in a work of this scope as Latin-American relations, despite the greater variety of the latter and their more difficult nature. If Canada, because of her relationship both to Great Britain and to the United States, has such an influence on the destiny of the New World, why then has she not been a member of the Pan American Union?

During the First World War, in 1916, it had been the idea of Colonel House to commit the British Empire, on behalf of Canada, to the Pan-American Pact which President Wilson and he were then preparing. He suggested as much indirectly to the British Government, through Sir Edward Grey, then recently resigned from the Foreign Office and serving as a member of Parliament. "This, I told him, was one way [for Great Britain] to bring about a sympathetic alliance not only with the United States but with the entire Western Hemisphere. In my opinion it was an opportunity not to be disregarded, and its tendency would be to bring together an influence which could control the peace of the world." [2]

Grey thought it should be done, and agreed to try to arrange an interpellation in the House of Commons on the subject. But the Government demurred on the ground that "it would be somewhat hasty to have the question asked in the House of Commons, and an answer given just now, about the Pan-American Pact." Bonar Law, Secretary of State for the Colonies, cabled the Canadian Prime Minister and promised that "the matter will be brought out at the time considered most opportune." The intervention of the United States in the First World War, and President Wilson's taking over into the Covenant of the League of Nations his principles for the proposed Pan-American Pact, caused this suggestion to be lost from sight. Canada has evidenced relatively little interest in the Pan-American system, preferring to attach all her aspirations for peace to the League of Nations and the British Commonwealth of Nations,[3] and, more latterly, to the United Nations and the North Atlantic regional arrangement.

Canada's isolation from the Pan-American movement has suited perfectly the Latin-American policy of the United States. As long as the slender umbilical cord still remained which binds Canada to a non-Ameri-

---

[1] Cf. Chapters I, II, V, VI, IX, X, XV, XVI, XVII, XXII, XXIII, XXXVIII, XL, versus III, V, VI, VIII, XI, XII, XIII, XIV, XIX, XXII, XXIV, XXVIII, XXIX, XXX, XXXVIII, XXXIX.

[2] Intimate Papers, op. cit., I, 228-230.

[3] John P. Humphrey in a useful study of The Inter-American System, a Canadian View (Canadian Institute of International Affairs, Toronto, 1942), concluded that Canada should co-operate fully and wholeheartedly in an organized international American community.

can political group through the person of the British Crown, the Department of State resisted any movement to bring Canada into the purely American family, as some Latin-American spokesmen have thought of doing possibly as a fancied make-weight against the United States in inter-American councils. Such opposition has now ceased. Membership in the Organization of American Nations awaits Canada's convenience.

A word must now be said about purely Canadian-American diplomatic relations. They have been comparatively tranquil, like the relations of the Scandinavian nations. The heavy investment of United States capital in Canada—approximately $5,150,000,000 [1] as of January 1, 1948, more than in any other foreign land (and safer)—has created no political problems, has led to no cry of "economic imperialism." The highly important questions of boundaries, fisheries, commerce, and navigation have already occupied the reader of previous pages of this volume. We have left to this place the subject of the regulation of waterways along the ocean-to-ocean frontier. It affords a distinctly Canadian-American contribution to the system of collective security in the New World.

The regulation of Canadian-American international waterways through commissions goes back to the period of British administration of Canadian foreign affairs, which continued until 1927. Joint commissions have been a favorite Anglo-American device for the settlement of Canadian-American questions. We have noted several such commissions which determined the arbitration of disputes over boundaries and fisheries. The Treaty of Washington of 1871, which involved many Canadian questions, was worked out by a joint commission of Canadians, Americans and Englishmen. In 1899 another joint commission, of ten members, similar to the one of 1871, met at Washington and at Quebec to draw up a treaty for the adjustment of the Alaska boundary controversy and for the settlement of all outstanding questions, among them the regulation of waterways. Disagreement on the boundary question terminated the labors of this commission, without any disposition of the other questions. Following the settlement of the Alaska boundary question by the joint commission created in 1903, the remaining significant diplomatic issues between the United States and Canada were the North Atlantic fisheries controversy, the dispute over title to little islands in Passamaquoddy Bay, and the various questions constantly arising in regard to the common waterways along the northern frontier. The fisheries dispute, we recall, was referred to the arbitration of the Hague Court by a treaty of 1909, and a special boundary commission was established in

---

[1] Information from Division of Commercial Policy, Department of State (1949).

1910 which settled the question of the disputed islands. Contemporaneously with the disposal of these issues Great Britain and the United
States agreed to a convention, in 1909, providing for the regulation of
boundary waters and setting up permanent machinery for the settlement
of future controversies.[1] Since there is no special treaty for conciliation,
or for arbitration, between Canada and the United States, this convention takes the place, in respect of Canada, of the bilateral and multilateral treaties which the United States has with most other nations.

The convention provides for the free and equal navigation, by nationals
of both parties, of the boundary waters, and also of the American Lake
Michigan, and sets up an International Joint Commission of six members
to regulate obstructions or diversions to the flow and level of boundary
waters, with particular regulations for the flow of water in the Niagara
River (much used for hydroelectric power), and in the St. Marys River
(much used for navigation between the Upper Lakes) and the Milk River
(used for irrigation in Montana, Saskatchewan and Alberta). For these
purposes the Commission has administrative, investigative, and judicial
powers, deciding by a majority vote, or referring the question back to the
governments in case of a deadlock. In addition, the Commission has certain conciliatory and arbitral functions. Any other questions or matters
of difference (other than the regulation of waterways) arising between
them involving the rights, obligations or interests of either in relation to
the other or to the inhabitants of the other *along the common frontier,*
shall be referred to the Commission for examination, and possible recommendation whenever either party so requests, the report and recommendation not to have the character of an arbitral award. Further, any questions or matters of difference involving the rights, obligations or interests
of either party in relation to each other or to their respective inhabitants
may be referred with the consent of both parties (by and with the advice
and consent of the United States Senate, and His Majesty's Governor
General in Council) to the Commission *for decision* by a majority vote;
in case of a deadlock, to an umpire chosen according to the relevant rules
of the Hague Convention establishing the Permanent Court of Arbitration.

It was to this Commission that both governments referred in 1920 the

---

[1] The preamble states the desire of the parties "to prevent disputes regarding the use
of boundary waters and to settle all questions which are now pending between the
United States and the Dominion of Canada involving the rights, obligations, or interests
of either in relation to the other or to the inhabitants of the other, along their common
frontier, and to make provision for the adjustment and settlement of all such questions
as may hereafter arise."

study of an international improvement of the St. Lawrence waterway between Montreal and Lakes Ontario and Erie, so as to make ocean-going navigation possible to the Upper Lakes, and to divide the immense hydroelectric power resources of the St. Lawrence River. The report of the Commission prepared the way for the negotiation of the St. Lawrence deep-waterway treaty between Canada and the United States (signed July 18, 1932). This treaty provided for co-operation by the United States and Canada to complete by a uniform plan, each country working within its own jurisdiction but under the general direction of a special joint commission, a twenty-seven-foot channel in the St. Lawrence River and around the rapids, and improvements in the channels of the Upper Lakes; and a provision for the construction of hydroelectric plants, with equal division of the flow of water for power development. The total estimated cost, past and future, was $543,429,000. The expense was to be equally shared, with the stipulation that each country would receive credit for the cost of past works which entered into the project. This made the new costs to the United States $257,992,000 and to Canada only $38,071,500—Canada having just completed at immense cost the Welland Canal, between Lakes Ontario and Erie, as well as other important works which were to be a part of the general waterway.

This treaty also attempted to settle a dormant issue between Canada and the United States concerning the diversion of waters from Lake Michigan, which is not a "boundary water" within the meaning of the treaty of 1909, and which had therefore remained under exclusive American jurisdiction, except for the treaty servitude of 1909 which allows free navigation there to Canadian shipping. Lake Michigan is, of course, nevertheless a part of the Great Lakes system. The city of Chicago in 1900 tapped the waters of the Lake to flush out its sewage into the Illinois River and down the Mississippi. The increasing use of the waters, which eventually worked up toward 8,500 cubic feet a second, threatened to lower seriously the general lake level and the power flow of the Niagara River. Alarmed, several of the lake states and Mississippi River states [1] sued the Chicago Sanitary District in a case appealed to the Supreme Court of the United States, to prevent the diversion. The Court in 1930 decreed that Chicago must taper down the taking of water to 1,500 cubic feet a second by 1938. This was a purely domestic affair. But in 1926 the British Ambassador at Washington had complained that excessive

---

[1] Wisconsin, Ohio, Pennsylvania, Missouri, New York, Michigan, Kentucky, Tennessee, Louisiana, Arkansas. See note by J. W. Garner in *Am. Jour. International Law*, XXII (1928), 837-840.

diversion from Lake Michigan was a violation of Article III of the waterways treaty of 1909. This treaty, we have just noted, prohibited diversion from "boundary waters" without authorization of the International Joint Commission. The lake states had really been pleading Canada's cause, in fact but not in law; and the Supreme Court's decree mitigated the grievance of Canada without recognizing it. The treaty signed in 1932, however, specifically agreed in Article VIII to limit diversion of water from "the Great Lakes system," by December 31, 1938, to the quantity permitted by the Supreme Court's decree of April 21, 1930. In case the Government of the United States should propose an emergency diversion, and the Government of Canada should take exception, the issue might be submitted to an arbitral tribunal empowered to determine any just and equitable diversion during an emergency. No other diversion from "the Great Lakes system," than that just provided, was to be authorized except by the International Joint Commission.[1] The treaty of 1932 would thus create, for better or worse, an additional servitude on the sovereignty of the United States over Lake Michigan, and thereby would place the Chicago drainage issue definitely in the international field.

The idea of a new servitude, of definitely merging Lake Michigan, a recognized American lake, into the treaty formula of "the Great Lakes system," created understandable if not justifiable opposition to the ratification. There was further objection to the much greater *new* American expenditure. Strong sectional opposition also manifested itself both in Canada and in the United States. Impartial economic analysis of the advantages and disadvantages to the United States of the navigation and power features of the project, as presented by the Brookings Institution in 1929,[2] was also adverse in its conclusions. The treaty came first to a decision on ratification in the Republic, where it was defeated in the Senate (March 14, 1934) by a vote of 46 for and 42 against, the negative votes coming particularly from New England, New York, the South, and the Mississippi navigation states.

What could not be arranged by treaty President Roosevelt tried, like President Tyler in the case of Texas, and President McKinley in the case of Hawaii, to carry by a majority vote of Congress. An executive agreement between "The President of the United States and His Majesty the King of Great Britain, Ireland and the British Dominions beyond the

---

[1] *Great Lakes-St. Lawrence Deep Waterway Treaty* (Department of State Publication 347, Washington, 1932). See also *Canadian Annual Review, 1932-1933.*

[2] H. G. Moulton, Charles S. Morgan, and Adah L. Lee, *The St. Lawrence Navigation and Power Project* (Brookings Institution, Washington, 1929).

seas, Emperor of India, in respect of Canada," signed at Ottawa, March 19, 1941, created a Great Lakes-St. Lawrence Basin Commission, of five members from each country, to carry the great project through to completion. Nothing in the Agreement "shall confer upon either of them proprietary rights, or legislative, administrative, or other jurisdiction in the territory of the other, and the works constructed under the provisions of this Agreement shall constitute a part of the territory in which they are situated." This keeps Lake Michigan inviolate; and the Agreement extends, indefinitely, reciprocal navigation rights in Lake Michigan and in the St. Lawrence River which otherwise might be terminated by due notice under existing treaties. The Agreement has not yet been approved by the Congress of the United States and the Parliament of Canada.[1]

The International Joint Commission became a prototype for other Canadian-American commissions in a modern network of agencies for peaceful settlement and regulation of common concerns: the Wild-Life Services (1916); the International Halibut Commission (1924) for conservation of fisheries on the Pacific Coast; the Salmon Commission (1930); not to mention yet the later Permanent Joint Defense Board, and other wartime and later agencies.

To come back to the older International Joint Commission: it has, in addition to its powers for the regulation and investigation of the use of boundary waterways, contingent functions of conciliation and of arbitration. The conciliatory function may be invoked by only one party to suggest a settlement. The arbitral function may be invoked by both parties jointly to decide a dispute. To date it is only the administrative, investigative and judicial powers of the Commission for the regulation of the boundary waterways which have been put to service—most effectively in numerous cases. But the machinery of conciliation and arbitration stands steadily available, whenever called for, just as does the apparatus of the multilateral treaties for peace provided for among the United States and the Pan-American nations. The Canadian-American International Joint Commission is thus a worthy adjunct to the system of collective security in the New World, a system which rests on the out-

---

[1] The President supported himself by opinions from the Solicitor of the Department of State, and the Attorney General of the United States, that an agreement of this kind, subject to ratification by a majority vote of both Houses of Congress, would be constitutional.

For text of the Agreement, and the legal opinions, see S. Shepard Jones and Denys P. Myers, *Documents on American Foreign Relations*, III (July, 1940-June, 1941), 187-199 (World Peace Foundation, Boston, 1939).

A vast amount of data is included in the publication compiled for the Department of Commerce by N. R. Danielian, director of the St. Lawrence Survey, in a report on *The St. Lawrence Survey* (7 vols., Washington, G.P.O., 1941-1942).

lawry of war and the pledge, without compulsion, to peaceful means for the settlement of international disputes. Further than this, both the United States and Canada have ratified the optional clause of the International Court of Justice, judicial organ of the United Nations, obligating each party to submit definitively all "legal" questions to the judgment of that court. For the perfection of peace and justice between them the United States and Canada still await a keystone treaty agreeing to submit *all* disputes to a standing tribunal of the best judicial talent in both countries,[1] to guarantee the heritage of freedom of both peoples.[2]

The First World War did very little to cement Canadian-American solidarity; on the contrary, it rather loosened traditional bonds. American neutrality, 1914-1917, tended to antagonize the Canadian people against their neighbors to the south notwithstanding an inveterate admiration by people in the United States for the gallant qualities of Canadians and for their highly successful democracy. Somehow the Canadians were convinced that it was the United States's war as much as Canada's. They resented the slowness, so it seemed to them, with which the Republic turned to the Allied cause. After American intervention it was galling to some to think that the war would have been lost except for the belated, as they thought, entry of the United States. Later, others were convinced that the United States had deserted a noble cause in failing to accept the League of Nations, thus, in their opinion, crippling it from the start, though in 1936 Canada and the other Dominions themselves proved reluctant to support Britain in stopping remilitarization of the Rhineland, which placed Germany in a position to begin her program of conquest. Canadians further felt that the United States was immoral in expecting the "war debts" of the European Allies to be paid even according to capacity to pay; but Canada held none of their paper. This bitter distaste,[3] which was so difficult for Americans to realize, and which was not reciprocated by them, persisted to some degree after the common victory of 1919. Added to it was a curious but understandable culture complex. As a highly intelligent people, surpassed by no nation anywhere, Canadians resented the greater force of American culture coming from mere power of territory, natural resources and infinitely greater population. They fancied that the United

[1] P. E. Corbett has published a critical study of methods and results in *The Settlement of Canadian-American Disputes* (Canadian-American Series, Carnegie Endowment for International Peace, Yale University Press, 1937).

[2] James T. Shotwell has described *The Heritage of Freedom,* in the Marfleet Lectures at the University of Toronto in 1932 (New York, 1934).

[3] Hugh L. Keenleyside discusses it temperately in his *Canada and the United States, op. cit.*

States did not pay enough attention to them, and even complained that Canadian events did not take up more space in metropolitan American newspapers!

In such murky atmosphere economic grievances quickly took root on both sides of the boundary and spread themselves like bad weeds. New tariffs of the United States in 1922 and 1930 were followed by the Canadian high tariffs of 1927 and 1930. The American tariffs restricted the market for Canadian products—hard wheat, lumber, cattle, dairy products, maple sugar—in the United States. The Canadian tariffs cut down, or at least heavily taxed, the importation of American manufactured products. By the Ottawa intra-imperial treaties of 1932 Canada took her place in a system of reciprocal preferences within the British Empire, and continued a tariff schedule of three rates: most-favored rates to the imperially preferred Dominions of the Ottawa inter-commonwealth agreements of 1932; next-favored rates to those nations which had treaties of commerce with Canada; highest rates of all on goods coming from nations which had no treaties of commerce, that was, principally the United States. A tariff war sharpened psychological differences between two friendly nations while the non-American world teetered on the edge of the abyss. This was more than intellectual leaders and good folk on both sides of the weed-grown frontier could tolerate.

How a group of anxious scholars in the United States and Canada set about pulling these bad weeds and cultivating the traditional affinity on the eve of world crisis is one of the most inspiring examples of intellectual and moral co-operation in the history of American diplomacy. With the support of the Carnegie Endowment for International Peace, a series of biennial conferences (1935, 1937, 1939, 1941) on Canadian-American Affairs, meeting alternately at St. Lawrence University, Canton, New York, and Queen's University, Kingston, Ontario, brought together statesmen, scholars, philanthropists, diplomatists, and journalists of both nations, to hammer out common problems on the anvil of determined friendship, with such utter frankness as is possible only between Canadians and Americans who, let it be repeated, regard themselves as independent of each other rather than foreign to each other. These extra-official conferences, and the continuing studies that they helped . put in motion,[1] restored the old tone of fellowship, and made themselves felt in official policy.

[1] The proceedings of the four *Conferences on Canadian-American Affairs* have been printed by the Carnegie Endowment for International Peace (N. Y., 1936, 1938, 1939, 1940), edited by Professors Walter W. McLaren, Albert B. Corey, and Reginald G. Trotter.

One of the most notable products of this Canadian-American intellectual collaboration was a comprehensive historical study, in twenty-five volumes, on all phases, economic, cultural, social, and diplomatic, of *The Relations of Canada and the United States*. This unusually successful series was unprecedented in the field of internationl intellectual co-operation and was to be of continuing influence for peace with freedom. Capstone of the series was a volume focused on *The North Atlantic Triangle, The Inter-Play of Canada, The United States and Great Britain*.[1]

First fruit of the new feeling was the reciprocal trade agreement of January 1, 1936. Though this did not altogether overcome the imperial preferences of the Ottawa agreements, it nevertheless lowered tariffs radically on both sides. Impelled by the circumstances of the Second World War, Great Britain and Canada made simultaneous but separate reciprocal trade agreements with the United States, December 20, 1940. (Most detailed and sweeping in their nature, they had the effect of doing away with the discriminations which either Canada or Great Britain hitherto had practiced against the United States, on the one hand, and of lowering United States tariffs drastically to both nations, daughter and mother.) (Undoubtedly there was a political motive as well as an economic impulse in the negotiation of these salutary trade agreements, the motive of Anglo-American solidarity. Once more Canada fulfilled her role of political accouplement between Great Britain and the United States.)

Conclusion of the first trade agreement, in 1936, made it easier for President Franklin D. Roosevelt to put the coupling-pin in place on the occasion of a visit (certainly not casual) to Queen's University, Kingston, Ontario, one of the homes of the Canadian-American Conferences to which we have referred. "The Dominion of Canada," he said apparently gratuitously, "is part of the sisterhood of the British Empire. I give to you assurances that the people of the United States will not stand idly by if domination of Canadian soil is threatened by any other Empire." [2] The Canadian Prime Minister, Mr. Mackenzie King, acknowledged this assurance with appropriate expressions, but made no pledges on his part.[3]

---

[1] By the general editor, Professor J. Bartlett Brebner of Colombia University. The twenty-five volumes were published, 1940-1945, by the Yale University Press, the Ryerson Press of Toronto, and the Oxford University Press, for the Carnegie Endowment for International Peace. A list of titles and authors may be found on the inside rear flap of the folder to Brebner's capstone volume.

[2] Department of State *Press Releases*, XIX, No. 464 (August 20, 1938).

[3] F. R. Scott, *Canada and the United States* (World Peace Foundation, Boston, 1941), 53.

Canadian foreign policy before the war aimed at: (1) preserving Canadian neutrality in case of war between the United States and Japan,[1] (2) appeasement, if possible, of the European situation—this spirit disappeared after Munich, (3) reliance on the British navy and the Monroe Doctrine to protect the Canadian homeland in any event, (4) in the last analysis, to support Great Britain if she found herself at war in the Old World, mobilizing Canada's whole resources after the event. In line with this policy, Mr. King could do no more than say thank-you to Mr. Roosevelt in 1938, before Munich.

The outbreak of the Second World War put Canadian policy into motion. The fall of Denmark and Norway, the Low Countries and France in the spring of 1940, and the terrible danger to England, threw Canada and the United States closer together.[2] In a meeting at Ogdensburg, New York, on August 17, 1940, during maneuvers of the United States Army, to which President Roosevelt invited Prime Minister King, the two executives announced an agreement—an executive agreement, not a treaty—to set up a Permanent Joint Board of Defense "to consider in the broad sense the defense of the northern half of the Western Hemisphere." The Agreement by Great Britain, September 2, 1940, to cede to the United States a naval and air base in Newfoundland punctuated Canadian-American collaboration for joint defense in a dramatic manner.[3]

After Ogdensburg, Canadian-American relations drew even more tightly together as German conquests in Europe became rapidly more threatening to both countries. The President and the Canadian Prime Minister in a meeting at the former's home on the Hudson laid down general principles for mobilizing the resources of the North American continent for the defense of Great Britain, in line with the "lend-lease" act of Congress of March 11, 1941. In the Hyde Park Declaration (April 20, 1941) they announced that the two governments would gear their production programs to fit each other, and that the United States would pay

---

[1] C. P. Stacey, "A Canadian View" of Defense and External Obligations, at *Conference on Canadian American Affairs,* St. Lawrence University, Canton, N. Y., June 19-22, 1939, 190-193 (Carnegie Endowment for International Peace, N. Y., 1939), 182-197.

[2] We are, of course, alluding to events narrated more in detail in Chapter XLIII below.

[3] A tripartite protocol signed by the United States, Canada and Great Britain, March 27, 1941, on the occasion of the signing on the same date of the final lease agreement for United States bases in Newfoundland (see below, p. 854) "recognized that the defense of Newfoundland was an integral part of the Canadian scheme of defense and as such a matter of special concern to the Canadian Government." Nothing in this agreement was to affect arrangements already taken by the Joint Board of Defense, United States and Canada, relative to the defense of Newfoundland. In the future the Newfoundland Government was to participate in all consultations.

Canada $200,000,000 to $300,000,000 during the next twelve months for certain supplies, complementary to the American defense program, but a "small fraction of it." This payment would assist Canada in meeting part of her defense purchases in the United States. Further, the United States would furnish to Great Britain, under the lend-lease program, certain parts to be made up in Canada into finished products to go forward directly to Great Britain.[1] Thus the vast reservoirs of American cash and supplies were opened up to Canada for help to Great Britain in her hour of greatest peril—in order to keep that peril away from North American shores, if possible.

If United States help to Canada and Great Britain should lead to war with Germany, as it speedily did, in undeclared form, and that should bring Japan into war against the United States, according to the terms of the Triple Alliance of Germany, Italy, and Japan, of September 27, 1940, what would be the position of Canada toward Japan? That was the principal question of Canadian-American relations as a real shooting war began between American and German naval forces on the Atlantic.[2]

Japan answered the question. After her staggering surprise attack on Pearl Harbor, December 7, 1941, she declared war on the United States *and* Great Britain. Canada, perforce, and the other Dominions, declared war in turn on Japan. Promptly the United States and Canada announced a joint declaration, by their War Production Committees, of a policy of all-out war production and the removal of any and all barriers (legislative, administrative, tariff, customs "or restriction of any character") standing in the way of total war effort.[3] Canada signed the Declaration of the United Nations in Washington, January 2, 1942. Both nations and the British Commonwealth, and their Allies, joined their destinies in the greatest and most fateful war of history. Throughout the great conflict the bars of nationality were let down, so to speak, for cooperation in a common military effort, without impairment of the sovereignty or national integrity of either nation.

At the close of the Second World War both the United States and Canada committed themselves unreservedly to the Charter and program of the United Nations. But the increasing insecurity of North America in the new unbalance of power, and the failure so far of the Security

---

[1] S. Shepard Jones and Denys P. Myers, *Documents on American Foreign Relations,* III, July, 1940-June, 1941 (World Peace Foundation, Boston, 1941), 161-169.

[2] For discussion of this vital question, see *Conference on Canadian-American Affairs, Queen's University, Kingston, Ontario, June 23-26, 1941* (New York, 1941), 241-242.

[3] Department of State *Bulletin,* V, No. 131 (December 27, 1941), 578-579. R. Warren James has published a study of the United States and Canada in the field of *Wartime Economic Cooperation* (Canadian Institute of International Affairs, Toronto, 1949).

Council to reconcile the great crisis of thought and action between the East and the West, kept the two independent countries ever more closely together, within the integrity of each people's sovereignty, notwithstanding complicated and vexing minor problems of imperial preference treaties, aerial navigation, and numerous other technical puzzles. In 1947 the two Governments announced their decision to continue indefinitely the Permanent Board of Joint Defense, first established in 1940 as a war measure. This common defense planning depended on no treaty, no executive agreement, no contractual obligation.[1] It rested on the anxiety of each party for the maintenance of its own security and freedom in an uncertain and dangerous world.

More than ever each people realizes that its independence and liberty depend on the independence and liberty of the other. In the North Atlantic Security Pact of 1949 Canada became in very firmest fit the coupling-pin of Anglo-American solidarity for the defense of the freedom of both the Old World and the New.

[1] Department of State *Bulletin*, XVI, No. 339 (February 23, 1947), 361.

CHAPTER XLI

THE UNITED STATES AND THE FAR EAST

(1922-1939)

THE Washington treaties of 1922 left Japan in a position of paramount military and naval power in the Far East, but they pledged the powers, including Japan, against *further* imperialism in China, to the maintenance of the Open Door and the political independence and territorial integrity of China, and to the continuance of the *status quo* in the region of the Pacific Ocean. These traditional American—and British—policies were thus written into multilateral pacts. Nobody could foresee the Great Depression and the rise of the European dictators, phenomena which would present tempting advantages and opportunities for Japanese power at the expense of the plighted word of her rulers. For nearly a decade Japan pursued loyally the policy of the Washington treaties. These years witnessed the crystallization and spread of a new Chinese national movement of profound significance to Japan's ambitions for the future of Asia.

The Chinese Nationalist movement took new shape at Canton in 1923 under the leadership of Dr. Sun Yat-sen, who turned for material support to the Russian Bolshevists. An understanding between Sun and the Soviet Commissioner, Joffe, agreed that the Soviet system could not actually be introduced into China because conditions were lacking for the successful establishment of communism or sovietism. In 1924 a diplomatic agreement and sequent treaty were reached between China and Russia, by which China recognized the Soviet Government. Russia abandoned all the special treaty rights and concessions procured from China under the Czarist régime, including extraterritoriality. This meant another step [1] in freeing China of the burden of "unequal treaties." The Sino-Soviet treaty regulated the Chinese Eastern Railway, hitherto a joint Sino-Russian enterprise, financed by Russia, by making it a purely commercial affair controlling its own business operations, with all other matters affecting the national and local governments of China to be administered by Chinese authorities. This divested the railroad of

---

[1] The "unequal treaties" with Germany and Austria-Hungary had been thrown off in the peace settlement of 1919.

the political attributes originally granted to the Czarist Government, including the right to guard it with armed guards.[1] Russian assistance in the form of military training, supplies, and funds now streamed into South China to support the campaign for national unity and control by the Kuomintang (Nationalist Party) of all China, this as a first step to the economic, social and moral regeneration and national galvanization of that chaotic republic under modern, and eventually Soviet, ideas.

Notwithstanding the terms of the working agreement between Russian communism and Chinese nationalism, the destitute condition of the Chinese people presented a favorable. medium for the cultivation of communist principles; behind the Kuomintang armies developed a wave of social and labor unrest, strikes and industrial violence particularly against foreign-owned factories. In 1927, however, after evidence was received that the Soviet mentors were plotting the overthrow of the Kuomintang in order to establish a thoroughly communist government, the Nationalists expelled the Bolshevik comrades and took reprisals on their native followers. Rapidly breasting the tide and confusion of Chinese political life, the Nationalist armies pressed northward until by 1928 they had established an enthusiastic but loose authority over all of China south of the Great Wall, with a new capital at Nanking. North of the Great Wall, the Manchurian provinces had lain under the control of warlord Chang Tso-lin, hitherto politically backed by Japan, but increasingly sympathetic to the Nationalists. Murderously the Japanese got rid of him in 1928 by blowing up his railway coach in a trackage area under their military guard. Next step in the Nationalist program of unification was control over the Manchurian provinces of China, long a theater of international rivalry, particularly between Russia and Japan.[2] Japan viewed with disfavor this territorial extension of authority by the Chinese Nationalist Government and made overt but unsuccessful efforts to prevent it.

The advance of the Nationalist movement was accompanied by some revival of animosity against the imperialist powers, a limited reincarnation of the Boxer revolt animated by more modernistic sentiment. It was convenient for the leaders to attribute the troubles of China not to their essential internal causes, but to the unequal treaties, and to sustain enthusiasm by exciting their followers to a frenzy of criticism and un-

---

[1] R. T. Pollard, *China's Foreign Relations, 1917-1931* (New York, 1933), 160-204.

[2] This account of the Chinese Nationalist Revolution is of course vastly simplified, based on the summaries in Morse and McNair, *Far Eastern International Relations, op. cit.,* and George N. Steiger, *History of the Far East* (New York, 1936).

rest against the foreigners and their concessions. Meanwhile the events of the First World War had weakened the white man's prestige, so powerful in China before 1914. Clashes with foreigners (at Shanghai, May 30, 1925, and also at Canton, June, 1925; Wanhsien incident on the upper Yangtze River, September, 1926) culminated in the premeditated and organized attack on foreign nationals in Nanking (March 24, 1927) resulting in the deaths of three British, one American, one French and one Italian national, the assault on many others without distinction as to sex or nationality, and the violation of the American, British and Japanese consulates. Only the laying down of a barrage of shells from British and American destroyers in the river made possible the evacuation of foreigners without more general slaughter. The affair at Nanking led to a demand, presented in identic notes (April 11, 1927) by the American, British, French, Italian and Japanese Governments for punishment of the commanders of troops responsible for the outrage, complete reparation, and apology in writing by the commander in chief of the Nationalist armies, including an express written undertaking to refrain from all forms of violence and agitation against foreign lives and property. Contingents of foreign forces from the protesting powers arrived, including a regiment of American marines, and hastened to Shanghai for the protection of the foreign settlement and the refugees clustered there. Of the total of 40,000 troops, there were about 11,000 British. Meanwhile there was almost a complete evacuation of foreign nationals from the interior of the Yangtze Valley and South China.

The Nationalist Government, then under the control of radicals at Hankow, undertook to reply to the powers individually, and at first offered no adequate satisfaction. Great Britain, France and Italy wished that the aggrieved powers jointly adopt measures to enforce compliance with their demands. Japan, before the fall of Baron Shidehara, was willing to follow. The United States refused to go that far, or to join in an ultimatum. After the establishment of the government at Nanking, the leadership of the Nationalists fell into more conservative hands, and the powers were able to make a friendly settlement without the use of force, involving mutual apologies, reparations, and guaranties by the Nationalist Government.[1] In this incident, as traditionally, the United States took a stand which bolstered the integrity of China.

Unlike the Boxer agitation, the Nationalist movement was not stimu-

[1] R. T. Pollard, *China's Foreign Relations, op. cit.*, 293-307. The terms of settlement in 1928 may be found in G. H. Blakeslee's *The Pacific Area; an International Survey* (World Peace Foundation Pamphlets, XII, No. 3, Boston, 1929), 155-159.

lated by threatened encroachments of the powers. It was directed against the accumulation of privileges forced from China in the past. It came to a head after the Washington Conference when the powers under American impulsion were pledged to a policy of patience and sympathy with China. In November, 1927, the commander of the Nationalist forces, General Chiang Kai-shek, announced: "We will execute no treaties such as were signed by former governments, nor will we at any time recognize any treaties or agreements which were made with other nations by any government in China previous to that of the Nationalist forces." These bold words went further than actual accomplishment, but the Kuomintang did secure the abolition of the old tariff treaties, and a diminution of concessions (notably the British relinquishment of concessions at Hankow, Kiukiang, Chinkiang, Amoy, and the restoration of Weihaiwei). It did not succeed in throwing off the trammels of extraterritoriality. A powerful instrument in its program of liberation was the device of boycotts. These menaced the security of foreign trade, first British, later Japanese. During these boycotts American trade prospered at the expense of the boycotted nations.

Particularly to Japan did the Nationalist movement assume an alarming aspect. Japanese leaders feared that the moral and political regeneration of China would block any plans of Japan for eventual control of that vast country. The increasing population of Japan (at the rate of 1,000,000 a year) depended for its support on the industrialization of the islands. This required expanding markets, of which China was the nearest and greatest. Few things could be a more painful blow to Japan in time of peace than a successful Chinese boycott of her exports. To all China also, particularly to the provinces of Manchuria, Japan looked for a continuing supply of raw materials to sustain her own island people, and for a possible (but not proven) outlet for her pressure of population.[1] Should the Nationalists establish themselves strongly, and extend their authority over Manchuria, Japan's career of future expansion on the continent of Asia might be permanently blocked.

Whether to continue the policy of conciliation with China became the paramount question of Japanese politics. Baron Shidehara, Japanese Minister of Foreign Affairs, 1924-1927, endeavored against increasing opposition to pursue conciliation and friendly co-operation based upon the Washington treaties. Those treaties, it is recalled, had not con-

[1] Tatsuji Takeuchi has the best presentation available in English of the Japanese point of view in Chapter XXVI of his *War and Diplomacy in the Japanese Empire* (New York, 1935).

tested Japan's treaty rights in Manchuria. It was Shidehara's belief
that this policy would win China's confidence and the confidence of the
world in Japan's motives toward China, and that a policy of moderation
generally in foreign affairs would increase the markets for Japan's expanding industries on which her growing population depended so im-
periously. Under his guidance, for example, Japan did not participate
in the protective barrage laid down by British and American naval forces
at Nanking in 1927, despite the fact that the Japanese consulate was
fired on, and several Japanese subjects wounded; and it was the British
rather than the Japanese who bore the brunt of that incident before the
Chinese boycotts. While Shidehara's policy reigned there was no special
feeling against Japan, and Japanese commerce flourished.

The Nanking incident fired Japanese public opinion against Shidehara's
friendly policy. His government was immediately overthrown in April,
1927, by Baron General Tanaka, personification of a more "positive"
policy, spokesman at that time of the army which was constantly pressing against the more liberal and conciliatory elements. The displaced
moderates were allied with "big business" in Japan and wanted peace.
The army in turn appealed strongly to the small landowners and peas-
ants, an agrarian class increasingly ground down by the rapid industrialization and urbanization of Japan. This class furnished many of the
officers. Supporting the army, and firing public sentiment by appeals to
a fanatical patriotism, stood various fraternal chauvinistic societies de-
votedly militaristic in nature and closely akin to fascist thought and
action.

The Tanaka Government came into power in Japan as the Kuomintang
forces were pushing north from the Yangtze Valley toward Peking.
Japan landed troops in Shantung, in 1927, and again in 1929, to keep
the civil war out of that province and to protect her interests there, as
well as to deflect and embarrass the northward movement of the Nationalists. These interventions, though withdrawn, brought on costly
and persisting boycotts on Japanese imports. In May, 1928, the Japanese Government declared to the rival Chinese groups in Nanking and
Peking that it would not tolerate the extension of the war into Manchuria and Mongolia; that if the disturbances should spread Japan would
"be constrained to take appropriate and effective steps for the maintenance of peace and order in Manchuria." In December of that year
Chang Hsueh-liang, war lord of Manchuria, son of Chang Tso-lin, acknowledged allegiance to the Nanking Government. The following spring
(1929) Chinese forces in Manchuria seized the Chinese Eastern Railway,

hitherto under joint Chinese-Russian management, and arrested the Russian officials and employees of the road. Diplomatic relations broke off. Border clashes began. War appeared imminent, although both China and Russia had just become parties to the Pact of Paris of 1928 for the renunciation of war. It became evident, however, that China could not withstand Russia in any conflict in Manchuria. The American Secretary of State, Henry L. Stimson, and Mr. Briand, the French Minister of Foreign Affairs, representing the two governments originally sponsors of the Pact of Paris, reminded the two disputants of their obligations under it. China, realizing her weak military position, hastened to accept a peaceful settlement based on the restoration of the *status quo ante*. Russia took occasion to snub the United States for venturing to apply to the Soviet Government with advice and counsel, when by its own choice it had no official relations with it; but the Soviets accepted a peaceful solution which was really a check to China.

Japan applauded the invocation of the Pact of Paris to keep the peace between Russia and China in Manchuria. China's action toward Russia was an earnest of what might confront Japan's treaty position in those provinces, were the Chinese successful. On the other hand, Soviet successes might strengthen Russia's position in an area which Japan coveted for herself. The Nationalists were as desirous of redeeming South Manchuria, where existed the Kwantung (southern tip of the Liaotung peninsula) leased area and the Japanese railway and ancillary concessions,[1] as they were to restore their sovereignty over North Manchuria *vis-à-vis* Russia. As the Nationalists spread their authority into Manchuria they began to contest the broad interpretations attached by Japan to her special treaty rights in that region: particularly the right to station a limited number of guards along the South Manchuria Railway; the administrative powers which that state railway enjoyed over areas which had passed under its proprietorship or lease; the police powers and juris-

---

[1] See above, pp. 493 ff. These treaty rights were based upon the transfer from Russia to Japan by the Peace of Portsmouth (1905) of all Russian rights south of Changchun, which was in turn ratified by the Sino-Japanese Treaty of Peking (1905), and extended by the Sino-Japanese treaties of 1915, following the presentation of the Twenty-One Demands. Extensive areas tributary to the South Manchuria Railway had been acquired before and after 1915, when such leases were regularized and placed under the semi-political jurisdiction of the railroad, which was in itself an instrument of the Japanese Government. C. Walter Young's elaborate studies of *Japan's Special Position in Manchuria; The International Legal Status of the Kwantung Leased Territory;* and *Japanese Jurisdiction in the South Manchuria Railway Areas* (all three published by the Johns Hopkins Press, 1931) are conveniently digested by T. A. Bisson's analysis of "Basic Treaty Issues in Manchuria Between China and Japan," in *Foreign Policy Reports,* VII, No. 21 (Dec. 23, 1931).

dictional powers which Japan assumed in these "railway areas" outside the Kwantung leasehold, and the expanding consular police which Japan set up in Manchuria, even in regions distant from the railway areas. Similar powers to these in North Manchuria the Soviet Government had already relinquished in 1924. The Chinese endeavored to undermine the power of the Japanese South Manchuria Railway by setting up a system of competing parallel roads, financed through foreign loans, which would drain away Manchurian commerce, at fares payable in cheap currency, to a new Chinese port (Hulutao) at the head of the Gulf of Pechili. On other feeder roads, previously constructed by Japanese capital, they defaulted in their loans. They also interposed difficulties in the way of leasing lands by Japanese subjects, who by the treaties of 1915 were enabled to make such leases.

If Japan were to have Manchuria some day for her own, as the proponents of the "positive" policy so ardently advocated,[1] or if she were to continue to control its destiny (as nearly all Japanese leaders desired), she must act before either Russia or China became too strong there. The situation was exacerbated by the occurrence of provocative affairs of the sort which lead up to conflict. One incident which incensed the Japanese military was the arrest and execution, in the interior of China, of a Japanese officer, one Major Nakamura, who was making a military reconnaissance there in civilian attire. Bitter anti-Chinese riots then followed in Japanese Korea, which in turn intensified anti-Japanese boycotts in China. Baron Shidehara, who had been called back to the

---

[1] Japanese policy after 1931 in Manchuria, Mongolia, and other adjacent provinces of China exhibited a striking similarity to the policy and action advocated in alleged official documents given to the world through Chinese channels after the outbreak of hostilities. One of these was a confidential memorial of July 25, 1927, to the Throne attributed to Baron Tanaka. It advocated the economic and political penetration and conquest of Manchuria and Mongolia, particularly through the construction and control of strategic railways, as a means of ensuring Japan an abundant supply of natural resources and an outlet for population, and as a first step for the control of all China. The Honjo Memorial, alleged to have been directed by the commander of Japanese forces in Manchuria to the Minister of War, General Minami, projected plans beyond this: it outlined an eventual conquest of the Philippines, Malaya, Australia, and a subjugation of Western Europe and Africa "until we would share equally with the United States the good things of this world." The Japanese Government has declared these documents to be forgeries by a venal subject, and has been able to point out obvious impossibilities in some of their details; but the array of carefully organized information (particularly in the so-called Tanaka Memorial) is astonishing; and the sequence of actual events in Manchuria, examined in the light of that memorial, is startling. For discussion of authenticity see debate between Japanese and Chinese delegates before the League of Nations in *Official Journal* of League of Nations, XIII (July-December, 1932), pp. 1882, 1893, 1895, 1898, 1902. J. W. Ballantine found no evidence in Tokyo War Criminals Trials to substantiate it. *Foreign Affairs*, XXVII, 652.

Ministry of Foreign Affairs in 1929,[1] found himself overwhelmed by mounting demands for a stronger policy toward China.

In Japan the army, like the navy, was responsible only to the Emperor directly, not to the government which rested on a parliamentary support. Demands for a "positive policy" meant a challenge to the League of Nations, to the Nine-Power Treaty of Washington of 1922, and to the Pact of Paris of 1928, and ultimately to the accompanying naval treaties of 1922 and 1930, all of which Japan had accepted freely. For such a challenge the world situation of international politics was propitious. In Europe the peace edifice of Versailles was beginning to show signs of cracks, and the international economic structure was collapsing. The Hoover standstill agreement for a year's moratorium on inter-governmental debts had just been proclaimed. Great Britain had gone off the gold standard, and the United States was pressed. The Great Depression gripped and paralyzed the nations of the western world. In the ensuing intervention which was precipitated by the Japanese army command in South Manchuria and which led to the establishment of the unrecognized puppet state of Manchukuo, the world came to realize what the reader must constantly bear in mind: that it was the army and navy authorities, not the Cabinet, which directed and controlled Japanese military policy; that the Foreign Office proposed, professed, and pretended, *vis-à-vis* the world, but the army command really defined, determined, and disposed for the destiny of Japan's continental policy in Asia, leaving it to the Foreign Office to smooth over things as best it could with the foreign treaty powers. The military were confident that a patriotic and warlike people would sustain them. They scorned the façade of treaties for the Open Door, the political independence and territorial integrity of China. They contemned the naval limitations of Washington and London. Theirs was the power. To them appeared the opportunity: the distresses of the Occident were obviously the advantage of Japan. They continued to be so, even more, perhaps, than Japanese radical militarists could have foreseen in 1931.

The military command in the Kwantung leased area took matters into its own hands on the night of September 18-19, 1931. Following a minor explosion on the railway, the Japanese army occupied "with swiftness and precision" [2]—as if it had been prepared and waiting for such

[1] He remained in that office in the ensuing Hamaguchi and Wakatsuki Cabinets until December 13, 1931.

[2] The phrase is from the *Report of the Commission of Enquiry* of the League of Nations (Lytton Report) which analyzes the evidence.

an event—the principal cities in Southern Manchuria (excepting, for the time being, Chinchow and Harbin), and took over the public services. Notwithstanding professions of the Foreign Office to the United States that there was no intention to occupy Chinchow, they followed (after the fall of the moderate *Minseito* Party, including Baron Shidehara) with further operations so that by the end of 1932 all of Manchuria was under their control. The Chinese troops withdrew with little fighting. In February, 1932, under Japanese tutelage the "independent" state of Manchukuo declared itself under the regency of "Mr. Henry Pu-Yi"— former Manchu boy-emperor of China, who had been living under Japanese patronage since leaving Peking in 1924. With the "new state" of Manchukuo, Japan negotiated a treaty, September 15, 1932. It confirmed and guaranteed all rights and interests possessed by Japan or her subjects within the territory of Manchukuo by virtue of Sino-Japanese treaties, agreements or other arrangements, or of Sino-Japanese contracts, *private as well as public.* "Japan and Manchukuo, recognizing that any threat to the territory or to the peace and order of either of the High Contracting Parties constitutes at the same time a threat to the safety and existence of the other, agree to co-operate in the maintenance of their national security; it being understood that such Japanese forces as may be necessary for this purpose shall be stationed in Manchukuo."

Manchukuo was to remain under *de facto* Japanese control until September, 1945. The Japanese crowned Henry Pu-Yi as Emperor Kang Te, March 1, 1934. Japanese troops meanwhile had pushed the boundaries of the new puppet state west and south to the Great Wall, including within it the additional Chinese province of Jehol, and leaving open the frontiers into Mongolia for further expansion. China, unable to secure help from the outside world, was forced to acquiesce, by the military truce of Tangku (May 31, 1933), signed in the outskirts of Tientsin. The Chinese Nationalist Government agreed to evacuate a demilitarized zone south of the Great Wall. Only when the Japanese authorities were sure that the Chinese were completely withdrawn were they to remove their forces out of the zone. The terms of the truce left Japan free to do as it pleased north of the Great Wall. This armistice—for technically it was only such—amounted to a *de facto* acceptance of the supremacy of Japan in Manchukuo. As if there were other, unpublished terms, the Chinese began immediately the suppression of anti-Japanese propaganda and boycotts. Any tendency to their renewal met a threat of the occupation of Peiping and the immediate detachment of more provinces.

This "positive" action of Japan in Manchuria was a clean-cut violation of the Covenant of the League of Nations, of the Nine-Power Treaty, and of the Pact of Paris. It took place over the impotent protests of China and the western world, of the League of Nations and the United States. We must now turn back to the reaction brought about by this challenge to the machinery of peace to which the nations of the world had pledged themselves since 1919 under the New Dispensation, and to the relation of the United States thereto.

China immediately appealed Japanese aggression in Manchuria to the Council of the League of Nations under Article XI of the Covenant (which declares "any war or threat of war" a "matter of concern"). The Council asked the two disputants not to aggravate the situation while peaceful measures were being sought. Secretary of State Stimson (September 22, 1931) told the Japanese Ambassador in Washington that the United States was profoundly concerned on account of the Nine-Power Treaty and Pact of Paris. Trusting that the civilian element in the Japanese Government represented by the Foreign Office could restrain the aggressive military leaders from making way with Manchuria, Stimson at first inclined to encourage China and Japan to settle the controversy directly.[1] This only emboldened Japan. The Council (i.e., including China and Japan) passed a resolution (September 30, 1931), requesting both China and Japan to do all in their power to hasten the restoration of normal relations, but Japan blocked the unanimity of another resolution (October 24, 1931) which called for the withdrawal of her troops.[2] Meanwhile the Council, as if anxious to take advantage of an opportunity to bring the United States into close co-operation with the League in a crisis, invited (over the protests of Japan) the United States to sit in on the case. Secretary Stimson immediately appointed Mr. Prentiss Gilbert, consul of the United States at Geneva, to be present at public sessions of the Council, but instructed him not to participate in discussions except when the subject of the Pact of Paris had been raised by someone else; then he could take a part in helping to mobilize world opinion against war. To this degree only did American participa-

---

[1] Sara S. Smith has analyzed *The Manchurian Crisis, 1931-1932* as *A Tragedy in International Relations* (Columbia University Press, 1948). Apparently she completed her study before the publication by the Department of State of voluminous official documents in *Foreign Relations of the United States, 1931*, Vol. III (Washington, G.P.O., 1946) and *ibid., 1932*, Vols. III and IV (1948). Richard W. Van Alstyne in *Far Eastern Quarterly*, VIII (1949), 222-225, feels that the materials in the *1931* Vol. III support Miss Smith's thesis that the incompetence of the American foreign service at this juncture, together with Stimson's confusion of policy, encouraged Japan's contumacy.

[2] The resolution of September 30 was unanimous, including Japan and China. The resolution of October 24 was voted over the dissent of Japan.

tion extend in the functioning of the League on the Manchurian question; the Government of the United States was careful not to appoint any delegate to any of the committees of the League which dealt with the Sino-Japanese disputes. Nevertheless, in supplementary diplomatic conversations the United States made plain its willingness to "reinforce" any action by the Council and to co-operate with the Council Powers in their effort to find a formula for peace which could be resolved by the Council. This formula, to which the representatives of both Japan and China agreed, was adopted by the Council in a resolution of December 10, 1931, providing for the appointment of a neutral commission of investigation to study the dispute on the spot and to report back to the Council. The members of this commission, which included an American army officer, Major General Frank McCoy, with an Englishman, Lord Lytton, as chairman, did not represent any particular government: they were employed by the Council only.

President Hoover was resolved not to let the League leave the abandoned Chinese "baby" on America's doorstep. He would not have the United States join in any sanctions against Japan, lest they lead to war. Nor, for that matter, was the League ready to resort to such. Secretary Stimson wanted to keep Japan guessing about the attitude of the United States, fearful of sanctions.[1] But Japan would not be bluffed. Her forces moved all the way into Manchuria.

Dismayed by the power of the Japanese military, Secretary Stimson proceeded to draw up a caveat, like that of Secretary Bryan in 1915,[2] notifying both China and Japan that the United States did not intend to recognize any treaties, understandings, or situations which Japan and China might enter into impairing the treaty rights of the United States or their citizens in China or impairing the sovereignty, independence or territorial or administrative integrity of China, or affecting the Open Door policy, or which might be arrived at by steps contrary to the Kellogg-Briand Pact of Paris. He called in the British and French Ambassadors separately and read each a draft of his proposed note. He suggested that Great Britain—and France—might take similar steps. Such parallel statements [3] he thought might tide over a bad situation until a future

---

[1] *Foreign Relations of the United States, 1931*, Vol. III, and *ibid., 1932*, vol. IV. Ernest Ralph Perkins has used these documents in his careful analysis of "The Non-application of Sanctions against Japan, 1931-1932," in *Essays in History and International Relations in Honor of George Hubbard Blakeslee* (Clark University Publication, 1949), pp. 215-233.

[2] Above, p. 682.

[3] Memorandum by the Secretary of State, January 5, 1932. *Foreign Relations, 1932*, III, 3-4.

occasion could redeem it. Without waiting for the reply of either Great Britain or France, Stimson independently dispatched his note to Japan and China, the "Stimson Doctrine." After observing that with the recent operations about Chinchow the last remaining administrative authority of the government of the Chinese Republic in South Manchuria as it existed prior to September 18, 1931, had been destroyed, the note went on to state (January 7, 1932):

The American Government continues confident that the work of the neutral commission recently authorized by the Council of the League of Nations will facilitate an ultimate solution of the difficulties now existing between China and Japan. But in view of the present situation and of its own rights and obligations therein, the American Government deems it to be its duty to notify both the Imperial Japanese Government and the Government of the Chinese Republic that it cannot admit the legality of any situation *de facto* nor does it intend to recognize any treaty or agreement entered into between those governments, or agents thereof, which may impair the treaty rights of the United States or its citizens in China, including those which relate to the sovereignty, the independence, or the territorial and administrative integrity of the Republic of China, or to the international policy relative to China, commonly known as the open-door policy; and that it does not intend to recognize any situation, treaty, or agreement which may be brought about by means contrary to the covenants and obligations of the Pact of Paris of August 27, 1928, to which treaty both China and Japan, as well as the United States, are parties.

To this note the Japanese Government replied (January 12, 1932) intimating that a new state would be set up in Manchuria by the Chinese people there who were "not destitute of the power for self-determination."

Neither Great Britain nor France was willing to take any such parallel step. From the British—not to mention the French Government—the United States met a pointed rebuff, communicated to the world at large in the form of a press communiqué: in view of former statements by Japanese representatives that Japan would adhere to the Open Door policy and would welcome participation and co-operation in Japanese enterprise, the British Government did not consider it necessary to address any formal note to Japan on the lines of the American note, but had requested the Japanese Ambassador to obtain confirmation of these early assurances from his Government.[1]

While the Lytton Commission was proceeding to the scene of the trouble in the Far East, Japan, undismayed, proceeded with her "positive policy" and set up the "independent" state of Manchukuo. To stamp

[1] Henry L. Stimson, *The Far Eastern Crisis* (New York, 1936), 98-104.

out the disastrous boycott to which the Nationalists had resorted as a defensive measure, Japanese military and naval forces attacked and occupied Shanghai, after severe and prolonged fighting (January 28-March 3, 1932) followed, with great loss of life [1] and destruction of property.

The attack on Shanghai, and the refusal of Great Britain to co-operate with the United States, led to a significant restatement of the Stimson Doctrine by the Secretary of State of the United States, and it impelled China to appeal her dispute with Japan from the Council to the Assembly of the League, according to the provisions of Article XV. The restatement of Mr. Stimson's doctrine was contained in a public letter addressed to Senator William E. Borah, chairman of the Senate Committee on Foreign Relations, February 24, 1932. He stated that the treaties of Washington were all dependent on each other, and intimated that a party to the Nine-Power Treaty could not ignore its obligations under that treaty and continue to enjoy the advantages of the others.

The appeal to the Assembly mobilized the judgment of the small states of the League. In the Council the great powers had been less eager to pronounce against Japan. In the Assembly they could not withstand the moral pressure of the small powers, who for their own future safety were anxious to secure small or weak states from the aggression of great powers. The result was a resolution of the Assembly (March 11, 1932) by the unanimous vote of 45 delegates (China and Japan abstaining) which:

1. Proclaimed the binding nature of the Covenant and of the Pact of Paris.
2. Declared: "that it is incumbent upon the members of the League of Nations not to recognize any situation, treaty, or arrangement which may be brought about by means contrary to the Covenant of the League of Nations or to the Pact of Paris."

This resolution meant the implementing of the League of Nations and the Pact of Paris with the peaceful weapon of non-recognition. It was equivalent to a statement that if the Lytton Commission should find Japan in the wrong, or that if Japan should not accept the recommendation of the League made after the report was rendered, then the League members would not recognize Manchukuo, for to do so would stamp Japan's conquest with the seal of international validity. The League resolution was not as sweeping as the Stimson Doctrine which had preceded it. That Doctrine rested on agreement and treaties between

---

[1] The Lytton Report cites estimates by the Chinese as 24,000 officers, men, and civilians, and $1,500,000,000 Mex.

Japan and the United States as well as on the multilateral treaties of Washington and the Pact of Paris. It implemented the League of Nations only indirectly.

The Lytton Commission finished its labors in September, 1932. The League published its report on October 2. An expert, conscientious and unbiased inquiry, it is the most authoritative history and analysis which exists of the whole issue between Japan and China to that time. Briefly summarized, its conclusions were:

(1) In regard to the original attack on South Manchuria the night of September 18-19, 1931: "The military operations of the Japanese troops . . . cannot be regarded as measures of legitimate self-defence."

(2) "The present regime [Manchukuo] cannot be considered to have been called into existence by a genuine and spontaneous independence movement," and the Japanese were in actual control.

(3) The maintenance of the present regime in Manchuria would be unsatisfactory, and not "compatible with the fundamental principle of existing international obligations, nor with the good understanding between the two countries upon which peace in the Far East depends."

(4) A mere restoration of the *status quo* would be no solution.

(5) A recommendation for the creation of an autonomous Manchuria within the Chinese Republic; a recognition of the rights and interests of Japan in a new Sino-Japanese treaty which would restate those rights and interests; negotiation of a new Sino-Japanese commercial treaty; and, finally, temporary international co-operation in the internal reconstruction of China, as suggested by the late Dr. Sun Yat-sen.

After a committee of nineteen of the Assembly had endeavored to persuade Japan to accept a settlement along these lines (for which China was willing), the League unanimously [1] voted a resolution, framed by the committee:

1. That any plan of agreement should observe the principles of the League Covenant, the Pact of Paris, and the Nine-Power Treaty of Washington.

2. It should observe the provisions of the Assembly's resolution of March 11, 1932, especially those concerning a scrupulous regard for treaties and the mutual obligations of the League Members to respect and preserve their territorial integrity and political independence against external aggression, and the submission of disputes arising among them to methods of peaceful settlement.

3. It should conform to the principles and conditions laid down in the Lytton Report.

---

[1] China voted for the adoption of the report, Japan against it, and Siam abstained from voting. The President of the Assembly of the League of Nations announced that under Article XV of the Covenant the votes of the parties to a dispute did not count in reckoning unanimity.

After the Japanese attack on Shanghai, in the British sphere of the Yangtse Valley, Great Britain was more anxious than she had been when Manchuria alone was the prey of Japan. In the Assembly she supported the above resolution.

Following the adoption of the resolution Mr. Matsuoka, the Japanese delegate, and his staff walked out of the Assembly. Soon thereafter his government gave the required notice (March 27, 1933) for withdrawal from the League, which became effective March 27, 1935. Japan quitted that League of Nations which her greatest diplomatist, Viscount Ishii, had so recently extolled in his *Diplomatic Commentaries* as "a house of correction for disturbers of world peace."

The League sat in legal judgment only. It resorted to no sanctions against contumacious Japan. It did not do so, because the great powers who were members were not willing to make the necessary sacrifices of trade and treasure, perhaps of men, in a region of the world where their interests seemed not sufficiently vital.[1] This was also true in two great tests of the League after Manchukuo: the Italo-Ethiopian War in 1935-1936, and the German garrisoning of the demilitarized Rhineland in 1936.

Except for nonrecognition [2] the League did nothing about the violation of the Covenant, the Nine-Power Treaty and the Pact of Paris. Except for the pronouncement of the "Stimson Doctrine" the United States also did nothing. That doctrine had been a signal to the League that the United States was on the same track.

Secretary Stimson in the restatement of the "Stimson Doctrine" in the letter to Senator Borah, noted above, made the point that the treaty structure of Washington must stand or fall as a whole. Japan had taken a passage from that book of treaties to create a doctrine to her particular advantage, while ignoring the obligations which she took upon herself so solemnly, along with other powers, when ratifying those treaties. The secret protocol to the Lansing-Ishii Agreement of 1917 had stated that the two governments would not "take advantage of the present [i.e., First World War] conditions in China in order to seek spe-

---

[1] See some very perspicuous comments in the late Frank H. Simonds' *American Foreign Policy in the Post-War Years* (Johns Hopkins Press, 1935).

[2] El Salvador and Germany (after she quitted the League) were the only states before 1936 to recognize Manchukuo *de jure*. Soviet Russia was not a member at the time of its judgment on the Sino-Japanese crisis and hence was not a party to the non-recognition resolution. In 1935 Russia sold the Chinese Eastern Railway to Manchukuo, for *yen* 140,000,000, one-third in cash, two-thirds in goods, the payments guaranteed by Japan. China filed a protest. This agreement between Russia and Manchukuo might be argued to constitute at least a *de facto* recognition.

cial rights or privileges which would abridge the rights of citizens or subjects of friendly states." Paragraph 4 of Article I of the Nine-Power Treaty of 1922 had stipulated that the contracting parties would "refrain from taking advantage of conditions in order to seek special rights or privileges in China which would abridge the rights of the subjects or citizens of other friendly states, *and from countenancing action inimical to the security of such States.*" [1] The Nine-Power Treaty thus took over, multilaterally, and continued beyond the period of the First World War, the obligation previously but secretly agreed upon by the United States and Japan to be in perfect accord with the *declared* policy of the two governments in regard to China. In thus embodying in the Nine-Power Treaty of 1922 the formula of the secret Lansing-Ishii protocol of 1917, the diplomatists at Washington had added the words just italicized.

Japan ignored those portions of the Nine-Power Treaty which had been inconvenient to her, but clung to the italicized phraseology of the article here quoted in an effort to construct for the Far East a new and exclusive policy. During the London Naval Conference in 1930 reference was made in Japan to the role of that Empire as "guardian of peace in the Pacific." Before Japan quitted the League, the Japanese delegation at Geneva stated to the Assembly (February 21, 1933) : "Japan is responsible for the maintenance of peace and order in the Far East." Shortly afterward (February 25, 1933) her representative at the League of Nations announced "the insistence of Japan not to allow any party to intervene in the Manchurian problem." Successive Japanese spokesmen repeated this statement of policy and expanded it to include the rest of China,[2] then Eastern Asia, next "Greater Eastern Asia," finally "Japan's Co-Prosperity Area," whatever those descriptions might comprise.

[1] Italics inserted. Notice that in the Nine-Power Treaty the word "present" is omitted, but the word "friendly" retained. Presumably the retention of "friendly" at that time excluded Russia.

[2] One of the most conspicuous utterances of this nature was by Mr. Eijii Amau, referred to by the newspapers as the "spokesman of the Foreign Office" at Tokyo, in 1934. Although the Amau pronouncement was not a state paper, its validity was confirmed by a statement attributed to the Japanese Ambassador in Washington, Mr. Saito, in the New York *Times* (April 24, 1934) and by a statement by Foreign Minister Hirota to the United States Embassy, reported in the *Times* (April 26, 1934). Said Amau in a long statement: "We oppose any attempt on the part of China to avail herself of the influence of any other country in order to resist Japan. . . . The supplying to China of war planes, the building of airdromes in China and the detailing of military instructors and advisers to China, or the contracting of a loan to provide funds for political uses would obviously tend to alienate the friendly relations between Japan and China and other countries and to disturb the peace and order of Eastern Asia. Japan will oppose such projects."

Under this concept Japan even objected to a League of Nations technical mission for reconstruction and internal improvements in China, including roads, waterways, education, rural credit, hygiene, and flood control.

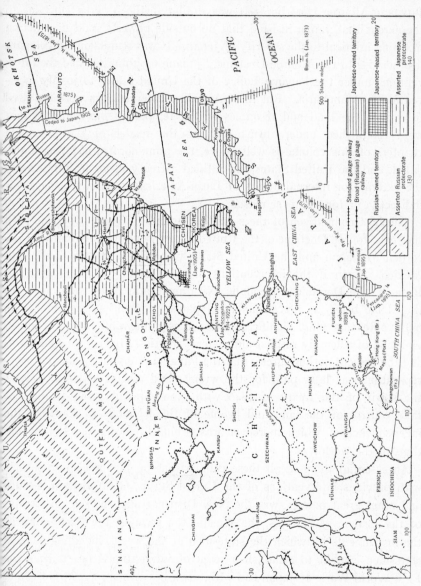

Map 36. Japan and Russia in Eastern Asia, 1936.

This expression of a policy of hegemony over "Greater Eastern Asia" was frequently referred to by Japanese spokesmen as the Asiatic or Japanese Monroe Doctrine.[1] It was similar to the Monroe Doctrine to the extent that Japan insisted that no outside power should take action in China inimical to the security of Japan. It was scandalous to compare it otherwise to the Monroe Doctrine. Japanese publicists cited the interventions under the Panama Policy of the United States to justify intervention in Manchuria. But these American interventions were not used to exploit the land and resources of the temporary protectorates that were established under them; and, as the reader of the preceding chapters of this volume is well aware, the protectorates had been liquidated, and the United States had ratified a treaty never to intervene in the external or internal affairs of Latin-American republics, directly or indirectly, or for whatever reason.

The best comparison of the so-called Japanese Monroe Doctrine with the real Monroe Doctrine of the United States would be the treatment accorded by Japan and the United States respectively to Manchuria and Mexico. Even if the interventions of the United States in Cuba, in Panama, the Dominican Republic, Nicaragua, and Haiti were cited—as they have been—as precedents for Japan's interventions in China, one must note this most significant fact: these interventions were not in violation of solemnly ratified multilateral treaties. It may be contended, and the present author agrees, that the Panama intervention was unjust—reparation was later paid for the wrong—and that it violated at least the spirit of the treaty of 1846 with New Granada; but it did not take control of the land and people of the Republic of Panama, the independence of which moreover was promptly recognized by the nations of the world.

An essential thing in all these comparisons of Japanese interventions with previous interventions of the United States, Great Britain, France and other great powers, was the New Dispensation: the solemn treaties of the League of Nations, the Washington treaties, the Pact of Paris, the instruments by which the statesmen of the world, including Japan's statesmen, sought to establish a reign of international peace after the First World War. If Japan had withdrawn her armed forces from China and had agreed with the recognized states of Asia as the United States had agreed with Latin America, that no one state has a right to intervene in the internal or external affairs of another state; if she had

---

[1] George H. Blakeslee has described the development of "The Japanese Monroe Doctrine," in *Foreign Affairs*, XI (1932-1933), 670-681.

observed the obligations of the Washington treaties as well as enjoyed their advantages; if she had accepted the recommendations of the League of Nations on the Manchurian and Shanghai and other issues with China, then the world might well have applauded the Japanese claim to an Asiatic Monroe Doctrine.

For the New Dispensation Japan had only hatred and contempt. Further, she interpreted the Philippine independence act of March 3, 1934,[1] and the efforts of the United States to bring about limitation of naval armament, not as evidence of good will and peaceful ideals, but rather as an indication of softness. The distresses of the Occident, signalized by the continuing Great Depression and the rise of Italian and German power in Europe, encouraged Japanese militarists to go ahead rapidly with the conquest of China while the Western powers were unable to stop them. Japan next attacked Peiping [2] (July 7, 1937) and extended the Second Sino-Japanese War for the thorough conquest of that vast country. She had now entered with spectacular earnestness a further phase of the designs expressed by Lord Hotta to the Shogun back in 1858: "to command universal vassalage" and "hegemony over all nations."

Such an empire, erected on the ruins of ancient China, accompanied by a German empire built on the ruins of a conquered Europe, presaged an unbalance of power in the Old World which ought to be the nightmare of every anxious American student of international affairs. It brought back the danger that had been removed for a generation by American intervention in the First World War. It cast power politics in the shape of a future totalitarian vise pressing out the life of the republican New World. It foreshadowed the possibility of a two-ocean war to be fought with a one-ocean navy. It signalized the close of that foolproof period of American diplomatic history when the distresses of the Old World had been uniformly the advantages of the New World. It meant the end of the long period of isolation and peace in which the

[1] This law provided that the Philippine Islands, after a period of ten years as an autonomous commonwealth under the protection of the United States, should become an absolutely independent republic. At the end of the ten-year period, which began with the inauguration in 1936 of the new commonwealth of the Philippines, all American military forces were to be withdrawn from the islands, and the two governments jointly were to decide whether, and on what terms, the United States should maintain a naval base in the islands. This act seemed to indicate a withdrawal for good and all by the United States from the Philippines at the end of the prescribed decade. Notwithstanding Japan's temporary conquest of the Philippines in 1942, Philippine independence went into effect as scheduled, July 4, 1946, following the defeat and surrender of Japan.

[2] Historical usage sanctions the name Peking for the capital of China before 1928, when the Nationalists shifted it to Nanking and renamed the former capital Peiping. In 1949 the Communists established Peking, with the old spelling, as their capital.

Continental Republic had been created in the empty spaces of North America, working out its Manifest Destiny between wide ocean barriers.

In the face of such doubly ominous portents President Roosevelt tried to thwart German aggression in Europe and Japanese aggression in Asia by throwing the weight of American neutrality in favor of the victims of aggression, and at the same time keeping the United States out of war in either Asia or Europe. To do this, first in the case of Japan, later in the case of Germany, he had to get around some of the apparent obstacles of the neutrality resolution of April 30, 1937, designed, so to speak, to keep the United States out of the First World War rather than the Second World War. We recall that the law stipulated a mandatory embargo on the export of arms, ammunition, and implements of warfare, and credits, from the neutral United States to belligerent countries, but left it to the discretion of the President to "find" or not to "find" a war in existence which required the application of this domestic law.

President Roosevelt hesitated to proclaim neutrality, in this phase of the Second Sino-Japanese War.[1] Under the domestic law of May 1, 1937, this would have instantly embargoed the export of arms, ammunition, and implements of war to both China and Japan, and would have given the President discretionary power to prohibit the export to *both* belligerents of other articles [2] *in American ships,* but not in foreign ships. Japan had ships. China had no ships. So Japan would continue in any event to import from the neutral United States other war material than arms, ammunition, and implements of war, that is, gasoline, oil, and scrap iron, to feed her war machines in China.

Such a neutrality, flowing from the mandatory provision of the law of May 1, 1937, was distasteful to the President because it would operate more favorably to Japan, considered to be the aggressor, than to China, esteemed to be the victim. He preferred that circumstances might not oblige him to "find" a war in existence. As the Sino-Japanese War developed, Japan proved equally unwilling to be involved in further "international difficulties" as long as the Western powers were not fully occupied by distresses in the Occident. She was not prepared to assert belligerent rights against neutral shipping on the high seas. Thereupon

---

[1] The First Sino-Japanese War was in 1895. The Second Sino-Japanese War may be said to have begun in 1931 with the conquest of Manchuria, and to have been in existence, with short truces, to 1945.

[2] This provision of the Act covering the export in American ships of articles other than arms, ammunition, and implements of warfare was on the statutes only between May 1, 1937, and May 1, 1939.

the Government began to license the export, in privately owned ships of the United States, of arms to Hong Kong to be trans-shipped to China. It also furnished credit to the Chinese Government for the stabilization of exchange and the purchase of supplies, as did European governments.[1] By "moral embargoes" it endeavored to persuade American exporters not to export arms, ammunition or implements of warfare to nations (like Japan) which bombed civilian populations in open cities.

President Roosevelt now took another look across the Pacific Ocean. He could not, for the life of the United States, see a war anywhere. Hostilities, battles, marches and counter-marches of invading armies, the bombing of civilian populations, the sack of great cities, indescribable human suffering and death, all this he could see clearly, but no war that required the proclamation of neutrality according to the Act of April 30, 1937.[2]

It is not a duty of neutrality to keep the weight of power even between two belligerents locked in mortal combat, and accordingly to regulate the flow of supplies so as to make up for the deficiencies of the one

[1] At first, beginning July, 1937, the $2,000,000,000 "gold profit" stabilization fund created as a result of the gold devaluation act of 1934, was used to stabilize the Chinese currency, to buy and sell dollars and *yuan*. On December 13, 1938, the Export-Import Bank, a government corporation, extended a commercial credit of $25,000,000, and on March 7, 1940, a second credit of $20,000,000, to the Universal Trading Company of New York, guaranteed in both instances by the Central Bank of China, for the purchase of agricultural, industrial and manufactured articles (including motor trucks).

These loans were paralleled by loans for the purchase of supplies, from the British, French, Russian, Czechoslovakian, and Belgian Governments. In the case of the French Government the loans were also for construction of the railway between Szechuan and Yunnan. See *Documents on American Foreign Relations*, III (1940-1941), 245-246.

[2] "We have not put into effect the neutrality proclamation," he explained in a then off-the-record special press conference with members of the American Society of Newspaper Editors, April 21, 1938, "for the very simple reason that if we could find a way of not doing it, we would be more neutral than if we did.

"Now, if we declared neutrality, what would happen? Japan could not buy any munitions from us, but they are not buying them anyway. China is buying munitions from us via England, via Singapore, via Hong Kong—not direct—through English purchases and, undoubtedly, American munitions are going into China today. But, on the other hand, Japan has complete, free access to all of our raw material markets because they dominate the ocean. They are buying their copper, their oil, their cotton—they are buying all kinds of things, scrap metal by the shiploads, which is going into munitions, and they would be able, under the Neutrality Act, to continue to buy oil and copper and scrap metal.

"Therefore, by virtue of this excuse [of the Japanese] that they are not at war—it is only an excuse—we are maintaining, in fact, a neutral position."

"We are achieving that, despite the neutrality?" asked one of his listeners.

"Despite the neutrality law," continued the President, "and that is the trouble with a neutrality law that attempts to tie the hands of an administration for future events and circumstances that no human being can possibly guess." *Public Papers and Addresses of Franklin D. Roosevelt*, 1937 volume: *The Constitution Prevails* (New York, 1941), 287.

which is weaker in seapower, or armament, or money, or manpower. But it may be imperative as a matter of policy to sacrifice a juridical neutrality to help one of the belligerents sustain itself against an aggressor lest the triumph of the aggressor build up an irresistible power to be turned against the whilom neutral. President Roosevelt's use of his discretion, under the letter of the neutrality law of April 30, 1937, was a diplomatic, not a juridical decision, a grave diplomatic step, let it be said, which was supported by the nation. The House of Representatives made no move to question, much less to challenge, the President.

Soon after the Second Sino-Japanese War broke out, Secretary of State Hull made a broad pronouncement (July 16, 1937) of general foreign policy invoking the principles of the Good Neighbor Policy, which the Secretary now applied to the Far East.

"We avoid entering into alliances or entangling commitments," he said, "but we believe in co-operative effort by peaceful and practicable means in support of the principles hereinbefore stated." [1]

Secretary Hull did not stress or mention the integrity of China. He did express willingness, as he had offered since 1934, to modify treaties, when need arose for it, "by orderly processes carried out in a spirit of mutual helpfulness and accommodation." He left the door open for peaceful negotiations to settle the China question, either by another conference, or by negotiation between the United States and Japan.

Once more China appealed to the League of Nations (September 12, 1937), and once more the United States accepted the League's invitation to sit in on its consideration of the conflict without voting. A committee of the League reported Japan guilty of violating the Pact of Paris and the Nine-Power Treaty, and called upon the signatories of the latter treaty, including Japan, to meet in conference to seek some method of ending the Sino-Japanese conflict by agreement.[2] The same day (October 5, 1937) President Roosevelt in a sensational public address at Chicago appealed to the "peace-loving nations" to make a concerted effort "in opposition to those violations of treaties and those ignorings of human instincts which today are creating a state of international anarchy and

---

[1] In a supplemental statement on August 23, 1937, Mr. Hull explained that the principles expressed on July 16 applied in the Pacific area as elsewhere. "It embraces the principles embodied in many treaties, including the Washington Conference treaties and the Kellogg-Briand Pact of Paris. . . . This Government is endeavoring to see kept alive, strengthened, and revitalized, in reference to the Pacific area and to the world these fundamental principles." Department of State *Press Releases*, XVII, No. 407 (July 17, 1937) and XVII, No. 413 (August 28, 1937). See also F. D. Roosevelt, *Public Addresses and Papers, 1940*, 589, 590.

[2] A. W. Griswold, *Far Eastern Policy of the United States* (New York, 1938), 456-460.

instability from which there is no escape through mere isolation or neutrality." War, he said, should be quarantined like an epidemic disease. The next day Secretary Hull declared that Japan's action in China was inconsistent with the Nine-Power Treaty and the Kellogg-Briand Pact of Paris, and that the Government of the United States was in general accord with the conclusion of the Assembly of the League of Nations on these points.

Given the dangerous international situation in Europe, none of the great European powers parties to the broken Nine-Power Treaty dared to call a conference to mend it. They prevailed on little Belgium to extend the invitation. If any government expected the United States to take the lead at Brussels in quarantine measures against Japan, it was disappointed. The President himself explained that the delegation of the United States went to Brussels without any commitments to any other governments. In the conference Japan declared she would tolerate no outside interference in the settlement of her dispute with China. Italy, who had left the League after its rebuke to her on Ethiopia, could be counted on to block unanimity of resolve on any action that might be proposed against Japan. The meeting adjourned without accomplishing anything more than an empty reaffirmation of the principles of the demolished Nine-Power Treaty.

After the failure of the Brussels Conference the United States began to evacuate its nationals and its forces [1] from Chinese territory, in order to avoid incidents that might lead to war. Japanese militarists took this as a sign of weakness. Some irresponsible officers bombed from the air and destroyed the U. S. gunboat *Panay* (December 12, 1937) in the Yangtze River. The United States was quick to protest and demand reparations. Japan even more quickly apologized in advance, and paid the reparations demanded without question: $2,214,007.36.[2] She did not want war with the United States while Europe was still at peace.

The United States continued to keep a list of Japanese violations of the treaty rights of American citizens, their persons and property, and to file protests and caveats against a future reckoning. Japan on her part continued her conquests deep in China. Wherever she went she

---

[1] Since the Boxer Protocol of 1901 the United States and other powers had maintained small detachments of marines to guard the legations, as long as they existed at Peking, and since 1927 they had contributed small forces to defend the international settlement at Shanghai. The United States also had maintained, in company with Great Britain and France, nine small gunboats to patrol Chinese rivers against depredations to American citizens and commerce. In 1937 there were 528 marines at Peiping (Peking), 814 infantry at Tientsin, 2,555 marines at Shanghai. Griswold, *op. cit.*, 462.

[2] No punitive reparations were assessed.

slammed shut, in the face of the Washington treaties of 1922 and all other treaties, the old Open Door, and locked it tight with all sorts of devices: discriminatory tariffs, taxes and railroad rates, exchange controls, import and export controls, restrictions on shipping and port facilities, monopolies, and other contrivances in violations of treaties.[1] As to the integrity of China, her armies tore it to pieces.

Japanese-American relations by now were raising greater questions than the Open Door or the treaty rights of American citizens in China. They were testing right and wrong, according to the respective lights of the two governments, in what was coming slowly to be interpreted as a challenge of power to the principles of liberty everywhere.[2]

The diplomatic capitulation of Great Britain and France to Germany at Munich in September, 1938, and the certainty that they would be involved indefinitely and deeply in European dangers, encouraged Japan in her Asiatic policy and sharpened her effrontery toward those powers in the Far East, although for the time being she dealt more cautiously with the United States and its nationals as long as that Pacific power was not definitely involved in Europe. While the United States protested to Japan against indiscriminate slaughter of civilian populations by the bombing of undefended cities in violation of Hague Conventions, Japan was making in the United States huge purchases of oil and gasoline with which to lubricate and fuel her growing fleets of warships and planes, and of scrap iron with which to perfect her armaments against any or all comers. Public opinion in the United States, incensed at Japanese bombings of civilians and conscience-stricken at the provenance of Japan's supplies, increasingly demanded an embargo on exports of war materials to Japan. Such an embargo, at least in time of peace (i.e., no recognized war between China and Japan, as testified

[1] William C. Johnstone has listed and analyzed these treaty violations in his study of *The United States and Japan's New Order* (American Council of the Institute of Pacific Relations, New York, 1941).

[2] So wrote Secretary Hull, in a public letter to Vice President Garner, January 10, 1938: "The interest and concern of the United States in the Far Eastern situation, in the European situation, and in situations on this continent, are not measured by the number of American concerns residing in a particular country at a particular moment nor by the amount of investment of American citizens there, nor by the volume of trade. There is a broader and more fundamental interest—which is that orderly processes in international relations must be maintained. Referring expressly to the Far East, an area which contains approximately half the population of the world, the United States is deeply interested in supporting *by peaceful means* influences contributory to preservation and encouragement of orderly processes. This interest far transcends in importance the value of American trade with China or American interests in China, it transcends even the question of safeguarding the immediate welfare of American citizens in China." Department of State *Press Releases*, XVIII, No. 433 (January 15, 1938). Italics inserted.

by the inanimity of the neutrality laws), would have been unquestionably in violation of the treaty of commerce of 1911. If the United States was standing for the sanctity of treaties all over the world it could not very consistently violate this one by imposing an embargo, not to mention political reasons for hesitating to discriminate against Japanese commerce. Widespread demand for abrogation of the treaty, with the stipulated six months' notice according to its terms, brought up proposed resolutions in Congress urging such a step on the executive. Before a resolution could be passed, Secretary Hull announced, as an executive act, that the requisite notice had been given, July 26, 1939. The treaty accordingly expired January 26, 1940, four months after the beginning of the European war. It left the way open for commercial discriminations and embargoes against Japan.[1]

In the next two chapters of this volume, we shall see how the unbalance of power in Europe and Asia and its mounting danger to the New World merged to break down the neutrality of the United States for the third time in its history. During that great conflict China was to rise suddenly to unheard-of prestige. As ally of the United States she succeeded in abolishing American extraterritorial rights by the treaty of January 11, 1943, thus accompanying the termination of the unequal treaties by the last of the other powers. The United States further recognized the new position of China by repealing the Chinese exclusion acts, admitting Chinese citizens to an immigration quota, and making Chinese aliens resident in the United States eligible at last for citizenship.[2] Entering the United Nations as a charter member, China became one of the five permanent members of the all-powerful Security Council along with the United States, Great Britain, France, and the Soviet Union. It seemed that a new day of equality and prosperity had come for that great nation, most populous state on the globe, vast seat of the world's oldest civilization. In the penultimate chapters of this book we shall have to read the sad climax for China of the Second World War : the Yalta agreement, the entrance of Russia into the war, the surprising surrender of Japan, which caught the Chinese off guard, so to speak ; the Communist Civil War ; and defeat in victory for the Nationalist Government.

[1] For pre-Pearl Harbor studies of Japanese-American relations and Far Eastern issues see: Harold S. Quigley and George H. Blakeslee, *The Far East, an International Survey* (World Peace Foundation, 1938) ; T. A. Bisson, *American Policy in the Far East, 1931-1940* (Institute of Pacific Relations, New York, 1940) ; W. W. Willoughby, *Japan's Case Examined* (Johns Hopkins Press, 1940). M. Royama, *Foreign Policy of Japan, 1914-1939* (Japanese Council, Institute of Pacific Relations, Tokyo, 1941).

[2] For the treaty and the act of December 17, 1943, repealing the exclusion acts, see *Documents on American Foreign Relations* (World Peace Foundation, 1944, 1945), V, 485-500, VI, 607-19.

COMPARATIVE NAVAL STRENGTH OF THE SEVEN PRINCIPAL POWERS IN JULY, 1939

TYPE	TOTAL BUILT		UNDER AGE		OVER AGE		BUILDING AND APPROPRIATED FOR	
	NUMBER	TONS	NUMBER	TONS	NUMBER	TONS	NUMBER	TONS
UNITED STATES								
CAPITAL SHIPS	15	464,300	14	438,200	1	26,100	8	300,000
AIRCRAFT CARRIERS	5	120,100	5	120,100	0	0	2	34,500
CRUISERS A	17	161,200	17	161,200	0	0	1	10,000
CRUISERS B	17	137,775	17	137,775	0	0	8	60,000
DESTROYERS	221	273,490	54	84,190	167	189,300	43	68,380
SUBMARINES	89	83,175	22	34,435	67	48,740	25	35,250
BRITISH EMPIRE								
CAPITAL SHIPS	18	495,500	18	495,500	0	0	9	335,000
AIRCRAFT CARRIERS	9	148,600	7	127,700	2	20,900	7	138,000
CRUISERS A	15	145,620	15	145,620	0	0	0	0
CRUISERS B	47	294,635	24	185,945	23	108,690	25	146,500
DESTROYERS	178	233,359	107	154,114	71	79,245	37	37,350
SUBMARINES	55	56,919	45	52,469	10	4,450	18	15,690
JAPAN *								
CAPITAL SHIPS	11	308,480	10	301,400	1	7,080	3	121,000
AIRCRAFT CARRIERS	11	146,520	11	146,520	0	0	2	25,000
CRUISERS A	17	153,050	12	107,800	5	45,250	0	0
CRUISERS B	23	132,635	15	97,555	8	35,080	5	44,000
DESTROYERS	111	141,748	75	106,798	36	34,950	9	14,900
SUBMARINES	59	76,863	40	59,261	19	17,602	3	6,000
FRANCE								
CAPITAL SHIPS	7	163,945	7	163,945	0	0	4	140,000
AIRCRAFT CARRIERS	2	32,146	2	32,146	0	0	2	36,000
CRUISERS A	7	70,000	7	70,000	0	0	0	0
CRUISERS B	11	79,725	11	79,725	0	0	3	24,000
DESTROYERS	71	121,201	70	120,286	1	915	30	46,776
SUBMARINES	75	72,709	75	72,709	0	0	27	24,252
ITALY								
CAPITAL SHIPS	10	108,730	9	99,498	1	9,232	4	140,000
AIRCRAFT CARRIERS	0	0	0	0	0	0	0	0
CRUISERS A	7	70,000	7	70,000	0	0	0	0
CRUISERS B	14	80,918	12	74,488	2	6,430	14	56,344
DESTROYERS	130	133,163	100	111,936	30	21,227	12	15,200
SUBMARINES	105	79,704	98	77,248	7	2,456	28	30,986
GERMANY								
CAPITAL SHIPS	7	108,080	5	82,000	2	26,000	4	150,000
AIRCRAFT CARRIERS	0	0	0	0	0	0	2	38,500
CRUISERS A	2	20,000	2	20,000	0	0	3	30,000
CRUISERS B	6	35,600	6	35,600	0	0	4	28,000
DESTROYERS	44	51,081	32	42,844	12	8,237	10	18,110
SUBMARINES	50	19,709	50	19,709	0	0	21	11,573
RUSSIA **								
CAPITAL SHIPS	3	69,878	3	69,878	0	0	3	105,000
AIRCRAFT CARRIERS	1	9,000	1	9,000	0	0	2	24,000
CRUISERS A	3	24,030	3	24,030	0	0	5	40,000
CRUISERS B	5	28,994	3	17,034	2	11,960	0	0
DESTROYERS	37	40,907	23	25,024	14	15,883	10	26,295
SUBMARINES	122	64,265	114	59,897	8	4,368	19	12,158

* Best obtainable data due to the fact that the Japanese Government did not release figures. Japanese tonnage was probably greater than indicated above, and particularly so in the categories of aircraft carriers, cruisers, destroyers, and submarines.

** Best obtainable data due to the fact that the Soviet Government did not release figures. Soviet tonnage was probably greater than indicated above, and particularly so in the categories of destroyers and submarines.

SOURCE: Compiled from figures furnished by United States Navy Department to House of Representatives indicating comparative naval strength of the seven principal powers as of 2 July, 1939. To be found in Congressional Record, 76th Congress, 2nd Session, Volume 85, Part I, pages 1065-66.

Compiled by Anthony C. J. Davidonis

STATUS OF THE WORLD'S SEVEN PRINCIPAL NAVIES ON 1 JULY, 1939

| CAPITAL SHIPS | AIRCRAFT CARRIERS | CRUISERS A | CRUISERS B | DESTROYERS | SUBMARINES |

UNITED STATES

BRITISH EMPIRE

JAPAN

FRANCE

ITALY

GERMANY

RUSSIA

[None building]

[None building ??]

[None building]

[None built]

[None building]

[None built]

In each ship-figure above, the hull length represents tonnage on the following basis:

1 Tonnage under age on 1 July, 1939
2 Tonnage over age on 1 July, 1939
3 Tonnage building on 1 July, 1939.
4 Unknown amount of tonnage secretly built or building.

Note: Soviet Government did not publish figures.
Japanese Government did not publish figures,

Compiled by Anthony C.J. Davidonis

CHAPTER XLII

ISOLATION AND NEUTRALITY

(1937-1939)

WHAT caused the second war in Europe, twenty-five years after the beginning of the First World War, was the recrudescence of German military power and will to conquest under a new Napoleonic genius, Adolf Hitler. Taking advantage of the apathy and division of the nations that had checked and beaten Germany in the First World War, he fired the German people with a religiously fanatical nationalism determined to avenge the defeat of 1918 and to conquer Europe: today Europe, tomorrow the entire world. He moulded them into a totalitarian folk under his own dictatorship, resting on revolutionary repudiations of popular sovereignty and democracy, a military technocracy called National Socialism. Before Great Britain and France [1] could fully awake to the swift and deadly facts of German power, Hitler had rearmed and fortified the Rhineland, had united Austria with Germany by force, and had built up a mighty mechanized army and overwhelming armadas of the air.

By threatening the Allies with war in the summer of 1938, Hitler achieved the greatest success possible in diplomacy: he won the fruits of a war without fighting one. He made the Allied leaders come to Munich and sign a peace with him and his new fascist ally, Premier Mussolini of Italy, a peace which at one stroke shattered the treaty of Versailles in Europe and broke up the alliances of France that had protected the small countries in the central and eastern parts of that continent against another eruption of German power. Helpless at Munich, Britain and France tried to divert the German lightnings away from their own dooryards by opening a field for German conquest in middle Europe and in Russia: in Russia, the actual ally of France, excluded at Munich!

Vainly Prime Minister Chamberlain and Premier Daladier hoped against hope that Munich would bring peace in their time in the west. Foolishly they put faith in Hitler's pledge that he would never change

---

[1] Arnold Wolfers has analyzed conflicting strategies of peace since Versailles in *Britain and France between Two Wars* (Yale Institute of International Studies, 1940).

another frontier in Europe. But the thunderbolts had been forged, and now they could be hurled in any direction from the mountaintop of Berchtesgaden. Too late the men of Munich woke up to this when they saw Czechoslovakia, sacrificed in 1938 by cession of her northern "Sudeten" provinces, next trampled, under the treads of German tanks in the spring of 1939 and annihilated, her vast stocks of armaments added to the conqueror's arsenals for use against the next victim. The League of Nations, which had guaranteed the political independence and territorial integrity of each covenanting party, was not even consulted in this dismemberment and extinction of a signatory state.

Belatedly Great Britain and France prepared for the war that was certain soon to come when Hitler's avalanche of armaments should move against another nation. Not to resist the next time would mean definitive surrender to a power that could not afterward be checked. It would mean the death of the British and French Empires and the democracies on which they rested at home, the end of the small nations of the continent, the unification of Europe by that conquest which successive captains of war had tried and failed to accomplish during the last three hundred years, and its enfeoffment to German Nazism.

As soon as the crops had been harvested, Hitler struck again, on September 1, 1939, this time at Poland, immediately after signing a dramatic non-aggression pact with Russia, the outcast of Munich, the only one of the former Allies of 1938 who had been willing to fight for Czechoslovakia, the former ally whom Great Britain had wooed again in vain. In desperation Great Britain and France declared war on Germany, September 3, rather than by neutrality to contribute to their own certain destruction. By fighting there was some chance to save themselves; by not fighting, none. From a bedeviled continent the holocaust flamed up, to light the whole world in its lurid glare.

Unlike the days of 1914, when the American public, and even the United States Government was taken by surprise by the sudden outbreak of war in Europe, the advent of war in 1939 was not unexpected either by the people or by the Government. They were watching for it. They had been dreading it for years.

The Roosevelt Administration came into power almost simultaneously with the accession of Hitler to the Chancellorship of Germany. Although at first absorbed with the economic debacle at home, the new President continued the efforts of the Hoover Administration to further international agreements for disarmament in order to promote peace. As early as May 27, 1933, the United States delegate to the disarmament conference at Geneva declared that his Government was willing "to consult the other States" in case of a threat to peace, with a view to averting conflict.

"Further than that," he declared, "in the event that the States, in conference, determine that a State has been guilty of a breach of the peace in violation of its international obligations and take measures against the violator, then, *if we concur in the judgment rendered* as to the responsible and guilty party, we will refrain from any action tending to defeat such collective effort which these States may thus make to restore peace." [1]

President Roosevelt made it plain at the time of the Ethiopian crisis of 1935, and again on the occasion of Japan's next attack on China in 1937, that the United States did concur in the judgment made by the League and would respect any sanctions that it might take to block aggression. In May, 1936, he appealed to all the chiefs of state the world over to enter into non-aggression pacts. He declared publicly at Chicago, October 5, 1937, after mentioning the Kellogg-Briand Pact of Paris, the Covenant of the League of Nations, the Nine-Power Treaty, and the new Pan-American treaties outlawing aggression and intervention in the New World, that aggressor states ought in effect to be quarantined. [2]

All these speeches, and numerous other expressions, indicated a disposition to co-operate for the maintenance of international peace, in order, as the President put it, to keep the United States out of war and to cut the expense of armament. They indicated also anxiety as to whether the United States could avoid involvement in any war that did come in Europe. No such anxiety existed in the Government of the United States in the years before the First World War. The new concern was reflected in the rising appropriations for army and navy bills.

Whatever the anxiety of the Government may have been as to the ultimate effect of another European war, there was no question of its policy of keeping out of war in the Old World, whether in Europe or Asia. That policy had been fixed in the neutrality legislation of 1935-1937, written on the statutes and signed by the President, in a wave of disillusionment arising from a review of the last war, and of fear that the United States might be "dragged" into another one like it. The

[1] Statement of Mr. Norman Davis to the General Commission of the Disarmament Conference, May 22, 1933. Italics inserted. Department of State *Press Releases* (May 27, 1933).

[2] *Public Papers and Addresses of Franklin D. Roosevelt*, 1937 volume, 406-411.

President favored the new neutrality laws in principle, but felt that they were too rigid, that situations might arise in which the wholly inflexible embargo might have exactly the opposite effect from that intended.[1] The people did not realize that the next war might not be like the last one. They were largely isolationist.

When during the European war crisis of September, 1938, all the peace machinery of the times seemed to have failed, President Roosevelt at the eleventh hour appealed to Great Britain, Germany, France, and Czechoslovakia, and to Hitler and Mussolini personally, to save the peace of Europe. This was more than Woodrow Wilson had done in 1914. Until archives are opened up years hence, it is not possible to say, probably it will never be possible to say, precisely what influence, if any, the President's appeal had in bringing about the Munich Conference. The motive of the Government was to insure the safety of the United States by preserving the peace of Europe. Every man and woman in the United States, it was explained officially, shared in the universal feeling of relief that war had been averted.[2] Roosevelt's reaction to the crisis of September, 1938, as contrasted with Wilson's passivity in July, 1914, is a gauge of the extent to which a quarter century of contemporary history had tightened up the relationships of the Old World and the New, for good or ill, in our age of Great Technology.

After Czechoslovakia had ceased to exist, if such a euphemism is permissible, President Roosevelt in the spring of 1939 addressed identic notes to Chancellor Hitler and Premier Mussolini stating that the possibility of a new war was of definite concern to the people of the United States, for whom he spoke, "as it must be also to the peoples of the other nations of the entire Western Hemisphere."[3] "All of them know," he continued, "that any major war, *even if it were confined to other continents,* must bear heavily on them during its continuance and for many generations to come." Speaking for the United States as one of the nations of the Western Hemisphere "not involved in the *immediate* con-

---

[1] Note by President Roosevelt, *Public Papers and Addresses,* 1939 volume, p. 523.

[2] Message to Czechoslovakia, Germany, Great Britain, and France, September 26, 1938. To Chancellor Adolf Hitler, September 27, 1938. *Ibid.,* 531-538. Department of State *Press Releases,* XIX, Nos. 470, 471 (October 1, October 8, 1938) for the correspondence. Undersecretary of State Sumner Welles summarizes the correspondence with Mussolini, which is not printed in the President's *Papers and Addresses.* The last two sentences of the above text are taken almost *verbatim* from Mr. Welles's radio address of October 3, 1938, explaining the crisis.

[3] "You will note that I did not assume to speak for them," he explained to the Press Conference of April 15, 1939, in a running exegesis of the note, which went out on April 14. *Papers and Addresses,* 1939 volume, 208-217. I have inserted italics in quoted passages.

troversies which have arisen in Europe," he challenged the dictators to make good their professions of peace by asking them outright if they were willing to give assurances that their armed forces would not attack or invade the territory or possessions of the following independent nations: Finland, Estonia, Latvia, Lithuania, Sweden, Norway, Denmark, the Netherlands, Belgium, Great Britain and Ireland, France, Portugal, Spain, Switzerland, Lichtenstein, Luxemburg, Poland, Hungary, Rumania, Yugoslavia, Russia, Bulgaria, Greece, Turkey, Iraq, the Arabias, Syria, Palestine, Egypt, and Iran.

In case Germany and Italy would engage in "reciprocal assurances" with the enumerated governments, Roosevelt offered to participate, in the resulting peaceful surroundings, in a general international discussion for the limitation of armaments and the elimination of international trade barriers—in other words a great international conference with guns "parked" outside.

The dictators did not deign to answer this plain proposal, except by tirades from their own rostra. It was evident they intended to make war.

In case of another European war and consequent proclamation of the neutrality of the United States under the Act of April 30, 1937, a mandatory embargo would immediately go into effect on the shipment of arms, ammunition and implements of warfare,[1] directly or indirectly from the United States to any of the belligerent powers. Included in such category, by official listing under the act, were airplanes and their component parts. Similarly the granting of credits to belligerent governments, other than for ordinary current transactions, would be blocked by domestic law. The neutrality law also prohibited citizens of the United States from traveling on belligerent merchant ships; and it prohibited the arming of neutral United States merchant ships. From the then current disillusionist historiography of American intervention in the First World War, the nation had drawn the conclusion that it had been impolitic to insist on traditional and indubitable neutral rights. To do so again might get the country into another war.

Thus had been forsworn in a trice, as it were, the American birthright of Freedom of the Seas, written into the early treaty structure of the United States, and subsequently into international law, doctrines which the great Republic of the West had championed in two previous major wars.

[1] The Act of 1937 had contained a two-year section authorizing the President, at his discretion, to embargo the export overseas in American ships of other articles than arms, ammunition and implements of warfare; and to forbid the export of any *American-owned* property in such articles or materials on foreign ships; but this section of the act expired on May 1, 1939. See above, pp. 666-667.

This was not only a discouragement to the small nations of the world who hoped to be neutrals and to have neutral rights in the next war. It was also an ominous portent for Great Britain and France. It would make it impossible for those powers to draw upon the neutral United States as a storehouse for munitions as they had done in the First World War. We have seen that without that neutral reservoir, and seapower to protect trans-Atlantic imports, the Allies could not have armed themselves adequately in 1914-1917 to resist their enemies. The neutrality laws of 1935 and 1937 closed this neutral storehouse to the powers that controlled the seas. The mandatory embargo on munitions, announced to the world by the United States for application automatically to the next war, was in effect an assurance to Germany that if her ruler attacked a European State, and thus provoked a general war, his enemies, Great Britain and France, could not rely on these vital succors from the United States as they had done in the last war. Given the greater preparation of Germany, the neutrality of the United States under the new *domestic* legislation of 1937 would ensure the defeat of the Allies, laggard as they had been in preparing themselves for a new attack by Germany. The existence of this legislation was thus a powerful advantage to Adolf Hitler. At the same time it was perfectly obvious that in another war, as in the last war, the United States had nothing to fear or to lose from a victory of the Allies, but much to fear and to lose from a German victory.

President Roosevelt saw this. Vainly he strove, in the summer of 1939, following an unprecedented visit of the British monarchs to Washington and Hyde Park, to get the neutrality statute amended before war should break out in Europe. To alter it radically *after* the outbreak of war, by a change that would operate in favor of one belligerent side, would be unneutral. The President did not ask for the repeal of the entire law, including embargo on credits, prohibition to American citizens to travel on belligerent ships, and prohibition of the arming of American merchant ships. It was only the mandatory, inflexible embargo that he urged Congressional leaders to repeal, retaining the other features calculated to keep the United States out of war. To go "back to international law" on the export of munitions, he felt, would be to benefit the friends of the United States rather than to help those powers who were not its friends.

There is as yet no evidence to show that the President insisted upon a diplomatic equivalent from Great Britain and France—such as cession of island bases or continental territory vital to the defense of the United

States and the New World—before he urged Congress to repeal the embargo. He advocated it gratuitously, in the interests of the United States. So vital was the interest of the Allies in a repeal of the embargo that undoubtedly they would have given much to obtain it, if they had to.

An amendment to the Neutrality Act repealing the embargo passed the House of Representatives in the summer of 1939, but stuck in the Senate. Despite the warnings of Secretary of State Hull that war was imminent, the disillusionists were able to block the amendment. Senator Borah of Idaho, distinguished isolationist and former leader of the irreconcilables of 1919, assured his colleagues that he had his own sources of information which made it clear that there would be no war. The Senate listened to him rather than to the Secretary of State or to the President. Congress adjourned without the amendment having passed. In a certain sense that body had "bet" that war would not break out in Europe before Congress reconvened in January, 1940.[1]

President Roosevelt promptly (September 5, 1939) proclaimed the neutrality of the United States, putting into effect recognized obligations under international law, and other obligations under the domestic neutrality laws including the embargo on arms, ammunition and implements of warfare. "The laws and treaties of the United States," he declared in the preamble of the proclamation, *"without interfering with the free expression of opinion and sympathy,"*[2] nevertheless impose upon all persons who may be within their territory and jurisdiction the duty of an impartial neutrality during the existence of the contest."

In a separate radio address to the people the President said: "This Nation will remain a neutral nation, but I cannot ask that every American remain neutral in thought as well. . . . I hope the United States will keep out of this war. I believe that it will. And I give you assurances that every effort of your Government will be directed toward that end. As long as it remains within my power, there will be no blackout of peace in the United States."[3]

The overwhelming majority of the American people, 99 and 44/100

---

[1] "The action of the majority of the members of Congress in refusing to amend the 'neutrality' legislation and thus permit this country to throw its influence in favor of peace constituted, in a sense, a 'bet' by them that there would be no war until after Congress reconvened in January, 1940." Note by President Roosevelt, *Public Papers and Addresses, op. cit.,* 1939 volume, p. 524.

[2] Italics inserted.

[3] *The Neutrality of the United States, Laws, Proclamations, Orders, Regulations, and Inter-American Declarations Applicable during the Present War in Europe.* Documents covering the period September 3-December 14, 1939. (World Peace Foundation, Boston 1939.)

per cent of them, favored neutrality. Even if they had wanted to go to war, the nation was hopelessly unprepared. The army, antiquated in matériel by the standards of 1939, was smaller than that of third-rate European powers. Despite renewed naval building at exorbitant cost the aim of naval construction had been "a treaty navy by 1942." This meant that by 1942, six years after the expiration of the Washington and London naval treaties, the United States might catch up to the limits allowed by those long-dead treaties! During the interval the rival powers had built far beyond those now ancient treaty ratios.

About ninety per cent of the American people ardently wanted the Allies to defeat Germany. They had desired Great Britain and France to take steps to stop Hitler and Mussolini in Europe, just as the British and French people had wanted the United States to take steps to stop Japan in Asia! Peace was the American passion, nevertheless. The people said and sang God Bless America and pasted those words on their windshields and were glad they were not like other less favored lands and peoples. They took comfort in the wise neutrality legislation, so they conceived it, that would keep their peaceful nation from being dragged or "colonel-housed" into a repetition of the events of 1914-1917.

So convinced was public opinion that the United States would and could keep out of the new war by applying the putative lessons of the last war that the President would have risked impeachment had he failed to "find" a war in existence in Europe which required the proclamation of neutrality.[1] Nor was the argument brought forth that already had been suggested by theorists, and which was to gather influence as the war developed: that a State which violated the Kellogg-Briand Pact of Paris, as Germany had in 1939, had deprived herself of any right to

---

[1] "When the war actually broke out, I was bound by the terms of the 'Neutrality' Act [of 1937] to impose an embargo upon the shipment of arms and munitions." Note by President Roosevelt in his *Public Papers and Addresses, op. cit.,* 1939 volume, p. 524. Compare his attitude toward the Sino-Japanese War, or toward the first Russo-Finnish War that began in 1939, in which the neutrality laws were not invoked. Loans were made through the Export-Import Bank to help Finland, a victim of aggression, as they were being made to help China, a victim of aggression; and "moral embargoes" were resorted to to dissuade American exporters from selling to governments that were bombing civilian populations (i.e., Russia and Japan), war materials other than arms, ammunition, and implements of warfare (i.e., airplanes, aviation gasoline, molybdenum, aluminum, etc.). Public opinion was overwhelmingly indignant at this unprovoked Russian attack on Finland, despite a previous treaty of non-aggression of 1932; and Finland had a warm place in American sympathies if only because of its unique record of paying to the United States Government its schedule of war debts.

On the other hand, when Germany, Italy and other allies, including Finland, declared war on Russia in June, 1941, President Roosevelt did not proclaim the neutrality of the United States. *Documents on American Foreign Relations,* II (1939-1940), 381-392, 725-727; III (1940-1941), 769-772.

the obligations of neutrals—that there could no longer be any real neutrality.[1] To ensure neutrality the President proclaimed (September 8, 1939) a limited national emergency to exist—to the extent necessary for the proper observance, safeguarding, and enforcement of the neutrality of the United States and the strengthening of national defense within the limits of peacetime authorizations.[2]

The uncomfortable truth kept staring people and President in the face: neutrality, with its embargo, would help Hitler defeat Great Britain and France because they could not buy munitions in the United States as they did in the First World War. Accordingly Roosevelt summoned a special session of Congress to repeal the embargo and prohibit American ships from entering such war zones as the Chief Executive should map out. At the same time, the Government of Panama, called for a significant Meeting of Foreign Ministers of the American Republics to take place at the capital of that isthmian state. It was a striking coincidence that the meeting at Panama occurred simultaneously with the special session of the 76th Congress of the United States.[3]

The "Neutrality Act of 1939" became law on November 4 of that year, after six weeks of thorough debate within Congress and without. It had the approval of the public notwithstanding the warning of international lawyers that to change the domestic rules of neutrality *during the course of a war*, so as to benefit one side—in this instance the naval powers—was a departure from neutrality,[4] even though it was a "return to international law." The title of the Act showed that it had a wider purpose than strict juridical neutrality. It was a "Joint Resolution to Preserve the Neutrality and the Peace of the United States *and to Secure the Safety of its Citizens and Their Interests.*"[5] Thus did Government essay to combine neutrality and peace with safety and interest while German and Russian armies overran Poland and the modern Alexander planned his next strokes against the western powers, enemy and neutral alike.

The Neutrality Act of 1939 repealed the embargo on arms, ammunition and implements of war. Such foreign nationals as could cross the

[1] Former Secretary of State Stimson argued so, most plausibly, in 1935. *Proc. Am. Soc. International Law*, 29th Annual Meeting, Washington, D. C., April 25-27, 1935 (Washington, 1935), p. 127.

[2] The legal character of such an emergency is difficult to appraise.

[3] See above, p. 773.

[4] *Research in International Law under the Auspices of the Harvard Law School*, published as a Supplementary Section to the *American Journal of International Law*, Vol XXXIII (1939), 316-317.

[5] Italics inserted.

seas, belligerent and neutrals, could come, buy for cash, and take away anything they wanted; hence this feature of the Act was dubbed the "cash-and-carry" section.[1] American ships were forbidden to carry arms, or to take goods or passengers to any state named in the President's proclamation, or to enter such combat zones as he should mark out. Otherwise the principal features of the old legislation were retained. By abandoning the traditional freedom of the seas for American citizens, ships and cargoes, the United States strove to avoid that choice of neutral policy which had led Woodrow Wilson step by step along the road to war in 1914-1917. At the same time it opened to the maritime Allies, Great Britain and France, *after the war began,* the resources of its private industry for their armament, an arsenal that had been closed to them at the beginning of the war. In this respect American neutral policy turned back, while the war was in progress, to where it was before 1935—to the advantage of the democratic sea powers of Europe so far as control of exports was concerned.[2] But it did not go back to the Freedom of the Seas.

Immediately after the passage of the Neutrality Act of 1939 the President lifted the embargo and proclaimed "combat zones," shown on the accompanying map,[3] into which American ships were forbidden to take cargoes or passengers. These zones were arranged to administer the law in such a way as to make impossible under any pretext such

[1] A limited "cash-and-carry" feature had existed by the Act of May 1, 1937. This act gave a two-year discretionary power to the President to forbid the export *in American ships* of articles other than arms, ammunitions, and implements of warfare, further to prohibit the export of such articles in foreign ships unless all title to the articles had passed from American owners previous to their being carried away from American jurisdiction. Present usage of the phrase "cash-and-carry" applies to the later Neutrality Act of 1939 rather than to the temporary provisions of the act of 1937, which had expired on May 1, 1939.

[2] In requesting a repeal of the embargo features of the neutrality laws of 1935-1937, President Roosevelt thus explained the way in which they had reversed the traditional neutral position of the United States: "The enactment of the embargo provisions did more than reverse our traditional policy [of neutrality under international law]. It had the effect of putting land powers on the same footing as naval powers, so far as sea-borne commerce was concerned. A land power which threatened war could thus feel assured in advance than any prospective sea-power antagonist would be weakened through denial of its ancient right to buy anything anywhere. This, four years ago, gave a definite advantage to one belligerent as against another, not through his own strength or geographical position, but through an affirmative act of ours. . . . The step I recommend is to put this country back on the solid footing of real and traditional neutrality." *Public Papers and Addresses, op. cit.,* 1939 volume, pp. 512-525. This includes the President's own notes of explanation of his address of September 21, 1939, to the Congress.

[3] Map 37.

Map 37. Neutrality Act Zone Map

ZONE 1—Combat Areas Proclaimed by the President (Indicated by crosshatching)

(a) It is unlawful for any citizen of the United States or American watercraft or aircraft to go into or through this area except under rules and regulations as may be prescribed. (Sec. 3.)

(b) Goods, except copyrighted articles or materials, must not leave the United States bound for a belligerent country in Zone 1, even on a foreign vessel, unless all right, title, and interest has been transferred to a foreign government, agent, or person, and a declaration under oath to that effect filed with the collector of the port of export. (Sec. 2(a).)

ZONE 2—Restrictions in this area relate solely to belligerent countries and their possessions, which are indicated by feathered shading

(a) It is unlawful for American vessels to carry any passengers or any articles or materials to belligerent ports in this zone. It is lawful for American vessels to travel in this zone provided they go to neutral ports and provided their voyage does not penetrate Zone 1.

(b) It is unlawful for American vessels to carry any passengers or any articles or materials to ports in Canada east of 66° west longitude. (Sec. 2(g).)

(c) It is lawful to extend credit on all goods for shipment to neutral countries in Zone 2.

ZONE 3—Covers rest of the world

(a) It is lawful to extend credit on goods other than arms, ammunition, and implements of war, shipped to Canada (except that portion of Canada in Zone 2) by inland waterway, railroad, or other vehicle, or aircraft, provided the goods are not purchased by a belligerent Government, its political subdivisions, or their agents, or a belligerent Government monopoly or its agents, and it is not necessary to pass all right, title, and interest in the goods. (Sec. 2(f).)

(b) American vessels and citizens may carry on commerc trade in any part of the world not included in Zo and 2 without passing title to the goods, except considered arms, ammunition, or implements of war tined for a belligerent country.

840

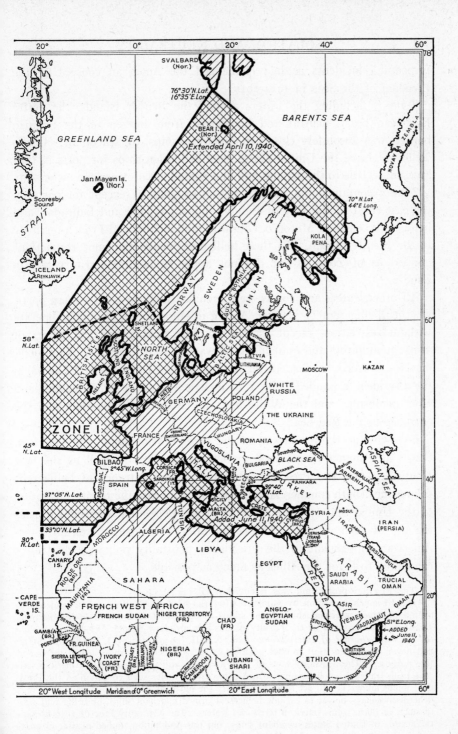

20° West Longitude   Meridian of 0° Greenwich   20° East Longitude

torpedoing incidents as had challenged the American concept of the Freedom of the Seas in 1914-1917.

Zone 1, including the waters around the British Islands, the entire European coast, neutral and belligerent from Bergen to the Spanish border, was absolutely closed to American ships, by sea or air. Goods could not leave the United States even in foreign ships for ports in that area unless title to the articles had first passed out of American ownership.

Zone 2 contained the Atlantic coasts of Canada (except for ports on the east coast of the Bay of Fundy), Newfoundland and Labrador, and belligerent coasts of Morocco, Gibraltar, and British and French territory in the Mediterranean. To these belligerent coasts the same restrictions applied as of Zone 1, but did not apply to neutral territory within Zone 2.

All other waters and coasts were included in Zone 3. To these ports, whether belligerent or neutral, American ships and trade might operate without restriction, except for the absolute embargo on the export of arms, ammunition and implements of warfare to belligerents. By proclamations of April 11, 1940 (after the invasion of Denmark and Norway), the President expanded Zone 1 to include the entire Scandinavian and Kola peninsulas and the White Sea, the entire Mediterranean, and the entrance to the Red Sea.[1]

Following up the resolutions of the Foreign Ministers of the American States at Panama (September 23-October 3, 1939) as well as the new Neutrality Act, the President also forbade the entrance of belligerent submarines (both commercial and ships of war) into the territorial waters of the United States, while allowing armed belligerent merchant vessels the use of such waters.[2] The consultation of Panama[3] was an inter-American supplement to the President's neutrality policy: a neutrality calculated to favor the Allies as much as possible.

---

[1] The Red Sea prohibition was removed April 11, 1941.

[2] Despite much discussion by publicists after the First World War, and a tendency to assimilate armed merchant ships to the status of warships (see Research in International Law under the auspices of the Faculty of the Harvard Law School, Supplement Section to American Journal of International Law, XXIII [1939], 222-231), the United States had never committed itself to that position as regards merchant ships armed for defensive purposes. The neutrality laws of 1935 and 1937 and 1939 prohibited American citizens from traveling on belligerent armed ships except under such condition as the President might allow (i.e., to get them home after the outbreak of war), and gave the President discretionary power to exclude belligerent armed merchant ships, or belligerent submarines, or both, from American territorial waters. The Neutrality Law of 1939 forbade the arming of United States merchant ships; but this prohibition applied to time of peace and neutrality; it was repealed, November 17, 1941. When war began the United States as a belligerent armed its merchant ships as fast as it could.

[3] See above, p. 773.

The Neutrality Act of 1939 and its sequels demonstrate that it was not possible, in this war, to reconcile peace and neutrality with safety and interest, even by forswearing the American birthright of the Freedom of the Seas. The new law was also a signal to Great Britain and France that the United States was on their side as much as a neutral could be, that they need not fear any very strenuous protests to their own belligerent practices.

Before we observe the successive developments that followed this first deviation until the ultimate collapse of neutrality, after Hitler had overrun the scrupulously neutral kingdoms of Europe, let us turn to the development, in the initial years of the Second World War, of the opposing belligerent maritime systems and to the position of the neutral United States between them. It is at least the third time which we have been required to do so in the course of this History.

CHAPTER XLIII

THE THIRD COLLAPSE OF NEUTRALITY

(1939-1941)

THE victory of the United States and the Allies in the First World War had greatly strengthened the validity of the naval measures which Great Britain had taken in 1914-1917 *vis-à-vis* the neutral United States, and which she was prepared to put into effect again in 1939. After entering the war in 1917 the United States had proclaimed a sweepingly expansive definition of contraband, had thrown aside all distinction between absolute and conditional contraband, and had applied the doctrine of continuous voyage and ultimate destination to all contraband.[1] In consequence, Great Britain in 1939 did not proclaim "measures of blockade" such as she had instituted against Germany by way of retaliation on March 1, 1915. Instead she proclaimed, at the outset of the war, a "contraband control" which served the same purpose, was easier to maintain, more effective, and less subject to objections on the ground of imperfect blockade.

All neutral ships bound for Europe were "invited" to call at designated ports (Weymouth, Ramsgate, Kirkwall, Gibraltar, and Haifa) for examination and clearance to a neutral destination. Or, on leaving their home port, they could, if they were that obliging, obtain from British consuls certificates of innocent character, called "navicerts." [2] This was a British practice initiated in 1916 at the suggestion of the neutral United States Government.[3] If a neutral ship ignored this control she was brought by force into a British port, under the doctrine of continuous voyage and ultimate destination applied to an all-inclusive definition of contraband. There she was searched and handed over to the prize courts

[1] Instructions for the Navy of the United States Governing Maritime Warfare, June 30, 1917, Savage, *Policy of the United States toward Maritime Commerce in War, op. cit.*, II, 615-638. Note paragraphs 23, 24, 69, 70, 71. The Secretary of the Navy to the Secretary of State, June 18, 1918, *ibid.*, II, 779.

[2] *Commerce Clearing House War Law Service*, nos. 40,620, 65,501, 65,502, 65,556, 66,005, and 66,015, cited by C. H. McLaughlin in his pioneer scholarly review of "Neutral Rights under International Law in the European War, 1939-1941," *Minnesota Law Review*, XXVI (1941-1942), 1-49, 177-222.

[3] H. Ritchie has described the origin and development of The *"Navicert"* System during the [First] World War (Carnegie Endowment for International Peace, 1938).

if alleged to be carrying contraband. While the neutral ship was in a British control port, whether voluntarily or by compulsion, the neutral mail bags were examined for contraband (including money and securities) and the letters censored.

The next step was to stop German exports. In retaliation against alleged German violations of international law—torpedoing or aerial bombing of merchant ships without warning and indiscriminate sowing of mines on the high seas—Great Britain by an Order in Council of November 27, 1939, proclaimed the "detention" of all goods of German origin, even if neutral property.[1] This was contrary to the ancient doctrine of free ships free goods, universally accepted in international law since the Declaration of Paris of 1856, to be excused if at all only under the principle of retaliation.

Thus by her contraband control Great Britain stopped all goods destined for Germany; by her retaliation she stopped all goods being exported across the seas from Germany. Further, she prohibited her own subjects from any relations with a published blacklist of neutral firms suspected of trading with the enemy.[2] To enforce these regulations the British Government established a Ministry of Economic Warfare, significant appellation.

France followed very closely the practice of her ally and tutor in these naval measures.[3]

The United States could not very well protest the British definition of contraband as it did in the previous war, because in 1939 the British employed almost word for word the same definition that the United States had used as a belligerent in 1917![4] So did Germany. The category of contraband simply evaporated, for all practical purposes, by being expanded to include anything useful to the enemy. With it, and with the neutrality acts of 1935-1939, disappeared almost the last vestiges of the traditional Freedom of the Seas, so dear to American diplomacy during the first century and a half of the independence of the United States. Nor could the United States any more protest the British blacklists, because it had used them itself in 1917-1918. The Secretary of State did protest against the detention of goods of German origin, against diversion of American ships into the war zones for examination at

---

[1] McLaughlin, op. cit., 47.

[2] September 13, 1939. Halsbury's Statutes of England, XXXII, 1095.

[3] All the belligerents in their first contraband lists observed a theoretical distinction between absolute and conditional contraband.

[4] Department of State Bulletin, I, No. 12 (September 16, 1939), 250, cf. Savage, op. cit. II, 615-638.

British control ports, and against search and censorship of neutral mail bags on board American ships in British ports.[1]

The strongest of these protests was against the last-mentioned grievance: diversion for search. Since the Neutrality Act of 1939 had forbidden American ships to visit European belligerent ports at all, and the President's accompanying proclamation of war-zones had blocked off entry also to Scandinavian neutral ports below Bergen, all American ships by necessity were carrying cargo only between neutral ports. "Such cargo," said the Secretary of State, "is entitled to the presumption of innocent character, in the absence of substantial evidence justifying a suspicion to the contrary." The State Department argued that because United States ships en route to neutral ports had voluntarily cooperated with British control by "putting aside certain of their rights under international law" they should be entitled to "a corresponding degree of accommodation and flexibility" so as not to give occasion for forcible diversion of American vessels to British control ports which the law of the United States forbade them to enter. It thus admitted by implication the propriety of diversion to control ports, particularly if there were reasonable grounds to suspect the ships of carrying contraband ultimately destined to the enemy.

Pending further examination and action, said the protest of December 14, 1939, the United States reserved for itself and its nationals all its and their rights in the matter and expected that compensation for losses and injuries resulting from the infraction of such rights would be made as a matter of course.

This perfunctory caveat left the door open for further argument throughout the war and possible adjudication after the war. At most the argument was directed against details that had been moot in the last war. For the implacable essentials of British practice the Governments of George VI and his ally had abundant United States precedent, that is, for their interpretation of contraband and the doctrine of continuous voyage to ultimate enemy destination. The State Department's notes encouraged rebuttal. As to mails, was it not worse, the British promptly asked, what Germany was now doing: not even examining ships to see whether they were neutral or belligerent, but sinking them mail and all by torpedo or bombs from the air?[2] To this question, and to other

[1] In notes of December 8, 1939 (re detention of goods of German origin); and December 14, 1939, and January 20, 1941 (re diversion); and December 27, 1939 (re mails) Documents on American Foreign Relations, op. cit. (1939-1940), pp. 705-719.

[2] Department of State Bulletin, II, No. 31 (January 27, 1940), 91-93.

British replies, the United States made no rejoinder. Soon it was co-operating with the British in these very practices, while still a nominal neutral.

We recall that after the First World War multilateral treaties, like the Inter-American Convention of Maritime Neutrality of 1928 and the London Naval Treaty of 1930, had applied to submarines the rules of surface warships: the necessity of visit and search, and provision for the safety of passengers and crew and ship's papers before destroying a merchant ship.[1] Only in case of persistent refusal to stop or of active resistance to visit or search could a warship, whether surface vessel or submarine, sink the ship or render it incapable of navigation without first having observed these precautions. Of her own free will Germany accepted these rules in 1937 by adhering to a special protocol of November 6, 1936, that had continued them after the expiration of the London treaty.

Did this mean that an armed merchantman—which could, if it chose, sink a submarine that stopped to visit and search—had all the treaty privileges of a merchant ship? International law had not settled that vitally important point. Only one multilateral treaty, the Inter-American Convention of Maritime Neutrality of 1928, just mentioned, had declared armed merchant ships to be ships of war, and this article had not been ratified by any naval power.[2]

The United States had avoided such a commitment, anticipating a day when it might want to arm its own merchant ships in defense against enemy submarines that would not obey international law. But by the Neutrality Act of 1939 it had forbidden the arming of its neutral merchant ships, so that it could never be alleged, as a pretext for submarine attack, that the belligerent warship could not in its own safety take the risk of visit and search of an American ship. Since no American ship was allowed to enter the war zone proclaimed by the President and all American merchant ships on the high seas were conspicuously marked

---

[1] Of course, a prize cannot be taken legally unless there is evidence of enemy owner-ship or of a neutral carrying contraband or of violating contraband. Even then the captor must take the ship into his prize court for judgment, unless imperious circumstances pre-vent; in that case he may destroy the prize, after making proper provisions for the safety of passengers and crew, keeping the ship's papers as evidence.

[2] Only Bolivia, Ecuador, Haiti, Nicaragua, Panama, and the Dominican Republic had ratified the Convention without reservation of this article on armed merchant ships. The United States ratified the convention with a reservation of the article. It is recalled (p. 773 above) that the Declaration of Panama of October 3, 1939, nullified this obliga-tion on the part of these Caribbean States that had ratified.

and lighted, there could be no reasonable pretext for mistaking them for armed enemy merchant ships.

Great Britain never renounced the ancient custom of arming merchant ships for defensive purposes. During the last war, after Germany had declared her submarine blockade of the British Islands—for which Woodrow Wilson chose to hold her to strict accountability as regarded American nationals or ships—the British Admiralty had instructed captains of merchant ships to ram or fire upon submarines if they showed "hostile intent." After the German announcement of February 4, 1915, no British sea captain could see an enemy submarine, certainly not one in the "blockade" zone which did not manifest hostile intent. Immediately upon the outbreak of the war in 1939 the unarmed British ship *Athenia*, en route from Scotland to Canada with about 1400 passengers of whom approximately one-half were Americans, was sunk September 3, 1939, by an exterior explosion, in the presence, it was alleged, of a German submarine. Twenty-eight American citizens lost their lives. The German Government denied responsibility and asserted that a British submarine had sunk the ship in order to accuse Germany of the crime and get the United States into the war. The naval records of Hitler's Government later captured by the American Army prove that this was a deliberate lie, but in 1939 the momentum of "neo-neutrality" was still so powerful that President Roosevelt's Government did not consider the evidence of torpedoing conclusive enough to warrant a protest to Germany! Actually it was in principle a repetition of the *Lusitania* affair, if possible even more heinous because in studious violation of solemn treaty pledges by the Third Reich not to torpedo passenger ships without summons, visit and search.

The British Government took speedy action for protection of its ships and subjects against dreaded torpedoing without warning. Winston Churchill, First Lord of the Admiralty at the outbreak of war in 1939, as he had been at the beginning of the previous conflict, stated in the House of Commons, September 26, 1939, that the whole British merchant marine would be armed defensively against attack by submarines and aircraft. Britain, with her experience of the last war, and the *Athenia* tragedy recently to remind her of it, would not trust German promises not to attack without visit and search.

During the first two months of the war, as long as it was possible that United States neutral ships might be in British or French waters or near them, Germany professed to follow the rules of surface warfare (unless an exception be recorded for the *Athenia* tragedy); that is, her submarine commanders tried to let crews and passengers get into lifeboats before sinking ships; in some cases commanders actually towed the boats toward safety.[1] During the few weeks of war before the passage of the Neutrality Act of November 4, 1939, German submarines observed the law toward American ships going to the British Islands;[2] the Neutrality Law of 1937 prohibited these neutral vessels from carrying arms, ammunition and implements of warfare. But after the Neutrality Act of 1939 became law, German submarines and aviators began to sink without warning any ship, neutral or belligerent, that was proceeding to or from the British Islands, or believed to be submitting to British contraband control, or accepting enemy convoy. Germany justified this practice on grounds of retaliation. She proclaimed a "blockade" of the British Islands, similar to that of 1915.[3] "Any neutral ship which in the future enters those waters is likely to be destroyed."[4]

Again, as in the other historical struggles between the Leviathan of the Seas and the Colossus of the Land (1793-1802; 1803-1815; 1914-1918), each mighty belligerent had reached for his most deadly weapon of war in a bitter struggle for life or death, with only incidental concern for the technicalities of international law. Great Britain resorted to her maritime measures to cut off German contact with overseas neutrals by her contraband control and retaliatory detention of neutral goods of German origin; Germany reverted to her use of unrestricted submarine warfare, the employment of mines of all sorts, and started bombing merchant ships from the air.

British measures had the weight of Anglo-American precedent back of them; German submarine action was in violation of a treaty, that is, if defensively armed merchant ships were not to be regarded as warships; even then Germany did not stop to see whether a ship was armed or not, or neutral or not. Since the last war devices had been perfected by which a submarine did not have to stick its periscope above the water to "see" its prey and aim its torpedo; now it could aim accurately and destroy from beneath the surface, guided by "hearing" apparatus. By

---

[1] This was not, of course, a perfect compliance with the treaty.

[2] On September 11, 1939, a German submarine detained the S.S. *Wacosta*, American flag, bound from New York to Glasgow with general cargo and a few passengers, for three hours of searching, and allowed it to proceed. Department of State *Bulletin*, I, No. 12 (September 16, 1939), 249.

[3] See Map 31, B, p. 599.

[4] New York *Times*, August 18, 1940, for text, p. 25.

the use of mines, greatly perfected since the last conflict, Germany also took an alarming toll of belligerent and even more of neutral merchant ships in the waters around the British Islands.[1] This led to protests by the Scandinavian neutrals, but not by the United States. It had been too deeply involved in mine laying during the previous war to justify a protest. Besides that, the Neutrality Act of 1939 prohibited American merchant ships from entering the war zones.

Unlike the period of American neutrality in 1914-1917, no serious controversies arose with either belligerent side during the latest war until after American neutrality had collapsed for other reasons than violations of neutral rights. The weight of Anglo-American precedent was too greatly in favor of British maritime practice by 1939 to justify a very effective protest to Great Britain, not to mention the strength of public opinion and sympathy in favor of the cause of Great Britain and France. So far as Germany was concerned, the Neutrality Act of 1939, forswearing for expediency's sake the Freedom of the Seas, kept American neutral ships out of harm's way.

The overrunning by German armies of neutral Denmark, Norway, the Netherlands and Belgium, and the fall of belligerent France, all in the spring and summer of 1940, put a different aspect on the war for the United States. Adhering to the doctrine of nonrecognition of the fruits of aggression, the Washington Government refused to recognize any change of sovereignty in those conquered kingdoms and continued diplomatic relations with their exiled governments, as with Poland's.

The conquest of England itself seemed alarmingly close in June, 1940, when Italy characteristically entered the war at what appeared the last hour of the enemy's resistance. Germany's military successes now threatened to destroy the balance of power in Europe and the supremacy of British seapower, behind which the United States, because of its peculiar position in reference to Canada, had rested in such security for a century. Then Hitler might either possess himself of the British navy, or, in possession of the combined ship-building resources of all Europe outside of Russia, be speedily in the way of building the instruments of invasion of the New World before the United States could brace itself adequately to meet the shock in the Atlantic while required to maintain at the same time a defensive fleet in the Pacific.

It was at this hour of history that the United States, in desperate disregard of neutral obligations, reached hastily into its own national

[1] McLaughlin, *op. cit.*, p. 7, note 20.

arsenals and sent arms to Englishmen—and Canadians—with which to defend themselves. Already it had been doing so furtively by rigging the neutrality laws so as to permit the export of airplanes to Canada and Great Britain while making it impossible to Germany. Beginning in the summer of 1940 a series of further steps led during the course of the next twelve months to the collapse of American neutrality and to undeclared naval hostilities with Germany: (1) Facilitation of purchase of military aircraft by Great Britain and France by giving increasing priorities to them over military orders from the United States Government with American manufacturers. (2) Gradual dropping of the encumbrances of neutrality on the export of military aircraft under their own locomotion, driven by belligerent pilots within the United States or by American pilots over belligerent territory. Great armadas of flying ships of war built in the United States sped on their way across the Atlantic ultimately destined to bomb military objectives in Germany. (3) Rushing from United States Government arsenals in the summer of 1940, through the intermediary of private corporations, of large supplies of rifles, machine guns, anti-aircraft guns, trench mortars, field pieces and other military equipment to England's new levies of men in her hour of vital need. (4) The executive agreement of September 6, 1940, with Great Britain, trading fifty United States destroyers of First World War age for American naval bases in British islands of the western Atlantic and Caribbean and in British Guiana. (5) Sale of 229 old First World War tanks to Canada in September, 1940. (6) The sale by the United States Maritime Commission of old First World War merchant ships to Great Britain in December, 1940. (7) President Roosevelt's speech of December 29, 1940, declaring that the United States would be the "arsenal of democracy" for the defense of Great Britain and her allies against Germany and her allies. (8) Successive statements by the Secretary of State and the President that it was the policy of the United States to aid any victim of aggression who would defend itself against the aggressor. (9) Passage of the Lend-Lease Act of March 11, 1941. (10) Seizure of merchant ships belonging to Germany, her allies, and captive countries, and their transfer to Great Britain, during March-July, 1941. (11) Measures for the defense of Greenland, April 7, 1941, taken under the Act of Havana.[1] (12) Proclamation by the President of an unlimited national emergency (May 27, 1941) because of the plain objectives of the Axis belligerents to overthrow exist-

[1] See above, p. 775.

ing democratic order throughout the world and to establish a worldwide domination of peoples and economies through the destruction of all resistance on land and sea and in the air.[1] (13) Establishment of direct relations with the independent Government of Iceland, April, 1941, and military occupation of Iceland at first jointly with British and Canadian troops, July, 1941. (14) Announcement, July 7, 1941, that the sea lanes to Iceland would be kept open by the American navy to prevent threats to Greenland and the northern part of the American Continent, and to protect the flow of munitions to Great Britain. (15) Construction, under outright ownership [2] of the British Government, of armament factories in the United States. (16) Blacklisting throughout the other American republics of persons and firms deemed to be acting for the benefit of Germany or Italy, and forbidding exports from the United States to them, in the interests of national defense. (17) Building, as if by anticipation, of a naval base in Northern Ireland, under nominal British auspices.

Most spectacular and far-reaching of these deviations from neutrality for the purpose of securing the defense of the United States [3] were: (18) the destroyer-naval base deal with Great Britain; and (19) the Lend-Lease Act, the former effected by an executive agreement before the presidential election of 1940, the latter enacted by Congress after the re-election of President Roosevelt for a third term.

Faced with imminent invasion of her unfortified island in the late summer of 1940, Great Britain needed more naval defense than ever before in her history, not only to defend the Channel, but also to protect the Atlantic transit for the armaments that were being sent from United States arsenals and factories. On the other hand, the downfall of England would have given Germany and Italy control of the Atlantic and would have opened up the New World to invasion by the Axis powers (as Germany and her allies had come to be designated). Against such a menace the United States realized the vital need of naval bases in the British islands of the Western Atlantic and the Caribbean Sea

---

[1] In response to a Senate Resolution requesting definition of the executive powers under such an emergency, the Attorney General declined to give an opinion, but transmitted a list of relevant statutes. *Documents on American Foreign Relations*, III (1940-1941), 754-755.

[2] The British Government refused to pay local taxes on such properties in Connecticut on the ground that the property of a foreign sovereign was not subject to taxation, in international law.

[3] "We have made no pretense about our self-interest in this aid. Great Britain understands it—and so does Nazi Germany." Address by President F. D. Roosevelt, May 27, 1941. *Documents on American Foreign Relations, op. cit.*, III (1940-1941), 49.

for the protection of the continental homeland, even as the Hawaiian Islands served that purpose in the Pacific. American diplomacy, in the midst of an opportunity in the first part of 1939, had been negligent on that score. The Government must now act quickly or it might be too late. There was grave doubt whether the President had constitutional power [1] by executive agreement to trade away any or all of the navy for naval bases in foreign territory; in fact, Congress had just passed a law preventing him from giving or trading certain new naval units to Great Britain. To negotiate a treaty with Great Britain and get it through the Senate was practically impossible, so confused was the state of public opinion. Even if ratified, a treaty would take so much debate and time that it might be too late. The danger of inaction or delay was much greater than the danger from doubt of executive powers.

In this predicament the President turned to the Attorney General for assurance that he had the powers to make such a deal by executive agreement. To these demands for advice Attorney General Robert H. Jackson responded with what might be called at any rate resourcefulness and ingenuity: it was he who called upon a comma to save a kingdom.[2] The resulting executive agreement was another devastating encroachment upon the treaty-making power of the Senate.

A mere exchange of notes, September 2, 1940, between Secretary of State Hull and the British Ambassador, "consummated an arrangement" far more important than most of the seven or eight hundred treaties that the Senate has ever ratified. In exchange for the immediate transfer of fifty destroyers, the British Government agreed to lease to the United States for ninety-nine years naval bases, with all rights for their operation and protection, in the Bahama Islands, Jamaica, Santa Lucia, Trinidad, Antigua, and British Guiana. These were only agreements to lease; the leases themselves with their conditions, still had to be negotiated in more time; [3] but the destroyers were handed over immediately. In addition, the British Government agreed to secure for the United States,

---

[1] "The Congress shall have Power to dispose of and make all needful Rules and Regulations respecting the Territory or other Property of the United States; and nothing in this Constitution shall be so construed as to prejudice any claims of the United States, or of any particular State." Article IV, Section 3, Paragraph 2, of the Constitution of the United States.

[2] The opinion of the Attorney General of August 27, 1941, is conveniently printed, along with other documents pertaining to the Agreement in *Documents on American Foreign Relations*, III (1940-1941), pp. 207-228. For critical analysis of the legal merit of the Attorney General's opinion see Quincy Wright (*pro*) and Edwin M. Borchard (*con*) in *Am. Jour. International Law*, XXXIV (October, 1940), 680-697.

[3] The supplementary lease agreements were signed March 27, 1941.

freely and without consideration, similar leases for naval bases in
Bermuda and Newfoundland.[1]

How could the Government be sure that this fleet of destroyers, built

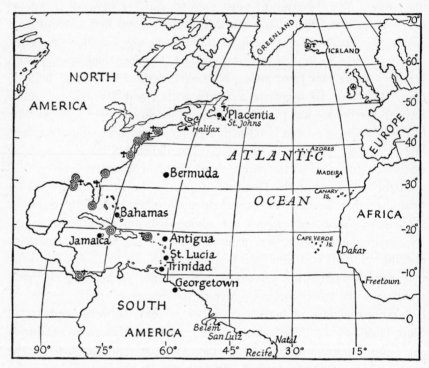

Map 38. New Bases Acquired from Great Britain, 1940
◎ Old bases, home waters.   ⊤ New air bases, home coasts.
▲ British bases.   ◉ British-American bases later established, 1941.
● The new bases, 1940.   (*See also* Map 32 for old bases)

by the United States and hitherto a part of its own navy, would not be
used against itself in case Germany conquered England? It could not
be sure that this would not happen, though the purpose of the transfer
was to prevent the defeat of England; but before he signed the bargain
Secretary Hull secured a statement from the British Ambassador that
it was "the settled policy of His Majesty's Government" never to sur-

---

[1] See Map 38. Rather than make a formal contract in an exchange of letters, by
which Great Britain would pay for the destroyers such undefined concessions as might
be required in the judgment of the United States, in the islands and places mentioned
for American naval bases, Prime Minister Churchill would have preferred to make
outright gifts of well-defined facilities, Great Britain the final judge of what she gave.
Winston Churchill, *The Second World War*, II *Their Finest Hour* (Boston, 1949),
399-416.

render or sink the British fleet in the event of the waters around the British Islands becoming untenable. Having made the deal by executive agreement, President Roosevelt tersely and triumphantly informed Congress about it: "the most important action in the reinforcement of our national defense that has taken place since the Louisiana Purchase."

The Senate did not demur. The House did not object. The people approved the deal. In the presidential election campaign of 1940 Mr. Wendell Willkie, Republican candidate, made no issue on this point of executive procedure. Both candidates favored "all-out" aid to Great Britain "short of war." Both advocated a conscription law (passed September 16, 1940) and full preparedness. Both party platforms pledged against entry into foreign wars, or sending American forces to fight in foreign lands outside America—unless attacked, said the Democratic platform. Both Roosevelt and Willkie pledged against leading the United States into a foreign war, against sending American forces overseas under any circumstances.[1] The conscription law had prohibited the use of the new army outside the Western Hemisphere. The principal issue of the election of 1940 was not peace or war: it was whether Wendell Willkie would make a more capable and more reliable President than Franklin Delano Roosevelt in the critical times immediately ahead.

A strong minority of anti-interventionists, under the national leadership of Charles A. Lindbergh, the eminent aviator and conqueror of the Atlantic, still favored strict neutrality in the European war. Only by arming to the teeth and conserving military strength at home, argued Lindbergh, could the United States be safe from Europe's wars. He was against extending aid to England. He lamented not so much the fact that Hitler was conquering Europe as that the occidental nations were bleeding each other to death for the advantage of Japan and Russia. The election of 1940 was a measure of persistence in the United States of this isolationist sentiment that had been so strong in 1939.

Following the election of 1940 Prime Minister Churchill addressed a long, confidential letter, made public first in 1949, and already famous, setting forth in forceful detail Great Britain's needs for survival, in terms of implements of war and munitions, airplanes, cargo ships and warships and convoys—he did not then think it was the kind of war in which Great Britain would be able to match the great armies of Germany in

[1] Charles A. Beard, *American Foreign Policy in the Making, 1932-1940; a Study in Responsibilities* (Yale University Press, 1946).
Secretary Hull was much more cautious in his campaign speeches on behalf of the Administration. He made no promises of this kind.

any field where their main power could be brought to bear.[1] Roosevelt responded with his renowned speech of December 30, 1940, calling for "all-out aid" to Great Britain and her allies, the captive kingdoms of Europe, by the United States as an "arsenal of democracy." At his impulse the Lend-Lease bill HR 1776 was immediately introduced into Congress. In the interests of national defense it overrode many of the prohibitions of the Neutrality Act of 1939 and of other statutes, and it disregarded the obligations of neutrality under international law.[2] Subject to the necessary appropriations by Congress (which were promptly forthcoming), this unprecedented law gave the President full powers at his discretion, and under his direction, and on terms to be arranged by him, to put the material resources of the Government (but not yet the nation's ships or manpower) at the disposal of countries whose defense he believed vital to the defense of the United States. Never in history had a President, even in times of war, received such a grant of power as this.[3] It was a measure of the alarm that the people felt in the midst of

---

[1] Churchill to Roosevelt, 10 Downing St., Whitehall, December 8, 1940. *Their Finest Hour*, pp. 558-569.

[2] For example, the Rules of Due Diligence. See above, p. 409.

[3] These were the powers which it gave to the President:

(1) To manufacture in arsenals, factories and shipyards under their jurisdiction, or otherwise procure, to the extent to which funds are made available therefore, or contracts are authorized from time to time by the Congress, or both, any defense article for the government of any country whose defense the President deems vital to the defense of the United States.

(2) To sell, transfer title to, exchange, lease, lend or otherwise dispose of to any such government any defense article, as described by the act, but only after consultation with the Chief of Staff of the Army or the Chief of Naval Operations of the Navy, or both.

(3) To test, inspect, prove, repair, outfit, recondition, or otherwise to place in good working order, any defense article for any such government, under appropriations or contracts authorized by Congress, or to procure any or all such services by private contract.

(4) To communicate to any such government any defense information, pertaining to any defense article furnished to such government under paragraph (2) of this subsection.

(5) To release for export any defense article disposed of in any way under this subsection to any such government.

The act further enabled the President to arrange terms, conditions, and benefits, direct or indirect, to be rendered by governments receiving such aid. Under this power the colossal aid to Great Britain was soon written off as subsidies, by an executive agreement of February 25, 1942, after certain understandings had been reached by the two Governments as to the nature of the principles that should govern the future peace.

The act further stipulated that nothing in its provisions should be construed to authorize or permit convoying of vessels by the naval forces of the United States. This was more of a gesture than a prohibition, because the Executive had the power of convoy, as Commander-in-Chief.

More authoritative was another stipulation that nothing in the act should authorize or permit the entry of an American vessel into a combat area in violation of the Neutrality Act of 1939; but even here the President had the power to make or unmake the combat zones.

their confusion at what might happen to them if Germany should defeat Great Britain before the United States had armed itself adequately.

It would have been folly to make of the nation this arsenal of democracy only to have the armaments sunk before they reached the hands of a fighting friend. The occupation of Iceland was a step to strengthen the shipping lanes of the North Atlantic against rupture by German naval and aerial forces. Iceland had proclaimed its complete independence from the crown of Denmark following the German occupation of that little neutral kingdom. But under British occupation Iceland was belligerent territory like Denmark under German occupation. Germany (March 25, 1941) expanded her retaliatory "blockade" of the British Islands to include Iceland, even as far as Greenland's icy waters,[1] and began to torpedo neutral ships going to Iceland as well as to the British Islands.

President Roosevelt had not included Iceland within the Class I combat zone proclaimed by him under the Neutrality Act of 1939, the zone into which American ships were forbidden to take passengers and cargo of any kind. That strategic island lay within Zone 2 where American ships could go to neutral countries with cargo and passengers, but not with arms, ammunition and implements of warfare.[2] Once American troops were in Iceland a service of supply ships was necessary. This led to the convoy of American ships, then of other neutral ships, finally of belligerent British ships along the way. Convoys led to naval engagements between American destroyers and German submarines.[3] An undeclared shooting war began on the North Atlantic in the summer of 1941.

Before these engagements occurred a German submarine had sunk, May 21, 1941, an unarmed American merchant ship, the *Robin Moor*, New York to Capetown with a mixed cargo not containing arms, ammunition or implements of warfare, prohibited to American ships by the Neutrality Act. The attack took place in the middle of the South Atlantic, far outside any war zone proclaimed by belligerent or neutral. There was no visit or search, although crew and passengers, including

---

[1] See Map 39.

[2] See Map 37.

[3] There were preliminary engagements as early as May, without casualties. On September 4, 1941, the United States Government announced that the destroyer U.S.S. *Greer* (which had been tracking a German submarine while a British plane dropped depth charges) had been attacked by torpedoes which missed their mark. On the night of October 16-17, 1941, a submarine attacked the destroyer U.S.S. *Kearny* while engaged in convoy work to Iceland, with the resulting loss of 11 men of the destroyer's crew. On October 31 the destroyer U.S.S. *Reuben James*, also engaged in convoy duty, was torpedoed off Iceland with a loss of 96 men and officers.

women and children, were allowed to take to open life-boats. After many days of suffering they were saved, fortunately and fortuitously, by friendly vessels. This incident was a flagrant violation of treaty

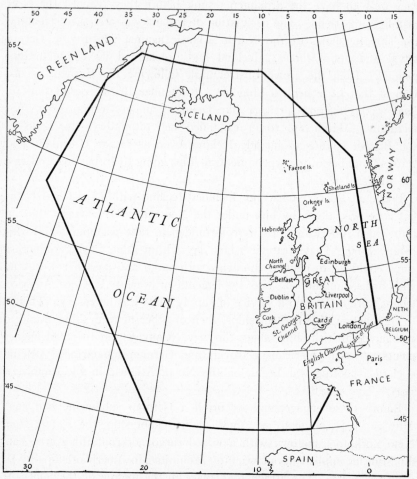

Map 39. German Blockade Area Proclaimed March 25, 1941

obligation. The United States demanded full reparation. Germany did not reply but did the same thing over again.[1] By this time [2] the neutrality of the United States already had collapsed from other reasons.

[1] The *Lehigh*, cargo ship under the American flag, sunk in the South Atlantic, just south of the Equator, off the African coast, October 19, 1941.

[2] After the passage of the Lend-Lease Act the President revoked (April 11, 1941) the combat zone of his proclamation of June 11, 1940, barring off the Red Sea, in order to allow American-flag ships to deliver lend-lease material to British armies in Egypt. In this maritime back-doorway one of them, the U.S.S. *Steelseafarer* was sunk by an aerial bomb, September 5, 1941.

Armed with the Lend-Lease Act, President Roosevelt had it within his power to reach an understanding with Great Britain on the principles of a future peace settlement before he opened wide the sluiceways of American supplies. Meanwhile most momentous problems had arisen calling for joint attention and anxiety of the United States and Britain: the islands of the Eastern Atlantic, and the menace of Japan in the Western Pacific: if Germany occupied Spain as a causeway to North Africa, someone would have to occupy the Spanish Canaries and Cape Verdes and the Portuguese Azores lest they fall into the hands of Hitler and become submarine bases to cut Britain's remaining route around Africa to Egypt and also menace the security of the Western Hemisphere. Japan's advance from China into French Indo-China threatened Singapore and menaced the Philippines: should the United States and Great Britain serve joint notice on Japan to stop?

In the summer of 1941 President Roosevelt had a meeting off the coast of Newfoundland with Prime Minister Winston Churchill, who was dreaming and working for the day when the United States might come into the war at Britain's side.[1] The two statesmen, after visiting back and forth to their respective flagships in Argentia Bay, announced eight principles of policy on which they based the hopes, the desires, the beliefs, the endeavors, and the promises of the Governments of the United States and Great Britain for a better future for the world: the Atlantic Charter, August 14, 1941.

As in the case of the Fourteen Points of President Wilson of 1918, the historian may well underline the carefully chosen verbs and their auxiliaries.

First, their countries seek no aggrandizement, territorial or other;

Second, they *desire* to see no territorial changes that do not accord with the freely expressed wishes of the peoples concerned;

Third, they respect the right of all peoples to choose the form of government under which they will live; and they *wish* to see sovereign rights and self-government restored to those who have been forcibly deprived of them;

Fourth, they *will endeavor*, with *due respect for their existing obligations,* to further the enjoyment by all States, great or small, victor or vanquished, of access, on equal terms, to the trade and to the raw materials of the world which are needed for their economic prosperity;

Fifth, they *desire* to bring about the fullest collaboration between all

[1] "That ['the United States unitedly and wholeheartedly in the war with us'] is what I have dreamed of and worked for, and now it is come to pass." Speech of Prime Minister Winston Churchill to the House of Commons announcing the fall of Singapore, February 15, 1942.

nations in the economic field with the object of securing, for all, improved labor standards, economic advancement, and social security;

Sixth, after the final destruction of the Nazi tyranny, they *hope* to see established a peace which will afford to all nations the means of dwelling in safety within their own boundaries, and which will afford assurance that all the men in all the lands may live out their lives in freedom from fear and want;

Seventh, such a peace *should* enable all men to traverse the high seas and oceans without hindrance;

Eighth, they *believe* that all of the nations of the world, for realistic as well as spiritual reasons, must come to the abandonment of the use of force. Since no future peace can be maintained if land, sea, or air armaments continue to be employed by nations which threaten, or may threaten, aggression outside of their frontiers, they *believe*, pending the establishment of a wider and permanent system of general security, that the disarmament of such nations is essential. They will likewise aid and encourage all other practicable measures which will lighten for peace-loving peoples the crushing burden of armaments.[1]

The use of the word Charter implied a treaty or an agreement of the most solemn kind. The Atlantic Charter was not a treaty, not a signed document, not even a state paper. It was only a press release,[2] carefully phrased by the two statesmen. It was nonetheless a most solemn and significant understanding, later incorporated in the signed Declaration of United Nations—testament of the grand alliance against the Axis powers—and in subsequent bilateral agreements on Lend-Lease for the winning of the war.

Hitler's decision not to invade Spain relieved Roosevelt and Churchill of the necessity of announcing any agreement they may have reached at that time regarding the Spanish and Portuguese islands of the Eastern Atlantic. As we shall see in the next chapter, they agreed at the Argentia

---

[1] Department of State *Bulletin*, V, No. 112 (August 16, 1941), 125. Italics inserted.

[2] See statement of President Roosevelt in press conference of December 18, 1944. New York *Times*, December 19, 1944. There is a growing literature on the Atlantic Conference: Forrest E. Davis and Ernest K. Lindley, *How the War Came* (New York, 1942), pp. 250-285; Sumner Welles, *Where Are We Heading* (New York, 1946), pp. 6-18; Elliott Roosevelt, *As He Saw It* (New York, 1946), Ch. II; Robert E. Sherwood, *Roosevelt and Hopkins* (New York, 1948), pp. 349-365; *Memoirs of Cordell Hull*, II, 974-976, 1012-1027; see also Sumner Welles's "Memoranda" on Atlantic Conferences in *Pearl Harbor Attack*, joint Congressional Committee hearings, Part 14, pp. 1268-1299, exhibits 22B, 22C, 22D (Committee Print, Washington, G.P.O., 1946). Derogatory are: George Morgenstern, *Pearl Harbor, the Story of the Secret War* (New York, 1947), 117-126; John T. Flynn, *The Roosevelt Myth* (New York, 1948), 299-303, 332-338, 385-386; Charles A. Beard, *President Roosevelt and the Coming of the War* (New Haven, 1948), 118-133.

Students of the subject looked forward to the third volume of Winston Churchill's matchless memoirs, *The Grand Alliance* (Boston, 1950).

Conference on a war warning to be sent to Japan, but Secretary of State Cordell Hull turned it into an olive branch.

Neutrality collapsed altogether in the Atlantic during the autumn months. On November 17, 1941, Congress, at the behest of the Administration, repealed the most essential features of the Neutrality Act of 1939: it permitted American merchant ships to carry goods of any kind, including arms, ammunition and implements of warfare, to belligerent ports; and it removed the prohibition to arm American merchant ships. After consultation with the exiled Dutch Government, United States forces occupied Surinam (Dutch Guiana), on November 24, 1941, the Brazilian Government being also invited to assist in the defense of that colony.

The United States and Germany by then had drifted into an undeclared state of hostilities as yet confined to naval action.[1] An interesting feature of this conflict, to the historian of American diplomacy, is that it came to pass despite the neutrality legislation of 1935-1937. The disillusionists had told their fellow-countrymen that they had been unnecessarily "dragged" into the First World War. Congress had taken these seers and prophets at their word. It had passed neutrality laws that repudiated completely Woodrow Wilson's choice of neutral policy of 1914-1917. A pacifist people, anxious to keep out of the next war, applied to its foreign policy the lessons of the last war, without success. The United States did not get into war again with Germany and her allies in 1941 because of torts against American citizens traveling on belligerent ships; they were prohibited from embarking on them. The munitions makers did not involve the country in the European conflict; their business was strictly licensed. Loans to belligerent governments were not a cause; they were prohibited by law. American merchant ships had been forbidden to go into danger zones. They were not allowed to arm themselves lest they get into trouble with belligerents outside the war zones. Propagandists had been registered. One by one the disillusionists had picked out and quarantined the causes of the last war, only to find themselves lost in academic and legal theory as the modern conquerors sprang upon their victims.

Despite and notwithstanding the neutrality acts, the United States drifted into war with Germany at the end of 1941 because it was scared

[1] Diplomatic representatives still remained in the respective capitals. The United States expelled German and Italian consular agents, and "froze" the assets of the European nations in the United States, in June, 1941. Reciprocal measures followed immediately in Germany and Italy. Russian assets in the United States were frozen at the same time but released after the German attack on Russia.

for its own national safety. It resorted to unneutral action to prevent the defeat of Great Britain whilst it armed itself to meet the mounting danger. The people of the New World had seen the scrupulous neutrals of Europe go down one by one under the heel of the conqueror: Denmark, Norway, the Netherlands, Belgium, Luxemburg, Albania, Yugoslavia, and Greece. Then they had seen Hitler attack Russia in unblushing violation of the treaty of nonaggression that he had concluded with that power on August 23, 1939, a week before he began the war. The United States feared that if Great Britain fell its turn would come next. In this desperate fear for its own safety it had come to throw its lot in gradually with the British Empire, including Canada.

But how about the Pacific War, the Japanese blow that brought the United States formally into the Second World War? This was caused by a collision of Japan's conquest in Asia with the Far Eastern policy of the United States, to which subject we must now turn again.

CHAPTER XLIV

PEARL HARBOR AND THE UNITED NATIONS

(1941-1942)

IN PREVIOUS chapters we have seen how skillfully Japan's diplomacy since 1902 had taken advantage of the divisions and conflicts of the Western powers in order to advance her interests and conquests in Asia. To the Japanese the revolution of the European situation after Munich and the ensuing war came as a divine wind richly laden with further opportunities for lavish successes. At last Japan was in a position to cut off the supplies which China had been importing from the United States and Europe to sustain her defense against the neighboring island empire.

Desperately resisting Japan's invasion, China had been equipping her armies largely with articles imported from overseas through the adjacent colonies of British Hong Kong and French Indo-China, and by way of British Burma over the new Burma motor road. Other succors came overland from Soviet Russia. Japan now laid plans to stop these. Immediately after Munich, Japanese forces occupied South China, including Canton and the coast behind British Kowloon; this cut off supplies coming in by way of Hong Kong. Other actions followed at the expense of the European powers, as fast as opportunities presented themselves. Thus when Hitler took over the remainder of Czechoslovakia in 1939, Japan promptly occupied the large Chinese island of Hainan, controlling the Gulf of Tonkin; next she took possession of the strategic Spratly Islands in the midst of the South China Sea, equidistant from the Philippines, Indo-China, Siam, Borneo, Java and Singapore. Again as German armies were turning the Maginot Line in June, 1940, Japan made a treaty of amity and guaranty of territorial integrity with Thailand (Siam), providing for the exchange of information and mutual consultation on matters of common interest. After the actual fall of France, Japan occupied northern French Indo-China (September, 1940), thus stopping up that source. These conquests enabled Japan to shut off supplies coming to China through the Pacific littoral. The next step was to cut off the Burma Road.

Following the passage of the Lend-Lease Act in the United States, Japan stirred up hostilities between Thailand and remaining French forces in Indo-China in order to fashion an opportunity for a mediation which gave her a further hold on Thailand (March, 1941) from which she might reach into Burma. After Hitler's surprise attack on Russia, Japanese forces proceeded to occupy southern Indo-China (July, 1941). With naval bases and air bases in this French territory, Japan was in a position to outflank Singapore from the land, as well as to move on Burma. In building their base at Singapore British policy had never counted on Japanese power rushing into a vacuum in French Indo-China and flowing down the narrow Malay peninsula to attack that key to the Empire in Asia, Malaysia, and Australasia. Singapore's costly fixed defenses all pointed out to sea!

In Europe the fall of the Low Countries and of France and the peril of England not only had provided Japan with an opportunity to prepare a blow against Singapore that might break up the British Empire as well as end the China War; it had also opened a menace. A German triumph in Europe might lead Hitler into Iran and India, to repossession of the former German islands of the Pacific, abandoned at Versailles, even to China where German generals were training Chinese armies; more than that, to sovereignty over the Dutch East Indies, richest tropical archipelago in the world, with their vast stores of petroleum and rubber. Therefore Japanese policy had to guard against substituting a German for a British Empire in the Far East. Accordingly Japan struck a bargain with Germany and her satellite Italy: an alliance (September 27, 1940) to confirm a German "new order" in Europe, that is, a German conquest of that continent, in return for a Japanese "new order" in the Far East, which meant a Japanese conquest of the Far East and the expulsion of occidental power from the protean area of "Greater East Asia." The alliance further stipulated that in case either of the three contracting parties were attacked by a power (other than Russia) not at present involved in the European war or the Sino-Japanese conflict, the other parties would come to its assistance.[1]

---

[1] The Triple Alliance of Germany, Italy and Japan, signed on September 27, 1940, stipulated:

"Article 1. Japan recognizes and respects the leadership of Germany and Italy in the establishment of a new order in Europe.

"Article 2. Germany and Italy recognize and respect the leadership of Japan in the establishment of a new order in Greater East Asia.

"Article 3. Germany, Italy and Japan agree to cooperate in their efforts on aforesaid lines. They further undertake to assist one another with all political, economic and military means if one of the three Contracting Powers is attacked by a Power at present not involved in the European War or in the Chinese-Japanese conflict.

"Article 4. With the view to implementing the present pact, joint technical commis-

In preparing herself for this division of the Old World into a New German Order and a New Japanese Order, of totalitarian empires, Japan could not ignore the position of Russia, her only really dangerous neighbor, the sharp edge of whose armament she had tested out recently in informal but bloody battles on the Manchurian border, a power which was well armed and in a position to strike with deadly effect by sea and air from Vladivostok. Russia needed to cover her Siberian front against the menace of a German attack in Europe; Japan needed to protect herself against conflict with Russia while she planned her war in the Pacific. Like Germany under Hitler, and unlike the United States, neither Japan nor Russia chose to involve herself in a war on two fronts at the same time. So they signed a five-year pact of non-aggression and neutrality, at Moscow, April 13, 1941, resembling the first Anglo-Japanese alliance of 1902.[1] It protected Japan from attack in the north while she herself prepared to attack the western powers in the south; but the articles as published did not forbid Russian aid to China. When Germany attacked Russia in June, 1941, another source of succor dried up for China—the overland source.

The Triple Alliance was directed against the United States, now committed to all-out aid to Great Britain "short of war" with Germany, and still sponsor of the Open Door and the integrity of China. It left it to the two greatest potential enemies of the United States to choose the moment when together they and their satellites would regard American aid to Britain or China to have crossed beyond the boundary short of war. Meanwhile Japan prepared for that day by the purchase of vast stores of gasoline, fuel oil, and scrap iron. Avidly she bought these and other war materials in the United States as long as that Government hesitated to restrict exports, particularly petroleum products, for fear

---

sions, to be appointed by the respective Governments of Germany, Italy and Japan, will meet without delay.

"Article 5. Germany, Italy and Japan affirm that the above agreement affects in no way the political status existing at present between each of the three Contracting Parties and Soviet Russia.

"Article 6. The present pact shall become valid immediately upon signature and shall remain in force ten years from the date on which it becomes effective." *Documents on American Foreign Relations, 1940-1941*, pp. 304-305.

[1] "Article I. Both Contracting Parties undertake to maintain peaceful and friendly relations between them and mutually respect the territorial integrity and inviolability of the other Contracting Party.

"Article II. Should one of the Contracting Parties become the object of hostilities on the part of one or several third Powers, the other Contracting Party will observe neutrality throughout the duration of the conflict." *Documents on American Foreign Relations*, III (1940-1941), 291.

such an embargo might impel Japan to seize the latter in the Dutch East Indies.[1]

Before the conclusion of the Triple Alliance the United States had been, generally speaking, in process of retirement from the Far East. It had pledged the independence of the Philippine Islands for 1946. It had responded only with protests and caveats to Japan's progressive violations of the Nine-Power Treaty and the Open Door. Repeatedly the Secretary of State had expressed the readiness of the United States to adjust Japanese-American relations, even existing treaties, by peaceful diplomacy; this had signified a willingness to reappraise and repair the Far Eastern situation in a diplomatic settlement with Japan. The White House at one time even went so far in the critical summer of 1940, when it seemed that England might go under, as to throw out indirectly a suggestion that there might be distinct and separate Monroe Doctrines for Europe, Asia and for the American World.[2] But a general Japanese-American diplomatic settlement became extremely difficult when, by signing the Triple Alliance, Japan stepped from the back yard of American diplomacy to take a place in the front yard too. By this act she projected herself into the affairs of the Atlantic, where American policy had pitched its all on an effort to hold England's head above water while preparing the defense of the United States and the Western Hemisphere amidst a world revolution of power. Japan's action after the fall of the Netherlands and France made it evident that compliance in her grand design of conquest would further weaken the British Empire at a time when the United States was taking all measures to sustain that Empire against Germany. It would completely unbalance both Europe and Asia against the United States. From then on American policy toward Japan stiffened uncompromisingly.

As Japan advanced through Indo-China toward Singapore and Burma,

[1] Statement of President Roosevelt, New York *Times*, July 25, 1941.

[2] Statement of Stephen A. Early, Secretary to the President, attributed to the President, printed in the New York *Times*, July 7, 1940, p. 1. The statement was actually made from Hyde Park. It was immediately welcomed by German and Japanese spokesmen and opposed by Generalissimo Chiang Kai-shek. Secretary Hull in a press statement on July 6 (New York *Times*, July 7) declared that the Monroe Doctrine contained "not the slightest vestige of any implication, much less assumption of hegemony on the part of the United States. It has never resembled, and does not today resemble, policies which appear to be arising in other geographical areas of the world, which are alleged to be similar to the Monroe Doctrine, but which, instead of resting on the sole policies of self-defense and of respect for existing sovereignties, as does the Monroe Doctrine, would in reality seem to be only the pretext for the carrying of conquest by the sword. . . ."

Mr. Early modified his statement (July 7) more in the direction of Secretary Hull's exegesis. See Arthur Krock in New York *Times*, July 9, 1940, p. 20.

and thus threatened increasingly the Dutch East Indies and the Philippines, the Secretary of State and the President uttered expressions and warnings against these aggressive steps and sought in various ways to counter them. More loans [1] were issued to China. When Great Britain, to appease Japan, closed the Burma Road for three months during the rainy season of 1940, the United States frowned on the closure.[2] In the following months American exports of war materials, including aviation gasoline, scrap iron, and ultimately petroleum were embargoed or licensed, not against Japan specifically, but in the interest of national defense.[3] In July, 1941, Japanese credits in the United States were blocked, and reciprocally American credits in Japan. In August, 1941, an American lend-lease mission was sent to China, and supplies of all kinds began to go forward to that country by way of Rangoon and the Burma Road, under the Lend-Lease Act.[4] Finally, when Japanese aviators from Thailand and Indo-China began to bomb the Burma Road, the United States furnished China with military planes and allowed trained aviators to resign their commissions in order to take service under China to give air protection to that lifeline of military and other supplies.

The United States and Japan were on the verge of open war from the summer of 1941, as were the United States and Germany. Curiously enough, the American public did not appear greatly alarmed over what had been a matter of deepest concern to students of American diplomatic history: the possibility of a two-ocean war with a one-ocean navy to fight it with. Instead of scanning the two oceans of world politics with national binocular vision, the people looked out from their Continental Republic under the impairment of a peculiar political strabismus. They beheld now with one eye the Atlantic scene while blind to the Pacific, and now again they viewed the panorama of conflict across the Pacific while the Atlantic war picture remained occluded. In the proprietary polls which purported to sample if not to guide the trend of public opin-

---

[1] March 7, 1940, the Export-Import Bank authorized a loan of $20,000,000, to be repaid in tin, on September 25, 1940, a loan of $25,000,000 guaranteed by the Bank of China; and in addition a $30,000,000 purchase of tungsten by the Metals Reserve Corporation, a subsidiary of the United States Reconstruction Finance Corporation. A further loan of $60,000,000 was announced November 30, 1940, in connection with a plan of the Metals Reserve Company to purchase a stock of wolframite, antimony, and tin from the National Resources Commission of China. *Public Papers and Addresses of Franklin D. Roosevelt,* 1940 volume, p. 595.

[2] See statement made by Secretary Hull to the Press, July 16, 1940. *Documents on American Foreign Relations,* III (1940-1941), 269.

[3] For a list of the restrictions to June 5, 1941, see *ibid.,* 473-495.

[4] Department of State *Bulletin,* V, No. 114 (August 30, 1941), 166; V, No. 122 (October 25, 1942), 313.

ion on vital political issues, professional pollsters never put the question:. "Are you in favor of going to war with Japan, Germany and Italy at one and the same time if necessary to prevent the defeat of England?"

Any war was certain to be a double war, a two-ocean war. If there had remained any doubt of what Japan would do in case the United States went to war with Germany, there was the Triple Alliance of September 27, 1940, to make the answer unmistakable. Yet the question which these ministers of public opinion asked was: "Are you in favor of going to war against Germany if necessary to prevent the defeat of England?" Increasingly the citizens were reported to answer yes, their gaze fixed primarily across the Atlantic.

Throughout the year 1941 Secretary of State Cordell Hull strove to work out with Japan some broad-gauged program of peace for the entire Pacific area, including the Far East, a settlement to be based really on recently established principles of inter-American diplomacy. Secretary Hull's "exploratory conversations" with the new Japanese Ambassador, Admiral Nomura, later joined by a second plenipotentiary, a Mr. Kurusu, remind one of the Lansing-Ishii conversations of 1917, but with this difference: during the First World War, Japan had threatened to switch to the enemy Germany if the United States would not, like the other powers, recognize her "special interests" in China; during the Second World War, Japan was already allied with Germany (not to mention Italy) and implicitly threatened war with the United States if her paramount interest, military, economic, and political, in China and "Greater East Asia" were not recognized. If she could get this by diplomacy, if she could win the fruits of war without going to war, she was willing to interpret *defensively* [1] her obligations to Germany—and Italy—in the Tripartite Pact: i.e., not to consider hostilities between the United States and Germany in the Atlantic as an "attack" which would bring Japan into war against the United States in the Pacific. To Japan time was of the essence. She must win a diplomatic triumph over the United States before Germany invoked the *casus foederis* of the Tripartite Pact. In case the negotiations should prove unsuccessful, Japan was preparing with all her might and main for a Pacific War, to be opened by a carefully drilled surprise attack on Pearl Harbor.

At the Atlantic Conference, in August, 1941, Roosevelt and Churchill had drafted identical warnings for their two Governments to deliver to Japan: (1) that "any further encroachment by Japan in the Southwestern Pacific would produce a situation in which the United States Government

[1] See Article 2 of the Pact, above, p. 864, n. 1.

[His Majesty's Government] would be compelled to take counter measures even though these might lead to war between the United States [Great Britain] and Japan"; and (2) "If any third power becomes the object of aggression by Japan in consequence of such counter measures or of their support of them, the President would have the intention to seek authority from Congress to give aid to such Power [His Majesty's Government would give all possible aid to such Power]." [1] This would have been practically a war ultimatum. Secretary Hull, engaged in conversation with Japan, succeeded in toning down the reference to contingent conflict and holding forth in its place an olive branch.[2]

Prince Konoye, Premier of Japan—he whose Government had used a lead pencil to answer Secretary Hull's patient expostulations against Japanese advances into French Indo-China—suggested a Pacific Conference (at Honolulu, or elsewhere) between Roosevelt and him, like the Atlantic Conference between Roosevelt and Churchill. Ambassador Grew, hoping to avoid a double war, urged such a conference, and Roosevelt toyed with the idea, but he was unwilling to go unless terms of a peaceful settlement could be agreed on in advance without selling China down the river. Japan's insistence on keeping troops in China and her military occupation of all of Indo-China (July 21, 1941) in the midst of these parleys made a meeting impossible.

Historians [3] will linger for centuries over the character and details of the Hull-Nomura negotiations of 1941. We can only summarize the position of each party.

The Japanese demands for a general peaceful settlement were included

---

[1] *Roosevelt and Hopkins, op. cit.*, p. 354.

[2] *Memoirs of Cordell Hull, op. cit.*, II, pp. 1018-1020.

[3] Already a massive literature has been built up. Forrest Davis and Ernest K. Lindley were favored with a limited inside official knowledge to write their book on *How War Came* (New York, 1942). Ambassador Joseph C. Grew's account of his *Ten Years in Japan* (New York, 1944) rests on his contemporary diaries and official correspondence. Two publications present the official documents on the American side: *Peace and War: United States Foreign Policy, 1931-1941* (Department of State Publication No. 1983, Washington, G.P.O., 1943); *Foreign Relations of the United States: Japan, 1931-1941* (Department of State Publication Nos. 2008 and 2016, 2 vols., Washington, G.P.O., 1943). Of the successive reports of investigations into the Pearl Harbor disaster, the most complete is *Pearl Harbor Attack*: hearings before the Joint Committee, 79th Cong., 1st Sess. (39 vols., Washington, G.P.O., 1946). The Majority and Minority Committee Reports are in Sen. Doc. 244, 79th Cong., 2d Sess. (Washington, G.P.O., 1946). Two disillusionist studies are: George Morgenstern, *Pearl Harbor, The Story of the Secret War* (New York, 1947), and C. A. Beard, *President Roosevelt and the Coming of the War, 1941; A Study in Appearances and Realities* (New Haven, 1948). A later corrective is Basil Rauch's study of *Roosevelt from Munich to Pearl Harbor* (New York, 1950). See also H. L. Stimson and McGeorge Bundy, *On Active Service in Peace and War* (New York, 1947), and, most important, *The Memoirs of Cordell Hull, op. cit.*, II, pp. 982-1083.

in a memorandum handed to the Secretary of State on November 20, 1941:

(1) The Governments of Japan and the United States undertake not to dispatch armed forces into any of the regions, excepting French Indo-China, in the Southeastern Asia and the Southern Pacific area.

(2) Both Governments shall cooperate with the view to securing the acquisition in the Netherlands East Indies of those goods and commodities of which the two countries are in need.

(3) Both Governments mutually undertake to restore commercial relations to those prevailing prior to the freezing of assets. The Government of the United States shall supply Japan the required quantity of oil.

(4) The Government of the United States undertakes not to resort to measures and actions prejudicial to the endeavours for the restoration of general peace between Japan and China.

(5) The Japanese Government undertakes to withdraw troops now stationed in French Indo-China upon either the restoration of peace between Japan and China or the establishment of an equitable peace in the Pacific Area; and it is prepared to remove the Japanese troops in the southern part of French Indo-China to the northern part upon the conclusion of the present agreement.

These demands show the vast gulf, as wide as the Pacific Ocean, that separated the principles of the good neighbors of the American world, and the rule of force in the Far East. Japanese forces presented a definite challenge to those principles for the governance of Asia.

There was no ultimatum attached to the Japanese demands. The Japanese representatives at Washington, the Ambassador, Admiral Nomura, and the Special Plenipotentiary, Mr. Kurusu, recently arrived as an Envoy Extraordinary, professed to be willing to explore further the possibilities of an agreement, at least for a couple of weeks more. Already Japanese naval forces, with air complements, had left their home bases for the neighborhood of the Hawaiian Islands, timed to strike without warning on Sunday morning, December 7, before negotiations were broken off.

The United States replied to Japan's demands with a tentative Outline of Proposed Basis for Agreement, dated November 26, 1941. After repeating the general American principles of territorial integrity, nonintervention, equality, and conciliation, Secretary Hull proposed that the two nations govern themselves in their *economic* relations with each other and with other nations and peoples by the following principles:

(1) The principle of non-discrimination in international commercial relations.

(2) The principle of international economic cooperation and abolition of extreme nationalism as expressed in excessive trade restrictions.

(3) The principle of non-discriminatory access by all nations to raw material supplies.

(4) The principle of full protection of the interests of consuming countries and populations as regards the operation of international commodity agreements.

(5) The principle of establishment of such institutions and arrangements of international finance as may lend aid to the essential enterprises and the continuous development of all countries and may permit payments through processes of trade consonant with the welfare of all countries.

As specific steps to be taken by the Governments of the United States and Japan to carry out these principles in a broad settlement of existing issues, the United States outline further proposed:

1. The Government of the United States and the Government of Japan will endeavor to conclude a multilateral non-aggression pact among the British Empire, China, Japan, the Netherlands, the Soviet Union, Thailand and the United States.

2. Both Governments will endeavor to conclude among the American, British, Chinese, Japanese, the Netherland and Thai Governments an agreement whereunder each of the Governments would pledge itself to respect the territorial integrity of French Indo-China and, in the event that there should develop a threat to the territorial integrity of Indo-China, to enter into immediate consultation with a view to taking such measures as may be deemed necessary and advisable to meet the threat in question. Such agreement would provide also that each of the Governments party to the agreement would not seek or accept preferential treatment in its trade or economic relations with Indo-China and would use its influence to obtain for each of the signatories equality of treatment in trade and commerce with French Indo-China.

3. The Government of Japan will withdraw all military, naval, air and police forces from China and from Indo-China.

4. The Government of the United States and the Government of Japan will not support—militarily, politically, economically—any government or regime in China other than the National Government of the Republic of China with capital temporarily at Chungking.

5. Both Governments will give up all extra-territorial rights in China, including rights and interests in and with regard to international settlements and concessions, and rights under the Boxer Protocol of 1901.

Both Governments will endeavor to obtain the agreement of the British and other governments to give up extra-territorial rights in China, including rights in international settlements and in concessions and under the Boxer Protocol of 1901.

6. The Government of the United States and the Government of Japan will enter into negotiations for the conclusion between the United States

and Japan of a trade agreement, based upon reciprocal most-favored-nation treatment and reduction of trade barriers by both countries, including an undertaking by the United States to bind raw silk on the free list.

7. The Government of the United States and the Government of Japan will, respectively, remove the freezing restrictions on Japanese funds in the United States and on American funds in Japan.

8. Both Governments will agree upon a plan for the stabilization of the dollar-yen rate, with the allocation of funds adequate for this purpose, half to be supplied by Japan and half by the United States.

9. Both Governments will agree that no agreement which either has concluded with any third power or powers shall be interpreted by it in such a way as to conflict with the fundamental purpose of this agreement, the establishment and preservation of peace throughout the Pacific area.

10. Both Governments will use their influence to cause other governments to adhere to and to give practical application to the basic political and economic principles set forth in this agreement.

A week passed without any response from Japan, ten days, eleven, twelve. Then on Saturday, December 6, President Roosevelt made a fervent personal appeal to the Emperor of Japan to give thought in this definite emergency to ways of dispelling the "dark clouds." "None of the peoples of whom I have spoken [inhabitants of Indo-China, Philippines, East Indies, Malaya, Thailand]," the President cabled, "can sit either indefinitely or permanently on a keg of dynamite."

Before the Emperor could respond, the Japanese Government's reply to the United States, timed to be delivered after war had commenced without declaration,[1] was handed in at Washington. After lengthy recrimination, it declared that in view of the attitude of the American Government, Japan could not but consider that it was impossible to reach an agreement through further negotiations.

Already Japan had struck her first blows at Pearl Harbor, Manila, and Hong Kong. Characteristically the American Government had shown the resourcefulness to "crack" the Japanese secret code and read the diplomatic and military correspondence of the Japanese Government on the eve of Pearl Harbor. Characteristically it neglected to make full and vigilant use of that valuable intelligence in order to ward off a well-nigh fatal surprise blow. By this one stroke Japan caught a careless democratic nation inexcusably off-guard on a sleepy Sunday morning.

---

[1] "The Contracting Powers recognize that hostilities between them must not commence without a previous and unequivocal warning, which shall take the form either of a declaration of war, giving reasons, or of an ultimatum with a conditional declaration of war." Article I of Hague Convention III, of 1907, Relative to the Commencement of Hostilities. The United States, Great Britain, Germany, Italy and Japan were all parties to this Convention in 1941.

At the start Japan crippled the American navy and air-force in the Hawaiian Islands and turned to the conquest of the Philippines, the Dutch Indies, Malaya, and Burma as the first phase of the war. It was the greatest defeat and humiliation in American history.

In a trice, by December 11, 1941, the United States, Great Britain and her Dominions were formally at war with Japan, Germany and Italy. The satellites of the Triple Alliance, Hungary, Roumania and Bulgaria, declared war on the United States December 13; another one, Thailand, on January 25, 1942. The United States returned the compliment, June 4, 1942, to Hungary, Bulgaria and Roumania.

In previous years the United States had been unwilling to stand fast at all costs for the Open Door and the integrity of China. For the security of the Philippine Islands it had made repeated concessions on its Far Eastern policy to Japan since the Russo-Japanese War (1905, 1908, 1915, 1917). From 1931 to 1941, during the various phases of the Second Sino-Japanese War, the United States had not been willing, for the sake of the Open Door and the integrity of China, to risk a war with Japan, even when Japan had no allies. Why then in 1941, after Japan had secured the most powerful allies possible for her to get in a war with the United States, and in addition had neutralized Russia, did the United States for the first time take an unflinching stand not only for the Open Door and the integrity of China, but also for the integrity of French Indo-China, British Malaya and the Dutch East Indies, actually urging the evacuation of Japanese forces from China, where they had been during ten years of conquest, and from French Indo-China?

The answer to this staggering question is that the German conquests in Europe and the Japanese conquests in Asia, and the Triple Alliance between the conquerors forbidding the United States to come into the war to save England or China from defeat, had so completely upset the balance of power in the Old World [1] and with it the whole basis of American foreign policy—Europe's distresses America's advantage—that if the United States was to defend itself and its principles, and the whole global cause of freedom, against the merging torrents of conquest it must do so *while still there was time, while there were left alive effective allies to fight with,* Great Britain, China, and Russia. Otherwise it would surely have to face alone in the New World and in its own homeland the victorious conquerors of the Old World. On the eve of Pearl Harbor,

[1] Nicholas J. Spykman has given us a perspicuous analysis of the United States and the balance of power in *America's Strategy in World Politics* (Yale Institute of International Studies, 1942).

Roosevelt had prepared a war message to Congress in response to Japan's moves against British Malaya and the Dutch East Indies.[1]   The perfidious Japanese blow, before a declaration of war, in violation of Hague Convention III of 1907, made this unnecessary.

Within seven hours after the faithless Japanese attack on Pearl Harbor naval orders went out from Washington: "Execute unrestricted air and submarine warfare against Japan," in violation of the London Naval Treaty of 1930.[2]   During the war against Japan, 1941-1945, American submarines sank 1,750 Japanese merchant ships and took the lives of 105,000 Japanese civilians.[3]   Thus did the United States forswear and throw overboard its ancient birthright, the Freedom of the Seas, for which it went to war with Germany in 1917 and collected adjudicated indemnities, after the victory, for torts against its own citizens by illegal German submarine warfare, 1914-1918.[4]

Pearl Harbor ended in one hour all previous debate in the United States on "measures short of war," or on the wisdom of intervention or nonintervention.   At the cost of a terrible defeat and national humiliation it welded the United States into an immediate union with the other nations, conquered and still unconquered, who were fighting for their existence as free men against the power and skill of the conquerors in Europe and Asia.   During a dramatic visit to Washington of Winston

[1] George Morgenstern, *Pearl Harbor, The Story of the Secret War* (New York, 1947), pp. 296, 403.   American, British, and Canadian military staff conversations in Washington in January-March, and American, British and Dutch conversations in Singapore in April, 1941, had envisaged the possibility of such a message in case Japanese forces should cross designated lines of defense (Japan crossed them December 5, 1941), but this was not a "secret alliance," or any "alliance" at all, as Morgenstern avers. These staff conversations did not constitute a treaty. They were not even an executive agreement, unless by some secret understanding with Prime Minister Churchill not yet revealed. They could not bind Congress. They were more like the Anglo-French staff conversations which planned defensive measures to meet any German invasion of Belgium in 1914.
Admiral Stark and General Marshall rejected the ABD staff plan of Singapore. "Nevertheless, on November 5, 1941, the United States chiefs-of-staff passed on to President Roosevelt the exact recommendations made by the Singapore Conference as to the three contingencies any one of which should be met by an American declaration of war on Japan." Samuel Eliot Morison, *The Rising Sun in the Pacific* (Boston, 1948), pp. 55-56.
[2] For text, see above, p. 665.
[3] Navy Department News Release, February 2, 1946.   See also New York *Times*, February 3, 1946.
[4] In answer to formal interrogations by former Gross Admiral Doenitz, at the request of the International Military Tribunal at Nuremberg, Germany, where Doenitz was tried as a war criminal, Fleet Admiral Chester W. Nimitz, Chief of Naval Operations, U.S.N., testified as follows: "The unrestricted submarine and air warfare ordered by the Chief of Naval Operations on 7 December 1941 was justified by Japanese attacks on that date on U.S. bases, and on both armed and unarmed ships and nationals, without warning or declaration of war." Navy Department Press Release. May 24, 1946.

Churchill, President and Prime Minister announced the terms of an alliance of the two English-speaking powers and all who cared to join it. This international agreement, the most important and far-reaching since the treaty of peace and independence of 1783, was not a treaty made by and with the advice and consent of the Senate. It was another executive agreement, signed by the executive authorities of twenty-six governments, in the form of a joint declaration, January 1, 1942, for the overthrow of Hitlerism and its allied forces and for ultimate peace on the basis of the Atlantic Charter. Mexico and the newly established Philippine Republic later signed this joint agreement in an impressive ceremony at Washington on June 14, 1942.

DECLARATION BY UNITED NATIONS

A Joint Declaration by The United States of America, The United Kingdom of Great Britain and Northern Ireland, The Union of Soviet Socialist Republics, China, Australia, Belgium, Canada, Costa Rica, Cuba, Czechoslovakia, Dominican Republic, El Salvador, Greece, Guatemala, Haiti, Honduras, India, Luxembourg, Netherlands, New Zealand, Nicaragua, Norway, Panama, Poland, South Africa, Yugoslavia.

The Governments signatory hereto,

Having subscribed to a common program of purposes and principles embodied in the Joint Declaration of the President of the United States of America and the Prime Minister of the United Kingdom of Great Britain and Northern Ireland dated August 14, 1941, known as the Atlantic Charter,

Being convinced that complete victory over their enemies is essential to defend life, liberty, independence and religious freedom, and to preserve human rights and justice in their own lands as well as in other lands, and that they are now engaged in a common struggle against savage and brutal forces seeking to subjugate the world, *Declare:*

(1) Each Government pledges itself to employ its full resources, military or economic, against those members of the Tripartite Pact and its adherents with which such government is at war.

(2) Each Government pledges itself to cooperate with the Governments signatory hereto and not to make a separate armistice or peace with the enemies.

The foregoing declaration may be adhered to by other nations which are, or which may be, rendering material assistance and contributions in the struggle for victory over Hitlerism.[1]

[1] Department of State *Bulletin*, VI, No. 132 (January 3, 1942), pp. 3-4.

CHAPTER XLV

AMERICAN DIPLOMACY DURING THE SECOND WORLD WAR

(1942-1945)

THE principal concern of the United States in the diplomacy of the Second World War was, of course, the winning of the war as soon as possible. All diplomatic goals were sighted to that surviving purpose: to sustain and fortify the tottering British Empire; to keep alive the defeated French nation, almost inanimate under Hitler's heel but still alive and stirring in North Africa; to arm and accouter the swarming Russian legions; and to prevent the remaining neutrals, Spain, Portugal, Sweden, Switzerland, and Turkey, from falling prey to the enemy: in short to win the war in Europe, then with Russia's hoped-for aid to knock out Japan in Asia: first VE-Day, then VJ-Day.

Thanks to the Good Neighbor Policy, the republics of the Western Hemisphere, all except Argentina, had already lined up on the side of the United States and the United Nations.[1]

In Europe, amidst the uncertainty and anxiety following the military collapse of France and the Franco-German armistice of June 22, 1940, the United States remained in formal diplomatic relations with the Vichy Government, despite the rupture between Great Britain and France. As President George Washington had refused to break with the French Revolutionary Government of the First Republic after the overthrow of the monarchy of Louis XVI, so President Roosevelt kept up a formal contact with the "neutral" National Revolutionary Government of Marshal Pétain long after the downfall of the Third Republic, even until after American entrance into the European war.

The reason for this connection with an unrespected regime was not so much perfect propriety under international law as convenience for American purposes: (1) to prevent, if possible, the French fleet (demobilized by the Franco-German armistice) from being turned over to the Germans to be used against Great Britain—and the United States; (2) to try to prevent Vichy from yielding to Germany or Italy any bases in French Africa or French colonies in the New World; [2] (3) generally

---

[1] See above, pp. 776-777.

[2] In October, 1940, Admiral Greenslade, U.S.N., entered into a separate understanding with the French High Commissioner at Martinique, Admiral Robert, em-

to stiffen Marshal Pétain's Government against co-operation and collaboration with Germany and Italy beyond the terms of the armistice.
During 1940-1942 the United States, still unprepared for war on a sufficient scale, could exert little military pressure on the situation, but its
diplomatic influence was by no means negligible: for France to lose the
historical friendship and potential support of the United States might
extinguish her last hope of resurrection from German conquest. The
American Ambassador to Vichy, Admiral William D. Leahy—succeeding
William C. Bullitt—was at least a bare rock to cling to after the Nazi tide
swirled over France.

Aside from the French Navy, which the Pétain Government pledged
itself to scuttle rather than make over to the Germans, North Africa was
the vital concern of the United States. It was a springboard for an Axis
invasion of the New World, not to mention advanced Atlantic submarine bases for Germany. By the same token it was a coveted military
platform on which the United States might some day stage a Mediterranean invasion of Italy and the German fortress of Europe.

The first American implement for the security of French North Africa
was the Murphy-Weygand agreement of February 26, 1941, made in
the name of the President by Robert D. Murphy, counselor of the United
States Embassy in France, with the French commander in North Africa,
and countenanced by Vichy. Under its terms the United States agreed
to provide a small revictualing of Morocco and Algeria to be controlled
and administered by an increased number of American vice-consuls. The
real function of these numerous officials was to maintain contact with
General Weygand, encourage resistance to German intrusion, and furnish
intelligence in preparation for a military occupation not to be resisted,
perhaps even to be assisted, by the French North African army.

Germany checkmated the American design for French North Africa by
bringing about the removal of General Weygand, but (thanks to Hitler's
war and disaster in Russia) was not able to invade the southern continent
before the United States and Great Britain landed massive forces in
Morocco and Algeria, November 8, 1942. This led to German occupa-

bodying guarantees immobilizing French war vessels in American waters and holding
at the island heavy shipments of gold en route to France from the United States—also
allowing an American observer and naval and air patrol to enforce the understanding.
Secretary of State Cordell Hull to Senator James M. Mead, June 2, 1941. *Documents
on American Foreign Relations* (World Peace Foundation, Boston, 1941), III, 95-6.
The agreement did not survive the rupture of relations between the United States and
Vichy in November, 1942, after which the United States Navy had to take the
problem into its own hands. *Ibid.*, V, 470-73. *Memoirs of Cordell Hull* (New York,
1948), II, 1160, 1223.

tion of all of metropolitan France and to a final rupture of the Allies with Pétain and the other men of Vichy, including the precious German tool, Pierre Laval—all of them by then discredited in their own country. Henceforth the French people put their faith in "underground" resistance inspired and led by General Charles de Gaulle in exile, supported by Allied military efforts. Pending the liberation of France and the establishment of a provisional government by the choice of free Frenchmen, the United States tried to sustain and unite the dissident overseas groups into one French Committee of National Liberation recognized by the Allies as administering such territories of France as acknowledged its authority.[1] At best our Vichy policy was an opportunist gamble with fate to cover the successful landing of an American army in North Africa and the turn of the tide of war.[2]

Allied operations in North Africa, prelude to a strike at *Festung Europa* from the Mediterranean, depended to a considerable degree on the attitude of Falangist Spain. There the dictator General Francisco Franco owed the success of his revolt against the established republican government, in the Spanish Civil War of 1936-1939, to the intervention of Fascist Italy and Nazi Germany, unsuccessfully opposed by the intervention of Soviet Russia—rehearsal for larger wars soon to come. But he could also burn a candle of thanks to the unprecedented attitude of the United States along with fellow democracies, Great Britain and France. By applying the new neutrality legislation to civil as well as international wars, the United States had reversed the old rule of the law of nations which permitted established governments to buy munitions

[1] Statement of President Roosevelt, August 26, 1943. *Docs. Am. Foreign Relations*, VI, 666.

[2] William L. Langer has written a scholarly history of *Our Vichy Gamble* (New York, 1947) with the aid of documents furnished uniquely to him by President Roosevelt and the Department of State. See also *Memoirs of Cordell Hull*, I, 844-855, II, 948-967, 1127-1165. Langer judges the North African phase of our Vichy diplomacy to have been an "unqualified success" (p. 388), but admits that it was not the deciding factor either in preventing parts of the French Empire, or the French fleet at Toulon (scuttled, November 27, 1942), from falling into the hands of the enemy. He considers its principal significance was that of providing military intelligence and contacts with French officers to lay the groundwork for the allied invasion. But General Eisenhower found our intelligence none too good upon launching the campaign in North Africa. Louis Gottschalk, reviewing Langer's book and thesis at length, contends from the evidence therein presented that "Our Vichy Gamble" was really "Our Vichy Fumble," in *Journal of Modern History*, XX (No. 1, March, 1948), 47-57. He alludes to the considerable body of literature already building up on this question. See also Eugene Rostow, "Wartime Policies toward Vichy and Franco," *World Politics*, I (No. 3, April, 1949), 389-394. For the naval and military history of the landings see: Samuel Eliot Morison, *History of United States Naval Operations, II: Operations in North African Waters* (Boston, 1947), and Dwight D. Eisenhower, *Crusade in Europe* (New York, 1948). See also Winston Churchill, *The Grand Alliance, op. cit.*

of war from the citizens of a neutral nation.[1] Now in 1940 after the
fall of France, Franco's heavy-caliber shore batteries commanded the
Straits of Gibraltar and the Rock itself. Across the Straits there were
150,000 Spanish troops in the Rif, resting on the immediate left flank
of the American invasion route. The Canary and Cape Verde Islands
could make an ideal base for the German *Luftwaffe* and U-boats. And
the Spanish peninsula could become an easy causeway for German
armored might rolling down from France to Algeciras to be ferried across
to Africa under the protection of Spanish guns.

At the outbreak of the war in Europe, General Franco had proclaimed
a strict neutrality. When Germany conquered France and Mussolini's
Italy entered the war like a jackal, the Spanish Caudillo changed suddenly from neutrality to "non-belligerency" in order to be more
benevolent to his fellow-dictator friends against his old enemy Soviet
Russia. He had to face the German Führer in a personal meeting at
Hendaye on the French frontier, October 23, 1940. Exhausted by the
recent civil war at home, which had bled Spain a million lives, Franco
seems not to have wanted another war, unless it were short and sure,
without peril, bringing great rewards. But Hitler's astonishing victories
might make it unsafe to stay out. In a spirit of appeasement rather
than determined bellicosity, Franco offered a pact with the devil. He
proposed to come in on Hitler's side, and had already named his price:
Gibraltar, traditional Spanish gauge of war with England; French
Morocco; the province of Oran in Algeria; plus additions to the colony
of Rio de Oro on the west coast of Africa south of Morocco; also Spain
to be supplied with food and armament.[2] When Hitler refused to meet
these terms unequivocally and continued his efforts to reduce England
first, Franco was relieved;[3] doubly so when, failing to conquer England,

[1] Compare the situation in 1948 when the United States Government having repealed
the neutrality legislation of 1935-1937, furnished the Chinese Government with economic
aid, military supplies and equipment for defense of "individual liberty, free institutions,
and genuine independence" during the communist revolt and civil war. See Foreign
Assistance Act of 1949, Title IV, approved April 3, 1948. For economic and military
aid rendered under this act, see New York *Times*, October 12, 14, November 13, December 16, 19, 1948.

[2] Langer, *Vichy Gamble,* pp. 90-100.

[3] So opines Professor Carlton J. H. Hayes, Ambassador of the United States to Spain,
1942-1945, in his *War Time Mission in Spain* (New York, 1945), pp. 64-66. Franco's
Foreign Minister, the Falangist commander, Serrano Suñer, was more eager for an
alliance on Hitler's terms than Franco. Langer, *op. cit.,* p. 91. Franco dropped
Serrano Suñer in September, 1942. Herbert Feis's account of *The Spanish Story* (New
York, 1948), pp. 93-111, affirms that a secret Spanish protocol with the Axis was
actually signed November 11, 1940, and endorsed by Franco, stipulating in principle
that Spain would enter the war, but not saying when, and vague as to particulars.
When later Hitler pressed Franco to set a date, the Caudillo managed to put him off

Hitler madly attacked Russia in June, 1941. All Spain breathed easier as the storm veered from the direction of the Iberian Peninsula to those roomy Scythian steppes that had lured the French Napoleon to his fate over a century before.

After Hitler's and Mussolini's declarations of war on Russia and six months later on the United States, Franco explained that Spain's "non-belligerency" applied only to the war between Hitler and Franco's old enemy Soviet Russia; in the war between the Western Allies and the Axis Powers he professed still to be neutral. It was the task of American Ambassadors at Madrid, successively Alexander C. Weddell and Professor Carlton J. H. Hayes, to keep uncertain Spain really neutral. In the dark days of 1940-1942, when American forces were still insufficient for a two-ocean war, about all that these diplomats had to rely on was poise and propaganda, manipulation of overseas exports, particularly petroleum, to the Peninsula, and costly "preclusive" buying of war materials—like tungsten ore (wolfram)—to prevent their going to Germany. Spain's real attitude finally became clear when her shore batteries remained silent as the Allies marshalled their planes and ships under range at Gibraltar and in the Bay of Algeciras.[1]

As the tide of war turned against Italy and Germany, Franco, despite continuing diplomatic problems, became more and more friendly, finally benevolently neutral to the Allies. At American behest the Spanish Government drastically reduced the shipment of vital products to Germany. Spain became not a causeway for German invasion but a vestibule for the escape of thousands of Allied airmen and able-bodied refugees out of France for service in the armies fighting Hitler and Mussolini in Africa and Italy. It was also an American listening-post for German military movements in France before the Normandy invasion. The signed photo-

---

with one reason or another. Captured German archives have not yet revealed the full text.

[1] Winston Churchill acknowledged in a speech to the House of Commons, May 24, 1944, that Spain on this occasion had made full amends for her former unfriendly attitude: "We had sometimes 600 airplanes crowded on this [Gibraltar] airfield in full range and full view of Spanish batteries . . . . apart from the aircraft, enormous numbers of ships were anchored far outside of the neutral waters inside the Bay of Algeciras, always under the command of Spanish shore guns. We would have suffered the greatest inconvenience if we had been ordered to move those ships. Indeed, I do not know how the vast convoys would have been marshalled and assembled." *Parliamentary Debates, House of Commons*, Vol. 400, p. 700.

At the time of the landings in North Africa, President Roosevelt conveyed written assurances to the Chiefs of State of Portugal (November 8, 1942) and Spain (November 13, 1942) of complete respect for the continental or island possessions of each power. In turn Franco's Ambassador in Washington assured the United States of continued maintenance of Spain's "absolute neutrality." *Docs. Am. Foreign Relations*, V, 592-594.

graphs of Mussolini and Hitler disappeared from the walls of General Franco's reception room; only the Pope's autographed portrait remained.[1]

Portugal, though at first anticipating German victory, did not desert her ancient British ally, but for a long time she stayed neutral. After the entrance of the United States into the war, and on British nomination, she allowed the establishment of an American air base in the Azores Islands,[2] under auspices of the ancient Anglo-Portuguese Alliance.

In the eastern Mediterranean and the Near East, Turkey was a strategic complement to Spain and Portugal in the West. Likewise the neutrality of Turkey depended not so much on the diplomacy of the Allies as it did upon the strategical decisions of Adolf Hitler and his consequent fatal invasion of Russia. As the war turned against Mussolini and Hitler, Turkey too became more and more benevolently neutral toward the United Nations, and finally embargoed the export of much needed chrome ore to the Axis and its satellites. As Hitler's edifice of power and hate began to crumble into rubble around the bunkers of Berlin, Turkey technically declared war on Germany and Japan (February 23, 1945) and entered the company of the United Nations.

Switzerland and Sweden remained neutral to the end of the war, thanks to their own location and convenient resources, so open to Germany; but even there the United Nations were able to prevail on those governments, as the twilight of the war descended on the false gods of Fascism and Nazism, to embargo war materials, like ball bearings, for Germany, and to close their frontiers, like the other neutrals Spain and Portugal, to escaping war criminals.

The Second World War was a war of dramatic personal conferences between Chiefs of State almost as much as it was a war of colossal battles on land, on sea, and in the air. The Allied leaders winged their way over the oceans to cement unity face to face in quick decisions on problems of high strategy. We recall that, during the First World War, Woodrow Wilson had stayed at home until the final peace conference at Paris, but had used a representative without office, Colonel Edward M. House, for the purpose of personal collaboration with the Associated war chiefs. President Franklin D. Roosevelt found his *alter ego* in Harry L. Hopkins, a New York social-service worker who had risen rapidly to high rank in the administration and familiar councils of the New Deal and had served for a while as Secretary of Commerce. For three and a half years he lived

[1] Hayes, *Wartime Mission,* p. 242.
[2] Still allowed and maintained for other purposes (1950).

in the Lincoln Study in the White House. It was Hopkins, acting without portfolio, who made the first personal contacts for Roosevelt with Churchill in London and Stalin in Moscow, preparing the way for the President's later conferences on both sides of the Atlantic.

Harry Hopkins all but set aside the higher responsibilities of the Secretary of State, and President Roosevelt as Commander in Chief of the armed forces all but usurped the treaty-making power of the Senate. A liaison officer had to be appointed to serve between the White House and the Department of State! In personal conferences Roosevelt made international agreements on subjects of the greatest possible significance, reserving for treaties only the new league of nations and the final peace settlement.[1] The Argentia (Atlantic Charter) and Arcadia [2] (United Nations Declaration) conferences of Roosevelt and Churchill were the first of eight meetings of the two statesmen for the conduct of the war and the promise of the peace, climaxed by their conferences with Stalin at Teheran and Yalta.

Hopkins's earlier confabulations had secured British agreement to General Marshall's plan for an Anglo-American second front to take shape on the Channel coast of France (after the collapse of the first second front during Soviet Russia's non-aggression agreement of 1939 with Hitler) to relieve German pressure on Russia in the year 1942, later to be extended into the heart of Germany by more extensive operations during 1943. President Roosevelt authorized V. M. Molotov, on the occasion of that Russian envoy's secret visit to Washington during the last days of May, 1942, to tell Joseph Stalin to expect a second front that very year. To suffering Soviet Russia, ravaged by Hitler's legions so deep within her frontiers, this was the most important factor in Allied diplomacy, and it meant to the Russians one thing: a second front *in France*.

A second front in France in 1942 was too big a promise to make and keep in the military situation that followed. Germany and Japan spoiled the plans. They seemed to be winning the war on every side. Military disasters in all theaters led to conferences between Roosevelt and Churchill at Hyde Park and Washington (June, 1942) that shifted the

---

[1] Robert E. Sherwood has written from forty boxes of Hopkins's personal papers an intimate history of *Roosevelt and Hopkins* (New York, 1948), which is as important to the historian of American diplomacy during the Second World War as is Charles Seymour's *Intimate Papers of Colonel House* for the First World War. Sherwood writes history like a playwright, selecting and excluding his materials to throw his characters into dramatic highlights, and exhibiting high disdain for precise documentation.

For Charles E. Bohlen, whom Hopkins persuaded Roosevelt to appoint to a post in the White House where he could act as liaison with the Department of State, see Sherwood, pp. 774-775.

[2] See above, pp. 859, 874.

projected invasion from the English Channel to North Africa. The Prime Minister undertook the difficult duty of explaining the decision personally to Stalin in Moscow (August, 1942). The mistrustful Russian leader acceded to the change only because he could not help it.

As the enemies' lightnings quivered and flashed through black clouds on every horizon, neither England, nor Russia, nor the United States faltered, nor did their war leaders. At length for stout hearts the tide of war turned. The first, isolated naval and air Battle of Midway put Japanese strategy on the defensive in the Pacific and made it safer for the United States to devote its principal war effort to the European arena. In November, 1942, came by a narrow margin the next victories: at El Alamein before the gates of Egypt; at Stalingrad on the Volga; in the waters of the distant Solomon Islands; and with the successful landings of American and British armies in Morocco and Algeria. Thenceforth the Allies could look forward not to defeat and slavery but to victory and freedom. The later great personal conferences took place in a spirit of increasing confidence.

At Casablanca (January, 1943) Roosevelt and Churchill met behind the new front in North Africa and made their military decisions for carrying the war into Sicily and Italy. It was at Casablanca that the President, in a joint press conference with the Prime Minister, announced to the world that the Allies would fight on implacably until the "unconditional surrender" of their enemies.[1] This time there would be no Fourteen Points. At Quebec in August, 1943, the two statesmen prepared for the surrender of Italy [2] and for a second front at last in France.

Secretary of State Cordell Hull, for once allowed to participate in an international war conference in Europe, conveyed such plans and as-

---

[1] Roosevelt later explained that the phrase "popped into his mind" from thoughts about General Grant and Lee during the American Civil War, but Sherwood, *op. cit.*, pp. 695-697, shows that the President used the phrase deliberately, reading from prepared notes. And Churchill, backed by the British Cabinet, had already agreed with the President on unconditional surrender—at least for Germany. See parliamentary exchange between Foreign Secretary Ernest Bevin and former Prime Minister Winston Churchill, November 17, 1949, printed in New York *Times,* November 18, 1949.

[2] Strictly speaking, the surrender of Italy, although it followed the formula of unconditional surrender in regard to full powers over the internal, financial, economic, and military life of Italy, left the Italian royal house (soon deposed by internal protest) in authority. Later, the provisional Italian government declared war on Germany, October 13, 1943, and on Japan, February 27, 1945.

For terms of Armistice between General Eisenhower, "acting by authority of the United States and Great Britain and in the interest of the United Nations" and Marshal Pietro Badoglio, "Head of the Italian Government," see Department of State *Bulletin,* XIII, No. 333 (November 11, 1945), 748-760. Howard McGaw Smith has written a history of "The Armistice of Cassibile," in *Military Affairs,* XII (No. 1, Spring, 1948), 12-36.

surances to Marshal Stalin in Moscow at the first meeting of foreign ministers and chiefs of staff of the Big Three (October, 1943). The Russian leader reciprocated by stating gratuitously and unequivocally, for delivery to President Roosevelt, that as soon as the Allies had succeeded in vanquishing Germany the Soviet Union would then join them in defeating Japan. The representatives of the three Allied Governments then proclaimed a solemn warning to all Nazis guilty of war atrocities that they would be brought back to the scene of their abominations to be charged and punished according to the laws of the countries that had suffered them. They set up an European Advisory Commission in London to examine European questions as they should arise and make joint recommendations to the three Governments—this Commission later was given the task of preparing the conditions to be imposed on Germany and Austria after the surrender, as well as delimitation of the zones of Allied occupation.[1] They also declared for a democratic regime in Italy and for the independence of Austria after the war. Most important of all for prevailing opinion in America was a Four-Power Declaration, sponsored by the American Secretary of State, pledging the United States, China,[2] Great Britain, and Russia to take the necessary steps for the establishment of a general international organization to insure world peace. What the Secretary of State then had in mind was inter-American principles of international co-operation applied on a world scale;[3] the structure of the new United Nations organization had not been drafted; but Hull wanted to get it going even during the war, lest post-war debate frustrate its inception.

The Four-Power Declaration of Moscow had the effect of joining a movement in both political parties in the United States for a new league of nations, only they would not call it that. It led to the passage by the Senate of the Connally Resolution, presented by the Committee on Foreign Relations, Tom Connally of Texas chairman, by a vote of 85 yeas, 5 nays (six Senators not voting). This epoch-making resolution, foreshadowing a diplomatic revolution in the history of the United States, looked to the consummation of a treaty "under constitutional process" with free and sovereign nations for the "establishment and maintenance

[1] Hajo Holborn has described the work of this Commission and other diplomatic antecedents of *American Military Government* (Washington, 1947).

[2] The Chinese Ambassador was empowered to sign the Declaration originally, thus making it a four-power document and considerably enhancing the prestige of China then in the eighth year of resistance to the invasion of Japan.

[3] *Memoirs of Cordell Hull*, pp. 1274-1318, notably p. 1281, p. 1298 and p. 1309. *Docs. Am. Foreign Relations*, VI, 225-32.

of international authority with power to prevent aggression and to preserve the peace of the world."

Thus did the Senate of the United States, which had four times refused the Treaty of Versailles, and which had joined with the House of Representatives in the passage of the neutrality legislation of 1935-1937, repudiating American intervention in the First World War, come back at last to Woodrow Wilson—Congress had already repealed the neutrality laws. At last, for the first time since 1920 an American political party, both American political parties, advocated the entry of the United States into an international organization for the maintenance of world peace. In the party conventions of 1944 the only debate was how to enforce the peace to come, whether the police force was to be an international army, or navy, or air force.

It was Roosevelt's ardent wish to meet Stalin face to face and convince him of the good faith and comradeship of the United States and Great Britain with Russia for the winning of the war and a future reign of peace. He had a "hunch" that he could treat him trustingly and not suspiciously.[1] But repeated postponements of the second front had chilled the Soviet Marshal. Only after the new assurances at Moscow did Stalin give Secretary Hull to understand that he would meet with the other two Chiefs of State if the place could be no farther away from the pressing Russian front than Teheran. (Roosevelt had suggested Basra on the Euphrates River, in Iraq.) Promptly the President and Prime Minister decided to pack their bags and fly[2] to the distant Iranian capital. But no place in the world was distant any more. At Oran, Tunis, Malta, Egypt, even in the Persian rendezvous of fabulous Teheran, the President signed or vetoed bills of Congress and returned them within the ten days prescribed by the Constitution.

In Cairo, en route to Teheran, Roosevelt and Churchill and their military and political advisers (including always the faithful Harry Hopkins) held a pre-arranged conference with Chiang Kai-shek, Generalissimo of the embattled Chinese Republic, now desperately at bay against the Japanese invaders. Since Russia was not yet a party to the war with Japan, no Soviet representative participated. At the Con-

---

[1] According to an undated conversation with William C. Bullitt, recounted by the latter in his article on "How We Won the War and Lost the Peace," *Life* Magazine for August 30 and September 6, 1948, Vol. XXV, Nos. 9 and 10.

[2] Roosevelt and Hopkins went as far as Oran on the new U.S.S. *Iowa*. They flew from there via Tunis to Cairo, and from Cairo to Teheran and back. From Cairo they returned by air to Tunis, where the President apprised General Eisenhower of his appointment to command the whole Allied second front; then to Malta and Sicily, and back from Malta by battleship to the United States.

ference of Cairo (November 22-26, 1943) the Sphinx and the Pyramids, not to mention the chic costumes of the Wellesley College alumna, Mrs. Chiang Kai-shek, illustrious spouse and interpreter to the Generalissimo, lent romantic color to the grim realities of war.[1] After the several military missions agreed upon future operations against Japan, Roosevelt, Churchill, and Chiang Kai-shek made a joint statement of purpose: to strip Japan of all the islands in the Pacific which she had seized or occupied since the beginning of the First World War in 1914 (this, of course, included the islands under mandate to the League of Nations), and to restore all the territory stolen from China, such as Manchuria, Formosa and the Pescadores Islands. They further declared: "The aforesaid three great powers, mindful of the enslavement of the people of Korea, are determined that in due course Korea shall become free and independent."

Explaining Cairo in a radio address on December 24, 1943, President Roosevelt further said that the three Chiefs of State had "discussed" simple and fundamental long-range principles that recognized "the right of millions of people in the Far East to build up their own forms of self-Government without molestation." Generalissimo Chiang in a message to the Chinese people referred to "absolute assurances" received at Cairo that all the oppressed and maltreated Asiatic peoples both in the Pacific and the Asiatic mainland might look forward with hope for liberation.[2] Prime Minister Churchill did not elaborate.

These statements were calculated to offset deceptive Japanese propaganda addressed with much effect to the subordinated peoples of Asia: that Japan was the real sponsor of freedom in the Far East. Roosevelt was constantly stressing the example of the United States in the Philippines as a model for all the great powers of the West. And China, enjoying for the time being her novel classification as a great power, relished also the temporary role of liberator. The statements seemed to imply a willingness on the part of the white man to ease himself as soon as he could after the war of the burden of a century of imperialism. But only one white man elaborated the promise of Cairo. Nevertheless, the action of Great Britain since Cairo speaks louder than the proverbial silence of the Sphinx of Ghizeh.

From Cairo, Roosevelt and Churchill flew on to meet at Teheran the other great partner in the European war. In order to win the war the Big Three had to agree among themselves. At the Persian capital (No-

[1] *Roosevelt and Hopkins*, p. 771.
[2] For the public statements on the Cairo Conference, see *Docs. Am. Foreign Relations*, VI, 232-234.

vember 28-December 1, 1943) the Big Three laid their plans for war and peace on this planet while about them hovered the envious ghost of Alexander the Great.

Stalin's most anxious question was about the second front. The two Western statesmen described their concerted plans in detail, not only for the second front in Europe, but also their recent conference with Chiang Kai-shek and their plans for concerted campaigns in Asia. Stalin repeated the assurance he had given to Hull in Moscow: that, when the Allies had defeated Germany, Russia would begin a second front of her own against Japan in Manchuria. This looked like a promise of one Russian Eastern second front against Japan on the Pacific in return for one Western second front against Germany on the Atlantic.

"Who will command OVERLORD?" the Russian Marshal asked, referring to the code name for the second front already in preparation. "Until that is done, OVERLORD cannot be said to be really in progress." [1] Stalin did not insist then and there on a specific answer to that vital question. Roosevelt appointed the commander before he got home.

The declaration of the Three Powers at Teheran (December 1, 1943) was brief: they had concerted plans for the destruction of German forces; as to the future "enduring peace" they said: "We shall seek the co-operation and active participation of all nations, large and small, whose peoples are in heart and mind dedicated, as are our own peoples, to the elimination of tyranny and slavery, oppression and intolerance. We welcome them, as they may choose to come, into a *world family of democratic nations*." [2] Nobody paused to define democracy—the Americans and British did not think it necessary to make clear the obvious. Was it not implicit in the Atlantic Charter?

There was also a declaration of the same date respecting Iran (Persia), to which the Big Three had referred in the earlier declaration as "our ally." [3] They expressed a common "desire" to maintain the "inde-

---

[1] *Roosevelt and Hopkins*, 787-788.

[2] Italics inserted.

A few days before at a Thanksgiving Day dinner of the British and American delegations at Cairo President Roosevelt had alluded to the family tradition in the American Thanksgiving, and said that this year America and Great Britain formed one family, which was more united than ever before. Roosevelt had opened the formal meetings of the Conference of Teheran by saying that he was glad to welcome the Russians as new members of "the family circle."

"If there was any supreme moment in Roosevelt's career," remarks the playwright Sherwood, "I believe that it will be fixed at this moment, at the end of the Teheran Conference. It certainly represents the peak for Harry Hopkins." *Roosevelt and Hopkins*, pp. 775, 778, 799.

[3] Iran declared war on January 16, 1943, against Germany, Italy and Japan.

pendence, sovereignty, and territorial integrity of Iran." "They count upon the participation of Iran together with all other peace-loving nations in the establishment of international peace, security and prosperity after the war in accordance with the principles of the Atlantic Charter, *to which all four governments have continued to subscribe.*" [1]

Such were the public "declarations" of Teheran. They were not treaties or even formal executive agreements but they had the import of treaties. Behind the scenes much more went on. The Three talked about getting the Turks into the war, but Stalin was unenthusiastic. Churchill mentioned possibilities of an Allied military diversion from the Adriatic via the Balkans into the Danube basin. Neither Roosevelt nor Stalin responded to that.[2] Churchill told Stalin he would welcome a warm-water port for Russia and the sight of her merchant marine and navy on every sea; Roosevelt proposed some kind of an international trusteeship that would ensure free passage to and from the Baltic Sea. The President also thought that Dairen, in Manchuria, might be made a free port under international guaranty, to which Russia might have access; he thought China would not object to the proposal.[3] Of course the Russian Marshal had no objections to such thoughts; in his turn he suggested that the islands in the vicinity of Japan would have to be used —he did not yet say by whom—to contain Japan against future aggression. And Roosevelt ventilated his ideas about a future United Nations organization for peace: an Assembly, an Executive Committee, and Four Policemen.

[1] Italics inserted.

[2] "I never at any time heard Mr. Churchill urge or suggest complete abandonment of the Overlord plan. His conviction, so far as I could interpret it, was that at some time in the indefinite future the Allies would have to cross the Channel. But he seemed to believe that our attack should be pushed elsewhere until the day came when the enemy would be forced to withdraw most of his troops from northwest Europe, at which time the Allies could go in easily and safely." Eisenhower, *Crusade in Europe*, p. 198.

It is fortunate for England, as well as for the entire Allied cause that Churchill's urgings did not succeed in diverting American military strategy from piercing directly to the heart of Germany from a second front in France based on England. Without stopping to discuss the difficulties of mountainous terrain in Yugoslavia (Tyrol, Styria, Carniola, Bosnia) so far from a major Allied base, it seems certain that Hitler would have pulverized England as a base and pounded it into surrender with V-2 projectiles if the American and British armies had not captured his launching platforms in the Low Countries barely in the nick of time. See *General Marshall's Report* (Washington, 1945).

See also Hajo Holborn, "The Collapse of the European Political System, 1914-45." *World Politics*, I (No. 4, July, 1949), 442-466.

[3] "It is my understanding," states Sherwood, who had access to the record of Teheran in the Hopkins Papers, "that Roosevelt was not merely guessing at this—that he had, in fact, discussed this very point with Chiang Kai-shek at Cairo a few days previously." *Roosevelt and Hopkins*, p. 792.

"Would this Executive Committee have the right to make decisions which would be binding on all the nations?" asked Stalin, anticipating his attitude toward a new league of nations.

They deliberated on the possible dismemberment of Germany. Stalin remarked that Poland's western boundary should be the Oder; he was less clear about the eastern boundary—he and Churchill had a conference separately on that question.

On the way back from Teheran, Roosevelt, Churchill, Harry Hopkins, and Anthony Eden met with the President and Foreign Minister of the Turkish Republic at Cairo (December 4-6, 1943) [1] but despite "useful" and "fruitful" discussions the Turkish officials would not commit themselves to entering the war while there was still danger of the destruction of Constantinople. The Second Cairo Conference was more important for further military deliberations between the leaders and staffs of the United States and Great Britain, preparing for the Normandy invasion, than it was for the talks with the Turks; [2] shortly afterwards President Roosevelt announced the appointment of General Eisenhower to command OVERLORD.[3]

Roosevelt and Churchill did not meet again until after the second front had been mounted successfully and France liberated. This interval was the period of greatest strain between the two Atlantic Allies. Finally in a second Quebec Conference (August 11-24, 1944) President and Prime Minister and numerous military, naval, financial and diplomatic staffs— Harry Hopkins instead of the Secretary of State—reached decisions with regard to the completion of the war in Europe and the "destruction of the barbarians in the Pacific," the United States to bear the principal burden of the last-named assignment.[4]

---

[1] Docs. Am. Foreign Relations, VI, 237-38.

[2] Roosevelt and Hopkins, pp. 798-804.

[3] Decided on, December 7, 1943. Crusade in Europe, p. 208.

[4] Joint Statement of the President and Prime Minister, September 16, 1944. Docs. Am. Foreign Relations, VII, 347. It was at this conference that Secretary of the Treasury Morgenthau, invading the province of the Secretary of State, Cordell Hull, who did not attend, secured adoption of his plan for dismantling Germany to an agrarian economy as a means of ensuring the future peace of Europe. The Secretary of State, Cordell Hull, and the Secretary of War, Henry L. Stimson, were unalterably opposed to the plan, but Roosevelt OK'd it and Churchill acquiesced, apparently in return for a promise by Morgenthau of a huge postwar subsidy to Great Britain: $3,500,000,000 cash, and $3,000,000,000 more later. Roosevelt later acknowledged that he had initialed this proposal without thinking enough about it, and soon dropped it: "I dislike making detailed plans for a country which we do not occupy." Memorandum of Roosevelt to Hull, October 20, 1944. Five years later Churchill said in Parliament (July 21, 1949): "I did not agree with it [the Morgenthau Plan], and I am sorry I put my initials to it." New York Times, July 22, 1949. See also Memoirs

The most vexing Anglo-American problem resolved at Quebec was the respective zones of occupation for American and British armies after the surrender of Germany. This had to be settled before the two governments could finally agree with Russia about the eastern Soviet zone. Roosevelt wanted the northwestern zone of Germany nearest to the sea. Churchill was happy to see American armies involved as deeply and constructively as possible in the heart of the continent for the protection of England and the salvation of Europe.[1] He naturally preferred that British armies should occupy the regions nearest to England as a buffer between Russia and the North Sea, and where Britain could do a thorough job of demolishing all naval works and destroying or at least controlling industrial war potential. The President finally gave in to Churchill and agreed that Britain should have the northwestern area, including the Ruhr Valley, the sea coasts, and the Kiel Canal; the United States would have all of southern Germany, including Bavaria, with Bremen in the north as an American port of entry enclaved in the British zone.[2] In southern Germany the American army forces would find themselves between the Soviet and the later French Zone, at the end of a long corridor, through British-held territory, from the sea. If a liberated France should go communist it would be an untenable military position.

Stalin did not attend this conference if only because Russia was not yet an enemy of Japan.[3] As a matter of fact, he was not anxious for a conference anyway. The second front in the West was an accomplished fact and success. Everything was now going Russia's way. Therefore why limit one's freedom of action for revolutionary reshaping of a

of *Cordell Hull*, 1602-1622; *Roosevelt and Hopkins*, 817-819; Henry L. Stimson and McGeorge Bundy, *On Active Service in Peace and War* (New York, 1947), pp. 568-583.

[1] "The United States has entered deeply and constructively into the life and salvation of Europe. We all three set our hands to far-reaching engagements, at once practical and solemn." Speech of Winston Churchill in House of Commons, Feb. 27, 1945. New York *Times*, Feb. 28, 1945, pp. 14-15. Announcement of the zones was not made until June 5, 1945. Department of State *Bulletin*, XII, No. 311 (June 10, 1945), p. 1052, and even then the boundaries were not described. They were later indicated on a map in *ibid.*, XIII (No. 321, Aug. 19, 1945), 275.

[2] *Memoirs of Cordell Hull*, pp. 1609-1616. According to Hull, "the United States Chiefs of Staff, however, proposed that the British and American spheres be exactly reversed" from what Churchill (and the Combined Chiefs of Staff) had proposed. Whatever the United States Chiefs of Staff had proposed, the Secretary of War Henry L. Stimson certainly opposed American instead of British occupation of the north-western zone. "He [Roosevelt] is hell-bent to occupy the northern portion. We all think that this is a mistake—that it will only get us into headlong collision with the British." *Active Service*, pp. 568-569.

[3] To protect its eastern flank against the possibility of a war with Germany, the USSR had signed (April 13, 1941) a five-year nonaggression pact with Japan; this was not due to terminate until April 13, 1946, and even then it would continue unless specifically denounced by either party on one year's notice.

Map 40. Zones of Military Occupation in Europe, beginning 1945.

NOTE: The Ruhr area has no accepted geographical definition but is generally taken to include the industrial cities of Duisburg, Essen, Bochum, Dortmund, Wuppertal and Düsseldorf. A French proposal for an international economic regime for the Ruhr included a precise geographical description of the area involved (text in *New York Times,* February 5, 1947). The Saar territory shown on the map covers the area which was under the League of Nations from 1920 to 1935, to which France added, in July 1946, the Rhineland districts of Saarburg and Wadern, thus extending it as far as the Luxemburg border. (Reproduced by permission of Council on Foreign Relations from their book, *The United States in World Affairs, 1945-1947,* by John C. Campbell, New York, 1947, p. 168.)

ruined continent? There was, however, one answer to give pause to Stalin: the Western Allies were reaching the peak of their military power in Europe. It might be best for the time being to play along with them until the United States should retire back across the ocean after the defeat of Germany.

A formidable group of questions now faced the Big Three. Although there seemed to be firm assurances, since Moscow and Teheran, that Russia would join the United States and Great Britain in the war against Japan as soon as Germany surrendered in Europe, there was not any agreement on what to do with Germany after the war. What would be the boundaries of the fourth Reich? Or should the Reich continue to exist at all as a state? Ought France, now liberated and functioning under the provisional government of General Charles de Gaulle, be admitted to a share of the occupation and control of defeated Germany? Stalin objected to French participation; Churchill desired it in order to bolster the West. And how should the victors deal with the other liberated countries, notably those in eastern and central Europe into which Russian influence and armed forces were now pouring?

Czechoslovakia had already made her own fateful choice. Deserted at Munich in 1938, and most likely to be occupied by Russian troops upon the defeat of Germany, she had been first to link her destiny to Moscow, hoping and trusting to keep her freedom. President Beneš in exile had signed in Moscow an alliance offensive and defensive with Russia (December 12, 1943) against the day of liberation from Hitler's power. In Poland and Yugoslavia, Soviet Russia refused to extend a helping hand to the old-line nationalist patriots under General Bor and General Mikhailovich, and insisted that the Western Allies ignore them in favor of the revolutionary partisans. Stalin was determined to make these Slavic border countries Russian satellites under communistic governments subject to leaders of his own appointment already schooled in Moscow. There was still no agreement among the Three on the future frontiers of Poland, through which invading armies had advanced for the conquest of Russia ever since the time of Napoleon Bonaparte. The United States had taken the position that the fixing of frontiers (there were thirty of them unsettled in Europe alone) [1] must await the final peace settlement, and that it would not guarantee any frontier except collectively as a member of the world peace organization agreed to in principle at Moscow in October, 1943, and already being formulated at Washington under the fatherly countenance of Cordell Hull (Dumbarton

[1] *Memoirs of Cordell Hull*, p. 1438.

Oaks Conference, August 21-October 7, 1944). Finally, how would the big powers (the United States, Great Britain, Russia, China; perhaps France) vote on decisive matters in the Security Council of the new league of nations? Would they have to be unanimous? Would each therefore have in effect an absolute check on the others, a *liberum veto*?

With all these issues brooding under the spreading Soviet wing, Prime Minister Churchill wanted another conference of the Big Three to settle the future of Europe before things got out of hand for England. But Roosevelt held off until after the national election, scheduled over a century before to take place the first Tuesday after the first Monday of November, 1944. Churchill could not wait. He and his Foreign Minister Anthony Eden flew to Moscow and made an agreement with Stalin (Anglo-Russian Conference of October 9-18, 1944) on the future boundaries of Poland (in the east approximately the Curzon Line recommended by British diplomacy in 1919; in the west the line of the River Oder, deep in the heart of Prussia) and on spheres of influence in the Balkans (predominantly for Russia in Roumania, Bulgaria and Hungary; for Great Britain in Greece; jointly for both in Yugoslavia).[1] Roosevelt let it be known that he would not be bound by anything decided by Russia and Great Britain in the Moscow Conference.[2] As the aurora of victory began to light up the horizon of Europe, the Allies seemed to be drifting apart.

It was in this uncertain dawn that Roosevelt and Hopkins and top American military advisers, and the new [3] Secretary of State, Edward R. Stettinius, Jr., and James F. Byrnes, Director of the Office of War Mobilization and Reconversion, chief "trouble-shooter" for the Administration, set forth for the Russian Crimea immediately after the President's fourth inauguration. They were on their way to the Crimean —Yalta—Conference, most famous in the annals of American secret diplomacy. For during the Second World War the United States, through the power of the Commander in Chief of the armed forces of the nation to make "military" agreements, had become engaged for better or worse

---

[1] The Anglo-Soviet communiqué of October 21, 1944, describes the discussion only in veiled terms. *Docs. Am. Foreign Relations*, VII, 347. *Memoirs of Cordell Hull*, p. 1485. The documentation is not fully available for these temporary arrangements. Vernon Van Dyke summarizes the evidence in his memorandum on "American Support of Free Institutions in Eastern Europe." *Yale Institute of International Studies*, No. 28 (August 10, 1948).

[2] *Roosevelt and Hopkins*, p. 834.

[3] Cordell Hull, who had held that office with great distinction since March 4, 1933, longer than any other Secretary of State in American history, resigned in a collapse of health on November 30, 1944.

in the practice of secret diplomacy,[1] hitherto a relatively unknown phenomenon in American history.

The Yalta Conference (February 4-11, 1945) was one of the most dramatic personal parleys in modern history, rivaling in that respect the memorable meeting of Napoleon and Alexander I on a raft in the middle of the Niemen River. There, amidst the soft airs of the ravaged Crimea, on the seats of the mighty in the old Livadia palace of the Czars, sat in joyful situation Joseph Stalin, the man of steel, dictator of the Russian proletariat, father of a new Pan-Slavism, implacable *Realpolitiker* of the Revolution, sponsor of a future WUSSR. On the other end of the row of three sat Winston Churchill, dauntless leader of large enterprises, greatest statesman of English history, somber man of blood and tears and toil and sweat, and now of smiling victory, striving for a peace that would make the world safe for a disintegrating British Empire. Between them sat the amiable Roosevelt, civilian Commander in Chief[2] of the armies and navies and airfleets of the United States, new dealer of good will and promises to the common man and voter, would-be good neighbor to all the world, preacher of the four freedoms to all the men in all the lands. Graven on his anxious visage were the fatal ravages of illness and fatigue. The last task of his life was to wean Stalin away from the inexorable revolutionary goal of a World Union of Soviet Socialist Republics into a peaceful World Family of Democratic Nations.

The joint public announcement of the results of the Yalta Conference masked the secret agreements of the three Chiefs of State. They told the world that they had agreed on the timing, scope, and co-ordination of military plans for the defeat and unconditional surrender of Germany and enforcement by military occupation by the United States, Great Britain, Russia, and France, in separate zones, with a joint Allied Control Commission of their respective commanders in that field. They declared that they would root out all vestiges of Nazism in order to give hope for a future decent life for Germans and a place for them in the comity of nations. They made known that they would call a conference of the

---

[1] By this is meant not secret and confidential discussions or negotiations, but secret international agreements not even known to the Senate, or the House of Representatives. The American delegation, listed in the joint Report on the Crimean Conference, included no member of either house of Congress.

[2] "Following Pearl Harbor, he preferred to be called Commander in Chief rather than President. He relished the title. He may have felt that this all-important position was now more essential than that of President.

"At a Cabinet dinner, probably in 1942, where I was to propose the toast, the President asked me, before I rose to speak:

"'Please try to address me as Commander in Chief, not as President.'" *Memoirs of Cordell Hull*, p. 1111.

THE BIG THREE AT YALTA, 1945

(Left to right: Churchill, Roosevelt, Stalin. Admiral Leahy is standing behind the President.)

signatories of the United Nations Declaration to meet at San Francisco
April 25, 1945, to agree upon a world peace organization on the basis
of the proposals of Dumbarton Oaks. They revealed that they had
reached an agreement, to be announced in due course, on the voting
formula of the big powers within the Security Council of such an organization. They broadcast their resolution to endow the liberated nations of
Europe with provisional governments representative of all the democratic
elements in the population pledged to free elections of *de jure* governments responsible to the will of the people. They did not define democracy, any more than they had done at Teheran, but they reaffirmed
their faith in the principles of the Atlantic Charter.

They conceded that a new situation had been created in Poland, as a
result of her complete liberation by the Red Army, that called for the
establishment of a more broadly based Provisional Government, to include democratic leaders from Poland itself and from Poles abroad; this
government would be pledged to hold free and unfettered elections as
soon as possible on the basis of universal suffrage and secret ballot to be
participated in by all democratic and anti-Nazi parties. They recognized
that the eastern boundary of Poland "should" follow the Curzon Line,
with minor deviations in favor of Poland, and that Poland "must" receive
substantial accessions of territory in the north and west—as compensation
for her losses in the east. They agreed to the establishment of a new
government in Yugoslavia under Marshal Tito—the Soviet protégé—but
with a broader basis including former members of parliament who had
not compromised themselves by collaboration with the enemy. They provided for periodic meetings of the foreign secretaries of their respective
governments, by rotation in the three capitals, to follow after the United
Nations Conference on World Organization.

The most important products of Yalta were the three secret supplementary agreements, not included in the public declaration of
February 11, 1945, but of the same date: (1) an agreement on the re-
patriation of citizens of the USA and the USSR, and on prisoners of war
and civilians liberated by American and Soviet forces respectively; (2)
on the voting formula for the Big Four in the Security Council kept
secret only until cleared with France and China; [1] and (3) conditions
agreed upon for the entrance of Russia into the war with Japan "in
two or three months after Germany has surrendered."

[1] Secretary Stettinius made a public announcement of the Yalta voting formula during
the Chapultepec Conference at Mexico City, March 5, 1945.

The latter agreement pledged the United States and Great Britain "unquestionably" to fulfill for Russia, after Japan's defeat: (1) the *status quo* of outer-Mongolia—named as The Mongolian Peoples' Republic—which had severed itself from China and accepted Russian protection; (2) restoration to Russia of her former status in Manchuria before the Russo-Japanese War of 1904-1905, with specific safeguarding of the "pre-eminent interests" [1] of Soviet Russia in the internationalized free port of Dairen, in a naval base (by lease) at Port Arthur, and in joint Sino-Russian control and operation of the Chinese-Eastern and South Manchurian Railroads; (3) the Kurile Islands and the southern half of the island of Sakhalin to be handed over to the USSR. [2]

The pledges at Yalta to Stalin, which the Russian leader was careful to have written down explicitly over the signatures of the Big Three, ran directly counter to the promises which Roosevelt and Churchill had made to Chiang Kai-shek in the Cairo Declaration. They placed the President under the "unquestionable" requirement of obtaining from the Generalissimo his consent, [3] a most mortifying function for the United States. Further, by failing to stipulate the Open Door for the USA along with the "preeminent interests" of the USSR in Manchuria, Roosevelt overlooked a fundamental of American foreign policy in the very region that originally called forth that doctrine and led to its pronouncement for all of China in 1899. [4]

Roosevelt signed the last, secret pact of Yalta—relating to Russia's entry into the war with Japan—while personally closeted with Stalin and Churchill. It was this agreement which provoked the most severe animadversions among the President's countrymen when the text became

[1] Compare this phrase with the words "paramount interests" which Viscount Ishii attempted unsuccessfully to substitute for "special interests" in the Lansing-Ishii Agreement of 1917. See above, pages 685-686.

[2] For the text of the Yalta Three-Power Declaration of February 12, 1945, and the supplementary agreements signed on February 11, and official explanations by President Roosevelt and Secretary of State Stettinius, see *Documents on Am. Foreign Relations*, VII, 360-364; VIII, 919-924.

According to Sherwood, Stalin asked Roosevelt whether any foreign troops would be stationed in Korea, and Roosevelt replied in the negative, whereupon Stalin expressed his approval. *Roosevelt and Hopkins*, p. 868.

[3] This was given in the Sino-Soviet Treaty of Friendship and Alliance, signed at Moscow, August 14, 1945, the very day of Japan's capitulation, formally attested in the instrument of surrender, September 2, 1945. The text of the Alliance is in *Docs. Am. Foreign Relations*, VIII, 826-29.

[4] Russia had never unequivocally accepted the Open Door and was not a party to the Nine-Power Treaty of 1922. See above, p. 692. In conversations in Moscow in May, 1945 (after Yalta), Stalin remarked to Harry Hopkins that he agreed with America's Open Door policy. *Roosevelt and Hopkins*, p. 903.

known.[1] Roosevelt had led the United States into a double war in order
to preserve a global balance of power. At Yalta, on the eve of certain
victory, he made concessions to Stalin at the expense of China which unhinged the balance of power in both Asia and Europe. Yet it is difficult
to see how, short of turning on the ally Russia in actual war, either the
United States or Great Britain could have prevented in fact the flow of
Russian power into the vacuums east and west that were being created
by the defeat of Germany and Japan. To be sure, in return for these concessions Stalin pledged support to the Chinese Nationalist government
and to uphold democratic principles in the liberated states in Eastern
Europe and elsewhere—just as Chamberlain received guaranties from
Hitler at Munich not to advance any farther in Europe after taking part
of Czechoslovakia. Placing this promise of Stalin's on record for these
principles was a most important factor in the great issues that were to
follow. Nevertheless, in its aftermath of deception, Yalta was in a
sense equivalent to another Munich.

President Roosevelt's top military advisers, present at Yalta, must
bear with him the heavy responsibility. They thought it greatly necessary to induce Russia to enter the Japanese war to save perhaps a million
American casualties and another year of war in a direct assault on the
islands of Japan then being planned.[2] But former Secretary of State

[1] James F. Byrnes, who was present at Yalta and took stenographic notes of the
deliberations did not know of this secret agreement when he became Secretary of
State on July 3, 1945. He first learned of it from Russia, and then he went to the
White House to find out, as he tells it, how many IOU's were outstanding against
the United States. Admiral Leahy got the text of the agreement for him out of a
safe in the Map Room of the White House, and Byrnes took it to the Department
of State. *Speaking Frankly*, p. 43. Edward R. Stettinius, Jr., Hull's successor as
Secretary of State, was present at the Crimea Conference and knew about the signed
agreement on the Far East. Harry Hopkins had told him about it before the
Conference convened, and President Roosevelt and Ambassador (to Russia) W. Averell
Harriman discussed the subject with him during the Conference. The State Department,
however, did not handle this matter, despite Harriman's participation. Harriman at
that time was more than an ambassador: he was the co-ordinator of all civilian
and military activities. I am indebted for this information to the late Mr. Stettinius and
to Professor Walter Johnson, his historical collaborator. Mr. Stettinius's account of
Roosevelt and the Russians: the Yalta Conference was published posthumously (New
York, 1949).
[2] Rear Admiral Ellis M. Zacharias has explained "The Inside Story of Yalta," in
United Nations World (January, 1949), pp. 12-16, in terms of poor intelligence furnished to Roosevelt by the Combined Chiefs of Staff grossly exaggerating Japan's army
strength at 5,000,000 effectives instead of 2,000,000 men of all kinds. As late as July,
1945, scarcely a month before VJ-Day, Secretary of War Stimson believed that the
United States would need 5,000,000 men to defeat Japan in her own islands. *On Active
Service*, pp. 618-619. This was after the Japanese Navy had been all but destroyed and
the main Japanese archipelago cut off from the island conquest and connections endangered even with the continent of Asia!

Hull has indicated that Stalin had already pledged the USSR to come into that war as soon as Germany was defeated and has suggested that it was scarcely necessary to tender equivalents to perform what he had already agreed to do.[1] It is too early, and we have too inadequate a record, to pass secure judgment on Roosevelt's diplomacy at Yalta. Perhaps the best explanation is that the President, realizing there could be no future world peace without Russian-American co-operation and reciprocal good will, went more than half way to get it. That the effort failed because of Soviet Russia's subsequent violations of the agreement does not disprove that it was a persevering attempt to convince Marshal Stalin of the sincerity of American intentions.[2]

Roosevelt and Hopkins, and the whole American delegation, left Yalta in a mood of supreme exultation. They felt that they could live with the Russians and get along with them in as far a future as any one of them could imagine.[3] The President persisted against mounting mistrust in his sanguine expectations of Russian good will, until the day of his death, April 12, 1945. Only an hour before he collapsed from a sudden cerebral hemorrhage, Roosevelt dictated this last message, to Winston Churchill:

I would minimize the general Soviet problem as much as possible because these problems, in one form or other, seem to arise every day and most of them straighten out as in the case of the Berne meeting.

We must be firm, however, and our course thus far is correct.[4]

ROOSEVELT'S INTERVIEWS WITH EMPEROR HAILE SELASSIE, KING FAROUK, AND KING IBN SAUD, 1945

On the way home from Yalta the President stopped at Suez to meet personally the Emperor Haile Selassie of Ethiopia, King Farouk of Egypt, and King Ibn Saud of Saudi Arabia.

In the ceremonial exchange of gifts that accompanied the interview with

---

[1] *Memoirs of Cordell Hull*, p. 1310. Harry Hopkins, Roosevelt's principal confidant, admits that, at Teheran, Stalin had made a first commitment insofar as Soviet participation in the war against Japan was concerned, but says it "needed to be clarified as to precise dates and the extent of Soviet participation." *Roosevelt and Hopkins*, p. 842. But the Yalta secret protocol clarified neither the one nor the other, except in the loose phrase "two or three months."

[2] Rudolph A. Winnacker asks the question: "Yalta—Another Munich?" in the *Virginia Quarterly Review*, XXIV (No. 4, Autumn, 1948), 520-537.

[3] *Roosevelt and Hopkins*, pp. 870-73.

[4] Byrnes, *Speaking Frankly*, pp. 56-59. The reference to the Berne meeting is to a contretemps between Roosevelt and Stalin arising from the latter's unjustified accusations that the Allies had parleyed with German officers for a surrender of German forces in Italy without participation of Soviet representatives.

Ibn Saud on board the U.S.S. *Quincy* the King presented Roosevelt with a freshly slaughtered sheep, and the President gave his own wheel-chair—plus a United States naval plane—to the King. He asked Ibn Saud, as a spokesman for the Arab world, to agree to admit more Jews into Palestine, but ended up by promising himself to take no step in Palestine without full consultation of both Arabs and Jews. "I will take no action in my capacity as Chief of the Executive branch of the Government," he further declared, "which might prove hostile to the Arab people." [1] Thus did the United States make dubious entry into the Palestine question.[2]

[1] New York *Times*, March 14, October 19, 1945.
[2] The scope of this History does not include the issues raised before the United Nations Organization, like Palestine, Greece, Iran, Indonesia, etc.

CHAPTER XLVI

WORLD FAMILY OF DEMOCRATIC NATIONS

VERSUS

WORLD UNION OF SOVIET SOCIALIST REPUBLICS

(1945-1950)

THE immediate purpose of the United Nations, in their diplomacy as in their military effort, great or small or merely nominal, had been to win the global war by complete defeat of Germany and Japan, not to mention Italy and the lesser captives of the Axis powers. After that, to win the peace. Here the policies of the greater powers diverged radically into two postwar worlds.

There was the One World [1] of general Western preference and renewed American fancy. It rested on the political thought of Burke and Bagehot and Woodrow Wilson. It was what Franklin D. Roosevelt thought of as a World Family of Democratic Nations. It envisaged collective security for individual liberty and political democracy, functioning nationally and constitutionally under a new league of nations, backed this time by an international force of righteousness.

On the other hand there was the Revolutionary world of Marx and Lenin and Joseph Stalin. It was based on totalitarian power, to be seized and wielded in the name of the proletariat. It sacrificed the freedom of the individual to the omnipotence of the state. The Marxian World, under its mighty Russian dictatorship, avowed an irreconcilable conflict between capitalism and communism. The First and the Second World Wars were classic convulsions, already marked down in the primer of revolution, to be encountered along the rapidly shortening way to the collapse of capitalism. The Strange Alliance [2] with the Western democracies against the Axis powers was a profitable episode in

---

[1] The phrase captivated public opinion following the publication of the quick brochure *One World* (New York, 1943) by Wendell Willkie, Roosevelt's Republican contender in 1940, who in 1942 made a flying trip around the world in the interests of Allied unity.

[2] General John R. Deane, head of the United States Military Mission in Moscow, 1943-1945, told the history of American efforts at wartime co-operation with Moscow in *The Strange Alliance* (New York, 1947).

more ways than one. To Soviet statesmen winning the peace did not mean collective security for peace-loving political democracies under a new league of nations. Russia had just been expelled summarily from the old League for the attack on Finland in 1939. To the leaders of the USSR victory meant not only defense of Holy Russia in a great patriotic war. It also warranted the prestige and power of the Soviet Union all over the globe. It presented a world-shaking opportunity to expand out of the Asiatic Heartland into the places of Germany and Japan west and east in the World Island of Eurasia, massive pedestal for world power in the complete sense of the word. The ultimate end would justify any means. The end in view was a revolutionary World Union of Soviet Socialist Republics. That was the one world of Lenin and Stalin.

It was otherwise among the Western democracies, particularly in America. To them victory meant world peace. Amidst the heartily unwanted anxieties, agonies, and responsibilities which a new World War had thrust upon them, thoughtful Americans began to talk remorsefully of the "lost peace"—meaning that of 1919! Actually no peace had been lost *then*. The United States and its Associates had emerged from the First World War altogether victorious. They had dictated a peace—a very fair peace, all things considered—to their own liking. That peace was lost in Europe in 1936, not in Washington in 1919. Great Britain and France, jealous of each other,[1] had allowed Adolf Hitler to re-arm Germany and tear up the Treaty of Versailles while Uncle Sam, entranced by a disillusionist historiography, had buried his addled head and strong shoulders in the drifting sands of pacifism and neutrality legislation. Good folk suddenly found themselves believing fondly that if only the great Republic of the West and its vanished army had been all along a member of the League of Nations the world would not have got so speedily unhinged.

In the black spring of 1942 old college grads, veterans of the First World War, came back to their twenty-fifth reunions to do honor to their alma maters. Their own sons had just gone forth to the wars to fight over again on a large scale what they battled for in their own youth. Military boots had worn bare the campus greens. Motors and propel-

[1]Arnold Wolfers, *Britain and France between Two Wars; Conflicting Strategies of Peace since Versailles* (New York, 1940); Harold Butler, *The Lost Peace, a Personal Impression* (New York, 1942); Leopold Schwartzschild, *The World in Trance* (London, 1942).

lers and anti-aircraft parts crowded the classrooms. The blackboards were covered with military logistics. "It must not happen again!" declaimed the men of 1917, Commencement orators of 1942. So said the teachers and the preachers everywhere. So felt the man in the street.[1] The politicians echoed the universal thought. They called for a new league of nations as Professor Wilson had called for one when President, got it, and lost it.

As the war progressed, a new school of historiography, students of the "lost peace," who had written their books in recent anxious years, held forth their warnings on President Wilson's mistakes with the Senate.[2] But the historians of Woodrow Wilson's supposedly lost peace were no more successful in teaching President Franklin D. Roosevelt how not to lose the next peace than their predecessors, the historians of Wilsonian neutrality, had been in teaching him how not to become involved in the Second World War. They and the American people about them, engrossed in their war against the two colossi of Europe and Asia, had too little comprehension of the changing balance of power and the consequently shifting strategy of American defense and diplomacy. They did not realize how quickly the totalitarian power of Soviet Russia would fill the vacuums left by the collapse of Germany and Japan, how mightily it would congeal there, what new dangers it would produce.

New historical prophets made the American people League-of-Nations-conscious again, if they had not made them conscious of the possibilities of new problems of power. Complete defeat of the enemies and collective security under the United Nations in a charter to be forged while the Allied arms still smoked hot on land, at sea, and in the air, became the most cherished goal of the United States and that of the Western Allies. They expected Russia after the war to sit down like a good neighbor to the bourgeois board of peace in a brave new world at ease from totalitarian dictators.

The United Nations Conference on International Organization, scheduled at Yalta, took place on time at San Francisco, April 25-June

[1] Thomas A. Bailey would fain educate *The Man in the Street* (New York, 1948) to cope responsibly with major problems of foreign policy and diplomacy. As a step towards this competence the Man might well read Professor Bailey's many books on the subject, including *A Diplomatic History of the American People* (New York, 1946).

[2] Paul Birdsall, *Versailles Twenty Years After* (New York, 1941). Thomas A. Bailey, *Woodrow Wilson and the Lost Peace* (New York, 1944), and *Woodrow Wilson and the Great Betrayal* (New York, 1945). Sumner Welles, *The Time for Decision* (New York, 1944). H. C. F. Bell, *Woodrow Wilson and the People* (New York, 1945).

26, 1945, called to order by Franklin D. Roosevelt's successor, President Harry S. Truman. Already a rift had appeared between the East and the West, over the democratization of Poland, over the amount of reparation in kind to be extracted from surrendered Germany and shared by the victors, and over the apparent lack of interest and enthusiasm manifested by Soviet Russia for the San Francisco Conference.[1]

The other United Nations met at San Francisco in a general fervor of conviction. Nowhere was this evangelism at higher pitch than in the United States. The Government fanned the fervor and galvanized it. From all over the land it brought teachers and civic leaders to the Golden Gate of World Peace as consultants or secretaries or assistants or advisers. They returned home as apostles to gather up and focus public opinion on the Senate of the United States. Foreign negotiators at San Francisco—notably the Soviet delegates—capitalized upon this popular insistence for the new league, as they had done at Paris in 1919, in Woodrow Wilson's time.

Most of the constructive work for the new league of nations had been done already by professional diplomatists and specialists at Dumbarton Oaks, and at Yalta the Big Three had compromised the vital controversial questions hitherto raised by Russia: (1) representation in the Assembly, (2) voting procedure in the Security Council. Stalin at first had talked about one membership in the Assembly for each one of the sixteen Soviet Republics, but he came down to three at Yalta, one for the USSR and one each for two of the components, Byelorussia, and the Ukraine. To match Stalin, Roosevelt had in mind before he went to Yalta to ask for one membership and vote for each one of the forty-eight states of the United States. Actually at Yalta he agreed to three for Russia, but wanted a certain "insurance" understanding, to which Stalin assented; in case the Senate objected (the President doubtless remembered the Great Debate of 1919-1920) to the three votes of Russia, the United States could have at least three votes too,[2] if desired, in the Assembly.

The Charter of United Nations, completed at San Francisco, June 26, 1945, attempted to remedy the defects of the Covenant of the League of

---

[1] In contrast to the other nations big and little, the Soviet Government did not attach enough vital importance to the conference to think it worthwhile to send its Minister of Foreign Affairs, Molotov, to San Francisco. Only after much urging by the United States and other powers did Stalin finally send Molotov, who was there for the opening of the Conference and during the first two weeks. Anthony Eden, the British Foreign Minister, left on May 13, four days after Molotov. New York Times.

[2] Roosevelt and Hopkins, pp. 854-57, 876-77.

Nations. As originally framed at Dumbarton Oaks, the Charter had endowed the Security Council (composed permanently of the United States, the United Kingdom of Great Britain and Northern Ireland, the Union of Soviet Socialist Republics, France, and China, plus six small powers elected in rotation by the General Assembly from the other members) with control over any question affecting the peace of the world. On all but procedural matters a decision of the Council required seven votes, including *unanimity of the five permanent members*. This gave a veto to each one of the Big Five.

At first Stalin had insisted, at Yalta, that this veto power apply even to admission of any question for consideration by the Council, but had finally conceded that unanimity of the Big Five need not be required merely to discuss a question, and that disputant parties could not vote in judgment on themselves in the Council. The President and the British Minister esteemed this Russian concession to be a great victory for peace; in turn they agreed that for any *action* by the Security Council there must be unanimity among the five major powers.[1] It meant, in brief, that there could be no enforcement of world peace except the Big Five agree.[2] This merely enacted a fact of life. The United States clung to the veto power on enforcement action if only to protect the Monroe Doctrine and matters of domestic jurisdiction from outside intervention. As revolution has spread since then in the world the veto power has become more and more of a comfort against the possibility of members of the Security Council, even permanent members, going communist.

The most important addition to the Charter at San Francisco came by way of the Chapultepec meeting of the American republics,[3] voicing a desire for more immediate security, individually or collectively, for the states of the New World. With the support of the United States the small nations succeeded in inserting Article 51, which declared that nothing in the Charter should impair the inherent right of individual or collective self-defense, if an armed attack should occur against a member of the United Nations, until the Security Council should have taken measures necessary to maintain international peace and security.[4] This

[1] *Roosevelt and Hopkins*, pp. 854-855.

[2] See William T. R. Fox, "The United States and the Other Great Powers," in *A Foreign Policy for the United States* (University of Chicago Press, 1947), p. 316.

[3] See above, p. 778.

[4] It meant that the Security Council could take no action against an American republic until the United States, sponsor of the Monroe Doctrine and party to the Inter-American Doctrine of Nonintervention, agreed to it as a permanent member of

made possible the regional inter-American defensive pact of Rio de Janeiro of 1947 [1] ; but it could apply, of course, to any region of the world, like the Middle East, the Balkans, Eastern Europe, or the North Atlantic countries. Article 51 of the Charter made the United States the watchdog within the Security Council for the liberties of the American republics, because the Council could take no action, like intervention in the Western Hemisphere, without consent of the United States. *Per contra,* the USSR built up regional pacts among its satellite states.[2]

Another feature added at San Francisco was a broader forum function for ventilation in the Assembly of problems which the Security Council might not be considering at the moment or, conceivably, might not even be willing to consider. But when all was said and done, whether at Dumbarton Oaks, or at Yalta, or at San Francisco, the future peace of the world depended on co-operation and agreement among the superpowers, particularly between the USA, exponent of the Four Freedoms in a World Family of Democratic Nations, and the USSR, dictator for the proletariat in a World Union of Soviet Socialist Republics.

"It must not happen again!" The Charter of United Nations, in treaty form, and the Court of International Justice, as a statute annexed thereto, went through the Senate of the United States with flying colors in less than a month, to be ratified overwhelmingly by a final vote of 89-2 (July 28, 1945), with not a single reservation. It was not necessary for President Truman to make use of the card which Stalin had let Roosevelt have at Yalta to keep up his sleeve in Washington: three votes for the USA in the Assembly.[3] The Senate advised and consented without demur to a new league of nations which might, through the Security Council (subject to the veto of the American representative) place armed forces of the United States (as part of an United Nations police force) in action to preserve the peace anywhere in the world without a vote of the United States Congress.

The Senate further agreed (August 14, 1946) under an option of the statute, to submit in advance as compulsory *ipso facto,* and without

the Council. See the analysis of W. T. R. Fox, who participated in the Conference, of "The Super-Powers at San Francisco," *Review of Politics,* VIII (No. 1, Jan., 1946), 115-127.

[1] See above, p. 779.

[2] See below, p. 915.

[3] Whether President Truman knew of this reservation at the time of the Senate deliberations is not yet clear.

further special agreement (*compromis*) any purely "legal"[1] dispute with any nation which similarly registered in advance its agreement to accept the same obligation. This was the greatest step ahead ever made by the United States in the history of judicial settlement of international disputes.[2]

The United States had pinned its hopes to the banner of the United Nations.[3] "We have solemnly dedicated ourselves and all our will to the success of the United Nations Organization," President Truman declared to the Congress, January 14, 1946.

Impelled by a vast surge of public opinion, the United States, repudiator of Woodrow Wilson's League of Nations, had led the movement for a new league and set its seal to the Charter before the global war was finished. Already Hitler and his arch-prophet Goebbels had committed suicide in the bunkers of Berlin and Germany had surrendered unconditionally, May 5, 1945. Another personal conference of Chiefs of State was necessary to sit on the ruins of the Reich and fix in detail the terms of occupation and reparation, and to arrange for the expected European peace conference.

No man has ever been called more suddenly, and with less preparation, than Harry S. Truman to the exalted duty of Commander in Chief of the armed forces of a great power—at the moment perhaps the greatest military power in all history—who, with his military and political advisers, represented the United States at the Conference of Berlin (July 17-August 2, 1945). Clement Attlee, the new British Prime Minister who had succeeded Winston Churchill as a result of a staggering British election held in the middle of the Conference, had far more experience

---

[1] The language of the Senate Resolution of August 14, 1946, included a reservation declaring that the obligation did not apply to:

   a. Disputes entrusted to other tribunals by treaties already existing or by treaties which might be concluded in the future.

   b. Disputes with regard to matters "essentially within the jurisdiction of the United States of America as determined by the United States of America."

   c. Disputes arising under a multilateral treaty, unless (1) all parties to the treaty affected by the decision are also parties to the case before the Court, or (2) the United States of America agrees to the jurisdiction.

   Docs. Am. Foreign Relations, VIII, 516.

[2] The following countries have also accepted (1949) the compulsory jurisdiction of the International Court of Justice: Australia, Belgium, Bolivia, Brazil, Canada, China, Colombia, Denmark, Dominican Republic, El Salvador, France, Guatemala, Haiti, Honduras, India, Iran, Luxemburg, Mexico, Netherlands, New Zealand, Nicaragua, Norway, Pakistan, Panama, Paraguay, Philippines, Sweden, Switzerland, Thailand, Turkey, Union of South Africa, United Kingdom, Uruguay.

[3] Radio Address of Secretary of State James F. Byrnes to the Overseas Press Club, February 28, 1946. Department of State *Bulletin,* XIV, No. 349 (March 10, 1946), 355.

in politics [1] than the Vice President who succeeded Franklin D. Roosevelt. Truman followed the advice of his new Secretary of State, James F. Byrnes, and of his admirals and generals.

At Berlin it was not a question so much of what was done as of what was left undone or referred to subordinate commissions or councils. The zones of occupation had already been laid down by the European Advisory Commission [2] and agreed to by the three Governments, and the victors were seated there in all their might. At Potsdam the Big Three (though personally no longer the Big Three of Teheran and Yalta) dismissed the European Advisory Commission and set up a Council of Foreign Ministers to prepare, for submission to the United Nations, treaty drafts of peace with Italy, Roumania, Bulgaria, Austria, Hungary, and Finland. They looked forward to the ultimate admission of those states into the United Nations. The Council of Foreign Ministers also received the task of preparing terms of peace to be accepted by Germany when a German government adequate for that purpose should be established—nobody could say when that would be. The Big Three meanwhile agreed that supreme authority in Germany would be exercised by each occupational commander (American, Russian, British, French) within his respective zone, and by a Control Council of all four commanders in matters affecting Germany as a whole—the Control Council set up zones for each of the four powers respectively in the jointly occupied city of Berlin, embedded deeply within the Russian zone. The three Chiefs of State came together on principles to govern the treatment of Germany in the initial period of control: the rooting out of all traces of Nazi power and authority in German life and complete disarmament and demilitarization of Germany, to prepare for the eventual reconstruction of the Reich on a "democratic basis"—again no definition of democracy—but was it not in the Atlantic Charter? They agreed to share equally—among the Three—what was left of the German navy and ocean-going merchant marine. They provided that during the occupation period Germany should be treated as a single economic unit, and primary emphasis given to the development of agriculture and peaceful domestic industries. They left German frontiers to be fixed in the future peace treaty; but pending final delimitation of Poland's western frontier in the peace settlement they agreed on a line running from the Baltic Sea immediately west of Swinemünde and thence up the Oder River to the confluence of the

---

[1] Winston Churchill had brought him along to Berlin to be familiar with the proceedings, just in case!

[2] Announced June 5, 1945. See Map 40.

western Neisse and to the Czechoslovak frontier—Stalin's maximum desire for Poland. They left the city of Königsberg and a large part of East Prussia meanwhile under Soviet control.

At the Yalta Conference the Big Three had laid down as a "basis of discussion" reparations of $20,000,000,000 "in kind" (including German labor to restore damage), 50 per cent to go to Russia. Much discussion had taken place since then, including the deliberations of a reparations commission, but no further agreement had been reached; for one thing the Russians, under the guise of war "booty" rather than accounted reparations, were stripping Germany, Austria, and Hungary of movable property (including American-owned property previously confiscated by the Nazi forces). At Berlin it finally was stipulated that the reparation claims of the United States and the United Kingdom and other Western countries should be met from the Western zones, plus appropriate German external assets; reparations and assets for Russia (and for Poland) should come from the Eastern zone, plus 10 per cent for Russia of the usable and complete capital equipment available for the purpose in the Western zone, furthermore another 15 per cent in exchange for an equivalent value of commodities more plentiful in the Russian zone. Austria would not be required to pay reparations.[1]

Looking out from the rubble of Berlin over a ravished Europe, Truman, Churchill, and Stalin reaffirmed their determination to bring to "sure and swift" justice the major war criminals whose crimes had no particular geographical localization—this was already being arranged in discussions by American, British, French, and Russian representatives in London.[2]

[1] Control machinery and zones of control for Austria, similar to those in Germany, were later agreed to by the Governments of the United States, the United Kingdom, Soviet Russia, and the provisional government and released to the press by the Department of State, August 8, 1945. Department of State Bulletin, XIII, No. 320 (Aug. 12, 1945), pp. 221-22.

[2] The agreement setting up the International Military Tribunal at Nuremberg for the trial of major German war criminals was signed at London, August 8, 1945. For text see Department of State Bulletin, VI, No. 320 (August 12, 1945), pp. 222-28. The Nuremberg trials lasted from October 14, 1945 to October 1, 1946. The surviving major German war criminals who were convicted and received the death sentence, and were hanged on October 15, 1947, were: Von Ribbentrop, Keitel, Kaltenbrunner, Rosenberg, Frank, Frick, Streicher, Sauckel, Jodl, Seyss-Inquart. Göring succeeded in committing suicide the night before. Martin Bormann, never apprehended, was condemned to death in absentia. Those who received less than the death sentence were: Hess, Funk, Raeder, life imprisonment; von Schirach, Speer, twenty years imprisonment; von Neurath, fifteen years; Dönitz, ten years. Acquitted were: Schacht, von Papen, and Fritzsche.

For the voluminous record of the trials see: Trial of the Major War Criminals Before the International Military Tribunal, Nuremberg, October, 1945-October, 1946 (pub-

Berlin was the last of the spectacular conferences of the Chiefs of State of the United States, Great Britain, and Soviet Russia,[1] and the final chapter of Allied unity.

President Truman hopefully reported to his fellow-Americans that the three great powers were now more closely bound than ever before in their determination to achieve a just and lasting peace. But the American delegation left Berlin far less sanguine than the group which came back with such exaltation from Yalta. Stalin and Molotov and Vishinsky had revealed a disturbing disposition to lay down the law as much as to co-operate—an ominous portent for the future. In the later words of James F. Byrnes, Potsdam was a success that failed.[2]

During the Conference, President Truman and Prime Minister Attlee, with the concurrence of Generalissimo Chiang Kai-shek, proclaimed the

lished at Nuremberg, Germany, 42 vols., 1946-1949). The documents in the exhibit are of greatest historical importance. The American case of prosecution is published in *Nazi Conspiracy and Aggression* (8 vols., Washington, G.P.O., 1946).

UNITED STATES WAR CRIMES PROGRAM FOR ALL THEATERS, AS OF OCTOBER 1, 1949

	Germany		Japan					
	Nurem-berg*	Dachau†	IMTFE‡	Yoko-hama	China	Manila	Italy	Navy
No. of cases......	12	491	1	317	11	97	9	25
No. of defendants tried..........	177	1,682	25	993	75	215	14	116
No. of defendants convicted......	142	1,416	25	850	67	195	11	108
No. of defendants acquitted......	35	266	0	143	8	20	3	8
No. of defendants on trial or await-ing sentence....	0	0	0	2§	0	0	0	2
No. of death sen-tences adjudged	24	428	7	124	10	92	5	28
No. of confirmed death sentences executed.......	7	259	7	43	6	52	5	11

* Does not include trial of Göring, et al., which was concluded on October 1, 1946.
† Includes cases tried in Austria.
‡ IMTFE = International Military Tribunal for the Far East.
§ During October these two remaining cases were tried, the defendants found guilty, and sentenced to a term of years.
Sentences other than capital punishment were imprisonment for various periods of years. One death sentence commuted.

[1] Report on the Tripartite Conference at Berlin, released to the press by the White House, August 2, 1945. Department of State *Bulletin*, XIII, No. 319 (August 5, 1945), 153-61. See also *Docs. Am. For. Relations*, VII, 924-38. This, and the comments in Secretary Byrnes's *Speaking Frankly* and Edward R. Stettinius, Jr.'s *Roosevelt and the Russians* are all we know at the present writing (1949) of the proceedings of the Conference.

[2] *Speaking Frankly*, 67-87.

Potsdam Declaration (July 26, 1945) of acceptable terms for Japanese surrender, thus altering, for the now impotent Pacific colossus, the formula of unconditional surrender:

Elimination for all time of Japanese militarism and the authority and influence of those who had deceived the Japanese people into embarking on world conquest.

Allied military occupation of Japan.

The terms of the Cairo declaration shall be carried out and Japanese sovereignty shall be limited to the islands of Honshu, Hokkaido, Kyushu, Shikoku, and such minor islands as might be determined by the victors.

Japanese military forces after being completely disarmed to be permitted to return to their homes with the opportunity to lead peaceful and productive lives.

No intention to enslave or destroy the Japanese as a nation, but stern justice to be meted out to war criminals.[1]

The Japanese Government to remove all obstacles to the revival and strengthening of democratic tendencies among the Japanese people. Freedom of speech, of religion, and of thought, as well as respect for the fundamental human rights, to be established.

Japan to be restricted to an economy of peace.

"The occupying forces of the allies shall be withdrawn from Japan as soon as these objectives have been accomplished and there has been established in accordance with the freely established will of the Japanese people a peacefully inclined and responsible government."

Russia, not having yet entered the war, was not a party to the Declaration. At Potsdam, Generalissimo Stalin had told President Truman about peace feelers he had received from Japan, and Truman had revealed to Stalin the perfection of the atomic bomb (first secretly demonstrated at Alamogordo, New Mexico, July 16, 1945). The Russian leader pretended not to be impressed.[2] We now know that his informers were even then busy spying out the secrets of Los Alamos.

The USSR had given on April 6, 1945, the required one year notice for the termination of the Russo-Japanese non-aggression pact of 1941,[3]

---

[1] The major war criminals were tried before a military international tribunal, sitting two and a half years from May 3, 1946, to November 12, 1948. The following were found guilty, sentenced to death and executed by hanging on December 23, 1948: Hideki Tojo, Prime Minister at the time of the Pearl Harbor attack, and the following other high officials: Koki Hirota, General Kenji Dohihara, General Iwane Matsui, General Akira Muto, Seishiro Itagaki, General Heitaro Kimura. Sixteen others received life imprisonment, one twenty years, and one seven years.

For summary of trials and judgments by United States military courts of all Japanese war criminals, see above, pp. 908-909, note 1.

[2] Byrnes, *Speaking Frankly*, p. 263.

[3] See above, p. 865.

explaining that circumstances had changed because of Japan having gone to war against the United States and Great Britain, allies of the Soviet Union. But the pact had still nearly a year to run. To make the Allies complicitous to the abrupt break-off of the treaty Stalin suggested that the USSR be requested by the Allies in the name of the United Nations to join them in the war against Japan in order to maintain world peace and security. President Truman made the request as suggested.[1]

While Japan was delaying and pondering surrender, the two atomic bombs were dropped successively over Hiroshima (August 6, 1945) and Nagasaki (August 8, 1945). Russia hastened to declare war on Japan (August 9, 1945). This happened to be three months to a day after the surrender of Germany, according to Stalin's promise at Yalta.[2]

Within a week the Red armies engulfed Manchuria. They were already there when Russia concluded (August 14, 1945) the Sino-Soviet treaty of alliance, draped with the Soviet servitudes coming from Yalta.[3] Russia in the nick of time barely managed to get in on the war and its booty. Another week and it might have been too late, at least with any Allied agreement.

Faced with utter destruction, Japan already had opened up negotiations with the Allies via neutral Switzerland. She accepted the Potsdam Declaration (August 14, 1945), but without prejudice to the prerogative of the Emperor as sovereign ruler. In answer the Allies (the USA, Great Britain, the USSR, and China) by implication allowed the Emperor to stay on his throne, but required him to authorize and ensure surrender terms necessary to carry out the provisions of the Potsdam Declaration.[4]

Such were the commanding terms of the definitive instrument of Japanese surrender, signed on the USS *Missouri* in Tokyo Bay at 0908 o'clock on September 2, 1945, almost a century after the Japanese soldier had shoved Commodore Biddle on the occasion of the first, friendly visit of the American Navy to Japan in 1846.[5]

Soviet Russia's acceptance of the surrender terms along with the other Allies made the USSR a party to the Potsdam Declaration, and thereby to the Cairo Declaration.

The Second World War had ended, so far as actual fighting was concerned. Military movements connected with the occupation of Italy,

---

[1] Byrnes, *Speaking Frankly,* pp. 208-209.

[2] See above, p. 895.

[3] See above, p. 896.

[4] For Potsdam Declaration, and documents relating to the Japanese surrender, see *Docs. Am. Foreign Relations*, VIII, 105-111.

[5] See above, p. 354.

Germany, Austria, and Japan, including Korea, prolonged a technical state of hostilities until December 31, 1946.[1] The vacuum of power left in Korea by Japan's surrender attracted the occupation of American and Russian armies if only to keep order in that liberated country. Pending the re-establishment of Korea as an independent state with a democratic government, the United States and Russia partitioned the country into two zones of Japanese surrender, divided by the line of 38° N.L., under general authority of a Soviet-American Joint Commission.[2] Soviet troops withdrew from North Korea in October, 1948, after setting up a communist Korean Government there with the aim of extending it by revolutionary force into all Korea. United States troops evacuated South Korea in June, 1949, after the Assembly of the United Nations had sponsored a Korean republic under fair and free elections. Korea remained a potential battlefield of the "cold war" that followed the Second World War.

Russia proceeded to take over the Kurile Islands and Southern Sakhalin, promised to her at Yalta. The United States occupied all the other Japanese islands in the Pacific. The Security Council of the United Nations by an unanimous vote (April 2, 1947) approved a trusteeship for the former German islands north of the Equator, later under mandate to Japan by the League of Nations, now placed under the full strategic authority and control of the United States.[3] The other Japanese islands (like Okinawa, Iwo Jima, etc.) occupied by the United States still await (1950) disposition by the eventual Treaty of Peace.

Hostilities had ceased with the surrender and occupation of the enemy countries, but peace could not come to the world until the final treaties of peace were signed and ratified. Even then it would not be possible without the sincere desire and common collaboration of the remaining superpowers, particularly of the USA and the USSR. The Council of Foreign Ministers in one meeting after another wrangled over the provisions of the minor peace treaties until December, 1946, with the Soviet representative trying to secure heavy reparations from Italy (to be pumped out of that prostrate state as expected American relief money poured in), to get the port of Trieste for Yugoslavia, to obtain for Russia

[1] President Truman formally proclaimed "the cessation of hostilities of World War II" as of twelve o'clock noon, December 31, 1946. *Docs. Am. Foreign Relations*, II, 112.

[2] *Docs. Am. Foreign Relations*, VIII, 834-42.

[3] Department of State *Bulletin*, XVI, No. 409 (May 4, 1947), 783-92.

Russia voted in favor of this trusteeship, possibly as a result of an understanding reached at Yalta in exchange for the Kuriles; but, if so, the text of such an agreement has never been revealed.

a trusteeship over Italian colonies in North Africa, and to keep the Western Allies from any free navigation of the Danube River. The five peace treaties finally concluded with Bulgaria, Finland, Hungary, Italy, and Roumania, made relatively small territorial changes in the map of Europe, already vastly altered *de facto* by Russian absorption of the Baltic states, the coast of East Prussia, eastern Poland, northern Bucovina, and Bessarabia.[1] The former satellites of Germany were laid under heavy indemnities to Russia,[2] Yugoslavia, and Greece, with token indemnities to Albania and Ethiopia. Trieste became a provisional Free Territory under the guaranty of the United Nations, occupied by American, British and Yugoslav troops until a neutral (i.e., not Yugoslav or Italian or Trentino) governor, to be appointed by the Security Council, should decide upon their withdrawal.[3] The Italian treaty left the disposition of Italian colonies in Africa to the Council of Foreign Ministers the more to dispute about, with the provision that if it was not settled by September 1, 1948, it should be determined by the General Assembly of the United Nations. (On November 22, 1949, the Assembly voted to establish Libya as an independent state not later than January 1, 1952;

[1] For map and tabulation of territorial changes in eastern Europe, and Finland, see *The United States in World Affairs, 1945-1947* (Council on Foreign Relations, 1947), 445-53.

[2] The five minor peace treaties levied the following indemnities by way of reparations:

Against Finland:
  $300,000,000 to USSR

Against Hungary:
  $200,000,000 to USSR (lowered to $100,000,000 in 1948)
  70,000,000 to Czechoslovakia
  30,000,000 to Yugoslavia

Against Roumania:
  $300,000,000 to USSR (lowered to $150,000,000 in 1948)

Against Bulgaria:
  $25,000,000 to Yugoslavia (canceled in 1947)
  45,000,000 to Greece (Bulgaria refused to pay because she would not recognize the Greek Government!)

Against Italy:
  $125,000,000 to Yugoslavia
  125,000,000 to Greece
  100,000,000 to USSR
  25,000,000 to Ethiopia
  5,000,000 to Albania

  $380,000,000 (total)

The above noted reductions by Russia are largely nominal because the countries had already been stripped in kind under the sense of "war booty." They however had a certain propaganda value. The other cancellations are parts of the political treaties between the new communist states of the Balkans.

[3] The Security Council, not being able to agree on the setting up of the Free Territory, a *status quo* of military occupation has continued in Trieste (1949).

to give independence to Somaliland after ten years under Italian trusteeship; and deferred the disposition of Eritrea pending further study.) It was agreed to call a conference of the Big Four plus the riparian states to regulate freedom of navigation on the Danube River. (It assembled at Belgrade in the summer of 1948, where seven of the eleven states signed a convention excluding nonriparian states from the International Danubian Commission, which was equivalent to excluding them from navigation.) [1]

The minor treaties disarmed the Balkan states and Italy and thus left Yugoslavia a heavily preponderant military power in southeastern Europe. They were far from satisfactory to the United States, but the Senate ratified them and the President proclaimed them,[2] obstinately hoping thereby to introduce some element of stability into European affairs and to make way for peace treaties with Austria and Germany.

What appealed most to the people and Government of the United States was the article common to all the minor treaties by which the former enemy state solemnly guaranteed to "take all measures necessary to secure to all persons under [its] jurisdiction, without distinction as to race, language, or religion, the enjoyment of human rights and of the fundamental freedoms, including freedom of expression, of press and of publication, of religious worship, of political opinion and of public meeting."

Trustful Americans hoped that the minor peace treaties would be the forerunner of a general peace, first in Europe and then in the Far East, protected and administered by a World Family of Democratic Nations. This hope crumbled slowly in the following months and years. Soviet Russia carried forward her revolutionary program, first in contiguous states, next in remoter regions, finally through fifth columns of com-

---

[1] This shut-out of the nonriparian states was a victory for Vishinsky, leader of the Russian delegation. Since the USSR controlled state navigation corporations of the Danubian states, the practical result of such a convention was Russian control of the Danube. It was a humiliating blow to an age-long fundamental of American foreign policy, the freedom of navigation of international waterways, as guaranteed on the Danube River by pre-war treaty rights. The United States, the United Kingdom, France, and the provisional government of Austria registered a formal protest at the majority decision of the conference and refused to accept it. See United States Department of State, *Documents and State Papers*, Vol. I (Nos. 8 and 9, Nov. and Dec., 1948), 487-514; II (No. 4, July, 1948), 250-275, for treaties and conventions relating to navigation on the Danube River.

[2] The United States was the only one of Russia's allies which did not declare war on Finland after that nation became involved in war as a concomitant of Hitler's invasion of the USSR in 1941. Therefore the United States was not a party to the Finnish peace treaty of 1946.

munists all over the world. Russian power flowed irresistibly into the vacuums left by the collapse of German and Japanese authority in Europe and Asia. The USSR clenched its hold on the territorial occupations in Eastern Europe. Then it intervened with the force of revolution, syphoned out of Soviet military might, to overturn the principles of real democracy and free and unfettered elections agreed to at Teheran and Yalta. One by one it installed communist governments in the satellite states to the west and southwest and imposed upon them a structure of alliances and political and economic control in the form of "co-operation" and "collaboration" for cultural and economic purposes: with Czechoslovakia, Roumania, Yugoslavia, Hungary, Albania, Poland, Bulgaria.[1] In Eastern Europe the *Comintern* (Communist International, politely suspended during the Strange Alliance) reappeared in the shape of the *Cominform* to implement these Soviet alliances. It invoked the solidarity of the several states in their forthcoming struggle against "Anglo-American imperialism."[2] In Northern Europe, Finland, and behind Finland the Scandinavian countries, Sweden, Norway and Denmark trembled before the aggressive advances of the revolutionary colossus.

To the Far East, Soviet expansion thrust rapidly into the great continent of Asia. A mutual-assistance treaty (February 27, 1946)[3] brought the "Mongolian People's Republic" into the Russian power system; communistic revolutionary governments were installed in Manchuria, Inner Mongolia, Northern Korea, and for all practical purposes in

[1] It was not the formal content of these treaties that caused concern so much as it was increasing Russian control over the satellite states, despite the word-service of the treaties to the principle of nonintervention and to the peace organization of the United Nations. The general pattern of the articles as published provides for friendship, co-operation and mutual aid in cultural and economic matters, and mutual military assistance in case of aggression from Germany or other powers allying themselves directly or in any other way whatever. Each party agrees not to join any alliance or coalition erected against the other, and not to intervene in the internal affairs of the other party, and both invoke the international peace system of the United Nations charter. Texts of the treaties in "The Soviet Alliance System, 1942-1945," and "New Links in the Soviet System of Alliances, 1948-49," may be found in United States Department of State, *Documents and State Papers,* No. 4, July, 1945, 219-250, and Nos. 12 and 13, March and April, 1949, 681-685. I am indebted to Dr. Andrew Gyorgy of Yale University for the opportunity to read in manuscript the relevant pages of his *Governments of Danubian Europe* (New York, 1949) in which he describes the network of bilaterial treaties between the non-Russian states of Eastern Europe and the Balkans. The USSR and the remaining satellites denounced and abrogated unilaterally the Yugoslav treaty, September-October, 1949.

[2] Resolution of the *Cominform* on World Affairs, October 5, 1947, originally published in *For a Lasting Peace, For a People's Democracy,* Vol. I, No. 1. (Belgrade, November 10, 1947).

[3] This supplemented an earlier treaty of March 12, 1936, which became the prototype of similar pacts between the USSR and the Baltic States before the latter were occupied and annexed.

Sinkiang. The tiny territory of Tannu Tuva, on the border between Outer Mongolia and Russia—tiny by Asiatic standards, but with a thinly populated area as large as Great Britain—went through the whole cycle of Red imperialism: from Chinese province to autonomy, from autonomy to Soviet protectorate, from a "people's republic" to an actual province of the Soviet Union.[1] Beyond these former buffers of inner Asia lay the vast prize of China itself and the restive peoples to the south—India, Malaya, and the East Indies.

Thus the Iron Curtain closed down between the West and one Soviet satellite after another in Europe and Asia. Next might come Greece, where a communist revolt had been smoldering since the end of the war; then Turkey, and Iran; and still further to the south lay Africa, as tempting for the future as were China and the Indies to the east. Africa could be what it threatened to be if controlled by Nazi Germany, a springboard for a jump of power to South America. The Revolution, to use the words of its guides and fellow travelers, was "on the march" from the Heartland towards the Rimlands of the World Island. Beyond the Rimlands of the Old World, communist fifth columns, with leaders of revolution schooled in Moscow, mapped out the political terrain in every country everywhere. The United States, with its wide liberties and meager policing, afforded unparalleled facilities.

Meanwhile the Western Allies were demobilizing and putting their faith in the United Nations Organization, with its permanent headquarters established in New York as if to flatter the United States and hold it to the purpose of collective security. The United Nations proved to be but an international debating society like the first League of Nations, only more vituperative. Competent observers had generally agreed that it would need force to make it work, and the Charter had provided for national constituencies of armed forces, with a staff committee to put into effect the decisions of the Security Council. But the big powers had not shown the slightest indication of being able to agree on such a force, and even if they had done so each one held an absolute veto on its use. More and more the Security Council became merely a sounding-board for Russia's aggressive diplomacy and the Western democracies' coalescing resistance. The issues of a troubled world produced a series of spectacular deadlocks in the Council while the various peace organs of the Organization proceeded to form their special councils and commissions: the professional Secretariat; the

[1] David J. Dallin has portrayed the expansion of *Soviet Russia in the Far East* (Yale University Press, 1948).

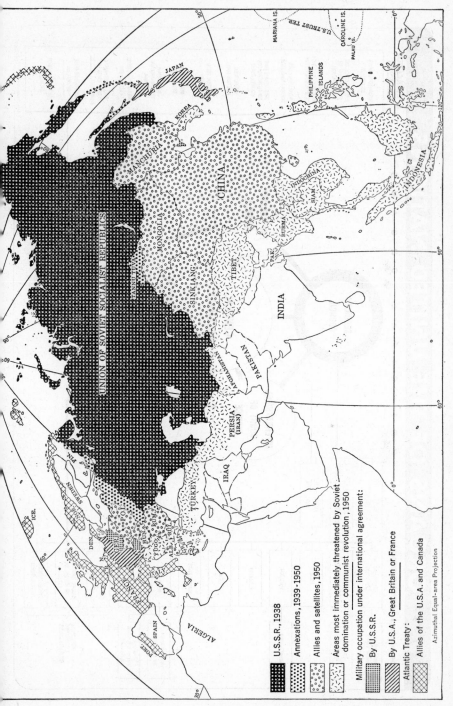

Map 41. Expansion of Soviet Power in Eurasia, 1939-1950.

U.S.S.R., 1938

Annexations, 1939-1950

Allies and satellites, 1950

Areas most immediately threatened by Soviet
domination or communist revolution, 1950

Military occupation under international agreement:

By U.S.S.R.

By U.S.A., Great Britain or France

Atlantic Treaty:

Allies of the U.S.A. and Canada

Azimuthal Equal-area Projection

917

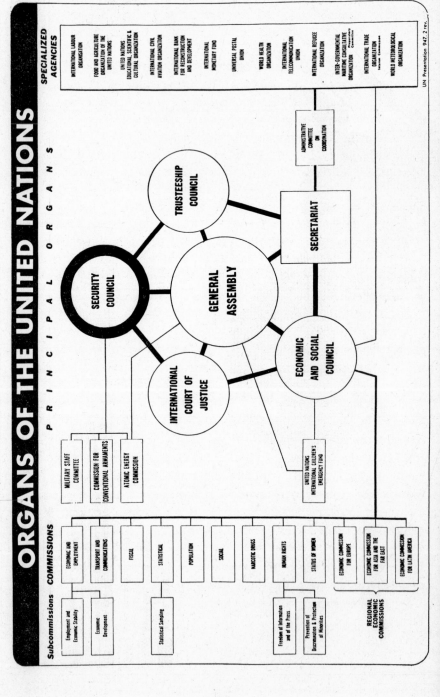

ORGANS OF THE UNITED NATIONS

Trusteeship Council; the Economic and Social Council, with its twelve permanent commissions; and the thirteen specialized agencies appending to the Secretariat, including the Educational, Scientific and Cultural Organization (UNESCO).

Most spectacular of all the deadlocks was that relating to the control of atomic weapons and energy. The USA presented to the Security Council a proposal for the outlawry of the atomic bomb and placing the manufacture of atomic energy under international control *and inspection*. The USSR proposed to outlaw and destroy the bombs first and create an international control next but not to submit to any international inspection.[1] It proposed an all-round reduction of armaments by one-third, well knowing that such a program would leave unchanged the relative strength of the rival powers. The aggressive antagonism of the USSR within the United Nations made it terrifyingly clear to the Western world that despite the five little peace treaties no real peace existed, that a far greater totalitarian power [2] had taken the place of Germany, Italy, and Japan to menace national independence and democratic liberty and the rights of man.

The agreements of Teheran, Yalta, and Berlin had invoked democratic principles as the basis of the coming peace. To the Soviet authorities democracy meant communism enforced only in the name of the people, without their free consent, by a dictatorship, with ruthless suppression of the freedom of speaking, meeting, publishing and voting. To the Western countries democracy meant the rights of man won from divine-right monarchy through centuries of constitutional struggle. It rested on universal suffrage freely expressed by secret ballot. It meant freedom of the common man, worker or drone, to speak, meet, print, and vote on perfect equality with the uncommon man, everybody equal before the law, as interpreted by independent courts of justice, enforced by a government of the people's own free choice. Such a government could regulate the people's economy as the voters desired, whether by capitalism and free enterprise or by socialistic or communistic collectivism—the fundamental principle of this democracy was a government truly of the people by the people and for the people.

Soviet intervention in the satellite states, the new Soviet alliances in Eastern Europe, and the increasing preponderance of Russian armed force, and gradual realization by the Western nations of the Soviet

---

[1] *The International Control of Atomic Energy; Growth of a Policy* (Department of State Publication No. 2702, Washington, G.P.O., 1947 [?]).

[2] Edmund J. Walsh, *Total Power* (New York, 1948).

program for world revolution,[1] frightened the democracies fringing on the Atlantic. Their heritage of freedom, so recently and so valiantly preserved, with Russia's aid, against the fascist conquest, seemed doomed to another even more formidable trial from their Ally of yesteryear.

The new fear focused first and foremost on the German Question. It became all too obvious that the Soviet Union intended to make Germany and its decisive war potential another satellite of Soviet power, a dominating thrust of the Revolution into Western Europe—to set up a communist Reich as an unchallengeable menace to western democracy. Secretary of State James F. Byrnes tried to neutralize that danger by proposing a four-power treaty (United States, France, Great Britain, Russia) designed to hold Germany to military impotence for twenty-five, even forty years, and thus make possible Allied evacuation and a German peace treaty safe to all.[2] But Russia would have none of it.

The next reaction, this time from the war-weary and semi-socialist democracies of Western Europe, was the Anglo-French alliance, the Treaty of Dunkirk (March 4, 1947), a regional security pact within the framework of the United Nations Charter, Article 51. Waiting for the other powers to make such a treaty as proposed by Secretary Byrnes, they joined in a military alliance of mutual defense in the event of any threat to the security of either "arising from the adoption by Germany of a policy of aggression, *or from action by Germany designed to facilitate such a policy.*"[3] The words italicized could, of course, envisage the action of a communist Germany set up by Russia, just as the Soviet alliances with the border satellite states looked toward action by states allied directly with Germany "or in any other way."

Germany and Austria were all that stood between the Western democracies and the colossus of the Soviet Revolution. Germany and the democracies of Western Europe were all that stood between the USA and the USSR to the east of the New World, even as Japan and China were all that stood across the Pacific between the two super-powers.

Closely following the Treaty of Dunkirk, President Truman declared to a joint session of Congress (March 12, 1947) that it was the policy of the United States "to support free peoples who are resisting attempted subjugation by armed minorities or by outside countries."

[1] Synthesized from Stalin's writings and speeches in a remarkable anonymous essay "Stalin on Revolution," by "Historicus," in *Foreign Affairs*, XXVII (January, 1949), 175-214, which was widely reprinted in digested form in the United States.

[2] For draft of treaty proposed, April 29, 1946, to the Council of Foreign Ministers, by Secretary Byrnes, and subsequent Stuttgart Speech, September 6, 1946, see *Docs. Am. Foreign Relations*, VIII, 205-221.

[3] Text in New York *Times*, March 5, 1947.

Specifically he asked for appropriations of $400,000,000 (enacted July 30, 1947) to provide economic assistance to Greece, struggling against a communist revolt sustained from the north, and to fortify Turkey to hold the line of the Near East against the threatened advance of Soviet power. The action of the United States Government ("Truman Doctrine") in furnishing loans, military and naval equipment, not to mention military and naval staff personnel, to the Government of Greece, and also to the Government of China, when they were engaged in domestic strife against communistic revolts, was without doubt an intervention in these civil wars, like similar action already taken, less openly, by the USSR and satellites to foment and sustain the revolts.[1] The pattern of American resistance to the Soviet menace was beginning to resemble that of President Roosevelt's build-up of defense against Nazi Germany in 1939-41, with public opinion, lulled by the earnest vision of collective security, following reluctantly but determined. It was what the journalists called a "cold war."[2]

The next step of the United States to stiffen overseas democracies against the Soviet menace was the European Recovery Program. Originally proposed by Secretary of State George C. Marshall (June 5, 1947), it offered a $20,000,000,000 five-year program to the co-operation of all the nations of Europe (except Falangist Spain) to transfuse their war-famished continent with American (i.e., United States Government) capital, livestock, new machinery and raw material, calculated to raise the national economies to 25 per cent above the pre-war level and make them impervious to communistic revolution. It was a gigantic continuation and expansion of lend-lease in time of peace, including even tobacco and cigarettes, supported by the American taxpayer. The Soviet Government refused to participate or allow its satellites to do so, but the program went into effect with sixteen other nations (Act of June 28, 1948). The huge purchases from outside the United States necessary to carry out this unprecedented departure spilled out largesses into Canada and Latin America and splashed all over the world outside and even inside the Soviet area. Congress added to the European Recovery appropriation $400,000,000 for aid to China—too late to prevent the collapse of Chiang

[1] Technically there was no violation of neutrality. The belligerency of the communist insurrection had not been recognized. The provisions of the joint resolutions of Congress of January 8, 1937, and May 1, 1937, enabling the President to proclaim an embargo on arms, ammunition, and implements of war to a state wherein civil strife existed, when necessary to promote the security or protect the lives or commerce of citizens of the United States, were repealed by Section 19 of the Neutrality Act of 1939.

[2] Walter Lippmann, *The Cold War* (New York, 1947).

Kai-shek's Nationalist Government before the onslaughts of the communist revolution encouraged and guided from Russia.

The rather belated Soviet reply (January 25, 1949) to the European
Recovery Program was the formation among the western satellites (ex-
clusive of seceded Yugoslavia) of an opposing Council for Economic
Mutual Assistance, open like the ERP to the other countries of Europe.

The European Recovery Program,[1] or the "Marshall Plan," as this
American succor was popularly called, stiffened Italy and France successfully to resist revolutions at least for the time being. It encouraged
Great Britain, France, the Netherlands, Belgium and Luxemburg—all
alarmed at the communist *coup d'état* in Czechoslovakia (February 20-25,
1948)—to expand the Dunkirk idea into the Western Union, a military
regional defensive alliance based on Article 51 of the United Nations
Charter against an "armed attack" on any one of them "in Europe." [2]

Soviet Russia's reply to the Pact of Brussels (March 17, 1948) setting
up the new regional alliance was to walk out (June 16, 1948) of the
joint Allied Control Council or *Kommandatura* of Berlin and, in violation
of previous occupation agreements,[3] to blockade (June 23, 1948) passage
of Allied personnel and matériel through the general Soviet zone of occupation into the American, British and French zones of the enclaved city.
It was a measure designed to maneuver the Western Allies out of the
German capital and make of it a metropolitan magnet in the communist
field of all Germany, under Soviet control and manipulation. Faced by
this blow, the American and British forces resorted to a costly air lift of
foodstuff and fuel from their Western zones into their respective areas
of Berlin, barely enough to keep the people there from starving or freezing during the blockade. Efforts to adjust the ugly impasse by a Conference of Foreign Ambassadors at Moscow collapsed in the summer
of 1948.[4] Further attempts to conciliate the controversy in the United
Nations Security Council also failed. But a vital minimum of truce
was reached by the Council of Foreign Ministers when the Soviet Government lifted the blockade of Berlin, May 12, 1949, restored the joint
Kommandatura and revived hopes for an Austrian treaty. After this the
United States and Great Britain eased off the air lift.

[1] *The European Recovery Program.* Sen. Doc. 111, 80th Cong., 1st Sess. (Washington,
G.P.O., 1947).

[2] Text in New York *Times,* March 18, 1948.

[3] For a list of Soviet violations of treaty and other agreements, see Department of
State *Bulletin,* XVIII, No. 466 (June 6, 1948), 738-744.

[4] *The Berlin Crisis. A Report on the Moscow Discussions, 1948.* (Department of
State Publication 3298, September, 1948). See also Walter Bedell Smith, *My Three
Years in Moscow* (Philadelphia, 1950).

Meanwhile Soviet forces had set up a German communist administration and militia in their Eastern Zone of occupation, while the United States, Great Britain, and France recruited democratic German officials to administer their respective zones. Then the Allies set up in all the Western Zones of occupation a single German Federal Republic (September, 1949) on a democratic basis, hoping that a government of the German people by the German people and for the German people, with individual freedom and human rights anchored in a republican constitution, would some day prevail all over the prostrate Reich, out of the hands of Russia. In turn the USSR set up a communist state (October, 1949)—a "German Democratic Republic"—in their Eastern Zone, on the model of similar communist governments installed after revolution in Poland, Czechoslovakia, Hungary, Roumania, Bulgaria, Albania and Yugoslavia, hoping that it would some day extend over all of Germany, out of control of the Allies. Germany and its future war potential remained the biggest battlefield of the "cold war."

Unexpectedly fortunate for the American policy of containment all round the circle [1] of Soviet aggression, revolutionary expansion, and Red imperialism, was the defection (June 28, 1948) of Marshal Tito, Moscow-schooled communistic dictator of Yugoslavia, from the *Cominform*, and his denunciation of the Soviet-Yugoslav Alliance of June 8, 1946. It was the initial crack in the Soviet system of alliances against the Western democracies. It held out encouragement to suppressed nationalist majorities in the other satellite states. It withdrew twenty ready military divisions from the Soviet bloc of power. It eased the Trieste Question and the Italian Question, if not the Greek Question (still sustained from Bulgaria and Albania). It gave pause to any plans that the USSR might have had for a hot war in the summer of 1948. It gave time for the further coagulation of Western resistance. But the communist military triumph in 1949 in the Chinese Civil War that had continued after the fall of Japan overbalanced the relief brought by Yugoslavia's secession from Moscow. And Soviet achievement of their first atomic explosion (announced by President Truman, September 23, 1949) weakened the American policy of containment in Europe as well as in Asia.

The communist victory in China, and affiliation in their new revolutionary constitution [2] (October, 1949) with the foreign policy of the USSR, unhinged American policy in the Far East. The United States had risked

[1] The articulator of this policy was "X" in his essay "Sources of Soviet Conduct," *Foreign Affairs*, XXV (No. 4, July, 1947), 566-582. "X" is widely believed to be George Kennan of the Department of State; and the assertion has never been denied.

[2] The USSR recognized the new communist government of China, October 1, 1949.

and won a double war in 1941-1945 in order to prevent China and the British Commonwealth of Nations from conquest in the East by Japan while America for its own security was trying to hold Britain up in the West as a buffer against Germany. After the Second World War the British Empire was disintegrating in the East and the component Commonwealths were threatened by a bloc of Russian power, actual and potential, following the communist conquest of China, larger than ever Japan had been able to mass on the continent of Asia. These revolutionary developments negated the American victory over Japan, one-half the victory of the double war. Reappraising its China policy,[1] the Department of State decided not to interfere further in the Chinese Civil War, hoping that China under Mao Tse-tung, sworn enemy of the United States, would "go Tito" like Yugoslavia, once the Chinese people realized how Soviet imperialism was depriving China of her fairest provinces in the north and west. Accordingly the American delegate to the United Nations, Dr. Philip C. Jessup, sought to pledge the powerless Assembly to the traditional American principles of self-determination for China and the political, territorial and administrative integrity of that nation.[2]

It was under circumstances of the increasingly bitter "cold war," and at the outset of the presidential campaign of 1948 in the United States, that the Senate passed (June 11, 1948) the bipartisan Vandenberg Resolution, outstanding signal of the reorientation of American foreign policy to a system of defensive alliances within the United Nations. It pledged the United States to associate itself by constitutional process, that is *by treaty requiring the advice and consent of the Senate,* with "regional and other collective arrangements"—the Senate still eschewed the traditionally forbidding word "alliance"—for individual or collective self-defense in case of an "armed attack" threatening the national security. This took the "cold war" out of the Truman-Dewey presidential campaign of 1948, except for the exhortations of Henry Wallace, candidate of the Progressive Party, who, reflecting the Soviet line of propaganda, vigorously but ineffectually attacked in Europe as well as

---

[1] *United States Relations with China, with Special Reference to the Period 1944-1949,* based on the files of the Department of State (Department of State Publication 3573, Far Eastern Series 30, released August 1949) presents official documents apparently intended to demonstrate that "nothing this country did or could have done within the limits of its capabilities could have changed that result [the communist triumph in China]; nothing that was left undone by this country has contributed to it."

[2] Statement of Dr. Philip C. Jessup, United States Ambassador at Large, to the Political and Security Committee of the United Nations General Assembly at Lake Success, N. Y., November 28, 1949.

in the United States the current foreign policy of his own country. Backed by the Vandenberg Resolution, Secretary of State George C. Marshall began the negotiation of a treaty to expand the Western Union into defensive military alliance along the lines of the Rio Pact of 1947, based on Article 51 of the United Nations Charter.[1] The collapse of General Marshall's health left the completion of the task to his successor, Secretary of State Dean Acheson. President Truman greeted the plenipotentiaries when they assembled at Washington (April 4, 1949) to sign the North Atlantic Treaty, following two World Wars of aggression. "Our peoples, to whom our Governments are responsible," he told the diplomatists, "are determined that *these things shall not happen again.*"[2]

The President sent the Treaty to the Senate on April 12, 1949. It provided (Article 1) that the signatories, Belgium, Canada, Denmark, France, Iceland, Italy, Luxemburg, Netherlands, Norway, Portugal, the United Kingdom, the United States, would consult together whenever the territorial integrity, political independence or security of any one of them were threatened; this was hardly more than they would do anyway. Key to the new ten-year alliance, completing a revolution in American foreign policy, was Article 5:

> The Parties agree that an armed attack against one or more of them in Europe or North America shall be considered an attack against them all; and consequently they agree that, if such an attack occurs, each of them, in exercise of the right of individual or collective self-defense recognized by Article 51 of the Charter of the United Nations, will assist the Party or Parties so attacked by taking forthwith, individually and in concert with the other Parties, *such action as it deems necessary,*[2] including the use of armed force, to restore and maintain the security of the North Atlantic area.
>
> Any such armed attack and all measures taken as a result thereof shall immediately be reported to the Security Council. Such measures shall be terminated when the Security Council has taken the measures necessary to restore and maintain international peace and security.

Article 6 specifically defined the territorial purview of the alliance:

> For the purpose of Article 5 an armed attack on one or more of the Parties is deemed to include an armed attack on the territory of any of the Parties in Europe or North America, on the Algerian departments of France, on the occupation forces of any Party in Europe, on the islands under the jurisdiction of any Party in the North Atlantic area north of the Tropic of Cancer or on the vessels or aircraft in this area of any of the Parties.

[1] The Department of State prepared a background statement on *Collective Security in the North Atlantic Area.* (Foreign Affairs Outlines, *Building the Peace,* Spring, 1949). Department of State Publication 3377.

[2] Italics inserted.

The North Atlantic Treaty, ratified by the Senate without reservation, July 21, 1949 (by a vote of 82 yeas, 13 nays), left uncovered the Near East, the Far East, and the islands of the Pacific Ocean. The United States alone would have to cope—so far as any pledges of the Alliance were concerned—with an attack on its territory, such as the islands of the Pacific, or its occupation forces in those areas.

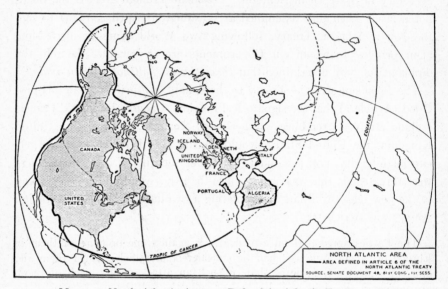

Map 42. North Atlantic Area, as Defined in Atlantic Treaty, 1949.[1]

Even in the North Atlantic area the pledges of the Allies were not absolute and automatic: each Party pledged itself only to *such action as it deemed necessary*. If and when the attack should come, how much action would each of the twelve allies "deem necessary"?

One of the reasons for the qualified nature of the pledge was the inability of the executive branch of the Government of the United States to bind Congress to vote to take any action, including the use of armed force, in advance of any situation. Despite the inroads of executive agreements by-passing the Senate, that body's advice and consent was still considered necessary for a treaty of alliance, and the Senate would not have advised and consented to a treaty that ignored the power of Congress to appropriate moneys and to declare war.

The qualifications introduced into the treaty in deference to the Con-

[1] Reproduced from *Major Problems of United States Foreign Policy, 1949-1950*, p. 270, with permission of Brookings Institution.

gress of the United States also served as "outs" for each of the other eleven Parties.

The North Atlantic Treaty was thus an uncertain alliance, which circumstance might further debilitate—*or further strengthen.* Congress implemented it (September, 1949) with an appropriation of $1,314,010,000 for military assistance to the Atlantic Allies; to Greece and Turkey; to Iran, "right flank" of the Atlantic defense line; to China (within the President's discretion); to Korea, the only remaining continental citadel of the rear guard in Asia; and to the island outposts of the Philippine Republic.

Such was the posture of American foreign affairs as the first half of our century drew to a disheartening close. The United States and its Allies had fought the Second World War to a brilliant military triumph. Five years later it looked like defeat in victory. The Republic of the West had spent 352,799 lives in the war. It had 668,653 wounded service [1] men and dependents to care for, and hundreds of thousands more invalided, not to mention pensions and allowances for millions of others, totaling, for veterans of all wars of the United States $6,495,232,236 in the year 1949 alone.[2] In the Second World War it had spent a third of a

---

[1] However tragic for individuals and families, the comparatively small loss of life and other military casualties to the United States in the two World Wars were by no means serious to the nation. Compare the equally sanguinary casualties from automobile accidents within the United States during the years of the Second World War, men, women and children killed, crippled, or maimed, a toll of death and injury which the public bears without revolt—and speeds on:

Year	Deaths	Nonfatal Injuries
1941	39,969	1,400,000
1942	28,309	1,000,000
1943	23,823	800,000
1944	24,282	850,000
1945	28,076	1,000,000
	144,459	5,055,000

Accident Facts (published by the National Safety Council, 20 North Wacker Drive, Chicago, 1948).

[2] An Associated Press despatch from Washington, February 15, 1949, doubtless a news release from the Veterans Administration, presented the following historical summary of pensions and other compensations to veterans of the armed forces of the United States in previous wars:

Veterans, their dependents or heirs from World War II back to the Mexican War received a total of $6,495,232,236 in various benefits during the fiscal year ending June 30, 1948.

This amount is roughly one billion less than the all-time high of the previous fiscal year.

Compensation or pension benefits for 2,918,325 veterans totaled $1,827,641,507. The

trillion dollars ($330,000,000,000) in military efforts and lend-lease. As in the case of all previous wars, pension costs in future years will multiply the first cost, and may bring the total perhaps to a trillion dollars. It had acquired a national debt of $258,286,383,109 (1947 peak) as compared with $48,961,443,536 in 1941. It had come to military conscription in time of peace. It was maintaining an armed force of 1,991,096 men in 1949 as contrasted with 683,591 in 1939, and a total military budget of $11,745,000,000 in 1949 as contrasted with $1,068,854,207 in 1939. It had become really a debtor in the disguise of a creditor nation in the balance of international payments. It had dipped deep into its depleted natural resources. In postwar relief and rehabilitation of friend and foe it had spent a larger amount of treasure than any indemnity ever squeezed out of a defeated people by a victorious conqueror—and the stream of hopeful tribute continued to flow out and out from the victor: $5,809,-990,000 for the European Recovery Program for the fiscal year July 1, 1949, to June 30, 1950, and $1,314,010,000 more for military assistance to the Atlantic Treaty Allies; and to Greece and Turkey and the others: total in grants and credits since V-J Day, $43,000,000,000.

To give still more generous gush to the outflow President Truman, apparently taking his cue from an earlier suggestion of Henry A. Wallace,[1] proposed as Point Four of his inaugural address of January 20, 1949, a "bold new program" for making the benefits of American scientific advances and industrial progress available for the growth of undeveloped areas of the world. Point Four awaits (1950) legislative enactment including, among other implementation, government guaranties for American private loans to foreign governments wishing to co-operate and otherwise unable to borrow money.[2]

---

rest went for subsistence, tuition, unemployment allowances and insurance payments.

The lingering cost of wars is shown by the following breakdown of compensation and pension payments:

Mexican War—$22,440 to the heirs of 36 veterans.

Indian Wars—$757,444 to 710 living veterans; $1,135,869 to heirs and dependents of 2,090 dead veterans.

Civil War—$94,491 to 49 living; $8,924,774 to 16,323 dead.

Spanish-American War—$126,906,930 to 106,698 living; $38,190,878 to 776,336 dead.

World War I—$317,396,870 to 449,609 living; $154,444,088 to 252,626 dead.

World War II—$974,139,086 to 1,714,535 living; $1,759,121,779 to 241,362 dead.

Regular Establishment—$23,378,857 to 43,438 living; $6,226,601 to 13,513 dead.

Congress may have raised pension costs further by the time the reader peruses this astonishing note!

[1] Address of Vice President Henry A. Wallace to the Free World Association, New York City, May 8, 1942. *International Conciliation*, No. 381 (June, 1942), 369-376.

[2] The Brookings Institution has analysed "The Problem of United States Assistance to Underdeveloped Areas," as one of the *Major Problems of American Foreign Policy, 1949-1950* (Washington, 1949), pp. 295-350.

Convinced that "it must not happen again," the American people and their Government had led the way into a new league of nations, putting their large-hearted faith in the trust that their Allies would co-operate for peace as they had worked for war. Disconsolately they faced the fact that the peace was all but lost, that the freedom-loving nations were outbalanced by the power of the USSR.

The revolutionary USSR would not clasp the proffered hand of friendship. It stood firmly based in the Heartland of Eurasia, one mighty foot by 1950 planted on the Asiatic Rimland of the World Island, the other poised to tread Atlantic shore.

> WHO RULES EAST EUROPE COMMANDS THE HEARTLAND:
> WHO RULES THE HEARTLAND COMMANDS THE WORLD-ISLAND:
> WHO RULES THE WORLD-ISLAND RULES THE WORLD.[1]

Within the United Nations Organization a new opposition of alliances and counteralliances had arisen. The best that men could hope for seemed a long armed peace. Only a political miracle could resolve truly and peaceably the issue between a World Family of Democratic Nations and a World Union of Soviet Socialist Republics. America had never faced so great a challenge to her heritage of freedom. America had arisen before triumphantly to meet great challenges at home and abroad—when there had been time to rise. Would there be time, once more?

[1] H. J. Mackinder, *Democratic Ideals and Reality: A Study in the Politics of Reconstruction* (New York, 1919, 1942).

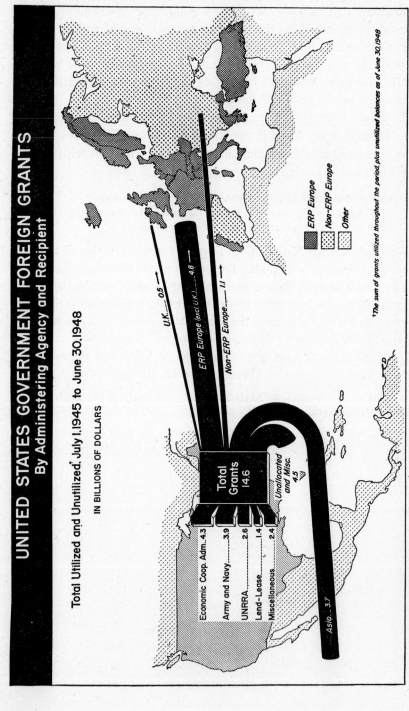

UNITED STATES GOVERNMENT FOREIGN GRANTS
By Administering Agency and Recipient

Total Utilized and Unutilized, July 1,1945 to June 30,1948

IN BILLIONS OF DOLLARS

Economic Coop. Adm.__4.3
Army and Navy_____3.9
UNRRA_____2.6
Lend-Lease_____1.4
Miscellaneous_____2.4

Total Grants 14.6

Unallocated and Misc. 4.5

U.K.____0.5
ERP Europe (excl. U.K.)____4.8
Non-ERP Europe_____1.1

Asia__3.7

ERP Europe
Non-ERP Europe
Other

*The sum of grants utilized throughout the period, plus unutilized balances as of June 30,1948

From *Report of Activities of the National Advisory Council on International and Financial Problems April 1, 1948-September 30, 1948.*

930

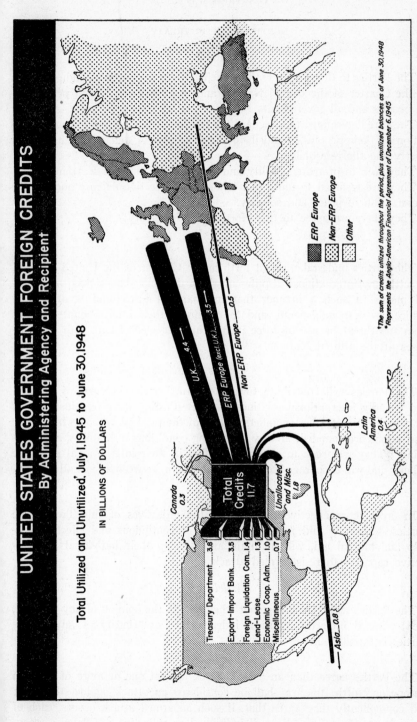

UNITED STATES GOVERNMENT FOREIGN CREDITS
By Administering Agency and Recipient

Total Utilized and Unutilized, July 1, 1945 to June 30, 1948

IN BILLIONS OF DOLLARS

Canada 0.3

U.K. —— 4.4

ERP Europe (excl. U.K.) —— 3.5

Non-ERP Europe —— 0.5

Latin America 0.4

Asia —— 0.8

Total Credits 11.7

Treasury Department 3.8
Export-Import Bank 3.5
Foreign Liquidation Com. 1.4
Lend-Lease 1.3
Economic Coop. Adm. 1.0
Miscellaneous 0.7

Unallocated and Misc. 1.8

ERP Europe
Non-ERP Europe
Other

*The sum of credits utilized throughout the period, plus unutilized balances as of June 30, 1948
†Represents the Anglo-American Financial Agreement of December 6, 1945

From *Report of Activities of the National Advisory Council on International and Financial Problems April 1, 1948–September 30, 1948.*

NORTH ATLANTIC TREATY

Preamble

The Parties to this Treaty reaffirm their faith in the purposes and principles of the Charter of the United Nations and their desire to live in peace with all peoples and all governments.

They are determined to safeguard the freedom, common heritage and civilization of their peoples, founded on the principles of democracy, individual liberty and the rule of law.

They seek to promote stability and well-being in the North Atlantic area.

They are resolved to unite their efforts for collective defense and for the preservation of peace and security.

They therefore agree to this North Atlantic Treaty:

Article 1

The Parties undertake, as set forth in the Charter of the United Nations, to settle any international disputes in which they may be involved by peaceful means in such a manner that international peace and security, and justice, are not endangered, and to refrain in their international relations from the threat or use of force in any manner inconsistent with the purposes of the United Nations.

Article 2

The Parties will contribute toward the further development of peaceful and friendly international relations by strengthening their free institutions, by bringing about a better understanding of the principles upon which these institutions are founded, and by promoting conditions of stability and well-being. They will seek to eliminate conflict in their international economic policies and will encourage economic collaboration between any or all of them.

Article 3

In order more effectively to achieve the objectives of this Treaty, the Parties, separately and jointly, by means of continuous and effective self-help and mutual aid, will maintain and develop their individual and collective capacity to resist armed attack.

Article 4

The Parties will consult together whenever, in the opinion of any of them, the territorial integrity, political independence or security of any of the Parties is threatened.

Article 5

The Parties agree than an armed attack against one or more of them in Europe or North America shall be considered an attack against them all; and consequently they agree that, if such an armed attack occurs, each of them, in exercise of the right of individual or collective self-defense recognized by Article 51 of the Charter of the United Nations, will assist the Party or Parties so attacked by taking forthwith, individually and in concert with the other Parties, such action as it deems necessary, including the use of armed force, to restore and maintain the security of the North Atlantic area.

Any such armed attack and all measures taken as a result thereof shall immediately be reported to the Security Council. Such measures shall be terminated when the Security Council has taken the measures necessary to restore and maintain international peace and security.

Article 6

For the purpose of Article 5 an armed attack on one or more of the Parties is deemed to include an armed attack on the territory of any of the Parties in Europe or North America, on the Algerian departments of France, on the occupation forces of any Party in Europe, on the islands under the jurisdiction of any Party in the North Atlantic area north of the Tropic of Cancer or on the vessels or aircraft in this area of any of the Parties.

Article 7

This Treaty does not affect, and shall not be interpreted as affecting, in any way the rights and obligations under the Charter of the Parties which are members of the United Nations, or the primary responsibility of the Security Council for the maintenance of international peace and security.

Article 8

Each Party declares that none of the international engagements now in force between it and any other of the Parties or any third state is in conflict with the provisions of this Treaty, and undertakes not to enter into any international engagement in conflict with this Treaty.

Article 9

The Parties hereby establish a council, on which each of them shall be represented, to consider matters concerning the implementation of this Treaty. The council shall be so organized as to be able to meet promptly at any time. The council shall set up such subsidiary bodies as may be necessary; in particular it shall establish immediately a defense committee which shall recommend measures for the implementation of Articles 3 and 5.

Article 10

The Parties may, by unanimous agreement, invite any other European state in a position to further the principles of this Treaty and to contribute to the security of the North Atlantic area to accede to this Treaty. Any state so invited may become a party to the Treaty by depositing its instrument of accession with the Government of the United States of America. The Government of the United States of America will inform each of the Parties of the deposit of each such instrument of accession.

Article 11

This Treaty shall be ratified and its provisions carried out by the Parties in accordance with their respective constitutional processes. The instruments of ratification shall be deposited as soon as possible with the Government of the United States of America, which will notify all the other signatories of each deposit. The Treaty shall enter into force between the states which have ratified it as soon as the ratifications of the majority of the signatories, including the ratifications of Belgium, Canada, France, Luxembourg, the Netherlands, the United Kingdom and the United States, have been deposited and shall come into effect with respect to other states on the date of the deposit of their ratifications.

Article 12

After the Treaty has been in force for ten years, or at any time thereafter, the Parties shall, if any of them so requests, consult together for the purpose of reviewing the Treaty, having regard for the factors then affecting peace and security in the North Atlantic area, including the development of universal as well as regional arrangements under the Charter of the United Nations for the maintenance of international peace and security.

Article 13

After the Treaty has been in force for twenty years, any Party may cease to be a party one year after its notice of denunciation has been given to the Government of the United States of America, which will inform the Governments of the other Parties of the deposit of each notice of denunciation.

Article 14

This Treaty, of which the English and French texts are equally authentic, shall be deposited in the archives of the Government of the United States of America. Duly certified copies thereof will be transmitted by that Government to the Governments of the other signatories.

In witness whereof, the undersigned plenipotentiaries have signed this Treaty.

Done at Washington, the fourth day of April, 1949.[1]

[1] For original twelve signatories see above, p. 925.

CHAPTER XLVII

EPILOGUE

(1776-1950)

FOLLOWING the achievement of sovereign independence by the successful American Revolution the fundamental principles of American foreign policy were classically defined and successfully worked out in the eighteenth and nineteenth centuries in the teeth of a hostile world. They were:

1. Freedom of the Seas, and freedom of international straits and rivers.

2. Freedom of commerce and navigation: that is, reciprocal equality of treatment without discrimination against the subjects or ships of any nation, whether in homeland or colonies, or spheres of protection or influence; later, this developed into the Open Door Doctrine.

3. Abstention from the *ordinary* vicissitudes and the *ordinary* combinations and collisions of European politics and wars. This maxim of Washington's Farewell Address was later included in the Monroe Doctrine of 1823.

4. The Non-Transfer principle of 1811: opposition to the transfer of adjacent, later of any European colonial dominions in the New World from one European sovereign to another. President Grant attached this principle to the Monroe Doctrine in 1869.

5. Continental expansion: the Manifest Destiny—a feeling of deep inner reality—of the United States to become a Continental Republic in dimension and significance.

6. Selfdetermination of peoples, exemplified by early recognition of the independence of the revolted peoples of Latin America, and championing of the independence of Latin America ever since.

7. No further European colonization in the New World—as pronounced in the Monroe Doctrine.

8. Nonintervention, also proclaimed in the Monroe Doctrine: to Europe, Hands Off the New World; to the United States itself (as illustrated in the instructions of Henry Clay to the intended plenipotentiaries to the Congress of Panama) nonintervention in the internal affairs of other free nations.

9. The right of expatriation and the wrong of impressment.

935

10. Suppression of the African slave trade (belatedly).

11. Pan Americanism, or "Good Neighborhood," to use the phrase of Henry Clay's instructions to the plenipotentiaries appointed in 1826 to attend the Congress of Panama.

12. International arbitration by voluntary agreement; this grew into the pledge to settle all controversies by peaceful means (1928) and the obligation towards many countries (1945) to submit all "legal" disputes, excepting those involving domestic jurisdiction, to the International Court of Justice.

Implicit in all these fundamentals was anti-imperialism, stemming from the Anglo-American Revolution itself and also from the Latin-American Revolution.[1]

Although isolation in a foolproof continent is no longer possible in the Atomic Age and the science-shrunken spaces of our globe, most of these fundamentals—except isolation—remain the foreign policy of the United States. That indeed is a test of their virtue. Some of them, like the Non-Transfer Policy, and Hands Off the New World, are so well established that like independence itself they no longer need mention. And when the United States finally became the largest naval power it did only lip service to that historic "birthright" of American independence, the Freedom of the Seas.

The reader may compare the twelve classic fundamentals here reviewed with the twelve "guiding principles" of American foreign policy reoriented from isolation to collective security and enunciated by President Harry S. Truman in his Navy Day Address of October 27, 1945, after the Second World War.[2] He will see that, except for isolation, the historical fundamentals are the basis of today's guiding principles.

We must not confuse foreign policy, the objectives and the guiding principles, with diplomacy, the means by which foreign policy is carried out. The United States made no serious mistake in its diplomacy, and committed few minor errors, from 1775 to 1898. Its impressive successes in that long period were due to taking advantage, without much deliberate calculation, of the rivalries, wars, and other distresses of a divided Europe and Asia, in other words to the balance of power in the Old World; to

[1] See the writer's *John Quincy Adams and the Foundations of American Foreign Policy* (Alfred A. Knopf, Inc., New York, 1949), Ch. XXVII. There, fourteen fundamentals (including sovereign independence and anti-imperialism) are listed. Here we stress sovereign independence and anti-imperialism, but explicitly enumerate only the other twelve as guiding principles. The principles of Pan Americanism or "Good Neighborhood," developed in Henry Clay's instructions of 1826 to the plenipotentiaries appointed to the Panama Congress, are explained more in the above-cited work than in this History.

[2] See note at end of this chapter.

its detached and distant position, almost foolproof; and to the fact that the main objectives of its policy then as now—freedom, peace, and fair trade with all the world—were perfectly compatible with its security and with the genius and interests of its people. At the close of the nineteenth century the foolproof position of the United States began to change. The rise of Germany and Japan as world powers, simultaneously with the United States, brought immense shifts in the strategy of American defense and diplomacy, forcing the United States reluctantly out of its happy isolation. The Continental Republic emerged into the arena of world power.

Students of the new position of the United States as a world power tended to chart American diplomacy by the three-way formula of Captain Alfred T. Mahan, the illustrious historian of sea power: in Europe, abstention; in Asia, co-operation; in the Caribbean, predominance.

It is unlikely that the United States would have embarked upon co-operation in the Far East—to preserve the Open Door and the integrity of China—if it had not been for the acquisition of the Philippine Islands. Co-operation proved imperfectly effective as a means of achieving that policy, first, because all the powers were not always willing to co-operate, and, secondly, because the European powers were increasingly paralyzed at home. Independent action to preserve the Open Door and the integrity of China proved to be more than the American people were willing to fight for *unless these objectives were coupled with some far more vital interest,* as happened in 1941-1945.

In the Caribbean, the United States was clearly pursuing its vital interests. It could have secured them, following the liberation of Cuba and the conquest of Puerto Rico, without intervention. The Panama Canal Zone did not need to be "taken." This move was an egregious mistake, by which the nation "coming of age" blackened its good will throughout South America.

In Europe, the policy of abstention could suit American interests only as long as Europe was balanced in power.

The intervention of the United States in the First World War in 1917 preserved the balance of power in Europe in favor of Great Britain and behind Great Britain in favor of the United States, which could always balance the exposed position of Canada against British sea power: the preservation of that balance was the real victory of the United States. The avoidable mistakes of American diplomacy during the First World War came from *unconditional* entry into full military and financial co-operation with the Allies without agreement as to the terms of peace.

Although not clearly foreseen as a reason for intervention, the profit of that war came from reducing the only great occidental naval power which was likely to unite with a large oriental naval power to crush the United States between their two jaws biting on both coasts.

For a time it appeared as if the idealistic diplomacy of Woodrow Wilson might override the traditional counsels of President Washington and merge the balance of power, "forever discredited," in a world system of collective security. It really did seem that the nations were ready to unite to prevent another such terrible conflict and the collapse it might bring to western civilization. The American people were ready for a League of Nations, and doubtless the Senate would have accepted the League, with the Lodge reservations, if President Wilson had approved them. When, because of partisan quarrels, the United States failed to ratify the Treaty of Versailles and the League of Nations, many of us thought that the fruits of victory had been tragically spilled away. We did not foresee the bogging-down of democracy, the rise of the dictators, the Great Depression, developments that were to palsy the League and lead to the renewal of war in Europe a generation later. We supposed that the great powers would be willing to make sacrifices in lives and in treasure to enforce the sanctions of the League against outlaw nations in regions where they had no vital interests. We naïvely believed this, although we ourselves were not willing in advance to sign up for any such definite responsibilities. We can see now in the embers of Europe and Asia the bitter truth that the world had to pass through a dreadful vale of human suffering before the nations could be willing to ensure collective security for all. It may have to pass through still another valley of the shadow of death before the nations and peoples, what are left of them, can agree to enforce world peace. Meanwhile the only security for the United States seems to rest in a safe balance of power.

The First World War passed without the United States deserting, definitively, the traditional principles of the Fathers: not to make foreign alliances, not to involve itself in the wars of European nations in matters relating to themselves.

Following the rejection of the League of Nations, United States foreign policy took on a pattern of satiated contentment, peace and pacifism. The Continental Republic seemed to be secure behind its ocean ramparts.

The Atlantic Ocean seemed safe because, after Versailles, Europe continued balanced in power behind the British Navy, and the British Navy was no menace if only because of the historic position of Canada as a hostage for Anglo-American amity; witness the attitude of Canada toward the Anglo-Japanese alliance and the problems of the Pacific and the Far East. The Pacific Ocean seemed safe after the Washington Conference of 1921-1922 had written the Far Eastern Policy of the United States for the first time into a strict international agreement freezing the *status quo* into a generation of peace. It left Japanese power supreme in its own waters and the American Navy in control of the eastern half of the ocean. It shifted responsibility for the China policy of the United States to the shoulders jointly of all parties to the Nine-Power Treaty and the other treaties of Washington. Before the expiration of the Washington Period—it proved to be a truce—the United States had emancipated the Philippine Islands, by a law that made them independent in 1946. The Continental Republic of North America was evidently preparing honorably to back out of the Far East when the new conquests of Japan upset the balance of power there. Even then the United States did not take it upon itself to go further than any of the other treaty parties to hold Japan to her freely pledged word.

In the interval of apparent security between the two world wars, when both oceans seemed entirely safe, the United States liquidated that imperialism which had thrown up the Panama Policy in the New World as a means of protecting naval communications between the Republic's two populous seacoasts. It renounced war as an instrument of national policy; it repudiated the Corollary of Theodore Roosevelt to the Monroe Doctrine; it all but pan-Americanized the Monroe Doctrine; it accepted the Doctrine of Nonintervention as a principle of inter-American public law; it gave up its Caribbean protectorates; it proclaimed as its own the inter-American doctrine of nonrecognition of territorial changes in sovereignty caused by conquest or the use of force; it urged the settlement of international controversies by peaceful means; and it ratified treaties of conciliation and arbitration, multilateral for the American republics, bilateral with as many other nations as would accept them.

The United States held forth this inter-American design as a model for world peace: the New World as exemplar to the Old. It strove continually for disarmament by international agreement. It even resorted to disarmament by example, beyond treaty requirements, during the Washington Period. In sponsoring this new program for peace the United States had the satisfaction that, unlike certain other major powers (Japan, Italy, Germany), it was to its real interests to have peace in a politically balanced world, to conserve its established, continental position, and to further world trade from that basis. It did not realize that such a peace could not be secure for a rich and satisfied power without heavy armaments to defend an enviable position.

Highlight in the new design for peace was the neutrality legislation of 1935-1937 to keep the country out of the next war that was suddenly threatening Europe again. It served, so to speak, only to keep the nation out of the previous war, already fought and won.

The interbella era of security suddenly vanished when Germany under Hitler rose to overrun Europe, while Japan took advantage of the distresses of the Occident to conquer Asia.

At first the United States stood confirmed again in its isolation, resolved to keep out of another war, whether in Europe or in Asia, slow to see, before June, 1940, that its own continental position was imperiled by the unbalancing of power through the rise of great conquering empires across both oceans. Traditional isolation had ever rested on a balance of power in Europe and Asia, a balance older than American independence itself. When that balance threatened to break down, as it did in 1917, and doubly so in 1940, isolation broke down with it.

A new school of historiography, which believed that the United States had lost the peace after the First World War, cautioned President Franklin D. Roosevelt not to make the mistake of Woodrow Wilson in dealing with Congress and thereby lose the next peace at the close of the Second World War. Roosevelt built up a bipartisan foreign policy only to win the previous peace, so to speak, even as the disillusionists of 1935-1939 succeeded in keeping the United States only out of the last war. The United States won the Second World War but in the victory lost the peace because its leaders and its people did not sense adequately the revolutionary impulse of Soviet policy and the new shift in the balance of power caused by the total defeat of Germany, Italy, and Japan.

A triple phenomenon of world politics resulted from the victory of the Allies:

(1) The potential supremacy of Russia on the World Island of power.

(2) The disintegration of the British Empire.

(3) The demoralization (at least temporary) of the United States in the Great Let-Down of 1945-1948.

None of these events served to offset either of the others. They all supplemented each other to support Russia's totalitarian power in the world to the menace of Western democracy. They brought into actual being the recurring nightmare of American diplomatists: an agglomeration of power united in Europe and Asia to encircle the Western Hemisphere and threaten it at once from north, east, and west in the age of airborne armies, trans-oceanic missiles, and atomic warfare.[1]

The new and forboding picture of power and politics that closed the first half of the twentieth century produced nothing less than a diplomatic revolution in the history of the United States. Hitherto a basic assumption of American foreign policy had been a divided Europe and a divided Asia, each balanced behind the supremacy of first the British Navy and finally the British and American Navies, Canada serving as lynch-pin for Anglo-American peace and amity. Europe's distresses were America's advantage. A United States of Europe was not to be desired, either by peaceful change or forceful compulsion. The First World War left Europe thus safely divided and balanced, and Asia too, and the United States lapsed back into its traditional isolation and neutrality. The Second World War threatened to break down this balance by uniting Europe and Asia in an Axis partnership of conquest and tyranny. To prevent such a combination the United States fought for its own security the greatest war of history. The unexpected phenomena of victory proved that Europe's distresses, and those of Asia too, had become America's distresses. The North American Continent was no longer secure. Thenceforth the United States would strive to unite Western Europe to resist the land-mass of Soviet power. There followed the European Recovery Program and the North Atlantic Treaty of 1949, seeking to couple, partially at least, the defense of the Old World with the defense of the New World as aligned in the Pact of Rio de Janeiro of 1947.

In the great crisis of thought and action that ushered in the Atomic Age it remained to be seen whether the uncertain formula of the North Atlantic Treaty, all within the individual constitutional decision and competence of each contracting party, would be strong enough to hold together the democracies of the Western World so that government of the people by the people and for the people might not perish from the earth.

AMERICAN FOREIGN POLICY AS OFFICIALLY DEFINED IN 1945 [2]

The foreign policy of the United States is based firmly on fundamental principles of righteousness and justice. In carrying out those principles we shall firmly adhere to what we believe to be right; and we shall not give our approval to any compromise with evil.

[1] See the maps in the late Nicholas John Spykmann's *The Geography of the Peace* (New York, 1944).
[2] Address of President Harry S. Truman, Navy Day, October 27, 1945, at New York City. Department of State *Bulletin*, XIII, No. 331 (October 28, 1945), pp. 654-55.

But we know that we cannot attain perfection in this world overnight. We shall not let our search for perfection obstruct our steady progress toward international cooperation. We must be prepared to fulfil our responsibilities as best we can, within the framework of our fundamental principles, even though we recognize that we have to operate in an imperfect world.

Let me restate the fundamentals of that foreign policy of the United States:

1. We seek no territorial expansion or selfish advantage. We have no plans for aggression against any other state, large or small. We have no objective which need clash with the peaceful aims of any other nation.

2. We believe in the eventual return of sovereign rights and self-government to all peoples who have been deprived of them by force.

3. We shall approve no territorial changes in any friendly part of the world unless they accord with the freely expressed wishes of the people concerned.

4. We believe that all peoples who are prepared for self-government should be permitted to choose their own form of government by their own freely expressed choice, without interference from any foreign source. That is true in Europe, in Asia, in Africa, as well as in the Western Hemisphere.

5. By the combined and cooperative action of our war Allies, we shall help the defeated enemy states establish peaceful, democratic governments of their own free choice. And we shall try to attain a world in which Nazism, Fascism, and military aggression cannot exist.

6. We shall refuse to recognize any government imposed upon any nation by the force of any foreign power. In some cases it may be impossible to prevent forceful imposition of such a government. But the United States will not recognize any such government.

7. We believe that all nations should have the freedom of the seas and equal rights to the navigation of boundary rivers and waterways and of rivers and waterways which pass through more than one country.

8. We believe that all states which are accepted in the society of nations should have access on equal terms to the trade and the raw materials of the world.

9. We believe that the sovereign states of the Western Hemisphere, without interference from outside the Western Hemisphere, must work together as good neighbors in the solution of their common problems.

10. We believe that full economic collaboration between all nations, great and small, is essential to the improvement of living conditions all over the world, and to the establishment of freedom from fear and freedom from want.

11. We shall continue to strive to promote freedom of expression and freedom of religion throughout the peace-loving areas of the world.

12. We are convinced that the preservation of peace between nations requires a United Nations Organization composed of all the peace-loving

nations of the world who are willing jointly to use force if necessary to insure peace.

That is the foreign policy which guides the United States now. That is the foreign policy with which it confidently faces the future.

It may not be put into effect tomorrow or the next day. But none the less, it is our policy; and we shall seek to achieve it. It may take a long time, but it is worth waiting for, and it is worth striving to attain.

INDEX

(including authors cited)